Literature CourseMate

The Literature CourseMate brings literature to life with interactive learning, study, and exam preparation tools that support LIT.

INCLUDES:

Interactive teaching and learning tools, such as tutorials on key literary concepts that guide students through the explication of selected works; podcast interviews with literature professors on canonical works; video activities based on *The Wadsworth Original Film Series in Literature*; and **Engagement Tracker,** a first-of-its-kind tool that monitors student engagement in the course.

ON THE WEB

LIT
Are you in?

ONLINE RESOURCES INCLUDED!

FOR INSTRUCTORS:
- Custom Options through 4LTR+ Program
- Test Bank
- Instructor Prep Cards
- Student Review Cards
- Engagement Tracker

FOR STUDENTS:
- Quizzes
- Flashcards
- Interactive Writing Projects
- Literary Concept Tutorials
- Podcast Interviews
- Audio Readings
- Literary Glossary
- Video Activities
- Research Guidance

Students sign in at **login.cengagebrain.com**

LIT
Laurie G. Kirszner &
Stephen R. Mandell

Senior Publisher: Lyn Uhl

Publisher: Michael Rosenberg

Development Editor: Karen Mauk

Assistant Editor: Erin Bosco

Editorial Assistant: Rebecca Donahue

Associate Media Editor: Janine Tangney

Marketing Manager: Melissa Holt

Marketing Director: Jason Sakos

Marketing Coordinator: Brittany Blais

Executive Marketing Manager: Stacey Purviance

Marketing Communications Manager:
Glenn McGibbon

Content Project Manager: Corinna Dibble

Senior Art Directors: Marissa Falco/
Cate Rickard Barr

Senior Print Buyer: Betsy Donaghey

Senior Rights Acquisition Specialist, Image:
Jen Meyer-Dare

Senior Rights Acquisition Specialist, Text:
Katie Huha

Production Service: Nesbitt Graphics, Inc.

Text Designer: Nesbitt Graphics, Inc.

Cover Designer: Studio Montage

Cover Images: Christopher Kontoes / Getty
Images; Marili Forastieri / Getty Images;
quilt: Greta Vaught

Compositor: Nesbitt Graphics, Inc.

For product information and technology assistance, contact us at
Cengage Learning Customer & Sales Support, 1-800-354-9706
For permission to use material from this text or product,
submit all requests online at **cengage.com/permissions**
Further permissions questions can be emailed to
permissionrequest@cengage.com

Library of Congress Control Number: 2010941412

ISBN-13: 978-1-111-34883-0

ISBN-10: 1-111-34883-9

Wadsworth
20 Channel Center Street
Boston, MA 02210
USA

Cengage Learning is a leading provider of customized learning solutions with office locations around the globe, including Singapore, the United Kingdom, Australia, Mexico, Brazil, and Japan. Locate your local office at:
international.cengage.com/region

Cengage Learning products are represented in Canada by Nelson Education, Ltd.

For your course and learning solutions, visit **www.cengage.com**

Purchase any of our products at your local college store or at our preferred online store **www.cengagebrain.com**

Printed in the United States of America
4 5 6 7 16 15 14

Brief Contents

Contents

>> *Westminster Bridge*, London (1886)
by Claude Thomas Stanfield Moore

>> Maya Angelou

4 THINKING CRITICALLY ABOUT YOUR WRITING 45

5 WRITING LITERARY ARGUMENTS 51

>> Scene from Alice Walker's "Everyday Use"

© Denna Bendall/Worn Path Productions

PART 2 FICTION 90

9 UNDERSTANDING FICTION 91

>> Ernest Hemingway

© Photo courtesy John F. Kennedy Presidential Library and Museum, Boston

10 FICTION SAMPLER: THE SHORT-SHORT STORY 100

>> ZZ Packer

© Marc Brasz/Corbis

11 PLOT 109

>> Kate Chopin

Courtesy of Missouri Historical Society

12 CHARACTER 127

>> Katherine Mansfield

13 SETTING 147

>> Sherman J. Alexie

14 POINT OF VIEW 169

>> Shaun Tan

>> Tim O'Brien

>> Alice Walker

>> DH Lawrence

>> Nathaniel Hawthorne

>> Nikki Giovanni

>> *Self Portrait with Monkey and Parrot* (1938) by Frida Kahlo

>> Janice Mirikitani

22 WORD CHOICE, WORD ORDER 381

>> Gwendolyn Brooks

25 SOUND 426

>> Alfred, Lord Tennyson

26 FORM 442

>> Pat Mora

Courtesy Pat Mora. Photo © Cheron Bayna

27 SYMBOL, ALLEGORY, ALLUSION, MYTH 461

>> Edgar Allan Poe

© AP Photo

28 DISCOVERING THEMES IN POETRY 479

>> Dylan Thomas

© AP Photo

29 POETRY FOR FURTHER READING 497

>> John Donne

© The Granger Collection, New York

PART 4 DRAMA **524**

30 UNDERSTANDING DRAMA 525

>> Anton Chekhov

© Bettmann/Corbis

>> Zora Neale Hurston

>> Henrik Ibsen

>> Arthur Miller

>> Sophocles

35 THEME   721

>> August Wilson

PART I
A GUIDE TO WRITING ABOUT LITERATURE

Maya Angelou (1928–   )

My Arkansas (1978)

There is a deep brooding
in Arkansas.
Old crimes like moss pend
from poplar trees.
The sullen earth
is much too
red for comfort.
Sunrise seems to hesitate
and in that second
lose its
incandescent aim, and
dusk no more shadows
than the noon.
*The past is brighter yet.
Old hates and
ante-bellum lace are rent
but not discarded.
*Today is yet to come
in Arkansas,
It writhes. It writhes in awful
waves of brooding.

Note repetition

Look up this word

*Note contrast betw.
past and present*

Look up this word

More repetition

Understanding Literature

Learning Outcomes

After reading this chapter, you should be able to do the following:

LO1 Understand imaginative literature

LO2 Recognize conventional themes

LO3 Understand the literary canon

LO4 Interpret literature

LO5 Evaluate literature

LO6 Understand the function of literary criticism

LO1 Understand Imaginative Literature

Imaginative literature begins with a writer's need to convey a personal vision to readers. Consider, for example, how William Wordsworth uses language in these lines from his poem "Composed upon Westminster Bridge, September 3, 1802":

> This City now doth, like a garment, wear
> The beauty of the morning; silent, bare,
> Ships, towers, domes, theatres, and temples lie
> Open unto the fields, and to the sky;
> All bright and glittering in the smokeless air.

Wordsworth does not try to present a picture of London that is topographically or sociologically accurate. Instead, by comparing the city at dawn to a person wearing a beautiful garment, he creates a striking picture that has its own kind of truth. By using a vivid, original comparison, the poet is able to suggest the oneness of the city, nature, and himself.

Even when writers of imaginative literature use factual material—historical documents, newspaper stories, or personal experience, for example—their primary purpose is to present their unique view of experience, one that has

>> *Westminster Bridge, London* (1886) by Claude Thomas Starfield Moore

significance beyond the moment. (As the poet Ezra Pound said, "Literature is the news that *stays* news.") To convey their views of experience, these writers often manipulate facts—changing dates, creating characters and events, and inventing dialogue. For example, when Herman Melville wrote his nineteenth-century novella *Benito Cereno*, he drew many of his facts from an account of an actual slave revolt. In his story, he reproduces court records and uses plot details from this primary source, but he leaves out some incidents, and he adds material of his own. The result is an original work of literature. Wanting to do more than retell the original story, Melville used the factual material as "a skeleton of actual reality" on which he built a story that attacks the institution of slavery and examines the nature of truth.

Imaginative literature is more likely than other types of writing to include words chosen not only because they communicate the writer's ideas, but also because they are memorable. Using vivid imagery and evocative comparisons, writers of imaginative literature often stretch language to its limits. By relying on the multiple connotations of words and images, a work of imaginative literature encourages readers to see the possibilities of language and to move beyond the factual details of an event.

Even though imaginative literature can be divided into types called **genres**—fiction, poetry, and drama—the nature of literary genres varies from culture to culture. In fact, some literary forms that Western readers take for granted are alien to other literary traditions. The sonnet, though fairly common in the West, is not a conventional literary form in Chinese or Arabic poetry. Similarly, the most popular theatrical entertainment in Japan since the mid-seventeenth century, the Kabuki play, has no counterpart in the West. (In a Kabuki play, which includes stories, scenes, dances, music, acrobatics, and elaborate costumes and stage settings, all of the actors are men, some of whom play the parts of females. Many Kabuki plays have little plot and seem to be primarily concerned with spectacle. One feature of this form of drama is a walkway that extends from the stage through the audience to the back of the theater.)

Conventions of narrative organization and character development can also vary considerably from culture to culture, especially in literature derived from oral traditions. For example, narrative organization in some Native American stories (and, even more commonly, in some African stories) can be very different from what contemporary Western readers are accustomed to. Events may be arranged spatially

instead of chronologically: first a story presents all the events that happened in one place, then it presents everything that happened in another location, and so on. Character development is also much less important in some traditional African and Native American stories than it is in modern short fiction. In fact, a character's name, description, and personality can change dramatically (and without warning) during the course of a story.

Despite such differences, the imaginative literature of all cultures has similar effects on readers: memorable characters, vivid descriptions, imaginative use of language, and compelling plots can fascinate and delight. Literature can take readers where they have never been before and, in so doing, can create a sense of adventure and wonder.

At another level, however, readers can find more than just pleasure or escape in literature. Beyond transporting readers out of their lives and times, literature can enable readers to see their own lives and times more clearly. Whether a work of imaginative literature depicts a young girl as she experiences the disillusionment of adulthood for the first time, as in David Michael Kaplan's "Doe Season" (p. 290), or examines the effect of discrimination on a black African who is looking for an apartment, as in Wole Soyinka's "Telephone Conversation" (p. 7), it can help readers to understand their own experiences and the experiences of others. In this sense, literature offers readers increased insight into the human condition. As the Chilean poet Pablo Neruda said, works of imaginative literature fulfill "the most ancient rites of our conscience in the awareness of being human and of believing in a common destiny."

LO2 Recognize Conventional Themes

The **theme** of a work of literature is its central or dominant idea. This idea is seldom stated explicitly. Instead, it is conveyed through the selection and arrangement of details; through the emphasis of certain words, events, or images; and through the actions and reactions of characters.

Although one central theme may dominate a literary work, many works explore a number of different themes or ideas. For example, the central theme of Mark Twain's *Adventures of Huckleberry Finn* might be the idea that an individual's innate sense of right and wrong is superior to society's artificial and sometimes unnatural values. The main character, Huck, gains a growing awareness of this idea by witnessing feuds, duels, and all manner of human folly. As a result, he makes a decision to help his friend Jim escape from slavery despite the fact that society, as well as his own conscience, condemns this action. However, *Huckleberry Finn* also examines other themes. Throughout his novel, Twain criticizes many of the ideas that prevailed in the pre–Civil War South, such as the racism and religious hypocrisy that pervaded the towns along the Mississippi.

Although a literary work can explore any theme, certain themes have recurred so frequently over the years that

>> *On the Raft*, from Mark Twain's *Adventures of Huckleberry Finn*

they have become conventions. One **conventional theme**—a character's loss of innocence—appears in the biblical story of Adam and Eve and later finds its way into works such as Nathaniel Hawthorne's 1835 short story "Young Goodman Brown" (p. 320) and James Joyce's 1914 short story "Araby" (p. 220). Another conventional theme—the conflict between an individual's values and the values of society—is examined in the ancient Greek play *Oedipus* by Sophocles (p. 701). Almost two thousand years later, Norwegian playwright Henrik Ibsen deals with the same theme in *A Doll House* (p. 562).

Other conventional themes examined in literary works include the individual's quest for spiritual enlightenment, the *carpe diem* ("seize the day") philosophy, the making of the artist, the nostalgia for a vanished past, the disillusionment of adulthood, the pain of love, the struggle of women for equality, the conflict between parents and children, the clash between civilization and the wilderness, the evils of unchecked ambition, the inevitability of fate, the impact of the past on the present, the conflict between human beings and machines, and the tension between the ideal and the actual realms of experience.

Many cultures explore similar themes, but writers from different cultures may develop these themes differently. A culture's history, a particular region's geography, or a country's social structure can suggest unique ways of developing conventional themes. In addition, the assumptions, concerns, values, ideals, and beliefs of a particular country or society—or of a particular group within that society—can help to determine the themes writers choose to explore and the manner in which they do so.

In American literature, for instance, familiar themes include the loss of innocence, rites of passage, childhood epiphanies, and the ability (or inability) to form relationships. American writers of color may use these themes to express their frustration with racism or to celebrate their cultural identities. For example, the theme of loss of innocence may be presented as a first encounter with racial prejudice; a conflict between the individual and society may be presented as a conflict between a minority view and the values of the dominant group; and the theme of failure or aborted relationships may be explored in a work about cultural misunderstandings.

Finally, modern works of literature sometimes treat conventional themes in new ways. For example, in *1984* George Orwell explores the negative consequences of unchecked power by creating a nightmare world in which the government controls and dehumanizes a population. Even though Orwell's novel is set in an imaginary future (it was written in 1948), its theme echoes ideas frequently examined in the plays of both Sophocles and Shakespeare.

"In American literature, . . . familiar themes include the loss of innocence, rites of passage, childhood epiphanies, and the ability (or inability) to form relationships."

LO3 Understand the Literary Canon

Originally, the term *canon* referred to the accepted list of books that made up the Christian Bible. More recently, the term **literary canon** has come to denote a group of works generally agreed upon by writers, teachers, and critics to be worth reading and studying. Over the years, as standards have changed, the definition of "good" literature has also changed, and the literary canon has been modified accordingly. For example, at various times, critics have characterized Shakespeare's plays as mundane, immoral, commonplace, and brilliant. The eighteenth-century critic Samuel Johnson said of Shakespeare that "in his comick scenes he is seldom very successful" and in tragedy "his performance seems constantly to be worse, as his labor is more." Many people find it difficult to believe that a writer whose name today is synonymous with great literature could ever have been judged so harshly. Like all aesthetic works, however, the plays of Shakespeare affect individuals in different periods of history and in different societies in different ways.

Some educators and literary scholars believe that the traditional literary canon, like a restricted club, arbitrarily admits some authors and excludes others. This fact is borne out, they say, by an examination of the literature curriculum that until recently was standard at many North American universities. This curriculum typically began with Homer, Plato, Dante, and Chaucer, progressed to Shakespeare, Milton, the eighteenth-century novel, the Romantics, and the Victorians, and ended with some of the "classics" of modern British and American literature. Most of the authors of these works are white and male, and their writing for the most part reflects Western values.

Missing from the literature courses in North American universities for many years were South American, African, and Asian writers. Students of American literature were not encouraged to consider the perspectives of women, of gay and lesbian writers, or of Latinos, Native Americans, or other ethnic or racial groups. During the past four decades, however, most universities have expanded the traditional canon by including more works by women, people of color, and writers from a variety of cultures. These additional works, studied alongside those representing the traditional canon, have opened up the curriculum and redefined the standards by which literature is judged.

One example of a literary work that challenged the traditional canon is "All about Suicide" by Luisa Valenzuela, an Argentinean writer. Currently, she is one of the most widely translated South American writers. This brief, shocking story is part of a large and growing body of literature from around the world that purposely violates our standard literary expectations to make its point—in this case, a point about the political realities of Argentina in the 1960s.

Luisa Valenzuela (1938–   )

All about Suicide (1967)

Translated by Helen Lane

Ismael grabbed the gun and slowly rubbed it across his face. Then he pulled the trigger and there was a shot. Bang. One more person dead in the city. It's getting to be a vice. First he grabbed the revolver that was in a desk drawer, rubbed it gently across his face, put it to his temple, and pulled the trigger. Without saying a word. Bang. Dead.

Let's recapitulate: the office is grand, fit for a minister. The desk is ministerial too, and covered with a glass that must have reflected the scene, the shock. Ismael knew where the gun was, he'd hidden it there himself. So he didn't lose any time, all he had to do was open the right-hand drawer and stick his hand in. Then he got a good hold on it and rubbed it over his face with a certain pleasure

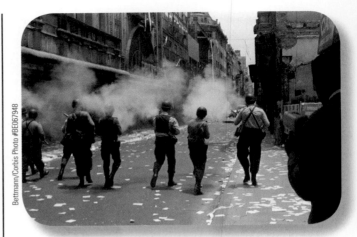

>> Police use tear gas on demonstrators, Buenos Aires, 1970

before putting it to his temple and pulling the trigger. It was something almost sensual and quite unexpected. He hadn't even had time to think about it. A trivial gesture, and the gun had fired.

There's something missing: Ismael in the bar with a glass in his hand thinking over his future act and its possible consequences.

We must go back farther if we want to get at the truth: Ismael in the cradle crying because his diapers are dirty and nobody is changing him.

Not that far.

Ismael in the first grade fighting with a classmate who'll one day become a minister, his friend, a traitor.

No, Ismael in the ministry without being able to tell what he knew, forced to be silent. Ismael in the bar with the glass (his third) in his hand, and the irrevocable decision: better death.

Ismael pushing the revolving door at the entrance to the building, pushing the swinging door leading to the office

>> Police action in Argentina, 1970

section, saying good morning to the guard, opening the door of his office. Once in his office, seven steps to his desk. Terror, the act of opening the drawer, taking out the revolver, and rubbing it across his face, almost a single gesture and very quick. The act of putting it to his temple and pulling the trigger—another act, immediately following the previous one. Bang. Dead. And Ismael coming out of his office (the other man's office, the minister's) almost relieved, even though he can predict what awaits him.

*   *   *

The Nigerian poet and playwright Wole Soyinka is another writer whose works were not part of the traditional Western canon—until, in 1986, he won the Nobel Prize in Literature. The subject of the following poem may not seem "relevant" to European audiences, and the language ("pillar-box," "omnibus") may not be familiar to Americans. Still, as a reading of the poem demonstrates, Soyinka's work makes a compelling plea for individual rights and self-determination—a theme that transcends the boundaries of time and place.

Wole Soyinka (1934–   )

Telephone Conversation (1962)

The price seemed reasonable, location
Indifferent. The landlady swore she lived
Off premises. Nothing remained
But self-confession. "Madam," I warned
"I hate a wasted journey—I am—African."   5
Silence. Silenced transmission of
Pressurized good-breeding. Voice, when it came,
Lip-stick coated, long gold-rolled
Cigarette-holder pipped. Caught I was, foully.
"HOW DARK?" . . . I had not misheard . . .   10
    "ARE YOU LIGHT
OR VERY DARK?" Button B. Button A. Stench
Of rancid breath of public-hide-and-speak.
Red booth. Red pillar-box. Red double-tiered
Omnibus squelching tar. It *was* real! Shamed   15
By ill-mannered silence, surrender
Pushed dumbfoundment to beg simplification.
Considerate she was, varying the emphasis—
"ARE YOU DARK? OR VERY LIGHT?" Revelation came.
"You mean—like plain or milk chocolate?"   20
Her assent was clinical, crushing in its light,
Impersonality. Rapidly, wave-length adjusted,
I chose, "West African sepia"—and as an afterthought,
"Down in my passport." Silence for spectroscopic
Flight of fancy, till truthfulness clanged her accent   25
Hard on the mouthpiece. "WHAT'S THAT?" conceding
"DON'T KNOW WHAT THAT IS." "Like brunette."
"THAT'S DARK, ISN'T IT?" "Not altogether.
Facially, I am brunette, but madam, you should see
The rest of me. Palm of my hand, soles of my feet   30
Are a peroxide blond. Friction, caused—
Foolishly madam—by sitting down, has turned
My bottom raven black—One moment madam!"—sensing
Her receiver rearing on the thunder clap
About my ears—"Madam," I pleaded, "Wouldn't you rather   35
See for yourself?"

>> Red London phone booth

*   *   *

Certainly canon revision is not without problems—for example, the possibility of including a work more for political or sociological reasons than for its literary merit. Nevertheless, if the debate about the literary canon has accomplished anything, it has revealed that the canon is not fixed and that many works formerly excluded—African-American slave narratives and eighteenth-century women's diaries, for example—deserve to be read.

LO4 Interpret Literature

When you **interpret** a literary work, you explore its possible meanings. One commonly held idea about reading a literary work is that its meaning lies buried somewhere within it, waiting to be unearthed. This reasoning suggests that a clever reader has only to discover the author's intent to find out what a story or poem means, and that the one actual meaning of a work is hidden "between the lines," unaffected by a reader's experiences or interpretations. More recently, however, a different model of the reading process—one that takes into consideration the reader as well as the work he or she is interpreting—has emerged.

Many contemporary critics see the reading process as **interactive.** In other words, meaning is created through the reader's interaction with a text. Thus, the meaning of a particular work comes alive in the imagination of an individual reader, and no reader can determine a work's meaning without considering his or her own reaction to the text. Meaning, therefore, is created partly by what is supplied by a work and partly by what is supplied by the reader.

The most obvious thing a work supplies is **facts,** the information that enables a reader to follow the plot of a story, the action of a play, or the development of a poem. The work itself will provide factual details about the setting; about the characters' names, ages, and appearances; about the sequence of events; and about the emotions and attitudes of a poem's speaker, a story's narrator, or the characters in a play or story. This factual information cannot be ignored: if a play's stage directions identify its setting as nineteenth-century Norway or the forest of Arden, that is where the play is set.

In addition to facts, a work also conveys the social, political, class, and gender **attitudes** of the writer. Thus, a work may have an overt feminist or working-class bias or a subtle (or obvious) political agenda; it may confirm or challenge contemporary attitudes; it may communicate a writer's nostalgia for a vanished past or outrage at a corrupt present; it may take an elitist, distant view of characters and events or present a sympathetic perspective. A reader's understanding of these attitudes will contribute to his or her interpretation of the work.

Finally, a work also includes **assumptions** about literary conventions. A poet, for example, may have definite ideas about whether a poem should be rhymed or unrhymed or about whether a particular subject is appropriate or inappropriate for poetic treatment. Therefore, a knowledge of the literary conventions of a particular period or the preferences of a particular writer can provide a starting point for your interpretation of literature.

As a reader, you bring to a work your own **personal perspectives.** Your experiences, your beliefs, your ideas about the issues discussed in the work, and your assumptions about literature color your interpretations. In fact, nearly every literary work has somewhat different meanings for different people, depending on their age, gender, nationality, political and religious beliefs, ethnic background, social and economic class, education, knowledge, and personal experiences. Depending on your religious beliefs, for instance, you can react to a passage from the Old Testament as literal truth, symbolic truth, or fiction. Depending on your race, where you live, your biases, and the nature of your experience, a story about racial discrimination can strike you as accurate and realistic, exaggerated and unrealistic, or understated and restrained.

In a sense, then, the process of determining meaning is like a conversation, one in which both you and the text have a voice. Sometimes, by clearly dictating the terms of the discussion, the text determines the direction of the conversation; at other times, by using your knowledge and experience to interpret the text, you dominate. Thus, because every reading of a literary work is actually an interpretation, it is a mistake to look for a single "correct" reading.

The 1923 poem "Stopping by Woods on a Snowy Evening" (p. 509), by the American poet Robert Frost, illustrates how a single work can have more than one interpretation. Readers may interpret the poem as being about the inevitability of death, as suggesting that the poet is tired or world

> "In a sense ... the process of determining meaning is like a conversation, one in which both you and the text have a voice."

Whose woods these are I think I know.

>> Opening pages from Susan Jeffers's illustrated children's book *Stopping by Woods on a Snowy Evening* (1978)

weary, or as making a comment about duty and the need to persevere, or about the conflicting pulls of life and art. Beyond these possibilities, readers' own associations of snow with quiet and sadness could lead them to define the mood of the poem as sorrowful or melancholy. Information about Robert Frost's life or his ideas about poetry could add to readers' understanding of the poem, and they might even develop ideas about the poem that are quite different from the poet's. In fact, on several occasions, Frost himself gave strikingly different—even contradictory—interpretations of "Stopping by Woods on a Snowy Evening," sometimes insisting that the poem had no hidden meaning and at other times saying that it required a good deal of explication. (Literary critics also disagree about its meaning.) When reading a work of literature, then, keep in mind that the meaning of the text is not fixed. Your best strategy is to open yourself up to the text's many possibilities and explore the full range of your responses.

Although no single reading of a literary work is "correct," some readings are more defensible than others. Like a scientific theory, a literary interpretation must have a basis in fact, and the text supplies the facts against which your interpretation should be judged. For example, after you read Shirley Jackson's "The Lottery" (p. 251), a 1948 short story in which a randomly chosen victim is stoned to death by her neighbors, it would be reasonable to conclude that the ceremonial aspects of the lottery suggest a pagan ritual. Your understanding of what a pagan ritual is, combined with your observation that a number of details in the text suggest ancient fertility rites, might lead you to this conclusion. Another possibility is that "The Lottery" provides a commentary on mob psychology. The way characters reinforce one another's violent tendencies lends support to this interpretation. However, the interpretation that the ritual of the lottery is a thinly veiled attack on the death penalty would be difficult to support. Certainly a character in the story is killed, but she is not accused of a crime, nor is she tried or convicted; in fact, the killing is random and seemingly without motivation. Still, although seeing "The Lottery" as a comment on the death penalty may be far-fetched, this interpretation could be a starting point. A second, closer reading of the story would allow you to explore other, more plausible, interpretations.

As you read, do not be afraid to develop unusual or creative interpretations. A **safe reading** of a work is likely to result in a dull paper that simply states the obvious, but an aggressive or **strong reading** of a work—one that challenges generally held assumptions—can lead to interesting and intellectually challenging conclusions. Even if your reading differs from established critics' interpretations, you should not automatically assume it has no merit. Your own special knowledge of the material discussed in the text—a regional practice, an ethnic custom, a personal experience—may give you a unique perspective from which to view the work. Whatever interpretation you make, be sure that you support it with specific references to the text. If your interpretation is based on your own experiences, explain those experiences and relate them clearly to the work you are discussing. As long as you can make a reasonable case, you have the right (and perhaps the obligation) to present your ideas. By doing so, you may give your fellow students and your instructor new insight into the work.

LO5 Evaluate Literature

When you **evaluate** a work of literature, you do more than interpret it; you make a judgment about it. You reach conclusions not simply about whether the work is "good" or "bad," but also about how effectively the work presents itself to you, the reader. To evaluate a work, you **analyze** it, breaking it apart and considering its individual elements. As you evaluate a work of literature, remember that different works are designed to fulfill different needs—entertainment, education, or enlightenment, for example. Before you begin to evaluate a work, be sure you understand its purpose; then, follow these guidelines:

- *Begin your evaluation by considering how various literary elements function within a work.* Fiction may be divided into chapters and use flashbacks and foreshadowing; plays may be divided into scenes and acts and include dialogue and special staging techniques; poems may be arranged in regularly ordered groups of lines and use poetic devices such as rhyme and meter. Understanding the choices writers make about these and other literary elements can help you form judgments about a work. For example, why does Alberto Alvaro Ríos use a first-person narrator in his story "The Secret Lion" (p. 333)? Would the story have been different had it been told in the third person by a narrator who was not a character in the story? How does unusual staging contribute to the effect Milcha Sanchez-Scott achieves in her play *The Cuban Swimmer*? How would a more realistic setting change the play? Naturally, you cannot focus on every element of a particular story, poem, or play. But you can and should focus on those aspects that determine your responses to a work. For this reason, elements such as the unusual stanzaic form in E. E. Cummings's poem "Buffalo Bill's" and the very specific stage directions in Arthur Miller's play *Death of a Salesman* (p. 605) should be of special interest to you.

Note Keep in mind that some interpretations are *not* reasonable. You may contribute ideas based on your own perspectives, but you cannot ignore or contradict evidence in the text to suit your own biases. As you read and reread a text, continue to question and reexamine your judgments. The conversation between you and the text should be a dialogue, not a monologue or a shouting match.

As you read, then, you should ask questions. Do the characters in a short story seem real, or do they seem like cardboard cutouts? Are the images in a poem original and thought provoking, or are they clichéd? Are the stage directions of a play minimal or very detailed? The answers to these and other questions will help you to shape your evaluation.

- *As you continue your evaluation, decide whether the literary elements of a work interact to achieve a common goal.* Good writers are like master cabinetmakers: their skill disguises the actual work that has gone into the process of creation. Thus, the elements of a well-crafted literary work often fit together in a way that conceals the craft of the writer. Consider the subtlety of the following stanza from the 1862 poem "Echo" by Christina Rossetti:

> Come to me in the silence of the night;
> Come to me in the speaking silence of a dream;
> Come with soft round cheeks and eyes as bright
> As sunlight on a stream;
> Come back in tears,
> O memory, hope, love of finished years.

Throughout this stanza, Rossetti repeats words ("Come to me . . . / Come with soft . . . / Come back . . .") and initial consonants ("speaking silence"; "sunlight on a stream"), using sound to create an almost hypnotic mood. The rhyme scheme (*night/bright, dream/stream,* and *tears/years*) reinforces the mood by establishing a musical undercurrent that extends throughout the poem. Thus, this stanza is effective because its repeated words and sounds work together to create a single lyrical effect.

The chorus in *Antigone* by Sophocles (p. 701) also illustrates how the elements of a well-crafted work of literature function together. In ancient Greece, plays were performed by masked male actors who played both male and female roles. A chorus of fifteen men remained in a central circle called the *orchestra* and commented on and reacted to the action taking place around them. The chorus expresses the judgment of the community and acts as a moral guide for the audience. Once modern audiences grow accustomed to the presence of the chorus, it becomes an important part of the play. It neither distracts the audience nor intrudes on the action. In fact, eliminating the chorus would diminish the impact of the play.

- *Next, consider whether a work reinforces or calls into question your ideas about the world.* Works of **popular fiction**—those aimed at a mass audience—usually do little more than reassure readers that what they believe is correct. Catering to people's desires (for wealth or success, for example), to their prejudices, or to their fears, these works serve as escapes from life. More serious fiction, however, often goes against the grain, challenging cherished beliefs and leading readers to reexamine long-held assumptions. For instance,

in the 1957 short story "Big Black Good Man" (p. 184), Richard Wright's protagonist, a night porter at a hotel, struggles with his consuming yet irrational fear of a "big black" sailor and with his inability to see beyond the sailor's size and color. Only at the end of the story do many readers see that they, like the night porter, have stereotyped and dehumanized the sailor.

- *Now, consider whether a work is intellectually challenging.* The extended comparison between the legs of a compass and two people in love in "A Valediction: Forbidding Mourning" (p. 414) by the seventeenth-century English poet John Donne illustrates how effectively an image can communicate complex ideas to readers. Compressed into this comparison are ideas about the perfection of love, the pain of enforced separation, and the difference between sexual and spiritual love. As intellectually challenging as the extended comparison is, it is nonetheless accessible to the careful reader. After all, many people have used a compass to draw a circle and, therefore, are able to understand the relationship between the two legs of the compass (and the two lovers).

A fine line exists, however, between works that are intellectually challenging and those that are simply obscure. An **intellectually challenging** work requires effort from readers to unlock ideas that enrich and expand their understanding of themselves and the world. Although complex, the work gives readers a sense that they have gained something by putting forth the effort to interpret it. An **obscure** work exists solely to display a writer's erudition or intellectual idiosyncrasies. Allusions to other works and events are so numerous and confusing that the work may seem more like a private code than an effort to enlighten readers. Consider the following excerpt from "Canto LXXVI" by the twentieth-century American poet Ezra Pound:

> Le Paradis n'est pas artificiel
> States of mind are inexplicable to us.
> δακρύων   δακρύων   δακρύων
> L.   P. gli onesti
> J'ai eu pitié des autres
> probablement pas assez, and at moments that
> suited my own
> convenience
> Le paradis n'est pas artificiel,
> l'enfer non plus.
> Came Eurus as comforter
> and at sunset la pastorella dei suini
> driving the pigs home, benecomata dea
> under the two-winged cloud
> as of less and more than a day

This passage contains lines in French, Greek, and Italian, as well as a reference to Eurus, the ancient Greek personification of the east wind, and the initials L. P. (Loomis Pound?). It demands a lot from readers; the question is whether or not the reward is worth the effort.

No hard-and-fast rule exists for determining whether a work is intellectually challenging or simply obscure. Just as a poem has no fixed meaning, it also has no fixed value. Some readers would say that the passage from "Canto LXXVI" is good, even great, poetry. Others would argue that those lines do not yield enough pleasure and insight to justify the effort needed to analyze them. As a reader, you must draw your own conclusions and justify them in a clear and reasonable way. Do not assume that just because a work is difficult, it is obscure. (Nor should you assume that all difficult works are great literature or that all accessible literature is trivial.) Some of the most beautiful and inspiring literary works demand a great deal of effort. Most readers would agree, however, that the time spent exploring such works yields tremendous rewards.

- *Consider whether a work gives you pleasure.* One of the primary reasons literature endures is that it gives readers enjoyment. As subjective as this assessment is, it is a starting point for critical judgment. When readers ask themselves what they liked about a work, why they liked it, or what they learned, they begin the process of evaluation. Although this process is largely uncritical, it can lead to an involvement with the work and to a valid critical response. When you encounter great literature, with all its complexities, you may lose sight of the idea of literature as a source of pleasure. But literature should touch you on a deep emotional or intellectual level. If it does not—despite its technical perfection—it fails to achieve one of its primary aims.

LO6 Understand the Function of Literary Criticism

Sometimes your personal reactions and knowledge cannot give you enough insight into a literary work. For example, archaic language, references to mythology, historical

literary criticism Descriptions, analyses, interpretations, or evaluations of works of literature by experts in the field.

allusions, and textual inconsistencies can make reading a work difficult. Similarly, an intellectual or philosophical movement such as Darwinism, Marxism, naturalism, structuralism, or feminism may influence a work, and if this is the case, you need some knowledge of the movement before you can interpret the work. In addition, you may not have the background to appreciate the technical or historical dimensions of a work. To increase your understanding, you may choose to read **literary criticism**— books and journal articles written by experts who describe, analyze, interpret, or evaluate a work of literature. Reading literary criticism enables you to expand your knowledge of a particular work and to participate in ongoing critical discussions about literature. In a sense, when you read literary criticism, you become part of a community of scholars who share their ideas and who are connected to one another through their writing.

Literary criticism is written by experts, but this does not mean you must always agree with it. You have to evaluate literary criticism just as you would any new opinion that you encounter. Not all criticism is sound, timely, or responsible (and not all literary criticism is pertinent to your assignment or useful for your purposes). Some critical comments will strike you as plausible; others will seem unfounded or biased.

Quite often, two critics will reach strikingly different conclusions about the quality or significance of the same work or writer, or they will interpret a character, a symbol, or even the entire work quite differently. Although critics may disagree, even conflicting ideas can help you reach your own conclusions about a work. It is up to you to sort out the various opinions and decide which have merit and which do not.

CHECKLIST

EVALUATING LITERARY CRITICISM

- ☐ What is the main point of the book or article you are reading?
- ☐ Does the critic supply enough examples to support his or her conclusions?
- ☐ Does the critic acknowledge and refute the most obvious arguments against his or her position?
- ☐ Does the critic ignore any information in the text that might call his or her conclusions into question?
- ☐ Does the critic present historical information? biographical information? literary information? How does this information shed light on the work or works being discussed?
- ☐ Does the critic hold any beliefs that might interfere with his or her critical judgment?
- ☐ Does the critic slant the facts, or does he or she approach the text critically and objectively?
- ☐ Does the critic support conclusions with references to other sources? Does the critic provide documentation and a list of works cited?
- ☐ Does the critic take into consideration the most important critical books and articles on his or her subject? Are there works that should have been mentioned but were not?
- ☐ Do other critics mention the source you are reading? Do they agree or disagree with its conclusions?
- ☐ Is the critic identified with a particular critical school of thought—deconstruction or Marxism, for example? What perspective does this school of thought provide?
- ☐ Is the critic well known and respected?
- ☐ Is the critical work's publication date of any significance?

Glossary Terms

conventional theme Theme that has occurred frequently over the years—for example, a character's loss of innocence.

genre Category of literature. Fiction, drama, and poetry are the three major genres; subgenres include the novel, the farce, and the lyric poem.

literary canon Group of literary works generally acknowledged by critics and teachers to be the best and most significant to have emerged from our history. Many contemporary teachers and critics have attempted to expand the canon to include works by women and by writers of color.

literary criticism Descriptions, analyses, interpretations, or evaluations of works of literature by experts in the field.

theme Central or dominant idea of a piece of literature, made concrete by the details and emphasis in the work itself.

2

Reading and Writing about Literature

Learning Outcomes

After reading this chapter, you should be able to do the following:

LO1 Read literature

LO2 Write about literature

LO1 Read Literature

Much of the time, readers are passive; they expect the text to give them everything they need, and they do not expect to contribute much to the reading process. In contrast, **active reading** means participating in the reading process: thinking about what you read, asking questions, and challenging ideas. Active reading is excellent preparation for the discussion and writing you will do in college literature classes. And, because it helps you understand and appreciate the works you read, active reading will continue to be of value to you long after your formal classroom study of literature has ended.

PREVIEWING

You begin active reading by **previewing** a work to get a general idea of what to look for later, when you read it more carefully.

Start previewing by observing the work's most obvious physical characteristics. How long is a short story? How many acts and scenes does a play have? Is a poem divided into stanzas? The answers to these and similar questions will help you begin to notice more subtle aspects of the

work's form. For example, previewing may reveal that a contemporary short story is presented entirely in a question-and-answer format, that it is organized as diary entries, or that it is divided into sections by headings. Previewing may identify poems that seem to lack formal structure, such as E. E. Cummings's unconventional "l(a" (p. 351); poems written in traditional forms (such as **sonnets**) or in experimental forms, such as the numbered list of questions and answers in Denise Levertov's "What Were They Like?" (p. 494); or **concrete poems,** such as George Herbert's

---

sonnet Fourteen-line poem, usually a **lyric** in *iambic pentameter*. It has a strict rhyme scheme in one of two forms: the *Italian,* or **Petrarchan sonnet** (an eight-line **octave** rhymed *abba/abba* with a six-line **sestet** rhymed *cdc/cdc* or a variation) and the *English,* or **Shakespearean sonnet** (three quatrains rhymed *abab/cdcd/efef* with a concluding couplet rhymed *gg*).

concrete poem Poem whose typographical appearance on the page reinforces its theme, as with George Herbert's "Easter Wings."

1633 poem "Easter Wings." Your awareness of these and other distinctive features at this point may help you gain insight into a work later on.

Perhaps the most physically distinctive element of a work is its title. Not only can the title give you a general idea of what the work is about, as straightforward titles like "Miss Brill" and "The Cask of Amontillado" do, but it can also isolate (and thus call attention to) a word or phrase that emphasizes an important idea. For example, the title of Amy Tan's short story "Two Kinds" (p. 336) refers to two kinds of daughters—Chinese and American—suggesting the two perspectives that create the story's conflict. A title can also be an allusion to another work. Thus, *The Sound and the Fury*, the title of a novel by William Faulkner, alludes to a speech from Shakespeare's *Macbeth* that reinforces a major theme of the novel. Finally, a title can introduce a symbol that will gain meaning in the course of a work—as the quilt does in Alice Walker's "Everyday Use" (p. 256).

Other physical elements—such as paragraphing, capitalization, italics, and punctuation—can also provide clues about how to read a work. In William Faulkner's short story "Barn Burning" (p. 194), for instance, previewing would help you to notice passages in italic type, indicating the protagonist's thoughts, which occasionally interrupt the narrator's story.

Finally, previewing can enable you to see some of the more obvious stylistic and structural features of a work—the point of view used in a story, how many characters a play has and where it is set, or the repetition of certain words or lines in a poem, for example. Such features may or may not be important; at this stage, your goal is to observe, not to analyze or evaluate.

Previewing is a useful strategy not because it provides answers but because it suggests questions to ask later, as you read more closely. For instance, *why* does Faulkner use italics in "Barn Burning," and *why* does Herbert shape his poem like a pair of wings? Elements such as those described above will gain significance as you read more carefully.

HIGHLIGHTING

When you read a work closely, you will notice additional, more subtle, elements that you may want to examine further. At this point, you should begin **highlighting**—physically marking the text to identify key words or details and to note relationships among ideas.

For example, you might notice that particular words or phrases are repeated, as in Tim O'Brien's short story "The Things They Carried" (p. 232), in which the word *carried* appears again and again. Because this word appears so frequently, and because it appears at key points in the story, it helps to reinforce a key theme: the burdens and responsibilities soldiers carry in wartime. Repeated words and phrases are particularly important in poetry. In Dylan Thomas's "Do not go gentle into that good night" (p. 484), for example, the repetition of two of the poem's nineteen lines four times each enhances the poem's rhythmic, almost monotonous, cadence. As you read, highlight your text to identify such repeated words and phrases. Later, you can consider *why* these elements are repeated.

During the highlighting stage, you might also pay particular attention to **patterns of imagery** that can help you to interpret the work. When highlighting Robert Frost's "Stopping by Woods on a Snowy Evening" (p. 509), for instance, you might identify the related images of silence, cold, and darkness. Later, you can consider their significance.

The following poem by Maya Angelou has been highlighted by a student preparing to write about it. Notice how the student uses highlighting symbols to help him identify stylistic features, key ideas, and patterns of repetition that he plans to examine later. This student identifies repeated words and phases ("brooding"; "It writhes") and places question marks beside the two words ("pend" and "rent") whose meanings he needs to check. He also boxes two phrases—"Old crimes" and "ante-bellum lace"—that he needs to think more about. Finally, he stars what he tentatively identifies as the poem's key ideas. When he rereads the poem, his highlighting will make it easier for him to react to and interpret the writer's ideas.

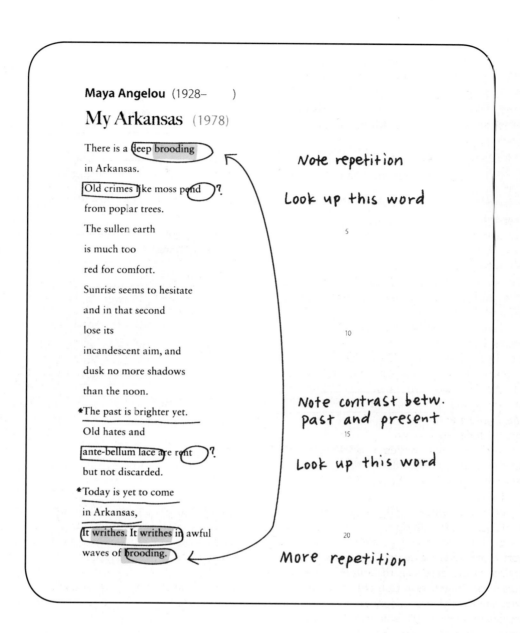

Maya Angelou (1928–　　)

My Arkansas (1978)

There is a deep brooding   *Note repetition*

in Arkansas.

Old crimes like moss pond ?   *Look up this word*

from poplar trees.

The sullen earth   5

is much too

red for comfort.

Sunrise seems to hesitate

and in that second

lose its   10

incandescent aim, and

dusk no more shadows

than the noon.

The past is brighter yet.   *Note contrast betw. past and present*

Old hates and   15

ante-bellum lace are rent ?   *Look up this word*

but not discarded.

Today is yet to come

in Arkansas,

It writhes. It writhes in awful   20

waves of brooding.   *More repetition*

ANNOTATING

At the same time you highlight a text, you should also **annotate** it, recording your reactions in the form of marginal notes. In these notes, you may define new words, identify **allusions** and patterns of language or imagery, summarize key events, list a work's possible themes, suggest a character's motivation, examine the possible significance of a particular symbol, or record questions that occur to you as you read. Ideally, your annotations will help you find ideas to write about.

The paragraph on the next page is from John Updike's 1961 short story "A&P" (p. 131) and was highlighted and annotated by a student in an Introduction to Literature course who was responding to the question, "Why does Sammy really quit his job?"

> **allusion** Reference, often to literature, history, mythology, or the Bible, that is unacknowledged in the text but that the author expects a reader to recognize. An example of allusion in a title is Charles Baxter's "Gryphon" (a mythical beast).

> **[margin note, left]** Action isn't the result of thought. Sammy reacts to the girl's embarrassment.

Lengel sighs and begins to look very patient and old and gray. He's been a friend of my parents for years. "Sammy, you don't want to do this to your Mom and Dad," he tells me. It's true, I don't. But it seems to me that once you begin a gesture it's fatal not to go through with it. I fold the apron, "Sammy" stitched in red on the pocket, and put it on the counter, and drop the bow tie on top of it. The bow tie is theirs, if you've ever wondered. "You'll feel this for the rest of your life," Lengel* says, and I know that's true, too, but remembering how he made the pretty girl blush makes me so scrunchy inside I punch the No Sale tab and the machine whirs "pee-pul" and the drawer splats out. One advantage to this scene taking place in summer, I can follow this up with a clean exit, there's no fumbling around getting your coat and galoshes, I just saunter into the electric eye in my white shirt that my mother ironed the night before, and the door heaves itself open, and outside the sunshine is skating around on the asphalt.

> **[margin note, right]** Need for a clean exit—romantic idea.

> **[margin note, bottom]** Romantic cowboy, but his mother irons his shirt (irony).

Because the instructor had discussed the story in class and given the class a specific assignment, the student's annotations are quite focused. In addition to highlighting important information, she notes her reactions to the story and tries to interpret the main character's actions.

Sometimes, however, you annotate a work before you have decided on a topic. In fact, the process of reading and responding to the text can help you find a topic to write about. If you don't yet have a topic, your annotations are likely to be somewhat unfocused, so you will probably need to annotate again when your paper's direction is clearer.

LO2 Write about Literature

Writing about literature—or about anything else—is an idiosyncratic process during which many activities occur at once: as you write, you think of ideas; as you think of ideas, you clarify the focus of your essay; and as you clarify your focus, you reshape your paragraphs and sentences and refine your word choice. Even though this process may sound disorganized, it has three distinct stages: *planning*, *drafting*, and *revising and editing*.

Planning an Essay

Considering Your Audience

Sometimes you write primarily for yourself—for example, when you write a journal entry. At other times, you write for others. As you write an essay, consider the special requirements of your **audience**. Is your audience your classmates or your instructor? Can you assume your readers are familiar with your paper's topic and with any technical terms you will use, or should you include brief plot summaries or definitions of key terms? If your audience is your instructor, remember that he or she is a representative of a larger academic audience and therefore expects accurate information,

> *"Writing about literature—or about anything else—is an idiosyncratic process during which many activities occur at once...."*

logical arguments, and a certain degree of stylistic fluency—as well as standard English and correct grammar, mechanics, and spelling. In addition, your instructor expects you to support your statements with specific information, to express yourself clearly and unambiguously, and to document your sources. In short, your instructor wants to see how clearly you think and whether you are able to arrange your ideas into a well-organized, coherent essay.

In addition to being a member of a general academic audience, your instructor is also a member of a particular community of scholars—in this case, those who study literature. By writing about literature, you engage in a dialogue with this community. For this reason, you need to follow certain specific **conventions**—procedures that by habitual use have become accepted practice. Many of the conventions that apply specifically to writing about literature—matters of style, format, and the like—are discussed in this book. (The checklist on p. 28 addresses some of these conventions.)

Understanding Your Purpose

Sometimes you write with a single **purpose** in mind. At other times, you may have more than one purpose. In general terms, you may write for any of the following three reasons:

1. *Writing to respond* When you write to **respond**, your goal is to discover and express your reactions to a work. To record your responses, you engage in relatively informal activities, such as brainstorming and journal writing (see p. 18). As you write, you explore your own ideas, forming and re-forming your impressions of the work.

2. *Writing to interpret* When you write to **interpret**, your aim is to explain a work's possible meanings. As you interpret a work of literature, you may summarize, give examples, or compare and contrast the work to other works or to your own experiences. Then, you may go on to analyze the work: as you discuss each of its elements, you put complex statements into your own words, define difficult concepts, and place ideas in context.

3. *Writing to evaluate* When you write to **evaluate**, your purpose is to assess a work's literary merits. You may consider not only its aesthetic appeal but also its ability to retain that appeal over time and across national or cultural boundaries. As you write, you use your own critical sense and the opinions of experts to help you make judgments about the work.

Note When you write a **literary argument**, your purpose is to persuade. See Chapter 5.

convention A practice or device that is so widely used that authors can expect their audiences to accept and comprehend it unquestioningly—for example, the division of plays into acts or the fact that stepmothers in fairy tales are likely to be wicked.

Choosing a Topic

When you write an essay about literature, you develop and support an idea about one or more literary works. Before you begin writing, you should make certain that you understand your assignment. Do you know how much time you have to complete your essay? Are you expected to rely on your own ideas, or are you able to consult outside sources? Is your essay to focus on a specific work, or on a particular element of literature? Do you have to write on an assigned topic, or are you free to choose a topic? About how long should your essay be? Do you understand exactly what the assignment is asking you to do?

Sometimes your assignment limits your options by telling you what you should discuss:

- Write an essay analyzing Thomas Hardy's use of irony in his poem "The Man He Killed."
- Discuss Hawthorne's use of allegory in his short story "Young Goodman Brown."
- Write a short essay explaining Nora's actions at the end of Ibsen's *A Doll House*.

At other times, your instructor may give you few guidelines other than a paper's required length and format. In such situations, when you must choose a topic on your own, you can often find a topic by brainstorming or by writing journal entries. As you engage in these activities, keep in mind that you have many options to choose from:

- You can **explicate** a poem or a passage of a play or short story, doing a close reading and analyzing the text.
- You can **compare two works** of literature. (The Related Works lists that follow some of the readings in this book suggests possible connections.)
- You can **compare two characters** or discuss some trait those characters share.
- You can **trace a common theme**—jealousy, revenge, power, coming of age—in two or more works.
- You can **discuss a common subject**—war, love, nature—in two or more works.
- You can **analyze a single literary element** in one or more works—for instance, plot, point of view, or character development.
- You can **focus on a single aspect** of a literary element, such as the use of flashbacks, the effect of a

shifting narrative perspective, or the role of a minor character.

- You can **apply a critical theory** to a work of literature—for instance, a feminist perspective to Tillie Olsen's "I Stand Here Ironing" (p. 162).
- You can **consider a work's cultural context,** examining connections between an issue treated in a work of literature—for instance, postpartum psychosis in Charlotte Perkins Gilman's "The Yellow Wallpaper" (p. 313)—and that same issue as it is treated in a professional journal or in the popular press.
- You can **examine some aspect of history or biography** and consider its relationship to a literary work—for instance, the influence of World War I on Wilfred Owen's poems.
- You can **explore a problem within a work and propose a possible solution**—for example, consider Montresor's possible motives for killing Fortunato in Edgar Allan Poe's "The Cask of Amontillado" (p. 190) and suggest the most likely one.
- You can **compare fiction and film,** exploring similarities and differences between a literary work and a film version of the work—for example, the different endings in Joyce Carol Oates's short story "Where Are You Going, Where Have You Been?" (p. 325) and *Smooth Talk,* the film version of the story.

Finding Something to Say

Once you have a topic, you have to find something to say about it. The ideas you came up with as you highlighted and annotated will help you formulate a statement that will be the central idea of your essay and will help you find material that can support that statement.

You can use a variety of strategies to find supporting material:

- You can discuss ideas with others—friends, classmates, instructors, parents, and so on.
- You can ask questions.
- You can do research, either in the library or on the Internet.
- You can **freewrite**—that is, write on a topic for a given period of time without pausing to consider style, structure, or content.

Two additional strategies—*brainstorming* and *keeping a journal*—are especially helpful at this stage of the writing process.

Brainstorming   When you **brainstorm,** you record ideas—single words, phrases, or sentences (in the form of statements or questions)—as they occur to you, moving as quickly as possible. Your starting point may be a general assignment, a particular work (or works) of literature, or a specific topic. You can brainstorm at any stage of the writing process—alone or in a group—and you can repeat this activity as often as you like.

A student preparing to write a paper on the relationships between children and parents in four poems brainstormed about each poem. The following excerpt from her notes shows her preliminary reactions to one of the four poems, Adrienne Rich's "A Woman Mourned by Daughters":

Memory: then and now

   Then: leaf, straw, dead insect (= light);
      ignored

   Now: swollen, puffed up, weight (= heavy);
      focus of attention controls their
      movements.

*Kitchen = a "universe"

   Teaspoons, goblets, etc. = concrete
      representations of mother; also =
      obligations, responsibilities (like plants
      and father)
   (weigh on them, keep them under her spell)

Milestones of past: weddings, being fed as

children, "You breathe upon us now"

   PARADOX? (Dead, she breathes, has

   weight, fills house and sky. Alive, she was a

   dead insect, no one paid attention to her.)

Keeping a Journal   You can record ideas in a journal (a notebook, a small notepad, or a computer file)—and, later, you can use these ideas in your paper. In a **journal,** you expand your marginal annotations, recording your responses to works you have read, noting questions, exploring emerging ideas, experimenting with possible paper topics, trying to paraphrase or summarize difficult concepts, or speculating about a work's ambiguities. A journal is the place to take chances, to try out ideas that may initially seem frivolous or irrelevant; here you can think on paper (or on your computer) until connections become clear or ideas crystallize. You can also use your journal as a convenient place to collect your brainstorming notes.

As he prepared to write a paper analyzing the role of Jim, the "gentleman caller" in Tennessee Williams's 1945 play *The Glass Menagerie,* a student explored ideas in the journal entry on the following page.

Seeing Connections

As you review your notes, you try to discover patterns—to see repeated images, similar characters, recurring words and phrases, and interrelated themes or ideas. Identifying these patterns can help you to decide which

When he tells Laura that being disappointed is not the same as being discouraged, and that he's disappointed but not discouraged, Jim reveals his role as a symbol of the power of newness and change—a "bulldozer" that will clear out whatever is in its path, even delicate people like Laura. But the fact that he is disappointed shows Jim's human side. He has run into problems since high school, and these problems have blocked his progress toward a successful future. Working at the warehouse, Jim needs Tom's friendship to remind him of what he used to be (and what he still can be?), and this shows his insecurity. He isn't as sure of himself as he seems to be.

points to make in your paper and what information you will use to support these points.

A student preparing a paper about D. H. Lawrence's short story "The Rocking-Horse Winner" (p. 297) made the following list of related ideas:

Secrets
    Mother can't feel love
    Paul gambles
    Paul gives mother money
    Family lives beyond means
    Paul gets information from horse
Religion
    Gambling becomes like a religion
    They all worship money
    Specific references: "serious as a church";
       "It's as if he had it from heaven"; "secret,
       religious voice"
Luck
    Father is unlucky
    Mother is desperate for luck
    Paul is lucky (ironic)

Deciding on a Thesis

Whenever you are ready, you should try to express the main idea of your emerging essay in a **thesis statement**—

an idea, usually expressed in a single sentence, that the rest of your essay will support. This idea should emerge logically out of your highlighting, annotating, brainstorming notes, journal entries, and lists of related ideas. Eventually, you will write a **thesis-and-support paper**: stating your thesis in your introduction, supporting the thesis in the body paragraphs of your essay, and reinforcing the thesis or summarizing your paper's key points in your conclusion.

An effective thesis statement tells readers what your essay will discuss and how you will approach your material. For this reason, it should be precisely worded, making its point clear to your readers, and it should contain no vague words or imprecise phrases that will make it difficult for readers to follow your discussion.

In addition to being specific, your thesis statement should give your readers an accurate sense of the scope and direction of your essay. It should not make promises that you do not intend to fulfill or include extraneous details that might confuse your readers. If, for example, you are going to write a paper about the dominant image in a poem, your thesis should not imply that you will focus on the poem's setting or tone.

Remember that as you organize your ideas and as you write, you will probably modify and sharpen your thesis. Sometimes you will even begin planning your essay with one thesis in mind and end up with an entirely different one. If this happens, be sure to revise your body paragraphs so that they support your new thesis. If you find that your ideas about your topic are changing, don't be concerned; this is how the writing process works.

> "Whenever you are ready, you should try to express the main idea of your emerging essay in a thesis statement—an idea, usually expressed in a single sentence, that the rest of your essay will support."

Preparing an Outline

Once you have decided on a thesis and have some idea how you will support it, you can begin to plan your essay's structure. At this stage of the writing process, an **outline** can help you to clarify your ideas and show how these ideas relate to one another.

A **scratch outline** is perhaps the most useful kind of outline for a short paper. An informal list of the main points you will discuss in your essay, a scratch outline is more focused than a simple list of related ideas because it presents ideas in the order in which they will be introduced. As its name implies, however, a scratch outline lacks the detail and the degree of organization of a more formal outline. The main purpose of a scratch outline is to give you a sense of the shape and order of your paper and thus enable you to begin writing.

A student writing a short essay on Edwin Arlington Robinson's use of irony in his 1910 poem "Miniver Cheevy" used the following scratch outline as a guide.

<u>Speaker's Attitude</u>
    Ironic
    Cynical
    Critical
<u>Use of Diction</u>
    Formal
    Detached
<u>Use of Allusions</u>
    Thebes
    Camelot
    Priam
    Medici
<u>Use of Repetition</u>
    "Miniver"
    "thought"
<u>Regular Rhyme Scheme</u>

Once this outline was complete, the student was ready to write a first draft.

DRAFTING AN ESSAY

A first draft is a preliminary version of your paper, something to react to and revise. Even before you actually begin drafting your paper, however, you should review the material you have collected. To make sure you are ready to begin drafting, take the following three steps:

1. *Make sure you have collected enough information to support your thesis.* The points you make are only as convincing as the evidence you present to support them. As you read and take notes, you collect supporting examples from the work or works about which you are writing. How many of these examples you need to use in your draft depends on the scope of your thesis. In general, the broader your thesis, the more material you need to support it. For example, if you were supporting the rather narrow thesis that the speech of a certain character in one scene of a play reveals important information about his motivation, only a few examples would be needed. However, if you wanted to support the broader thesis that Nora and Torvald Helmer in Henrik Ibsen's *A Doll House* (p. 562) are trapped in their roles, you would need to present a wide range of examples.

2. *See if the work includes any details that contradict your thesis.* Before you begin writing, test the validity of your thesis by looking for details that contradict it. For example, if you plan to support the thesis that in *A Doll House*, Ibsen makes a strong case for the rights of women, you should look for counterexamples. Can you find subtle hints in the play that suggest women should remain locked in their traditional roles and continue to defer to their fathers and husbands? If so, you will want to modify your thesis accordingly.

3. *Consider whether you need to use outside sources to help you support your thesis.* You could, for example, strengthen the thesis that *A Doll House* challenged contemporary attitudes about marriage by including the information that when the play first opened, Ibsen was convinced by an apprehensive theater manager to write an alternative ending. In this new ending, Ibsen had Nora decide, after she stopped briefly to look in at her sleeping children, that she could not leave her family. Sometimes information from another source can even lead you to change your thesis. For example, after reading *A Doll House*, you might have decided that Ibsen's purpose was to make a strong case for the rights of women. In class, however, you might learn that Ibsen repeatedly said that his play was about the rights of all human beings, not just of women. This information could lead you to a thesis that suggests Torvald is just as trapped in his role as Nora is in hers. Naturally, Ibsen's interpretation of his own work does not invalidate your first judgment, but it does suggest another conclusion that is worth investigating.

After carefully evaluating the completeness, relevance, and validity of your supporting material, you can begin drafting your essay, using your scratch outline as a guide. In this first draft, your focus should be on the body of your essay; this is not the time to worry about constructing the "perfect" introduction and conclusion. (In fact, many writers, knowing that their ideas will change as they write, postpone writing these paragraphs until a later draft, preferring instead to begin simply by stating their thesis.) As you write, remember that your first draft is going to be rough and will probably not be as clear as you would like it to be; still, it will enable you to see your ideas begin to take shape.

REVISING AND EDITING AN ESSAY

Revision

When you **revise**, you literally "re-see" your draft; in many cases, you go on to reorder and rewrite substantial portions of your essay. Before you are satisfied with your essay, you will probably write several drafts—each more closely focused and more coherent than the previous one.

STRATEGIES FOR REVISION

Two strategies can help you to revise your drafts: *peer review* and *a dialogue with your instructor*:

1. **Peer review** is a process in which students assess each other's work-in-progress. This activity may be carried out in informal sessions during which one student comments on another's draft, or it may be a formal process in which students respond to specific questions on a form supplied by the instructor or participate in an electronic exchange. In either case, one student's reactions can help another student revise.

2. **A dialogue with your instructor**—in conference or by email—can give you a sense of how to proceed with your revision. Establishing such an oral or written dialogue can help you learn how to respond critically to your own writing, and your reactions to your instructor's comments on any draft can help you to clarify your essay's goals and write drafts that are increasingly consistent with these goals. (If your instructor is not available, try to schedule a conference with a writing center tutor.)

As you move through successive drafts, the task of revising your essay will be easier if you follow a systematic process. As you read and react to your essay, begin by assessing the effectiveness of the larger elements—for example, your thesis statement and your key supporting ideas—and then move on to examine increasingly smaller elements.

Thesis Statement   First, reconsider your **thesis statement**. Is it carefully and precisely worded? Does it provide a realistic idea of what your essay will cover? Does it make a point that is worth supporting?

> **Vague:**   Many important reasons exist to explain why Margot Macomber's shooting of her husband was probably intentional.

> **Revised:**   Although Hemingway's text states that Margot Macomber "shot at the buffalo," a careful analysis of her relationship with her husband suggests that in fact she intended to kill him.

> **Vague:**   Dickens's characters are a lot like those of Addison and Steele.

> **Revised:**   With their familiar physical and moral traits, Charles Dickens's minor characters are similar to the "characters" created by the eighteenth-century essayists Joseph Addison and Richard Steele for the newspaper the *Spectator*.

Supporting Ideas   Next, assess the appropriateness of your **supporting ideas**, considering whether you present enough support for your thesis and whether all the details you include are relevant to that thesis. Make sure you have supported your key points with specific, concrete examples from the work or works you are discussing, briefly summarizing key events, quoting dialogue or description, and describing characters or settings. Make certain, however, that your own ideas are central to the essay and that you have not substituted plot summary for analysis and interpretation. Your goal is to draw a conclusion about one or more works and to support that conclusion with pertinent details. If an event in a story you are analyzing supports a point you wish to make, include a *brief* summary; then, explain its relevance to the point you are making.

In the following excerpt from a paper on a short story by James Joyce, the first sentence briefly summarizes a key event, and the second sentence explains its significance.

> At the end of James Joyce's "Counterparts," when Farrington returns home after a day of frustration and abuse at work, his reaction is to strike out at his son Tom. This act shows that although he and his son are similarly victimized, Farrington is also the counterpart of his tyrannical boss.

Topic Sentences   Now, turn your attention to the **topic sentences** that present the main ideas of your body paragraphs. Make sure that each topic sentence is clearly worded and that it signals the direction of your discussion.

Be especially careful to avoid abstractions and vague generalities in topic sentences. Also avoid words and phrases like *involves, deals with, concerns,* and *pertains to,* which are likely to make your topic sentences wordy and imprecise.

> **Vague:** One similarity involves the dominance of the men by women. (What is the similarity?)

> **Revised:** In both stories, a man is dominated by a woman.

> **Vague:** There is one reason for the fact that Jay Gatsby remains a mystery. (What is the reason?)

> **Revised:** Because *The Great Gatsby* is narrated by the outsider Nick Carraway, Jay Gatsby himself remains a mystery.

When revising topic sentences that are intended to move readers from one point (or one section of your paper) to another, be sure the relationship between the ideas they link is clear. A topic sentence should include transitions that look back at the previous paragraphs as well as ahead to the paragraph it introduces.

> **Unclear:** Now, the poem's imagery will be discussed.

> **Revised:** <u>Another reason</u> for the poem's effectiveness is its unusual imagery.

> **Unclear:** The sheriff's wife is another interesting character.

> **Revised:** <u>Like her friend Mrs. Hale,</u> the sheriff's wife also has mixed feelings about what Mrs. Wright has done.

Introduction and Conclusion   When you are satisfied with the body of your essay, you can turn your attention to your paper's *introduction* and *conclusion.*

The **introduction** of an essay about literature should identify the works to be discussed and their authors and indicate the emphasis of the discussion to follow. Depending on your purpose and on your paper's topic, you may want to provide some historical background or biographical information or briefly discuss the work in relation to similar works. Like all introductions, the one you write for an essay about literature should create interest in your topic and should include a clear thesis statement.

The following introduction, though acceptable for a first draft, is in need of revision.

> **Draft:** *Revenge*, which is defined as "the chance to retaliate, get satisfaction, take vengeance, or inflict damage or injury in return for an injury, insult, etc.," is a major theme in many of the stories we have read. The stories that will be discussed here deal with a variety of ways to seek revenge. In my essay, I will consider some of these differences.

Although the student clearly identifies her paper's topic, she does not identify the works she will discuss or the particular point she will make about revenge. Her tired opening strategy, a dictionary definition, is not likely to create interest in her topic, and her announcement of her intention in the last sentence is awkward and unnecessary. The following revision is much more effective.

> **Revised:** In Edgar Allan Poe's "The Cask of Amontillado," Montresor vows revenge on Fortunato for an unspecified "insult" (190); in Ring Lardner's "Haircut," Paul, a young retarded man, gets even with a cruel practical joker who has taunted him for years. Both of these stories present characters who seek revenge, and both stories end in murder. However, the murderers' motivations are presented very differently. In "Haircut," the narrator is unaware of the significance of many events, and his ignorance helps to create sympathy for the murderer; in "The Cask of Amontillado," where the narrator is the murderer himself, Montresor's inability to offer a convincing motive turns the reader against him.

In your **conclusion,** you restate your thesis and perhaps sum up your essay's main points; then, you make a graceful exit.

The concluding paragraph that follows is acceptable for a first draft, but it needs further development.

> **Draft:** Although the characters of Montresor and Paul were created by different authors at different times, they do have similar motives and goals. However, they are portrayed very differently.

The following revision reinforces the essay's main point, effectively incorporating a brief quotation from "The Cask of Amontillado" (p. 190):

> **Revised:** What is significant is not whether each murderer's act is justified, but rather how each murderer, and each victim, is portrayed by the narrator. Montresor—driven by a thirst to avenge a "thousand injuries" (190) as well as a final insult—is shown to be sadistic and unrepentant; in "Haircut," it is Jim, the victim, whose sadism and lack of remorse are revealed to the reader.

Sentences and Words Now, focus on the individual sentences and words of your essay. Begin by evaluating your **transitions,** the words and phrases that link sentences and paragraphs. Be sure that every necessary transitional element has been supplied and that each word or phrase you have selected accurately conveys the exact relationship (sequence, contradiction, and so on) between ideas.

When you are satisfied with the clarity and appropriateness of your paper's transitions, consider sentence variety and word choice:

- Be sure you have varied your sentence structure. You will bore your readers if all your sentences begin with the subject ("He.... He...."; "The story.... The story....").
- Make sure that all the words you have selected communicate your ideas accurately and that you have not used vague, inexact diction. For example, saying that a character is *bad* is a lot less helpful than describing him or her as *ruthless, conniving,* or *malicious.*

- Eliminate subjective expressions, such as *I think, in my opinion, I believe, it seems to me,* and *I feel.* These phrases weaken your essay by suggesting that its ideas are "only" your opinions and have no objective validity.

Using and Documenting Sources   Make certain that all references to sources are integrated smoothly into your sentences and that all information that is not your own is documented appropriately. For specific information on documenting sources, see Chapter 7.

Editing and Proofreading

Once you have finished revising, you **edit**—that is, you make certain that your paper's grammar, punctuation, spelling, and mechanics are correct. Always run a spell check, but remember that you still have to **proofread**—look carefully for errors that the spell checker will not identify. These include homophones (*brake* incorrectly used instead of *break*), typos that create correctly spelled words (*work* instead of *word*), and words (such as a technical or foreign term or a writer's name) that may not be in your computer's dictionary. If you use a grammar checker, remember that although grammar programs may identify potential problems—long sentences, for example—they may not be able to determine whether a particular long sentence is grammatically correct (let alone stylistically pleasing). Always keep a style handbook nearby so that you can double-check any problems a spell checker or grammar checker highlights in your writing.

As you edit, pay particular attention to the special conventions of literary essays, some of which are addressed in the checklist below. When your editing is complete, give your essay a descriptive title. Before you print your final copy, be sure that its format conforms to your instructor's requirements.

> *"Always run a spell check, but remember that you still have to proofread—look carefully for errors that the spell checker will not identify."*

EXERCISE: TWO STUDENT PAPERS

The following student papers, "Initiation into Adulthood" and "Hard Choices," were written for the same Introduction to Literature class. Both consider the initiation theme in the same three short stories: James Joyce's "Eveline," John Updike's "A&P" (p. 131), and William Faulkner's "Barn Burning" (p. 194). "Hard Choices" conforms to the conventions of writing about literature discussed in this chapter. "Initiation into Adulthood" does not.

Read the two essays. Then, guided by this chapter's discussion of writing about literature and by the checklists on page 28, identify the features that make "Hard Choices" the more effective essay, and decide where "Initiation into Adulthood" needs further revision. Finally, suggest some possible revisions for "Hard Choices."

Essay 1

Initiation into Adulthood

At an early age, the main focus in a child's life is his parents. But as this child grows, he begins to get his own view of life, which may be, and usually is, different from that of his parents. Sooner or later, there will come a time in this child's life when he must stand up for what he truly believes in. At this point in his life, he can no longer be called a child, and he becomes part of the adult world. In literature, many stories—such as James Joyce's "Eveline," John Updike's "A&P," and William Faulkner's "Barn Burning"—focus on this initiation into adulthood.

James Joyce's "Eveline" is a story that describes a major turning point in a woman's life. At home, Eveline's life was very hard. She was responsible for keeping the house together and caring for the younger children after her mother's death. Unfortunately, the only thoughts that ran through her mind were thoughts of escape, of leaving her unhappy life and beginning a new life of her own.

> Introduction

> Thesis statement

> Discussion of first story: "Eveline"

The night before she was to secretly leave with Frank on a boat to Buenos Ayres, a street organ playing reminded her of her promise to her dying mother to keep the home together as long as she could. She was now forced to make a decision between life with Frank and her present life, which didn't look wholly undesirable now that she was about to leave. The next night, just as she was about to step on the boat, she realized she could not leave. The making of this decision was in essence Eveline's initiation into adulthood.

John Updike's "A&P" presents the brief infatuation of a young boy, Sammy, and the consequences that follow. Sammy's home was a small quiet town a few miles from the shore. He worked in the local A&P as a cashier, a job his father had gotten for him. One day, three girls in nothing but bathing suits walked through the front door. Immediately they caught Sammy's eye, especially the leader, the one he nicknamed "Queenie." After prancing through the store, they eventually came to Sammy's checkout with an unusual purchase. It was not long before they caught the attention of Mr. Lengel, the manager. Unpleasant words were exchanged between the manager and Queenie pertaining to their inappropriate shopping attire. Before the girls left the store, Sammy told Lengel that he quit, hoping they would stop and watch him, their unsuspected hero. But they kept walking, and Sammy was faced with the decision of whether or not to follow through with his gesture. Knowing that it is "fatal" not to follow through with a gesture once you've started, he removed his apron and bow tie and walked out the door, realizing how hard the world was going to be to him hereafter. The making of this decision, to leave the mundane life of the A&P and enter the harsh world, was in essence Sammy's initiation into adulthood.

William Faulkner's "Barn Burning" is a story about Sarty Snopes, an innocent young boy who must make a decision between his family and his honor. Because Abner Snopes, Sarty's father, had so little, he tried to hurt those who had more than he had—often by burning down their barns. These acts forced the Snopes family to move around quite a bit. The last time Snopes burned a barn, he did it without warning his victim, making Sarty realize how cruel and dishonest his father really was. Because of this realization, Sarty decided to leave his family. This decision of Sarty's not to stick to his own blood was his initiation into adulthood.

"Eveline," "A&P," and "Barn Burning" all deal with a youth maturing to adulthood in the process of deciding whether to stay unhappy or to go and seek a better life. Sammy and Sarty leave their unpleasant situations because of something done unfairly. Eveline, on the other hand, decides to stay, remembering a promise to her mother. The decisions of these characters presented in their respective stories are focal points in the literary works and pertain to initiation into adulthood.

> Discussion of second story: "A&P"

> Discussion of third story: "Barn Burning"

> Conclusion

Essay 2

Hard Choices

Introduc-
tion

Although William Faulkner's "Barn Burning" focuses on a young boy in the American South, John Updike's "A&P" on a teenager in a town north of Boston, and James Joyce's "Eveline" on a young woman in Dublin, each of the three stories revolves around a decision the central character must make. These decisions are not easy ones; in all three cases, family loyalty competes with a desire for individual freedom. However, the difficult decision-making process helps each character to mature, and in this sense, all three works are initiation stories.

For Sarty Snopes in "Barn Burning," initiation into adulthood means coming to terms with his father's concept of revenge. Mr. Snopes believes that a person should take revenge himself if he cannot get justice in court. Revenge, for this bitter man, means burning down barns. Sarty knows that his father is doing wrong, but Mr. Snopes drills into his son's mind the idea that "You got to learn to stick to your own blood or you ain't going to have any blood to stick to you" (Faulkner 196), and for a long time Sarty believes him. Naturally, this blood tie makes Sarty's decision to leave his family extremely difficult. In the end, though, Sarty decides to reject his father's values and remain behind when his family moves.

Like Sarty, Sammy must choose between his values and his parents' values (reflected in his job at the supermarket). While Sammy is working in the A&P, he notices how much like sheep people are. Most customers have a routine life that they never consider changing, and Sammy does not want to end up like them. When three seemingly carefree girls enter the store and exhibit nonconformist behavior—such as going against the flow of people in the aisles, not having a grocery list, and wearing bathing suits—Sammy sees them as rebels, and he longs to escape through them from his humdrum world. In the end, he chooses to defend the girls and quit the job his parents helped him to get.

Likewise, Eveline has to decide between a new life with her boyfriend, Frank, in South America and her dull, hard life at home with her father. The new life offers change and freedom, while her life at home is spent working and keeping house. Still, when given the chance to leave, she declines because she promised her dying mother that she would try to keep the family together.

All three characters enter adulthood by making difficult decisions. Sarty realizes that in order to grow, he must repudiate his father's wrongdoings. He stands up for his values and rejects his "blood." Sammy makes the same decision although with less extreme consequences: knowing that he will have to confront his parents, he still defends the three girls and stands up to his boss, rejecting a life of conformity and security. Unlike the other two, Eveline does not reject her parents' values. Instead, she decides to sacrifice her own future by remaining with her father. She keeps her promise to her mother and puts her father before herself because she believes that caring for him is her duty.

Each of the three characters confronts a challenging future. Sarty must support himself and make a new life. Because he is very young and because he has no one to help him, his future is the most uncertain of the three. Unlike Sammy and Eveline, who still have homes, Sarty has only his judgment and his values to guide him. Sammy's future is less bleak but still unpredictable:

Thesis statement

Discussion of first story: "Barn Burning"

Discussion of second story: "A&P"

Discussion of Third story: "Eveline"

Compara-tive analysis of the three stories

Further analysis of the three stories

he knows that the world will be a harder place for him from now on (Updike 134) because now he is a man of principle. Unlike the other two, Eveline knows exactly what her future holds: work, pain, and boredom. She has no fear or uncertainty—but no hope for a better tomorrow either.

"Barn Burning," "A&P," and "Eveline" are stories of initiation in which the main characters struggle with decisions that help them to grow up. All three consider giving up the known for the unknown, challenging their parents and becoming truly themselves, but only Sarty and Sammy actually do so. Both boys defy their parents and thus trade difficult lives for uncertain ones. Eveline, however, decides to stay on in her familiar life, choosing the known—however deadening—over the unknown. Still, all three, in confronting hard choices and deciding to do what their values tell them they must do, experience an initiation into adulthood.

Conclusion

CHECKLIST

USING HIGHLIGHTING SYMBOLS

Here are some other ways to use highlighting:

- ☐ Underline important ideas.
- ☐ Box or circle words, phrases, or images that you want to think more about.
- ☐ Put question marks beside confusing passages, unfamiliar references, or words that need to be defined.
- ☐ Circle related words, ideas, or images and draw lines or arrows to connect them.
- ☐ Number incidents that occur in sequence.
- ☐ Identify a key portion of the text with a vertical line in the margin.
- ☐ Place stars beside particularly important ideas.

 CHECKLIST

CONVENTIONS OF WRITING ABOUT LITERATURE

- ☐ Use present-tense verbs when discussing works of literature: **The character of Mrs. Mallard's husband is not developed. . . .**
- ☐ Use past-tense verbs only when discussing historical events (**Owen's poem conveys the destructiveness of World War I, which at the time the poem was written was considered to be . . .**); when presenting historical or biographical data (**Her first novel, which was published in 1811 when Austen was thirty-six, . . .**); or when identifying events that occurred prior to the time of the story's main action (**Miss Emily is a recluse; since her father's death she has lived alone except for a servant**).
- ☐ Avoid unnecessary plot summary. Your goal is to draw a conclusion about one or more works and to support that conclusion with pertinent details. If a plot detail supports a point you wish to make, a *brief* summary is acceptable. But remember, plot summary is no substitute for analysis.
- ☐ Use literary terms accurately. For example, be careful not to confuse *narrator* or *speaker* with *author*; feelings or opinions expressed by a narrator or character do not necessarily represent those of the author. You should not say, "**In the poem's last stanza, *Frost* expresses his indecision**" when you mean that the poem's *speaker* is indecisive.
- ☐ Italicize titles of novels and plays; place titles of short stories and poems within quotation marks.
- ☐ Refer to authors of literary works by their full names (***Edgar Allan Poe***) in your first reference to them and by their last names (***Poe***) in subsequent references. Never refer to authors by their first names, and never use titles that indicate marital status (***Flannery O'Connor or O'Connor, never Flannery or Miss O'Connor***).

Glossary Terms

allusion Reference, often to literature, history, mythology, or the Bible, that is unacknowledged in the text but that the author expects a reader to recognize.

concrete poem Poem whose typographical appearance on the page reinforces its theme, as with George Herbert's "Easter Wings."

convention A practice or device that is so widely used that authors can expect their audiences to accept and comprehend it unquestioningly—for example, the division of plays into acts or the fact that stepmothers in fairy tales are likely to be wicked.

pattern of imagery Group of related images developed throughout a work. **Synesthesia** is a form of imagery that mixes the experience of the senses (hearing something visual, smelling something audible, and so on): "He smelled the blue fumes of her scent." **Static imagery** freezes the moment to give it the timeless quality of painting or sculpture. **Kinetic imagery** attempts to show motion or change.

sonnet Fourteen-line poem, usually a **lyric** in *iambic pentameter*. It has a strict rhyme scheme in one of two forms: the *Italian*, or **Petrarchan sonnet** (an eight-line **octave** rhymed *abba/abba* with a six-line **sestet** rhymed *cdc/cdc* or a variation) and the *English*, or **Shakespearean sonnet** (three quatrains rhymed *abab/cdcd/efef* with a concluding couplet rhymed *gg*).

3

Writing Special Kinds of Papers

Learning Outcomes

After reading this chapter, you should be able to do the following:

LO1 Write a response paper

LO2 Write a comparison-contrast

LO3 Write an explication

LO4 Write a character analysis

LO5 Write about a work's cultural context

When you write a paper about literature, you have many options (some of these are listed in Chapter 2, pp. 17–18). Often, however, you will be asked to respond to one of five special assignments: to write a *response paper,* to write a *comparison-contrast,* to write an *explication,* to write a *character analysis,* or to write about a work's *cultural context.* The pages that follow offer guidelines for responding to each of these assignments as well as annotated model student papers.

LO1 Write a Response Paper

When you write a **response paper,** you explore and explain your reactions to a short story, poem, or play by focusing on one or more of the work's elements. This kind of assignment can help you to discover how a work's elements contribute to its overall effectiveness, meaning, and impact. For example, a controversial theme in a particular work may elicit a strong response, or a character's actions might amuse, enrage, or enlighten you. Probing your own personal reactions to various elements can help you begin to understand the work as a whole and bring the work to life in a meaningful way. Writing a response paper allows you to shape and reshape your impressions of a story, poem, or play. As you consider how a particular literary work relates to others you have read and to your own experiences, you create your own interpretation of the work.

Eventually, you may develop a response paper into a longer, more formal paper. In fact, a response paper is often assigned as an initial step toward formulating a thesis statement for a more complex assignment. A response paper, sometimes written as a **journal entry** (see p. 18), is generally less formal than other types of writing about literature, and it can incorporate freewriting, brainstorming, and informal outlining techniques. Remember, however, that although your response paper may use an informal—even personal—style and tone, it cannot be based solely on your personal opinions. You must always include examples and details from the work to support your reactions to it.

RESPONDING TO A SHORT STORY

The following student paper is a response to questions about Tim O'Brien's story "The Things They Carried" (p. 232).

> At the end of the story, what has Lieutenant Cross learned? What more do you think he still has to learn?

Note that this paper does not include a works-cited list because the instructor did not require one for this informal assignment.

Brad Russell

Professor Chu

English 102

12 January 2011

Response to Tim O'Brien's "The Things They Carried"

Tim O'Brien's "The Things They Carried" is a coming-of-age story, and Lieutenant Cross, a young soldier, learns the hard way that war can have serious consequences. Throughout the story, the narrator lists all the weapons and tools and mementos that the soldiers carry, and having to read about all the technical specifications of guns, ammunition, and other machinery that the men carry got to be really boring after a while. I actually felt like I was carrying these things as I read about them, but I couldn't figure out why all this information was in the story. I looked forward to the short paragraphs where the narrator describes the men's emotions and the deeper impact of the war.

It didn't occur to me until I read the story a second time that what I was experiencing as a reader is similar to what Lieutenant Cross experiences. He feels the burden of all the monotonous details, and they prevent him from seeing the big picture. Some details show how dull and uneventful war can be, like when the narrator describes "moving on to the next village, then other villages, where it would always be the same" (236). Other details are shocking; for example, the narrator describes in a flat, detached way how Norman Bowker carries around a dead Vietcong soldier's severed thumb that is "dark brown, rubbery to the touch," (236) and how Ted Lavender gets shot and "[t]he cheekbone was gone" (236). I understand that all these details are supposed to show readers the heavy burden war places on the soldiers, but I wanted to get past the details. I wanted to know what these things and events mean to the men, and especially to Lieutenant Cross.

For a long time, Lieutenant Cross relies on the details of his job—and on his memories of home—to help him survive. He is unable to focus on the brutal reality of war, and he slips into daydreams about Martha and the New Jersey shore when he and his men are on long missions, or when they face danger (like when one of them gets picked to search out a tunnel they're about to destroy).

Lieutenant Cross blames himself for Lavender's death because he was unable to focus on his men's safety and on the dangers all around them, but eventually he learns that blaming himself will not make the situation better or bring Ted Lavender back. What he needs to do now is stop focusing on the endless burdens he and his men carry, or on the monotony and pointlessness of the daily struggle to survive, or on "all the emotional baggage of men who might die" (238). Now, he has to focus on being a leader.

Lieutenant Cross finally realizes that war "was another world, where there were no pretty poems or midterm exams, a place where men died because of carelessness and gross stupidity" (239). He learns that he has to "dispense with love; it was not now a factor" (239). But I think Lieutenant Cross still has more to learn. What I learned while reading the story is that we *need* the "pretty poems" and "midterm exams" and especially the "love" that make us human; we need to carry these things with us to survive in times, such as wartime, when these things are absent. Although Lieutenant Cross doesn't realize it by the end of the story, he still must carry these memories with him in order to "[c]arry on" and to get back to a place where people are allowed to dream and love (239).

LO2 Write a Comparison-Contrast

Writing a **comparison-contrast,** one of the most common assignments in literature classes, offers many possibilities. For example, you can compare two stories, two poems, or two plays—or you can cross genres, comparing a story with a poem or a play on a similar topic. Alternatively, you can compare two characters, two works by the same author, a poem to a work of fine art, a conventional print story to a graphic story, or a literary work to a film.

> *"When you write a comparison-contrast, you look first for significant similarities between your two subjects."*

When you write a comparison-contrast, you look first for significant similarities between your two subjects. For example, two characters may have a similar motivation or similar goals or flaws; two stories may have similar settings; two plays may have similar plots; and two poems may have parallels in their use of sound or imagery. Once you have identified the key similarities, you can consider why these similarities are important and what they reveal about the works.

There are two ways to arrange material in a comparison-contrast essay. When you write a **point-by-point comparison,** you discuss one point of similarity at a time, alternating between subjects. When you write a **subject-by-subject comparison,** you approach each subject separately, discussing all your points first for one subject and then for the other. The outlines that follow illustrate how you could use either a point-by-point or a subject-by-subject strategy to support the same thesis statement.

Thesis Statement: Both David Michael Kaplan's "Doe Season" and Alice Munro's "Boys and Girls" focus on a young girl who learns that her gender limits her and comes to accept that such limitations are inevitable.

Point-by-Point Comparison

First point: In both stories, the girls are tomboys who like being with their fathers.

"*Doe Season*": Andy goes hunting with her father.
"*Boys and Girls*": The narrator does farm chores with her father.

Second point: In both stories, the girls struggle against the expectations of others.
"*Doe Season*": Mac and Charlie challenge Andy's right to hunt.
"*Boys and Girls*": Narrator's mother expects her to do household chores.

Third point: In both stories, the girls learn that they are limited by their gender.
"*Doe Season*": Andy shoots the deer but runs away, thinking of her mother.
"*Boys and Girls*": The narrator fails to save the horse and realizes she is "only a girl."

Subject-by-Subject Comparison

First subject: "Doe Season"
First point: Andy is a tomboy who is excited about going hunting with her father.

Second point: Charlie and Mac challenge her right to hunt.
Third point: Through her encounter with the deer, she learns that she is not as brave as she thought she was.

Second subject: "Boys and Girls"
First point: Like Andy, the narrator likes being with her father and is glad not to be in the house with her mother.
Second point: Like Andy, she is criticized by others.
Third point: Like Andy, she learns through her encounter with an animal—in her case, the horse whose life she cannot save—that she is limited by her gender.

COMPARING A SHORT STORY AND A FILM

The following student paper, "Two Cathedrals," is a point-by-point comparison of Raymond Carver's short story "Cathedral" (p. 261) and a film version of the story.

Jason Townsend
Professor Blair
English 102
13 January 2011

Two Cathedrals

In many ways, the movie of Raymond Carver's "Cathedral" is very similar to the short story on which it is based. The plots are the same, the characters are the same, and much of the movie's dialogue is taken directly from the story. Still, there are a number of differences in how the characters' relationships, and other important information, are presented, and these differences help to explain the very different impacts of the endings.

Early in the story, the first-person narrator tells about his wife's first marriage. The subject comes up as part of his explanation of how his wife came to work for Robert, the blind man who is about to visit. But the narrator describes her first marriage in a way that raises questions about the strength of their current marriage, saying, "she was in love with the guy, and he was in love with her, etc." (261). In the movie, on the other hand, the wife's first husband is not mentioned until after Robert's arrival. Here, the first husband is brought up to explain the wife's suicide attempt rather than to explain how she met Robert. As a result, the importance of the wife's first marriage is diminished in the movie, and the possibility of her romantic connection with Robert is heightened.

Thesis statement

First point of contrast: importance of past relationships

This relationship is reinforced in the movie when Robert reminisces about how they sometimes drank Scotch together at the end of the workday—a memory that does not exist in the story.

Throughout the story, the narrator has no name. In addition, he refuses to use the name of his wife's first husband, asking, "why should he have a name? he was the childhood sweetheart, and what more does he want?"(261). The wife is also unnamed. Only Robert has a name and, thus, only he has an identity, a distinctive self. However, in the movie the wife calls the narrator Ed on one occasion; only she herself remains nameless. As a result, any notion that the story is about namelessness or identity is lost. Moreover, the wife's use of her husband's name in the film makes Robert's tendency to call him "Bub" hard to understand. In the story, this familiar usage makes sense, following logically from Robert's statement when they first meet: "'I feel like we've already met'" (262).

For years, Robert and the wife have stayed in touch through an exchange of audio tapes, and these tapes have different purposes in the story and the film. In the story, this exchange of tapes is used to emphasize the relationship, or potential relationship, between Robert and the husband. The narrator concludes his discussion of the tapes with a memory of his wife and himself listening to a tape from Robert. The narrator says they were interrupted just as Robert was about to say what he thought of the husband: "'From what you've said about him, I can only conclude —.'" The husband never listened to Robert's conclusion; he admits, "I'd heard all I wanted to" (262). In the movie, however, the tapes are used to emphasize the relationship between the husband and the wife. In a flashback in which the husband listens alone to a tape his wife had made for Robert, she tells Robert why she will probably remarry. The husband turns the recorder off in anger at the thought that he had been "settled for."

Robert's own marriage is also treated differently in the story and the film. In the story, the wife has two reasons for telling her husband about the death of Robert's wife. First, she uses it in connection with her attempt to make the husband's reaction to Robert a kind of test of their own relationship: "'If you love me,'" she tells him, "'you can do this for me'" (262). Second, she tells the story of Robert's wife dying as Robert held her hand to increase the husband's sympathy for Robert. In the movie, however, Robert himself tells the husband and the wife about his wife's death, and he presents information that does not exist in the story at all. Robert says that at the end his wife "lost her voice" and could only communicate by squeezing his hand, one squeeze for "yes" and two for "no." This discussion of touch as a means of communication, absent in the story, tends to decrease the surprise (and, therefore, diminish the power) of the joined hands that draw the cathedral at the story's end.

Similarly, Robert's touching of the wife's face with his hands on her last day of work is merely described by the narrator of the story. The narrator reports that his wife wrote a poem about this experience that he did not think much of, although he admits, "Maybe I just don't understand poetry" (261). A flashback in the movie actually shows Robert's hands feeling the features of the wife's face while the wife's voice reads the poem aloud. In short, what the reader of the story is encouraged to imagine is actually depicted in visual and audio images for a viewer of the movie. The film's ability to show rather than suggesting is one of the things that makes the endings of the story and the film so different.

Second point of contrast: use of names

Third point of contrast: role of audio tapes

Fourth point of contrast: treatment of Robert's marriage

Fifth point of contrast: showing vs. suggesting

In the story, the narrator seeks out some ballpoint pens and a brown paper shopping bag in preparation for drawing a cathedral as Robert has suggested. When the narrator returns to the living room, he puts the paper bag on the coffee table and sits on the floor. At this point, the narrator says, "The blind man got down from the sofa and sat next to me on the carpet" (267). The description of the two men sitting together on the floor to draw almost suggests boys at play, childlike innocents who are more or less equals. In the movie, however, the husband returns to the dining room and sits in a chair to work at the table. Robert stands behind him, blind but still "looking" over his shoulder, suggesting a teacher and a student or a parent and a child—people who are unequal.

> Sixth point of contrast: staging of drawing scene

The greatest single difference between the story and the movie is the treatment of the actual picture of a cathedral that the men draw. Viewers of the movie see it being drawn and see it in its finished state. When the husband—with his eyes still closed—judges the work he has done with Robert and says, "'It's really something,'" viewers know exactly what the picture looks like. Readers of the story, on the other hand, must imagine the picture and the experience of creating the drawing—an experience that is, the narrator says, "like nothing else in my life up to now" (267). Their own inability to see the finished product makes it possible for readers to understand both the limitations and the power of Robert's blindness.

> Last (and most important) point of contrast: treatment of cathedral picture

Because the story is about blindness and sight, the visual capabilities of the movie are important. However, rather than strengthening the story, the film's visual images are to some extent intrusive. The substitution of an actual visual image of the cathedral for readers' own imagined image changes everything. In fact, those who read the story are more likely to understand Robert's perspective, and to sense what the narrator experienced, than those who see the movie are.

> Conclusion

Works Cited

Carver, Raymond. "Cathedral." *LIT*. Ed. Laurie G. Kirszner and Stephen R. Mandell. Boston: Wadsworth, 2012. 261–67. Print.

The Heinle Original Film Series in Literature: Raymond Carver's "Cathedral." Dir. Bruce R. Schwartz. Wadsworth, 2003. DVD.

LO3 Write an Explication

When you write an **explication** (of a poem, a short story, or a scene in a play), you do a close reading of a work or a portion of a work, carefully analyzing one or more of its elements. For example, you might decide to analyze a story's characters, symbols, or setting; a poem's language, rhyme scheme, meter, or form; or a play's dialogue or staging.

When you organize your material in an explication, you should proceed systematically. If you are focusing on a single element, analyze its importance in one section of the work at a time. If you are analyzing several elements, consider each—plot, setting, point of view, and so on—in turn. You will probably choose to group the less significant elements together in a single paragraph or section of your paper and then devote several paragraphs to one particularly important element, carefully considering how symbols, for example, shed light on the work. For each element you discuss, you will give examples from the work you are explicating, quoting words, phrases, lines, and passages that illustrate each point you are making.

Explicating a Poem

The following student paper, "A Lingering Doubt," is an explication of Robert Frost's poem "The Road Not Taken" (p. 509).

Craff 1

Jeanette Craff
Professor Rosenberg
English 102
14 January 2011

A Lingering Doubt

Sometimes it is tempting to look back on a lifetime of choices and decisions and to think, "What if? What if I had made a different choice? Would my life be better? Worse? More interesting?" In Robert Frost's poem "The Road Not Taken," the speaker does just this: he looks back at a time in his life when he came to a fork in the road and chose one path over another. He tells readers that he "took the one less traveled by, / And that has made all the difference" (lines 19-20). At first, this statement seems to suggest that the speaker is satisfied with the decision he made long ago. However, certain elements in the poem—its structure, its language, and even its title—suggest that the speaker is regretting his decision, not celebrating it.

The title of the poem, "The Road Not Taken," immediately suggests that the speaker is focusing not on the choice he *did* make long ago but on the road he chose *not* to take. The poem's language supports this interpretation. Frost begins his poem with the speaker recalling that "Two roads diverged in a yellow wood" and saying that he is "sorry [he] could not travel both" (1-2). The image Frost uses of the two roads diverging is an obvious metaphor for the choices a person

Introduction

Thesis statement

Overview of poem's language and theme

has to make in the course of a lifetime. As a young man, the speaker was not aware of any major difference between the two roads. He says that he saw one as "just as fair" (6) as the other, and he uses words and phrases such as "equally" (11) and "really about the same" (10). However, in the third stanza of the poem, the older and wiser speaker, looking back on that period of his life, says that he still might take the other road "another day" (13). That the mature speaker still continues to examine a decision he made earlier in life suggests that he may not be completely satisfied with that decision.

A close look at the poem suggests that it is the departures from the expected structure and meter that make its meaning clear. The poem is divided into four stanzas, each made up of five lines. The regular meter of these four stanzas conveys a sense of tranquillity and certainty. The regularity of the poem's rhyme scheme (a, b, a, a, b) also contributes to the poem's natural fluidity. This fluidity is evident, for example, in the first stanza:

> Two roads diverged in a yellow wood,
>
> And sorry I could not travel both
>
> And be one traveler, long I stood
>
> And looked down one as far as I could
>
> To where it bent in the undergrowth; (1-5)

Here, the end rhyme of lines 1, 3, and 4 and of lines 2 and 5, as well as the even line lengths (each line contains nine syllables), make the poem flow smoothly.

However, the poem does not maintain this fluidity. In other stanzas, lines range from eight to ten syllables, and the important final stanza ends with a line that is an awkward metrical departure from the rest of the poem:

> I shall be telling this with a sigh
>
> Somewhere ages and ages hence:
>
> Two roads diverged in a wood, and I—
>
> I took the one less traveled by, And
>
> that has made all the difference. (16-20)

In this stanza, line 20 has nine syllables as lines 16 and 18 do, but unlike them, it also has an irregular meter ("And that has made all the difference"), which forces readers to hesitate on the word "all" before landing on "difference." This hesitation, coupled with the hesitation signaled by the dash that ends line 18, suggests the speaker's doubts about his decision. When the speaker was young, he did not notice any significant difference between the two roads, or the two life choices, presented to him. Now, looking back, he believes that there was a difference, and he may be lamenting the fact that he will never know where life would have taken him had he chosen differently.

Departure from expected meter is not the only strategy Frost uses to convey a sense of hesitation and an air of regret. Frost's choice of words also plays an important part in helping readers understand the poem's theme. In the first stanza, for example, the speaker thinks back to the period of his life in which he had to choose between two separate paths, and he says that he was "sorry [he] could not travel both" (2). The word "sorry" helps to establish the tone of regret that pervades the poem.

Analysis of poem's structure and meter

Further analysis of poem's structure and meter

Analysis of poem's language

In the second stanza, Frost begins to use words and phrases to convey indecision and doubt in the speaker's voice. The speaker attempts to pacify himself by saying that the road he chose had "perhaps the better claim" (7), but then he is quick to say that the passage of time has worn both roads "really about the same" (10). The words "perhaps" and "really" suggest indecision, and Frost's choice of these words helps to convey the doubt in the speaker's mind.

The speaker's sense of regret deepens in the third stanza as he continues to think back on his decision. When the speaker says, "Oh, I kept the first for another day!" (13), the word "Oh" expresses his regret. The exclamation point at the end of the statement helps reinforce the finality of his decision. When the speaker continues, "Yet knowing how way leads on to way, / I doubted if I should ever come back" (14-15), the word "Yet" is filled with uncertainty.

In the poem's final stanza, the speaker suddenly leaves his thoughts of the past and speaks in the future tense: "I shall be telling this [story] with a sigh" (16). Frost's use of the word "sigh" here is very revealing because it connotes resignation or regret. The speaker concludes, "Two roads diverged in a wood, and I— / I took the one less traveled by, / And that has made all the difference" (18-20). Both the dash and the repetition of the word "I" convey hesitation and thus communicate his lingering doubts over the decision he made long ago.

Although this doubt is evident throughout the poem, "The Road Not Taken" has frequently been interpreted as optimistic because of the speaker's final statement that the choice he made "has made all the difference" (20). However, "made all the difference" can be interpreted as neutral (or even negative) as well as positive, and so the speaker's statement at the end of the poem may actually be a statement of regret, not celebration. The "difference" mentioned in the final line has left a doubt in the speaker's mind, and, as Frost suggests in the title of his poem, the speaker is left thinking about the road he did not take—and will never be able to take.

Conclusion

Work Cited

Frost, Robert. "The Road Not Taken." *LIT.* Ed. Laurie G. Kirszner and Stephen R. Mandell. Boston: Wadsworth, 2012. 509. Print.

Note For a model student paper that explicates a short story, see "And Again She Makes the Journey: Character and Act in Eudora Welty's 'A Worn Path'" (p. 66).

LO4 Write a Character Analysis

When you write a **character analysis** of a character in a short story or play, you can focus on a major or a minor character, examining the character's language, behavior, background, interaction with other characters, and reaction to his or her environment. Everything you are told about a character—and everything you can reasonably infer about him or her from words, actions, or appearance—can help you to understand the character. In your analysis, you can focus on the influences that shaped the character, the character's effect on others, how the character changes during the course of the story or play, or what motivates him or her to act (or not to act).

ANALYZING A CHARACTER IN A PLAY

The following student paper, "Linda Loman: Breaking the Mold," analyzes a character in Arthur Miller's play *Death of a Salesman* (p. 605).

Dube 1

Caroline Dube

Professor Nelson

English 1302

15 January 2011

Linda Loman: Breaking the Mold

In many ways, Linda Loman appears to play the part of the stereotypical dutiful and loving wife in Arthur Miller's *Death of a Salesman*. She eagerly greets her husband, ignores his shortcomings, and maintains an upbeat attitude, all while managing the bills, waxing the floors, and mending the clothes. Her kindness and infinite patience seem to establish her as a foil for Willy, with his turbulent temperament. In addition, most of her actions seem to be only reactions to the other characters in the play. However, a closer look at Linda reveals a more complex woman: a fully developed character with dreams, insights, and flashes of defiance.

> **Thesis statement**

Unlike stock characters, whose motivations seem transparent and obvious, Linda has dreams that are both complex and realistically human. The stage directions that introduce Linda describe her as sharing Willy's "turbulent longings" but lacking the temperament to pursue them (605). It seems she has applied the wisdom she shares with Willy, that "life is a casting off," to her own cast-away dreams (607). Linda's hopes seem more realistic than Willy's. She wants Biff to settle down, the mortgage to be paid off, and the members of her family to coexist happily. These modest aspirations are the product of Linda's long experience. The fact that Linda does not pursue unrealistic goals, as Willy does, does not make her a flat character (or even a less interesting one); instead, her weaknesses give her character a degree of depth and human realism.

> **Linda's hopes and dreams**

At times, Linda takes on the role of family peacemaker—a role we would expect her to play consistently throughout the play if she were simply a stock character. But Linda breaks out of the

> **Linda's actions**

obedient wife mode on several occasions. When Willy insists that she stop mending her stockings, Linda quietly puts them into her pocket to resume her mending later. When Biff and Happy show they are ashamed of their father, Linda fiercely lashes out at them in his defense, calling Happy a "philandering bum" and threatening to kick Biff out of the house for good (620). Although at first she cannot bring herself to remove the rubber pipe that Willy used to commit suicide, Linda says she had finally decided to destroy the pipe when Biff removed it. She does not always have an opportunity to follow through on her threats, but Linda demonstrates clearly that she will not always follow orders—especially when she is protecting Willy.

Linda seems to be the cheerful voice of the family, but beneath the surface, she is keenly aware of the ongoing problems. She knows that Charley has been giving money to Willy every week, but she says nothing for fear of embarrassing Willy. She senses Willy's suicidal tendencies and even finds physical evidence of his plans. Linda is the first to raise doubts about Biff's plans to ask Mr. Oliver for money, suggesting that he may not remember Biff. Above all, Linda understands human nature and how the minds of those around her work. She gives an honest description of her husband and his situation:

> I don't say he's a great man. Willy Loman never made a lot of money. His name was never in the paper. He's not the finest character that ever lived. But he's a human being, and a terrible thing is happening to him. So attention must be paid. (619)

Linda sees past her sons' exaggerated lies and is not afraid to criticize them for their selfish choices. She pretends to be unaware of their shortcomings, but her feigned obliviousness is simply another layer in her multifaceted personality.

Linda appears to be the steadiest character in the play, providing stability for the other characters, but her constant brushing aside of problems actually makes her the most responsible for the ultimate tragedy of the play. She lies to Willy in order to soothe him, telling him he has "too much on the ball to worry about" (607) and is "the handsomest man in the world" (614). In the process, she allows him to continue believing in the unattainable dreams that ultimately lead him to self-destruct. She also makes exceptions for her sons, suggesting Willy can simply talk to Biff's teacher to change his grade and encouraging Biff's business plans even when she knows he will not succeed. As a result, failure hits Biff hard because he has not been forced to think realistically.

In the end, Linda goes beyond the stereotypical boundaries of her role as ever-supportive wife and mother. There are many layers to her character: beneath her simple goals of owning her home and living happily with her family lie years of disappointments and failed dreams. Hidden beneath her eagerness to please is her willingness to defy orders to defend her husband. And, although she seems not to notice what is going on, she is perceptive about the family's problems long before others show awareness. Her actions clearly show that she is more than a minor supporting character. Linda is deeply involved in the actions and impulses of the other characters in the play. As a fully developed character, she has complex motivations and human qualities (including faults) that set her apart from stock characters. As her son Happy notes, "They broke the mold when they made her" (622).

Linda's awareness of family problems

Linda's failure to confront family problems

Conclusion

Work Cited

Miller, Arthur. *Death of a Salesman. LIT.* Ed. Laurie G. Kirszner and Stephen R. Mandell. Boston: Wadsworth, 2012. 605–43. Print.

Note For a model student paper analyzing a major character in a short story, see "And Again She Makes the Journey: Character and Act in Eudora Welty's 'A Worn Path'" (p. 66).

LO5 Write about a Work's Cultural Context

When you explore the **cultural context** of a short story, poem, or play, you set the work in a particular time and place. Acknowledging that literary works do not exist in a vacuum, you consider factors such as the characters' social class and cultural or racial background as well as specific events that occurred at the time in which the story is set or written. You can also consider practices and situations that were characteristic of the time—for example, the wife's subservient role in Arthur Miller's *Death of a Salesman* (p. 605) or racial discrimination in Richard Wright's "Big Black Good Man" (p. 184).

> "When you explore the cultural context of a short story, poem, or play, you set the work in a particular time and place."

Note For additional possibilities for writing about a work's cultural context, see the **cultural context** paragraphs that accompany many of the selections in this text.

When you write your paper, you examine the connections between the work's cultural setting and the work itself, considering how particular situations and events influence the characters' actions. For example, you might see that a character in a story or play is limited—or inspired to act—by his or her race or class or gender; or by a social movement, such as feminism; or a particular event, such as a war. To set the work in context, you will probably need to do some research—perhaps reading contemporary newspapers, diaries, and letters as well as current critical interpretations of the cultural period on which you are focusing. You might even want to interview someone who lived through the events that influenced the work—for example, someone who lived through the Great Depression, which has a great impact on the lives of the characters in "I Stand Here Ironing" (p. 162).

It usually makes sense to begin your paper with an overview to help orient readers who are not familiar with the work's background. You might also **explicate** the work (see p. 35), systematically exploring specific parallels between the historical setting and the work. Alternatively, you might focus on one character in a story or play, examining how that character is shaped by the events or conventions of a particular cultural time—for example, how Ab Snopes in William Faulkner's "Barn Burning" (p. 194) has been affected by the Civil War—and by his inferior station in life.

WRITING ABOUT A POEM'S CULTURAL CONTEXT

The following student paper, "Dreaming of Home," sets Louise Erdrich's poem "Indian Boarding School: The Runaways" (p. 507) in the context of the events that inspired it.

Matt Monteleone

Professor Kennedy

Composition 101

16 January 2011

Dreaming of Home

Louise Erdrich's poem "Indian Boarding School: The Runaways" describes the experiences of Native American children who have been sent to a US-government-sponsored boarding school. Although the experiences themselves are traumatic and heart wrenching, the full impact of the poem comes only with an understanding of the United States government's motivation for creating these schools and of their treatment of the Native American children who lived there during the late nineteenth and early twentieth centuries. With this background, Erdrich's work becomes not only a moving description of the painful experience of Native American children at federal boarding schools, but also a political statement about the treatment of Native Americans in the United States—and, perhaps, a statement about the pain of forced cultural assimilation.

"Indian Boarding School: The Runaways" relates the experience of Indian children struggling to maintain their cultural identities and preserve their cherished memories of home despite a series of efforts to purge them of their Indian heritage. Erdrich uses haunting language to explain that, for these children, the world they once knew has changed to such an extent that it exists only in their imaginations. Therefore, the children can escape to their home only when they go to sleep, and dream. In the first stanza, the narrator conveys her longing when she says, "Home's the place we head for in our sleep. / Boxcars stumbling north in dreams / don't wait for us. We catch them on the run" (lines 1-3). At night, the children dream of making their way home. In the daytime, they are "cold in regulation clothes" (11), forced to wear "dresses, long green ones" (17) and to engage in "shameful" manual labor (19). To fight the assimilation being forced upon them, the children have only their memories.

By relating the experiences of these "runaways" and their dreams of home, Erdrich recreates the emotional experience of Native American children sent to the US government's boarding schools. The history of these Indian schools further explains the experience described in the poem and sheds light on the consequences of America's policy of forced assimilation.

During the late 1800s and early 1900s, the United States government sponsored a variety of initiatives aimed at assimilating Native Americans into white culture. Although some government officials genuinely believed that assimilation was the best way for Native Americans to live better, happier lives, this policy was grounded in the assumption that white culture is superior to Indian culture. As a result, government officials used a variety of methods to encourage assimilation, and the establishment of the non-reservation boarding school was one of them. According to the *Modern American Poetry* Web site, the Carlisle Indian Industrial School, established in 1879 with 139 students from the Rosebud and Pine Ridge nations, was one of the first of these schools. A description of the Carlisle Indian Industrial School reveals that Erdrich's poem is rooted in actual events. As Tim Alan Garrison explains, this school was "designed to erase the child's tribal influence and inculcate Anglo-American mores."

Introduction

Thesis statement

Explication of poem's theme

Transitional paragraph

Background: Rationalization for US government's Indian boarding schools

According to the Cumberland County Historical Society in Pennsylvania, where the Carlisle Industrial School was located, in 1879 General Richard Henry Pratt received permission from the United States government to use a former military base as the site of the first Indian boarding school. Although the school closed in 1918, Carlisle served as a model for many of the other Indian boarding schools around the United States. Consequently, an examination of its policies and practices will explain how most Indian boarding schools operated.

After receiving permission from the government, Pratt traveled to the Rosebud and Pine Ridge reservations to recruit students. According to the *Carlisle Indian Industrial School,* the chief of the Rosebud reservation, although initially reluctant, eventually agreed to send some children from the reservation to the school. Pratt soon convinced other Indian nations, including the Cheyenne, Kiowa, and Lakota, to send their children to the school as well. At the Carlisle school, the teachers used a variety of methods to "civilize" the Native American students.

For example, as the *Modern American Poetry* Web site explains, students were given new names, their hair was cut, and they were forced to speak English instead of their tribal languages. (The *Carlisle Indian Industrial School* notes that members of the Lakota nation cut hair to symbolize mourning, so this practice was particularly upsetting to the Lakota children.) Figure 1 shows a group of Indian children at the Carlisle school. Like the girls being forced to wear long green dresses in Erdrich's poem, these Indian students are dressed in school uniforms, not in their native clothing.

Fig. 1. Apache children four months after arriving at the Carlisle Indian Industrial School in Pennsylvania; Owen Lindauer, "Archaeology of the Phoenix Indian School," *Archaeology* (Archaeological Inst. of Amer., 27 Mar. 1998; Web; 13 Jan. 2011).

Parents did not always send their children to Carlisle willingly. The *Carlisle Indian Industrial School* explains that when Geronimo, chief of the Apache nation, was arrested, Pratt traveled to Fort Mario prison, where the Apache children were being held. Pratt then picked sixty-two of the children to be sent to Carlisle, despite pleas from their parents. In an effort to prevent them from leaving, several of the parents hid the children, but Pratt eventually found them, and the children were sent to the school.

Erdrich closes her poem by explaining how the children try to remember their cultural heritage even as they are being forced to adopt the customs of white America:

> Our brushes cut the stone in watered arcs
>
> and in the soak frail outlines shiver clear
>
> a moment, things us kids pressed on the dark
>
> face before it hardened, pale, remembering
>
> delicate old injuries, the spines of names and leaves. (20-24)

The history of the Indian boarding schools, and how they worked to rid children of their Native American identities, clearly informs this poem. In this sense, Erdrich's work is not only literary; it is also political. By invoking an emotional response in her readers, Erdrich is able to expose a dark side of United States history and its treatment of Native Americans.

> Conclusion (poem set in cultural context)

Works Cited

"Carlisle Indian Industrial School." *Cumberland County Historical Society*. PaDotNet, n.d. Web. 13 Jan. 2011

Erdrich, Louise. "Indian Boarding School: The Runaways." *LIT*. Ed. Laurie G. Kirszner and Stephen R. Mandell. Boston: Wadsworth, 2012. 507. Print.

Garrison, Tim Alan. "Indian Removal and Response." *Americans at War*. Ed. John P. Resch. Vol. 2: 1816–1900. Detroit: Macmillan Reference USA, 2005. N. pag. *CourseReader: Introduction to Literature*. Web. 13 Jan. 2011.

Landis, Barbara. "History." *Carlisle Indian Industrial School*. N.p., 1996. Web. 10 Jan. 2010.

Nelson, Cary, comp. "About Indian Boarding Schools: Key Issues and Challenges." *Modern American Poetry*. Dept. of English, U of Illinois, Urbana-Champaign, 2002. Web. 13 Jan. 2011.

CHECKLISTS

WRITING A RESPONSE PAPER

- ☐ Have you focused your responses in an interesting and meaningful way?
- ☐ Have you clearly explained how one or more of the work's elements relate to the overall effectiveness of the work?
- ☐ If your response paper analyzes more than one literary element, have you paid enough attention to each element in your response?
- ☐ Do you use examples and details—including paraphrases and quotations—from the work to illustrate your points and to support your reactions?
- ☐ Have you followed your instructor's format and documentation guidelines?

WRITING A COMPARISON-CONTRAST

- ☐ Have you chosen two subjects that have significant similarities?
- ☐ Does your thesis statement identify the two subjects you are comparing and tell why they are alike (and perhaps also briefly acknowledge their differences)?
- ☐ Does your paper's structure follow either a point-by-point or a subject-by-subject pattern?
- ☐ Do each of your topic sentences identify the subject you are discussing and the point you are focusing on in the paragraph?
- ☐ Do transitional words and phrases clearly lead readers from subject to subject and from point to point?
- ☐ Have you followed your instructor's format and documentation guidelines?

WRITING AN EXPLICATION

- ☐ Is the work you have chosen sufficiently rich to support an explication?
- ☐ Do topic sentences make clear which element (or elements) you are focusing on in each paragraph?
- ☐ Do you use quotations from the work to illustrate your points?
- ☐ Does your thesis state the central point about the work that your explication supports?
- ☐ Have you followed your instructor's format and documentation guidelines?

WRITING A CHARACTER ANALYSIS

- ☐ Have you chosen a character who is interesting enough to serve as the focus of your paper?
- ☐ Have you considered the character's words, actions, appearance, and interactions with others?
- ☐ Have you considered how and why the character changes—or why he or she fails to change?
- ☐ Have you considered how the work would be different if the character had made different choices?
- ☐ Have you considered how the work would be different without the character?
- ☐ Have you considered what motivates the character to act (or not to act)?
- ☐ Have you followed your instructor's format and documentation guidelines?

WRITING ABOUT A WORK'S CULTURAL CONTEXT

- ☐ Is a particular figure or event an important influence on the work?
- ☐ Is a cultural movement an important influence on the work?
- ☐ Do you summarize and explain the relevant cultural background?
- ☐ Do you clearly explain the relationship between the cultural background and the literary work?
- ☐ Do you use examples and quotations from the literary work to illustrate specific parallels between the work of literature and its cultural context?
- ☐ Have you followed your instructor's format and documentation guidelines?

4

Thinking Critically about Your Writing

Learning Outcomes

After reading this chapter, you should be able to do the following:

LO1 Distinguish fact from opinion

LO2 Evaluate supporting evidence

LO3 Detect bias in your writing

LO4 Understand logic

As you write about literature, you should carefully assess the strength of the ideas you present to readers. This is especially true in **literary arguments**, essays in which you take a stand on a debatable topic and try to convince readers to accept your position (see Chapter 5). If you learn to **think critically** about your writing, you will be able to distinguish fact from opinion, evaluate the usefulness and appropriateness of your supporting evidence, and keep any biases you have out of your writing. Then, guided by the basic principles of inductive and deductive reasoning, you will be able to structure your literary argument in a way that will encourage readers to accept (or at least acknowledge) the strengths of your ideas.

LO1 Distinguish Fact from Opinion

A **fact** is a verifiable statement that something is true or that something occurred. An **opinion** is a personal judgment or belief that can never be substantiated beyond any doubt and is, therefore, debatable.

> Fact: Langston Hughes mentions four rivers in his poem "The Negro Speaks of Rivers."

Opinion: Rivers have symbolic significance in Langston Hughes's poem "The Negro Speaks of Rivers."

An opinion may be *unsupported* or *supported*.

Unsupported Opinion: Rivers have symbolic significance in Langston Hughes's poem "The Negro Speaks of Rivers."

Supported Opinion: Rivers have symbolic significance in Langston Hughes's poem "The Negro Speaks of Rivers." In the poem, the speaker mentions four rivers—the Euphrates, the Congo, the Nile, and the Mississippi. According to the speaker, these rivers are as "ancient as the world and as old as the flow of human blood in human veins" (line 2). Through their associations with the black experience, these particular rivers are linked not only to the speaker's African roots but also to the racial situation in America at the time the poem was written.

As the above examples show, supported opinion is more convincing than unsupported opinion.

SUPPORTING YOUR OPINIONS

Your opinions can be supported with **examples, quotations,** or **expert opinion.**

Examples:

In the play *The Glass Menagerie,* Jim's focus on the future challenges Amanda's unrealistic romantic dreams of the past. For example, when Jim comes to dinner, she dreams of entertaining him in the old Southern tradition, but he talks enthusiastically of the promise the future holds.

Quotations:

Although Gertrude is queen of Denmark, she is also a devoted mother. In her efforts to console her son, she speaks tenderly: "Good Hamlet, cast thy knighted color off" (1.2.68). She also conveys her wisdom about life: "Thou know'st 'tis common,—all that live must die, / Passing through nature to eternity" (1.2.72-73).

Expert Opinion (From Literary Criticism):

Throughout the short story "The Yellow Wallpaper," a number of clues suggest that the narrator has lost her hold on reality. According to Sandra Gilbert and Susan Gubar in *Madwoman in the Attic: The Woman Writer and the Nineteenth-Century Literary Imagination,* the extent of the narrator's dislike for the wallpaper should serve as an early warning that she is not responding well to her treatment and that she may in fact be losing her mind (464).

LO2 Evaluate Supporting Evidence

The examples, quotations, and opinions of literary critics that you use to support your statements constitute **evidence.** The more **reliable** your supporting evidence, the more willing your readers will be to accept a statement. Remember, though, that to be reliable the evidence you use must be *accurate, sufficient, representative,* and *relevant.*

For your evidence to be **accurate,** it must come from a trustworthy source. Such a source quotes *exactly* and does not present information out of context. It also presents examples, quotations, and expert opinion fairly, drawing them from other reliable sources.

For your evidence to be **sufficient,** you must present an adequate amount of evidence. It is not enough, for instance, to cite just one example from a Joyce Carol Oates short story in an attempt to demonstrate that her experiments with literary form and subject matter give her work universal appeal. Moreover, the opinions of a single literary critic, no matter how reputable, are not enough to support this position.

For your evidence to be **representative,** it must reflect a range of sources and viewpoints. You should not choose evidence that simply supports your thesis and ignore evidence that does not. For example, if you are making the point that the structure of Emily Dickinson's poems changed over the course of her career, you cannot disregard compelling evidence that, in fact, her poetic structure remained consistent over the years.

Finally, for your evidence to be **relevant**, it must apply to the case being discussed. For example, you cannot support the assertion that Arthur Miller's *Death of a Salesman* critiques post–World War II American society by citing examples from Miller's *The Crucible*.

LO3 Detect Bias in Your Writing

A **bias** is an opinion, usually unfavorable, based on preconceived ideas rather than on evidence. As a critical thinker, you should be aware that your biases can sometimes lead you to see just what you want to see and to select evidence that is consistent with these biases.

DETECTING BIAS IN YOUR WRITING

When you write, be on the lookout for the following kinds of biases:

- **Slanted language:** Avoid slanted language—language that is inflammatory or confrontational. For example, do not say that a literary critic's article is stupid or that a character in a short story is immoral. Instead, use language that clearly and accurately conveys your ideas.

- **Biased tone:** Avoid using a tone that communicates bias toward your subject (for example, anger or sarcasm).

- **Stereotypes:** Avoid statements that perpetuate stereotypes. For example, be careful not to make unwarranted assumptions about gender roles or about a particular groups' attributes or shortcomings and then criticize characters on the basis of these generalizations. For example, saying that Andy in "Doe Season" gets what she deserves because a deer hunt is no place for girls stereotypes the character and reveals gender bias.

- **Preconceived ideas:** Don't let your own beliefs or attitudes prevent you from fairly evaluating a work of literature. For example, you may believe strongly that husbands and wives should be faithful to each other, but you should not let this belief prevent you from appreciating the literary strengths of Kate Chopin's "The Storm," a short story in which two characters commit adultery, apparently with no consequences.

LO4 Understand Logic

All argumentative essays, including literary arguments, rely on **logic**—inductive and deductive reasoning—to reach conclusions in a systematic way. If you understand the basic principles of inductive and deductive reasoning, you will be able to write clearer, more convincing essays.

INDUCTIVE REASONING

Inductive reasoning is a process that moves from specific facts, observations, or experiences to a general conclusion. You use inductive reasoning in your writing when you want to lead readers from a series of specific observations to a general conclusion. You can see how inductive reasoning operates by studying the following list of statements about John Updike's short story "A&P":

- Sammy, the main character in "A&P," is nineteen and works as a cashier in a supermarket in a small New England town.
- Sammy sees the A&P's customers as sheep, with no individuality.
- Sammy's fellow workers include Stokesie, a married twenty-two-year-old with two children, and Lengel, the store manager.
- Stokesie and Lengel lead boring, predictable lives.
- On the day the story takes place, three girls in bathing suits walk into the store and change Sammy's life.
- Sammy fantasizes about the girls' lives and imagines what a party at one girl's home would be like.
- When Lengel scolds the girls for dressing inappropriately, Sammy abruptly quits his job.
- At the end of the story, Sammy realizes that although some people think he was foolish to quit his job, he did the right thing.

After reading the statements above, you can use inductive reasoning to reach a general conclusion about the theme of Updike's story: that someone who wants to escape a confining life must sometimes make a break with his community's values.

No matter how much evidence you present, an inductive conclusion is never certain, only probable. You arrive at an inductive conclusion by making an **inference**, a statement about the unknown based on the known. In order to bridge the gap that exists between your specific observations and your general conclusion, you have to make an **inductive leap.** If you have presented enough specific evidence, this gap will be relatively small and your readers will accept your conclusion. If the gap is too wide, your readers will accuse you of making a **hasty generalization**—a conclusion based on too little evidence.

DEDUCTIVE REASONING

Deductive reasoning is a process that moves from a general statement believed to be true or self-evident (so obvious that it needs no proof) to a specific conclusion. Writers use deductive reasoning when they think their audience is more likely to be influenced by logic than by evidence. The process of deduction has traditionally been illustrated by a **syllogism**, a three-part set of statements or propositions that includes a *major premise*, a *minor premise*, and a *conclusion*.

> **Major Premise:** All tragic heroes have tragic flaws.
> **Minor Premise:** Hamlet is a tragic hero.
> **Conclusion:** Therefore, Hamlet has a tragic flaw.

> *"A syllogism is valid when its conclusion logically follows from its premises. A syllogism is true when the information it contains is consistent with the facts."*

The **major premise** of a syllogism makes a general statement that the writer believes to be true or self-evident. The **minor premise** presents a specific example of the belief that is stated in the major premise. If the reasoning is sound, the **conclusion** should follow from the two premises. (Note that the conclusion should introduce no terms that have not already appeared in the major and minor premises.) The advantage of a deductive argument is that if readers accept the premises, they usually grant the conclusion.

A syllogism is **valid** when its conclusion logically follows from its premises. A syllogism is **true** when the information it contains is consistent with the facts. To be **sound**, a syllogism must be *both* valid and true. However, a syllogism can be valid without being true or true without being valid. The following syllogism, for example, is valid but not true.

> **Major Premise:** All poems contain rhymed lines.
> **Minor Premise:** Walt Whitman's "Had I the Choice" is a poem.
> **Conclusion:** Therefore, Walt Whitman's "Had I the Choice" contains rhymed lines.

This syllogism is valid. In the major premise, the phrase *all poems* establishes that the entire class *poems* contains rhymed lines. After Walt Whitman's "Had I the Choice" is identified as a poem, the conclusion that it contains rhymed lines logically follows. However, Whitman's poem, like many others, is unrhymed. Because the major premise of this syllogism is not true, no conclusion based on it can be true. For this reason, even though the logic of the syllogism is correct, its conclusion is not.

TOULMIN LOGIC

Stephen Toulmin, a philosopher and rhetorician, has formulated another way to understand logical thinking. According to Toulmin, the traditional syllogism, while useful for identifying flaws in logic, is not useful for analyzing arguments that occur in the real world. To address this shortcoming, Toulmin divides arguments into three parts: the *claim*, the *grounds*, and the *warrant*:

- **The claim** is your thesis, the main point that you want to make in your essay.
- **The grounds** are the facts, examples, and opinions of experts that support your claim. In essays about literature, the grounds can come from a work of literature or from literary criticism.
- **The warrant** is an assumption that underlies both the claim and the grounds. Keep in mind that some warrants are explicitly stated while others may be simply implied.

In its simplest terms, an argument following Toulmin's structure would look like this:

- **The claim:** Phoenix Jackson, the main character in Eudora Welty's "A Worn Path," challenges the racial restrictions of her community.
- **The grounds:** Phoenix Jackson defies the man with the gun; she asks a white woman to tie her shoe; she steals a nickel; she gets free medicine from the doctor.
- **The warrant:** At the time "A Worn Path" takes place, racial segregation limited the actions of African Americans.

Notice that the claim presents a specific situation; the warrant, however, is a general principle that could apply to a number of situations. In a sense, the warrant is similar to the major premise of a syllogism, and the claim is similar to the conclusion. The grounds consist of the evidence that supports the claim.

RECOGNIZING LOGICAL FALLACIES

Logical fallacies are flawed arguments. A writer who inadvertently uses such fallacies is not thinking clearly or logically; a writer who intentionally uses them is trying to deceive readers. Learn to recognize them so you can avoid them when you write.

COMMON LOGICAL FALLACIES

- **Hasty Generalization:** A form of induction that reaches a conclusion on the basis of too little evidence. For example, one appearance of a river in a poem is not enough to support the statement that it is an important symbol. Several mentions, however, might justify this conclusion.

- **Sweeping Generalization:** A generalization that cannot be supported no matter how much evidence is supplied. For example, the statement "All literary critics like August Wilson's plays" is a sweeping generalization. Certainly, many critics like Wilson's plays, but it is virtually impossible to prove that all do. To avoid making statements that cannot be supported, qualify your statements with words such as *some, many, often,* or *most.*

- *Ad Hominem* **(Argument to the Person):** A fallacy that occurs when you attack a person rather than the issue, as in the following argument: "Many critics see imagism as a very important literary movement. However, the fact that its founder, Ezra Pound, was a Nazi sympathizer challenges that assessment." Although you may find Pound's Nazi sympathies repugnant, his political ideas are not relevant to your evaluation of imagism.

- **Non Sequitur:** A conclusion that does not logically follow from what comes before it, as in the following statement: "John Updike writes critically acclaimed novels, so he must be a gifted poet." It does not logically follow that just because Updike can write good novels, he can also write good poetry.

- **Either/Or Fallacy:** A fallacy that occurs when a complex issue is presented as if it has only two sides. If you ask your readers to consider whether a character is good or evil, you commit this fallacy. In fact, a complex character may possess both positive and negative qualities.

- **Begging the Question:** A fallacy that occurs when you present a debatable premise as if it were true, as in the following statement: "Hemingway's negative portrayals of women have caused his popularity to decline in recent years." Hemingway's portrayals of women may be negative, but readers do not have to accept this statement as fact just because you say it is true. Before you can make a judgment based on this assertion, you must support it with examples from Hemingway's work as well as with statements from a fair range of literary critics.

- **Bandwagon:** A fallacy that occurs when you try to establish that something is true just because everyone believes it is. You commit this fallacy when you say, for example, that a certain literary work must be good because it is so popular.

✔ CHECKLIST

DETECTING BIAS

☐ Have you chosen evidence that presents a balanced view of your topic?

☐ Have you cited experts? If so, do they represent a range of opinion?

☐ Have you avoided slanted language?

☐ Have you been careful not to convey your bias through your tone?

☐ Have you avoided statements that perpetuate stereotypes?

5

Writing Literary Arguments

Learning Outcomes

After reading this chapter, you should be able to do the following:

LO1 Plan a literary argument

LO2 Use evidence effectively

LO3 Organize a literary argument

Many of the essays you write about literature are **expository**—that is, you write to give information to readers. For example, you might discuss the rhyme or meter of a poem or examine the interaction of two characters in a play. Other essays you write, however, may be **literary arguments**—that is, you take a position on a debatable topic and attempt to change readers' minds about it. For example, you might argue that the boy's quest in James Joyce's short story "Araby" (p. 220) has symbolic meaning or that Sammy, the main character in John Updike's short story "A&P" (p. 131) is sexist.

When you write a literary argument, you follow the same process you do when you write any essay about a literary topic. However, because the purpose of an argument is to convince readers, you need to use some additional strategies to pre-sent your ideas.

LO1 Plan a Literary Argument

CHOOSING A TOPIC

Your first step in writing a literary argument will be to decide on a topic to write about. Ideally, your topic should

be one that you want to explore further. It stands to reason that the more your topic excites you, the more willing you will be to do serious research and some hard thinking. As a result, you are more likely than not to formulate an interesting and persuasive argument.

Your topic should also be narrow enough for you to develop within your page limit. After all, in an argumentative essay, you will have to present your own ideas and supply convincing support while possibly also addressing opposing arguments. If your topic is too broad, you will not be able to discuss it in enough detail.

Finally, your topic should be interesting. Keep in mind that some topics—such as the significance of the wall in Robert Frost's poem "Mending Wall"—have been written about so often that you will probably not be able to say anything new or interesting about them. Instead of relying on an overused topic, choose one that allows you to write something original.

DEVELOPING AN ARGUMENTATIVE THESIS

After you have chosen a topic, your next step is to develop an **argumentative thesis**—one that takes a strong stand.

Because an argumentative essay attempts to change the way readers think, it must focus on a thesis about which reasonable people disagree. In other words, it must be **debatable**; that is, it must have at least two sides. A factual statement—one about which reasonable people do not disagree—is therefore not appropriate as a thesis for argument.

Factual Statement: Linda Loman is Willie's long-suffering wife in Arthur Miller's play *Death of a Salesman.*

Argumentative Thesis: More than a stereotype of the long-suffering wife, Linda Loman in Arthur Miller's play *Death of a Salesman* is a complex character.

One way to make sure that your thesis actually does take a stand is to try to formulate an **antithesis**—a statement that takes an arguable position opposite from yours. If you can construct an antithesis, you can be certain that your thesis statement is debatable. If you cannot, your thesis statement needs further revision.

Thesis Statement: The last line of Richard Wright's short story "Big Black Good Man" indicates that Jim was fully aware all along of Olaf's deep-seated racial prejudice.

Antithesis: The last line of Richard Wright's short story "Big Black Good Man" indicates that Jim remained unaware of Olaf's feelings toward him.

Note Your thesis statement is an assertion that your entire essay supports. Keep in mind, however, that you can never prove an argumentative thesis conclusively—if you could, there would be no argument. The best you can do is provide enough evidence to establish a high probability that your thesis is reasonable

Defining Your Terms

You should always define the key terms you use in your argument. For example, if you are using the term *narrator* in an essay, make sure that readers know whether you are referring to a first-person or a third-person narrator. In addition, you may need to clarify the difference between an **unreliable narrator**—someone who misrepresents or misinterprets events—and a **reliable narrator**—someone who accurately describes events. Without a clear definition of the terms you are using, readers may have a difficult time understanding the point you are making.

DEFINING YOUR TERMS

Be especially careful to use precise terms in your thesis statement. Avoid vague and judgmental words, such as *wrong, bad, good, right,* and *immoral.*

Vague: The poem "Birmingham Sunday (September 15, 1963)" by Langston Hughes shows how bad racism can be.

Clearer: The poem "Birmingham Sunday (September 15, 1963)" by Langston Hughes makes a moving statement about how dehumanizing racism can be.

Considering Your Audience

As you plan your essay, keep your audience in mind. For example, if you are writing about a work that has been discussed in class, you can assume that your readers are familiar with it; include plot summary only when it is needed to explain a point you are making. Keep in mind that you will be addressing an academic audience—your instructor and possibly some students. For this reason, you should be sure to follow the conventions of writing about literature as well as the conventions of standard written English. (For information on the conventions of writing about literature, see the checklist in Chapter 2, p. 28.)

When you write an argumentative essay, assume that you are addressing a skeptical audience—one that is not easily convinced. Remember, your thesis is debatable, so not everyone will agree with you—and even if your readers are sympathetic to your position, you cannot assume that they will accept your ideas without question.

The strategies you use to convince your readers will vary according to your relationship with them. Somewhat skeptical readers may need to see only that your argument is logical and that your evidence is solid. More skeptical readers, however, may need to see that you understand their reservations and that you concede some of their points. Of course, you may never be able to convince hostile readers that your conclusions are legitimate. The best you can hope for is that these readers will acknowledge the strengths of your argument even if they do not accept your conclusion.

REFUTING OPPOSING ARGUMENTS

As you develop your literary argument, you may need to **refute**—that is, to disprove—opposing arguments by demonstrating that they are false, misguided, or illogical. By summarizing and refuting opposing views, you make opposing arguments seem less credible to readers; thus, you strengthen your case. When an opposing argument is so strong that it cannot be easily dismissed, however, you should **concede** (admit the strength of) the argument and then point out its limitations.

Notice in the following paragraph how a student refutes the argument that Homer Barron, a character in William Faulkner's short story "A Rose for Emily," is gay.

> **Opposing argument** — A number of critics have suggested that Homer Barron, Miss Emily's suitor, is gay. Actually, there is some evidence in the story to support this interpretation. For example, the narrator points out that Homer "liked men" and that he was not "a marrying man" (Faulkner 124).
>
> **Concession** — In addition, the narrator describes Homer as wearing yellow gloves when he took Emily for drives. According to the critic William Greenslade, in the 1890s yellow was associated with homosexuality (24).
>
> **Refutation** — This evidence does not prove that Homer is gay, however. During the nineteenth century, many men preferred the company of other men (as many do today). This, in itself, did not mean they were gay. Neither does the fact that Homer wore yellow gloves. According to the narrator, Homer was a man who liked to dress well. It is certainly possible that he wore these gloves to impress Miss Emily, a woman he was trying to attract.

LO2 Use Evidence Effectively

SUPPORTING YOUR LITERARY ARGUMENT

Many literary arguments are built on **assertions**—statements made about a debatable topic—backed by **evidence**—supporting examples in the form of references to the text, quotations, and the opinions of literary critics. For example, if you stated that Torvald Helmer, Nora's husband in Henrik Ibsen's play *A Doll House,* is as much a victim of society as his wife is, you could support this assertion with relevant quotations and examples from the play. You could also paraphrase, summarize, or quote the ideas of literary critics who also hold this opinion. Remember, only assertions that are **self-evident** (All plays include characters and dialogue) or **factual** (*A Doll House* was published in 1879) need no supporting evidence. All other kinds of assertions require support.

> *"Many literary arguments are built on assertions— statements made about a debatable topic—backed by evidence—supporting examples."*

ESTABLISHING CREDIBILITY

Some people bring **credibility** with them whenever they write. When a well-known literary critic evaluates the contributions of a particular writer, you can assume that he or she speaks with authority. (Although you might question the critic's opinions, you do not question his or her expertise.) But most people do not have this kind of credibility. When you write a literary argument, you must constantly work to establish credibility. You do this by *demonstrating knowledge, maintaining a reasonable tone,* and *presenting yourself as someone worth listening to.*

Demonstrating Knowledge   One way to establish credibility is by presenting your own carefully considered ideas about a subject. A clear argument and compelling support can demonstrate to readers that you know what you are talking about.

You can also show readers that you have thoroughly researched your subject. By referring to important sources and by providing accurate documentation for your information, you present evidence that you have done the necessary background reading. Including a range of sources—not just one or two—suggests that you are well acquainted with your subject. Remember, however, that questionable sources, inaccurate (or missing) documentation, and factual errors can

tone Attitude of the speaker or author of a work toward the subject or the audience, as determined by the word choice and arrangement of ideas.

undermine your credibility. For many readers, an undocumented quotation or even an incorrect date can call an entire argument into question.

Maintaining a Reasonable Tone Your **tone**—your attitude toward your readers or subject—is almost as important as the information you convey. Talk *to* your readers, not *at* them. If you lecture your readers or appear to talk down to them, you will alienate them. Generally speaking, readers are more likely to respond to a writer who seems fair and respectful than one who seems strident or condescending.

As you write your essay, use moderate language and qualify your statements so that they seem reasonable. Try to avoid words and phrases such as *all, never, always,* and *in every case,* which can make your points seem simplistic, exaggerated, or unrealistic. Also, avoid absolute statements. For example, the statement, In *"Doe Season,"* the ocean obviously symbolizes Andy's attachment to her mother, leaves no room for other possible interpretations. A more measured and accurate statement might be, In *"Doe Season,"* the use of the ocean as a symbol suggests Andy's identification with her mother and her realization that she is becoming a woman.

Presenting Yourself as Someone Worth Listening To When you write a literary argument, you should present yourself as someone your readers will want to listen to. Make your argument confidently, and don't apologize for your views. For example, do not use phrases such as "In my opinion" and "It seems to me," which undercut your credibility. Be consistent, and be careful not to contradict yourself. Finally, avoid the use of *I* (unless you are asked to give your opinion or to write a response paper), and avoid slang and colloquialisms.

Being Fair

Argument promotes one point of view over all others, so it is seldom objective. However, college writing requires that you stay within the bounds of fairness and that you avoid **bias**—opinions based on preconceived ideas rather than on evidence (see p. 47, 50). To make sure that the support for your argument is not misleading or distorted, follow these guidelines:

- *Avoid misrepresenting evidence.* Be careful not to misrepresent the extent to which critical opinion supports your thesis. For example, don't try to make a weak case stronger than it actually is by saying that

"many critics" think that something is so when only one or two do.

- *Avoid quoting out of context.* When you take words from their original setting and use them in another, you run the risk of quoting out of context. When you quote a source's words out of context, you can change the meaning of what someone has said or suggested. For example, you are quoting out of context if you say, "Emily Dickinson's poems are so idiosyncratic that they do not appeal to readers" when your source says, "Emily Dickinson's poems are so idiosyncratic that they do not appeal to readers *who are accustomed to safe, conventional subjects.*" By eliminating a key portion of the sentence, you alter the meaning of the original.

- *Avoid slanting.* When you select only information that supports your case and ignore information that does not, you are guilty of slanting. You can eliminate this problem by including a full range of examples, not just examples that support your thesis. Be sure to consult books and articles that represent a cross-section of critical opinion about your subject.

- *Avoid using unfair appeals.* Traditionally, writers of arguments use three types of appeals to influence readers: **logical appeals**, which address a reader's sense of reason, **emotional appeals**, which play on a reader's emotions, and **ethical appeals**, which emphasize the credibility of the writer. Problems arise, however, when these appeals are used unfairly. For example, writers can use **logical fallacies**—flawed arguments—to fool readers into thinking a conclusion is logical when it is not (see Chapter 4 for a discussion of logical fallacies). Writers can also use inappropriate emotional appeals—appeals to prejudice, for example—to influence readers. And finally, writers can undercut their credibility if they use questionable support—books and articles written by people who have little or no expertise on the topic. This is especially true when information is obtained from the Internet, where the credentials of the writer may be difficult or impossible to assess. If you want your readers to accept your position, you must be careful to avoid logical fallacies and unfair appeals.

Using Visuals as Evidence

Visuals—pictures, drawings, diagrams, and the like—can add a persuasive dimension to your essay. Because visual images have an immediate impact, they can sometimes make a strong literary argument even stronger. In a sense, visuals are another type of evidence that can support your thesis. For example, suppose you are writing an essay about the play *Trifles* in which you argue that Mrs. Wright's quilt is an important symbol in the play. In fact, your research leads you to conclude that the process of creating the quilt by piecing together its log cabin pattern parallels the process by

- **Introduction:** The introduction should orient readers to the subject of your essay, presenting the issue you will discuss and explaining its significance.

- **Thesis statement:** In most literary arguments, you will present your thesis statement in your introduction. However, if you think your readers may not be familiar with the issue you are discussing (or if it is very controversial), you may want to postpone stating your thesis until later in the essay.

- **Background:** In this section, you can survey critical opinion about your topic, perhaps pointing out the shortcomings of these opinions. You can also define key terms, review basic facts, or briefly summarize the plot of the work or works you will discuss.

- **Arguments in support of your thesis:** Here you present your arguments and the evidence to support them. It makes sense to move from the least controversial to the most controversial point or from the most familiar to the least familiar idea. In other words, you should begin with arguments that your readers are most likely to accept and then deal with those that require more discussion and more evidence.

- **Refutation of opposing arguments:** In a literary argument, you should summarize and refute the most obvious arguments against your thesis. If you do not address these opposing arguments, doubts about your position will remain in your readers' minds. If the opposing arguments are relatively weak, refute them after you have presented your own arguments. However, if the opposing arguments are strong, you may want to concede their strengths and discuss their limitations *before* you present your own arguments.

- **Conclusion:** Your conclusion will often restate your thesis as well as summarize the major arguments you have made in support of it. Your conclusion can also summarize key points, remind readers of the weaknesses of opposing arguments, or underscore the logic of your position. Many writers like to end their essays with a strong last line—for example, a quotation or a memorable statement that they hope will stay with readers after they finish the essay.

> *"Visuals are another type of evidence that can support your thesis."*

which the two female characters in the play determine why Mrs. Wright murdered her husband. The addition of a photograph of a quilt with a log cabin pattern could not only eliminate several paragraphs of description but also help support your conclusion.

Of course, not all visuals will be appropriate or effective for a literary argument. Before using a visual, make certain it actually supports the point you want to make. If it does not, it will distract readers and undercut your argument. To ensure that readers understand the purpose of the visual, introduce it with a sentence that establishes its context; then, discuss its significance, paying particular attention to how it helps you make your point. Finally, be sure to include full documentation for any visual that is not your original creation.

(See pages 42 and 56 for examples of visuals used as evidence in a student paper.)

LO3 Organize a Literary Argument

In its simplest form, a literary argument—like any argumentative essay—consists of a thesis statement and supporting evidence. Literary arguments, however, frequently use additional strategies to win audience approval and to overcome potential opposition.

WRITING A LITERARY ARGUMENT

The following student paper presents a literary argument about Dee, a character in Alice Walker's short story "Everyday Use." The student author supports her thesis with ideas she developed as she read the story as well as with information she found when she did research. She also includes two visuals from a DVD version of the story.

Margaret Chase

Professor Sierra

English 1001

20 January 2011

The Politics of "Everyday Use"

Alice Walker's "Everyday Use" focuses on a mother, Mrs. Johnson, and her two daughters, Maggie and Dee, and how they view their heritage. The story's climax comes when Mrs. Johnson rejects Dee's request to take a hand-stitched quilt with her so that she can hang it on her wall. Knowing that Maggie will put the quilt to "everyday use," Dee is horrified, and she tells her mother and Maggie that they do not understand their heritage. Although many literary critics see Dee's desire for the quilt as materialistic and shallow, a closer examination of this story, written in 1973, suggests a more positive interpretation of Dee's character.

On the surface, "Everyday Use" is a story about two sisters, Dee and Maggie, and Mrs. Johnson, their mother. Mrs. Johnson tells the reader that "Dee, . . . would always look anyone in the eye. Hesitation was no part of her nature" (256). Unlike her sister, Maggie is shy and introverted. She is described as looking like a lame animal that has been run over by a car. According to the narrator, "She has been like this, chin on chest, eyes on ground, feet in shuffle" (256) ever since she was burned in a fire.

Unlike Dee, Mrs. Johnson never got an education. After second grade, she explains, the school closed down. She says, "Don't ask me why: in 1927 colored asked fewer questions than they do now" (257). Mrs. Johnson admits that she accepts the status quo even though she knows that it is unjust. This admission further establishes the difference between Mrs. Johnson and Dee: Mrs. Johnson has accepted her circumstances, while Dee has worked to change hers. Their differences are illustrated in a film version of the story by their contrasting dress. As shown in fig. 1, Dee and her boyfriend

Source © Denna Bendall/Worn Path Productions

Fig. 1. Dee and Hakim-a-barber arrive at the family home; *The Wadsworth Original Film Series in Literature: "Everyday Use,"* dir. Bruce R. Schwartz; Wadsworth, 2005; DVD.

Introduction

Thesis statement

Background

Hakim-a-barber dress in a style that celebrates their African heritage; Mrs. Johnson and Maggie dress in plain, conservative clothing.

When Dee arrives home with her new boyfriend, other differences soon become obvious. As she eyes her mother's belongings and asks Mrs. Johnson if she can take the top of the butter churn home with her, it is clear that she is very materialistic. However, her years away from home have also politicized her. Dee now wants to be called "Wangero" because she believes (although mistakenly) that her given name comes from whites who owned her ancestors. In addition, she talks about how a new day is dawning for African Americans.

The meaning and political importance of Dee's decision to adopt an African name and wear African clothing cannot be fully understood without a knowledge of the social and political context in which Walker wrote this story. Walker's own comments about this time period explain Dee's behavior and add meaning to it. In her interview with White, Walker explains that the late 1960s was a time of cultural and intellectual awakening for African Americans. Many turned ideologically and culturally to Africa, adopting the dress, hairstyles, and even the names of their African ancestors. Walker admits that as a young woman she too became interested in discovering her African heritage. (In fact, she herself was given the name *Wangero* during a visit to Kenya in the late 1960s.) Walker tells White that she considered keeping this new name but eventually realized that to do so would be to "dismiss" her family and her American heritage. When she researched her American family, she found that her great-great-grandmother had walked from Virginia to Georgia carrying two children. "If that's not a Walker," she says, "I don't know what is." Thus, Walker realized that, over time, African Americans had actually transformed the names they had originally taken from their enslavers. To respect the ancestors she knew, Walker says, she decided it was important to keep her name.

Along with adopting symbols of their African heritage, many African Americans also elevated these symbols, such as the quilt shown in fig. 2, to the status of art. According to Salaam, one way of doing this was to put these objects in museums; another was to hang them on the walls of their homes. Such acts were aimed at convincing whites that African Americans had an old and rich culture and that, consequently, they deserved not only basic civil rights but also respect. These gestures were also meant to improve self-esteem and pride within black communities (Salaam 42-43).

Admittedly, as some critics have pointed out, Dee is more materialistic than political. For example, although Mrs. Johnson makes several statements throughout the story that suggest her admiration of Dee's defiant character, she also identifies incidents that highlight Dee's materialism and selfishness. When their first house burned down, Dee watched it burn while she stood under a tree with "a look of concentration" (257) rather than grief. Mrs. Johnson knows that Dee hated their small, dingy house, and she knows too that Dee was glad to see it destroyed. Furthermore, Walker acknowledges in an interview with her biographer, Evelyn C. White, that as she was writing the story, she imagined that Dee might even have set the fire that destroyed the house and scarred her sister. Even now, Dee is ashamed of the tin-roofed house her family lives in, and she has said that she would never bring her friends there.

Back-ground continued

First argument in support of thesis

Refutation of opposing argument

©Suzanne English/Worn Path Productions

Fig. 2. Traditional hand-stitched quilt; Evelyn C. White, "Alice Walker: Stitches in Time," interview, *The Wadsworth Original Film Series in Literature: "Everyday Use,"* dir. Bruce R. Schwartz; Wadsworth, 2005; DVD.

Mrs. Johnson has always known that Dee wanted "nice things" (257); even at sixteen, "she had a style of her own: and knew what style was" (257). However, although Dee is materialistic and self-serving, she is also proud and strong willed. Knowing that she will encounter opposition wherever she goes, she works to establish power. Thus, her desire for the quilt can be seen as an attempt to establish herself and her African-American culture in a society dominated by whites.

Refutation of opposing argument

Even though Mrs. Johnson knows Dee wants the quilt, she gives it to Maggie. According to literary critics Houston Baker and Charlotte Pierce-Baker, when Mrs. Johnson decides to give the quilt to Maggie, she is challenging Dee's understanding of her heritage. Unlike Dee, Mrs. Johnson recognizes that quilts signify "sacred generations of women who have made their own special kind of beauty separate from the traditional artistic world." According to Baker and Pierce-Baker, Mrs. Johnson realizes that her daughter Maggie, whom she has long dismissed because of her quiet nature and shyness, understands the true meaning of the quilt in a way that Dee never will (Piedmont-Marton 45).

Analysis of Mrs. Johnson's final act

Unlike Dee, Maggie has paid close attention to the traditions and skills of her mother and grandmother: she has actually learned to quilt. More important, by staying with her mother instead of going to school, she has gotten to know her family. She underscores this fact when she tells her mother that Dee can have the quilt because she does not need it to remember her grandmother. Even though Maggie's and Mrs. Johnson's understanding of heritage may be more emotionally profound than Dee's, it is important not to dismiss Dee's interest in elevating the quilt to the level of high art. The political stakes of defining an object as art in the late 1960s and early 1970s were high, and the fight for equality went beyond basic civil rights.

Although there is much in the story that indicates Dee's materialism, her desire to hang the quilt should not be dismissed as a selfish act. Like Mrs. Johnson and Maggie, Dee is a complicated

Conclusion (restating thesis)

character. In 1973, when "Everyday Use" was written, displaying the quilt would have been not only a personal act, but also a political act—an act with important implications. The final message of "Everyday Use" may just be that an accurate understanding of the quilt (and, by extension, of African-American culture) requires both views—Maggie's and Mrs. Johnson's "every day use" and Dee's elevation of the quilt to art.

Works Cited

Piedmont-Marton, Elisabeth. "An Overview of 'Everyday Use.'" *Short Stories for Students* 2 (1997): 42-45. *Literature Resource Center.* Web. 18 Jan. 2011.

Salaam, Kalamu Ya. "A Primer of the Black Arts Movement: Excerpts from *The Magic of Juju: An Appreciation of the Black Arts Movement.*" *Black Renaissance/Renaissance Noire* (2002): 40-59. *Expanded Academic ASAP.* Web. 18 Jan. 2011.

Walker, Alice. "Alice Walker: Stitches in Time." Interview by Evelyn C. White. *The Wadsworth Original Film Series in Literature: "Everyday Use."* Dir. Bruce R. Schwartz. Wadsworth, 2005. DVD.

---. "Everyday Use." *LIT*. Ed. Laurie G. Kirszner and Stephen R. Mandell. Boston: Wadsworth, 2012. 256–60. Print.

CHECKLIST

DEVELOPING AN ARGUMENTATIVE THESIS

☐ Can you formulate an antithesis?

☐ Does your thesis statement make clear to readers what position you are taking?

☐ Can you support your thesis with evidence from the text and from research?

CHECKLIST

BEING FAIR

☐ Have you distorted evidence?

☐ Have you quoted material out of context, changing the meaning of a statement by focusing on certain words and ignoring others?

☐ Have you slanted information, selecting material that supports your points and ignoring information that does not?

☐ Have you used any unfair appeals?

Glossary Terms

tone Attitude of the speaker or author of a work toward the subject or the audience, as determined by the word choice and arrangement of ideas.

6

Using Sources in Your Writing

Learning Outcomes

After reading this chapter, you should be able to do the following:

LO1 Choose a topic

LO2 Do exploratory research

LO3 Narrow your topic

LO4 Do focused research

LO5 Take notes

LO6 Integrate sources

LO7 Draft a thesis statement

LO8 Make a formal outline

LO9 Draft your paper

LO10 Evaluate a model literature paper with MLA documentation

When you write a paper about a literary topic, you often do **research**, supplementing your own interpretations with information from other sources. These sources may include works of literature as well as books and journal articles by literary critics (see p. 11). You may get this information from print sources, from electronic databases in the library, or from the Internet. When you write a literary research paper, follow the process discussed in this chapter.

LO1 Choose a Topic

Your instructor may assign a topic or allow you to choose one. If you choose a topic, make sure it is narrow enough for your paper's length, the amount of time you have for writing, and the number of sources your instructor expects you to use.

Daniel Collins, a student in an Introduction to Literature course, was given three weeks to write a four- to six-page research paper on one of the short stories the class had read. Daniel chose to write about Eudora Welty's short story "A Worn Path" because the main character, Phoenix Jackson, interested him. He knew, however, that he would have to narrow his topic before he could begin. In class, Daniel's instructor had asked some provocative questions about the significance of Phoenix Jackson's journey. Daniel thought that this topic might work well because he could explore it in a short paper and could complete the paper within the three-week time limit.

LO2 Do Exploratory Research

To see whether you will be able to find enough material about your topic, you should do some **exploratory research** by taking a quick survey of your library's resources. Your goal at this stage is to formulate a **research question**, the question that you want your research to answer. This question will help you decide which sources to look for, which to examine first, and which to skip entirely.

You can begin your exploratory research by consulting your library's **online central information system**. This system usually includes the library's **catalog** as well as a number of **bibliographic databases**, such as *Readers' Guide to Periodical Literature* and *Humanities Index*. Then you can consult Internet sources as well as **general reference works** like encyclopedias and specialized dictionaries and browse your search engine's subject guides to get an overview of your subject.

A quick look showed Daniel that his library's central information system included several books and a number of articles on Eudora Welty. He noted the titles of the most promising sources so he could find them later. After consulting some additional sources on the Internet and thinking more about his topic, Daniel came up with the following research question: What enabled Phoenix Jackson to continue her journey despite the many obstacles she faced?

LO3 Narrow Your Topic

As you survey library and Internet resources, the titles of books and articles should help you to narrow your topic.

Daniel found two critical articles that discussed the significance of Phoenix Jackson's journey, and he hoped they would help him to understand why this character continued her journey despite all the hardships she encountered. However, Daniel knew that he would have to do more than just summarize his sources; he would have to make a point about the journey, one that he could support with examples from the story as well as from his research.

LO4 Do Focused Research

Once you have completed your exploratory research and formulated your research question, you are ready to begin **focused research**—the process of looking in the library and on the Internet for the specific information you need.

LIBRARY RESEARCH
Using the Library

The first step is to go back to the library and check out any books that you think will be useful. Then, consult **specialized reference works**—indexes, bibliographies, and specialized encyclopedias, for example—to find relevant articles. If you find print articles, photocopy them (and make sure to copy all the publication information you will need to document these sources).

Your library's **databases** (usually accessed through the library's Web site) will help you find information in periodicals. A **periodical** is a newspaper, magazine, or scholarly journal published at regular intervals. **Periodical indexes** are databases that list articles from a selected group of periodicals. Although you may occasionally

find scholarly articles on the Internet, the easiest (and most reliable) way to access scholarly journals is through the databases to which your college library subscribes. These databases are updated frequently, and the articles they include usually provide current, reliable information.

Choosing the right database for your research is important. Each database has a different focus and lists different magazines or journals. In addition, some indexes include just citations while others contain the full text of articles. Using the wrong database can lead to wasted time and frustration. For example, searching a database that focuses on business will not help you much if you are looking for information on a literary topic. Be sure to ask a reference librarian which database will be most helpful.

> "Choosing the right database for your research is important. Each database has a different focus and lists different magazines or journals."

FREQUENTLY USED DATABASES

The following databases are useful for literary research.

EBSCOhost	Includes thousands of periodical articles on many subjects
Expanded Academic ASAP	Largely full-text database covering all subjects in thousands of magazines and journals
FirstSearch	Full-text articles in many popular and scholarly periodicals

Evaluating Library Sources

Whenever you find a library source (print or electronic), take the time to **evaluate** it—to assess its usefulness and reliability.

EVALUATING LIBRARY SOURCES

- [ ] *Does the source treat your topic in enough detail?* To be of real help, a book should include a section or a chapter on your topic. An article should have your topic as its central subject or at least one of its main concerns.

- [ ] *Is the source current?* Although currency is not as important for literary research as it is in the sciences, it should still be a consideration. Check the date of publication to see whether the information in a book or article is up to date.

- [ ] *Is the source respected?* A contemporary review of a source can help you make this assessment. You can find reviews in *Book Review Digest*, available in print and online.

- [ ] *Is the source reliable?* Does the author support his or her opinions? Does the author include documentation? Does the author have a particular agenda to advance? Compare a few statements with a more neutral source—an encyclopedia or a textbook, for example—to see whether the author seems to be slanting facts. If you have difficulty making this assessment, ask your instructor or a reference librarian for help.

INTERNET RESEARCH
Using the Internet

As you can imagine, the Internet has revolutionized the way scholars conduct research, offering instant access to a host of useful sources. Keep in mind, however, that the Internet does not give you access to the large number of high-quality print and electronic sources that you find in your college library.

Some search engines are more user friendly than others, some allow for more sophisticated searching, and some are more comprehensive. As you try out various search engines, you will eventually settle on one that you will turn to when you need to find information.

In addition to the general-purpose search engines listed above, you can use **specialized search engines**—search sites that are especially useful during focused research when you are looking for in-depth information about a specific topic.

Evaluating Web Sites

Anyone can operate a Web site and thereby publish anything. For this reason, it is important to determine the quality of a Web site before you use it as a source. Asking the questions below will help you evaluate Web sites and the information they contain.

Daniel Collins, the student writing about Phoenix Jackson's journey, was lucky enough to find everything he needed in his college library. He found two print articles about the Welty story, and he found two more articles in the *Humanities Index* database. Finally, a search of his library's online central information system revealed that among the library's holdings was a DVD dramatization of "A Worn Path" that included an interview with the author.

LO5 Take Notes

Once you have located your sources, you should record information that you think will be useful. There is no single correct way to take notes. Some writers store information in a computer file; others keep their notes on index cards. Whatever system you use, be sure to record the author's full name as well as *complete* publication information. You will need this information later on to compile your works-cited list (see p. 76).

When you take notes from a source, you have three options: you can *paraphrase, summarize,* or *quote.*

When you **paraphrase,** you put the author's main points into your own words, keeping the emphasis of the original.

You paraphrase when you want to make a difficult or complex discussion accessible to readers so that you can comment on it or use it to support your own points. Here is a passage from a critical article, followed by Daniel's paraphrase.

Original

The assumption that the grandson is dead helps explain Phoenix Jackson's stoical behavior in the doctor's office. She displays a "ceremonial stiffness" as she sits "bolt upright" staring "straight ahead, her face solemn and withdrawn into rigidity." This passiveness suggests her psychological dilemma—she cannot explain why she made the journey. Her attempt to blame the lapse of memory on her illiteracy is unconvincing. Her lack of education is hardly an excuse for forgetting her grandson, but it goes a long way toward explaining her inability to articulate her subconscious motives for her journey. (Bartel, Roland. "Life and Death in Eudora Welty's 'A Worn Path.'" *Studies in Short Fiction* 14.1 (1977): 288-90. Print.)

Paraphrase

As Roland Bartel points out in "Life and Death in Eudora Welty's 'A Worn Path,'" Phoenix Jackson's "stoical behavior" at the doctor's office makes sense if her grandson is actually dead. Although she says that her forgetfulness is due to her lack of education, Bartel does not accept this excuse. According to him, the fact that Phoenix is uneducated cannot fully explain her forgetting about her grandson—although it might explain why she cannot communicate her reasons for her trip (289).

When you write a **summary,** you also put an author's ideas into your own words, but you convey just the main idea of a passage. For this reason, a summary is always much shorter than the original. Here is Daniel's summary of the passage from Bartel's article.

Summary

As Roland Bartel points out in "Life and Death in Eudora Welty's 'A Worn Path,'" Phoenix Jackson's actions make sense if we assume that her grandson is dead and that she does not have the skill to explain her motive (289).

When you **quote,** you reproduce a passage exactly, word for word and punctuation mark for punctuation mark, enclosing the entire passage in quotation marks. Because a large number of quotations will distract readers, use a quotation only when you think that the author's words will add something—memorable wording, for example—to your paper.

LO6 Integrate Sources

To integrate a paraphrase, summary, or quotation smoothly into your paper, use a phrase that introduces your source and its author—*Bartel points out, according to Bartel, Bartel claims,* or *Bartel says,* for example. You can place this identifying phrase at various points in a sentence.

According to Roland Bartel, "The assumption that the grandson is dead helps explain Phoenix Jackson's stoical behavior in the doctor's office" (289).

"The assumption that the grandson is dead helps explain Phoenix Jackson's stoical behavior in the doctor's office," observes Roland Bartel in his article "Life and Death in Eudora Welty's 'A Worn Path'" (289).

"The assumption that the grandson is dead," notes the literary critic Roland Bartel, "helps explain Phoenix Jackson's stoical behavior in the doctor's office" (289).

EXERCISE: INTEGRATING QUOTATIONS

For each of the quotations below, write three sentences: one that integrates the complete quotation into your sentence, one that integrates part of the quotation into your sentence, and one that quotes just a distinctive word or phrase.

Example

- **Original quotation:** "But it seems to me that once you begin a gesture it's fatal not to go through with it" (Updike 134).
- **Sentence integrating complete quotation:** Readers understand Sammy's determination to stand up to Lengel when he says, "But it seems to me that once you begin a gesture it's fatal not to go through with it" (Updike 134).
- **Sentence integrating part of the quotation:** Sammy has mixed feelings about quitting his job but feels that "once you begin a gesture it's fatal not to go through with it" (Updike 134).
- **Sentence quoting one distinctive word:** Sammy considers changing his mind but decides that to do so would be "fatal" (Updike 134).

Quotations

1. "We remembered all the young men her father had driven away, and we knew that with nothing left she would have to cling to that which had robbed her, as people will" (Faulkner 123).
2. "And so the house came to be haunted by the unspoken phrase: *There must be more money! There must be more money!*" (Lawrence 298).
3. "That moment she was mine, mine, fair" (Browning, line 36)
4. "But I have promises to keep, / And miles to go before I sleep / and miles to go before I sleep" (Frost, lines 14–16).
5. "We live close together and we live far apart. We all go through the same things—it's just a different kind of the same thing" (Glaspell 561).

> **Note** Remember to document all paraphrases, summaries, and quotations that you use in your essays. (See Chapter 7, Documenting Sources and Avoiding Plagiarism.)

LO7 Draft a Thesis Statement

After you have taken notes, review the information you have gathered, and use it to help you draft a **thesis statement**—a single sentence that states the main idea of your paper. You will support this thesis with a combination of your own ideas and the ideas you have drawn from your research.

After reviewing his notes, Daniel developed the following thesis statement about Eudora Welty's "A Worn Path."

Thesis Statement: What is most important in the story is the spiritual and emotional strength of Phoenix Jackson and how this strength enables her to continue her journey.

As you draft and revise your paper, your thesis statement will probably change. At this point in the writing process, however, it gives your ideas focus and enables you to organize them into an outline.

LO8 Make a Formal Outline

Once you have drafted a thesis statement, you can construct a formal outline from your notes. Begin by writing your thesis statement at the top of the page. Then, review your notes, and arrange them in the order in which you plan to use them. As you construct your outline, group these points under appropriate headings.

When it is completed, your outline will show you how much support you have for each of your points, and it will guide you as you write a draft of your paper. Your outline, which covers the body paragraphs of your essay, can be a **sentence outline,** in which each idea is expressed as a sentence, or a **topic outline,** in which each idea is expressed in a word or a short phrase.

After reviewing his notes, Daniel constructed the following topic outline. Notice that he uses roman numerals for first-level headings, capital letters for second-level headings, and arabic numerals for third-level headings. Notice too that all points in the outline are expressed in parallel terms.

> Thesis Statement: What is most important in the story is the spiritual and emotional strength of Phoenix Jackson and how this strength enables her to continue her journey.
>
> I. Critical interpretations of "A Worn Path"
>   A. Heroic act of sacrifice
>   B. Journey of life
>   C. Religious pilgrimage
> II. Focus on journey
>   A. Jackson and her grandson
>   B. Nurse's question
>   C. Jackson's reply

III. Jackson's character
    A. Interaction between Jackson's character and journey
        1. Significance of Jackson's first name
        2. Jackson as a complex character
    B. Jackson's physical problems
        1. Failing eyesight
        2. Difficulty walking
IV. Jackson's spiritual strength
    A. Belief in God
    B. Child of nature
V. Jackson's emotional strength
    A. Love for grandson
    B. Fearlessness and selflessness
    C. Determination

LO9 Draft Your Paper

Once you have constructed your outline, you can draft your paper. Follow your outline as you write, using your notes as the need arises.

Your paper's **introduction** will usually be a single paragraph. In addition to identifying the work (or works) you are writing about and stating your thesis, the introduction to a literary research paper may present an overview of your topic or necessary background information.

> "Remember, the purpose of your first draft is to get ideas down on paper so that you can react to them. You should expect to revise, possibly writing several drafts."

The **body** of your paper supports your thesis statement, with each of your paragraphs developing a single point. Support your points with examples from the literary work you are discussing or with summaries, paraphrases, and quotations from your sources. In addition, be sure to include your own observations and inferences.

Your paper's **conclusion,** usually a single paragraph (but sometimes more), restates your main points and reinforces your thesis statement.

Remember, the purpose of your first draft is to get ideas down on paper so that you can react to them. You should expect to revise, possibly writing several drafts.

The final draft of Daniel Collins's paper on Eudora Welty's "A Worn Path" appears on the pages that follow.

LO10 Evaluate a Model Literature Paper with MLA Documentation

Collins 1

Daniel Collins

Professor Smith

English 201

11 January 2011

    And Again She Makes the Journey: Character and Act in Eudora Welty's "A Worn Path"

    Since it was published in 1940, Eudora Welty's "A Worn Path," the tale of an elderly black woman, Phoenix Jackson, traveling to the city to obtain medicine for her sick grandson, has been the subject of much critical interpretation. Critics have wondered about the meaning of the many death and rebirth symbols, including the scarecrow, which the old woman believes is a ghost; the buzzard who watches her travel; the skeleton-like branches that reach out to slow her; and her first name, Phoenix. Various critics have concluded that "A Worn Path" is either a "heroic act of sacrifice," "a parable for the journey of life," or "a religious pilgrimage" (Piwinski 40). It is certainly true that Phoenix Jackson's journey has symbolic significance. However, what is most important in the story is the spiritual and emotional strength of Phoenix Jackson and how this strength enables her to continue her journey.

Eudora Welty discusses Phoenix Jackson in a DVD interview with Beth Henley. Welty points out that Jackson's first name refers to a mythical bird that dies and is reborn every five hundred years. She explains, however, that despite her symbolic name, Phoenix Jackson is more than a symbol: she is a complex character with human frailties and emotions.

Phoenix Jackson has a number of physical problems that make it difficult for her to perform daily tasks. Because of her age, she has failing eyesight, which distorts her perception of the objects she encounters during her journey. For example, Phoenix mistakes a patch of thorns for "a pretty little *green bush*" (286), and she believes a scarecrow is the ghost of a man. She also has difficulty walking, so she must use a cane; at one point, she is unable to bend and tie her own shoes. Because of these physical problems, readers might expect her to fail in her attempt to reach town; as the narrator points out, the journey is long and difficult. So what gives Phoenix Jackson the energy and endurance for the journey?

Although Phoenix Jackson's body is weak, she has great spiritual and emotional strength. According to James Saunders, her oneness with nature helps her overcome the challenges that she encounters. Because Phoenix Jackson is "a child of nature," her impaired vision, although it slows her journey, does not stop it. As Saunders explains, "mere human vision would not have been sufficient for the journey" (67). Instead, Phoenix Jackson relies on her spiritual connection with nature; thus, she warns various animals to "Keep out from under these feet . . ." (285). Her spiritual strength also comes from her belief in God—a quality seen when she refers to God watching her steal the hunter's nickel.

Phoenix Jackson's spiritual strength is matched by her emotional strength. Her love for her grandson compels her to endure any difficulty and to defy any danger. Therefore, throughout her journey, she demonstrates fearlessness and selflessness. For example, when the hunter threatens her with his gun, she tells him that she has faced worse dangers. And, despite her need for new shoes, she buys a paper windmill for her grandson instead.

In her interview with Beth Henley, Eudora Welty explains how she created Phoenix Jackson—outwardly frail and inwardly strong. Welty tells how she noticed an "old lady" slowly making her way across a "silent horizon,"[1] driven by an overwhelming need to reach her destination; as Welty says, "she had a purpose." Welty created Phoenix Jackson in the image of this determined woman. In order to emphasize the character's strength, Welty had her make the journey to Natchez to get medication for her grandson.

Because the act had to be performed repeatedly, the journey became a ritual that had to be completed at all costs. Thus, as Welty explains in the interview, the act of making the journey—not the journey itself—is the most important element in the story.

In order to emphasize the importance of the journey, Welty gives little information about the daily life of the boy and his grandmother or about the illness for which the boy is being treated. Regardless of the boy's condition—or even whether he is alive or dead—Jackson must complete her journey. The nurse's statement—"The doctor said as long as you came to get it [the medicine], you could have it" (289)—reinforces the ritualistic nature of Jackson's journey, a journey that Bartel suggests is a "subconscious" act (289). Thus, Phoenix Jackson cannot answer the nurse's questions because she does not consciously know what forces her to make the journey. Nevertheless, next Saturday, Phoenix Jackson will again walk, and "will continue to do so, regardless of the difficulties facing her, along the worn path that leads through the wilderness of the Natchez Trace, cheerfully performing her labor of love" (Howard 84).

Clearly, the interaction of character (Phoenix Jackson) and act (the ritual journey in search of medication) is the most important element of Welty's story. By describing Phoenix Jackson's difficult encounters during her ritual journey to town, Welty emphasizes how spiritual and emotional strength can overcome physical frailty and how determination and fearlessness can overcome any danger (Bethea 37). These moral messages become clear by the time Jackson reaches the doctor's office. The image of the elderly woman determinedly walking across the horizon, the image that prompted Welty to write the story, remains in the minds of readers.

Note

1. Unlike the written version of "A Worn Path," the DVD version of the short story ends not at the doctor's office but with a vision similar to the one that inspired Welty to write the story—the elderly African-American woman silently walking along the horizon at dusk.

Works Cited

Bartel, Roland. "Life and Death in Eudora Welty's 'A Worn Path.'" *Studies in Short Fiction* 14.1 (1977): 288-90. Print.

Bethea, Dean. "Phoenix Has No Coat: Historicity, Eschatology, and Sins of Omission in Eudora Welty's 'A Worn Path.'" *International Fiction Review* 27.5 (2001): 32-38. *Expanded Academic ASAP*. Web. 9 Jan. 2011.

Howard, Zelma Turner. *The Rhetoric of Eudora Welty's Short Stories*. Jackson: UP of Mississippi, 1973. Print.

Piwinski, David J. "Mistletoe in Eudora Welty's 'A Worn Path.'" *ANQ* 16.1 (2003): 40-43. *Expanded Academic ASAP*. Web. 9 Jan. 2011.

Saunders, James Robert. "'A Worn Path': The Eternal Quest of Welty's Phoenix Jackson." *Southern Literary Journal* 25.1 (1992): 62-73. Print.

Welty, Eudora. Interview by Beth Henley. *The Heinle Original Film Series in Literature: Eudora Welty's "A Worn Path."* Dir. Bruce R. Schwartz. Wadsworth, 2003. DVD.

---. "A Worn Path." *LIT*. Ed. Laurie G. Kirszner and Stephen R. Mandell. Boston: Wadsworth, 2012. 285-89. Print.

CHECKLIST

USING SOURCES

☐ Acknowledge all material from sources, including the literary work or works under discussion, using the documentation style of the Modern Language Association (MLA).

☐ Combine paraphrases, summaries, and quotations with your own interpretations, weaving quotations smoothly into your paper. Introduce the words or ideas of others with a phrase that identifies their source (**According to Richard Wright's biographer, . . .**), and end with appropriate parenthetical documentation.

☐ Use quotations *only* when something vital would be lost if you did not reproduce the author's exact words.

☐ Integrate short quotations (four lines or fewer of prose or three lines or fewer of poetry) smoothly into your paper. Use a slash (/) with one space on either side to separate lines of poetry. Be sure to enclose quotations in quotation marks.

☐ Set off quotations of more than four lines of prose or more than three lines of poetry by indenting one inch from the left-hand margin. Double-space, and do not use quotation marks. If you are quoting just one paragraph, do not indent the first line.

☐ Use ellipses—three spaced periods—to indicate that you have omitted material within a quotation (but never use ellipses at the beginning of a quoted passage).

☐ Use brackets to indicate that you have added words to a quotation: **As Earl notes, "[Willie] is a modern-day Everyman" (201).** Use brackets to alter a quotation so that it fits grammatically into your sentence: **Wilson says that Miller "offer[s] audiences a dark view of the present" (74).**

☐ Place commas and periods *inside* quotation marks: **According to Robert Coles, the child could "make others smile."**

☐ Place punctuation marks other than commas and periods *outside* quotation marks: **What does Frost mean when he says, "a poem must ride on its own melting"?** If the punctuation mark is part of the quoted material, place it inside the quotation marks: **In "Mending Wall," Frost asks, "Why do they make good neighbors?"**

☐ When citing part of a short story or novel, supply the page number (143). For a poem, supply line numbers (3-5), including the word *line* or *lines* just in the first reference. For a play, supply act, scene, and line numbers (2.2.17-22).

☐ Include a works-cited list (unless your instructor tells you not to).

7

Documenting Sources and Avoiding Plagiarism

Learning Outcomes

After reading this chapter, you should be able to do the following:

LO1 Avoid plagiarism

LO2 Document sources

Documentation is the formal acknowledgment of the sources in a research paper. This chapter explains and illustrates the documentation style recommended by the Modern Language Association (MLA), the style used by students of literature.

WHAT TO DOCUMENT

In general, you must document the following types of information from a source (print or electronic):

- *All word-for-word quotations from a source.* Whenever you use a writer's exact words, you must document them. Even if you quote only a word or two within a paraphrase or summary, you must document the quoted words separately, after the final quotation marks.

- *All ideas from a source that you put into your own words.* Be sure to document all paraphrases or summaries of a source's ideas, including the author's judgments, conclusions, and debatable assertions.

- *All visuals—tables, charts, and photographs—from a source.* Because visuals are almost always someone's original creation, they must be documented.

LO1 Avoid Plagiarism

Plagiarism is the presentation of another person's words or ideas as if they were your own. Most plagiarism is **unintentional plagiarism**—for example, pasting a passage from a downloaded document directly into your paper and forgetting to include quotation marks and documentation. However, there is a difference between an honest mistake and **intentional plagiarism**—for example, copying sentences from a journal article or submitting as your own an essay that someone else has written. The penalties for unintentional plagiarism may sometimes be severe, but intentional plagiarism is intellectual theft and is almost always dealt with harshly.

The best way to avoid unintentional plagiarism is to keep careful notes and to make sure you differentiate your words and ideas from those of your sources.

The guidelines that follow can help you avoid mistakes that lead to unintentional plagiarism.

Certain items do not require documentation: **common knowledge** (information most readers probably know), facts available from a variety of reference sources, familiar sayings and well-known quotations, and your own ideas and conclusions.

DOCUMENT ALL MATERIAL THAT REQUIRES DOCUMENTATION

Original: In Oates's stories there are no safe relationships, but the most perilous of all possibilities is sex. Sex is always destructive. (Tierce, Mike, and John Michael Crafton. "Connie's Tambourine Man: A New Reading of Arnold Friend.")

Plagiarism: In many of Oates's stories, relationships—especially sexual relationships—are dangerous.

In the example above, the writer uses an idea from a source but does not include documentation. As a result, she gives readers the mistaken impression that the source's idea is actually her own.

Correct: Tierce and Crafton point out that in many of Oates's stories, relationships—especially sexual relationships—are dangerous (220).

ENCLOSE BORROWED WORDS IN QUOTATION MARKS

Original: "The Yellow Wallpaper," which Gilman herself called "a description of a case of nervous breakdown," recalls in the first person the experiences of a woman who is evidently suffering from postpartum psychosis. (Gilbert, Sandra M., and Susan Gubar. *The Madwoman in the Attic: The Woman Writer and the Nineteenth-Century Literary Imagination.*)

Plagiarism: As Gilbert and Gubar point out, the narrator in "The Yellow Wallpaper" is evidently suffering from postpartum psychosis (212).

Even though the writer documents the passage, he uses the source's exact words without putting them in quotation marks.

Correct: As Gilbert and Gubar point out, the narrator in "The Yellow Wallpaper" is "evidently suffering from postpartum psychosis" (212).

Do Not Imitate a Source's Syntax and Phrasing

> **Original:** Tennessee Williams's *The Glass Menagerie*, though it has achieved a firmly established position in the canon of American plays, is often distorted, if not misunderstood, by readers, directors, and audiences. (King, Thomas. "Irony and Distance in *The Glass Menagerie*.")

> **Plagiarism:** Although *The Glass Menagerie* has a well-established place in the American theater, it is frequently misinterpreted by those who read it, direct it, and see it (King 125).

Although the student does not use the exact words of the source, he closely follows the sentence structure of the original and simply substitutes synonyms for the writer's key words. Remember, acceptable paraphrases and summaries do more than change words; they use original phrasing and syntax to convey the source's meaning.

> **Correct:** According to Thomas King, although *The Glass Menagerie* has become an American classic, it is still not fully appreciated (125).

Differentiate Your Words from Those of Your Source

> **Original:** At some colleges and universities, traditional survey courses of world and English literature . . . have been scrapped or diluted. . . . What replaces them is sometimes a mere option of electives, sometimes "multicultural" courses introducing material from Third World cultures and thinning out an already thin sampling of Western writings, and sometimes courses geared especially to issues of class, race, and gender. (Howe, Irving. "The Value of the Canon.")

> **Plagiarism:** At many universities, the Western literature survey courses have been edged out by courses that emphasize minority concerns. These courses are "thinning an already thin sampling of Western writings" in favor of courses geared especially to issues of "class, race, and gender" (Howe 40).

Because the student writer does not differentiate his ideas from those of his source, it appears that only the two quotations in the last sentence are borrowed when, in fact, the first sentence also borrows ideas from the original. The student should have identified the boundaries of the borrowed material by introducing it with an identifying phrase and ending with documentation. (Note that a quotation always requires its own documentation.)

Correct: According to Irving Howe, at many universities the Western literature survey courses have been edged out by courses that emphasize minority concerns (41). These courses, says Howe, are "thinning an already thin sampling of Western writings" in favor of courses geared especially to issues of "class, race, and gender" (40).

LO2 Document Sources

MLA documentation has three parts: *parenthetical references in the body of the paper* (also known as *in-text citations*), a *works-cited list*, and *content notes*.*

PARENTHETICAL REFERENCES IN THE TEXT

MLA documentation style uses parenthetical references within the text to refer to an alphabetical works-cited list at the end of the paper. A parenthetical reference should contain just enough information to guide readers to the appropriate entry on your works-cited list.

A typical parenthetical reference consists of the author's last name and a page number.

Gwendolyn Brooks uses the sonnet form to create poems that have a wide social and aesthetic range (Williams 972).

If you mention the author's name or the title of the work in your paper, only a page reference is needed.

According to Gladys Margaret Williams in "Gwendolyn Brooks's Way with the Sonnet," Brooks combines a sensitivity to poetic forms with a depth of emotion appropriate for her subject matter (972-73).

If you use more than one source by the same author, include a shortened title in the parenthetical reference.

Brooks knows not only Shakespeare, Spenser, and Milton, but also the full range of African-American poetry (Williams, "Brooks's Way" 972).

Sample Parenthetical References

An entire work
When citing an entire work, state the name of the author in your paper instead of in a parenthetical reference.

August Wilson's play *Fences* treats many themes frequently expressed in modern drama.

A work by two or three authors

Myths cut across boundaries and cultural spheres and reappear in strikingly similar forms from country to country (Feldman and Richardson 124).

The effect of a work of literature depends on the audience's predispositions that derive from membership in various social groups (Hovland, Janis, and Kelley 87).

*For more information, see the *MLA Handbook for Writers of Research Papers*, 7th ed. (New York: MLA, 2009). You can also consult the MLA Web site at <http://www.mlahandbook.org>.

A work by more than three authors
State the last name of the first author, and use the abbreviation *et al.* (Latin for "and others") for the rest.

> Hawthorne's short stories frequently use a combination of allegorical and symbolic methods (Guerin et al. 91).

A work in an anthology

> In his essay "Flat and Round Characters," E. M. Forster distinguishes between one-dimensional characters and those that are well developed (Stevick 223-31).

Note that the parenthetical reference cites the anthology (edited by Stevick) that contains Forster's essay; full information about the anthology appears in the works-cited list.

A work with volume and page numbers

> Critics consider *The Zoo Story* to be one of Albee's best plays (Eagleton 2: 17).

An indirect source
Use the abbreviation qtd. in ("quoted in") to indicate that the quoted material was not taken directly from the original source.

> Wagner observed that myth and history stood before him "with opposing claims" (qtd. in Winkler 10).

A play with numbered lines
The parenthetical reference should contain the act, scene, and line numbers (in arabic numerals), separated by periods. When included in parenthetical references, titles of the books of the Bible and well-known literary works are often abbreviated—Gen. for Genesis and *Ham.* for *Hamlet*, for example.

> "Give thy thoughts no tongue," says Polonius, "Nor any unproportioned thought his act" (*Ham.* 1.3.64-65).

A poem
Use a slash (/) to separate lines of poetry run in with the text. (The slash is preceded and followed by one space.) The parenthetical reference should cite the lines quoted. Include the word line or lines in the first reference but just the numbers in subsequent references.

> "I muse my life-long hate, and without flinch / I bear it nobly as I live my part," says the speaker in Claude McKay's bitterly ironic poem "The White City" (lines 3-4).

An electronic source
If you are citing a source from the Internet or from an online database, use page numbers if possible. If the source uses paragraph, section, or screen numbers, use the abbreviation par. or sec. or the full word screen.

> The earliest type of movie censoring came in the form of licensing fees, and in Deer River, Minnesota, "a licensing fee of $200 was deemed not excessive for a town of 1000" (Ernst, par. 20).

If an Internet source has no page, paragraph, section, or screen markers, cite the entire work. (When readers consult your works-cited list, they will be able to determine the nature of the source.)

> In her article "Limited Horizons," Lynne Cheney says that schools do best when students read literature not for practical information but for its insights into the human condition.

> Because of its parody of communism, the film *Antz* is actually an adult film masquerading as a child's tale (Clemin).

THE WORKS-CITED LIST

Parenthetical references refer to a **works-cited list** that includes all the sources you refer to in your paper:

- Begin the works-cited list on a new page, continuing the page numbers of the paper. For example, if the text of the paper ends on page 6, the works-cited list will begin on page 7.
  - Center the title Works Cited one inch from the top of the page.
  - Arrange entries alphabetically, according to the last name of each author. Use the first word of the title if the author is unknown (articles—*a*, *an*, and *the*—at the beginning of a title are not considered first words).

> *"Each works-cited entry has three divisions—author, title, and publishing information— separated by periods."*

- Double-space the entire works-cited list between and within entries.
- Begin typing each entry at the left margin, and indent subsequent lines one-half inch.
- Each works-cited entry has three divisions—*author*, *title*, and *publishing information*—separated by periods. The *MLA Handbook for Writers of Research Papers* shows a single space after all end punctuation.

Below is a directory listing the sample MLA works-cited list entries that begin on page 77.

Directory of MLA Works-Cited List Entries

Print Sources: Entries for Articles

1. An article in a journal
2. An article in a magazine
3. An article in a daily newspaper
4. An article in a reference book

Print Sources: Entries for Books

5. A book by a single author
6. A book by two or three authors
7. A book by more than three authors
8. Two or more works by the same author
9. An edited book
10. A book with a volume number
11. A short story, poem, or play in a collection of the author's work
12. A short story in an anthology
13. A poem in an anthology
14. A play in an anthology
15. An article in an anthology
16. More than one article from the same anthology
17. A translation

Entries for Other Sources

18. An interview
19. A lecture or an address

Electronic Sources: Entries from Internet Sites

20. A scholarly project or information database on the Internet
21. A document within a scholarly project or information database on the Internet
22. A personal site on the Internet
23. A book on the Internet
24. An article in a scholarly journal on the Internet
25. An article in an encyclopedia on the Internet
26. An article in a newspaper on the Internet
27. An article in a magazine on the Internet
28. A painting or photograph on the Internet
29. An email
30. An online posting

Electronic Sources: Entries from Online Databases

31. A scholarly journal article from an online database
32. A monthly magazine article from an online database
33. A newspaper article from an online database
34. A reference book article from an online database
35. A dictionary definition from an online database

Entries for Other Electronic Sources

36. A nonperiodical publication on DVD-ROM or CD-ROM
37. A periodical publication on DVD-ROM or CD-ROM
38. A film, videocassette, DVD, or CD-ROM

MLA PRINT SOURCES • Entries for Articles

Article citations include the author's name; the title of the article (in quotation marks); the name of the periodical (italicized); the volume and issue numbers (if applicable; see below); the month, if applicable (abbreviated, except for May, June, and July), and the year; the pages on which the full article appears (without the abbreviations *p.* or *pp.*); and the publication medium.

1. An article in a journal

> Grossman, Robert. "The Grotesque in Faulkner's 'A Rose for Emily.'" *Mosaic* 20.3 (1987): 40-55. Print.

Note that 20.3 signifies volume 20, issue 3.

2. An article in a magazine

> Milosz, Czeslaw. "A Lecture." *New Yorker* 22 June 1992: 32. Print.

An article with no listed author is entered by title on the works-cited list.

> "Solzhenitsyn: An Artist Becomes an Exile." *Time* 25 Feb. 1974: 34+. Print.

Note that *34+* indicates that the article appears on pages that are not consecutive; in this case, the article begins on page 34 and continues on page 37.

3. An article in a daily newspaper

Omit the article *the* from the title of a newspaper even if the newspaper's actual title includes the article.

> Oates, Joyce Carol. "When Characters from the Page Are Made Flesh on the Screen." *New York Times* 23 Mar. 1986, late ed.: C1+. Print.

Note that *C1+* indicates that the article begins on page 1 of Section C and continues on a subsequent page.

4. An article in a reference book

Do not include full publication information for well-known reference books.

> "Dance Theatre of Harlem." *The New Encyclopaedia Britannica: Micropaedia.* 2008 ed. Print.

Include full publication information when citing reference books that are not well known.

> Grimstead, David. "Fuller, Margaret Sarah." *Encyclopedia of American Biography.* Ed. John A. Garraty. New York: Harper, 1996. Print.

MLA PRINT SOURCES • Entries for Books

Book citations include the author's name; book title (italicized); and publication information (place, publisher, date, publication medium). Capitalize all major words in the title except articles, prepositions, and the *to* of an infinitive (unless it is the first or last word of the title or subtitle). MLA requires that you abbreviate publishers' names—for example, *Basic* for Basic Books and *Oxford UP* for Oxford University Press.

5. A book by a single author

> Kingston, Maxine Hong. *The Woman Warrior: Memoirs of a Girlhood among Ghosts.* New York: Knopf, 1976. Print.

6. A book by two or three authors

> Feldman, Burton, and Robert D. Richardson. *The Rise of Modern Mythology*. Bloomington: Indiana UP, 1972. Print.

Note that only the *first* author's name is in reverse order.

7. A book by more than three authors

> Guerin, Wilfred, et al., eds. *A Handbook of Critical Approaches to Literature*. 5th ed. New York: Harper, 2004. Print.

Note that instead of using et al., you may list all the authors' names in the order in which they appear on the title page.

8. Two or more works by the same author

List two or more works by the same author in alphabetical order by *title*. Include the author's full name in the first entry; use three unspaced hyphens followed by a period to take the place of the author's name in second and subsequent entries.

> Novoa, Juan-Bruce. *Chicano Authors: Inquiry by Interview*. Austin: U of Texas P, 1980. Print.
> ---. "Themes in Rudolfo Anaya's Work." Literature Colloquium. New Mexico State U, Las Cruces. 11 Apr. 2002. Address.

9. An edited book

> Oosthuizen, Ann, ed. *Sometimes When It Rains: Writings by South African Women*. New York: Pandora, 1987. Print.

Note that here the abbreviation *ed.* stands for *editor*.

10. A book with a volume number

When all the volumes of a multivolume work have the same title, list the number of the volume you used.

> Eagleton, T. Allston. *A History of the New York Stage*. Vol. 2. Englewood Cliffs: Prentice, 1987. Print.

When each volume of a multivolume work has a separate title, list the title of the volume you used.

> Durant, Will, and Ariel Durant. *The Age of Napoleon: A History of European Civilization from 1789 to 1815*. New York: Simon, 1975. Print.

(*The Age of Napoleon* is volume 2 of *The Story of Civilization*. You need not provide documentation for the entire multivolume work.)

11. A short story, poem, or play in a collection of the author's work

> Gordimer, Nadine. "Once upon a Time." *"Jump" and Other Stories*. New York: Farrar, 1991. 23-30. Print.

12. A short story in an anthology

> Salinas, Marta. "The Scholarship Jacket." *Nosotros: Latina Literature Today*. Ed. Maria del Carmen Boza, Beverly Silva, and Carmen Valle. Binghamton: Bilingual, 1986. 68-70. Print.

Note that here the abbreviation *Ed.* stands for *Edited by.* The inclusive page numbers follow the year of publication.

13. A poem in an anthology

Simmerman, Jim. "Child's Grave, Hale County, Alabama." *The Pushcart Prize, X: Best of the Small Presses.* Ed. Bill Henderson. New York: Penguin, 1986. 198-99. Print.

14. A play in an anthology

Hughes, Langston. *Mother and Child. Black Drama Anthology.* Ed. Woodie King and Ron Miller. New York: NAL, 1986. 399-406. Print.

15. An article in an anthology

Forster, E. M. "Flat and Round Characters." *The Theory of the Novel.* Ed. Philip Stevick. New York: Free, 1980. 223-31. Print.

16. More than one article from the same anthology

If you are using more than one article from an anthology, cite the anthology in a separate entry. Then, list each individual selection separately, including the author and title of the selection, the anthology editor's last name, and the inclusive page numbers.

Baxter, Charles. "Gryphon." Kirszner and Mandell 138–45.

Kirszner, Laurie G., and Stephen R. Mandell, eds. *LIT.* Boston: Wadsworth, 2012. Print.

Rich, Adrienne. "Diving into the Wreck." Kirszner and Mandell 469-70.

17. A translation

Carpentier, Alejo. *Reasons of State.* Trans. Francis Partridge. New York: Norton, 1976. Print.

Entries for Other Sources
18. An interview

Brooks, Gwendolyn. "An Interview with Gwendolyn Brooks." *Triquarterly* 60 (1984): 405-10. Print.

19. A lecture or an address

Novoa, Juan-Bruce. "Themes in Rudolfo Anaya's Work." Literature Colloquium. New Mexico State U, Las Cruces. 11 Apr. 2002. Address.

MLA ELECTRONIC SOURCES: • Entries from Internet Sites

MLA style recognizes that full publication information is not always available for electronic sources. Include in your citation whatever information you can reasonably obtain: the author or editor of the site (if available); the title of the Internet site (italicized); the version number of the source (if applicable); the name of any sponsoring institution (if unavailable, include the abbreviation N.p. for "no publisher"); the date of electronic publication or update (if unavailable, include the abbreviation n.d. for "no date of publication"); the publication medium (Web); and the date of access. MLA recommends omitting the URL from the citation unless it is necessary to find the source. If a URL is necessary, MLA requires that you enclose it within angle brackets. If you have to carry the URL over to the next line, divide it after a slash.

20. A scholarly project or information database on the Internet

> Nelson, Cary, ed. *Modern American Poetry*. Dept. of English, U of Illinois, Urbana-Champaign, 2002. Web. 26 May 2010.

21. A document within a scholarly project or information database on the Internet

> "D-Day: June 6th, 1944." *History.com.* History Channel, 1999. Web. 7 June 2010.

22. A personal site on the Internet

> Yerkes, James. *The Centaurian: John Updike Home Page.*Prexar, 15 June 2009. Web. 19 June 2010. <http://userpages.prexar.com/joyerkes/>.

23. A book on the Internet

> Douglass, Frederick. *My Bondage and My Freedom*. Boston, 1855. *Google Book Search*. Web. 8 June 2010.

24. An article in a scholarly journal on the Internet

> DeKoven, Marianne. "Utopias Limited: Post-Sixties and Postmodern American Fiction." *Modern Fiction Studies* 41.1 (1995): 75-97. Web. 17 Mar. 2010.

When you cite information from the print version of an electronic source, include the publication information for the printed source, the inclusive page numbers (if available), the publication medium, and the date of access.

25. An article in an encyclopedia on the Internet

> "Hawthorne, Nathaniel." *Encyclopaedia Britannica Online*. Encyclopaedia Britannica, 2007. Web. 16 May 2010.

26. An article in a newspaper on the Internet

> Cave, Damien. "Election Day May Look Familiar." *New York Times*. New York Times, 28 Apr. 2008. Web. 29 Apr. 2010.

27. An article in a magazine on the Internet

> Weiser, Jay. "The Tyranny of Informality." *Time*. Time, 26 Feb. 1996. Web. 1 Mar. 2010.

28. A painting or photograph on the Internet

> Lange, Dorothea. *Looking at Pictures*. 1936. Museum of Mod. Art, New York. *MoMA. org*. Web. 17 July 2010.

29. An email

> Mauk, Karen. Message to the author. 28 June 2010. E-mail.

30. An online posting

> Berg, Kirsten. "Bright Angel." Online posting. *PowellsBooks.Blog*. Powells, 17 June 2009. Web. 18 June 2010.

MLA ELECTRONIC SOURCES: • Entries from Online Databases

To cite information from an online database, supply the publication information (including page numbers, if available; if unavailable, use n. pag.) followed by the italicized name of the database, the publication medium (Web), and the date of access.

> Luckenbill, Trent. "Environmental Litigation: Down the Endless Corridor." *Environment* 17 July 2001: 34-42. *ABI/INFORM GLOBAL*. Web. 12 Oct. 2010.

31. *A scholarly journal article from an online database*

> Schaefer, Richard J. "Editing Strategies in Television News Documentaries." *Journal of Communication* 47.4 (1997): 69-89. *InfoTrac OneFile Plus*. Web. 2 Oct. 2010.

32. *A monthly magazine article from an online database*

> Livermore, Beth. "Meteorites on Ice." *Astronomy* July 1993:54-58. *Expanded Academic ASAP Plus*. Web. 2 Oct. 2010.

33. *A newspaper article from an online database*

> Meyer, Greg. "Answering Questions about the West Nile Virus." *Dayton Daily News* 11 July 2002: Z3-7. *LexisNexis*. Web. 2 Oct. 2010.

34. *A reference book article from an online database*

> Laird, Judith. "Geoffrey Chaucer." *Cyclopedia of World Authors*. 1997. *MagillOnLiterature*. Web. 2 Oct. 2010.

35. *A dictionary definition from an online database*

> "Migraine." *Mosby's Medical, Nursing, and Allied Health Dictionary*. 1998 ed. *Health Reference Center*. Web. 2 Oct. 2010.

MLA ELECTRONIC SOURCES • Entries from Other Electronic Sources

36. *A nonperiodical publication on DVD-ROM or CD-ROM*

> "Windhover." *Concise Oxford English Dictionary*. 11th ed. Oxford: Oxford UP, 2009. CD-ROM.

37. *A periodical publication on DVD-ROM or CD-ROM*

> Zurbach, Kate. "The Linguistic Roots of Three Terms." *Linguistic Quarterly* 37 (1994): 12-47. CD-ROM. *InfoTrac: Magazine Index Plus*. Information Access. Jan. 2011.

38. A film, videocassette, DVD, or CD-ROM

> *The Heinle Original Film Series in Literature:*
> *Eudora Welty's "A Worn Path."* Dir. Bruce
> R. Schwartz. Wadsworth, 2003. DVD.

CONTENT NOTES

Use **content notes**, indicated by a superscript (a raised number) in the text, to cite several sources at once or to provide commentary or explanations that do not fit smoothly into your paper. The full text of these notes appears on the first numbered page following the last page of the paper. (If your paper has no content notes, the works-cited page follows the last page of the paper.) Like works-cited entries, content notes are double-spaced within and between entries. However, the first line of each explanatory note is indented one-half inch, and subsequent lines are flush with the left-hand margin.

> "Use content notes, indicated by a superscript (a raised number) in the text, to cite several sources at once or to provide commentary or explanations that do not fit smoothly into your paper."

To Cite Several Sources

In the paper

> Surprising as it may seem, there have been many attempts to define literature.[1]

In the note

> 1. For an overview of critical opinion, see Arnold 72; Eagleton 1-2; Howe 43-44; and Abrams 232-34.

To Provide Explanations

In the paper

> In recent years, gothic novels have achieved great popularity.[3]

In the note

> 3. Gothic novels, works written in imitation of medieval romances, originally relied on supernatural occurrences. They flourished in the late eighteenth and early nineteenth centuries.

CHECKLISTS

PLAGIARISM AND INTERNET SOURCES

To avoid accidental plagiarism with Internet sources, follow these guidelines:

- ☐ Download material into individual files so you can easily keep track of your sources.
- ☐ Do not cut and paste blocks of downloaded text directly into your paper. Summarize or paraphrase this material first.
- ☐ If you use the exact words of a source, enclose them in boldface quotation marks. If you do this, you will know that you need to document this material.
- ☐ Record full documentation information for emails, Web sites, and online postings.

GUIDELINES FOR PUNCTUATING PARENTHETICAL REFERENCES

Paraphrases and Summaries

Place the parenthetical reference *after* the last word of the sentence and *before* the final punctuation.

> In her poems, Brooks combines the pessimism of modernist poetry with the optimism of the Harlem Renaissance (Smith 978).

Direct Quotations Run in with the Text

Place the parenthetical reference *after* the quotation marks and *before* the final punctuation.

> According to Gary Smith, Brooks's *A Street in Bronzeville* "conveys the primacy of suffering in the lives of poor Black women" (980).
>
> According to Gary Smith, the poems in *A Street in Bronzeville* "served notice that Brooks had learned her craft . . ." (978).
>
> Along with Thompson, we must ask, "Why did it take so long for critics to acknowledge that Gwendolyn Brooks is an important voice in twentieth-century American poetry" (123)?

Quotations Set Off from the Text

Omit the quotation marks, and place the parenthetical reference one space *after* the final punctuation. (For guidelines for setting off long quotations, see p. 70.)

> For Gary Smith, the identity of Brooks's African-American women is inextricably linked with their sense of race and poverty:
>
> > For Brooks, unlike the Renaissance poets, the victimization of poor Black women becomes not simply a minor chord but a predominant theme of *A Street in Bronzeville*. Few, if any, of her female characters are able to free themselves from a web of poverty that threatens to strangle their lives. (980)

8

Writing Essay Exams about Literature

Learning Outcomes

After reading this chapter, you should be able to do the following:

LO1 Plan an essay exam answer

LO2 Shape an essay exam answer

LO3 Draft and revise an essay exam answer

Taking exams is a skill that you have been developing throughout your career as a student. Short-answer exams and essay exams require you to study, to recall what you know, and to budget your time carefully as you write your answers. Only essay questions, however, ask you to synthesize information and to arrange ideas in a series of clear, logically connected sentences and paragraphs. For this reason, taking essay exams requires writing skills. To write an essay exam—or even a paragraph-length response—you must do more than memorize facts; you must identify the relationships among them. In other words, you must **think critically** about your subject, and you must plan, shape, draft, and revise an essay that clearly communicates your ideas to your audience.

LO1 Plan an Essay Exam Answer

Because you are under pressure during an exam and tend to write quickly, you may be tempted to skip the planning and revision stages of the writing process. But if you write in a frenzy and hand in your exam without a second glance, you are likely to produce a disorganized (or even incoherent)

answer. With careful planning, you can write an essay that demonstrates your understanding of the material.

REVIEW YOUR MATERIAL

Be sure you know beforehand the scope and format of the exam. How much of your textbook and class notes will the exam cover—the entire semester's work or only the material covered since the last test? Will you have to answer every question, or will you be able to choose among alternatives? Will the exam test your ability to recall specific facts, or will it require you to demonstrate your understanding of the course material by drawing original conclusions?

Exams challenge you to recall and express in writing what you already know—what you have read, what you have heard in class, what you have reviewed in your notes. Before you even begin an exam, you must study: reread your textbook and class notes, highlight key points, and perhaps outline particularly important sections of your notes. When you prepare for a short-answer exam, you may memorize facts without analyzing their relationship to one another or their relationship to a body of knowledge as a whole: the definition of romanticism, the date of

> *"When you prepare for an essay exam, . . . you must do more than remember bits of information; you must also make connections among ideas."*

Queen Victoria's death, two examples of irony, four characteristics of a villanelle. When you prepare for an essay exam, however, you must do more than remember bits of information; you must also make connections among ideas.

When you are sure you know what to expect, try to anticipate the essay questions your instructor might ask. Try out likely questions on classmates, and see whether you can do some collaborative brainstorming to outline answers to possible questions. If you have time, you might even practice answering one or two in writing.

CONSIDER YOUR AUDIENCE AND PURPOSE

The audience for any exam is the instructor who prepared it. As you read the questions, think about what your instructor has emphasized in class. Although you may certainly arrange material in a new way or use it to make an original point, keep in mind that your purpose is to demonstrate that you understand the material, not to make clever remarks or introduce irrelevant information. In addition, you should make every effort to use the vocabulary of the discipline for which you are writing and to follow the specific **conventions** for writing about literature (p. 28).

READ THROUGH THE ENTIRE EXAM

Your time is usually limited when you take an exam, so plan carefully. How long should a "one-paragraph" or "essay-length" answer be? How much time should you devote to answering each question? The exam question itself may specify the time allotted for each answer, so look for that information. More often, the point value of each question or the number of questions on the exam indicates how much time to spend on each answer. If an essay question is worth 50 out of 100 points, for example, you will probably have to spend at least half of your time planning, writing, and revising your answer.

Before you begin to write, read the entire exam carefully to determine your priorities and your strategy. First, be sure that your copy of the test is complete and that you understand exactly what each question requires. If you need clarification, ask your instructor or proctor for help. Then, decide where to start. If there is more than one question on the exam, responding first to the one you feel most confident about is usually a good strategy. This approach ensures that you will not become bogged down responding to a question that baffles you

and have too little time to write a strong answer to a question that you understand well.

READ EACH QUESTION CAREFULLY

To write an effective answer, you need to understand the question. As you read any essay question, you may find it helpful to underline key words and important terms.

<u>Summarize in detail</u> the contributions of American <u>writers</u> of the <u>Harlem Renaissance,</u> <u>briefly outlining</u> the contributions of <u>artists and musicians.</u>

Look carefully at the question's wording. If the question calls for a comparison and contrast of two works of literature, a description or analysis of *one* work, no matter how comprehensive, will not be acceptable. If a question asks for causes *and* effects, a discussion of causes alone will be insufficient.

KEY WORDS IN EXAM QUESTIONS		
Analyze	Describe	Interpret
Clarify	Discuss	Justify
Classify	Evaluate	Relate
Compare	Explain	Summarize
Contrast	Identify	Support
Define	Illustrate	Trace

As its key words indicate, the following question calls for a very specific kind of response.

Question

Identify <u>three differences</u> between the <u>hard-boiled detective story</u> and the <u>classical detective story.</u>

The following response to the question simply *identifies* three characteristics of *one* kind of detective story and is therefore not acceptable.

Unacceptable Answer

The hard-boiled detective story, popularized in *Black Mask* magazine in the 1930s and 1940s, is very different from the classical detective stories of Edgar Allan Poe or Agatha Christie. The hard-boiled stories feature a down-on-his-luck detective who is constantly tempted and betrayed. His world is dark and chaotic, and the crimes he tries to solve are not out-of-the-ordinary occurrences; they are the norm. These stories have no happy endings; even when the crime is solved, the world is still corrupt.

The answer below, which *contrasts* the two kinds of detective stories, is acceptable.

Acceptable Answer

The hard-boiled detective story differs from the classical detective story in its characters, its setting, and its plot. The classical detective is usually well educated and well off; he is aloof from the other characters and therefore can remain in total control of the situation. The hard-boiled detective, on the other hand, is typically a decent but down-on-his-luck man who is drawn into the chaos around him, constantly tempted and betrayed. In the orderly world of the classical detective, the crime is a temporary disruption. In the hard-boiled detective's dark and chaotic world, the crimes he tries to solve are the norm. In the classical detective story, order is restored at the end. Hard-boiled stories have no happy endings; even when the crime is solved, the world is still a corrupt and dangerous place.

BRAINSTORM TO FIND IDEAS

Once you understand the question, you need to find something to say. Begin by **brainstorming**—quickly listing all of the relevant ideas you can remember about a topic. Then, identify the most important points on your list, and delete the others. A quick review of the exam question and your supporting ideas should lead you toward a workable thesis for your essay.

LO2 Shape an Essay Exam Answer

STATE YOUR THESIS

Often, you can rephrase the exam question as a **thesis statement**. For example, the question "Discuss in detail the contributions of American writers of the Harlem Renaissance, briefly outlining the contributions of artists and musicians" suggests the following thesis statement.

Effective Thesis Statement

Writers of the Harlem Renaissance—notably Richard Wright, Gwendolyn Brooks, Zora Neale Hurston, and Langston Hughes—made significant contributions to American literature; artists and musicians of the movement also left an important legacy.

An effective thesis statement addresses all aspects of the exam question but highlights only relevant concerns. The following thesis statements are not effective.

Vague Thesis Statement

The Harlem Renaissance produced many important writers, artists, and musicians.

Incomplete Thesis Statement

The writers of the Harlem Renaissance, such as Richard Wright, Gwendolyn Brooks, Zora Neale Hurston, and Langston Hughes, made significant contributions to American literature.

Irrelevant Thesis Statement

The writers of the Harlem Renaissance had a greater impact on American literature than the writers of the Beat generation, such as Jack Kerouac.

MAKE A SCRATCH OUTLINE

Because time is limited, you should plan your answer before you begin to write it. Therefore, once you have decided on a suitable thesis, you should make a **scratch outline** that lists the points you will use to support your thesis.

On the inside cover of your exam book, arrange your supporting points in the order in which you plan to discuss them. Once you have completed your outline, check it against the exam question to make certain it covers everything the question calls for—and *only* what the question calls for.

A scratch outline for an answer to the question "Discuss in detail the contributions of American writers of the Harlem Renaissance, briefly outlining the contributions of artists and musicians" might look like this.

Thesis statement:

Writers of the Harlem Renaissance—notably Richard Wright, Gwendolyn Brooks, Zora Neale Hurston, and Langston Hughes—made significant contributions to American literature; artists and musicians of the movement also left an important legacy.

Writers

Wright—*Uncle Tom's Children, Black Boy, Native Son*

Brooks—poetry (classical forms; social issues)

Hurston—*Their Eyes Were Watching God,* essays, autobiography

Hughes—poetry (ballads, blues); "Simple" stories

Artists and Musicians

Henry Tanner

Duke Ellington

LO3 Draft and Revise an Essay Exam Answer

Referring to your outline, you can now begin to draft your answer. Don't bother crafting an elaborate or unusual **introduction**; your time is precious, and so is your reader's. A simple statement of your thesis that summarizes your answer is your best introductory strategy. This approach is efficient, and it reminds you to address the question directly.

To develop the **body** of the essay, follow your outline point by point, using specifically worded topic sentences to introduce your supporting points and clear transitions to indicate your progression from point to point (and to help your instructor see that you are answering the question in

full). Such signals, along with parallel sentence structure and repeated words, will make your essay easy to follow.

The most effective **conclusion** for an essay exam is a clear, simple restatement of the thesis or a summary of the essay's main points.

Essay answers should be complete and detailed, but they should not contain irrelevant material. Every unnecessary fact or opinion increases your chance of error, so don't repeat yourself or volunteer unrequested information, and don't express your own feelings or opinions unless such information is specifically called for. Finally, be sure to support all your general statements with specific examples.

Don't forget to leave enough time to reread and revise what you have written. When you reread, try to view your answer from a fresh perspective. Is your thesis statement clearly worded? Does your essay support your thesis and answer the question? Are your facts correct, and are your ideas presented in a logical order? Review your topic sentences and transitions, and check sentence structure and word choice, spelling and punctuation. If a sentence—or even a whole paragraph—seems irrelevant, cross it out. If you suddenly remember something you want to add, you can insert a few additional words with a caret (^). Neatly insert a longer addition at the end of your answer, box it, and label it so your instructor will know where it belongs. Finally, be sure that you have written legibly and that you have not inadvertently left out any words.

MODEL STUDENT ESSAY
EXAM ANSWER

The essay exam answer on page 88 was written in response to the following question.

Question

Fictional characters (like real people) do not always behave as others want them to. Sometimes they rebel against the expectations of their family or their society. In a clearly written and supported essay, explain how the specific actions of any three characters in works we have read this semester defy the expectations of those around them. Then, briefly consider the consequences of each character's decision to rebel.

As you read the following response to the question, notice that the student writer does not include any irrelevant information. She does not, for example, provide unnecessary plot summary or discuss more than three characters; she covers only what the question asks for. Guided by the question's key words—*explain* and *briefly consider*—she describes how each character's actions are defiant and outlines the consequences of those actions.

Thesis statement

Many characters we have read about this semester do not behave as others believe they should behave. This is apparent in the actions of Connie in Joyce Carol Oates's short story "Where Are You Going, Where Have You Been?," Nora in Henrik Ibsen's play *A Doll House*, and Marty in Paddy Chayefsky's play *Marty*. For each of these characters, rebellion comes with a significant sacrifice.

Introduction echoes wording of exam question and introduces three characters to be discussed

Connie's rebellion is somewhat typical for a teenager: she rebels against the constraints her parents put on her to be a "good girl" by being a "bad girl" (at least in their terms). The makeup and style of clothing that Connie wears when she is away from home reinforce this "bad girl" image. Her behavior—staying out late, lying about where she is going, having "trashy daydreams"—creates a problem for her parents because she is not conforming to their standards and because she is not conducting herself in a manner they consider appropriate. Her actions also put a strain on the relationship between her and her sister, who is the perfect example of a "good girl." Her determination to rebel ultimately makes her stay home from the family outing, and this in turn leaves her alone and vulnerable to Arnold's advances. Thus, her rebellious actions lead to probable violence (she goes with Arnold, who we know has frightening plans for her). The ending of the story is ambiguous. We do not know if she ever comes back; possibly, her innocent rebellion leads to her death.

First character's actions explained

Conse-quences of actions

Nora in *A Doll House* rebels only after she understands the conflict between her duty to herself to be a "real" person and her duty to her husband and children. Throughout the play, we see this conflict escalating until Nora has no choice but to act to resolve it, choosing to go against the norms of society and against how others think she should act. This behavior creates a problem for Torvald because of the image it presents to others. Torvald's greatest fear is that society will not accept him, and when Nora admits what she has done, he panics. At the end of the play, Nora chooses to be true to herself even though the person closest to her does not approve—and even though she will lose her children. She will be a stronger person because she has found the courage to stand up for herself.

Second character's actions explained

Conse-quences of actions

Marty's rebellious act is simply his decision to call Clara even though his friends and his mother do not approve. Although Marty is an adult, he is very much still an adolescent in some ways. He has not yet broken away from his mother, and he continues to seek approval from her (and from his friends). He struggles to please his mother—by going to the dance, by allowing Aunt Catherine to move in with them—even when her desires are in conflict with his own. Marty's action at the play's end—calling Clara—will create a problem for his mother and for his friends, who fear his growing independence and fight his decision to pursue a relationship with Clara. But Marty, like Nora, chooses to be true to himself and to do what he thinks is the right thing for him, rather than what others force upon him. He risks hurting his mother, alienating his friends, and losing the only life he knows. But for Marty, the potential gains seem worth the risk.

Third character's actions explained

Conse-quences of actions

Connie, Nora, and Marty all break with family and society; all struggle to be independent. For all three, this independence has a cost. Connie may lose her life, Nora gives up her marriage and her children, and Marty leaves behind the comforting, secure existence he has known. Although each character deals with conflict and rebellion in a different way, all three struggle within themselves when decisions they must make are in conflict with the norms and expectations of society. For all three, rebellion leads to sacrifice.

Conclu-sion

✔ CHECKLIST

GUIDELINES FOR WRITING ESSAY EXAMS ABOUT LITERATURE
☐ Be sure you understand the scope and format of the exam.
☐ Be sure you understand your purpose and your audience's expectations.
☐ Read and highlight the exam question before you begin to write.
☐ Use the wording of the exam question to help you write your thesis statement.
☐ Include plenty of specific supporting facts and examples—and no irrelevant material.
☐ Leave enough time to reread your essay so you can revise it if necessary.

PART 2
FICTION

9

Understanding Fiction

Learning Outcomes

After reading this chapter, you should be able to do the following:

LO1 Identify the origins of modern fiction

LO2 Define the short story

LO3 Understand the boundaries of fiction

narrative tells a story by presenting events in some logical or orderly way. A work of **fiction** is a narrative that originates in the imagination of the author rather than in history or fact. Certainly some fiction—historical or autobiographical fiction, for example—focuses on real people and is grounded in actual events, but the way the characters interact, what they say, and how the plot unfolds are largely the author's invention.

Even before they know how to read, most people learn how narratives are structured. As children learn how to tell a story, they start to experiment with its form, learning the value of exaggerating, adding or deleting details, rearranging events, and bending facts. In other words, they learn how to *fictionalize* a narrative to achieve a desired effect. This kind of informal personal narrative is similar in many respects to more structured literary narratives.

LO1 Identify the Origins of Modern Fiction

The earliest examples of narrative fiction are linked with our understanding of stories in general. People have always had stories to tell, and as we evolved, so did our

> **narrative** The "storytelling" of a piece of fiction; the forward-moving recounting of episode and description. When an event that occurred earlier is told during a later sequence of events, it is called a **flashback**; suggesting earlier in a narration something that will occur later on is called **foreshadowing**.
>
> **fiction** Form of narrative that is primarily imaginative, though its form may resemble that of factual writing like history and biography.

rhyme Repetition of concluding sounds in different words, often intentionally used at the ends of poetic lines.

alliteration Repetition of consonant sounds (usually the initial sounds) in a series of words, as in Blake's "The Chimney Sweeper": "So your chimneys I sweep, and in soot I sleep." Alliteration may be reinforced by repeated sounds within and at the ends of words.

epic Long narrative poem, such as the *Iliad* or the *Aeneid*, recounting the adventures of heroes on whose actions the fate of a nation or race depends. Frequently the gods or other supernatural beings take active interest in the events.

romance Type of narrative that deals with love and adventure in a nonrealistic way, most popular in the Middle Ages but sometimes used by more modern authors, such as Hawthorne.

means of self-expression. Our early ancestors depicted the stories of their daily lives and beliefs in primitive drawings that used pictures as symbols. As language evolved, so too did our means of communicating—and our need to preserve what we understood to be our past.

Stories and songs emerged as an oral means of communicating and preserving the past: tales of heroic battles or struggles, myths, or religious beliefs. In a society that was not literate, and in a time before mass communication, the oral tradition enabled people to pass down these stories, usually in the form of long rhyming poems. These poems used various literary devices—including **rhyme** and **alliteration** as well as **anaphora** (the repetition of key words or phrases)—

to make them easier to remember. Thus, the earliest works of fiction were in fact poetry.

Eventually written down, these extended narratives developed into **epics**—long narrative poems about heroic figures whose actions determine the fate of a nation or of an entire race. Homer's *Iliad* and *Odyssey*, the ancient Babylonian *Epic of Gilgamesh*, the Hindu *Bhagavad Gita*, and the Anglo-Saxon *Beowulf* are examples of epics. Many of the tales of the Old Testament also came out of this tradition. The setting of an epic is vast—sometimes worldwide or cosmic, including heaven and hell—and the action commonly involves a battle or a perilous journey. Quite often, divine beings participate in the action and influence the outcome of events, as they do in the Trojan War in the *Iliad* and in the founding of Rome in Virgil's *Aeneid*.

During the Middle Ages, these early epics were supplanted by the **romance.** Written initially in verse and later in prose, the romance replaced the gods, goddesses, and central heroic characters of the epic with knights, kings, and damsels in distress. Events were controlled by enchantments rather than by the will of divine beings. The anonymously written *Sir Gawain and the Green Knight* and Thomas Malory's *Le Morte d'Arthur* are romances based on the legend of King Arthur and the Knights of the Round Table.

Other significant texts of the Middle Ages are Geoffrey Chaucer's *The Canterbury Tales* and Giovanni Boccaccio's *The Decameron*, both written in the fourteenth century. These works are made up of poems and stories, respectively, integrated into a larger narrative framework. They have much in common with modern collections of linked short stories, such as Sherwood Anderson's 1919 *Winesburg, Ohio*.

© Bettmann/Corbis

>> Engraving of Ulysses slaying Penelope's suitors, from Homer's *Odyssey*.

© Bettmann/Corbis

>> Engraving of the Trojan horse from Homer's *Iliad*.

THE HISTORY OF THE NOVEL

The evolution of the **novel** has been a gradual but steady process. Early forms of literature share many of the characteristics of the novel (although not necessarily sharing its recognizable form). Epics and romances, for instance, often had unified plots, developed characters, and complex themes, and in this way, they were precursors of what we call the novel today.

Perhaps the most notable event in the development of the novel, and of literature as a whole, was the invention of the printing press by Johannes Gutenberg in 1440. Before this milestone, printing was a costly and impractical process that was largely reserved for medical books and sacred texts. In fact, this invention made the production and distribution of longer works a practical possibility and forever expanded the scope of what we consider literature to be—and how we access it. In fact, the printing press was one of the factors that made the Renaissance possible. During this period, philosophy, science, literature, and the arts flowered. The **pastoral romance,** a prose tale set in an idealized rural world, and the **character,** a brief satirical sketch illustrating a type of personality, both became popular in Renaissance England. The **picaresque novel,** an episodic, often satirical work about a rogue or rascal (such as Miguel de Cervantes's *Don Quixote*), emerged in seventeenth-century Spain. Other notable Renaissance-era texts included Sir Philip Sidney's *Arcadia*, Edmund Spenser's *The Faerie Queen*, and John Bunyan's *The Pilgrim's Progress*. Each of these texts included features now associated with the novel—longer narratives, extended plots, the development of characters over time, and a hero/protagonist—and the form continued to evolve.

The English writer Daniel Defoe is commonly given credit for writing the first novel. His *Robinson Crusoe* (1719) is an episodic narrative similar to a picaresque but unified by a single setting as well as by a central character. Another early novel, Jonathan Swift's *Gulliver's Travels* (1726), is a satirical commentary on the undesirable outcomes of science. During this time, the **epistolary novel** also flourished. This kind of novel told a story in letters or included letters as a means of disseminating information. Samuel Richardson's *Clarissa* (1748) is an example from the eighteenth century; a contemporary example is Alice Walker's *The Color Purple*.

By the nineteenth century, the novel had reached a high point in its development, and its influence and importance were widespread. During the Victorian era in England (1837–1901), many novels reflected the era's preoccupation with propriety and manners. The most notable examples of these **novels of manners** were Jane Austen's *Sense and Sensibility* and *Pride and Prejudice*. Beyond the world of the aristocracy, members of the middle class clamored for novels that mirrored their own experiences, and writers such as George Eliot, Charles Dickens, William Thackeray, and Charlotte and Emily Brontë appealed to this desire by creating large fictional worlds populated by many different characters who reflected the complexity—and at times the melodrama—of Victorian society.

novel Fictional narrative, traditionally realistic, relating a series of events or following the history of a character or group of characters through a period of time.

pastoral romance Prose tale set in an idealized rural world; popular in Renaissance England.

character Fictional representation of a person, usually but not necessarily in a psychologically realistic way. E. M. Forster classified characters as **round** (well developed, closely involved in the action and responsive to it) or **flat** (static, stereotypical, or operating as **foils** for the protagonist). Characters can also be classified as **dynamic** (growing and changing in the course of the action) or **static** (remaining unchanged).

picaresque Episodic, often satirical work presenting the life story of a rogue or rascal—for example, Cervantes's *Don Quixote*. The form emerged in sixteenth-century Spain.

realism Writing that stresses life as it really is. Realism relies on careful description of setting and the trappings of daily life, psychological probability, and the lives of ordinary people. Ibsen's *A Doll House* is an example.

Other writers addressed the dire consequences of science and ambition, as Mary Wollstonecraft Shelley did in her Gothic tale *Frankenstein* (1817).

In the United States, the early nineteenth century was marked by novels that reflected the concerns of a growing country with burgeoning interests. James Fenimore Cooper (*Last of the Mohicans*) and Nathaniel Hawthorne (*The Scarlet Letter*) wrote historical fiction, while Herman Melville (*Moby-Dick*) examined good and evil, madness and sanity. **Realism,** which strove to portray everyday events and people in a realistic fashion, began in France with Honoré de Balzac and Gustav Flaubert and spread to the United States, influencing writers such as Henry James, Stephen Crane, and Mark Twain. Other nineteenth-century writers addressed social and even feminist themes in their work. In the United States, writers who addressed such concerns included Harriet Beecher Stowe (*Uncle Tom's Cabin*) and Kate Chopin (*The Awakening*). Meanwhile, in Russia, novelists such as

© Bettmann/Corbis

>> Scene from the 1931 film *Frankenstein*, based on Mary Shelley's 1817 novel.

parable Story that teaches a lesson, such as the parable of the prodigal son in the New Testament.

fable Short tale, often involving animals or supernatural beings and stressing plot above character development, whose object is to teach a pragmatic or moral lesson.

folk tale/fairy tale Contemporary version of an old, even ancient, oral tale that can be traced back centuries through many different cultures. Folk tales include fairy tales, myths, and fables.

Fyodor Dostoyevsky (*Crime and Punishment*) and Leo Tolstoy (*War and Peace*) examined the everyday lives, as well as the larger political struggles and triumphs, of their people.

The early twentieth century marked the beginning of a literary movement known as **modernism**, in which writers reacted to the increasing complexity of a changing world and mourned the passing of old ways under the pressures of modernity. World War I, urbanization, and the rise of industrialism all contributed to a sense that new ideas needed to be expressed in new ways, and writers such as James Joyce (*Ulysses*), Virginia Woolf (*To the Lighthouse*), and D. H. Lawrence (*Sons and Lovers*) experimented with both form and content.

In the United States, the Roaring Twenties and the Great Depression inspired numerous novelists who set out to write the "Great American Novel" and capture the culture and concerns of the times, often in very gritty and realistic ways. These authors included F. Scott Fitzgerald (*The Great Gatsby*), Ernest Hemingway (*The Sun Also Rises*), William Faulkner (*The Sound and the Fury*), and John Steinbeck (*The Grapes of Wrath*). A little later, novelists such as Richard Wright (*Native Son*) and Ralph Ellison (*Invisible Man*) made important literary contributions by addressing the sociopolitical climate for African Americans in a segregated society.

In the aftermath of modernism, a movement called **postmodernism** emerged. Postmodern artists reacted to the confines and limitations placed on form and meaning. For them, the search for meaning in a text often became more important than the meaning itself. With these experimental techniques, postmodern novelists, such as Donald Barthelme, Margaret Atwood, Thomas Pynchon, Salman Rushdie, and Kurt Vonnegut, confronted the changing society and the future.

Contemporary fiction has been marked and influenced by the developments of the latter part of the twentieth century, including globalization, the rise of technology, and the advent of the Internet and the Age of Communication. As our ability to interact and communicate with other societies has increased exponentially, so too has our access to the literature of other cultures. Contemporary fiction is a world that mirrors the diversity of its participants in terms of form, content, themes, styles, and language. There are many writers worthy of mention, as each culture makes its own invaluable contributions. Some particularly noteworthy contemporary writers include the Nobel Prize–winning novelists Orhan Pamuk, José Saramago, Doris Lessing, Gabriel García Márquez, Nadine Gordimer, Saul Bellow, Toni Morrison, and V. S. Naipaul. As we continue into the twenty-first century, the only thing that remains certain about the future of the novel, and of fiction in general, is its past.

THE HISTORY OF THE SHORT STORY

Early precursors of the short story include **anecdotes, parables, fables, folk tales,** and **fairy tales.** What all of these forms have in common is brevity and a moral. The

>> Cover images of *The Great Gatsby, The Sun Also Rises,* and *The Sound and the Fury.*

ones that have survived, such as "Cinderella" and Aesop's *Fables*, are contemporary versions of old, even ancient, tales that can be traced back centuries through many different cultures.

Folktales and fairy tales share many characteristics. First, they feature simple characters who illustrate a quality or trait that can be summed up in a few words. Much of the appeal of "Cinderella," for example, depends on the contrast between the selfish, sadistic stepsisters and the poor, gentle, victimized Cinderella. In addition, the folktale or fairy tale has an obvious theme or **moral**—good triumphing over evil, for instance. The stories move directly to their conclusions, never interrupted by ingenious or unexpected plot twists. (Love is temporarily thwarted, but the prince eventually finds Cinderella and marries her.) Finally, these tales are anchored not in specific times or places but in "Once upon a time" settings, green worlds of prehistory filled with royalty, talking animals, and magic.

>> Undated woodcut of Cinderella.

© Bettmann/Corbis

The thematically linked stories in Giovanni Boccaccio's *The Decameron* and Geoffrey Chaucer's *The Canterbury Tales*, both written in the fourteenth century, were precursors of the modern short story. *Grimm's Fairy Tales* (1824–1826), an early collection of short narratives and folk stories, also helped to pave the way for the development of the genre, but it was not until the nineteenth century that the contemporary version of the short story emerged.

During the last quarter of the nineteenth century, a proliferation of literary and popular magazines and journals created a demand for short fiction (between 3,000 and 15,000 words) that could be published in their entirety rather than in serial installments, as most novels at the time were. Nathaniel Hawthorne's *Twice Told Tales* (1842) and Edgar Allan Poe's *Tales of the Grotesque and Arabesque* (1836) were early collections of short stories. Americans in particular hungrily consumed the written word, and short stories soared in popularity. In fact, because the short story was embraced so readily and developed so quickly in the United States, it is commonly (although not quite accurately) thought of as an American literary form.

short story Fictional narrative often centered on one event and usually developing only one character in depth; its scope is narrower than that of the **novel**, and it often uses setting and characterization more directly to make its theme clear.

epiphany Term first applied to literature by James Joyce to describe a sudden moment of revelation or insight such as the boy's realization at the end of "Araby."

short-short story Short fictional narrative that is generally under five pages (or fifteen hundred words) in length.

LO2 Define the Short Story

Like the novel, the short story evolved from various forms of narrative and has its roots in an oral tradition. However, whereas the novel is an extended piece of narrative fiction, the **short story** is distinguished by its relative brevity, which creates a specific set of expectations and possibilities as well as certain limitations. Unlike the novelist, the short story writer cannot devote a great deal of space to developing a highly complex plot or a large number of characters. As a result, the short story often begins close to or at the height of action and develops a limited number of characters. Usually focusing on a single incident, the writer develops one or more characters by showing their reactions to events. This attention to character development, as well as its detailed description of setting, is what distinguishes the short story from earlier short narrative forms.

In many contemporary short stories, a character experiences an **epiphany,** a moment of illumination in which something hidden or not understood becomes immediately clear. In other short stories, the thematic significance, or meaning, is communicated through the way in which the characters develop, or react. Regardless of the specifics of its format or its theme, a short story offers readers an open window to a world that they can enter—if only briefly.

The short story that follows, Ernest Hemingway's "Hills Like White Elephants" (1927), illustrates many of the characteristics of the modern **short story.** Although it is so brief that it might be more accurately called a **short-short story,** it uses its limited space to establish a distinct setting and develop two characters. From the story's first paragraph, readers know where the story takes place and whom it is about: "The American and the girl with him sat at a table in the shade, outside the building. It was very hot and the express from Barcelona would come in forty minutes." As time elapses and the man and woman wait for the train to Madrid, their strained dialogue reveals the tension between them and hints at the serious conflict they must resolve.

Ernest Hemingway (1898–1961)

grew up in Oak Park, Illinois, and after high school graduation began his writing career as a reporter on the *Kansas City Star*. While working as a volunteer ambulance driver in World War I, eighteen-year-old Hemingway was wounded. As Hemingway himself told the story, he was hit by machine-gun fire while carrying an Italian soldier to safety. (Hemingway biographer Michael Reynolds, however, reports that Hemingway was wounded when a mortar shell fell and killed the man next to him.)

Success for Hemingway came early, with publication of the short story collection *In Our Time* (1925) and his first and most acclaimed novel, *The Sun Also Rises* (1926), a portrait of a postwar "lost generation" of Americans adrift in Europe. This group was based on his own circle of friends and their experiences, and thus

the novel established Hemingway's ability to create fiction out of the reality of his own life. *A Farewell to Arms* (1929) harks back to his war experiences; *For Whom the Bell Tolls* (1940) emerged out of his experiences as a journalist in Spain during the Spanish Civil War. Later in life, he made his home in Key West, Florida, and then in Cuba, where he wrote *The Old Man and the Sea* (1952). In 1954, he won the Nobel Prize in Literature. In 1961, plagued by poor health and mental illness—and perhaps also by the difficulty of living up to his own image—Hemingway took his own life.

Hills Like White Elephants (1927)

The hills across the valley of the Ebro° were long and white. On this side there was no shade and no trees and the station was between two lines of rails in the sun. Close against the side of the station there was the warm shadow of the building and a curtain, made of strings of bamboo beads, hung across the open door into the bar, to keep out flies. The American and the girl with him sat at a table in the shade, outside the building. It was very hot and the express from Barcelona would come in forty minutes. It stopped at this junction for two minutes and went on to Madrid. *— Setting: train station*

"What should we drink?" the girl asked. She had taken off her hat and put it on the table.

"It's pretty hot," the man said.

"Let's drink beer."

"Dos cervezas," the man said into the curtain. 5

"Big ones?" a woman asked from the doorway.

"Yes. Two big ones."

The woman brought two glasses of beer and two felt pads. She put the felt pads and the beer glasses on the table and looked at the man and the girl. The girl was looking off at the line of hills. They were white in the sun and the country was brown and dry. *— A dessert plain*

"They look like white elephants," she said.

"I've never seen one," the man drank his beer. 10

"No, you wouldn't have."

"I might have," the man said. "Just because you say I wouldn't have doesn't prove anything."

The girl looked at the bead curtain. "They've painted something on it," she said. "What does it say?"

"Anis del Toro.° It's a drink."

"Could we try it?" 15

The man called "Listen" through the curtain. The woman came out from the bar.

"Four reales."°

"We want two Anis del Toro."

"With water?"

"Do you want it with water?" 20

"I don't know," the girl said. "Is it good with water?"

"It's all right."

"You want them with water?" asked the woman.

"Yes, with water."

"It tastes like licorice," the girl said and put the glass 25 down.

"That's the way with everything."

° **Ebro** A river in northern Spain.

° **Anis del Toro** A dark alcoholic drink made from anise, an herb that tastes like licorice.

° **reales** Spanish coins.

Cultural Context

At the time this story was written, Ernest Hemingway was part of a group of American expatriates living in Paris. Disillusioned by World War I and seeking a more bohemian lifestyle, free from the concerns of American materialism, this group of artists, intellectuals, poets, and writers were known as the "Lost Generation." Some of the group's most famous members included F. Scott Fitzgerald, Gertrude Stein, and John Dos Passos. The literary legacy they left behind is arguably one of the greatest of the twentieth century.

"Yes," said the girl. "Everything tastes of licorice. Especially all the things you've waited so long for, like absinthe."

"Oh, cut it out."

"You started it," the girl said. "I was being amused. I was having a fine time."

"Well, let's try and have a fine time." 30

"All right I was trying. I said the mountains looked like white elephants. Wasn't that bright?"

"That was bright."

"I wanted to try this new drink. That's all we do, isn't it—look at things and try new drinks?"

"I guess so."

The girl looked across at the hills. 35

"They're lovely hills," she said. "They don't really look like white elephants. I just meant the coloring of their skin through the trees."

"Should we have another drink?"

"All right."

The warm wind blew the bead curtain against the table.

"The beer's nice and cool," the man said. 40

"It's lovely," the girl said.

change subject

"It's really an awfully simple operation, Jig," the man said. "It's not really an operation at all."

The girl looked at the ground the table legs rested on.

"I know you wouldn't mind it, Jig. It's really not anything. It's just to let the air in."

The girl did not say anything. 45

"I'll go with you and I'll stay with you all the time. They just let the air in and then it's all perfectly natural."

"Then what will we do afterward?"

"We'll be fine afterward. Just like we were before."

"What makes you think so?"

"That's the only thing that bothers us. It's the only 50 thing that's made us unhappy."

>> Spanish landscape in La Rioja region

The girl looked at the bead curtain, put her hand out and took hold of two of the strings of beads.

"And you think then we'll be all right and be happy."

"I know we will. You don't have to be afraid. I've known lots of people that have done it."

"So have I," said the girl. "And afterward they were all so happy."

"Well," the man said, "if you don't want to you don't 55 have to. I wouldn't have you do it if you didn't want to. But I know it's perfectly simple."

"And you really want to?"

"I think it's the best thing to do. But I don't want you to do it if you don't really want to."

"And if I do it you'll be happy and things will be like they were and you'll love me?"

"I love you now. You know I love you."

"I know. But if I do it, then it will be nice again 60 if I say things are like white elephants, and you'll like it?"

"I'll love it. I love it now but I just can't think about it. You know how I get when I worry."

"If I do it you won't ever worry?"

"I won't worry about that because it's perfectly simple."

"Then I'll do it. Because I don't care about me."

"What do you mean?" 65

"I don't care about me."

"Well, I care about you."

"Oh, yes. But I don't care about me. And I'll do it and then everything will be fine."

"I don't want you to do it if you feel that way."

The girl stood up and walked to the end of the sta- 70 tion. Across, on the other side, were fields of grain and trees along the banks of the Ebro. Far away beyond the river, were mountains. The shadow of a cloud moved across the field of grain and she saw the river through the trees.

"And we could have all this," she said. "And we could have everything and every day we make it more impossible."

"What did you say?"

"I said we could have everything."

"We can have everything."

"No, we can't." 75

"We can have the whole world."

"No, we can't."

"We can go everywhere."

"No, we can't. It isn't ours any more."

"It's ours." 80

"No, it isn't. And once they take it away, you never get it back."

"But they haven't taken it away."

"We'll wait and see."

"Come on back in the shade," he said. "You mustn't feel that way."

"I don't feel any way," the girl said. "I just know things." 85

>> 1920's European train junction

© Andalucia Plus Image Bank/Alamy

"I don't want you to do anything that you don't want to do—."

"Nor that isn't good for me," she said. "I know. Could we have another beer?"

"All right. But you've got to realize—"

"I realize," the girl said. "Can't we maybe stop talking?"

They sat down at the table and the girl looked across 90 at the hills on the dry side of the valley and the man looked at her and at the table.

"You've got to realize," he said, "that I don't want you to do it if you don't want to. I'm perfectly willing to go through with it if it means anything to you."

"Doesn't it mean anything to you? We could get along."

"Of course it does. But I don't want anybody but you. I don't want any one else. And I know it's perfectly simple."

"Yes, you know it's perfectly simple."

"It's all right for you to say that, but I do know it." 95

"Would you do something for me now?"

"I'd do anything for you."

"Would you please please please please please please please stop talking?"

He did not say anything but looked at the bags against the wall of the station. There were labels on them from all the hotels where they had spent nights.

"But I don't want you to," he said, "I don't care any-100 thing about it."

"I'll scream," the girl said.

The woman came out through the curtains with two glasses of beer and put them down on the damp felt pads. "The train comes in five minutes," she said.

"What did she say?" asked the girl.

"That the train is coming in five minutes."

The girl smiled brightly at the woman, to thank her. 105

"I'd better take the bags over to the other side of the station," the man said. She smiled at him.

"All right. Then come back and we'll finish the beer."

He picked up the two heavy bags and carried them around the station to the other tracks. He looked up the tracks but could not see the train. Coming back, he walked through the barroom, where people waiting for the train were drinking. He drank an Anis at the bar and looked at the people. They were all waiting reasonably for the train. He went out through the bead curtain. She was sitting at the table and smiled at him.

"Do you feel better?" he asked.

"I feel fine," she said. "There's nothing wrong with 110 me. I feel fine."

*   *   *

LO3 Understand the Boundaries of Fiction

As noted earlier, a **short story** is a work of fiction that is marked by its brevity, its relatively limited number of characters, its short time frame, and its ability to achieve thematic significance in a relatively short space. A **novella** (such as Franz Kafka's "The Metamorphosis" and Herman Melville's "Bartleby, the Scrivener") is an extended short story that shares some characteristics (for example, concentrated action) with a short story while retaining some qualities of a novel, including greater character development. At the other end of the spectrum are **short-short stories**, which are under 1,500 words (about five pages) in length. (Examples of those very brief stories are included in Chapter 5 "Fiction Sampler: The Short-Short Story.") **Prose poems,** such as Carolyn Forché's, "The Colonel" (p. 485), are hybrid versions of literature that have characteristics of both prose (being written in paragraphs) and poetry (being written in verse form, often using imagery, meter, and rhyme to convey lyrical beauty). In addition, **graphic stories**— sometimes complete in themselves, sometimes part of **graphic novels**—have proliferated in recent years. Finally, the Internet offers endless possibilities for arranging, presenting, and disseminating text.

---

novella Extended short story, usually concentrated in episode and action (like a short story) but involving greater character development (like a novel); Franz Kafka's "The Metamorphosis" is a novella.

prose poem Open form poem whose long lines appear to be prose set in paragraphs — for example, Carolyn Forché's "The Colonel."

There are, it seems, as many different ways to tell a story as there are stories to be told. A short story may be comic or tragic; its subject may be growing up, marriage, crime and punishment, war, sexual awakening, death, or any number of other human concerns. The setting can be an imaginary world, the old West, rural America, the jungles of Uruguay, nineteenth-century Russia, precommunist China, or modern Egypt. The story may have a conventional form, with a definite beginning, middle, and end, or it may be structured as a letter, as a diary entry, or even as a collection of random notes. The story may use just words, or it may juxtapose conventional text with symbols, pictures, or empty space. The narrator of a story may be trustworthy or unreliable, involved in the action or a disinterested observer, sympathetic or deserving of scorn, extremely ignorant or highly insightful, limited in vision or able to see inside the minds of all the characters. As the selections in this anthology show, the possibilities of the short story are almost infinite.

10

Fiction Sampler:
The Short-Short Story

Learning Outcomes

After reading this chapter, you should be able to do the following:

LO1 Define the short-short story

Timeline

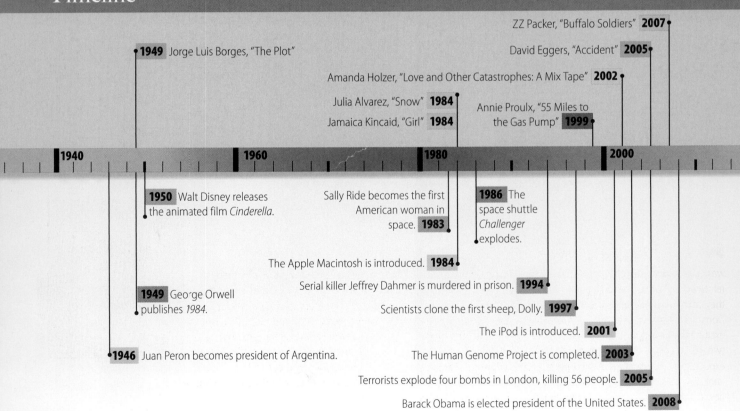

ZZ Packer, "Buffalo Soldiers" **2007**

David Eggers, "Accident" **2005**

1949 Jorge Luis Borges, "The Plot"

Amanda Holzer, "Love and Other Catastrophes: A Mix Tape" **2002**

Julia Alvarez, "Snow" **1984**

Jamaica Kincaid, "Girl" **1984**

Annie Proulx, "55 Miles to the Gas Pump" **1999**

1940   1960   1980   2000

1950 Walt Disney releases the animated film *Cinderella*.

Sally Ride becomes the first American woman in space. **1983**

1986 The space shuttle *Challenger* explodes.

The Apple Macintosh is introduced. **1984**

1949 George Orwell publishes *1984*.

Serial killer Jeffrey Dahmer is murdered in prison. **1994**

Scientists clone the first sheep, Dolly. **1997**

The iPod is introduced. **2001**

1946 Juan Peron becomes president of Argentina.

The Human Genome Project is completed. **2003**

Terrorists explode four bombs in London, killing 56 people. **2005**

Barack Obama is elected president of the United States. **2008**

100   PART 2: FICTION

LO1 Define the Short-Short Story

This chapter focuses on the **short-short story**, a short story that is fewer than 1,500 words in length. Short-shorts are often classified according to their overall length. For example, **micro fiction**, at approximately 250 words or fewer, is one of the shortest kinds of short-short fiction, followed by **flash fiction** (fewer than approximately 1,000 words) and then by **sudden fiction** (fewer than approximately 1,500 words). Short-shorts are sometimes also categorized according to how long they take to read or how long they take to write. Regardless of their individual characteristics, all short-shorts compress ideas into a small package and, to varying degrees, test the limits of the short story genre. Some short-shorts are quite conventional (that is, they include recognizable characters and have an identifiable beginning, middle, and end); others are experimental, perhaps lacking a definite setting or a clear plot. As defined by Robert Shapard (who, along with James Thomas, edited the short-short story collections *Sudden Fiction* and *New Sudden Fiction*), short-shorts are "Highly compressed, highly charged, insidious, protean, sudden, alarming, tantalizing"; they can "confer form on small corners of chaos, can do in a page what a novel does in two hundred." One of the most extreme examples is Ernest Hemingway's famous six-word story: "For sale: baby shoes, never worn."

The stories in this chapter represent a wide range of short-short fiction. Of the seven stories collected here, Julia Alvarez's "Snow" and ZZ Packer's "Buffalo Soldiers" most resemble traditional short stories in that they develop a main character and place that character in a distinct setting.

short-short story Short fictional narrative that is under five pages (or fifteen hundred words) in length.

stream of consciousness Form of narration controlled not by external events but by the thoughts and subjective impressions of the narrator, commonly found in modern literature, such as the work of Virginia Woolf and James Joyce.

Other stories in this chapter are more experimental. For example, Annie Proulx's "55 Miles to the Gas Pump" presents a stunning vignette, in a mere three sentences, of a married Wyoming couple. Jamaica Kincaid's "Girl," a **stream-of-consciousness** monologue, is also unusual in its style and form (the entire story is a single sentence), as is Amanda Holzer's "Love and Other Catastrophes: A Mix Tape," consisting entirely of a list of song titles. An example of **metafiction**, Jorge Luis Borges's "The Plot" explores the function of plot in certain literary works. Finally, Dave Eggers's "Accident" maintains narrative distance with an unusual point of view.

Despite their brevity, the stories in this chapter have much in common with the stories that appear elsewhere in this book. Each, in its own distinctive way, "tells a story."

The following short-short stories are included in this sampler:

Julia Alvarez (1950–   )

was born in New York City. Soon after her birth, Alvarez's family relocated to the Dominican Republic, where they lived for ten years until they emigrated back to New York. Alvarez describes herself as "a Dominican, hyphen, American. . . . As a fiction writer, I find that the most exciting things happen in the realm of that hyphen—the place where two worlds collide or blend together." Alvarez's works explore the experiences and emotions of immigrants, particularly female Hispanic immigrants, as they struggle to redefine themselves in the context of a new culture. She has published many highly regarded works of fiction and poetry, including *Homecoming* (1984 and 1996), *How the García Girls Lost Their Accents* (1991), *In the Time of Butterflies* (1995), and *¡Yo!* (1997). She is also the author of the forthcoming children's book *How Tía Lola Saved the Summer*. Alvarez is currently a writer-in-residence at Middlebury College in Vermont.

Snow (1984)

Our first year in New York we rented a small apartment with a Catholic school nearby, taught by the Sisters of Charity, hefty women in long black gowns and bonnets that made them look peculiar, like dolls in mourning. I liked them a lot, especially my grandmotherly fourth grade teacher, Sister Zoe. I had a lovely name, she said, and she had me teach the whole class how to pronounce it. *Yo-Ian-da.* As the only immigrant in my class. I was put in a special seat in the first row by the window, apart from the other children so that Sister Zoe could tutor me without distributing them. Slowly, she enunciated the new words I was to repeat: *laundromat, cornflakes, subway, snow.*

Soon I picked up enough English to understand holocaust was in the air. Sister Zoe explained to a wide-eyed classroom what was happening in Cuba. Russian missiles were being assembled, trained supposedly on New York City. President Kennedy, looking worried too, was on the television at home, explaining we might have to go to war against the Communists. At school, we had air-raid drills: an ominous bell would go off and we'd file into the hall, fall to the floor, cover our heads with our coats, and imagine our hair falling out, the bones in our arms going soft. At home, Mami and my sisters and I said a rosary for world peace. I heard new vocabulary: *nuclear bomb, radioactive fallout, bomb shelter.* Sister Zoe explained how it would happen. She drew a picture of a mushroom on the blackboard and dotted a flurry of chalk-marks for the dusty fallout that would kill us all.

The months grew cold, November, December. It was dark when I got up in the morning, frosty when I followed my breath to school. One morning as I sat at my desk daydreaming out the window, I saw dots in the air like the ones Sister Zoe had drawn—random at first, then lots and lots. I shrieked, "Bomb Bomb!" Sister Zoe jerked around, her full black skirt ballooning as she hurried to my side. A few girls began to cry.

But then Sister Zoe's shocked look faded. "Why, Yolanda dear, that's snow!" She laughed. "Snow."

"Snow," I repeated. I looked out the window warily. 5 All my life I had heard about the white crystals that fell out of American skies in the winter. From my desk I watched the fine powder dust the sidewalk and parked cars below. Each flake was different, Sister Zoe said, like a person, irreplaceable and beautiful.

Jorge Luis Borges (1899–1986)

was born in Buenos Aires, Argentina. Widely regarded as one of the most influential modernist and symbolist writers of his time, Borges wrote challenging and deeply metaphysical poetry and fiction. *Ficciones,* published in 1945, is perhaps his most famous collection of short stories. Borges also wrote essays, several screenplays, and a considerable volume of literary criticism, prologues, and reviews. In addition, he edited numerous anthologies and was a prominent translator of English, French, and German literature into Spanish.

The Plot (1949)

To make his horror perfect, Caesar,° hemmed about at the foot of a statue by his friends' impatient knives, discovers among the faces and the blades the face of Marcus Junius Brutus,° his ward, perhaps his very son—and so Caesar stops defending himself, and cries out *Et tu, Brute?°* Shakespeare and Quevedo° record that pathetic cry.

Fate is partial to repetitions, variations symmetries. Nineteen centuries later, in the southern part of the province of Buenos Aires, a gaucho° is set upon by other gauchos, and as he falls he recognizes a godson of his, and says to him in gentle remonstrance and slow surprise (these words must be heard, not read): *Pero, che!°* He dies, but he does not know that he has died so that a scene can be played out again.

°**Caesar** Julius Caesar (100 B.C.–44 B.C.), Roman dictator assassinated by a band of conspirators.

°**Marcus Junius Brutus** Roman politician (85 B.C.–42 B.C.) and the lead conspirator who assassinated Julius Caesar.

°**Et tu, Brute?** Latin for *"You too, Brutus?"*

°**Quevedo** Francisco Gómez de Quevedo y Villegas (1580–1645), Spanish poet and satirist.

°**gaucho** South American cowboy.

°**Pero, che!** Spanish expression expressing surprise.

Dave Eggers (1970–)

grew up near Chicago. In addition to many short stories, he has also published the memoir *A Heartbreaking Work of Staggering Genius* (2000), a finalist for the Pulitzer Prize, as well as three novels. His most recent novel, *The Wild Things* (2009), is based on the screenplay *Where the Wild Things Are*, which Eggers co-wrote with film director Spike Jonze. As the founder of McSweeney's (a literary group that publishes the journal *McSweeney's*, the magazine the *Believer*, and the DVD magazine *Wholphin*) and as editor of *The Best American Nonrequired Reading 2002, 2003*, and *2004*, Eggers has helped to popularize experimental, irreverent literature in print and electronic formats.

Accident (2005)

You all get out of your cars. You are alone in yours, and there are three teenagers in theirs, an older Camaro in new condition. The accident was your fault, and you walk over to tell them this.

Walking over to their car, which you have ruined, it occurs to you that if the three teenagers are angry teenagers, this encounter could be very unpleasant. You pulled into an intersection, obstructing them, and their car hit yours. They have every right to be upset, or livid, or even violence-contemplating.

As you approach, you see that their driver's side door won't open. The driver pushes against it, and you are reminded of scenes where drivers are stuck in submerged cars. Soon they all exit through the passenger side door and walk around the Camaro, inspecting the damage. None of them is hurt, but the car is wrecked. "Just bought this today," the driver says. He is 18, blond, average in all ways. "Today?" you ask.

You are a bad person, you think. You also think: what a dorky car for a teenager to buy in 2005. "Yeah, today," he says, then sighs. You tell him that you are sorry. That you are so, so sorry. That it was your fault and that you will cover all costs.

You exchange insurance information, and you find 5 yourself, minute by minute, ever more thankful that none of these teenagers has punched you, or even made a remark about your being drunk, which you are not, or being stupid, which you are, often. You become more friendly with all of them, and you realize that you are much more connected to them, particularly to the driver, than possible in perhaps any other way.

You have done him and his friends harm, in a way, and you jeopardized their health, and now you are so close you feel like you share a heart. He knows your name and you know his, and you almost killed him and, because you got so close to doing so but didn't, you want to fall on him, weeping, because you are so lonely, so lonely always, and all contact is contact, and all contact makes us so grateful we want to cry and dance and cry and cry.

In a moment of clarity, you finally understand why boxers, who want so badly to hurt each other, can rest their heads on the shoulders of their opponents, can lean against one another like tired lovers, so thankful for a moment of peace.

> *"Walking over to their car, which you have ruined, it occurs to you that if the three teenagers are angry teenagers, this encounter could be very unpleasant."*

Amanda Holzer (1981–)

is a graduate of Emerson College and co-owns the independent record label Not Not Fun. "Love and Other Catastrophes" was first published in 2002 in *Story Quarterly* and was reprinted in *The Best American Nonrequired Reading 2003*.

Love and Other Catastrophes: A Mix Tape (2002)

"All By Myself" (Eric Carmen). "Looking for Love" (Lou Reed). "I Wanna Dance With Somebody" (Whitney Houston). "Let's Dance" (David Bowie). "Let's Kiss" (Beat Happening). "Let's Talk About Sex" (Salt N' Pepa). "Like A Virgin" (Madonna). "We've Only Just Begun" (The Carpenters). "I Wanna Be Your Boyfriend" (The Ramones). "I'll Tumble 4 Ya" (Culture Club). "Head Over Heels" (The Go-Go's). "Nothing Compares To You"

(Sinéad O'Connor). "My Girl" (The Temptations). "Could This Be Love?" (Bob Marley). "Love and Marriage" (Frank Sinatra). "White Wedding" (Billy Idol). "Stuck in the Middle with You" (Steelers Wheel). "Tempted" (The Squeeze). "There Goes My Baby" (The Drifters). "What's Going On?" (Marvin Gaye). "Where Did You Sleep Last Night?" (Leadbelly). "Whose Bed Have Your Boots Been Under?" (Shania Twain). "Jealous Guy" (John Lennon). "Your Cheatin' Heart" (Tammy Wynette). "Shot Through the Heart" (Bon Jovi). "Don't Go Breaking My Heart" (Elton John and Kiki Dee). "My Achy Breaky Heart" (Billy Ray Cyrus). "Heartbreak Hotel" (Elvis Presley), "Stop, In the Name of Love" (The Supremes). "Try a Little Tenderness" (Otis Redding). "Try (Just a Little Bit Harder)" (Janis Joplin). "All Apologies" (Nirvana). "Hanging on the Telephone" (Blondie). "I Just Called to Say I Love You" (Stevie Wonder). "Love Will Keep Us Together" (Captain and Tennille). "Let's Stay Together" (Al Green). "It Ain't Over 'Till It's Over" (Lenny Kravitz). "What's Love Got To Do With It? (Tina Turner). "You Don't Bring Me Flowers Anymore" (Barbara Streisand and Neil Diamond). "I Wish You Wouldn't Say That" (Talking Heads). "You're So Vain" (Carly Simon). "Love Is a Battlefield" (Pat Benatar). "Heaven Knows I'm Miserable Now" (The Smiths). "(Can't Get No) Satisfaction" (Rolling Stones). "Must Have Been Love (But It's Over Now)" (Roxette). "Breaking Up is Hard to Do" (Neil Sedaka). "I Will Survive" (Gloria Gaynor). "Hit the Road, Jack" (Mary McCaslin and Jim Ringer). "These Boots Were Made for Walking" (Nancy Sinatra). "All Out of Love" (Air Supply). "All By Myself" (Eric Carmen).

Jamaica Kincaid (1949–   )

© Time & Life Pictures/Getty Images

was born Elaine Potter Richardson on the island of Antigua, where she received a British education and was often at the top of her class. In early childhood, she was very close to her mother, but when her mother gave birth to three sons in quick succession, it altered their relationship forever. According to Kincaid, she was treated badly and neglected, and she left Antigua in 1965 to work as an au pair in Westchester county, near New York City. She went on to study photography at the New School for Social Research and attended Franconia College in New Hampshire for a year. In 1973, after having begun her writing career, she changed her name to Jamaica Kincaid because her family disapproved of her writing. She soon began writing a regular column for the *New Yorker*. Her best-known works include the novel *Annie John* (1986) and the nonfiction book *A Small Place* (1988), which criticizes British Colonialism in Antigua. Her most recent books include *Talk Stories* (2001), *Among Flowers: A Walk in the Himalaya* (2005), and *My Favorite Tool* (2005).

Girl (1984)

Wash the white clothes on Monday and put them on the stone heap; wash the color clothes on Tuesday and put them on the clothesline to dry; don't walk barehead in the hot sun; cook pumpkin fritters in very hot sweet oil; soak your little clothes right after you take them off; when buying cotton to make yourself a nice blouse, be sure that it doesn't have gum on it, because that way it won't hold up well after a wash; soak salt fish overnight before you cook it; is it true that you sing benna° in Sunday School?; always eat your food in such a way that it won't turn someone else's stomach; on Sundays try to walk like a lady and not like the slut you are so bent on becoming; don't sing benna in Sunday School; you mustn't speak to wharf-rat boys, not even to give directions; don't eat fruits on the street— flies will follow you; *but I don't sing benna on Sundays at all and never in Sunday school;* this is how to sew on a button; this is how to make a buttonhole for the button you have just sewed on; this is how to hem a dress when you see the hem coming down and so to prevent yourself from looking like the slut I know you are so bent on becoming; this is how you iron your father's khaki shirt so that it doesn't have a crease; this is how you iron your father's khaki pants so that they don't have a crease; this is how you grow okra—far from the house, because okra tree harbors red ants; when you are growing dasheen, make sure it gets plenty of water or else it makes your throat itch when you are eating it; this is how you sweep a

---

° **benna** Calypso music.

corner; this is how you sweep a whole house; this is how you sweep a yard; this is how you smile to someone you don't like too much; this is how you smile to someone you don't like at all; this is how you smile to someone you like completely; this is how you set a table for tea; this is how you set a table for dinner; this is how you set a table for dinner with an important guest; this is how you set a table for lunch; this is how you set a table for breakfast; this is how to behave in the presence of men who don't know you very well, and this way they won't recognize immediately the slut I have warned you against becoming; be sure to wash every day, even if it is with your own spit; don't squat down to play marbles—you are not a boy, you know; don't pick people's flowers—you might catch something; don't throw stones at blackbirds, because it might not be a blackbird at all; this is how to make a bread pudding; this is how to make doukona;° this is how to make pepper pot; this is how to make a good medicine for a cold; this is how to make a good medicine to throw away a child before it even becomes a child; this is how to catch a fish; this is how to throw back a fish you don't like, and that way something bad won't fall on you; this is how to bully a man; this is how a man bullies you; this is how to love a man, and if this doesn't work there are other ways, and if they don't work don't feel too bad about giving up; this is how to spit up in the air if you feel like it, and this is how to move quick so that it doesn't fall on you; this is how to make ends meet; always squeeze bread to make sure it's fresh; *but what if the baker won't let me feel the bread?*; you mean to say that after all you are really going to be the kind of woman who the baker won't let near the bread?

°**doukona** Spicy plantain pudding.

ZZ Packer (1973–   )

was born in Chicago and raised in Atlanta and Louisville, Kentucky. Her stories have appeared in the *New Yorker, Harper's,* and *Zoetrope.* She has also published a collection of stories entitled *Drinking Coffee Elsewhere* (2003), a *New York Times* Notable Book and a PEN/Faulkner Award finalist. Packer's work, which focuses largely on the lives of young African-American girls, also explores universal themes of acceptance, belonging, and loss. "I like to discover things that I'm writing," Packer explains, "and I like to explore what I've seen in the world, through writing. And it doesn't have to be autobiographical or verbatim, but the sort of essential truth that I see in the world." Packer is currently at work on her first novel, *The Thousands,* from which the following story is excerpted.

Buffalo Soldiers° (2007)

It had seemed that just riding at a walk was difficult enough, but heading into the mountains meant slight drifts of fear at every incline, every pass. It was enough to make Lazarus realize that whatever little hillocks they'd encountered on their march from San Antonio to their headquarters at Fort Stockton were nothing. They tried to file two by two, but there were some places the scouts had led them where the men had to go through one at a time, and it was then that Lazarus feared that the horse in front of him would lose its footing and fall, smacking him with the might of an avalanche of horseflesh, or that Grey Bat, his own horse—who was a little too fond of leaping up or rushing down a slope—would miscalculate, and that would be the end of them both.

No one spoke. All that could be heard were the horses negotiating the passes with grunts and whinnies and the razor sharp zips of passing mosquitoes and horseflies, locusts bouncing at crazy angles as the horses crushed their hiding places. Lazarus had never heard the men so quiet, and still the scout Liege seemed quieter than the rest, separate from the other scouts, looking around occasionally as if he were the colonel himself, surveying his men.

They stood at the next pass, waiting—for what, Lazarus did not know. All he could think upon seeing the land was that it was somehow ugly and strangely beautiful at the same time. Then without so much as a word from Lieutenant Heyl, they were ascending again, and with each ascent, a shoulder of rock on his near side or far side would bring blessed shade and calm, so different from anything he'd seen in Mississippi or Louisiana that

---

°**Buffalo soldiers** African-American cavalry regiments of the United States Army stationed in the West from 1867–1896.

he sometimes forgot that it was home he wanted to be going towards. He could not make out the expressions on the faces of the scouts up ahead, but they were pacing back and forth on their horses, as if in confusion, and when he went to look at Liege, Liege looked worried.

"I think they want you to get on up there, Mr. Indian," Redbone said, but Liege didn't pay Redbone and mind. He just started sniffing and rolling his eyes up to the ceiling of the sky, figuring.

Then came the sound of shots, and the horses started, 5 and the men up front with Lieutenant Heyl fought to keep them under control. Along with shots came Indian whoops and cries, sounding like they were calling for the end of the world to commence.

"This is it, Niggers," Heyl called out, "This is it."

The men in front bounded forward, while Lazarus and the rest of the advance party manoeuvred behind. He could hear the front men returning fire but a blizzard of dust from the pounding of horse hooves made it impossible to see.

"Spread out you fucking niggers!" Heyl yelled, as if unaware that the men had already surged forward. Lazarus was deep in the middle of the men, and saw men in the very front line falling to an invisible enemy—all he saw were clouds of dust, and when the dust cleared just the sheer facing of rocks. He had to push his way against other men coming forward, the horses jostling each other, their flanks briefly caroming off one another while Lazarus sought partial protection by lying flush against Grey Bat's bristly mane.

The bullets came in little pings. One man was down already, his horse hit, whinnying and rearing before it fell on to the ground in a crash of meat, pinning his rider while everyone still upright sidestepped fallen horse and rider as if they were prickly cactus.

Heyl yelled out another command, and once again, 10 the men shuffled into a loose formation—not nearly as tight as before. He didn't know if the formation had loosened because all was just complete chaos and men simply couldn't hear, but he knew there would be hell to pay from Heyl later. Lazarus wanted to shoehorn everyone into place just so he wouldn't have to hear Heyl yelling everyday for the next week, and he even tried lining up behind the horse in front of him, but Liege reined his horse sideways so that his flanks

pushed at Grey Bat's. "Don't fall into no formation!" Liege yelled at him, then yelled it again, his toad's voice shouting.

"We got to follow orders!" Lazarus shouted to him over the din. Insubordination. The word he'd heard Hatch hissing over and over again to his officers, and the officers to any of the soldiers who dated complain.

"Don't fall into no goddamned formation," Liege said again, and though he didn't yell it, it had more force somehow, and all the men around him seemed to understand. His horse kept skittering sideways into Grey Bat, trying poor Grey Bat's patience. "I been fighting with Indians my whole life. Ain't no way to fight 'em by standing in line, clear and plain for them to see, waiting for them to kill us off. That ain't no Indian way of fighting."

Lazarus didn't know what Liege had in mind, but Liege kept his arm braced just inches in front of Lazarus, as if in ready to knock the carbine° out of his hand if need be. It was as if Liege knew that it would take these few but vital moments before Lazarus understood what was happening. Lazarus now saw the limited use of the formation point, advance party, support and reserve, if only because the Kickapoos° were not coming from some designated place the Ninth could see, but from all around, and there was no way of knowing how many were in front or back of them, due of their stealth. Instead of one army meeting another, Lazarus now saw their situation was more like a spider lured into an anthill, and he had no way of knowing how Liege proposed to get them out, if retreat had already been struck as an option.

Heyl was busy yelling again, but this time, only a few scampered into formation while the rest were all scattered and shooting, advancing towards the rocks whichever way they could get there while the Indians kept up fire, and in the few beats it took Lazarus to understand what was happening—that Leige was taking over and giving the commands instead of Heyl—Lazarus and the wave of men who'd listened to Liege were swept up into the advance from behind. Suddenly, all was clear to see, and Heyl came crashing down in the volley of fire coming from the rocks.

"Man down!" came the call, and though all was chaos 15 at first, with Heyl screaming for his life in one moment, and then in another—Lazarus charging forwards towards the rocks, and for the first time, sighting Indians. Not the roadside stumps he'd seen coming through San Antonio, drowsily biding their time with corn husks while their lethargic children wove baskets—and putted their leather balls about, but blurs of brown, a flash of some sort of animal pelt covering their loins, and streaming hair, straight as a horse's mane.

He had finally managed to unleash his carbine and cock it, but hadn't the chance to use it for fear of shooting one of his own in the back while they had still been prisoners to the dust cloud.

For a time, he hid his face behind Grey Bat's mane. Then, as the wave of men cleared and without the least bit

---

°**carbine** A short-barreled lightweight rifle.

°**Kickapoos** Native American tribe living in Kansas, Oklahoma, Texas, and northern Mexico.

of pressure on the reigns, Grey Bat took off with even greater speed straight towards the whoops and ululations of Indians. He could not believe it; he was heading into fire, headed straight towards the bullets, and so he aimed his carbine where the dust cloud had cleared before him—a straight shot with none of his own impeding the way—but when he went to shoot, there was nothing, nothing at all.

No bullet, no recoil, no shot.

They'd never used bullets for target practice, as the Army rationed out its ammunition with the coloured regiments. They'd all gotten their share of ammunition before heading out, and Lazarus had dutifully loaded his carbine as demonstrated, and yet, it did not fire.

He pumped his carbine furiously, and found to his 20 surprise that this was the first time since the skirmish began that he began to fear for his life. "Lord Jesus," he said, or thought he said, and looked round for Liege, but could not find him. The fear that pulsed through his body kept him moving and dodging, but he had no gun that worked, and he could not turn Grey Bat around lest he be stampeded, and even if no one blocked his path, he knew he could never retreat, or he'd get branded as yellow, and furthermore a traitor, and would have proven all the East Texas papers right: the Negro was not ready for battle.

Annie Proulx (1935–   )

lives in Wyoming, where most of her short stories are set. Many of Proulx's works reveal the ways in which geography and landscape influence a character's language, thoughts, and development. Her story collections include *Heart Songs and Other Stories* (1988), *Close Range: Wyoming Stories* (1999), *Bad Dirt: Wyoming Stories 2* (2004), and *Fine Just the Way It Is: Wyoming Stories 3* (2008). Proulx has also published four novels, including the PEN/Faulkner Award winner

Postcards (1992) and the Pulitzer Prize and National Book Award winner *The Shipping News* (1993). The critically acclaimed feature films *The Shipping News* (2001) and *Brokeback Mountain* (2005) are based on her novel and story of the same names.

© AP Photo/Daniel Ochoa de Olza

55 Miles to the Gas Pump (1999)

Rancher Croom in handmade boots and filthy hat, that walleyed cattleman, stray hairs like curling fiddle string ends, that warm-handed, quick-foot dancer on splintery boards or down the cellar stairs to a rack of bottles of his own strange beer, yeasty, cloudy, bursting out in garlands of foam, Rancher Croom at night galloping drunk over the dark plain, turning off at a place he knows to arrive at a canyon brink where he dismounts and looks down on tumbled rock, waits, then steps out, parting the air with his last roar, sleeves surging up windmill arms, jeans riding over boot tops, but before he hits he rises again to the top of the cliff like a cork in a bucket of milk.

Mrs. Croom on the roof with a saw cutting a hole into the attic where she has not been for twelve years thanks to old Croom's padlocks and warnings, whets to

her desire, and the sweat flies as she exchanges the saw for a chisel and hammer until a ragged slab of peak is free and she can see inside: just as she thought: the corpses of Mr. Croom's paramours°—she recognizes them from their photographs in the paper: MISSING WOMAN—some desiccated as jerky and much the same color, some moldy from lying beneath roof leaks, and all of them used hard, covered with tarry handprints, the marks of boot heels, some bright blue with the remnants of paint used on the shutters years ago, one wrapped in newspaper nipple to knee.

When you live a long way out you make your own fun.

°**paramours** Secret lovers.

CHAPTER 10 IN REVIEW
Fiction Sampler: The Short-Short Story

Reading and Reacting to the Short-Short Story

1. Which story in this chapter do you see as the most conventional? Which one seems *least* conventional? Why?

2. Does every story seem complete? What, if anything, seems to be missing from each story that might be present in a longer story?

3. If you were going to add material to "Snow," what would you add? Why?

4. How would "Accident" be different if the writer had used *I* instead of *you* to express the narrator's point of view?

5. Some stories in this chapter—such as "Buffalo Soldiers"—include dialogue; others include none (or very little). How would these stories—for example, "Girl"—be different if dialogue (or more dialogue) were added? What kind of dialogue would be useful?

Writing Suggestions: The Short-Short Story

1. Write a **response paper** (see Chapter 3) expressing your reactions to the ending of "55 Miles to the Gas Pump."

2. Write an **explication** (see Chapter 3) of "Girl" or of a short-short story located elsewhere in this book—for example, Kate Chopin's "Story of an Hour" (p. 115).

3. Write a **comparison-contrast** (see Chapter 3) comparing "Love and Other Catastrophes: A Mix Tape" with one of the love poems in Chapter 28.

4. Write a **character analysis** (see Chapter 3) of the narrator of "Accident."

5. Write an essay about the **cultural context** (see Chapter 3) of "Buffalo Soldiers."

6. Write a "mix tape" story about an experience in your own life.

Glossary Terms

short-short story Short fictional narrative that is under five pages (or fifteen hundred words) in length.

stream of consciousness Form of narration controlled not by external events but by the thoughts and subjective impressions of the narrator, commonly found in modern literature, such as the work of Virginia Woolf and James Joyce.

11

Plot

Learning Outcomes

After reading this chapter, you should be able to do the following:

LO1 Recognize conflict

LO2 Recognize stages of plot

LO3 Recognize order and sequence

Timeline

Ben Katchor, "The Goner Pillow Company" **2006**

1894 Kate Chopin, "The Story of an Hour" **1930** William Faulkner, "A Rose for Emily" Stephen Dobyns. "Kansas" **1999**

1890   **1910**   **1930**   **1950**   **1970**   **1990**

1897 The first subway opens in Boston, Massachusetts.

1935 The George Gershwin opera *Porgy and Bess* opens in New York City.

Diana, Princess of Wales, is killed in a car crash. **1997**

1895 Biologist Louis Pasteur dies.

1931 "The Star Spangled Banner" officially becomes the national anthem of the United States.

The Euro is introduced as a currency. **1999**

1894 American painter and illustrator Norman Rockwell is born.

George W. Bush is elected president of the United States. **2000**

1893 Women in Colorado become eligible to vote.

Hurricane Katrina strikes the Gulf Coast. **2005**

plot Way in which the events of the story are arranged. When there is more than one story but one string of events is clearly the most significant, the other stories are called **subplots**. Plot in fiction often follows the pattern of action in drama, rising toward a **climax** and then falling toward a **resolution**.

protagonist Principal character in a work of fiction.

antagonist Character who is in conflict with or opposition to the protagonist. Sometimes the antagonist may be a force or situation (war or poverty) rather than a person.

exposition First stage of a plot, where the author presents the information about characters or setting that a reader will need to understand the subsequent action.

Alfred Hitchcock's 1951 film *Strangers on a Train,* based on a suspense novel by Patricia Highsmith, offers an intriguing premise: two men, strangers, each can murder someone the other wishes dead; because they have no apparent connection to their victims, both can escape suspicion. Many people would describe this ingenious scheme as the film's "plot," but in fact it is simply the gimmick around which the complex plot revolves. Certainly a clever twist can be an important ingredient of a story's plot, but **plot** is more than "what happens": it is how what happens is revealed, the way in which a story's events are arranged.

Plot is shaped by causal connections—historical, social, and personal—by the interaction between characters, and by the juxtaposition of events. In *Strangers on a Train,* the plot that unfolds is complex: one character directs the events and determines their order while the other character is drawn into the action against his will. The same elements

>> Scene from Alfred Hitchcock's 1951 film *Strangers on a Train.*

that enrich the plot of the film—unexpected events, conflict, suspense, flashbacks, foreshadowing—can also enrich the plot of a work of short fiction.

LO1 Recognize Conflict

Readers' interest and involvement are heightened by a story's **conflict,** the struggle between opposing forces that emerges as the action develops. This conflict is a clash between the **protagonist,** a story's principal character, and an **antagonist,** someone or something presented in opposition to the protagonist. Sometimes the antagonist is a villain; more often, it is a character who represents a conflicting point of view or advocates a course of action different from the one the protagonist follows. Sometimes the antagonist is not a character at all but a situation (for instance, war or poverty) or an event (for example, a natural disaster, such as a flood or a storm) that challenges the protagonist. In some stories, the protagonist may struggle against a supernatural force, or the conflict may occur within a character's mind. It may, for example, be a struggle between two moral choices, such as whether to stay at home and care for an aging parent or to leave and make a new life.

LO2 Recognize Stages of Plot

A work's plot explores one or more conflicts, moving from *exposition* through a series of *complications* to a *climax* and, finally, to a *resolution*.

During a story's **exposition,** the writer presents the basic information readers need to understand the events that follow. Typically, the exposition sets the story in motion: it establishes the scene, introduces the major characters, and perhaps suggests the major events or conflicts to come.

Sometimes a single sentence can present a story's exposition clearly and economically, giving readers information vital to their understanding of the plot that will unfold. For example, the opening sentence of Amy Tan's "Two Kinds" (p. 336)—"My mother believed you could be anything you wanted to be in America"—reveals an important trait of a central character. Similarly, the opening sentence of Shirley Jackson's "The Lottery" (p. 251)—"The morning of June 27th was clear and sunny, with the fresh warmth of a full-summer day; the flowers were blossoming profusely and the grass was richly green"—introduces the picture-perfect setting that is essential to the story's irony. At other times, as in John Updike's "A&P" (p. 131), a more fully developed exposition section establishes the story's setting, introduces the main characters, and suggests possible conflicts. Finally, in some experimental stories, a distinct exposition component may be absent, as it is in and Amanda Holzer's "Love and Other Catastrophes: A Mix Tape" (p. 103).

As the plot progresses, the story's conflict unfolds through a series of complications that eventually lead

EXPLORE ONLINE >

To complete a tutorial of "Plot," visit your Literature
CourseMate, accessed through www.cengagebrain.com.

crisis Peak in the story's action.

climax Point of greatest tension or importance, where the decisive action of a play or story takes place.

resolution/denouement The final stage in the plot. Here the action comes to an end, and remaining loose ends are tied up.

deus ex machina Latin for "god from a machine": any improbable resolution of plot involving the intervention of some force or agent from outside the story.

in medias res Latin phrase describing works like Homer's *Iliad* that begin in the middle of the act on in order to catch a reader's interest.

flashback Variation on chronological order that presents an event or situation that occurred before the time in which the story's action takes place.

foreshadowing Presentation early in a story of situations, characters, or objects that seem to have no special importance but are later revealed to have great significance.

readers to the story's climax. As it develops, the story may include several crises. A **crisis** is a peak in the story's action, a moment of considerable tension or importance. The **climax** is the point of greatest tension or importance, the scene that presents a story's decisive action or event.

The final stage of plot, the **resolution,** or **denouement** (French for "untying of the knot"), draws the action to a close and accounts for all remaining loose ends. Sometimes this resolution is achieved with the help of a *deus ex machina* (Latin for "god from a machine"), an intervention of some force or agent previously extraneous to the story—for example, the sudden arrival of a long-lost relative or a fortuitous inheritance, the discovery of a character's true identity, or a last-minute rescue by a character not previously introduced. Usually, however, the resolution is more plausible: all the events lead logically and convincingly (though not necessarily predictably) to the resolution. Sometimes the ending of a story is indefinite—that is, readers are not quite sure what the protagonist will do or what will happen next. This kind of resolution, although it may leave some readers feeling cheated, has its advantages: it mirrors the complexity of life, where closure rarely occurs, and it can keep readers involved in the story as they try to understand the significance of its ending or to decide how conflicts should have been resolved.

LO3 Recognize Order and Sequence

A writer may present a story's events in strict chronological order, presenting each event in the sequence in which it actually takes place. More often, however, especially in relatively modern fiction, writers do not present events chronologically. Instead, they present incidents out of expected order, or in no apparent order. For example, a writer may choose to begin *in medias res* (Latin for "in the midst of things"), starting with a key event and later going back in time to explain events that preceded it, as Tillie Olsen does in "I Stand Here Ironing" (p. 162). Or, a writer can decide to begin a work of fiction at the end and then move back to reconstruct events that led up to the final outcome, as William Faulkner does in "A Rose for Emily" (p. 121). Many sequences are possible as the writer manipulates events to create interest, suspense, confusion, wonder, or some other effect.

Writers who wish to depart from strict chronological order use *flashbacks* and *foreshadowing*. A **flashback**

moves out of sequence to examine an event or situation that occurred before the time in which the story's action takes place. A character can remember an earlier event, or a story's narrator can re-create an earlier situation. For example, in Alberto Alvaro Ríos's "The Secret Lion" (p. 333), the adult narrator looks back at events that occurred when he was twelve years old and then moves further back in time to consider related events that occurred when he was five. In Edgar Allan Poe's "The Cask of Amontillado" (p. 190), the entire story is told as a flashback. Flashbacks are valuable because they can substitute for or supplement formal exposition by presenting background readers need to understand a story's events. One disadvantage of flashbacks is that, because they interrupt the natural flow of events, they may be intrusive or distracting. Such distractions, however, can be an advantage if the writer wishes to reveal events gradually and subtly or to obscure causal links.

Foreshadowing is the introduction early in a story of situations, events, characters, or objects that hint at things to come. Typically, a seemingly simple element—a chance remark, a natural occurrence, a trivial event—is eventually revealed to have great significance. For example, a dark cloud passing across the sky during a wedding can foreshadow future problems for the marriage. Foreshadowing allows a writer to hint provocatively at what is to come, so that readers only gradually become aware of a particular detail's role in a story. Thus, foreshadowing helps readers sense what will occur and grow increasingly involved as they see the likelihood (or even the inevitability) of a particular outcome.

In addition to using conventional techniques like flashbacks and foreshadowing, writers may experiment with sequence by substantially tampering with—or even dispensing with—chronological order. (An example is the scrambled chronology of "A Rose for Emily.") In such instances, the experimental form enhances interest and encourages readers to become involved with the story as they work to untangle or reorder the events and determine their logical and causal connections.

Today, the computer has given a new fluidity to the nature of plot, with hypertext stories appearing on the Internet, where stories may be constructed to permit readers to actually participate in the creation of plot.

Ben Katchor (1951–)

was born in Brooklyn, New York, and has published numerous comics, or "picture-stories," in a range of publications, including the Jewish-American newspaper the *Forward* and the monthly magazine *Metropolis*. Much of his work focuses on the Jewish-American immigrant experience and the humor surrounding cultural assimilation. His graphic novels include *Cheap Novelties: The Pleasures of Urban Decay* (1991); *Julius Knipl, Real Estate Photographer: Stories* (1996); *The Jew of New York* (1998); and *Julius Knipl, Real Estate Photographer: The Beauty Supply* *District* (2000). A fifth graphic novel, *The Cardboard Valise*, is forthcoming. Winner of a Guggenheim Memorial Foundation Fellowship and a MacArthur Foundation Fellowship, Katchor is currently an associate professor of illustration at Parsons The New School for Design in New York City.

The Goner Pillow Company (2006)

This graphic story starts on the next page.

 See Chapter 11 Review Card for Reading and Reacting questions about Ben Katchor, "The Goner Pillow Company."

Related Works

"The World Is Too Much with Us" (p. 373), "When I Heard the Learn'd Astronomer" (p. 383), *Trifles* (p. 555)

Cultural Context

Before air-conditioning window units became widespread in the 1950s, residents of urban apartment houses often kept their windows open to get some relief from the sweltering city heat. Open windows provided opportunities for apartment dwellers to socialize with neighbors and observe neighborhood goings-on, as depicted in this graphic story. Between 1948 and 1953, sales in the United States of air-conditioning window units spiked from 74,000 to 1,045,000. As a result, more and more apartment dwellers began shutting their windows, bringing the era of "window gossip" to a close.

The Goner Pillow Company by Ben Katchor

Source: ©2006 Ben Katchor. Used courtesy of The Wylie Agency.

Kate Chopin (1851–1904)

was born Katherine O'Flaherty, the daughter of a wealthy Irish-born merchant and his aristocratic Creole wife. She was married at nineteen to Oscar Chopin, a Louisiana cotton broker, who took her to live first in New Orleans and later on a plantation in central Louisiana. Chopin's representations of the Cane River region and its people in two volumes of short stories—*Bayou Folk* (1894) and *A Night in Arcadie* (1897)—are the foundation of her reputation as a local colorist, a writer dedicated to creating an accurate picture of a particular region and its people.

Her honest, sexually frank stories (many of them out of print for more than half a century) were rediscovered in the 1960s and 1970s, influencing a new generation of writers. Though she was a popular

contributor of stories and sketches to the magazines of her day, Chopin scandalized many critics with her outspoken novel *The Awakening* (1899), in which a woman seeks sexual and emotional fulfillment with a man who is not her husband. The book was removed from the shelves of the public library in St. Louis, where Chopin was born.

"The Story of an Hour" depicts a brief event in a woman's life, but in this single hour, Chopin reveals both a lifetime's emotional torment and the momentary joy of freedom.

Courtesy of Missouri Historical Society

The Story of an Hour (1894)

Knowing that Mrs. Mallard was afflicted with a heart trouble, great care was taken to break to her as gently as possible the news of her husband's death.

It was her sister Josephine who told her, in broken sentences, veiled hints that revealed in half concealing. Her husband's friend Richards was there, too, near her. It was he who had been in the newspaper office when intelligence of the railroad disaster was received, with Brently Mallard's name leading the list of "killed." He had only taken the time to assure himself of its truth by a second telegram, and had hastened to forestall any less careful, less tender friend in bearing the sad message.

She did not hear the story as many women have heard the same, with a paralyzed inability to accept its significance. She wept at once, with sudden, wild abandonment, in her sister's arms. When the storm of grief had spent itself she went away to her room alone. She would have no one follow her.

There stood, facing the open window, a comfortable, roomy armchair. Into this she sank, pressed down by a physical exhaustion that haunted her body and seemed to reach into her soul.

She could see in the open square before her house the 5 tops of trees that were all aquiver with the new spring life. The delicious breath of rain was in the air. In the street below a peddler was crying his wares. The notes of a distant song which some one was singing reached her faintly, and countless sparrows were twittering in the eaves.

There were patches of blue sky showing here and there through the clouds that had met and piled one above the other in the west facing her window.

She sat with her head thrown back upon the cushion of the chair, quite motionless, except when a sob came up into her throat and shook her, as a child who has cried itself to sleep continues to sob in its dreams.

She was young, with a fair, calm face, whose lines bespoke repression and even a certain strength. But now there was a dull stare in her eyes, whose gaze was fixed away off yonder on one of those patches of blue sky. It was not a glance of reflection, but rather indicated a suspension of intelligent thought.

There was something coming to her and she was waiting for it, fearfully. What was it? She did not know; it was too subtle and elusive to name. But she felt it, creeping out of the sky, reaching toward her through the sounds, the scents, the color that filled the air.

Now her bosom rose and fell tumultuously. She was 10 beginning to recognize this thing that was approaching to possess her, and she was striving to beat it back with her

> "It was he who had been in the newspaper office when intelligence of the railroad disaster was received, with Brently Mallard's name leading the list of 'killed.'"

POSTAL TELEGRAPH COMMERCIAL CABLES

TELEGRAM

>> Telegram

Jim Battaglia/Shutterstock.com

>> Interior of nineteenth-century home

EXPLORE ONLINE >

To listen to a podcast of "The Story of an Hour,"
visit your Literature CourseMate, accessed through
www.cengagebrain.com.

will—as powerless as her two white slender hands would have been.

When she abandoned herself a little whispered word escaped her slightly parted lips. She said it over and over under her breath: "Free, free, free!" The vacant stare and the look of terror that had followed it went from her eyes. They stayed keen and bright. Her pulses beat fast, and the coursing blood warmed and relaxed every inch of her body.

She did not stop to ask if it were not a monstrous joy that held her. A clear and exalted perception enabled her to dismiss the suggestion as trivial.

She knew that she would weep again when she saw the kind, tender hands folded in death; the face that had never looked save with love upon her, fixed and gray and dead. But she saw beyond that bitter moment a long procession of years to come that would belong to her absolutely. And she opened and spread her arms out to them in welcome.

There would be no one to live for during those coming years; she would live for herself. There would be no powerful will bending her in that blind persistence with which men and women believe they have a right to impose a private will upon a fellow creature. A kind intention or a cruel intention made the act seem no less a crime as she looked upon it in that brief moment of illumination.

And yet she had loved him—sometimes. Often she 15 had not. What did it matter! What could love, the unsolved mystery, count for in face of this possession of self-assertion which she suddenly recognized as the strongest impulse of her being.

"Free! Body and soul free!" she kept whispering.

Josephine was kneeling before the closed door with her lips to the key-hole, imploring for admission. "Louise, open the door! I beg; open the door—you will make yourself ill. What are you doing, Louise? For heaven's sake open the door."

"Go away. I am not making myself ill." No; she was drinking in a very elixir of life through that open window.

Cultural Context
During her marriage, Chopin lived in Louisiana, the only civil-law state in the United States. Whereas the legal systems of all other states are based on common law, the laws of Louisiana have their roots in the Napoleonic Code, the civil code enacted in France in 1804 to regulate issues of property, marriage, and divorce. This patriarchal code favored the husband in all domestic affairs and left women without many legal or fiscal rights. In "The Story of an Hour," the concept of freedom is closely tied to the prospect of escaping these restrictions.

>> Nineteenth-century train wreck

Her fancy was running riot along those days ahead of her. Spring days, and summer days, and all sorts of days that would be her own. She breathed a quick prayer that life might be long. It was only yesterday she had thought with a shudder that life might be long.

She arose at length and opened the door to her sister's 20 importunities. There was a feverish triumph in her eyes, and she carried herself unwittingly like a goddess of Victory. She clasped her sister's waist, and together they descended the stairs. Richards stood waiting for them at the bottom.

Some one was opening the front door with a latchkey. It was Brently Mallard who entered, a little travel-stained, composedly carrying his grip-sack and umbrella. He had been far from the scene of the accident, and did not even know there had been one. He stood amazed at Josephine's piercing cry; at Richards' quick motion to screen him from the view of his wife.

But Richards was too late.

When the doctors came they said she had died of heart disease—of joy that kills.

 See Chapter 11 Review Card for Reading and Reacting questions about Kate Chopin, "The Story of an Hour."

 Related Works

"The Storm" (p. 154), "The Yellow Wallpaper" (p. 313), *A Doll House* (p. 562)

Stephen Dobyns (1941–)

is a prolific writer in a variety of genres—poetry, novels, short stories, essays—whose work has been translated into numerous languages. Dobyns was educated at Wayne State University, and he went on to earn an MFA from the University of Iowa. Of his thirteen books of poetry and twenty novels, the most recent is *Winter's Journey* (2010). His collection of short stories, *Eating Naked*, was published in 2000; his essays appear in *Best Words, Best Order* (1996). The recipient of numerous literary awards, Dobyns has taught at the University of Iowa, Boston University, Sarah Lawrence College, Warren Wilson College, Syracuse University, and Emerson College.

© Dorothy Alexander

Kansas (1999)

The boy hitchhiking on the back-country Kansas road was nineteen years old. He had been dropped there by a farmer in a Model T Ford who had turned off to the north. Then he waited for three hours. It was July and there were no clouds. The wheat fields were flat and went straight to the horizon. The boy had two plums and he ate them. A blue Plymouth coupe° went by with a man and a woman. They were laughing. The woman had blond hair and it was all loose and blew from the window. They didn't even see the boy. The strands of straw-colored hair seemed to be waving to him. Half an hour later a farmer stopped in a Ford pick-up covered with a layer of dust. The boy clambered into the front seat. The farmer took off again without glancing at him. A forty-five revolver lay next to the farmer's buttocks on the seat. Seeing it, the boy felt something electric go off inside of him. The revolver was old and there were rust spots on the barrel. Black electrician's tape was wrapped around the handle.

"You seen a woman and a man go by here in a Plymouth coupe?" asked the farmer. He pronounced it "koo-pay."

The boy said he had.

"How long ago?"

"About thirty minutes." 5

The farmer had light blue eyes and there was stubble on his chin. Perhaps he was forty, but to the boy he looked old. His skin was leather-colored from the sun. The farmer pressed his foot to the floor and the pickup roared. It was a dirt road and the boy had to hold his hands against the dashboard to keep from being bounced around. It was hot and both windows were open. There was grit in the boy's eyes and on his tongue. He kept glancing sideways at the revolver.

"They friends of yours?" asked the boy.

The farmer didn't look at him. "That's my wife," he said. "I'm going to put a bullet in her head." He put a hand to the revolver to make sure it was still there. "The man too," he added.

The boy didn't say anything. He was hitchhiking back to summer school from Oklahoma. He was the middle of three boys and the only one who had left home. He had already spent a year at the University of Oklahoma and was spending the summer at Lawrence. And there were

---

° **coupe** A two-door car, often one that seats only people.

>> 1930s dust bowl farm

other places, farther places. The boy played the piano. He intended to go to those farther places.

"What did they do?" the boy asked at last. 10

"You just guess," said the farmer.

The pickup was going about fifty miles per hour. The boy was afraid of seeing the dust cloud from the Plymouth up ahead, but there was only straight road. Then he was afraid that the Plymouth might have pulled off someplace. He touched his tongue to his upper lip but it was just one dry thing against another. Getting into the pickup, the boy had had a clear idea of the direction of his life. He meant to go to New York City at the end of summer. He meant to play the piano in Carnegie Hall.° The farmer and his forty-five seemed to stand between him and that future. They formed a wall that the boy was afraid to climb over.

"Do you have to kill them?" the boy asked. He didn't want to talk but he felt unable to remain silent.

The farmer had a red boil on the side of his neck and he kept touching it with two fingers. "When you have something wicked, what do you do?" asked the farmer.

The boy wanted to say he didn't know or he wanted to 15 say he would call the police, but the farmer would have no patience with those answers. And the boy also wanted to say he would forgive the wickedness, but he was afraid of that answer as well. He was afraid of making the farmer angry and so he only shrugged.

° **Carnegie Hall**   A famous concert hall in New York City.

"You stomp it out," said the farmer. "That's what you do—you stomp it out."

The boy stared straight ahead, searching for the dust cloud and hoping not to see it. The hot air seemed to bend in front of them. The boy was so frightened of seeing the dust cloud that he was sure he saw it. A little puff of gray getting closer. The pickup went straight down the middle of the road. There was no other traffic. Even if there had been other cars, the boy felt certain that the farmer wouldn't have moved out of the way. The wheat on either side of the road was coated with layers of dust, making it a reddish color, the color of dried blood.

"What about the police?" asked the boy.

"It's my wife," said the farmer. "It's my problem."

The boy never did see the dust cloud. They reached Law- 20 rence and the boy got out as soon as he could. His shirt was stuck to his back and he kept rubbing his palms on his dungarees. He thanked the farmer but the man didn't look at him, he just kept staring straight ahead.

"Don't tell the police," said the farmer. His hand rested lightly on the forty-five beside him on the seat.

"No," said the boy. "I promise." He slammed shut the dusty door of the pickup.

The boy didn't tell the police. For several days he didn't tell anyone at all. He looked at the newspapers twice a day for news of a killing, but he didn't find anything. More than the farmer's gun, he had been frightened by the strength of the farmer's resolve. It had been like a chunk of stone and compared to it the boy had felt as soft as a piece of white bread. The boy never knew what happened. Perhaps nothing had happened.

The summer wound to its conclusion. The boy went to New York. He never did play in Carnegie Hall. His piano playing never got good enough. The war came and went. He wasn't a boy any longer. He was a married man with two sons. The family moved to Michigan. The man was a teacher, then a minister. His own parents died. He

Library of Congress public domain photo Photo #LC-DIG-fsa-8b32410

>> 1930s farmer standing beside pickup truck

told his sons the story about the farmer in the pickup. "What do you think happened?" they asked. Nobody knew. Perhaps the farmer caught up with them; perhaps he didn't. The man's sons went off to college and began their own lives. The man and his wife moved to New Hampshire. They grew old. Sixty years went by between that summer in Kansas and the present. The man entered his last illness. He stayed at home but he couldn't get out of bed. His wife gave him shots of morphine. He began to have dreams even when he was awake. The visiting nurse was always chipper. "Feeling better today?" she would ask. He tried to be polite, but he had no illusions. He went from one shot a day to two, and then three. The doctor said, "Give him as many as he needs." His wife started to ask about the danger of addiction, then she said nothing.

The man hardly knew when he was asleep or 25 awake. He hardly knew if one day had passed or many. He had oxygen. He didn't eat. The space between his eyes and the bedroom wall was always occupied with people of his invention, people of his past. He would lift his hand to wave them away, only to find his hand still lying motionless on the counterpane. Even music distracted him now. Always he was listening for something in the distance.

The boy was standing by the side of a dirt road. A Ford pickup stopped beside him and he got in. The farmer lifted a forty-five revolver. "I'm going to shoot my wife in the head."

"No," said the boy, "don't do it!"

The farmer drove fast. He had a red boil on the side of his neck and he kept touching it with two fingers. They found the Plymouth coupe pulled off into a hollow. There were shade trees and a brook. The farmer jammed down the brakes and the pickup slid sideways across the dirt. The man and woman were in the front seat of the Plymouth. Their clothes were half off. They jumped out of the car. The

woman had big red breasts. The farmer jumped out with his forty-five. "No!" shouted the boy. The farmer shot the man in the head. His whole head exploded and he fell down in the dust. His head was just a broken thing on the ground. The woman covered her face and tried to cover her breasts as well. The farmer shot her as well. Bits of dust floated on the surface of her blood. "One last for me," said the farmer. He put the barrel of the gun in his mouth. "No, no!" cried the boy.

The boy was standing by the side of a dirt road. A Ford pickup stopped beside him and he got in. "I'm going to shoot my wife," said the farmer. He had a big revolver on the seat beside him.

"You can't," said the boy. 30

They talked all the way to Lawrence. The farmer was crying. "I've always been good to her," he said. He had a red boil on the side of his neck and he kept touching it.

"Give the gun to the police," said the boy.

"I'm afraid," said the farmer.

"You needn't be," said the boy. "The police won't hurt you."

They drove to the police station. The boy told the desk 35 sergeant what had happened. The sergeant shook his head. He took the revolver away from the farmer. "We'll get her back, sir," he said. "Wife stealing's not permitted around here."

"I could have got in real trouble," said the farmer.

The boy was standing by the side of a dirt road. A pickup stopped beside him and he got in. The farmer said, "I'm going to kill my wife."

The boy was too frightened to say anything. He kept looking at the forty-five revolver. He was sure that he would be shot himself. He regretted not staying in Oklahoma, where he had friends and family. He couldn't imagine why he had moved away. The farmer drove straight to Lawrence. The boy was bounced all over the cab of the pickup but he didn't say anything. He was afraid that something would happen to his hands and he wouldn't be able to play the piano. It seemed to him that playing the piano was the only important thing in the entire world. The farmer had a red boil on the side of his neck and he kept touching it.

When they got to Lawrence, the boy jumped out of the pickup and ran. He saw a policeman and told him what had happened. An hour later he was getting a hamburger at a White Tower restaurant. He heard shooting. He ran out and saw the farmer's dusty pickup. There were police cars with their lights flashing. The boy pushed through the crowd. The farmer was hanging half out of the door of his pickup truck. There was blood all over the front of his work-shirt. The forty-five revolver lay on the pavement. The police-men were clapping each other on the back. They had big grins. The boy began cracking his knuckles. They made snapping noises.

The boy was standing by the side of a dirt road. A pickup 40 stopped beside him and he got in. The farmer pointed a forty-five revolver at his head. "Get in here," he said. They drove toward Lawrence.

"I'm going to shoot my wife for wickedness," said the farmer.

"No," said the boy, "you must forgive her."

"I'm going to kill her," said the farmer, "and her fancy man besides."

The boy said, "You can't take the law into your own hands."

The farmer raised his forty-five revolver. "They're as good 45 as dead." He had a red boil on the side of his neck.

The boy was a college student. It was the Depression. He wanted to go to New York and become a classical pianist. He had already been accepted by Juilliard.° "Justice does not be-long to you," said the boy.

"Wickedness must be punished," said the farmer.

They argued all the way to Lawrence. The boy stayed with the farmer. He could have jumped out of the pickup, but he didn't. The boy kept trying to convince him that he was wrong. The farmer drove to the train station.

The farmer's wife was in the waiting room with the man who had been driving the Plymouth coupe. She was very pretty, with blond hair and milky pink skin. She screamed when she saw the farmer. Her companion put his arms around her to protect her.

The boy hurried to stand between the woman and her 50 husband. "Think of what you are doing," he said. "Think how you are throwing your life away." The first bullet struck him in the shoulder and whipped him around. He could see

---

° **Juilliard** A highly respected school for the performing arts in New York City.

the woman open her mouth in a startled *Oh* of surprise. The second bullet caught him in the small of his back.

The man's family was with him in New Hampshire when he died: his wife and his two sons, neither of them young anymore. It was early evening in October at the very height of color. Even after sundown the maple trees seemed bright. The older son watched his father breathing. He kept twisting and trying to kick his feet. His face was very thin, his whole body was just a ridge under the middle of the sheet. He didn't talk anymore. He didn't want anyone to touch him. He seemed to be focusing his attention. He took a breath and they waited. He exhaled slowly. They continued to wait. He didn't breathe again. They waited several minutes. Then his wife removed the oxygen tubes from his nose, doing it quickly, as if afraid of doing some-thing wrong.

The older son went back into the bedroom with the two men from the funeral home. They had a collapsible stretcher which they put next to the bed. They unrolled a dark blue body bag. They shifted the dead man onto the stretcher and wrestled him into the body bag, one at his feet, one at his head. The son stood in the doorway. The men from the fu-neral home muttered directions to each other. They were breathing heavily and their hair was mussed. At last they got him into the body bag. The son watched closely as the zipper was drawn up and across his father's face. It was a large silver zipper and the son watched it being pulled across his father's forehead. All the days after that he kept seeing its glittering progress, a picture repeating itself in his mind.

 See Chapter 11 Review Card for Reading and Reacting questions about Stephen Dobyns, "Kansas."

 Related Works

"I Stand Here Ironing" (p. 162), "A Good Man Is Hard to Find" (p. 224), "Do not go gentle into that good night" (p. 484), "The Road Not Taken" (p. 509), *Beauty* (p. 541), *Tape* (p. 543)

William Faulkner (1897–1962)

was the winner of the 1949 Nobel Prize in Literature and the 1955 and 1963 Pulitzer Prizes for fiction. He was a Southern writer whose work continues to transcend the regional label. His nineteen novels, notably *The Sound and the Fury* (1929), *As I Lay Dying* (1930), *Light in August* (1932), *Absalom, Absalom!* (1936), and *The Reivers* (1962), explore a wide range of human experience—from high comedy to tragedy—as seen in the life of one community, the fictional Yoknapatawpha County (modeled on the area around Faulkner's own hometown of Oxford, Mississippi). Faulkner's Yoknapatawpha stories—a fascinating blend of complex Latinate prose and primitive Southern dialect—paint an extraordinary portrait of a community bound together by ties of blood, by a shared belief in moral "verities," and by an old grief (the Civil War). Faulkner's grandfather raised "Billy" on Civil War tales and local legends, including many about the "Old Colonel," the writer's great-grandfather, who was a

colorful Confederate officer. Although Faulkner's stories elegize the agrarian virtues of the Old South, they look unflinchingly at that world's tragic flaw: the "peculiar institution" of slavery.

Local legends and gossip frequently served as the spark for Faulkner's stories. As John B. Cullen, writing in *Old Times in Faulkner Country*, notes, "A Rose for Emily," Faulkner's first nationally published short story, was based on the tale of Oxford's aristocratic "Miss Mary" Neilson, who married Captain Jack Hume, the charming Yankee foreman of a street-paving crew, over her family's shocked protests. According to Cullen, one of Faulkner's neighbors said he created his story "out of fears and rumors"—the dire predictions of what *might* happen if Mary Neilson married her Yankee.

A Rose for Emily (1930)

I

When Miss Emily Grierson died, our whole town went to her funeral: the men through a sort of respectful affection for a fallen monument, the women mostly out of curiosity to see the inside of her house, which no one save an old manservant—a combined gardener and cook—had seen in at least ten years.

It was a big, squarish frame house that had once been white, decorated with cupolas and spires and scrolled balconies in the heavily lightsome style of the seventies, set on what had once been our most select street. But garages and cotton gins had encroached and obliterated even the august names of that neighborhood; only Miss Emily's house was left, lifting its stubborn and coquettish decay above the cotton wagons and the gasoline pumps—an eyesore among eyesores. And now Miss Emily had gone to join the representatives of those august names where they lay in the cedar-bemused cemetery among the ranked and anonymous graves of Union and Confederate soldiers who fell at the battle of Jefferson.

Alive, Miss Emily had been a tradition, a duty, and a care; a sort of hereditary obligation upon the town, dating from that day in 1894 when Colonel Sartoris, the mayor—he who fathered the edict that no Negro woman should appear on the streets without an apron—remitted her taxes, the dispensation dating from the death of her father on into perpetuity. Not that Miss Emily would have accepted charity. Colonel Sartoris invented an involved tale to the effect that Miss Emily's father had loaned money to the town, which the town, as a matter of business, preferred this way of repaying. Only a man of Colonel Sartoris' generation and thought could have invented it, and only a woman could have believed it.

When the next generation, with its more modern ideas, became mayors and aldermen, this arrangement created some little dissatisfaction. On the first of the year they mailed her a tax notice. February came, and there was no reply. They wrote her a formal letter, asking her to call at the sheriff's office at her convenience. A week later the mayor wrote her himself, offering to call or to send his car for her, and received in reply a note on paper of an archaic shape, in a thin, flowing calligraphy in faded ink, to the effect that she no longer went out at all. The tax notice was also enclosed, without comment.

They called a special meeting of the Board of Aldermen. A deputation waited upon her, knocked at the door through which no visitor had passed since she ceased giving china-painting lessons eight or ten years earlier. They were admitted by the old Negro into a dim hall from which a stairway mounted into still more shadow. It smelled of dust and disuse—a close, dank smell. The

5

> ## Cultural Context
> For many years, the pre–Civil War South was idealized as a land of prosperous plantations, large white houses, cultured and gracious people, and a stable economy based on farming. Central to the myth of the Old South was an adherence to the code of chivalry and a belief in the natural superiority of the white aristocracy, led by men who made their fortune by owning and running plantations that depended on slave labor. Once the South lost the Civil War, the idea of the Old South fell by the wayside, making room for the New South, which, like the North, was industrialized. In this story, Faulkner contrasts notions of the Old South and its decaying values with the newer ideas and innovations of the post-Reconstruction South.

Negro led them into the parlor. It was furnished in heavy, leather-covered furniture. When the Negro opened the blinds of one window, they could see that the leather was cracked; and when they sat down, a faint dust rose sluggishly about their thighs, spinning with slow motes in the single sun-ray. On a tarnished gilt easel before the fireplace stood a crayon portrait of Miss Emily's father.

They rose when she entered—a small, fat woman in black, with a thin gold chain descending to her waist and vanishing into her belt, leaning on an ebony cane with a tarnished gold head. Her skeleton was small and spare; perhaps that was why what would have been merely plumpness in another was obesity in her. She looked bloated, like a body long submerged in motionless water, and of that pallid hue. Her eyes, lost in the fatty ridges of her face, looked like two small pieces of coal pressed into a lump of dough as they moved from one face to another while the visitors stated their errand.

She did not ask them to sit. She just stood in the door and listened quietly until the spokesman came to a stumbling halt. Then they could hear the invisible watch ticking at the end of the gold chain.

Her voice was dry and cold. "I have no taxes in Jefferson. Colonel Sartoris explained it to me. Perhaps one of you can gain access to the city records and satisfy yourselves."

>> Civil War cemetery in the South

"But we have. We are the city authorities, Miss Emily. Didn't you get a notice from the sheriff, signed by him?"

"I received a paper, yes," Miss Emily said. "Perhaps he considers himself the sheriff . . . I have no taxes in Jefferson." 10

"But there is nothing on the books to show that, you see. We must go by the—"

"See Colonel Sartoris. I have no taxes in Jefferson."

"But, Miss Emily—"

"See Colonel Sartoris." (Colonel Sartoris had been dead almost ten years.) "I have no taxes in Jefferson. Tobe!" The Negro appeared. "Show these gentlemen out."

II

So she vanquished them, horse and foot, just as she had 15 vanquished their fathers thirty years before about the smell. That was two years after her father's death and a short time after her sweetheart—the one we believed would marry her—had deserted her. After her father's death she went out very little; after her sweetheart went away, people hardly saw her at all. A few of the ladies had the temerity to call, but were not received, and the only sign of life about the place was the Negro man—a young man then—going in and out with a market basket.

"Just as if a man—any man—could keep a kitchen properly," the ladies said; so they were not surprised when the smell developed. It was another link between the gross, teeming world and the high and mighty Griersons.

A neighbor, a woman, complained to the mayor, Judge Stevens, eighty years old.

"But what will you have me do about it, madam?" he said.

"Why, send her word to stop it," the woman said. "Isn't there a law?"

"I'm sure that won't be necessary," Judge Stevens 20 said. "It's probably just a snake or a rat that nigger of hers killed in the yard. I'll speak to him about it."

The next day he received two more complaints, one from a man who came in diffident deprecation. "We really must do something about it, Judge. I'd be the last one in the world to bother Miss Emily, but we've got to do something." That night the Board of Aldermen met—three graybeards and one younger man, a member of the rising generation.

"It's simple enough," he said. "Send her word to have her place cleaned up. Give her a certain time to do it in, and if she don't . . ."

"So she vanquished them, horse and foot, just as she had vanquished their fathers thirty years before. . . ."

>> Antebellum neighborhood, Charleston, SC

 EXPLORE ONLINE >

To listen to a podcast of "A Rose for Emily," visit your Literature CourseMate, accessed through www.cengagebrain.com.

"Dammit, sir," Judge Stevens said, "will you accuse a lady to her face of smelling bad?"

So the next night, after midnight, four men crossed Miss Emily's lawn and slunk about the house like burglars, sniffing along the base of the brickwork and at the cellar openings while one of them performed a regular sowing motion with his hand out of a sack slung from his shoulder. They broke open the cellar door and sprinkled lime there, and in all the outbuildings. As they recrossed the lawn, a window that had been dark was lighted and Miss Emily sat in it, the light behind her, and her upright torso motionless as that of an idol. They crept quietly across the lawn and into the shadow of the locusts that lined the street. After a week or two the smell went away.

That was when people had begun to feel really sorry 25 for her. People in our town, remembering how old lady Wyatt, her great-aunt, had gone completely crazy at last, believed that the Griersons held themselves a little too high for what they really were. None of the young men were quite good enough for Miss Emily and such. We had long thought of them as a tableau, Miss Emily a slender figure in white in the background, her father a spraddled silhouette in the foreground, his back to her and clutching a horsewhip, the two of them framed by the back-flung front door. So when she got to be thirty and was still single, we were not pleased exactly, but vindicated; even with insanity in the family she wouldn't have turned down all of her chances if they had really materialized.

When her father died, it got about that the house was all that was left to her; and in a way, people were glad. At last they could pity Miss Emily. Being left alone, and a pauper, she had become humanized. Now she too would know the old thrill and the old despair of a penny more or less.

The day after his death all the ladies prepared to call at the house and offer condolence and aid, as is our custom. Miss Emily met them at the door, dressed as usual and with no trace of grief on her face. She told them that her father was not dead. She did that for three days, with the ministers calling on her, and the doctors, trying to persuade her to let them dispose of the body. Just as they were about to resort to law and force, she broke down, and they buried her father quickly.

We did not say she was crazy then. We believed she had to do that. We remembered all the young men her father had driven away, and we knew that with nothing left, she would have to cling to that which had robbed her, as people will.

III

She was sick for a long time. When we saw her again, her hair was cut short, making her look like a girl, with a vague resemblance to those angels in colored church windows—sort of tragic and serene.

The town had just let the contracts for paving the 30 sidewalks, and in the summer after her father's death they began the work. The construction company came with niggers and mules and machinery, and a foreman named Homer Barron, a Yankee—a big, dark, ready man, with a big voice and eyes lighter than his face. The little boys would follow in groups to hear him cuss the niggers, and the niggers singing in time to the rise and fall of picks. Pretty soon he knew everybody in town. Whenever you heard a lot of laughing anywhere about the square, Homer Barron would be in the center of the group. Presently we began to see him and Miss Emily on Sunday afternoons driving in the yellow-wheeled buggy and the matched team of bays from the livery stable.

At first we were glad that Miss Emily would have an interest, because the ladies all said, "Of course a Grierson would not think seriously of a Northerner, a day laborer." But there were still others, older people, who said that even grief could not cause a real lady to forget *noblesse oblige*°— without calling it *noblesse oblige*. They just said, "Poor Emily. Her kinsfolk should come to her." She had some kin in Alabama; but years ago her father had fallen out with them over the estate of old lady Wyatt, the crazy woman, and there was no communication between the two families. They had not even been represented at the funeral.

And as soon as the old people said, "Poor Emily," the whispering began. "Do you suppose it's really so?" they said to one another. "Of course it is. What else could . . ." This behind their hands; rustling of craned silk and satin

---

° **noblesse oblige** The obligation of those of high birth or rank to behave honorably.

behind jalousies closed upon the sun of Sunday afternoon as the thin, swift clop-clop-clop of the matched team passed: "Poor Emily."

She carried her head high enough—even when we believed that she was fallen. It was as if she demanded more than ever the recognition of her dignity as the last Grierson; as if it had wanted that touch of earthiness to reaffirm her imperviousness. Like when she bought the rat poison, the arsenic. That was over a year after they had begun to say "Poor Emily," and while the two female cousins were visiting her.

"I want some poison," she said to the druggist. She was over thirty then, still a slight woman, though thinner than usual, with cold, haughty black eyes in a face the flesh of which was strained across the temples and about the eye-sockets as you imagine a lighthouse-keeper's face ought to look. "I want some poison," she said.

"Yes, Miss Emily. What kind? For rats and such? I'd 35 recom—"

"I want the best you have. I don't care what kind."

The druggist named several. "They'll kill anything up to an elephant. But what you want is—"

"Arsenic," Miss Emily said. "Is that a good one?"

"Is . . . arsenic? Yes, ma'am. But what you want—"

"I want arsenic." 40

The druggist looked down at her. She looked back at him, erect, her face like a strained flag. "Why, of course," the druggist said. "If that's what you want. But the law requires you to tell what you are going to use it for."

Miss Emily just stared at him, her head tilted back in order to look him eye for eye, until he looked away and went and got the arsenic and wrapped it up. The Negro delivery boy brought her the package; the druggist didn't come back. When she opened the package at home there was written on the box, under the skull and bones: "For rats."

IV

So the next day we all said, "She will kill herself"; and we said it would be the best thing. When she had first begun to be seen with Homer Barron, we had said, "She will marry him." Then we said, "She will persuade him yet," because Homer himself had remarked—he liked men, and it was known that he drank with the younger men in the Elks' Club—that he was not a marrying man. Later we said, "Poor Emily" behind the jalousies as they passed on Sunday afternoon in the glittering buggy, Miss Emily with her head high and Homer Barron with his hat cocked and a cigar in his teeth, reins and whip in a yellow glove.

Then some of the ladies began to say that it was a disgrace to the town and a bad example to the young people. The men did not want to interfere, but at last the ladies forced the Baptist minister—Miss Emily's people were Episcopal—to call upon her. He would never divulge what happened during that interview, but he refused to go back again. The next Sunday they again drove about the streets, and the following day the minister's wife wrote to Miss Emily's relations in Alabama.

>> Man driving buggy with two-horse team

So she had blood-kin under her roof again and we 45 sat back to watch developments. At first nothing happened. Then we were sure that they were to be married. We learned that Miss Emily had been to the jeweler's and ordered a man's toilet set in silver, with the letters H. B. on each piece. Two days later we learned that she had bought a complete outfit of men's clothing, including a nightshirt, and we said, "They are married." We were really glad. We were glad because the two female cousins were even more Grierson than Miss Emily had ever been.

So we were not surprised when Homer Barron—the streets had been finished some time since—was gone. We were a little disappointed that there was not a public blowing-off, but we believed that he had gone on to prepare for Miss Emily's coming, or to give her a chance to get rid of the cousins. (By that time it was a cabal, and we were all Miss Emily's allies to help circumvent the cousins.) Sure enough, after another week they departed. And, as we had expected all along, within three days Homer Barron was back in town. A neighbor saw the Negro man admit him at the kitchen door at dusk one evening.

And that was the last we saw of Homer Barron. And of Miss Emily for some time. The Negro man went in and out with the market basket, but the front door remained closed. Now and then we would see her at a window for a moment, as the men did that night when they sprinkled the lime, but for almost six months she did not appear on the streets. Then we knew that this was to be expected too; as if that quality of her father which had thwarted her woman's life so many times had been too virulent and too furious to die.

When we next saw Miss Emily, she had grown fat and her hair was turning gray. During the next few years it grew grayer and grayer until it attained an even pepper-and-salt iron-gray, when it ceased turning. Up to the day of her death at seventy-four it was still that vigorous iron-gray, like the hair of an active man.

Bettmann/Corbis Photo #F5715

From that time on her front door remained closed, save for a period of six or seven years, when she was about forty, during which she gave lessons in china-painting. She fitted up a studio in one of the downstairs rooms, where the daughters and granddaughters of Colonel Sartoris' contemporaries were sent to her with the same regularity and in the same spirit that they were sent to church on Sundays with a twenty-five-cent piece for the collection plate. Meanwhile her taxes had been remitted.

Then the newer generation became the backbone [50] and the spirit of the town, and the painting pupils grew up and fell away and did not send their children to her with boxes of color and tedious brushes and pictures cut from the ladies' magazines. The front door closed upon the last one and remained closed for good. When the town got free postal delivery, Miss Emily alone refused to let them fasten the metal numbers above her door and attach a mailbox to it. She would not listen to them.

Daily, monthly, yearly we watched the Negro grow grayer and more stooped, going in and out with the market basket. Each December we sent her a tax notice, which would be returned by the post office a week later, unclaimed. Now and then we would see her in one of the downstairs windows—she had evidently shut up the top floor of the house—like the carven torso of an idol in a niche, looking or not looking at us, we could never tell which. Thus she passed from generation to generation—dear, inescapable, impervious, tranquil, and perverse.

And so she died. Fell ill in the house filled with dust and shadows, with only a doddering Negro man to wait on her. We did not even know she was sick; we had long since given up trying to get any information from the Negro. He talked to no one, probably not even to her, for his voice had grown harsh and rusty, as if from disuse.

She died in one of the downstairs rooms, in a heavy walnut bed with a curtain, her gray head propped on a pillow yellow and moldy with age and lack of sunlight.

V

The Negro met the first of the ladies at the front door and let them in, with their hushed, sibilant voices and their quick, curious glances, and then he disappeared. He walked right through the house and out the back and was not seen again.

The two female cousins came at once. They held the [55] funeral on the second day, with the town coming to look at Miss Emily beneath a mass of bought flowers, with the crayon face of her father musing profoundly above the bier and the ladies sibilant and macabre; and the very old men—some in their brushed Confederate uniforms—on the porch and the lawn, talking of Miss Emily as if she had been a contemporary of theirs, believing that they had danced with her and courted her perhaps, confusing time with its mathematical progression, as the old do, to whom all the past is not a diminishing road but, instead, a huge meadow which no winter ever quite touches, divided from them now by the narrow bottle-neck of the most recent decade of years.

Already we knew that there was one room in that region above stairs which no one had seen in forty years, and which would have to be forced. They waited until Miss Emily was decently in the ground before they opened it.

The violence of breaking down the door seemed to fill this room with pervading dust. A thin, acrid pall as of the tomb seemed to lie everywhere upon this room decked and furnished as for a bridal: upon the valance curtains of faded rose color, upon the rose-shaded lights, upon the dressing table, upon the delicate array of crystal and the man's toilet things backed with tarnished silver, silver so tarnished that the monogram was obscured. Among them lay collar and tie, as if they had just been removed, which, lifted, left upon the surface a pale crescent in the dust. Upon a chair hung the suit, carefully folded; beneath it the two mute shoes and the discarded socks.

The man himself lay in the bed.

For a long while we just stood there, looking down at the profound and fleshless grin. The body had apparently once lain in the attitude of an embrace, but now the long sleep that outlasts love, that conquers even the grimace of love, had cuckolded him. What was left of him, rotted beneath what was left of the nightshirt, had become inextricable from the bed in which he lay; and upon him and upon the pillow beside him lay that even coating of the patient and biding dust.

Then we noticed that in the second pillow was the [60] indentation of a head. One of us lifted something from it, and leaning forward, that faint and invisible dust dry and acrid in the nostrils, we saw a long strand of iron-gray hair.

Related Works

"Miss Brill" (p. 135), "Barn Burning" (p. 194), "Porphyria's Lover" (p. 375), "Richard Cory" (p. 516), *Trifles* (p. 555)

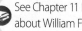

See Chapter 11 Review Card for Reading and Reacting questions about William Faulkner, "A Rose for Emily."

Writing Suggestions: Plot

1. Write a sequel to "The Story of an Hour," telling the story in the voice of Brently Mallard. Use **flashbacks** to provide information about his view of the Mallards' marriage.

2. "The Story of an Hour" includes a *deus ex machina,* an outside force or agent that suddenly appears to change the course of events. Consider the possible effects of a *deus ex machina* on the other stories in this chapter, including "The Goner Pillow Company." What might this outside force be in each story? How might it change the story's action? How plausible would such a dramatic turn of events be in each case?

3. In "Kansas," a character's actual life unfolds alongside his memories and fantasies. Write an essay in which you compare "Kansas" with another story in which a character's imaginative life is a significant part of the story—for example, "The Rocking-Horse Winner" (p. 297) or "The Yellow Wallpaper" (p. 313).

 CHECKLIST

WRITING ABOUT PLOT
☐ What happens in the story?
☐ Where does the story's formal exposition section end? What do readers learn about characters in this section? What do readers learn about setting? What possible conflicts are suggested here?
☐ What is the story's central conflict? What other conflicts are presented? Who is the protagonist? Who (or what) serves as the antagonist?
☐ Identify the story's crisis or crises.
☐ Identify the story's climax.
☐ How is the story's central conflict resolved? Is this resolution plausible? Satisfying?
☐ Which part of the story constitutes the resolution? Do any problems remain unresolved? Does any uncertainty remain? If so, does this uncertainty strengthen or weaken the story? Would another ending be more effective?
☐ How are the story's events arranged? Are they presented in chronological order? What events are presented out of logical sequence? Does the story use foreshadowing? flashbacks? Are the causal connections between events clear? logical? If not, can you explain why?

Glossary Terms

antagonist Character who is in conflict with or opposition to the protagonist. Sometimes the antagonist may be a force or situation (war or poverty) rather than a person.

climax Point of greatest tension or importance, where the decisive action of a play or story takes place.

crisis Peak in the story's action.

deus ex machina Latin for "god from a machine": any improbable resolution of plot involving the intervention of some force or agent from outside the story.

exposition First stage of a plot, where the author presents the information about characters or setting that a reader will need to understand the subsequent action.

flashback Variation on chronological order that presents an event or situation that occurred before the time in which the story's action takes place.

foreshadowing Presentation early in a story of situations, characters, or objects that seem to have no special importance but are later revealed to have great significance.

in medias res Latin phrase describing works like Homer's *Iliad* that begin in the middle of the action in order to catch a reader's interest.

plot Way in which the events of the story are arranged. When there is more than one story but one string of events is clearly the most significant, the other stories are called **subplots.** Plot in fiction often follows the pattern of action in drama, rising toward a **climax** and then falling toward a **resolution.**

protagonist Principal character of a drama or a work of fiction.

resolution/denouement The final stage in the plot. Here the action comes to an end, and remaining loose ends are tied up.

12

Character

Learning Outcomes

After reading this chapter, you should be able to do the following:

LO1 Recognize round and flat characters

LO2 Recognize dynamic and static characters

LO3 Understand motivation

Timeline

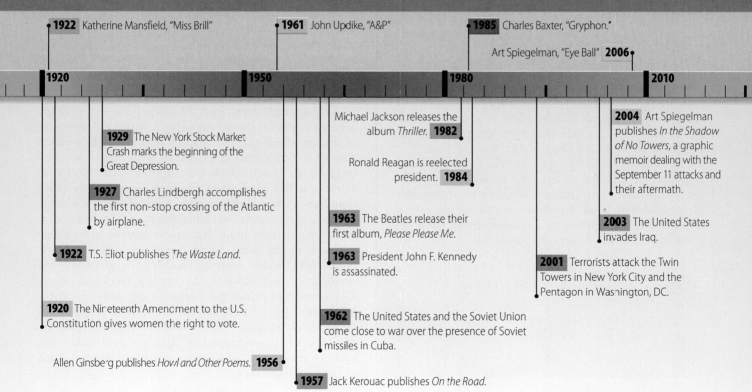

1922 Katherine Mansfield, "Miss Brill"

1961 John Updike, "A&P"

1985 Charles Baxter, "Gryphon."

Art Spiegelman, "Eye Ball" **2006**

1920 **1950** **1980** **2010**

Michael Jackson releases the album *Thriller.* **1982**

Ronald Reagan is reelected president. **1984**

2004 Art Spiegelman publishes *In the Shadow of No Towers*, a graphic memoir dealing with the September 11 attacks and their aftermath.

1929 The New York Stock Market Crash marks the beginning of the Great Depression.

1927 Charles Lindbergh accomplishes the first non-stop crossing of the Atlantic by airplane.

1922 T.S. Eliot publishes *The Waste Land.*

1963 The Beatles release their first album, *Please Please Me.*

1963 President John F. Kennedy is assassinated.

2003 The United States invades Iraq.

2001 Terrorists attack the Twin Towers in New York City and the Pentagon in Washington, DC.

1920 The Nineteenth Amendment to the U.S. Constitution gives women the right to vote.

1962 The United States and the Soviet Union come close to war over the presence of Soviet missiles in Cuba.

Allen Ginsberg publishes *Howl and Other Poems.* **1956**

1957 Jack Kerouac publishes *On the Road.*

LO1 Recognize Round and Flat Characters

In his influential 1927 work *Aspects of the Novel*, English novelist E. M. Forster classifies characters as either **round** (well developed, closely involved in and responsive to the action) or **flat** (barely developed or stereotypical). To a great extent, these categories are still useful. In an effective story, the major characters are usually complex and fully developed; if they are not, readers will not care what happens to them. Sometimes readers are encouraged to become involved with the characters, even to identify with them, and this empathy is possible only when we know something about the characters—their strengths and weaknesses, their likes and dislikes. In some cases, of course, a story can be effective even when its central characters are not well developed. Sometimes, in fact, a story's effectiveness is enhanced by an absence of character development, as in Shirley Jackson's "The Lottery" (p. 251).

Readers often expect characters to behave as "real people" in their situation might behave. Real people are not perfect, and realistic characters cannot be perfect either. The flaws that are revealed as round characters are developed—greed, gullibility, naïveté, shyness, a quick temper, or a lack of insight or judgment or tolerance or even intelligence—make them believable. In modern fiction, the protagonist is seldom if ever the noble "hero"; more often,

> **"Real people are not perfect, and realistic characters cannot be perfect either."**

he or she is at least partly a victim, someone to whom unpleasant things happen and someone who is sometimes ill equipped to cope with events.

Unlike major characters, minor characters are frequently not well developed. Often they are flat, perhaps acting as foils for the protagonist. A **foil** is a supporting character whose role in the story is to highlight a major character by presenting a contrast with him or her. For instance, in "A&P," Stokesie, another young checkout clerk, is a foil for Sammy. Because he is a little older than Sammy and seems to have none of Sammy's imagination, restlessness, or nonconformity, Stokesie suggests what Sammy might become if he were to continue to work at the A&P. Some flat characters are **stock characters,** easily identifiable types who behave so predictably that readers can readily recognize them. The kindly old priest, the tough young bully, the ruthless business executive, and the reckless adventurer are all stock characters. Some flat characters can even be **caricatures,** characterized by a single dominant trait, such as miserliness, or even by one physical trait, such as nearsightedness.

A character is a fictional representation of a person—usually (but not necessarily) a psychologically realistic depiction. Writers may develop characters through their actions, through their reactions to situations or to other characters, through their physical appearance, through their speech and gestures and expressions, and even through their names.

Generally speaking, characters' personality traits, as well as their appearances and their feelings and beliefs, are communicated to readers in two ways. First, readers can be told about characters. Third-person narrators can provide information about what characters are doing, saying, and thinking; what experiences they have had; what they look like; how they are dressed; and so on. Sometimes narrators also offer analysis of and judgments about a character's behavior or motivation. Similarly, first-person narrators can tell us about themselves or about other characters. Thus, Sammy in John Updike's "A&P" (p. 131) tells readers what he thinks about his job and about the girls who come into the supermarket where he works. He also tells us what various characters look like and describes their actions, attitudes, and gestures. (For more information about first-person narrators, see Chapter 14, "Point of View.")

Alternatively, aspects of a character's personality and beliefs may be revealed through his or her actions, dialogue, or thoughts. For instance, Sammy's vivid fantasies and his disapproval of his customers' lives suggest to readers that he is something of a nonconformist; however, Sammy himself does not actually tell us this.

EXPLORE ONLINE >

To complete a tutorial of "Character," visit your Literature CourseMate, accessed through www.cengagebrain.com.

LO2 Recognize Dynamic and Static Characters

Characters may also be classified as either dynamic or static. A **dynamic character** grows and changes in the course of a story, developing as he or she reacts to events and to other characters. In "A&P," for instance, Sammy's decision to speak out in defense of the girls—as well as the events that lead him to do so—changes him. His view of the world has changed at the end of the story, and as a result his position in the world may change too. A **static character** may face the same challenges a dynamic character might face but will remain essentially unchanged: a static character who was selfish and arrogant will remain selfish and arrogant, regardless of the nature of the story's conflict. In the fairy tale "Cinderella," for example, the title character is as sweet and good-natured at the end of the story—despite her mistreatment by her family—as she is at the beginning. Her situation may have changed, but her character has not.

Whereas round characters tend to be dynamic, flat characters tend to be static. But even a very complex, well-developed major character may be static; sometimes, in fact, the point of a story may hinge on a character's inability to change. A familiar example is the title character in William Faulkner's "A Rose for Emily" (p. 121), who lives a wasted, empty life, at least in part because she is unwilling or unable to accept that the world around her and the people in it have changed.

A story's minor characters are often static; their growth is not usually relevant to the story's development. Moreover, we usually do not learn enough about a minor character's traits, thoughts, actions, or motivation to determine whether the character changes significantly.

> **dynamic character** A character who grows and changes in the course of a story.
>
> **static character** A character who remains unchanged in the course of a story.
>
> **motivation** Reasons behind a character's behavior.

LO3 Understand Motivation

Because round characters are complex, they are not always easy to understand. They may act unpredictably, just as real people do. They wrestle with decisions, resist or succumb to temptation, make mistakes, ask questions, search for answers, hope and dream, rejoice and despair. What is important is not whether we approve of a character's actions but whether those actions are plausible—whether the actions make sense in light of what we know about the character. We need to understand a character's **motivation**—the reasons behind his or her behavior—or we will not believe or accept that behavior. In "A&P," for instance, given Sammy's age, his dissatisfaction with his job, and his desire to impress the young woman he calls Queenie, the decision he makes at the end of the story is perfectly plausible. Without having established his motivation, Updike could not have expected readers to accept Sammy's actions.

Of course, even when readers get to know a character, they still are not able to predict how a complex, round character will behave in a given situation; only a flat character is predictable. The tension that develops as readers wait to see how a character will act or react, and thus how a story's conflict will be resolved, is what holds readers' interest and keeps them involved as a story's action unfolds.

© Sean Gallup/Getty Images

Art Spiegelman (1948–   )

was born in Stockholm, Sweden, and raised in Queens, New York. He is arguably one of the most influential comic artists of the underground movement, which began (thanks in large part to R. Crumb) in the 1960s. In collaboration with his wife, Spiegelman founded the comics magazine *RAW* in 1980, and his comics have been featured in such publications as the *New Yorker*, the *New York Times*, and the *Village Voice*. His two-part masterpiece, the Pulitzer Prize–winning *Maus* (1986) and *Maus II* (1991), are based on his parents' struggle for survival during the Holocaust. Collections of his work include *In the Shadow of No Towers* (2004), one of the *New York Times* Book Review's 100 Notable Books of 2004.

Cultural Context

The young narrator of "Eye Ball" suffers from amblyopia, or "lazy eye," the most common cause of impaired vision in children. When one eye develops slowly or improperly, the stronger eye overcompensates, creating the kind of distorted vision depicted in this story. Amblyopia often develops in children before age seven, and early treatment (in the form of an eye patch or other device to help the brain relearn to use the weaker eye) is crucial to correct the problem.

Eye Ball (2006)

 See Chapter 12 Review Card for Reading and Reacting questions about Art Spiegelman, "Eye Ball."

Related Works

"A&P" (p. 131), "Cathedral" (p. 261)

John Updike (1932–2009)

was a prolific writer of novels, short stories, essays, poems, plays, and children's tales. Updike's earliest ambition was to be a cartoonist for the *New Yorker*. He attended Harvard hoping to draw cartoons for the *Harvard Lampoon*, studied drawing and fine art at Oxford, and in 1955 went to work for the *New Yorker*—not as a cartoonist but as a "Talk of the Town" reporter. Updike left the *New Yorker* after three years to write full-time but continued to contribute stories, reviews, and essays to the magazine until his death in 2009. Among his novels are *Rabbit, Run* (1960), *The Centaur* (1963), *Rabbit Redux* (1971), *Rabbit Is Rich* (1981), *The Witches of Eastwick* (1985), and *Rabbit at Rest* (1990). His last novels are *Seek My Face* (2002), *Villages* (2004), *Of the Farm* (2004), *Terrorist* (2006), and *The Widows of Eastwick* (2008). Updike received the National Book Foundation Medal for Distinguished Contribution to American Letters.

In early stories such as "A&P" (1961), Updike draws on memories of his childhood and teenage years for the sort of "small" scenes and stories for which he quickly became famous. "There is a great deal to be said about almost anything," Updike comments in an interview in *Contemporary Authors*. "All people can be equally interesting. . . . Now either nobody is a hero or everybody is. I vote for everybody. My subject is the American Protestant small-town middle class. I like middles. It is in middles that extremes clash."

A&P (1961)

In walks these three girls in nothing but bathing suits. I'm in the third check-out slot, with my back to the door, so I don't see them until they're over by the bread. The one that caught my eye first was the one in the plaid green two-piece. She was a chunky kid, with a good tan and a sweet broad soft-looking can with those two crescents of white just under it, where the sun never seems to hit, at the top of the backs of her legs. I stood there with my hand on a box of Hi Ho crackers trying to remember if I rang it up or not. I ring it up again and the customer starts giving me hell. She's one of these cash-register-watchers, a witch about fifty with rouge on her cheekbones and no eyebrows, and I know it made her day to trip me up. She'd been watching cash registers for fifty years and probably never seen a mistake before.

By the time I got her feathers smoothed and her goodies into a bag—she gives me a little snort in passing, if she'd been born at the right time they would have burned her over in Salem—by the time I get her on her way the girls had circled around the bread and were coming back, without a push-cart, back my way along the counters, in the aisle between the check-outs and the Special bins. They didn't even have shoes on. There was this chunky one, with the two-piece—it was bright green and the seams on the bra were still sharp and her belly was still pretty pale so I guessed she just got it (the suit)—there was this one, with one of those chubby berry-faces, the lips all bunched together under her nose, this one, and a tall one, with black hair that hadn't quite frizzed right, and one of these sunburns right across under the eyes, and a chin that was too long—you know, the kind of girl other girls think is very "striking" and "attractive" but never quite makes it, as they very well know, which is why they like her so much—and then the third one, that wasn't quite so tall. She was the queen. She kind of led them, the other two peeking around and making their shoulders round. She

didn't look around, not this queen, she just walked straight on slowly, on these long white prima-donna legs. She came down a little hard on her heels, as if she didn't walk in her bare feet that much, putting down her heels and then letting the weight move along to her toes as if she was testing the floor with every step, putting a little deliberate extra action into it. You never know for sure how girls' minds work (do you really think it's a mind in there or just a little buzz like a bee in a glass jar?) but you got the idea she had talked the other two into coming in here with her, and now she was showing them how to do it, walk slow and hold yourself straight.

She had on a kind of dirty-pink—beige maybe, I don't know—bathing suit with a little nubble all over it and, what got me, the straps were down. They were off her shoulders

>> Facade of 1950s A&P supermarket

looped loose around the cool tops of her arms, and I guess as a result the suit had slipped a little on her, so all around the top of the cloth there was this shining rim. If it hadn't been there you wouldn't have known there could have been anything whiter than those shoulders. With the straps pushed off, there was nothing between the top of the suit and the top of her head except just her, this clean bare plane of the top of her chest down from the shoulder bones like a dented sheet of metal tilted in the light. I mean, it was more than pretty.

She had sort of oaky hair that the sun and salt had bleached, done up in a bun that was unravelling, and a kind of prim face. Walking into the A&P with your straps down, I suppose it's the only kind of face you can have. She held her head so high her neck, coming up out of those white shoulders, looked kind of stretched, but I didn't mind. The longer her neck was, the more of her there was.

She must have felt in the corner of her eye me and over ⁵ my shoulder Stokesie in the second slot watching, but she didn't tip. Not this queen. She kept her eyes moving across the racks, and stopped, and turned so slow it made my stomach rub the inside of my apron, and buzzed to the other two, who kind of huddled against her for relief, and they all three of them went up the cat-and-dog-food-breakfast-cereal-macaroni-rice-raisins-seasonings-spreads-spaghetti-soft-drinks-crackers-and-cookies aisle. From the third slot I look straight up this aisle to the meat counter, and I watched them all the way. The fat one with the tan sort of fumbled with the cookies, but on second thought she put the packages back. The sheep pushing their carts down the aisle—the girls were walking against the usual traffic (not that we have one-way signs or anything)—were pretty hilarious. You could see them, when Queenie's white shoulders dawned on them, kind of jerk, or hop, or hiccup, but their eyes snapped back to their own baskets and on they pushed. I bet you could set off dynamite in an A&P and the people would by and large keep reaching and checking oatmeal off their lists and muttering "Let me see, there was a third thing, began with A, asparagus, no, ah, yes, applesauce!" or whatever it is they do mutter. But there was no doubt, this jiggled them. A few houseslaves in pin curlers even looked around after pushing their carts past to make sure what they had seen was correct.

You know, it's one thing to have a girl in a bathing suit down on the beach, where what with the glare nobody can look at each other much anyway, and another thing in the cool of the A&P, under the fluorescent lights, against all those stacked packages, with her feet paddling along naked over our checkerboard green-and-cream rubber-tile floor.

"Oh Daddy," Stokesie said beside me. "I feel so faint."

>> Queenie and her friends as pictured in DVD of "A&P"

© Steven Payne/Mom Path Productions

"Darling," I said. "Hold me tight." Stokesie's married, with two babies chalked up on his fuselage already, but as far as I can tell that's the only difference. He's twenty-two, and I was nineteen this April.

"Is it done?" he asks, the responsible married man finding his voice. I forgot to say he thinks he's going to be manager some sunny day, maybe in 1990 when it's called the Great Alexandrov and Petrooshki Tea Company or something.

What he meant was, our town is five miles from ¹⁰ a beach, with a big summer colony out on the Point, but we're right in the middle of town, and the women generally put on a shirt or shorts or something before they get out of the car into the street. And anyway these are usually women with six children and varicose veins mapping their legs and nobody, including them, could care less. As I say, we're right in the middle of town, and if you stand at our front doors you can see two banks and the Congregational church and the newspaper store and three real-estate offices and about twenty-seven old freeloaders tearing up Central Street because the sewer broke again. It's not as if we're on the Cape; we're north of Boston and there's people in this town haven't seen the ocean for twenty years.

The girls had reached the meat counter and were asking McMahon something. He pointed, they pointed, and they shuffled out of sight behind a pyramid of Diet Delight peaches. All that was left for us to see was old McMahon patting his mouth and looking after them sizing up their joints. Poor kids, I began to feel sorry for them, they couldn't help it.

Now here comes the sad part of the story, at least my family says it's sad but I don't think it's sad myself. The store's pretty empty, it being Thursday afternoon, so there was nothing much to do except lean on the register and wait for the girls to show up again. The whole store was like a pinball machine and I didn't know which tunnel they'd come out of. After a while they come around out of the far aisle, around the light bulbs, records at discount of the Caribbean Six or Tony Martin Sings or some such gunk you wonder they waste the wax on, sixpacks of candy bars, and plastic toys done up in cellophane that fall apart when a kid looks at them anyway. Around they come, Queenie still leading the way, and holding a little gray jar in her hand. Slots Three through Seven are unmanned and I could see her wondering between Stokes and me, but Stokesie with his usual luck draws an old party in baggy gray pants who stumbles up with four giant cans of pineapple juice (what do these bums do with all that pineapple juice? I've often asked myself) so the girls come to me. Queenie puts down the jar and I take it into my fingers icy cold. King-

© The Advertising Archives

<< Vintage magazine ad for A&P supermarket

fish Fancy Herring Snacks in Pure Sour Cream: 49. Now her hands are empty, not a ring or a bracelet, bare as God made them, and I wonder where the money's coming from. Still with that prim look she lifts a folded dollar bill out of the hollow at the center of her nubbled pink top. The jar went heavy in my hand. Really, I thought that was so cute.

"The whole store was like a pinball machine and I didn't know which tunnel they'd come out of."

Then everybody's luck begins to run out. Lengel comes in from haggling with a truck full of cabbages on the lot and is about to scuttle into that door marked MANAGER behind which he hides all day when the girls touch his eye. Lengel's pretty dreary, teaches Sunday school and the rest, but he doesn't miss that much. He comes over and says, "Girls, this isn't the beach."

Queenie blushes, though maybe it's just a brush of sunburn I was noticing for the first time, now that she was so close. "My mother asked me to pick up a jar of herring snacks." Her voice kind of startled me, the way voices do when you see the people first, coming out so flat and dumb yet kind of tony, too, the way it ticked over "pick up" and "snacks." All of a sudden I slid right down her voice into her living room. Her father and the other men were standing around in ice-cream coats and bow ties and the women were in sandals picking up herring snacks on toothpicks off a big plate and they were all holding drinks the color of water with olives and sprigs of mint in them. When my parents have somebody over they get lemonade and if it's a real racy affair Schlitz in tall glasses with "They'll Do It Every Time" cartoons stencilled on.

"That's all right," Lengel said. "But this isn't the beach." 15 His repeating this struck me as funny, as if it had just occurred

Courtesy, Vita Food Products, Inc.

>> Jars of herring snacks

to him, and he had been thinking all these years the A&P was a great big dune and he was the head lifeguard. He didn't like my smiling—as I say he doesn't miss much—but he concentrates on giving the girls that sad Sunday-school-superintendent stare.

Queenie's blush is no sunburn now, and the plump one in plaid, that I liked better from the back—a really sweet can—pipes up, "We weren't doing any shopping. We just came in for the one thing."

"That makes no difference," Lengel tells her, and I could see from the way his eyes went that he hadn't noticed she was wearing a two-piece before. "We want you decently dressed when you come in here."

"We *are* decent," Queenie says suddenly, her lower lip pushing, getting sore now that she remembers her place, a place from which the crowd that runs the A&P must look pretty crummy. Fancy Herring Snacks flashed in her very blue eyes.

"Girls, I don't want to argue with you. After this come in here with your shoulders covered. It's our policy." He turns his back. That's policy for you. Policy is what the kingpins want. What the others want is juvenile delinquency.

All this while, the customers had been showing up 20 with their carts but, you know, sheep, seeing a scene, they had all bunched up on Stokesie, who shook open a paper bag as gently as peeling a peach, not wanting to miss a word. I could feel in the silence everybody getting nervous, most of all Lengel, who asks me, "Sammy, have you rung up this purchase?"

I thought and said "No" but it wasn't about that I was thinking. I go through the punches, 4, 9, GROC, TOT—it's more complicated than you think, and after you do it often enough, it begins to make a little song, that you hear words to, in my case "Hello (bing) there, you (gung) hap-py pee-pul (splat)!"—the splat being the drawer flying out. I uncrease the bill, tenderly as you may imagine, it just having come from between the two smoothest scoops of vanilla I had ever known were there, and pass a half and a penny into her narrow pink palm, and nestle the herrings in a bag and twist its neck and hand it over, all the time thinking.

EXPLORE ONLINE >

To complete a video activity of "A & P," visit your Literature CourseMate, accessed through www.cengagebrain.com.

The girls, and who'd blame them, are in a hurry to get out, so I say "I quit" to Lengel quick enough for them to hear, hoping they'll stop and watch me, their unsuspected hero. They keep right on going, into the electric eye; the door flies open and they flicker across the lot to their car, Queenie and Plaid and Big Tall Goony-Goony (not that as raw material she was so bad), leaving me with Lengel and a kink in his eyebrow.

"Did you say something, Sammy?"

"I said I quit."

"I thought you did."   25

"You didn't have to embarrass them."

"It was they who were embarrassing us."

I started to say something that came out "Fiddle-de-doo." It's a saying of my grandmother's, and I know she would have been pleased.

"I don't think you know what you're saying," Lengel said.

"I know you don't," I said. "But I do." I pull the bow 30 at the back of my apron and start shrugging it off my shoulders. A couple customers that had been heading for my slot begin to knock against each other, like scared pigs in a chute.

Lengel sighs and begins to look very patient and old and gray. He's been a friend of my parents for years. "Sammy, you don't want to do this to your Mom and Dad," he tells me. It's true, I don't. But it seems to me that once you begin a gesture it's fatal not to go through with it. I fold the apron, "Sammy" stitched in red on the pocket, and put it on the counter, and drop the bow tie on top of it. The bow tie is theirs, if you've ever wondered. "You'll feel this for the rest of your life," Lengel says, and I know that's true, too, but remembering how he made that pretty girl blush makes me so scrunchy inside I punch the No Sale tab and the machine whirs "pee-pul" and the drawer splats out. One advantage to this scene taking place in summer, I can follow this up with a clean exit, there's no fumbling around getting your coat and galoshes, I just saunter into the electric eye in my white shirt that my mother ironed the night before, and the door heaves itself open, and outside the sunshine is skating around the asphalt.

I look around for my girls, but they're gone, of course. There wasn't anybody but some young married screaming with her children about some candy they didn't get by the door of a powder-blue Falcon station wagon. Looking back in the big windows, over the bags of peat moss and aluminum lawn furniture stacked on the pavement, I could see Lengel in my place in the slot, checking the sheep through. His face was dark gray and his back stiff, as if he'd just had an injection of iron, and my stomach kind of fell as I felt how hard the world was going to be to me hereafter.

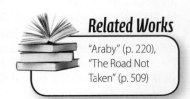

Related Works

"Araby" (p. 220), "The Road Not Taken" (p. 509)

See Chapter 12 Review Card for Reading and Reacting questions about John Updike, "A&P."

Katherine Mansfield (1888–1923)

was one of the pioneers of the modern short story. Mansfield was born in New Zealand and educated in England. Very much a "modern young woman," she began living on her own in London at the age of nineteen, soon publishing stories and book reviews in many of the most influential literary magazines of the day.

A short story writer of great versatility, Mansfield produced sparkling social comedies as well as more intellectually and technically complex works intended for "perceptive readers." According to one critic, her best works "[w]ith delicate plainness . . . present elusive moments of decision, defeat, and small triumph." Her last two story collections—*Bliss* and Other Stories (1920) and *The Garden Party and Other Stories* (1922)—were met with immediate critical acclaim, but Mansfield's career was cut short in 1923 when she died of complications from tuberculosis at the age of thirty-five.

One notable theme in Mansfield's work is the *dame seule,* the "woman alone," which provides the basis for the poignant "Miss Brill."

© Bettmann/Corbis

Miss Brill (1922)

Although it was so brilliantly fine—the blue sky powdered with gold and great spots of light like white wine splashed over the **Jardins Publiques°**—Miss Brill was glad that she had decided on her fur. The air was motionless, but when you opened your mouth there was just a faint chill, like a chill from a glass of iced water before you sip, and now and again a leaf came drifting—from nowhere, from the sky. Miss Brill put up her hand and touched her fur. Dear little thing! It was nice to feel it again. She had taken it out of its box that afternoon, shaken out the moth-powder, given it a good brush, and rubbed the life back into the dim little eyes. "What has been happening to me?" said the sad little eyes. Oh, how sweet it was to see them snap at her again from the red eiderdown! . . . But the nose, which was of some black composition, wasn't at all firm. It must have had a knock, somehow. Never mind—a little dab of black sealing-wax when the time came—when it was absolutely necessary. . . . Little rogue! Yes, she really felt like that about it. Little rogue biting its tail just by her left ear. She could have taken it off and laid it on her lap and stroked it. She felt a tingling in her hands and arms, but that came from walking, she supposed. And when she breathed, something light and sad—no, not sad, exactly—something gentle seemed to move in her bosom.

There were a number of people out this afternoon, far more than last Sunday. And the band sounded louder and gayer. That was because the Season had begun. For although the band played all year round on Sundays, out of season it was never the same. It was like someone playing with only the family to listen; it didn't care how it played if there weren't any strangers present. Wasn't the conductor wearing a new coat, too? She was sure it was new. He scraped with his foot and flapped his arms like a rooster about to crow, and the bandsmen sitting in the green rotunda blew out their cheeks and glared at the music. Now there came a little "flutey" bit—very pretty!—a little chain of bright drops. She was sure it would be repeated. It was; she lifted her head and smiled.

Only two people shared her "special" seat: a fine old man in a velvet coat, his hands clasped over a huge carved walking-stick, and a big old woman, sitting upright, with a roll of knitting on her embroidered apron. They did not speak. This was disappointing, for Miss Brill always looked forward to the conversation. She had become really quite expert, she thought, at listening as though she didn't listen, at sitting in other people's lives just for a minute while they talked round her.

She glanced, sideways, at the old couple. Perhaps they would go soon. Last Sunday, too, hadn't been as interesting as usual. An Englishman and his wife, he wearing a dreadful Panama hat and she button boots. And she'd gone on the whole time about how she ought to wear spectacles; she knew she needed them; but that it was no good getting any; they'd be sure to break and they'd never keep on. And he'd been so patient. He'd suggested everything—gold rims, the kind that curved round your ears, little pads inside the bridge. No, nothing would please her. "They'll always be sliding down my nose!" Miss Brill wanted to shake her.

The old people sat on the bench, still as statues. Never 5 mind, there was always the crowd to watch. To and fro, in front of the flower-beds and the band rotunda, the couples and groups paraded, stopped to talk, to greet, to buy a handful of flowers from the old beggar who had his tray fixed to the railings. Little children ran among them, swooping and laughing; little boys with big white silk bows under their chins, little girls, little French dolls, dressed up in velvet and lace. And sometimes a tiny staggerer came suddenly rocking into the open from under the trees, stopped, stared, as suddenly sat down "flop," until its small high-stepping mother, like a young hen, rushed scolding to its rescue. Other people sat on the benches and green chairs, but they were nearly always the same, Sunday after Sunday, and—Miss Brill had often noticed—there was something funny about nearly all of them. They were odd, silent, nearly all old, and from the way they stared they looked as though they'd just come from dark little rooms or even—even cupboards!

>> 1923 magazine cover showing woman in fox fur stole

° **Jardins Publiques** "Public Gardens" (French).

<< Couple sitting on park bench

Behind the rotunda the slender trees with yellow leaves down drooping, and through them just a line of sea, and beyond the blue sky with gold-veined clouds.

Tum-tum-tum tiddle-um! tiddle-um! tum tiddley-um tum ta! blew the band.

Two young girls in red came by and two young soldiers in blue met them, and they laughed and paired and went off arm-in-arm. Two peasant women with funny straw hats passed, gravely, leading beautiful smoke-colored donkeys. A cold, pale nun hurried by. A beautiful woman came along and dropped her bunch of violets, and a little boy ran after to hand them to her, and she took them and threw them away as if they'd been poisoned. Dear me! Miss Brill didn't know whether to admire that or not! And now an ermine **toque**° and a gentleman in grey met just in front of her. He was tall, stiff, dignified, and she was wearing the ermine toque she'd bought when her hair was yellow. Now everything, her hair, her face, even her eyes, was the same color as the shabby ermine, and her hand, in its cleaned glove, lifted to dab her lips, was a tiny yellowish paw. Oh, she was so pleased to see him—delighted! She rather thought they were going to meet that afternoon. She described where she'd been—everywhere, here, there, along by the sea. The day was so charming—didn't he agree? And wouldn't he, perhaps? . . . But he shook his head, lighted a cigarette, slowly breathed a great deep puff into her face, and, even while she was still talking and laughing, flicked the match away and walked on. The ermine toque was alone; she smiled more brightly than ever. But even the band seemed to know what she was feeling and played more softly, played tenderly, and the drum beat, "The Brute! The Brute!" over and over. What would she do? What was going to happen now? But as Miss Brill wondered, the ermine toque turned, raised her hand as though she'd seen some one else, much nicer, just over there, and pattered away. And the band changed again and played more quickly, more gaily than ever, and the old couple on Miss Brill's seat got up and marched away, and such a funny old man with long whiskers hobbled along in time to the music and was nearly knocked over by four girls walking abreast.

° **toque** Small, close-fitting woman's hat.

Oh, how fascinating it was! How she enjoyed it! How she loved sitting here, watching it all! It was like a play. It was exactly like a play. Who could believe the sky at the back wasn't painted? But it wasn't till a little brown dog trotted on solemn and then slowly trotted off, like a little "theatre" dog, a little dog that had been drugged, that Miss Brill discovered what it was that made it so exciting. They were all on the stage. They weren't only the audience, not only looking on; they were acting. Even she had a part and came every Sunday. No doubt somebody would have noticed if she hadn't been there; she was part of the performance after all. How strange she'd never thought of it like that before! And yet it explained why she made such a point of starting from home at just the same time each week—so as not to be late for the performance—and it also explained why she had quite a queer, shy feeling at telling her English pupils how she spent her Sunday afternoons. No wonder! Miss Brill nearly laughed out loud. She was on the stage. She thought of the old invalid gentleman to whom she read the newspaper four afternoons a week while he slept in the garden. She had got quite used to the frail head on the cotton pillow, the hollowed eyes, the open mouth and the high pinched nose. If he'd been dead she mightn't have noticed for weeks; she wouldn't have minded. But suddenly he knew he was having the paper read to him by an actress! "An actress!" The old head lifted; two points of light quivered in the old eyes. "An actress—are ye?" And Miss Brill smoothed the newspaper as though it were the manuscript of her part and said gently: "Yes, I have been an actress for a long time."

> *"It was like a play. It was exactly like a play. Who could believe the sky at the back wasn't painted?"*

The band had been having a rest. Now they started 10 again. And what they played was warm, sunny, yet there was just a faint chill—a something, what was it?—not

Cultural Context During the nineteenth century, the task of spinning wool was typically given to unmarried women as a way for them to earn their keep in the home. Thus, the term **spinster** came into existence. Over time, the word acquired a negative stereotype, conjuring up the image of a lonely, childless, frumpy middle-aged woman who longs to be like other "normal" women—wives and mothers. Today, the word spinster is rarely used, reflecting the changed perception of unmarried women and the wider lifestyle choices open to them.

>> 1900 band concert in the park

sadness—no, not sadness—a something that made you want to sing. The tune lifted, lifted, the light shone; and it seemed to Miss Brill that in another moment all of them, all the whole company, would begin singing. The young ones, the laughing ones who were moving together, they would begin, and the men's voices, very resolute and brave, would join them. And then she too, she too, and the others on the benches—they would come in with a kind of accompaniment—something low, that scarcely rose or fell, something so beautiful—moving. . . . And Miss Brill's eyes filled with tears and she looked smiling at all the other members of the company. Yes, we understand, we understand, she thought—though what they understood she didn't know.

Just at that moment a boy and a girl came and sat down where the old couple had been. They were beautifully dressed; they were in love. The hero and heroine, of course, just arrived from his father's yacht. And still soundlessly singing, still with that trembling smile, Miss Brill prepared to listen to them.

"No, not now," said the girl. "Not here, I can't."

"But why? Because of that stupid old thing at the end there?" asked the boy. "Why does she come here at all—who wants her? Why doesn't she keep her silly old mug at home?"

"It's her fu-fur which is so funny," giggled the girl. "It's exactly like a fried **whiting**."°

"Ah, be off with you!" said the boy in an angry whisper. Then: "Tell me, my **petite chérie**—"° 15

"No, not here," said the girl. "Not *yet*."

On her way home she usually bought a slice of honeycake at the baker's. It was her Sunday treat. Sometimes there was an almond in her slice, sometimes not. It made a great difference. And Miss Brill's eyes filled with tears and she looked smiling at all the other members of the company. Yes, we understand, we understand, she thought—though what they understood she didn't know. If there was an almond it was like carrying home a tiny present—a surprise—something that might very well not have been there. She hurried on the almond Sundays and struck the match for the kettle in quite a dashing way.

But to-day she passed the baker's by, climbed the stairs, went into the little dark room—her room like a cupboard—and sat down on the red eiderdown. She sat there for a long time Sundays and struck the match. The box that the fur came out of was on the bed. She unclasped the necklet quickly; quickly, without looking, laid it inside. But when she put the lid on she thought she heard something crying.

Related Works

"Rooming houses are old women" (p. 411), "Aunt Jennifer's Tigers" (p. 433), *The Stronger* (p. 602)

 See Chapter 12 Review Card for Reading and Reacting questions about Katherine Mansfield, "Miss Brill."

° **whiting** Food fish related to the cod.

° **petite chérie** "Little darling" (French).

Charles Baxter (1947–   )

was born in Minneapolis and educated at Macalester College and at the State University of New York, Buffalo. Currently teaching in the creative writing program at the University of Minnesota, Baxter is the author of four critically praised collections of short stories: *Harmony of the World* (1984), *Through the Safety Net* (1985), *A Relative Stranger: Stories* (1990), and *Believers: A Novella and Stories* (1997). His fifth collection, *Gryphon: New and Selected Stories,* is forthcoming. He is also the author of five novels, *First Light* (1987), *Shadow Play* (1993), *The Feast of Love* (2002), *Saul and Patsy* (2003), and *The Soul Thief* (2008), and one book of poetry, *Imaginary Paintings and Other Poems* (1989). Baxter has also written *Burning Down the House* (1997), a collection of essays on fiction.

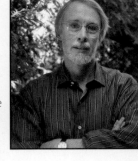

Baxter's critics often mention the compassion he shows in writing about his fictional characters: a couple who lose their child, a hospital worker who wants to be famous, a tired businessman who really wants to paint. In many of his short stories in *Through the Safety Net* (in which "Gryphon" appeared), unexpected events jar Baxter's characters out of their routines, forcing them to consider different choices, to call on inner strength, or to swim against the tide of "middle America's" conventions.

Gryphon (1985)

On Wednesday afternoon, between the geography lesson on ancient Egypt's hand-operated irrigation system and an art project that involved drawing a model city next to a mountain, our fourth-grade teacher, Mr. Hibler, developed a cough. This cough began with a series of muffled throat clearings and progressed to propulsive noises contained within Mr. Hibler's closed mouth. "Listen to him," Carol Peterson whispered to me. "He's gonna blow up." Mr. Hibler's laughter—dazed and infrequent—sounded a bit like his cough, but as we worked on our model cities we would look up, thinking he was enjoying a joke, and see Mr. Hibler's face turning red, his cheeks puffed out. This was not laughter. Twice he bent over, and his loose tie, like a plumb line, hung down straight from his neck as he exploded himself into a Kleenex. He would excuse himself, then go on coughing. "I'll bet you a dime," Carol Peterson whispered, "we get a substitute tomorrow."

Carol sat at the desk in front of mine and was a bad person—when she thought no one was looking she would blow her nose on notebook paper, then crumble it up and throw it into the wastebasket—but at times of crisis she spoke the truth. I knew I'd lose the dime.

"No deal," I said.

When Mr. Hibler stood us up in formation at the door just prior to the final bell, he was almost incapable of speech. "I'm sorry, boys and girls," he said. "I seem to be coming down with something."

"I hope you feel better tomorrow, Mr. Hibler," Bobby 5 Kryzanowicz, the faultless brown-noser said, and I heard Carol Peterson's evil giggle. Then Mr. Hibler opened the door and we walked out to the buses, a clique of us starting noisily to hawk and cough as soon as we thought we were a few feet beyond Mr. Hibler's earshot.

Five Oaks being a rural community, and in Michigan, the supply of substitute teachers was limited to the town's unemployed community college graduates, a pool of about four mothers. These ladies fluttered, provided easeful class days, and nervously covered material we had mastered weeks earlier. Therefore it was a surprise when a woman we had never seen came into the class the next day, carrying a purple purse, a checkerboard lunchbox, and a few books. She put the books on one side of Mr. Hibler's desk and the lunchbox on the other, next to the Voice of Music phonograph. Three of us in the back of the room were playing with Heever, the chameleon that lived in the terrarium and on one of the plastic drapes, when she walked in.

She clapped her hands at us. "Little boys," she said, "why are you bent over together like that?" She didn't wait for us to answer. "Are you tormenting an animal? Put it back. Please sit down at your desks. I want no cabals this time of the day." We just stared at her. "Boys," she repeated, "I asked you to sit down."

I put the chameleon in his terrarium and felt my way to my desk, never taking my eyes off the woman. With white and green chalk, she had started to draw a tree on the left side of the blackboard. She didn't look usual. Furthermore, her tree was outsized, disproportionate, for some reason.

"This room needs a tree," she said, with one line drawing the suggestion of a leaf. "A large, leafy, shady, deciduous . . . oak."

Her fine, light hair had been done up in what I would 10 learn years later was called a chignon, and she wore gold-rimmed glasses whose lenses seemed to have the faintest blue tint. Harold Knardahl, who sat across from me, whispered "Mars," and I nodded slowly, savoring the imminent weirdness of the day. The substitute drew another branch with an extravagant arm gesture, then turned around and said, "Good morning. I don't believe I said good morning to all of you yet."

Facing us, she was no special age—an adult is an adult—but her face had two prominent lines, descending vertically from the sides of her mouth to her chin. I knew where I had seen those lines before: *Pinocchio*. They were marionette lines. "You may stare at me," she said to us, as a few more kids from the last bus came into the room, their eyes fixed on her, "for a few more seconds, until the bell rings. Then I will permit no more staring. Looking I will permit. Staring, no. It is impolite to stare, and a sign of bad breeding. You cannot make a social effort while staring."

Harold Knardahl did not glance at me, or nudge, but I heard him whisper "Mars" again, trying to get more mileage out of his single joke with the kids who had just come in.

When everyone was seated, the substitute teacher finished her tree, put down her chalk fastidiously on the phonograph, brushed her hands, and faced us. "Good morning," she said. "I am Miss Ferenczi, your teacher for the day. I am fairly new to your community, and I don't believe any of you know me. I will therefore start by telling you a story about myself."

While we settled back, she launched into her tale. She said her grandfather had been a Hungarian prince; her mother had been born in some place called Flanders, had been a pianist, and had played concerts for people Miss Ferenczi referred to as "crowned heads." She gave us a knowing look. "Grieg," she said, "the Norwegian master, wrote a concerto for piano that was," she paused, "my mother's triumph at her debut concert in London." Her eyes searched the ceiling. Our eyes followed. Nothing up there but ceiling tile. "For reasons that I shall not go into, my family's fortunes took us to Detroit, then north to dreadful Saginaw, and now here I am in Five Oaks, as your substitute teacher, for today, Thursday, October the eleventh. I believe it will be a good day: All the forecasts coincide. We shall start with your reading lesson. Take out your reading book. I believe it is called *Broad Horizons*, or something along those lines."

Jeannie Vermeesch raised her hand. Miss Ferenczi 15 nodded at her. "Mr. Hibler always starts the day with the Pledge of Allegiance," Jeannie whined.

"Oh, does he? In that case," Miss Ferenczi said, "you must know it *very* well by now, and we certainly need not spend our time on it. No, no allegiance pledging on the premises today, by my reckoning. Not with so much sunlight coming into the room. A pledge does not suit my mood." She glanced at her watch. "Time *is* flying. Take out *Broad Horizons*."

She disappointed us by giving us an ordinary lesson, complete with vocabulary word drills, comprehension questions, and recitation. She didn't seem to care for the material, however. She sighed every few minutes and rubbed her glasses with a frilly perfumed handkerchief that she withdrew, magician style, from her left sleeve.

> "'Besides, I'm your substitute teacher, am I not?' We all nodded. 'Well, then, think of six times eleven equals sixty-eight as a substitute fact.'"

After reading we moved on to arithmetic. It was my favorite time of the morning, when the lazy autumn sunlight dazzled its way through ribbons of clouds past the windows on the east side of the classroom, and crept across the linoleum floor. On the playground the first group of children, the kindergartners, were running on the quack grass just beyond the monkey bars. We were doing multiplication tables. Miss Ferenczi had made John Wazny stand up at his desk in the front row. He was supposed to go through the tables of six. From where I was sitting, I could smell the Vitalis soaked into John's plastered hair. He was doing fine until he came to six times eleven and six times twelve. "Six times eleven," he said, "is sixty-eight. Six times twelve is . . ." He put his fingers to his head, quickly and secretly sniffed his fingertips, and said, "seventy-two." Then he sat down.

"Fine," Miss Ferenczi said. "Well now. That was very good."

"Miss Ferenczi!" One of the Eddy twins was waving 20 her hand desperately in the air. "Miss Ferenczi! Miss Ferenczi!"

"Yes?"

"John said that six times eleven is sixty-eight and you said he was right!"

"*Did* I?" She gazed at the class with a jolly look breaking across her marionette's face. "Did I say that? Well, what is six times eleven?"

"It's sixty-six!"

She nodded. "Yes. So it is. But, and I know some peo- 25 ple will not entirely agree with me, at some times it is sixty-eight."

"When? When is it sixty-eight?"

We were all waiting.

"In higher mathematics, which you children do not yet understand, six times eleven can be considered to be sixty-eight." She laughed through her nose. "In higher mathematics numbers are . . . more fluid. The only thing a number does is contain a certain amount of something. Think of water. A cup is not the only way to measure a certain amount of water, is it?" We were staring, shaking our heads. "You could use

Cultural Context
One of the key elements of this story is a character's use of a deck of tarot cards to predict the future. Originating more than 500 years ago in northern Italy in a game called "Triumphs," the Tarot was quickly adopted as a tool for divining the future. With deep roots in the symbolism of medieval and Renaissance Europe, the Tarot is today the singular most popular tool for spiritual introspection and prophesy. While the death card in particular is often feared, many interpreters argue that it hardly ever points to literal death but rather symbolizes the ending of something significant and the beginning of something new. In "Gryphon," the accuracy of the Tarot's prediction is less important than various characters' reactions to it.

saucepans or thimbles. In either case, the water *would be the same*. Perhaps," she started again, "it would be better for you to think that six times eleven is sixty-eight only when I am in the room."

"Why is it sixty-eight," Mark Poole asked, "when you're in the room?"

"Because it's more interesting that way," she said, 30 smiling very rapidly behind her blue-tinted glasses. "Besides, I'm your substitute teacher, am I not?" We all nodded. "Well, then, think of six times eleven equals sixty-eight as a substitute fact."

"A substitute fact?"

"Yes." Then she looked at us carefully. "Do you think," she asked, "that anyone is going to be hurt by a substitute fact?"

We looked back at her.

"Will the plants on the windowsill be hurt?" We glanced at them. There were sensitive plants thriving in a green plastic tray, and several wilted ferns in small clay pots. "Your dogs and cats, or your moms and dads?" She waited. "So," she concluded, "what's the problem?"

"But it's wrong," Janice Weber said, "isn't it?" 35

"What's your name, young lady?"

"Janice Weber."

"And you think it's wrong, Janice?"

"I was just asking."

"Well, all right. You were just asking. I think we've 40 spent enough time on this matter by now, don't you, class? You are free to think what you like. When your teacher, Mr. Hibler, returns, six times eleven will be sixty-six again, you can rest assured. And it will be that for the rest of your lives in Five Oaks. Too bad, eh?" She raised her eyebrows and glinted herself at us. "But for now, it wasn't. So much for that. Let us go to your assigned problems for today, as painstakingly outlined, I see, in Mr. Hibler's lesson plan. Take out a sheet of paper and write your names in the upper left-hand corner."

For the next half hour we did the rest of our arithmetic problems. We handed them in and went on to spelling, my worst subject. Spelling always came before lunch. We were taking spelling dictation and looking at the clock. "Thorough," Miss Ferenczi said. "Boundary." She walked in the aisles between the desks, holding the spelling book open and looking down at our papers. "Balcony." I clutched my pencil. Somehow, the way she said those words, they seemed foreign, Hungarian, mis-voweled and mis-consonanted. I stared down at what I had spelled. *Balconie*. I turned my pencil upside down and erased my mistake. *Balconey*. That looked better, but still incorrect. I cursed the world of spelling and tried erasing it again and saw the paper beginning to wear away. *Balkony*. Suddenly I felt a hand on my shoulder.

"I don't like that word either," Miss Ferenczi whispered, bent over, her mouth near my ear. "It's ugly. My feeling is, if you don't like a word, you don't have to use it." She straightened up, leaving behind a slight odor of Clorets.

At lunchtime we went out to get our trays of sloppy joes, peaches in heavy syrup, coconut cookies, and milk, and brought them back to the classroom, where Miss Ferenczi was sitting at the desk, eating a brown sticky thing she had unwrapped from tightly rubber-banded wax paper. "Miss Ferenczi," I said, raising my hand. "You don't have to eat with us. You can eat with the other teachers. There's a teachers' lounge," I ended up, "next to the principal's office."

"No, thank you," she said. "I prefer it here."

"We've got a room monitor," I said. "Mrs. Eddy." I 45 pointed to where Mrs. Eddy, Joyce and Judy's mother, sat silently at the back of the room, doing her knitting.

"That's fine," Miss Ferenczi said. "But I shall continue to eat here, with you children. I prefer it," she repeated.

"How come?" Wayne Razmer asked without raising his hand.

"I talked with the other teachers before class this morning," Miss Ferenczi said, biting into her brown food. "There was a great rattling of the words for the fewness of ideas. I didn't care for their brand of hilarity. I don't like ditto machine jokes."

"Oh," Wayne said.

"What's that you're eating?" Maxine Sylvester asked, 50 twitching her nose. "Is it food?"

"It most certainly is food. It's a stuffed fig. I had to drive almost down to Detroit to get it. I also bought some smoked sturgeon. And this," she said, lifting some green leaves out of her lunchbox, "is raw spinach, cleaned this morning before I came out here to the Garfield-Murry school."

"Why're you eating raw spinach?" Maxine asked.

"It's good for you," Miss Ferenczi said. "More stimulating than soda pop or smelling salts." I bit into my sloppy joe and stared blankly out the window. An almost invisible moon was faintly silvered in the daytime autumn sky. "As far as food is concerned," Miss Ferenczi was saying, "you have to shuffle the pack. Mix it up. Too many people eat . . . well, never mind."

"Miss Ferenczi," Carol Peterson said, "what are we going to do this afternoon?"

"Well," she said, looking down at Mr. Hibler's 55 lesson plan, "I see that your teacher, Mr. Hibler, has you scheduled for a unit on the Egyptians." Carol groaned. "Yessss," Miss Ferenczi continued, "that is what we will do: the Egyptians. A remarkable people. Almost as remarkable as the Americans. But not quite." She lowered her head, did her quick smile, and went back to eating her spinach.

After noon recess we came back into the classroom and saw that Miss Ferenczi had drawn a pyramid on the blackboard, close to her oak tree. Some of us who had been playing baseball were messing around in the back of the room, dropping the bats and the gloves into the playground box, and I think that Ray Schontzeler had just slugged me when I heard Miss Ferenczi's high-pitched voice quavering with emotion. "Boys," she said, "come to order right this minute and take your seats. I do not wish to waste a minute of class time. Take out your geography books." We trudged to our desks and, still sweating, pulled out *Distant Lands and Their People*. "Turn to page forty-two." She waited for thirty seconds, then looked over at Kelly Munger. "Young man," she said, "why are you still fossicking in your desk?"

Kelly looked as if his foot had been stepped on. "Why am I what?"

"Why are you . . . burrowing in your desk like that?"

"I'm lookin' for the book, Miss Ferenczi."

Bobby Kryzanowicz, the faultless brown-noser who sat 60 in the first row by choice, softly said, "His name is Kelly Munger. He can't ever find his stuff. He always does that."

"I don't care what his name is, especially after lunch," Miss Ferenczi said. "*Where is your book?*"

"I just found it." Kelly was peering into his desk and with both hands pulled at the book, shoveling along in front of it several pencils and crayons, which fell into his lap and then to the floor.

"I hate a mess," Miss Ferenczi said. "I hate a mess in a desk or a mind. It's . . . unsanitary. You wouldn't want your house at home to look like your desk at school, now, would you?" She didn't wait for an answer. "I should think not. A house at home should be as neat as human hands can make it. What were we talking about? Egypt. Page forty-two. I note from Mr. Hibler's lesson plan that you have been discussing the modes of Egyptian irrigation. Interesting, in my view, but not so interesting as what we are about to cover. The pyramids and Egyptian slave labor. A plus on one side, a minus on the other." We had our books open to page forty-two, where there was a picture of a pyramid, but Miss Ferenczi wasn't looking at the book. Instead, she was staring at some object just outside the window.

"Pyramids," Miss Ferenczi said, still looking past the window. "I want you to think about the pyramids. And what was inside. The bodies of the pharaohs, of course, and their attendant treasures. Scrolls. Perhaps," Miss Ferenczi said, with something gleeful but unsmiling in her face, "these scrolls were novels for the pharaohs, helping them to pass the time in their long voyage through the centuries. But then, I am joking." I was looking at the lines on Miss Ferenczi's face. "Pyramids," Miss Ferenczi went on, "were the repositories of special cosmic powers. The nature of a pyramid is to guide cosmic energy forces into a concentrated point. The Egyptians knew that; we have generally forgotten it. Did you know," she asked, walking to the side of the room so that she was standing by the coat closet, "that George Washington had Egyptian blood, from his grandmother? Certain features of the Constitution of the United States are notable for their Egyptian ideas."

Without glancing down at the book, she began to talk 65 about the movement of souls in Egyptian religion. She said that when people die, their souls return to Earth in the form of carpenter ants or walnut trees, depending on how they behaved—"well or ill"—in life. She said that the Egyptians believed that people act the way they do because of magnetism produced by tidal forces in the solar system, forces produced by the sun and by its "planetary ally," Jupiter. Jupiter, she said, was a planet, as we had been told, but had "certain properties of stars." She was speaking very fast. She said that the Egyptians were great explorers and conquerors. She said that the greatest of all the conquerors, Genghis Khan, had had forty horses and forty

>> Statue of gryphon

young women killed on the site of his grave. We listened. No one tried to stop her. "I myself have been in Egypt," she said, "and have witnessed much dust and many brutalities." She said that an old man in Egypt who worked for a circus had personally shown her an animal in a cage, a monster, half bird and half lion. She said that this monster was called a gryphon and that she had heard about them but never seen them until she traveled to the outskirts of Cairo. She said that Egyptian astronomers had discovered the planet Saturn, but had not seen its rings. She said that the Egyptians were the first to discover that dogs, when they are ill, will not drink from rivers, but wait for rain, and hold their jaws open to catch it.

* * *

"She lies."

We were on the school bus home. I was sitting next to Carl Whiteside, who had bad breath and a huge collection of marbles. We were arguing. Carl thought she was lying. I said she wasn't, probably.

"I didn't believe that stuff about the bird," Carl said, "and what she told us about the pyramids? I didn't believe that either. She didn't know what she was talking about."

"Oh yeah?" I had liked her. She was strange. I thought I could nail him. "If she was lying," I said, "what'd she say that was a lie?"

"Six times eleven isn't sixty-eight. It isn't ever. It's 70 sixty-six, I know for a fact."

"She said so. She admitted it. What else did she lie about?"

"I don't know," he said. "Stuff."

"What stuff?"

"Well." He swung his legs back and forth. "You ever see an animal that was half lion and half bird?" He crossed his arms. "It sounded real fakey to me."

"It could happen," I said. I had to improvise, to outrage 75 him. "I read in this newspaper my mom bought in the IGA about this scientist, this mad scientist in the Swiss Alps, and he's been putting genes and chromosomes and stuff together in test tubes, and he combined a human being and a hamster." I waited, for effect. "It's called a humster."

"You never." Carl was staring at me, his mouth open, his terrible bad breath making its way toward me. "What newspaper was it?"

"The *National Enquirer*," I said, "that they sell next to the cash registers." When I saw his look of recognition, I knew I had bested him. "And this mad scientist," I said, "his name was, um, Dr. Frankenbush." I realized belatedly that this name was a mistake and waited for Carl to notice its resemblance to the name of the other famous mad master of permutations, but he only sat there.

"A man and a hamster?" He was staring at me, squinting, his mouth opening in distaste. "Jeez. What'd it look like?"

When the bus reached my stop, I took off down our dirt road and ran up through the back yard, kicking the tire swing for good luck. I dropped my books on the back steps so I could hug and kiss our dog, Mr. Selby. Then I hurried inside. I could smell Brussels sprouts cooking, my unfavorite vegetable. My mother was washing other vegetables in the kitchen sink, and my baby brother was hollering in his yellow playpen on the kitchen floor.

"Hi, Mom," I said, hopping around the playpen to kiss her, "Guess what?" 80

"I have no idea."

"We had this substitute today, Miss Ferenczi, and I'd never seen her before, and she had all these stories and ideas and stuff."

"Well. That's good." My mother looked out the window behind the sink, her eyes on the pine woods west of our house. Her face and hair-

style always reminded other people of Betty Crocker, whose picture was framed inside a gigantic spoon on the side of the Bisquick box; to me, though, my mother's face just looked white. "Listen, Tommy," she said, "go upstairs and pick your clothes off the bathroom floor, then go outside to the shed and put the shovel and ax away that your father left outside this morning."

"She said that six times eleven was sometimes sixty-eight!" I said. "And she said she once saw a monster that was half lion and half bird." I waited. "In Egypt, she said."

"Did you hear me?" my mother asked, raising her arm 85 to wipe her forehead with the back of her hand. "You have chores to do."

"I know," I said. "I was just telling you about the substitute."

"It's very interesting," my mother said, quickly glancing down at me, "and we can talk about it later when your father gets home. But right now you have some work to do."

"Okay, Mom." I took a cookie out of the jar on the counter and was about to go outside when I had a thought. I ran into the living room, pulled out a dictionary next to the TV stand, and opened it to the G's. *Gryphon:* "variant of griffin." *Griffin:* "a fabulous beast with the head and wings of an eagle and the body of a lion." Fabulous was right. I shouted with triumph and ran outside to put my father's tools back in their place.

Miss Ferenczi was back the next day, slightly altered. She had pulled her hair down and twisted it into pigtails, with red rubber bands holding them tight one inch from the ends. She was wearing a green blouse and pink scarf, making her difficult to look at for a full class day. This time there was no pretense of doing a reading lesson or moving on to arithmetic. As soon as the bell rang, she simply began to talk.

She talked for forty minutes straight. There seemed 90 to be less connection between her ideas, but the ideas themselves were, as the dictionary would say, fabulous. She said she had heard of a huge jewel, in what she called the Antipodes, that was so brilliant that when the light shone into it at a certain angle it would blind whoever was looking at its center. She said that the biggest diamond in the world was cursed and had killed everyone who owned it, and that by a trick of fate it was called the Hope diamond. Diamonds are magic, she said, and this is why women wear them on their fingers, as a sign of the magic of womanhood. Men have strength, Miss Ferenczi said, but no true magic. That is why men fall in love with women but women do not fall in love with men; they just love being loved. George Washington had died because of a mistake he made about a diamond. Washington was not the first *true* President, but she did not say who was. In some places in the world, she said, men and women still live in the trees and eat monkeys for breakfast. Their doctors are magicians. At the bottom of the sea are creatures thin as pancakes which have never been studied by scientists because when you take them up to the air, the fish explode.

There was not a sound in the classroom, except for Miss Ferenczi's voice, and Donna DeShano's coughing. No one even went to the bathroom.

Beethoven, she said, had not been deaf; it was a trick to make himself famous, and it worked. As she talked, Miss Ferenczi's pigtails swung back and forth. There are trees in the world, she said, that eat meat: their leaves are sticky and close up on bugs like hands. She lifted her hands and brought them together, palm to palm. Venus, which most people think is the next closest planet to the sun, is not always closer, and, besides, it is the planet of greatest mystery because of its thick cloud cover. "I know what lies underneath those clouds," Miss Ferenczi said, and waited. After the silence, she said, "Angels. Angels live under those clouds." She said that angels were not invisible to everyone and were in fact smarter than most people. They did not dress in robes as was often claimed but instead wore formal evening clothes, as if they were about to attend a concert. Often angels *do* attend concerts and sit in the aisles where, she said, most people pay no attention to them. She said the most terrible angel had the shape of the Sphinx. "There is no running away from that one," she said. She said that unquenchable fires burn just under the surface of the earth in Ohio, and that the baby Mozart fainted dead away in his cradle when he first heard the sound of a trumpet. She said that someone named Narzim al Harradim was the greatest writer who ever lived. She said that planets control behavior, and anyone conceived during a solar eclipse would be born with webbed feet.

"I know you children like to hear these things," she said, "these secrets, and that is why I am telling you all this." We nodded. It was better than doing comprehension questions for the readings in *Broad Horizons*.

"I will tell you one more story," she said, "and then we will have to do arithmetic." She leaned over, and her voice grew soft. "There is no death," she said. "You must never be afraid. Never. That which is, cannot die. It will change into different earthly and unearthly elements, but I know this as sure as I stand here in front of you, and I swear it: you must not be afraid. I have seen this truth with these eyes. I know it because in a dream God kissed me. Here." And she pointed with her right index finger to the side of her head, below the mouth, where the vertical lines were carved into her skin.

Absent-mindedly we all did our arithmetic problems. 95 At recess the class was out on the playground, but no one was playing. We were all standing in small groups, talking about Miss Ferenczi. We didn't know if she was crazy, or what. I looked out beyond the playground, at the rusted cars piled in a small heap behind a clump of sumac, and I wanted to see shapes there, approaching me.

On the way home, Carl sat next to me again. He didn't say much, and I didn't either. At last he turned to me. "You know what she said about the leaves that close up on bugs?"

"Huh?"

"The leaves," Carl insisted. "The meat-eating plants. I know it's true. I saw it on television. The leaves have this icky glue that the plants have got smeared all over them and the insects can't get off, 'cause they're stuck. I saw it." He seemed demoralized. "She's tellin' the truth."

"Yeah."

"You think she's seen all those angels?"   100

I shrugged.

"I don't think she has," Carl informed me. "I think she made that part up."

"There's a tree," I suddenly said. I was looking out the window at the farms along County Road H. I knew every barn, every broken windmill, every fence, every anhydrous ammonia tank, by heart. "There's a tree that's . . . that I've seen . . ."

"Don't you try to do it," Carl said. "You'll just sound like a jerk."

I kissed my mother. She was standing in front of the 105 stove. "How was your day?" she asked.

"Fine."

"Did you have Miss Ferenczi again?"

"Yeah."

"Well?"

"She was fine. Mom," I asked, "can I go to my room?"   110

"No," she said, "not until you've gone out to the vegetable garden and picked me a few tomatoes." She glanced at the sky. "I think it's going to rain. Skedaddle and do it now. Then you come back inside and watch your brother for a few minutes while I go upstairs. I need to clean up before dinner." She looked down at me. "You're looking a little pale, Tommy." She touched the back of her hand to my forehead and I felt her diamond ring against my skin. "Do you feel all right?"

"I'm fine," I said, and went out to pick the tomatoes.

Coughing mutedly, Mr. Hibler was back the next day, slipping lozenges into his mouth when his back was turned at forty-five minute intervals and asking us how much of the prepared lesson plan Miss Ferenczi had followed. Edith Atwater took the responsibility for the class of explaining to Mr. Hibler that the substitute hadn't always done exactly what he would have done, but we had worked hard even though she talked a lot. About what? he asked. All kinds of things, Edith said. I sort of forgot. To our relief, Mr. Hibler seemed not at all interested in what Miss Ferenczi had said to fill the day. He probably thought it was woman's talk; unserious and not suited for school. It was enough that he had a pile of arithmetic problems from us to correct.

For the next month, the sumac turned a distracting red in the field, and the sun traveled toward the southern sky, so that its rays reached Mr. Hibler's Halloween display on the bulletin board in the back of the room, fading the scarecrow with a pumpkin head from orange to tan. Every three days I measured how much farther the sun had moved toward the southern horizon by making small marks with my black Crayola on the north wall, ant-sized marks only I knew were there, inching west.

And then in early December, four days after the first 115 permanent snowfall, she appeared again in our classroom. The minute she came in the door, I felt my heart begin to pound. Once again, she was different: this time, her hair hung straight down and seemed hardly to have been combed. She hadn't brought her lunchbox with her, but she was carrying what seemed to be a small box. She greeted all of us and talked about the weather. Donna DeShano had to remind her to take her overcoat off.

When the bell to start the day finally rang, Miss Ferenczi looked out at all of us and said, "Children, I have enjoyed your company in the past, and today I am going to reward you." She held up the small box. "Do you

>> Tarot card symbolizing death

know what this is?" She waited. "Of course you don't. It is a tarot pack."

Edith Atwater raised her hand. "What's a tarot pack, Miss Ferenczi?"

"It is used to tell fortunes," she said. "And that is what I shall do this morning. I shall tell your fortunes, as I have been taught to do."

"What's fortune?" Bobby Kryzanowicz asked.

"The future, young man. I shall tell you what your fu- 120 ture will be. I can't do your whole future, of course. I shall have to limit myself to the five-card system, the wands, cups, swords, pentacles, and the higher arcanes. Now who wants to be first?"

There was a long silence. Then Carol Peterson raised her hand.

"All right," Miss Ferenczi said. She divided the pack into five smaller packs and walked back to Carol's desk, in front of mine. "Pick one card from each of these packs," she said. I saw that Carol had a four of cups, a six of swords, but I couldn't see the other cards. Miss Ferenczi studied the cards on Carol's desk for a minute. "Not bad," she said. "I do not see much higher education. Probably an early marriage. Many children. There's something bleak and dreary here, but I can't tell what. Perhaps just the tasks of a housewife life. I think you'll do very well, for the most part." She smiled at Carol, a smile with a certain lack of interest. "Who wants to be next?"

Carl Whiteside raised his hand slowly.

"Yes," Miss Ferenczi said, "let's do a boy." She walked over to where Carl sat. After he picked his five cards, she gazed at them for a long time. "Travel," she said. "Much distant travel. You might go into the Army. Not too much romantic interest here. A late marriage, if at all. Squabbles. But the Sun is in your major arcana, here, yes, that's a very good card." She giggled. "Maybe a good life."

Next I raised my hand, and she told me my future. She 125 did the same with Bobby Kryzanowicz, Kelly Munger, Edith Atwater, and Kim Foor. Then she came to Wayne Razmer. He picked his five cards, and I could see that the Death card was one of them.

"What's your name?" Miss Ferenczi asked.

"Wayne."

"Well, Wayne," she said, "you will undergo a *great* metamorphosis, the greatest, before you become an adult. Your earthly element will leap away, into thin air, you sweet boy. This card, this nine of swords here, tells of suffering and desolation. "

"What about this one?" Wayne pointed to the Death card.

"That one? That one means you will die soon, my dear." 130 She gathered up the cards. We were all looking at Wayne. "But do not fear," she said. "It's not really death, so much as change." She put the cards on Mr. Hibler's desk. "And now, let's do some arithmetic."

At lunchtime Wayne went to Mr. Faegre, the principal, and told him what Miss Ferenczi had done. During the noon recess, we saw Miss Ferenczi drive out of the parking lot in her green Rambler. I stood under the slide, listening to the other kids coasting down and landing in the little depressive bowl at the bottom. I was kicking stones and tugging at my hair right up to the moment when I saw Wayne come out to the playground. He smiled, the dead fool, and with the fingers of his right hand he was showing everyone how he had told on Miss Ferenczi.

I made my way toward Wayne, pushing myself past two girls from another class. He was watching me with his little pinhead eyes.

"You told," I shouted at him. "She was just kidding."

"She shouldn't have," he shouted back. "We were supposed to be doing arithmetic."

"She just scared you," I said. "You're a chicken. You're 135 a chicken, Wayne. You are. Scared of a little card," I singsonged.

Wayne fell at me, his two fists hammering down on my nose. I gave him a good one in the stomach and then I tried for his head. Aiming my fist, I saw that he was crying. I slugged him.

"She was right," I yelled. "She was always right! She told the truth!" Other kids were whooping. "You were just scared, that's all!"

And then large hands pulled at us, and it was my turn to speak to Mr. Faegre.

In the afternoon Miss Ferenczi was gone, and my nose was stuffed with cotton clotted with blood, and my lip had swelled, and our class had been combined with Mrs. Mantei's sixth-grade class for a crowded afternoon science unit on insect life in ditches and swamps. I knew where Mrs. Mantei lived: she had a new house trailer just down the road from us, at the Clearwater Park. She was no mystery. Somehow she and Mr. Bodine, the other fourth-grade teacher, had managed to fit forty-five desks into the room. Kelly Munger asked if Miss Ferenczi had been arrested, and Mrs. Mantei said no, of course not. All that afternoon, until the buses came to pick us up, we learned about field crickets and two-striped grasshoppers, water bugs, cicadas, mosquitoes, flies, and moths. We learned about insects' hard outer shell, the exoskeleton, and the usual parts of the mouth, including the labrum, mandible, maxilla, and glossa. We learned about compound eyes and the four-stage metamorphosis from egg to larva to pupa to adult. We learned something, but not much, about mating. Mrs. Mantei drew, very skillfully, the internal anatomy of the grasshopper on the blackboard.

We learned about the dance of the honeybee, directing other bees in the hive to pollen. We found out about which insects were pests to man, and which were not. On lined white pieces of paper we made lists of insects we might actually see, then a list of insects too small to be clearly visible, such as fleas; Mrs. Mantei said that our assignment would be to memorize these lists for the next day, when Mr. Hibler would certainly return and test us on our knowledge.

Related Works

"A & P" (p. 131), "A Worn Path" (p. 256), "The Secret Lion" (p. 333), "When I Heard the Learn'd Astronomer" (p. 383), "On First Looking Into Chapman's Homer" (p. 447)

 See Chapter 12 Review Card for Reading and Reacting questions about Charles Baxter, "Gryphon."

Writing Suggestions: Character

1. In both "A&P," and "Gryphon," the main characters (Sammy and Tommy, respectively) struggle against rules, authority figures, and inflexible social systems. Compare and contrast the struggles in which these two characters are engaged.

2. Write an essay in which you contrast the character of Miss Brill (p. 135) with the character of Emily Grierson in "A Rose for Emily" (p. 121) or with Phoenix Jackson in "A Worn Path" (p. 285). Consider how each character interacts with those around her as well as how each seems to see her role or mission in the world.

3. Sammy, Miss Brill, and Miss Ferenczi all use their active imaginations to create scenarios that help get them through the day. None of them is able to sustain the illusion, however. As a result, all three find out how harsh reality can be. How are these scenarios alike, and how are they different? What steps could these three characters take to fit more comfortably into the worlds they inhabit? Should they take such steps? Are they able to do so?

4. Write an analysis of a minor character in one of this chapter's stories.

5. Several of the characters in this chapter's stories—for example, the narrator in "Eye Ball," and Tommy in "Gryphon"—are presented as outsiders struggling to understand and adapt to the dominant culture. In what sense is each outside the mainstream? Which characters do you think have the best chance of surviving (and thriving) in the larger world? Why?

✔ CHECKLIST

WRITING ABOUT A CHARACTER

- ☐ Who is the story's main character? Who are the other major characters?
- ☐ Who are the minor characters? What roles do they play in the story? How would the story be different without them?
- ☐ What do the major characters look like? Is their physical appearance important?
- ☐ What are the major characters' most notable personality traits?
- ☐ What are the major characters' likes and dislikes? their strengths and weaknesses?
- ☐ What are the main character's most strongly held feelings and beliefs?
- ☐ What are we told about the major characters' backgrounds and prior experiences? What can we infer?
- ☐ Are the characters round or flat?
- ☐ Are the characters dynamic or static?
- ☐ Does the story include any stock characters? Does any character serve as a foil?
- ☐ Do the characters act in a way that is consistent with how readers expect them to act?
- ☐ With which characters are readers likely to be most sympathetic? least sympathetic?

Glossary Terms

caricature Stock character with a single dominant trait, such as miserliness, or a single physical trait, like nearsightedness.

character Fictional representation of a person, usually but not necessarily in a psychologically realistic way.

dynamic character A character who grows and changes in the course of a story.

flat character Static, stereotypical character.

foil Minor character whose role is to highlight the main character by presenting a contrast with him or her.

motivation Reasons behind a character's behavior.

round character Well-developed character, closely involved in the action and responsive to it.

static character A character who remains unchanged in the course of a story.

stock character Stereotypical character who behaves consistently and whom the audience can recognize and classify instantly.

13
Setting

Learning Outcomes

After reading this chapter, you should be able to do the following:

LO1 Understand historical setting

LO2 Understand geographical setting

LO3 Understand physical setting

Timeline

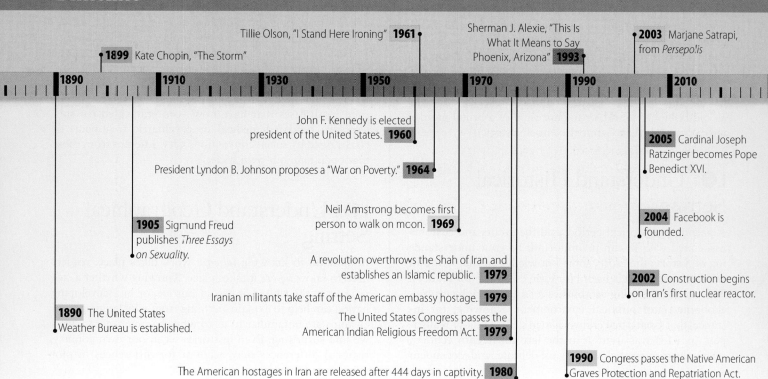

Tillie Olson, "I Stand Here Ironing" **1961**

1899 Kate Chopin, "The Storm"

Sherman J. Alexie, "This Is What It Means to Say Phoenix, Arizona" **1993**

2003 Marjane Satrapi, from *Persepolis*

1890 **1910** **1930** **1950** **1970** **1990** **2010**

John F. Kennedy is elected president of the United States. **1960**

2005 Cardinal Joseph Ratzinger becomes Pope Benedict XVI.

President Lyndon B. Johnson proposes a "War on Poverty." **1964**

1905 Sigmund Freud publishes *Three Essays on Sexuality*.

Neil Armstrong becomes first person to walk on moon. **1969**

2004 Facebook is founded.

A revolution overthrows the Shah of Iran and establishes an Islamic republic. **1979**

Iranian militants take staff of the American embassy hostage. **1979**

The United States Congress passes the American Indian Religious Freedom Act. **1979**

2002 Construction begins on Iran's first nuclear reactor.

1890 The United States Weather Bureau is established.

The American hostages in Iran are released after 444 days in captivity. **1980**

1990 Congress passes the Native American Graves Protection and Repatriation Act.

setting Background against which the action of a work takes place: the historical time, locale, season, time of day, weather, and so on.

 EXPLORE ONLINE >

To complete a tutorial of "Setting," visit your Literature CourseMate, accessed through www.cengagebrain.com.

The **setting** of a work of fiction establishes its historical, geographical, and physical context. *Where* a work is set—on a tropical island, in a dungeon, at a crowded party, in the woods—influences our reactions to the story's events and characters. *When* a work takes place—during the French Revolution, during the Vietnam War, today, or in the future—is equally important. Setting, however, is more than just the approximate time and place in which a work is set; setting also encompasses a wide variety of physical and cultural elements.

Clearly, setting is more important in some works than in others. In some stories, no particular time or place is specified or even suggested, perhaps because the writer does not consider a specific setting to be important or because the writer wishes the story's events to seem timeless and universal. This is the case in Nathaniel Hawthorne's "Young Goodman Brown" (p. 320), which is set in a forest in an unidentified location. In other stories, a writer may provide only minimal information about setting, telling readers little more than where and when the action takes place. Sometimes, however, a particular setting may be vital to the story, perhaps influencing characters' feelings or behavior, as it does in the stories in this chapter.

Sometimes a story's central conflict is between the protagonist and the setting—for example, *Alice in Wonderland*, a northerner in the South, an unsophisticated American tourist in an old European city, a sane person in a psychiatric hospital, a moral person in a corrupt environment, an immigrant in a new world, or a city dweller in the country. Such a conflict may drive the story's plot and also help to define the characters. (A conflict between events and setting—for example, the arrival of a mysterious stranger in a typical suburban neighborhood, the intrusion of modern social ideas into an old-fashioned world, or the intrusion of a brutal murder into a peaceful village—can also enrich a story.)

LO1 Understand Historical Setting

A particular historical period, and the events and customs associated with it, can be important to your understanding of a story; therefore, some knowledge of the period in which a story is set is useful (or even essential) for readers. The historical setting establishes a story's social, cultural, economic, and political environment. Knowing, for instance, that Charlotte Perkins Gilman's "The Yellow Wallpaper" (p. 313) was written in the late nineteenth century, when doctors treated women as delicate and dependent

creatures, helps to explain the narrator's emotional state. Likewise, it may be important to know that a story is set during a particularly volatile (or static) political era, during a time of permissive (or repressive) attitudes toward sex, during a war, or during a period of economic prosperity or recession. Any one of these factors may help to explain why events occur as well as why characters act as they do and what motivates them. Historical events or cultural norms may, for instance, limit or expand a character's options, and our knowledge of history may reveal to us a character's incompatibility with his or her milieu. For example, in F. Scott Fitzgerald's "Bernice Bobs Her Hair," set in the 1920s in a midwestern town, a young girl is goaded into cutting her long hair. To understand the significance of Bernice's act—and to understand the reactions of others to that act—readers must know that during that era only racy "society vampires," not nice girls from good families, bobbed their hair.

Knowing the approximate year or historical period during which a story takes place can help readers to better understand characters and events. This knowledge can explain forces that act on characters and account for their behavior, clarify circumstances that influence the story's action, and justify a writer's use of plot devices that might otherwise seem improbable. Thus, stories set before the development of modern transportation and communication systems may hinge on plot devices readers would not accept in a modern story. For example, in "Paul's Case," a 1904 story by Willa Cather, a young man who steals a large sum of money in Pittsburgh is able to spend several days enjoying it before the news of the theft reaches New York, where he has fled. In other stories, we see characters threatened by diseases that have now been eradicated (or subjected to outdated medical or psychiatric treatment) or constrained by social conventions very different from those that operate in our own society.

LO2 Understand Geographical Setting

In addition to knowing *when* a work takes place, readers need to know *where* it takes place. Knowing whether a story is set in the United States, in Europe, or in a developing nation can help to explain anything from why language and customs are unfamiliar to us to why characters act in ways we find surprising. Even in stories set in our own country, regional differences may account for differences in plot development and characters' motivation. For example, knowing that William Faulkner's "A Rose for Emily" (p. 121) is set in the post–Civil War American South helps to explain why the townspeople are so chivalrously protective of Miss Emily. Similarly, the fact that Bret Harte's classic story "The Outcasts of Poker Flat" (1869) is set in a California mining camp accounts for its varied cast of characters—including a gambler, a prostitute, and a traveling salesman.

The size of the town or city in which a story takes place may also be important. In a small town, for example, a character's problems are more likely to be subject to intense scrutiny by other characters, as they are in stories of small-town life such as those in Sherwood Anderson's 1919 novel *Winesburg, Ohio*. In a large city, characters may be more likely to be isolated and anonymous, like Mrs. Miller in Truman Capote's gothic short story "Miriam" (1945), who is so lonely that she creates an imaginary companion. Characters may also be alienated by their big-city surroundings, as Gregor Samsa is in Franz Kafka's classic novella "The Metamorphosis" (1915).

Of course, a story may not have a recognizable geographical setting: its location may not be specified, or it may be set in a fantasy world. Choosing unusual settings may free writers from the constraints placed on them by familiar environments, allowing them to experiment with situations and characters, unaffected by readers' expectations or associations with familiar settings.

LO3 Understand Physical Setting

Physical setting can influence a story's mood as well as its development. For example, *time of day* can be important. The gruesome murder described in Edgar Allan Poe's "The Cask of Amontillado" (p. 190) takes place in an appropriate setting: not just underground but in the darkness of night. Conversely, the horrifying events of Shirley Jackson's "The Lottery" (p. 251) take place in broad daylight, contrasting dramatically with the darkness of the society that permits—and even participates in—a shocking ritual. Many stories, of course, move through several time periods as the action unfolds, and changes in time may also be important. For instance, the approach of evening, or of dawn, can signal the end of a crisis in the plot.

Whether a story is set primarily *indoors* or *out-of-doors* may also be significant: characters may be physically constrained by a closed-in setting or liberated by an expansive landscape. Some interior settings may be psychologically limiting. For instance, the narrator in "The Yellow Wallpaper" feels suffocated by her room, whose ugly wallpaper comes to haunt her. In many of Poe's stories, the central character is trapped, physically or psychologically, in a confined, suffocating space. In other stories, an interior setting may have a symbolic function. For example, in "A Rose for Emily," the house is for Miss Emily a symbol of the South's past glory as well as a refuge, a fortress, and a hiding place. Similarly, a building or house may

atmosphere Tone or mood of a literary work, often established by the setting and language. Atmosphere is the emotional aura that determines readers' expectations about a work—for example, the sense of doom established at the beginning of Shakespeare's *Macbeth*.

mood Atmosphere created by the elements of a literary work (setting, characterization, imagery, tone, and so on).

represent society, with its rules, norms, and limitations, as in John Updike's "A&P" (p. 131), where the supermarket establishes social as well as physical limits.

Conversely, an outdoor setting can free a character from social norms of behavior, as it does for Ernest Hemingway's Nick Adams, a war veteran who, in "Big Two-Hearted River" (1925), finds order, comfort, and peace only when he is away from civilization. An outdoor setting can also expose characters to physical dangers, such as untamed wilderness, uncharted seas, and frighteningly empty open spaces, as is the case in Stephen Crane's "The Open Boat" (1897).

Weather can be another important aspect of setting. A storm can threaten a character's life or just make the character—and readers—*think* danger is present, distracting us from other, more subtle threats. Extreme weather conditions can make characters act irrationally or uncharacteristically, as in Kate Chopin's "The Storm" (p. 154), where a storm provides the story's complication and determines the characters' actions. In numerous stories set in hostile landscapes, where extremes of heat and cold influence the action, weather may serve as a test for characters, as it does in Jack London's "To Build a Fire" (1908), in which the main character struggles unsuccessfully against the brutally cold, hostile environment of the Yukon.

The various physical attributes of setting combine to create a story's **atmosphere** or **mood**. In "The Cask of Amontillado," for example, several factors work together to create the story's eerie, intense atmosphere: it is nighttime; it is the hectic carnival season; and the catacombs are dark, damp, and filled with the bones of the narrator's ancestors. Sometimes the mood or atmosphere that is created helps to convey a story's central theme—as the ironic contrast between the pleasant atmosphere and the shocking events that unfold communicates the theme of "The Lottery." A story's atmosphere may also be linked to a character's mental state, perhaps reflecting his or her mood. For example, darkness and isolation can reflect a character's depression, whereas an idyllic, peaceful atmosphere can express a character's joy. And, of course, a story's atmosphere can also *influence* the characters' state of mind, causing them to react one way in a crowded, busy, urban atmosphere but to react very differently in a peaceful rural atmosphere.

Marjane Satrapi (1969–   )

was raised in Tehran, Iran, and has published numerous graphic fiction books in both English and French, including the award-winning graphic memoir *Persepolis* (2003) and its sequel, *Persepolis 2* (2004). The *Persepolis* works, from which the following excerpt is taken, depict Satrapi's experiences growing up in Tehran during the Islamic Revolution and Iran's war with Iraq. Satrapi cowrote and codirected the animated feature film *Persepolis* (2007), which tied for a Special Jury Prize at the 2007 Cannes Film Festival and was nominated for an Academy Award for best animated feature film. Like *Persepolis,* Satrapi's latest graphic novel, *Embroideries* (2005), also portrays the female experience in modern-day Iran.

from Persepolis   (2003)

This graphic story starts on the next page.

 See Chapter 13 Review Card for Reading and Reacting questions about Marjane Satrapi, *Persepolis*.

Related Work

"Two Kinds" (p. 336)

Cultural Context   Persepolis is an ancient Persian city located in modern-day Iran. King of Persia from 522–486 B.C., Darius I named Persepolis the capital of Persia. The city is known for its monumental architecture, including several royal palaces and an audience hall, the ruins of which can still be seen today. Named after the ancient city, Satrapi's graphic novel, from which the following excerpt is taken, alludes to Iran's epic past and makes an ironic statement about the cultural climate of today.

FOR A YEAR NOW, THE FOOD SHORTAGE HAD BEEN RESOLVED BY THE GROWTH OF THE BLACK MARKET. HOWEVER, FINDING TAPES WAS A LITTLE MORE COMPLICATED. ON GANDHI AVENUE YOU COULD FIND THEM SOMETIMES.

ESTEVIE VONDER

ABBA, BEE GEES

YAZOO

JULIO IGLESIAS

PINK FLOYD

JIKAEL MACKSON

VIDEOS, MUSIC, CARDS, LIPSTICK, NAIL POLISH, CHESS SET, PANTYHOSE, CHOCOLATE, ...,...

I BOUGHT TWO TAPES: KIM WILDE AND CAMEL.

HOW MUCH?

110 TUMANS.

♪WE'RE THE KIDS IN AMERICA ♪WHOA...

YOU! STOP!

THEY WERE GUARDIANS OF THE REVOLUTION, THE WOMEN'S BRANCH. THIS GROUP HAD BEEN ADDED IN 1982, TO ARREST WOMEN WHO WERE IMPROPERLY VEILED. (LIKE ME, FOR EXAMPLE.)

AT THE COMMITTEE, THEY DIDN'T HAVE TO INFORM MY PARENTS. THEY COULD DETAIN ME FOR HOURS, OR FOR DAYS. I COULD BE WHIPPED. IN SHORT, ANYTHING COULD HAPPEN TO ME. IT WAS TIME FOR ACTION.

I'M SORRY MA'AM! I'LL NEVER DO IT AGAIN...

GET IN THE CAR!

MA'AM, MY MOTHER'S DEAD. MY STEPMOTHER IS REALLY CRUEL AND IF I DON'T GO HOME RIGHT AWAY, SHE'LL KILL ME...

SHE'LL BURN ME WITH THE CLOTHES IRON!

SHE'LL MAKE MY FATHER PUT ME IN AN ORPHANAGE

MAYBE SHE BELIEVED ME, MAYBE SHE JUST PRETENDED TO. BUT, MIRACULOUSLY, SHE LET ME GO.

BACK HOME...

MARJI! WHAT HAPPENED? HAVE YOU BEEN CRYING?

NO MOM. I'M JUST TIRED. I'M GOING TO MY ROOM.

THERE WAS NO WAY I COULD TELL THE TRUTH. SHE NEVER WOULD HAVE LET ME GO OUT ALONE AGAIN.

I GOT OFF PRETTY EASY, CONSIDERING. THE GUARDIANS OF THE REVOLUTION DIDN'T FIND MY TAPES.

♫ WE'RE THE KIDS IN AMERICA WHOAO ♫

TO EACH HIS OWN WAY OF CALMING DOWN.

Kate Chopin (1851–1904)

wrote in a style that was realistic yet infused with a dense, sensual texture that was perhaps, in part, her artistic response to her memories of the exotic Louisiana bayou country. Like her contemporary Gustave Flaubert (Chopin's short novel *The Awakening* has often been called a "Creole *Bovary*"), Chopin used the physical world—as in the charged atmosphere of "The Storm"—to symbolize the inner truths of her characters' minds and hearts. Unlike Flaubert, however, she depicted sex not as a frantic and destructive force but as a joyous, elemental part of life. Apparently Kate Chopin knew how daring "The Storm" was: she never submitted it for publication.

The Storm (c. 1899)

I

The leaves were so still that even Bibi thought it was going to rain. Bobinôt, who was accustomed to converse on terms of perfect equality with his little son, called the child's attention to certain sombre clouds that were rolling with sinister intention from the west, accompanied by a sullen, threatening roar. They were at Friedheimer's store and decided to remain there till the storm had passed. They sat within the door on two empty kegs. Bibi was four years old and looked very wise.

"Mama'll be 'fraid, yes," he suggested with blinking eyes.

"She'll shut the house. Maybe she got Sylvie helpin' her this evenin'," Bobinôt responded reassuringly.

"No; she ent got Sylvie. Sylvie was helpin' her yistiday," piped Bibi.

Bobinôt arose and going across to the counter purchased a can of shrimps, of which Calixta was very fond. Then he returned to his perch on the keg and sat stolidly holding the can of shrimps while the storm burst. It shook the wooden store and seemed to be ripping great furrows in the distant field. Bibi laid his little hand on his father's knee and was not afraid.

II

Calixta, at home, felt no uneasiness for their safety. She sat at a side window sewing furiously on a sewing machine. She was greatly occupied and did not notice the approaching storm. But she felt very warm and often stopped to mop her face on which the perspiration gathered in beads. She unfastened her white sacque at the throat. It began to grow dark, and suddenly realizing the situation she got up hurriedly and went about closing windows and doors.

Out on the small front gallery she had hung Bobinôt's Sunday clothes to air and she hastened out to gather them before the rain fell. As she stepped outside, Alcée Laballière rode in at the gate. She had not seen him very often since her marriage, and never alone. She stood there with Bobinôt's coat in her hands, and the big rain drops began to fall. Alcée rode his horse under the shelter of a side projection where the chickens had huddled and there were plows and a harrow piled up in the corner.

"May I come and wait on your gallery till the storm is over, Calixta?" he asked.

"Come 'long in, M'sieur Alcée."

His voice and her own startled her as if from a trance, and she seized Bobinôt's vest. Alcée, mounting to the porch, grabbed the trousers and snatched Bibi's braided jacket that was about to be carried away by a sudden gust of wind. He expressed an intention to remain outside, but it was soon apparent that he might as well have been out in the open: the water beat in upon the boards in driving sheets, and he went inside, closing the door after him. It was even necessary to put something beneath the door to keep the water out.

"As she stepped outside, Alcée Laballière rode in at the gate. She had not seen him very often since her marriage, and never alone."

"My! what a rain! It's good two years sence it rain' like that," exclaimed Calixta as she rolled up a piece of bagging and Alcée helped her to thrust it beneath the crack.

She was a little fuller of figure than five years before when she married; but she had lost nothing of her vivacity. Her blue eyes still retained their melting quality; and her yellow hair, dishevelled by the wind and rain, kinked more stubbornly than ever about her ears and temples.

The rain beat upon the low, shingled roof with a force and clatter that threatened to break an entrance and deluge them there. They were in the dining room—the sitting room—the general utility room. Adjoining was her bed room, with Bibi's couch along side her own. The door stood open, and the room with its white, monumental bed, its closed shutters, looked dim and mysterious.

Alcée flung himself into a rocker and Calixta nervously began to gather up from the floor the lengths of a cotton sheet which she had been sewing.

>> Levee near New Orleans, about 1900

"If this keeps up, *Dieu sait*° if the levees° goin' to stan' 15 it!" she exclaimed.

"What have you got to do with the levees?"

"I got enough to do! An' there's Bobinôt with Bibi out in that storm—if he only didn't left Friedheimer's!"

"Let us hope, Calixta, that Bobinôt's got sense enough to come in out of a cyclone."

She went and stood at the window with a greatly disturbed look on her face. She wiped the frame that was clouded with moisture. It was stiflingly hot. Alcée got up and joined her at the window, looking over her shoulder. The rain was coming down in sheets obscuring the view of far-off cabins and enveloping the distant wood in a gray mist. The playing of the lightning was incessant. A bolt struck a tall chinaberry tree at the edge of the field. It filled all visible space with a blinding glare and the crash seemed to invade the very boards they stood upon.

Calixta put her hands to her eyes, and with a cry, 20 staggered backward. Alcée's arm encircled her, and for an instant he drew her close and spasmodically to him.

"*Bonté!*"° she cried, releasing herself from his encircling arm and retreating from the window, "the house'll go

next! If I only knew w'ere Bibi was!" She would not compose herself; she would not be seated. Alcée clasped her shoulders and looked into her face. The contact of her warm, palpitating body when he had unthinkingly drawn her into his arms, had aroused all the old-time infatuation and desire for her flesh.

"Calixta," he said, "don't be frightened. Nothing can happen. The house is too low to be struck, with so many tall trees standing about. There! aren't you going to be quiet? say, aren't you?" He pushed her hair back from her face that was warm and steaming. Her lips were as red and moist as pomegranate seed. Her white neck and a glimpse of her full, firm bosom disturbed him powerfully. As she glanced up at him the fear in her liquid blue eyes had given place to a drowsy gleam that unconsciously betrayed a sensuous desire. He looked down into her eyes and there was nothing for him to do but to gather her lips in a kiss. It reminded him of Assumption.

"Do you remember—in Assumption, Calixta?" he asked in a low voice broken by passion. Oh! she remembered; for in Assumption he had kissed her and kissed and kissed her; until his senses would well nigh fail, and to save her he would resort to a desperate flight. If she was not an immaculate dove in those days, she was still inviolate; a passionate creature whose very defenselessness had made her defense, against which his honor forbade him to prevail. Now—well, now—her lips seemed in a manner free to be tasted, as well as her round, white throat and her whiter breasts.

They did not heed the crashing torrents, and the roar of the elements made her laugh as she lay in his arms. She was a revelation in that dim, mysterious chamber; as white as the couch she lay upon. Her firm, elastic flesh that was knowing for the first time its birthright, was like a creamy lily that the sun invites to contribute its breath and perfume to the undying life of the world.

The generous abundance of her passion, without guile or 25 trickery, was like a white flame which penetrated and found response in depths of his own sensuous nature that had never yet been reached.

When he touched her breasts they gave themselves up in quivering ecstasy, inviting his lips. Her mouth was a fountain of delight. And when he possessed her, they seemed to swoon together at the very borderland of life's mystery.

He stayed cushioned upon her, breathless, dazed, enervated, with his heart beating like a hammer upon her. With one hand she clasped his head, her lips lightly touching his forehead. The other hand stroked with a soothing rhythm his muscular shoulders.

The growl of the thunder was distant and passing away. The rain beat softly upon the shingles, inviting them to drowsiness and sleep. But they dared not yield.

Cultural Context In this story, which presumably takes place in Louisiana, the character Calixta expresses fear that the powerful storm will break the levees, the raised embankments kept in place to prevent the river from overflowing. In August 2005, more than one hundred years after this story was written, the levees in New Orleans gave way to the sheer force of Hurricane Katrina, which flooded the city, destroyed the area's economic and cultural foundation, and displaced hundreds of thousands of residents.

° *Dieu sait* "God knows" (French).

° **levees** Raised embankments designed to keep a river from overflowing.

° *Bonté* "Goodness!" (French).

>> Bayou country, Louisiana

The rain was over; and the sun was turning the glistening green world into a palace of gems. Calixta, on the gallery, watched Alcée ride away. He turned and smiled at her with a beaming face; and she lifted her pretty chin in the air and laughed aloud.

III

Bobinôt and Bibi, trudging home, stopped without at the 30 cistern to make themselves presentable.

"My! Bibi, w'at will yo' mama say! You ought to be ashame'. You oughtn' put on those good pants. Look at 'em! An' that mud on yo' collar! How you got that mud on yo' collar, Bibi? I never saw such a boy!" Bibi was the picture of pathetic resignation. Bobinôt was the embodiment of serious solicitude as he strove to remove from his own person and his son's the signs of their tramp over heavy roads and through wet fields. He scraped the mud off Bibi's bare legs and feet with a stick and carefully removed all traces from his heavy brogans. Then, prepared for the worst—the meeting with an over-scrupulous housewife, they entered cautiously at the back door.

Calixta was preparing supper. She had set the table and was dripping coffee at the hearth. She sprang up as they came in.

"Oh, Bobinôt! You back! My! but I was uneasy. W'ere you been during the rain? An' Bibi? he ain't wet? he ain't

hurt?" She had clasped Bibi and was kissing him effusively. Bobinôt's explanations and apologies which he had been composing all along the way, died on his lips as Calixta felt him to see if he were dry, and seemed to express nothing but satisfaction at their safe return.

"I brought you some shrimps, Calixta," offered Bobinôt, hauling the can from his ample side pocket and laying it on the table.

"Shrimps! Oh, Bobinôt! you too good fo' anything!" 35 and she gave him a smacking kiss on the cheek that resounded. "*J'vous réponds,*° we'll have a feas' tonight! umph-umph!"

Bobinôt and Bibi began to relax and enjoy themselves, and when the three seated themselves at table they laughed much and so loud that anyone might have heard them as far away as Laballière's.

IV

Alcée Laballière wrote to his wife, Clarisse, that night. It was a loving letter, full of tender solicitude. He told her not to hurry back, but if she and the babies liked it at Biloxi, to stay a month longer. He was getting on nicely; and though he missed them, he was willing to bear the separation a while longer—realizing that their health and pleasure were the first things to be considered.

V

As for Clarisse, she was charmed upon receiving her husband's letter. She and the babies were doing well. The society was agreeable; many of her old friends and acquaintances were at the bay. And the first free breath since her marriage seemed to restore the pleasant liberty of her maiden days. Devoted as she was to her husband, their intimate conjugal life was something which she was more than willing to forego for a while.

So the storm passed and everyone was happy.

Related Works

"Hills Like White Elephants" (p. 96), "What Lips My Lips Have Kissed" (p. 490), "General Review of the Sex Situation" (p. 490), *The Stronger* (p. 602)

See Chapter 13 Review Card for Reading and Reacting questions about Kate Chopin, "The Storm."

° *J'vous réponds* "I tell you" (French).

Sherman J. Alexie (1966–   )

is a Spokane/Coeur d'Alene Indian who grew up on the Spokane Indian
Reservation in Wellpinit, Washington, about fifty miles northwest of
Spokane, where approximately 2,400 Spokane Tribal members live.
Alexie has published short stories, novels, and poetry. He was named
one of Granta's Best of Young American Novelists, and his first novel,
Reservation Blues (1995), won the Before Columbus Foundation's
American Book Award and the Murray Morgan Prize. His second novel,
Indian Killer (1996), was named one of *People's* Best of Pages and was a
New York Times Notable Book. "This Is What It Means to Say Phoenix,
Arizona" (from his 1993 short story collection *The Lone Ranger and Tonto
Fistfight in Heaven*) eventually became the movie *Smoke Signals,* which
was released in 1998. His most recent books are the young adult novel

The Absolutely True Diary of a Part-Time Indian
(2007), for which he won the National Book
Award for Young People's Literature, the
novel *Flight* (2007), and the poetry collection
Face (2009).

Commenting on Native American
culture, Alexie has said, "One of the biggest
misconceptions about Indians is that we're
stoic, but humor is an essential part of our culture." "This Is What It
Means to Say Phoenix, Arizona" demonstrates this unique use of
humor to transcend the harsh realities of life on the reservation and
of the struggle to adapt to contemporary American life.

This Is What It Means to Say Phoenix, Arizona (1993)

Just after Victor lost his job at the Bureau of Indian Affairs,° he also found out that his father had died of a heart attack in Phoenix, Arizona. Victor hadn't seen his father in a few years, had only talked to him on the telephone once or twice, but there still was a genetic pain, which was as real and immediate as a broken bone. Victor didn't have any money. Who does have money on a reservation, except the cigarette and fireworks salespeople? His father had a savings account waiting to be claimed, but Victor needed to find a way to get from Spokane to Phoenix. Victor's mother was just as poor as he was, and the rest of his family didn't have any use at all for him. So Victor called the tribal council.

"Listen," Victor said. "My father just died. I need some money to get to Phoenix to make arrangements."

"Now, Victor," the council said, "you know we're having a difficult time financially."

"But I thought the council had special funds set aside for stuff like this."

"Now, Victor, we do have some money available for ⁵ the proper return of tribal members' bodies. But I don't think we have enough to bring your father all the way back from Phoenix."

"Well," Victor said. "It ain't going to cost all that much. He had to be cremated. Things were kind of ugly. He died of a heart attack in his trailer and nobody found him for a week. It was really hot, too. You get the picture."

"Now, Victor, we're sorry for your loss and the circumstances. But we can really only afford to give you one hundred dollars."

"That's not even enough for a plane ticket."

"Well, you might consider driving down to Phoenix."

"I don't have a car. Besides, I was going to drive my ¹⁰ father's pickup back up here."

"Now, Victor," the council said, "we're sure there is somebody who could drive you to Phoenix. Or could anybody lend you the rest of the money?"

"You know there ain't nobody around with that kind of money."

"Well, we're sorry, Victor, but that's the best we can do."

Victor accepted the tribal council's offer. What else could he do? So he signed the proper papers, picked up his check, and walked over to the Trading Post to cash it.

While Victor stood in line, he watched Thomas Builds- ¹⁵ the-Fire standing near the magazine rack talking to himself. Like he always did. Thomas was a storyteller whom nobody wanted to listen to. That's like being a dentist in a town where everybody has false teeth.

Victor and Thomas Builds-the-Fire were the same age, had grown up and played in the dirt together. Ever since Victor could remember, it was Thomas who had always had something to say.

Once, when they were seven years old, when Victor's father still lived with the family, Thomas closed his eyes and told Victor this story: "Your father's heart is weak. He is afraid of his own family. He is afraid of you. Late at night, he sits in the dark. Watches the television until there's nothing but that white noise. Sometimes he feels like he wants to buy a motorcycle and ride away. He wants to run and hide. He doesn't want to be found."

Thomas Builds-the-Fire had known that Victor's father was going to leave, known it before anyone. Now Victor stood in the Trading Post with a one-hundred-dollar check in his hand, wondering if Thomas knew that Victor's father was dead, if he knew what was going to happen next.

Just then, Thomas looked at Victor, smiled, and walked over to him.

"Victor, I'm sorry about your father," Thomas said.   ²⁰

° **Bureau of Indian Affairs**   The division of the U.S. Department of the
Interior that manages Native American matters; the bureau is operated
by government officials, not tribal leaders.

>> Spokane Indian Reservation in Wellpoint, Washington State, 1920

"How did you know about it?" Victor asked.

"I heard it on the wind. I heard it from the birds. I felt it in the sunlight. Also, your mother was just in here crying."

"Oh," Victor said and looked around the Trading Post. All the other Indians stared, surprised that Victor was even talking to Thomas. Nobody talked to Thomas anymore because he told the same damn stories over and over again. Victor was embarrassed, but he thought that Thomas might be able to help him. Victor felt a sudden need for tradition.

"I can lend you the money you need," Thomas said suddenly. "But you have to take me with you."

"I can't take your money," Victor said. "I mean, I 25 haven't hardly talked to you in years. We're not really friends anymore."

"I didn't say we were friends. I said you had to take me with you."

"Let me think about it."

Victor went home with his one hundred dollars and sat at the kitchen table. He held his head in his hands and thought about Thomas Builds-the-Fire, remembered little details, tears and scars, the bicycle they shared for a summer, so many stories.

* * *

Thomas Builds-the-Fire sat on the bicycle, waiting in Victor's yard. He was ten years old and skinny. His hair was dirty because it was the Fourth of July.

"Victor," Thomas yelled. "Hurry up. We're going to 30 miss the fireworks."

After a few minutes, Victor ran out of his family's house, vaulted over the porch railing, and landed gracefully on the sidewalk.

Thomas gave him the bike and they headed for the fireworks. It was nearly dark and the fireworks were about to start.

"You know," Thomas said, "it's strange how us Indians celebrate the Fourth of July. It ain't like it was our independence everybody was fighting for."

"You think about things too much," Victor said. "It's just supposed to be fun. Maybe Junior will be there."

"Which Junior? Everybody on this reservation is 35 named Junior."

The fireworks were small, hardly more than a few bottle rockets and a fountain. But it was enough for two Indian boys. Years later, they would need much more.

Afterward, sitting in the dark, fighting off mosquitoes, Victor turned to Thomas Builds-the-Fire.

"Hey," Victor said. "Tell me a story."

Thomas closed his eyes and told this story: "There were these two Indian boys who wanted to be warriors. But it was too late to be warriors in the old way. All the horses were gone. So the two Indian boys stole a car and drove to the city. They parked the stolen car in the front of the police station and then hitchhiked back home to the reservation. When they got back, all their friends cheered and their parents' eyes shone with pride. 'You were very brave,' everybody said to the two Indian boys. 'Very brave.'"

"Ya-hey," Victor said. "That's a good one. I wish I 40 could be a warrior."

"Me too," Thomas said.

Victor sat at his kitchen table. He counted his one hundred dollars again and again. He knew he needed more to make it to Phoenix and back. He knew he needed Thomas Builds-the-Fire. So he put his money in his wallet and opened the front door to find Thomas on the porch.

Cultural Context The United States policy of creating Native American reservations can be traced back to the administration of President Ulysses S. Grant, who determined that establishing such reservations was the best way to handle the "Indian problem" between white settlers and the Native Americans they encountered. (Even supporters of Native Americans believed that they were incapable of assimilating into the wider American society and that only on reservations would they be able to survive as a people.) Today, about half of America's 2.5 million Native Americans continue to live on reservations, where more than forty percent of the families live below the federal poverty line and the unemployment rate averages around seventy percent. At the same time, reservations are the one place where members of a tribe can live together and retain their culture, language, and heritage. The characters in "This Is What It Means to Say Phoenix, Arizona" experience both the positive and negative aspects of reservation life.

>> Victor and Thomas in scene from the film *Smoke Signals*, which is based on this story

"Ya-hey, Victor," Thomas said. "I knew you'd call me."

Thomas walked into the living room and sat down in Victor's favorite chair.

"I've got some money saved up," Thomas said. "It's enough to get us down there, but you have to get us back." 45

"I've got this hundred dollars," Victor said. "And my dad had a savings account I'm going to claim."

"How much in your dad's account?"

"Enough. A few hundred."

"Sounds good. When we leaving?"

When they were fifteen and had long since stopped be- 50 ing friends, Victor and Thomas got into a fistfight. That is, Victor was really drunk and beat Thomas up for no reason at all. All the other Indian boys stood around and watched it happen. Junior was there and so were Lester, Seymour, and a lot of others.

The beating might have gone on until Thomas was dead if Norma Many Horses hadn't come along and stopped it.

"Hey, you boys," Norma yelled and jumped out of her car. "Leave him alone."

If it had been someone else, even another man, the Indian boys would've just ignored the warnings. But Norma was a warrior. She was powerful. She could have picked up any two of the boys and smashed their skulls together. But worse than that, she would have dragged them all over to some tepee and made them listen to some elder tell a dusty old story.

The Indian boys scattered, and Norma walked over to Thomas and picked him up.

"Hey, little man, are you O.K.?" she asked. 55

Thomas gave her a thumbs-up.

"Why they always picking on you?"

Thomas shook his head, closed his eyes, but no stories came to him, no words or music. He just wanted to go home, to lie in his bed and let his dreams tell the stories for him.

Thomas Builds-the-Fire and Victor sat next to each other in the airplane, coach section. A tiny white woman had the window seat. She was busy twisting her body into pretzels. She was flexible.

"I have to ask," Thomas said, and Victor closed his 60 eyes in embarrassment.

"Don't," Victor said.

"Excuse me, miss," Thomas asked. "Are you a gymnast or something?"

"There's no something about it," she said. "I was first alternate on the 1980 Olympic team."

"Really?" Thomas asked.

"Really." 65

"I mean, you used to be a world-class athlete?" Thomas asked.

"My husband thinks I still am."

Thomas Builds-the-Fire smiled. She was a mental gymnast too. She pulled her leg straight up against her body so that she could've kissed her kneecap.

"I wish I could do that," Thomas said.

Victor was ready to jump out of the plane. Thomas, 70 that crazy Indian storyteller with ratty old braids and broken teeth, was flirting with a beautiful Olympic gymnast. Nobody back home on the reservation would ever believe it.

"Well," the gymnast said. "It's easy. Try it."

Thomas grabbed at his leg and tried to pull it up into the same position as the gymnast's. He couldn't even come close, which made Victor and the gymnast laugh.

"Hey," she asked. "You two are Indian, right?"

"Full-blood," Victor said.

"Not me," Thomas said. "I'm half magician on my 75 mother's side and half clown on my father's."

They all laughed.

"What are your names?" she asked.

"Victor and Thomas."

"Mine is Cathy. Pleased to meet you all."

The three of them talked for the duration of the flight. 80 Cathy the gymnast complained about the government, how they screwed the 1980 Olympic team by boycotting the games.

"Sounds like you all got a lot in common with Indians," Thomas said.

Nobody laughed.

After the plane landed in Phoenix and they had all found their way to the terminal, Cathy the gymnast smiled and waved goodbye.

"She was really nice," Thomas said.

"Yeah, but everybody talks to everybody on air- 85 planes," Victor said.

"You always used to tell me I think too much," Thomas said. "Now it sounds like you do."

"Maybe I caught it from you."

"Yeah."

Thomas and Victor rode in a taxi to the trailer where Victor's father had died.

"Listen," Victor said as they stopped in front of the 90 trailer. "I never told you I was sorry for beating you up that time."

"Oh, it was nothing. We were just kids and you were drunk."

"Yeah, but I'm still sorry."

"That's all right."

Victor paid for the taxi, and the two of them stood in the hot Phoenix summer. They could smell the trailer.

"This ain't going to be nice," Victor said. "You don't 95 have to go in."

"You're going to need help."

Victor walked to the front door and opened it. The stink rolled out and made them both gag. Victor's father had lain in that trailer for a week in hundred-degree temperatures before anyone had found him. And the only reason anyone found him was the smell. They needed dental records to identify him. That's exactly what the coroner said. They needed dental records.

"Oh, man," Victor said. "I don't know if I can do this."

"Well, then don't."

"But there might be something valuable in there."   100

"I thought his money was in the bank."

"It is: I was talking about pictures and letters and stuff like that."

"Oh," Thomas said as he held his breath and followed Victor into the trailer.

When Victor was twelve, he stepped into an underground wasps' nest. His foot was caught in the hole and no matter how hard he struggled, Victor couldn't pull free. He might have died there, stung a thousand times, if Thomas Builds-the-Fire had not come by.

"Run," Thomas yelled and pulled Victor's foot from 105 the hole. They ran then, hard as they ever had, faster than Billy Mills, faster than Jim Thorpe, faster than the wasps could fly.

Victor and Thomas ran until they couldn't breathe, ran until it was cold and dark outside, ran until they were lost and it took hours to find their way home. All the way back, Victor counted his stings.

"Seven," Victor said. "My lucky number."

*　　*　　*

Victor didn't find much to keep in the trailer. Only a photo album and a stereo. Everything else had that smell stuck in it or was useless anyway. "I guess this is all," Victor said. "It ain't much."

"Better than nothing," Thomas said.

"Yeah, and I do have the pickup."   110

"Yeah," Thomas said. "It's in good shape."

"Dad was good about that stuff."

"Yeah, I remember your dad."

"Really?" Victor asked. "What do you remember?"

Thomas Builds-the-Fire closed his eyes and told this 115 story: "I remember when I had this dream that told me to go to Spokane, to stand by the falls in the middle of the city and wait for a sign. I knew I had to go there but I didn't have a car. Didn't have a license. I was only thirteen. So I walked all the way, took me all day, and I finally made it to the falls. I stood there for an hour waiting. Then your dad came walking up. 'What the hell are you doing here?' he asked me. I said, 'Waiting for a vision.' Then your father said, 'All you're going to get here is mugged.' So he drove me over to Denny's, bought me dinner, and then drove me home to the reservation. For a long time, I was mad because I thought my dreams had lied to me. But they hadn't. Your dad was my vision. *Take care of each other* is what my dreams were saying. *Take care of each other.*"

Victor was quiet for a long time. He searched his mind for memories of his father, found the good ones, found a few bad ones, added it all up, and smiled.

"My father never told me about finding you in Spokane," Victor said.

"He said he wouldn't tell anybody. Didn't want me to get in trouble. But he said I had to watch out for you as part of the deal."

"Really?"

"Really. Your father said you would need the help. He 120 was right."

"That's why you came down here with me, isn't it?" Victor asked.

"I came because of your father."

Victor and Thomas climbed into the pickup, drove over to the bank, and claimed the three hundred dollars in the savings account.

Thomas Builds-the-Fire could fly.

Once, he jumped off the roof of the tribal school and 125 flapped his arms like a crazy eagle. And he flew. For a second he hovered, suspended above all the other Indian boys, who were too smart or too scared to jump too.

"He's flying," Junior yelled, and Seymour was busy looking for the trick wires or mirrors. But it was real. As real as the dirt when Thomas lost altitude and crashed to the ground.

He broke his arm in two places.

"He broke his wing, he broke his wing, he broke his wing," all the Indian boys chanted as they ran off, flapping their wings, wishing they could fly too. They hated Thomas for his courage, his brief moment as a bird. Everybody has dreams about flying. Thomas flew.

One of his dreams came true for just a second, just enough to make it real.

*　　*　　*

Victor's father, his ashes, fit in one wooden box with enough left over to fill a cardboard box.

"He always was a big man," Thomas said.

Victor carried part of his father out to the pickup, and Thomas carried the rest. They set him down carefully behind the seats, put a cowboy hat on the wooden box and a Dodgers cap on the cardboard box. That was the way it was supposed to be.

"Ready to head back home?" Victor asked.

"It's going to be a long drive."

"Yeah, take a couple days, maybe."

"We can take turns," Thomas said.

"O.K.," Victor said, but they didn't take turns. Victor drove for sixteen hours straight north, made it halfway up Nevada toward home before he finally pulled over.

"Hey, Thomas," Victor said. "You got to drive for a while."

"O.K."

Thomas Builds-the-Fire slid behind the wheel and started off down the road. All through Nevada, Thomas and Victor had been amazed at the lack of animal life, at the absence of water, of movement.

"Where is everything?" Victor had asked more than once.

Now, when Thomas was finally driving, they saw the first animal, maybe the only animal in Nevada. It was a long-eared jackrabbit.

"Look," Victor yelled. "It's alive."

Thomas and Victor were busy congratulating themselves on their discovery when the jackrabbit darted out into the road and under the wheels of the pickup.

"Stop the goddamn car," Victor yelled, and Thomas did stop and backed the pickup to the dead jackrabbit.

"Oh, man, he's dead," Victor said as he looked at the squashed animal.

"Really dead."

"The only thing alive in this whole state and we just killed it."

"I don't know," Thomas said. "I think it was suicide."

Victor looked around the desert, sniffed the air, felt the emptiness and loneliness, and nodded his head.

"Yeah," Victor said. "It had to be suicide."

"I can't believe this," Thomas said. "You drive for a thousand miles and there ain't even any bugs smashed on the windshield. I drive for ten seconds and kill the only living thing in Nevada."

"Yeah," Victor said. "Maybe I should drive."

"Maybe you should."

Thomas Builds-the-Fire walked through the corridors of the tribal school by himself. Nobody wanted to be anywhere near him because of all those stories. Story after story.

Thomas closed his eyes and this story came to him: "We are all given one thing by which our lives are measured, one determination. Mine are the stories that can change or not change the world. It doesn't matter which,

as long as I continue to tell the stories. My father, he died on Okinawa° in World War II, died fighting for this country, which had tried to kill him for years. My mother, she died giving birth to me, died while I was still inside her. She pushed me out into the world with her last breath. I have no brothers or sisters. I have only my stories, which came to me before I even had the words to speak. I learned a thousand stories before I took my first thousand steps. They are all I have. It's all I can do."

Thomas Builds-the-Fire told his stories to all those who would stop and listen. He kept telling them long after people had stopped listening.

Victor and Thomas made it back to the reservation just as the sun was rising. It was the beginning of a new day on earth, but the same old shit on the reservation.

"Good morning," Thomas said.

"Good morning."

The tribe was waking up, ready for work, eating breakfast, reading the newspaper, just like everybody else does. Willene LeBret was out in her garden, wearing a bathrobe. She waved when Thomas and Victor drove by.

"Crazy Indians made it," she said to herself and went back to her roses.

Victor stopped the pickup in front of Thomas Builds-the-Fire's HUD° house. They both yawned, stretched a little, shook dust from their bodies.

"I'm tired," Victor said.

"Of everything," Thomas added.

They both searched for words to end the journey. Victor needed to thank Thomas for his help and for the money, and to make the promise to pay it all back.

"Don't worry about the money." Thomas said. "It don't make any difference anyhow."

"Probably not, enit?"

"Nope."

Victor knew that Thomas would remain the crazy storyteller who talked to dogs and cars, who listened to the wind and pine trees. Victor knew that he couldn't really be friends with Thomas, even after all that had happened. It was cruel but it was real. As real as the ash, as Victor's father, sitting behind the seats.

"I know how it is," Thomas said. "I know you ain't going to treat me any better than you did before. I know your friends would give you too much shit about it."

Victor was ashamed of himself. Whatever happened to the tribal ties, the sense of community? The only real thing he shared with anybody was a bottle and broken dreams. He owed Thomas something, anything.

"Listen," Victor said and handed Thomas the cardboard box that contained half of his father. "I want you to have this."

° **Okinawa** Largest island of the Ryukyus, a chain of Japanese islands in the western Pacific Ocean.

° **HUD** The U.S. Department of Housing and Urban Development.

Thomas took the ashes and smiled, closed his eyes, and told this story: "I'm going to travel to Spokane Falls one last time and toss these ashes into the water. And your father will rise like a salmon, leap over the bridge, over me, and find his way home. It will be beautiful. His teeth will shine like silver, like a rainbow. He will rise, Victor, he will rise."

Victor smiled.   175

"I was planning on doing the same thing with my half," Victor said. "But I didn't imagine my father looking anything like a salmon. I thought it'd be like cleaning the attic or something. Like letting things go after they've stopped having any use."

"Nothing stops, cousin," Thomas said. "Nothing stops."

Thomas Builds-the-Fire got out of the pickup and walked up his driveway. Victor started the pickup and began the drive home.

"Wait," Thomas yelled suddenly from his porch. "I just got to ask one favor."

Victor stopped the pickup, leaned out the window, 180 and shouted back.

"What do you want?" he asked.

"Just one time when I'm telling a story somewhere, why don't you stop and listen?" Thomas asked.

"Just once?"

"Just once."

Victor waved his arms to let Thomas know that the 185 deal was good. It was a fair trade. That's all Thomas had ever wanted from his whole life. So Victor drove his father's pickup toward home while Thomas went into his house, closed the door behind him, and heard a new story come to him in the silence afterward.

Related Work

"Indian Boarding School: The Runaways" (p. 507)

See Chapter 13 Review Card for Reading and Reacting questions about Sherman J. Alexie, "This is What It Means to Say Phoenix, Arizona."

Tillie Olsen (1912 or 1913–2007)

is known for her works of fiction about working-class Americans. Her short stories and one novel are inhabited by those she called the "despised people"—coal miners, farm laborers, packinghouse butchers, and housewives. Olsen was born in Nebraska into a working-class family. According to an account in her nonfiction work *Silences* (1978), she was inspired at age fifteen to write about working-class people when she read Rebecca Harding Davis's *Life in the Iron Mills*, a tale of the effects of industrialization on workers, in an 1861 issue of *Atlantic Monthly* bought for ten cents in a junk shop.

Shortly after she left high school, Olsen was jailed for helping to organize packinghouse workers. Motivated by her experiences, she began to write a novel, *Yonnondio*. Under her maiden name, Tillie Lerner, she published two poems, a short story, and part of her novel during the 1930s. After her marriage, she did not publish again for twenty-two years, spending her time raising four children and working

at a variety of jobs. The collection of short stories *Tell Me a Riddle* (1961), which includes "I Stand Here Ironing" (originally titled "Help Her to Believe"), was published when she was fifty. Her only other work of fiction is *Yonnondio* (1974), which she pieced together from drafts she wrote in the 1930s and edited for publication in 1974.

In 1984, she edited *Mother to Daughter, Daughter to Mother: Mothers on Mothering*, a collection of poems, letters, short fiction, and diary excerpts written by famous and not-so-famous women, and in 1987, she collaborated with photographer Estelle Jussim on *Mothers & Daughters: An Exploration in Photographs*.

I Stand Here Ironing (1961)

I stand here ironing, and what you asked me moves tormented back and forth with the iron.

"I wish you would manage the time to come and talk with me about your daughter. I'm sure you can help me understand her. She's a youngster who needs help and whom I'm deeply interested in helping."

"Who needs help." . . . Even if I came, what good would it do? You think because I am her mother I have a key, or that in some way you could use me as a key? She

has lived for nineteen years. There is all that life that has happened outside of me, beyond me.

And when is there time to remember, to sift, to weigh, to estimate, to total? I will start and there will be an interruption and I will have to gather it all together again. Or I will become engulfed with all I did or did not do, with what should have been and what cannot be helped.

She was a beautiful baby. The first and only one of 5 our five that was beautiful at birth. You do not guess how new and uneasy her tenancy in her now-loveliness. You did not know her all those years she was thought homely, or see her poring over her baby pictures, making me tell her over and over how beautiful she had been—and would be, I would tell her—and was now, to the seeing eye. But the seeing eyes were few or nonexistent. Including mine.

I nursed her. They feel that's important nowadays. I nursed all the children, but with her, with all the fierce rigidity of first motherhood, I did like the books then said.

> "I was nineteen. It was the pre-relief, pre-WPA world of the depression."

Though her cries battered me to trembling and my breasts ached with swollenness, I waited till the clock decreed.

Why do I put that first? I do not even know if it matters, or if it explains anything.

She was a beautiful baby. She blew shining bubbles of sound. She loved motion, loved light, loved color and music and textures. She would lie on the floor in her blue overalls patting the surface so hard in ecstasy her hands and feet would blur. She was a miracle to me, but when she was eight months old I had to leave her daytimes with the woman downstairs to whom she was no miracle at all, for I worked or looked for work and for Emily's father, who "could no longer endure" (he wrote in his good-bye note) "sharing want with us."

I was nineteen. It was the pre-relief, pre-WPA° world of the depression. I would start running as soon as I got off the streetcar, running up the stairs, the place smelling sour, and awake or asleep to startle awake, when she saw me she would break into a clogged weeping that could not be comforted, a weeping I can hear yet.

After a while I found a job hashing at night so I could 10 be with her days, and it was better. But it came to where I had to bring her to his family and leave her.

>> Scene from the DVD, "I Stand Here Ironing": Narrator (as a young woman) at an ironing board

© Denna Bendall/Worn Path Productions

It took a long time to raise the money for her fare back. Then she got chicken pox and I had to wait longer. When she finally came, I hardly knew her, walking quick and nervous like her father, looking like her father, thin, and dressed in a shoddy red that yellowed her skin and glared at the pockmarks. All the baby loveliness gone.

She was two. Old enough for nursery school they said, and I did not know then what I know now—the fatigue of the long day, and the lacerations of group life in the kinds of nurseries that are only parking places for children.

Except that it would have made no difference if I had known. It was the only place there was. It was the only way we could be together, the only way I could hold a job.

And even without knowing, I knew. I knew the teacher that was evil because all these years it has curdled into my memory, the little boy hunched in the corner, her rasp, "why aren't you outside, because Alvin hits you? that's no reason, go out, scaredy." I knew Emily hated it even if she did not clutch and implore "don't go Mommy" like the other children, mornings.

She always had a reason why we should stay home. 15 Momma, you look sick. Momma, I feel sick. Momma, the teachers aren't there today, they're sick. Momma, we can't go, there was a fire there last night. Momma, it's a holiday today, no school, they told me.

But never a direct protest, never rebellion. I think of our others in their three-, four-year-oldness—the explosions, the tempers, the denunciations, the demands—and I feel suddenly ill. I put the iron down. What in me demanded that goodness in her? And what was the cost, the cost to her of such goodness?

The old man living in the back once said in his gentle way: "You should smile at Emily more when you look at her." What *was* in my face when I looked at her? I loved her. There were all the acts of love.

It was only with the others I remembered what he said, and it was the face of joy, and not of care or tightness or worry I turned to them—too late for Emily. She does not smile easily, let alone almost always as her brothers and sisters do. Her face is closed and sombre, but when she wants, how fluid. You must have seen it in her pantomimes, you spoke of her rare gift for comedy on the stage that rouses laughter out of the audience so dear they applaud and applaud and do not want to let her go.

Where does it come from, that comedy? There was none of it in her when she came back to me that second time, after I had had to send her away again. She had a new daddy now to learn to love, and I think perhaps it was a better time.

°**WPA** The Works Progress Administration, created in 1935 as part of President Franklin D. Roosevelt's New Deal program. The purpose of the WPA (renamed the Works Projects Administration in 1939) was to provide jobs for the unemployed during the Great Depression.

>> 1930s bread line

EXPLORE ONLINE >

To complete a video activity of "I Stand Here Ironing,"
visit your Literature CourseMate, accessed through
www.cengagebrain.com.

Except when we left her alone nights, telling ourselves 20
she was old enough.

"Can't you go some other time, Mommy, like tomorrow?" she would ask. "Will it be just a little while you'll be
gone? Do you promise?"

The time we came back, the front door open, the clock
on the floor in the hall. She rigid awake. "It wasn't just a
little while. I didn't cry. Three times I called you, just three
times, and then I ran downstairs to open the door so you
could come faster. The clock talked loud. I threw it away,
it scared me what it talked."

She said the clock talked loud again that night I went
to the hospital to have Susan. She was delirious with the
fever that comes before red measles, but she was fully
conscious all the week I was gone and the week after we
were home when she could not come near the new baby
or me.

She did not get well. She stayed skeleton thin, not
wanting to eat, and night after night she had nightmares.
She would call for me, and I would rouse from exhaustion
to sleepily call back: "You're all right, darling, go to sleep,

it's just a dream," and if she still called, in a sterner voice,
"now go to sleep, Emily, there's nothing to hurt you."
Twice, only twice, when I had to get up for Susan anyhow,
I went in to sit with her.

Now when it is too late (as if she would let me hold 25
and comfort her like I do the others) I get up and go to
her at once at her moan or restless stirring. "Are you
awake, Emily? Can I get you something?" And the answer is always the same: "No, I'm all right, go back to
sleep, Mother."

They persuaded me at the clinic to send her away to a
convalescent home in the country where "she can have the
kind of food and care you can't manage for her, and you'll
be free to concentrate on the new baby." They still send
children to that place. I see pictures on the society page of
sleek young women planning affairs to raise money for it,
or dancing at the affairs, or decorating Easter eggs or
filling Christmas stockings for the children.

They never have a picture of the children so I do not
know if the girls still wear those gigantic red bows and
the ravaged looks on the every other Sunday when parents can come to visit "unless otherwise notified"—as we
were notified the first six weeks.

Oh it is a handsome place, green lawns and tall trees
and fluted flower beds. High up on the balconies of each
cottage the children stand, the girls in their red bows and
white dresses, the boys in white suits and giant red ties.
The parents stand below shrieking up to be heard and the
children shriek down to be heard, and between them the
invisible wall: "Not to Be Contaminated by Parental
Germs or Physical Affection."

There was a tiny girl who always stood hand in hand
with Emily. Her parents never came. One visit she was
gone. "They moved her to Rose Cottage," Emily shouted in
explanation. "They don't like you to love anybody here."

She wrote once a week, the labored writing of a seven- 30
year-old. "I am fine. How is the baby. If I write my leter ni-
cly I will have a star. Love." There never was a star. We
wrote every other day, letters she could never hold or keep
but only hear read—once. "We simply do not have room for
children to keep any personal possessions," they patiently
explained when we pieced one Sunday's shrieking together
to plead how much it would mean to Emily, who loved so
to keep things, to be allowed to keep her letters and cards.

Each visit she looked frailer. "She isn't eating," they
told us.

(They had runny eggs for breakfast or mush with
lumps, Emily said later, I'd hold it in my mouth and not

Cultural Context During the Great Depression of
the 1930s, jobs were scarce throughout the United States, and
many people who managed to keep their jobs were forced to
take pay cuts. At the height of the Depression in 1933, almost
twenty-five percent of the total workforce—more than eleven
million people—were unemployed. The displacement of the
American worker and the destruction of farming communities
caused families such as the one in this story to split up or
migrate from their homes in search of work. In 1935, the Social
Security Act established public assistance, unemployment insurance, and social security, which offered economic relief to
American workers.

>> Scene from the DVD of, "I Stand Here Ironing": Emily as a child (in convalescent home)

swallow. Nothing ever tasted good, just when they had chicken.)

It took us eight months to get her released home, and only the fact that she gained back so little of her seven lost pounds convinced the social worker.

I used to try to hold and love her after she came back, but her body would stay stiff, and after a while she'd push away. She ate little. Food sickened her, and I think much of life too. Oh she had physical lightness and brightness, twinkling by on skates, bouncing like a ball up and down up and down over the jump rope, skimming over the hill; but these were momentary.

She fretted about her appearance, thin and dark and 35 foreign-looking at a time when every little girl was supposed to look or thought she should look a chubby blonde replica of Shirley Temple. The doorbell sometimes rang for her, but no one seemed to come and play in the house or be a best friend. Maybe because we moved so much.

There was a boy she loved painfully through two school semesters. Months later she told me how she had taken pennies from my purse to buy him candy. "Licorice was his favorite and I brought him some every day, but he still liked Jennifer better'n me. Why, Mommy?" The kind of question for which there is no answer.

School was a worry to her. She was not glib or quick in a world where glibness and quickness were easily confused with ability to learn. To her overworked and exasperated teachers she was an overconscientious "slow learner" who kept trying to catch up and was absent entirely too often.

I let her be absent, though sometimes the illness was imaginary. How different from my now-strictness about attendance with the others. I wasn't working. We had a new baby, I was home anyhow. Sometimes, after Susan grew old enough, I would keep her home from school, too, to have them all together.

Mostly Emily had asthma, and her breathing, harsh and labored, would fill the house with a curiously tranquil sound. I would bring the two old dresser mirrors and her boxes of collections to her bed. She would select beads and single earrings, bottle tops and shells, dried flowers and pebbles, old postcards and scraps, all sorts of oddments; then she and Susan would play Kingdom, setting up landscapes and furniture, peopling them with action.

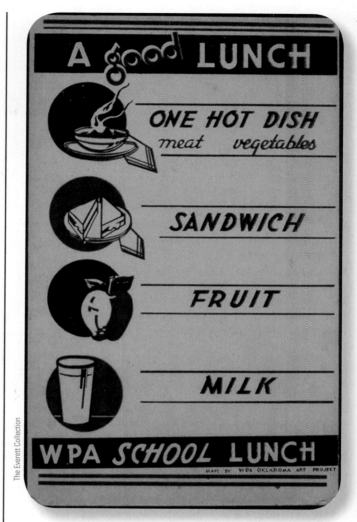

>> WPA sign from 1930's Depression era

Those were the only times of peaceful companionship 40 between her and Susan. I have edged away from it, that poisonous feeling between them, that terrible balancing of hurts and needs I had to do between the two, and did so badly, those earlier years.

Oh there are conflicts between the others too, each one human, needing, demanding, hurting, taking—but only between Emily and Susan, no, Emily toward Susan that corroding resentment. It seems so obvious on the surface, yet it is not obvious. Susan, the second child, Susan, golden- and curly-haired and chubby, quick and articulate and assured, everything in appearance and manner Emily was not; Susan, not able to resist Emily's precious things, losing or sometimes clumsily breaking them; Susan telling jokes and riddles to company for applause while Emily sat silent (to say to me later: that was *my* riddle, Mother, I told it to Susan); Susan, who for all the five years' difference in age was just a year behind Emily in developing physically.

I am glad for that slow physical development that widened the difference between her and her contemporaries, though she suffered over it. She was too vulnerable

EXPLORE ONLINE >

To watch a video interview with Tillie Olsen about "I Stand
Here Ironing," visit your Literature CourseMate accessed
through www.cengagebrain.com.

for that terrible world of youthful competition, of preen-
ing and parading, of constant measuring of yourself
against every other, of envy, "If I had that copper hair," "If
I had that skin. . . ." She tormented herself enough about
not looking like the others, there was enough of the un-
sureness, the having to be conscious of words before you
speak, the constant caring—what are they thinking of
me? without having it all magnified by the merciless physical drives.

Ronnie is calling. He is wet and I change him. It is rare
there is such a cry now. That time of motherhood is almost
behind me when the ear is not one's own but must always
be racked and listening for the child cry, the child call. We
sit for a while and I hold him, looking out over the city
spread in charcoal with its soft aisles of light. *"Shoogily,"*
he breathes and curls closer. I carry him back to bed,
asleep. *Shoogily.* A funny word, a family word, inherited
from Emily, invented by her to say: *comfort.*

In this and other ways she leaves her seal, I say aloud.
And startle at my saying it. What do I mean? What did I
start to gather together, to try and make coherent? I was
at the terrible, growing years. War years. I do not remember them well. I was working, there were four smaller
ones now, there was not time for her. She had to help be
a mother, and housekeeper, and shopper. She had to set
her seal. Mornings of crisis and near hysteria trying to get
lunches packed, hair combed, coats and shoes found, everyone to school or Child Care on time, the baby ready
for transportation. And always the paper scribbled on by
a smaller one, the book looked at by Susan then mislaid,
the homework not done. Running out to that huge school
where she was one, she was lost, she was a drop; suffering over the unpreparedness, stammering and unsure in
her classes.

There was so little time left at night after the kids were 45
bedded down. She would struggle over books, always eating (it was in those years she developed her enormous
appetite that is legendary in our family) and I would be
ironing, or preparing food for the next day, or writing
V-mail° to Bill, or tending the baby. Sometimes, to make
me laugh, or out of her despair, she would imitate hap-
penings or types at school.

°**V-mail**   Mail sent to or from members of the armed forces during
World War II. Letters were reduced onto microfilm and enlarged and
printed out at their destination.

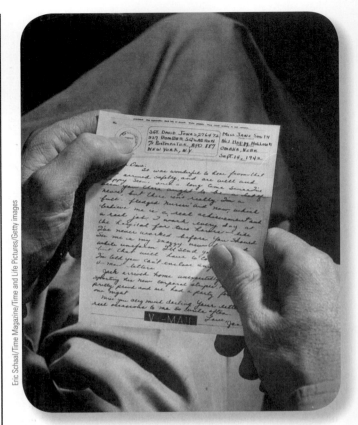

>> 1940s V-mail letter

I think I said once: "Why don't you do something like
this in the school amateur show?" One morning she
phoned me at work, hardly understandable through the
weeping: "Mother, I did it. I won, I won; they gave me first
prize; they clapped and clapped and wouldn't let me go."

Now suddenly she was Somebody, and as imprisoned
in her difference as she had been in anonymity.

She began to be asked to perform at other high
schools, even in colleges, then at city and statewide affairs.
The first one we went to, I only recognized her that first
moment when thin, shy, she almost drowned herself into
the curtains. Then: Was this Emily? The control, the command, the convulsing and deadly clowning, the spell, then
the roaring, stamping audience, unwilling to let this rare
and precious laughter out of their lives.

Afterwards: You ought to do something about her
with a gift like that—but without money or knowing how,
what does one do? We have left it all to her, and the gift
has as often eddied inside, clogged and clotted, as been
used and growing.

She is coming. She runs up the stairs two at a time 50
with her light graceful step, and I know she is happy tonight. Whatever it was that occasioned your call did not
happen today.

"Aren't you ever going to finish the ironing, Mother?
Whistler painted his mother in a rocker. I'd have to paint
mine standing over an ironing board." This is one of her

>> Scene from the film, *I Stand Here Ironing:* Emily performing at her school's amateur show

communicative nights and she tells me everything and nothing as she fixes herself a plate of food out of the icebox.

She is so lovely. Why did you want me to come in at all? Why were you concerned? She will find her way.

She starts up the stairs to bed. "Don't get me up with the rest in the morning." "But I thought you were having midterms." "Oh, those," she comes back in, kisses me, and says quite lightly, "in a couple of years when we'll all be atom-dead they won't matter a bit."

She has said it before. She *believes* it. But because I have been dredging the past, and all that compounds a human being is so heavy and meaningful in me, I cannot endure it tonight.

I will never total it all. I will never come in to say: 55 She was a child seldom smiled at. Her father left me before she was a year old. I had to work her first six years when there was work, or I sent her home and to his relatives. There were years she had care she hated. She was dark and thin and foreign-looking in a world where the prestige went to blondeness and curly hair and dimples, she was slow where glibness was prized. She was a child of anxious, not proud, love. We were poor and could not afford for her the soil of easy growth. I was a young mother, I was a distracted mother. There were other children pushing up, demanding. Her younger sister seemed all that she was not. There were years she did not want me to touch her. She kept too much in herself, her life was such she had to keep too much in herself. My wisdom came too late. She has much to her and probably little will come of it. She is a child of her age, of depression, of war, of fear.

Let her be. So all that is in her will not bloom—but in how many does it? There is still enough left to live by. Only help her to know—help make it so there is cause for her to know—that she is more than this dress on the ironing board, helpless before the iron.

 Related Works

"Kansas" (p. 117), "Everyday Use" (p. 256), "Two Kinds" (p. 336), "Those Winter Sundays" (p. 482)

 See Chapter 13 Review Card for Reading and Reacting questions about Tillie Olsen, "I Stand Here Ironing."

Writing Suggestions: Setting

1. In "The Storm," "I Stand Here Ironing," and the excerpt from *Persepolis*, social constraints determined by the story's historical setting limit a woman's options. Explore the options each woman might reasonably exercise in order to break free of the limits that social institutions impose on her.

2. Write an essay in which you consider how "This Is What It Means to Say Phoenix, Arizona" would be different if its geographical and physical setting were changed to a setting of your choice. In your essay, examine the changes (in plot development as well as in the characters' conflicts, reactions, and motivation) that might occur as a result of the change in setting.

3. Select a story from another chapter, and write an essay in which you consider how setting affects its plot—for example, how it creates conflict or crisis, how it forces characters to act, or how it determines how the plot is resolved.

4. "The Storm" uses rich descriptive language to create a mood that dominates the story. Analyze this use of language in this story, or explicate and compare two short passages from different stories. How does language help to create and enrich each story's setting?

✔ CHECKLIST

WRITING ABOUT SETTING

- ☐ Is the setting specified or unspecified? Is it fully described or only suggested?
- ☐ Is the setting just background, or is it a key force in the story?
- ☐ Are any characters in conflict with their environment?
- ☐ How does the setting influence the story's plot? Does it cause characters to act?
- ☐ In what time period does the story take place? How can you tell? What social, political, or economic situations or events of the historical period might influence the story?
- ☐ In what geographical location is the story set? Is this location important to the story?
- ☐ At what time of day is the story set? Is time important to the development of the story?
- ☐ Is the story set primarily indoors or out-of-doors? What role does this aspect of the setting play in the story?
- ☐ What role do weather conditions play in the story?
- ☐ What kind of atmosphere or mood does the setting create?
- ☐ How does the setting influence the characters? Does it affect (or reflect) their emotional state? Does it help to explain their motivation?
- ☐ Does the atmosphere change as the story progresses? Is this change significant?

Glossary Terms

atmosphere Tone or mood of a literary work, often established by the setting and language. Atmosphere is the emotional aura that determines readers' expectations about a work—for example, the sense of doom established at the beginning of Shakespeare's *Macbeth*.

mood Atmosphere created by the elements of a literary work (setting, characterization, imagery, tone, and so on).

setting Background against which the action of a work takes place: the historical time, locale, season, time of day, weather, and so on.

14

Point of View

Learning Outcomes

After reading this chapter, you should be able to do the following:

LO1 Recognize first-person narrators

LO2 Recognize third-person narrators

LO3 Understand the uses of point of view

Timeline

William Faulkner, "Barn Burning" **1939**

1957 Richard Wright, "Big Black Good Man"

1846 Edgar Allan Poe, "The Cask of Amontillado"

Shaun Tan, from *The Arrival* **2006**

1830 | **1860** | **1890** | **1920** | **1950** | **1980**

1849 Edgar Allan Poe dies at the age of 40.

1848 The Mexican–American War ends.

1846 The Mexican–American War begins.

1838 The first wine grapes are planted in Napa Valley.

German troops invade Czechoslovakia. **1938**

The character of Superman first appears in a comic book. **1938**

The character of Batman appears in a comic book for the first time. **1939**

President Dwight D. Eisenhower sends federal troops to enforce school desegregation in Little Rock, AK. **1957**

A massive earthquake and tsunami devastate the South Pacific. **2004**

NASA's *Phoenix* spacecraft lands on Mars. **2008**

EXPLORE ONLINE >

To complete a tutorial of "Point of View," visit your Literature CourseMate, accessed through www.cengagebrain.com.

One of the first choices writers make is who tells the story. This choice determines the story's **point of view**—the vantage point from which events are presented. The implications of this choice are far-reaching.

Consider the following scenario. Five people witness a crime and are questioned by the police. Their stories agree on certain points: a crime was committed, a body was found, and the crime occurred at noon. But in other ways their stories are different. The man who fled the scene was either tall or of average height; his hair was either dark or light; he either was carrying an object or was empty-handed. The events that led up to the crime and even the description of the crime itself are markedly different, depending on who tells the story. Thus, the **narrator**—the person telling the story—determines what details are included in the story and how they are arranged—in short, the plot. In addition, the perspective of the narrator affects the story's style, language, and themes.

The narrator of a work of fiction is not the same as the writer—even when a writer uses the first-person *I*.

point of view Perspective from which a story is told. The storyteller may be a major character in the story or a character who witnesses the story's events (*first-person narrator*) or someone who does not figure in the action at all (*third-person narrator*), in which case he or she may know the actions and thoughts of everyone in the story (*omniscient narrator*) or just know some part of these (*limited omniscient narrator*).

narrator Person who tells the story.

persona Narrator created by the writer to tell a story; in Greek tragedy, a persona was a mask worn by an actor.

irony/dramatic irony/situational irony/verbal irony Literary device or situation that depends on the existence of at least two separate and contrasting levels of meaning or experience. **Dramatic** or **tragic irony** depends on the audience's knowing something the protagonist has not yet realized. **Situational irony** exists when what happens is at odds with what the story's situation leads readers to expect will happen. **Verbal irony** occurs when what is said is in contrast with what is meant.

Writers create narrators to tell their stories. Often the personalities and opinions of narrators are far different from those of the author. The term **persona**—which literally means "mask"—is used for such narrators. By assuming this mask, a writer expands the creative possibilities of a work.

When deciding on a point of view for a work of fiction, a writer can choose to tell the story either in the **first person** or in the **third person**.

LO1 Recognize First-Person Narrators

Sometimes the narrator is a character who uses the **first person** (*I* or sometimes *we*) to tell the story. Often this narrator is a **major character**—Sammy in John Updike's "A&P" (p. 131) and the boy in James Joyce's "Araby" (p. 220), for example—who tells his or her own story and is the focus of that story. Sometimes, however, a first-person narrator tells a story that is primarily about someone else. Such a narrator may be a **minor character** who plays a relatively small part in the story or simply an **observer** who reports events experienced or related by others. The narrator of William Faulkner's "A Rose for Emily" (p. 121), for example, is an unidentified witness to the story's events. By using *we* instead of *I*, this narrator speaks on behalf of all the town's residents, expressing their shared views of their neighbor, Emily Grierson as the following excerpt illustrates:

> We did not say she was crazy then. We believed she had to do that. We remembered all the young men her father had driven away, and we knew that with nothing left, she would have to cling to that which had robbed her, as people will.

Writers gain a number of advantages when they use first-person narrators. First, they are able to present incidents convincingly. Readers are more willing to accept a statement like "My sister changed a lot after that day" than they are to accept the impersonal observations of a third-person narrator. The first-person narrator also simplifies a writer's task of selecting details. Only the events and details that the narrator could actually have observed or experienced can be introduced into the story.

Another major advantage of first-person narrators is that their restricted view can create **irony**—a discrepancy between what is said and what readers believe to be true. Irony may be *dramatic, situational,* or *verbal.* **Dramatic irony** occurs when a narrator (or a character) perceives less than readers do; **situational irony** occurs when what happens is at odds with what readers are led to expect; **verbal irony** occurs when the narrator says one thing but actually means another.

"Gryphon," by Charles Baxter (p. 138), illustrates all three kinds of irony. Baxter creates **dramatic irony** when he has his main character see less than readers do. For example, at the end of the story, the young boy does not yet realize what readers already know—that he has learned more from Miss Ferenczi's way of teaching than from Mr. Hibler's. The setting of the story—a conventional school—creates **situational irony** because it contrasts with the unexpected events that unfold there. In addition, many of the narrator's comments create **verbal irony** because they convey the opposite of their literal meaning. At the end of the story, for example, after the substitute, Miss Ferenczi, has been fired, the narrator relates another teacher's comment that life will now return to "normal" and that their regular teacher will soon return to test them on their "knowledge." This comment is ironic in light of all Miss Ferenczi has done to redefine the narrator's ideas about "normal" education and about "knowledge."

UNRELIABLE NARRATORS

Sometimes first-person narrators are self-serving, mistaken, confused, unstable, or even insane. These **unreliable narrators,** whether intentionally or unintentionally, misrepresent events and misdirect readers. In Edgar Allan Poe's "The Cask of Amontillado" (p. 190), for example, the narrator, Montresor, tells his story to justify a crime he committed fifty years before. Montresor's version of what happened is not accurate, and perceptive readers know it: his obvious self-deception, his sadistic manipulation of Fortunato, his detached description of the cold-blooded murder, and his lack of remorse lead readers to question his sanity and, therefore, to distrust his version of events. This distrust creates an ironic distance between readers and narrator.

The narrator of Charlotte Perkins Gilman's "The Yellow Wallpaper" (p. 313) is also an unreliable narrator. Suffering from "nervous depression," she unintentionally distorts the facts when she says that the shapes in her bedroom wallpaper are changing and moving. Moreover, she does not realize what is wrong with her or why, or how her husband's "good intentions" are hurting her. Readers, however, see the disparity between the narrator's interpretation of events and their own, and this irony enriches their understanding of the story.

Some narrators are unreliable because they are naive. Because they are immature, sheltered, or innocent of evil, these narrators are not aware of the significance of the events they are relating. Having the benefit of experience, readers interpret events differently from the way these narrators do. When we read a passage by a child narrator—such as the following one from J. D. Salinger's classic 1951 novel *The Catcher in the Rye*—we are aware of the narrator's innocence, and we know his interpretation of events is flawed:

> Anyway, I keep picturing all these little kids playing some game in this big field of rye and all. Thousands of little kids, and nobody's around—nobody big, I mean—

except me. And I'm standing on the edge of some crazy cliff. What I have to do, I have to catch everybody if they start to go over the cliff—I mean if they're running and they don't look where they're going I have to come out from somewhere and catch them. I'd just be the catcher in the rye. . . .

The irony in the preceding passage comes from our knowledge that the naive narrator, Holden Caulfield, cannot stop children from growing up. Ultimately, they all fall off the "crazy cliff" and mature into adults. Although Holden is not aware of the futility of trying to protect children from the dangers of adulthood, readers know that his efforts are doomed from the start.

A naive narrator's background can also limit his or her ability to understand a situation. The narrator in Sherwood Anderson's 1922 short story "I'm a Fool," for example, lies to impress a rich girl he meets at a racetrack. At the end of the story, the boy regrets the fact that he lied, believing that if he had told the truth, he could have seen the girl again. The reader knows, however, that the narrator (a laborer at the racetrack) is deceiving himself because the social gap that separates him and the girl could never be bridged.

Keep in mind that all first-person narrators are, in a sense, unreliable because they present a situation as only one person sees it. When you read, you should look for discrepancies between a narrator's view of events and your own. Discovering that a story has an unreliable narrator enables you not only to question the accuracy of the narrative but also to recognize the irony in the narrator's version of events. In this way, you gain insight into the story and learn something about the writer's purpose.

LO2 Recognize Third-Person Narrators

Sometimes a writer uses the **third person** (*he, she, they*) to tell the story from the point of view of a narrator who is not a character. Third-person narrators fall into three categories: **omniscient, limited omniscient,** and **objective.**

OMNISCIENT NARRATORS

Some third-person narrators are **omniscient** (all-knowing) narrators, moving at will from one character's mind to another's. One advantage of omniscient narrators is that they have none of the naïveté, dishonesty, gullibility, or mental instability that can characterize first-person narrators. In addition, because omniscient narrators are not characters in the story, their perception is not limited to what any one character can observe or comprehend. As a result, they can present a more inclusive view of events and characters than first-person narrators can.

Omniscient narrators can also convey their attitude toward their subject matter. For example, the omniscient narrator in "Once upon a Time," Nadine Gordimer's chilling 1991 story about South Africa under apartheid, uses sentence structure, word choice, and repetition to express distaste for the scene being described:

> In a house, in a suburb, in a city, there were a man and his wife who loved each other very much and were living happily ever after. They had a little boy, and they loved him very much. They had a cat and a dog that the little boy loved very much. They had a car and a caravan trailer for holidays, and a swimming-pool which was fenced so that the little boy and his playmates would not fall in and drown. They had a housemaid who was absolutely trustworthy and an itinerant gardener who was highly recommended by the neighbours. For when they began to live happily ever after they were warned, by that wise old witch, the husband's mother, not to take on anyone off the street.

Occasionally, omniscient narrators move not only in and out of the minds of the characters but also in and out of a **persona** (representing the voice of the author) who speaks directly to readers. This narrative technique was popular with writers during the eighteenth century, when the novel was a new literary form. It permitted writers to present themselves as masters of artifice, able to know and control all aspects of experience. Few contemporary writers would give themselves the license that Henry Fielding does in the following passage from *Tom Jones* (1749):

> And true it was that [Mr. Alworthy] did many of these things; but had he done nothing more I should have left him to have recorded his own merit on some fair freestone over the door of that hospital. Matters of a much more extraordinary kind are to be the subject of this history, or I should grossly misspend my time in writing so voluminous a work; and you my sagacious friend, might with equal profit and pleasure travel through some pages which certain droll authors have been facetiously pleased to call *The History of England*.

A contemporary example of this type of omniscient point of view occurs in Ursula K. LeGuin's "The Ones Who Walk Away from Omelas." This story presents a description of a city that in the narrator's words is "like a city in a fairy tale." As the story proceeds, however, the description of Omelas changes, and the narrator's tone changes as well: "Do you believe? Do you accept the festival, the city, the joy? No? Then let me describe one more thing." By undercutting her own narrative, the narrator underscores the ironic theme of the story, which suggests that it is impossible for human beings to ever achieve an ideal society.

LIMITED OMNISCIENT NARRATORS

Third-person narrators can have **limited omniscience**, focusing on only what a single character experiences. In other words, nothing is revealed that the character does not see, hear, feel, or think.

Limited omniscient narrators, like all third-person narrators, have certain advantages over first-person narrators. When a writer uses a first-person narrator, the narrator's personality and speech color the story, creating a personal or even an idiosyncratic narrative. Also, the first-person narrator's character flaws or lack of knowledge may limit his or her awareness of the significance of events. Limited omniscient narrators are more flexible: they take readers into a particular character's mind just as a first-person narrator does, but without the first-person narrator's subjectivity, self-deception, or naïveté. In the following example from Anne Tyler's 1984 story "Teenage Wasteland," the limited omniscient narrator presents the story from the point of view of a single character, Daisy:

> Daisy and Matt sat silent, shocked. Matt rubbed his forehead with his fingertips. Imagine, Daisy thought, how they must look to Mr. Lanham: an overweight housewife in a cotton dress and a too-tall, too-thin insurance agent in a baggy, frayed suit. Failures, both of them—the kind of people who are always hurrying to catch up, missing the point of things that everyone else grasps at once. She wished she'd worn nylons instead of knee socks.

Here the point of view gives readers the impression that they are standing off to the side watching Daisy and her husband Matt. However, at the same time that we have the advantage of this objective view, we are also able to see into the mind of one character.

OBJECTIVE NARRATORS

Third-person **objective narrators**, who tell a story from an objective (or dramatic) point of view, remain entirely outside the characters' minds. With objective narrators, events unfold the way they would in a play or a movie: narrators tell the story only by presenting dialogue and recounting events; they do not reveal the characters' (or their own) thoughts or attitudes. Thus, they allow readers to interpret the actions of the characters without any interference. Ernest Hemingway uses the objective point of view in his short story "A Clean, Well-Lighted Place" (1933):

> The waiter took the brandy bottle and another saucer from the counter inside the café and marched out to the old man's table. He put down the saucer and poured the glass full of brandy.
> "You should have killed yourself last week," he said to the deaf man. The old man motioned with his finger. "A little more," he said. The waiter poured on into the glass so that the brandy slopped over and ran down the

stem into the top saucer of the pile. "Thank you," the old man said. The waiter took the bottle back inside the café. He sat down at the table with his colleague again.

The story's narrator is distant, seemingly emotionless, and this perspective is consistent with the author's purpose: for Hemingway, the attitude of the narrator reflects the stunned, almost anesthetized condition of people in the post–World War I world.

LO3 Understand the Uses of Point of View

Writers of short stories often maintain a consistent point of view. The main criterion writers use when they decide on a point of view is how the point of view they select will affect their narrative. The stories that follow illustrate the options available to writers.

Shaun Tan (1974–)

was born in Ferth, Western Australia, and as a teenager began drawing illustrations for science fiction and horror stories. He has since become a critically acclaimed illustrator. Tan has collaborated on six picture book projects and is the author and illustrator of five picture books. A sixth, *Lost & Found: Three,* is forthcoming. With works such as *The Arrival* (2006), from which the following excerpt is taken, Tan captures fundamental human desires, needs, and behaviors in a stunning visual format. According to Tan, he chose migration as the subject for *The Arrival*

because "migration is a fundamental part of human history, both in the distant and recent past." Named Best Artist at the 2001 World Fantasy Awards in Montreal, Tan has also done illustration for film projects with Blue Sky and Pixar Studios.

© AP Photo/Ed Wray

Cultural Context
Shaun Tan's graphic novel belongs to the rich literary tradition of the epic journey. In Western literature, this tradition is largely defined by Homer's *Odyssey,* the tale of Odysseus, the king of Ithaca, returning home from the Trojan War on an epic nine-year journey. Since Homer's time, countless other writers—from Dante in *The Divine Comedy* to Miguel de Cervantes in *Don Quixote*— have used the hero's journey as a central theme in their work. As mythologist Joseph Campbell notes in his book *The Hero with a Thousand Faces* (1949), the "hero's journey" is a universal experience, one that cuts across times and cultures. Shaun Tan's graphic novel embodies a number of elements of the epic journey. Using the universal language of pictures, Tan tells the story of an immigrant making a journey to a new and mysterious place where he faces and overcomes challenges that suggest of the hero's journey that Campbell describes.

This graphic story starts on the next page.

from The Arrival (2006)

From THE ARRIVAL by Shaun Tan. Text and illustrations copyright © 2006 by Shaun Tan. Reprinted by permission of Scholastic, Inc.

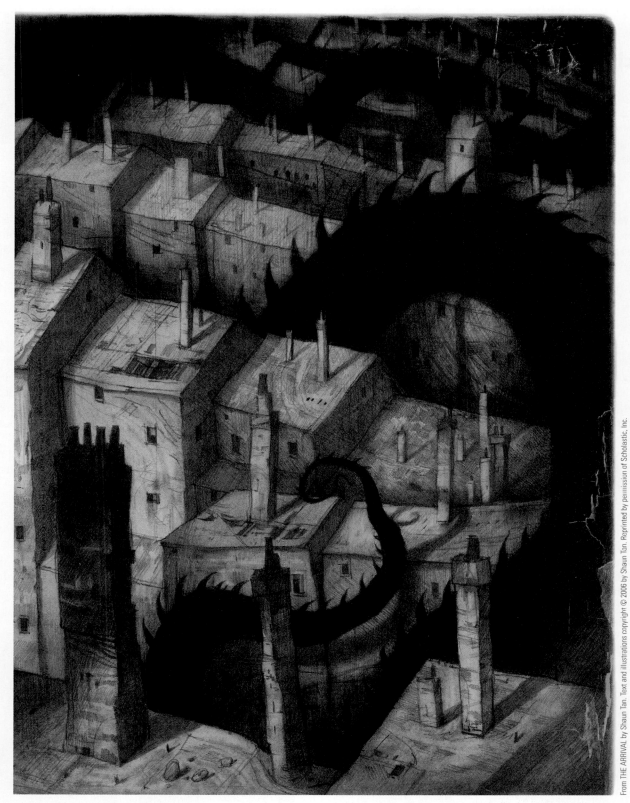

From THE ARRIVAL by Shaun Tan. Text and illustrations copyright © 2006 by Shaun Tan. Reprinted by permission of Scholastic, Inc.

Related Work

"Snow" (p. 102)

See Chapter 14 Review Card for Reading and Reacting questions about Shaun Tan, from *The Arrival*.

Richard Wright (1908–1960)

was born near Natchez, Mississippi, the son of sharecroppers. He had little formal schooling but as a young man was a voracious reader, especially of naturalistic fiction. Relocating to Chicago in the late 1920s, Wright worked as a postal clerk until 1935, when he joined the Federal Writers' Project, an association that took him to New York City. Deeply troubled by the economic and social oppression of African Americans, Wright joined the Communist Party in 1932, and his early poems and stories reflect a distinctly Marxist perspective. In 1944, he broke with the party because of its stifling effect on his creativity.

Wright began to reach a mainstream audience when a group of four long stories on the theme of racial oppression and violence was judged best manuscript in a contest sponsored by *Story* magazine; these stories were published as *Uncle Tom's Children* in 1938. Two years later,

Wright published his most famous work, *Native Son*, an angry and brutal novel exploring the moral devastation wrought by a racist society. The autobiographical *Black Boy* was published in 1945. Wright eventually left the United States for Paris in protest against the treatment of African Americans in his native country. His later work was concerned with national independence movements in Africa and elsewhere in the Third World.

The following story, published in the posthumous collection *Eight Men* (1961), is uncharacteristic of Wright's work in a number of ways—not least of which is that it is told through the eyes of a white protagonist.

Big Black Good Man (1957)

Through the open window Olaf Jenson could smell the sea and hear the occasional foghorn of a freighter; outside, rain pelted down through an August night, drumming softly upon the pavements of Copenhagen,° inducing drowsiness, bringing dreamy memory, relaxing the tired muscles of his work-wracked body. He sat slumped in a swivel chair with his legs outstretched and his feet propped atop an edge of his desk. An inch of white ash tipped the end of his brown cigar and now and then he inserted the end of the stogie° into his mouth and drew gently upon it, letting wisps of blue smoke eddy from the corners of his wide, thin lips. The watery gray irises behind the thick lenses of his eyeglasses gave him a look of abstraction, of absentmindedness, of an almost genial idiocy. He sighed, reached for his half-empty bottle of beer, and drained it into his glass and downed it with a long slow gulp, then licked his lips. Replacing the cigar, he slapped his right palm against his thigh and said half aloud:

"Well, I'll be sixty tomorrow. I'm not rich, but I'm not poor either . . . Really, I can't complain. Got good health. Traveled all over the world and had my share of girls when I was young . . . And my Karen's a good wife. I own my home. Got no debts. And I love digging in my garden in the spring . . . Grew the biggest carrots of anybody last year. Ain't saved much money, but what the hell . . . Money ain't everything. Got a good job. Night portering ain't too bad." He shook his head and yawned. "Karen and I could of had some children, though. Would of been good company . . . 'Specially for Karen. And I could of taught 'em languages . . . English, French, German, Danish, Dutch, Swedish, Norwegian, and Spanish . . ." He took the cigar

out of his mouth and eyed the white ash critically. "Hell of a lot of good language learning did me . . . Never got anything out of it. But those ten years in New York were fun . . . Maybe I could of got rich if I'd stayed in America . . . Maybe. But I'm satisfied. You can't have everything."

Behind him the office door opened and a young man, a medical student occupying room number nine, entered.

"Good evening," the student said.

"Good evening," Olaf said, turning. 5

The student went to the keyboard and took hold of the round, brown knob that anchored his key.

"Rain, rain, rain," the student said.

"That's Denmark for you," Olaf smiled at him.

"This dampness keeps me clogged up like a drainpipe," the student complained.

>> Waterfront, 1950s Copenhagen

° **Copenhagen** The capital of Denmark.
° **stogie** A cheap cigar.

> *"His chest bulged like a barrel; his rocklike and humped shoulders hinted of mountain ridges; the stomach ballooned like a threatening stone; and the legs were like telephone poles . . ."*

"That's Den-[10] mark for you," Olaf repeated with a smile.

"Good night," the student said.

"Good night, son," Olaf sighed, watching the door close.

Well, my tenants are my children, Olaf told himself. Almost all of his children were in their rooms now . . . Only seventy-two and forty-four were missing . . . Seventy-two might've gone to Sweden . . . And forty-four was maybe staying at his girl's place tonight, like he sometimes did . . . He studied the pear-shaped blobs of hard rubber, reddish brown like ripe fruit, that hung from the keyboard, then glanced at his watch. Only room thirty, eighty-one, and one hundred and one were empty . . . And it was almost midnight. In a few moments he could take a nap. Nobody hardly ever came looking for accommodations after midnight, unless a stray freighter came in, bringing thirsty, women-hungry sailors. Olaf chuckled softly. Why in hell was I ever a sailor? The whole time I was at sea I was thinking and dreaming about women. Then why didn't I stay on land where women could be had? Hunh? Sailors are crazy . . .

But he liked sailors. They reminded him of his youth, and there was something so direct, simple, and childlike about them. They always said straight out what they wanted, and what they wanted was almost always women and whisky . . . "Well, there's no harm in that . . . Nothing could be more natural," Olaf sighed, looking thirstily at his empty beer bottle. No; he'd not drink any more tonight; he'd had enough; he'd go to sleep . . .

He was bending forward and loosening his shoelaces [15] when he heard the office door crack open. He lifted his eyes, then sucked in his breath. He did not straighten; he just stared up and around at the huge black thing that filled the doorway. His reflexes refused to function; it was not fear; it was just simple astonishment. He was staring at the biggest, strangest, and blackest man he'd ever seen in all his life.

"Good evening," the black giant said in a voice that filled the small office. "Say, you got a room?"

Olaf sat up slowly, not to answer but to look at this brooding black vision; it towered darkly some six and a half feet into the air, almost touching the ceiling, and its skin was so black that it had a bluish tint. And the sheer bulk of the man! . . . His chest bulged like a barrel; his rocklike and humped shoulders hinted of mountain ridges; the stomach ballooned like a threatening stone; and the legs were like telephone poles . . . The big black cloud of a man now lumbered into the office, bending to get its buffalolike head under the door frame, then advanced slowly upon Olaf, like a stormy sky descending.

"You got a room?" the big black man asked again in a resounding voice.

Olaf now noticed that the ebony giant was well dressed, carried a wonderful new suitcase, and wore black shoes that gleamed despite the raindrops that peppered their toes.

"You're American?" Olaf asked him. [20]

"Yeah, man; sure," the black giant answered.

"Sailor?"

"Yeah. American Continental Lines."

Olaf had not answered the black man's question. It was not that the hotel did not admit men of color; Olaf took in all comers—blacks, yellows, whites, and browns . . . To Olaf, men were men, and, in his day, he'd worked and eaten and slept and fought with all kinds of men. But this particular black man . . . Well, he didn't seem human. Too big, too black, too loud, too direct, and probably too violent to boot . . . Olaf's five feet seven inches scarcely reached the black giant's shoulder and his frail body weighed less, perhaps, than one of the man's gigantic legs . . . There was something about the man's intense blackness and ungainly bigness that frightened and insulted Olaf; he felt as though this man had come here expressly to remind him how puny, how tiny, and how weak and how white he was. Olaf knew, while registering his reactions, that he was being irrational and foolish; yet, for the first time in his life, he was emotionally determined to refuse a man a room solely on the basis of the man's size and color . . . Olaf's lips parted as he groped for the right words in which to couch his refusal, but the black giant bent forward and boomed:

"I asked you if you got a room. I got to put up some- [25] where tonight, man."

"Yes, we got a room," Olaf murmured.

And at once he was ashamed and confused. Sheer fear had made him yield. And he seethed against himself for his involuntary weakness. Well, he'd look over his book and pretend that he'd made a mistake; he'd tell this hunk of

Cultural Context In 1957, the year "Big Black Good Man" was written, President Eisenhower sent paratroopers to Little Rock, Arkansas, to forestall violence over desegregation of the public schools. The crisis began on September 2, when Governor Orval Faubus ordered the Arkansas National Guard to blockade Central High School in Little Rock to prevent the entrance of nine black students. On September 20, NAACP lawyers Thurgood Marshall and Wiley Brandon obtained an injunction from the federal district court that ordered the troops removed. On September 25, the students entered the school, escorted by members of the 101st Airborne Division of the United States Army.

Peter Newark American Pictures/Bridgeman Art Library International

>> Parents and children protesting segregated schools in St. Louis, Missouri, 1957

blackness that there was really no free room in the hotel, and that he was so sorry ... Then, just as he took out the hotel register to make believe that he was poring over it, a thick roll of American bank notes, crisp and green, was thrust under his nose.

"Keep this for me, will you?" the black giant commanded. "Cause I'm gonna get drunk tonight and I don't wanna lose it."

Olaf stared at the roll; it was huge, in denominations of fifties and hundreds. Olaf's eyes widened.

"How much is there?" he asked. 30

"Two thousand six hundred," the giant said. "Just put it into an envelope and write 'Jim' on it and lock it in your safe, hunh?"

The black mass of man had spoken in a manner that indicated that it was taking it for granted that Olaf would obey. Olaf was licked. Resentment clogged the pores of his wrinkled white skin. His hands trembled as he picked up the money. No; he couldn't refuse this man ... The impulse to deny him was strong, but each time he was about to act upon it something thwarted him, made him shy off. He clutched about desperately for an idea. Oh yes, he could say that if he planned to stay for only one night, then he could not have the room, for it was against the policy of the hotel to rent rooms for only one night ...

"How long are you staying? Just tonight?" Olaf asked.

"Naw. I'll be here for five or six days, I reckon," the giant answered off handedly.

"You take room number thirty," Olaf heard himself 35 saying. "It's forty kroner a day."

"That's all right with me," the giant said.

With slow, stiff movements, Olaf put the money in the safe and then turned and stared helplessly up into the living, breathing blackness looming above him. Suddenly he became conscious of the outstretched palm of the black giant; he was silently demanding the key to the room. His eyes downcast, Olaf surrendered the key, marveling at the black man's tremendous hands ... He could kill me with one blow, Olaf told himself in fear.

Feeling himself beaten, Olaf reached for the suitcase, but the black hand of the giant whisked it out of his grasp.

"That's too heavy for you, big boy; I'll take it," the giant said.

Olaf let him. He thinks I'm nothing ... He led the 40 way down the corridor, sensing the giant's lumbering presence behind him. Olaf opened the door of number thirty and stood politely to one side, allowing the black giant to enter. At once the room seemed like a doll's house, so dwarfed and filled and tiny it was with a great living blackness ... Flinging his suitcase upon a chair, the giant turned. The two men looked directly at each other now. Olaf saw that the giant's eyes were tiny and red, buried, it seemed, in muscle and fat. Black cheeks spread, flat and broad, topping the wide and flaring nostrils. The mouth was the biggest that Olaf had ever seen on a human face; the lips were thick, pursed, parted, showing snow-white teeth. The black neck was like a bull's ... The giant advanced upon Olaf and stood over him.

"I want a bottle of whiskey and a woman," he said. "Can you fix me up?"

"Yes," Olaf whispered, wild with anger and insult.

But what was he angry about? He'd had requests like this every night from all sorts of men and he was used to fulfilling them; he was a night porter in a cheap, water-front Copenhagen hotel that catered to sailors and students. Yes, men needed women, but this man, Olaf felt, ought to have a special sort of woman. He felt a deep and strange reluctance to phone any of the women whom he habitually sent to men. Yet he had promised. Could he lie and say that none was available? No. That sounded too fishy. The black giant sat upon the bed, staring straight before him. Olaf moved about quickly, pulling down the window shades, taking the pink coverlet off the bed, nudging the giant with his elbow to make him move as he did so ... That's the way to treat 'im ... Show 'im I ain't scared of 'im ... But he was still seeking for an excuse to refuse. And he could think of nothing. He felt hypnotized, mentally immobilized. He stood hesitantly at the door.

"You send the whiskey and the woman quick, pal?" the black giant asked, rousing himself from a brooding stare.

"Yes," Olaf grunted, shutting the door. 45

Goddamn, Olaf sighed. He sat in his office at his desk before the phone. Why did *he* have to come here? ... I'm not prejudiced ... No, not at all ... But ... He couldn't think any more. God oughtn't make men as big and black as that . . . But what the hell was he worrying about? He'd sent women of all races to men of all colors . . . So why not a woman to the black giant? Oh, only if the man were small, brown, and intelligent-looking . . . Olaf felt trapped.

With a reflex movement of his hand, he picked up the phone and dialed Lena. She was big and strong and always cut him in for fifteen per cent instead of the usual ten per cent. Lena had four small children to feed and clothe. Lena was willing; she was, she said, coming over right now. She didn't give a good goddamn about how big and black the man was . . .

"Why you ask me that?" Lena wanted to know over the phone. "You never asked that before . . ."

"But this one is *big*," Olaf found himself saying.

"He's just a man," Lena told him, her voice singing stri- 50 dently, laughingly over the wire. "You just leave that to me. You don't have to do anything. *I'll* handle 'im."

Lena had a key to the hotel door downstairs, but tonight Olaf stayed awake. He wanted to see her. Why? He didn't know. He stretched out on the sofa in his office, but sleep was far from him. When Lena arrived, he told her again how big and black the man was.

"You told me that over the phone," Lena reminded him.

Olaf said nothing. Lena flounced off on her errand of mercy. Olaf shut the office door, then opened it and left it ajar. But why? He didn't know. He lay upon the sofa and stared at the ceiling. He glanced at his watch; it was almost two o'clock . . . She's staying in there a long time . . . Ah, God, but he could do with a drink . . . Why was he so damned worked up and nervous about a nigger and a white whore? . . . He'd never been so upset in all his life. Before he knew it, he had drifted off to sleep. Then he heard the office door swinging creakingly open on its rusty hinges. Lena stood in it, grim and businesslike, her face scrubbed free of powder and rouge. Olaf scrambled to his feet, adjusting his eyeglasses, blinking.

"How was it?" he asked her in a confidential whisper. Lena's eyes blazed. 55

"What the hell's that to you?" she snapped. "There's your cut," she said, flinging him his money, tossing it upon the covers of the sofa. "You're sure nosy tonight. You wanna take over my work?"

Olaf's pasty cheeks burned red.

"You go to hell," he said, slamming the door.

"I'll meet you there!" Lena's shouting voice reached him dimly.

He was being a fool; there was no doubt about it. But, 60 try as he might, he could not shake off a primitive hate for that black mountain of energy, of muscle, of bone; he envied the easy manner in which it moved with such a creeping and powerful motion; he winced at the booming and commanding voice that came to him when the tiny little eyes were not even looking at him; he shivered at the sight of those vast and clawlike hands that seemed always to hint of death . . .

Olaf kept his counsel. He never spoke to Karen about the sordid doings at the hotel. Such things were not for women like Karen. He knew instinctively that Karen would have been amazed had he told her that he was worried sick about a nigger and a blonde whore . . . No; he couldn't talk to anybody about it, not even the hard-bitten° old bitch who owned the hotel. She was concerned only about money; she didn't give a damn about how big and how black a client was as long as he paid his room rent.

Next evening, when Olaf arrived for duty, there was no sight or sound of the black giant. A little later after one o'clock in the morning he appeared, left his key, and went out wordlessly. A few moments past two the giant returned, took his key from the board, and paused.

"I want that Lena again tonight. And another bottle of whiskey," he said boomingly.

"I'll call her and see if she's in," Olaf said.

"Do that," the black giant said and was gone. 65

He thinks he's God, Olaf fumed. He picked up the phone and ordered Lena and a bottle of whiskey, and there was a taste of ashes in his mouth. On the third night came the same request: Lena and whiskey. When the black giant appeared on the fifth night, Olaf was about to make a sarcastic remark to the effect that maybe he ought to marry Lena, but he checked it in time . . . After all, he could kill me with one hand, he told himself.

Olaf was nervous and angry with himself for being nervous. Other black sailors came and asked for girls and Olaf sent them, but with none of the fear and loathing that he sent Lena and a bottle of whiskey to the giant . . . All right, the black giant's stay was almost up. He'd said that he was staying for five or six nights; tomorrow night was the sixth night and that ought to be the end of this nameless terror.

On the sixth night Olaf sat in his swivel chair with his bottle of beer and waited, his teeth on edge, his fingers drumming the desk. But what the hell am I fretting for? . . . The hell with 'im . . . Olaf sat and dozed. Occasionally he'd awaken and listen to the foghorns of freighters sounding as ships came and went in the misty Copenhagen harbor. He was half asleep when he felt a rough hand on his shoulder. He blinked his eyes open. The giant, black and vast and powerful, all but blotted out his vision.

"What I owe you, man?" the giant demanded. "And I want my money."

"Sure," Olaf said, relieved, but filled as always with 70 fear of this living wall of black flesh.

With fumbling hands, he made out the bill and received payment, then gave the giant his roll of money, laying it on the desk so as not to let his hands touch the flesh of the black mountain. Well, his ordeal was over. It was past two o'clock in the morning. Olaf even managed a wry smile and muttered a guttural "Thanks" for the generous tip that the giant tossed him.

° **hard-bitten** Stubborn, tough.

Then a strange tension entered the office. The office door was shut and Olaf was alone with the black mass of power, yearning for it to leave. But the black mass of power stood still, immobile, looking down at Olaf. And Olaf could not, for the life of him, guess at what was transpiring in that mysterious black mind. The two of them simply stared at each other for a full two minutes, the giant's tiny little beady eyes blinking slowly as they seemed to measure and search Olaf's face. Olaf's vision dimmed for a second as terror seized him and he could feel a flush of heat overspread his body. Then Olaf sucked in his breath as the devil of blackness commanded:

"Stand up!"

Olaf was paralyzed. Sweat broke on his face. His worst premonitions about this black beast were coming true. This evil blackness was about to attack him, maybe kill him . . . Slowly Olaf shook his head, his terror permitting him to breathe:

"What're you talking about?"   75

"Stand up, I say!" the black giant bellowed.

As though hypnotized, Olaf tried to rise; then he felt the black paw of the beast helping him roughly to his feet.

They stood an inch apart. Olaf's pasty-white features were glued to the giant's swollen black face. The ebony ensemble of eyes and nose and mouth and cheeks looked down at Olaf, silently; then, with a slow and deliberate movement of his gorillalike arms, he lifted his mammoth hands to Olaf's throat. Olaf had long known and felt that this dreadful moment was coming; he felt trapped in a nightmare. He could not move. He wanted to scream, but could find no words. His lips refused to open; his tongue felt icy and inert. Then he knew that his end had come when the giant's black fingers slowly, softly encircled his throat while a horrible grin of delight broke out on the sooty face . . . Olaf lost control of the reflexes of his body and he felt a hot stickiness flooding his underwear . . . He stared without breathing, gazing into the grinning blackness of the face that was bent over him, feeling the black fingers caressing his throat and waiting to feel the sharp, stinging ache and pain of the bones in his neck being snapped, crushed . . . He knew all along that I hated 'im . . . Yes, and now he's going to kill me for it, Olaf told himself with despair.

The black fingers still circled Olaf's neck, not closing, but gently massaging it, as it were, moving to and fro, while the obscene face grinned into his. Olaf could feel the giant's warm breath blowing on his eyelashes and he felt like a chicken about to have its neck wrung and its body tossed to flip and flap dyingly in the dust of the barnyard . . . Then suddenly the black giant withdrew his fingers from Olaf's neck and stepped back a pace, still grinning. Olaf sighed, trembling, his body seeming to shrink; he waited. Shame sheeted him for the hot wetness that was in his trousers. Oh, God, he's teasing me . . . He's showing me how easily he can kill me . . . He swallowed, waiting, his eyes stones of gray.

The giant's barrel-like chest gave forth a low, rum-   80
bling chuckle of delight.

"You laugh?" Olaf asked whimperingly.

"Sure I laugh," the giant shouted.

"Please don't hurt me," Olaf managed to say.

"I wouldn't hurt you, boy," the giant said in a tone of mockery. "So long."

And he was gone. Olaf fell limply into the swivel   85
chair and fought off losing consciousness. Then he wept. He was showing me how easily he could kill me . . . He made me shake with terror and then laughed and left . . . Slowly, Olaf recovered, stood, then gave vent to a string of curses:

"Goddamn 'im! My gun's right there in the desk drawer; I should of shot 'im. Jesus, I hope the ship he's on sinks . . . I hope he drowns and the sharks eat 'im . . ."

Later, he thought of going to the police, but sheer shame kept him back; and, anyway, the giant was probably on board his ship by now. And he had to get home and clean himself. Oh, Lord, what could he tell Karen? Yes, he would say that his stomach had been upset . . . He'd change clothes and return to work. He phoned the hotel owner that he was ill and wanted an hour off; the old bitch said that she was coming right over and that poor Olaf could have the evening off.

Olaf went home and lied to Karen. Then he lay awake the rest of the night dreaming of revenge. He saw that freighter on which the giant was sailing; he saw it springing a dangerous leak and saw a torrent of sea water flooding, gushing into all the compartments of the ship until it found the bunk in which the black giant slept. Ah, yes, the foamy, surging waters would surprise that sleeping black bastard of a giant and he would drown, gasping and choking like a trapped rat, his tiny eyes bulging until they glittered red, the bitter water of the sea pounding his lungs until they ached and finally burst . . . The ship would sink slowly to the bottom of the cold, black, silent depths of the sea and a shark, a *white* one, would glide aimlessly about the shut portholes until it found an open one and it would slither inside and nose about until it found that swollen, rotting, stinking carcass of the black beast and it would then begin to nibble at the decomposing mass of tarlike flesh, eating the bones clean . . . Olaf always pictured the giant's bones as being jet black and shining.

Once or twice, during these fantasies of cannibalistic revenge, Olaf felt a little guilty about all the many innocent people, women and children, all white and blonde, who would have to go down into watery graves in order that that white shark could devour the evil giant's black flesh . . . But, despite feelings of remorse, the fantasy lived persistently on, and when Olaf found himself alone, it would crowd and cloud his mind to the exclusion of all else, affording him the only revenge he knew. To make me suffer just for the pleasure of it, he fumed. Just to show me how strong he was . . . Olaf learned how to hate, and got pleasure out of it.

Summer fled on wings of rain. Autumn flooded Den-   90
mark with color. Winter made rain and snow fall on

Copenhagen. Finally spring came, bringing violets and roses. Olaf kept to his job. For many months he feared the return of the black giant. But when a year had passed and the giant had not put in an appearance, Olaf allowed his revenge fantasy to peter out, indulging in it only when recalling the shame that the black monster had made him feel.

Then one rainy August night, a year later, Olaf sat drowsing at his desk, his bottle of beer before him, tilting back in his swivel chair, his feet resting atop a corner of his desk, his mind mulling over the more pleasant aspects of his life. The office door cracked open. Olaf glanced boredly up and around. His heart jumped and skipped a beat. The black nightmare of terror and shame that he had hoped that he had lost forever was again upon him . . . Resplendently dressed, suitcase in hand, the black looming mountain filled the doorway. Olaf's thin lips parted and a silent moan, half a curse, escaped them.

"Hi," the black giant boomed from the doorway.

Olaf could not reply. But a sudden resolve swept him: this time he would even the score. If this black beast came within so much as three feet of him, he would snatch his gun out of the drawer and shoot him dead, so help him God . . .

"No rooms tonight," Olaf heard himself announcing in a determined voice.

The black giant grinned; it was the same infernal gri- 95 mace of delight and triumph that he had had when his damnable black fingers had been around his throat . . .

"Don't want no room tonight," the giant announced.

"Then what are you doing here?" Olaf asked in a loud but tremulous voice.

The giant swept toward Olaf and stood over him; and Olaf could not move, despite his oath to kill him . . .

"What do you want then?" Olaf demanded once more, ashamed that he could not lift his voice above a whisper.

The giant still grinned, then tossed what seemed the 100 same suitcase upon Olaf's sofa and bent over it; he zippered it open with a sweep of his clawlike hand and rummaged in it, drawing forth a flat, gleaming white object done up in glowing cellophane. Olaf watched with lowered lids, wondering what trick was now being played on him. Then, before he could defend himself, the giant had whirled and again long, black, snakelike fingers were encircling Olaf's throat . . . Olaf stiffened, his right hand clawing blindly for the drawer where the gun was kept. But the giant was quick.

"Wait," he bellowed, pushing Olaf back from the desk.

The giant turned quickly to the sofa and, still holding his fingers in a wide circle that seemed a noose for Olaf's neck, he inserted the rounded fingers into the top of the flat, gleaming object. Olaf had the drawer open and his sweaty fingers were now touching the gun, but something made him freeze. The flat, gleaming object was a shirt and the black giant's circled fingers were fitting themselves into its neck . . .

"A perfect fit!" the giant shouted.

Olaf stared, trying to understand. His fingers loosened about the gun. A mixture of a laugh and a curse struggled in him. He watched the giant plunge his hands into the suitcase and pull out other flat, gleaming shirts.

"One, two, three, four, five, six," the black giant in- 105 toned, his voice crisp and businesslike. "Six nylon shirts. And they're all yours. One shirt for each time Lena came . . . See, Daddy-O?"

The black, cupped hands, filled with billowing nylon whiteness, were extended under Olaf's nose. Olaf eased his damp fingers from his gun and pushed the drawer closed, staring at the shirts and then at the black giant's grinning face.

"Don't you like 'em?" the giant asked.

Olaf began to laugh hysterically, then suddenly he was crying, his eyes so flooded with tears that the pile of dazzling nylon looked like snow in the dead of winter. Was this true? Could he believe it? Maybe this too was a trick? But, no. There were six shirts, all nylon, and the black giant had had Lena six nights.

"What's the matter with you, Daddy-O?" the giant asked. "You blowing your top? Laughing and crying . . ."

Olaf swallowed, dabbed his withered fists at his 110 dimmed eyes; then he realized that he had his glasses on. He took them off and dried his eyes and sat up. He sighed, the tension and shame and fear and haunting dread of his fantasy went from him, and he leaned limply back in his chair . . .

"Try one on," the giant ordered.

Olaf fumbled with the buttons of his shirt, let down his suspenders, and pulled the shirt off. He donned a gleaming nylon one and the giant began buttoning it for him.

"Perfect, Daddy-O," the giant said.

His spectacled face framed in sparkling nylon, Olaf sat with trembling lips. So he'd not been trying to kill me after all.

"You want Lena, don't you?" he asked the giant in a 115 soft whisper. "But I don't know where she is. She never came back here after you left—"

"I know where Lena is," the giant told him. "We been writing to each other. I'm going to her house. And, Daddy-O, I'm late." The giant zippered the suitcase shut and stood a moment gazing down at Olaf, his tiny little red eyes blinking slowly. Then Olaf realized that there was a compassion in that stare that he had never seen before.

"And I thought you wanted to kill me," Olaf told him. "I was scared of you . . ."

"Me? Kill you?" the giant blinked. "When?"

"That night when you put your fingers around my throat—"

"What?" the giant asked, then roared with laughter. 120 "Daddy-O, you're a funny little man. I wouldn't hurt you. I like you. You a *good* man. You helped me."

Olaf smiled, clutching the pile of nylon shirts in his arms.

"You're a good man too," Olaf murmured. Then loudly, "You're a big black good man."

"Daddy-O, you're crazy," the giant said.

He swept his suitcase from the sofa, spun on his heel, and was at the door in one stride.

"Thanks!" Olaf cried after him.   125

The black giant paused, turned his vast black head, and flashed a grin.

"Daddy-O, drop dead," he said and was gone.

Related Works

"Buffalo Soldiers" (p. 105), "The Cask of Amontillado" (p. 190), *The Stronger* (p. 602)

 See Chapter 14 Review Card for Reading and Reacting questions about Richard Wright, "Big Black Good Man."

Edgar Allan Poe (1809–1849)

© AP Photo

profoundly influenced many writers all over the world. His tales of psychological terror and the macabre, his hauntingly musical lyric poems, and his writings on the craft of poetry and short story writing affected the development of symbolic fiction, the modern detective story, and the gothic horror tale. In most of Poe's horror tales (as in "The Cask of Amontillado"), readers vicariously "live" the story through the first-person narrator who tells the tale.

Poe was born in 1809, the son of a talented English-born actress who, deserted by her actor husband, died of tuberculosis before her son's third birthday. Although Poe was raised in material comfort by foster parents in Richmond, Virginia, his life was increasingly uncertain: his foster mother loved him, but her husband became antagonistic. He kept the young Poe so short of money at the University of Virginia (and later at West Point) that Poe resorted to gambling to raise money for food and clothing. Finally, disgraced and debt-ridden, he left school.

Poe found work as a magazine editor, gaining recognition as a literary critic. In 1836, he married his frail thirteen-year-old cousin, Virginia Clemm. Poe produced many of his most famous stories and poems in the next few years, working feverishly to support his tubercular wife, but although his stories were widely admired, he never achieved financial success. His wife died in 1847. Less than two years after her death, Poe was found barely conscious on a Baltimore street; three days later, he was dead at age forty.

The Cask of Amontillado (1846)

The thousand injuries of Fortunato I had borne as I best could, but when he ventured upon insult I vowed revenge. You, who so well know the nature of my soul, will not suppose, however, that I gave utterance to a threat. *At length* I would be avenged; this was a point definitely settled—but the very definitiveness with which it was resolved precluded the idea of risk. I must not only punish but punish with impunity. A wrong is unredressed when retribution overtakes its redresser. It is equally unredressed when the avenger fails to make himself felt as such to him who has done the wrong.

It must be understood that neither by word nor deed had I given Fortunato cause to doubt my good will. I continued, as was my wont, to smile in his face, and he did not perceive that my smile *now* was at the thought of his immolation.

He had a weak point—this Fortunato —although in other regards he was a man to be respected and even feared. He prided himself on his connoisseurship in wine. Few Italians have the true virtuoso spirit. For the most part their enthusiasm is adopted to suit the time and opportunity, to practise imposture upon the British and Austrian *millionaires*. In painting and gemmary, Fortunato, like his countrymen, was a quack, but in the matter of old wines he was sincere. In this respect I did not differ from him materially;—I was skillful in the Italian vintages myself, and bought largely whenever I could.

It was about dusk, one evening during the supreme madness of the carnival season, that I encountered my

Cultural Context Throughout antiquity, catacombs, such as those in Poe's story, were used to bury the dead. Catacombs are underground cemeteries composed of passages with recesses for tombs. The early Christian catacombs of Rome, consisting of approximately forty known chambers located in a rough circle about three miles from the center of the city, are the most extensive of all known catacombs. Funeral feasts were often celebrated in family vaults on the day of burial and on anniversary dates of the deaths of loved ones.

friend. He accosted me with excessive warmth, for he had been drinking much. The man wore motley.° He had on a tight-fitting parti-striped dress, and his head was surmounted by the conical cap and bells. I was so pleased to see him that I thought I should never have done wringing his hand.

I said to him—"My dear Fortunato, you are luckily 5 met. How remarkably well you are looking to-day. But I have received a pipe° of what passes for Amontillado,° and I have my doubts."

"How?" said he. "Amontillado? A pipe? Impossible! And in the middle of the carnival!"

"I have my doubts," I replied; "and I was silly enough to pay the full Amontillado price without consulting you in the matter. You were not to be found, and I was fearful of losing a bargain."

"Amontillado!"

"I have my doubts."

"Amontillado!" 10

"And I must satisfy them."

"Amontillado!"

"As you are engaged, I am on my way to Luchresi. If any one has a critical turn it is he. He will tell me—"

"Luchresi cannot tell Amontillado from Sherry."

"And yet some fools will have it that his taste is a 15 match for your own."

"Come, let us go."

"Whither?"

"To your vaults."

"My friend, no; I will not impose upon your good nature. I perceive you have an engagement. Luchresi—"

"I have no engagement;—come." 20

"My friend, no. It is not the engagement, but the severe cold with which I perceive you are afflicted. The vaults are insufferably damp. They are encrusted with nitre."°

"Let us go, nevertheless. The cold is merely nothing. Amontillado! You have been imposed upon. And as for Luchresi, he cannot distinguish Sherry from Amontillado."

Thus speaking, Fortunato possessed himself of my arm; and putting on a mask of black silk and drawing a *roquelaire°* closely about my person, I suffered him to hurry me to my palazzo.

There were no attendants at home; they had absconded to make merry in honor of the time. I had told them that I should not return until the morning, and had given them explicit orders not to stir from the house. These orders were sufficient, I well knew, to insure their immediate disappearance, one and all, as soon as my back was turned.

I took from their sconces two flambeaux, and giving 25 one to Fortunato, bowed him through several suites of rooms to the archway that led into the vaults. I passed down a long and winding staircase, requesting him to be cautious as he followed. We came at length to the foot of the descent, and stood together upon the damp ground of the catacombs of the Montresors.

>> Staircase to catacombs

The gait of my friend was unsteady, and the bells upon his cap jingled as he strode.

"The pipe," he said.

"It is farther on," said I; "but observe the white webwork which gleams from these cavern walls."

He turned towards me, and looked into my eyes with two filmy orbs that distilled the rheum of intoxication.

"Nitre?" he asked at length. 30

"Nitre," I replied. "How long have you had that cough?"

"Ugh! ugh! ugh!—ugh! ugh! ugh!—ugh! ugh! ugh!—ugh! ugh! ugh!—ugh! ugh! ugh!"

My poor friend found it impossible to reply for many minutes.

"It is nothing," he said at last.

° **motley** The many-colored attire of a court jester.

° **pipe** In the United States and England, a cask containing a volume equal to 126 gallons.

° **Amontillado** A pale, dry sherry; literally, a wine "from Montilla" (Spain)

° **nitre** Mineral deposits.

° *roquelaire* A short cloak.

>> A family coat of arms

"Come," I said, with decision, "we will go back; your health is precious. You are rich, respected, admired, beloved; you are happy, as once I was. You are a man to be missed. For me it is no matter. We will go back; you will be ill, and I cannot be responsible. Besides, there is Luchresi—"

"Enough," he said; "the cough is a mere nothing; it will not kill me. I shall not die of a cough."

"True—true," I replied; "and, indeed, I had no intention of alarming you unnecessarily—but you should use all proper caution. A draught of this Médoc° will defend us from the damps."

Here I knocked off the neck of a bottle which I drew from a long row of its fellows that lay upon the mould.

° **Médoc** A red wine from the Médoc district, near Bordeaux, France.

° ***Nemo me impune lacessit*** "No one insults me with impunity" (Latin); this is the legend on the royal coat of arms of Scotland.

° **puncheons** Barrels.

° **De Grâve** Correctly, "Graves," a light wine from the Bordeaux area.

° **masons** Freemasons (members of a secret fraternity). The trowel is a symbol of their alleged origin as a guild of stonemasons.

"Drink," I said, presenting him the wine.

He raised it to his lips with a leer. He paused and nodded to me familiarly, while his bells jingled.

"I drink," he said, "to the buried that repose around us."

"And I to your long life."

He again took my arm, and we proceeded.

"These vaults," he said, "are extensive."

"The Montresors," I replied, "were a great and numerous family."

"I forget your arms."

"A huge human foot d'or, in a field azure; the foot crushes a serpent rampant whose fangs are imbedded in the heel."

"And the motto?"

"*Nemo me impune lacessit.*"°

"Good!" he said.

The wine sparkled in his eyes and the bells jingled. My own fancy grew warm with the Médoc. We had passed through long walls of piled skeletons, with casks and puncheons° intermingling, into the inmost recesses of the catacombs. I paused again, and this time I made bold to seize Fortunato by an arm above the elbow.

"The nitre!" I said; "see, it increases. It hangs like moss upon the vaults. We are below the river's bed. The drops of moisture trickle among the bones. Come, we will go back ere it is too late. Your cough—"

"It is nothing," he said; "let us go on. But first, another draught of the Médoc."

I broke and reached him a flagon of De Grâve.° He emptied it at a breath. His eyes flashed with a fierce light. He laughed and threw the bottle upwards with a gesticulation I did not understand.

I looked at him in surprise. He repeated the movement—a grotesque one.

"You do not comprehend?" he said.

"Not I," I replied.

"Then you are not of the brotherhood."

"How?"

"You are not of the masons."°

"Yes, yes," I said; "yes, yes."

"You? Impossible! A mason?"

"A mason," I replied.

"A sign," he said, "a sign."

"It is this," I answered, producing from beneath the folds of my *roquelaire* a trowel.

"You jest," he exclaimed, recoiling a few paces. "But let us proceed to the Amontillado."

"Be it so," I said, replacing the tool beneath the cloak and again offering him my arm. He leaned upon it heavily. We continued our route in search of the Amontillado. We passed through a range of low arches, descended, passed on, and descending again, arrived at a deep crypt, in which the foulness of the air caused our flambeaux rather to glow than flame.

At the most remote end of the crypt there appeared another less spacious. Its walls had been lined with human remains, piled to the vault overhead, in the fashion of the great catacombs of Paris. Three sides of this interior crypt were still ornamented in this manner. From the fourth side the bones had been thrown down, and lay promiscuously upon the earth, forming at one point a mound of some size. Within the wall thus exposed by the displacing of the bones, we perceived a still interior crypt or recess, in depth about four feet, in width three, in height six or seven. It seemed to have been constructed for no especial use within itself, but formed merely the interval between two of the colossal supports of the roof of the catacombs, and was backed by one of their circumscribing walls of solid granite.

It was in vain that Fortunato, uplifting his dull torch, endeavored to pry into the depth of the recess. Its termination the feeble light did not enable us to see.

"Proceed," I said; "herein is the Amontillado. As for 70 Luchresi—"

"He is an ignoramus," interrupted my friend, as he stepped unsteadily forward, while I followed immediately at his heels. In an instant he had reached the extremity of the niche, and finding his progress arrested by the rock, stood stupidly bewildered. A moment more and I had fettered him to the granite. In its surface were two iron staples, distant from each other about two feet, horizontally. From one of these depended a short chain, from the other a padlock. Throwing the links about his waist, it was but the work of a few seconds to secure it. He was too much astounded to resist. Withdrawing the key I stepped back from the recess.

> *"In an instant he had reached the extremity of the niche, and finding his progress arrested by the rock, stood stupidly bewildered. A moment more and I had fettered him to the granite."*

"Pass your hand," I said, "over the wall; you cannot help feeling the nitre. Indeed, it is *very* damp. Once more let me *implore* you to return. No? Then I must positively leave you. But I must first render you all the little attentions in my power."

"The Amontillado!" ejaculated my friend, not yet recovered from his astonishment.

"True," I replied; "the Amontillado."

As I said these words I busied myself among the pile 75 of bones of which I have before spoken. Throwing them aside, I soon uncovered a quantity of building stone and mortar. With these materials and with the aid of my trowel, I began vigorously to wall up the entrance of the niche.

I had scarcely laid the first tier of the masonry when I discovered that the intoxication of Fortunato had in a great measure worn off. The earliest indication I had of this was a low moaning cry from the depth of the recess. It was *not* the cry of a drunken man. There was a long and obstinate silence. I laid the second tier, and the third, and the fourth; and then I heard the furious vibrations of the chain. The noise lasted for several minutes, during which, that I might hearken to it with the more satisfaction, I ceased my labors and sat down upon the bones. When at last the clanking subsided, I resumed the trowel, and finished without interruption the fifth, the sixth, and the seventh tier. The wall was now nearly upon a level with my breast. I again paused, and holding the flambeaux over the mason-work, threw a few feeble rays upon the figure within.

A succession of loud and shrill screams, bursting suddenly from the throat of the chained form, seemed to thrust me violently back. For a brief moment I hesitated, I trembled. Unsheathing my rapier, I began to grope with it about the recess; but the thought of an instant reassured me. I placed my hand upon the solid fabric of the catacombs, and felt satisfied. I reapproached the wall; I replied to the yells of him who clamoured. I re-echoed, I aided, I surpassed them in volume and in strength. I did this, and the clamourer grew still.

>> Illustration from Edgar Allan Poe's story, "The Cask of Amontillado"

It was now midnight, and my task was drawing to a close. I had completed the eighth, the ninth and the tenth tier. I had finished a portion of the last and the eleventh; there remained but a single stone to be fitted and plastered in. I struggled with its weight; I placed it partially in its destined position. But now there came from out the niche a low laugh that erected the hairs upon my head. It was succeeded by a sad voice, which I had difficulty in recognizing as that of the noble Fortunato. The voice said—

"Ha! ha! ha!—he! he! he!—a very good joke, indeed—an excellent jest. We will have many a rich laugh about it at the palazzo—he! he! he!—over our wine—he! he! he!"

"The Amontillado!" I said.

"He! he! he!—he! he! he!—yes, the Amontillado. But is it not getting late? Will not they be awaiting us at the palazzo, the Lady Fortunato and the rest? Let us be gone."

"Yes," I said, "let us be gone."

"For the love of God, Montresor!"

"Yes," I said, "for the love of God."

But to these words I hearkened in vain for a reply. I 85 grew impatient. I called aloud—

"Fortunato!"

No answer. I called again—

"Fortunato!"

No answer still. I thrust a torch through the remaining aperture and let it fall within. There came forth in return only a jingling of the bells. My heart grew sick; it was the dampness of the catacombs that made it so. I hastened to make an end of my labour. I forced the last stone into its position; I plastered it up. Against the new masonry I re-erected the old rampart of bones. For the half of a century no mortal has disturbed them. *In pace requiescat!*°

Related Works

"A Rose for Emily" (p. 121), "Porphyria's Lover" (p. 375), *Tape* (p. 543), *Trifles* (p. 555)

See Chapter 14 Review Card for Reading and Reacting questions about Edgar Allan Poe, "The Cask of Amontillado."

° *In pace requiescat* "May he rest in peace" (Latin).

William Faulkner (1897–1962)

(picture and biography on p. 121) "Barn Burning" (1939) marks the first appearance of the Snopes clan in Faulkner's fiction. These ruthless, conniving, and unappealing poor white tenant farmers and traders run roughshod over the aristocratic families of Yoknapatawpha County in three Faulkner novels: *The Hamlet* (1940), *The Town* (1957), and *The Mansion* (1959). According to Ben Wasson in *Count No Count*, Faulkner once told a friend that "somebody said I was a genius writer. The only thing I'd claim genius for is thinking up that name *Snopes*." In Southern literary circles, at least, the name "Snopes" still serves as a shorthand term for the graceless and greedy (but frequently successful) opportunists of the "New South."

Barn Burning (1939)

The store in which the Justice of the Peace's court was sitting smelled of cheese. The boy, crouched on his nail keg at the back of the crowded room, knew he smelled cheese, and more: from where he sat he could see the ranked shelves close-packed with the solid, squat, dynamic shapes of tin cans whose labels his stomach read, not from the lettering which meant nothing to his mind but from the scarlet devils and the silver curve of fish—this, the cheese which he knew he smelled and the hermetic° meat which his intestines believed he smelled coming in intermittent gusts momentary and brief between the other constant one, the smell and sense just a little of fear because mostly of despair and grief, the old fierce pull of blood. He could

not see the table where the Justice sat and before which his father and his father's enemy (*our enemy* he thought in that despair; *ourn! mine and hisn both! He's my father!*) stood, but he could hear them, the two of them that is, because his father had said no word yet:

"But what proof have you, Mr. Harris?"

"I told you. The hog got into my corn. I caught it up and sent it back to him. He had no fence that would hold it. I told him so, warned him. The next time I put the hog in my pen. When he came to get it I gave him enough wire to patch up his pen. The next time I put the hog up and kept it. I rode down to his house and saw the wire I gave him still rolled on to the spool in his yard. I told him he could have the hog when he paid me a dollar pound fee. That evening a nigger came with the dollar and got the hog. He was a strange nigger. He said, 'He say to tell you wood and hay kin burn.' I said, 'What?'

° **hermetic** Canned.

'That whut he say to tell you,' the nigger said. 'Wood and hay kin burn.' That night my barn burned. I got the stock out but I lost the barn."

"Where is the nigger? Have you got him?"

"He was a strange nigger, I tell you. I don't know what became of him." 5

"But that's not proof. Don't you see that's not proof?"

"Get that boy up here. He knows." For a moment the boy thought too that the man meant his older brother until Harris said, "Not him. The little one. The boy," and, crouching, small for his age, small and wiry like his father, in patched and faded jeans even too small for him, with straight, uncombed, brown hair and eyes gray and wild as storm scud, he saw the men between himself and the table part and become a lane of grim faces, at the end of which he saw the Justice, a shabby, collarless, graying man in spectacles, beckoning him. He felt no floor under his bare feet; he seemed to walk beneath the palpable weight of the grim turning faces. His father, stiff in his black Sunday coat donned not for the trial but for the moving, did not even look at him. *He aims for me to lie,* he thought, again with that frantic grief and despair. *And I will have to do hit.*

"What's your name, boy?" the Justice said.

"Colonel Sartoris Snopes," the boy whispered.

"Hey?" the Justice said. "Talk louder. Colonel Sarto- 10 ris? I reckon anybody named for Colonel Sartoris in this country can't help but tell the truth, can they?" The boy said nothing. *Enemy! Enemy!* he thought; for a moment he could not even see, could not see that the Justice's face was kindly nor discern that his voice was troubled when he spoke to the man named Harris: "Do you want me to question this boy?" But he could hear, and during those subsequent long seconds while there was absolutely no sound in the crowded little room save that of quiet and intent breathing it was as if he had swung outward at the end of a grape vine, over a ravine, and at the top of the swing had been caught in a prolonged instant of mesmerized gravity, weightless in time.

"No!" Harris said violently, explosively. "Damnation! Send him out of here!" Now time, the fluid world, rushed beneath him again, the voices coming to him again through the smell of cheese and sealed meat, the fear and despair and the old grief of blood:

Cultural Context

Tenant farming is a system of agriculture in which landowners contribute their land while tenants contribute labor. One form of tenant farming, known as sharecropping, required the landowner to furnish all the capital (and usually the food, clothing, and shelter) to the tenant in return for labor. Given the way the system worked, the sharecropper was lucky to end the year without owing money to the landowner. In "Barn Burning," Abner Snopes is a poor sharecropper who takes out his frustrations against the post–Civil War aristocracy of landowners.

"This case is closed. I can't find against you, Snopes, but I can give you advice. Leave this country and don't come back to it."

His father spoke for the first time, his voice cold and harsh, level, without emphasis: "I aim to. I don't figure to stay in a country among people who . . ." he said something unprintable and vile, addressed to no one.

"That'll do," the Justice said. "Take your wagon and get out of this country before dark. Case dismissed."

His father turned, and he followed the stiff black coat, 15 the wiry figure walking a little stiffly from where a Confederate provost's man's° musket ball had taken him in the heel on a stolen horse thirty years ago, followed the two backs now, since his older brother had appeared from somewhere in the crowd, no taller than the father but thicker, chewing tobacco steadily, between the two lines of grim-faced men and out of the store and across the worn gallery and down the sagging steps and among the dogs and half-grown boys in the mild May dust, where as he passed a voice hissed:

"Barn burner!"

Again he could not see, whirling; there was a face in a red haze, moonlike, bigger than the full moon, the owner of it half again his size, he leaping in the red haze toward the face, feeling no blow, feeling no shock when his head struck the earth, scrabbling up and leaping again, feeling no blow this time either and tasting no blood, scrabbling up to see the other boy in full flight and himself already leaping into pursuit as his father's hand jerked him back, the harsh, cold voice speaking above him: "Go get in the wagon."

It stood in a grove of locusts and mulberries across the road. His two hulking sisters in their Sunday dresses and his mother and her sister in calico and sunbonnets were already in it, sitting on and among the sorry residue of the dozen and more movings which even the boy could remember—the battered stove, the broken beds and chairs, the clock inlaid with mother-of-pearl, which would not run, stopped at some fourteen minutes past two o'clock of a dead and forgotten day and time, which had been his mother's dowry. She was crying, though when she saw him she drew her sleeve across her face and began to descend from the wagon. "Get back," the father said.

"He's hurt. I got to get some water and wash his . . ."

° **provost's man's** Military policeman's.

>> 1930s sharecropper cabin in the South

"Get back in the wagon," his father said. He got in too, over the tail-gate. His father mounted to the seat where the older brother already sat and struck the gaunt mules two savage blows with the peeled willow, but without heat. It was not even sadistic; it was exactly that same quality which in later years would cause his descendants to overrun the engine before putting a motor car into motion, striking and reining back in the same movement. The wagon went on, the store with its quiet crowd of grimly watching men dropped behind; a curve in the road hid it. *Forever* he thought. *Maybe he's done satisfied now, now that he has* . . . stopping himself, not to say it aloud even to himself. His mother's hand touched his shoulder.

"Does hit hurt?" she said.

"Naw," he said. "Hit don't hurt. Lemme be."

"Can't you wipe some of the blood off before hit dries?"

"I'll wash to-night," he said. "Lemme be, I tell you."

The wagon went on. He did not know where they were going. None of them ever did or ever asked, because it was always somewhere, always a house of sorts waiting for them a day or two days or even three days away. Likely his father had already arranged to make a crop on another farm before he . . . Again he had to stop himself. He (the father) always did. There was something about his wolf-like independence and even courage when the advantage was at least neutral which impressed strangers, as if they got from his latent ravening ferocity not so much a sense of dependability as a feeling that his ferocious conviction in the rightness of his own actions would be of advantage to all whose interest lay with his.

That night they camped, in a grove of oaks and beeches where a spring ran. The nights were still cool and they had a fire against it, of a rail lifted from a nearby fence and cut into lengths—a small fire, neat, niggard almost, a shrewd fire; such fires were his father's habit and custom always, even in freezing weather. Older, the boy might have remarked this and wondered why not a big

one; why should not a man who had not only seen the waste and extravagance of war, but who had in his blood an inherent voracious prodigality with material not his own, have burned everything in sight? Then he might have gone a step farther and thought that that was the reason: that niggard blaze was the living fruit of nights passed during those four years in the woods hiding from all men, blue or gray, with his strings of horses (captured horses, he called them). And older still, he might have divined the true reason: that the element of fire spoke to some deep mainspring of his father's being, as the element of steel or of powder spoke to other men, as the one weapon for the preservation of integrity, else breath were not worth the breathing, and hence to be regarded with respect and used with discretion.

But he did not think this now and he had seen those same niggard blazes all his life. He merely ate his supper beside it and was already half asleep over his iron plate when his father called him, and once more he followed the stiff back, the stiff and ruthless limp, up the slope and on to the starlit road where, turning, he could see his father against the stars but without face or depth—a shape black, flat, and bloodless as though cut from tin in the iron folds of the frockcoat which had not been made for him, the voice harsh like tin and without heat like tin:

"You were fixing to tell them. You would have told him." He didn't answer. His father struck him with the flat of his hand on the side of the head, hard but without heat, exactly as he had struck the two mules at the store, exactly as he would strike either of them with any stick in order to kill a horse fly, his voice still without fear or anger: "You're getting to be a man. You got to learn. You got to learn to stick to your own blood or you ain't going to have any blood to stick to you. Do you think either of them, any man there this morning, would? Don't you know all they wanted was a chance to get at me because they knew I had them beat? Eh?" Later, twenty years later, he was to tell himself, "If I had said they wanted only truth, justice, he would have hit me again." But now he said nothing. He was not crying. He just stood there. "Answer me," his father said.

"Yes," he whispered. His father turned.

"Get on to bed. We'll be there tomorrow."

Tomorrow they were there. In the early afternoon the wagon stopped before a paintless two-room house identical almost with the dozen others it had stopped before even in the boy's ten years, and again, as on the other dozen occasions, his mother and aunt got down and began to unload the wagon, although his two sisters and his father and brother had not moved.

"Likely hit ain't fitten for hawgs," one of the sisters said.

"Nevertheless, fit it will and you'll hog it and like it," his father said. "Get out of them chairs and help your Ma unload."

The two sisters got down, big, bovine, in a flutter of cheap ribbons; one of them drew from the jumbled wagon

>> Burning barn

bed a battered lantern, the other a worn broom. His father handed the reins to the older son and began to climb stiffly over the wheel. "When they get unloaded, take the team to the barn and feed them." Then he said, and at first the boy thought he was still speaking to his brother: "Come with me."

"Me?" he said.

"Yes," his father said. "You."

"Abner," his mother said. His father paused and looked back—the harsh level stare beneath the shaggy, graying, irascible brows.

"I reckon I'll have a word with the man that aims to begin tomorrow owning me body and soul for the next eight months."

They went back up the road. A week ago—or before last night, that is—he would have asked where they were going, but not now. His father had struck him before last night but never before had he paused afterward to explain why; it was as if the blow and the following calm, outrageous voice still rang, repercussed, divulging nothing to him save the terrible handicap of being young, the light weight of his few years, just heavy enough to prevent his soaring free of the world as it seemed to be ordered but not heavy enough to keep him footed solid in it, to resist it and try to change the course of its events.

Presently he could see the grove of oaks and cedars and the other flowering trees and shrubs, where the house would be, though not the house yet. They walked beside a fence massed with honeysuckle and Cherokee roses and came to a gate swinging open between two brick pillars, and now, beyond a sweep of drive, he saw the house for

the first time and at that instant he forgot his father and the terror and despair both, and even when he remembered his father again (who had not stopped) the terror and despair did not return. Because, for all the twelve movings, they had sojourned until now in a poor country, a land of small farms and fields and houses, and he had never seen a house like this before. *Hit's big as a courthouse* he thought quietly, with a surge of peace and joy whose reason he could not have thought into words, being too young for that: *They are safe from him. People whose lives are a part of this peace and dignity are beyond his touch, he no more to them than a buzzing wasp: capable of stinging for a little moment but that's all; the spell of this peace and dignity rendering even the barns and stable and cribs which belong to it impervious to the puny flames he might contrive* . . . this, the peace and joy, ebbing for an instant as he looked again at the stiff black back, the stiff and implacable limp of the figure which was not dwarfed by the house, for the reason that it had never looked big anywhere and which now, against the serene columned backdrop, had more than ever that impervious quality of something cut ruthlessly from tin, depthless, as though, sidewise to the sun, it would cast no shadow. Watching him, the boy remarked the absolutely undeviating course which his father held and saw the stiff foot come squarely down in a pile of fresh droppings where a horse had stood in the drive and which his father could have avoided by a simple change of stride. But it ebbed only for a moment, though he could not have thought this into words either, walking on in the spell of the house, which he could even want but without envy, without sorrow, certainly never with that ravening and jealous rage which unknown to him walked in the ironlike black coat before him: *Maybe he will feel it too. Maybe it will even change him now from what maybe he couldn't help but be.*

They crossed the portico. Now he could hear his father's stiff foot as it came down on the boards with clocklike finality, a sound out of all proportion to the displacement of the body it bore and which was not dwarfed either by the white door before it, as though it had attained to a sort of vicious and ravening minimum not to be dwarfed by anything—the flat, wide, black hat, the formal coat of broadcloth which had once been black but which had now that friction-glazed greenish cast of the bodies of old house flies, the lifted sleeve which was too large, the lifted hand like a curled claw. The door opened so promptly that the boy knew the Negro must have been watching them all the time, an old man with neat grizzled hair, in a linen jacket, who stood barring the door with his body, saying, "Wipe yo foots, white man, fo you come in here. Major ain't home nohow."

"Get out of my way, nigger," his father said, without heat too, flinging the door back and the Negro also and entering, his hat still on his head. And now the boy saw the prints of the stiff foot on the doorjamb and saw them appear on the pale rug behind the machinelike deliberation of the foot which seemed to bear (or transmit) twice the

35

40

>> Tommy Lee Jones as Ab Snopes in film version of "Barn Burning."

drag round the arc of the turning, leaving a final long and fading smear. His father never looked at it, he never once looked down at the rug. The Negro held the door. It closed behind them, upon the hysteric and indistinguishable woman-wail. His father stopped at the top of the steps and scraped his boot clean on the edge of it. At the gate he stopped again. He stood for a moment, planted stiffly on the stiff foot, looking back at the house. "Pretty and white, ain't it?" he said. "That's sweat. Nigger sweat. Maybe it ain't white enough yet to suit him. Maybe he wants to mix some white sweat with it."

Two hours later the boy was chopping wood behind the house within which his mother and aunt and the two sisters (the mother and aunt, not the two girls, he knew that; even at this distance and muffled by walls the flat loud voices of the two girls emanated an incorrigible idle inertia) were setting up the stove to prepare a meal, when he heard the hooves and saw the linen-clad man on a fine sorrel mare, whom he recognized even before he saw the rolled rug in front of the Negro youth following on a fat bay carriage horse—a suffused, angry face vanishing, still at full gallop, beyond the corner of the house where his father and brother were sitting in the two tilted chairs; and a moment later, almost before he could have put the axe down, he heard the hooves again and watched the sorrel mare go back out of the yard, already galloping again. Then his father began to shout one of the sisters' names, who presently emerged backward from the kitchen door dragging the rolled rug along the ground by one end while the other sister walked behind it.

"If you ain't going to tote, go on and set up the wash pot," the first said.

"You, Sarty!" the second shouted. "Set up the wash pot!" His father appeared at the door, framed against that shabbiness, as he had been against that other bland perfection, impervious to either, the mother's anxious face at his shoulder.

"Go on," the father said. "Pick it up." The two sisters stooped, broad, lethargic; stooping, they presented an incredible expanse of pale cloth and a flutter of tawdry ribbons.

"If I thought enough of a rug to have to git hit all the way from France I wouldn't keep hit where folks coming in would have to tromp on hit," the first said. They raised the rug. [50]

"Abner," the mother said. "Let me do it."

"You go back and git dinner," his father said. "I'll tend to this."

From the woodpile through the rest of the afternoon the boy watched them, the rug spread flat in the dust beside the bubbling wash-pot, the two sisters stooping over it with that profound and lethargic reluctance, while the father stood over them in turn, implacable and grim, driving them though never raising his voice again. He could smell the harsh home-made lye° they were using; he saw his mother come to the door once and look toward them with an expression not anxious now but very like despair; he saw his father turn,

weight which the body compassed. The Negro was shouting "Miss Lula! Miss Lula!" somewhere behind them, then the boy, deluged as though by a warm wave by a suave turn of carpeted stair and a pendant glitter of chandeliers and a mute gleam of gold frames, heard the swift feet and saw her too, a lady—perhaps he had never seen her like before either—in a gray, smooth gown with lace at the throat and an apron tied at the waist and the sleeves turned back, wiping cake or biscuit dough from her hands with a towel as she came up the hall, looking not at his father at all but at the tracks on the blond rug with an expression of incredulous amazement.

"I tried," the Negro cried, "I tole him to . . ."

"Will you please go away?" she said in a shaking voice. "Major de Spain is not at home. Will you please go away?"

His father had not spoken again. He did not speak [45] again. He did not even look at her. He just stood stiff in the center of the rug, in his hat, the shaggy iron-gray brows twitching slightly above the pebble-colored eyes as he appeared to examine the house with brief deliberation. Then with the same deliberation he turned; the boy watched him pivot on the good leg and saw the stiff foot

---

°**lye** A soap made from wood ashes and water, unsuitable for washing fine fabrics.

and he fell to with the axe and saw from the corner of his eye his father raise from the ground a flattish fragment of field stone and examine it and return to the pot, and this time his mother actually spoke: "Abner. Abner. Please don't. Please, Abner."

Then he was done too. It was dusk; the whippoorwills had already begun. He could smell coffee from the room where they would presently eat the cold food remaining from the mid-afternoon meal, though when he entered the house he realized they were having coffee again probably because there was a fire on the hearth, before which the rug now lay spread over the backs of the two chairs. The tracks of his father's foot were gone. Where they had been were now long, water-cloudy scoriations resembling the sporadic course of a Lilliputian mowing machine.

It still hung there while they ate the cold food and then 55 went to bed, scattered without order or claim up and down the two rooms, his mother in one bed, where his father would later lie, the older brother in the other, himself, the aunt, and the two sisters on pallets on the floor. But his father was not in bed yet. The last thing the boy remembered was the depthless, harsh silhouette of the hat and coat bending over the rug and it seemed to him that he had not even closed his eyes when the silhouette was standing over him, the fire almost dead behind it, the stiff foot prodding him awake. "Catch up the mule," his father said.

When he returned with the mule his father was standing in the black door, the rolled rug over his shoulder. "Ain't you going to ride?" he said.

"No. Give me your foot."

He bent his knee into his father's hand, the wiry, surprising power flowed smoothly, rising, he rising with it, on to the mule's bare back (they had owned a saddle once; the boy could remember it though not when or where) and with the same effortlessness his father swung the rug up in front of him. Now in the starlight they retraced the afternoon's path, up the dusty road rife with honeysuckle, through the gate and up the black tunnel to the drive to the lightless house, where he sat on the mule and felt the rough warp of the rug drag across his thighs and vanish.

"Don't you want me to help?" he whispered. His father did not answer and now he heard again that stiff foot striking the hollow portico with that wooden and clocklike deliberation, that outrageous overstatement of the weight it carried. The rug, hunched, not flung (the boy could tell that even in the darkness) from his father's shoulder struck the angle of wall and floor with a sound unbelievably loud, thunderous, then the foot again, unhurried and enormous; a light came on in the house and the boy sat, tense, breathing steadily and quietly and just a little fast, though the foot itself did not increase its beat at all, descending the steps now; now the boy could see him.

"Don't you want to ride now?" he whispered. "We kin 60 both ride now," the light within the house altering now, flaring up and sinking. *He's coming down the stairs now,* he thought. He had already ridden the mule up beside the horse block; presently his father was up behind him and he doubled the reins over and slashed the mule across the neck, but before the animal could begin to trot the hard, thin arm came round him, the hard, knotted hand jerking the mule back to a walk.

In the first red rays of the sun they were in the lot, putting plow gear on the mules. This time the sorrel mare was in the lot before he heard it at all, the rider collarless and even bareheaded, trembling, speaking in a shaking voice as the woman in the house had done, his father merely looking up once before stooping again to the hame° he was buckling, so that the man on the mare spoke to his stooping back:

"You must realize you have ruined that rug. Wasn't there anybody here, any of your women . . ." he ceased, shaking, the boy watching him, the older brother leaning now in the stable door, chewing, blinking slowly and steadily at nothing apparently. "It cost a hundred dollars. But you never had a hundred dollars. You never will. So I'm going to charge you twenty bushels of corn against your crop. I'll add it in your contract and when you come to the commissary you can sign it. That won't keep Mrs. de Spain quiet but maybe it will teach you to wipe your feet off before you enter her house again."

Then he was gone. The boy looked at his father, who still had not spoken or even looked up again, who was now adjusting the loggerhead in the hame.

"Pap," he said. His father looked at him—the inscrutable face, the shaggy brows beneath which the gray eyes glinted coldly. Suddenly the boy went toward him, fast, stopping as suddenly. "You done the best you could!" he cried. "If he wanted hit done different why didn't he wait and tell you how? He won't git no twenty bushels! He won't git none! We'll gether hit and hide hit! I kin watch . . ."

"Did you put the cutter back in that straight stock like 65 I told you?"

"No, sir," he said.

"Then go do it."

That was Wednesday. During the rest of that week he worked steadily, at what was within his scope and some which was beyond it, with an industry that did not need to be driven nor even commanded twice; he had this from his mother, with the difference that some at least of what he did he liked to do, such as splitting wood with the half-size axe which his mother and aunt had earned, or saved money somehow, to present him with at Christmas. In company with the two older women (and on one afternoon, even one of the sisters), he built pens for the shoat and the cow which were a part of his father's contract with the landlord, and one afternoon, his father being absent, gone somewhere on one of the mules, he went to the field.

They were running a middle buster now, his brother holding the plow straight while he handled the reins, and

---

° **hame** Harness.

walking beside the straining mule, the rich black soil shearing cool and damp against his bare ankles, he thought *Maybe this is the end of it. Maybe even that twenty bushels that seems hard to have to pay for just a rug will be a cheap price for him to stop forever and always from being what he used to be;* thinking, dreaming now, so that his brother had to speak sharply to him to mind the mule: *Maybe he even won't collect the twenty bushels. Maybe it will all add up and balance and vanish—corn, rug, fire; the terror and grief, the being pulled two ways like between two teams of horses— gone, done with for ever and ever.*

Then it was Saturday; he looked up from beneath the 70 mule he was harnessing and saw his father in the black coat and hat. "Not that," his father said. "The wagon gear." And then, two hours later, sitting in the wagon bed behind his father and brother on the seat, the wagon accomplished a final curve, and he saw the weathered paintless store with its tattered tobacco- and patent-medicine posters and the tethered wagons and saddle animals below the gallery. He mounted the gnawed steps behind his father and brother, and there again was the lane of quiet, watching faces for the three of them to walk through. He saw the man in spectacles sitting at the plank table and he did not need to be told this was a Justice of the Peace; he sent one glare of fierce, exultant, partisan defiance at the man in collar and cravat now, whom he had seen but twice before in his life, and that on a galloping horse, who now wore on his face an expression not of rage but of amazed unbelief which the boy could not have known was at the incredible circumstance of being sued by one of his own tenants, and came and stood against his father and cried at the Justice: "He ain't done it! He ain't burnt . . ."

"Go back to the wagon," his father said.

"Burnt?" the Justice said. "Do I understand this rug was burned too?"

"Does anybody here claim it was?" his father said. "Go back to the wagon." But he did not, he merely retreated to the rear of the room, crowded as that other had been, but not to sit down this time, instead, to stand pressing among the motionless bodies, listening to the voices:

"And you claim twenty bushels of corn is too high for the damage you did to the rug?"

"He brought the rug to me and said he wanted the 75 tracks washed out of it. I washed the tracks out and took the rug back to him."

"But you didn't carry the rug back to him in the same condition it was in before you made the tracks on it."

His father did not answer, and now for perhaps half a minute there was no sound at all save that of breathing, the faint, steady suspiration of complete and intent listening.

"You decline to answer that, Mr. Snopes?" Again his father did not answer. "I'm going to find against you, Mr. Snopes. I'm going to find that you were responsible for the injury to Major de Spain's rug and hold you liable for it. But twenty bushels of corn seems a little high for a man in your circumstances to have to pay. Major de Spain claims it cost a hundred dollars. October corn will be worth about fifty cents. I figure that if Major de Spain can stand a ninety-five dollar

loss on something he paid cash for, you can stand a five-dollar loss you haven't earned yet. I hold you in damages to Major de Spain to the amount of ten bushels of corn over and above your contract with him, to be paid to him out of your crop at gathering time. Court adjourned."

It had taken no time hardly, the morning was but half begun. He thought they would return home and perhaps back to the field, since they were late, far behind all other farmers. But instead his father passed on behind the wagon, merely indicating with his hand for the older brother to follow with it, and crossed the road toward the blacksmith shop opposite, pressing on after his father, overtaking him, speaking, whispering up at the harsh, calm face beneath the weathered hat: "He won't git no ten bushels neither. He won't git one. We'll . . ." until his father glanced for an instant down at him, the face absolutely calm, the grizzled eyebrows tangled above the cold eyes, the voice almost pleasant, almost gentle:

"You think so? Well, we'll wait till October anyway." 80

The matter of the wagon—the setting of a spoke or two and the tightening of the tires—did not take long either, the business of the tires accomplished by driving the wagon into the spring branch behind the shop and letting it stand there, the mules nuzzling into the water from time to time, and the boy on the seat with the idle reins, looking up the slope and through the sooty tunnel of the shed where the slow hammer rang and where his father sat on an upended cypress bolt, easily, either talking or listening, still sitting there when the boy brought the dripping wagon up out of the branch and halted it before the door.

"Take them on to the shade and hitch," his father said. He did so and returned. His father and the smith and a third man squatting on his heels inside the door were talking, about crops and animals; the boy, squatting too in the ammoniac dust and hoof-parings and scales of rust, heard his father tell a long and unhurried story out of the time before the birth of the older brother even when he had been a professional horsetrader. And then his father came up beside him where he stood before a tattered last year's circus poster on the other side of the store, gazing rapt and quiet at the scarlet horses, the incredible poisings and convolutions of tulle and tights and the painted leers of comedians, and said, "It's time to eat."

But not at home. Squatting beside his brother against the front wall, he watched his father emerge from the store and produce from a paper sack a segment of cheese and divide it carefully and deliberately into three with his pocket knife and produce crackers from the same sack. They all three squatted on the gallery and ate, slowly, without talking; then in the store again, they drank from a tin dipper tepid water smelling of the cedar bucket and of living beech trees. And still they did not go home. It was a horse lot this time, a tall rail fence upon and along which men stood and sat and out of which one by one horses were led, to be walked and trotted and then cantered back and forth along the road while the slow swapping and buying went on and the sun began to slant westward, they—the three of them—watching and listening, the older brother with his muddy eyes and his steady, inevitable to-bacco, the father commenting now and then on certain of the animals, to no one in particular.

It was after sundown when they reached home. They ate supper by lamplight, then, sitting on the doorstep, the boy watched the night fully accomplish, listening to the whippoorwills and the frogs, when he heard his mother's voice: "Abner! No! No! Oh, God. Oh, God. Abner!" and he rose, whirled, and saw the altered light through the door where a candle stub now burned in a bottle neck on the table and his father, still in the hat and coat, at once formal and burlesque as though dressed carefully for some shabby and ceremonial violence, emptying the reservoir of the lamp back into the five-gallon kerosene can from which it had been filled, while the mother tugged at his arm until he shifted the lamp to the other hand and flung her back, not savagely or viciously, just hard, into the wall, her hands flung out against the wall for balance, her mouth open and in her face the same quality of hopeless despair as had been in her voice. Then his father saw him standing in the door.

"Go to the barn and get that can of oil we were oiling 85 the wagon with," he said. The boy did not move. Then he could speak.

"What . . ." he cried. "What are you . . ."

"Go get that oil," his father said. "Go."

Then he was moving, running, outside the house, to-ward the stable: this the old habit, the old blood which he had not been permitted to choose for himself, which had been bequeathed him willy nilly and which had run for so long (and who knew where, battening on what of outrage and savagery and lust) before it came to him. *I could keep on,* he thought. *I could run on and on and never look back, never need to see his face again. Only I can't. I can't,* the rusted can in his hand now, the liquid sploshing in it as he ran back to the house and into it, into the sound of his mother's weeping in the next room, and handed the can to his father.

"Ain't you going to even send a nigger?" he cried. "At least you sent a nigger before!"

This time his father didn't strike him. The hand came 90 even faster than the blow had, the same hand which had set the can on the table with almost excruciating care flashing from the can toward him too quick for him to fol-low it, gripping him by the back of his shirt and on to tiptoe before he had seen it quit the can, the face stooping at him in breathless and frozen ferocity, the cold, dead voice speaking over him to the older brother who leaned against the table, chewing with that steady, curious, side-wise motion of cows:

"Empty the can into the big one and go on. I'll catch up with you."

"Better tie him to the bedpost," the brother said.

"Do like I told you," the father said. Then the boy was moving, his bunched shirt and the hard, bony hand between his shoulderblades, his toes just touching the floor, across the room and into the other one, past the sisters sitting with spread heavy thighs in the two chairs over the cold hearth, and to where his mother and aunt sat side by side on the bed, the aunt's arms about his mother's shoulders.

"Hold him," the father said. The aunt made a startled movement. "Not you," the father said. "Lennie. Take hold of him. I want to see you do it." His mother took him by the wrist. "You'll hold him better than that. If he gets loose don't you know what he is going to do? He will go up yonder." He jerked his head toward the road. "Maybe I'd better tie him."

"I'll hold him," his mother whispered. 95

"See you do then." Then his father was gone, the stiff foot heavy and measured upon the boards, ceasing at last.

Then he began to struggle. His mother caught him in both arms, he jerking and wrenching at them. He would be stronger in the end, he knew that. But he had no time to wait for it. "Lemme go!" he cried. "I don't want to have to hit you!"

"Let him go!" the aunt said. "If he don't go, before God, I am going up there myself!"

"Don't you see I can't?" his mother cried. "Sarty! Sar-ty! No! No! Help me, Lizzie!"

Then he was free. His aunt grasped at him but it was 100 too late. He whirled, running, his mother stumbled for-ward on to her knees behind him, crying to the nearest sister: "Catch him, Net! Catch him!" But that was too late too, the sister (the sisters were twins, born at the same time, yet either of them now gave the impression of being, encompassing as much living meat and volume and weight as any other two of the family) not yet having begun to rise from the chair, her head, face, alone merely turned, presenting to him in the flying instant an astonishing ex-panse of young female features untroubled by any sur-prise even, wearing only an expression of bovine interest. Then he was out of the room, out of the house, in the mild dust of the starlit road and the heavy rifeness of honey-suckle, the pale ribbon unspooling with terrific slowness under his running feet, reaching the gate at last and turn-ing in, running, his heart and lungs drumming, on up the drive toward the lighted house, the lighted door. He did not knock, he burst in, sobbing for breath, incapable for the moment of speech; he saw the astonished face of the Negro in the linen jacket without knowing when the Ne-gro had appeared.

"De Spain!" he cried, panted. "Where's . . ." then he saw the white man too emerging from a white door down the hall. "Barn!" he cried. "Barn!"

"What?" the white man said. "Barn?"

"Yes!" the boy cried. "Barn!"

"Catch him!" the white man shouted.

But it was too late this time too. The Negro grasped 105 his shirt, but the entire sleeve, rotten with washing, carried away, and he was out that door too and in the drive again, and had actually never ceased to run even while he was screaming into the white man's face.

Behind him the white man was shouting, "My horse! Fetch my horse!" and he thought for an instant of cutting across the park and climbing the fence into the road, but he did not know the park nor how high the vine-massed fence might be and he dared not risk it. So he ran on down the drive, blood and breath roaring; presently he was in the road again though he could not see it. He could not hear either: the galloping mare was almost upon him before he heard her, and even then he held his course, as if the very urgency of his wild grief and need must in a moment more find him wings, waiting until the ultimate instant to hurl himself aside and into the weed-choked roadside ditch as the horse thundered past and on, for an instant in furious silhouette against the stars, the tranquil early summer night sky which, even before the shape of the horse and rider vanished, stained abruptly and violently upward: a long, swirling roar incredible and soundless, blotting the stars, and he springing up and into the road again, running again, knowing it was too late yet still running even after he heard the shot and, an instant later, two shots, pausing now without knowing he had ceased to run, crying "Pap! Pap!", running again before he knew he had begun to run, stumbling, tripping over something and scrabbling up again without ceasing to run, looking backward over his shoulder at the glare as he got up, running on among the invisible trees, panting, sobbing, "Father! Father!"

At midnight he was sitting on the crest of a hill. He did not know it was midnight and he did not know how far he had come. But there was no glare behind him now and he sat now, his back toward what he had called home for four days anyhow, his face toward the dark woods which he would enter when breath was strong again, small, shaking steadily in the chill darkness, hugging himself into the remainder of his thin, rotten shirt, the grief and despair now no longer terror and fear but just grief and despair. *Father. My father,* he thought. "He was

brave!" he cried suddenly, aloud but not loud, no more than a whisper: "He was! He was in the war! He was in Colonel Sartoris' cav'ry!" not knowing that his father had gone to that war a private in the fine old European sense, wearing no uniform, admitting the authority of and giving fidelity to no man or army or flag, going to war as Malbrouck° himself did: for booty—it meant nothing and less than nothing to him if it were enemy booty or his own.

The slow constellations wheeled on. It would be dawn and then sunup after a while and he would be hungry. But that would be tomorrow and now he was only cold, and walking would cure that. His breathing was easier now and he decided to get up and go on, and then he found that he had been asleep because he knew it was almost dawn, the night almost over. He could tell that from the whippoorwills. They were everywhere now among the dark trees below him, constant and inflectioned and ceaseless, so that, as the instant for giving over to the day birds drew nearer and nearer, there was no interval at all between them. He got up. He was a little stiff, but walking would cure that too as it would the cold, and soon there would be the sun. He went on down the hill, toward the dark woods within which the liquid silver voices of the birds called unceasing—the rapid and urgent beating of the urgent and quiring heart of the late spring night. He did not look back.

Related Works

"A Worn Path" (p. 285), "Daddy" (p. 416), "For the Union Dead" (p. 492), *Fences* (p. 724)

See Chapter 14 Review Card for Reading and Reacting questions about William Faulkner, "Barn Burning."

° **Malbrouck** A character in a popular eighteenth-century nursery rhyme about a famous warrior.

Writing Suggestions: Point of View

1. How would Poe's "The Cask of Amontillado" be different if it were told by a minor character who observed the events? Rewrite the story from this point of view—or tell the story that precedes the story, explaining the "thousand injuries" and the "insult."

2. Assume that you are Jim, the sailor in "Big Black Good Man," and that you are keeping a journal of your travels. Write the journal entries for the time you spent in Copenhagen. Include your impressions of Olaf, Lena, the hotel, and anything else that caught your attention. Make sure you present your version of the key events described in the story—especially Olaf's reaction to you.

3. Both "The Cask of Amontillado" and "Barn Burning" deal with crimes that essentially go unpunished and with the emotions that accompany these crimes. In what sense does each story's use of point of view shape its treatment of the crime in question? For instance, how does point of view determine how much readers know about the motives for the crime, the crime's basic circumstances, and the extent to which the crime is justified?

 CHECKLISTS

SELECTING AN APPROPRIATE POINT OF VIEW: REVIEW

First-Person Narrators (use *I* or *we*)

Major character telling his or her own story "Every morning I lay on the floor in the front parlour watching her door." (James Joyce, "Araby")

Minor character as witness "And so she died. . . . We did not even know she was sick; we had long since given up trying to get information. . . ." (William Faulkner, "A Rose for Emily")

Third-Person Narrators (use *he, she,* and *they*)

Omniscient—able to move at will from character to character and comment about them "In a house, in a suburb, in a city, there were a man and his wife who loved each other very much. . . ." (Nadine Gordimer, "Once upon a Time")

Limited omniscient—restricts focus to a single character "The wagon went on. He did not know where they were going." (William Faulkner, "Barn Burning")

Objective (dramatic)—simply reports the dialogue and the actions of characters "'You'll be drunk,' the waiter said. The old man looked at him. The waiter went away." (Ernest Hemingway, "A Clean, We l-Lighted Place")

WRITING ABOUT POINT OF VIEW

- [ ] What is the dominant point of view from which the story is told?
- [ ] Is the narrator a character in the story? If so, is he or she a participant in the story's events or just a witness?
- [ ] Does the story's point of view create irony?
- [ ] If the story has a first-person narrator, is the narrator reliable or unreliable?
- [ ] If the story has a third-person narrator, is he or she omniscient? Does he or she have limited omniscience? Is the narrator objective?
- [ ] What are the advantages of the story's point of view? What are the disadvantages?
- [ ] Does the point of view remain consistent throughout the story, or does it shift?
- [ ] How might a different point of view change the story?

Glossary Terms

irony/dramatic irony/situational irony/verbal irony
Literary device or situation that depends on the existence of at least two separate and contrasting levels of meaning or experience. **Dramatic** or **tragic irony** depends on the audience's knowing something the protagonist has not yet realized. **Situational irony** exists when what happens is at odds with what the story's situation leads readers to expect will happen. **Verbal irony** occurs when what is said is in contrast with what is meant.

narrator Person who tells the story.

persona Narrator created by the writer to tell the story; in Greek tragedy, a persona was a mask worn by an actor.

point of view Perspective from which a story is told. The storyteller may be a major character in the story or a character who witnesses the story's events (*first-person narrator*) or someone who does not figure in the action at all (*third-person narrator*), in which case he or she may know the actions and thoughts of everyone in the story (*omniscient narrator*) or just know some part of these (*limited omniscient narrator*).

15

Style, Tone, and Language

Learning Outcomes

After reading this chapter, you should be able to do the following:

LO1 Understand style and tone

LO2 Understand the uses of language

LO3 Recognize formal and informal diction

LO4 Recognize imagery

LO5 Recognize figures of speech

Timeline

1914 James Joyce, "Araby"

Flannery O'Connor, "A Good Man is Hard to Find" **1955**

Tim O'Brien, "The Things They Carried" **1986**

1993 R. Crumb, "A Hunger Artist"

1910 · 1930 · 1950 · 1970 · 1990

1924 Franz Kafka, author of the story "The Hunger Artist," dies.

The signing of the Paris Peace Accords ends US involvement in the Vietnam War. **1973**

1996 Famine strikes North Korea.

1915 For the first time, German zeppelins bomb targets in the United Kingdom.

The International Criminal Police Organization is founded. **1956**

The Vietnam Veterans Memorial is dedicated in Washington, DC. **1982**

1991 The First Gulf War results in the expulsion of the Iraqi Army from Kuwait.

1991 The Soviet Union collapses.

1913 Woodrow Wilson is sworn in as president of the United States.

A disaster occurs at the Chernobyl Nuclear Power plant in Kiev, Ukraine. **1986**

LO1 Understand Style and Tone

One of the qualities that gives a work of literature its individuality is its **style,** the way in which a writer uses language, selecting and arranging words to say what he or she wants to say. Style encompasses elements such as word choice; syntax; sentence length and structure; and the presence, frequency, and prominence of imagery and figures of speech.

Closely related to style is **tone,** the attitude of the narrator or author of a work toward the subject matter, characters, or audience. Word choice and sentence structure help to create a work's tone, which may be intimate or distant, bitter or affectionate, straightforward or cautious, supportive or critical, respectful or condescending. (Tone may also be **ironic;** see Chapter 14, "Point of View," for a discussion of irony.)

LO2 Understand the Uses of Language

Language offers almost limitless possibilities to a writer. Creative use of language (such as unusual word choice, word order, or sentence structure) can enrich a story and add to its overall effect. Sometimes, in fact, a writer's use of language can expand a story's possibilities through its very inventiveness. For example, James Joyce's innovative **stream-of-consciousness** style mimics thought, allowing ideas to run into one another as random associations are made so that readers may follow and participate in the thought processes of the narrator. Here is a stream-of-consciousness passage from Joyce's experimental 1922 novel *Ulysses:*

> frseeeeeeeefronnnng train somewhere whistling the strength those engines have in them like big giants and the water rolling all over and out of them all sides like the end of Loves old sweet sonnnng the poor men that have to be out all the night from their wives and families in those roasting engines stifling it was today. . . .

Skillfully used, language can enhance a story's other elements. It may, for example, help to create an atmosphere that is important to the story's plot or theme, as Kate Chopin's lush, rhythmic sentences help to create the sexually charged atmosphere of "The Storm" (p. 154)—an atmosphere that overpowers the characters and thus drives the plot. Language may also help to delineate character, perhaps by conveying a character's mental state to readers. For instance, the breathless, disjointed style of Edgar Allan Poe's "The Tell-Tale Heart" (p. 331) suggests the narrator's increasing emotional instability: "Was it possible they heard not? Almighty God!—no, no! They heard!—they suspected!—they *knew!*—they were making a mockery of my horror!"

In his 1925 short story "Big Two-Hearted River," Ernest Hemingway uses sentences without transitions to

 EXPLORE ONLINE >

To complete a tutorial of "Style," and "Tone," visit your Literature CourseMate, accessed through www.cengagebrain.com.

style How an author selects and arranges words to express ideas.

tone Attitude of the speaker or narrator of a work toward the subject, the characters, or the audience, as determined by word choice, use of imagery, and so on.

stream of consciousness Form of narration controlled not by external events but by the thoughts and subjective impressions of the narrator.

alliteration Repetition of consonant sounds (usually the initial sounds) in a series of words. Alliteration may be reinforced by repeated sounds within and at the ends of words.

create a flat, emotionless prose style that reveals his character's alienation and fragility as he struggles to maintain control: "Now things were done. There had been this to do. Now it was done. It had been a hard trip. He was very tired. That was done. He had made his camp. He was settled. Nothing could touch him."

Language that places emphasis on the sounds and rhythm of words and sentences can also enrich a work of fiction. Consider the use of such language in the following sentence from James Joyce's "Araby" (p. 220):

> The light from the lamp opposite our door caught the white curve of her neck, lit up her hair that rested there and, falling, lit up the hand upon the railing.

Here the narrator is describing his first conversation with a girl who fascinates him, and the lyrical, almost musical language reflects his enchantment. Note in particular the **alliteration** (*l*ight/*l*amp; *c*aught/*c*urve; *h*air/*h*and), the repetition (lit up/lit up), and the rhyme (lit up her *hair*/that rested *there*) and **near rhyme** (falling/railing); these poetic devices connect the words of the sentence into a smooth, rhythmic whole.

Another example of this emphasis on sound may be found in the measured **parallelism** of this sentence from Nathaniel Hawthorne's 1843 story "The Birthmark":

> He had left his laboratory to the care of an assistant, cleared his fine countenance from the furnace smoke, washed the stain of acids from his fingers, and persuaded a beautiful woman to become his wife.

The style of this sentence, conveying methodical precision and order, reflects the compulsive personality of the character being described.

formal diction Diction that is lofty and elaborate, with a learned vocabulary and detached tone.

The following passage from Alberto Alvaro Ríos's story "The Secret Lion" (p. 333) illustrates the power of language to enrich a story:

> We had read the books, after all; we knew about bridges and castles and wildtreacherousraging alligator-mouth rivers. We wanted them. So we were going to go out and get them. We went back that morning into that kitchen and we said, "We're going out there, we're going into the hills, we're going away for three days, don't worry." She said, "All right."
>
> "You know," I said to Sergio, "if we're going to go away for three days, well, we ought to at least pack a lunch."
>
> But we were two young boys with no patience for what we thought at the time was mom-stuff: making sa-and-wiches. My mother didn't offer. So we got out little kid knapsacks that my mother had sewn for us, and into them we put the jar of mustard. A loaf of bread. Knivesforksplates, bottles of Coke, a can opener. This was lunch for the two of us. And we were weighed down, humped over to be strong enough to carry this stuff. But we started walking anyway, into the hills. We were going to eat berries and stuff otherwise. "Goodbye." My mom said that.

Through language, the adult narrator of the preceding paragraphs recaptures the bravado of the boys in search of "wildtreacherousraging alligatormouth rivers" even as he suggests to readers that the boys are not going far. The story's use of language is original and inventive: words are blended together ("getridofit," "knivesforksplates"), linked to form new words ("mom-stuff"), and drawn out to mimic speech ("sa-and-wiches"). These experiments with language show the narrator's willingness to move back into a child's frame of reference while maintaining the advantage of distance. The adult narrator uses sentence fragments ("A loaf of bread."), colloquialisms ("kid," "mom," "stuff"), and contractions. He also includes conversational elements such as *you know* and *well* in the story's dialogue, accurately recreating the childhood scene even as he sees its folly and remains aware of the disillusionment that awaits him. Thus, the unique style permits the narrator to bring readers with him into the child's world while he maintains his adult stance: "But we were two young boys with no patience for what we thought at the time was mom-stuff. . . ."

Although many stylistic options are available to writers, a story's language must be consistent with the writer's purpose and with the effect he or she hopes to create. Just as writers may experiment with point of view or manipulate events to create a complex plot, so they can adjust language to suit a particular narrator or character or to

EXPLORE ONLINE >

To complete a tutorial of "Levels of Diction," visit your Literature CourseMate, accessed through www.cengagebrain.com.

convey a particular theme. In addition to the creative uses of language described earlier, writers also frequently experiment with *formal and informal diction, imagery,* and *figures of speech.*

LO3 Recognize Formal and Informal Diction

The level of diction—how formal or informal a story's language is—can reveal a good deal about a story's narrator and characters.

Formal diction is characterized by elaborate, complex sentences; a learned vocabulary; and a serious, objective, detached tone. It does not generally include contractions, shortened word forms (like *phone*), regional expressions, or slang, and it may substitute *one* or *we* for *I.* At its most extreme, formal language is stiff and stilted, far removed from everyday speech.

When formal diction is used by a narrator or by a character, it may indicate erudition, a high educational level, a superior social or professional position, or emotional detachment. When one character's language is significantly more formal than others', he or she may seem old-fashioned or stuffy; when language is inappropriately elevated or complex, it may reveal the character to be pompous or ridiculous; when a narrator's language is noticeably more formal than that of the characters, the narrator may seem superior or even condescending. Thus, the choice of a particular level (or levels) of diction in a story can convey information about characters and about the narrator's attitude toward them.

The following passage from Hawthorne's "The Birthmark" illustrates formal style:

> In the latter part of the last century there lived a man of science, an eminent proficient in every branch of natural philosophy, who not long before our story opens had made experience of a spiritual affinity more attractive than any chemical one. He had left his laboratory to the care of an assistant, cleared his fine countenance from the furnace smoke, washed the stain of acids from his fingers, and persuaded a beautiful woman to become his wife. In those days when the comparatively recent discovery of electricity and other kindred mysteries of Nature seemed to open paths into the region of miracle, it was not unusual for the love of science to

rival the love of woman in its depth and absorbing energy. The higher intellect, the imagination, the spirit, and even the heart might all find their congenial ailment in pursuits which, as some of their ardent votaries believed, would ascend from one step of powerful intelligence to another, until the philosopher should lay his hand on the secret of creative force and perhaps make new worlds for himself.

The long and complex sentences, learned vocabulary ("countenance," "ailment," "votaries"), and absence of colloquialisms suit Hawthorne's purpose well, re-creating the formal language of the earlier era in which his story is set. The narrator is aloof and controlled, and his diction makes this clear to readers.

Informal diction, consistent with everyday speech, is characterized by slang, contractions, colloquial expressions like *you know* and *I mean*, shortened word forms, incomplete sentences, and a casual, conversational tone. A first-person narrator may use an informal style, or characters may speak informally; in either case, informal style tends to narrow the distance between readers and text.

Informal language can range from the distinctive contemporary style of the narrator's voice in T. Coraghessan Boyle's "Greasy Lake" (p. 306) to the regionalisms and dialect used in Flannery O'Connor's "A Good Man is Hard to Find" ("aloose"; "you all"; "britches"). In "Greasy Lake," the narrator's self-consciously slangy, conversational style reveals the naïveté, and false bravado that characterizes his adolescence; in "A Good Man is Hard to Find" (p. 224), speech patterns and diction help to identify the region in which the characters live and their social class. Informal language may also include language readers find offensive. In this case, a character's use of obscenities may suggest his or her crudeness or adolescent bravado, and the use of racial or ethnic slurs indicates that a character is insensitive and bigoted.

The following passage from John Updike's "A&P" (p. 131) illustrates informal style:

> She had sort of oaky hair that the sun and salt had bleached, done up in a bun that was unravelling, and a kind of prim face. Walking into the A&P with your straps down, I suppose it's the only kind of face you *can* have. She held her head so high her neck, coming out of those white shoulders, looked kind of stretched, but I didn't mind. The longer her neck was, the more of her there was.

Here, the first-person narrator, a nineteen-year-old supermarket checkout clerk, uses a conversational style, including colloquialisms ("sort of," "I suppose," "kind of"), contractions ("it's," "didn't"), and the imprecise, informal *you* ("Walking into the A&P with *your* straps down. . . ."). The narrator uses neither elaborate syntax nor a learned vocabulary.

 EXPLORE ONLINE >

To complete a tutorial of "Imagery," visit your Literature CourseMate, accessed through www.cengagebrain.com.

informal diction Diction that is idiomatic and relaxed, like everyday speech.

imagery Words and phrases that describe the five senses, most often sight. A **pattern of imagery** is a group of related images developed throughout a work.

figures of speech Expressions—such as **simile, metaphor, personification, hyperbole,** and **understatement**—that use words to achieve effects beyond ordinary language.

LO4 Recognize Imagery

Imagery—words and phrases that describe what is seen, heard, smelled, tasted, or touched—can have a significant impact in a story. A writer may use a pattern of repeated imagery to convey a particular impression about a character or situation or to communicate or reinforce a story's theme. For example, the theme of newly discovered sexuality can be conveyed through repeated use of words and phrases suggesting blooming or ripening.

In T. Coraghessan Boyle's "Greasy Lake" (p. 306), the narrator's vivid description of Greasy Lake uses rich visual imagery to evoke a scene:

> Through the center of town, up the strip, past the housing developments and shopping malls, street lights giving way to the thin streaming illumination of the headlights, trees crowding the asphalt in a black unbroken wall: that was the way out to Greasy Lake. The Indians had called it Wakan, a reference to the clarity of its waters. Now it was fetid and murky, the mud banks glittering with broken glass and strewn with beer cans and the charred remains of bonfires. There was a single ravaged island a hundred yards from shore, so stripped of vegetation it looked as if the air force had strafed it. We went up to the lake because everyone went there, because we wanted to snuff the rich scent of possibility on the breeze, watch a girl take off her clothes and plunge into the festering murk, drink beer, smoke pot, howl at the stars, savor the incongruous full-throated roar of rock and roll against the primeval susurrus of frogs and crickets. This was nature.

By characterizing a natural setting with surprising words like "fetid," "murky," and "greasy" and unpleasant images such

metaphor Concise form of comparison equating two things that may at first seem completely dissimilar, often an abstraction and a concrete image.

simile Comparison of two seemingly unlike things using the words *like* or *as*.

personification A figure of speech that endows inanimate objects or abstract ideas with life or human characteristics.

hyperbole Figurative language that depends on intentional overstatement.

understatement Intentional downplaying of a situation's significance, often for ironic or humorous effect.

allusion Reference, often to literature, history, mythology, or the Bible, that is unacknowledged in the text but that the author expects a reader to recognize.

EXPLORE ONLINE >

To complete a tutorial of "Figures of Speech," visit your Literature CourseMate, accessed through www.cengagebrain.com.

as the "glittering of broken glass," the "ravaged island," and the "charred remains of bonfires," Boyle creates a picture that is completely at odds with the traditional view of nature. The incongruous images are nevertheless perfectly consistent with the sordid events that take place at Greasy Lake.

LO5 Recognize Figures of Speech

Figures of speech—such as *similes*, *metaphors*, and *personification*—can enrich a story, subtly revealing information about characters and themes.

By using **metaphors** and **similes**—figures of speech that compare two dissimilar items—writers can indicate a particular attitude toward characters and events. Thus, Flannery O'Connor's many grotesque similes in "A Good Man Is Hard to Find" help to dehumanize her characters; the children's mother, for instance, has a face "as broad and innocent as a cabbage." In Tillie Olsen's "I Stand Here Ironing" (p. 162), an extended metaphor in which a mother compares her daughter to a dress waiting to be ironed expresses the mother's attitude toward her child, effectively suggesting to readers the daughter's vulnerability. Similes and metaphors are used throughout in Kate Chopin's "The Storm" (p. 154). In a scene of sexual awakening, Calixta's skin is "like a creamy lily," her passion is "like a white flame," and her mouth is "a fountain of delight"; these figures of speech add a lushness and sensuality to the story.

Personification—a figure of speech, closely related to metaphor, that endows inanimate objects or abstract ideas with life or with human characteristics—is used in "Araby" (p. 220), where houses, "conscious of decent lives within them, gazed at one another with brown imperturbable faces." This use of figurative language expands readers' vision of the story's setting and gives a dreamlike quality to the passage. (Other figures of speech, such as **hyperbole** and **understatement,** can also enrich works of fiction. See Chapter 24, "Figures of Speech," for further information.)

Allusions—references to familiar historical, cultural, literary, or biblical texts, figures, or events—may also expand readers' understanding and appreciation of a work. An allusion widens a work's context by bringing it into the context of a related subject or idea. For instance, in Charles Baxter's short story "Gryphon" (p. 138), the narrator's allusions to *Pinocchio* and Betty Crocker enable readers who recognize the references to gain a deeper understanding of what certain characters are really like.

Note In analyzing the use of language in a work of fiction, you may occasionally encounter obscure allusions (or foreign words and phrases or unfamiliar regional expressions), particularly in works treating cultures and historical periods other than your own. Frequently, such language will be clarified by the context, or by explanatory notes in your text. When it is not, you should consult a dictionary, encyclopedia, or other reference work.

R. Crumb (1943–)

is widely considered to be the founder of the underground or alternative comics movement, which emerged in the 1960s as a reaction against the popular superhero comics that had, until then, dominated and defined the comic book genre. Crumb and his underground contemporaries, including Art Spiegelman (p. 129), depicted taboo topics such as drugs and sex in a medium that had previously been perceived as a children's genre. He created the infamously risqué illustrated character Fritz the Cat, among others. With works such as *Introducing Kafka* (1993), in which he illustrates

© Oscar White/Corbis

Franz Kafka's life and work and from which the following selection is excerpted, Crumb helped to raise the graphic novel to the level of high art. His work appears in numerous collections, including the *R. Crumb Sketchbook* volumes (1978, 1981, 2005), *The Complete Crumb* (2005), and *The Sweeter Side of R. Crumb* (2010).

A Hunger Artist   (1993)

This graphic story starts on the next page.

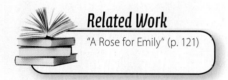

Related Work

"A Rose for Emily" (p. 121)

 See Chapter 15 Review Card for Reading and Reacting questions about R. Crumb, "A Hunger Artist."

Cultural Context
Throughout history, people have been fascinated with the effects of fasting on the human body and mind. In the early twentieth century, carnivals and freak shows throughout Europe featured "hunger artists," such as the one depicted in the following graphic story, who voluntarily starved themselves for the public's entertainment. Carnival goers would watch hunger artists, who were considered to be more oddities than "artists," while they would sit in a cage and do menial tasks, or nothing at all. Large crowds would often form when hunger artists, for whatever reason, decided to end their fast and finally eat.

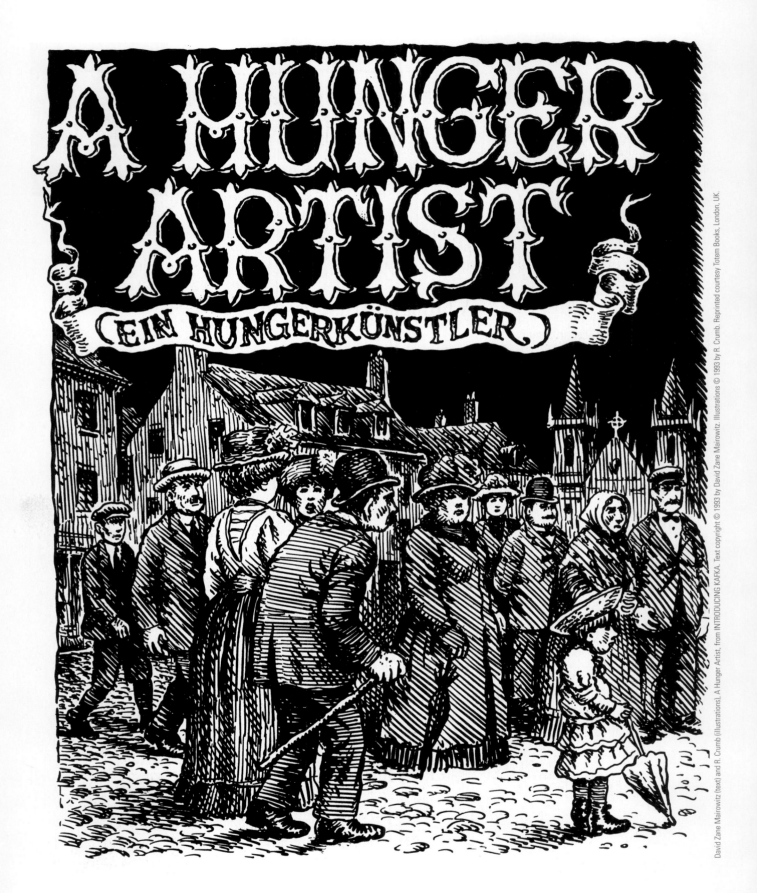

A HUNGER ARTIST

(EIN HUNGERKÜNSTLER.)

IN THE LAST FEW DECADES, THE INTEREST IN PROFESSIONAL HUNGER-ARTISTRY HAS GREATLY DIMINISHED. ONCE THE WHOLE TOWN CAME OUT TO SEE THE HUNGER-ARTIST. SOME EVEN BOUGHT SEASON TICKETS, AND AT NIGHT THE SCENE WAS BATHED IN THE LIGHT OF TORCHES.

GROUPS OF PROFESSIONAL WATCHERS, USUALLY BUTCHERS, WERE SENT TO WATCH HIM, IN CASE HE HAD SOME SECRET CACHE OF NOURISHMENT. BUT, DURING HIS FAST THE ARTISTE WOULD NEVER, EVEN UNDER COMPULSION, SWALLOW THE SMALLEST BIT OF FOOD; HIS PROFESSIONAL HONOR FORBADE IT. HE ALONE KNEW WHAT THE OTHERS DIDN'T: FASTING WAS THE EASIEST THING IN THE WORLD.

TICKETS
SEE THE HUNGER ARTIST

THE PERIOD OF FASTING WAS SET BY HIS IMPRESARIO AT FORTY DAYS MAXIMUM, BECAUSE AFTER THAT TIME THE PUBLIC BEGAN TO LOSE INTEREST. SO, ON THE FORTIETH DAY, WITH AN EXCITED CROWD FILLING THE ARENA AND A MILITARY BAND PLAYING, TWO YOUNG LADIES CAME TO LEAD THE HUNGER-ARTIST OUT OF HIS CAGE. WHEN THIS HAPPENED HE ALWAYS PUT UP SOME RESISTANCE...WHY STOP AFTER ONLY FORTY DAYS?!? WHY SHOULD THEY TAKE FROM HIM THE GLORY OF FASTING EVEN LONGER, OF SURPASSING EVEN HIMSELF TO REACH UNIMAGINABLE HEIGHTS, FOR HE SAW HIS ABILITY TO GO ON FASTING AS *UNLIMITED!*

David Zane Mairowitz (text) and R. Crumb (illustrations). A Hunger Artist, from INTRODUCING KAFKA. Text copyright © 1993 by David Zane Mairowitz. Illustrations © 1993 by R. Crumb. Reprinted courtesy Totem Books, London, UK.

James Joyce (1882–1941)

was born in Dublin but lived his entire adult life in self-imposed exile from his native Ireland. Though his parents sent him to schools that trained young men for the priesthood, Joyce saw himself as a religious and artistic rebel and fled to Paris soon after graduation in 1902. Recalled briefly to Dublin by his mother's fatal illness, Joyce returned to the Continent in 1904, taking with him an uneducated Irish country girl named Nora Barnacle, who became his wife in 1931. In dreary quarters in Trieste, Zurich, and Paris, Joyce struggled to support a growing family, sometimes teaching classes in Berlitz language schools.

Though Joyce never again lived in Ireland, he continued to write about Dublin. Publication of *Dubliners* (1914), a collection of short stories that included "Araby," was delayed for seven years because the Irish publisher feared libel suits from local citizens who were thinly disguised

as characters in the stories. Joyce's autobiographical *Portrait of the Artist as a Young Man* (1916) tells of a young writer's rejection of family, church, and country. *Ulysses* (1922), the comic tale of eighteen hours in the life of a wandering Dublin advertising salesman, was banned when the United States Post Office brought charges of obscenity against the book, and it remained banned in the United States and England for more than a decade. With *Ulysses,* Joyce began a revolutionary journey away from traditional techniques of plot and characterization to the interior monologues and stream-of-consciousness style that mark his last great novel, *Finnegans Wake* (1939).

Araby (1914)

North Richmond Street, being blind,° was a quiet street except at the hour when the Christian Brothers' School set the boys free. An uninhabited house of two storeys stood at the blind end, detached from its neighbours in a square ground. The other houses of the street, conscious of decent lives within them, gazed at one another with brown imperturbable faces.

The former tenant of our house, a priest, had died in the back drawing-room. Air, musty from having been long enclosed, hung in all the rooms, and the waste room behind the kitchen was littered with old useless papers. Among these I found a few paper-covered books, the pages of which were curled and damp: *The Abbot,* by Walter Scott, *The Devout Communicant* and *The Memoirs of Vidocq.*° I liked the last best because its leaves were yellow. The wild garden behind the house contained a central apple-tree and a few straggling bushes under one of which I found the late tenant's rusty bicycle-pump. He had been a very charitable priest; in his will he had left all his money to institutions and the furniture of his house to his sister.

When the short days of winter came dusk fell before we had well eaten our dinners. When we met in the street the houses had grown sombre. The space of sky above us was the colour of ever-changing violet and towards it the lamps of the street lifted their feeble lanterns. The cold air

stung us and we played till our bodies glowed. Our shouts echoed in the silent street. The career of our play brought us through the dark muddy lanes behind the houses where we ran the gauntlet of the rough tribes from the cottages, to the back doors of the dark dripping gardens where odours arose from the ash-pits, to the dark odorous stables where a coach-man smoothed and combed the horse or shook music from the buckled harness. When we returned to the street light from the kitchen windows had filled the areas. If my uncle was seen turning the corner we hid in the shadow until we had seen him safely housed. Or if Mangan's sister came out on the doorstep to call her brother in to his tea we watched her from our shadow peer up and down the street. We waited to see whether she would remain or go in and, if she remained, we left our shadow and walked up to Mangan's steps resignedly. She was waiting for us, her figure defined by the light from the half-opened door. Her brother always teased her before he obeyed and I stood by the railings looking at her. Her dress swung as she moved her body and the soft rope of her hair tossed from side to side.

> "The space of sky above us was the colour of ever-changing violet and towards it the lamps of the street lifted their feeble lanterns. The cold air stung us and we played till our bodies glowed."

° **blind** Dead-end.

° ***The Abbot . . . Vidocq*** Sir Walter Scott (1771–1832)—an English Romantic novelist; *The Devout Communicant*—a variant title for *Pious Meditations*, written by an eighteenth-century English Franciscan friar, Pacifus Baker; *The Memoirs of Vidocq*—an autobiography of François-Jules Vidocq (1775–1857), a French criminal turned police agent.

>> Early-twentieth-century Dublin street

>> Knight bowing to his lady

Every morning I lay on the floor in the front parlour watching her door. The blind was pulled down to within an inch of the sash so that I could not be seen. When she came out on the doorstep my heart leaped. I ran to the hall, seized my books and followed her. I kept her brown figure always in my eye and, when we came near the point at which our ways diverged, I quickened my pace and passed her. This happened morning after morning. I had never spoken to her, except for a few casual words, and yet her name was like a summons to all my foolish blood.

Her image accompanied me even in places the most 5 hostile to romance. On Saturday evenings when my aunt went marketing I had to go to carry some of the parcels. We walked through the flaring streets, jostled by drunken men and bargaining women, amid the curses of labourers, the shrill litanies of shop-boys who stood on guard by the barrels of pigs' cheeks, the nasal chanting of street-singers, who sang a *come-all-you* about O'Donovan Rossa,° or a ballad about the troubles in our native land. These noises converged in a single sensation of life for me: I imagined that I bore my chalice safely through a throng of foes. Her name sprang to my lips at moments in strange prayers and praises which I myself did not understand. My eyes were often full of tears (I could not tell why) and at times a flood from my heart seemed to pour itself out into my bosom. I thought little of the future. I did not know whether I would ever speak to her or not or, if I spoke to her, how I could tell her of my confused adoration. But my body was like a harp and her words and gestures were like fingers running upon the wires.

One evening I went into the back drawing-room in which the priest had died. It was a dark rainy evening and there was no sound in the house. Through one of the broken panes I heard the rain impinge upon the earth, the fine incessant needles of water playing in the sodden beds. Some distant lamp or lighted window gleamed below me. I was thankful that I could see so little. All my senses

seemed to desire to veil themselves and, feeling that I was about to slip from them, I pressed the palms of my hands together until they trembled, murmuring: "*O love! O love!*" many times.

At last she spoke to me. When she addressed the first words to me I was so confused that I did not know what to answer. She asked me was I going to *Araby*. I forgot whether I answered yes or no. It would be a splendid bazaar, she said she would love to go.

"And why can't you?" I asked.

While she spoke she turned a silver bracelet round and round her wrist. She could not go, she said, because there would be a retreat that week in her convent.° Her brother and two other boys were fighting for their caps and I was alone at the railings. She held one of the spikes, bowing her head towards me. The light from the lamp opposite our door caught the white curve of her neck, lit up her hair that rested there and, falling, lit up the hand upon the railing. It fell over one side of her dress and caught the white border of a petticoat, just visible as she stood at ease.

"It's well for you," she said. 10

"If I go," I said, "I will bring you something."

What innumerable follies laid waste my waking and sleeping thoughts after that evening! I wished to annihilate the tedious intervening days. I chafed against the work of

° **O'Donovan Rossa** Any popular song beginning "Come all you gallant Irishmen . . ."; O'Donovan Rossa was an Irish nationalist who was banished in 1870 for advocating violent rebellion against the British.

° **convent** Her convent school.

school. At night in my bedroom and by day in the classroom her image came between me and the page I strove to read. The syllables of the word *Araby* were called to me through the silence in which my soul luxuriated and cast an Eastern enchantment over me. I asked for leave to go to the bazaar on Saturday night. My aunt was surprised and hoped it was not some Freemason° affair. I answered few questions in class. I watched my master's face pass from amiability to sternness; he hoped I was not beginning to idle. I could not call my wandering thoughts together. I had hardly any patience with the serious work of life which, now that it stood between me and my desire, seemed to me child's play, ugly monotonous child's play.

On Saturday morning I reminded my uncle that I wished to go to the bazaar in the evening. He was fussing at the hallstand, looking for the hatbrush, and answered me curtly:

"Yes, boy, I know."

As he was in the hall I could not go into the front 15 parlour and lie at the window. I left the house in bad humour and walked slowly towards the school. The air was pitilessly raw and already my heart misgave me.

When I came home to dinner my uncle had not yet been home. Still it was early. I sat staring at the clock for some time and, when its ticking began to irritate me, I left the room. I mounted the staircase and gained the upper part of the house. The high cold empty gloomy rooms liberated me and I went from room to room singing. From the front window I saw my companions playing below in the street. Their cries reached me weakened and indistinct and, leaning my forehead against the cool glass, I looked over at the dark house where she lived. I may have stood there for an hour, seeing nothing but the brown-clad figure cast by my imagination, touched discreetly by the lamplight at the curved neck, at the hand upon the railings and at the border below the dress.

When I came downstairs again I found Mrs. Mercer sitting at the fire. She was an old garrulous woman, a pawnbroker's widow, who collected used stamps for some pious purpose. I had to endure the gossip of the tea-table. The meal was prolonged beyond an hour and still my uncle did not come. Mrs. Mercer stood up to go: she was sorry she couldn't wait any longer, but it was after eight o'clock and she did not like to be out late, as the night air was bad for her. When she had gone I began to walk up and down the room, clenching my fists. My aunt said:

"I'm afraid you may put off your bazaar for this night of Our Lord."

At nine o'clock I heard my uncle's latchkey in the halldoor. I heard him talking to himself and heard the hallstand

rocking when it had received the weight of his overcoat. I could interpret these signs. When he was midway through his dinner I asked him to give me the money to go to the bazaar. He had forgotten.

"The people are in bed and after their first sleep now," 20 he said.

I did not smile. My aunt said to him energetically:

"Can't you give him the money and let him go? You've kept him late enough as it is."

My uncle said he was very sorry he had forgotten. He said he believed in the old saying: "All work and no play makes Jack a dull boy." He asked me where I was going and, when I had told him a second time he asked me did I know *The Arab's Farewell to his Steed*.° When I left the kitchen he was about to recite the opening lines of the piece to my aunt.

I held a florin tightly in my hand as I strode down Buckingham Street towards the station. The sight of the streets thronged with buyers and glaring with gas recalled to me the purpose of my journey. I took my seat in a third-class carriage of a deserted train. After an intolerable delay the train moved out of the station slowly. It crept onward among ruinous houses and over the twinkling river. At Westland Row Station a crowd of people pressed to the carriage doors; but the porters moved them back, saying that it was a special train for the bazaar. I remained alone in the bare carriage. In a few minutes the train drew up beside an improvised wooden platform. I passed out on to the road and saw by the lighted dial of a clock that it was ten minutes to ten. In front of me was a large building which displayed the magical name.

I could not find any sixpenny entrance and, fearing 25 that the bazaar would be closed, I passed in quickly through a turnstile, handing a shilling to a weary-looking man. I found myself in a big hall girdled at half its height by a gallery. Nearly all the stalls were closed and the greater part of the hall was in darkness. I recognised a silence like that which pervades a church after a service. I walked into the centre of the bazaar timidly. A few people were gathered about the stalls which were still open. Before a curtain, over which the words *Café Chantant*° were

---

° **Freemason** At the time the story takes place, many Catholics in Ireland thought the Masonic Order was a threat to the church.

° ***The Arab's Farewell to his Steed*** A sentimental poem by Caroline Norton (1808–1877) that tells the story of a nomad's heartbreak after selling his much-loved horse.

° ***Café Chantant*** A Paris café featuring musical entertainment.

Cultural Context In the early twentieth century, as world travel and the shipment of goods around the globe expanded at a dizzying pace, the West experienced a fascination with the "Orient." To peddle their wares, immigrants from the East established bazaars reminiscent of the ones in their homelands, displaying a dazzling array of spices, foods, and material goods. This exotic appeal to the senses, representing the allure of the distant and unknown, became a highlight of many towns and cities. In this story, the bazaar represents the allure of the strange and exotic for the young narrator.

The Art Archive/University Library, Istanbul/Gianni Dagli Orti

>> Bazaar with stalls

written in coloured lamps, two men were counting money on a salver. I listened to the fall of the coins.

Remembering with difficulty why I had come I went over to one of the stalls and examined porcelain vases and flowered tea-sets. At the door of the stall a young lady was talking and laughing with two young gentlemen. I remarked their English accents and listened vaguely to their conversation.

"O, I never said such a thing!"
"O, but you did!"
"O, but I didn't!"
"Didn't she say that?"
"Yes. I heard her."
"O, there's a . . . fib!"

Observing me the young lady came over and asked me did I wish to buy anything. The tone of her voice was not encouraging; she seemed to have spoken to me out of a sense of duty. I looked humbly at the great jars that stood like eastern guards at either side of the dark entrance to the stall and murmured:

"No, thank you."

The young lady changed the position of one of the vases and went back to the two young men. They began to talk of the same subject. Once or twice the young lady glanced at me over her shoulder.

I lingered before her stall, though I knew my stay was useless, to make my interest in her wares seem the more real. Then I turned away slowly and walked down the middle of the bazaar. I allowed the two pennies to fall against the sixpence in my pocket. I heard a voice call from one end of the gallery that the light was out. The upper part of the hall was now completely dark.

Gazing up into the darkness I saw myself as a creature driven and derided by vanity; and my eyes burned with anguish and anger.

Related Works

"Snow" (p. 102), "A&P" (p. 131), "Gryphon" (p. 138), "Doe Season" (p. 290), "The Secret Lion" (p. 333), "Shall I compare thee to a summer's day?" (p. 408), *Beauty* (p. 541)

 See Chapter 15 Review Card for Reading and Reacting questions about James Joyce, "Araby."

(Mary) Flannery O'Connor
(1925–1964)

© AP Photo

was born to a prosperous Catholic family in Savannah, Georgia, and spent most of her adult life on a farm near the town of Milledgeville. She left the South to study writing at the University of Iowa, moving to New York to work on her first novel, *Wise Blood* (1952). On a train going south for Christmas, O'Connor became seriously ill; she was diagnosed as having lupus, the immune system disease that had killed her father and would cause O'Connor's death when she was only thirty-nine years old.

While her mother ran the farm, O'Connor spent mornings writing and afternoons wandering the fields with cane or crutches. Her short story collection *A Good Man Is Hard to Find* (1955) and an excellent French translation of *Wise Blood* established her international reputation, which was solidified with the publication of a second novel, *The Violent*

Bear It Away (1960), and a posthumously published book of short stories, *Everything That Rises Must Converge* (1965).

O'Connor, said a friend, believed that an artist "should face all the truth down to the worst of it." Yet however dark, her stories are infused with grim humor and a fierce belief in the possibility of spiritual redemption, even for her most tortured characters. A line from her short story "A Good Man Is Hard to Find" says much about what O'Connor perceived about both natural things and her characters: "The trees were full of silver-white sunlight and the meanest of them sparkled." In O'Connor's work, the "meanest" things and people can sparkle, touched by a kind of holy madness and beauty.

A Good Man Is Hard to Find (1955)

The grandmother didn't want to go to Florida. She wanted to visit some of her connections in east Tennessee and she was seizing at every chance to change Bailey's mind. Bailey was the son she lived with, her only boy. He was sitting on the edge of his chair at the table, bent over the orange sports section of the *Journal*. "Now look here, Bailey," she said, "see here, read this," and she stood with one hand on her thin hip and the other rattling the newspaper at his bald head. "Here this fellow that calls himself The Misfit is aloose from the Federal Pen and headed toward Florida and you read here what it says he did to these people. Just you read it. I wouldn't take my children in any direction with a criminal like that aloose in it. I couldn't answer to my conscience if I did."

Bailey didn't look up from his reading so she wheeled around then and faced the children's mother, a young woman in slacks, whose face was as broad and innocent as a cabbage and was tied around with a green headkerchief that had two points on the top like a rabbit's ears. She was sitting on the sofa, feeding the baby his apricots out of a jar. "The children have been to Florida before," the old lady said. "You all ought to take them somewhere else for a change so they would see different parts of the world and be broad. They never have been to east Tennessee."

The children's mother didn't seem to hear her but the eight-year-old boy, John Wesley, a stocky child with glasses, said, "If you don't want to go to Florida, why dontcha stay at home?" He and the little girl, June Star, were reading the funny papers on the floor.

"She wouldn't stay at home to be queen for a day," June Star said without raising her yellow head.

"Yes and what would you do if this fellow, the Misfit, 5 caught you?" the grandmother asked.

"I'd smack his face," John Wesley said.

"She wouldn't stay at home for a million bucks," June Star said. "Afraid she'd miss something. She has to go everywhere we go."

"All right, Miss," the grandmother said. "Just remember that the next time you want me to curl your hair."

June Star said her hair was naturally curly.

The next morning the grandmother was the first 10 one in the car, ready to go. She had her big black valise that looked like the head of a hippopotamus in one corner, and underneath it she was hiding a basket with Pitty Sing, the cat, in it. She didn't intend for the cat to be left alone in the house for three days because he would miss her too much and she was afraid he might brush against one of the gas burners and accidentally asphyxiate himself. Her son, Bailey, didn't like to arrive at a motel with a cat.

She sat in the middle of the back seat with John Wesley and June Star on either side of her.

> "'Here this fellow that calls himself The Misfit is aloose from the Federal Pen and headed toward Florida and you read here what it says he did to these people. Just you read it.'"

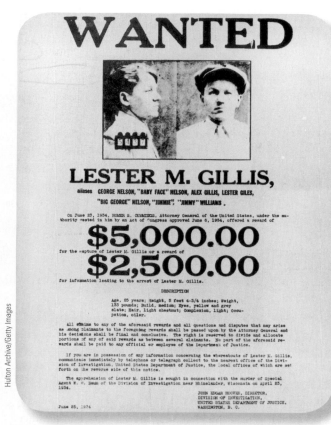

>> Wanted poster

clay banks slightly streaked with purple; and the various crops that made rows of green lace-work on the ground. The trees were full of silver-white sunlight and the meanest of them sparkled. The children were reading comic magazines and their mother had gone back to sleep.

"Let's go through Georgia fast so we won't have to look at it much," John Wesley said.

"If I were a little boy," said the grandmother, "I 15 wouldn't talk about my native state that way. Tennessee has the mountains and Georgia has the hills."

"Tennessee is just a hillbilly dumping ground," John Wesley said, "and Georgia is a lousy state too."

"You said it," June Star said.

"In my time," said the grandmother, folding her thin veined fingers, "children were more respectful of their native states and their parents and everything else. People did right then. Oh look at the cute little pickaninny!" she said and pointed to a Negro child standing in the door of a shack. "Wouldn't that make a picture, now?" she asked and they all turned and looked at the little Negro out of the back window. He waved.

"He didn't have any britches on," June Star said.

"He probably didn't have any," the grandmother ex- 20 plained. "Little niggers in the country don't have things like we do. If I could paint, I'd paint that picture," she said.

The children exchanged comic books.

The grandmother offered to hold the baby and the children's mother passed him over the front seat to her. She set him on her knee and bounced him and told him about the things they were passing. She rolled her eyes and screwed up her mouth and stuck her leathery thin face into his smooth bland one. Occasionally he gave her a faraway smile. They passed a large cotton field with five or six graves fenced in the middle of it, like a small island. "Look at the graveyard!" the grandmother said, pointing it out. "That was the old family burying ground. That belonged to the plantation."

"Where's the plantation?" John Wesley asked.

"Gone With the Wind,"° said the grandmother. "Ha. Ha."

When the children finished all the comic books they 25 had brought, they opened the lunch and ate it. The grandmother ate a peanut butter sandwich and an olive and would not let the children throw the box and the paper napkins out the window. When there was nothing else to do they played a game by choosing a cloud and making the other two guess what shape it suggested. John Wesley took one the shape of a cow and June Star guessed a cow and John Wesley said, no, an automobile, and June Star said he didn't play fair, and they began to slap each other over the grandmother.

The grandmother said she would tell them a story if they would keep quiet. When she told a story, she rolled her eyes and waved her head and was very dramatic. She

Bailey and the children's mother and the baby sat in front and they left Atlanta at eight forty-five with the mileage on the car at 55890. The grandmother wrote this down because she thought it would be interesting to say how many miles they had been when they got back. It took them twenty minutes to reach the outskirts of the city.

The old lady settled herself comfortably, removing her white cotton gloves and putting them up with her purse on the shelf in front of the back window. The children's mother still had on slacks and still had her head tied up in a green kerchief, but the grandmother had on a navy blue straw sailor hat with a bunch of white violets on the brim and a navy blue dress with a small white dot in the print. Her collars and cuffs were white organdy trimmed with lace and at her neckline she had pinned a purple spray of cloth violets containing a sachet. In case of an accident, anyone seeing her dead on the highway would know at once that she was a lady.

She said she thought it was going to be a good day for driving, neither too hot nor too cold, and she cautioned Bailey that the speed limit was fifty-five miles an hour and that the patrolmen hid themselves behind billboards and small clumps of trees and sped out after you before you had a chance to slow down. She pointed out interesting details of the scenery: Stone Mountain; the blue granite that in some places came up to both sides of the highway; the brilliant red

---

° **Gone with the Wind** *Gone with the Wind* is a 1936 novel by Margaret Mitchell about the Civil War.

>> Scene from *Gone with the Wind* (1939)

said once when she was a maiden lady she had been courted by a Mr. Edgar Atkins Teagarden from Jasper, Georgia. She said he was a very good-looking man and a gentleman and that he brought her a watermelon every Saturday afternoon with his initials cut in it, E. A. T. Well, one Saturday, she said, Mr. Teagarden brought the watermelon and there was nobody at home and he left it on the front porch and returned in his buggy to Jasper, but she never got the watermelon, she said, because a nigger boy ate it when he saw the initials, E. A. T.! This story tickled John Wesley's funny bone and he giggled and giggled but June Star didn't think it was any good. She said she wouldn't marry a man that just brought her a watermelon on Saturday. The grandmother said she would have done well to marry Mr. Teagarden because he was a gentleman and had bought Coca-Cola stock when it first came out and that he died only a few years ago, a very wealthy man.

They stopped at The Tower for barbecued sandwiches. The Tower was a part stucco and part wood filling station and dance hall set in a clearing outside of Timothy. A fat man named Red Sammy Butts ran it and there were signs stuck here and there on the building and for miles up and down the highway saying, TRY RED SAMMY'S FAMOUS BARBECUE. NONE LIKE FAMOUS RED SAMMY'S! RED SAM! THE FAT BOY WITH THE HAPPY LAUGH. A VETERAN! RED SAMMY'S YOUR MAN!

Red Sammy was lying on the bare ground outside The Tower with his head under a truck while a gray monkey about a foot high, chained to a small chinaberry tree, chattered nearby. The monkey sprang back into the tree and got on the highest limb as soon as he saw the children jump out of the car and run toward him.

Inside, The Tower was a long dark room with a counter at one end and tables at the other and dancing space in the middle. They all sat down at a board table next to the nickelodeon and Red Sam's wife, a tall burnt-brown woman with hair and eyes lighter than her skin, came and took their order. The children's mother put a dime in the machine and played "The Tennessee Waltz," and the grandmother said that tune always made her want to dance. She asked Bailey if he would like to dance but he only glared at her. He didn't have a naturally sweet disposition like she did and trips made him nervous. The grandmother's brown eyes were very bright. She swayed her head from side to side and pretended she was dancing in her chair. June Star said play something she could tap to so the children's mother put in another dime and played a fast number and June Star stepped out onto the dance floor and did her tap routine.

"Ain't she cute?" Red Sam's wife said, leaning over the 30 counter. "Would you like to come be my little girl?"

"No I certainly wouldn't," June Star said. "I wouldn't live in a broken-down place like this for a million bucks!" and she ran back to the table.

"Ain't she cute?" the woman repeated, stretching her mouth politely.

"Aren't you ashamed?" hissed the grandmother.

Red Sam came in and told his wife to quit lounging on the counter and hurry up with these people's order. His khaki trousers reached just to his hip bones and his stomach hung over them like a sack of meal swaying under his shirt. He came over and sat down at a table nearby and let out a combination sigh and yodel. "You can't win," he said. "You can't win," and he wiped his sweating red face off with a gray handkerchief. "These days you don't know who to trust," he said. "Ain't that the truth?"

"People are certainly not nice like they used to be," 35 said the grandmother.

"Two fellers come in here last week," Red Sammy said, "driving a Chrysler. It was a old beat-up car but it was a good one and these boys looked all right to me. Said they worked at the mill and you know I let them fellers charge the gas they bought? Now why did I do that?"

"Because you're a good man!" the grandmother said at once.

>> 1950s gas station

"Yes'm, I suppose so," Red Sam said as if he were struck with this answer.

His wife brought the orders, carrying the five plates all at once without a tray, two in each hand and one balanced on her arm. "It isn't a soul in this green world of God's that you can trust," she said. "And I don't count nobody out of that, not nobody," she repeated, looking at Red Sammy.

"Did you read about that criminal, The Misfit, that's 40 escaped?" asked the grandmother.

"I wouldn't be a bit surprised if he didn't attack this place right here," said the woman. "If he hears about it being here, I wouldn't be none surprised to see him. If he hears it's two cent in the cash register, I wouldn't be at all surprised if he . . ."

"That'll do," Red Sam said. "Go bring these people their Co'-Colas," and the woman went off to get the rest of the order.

"A good man is hard to find," Red Sammy said. "Everything is getting terrible. I remember the day you could go off and leave your screen door unlatched. Not no more."

He and the grandmother discussed better times. The old lady said that in her opinion Europe was entirely to blame for the way things were now. She said the way Europe acted you would think we were made of money and Red Sam said it was no use talking about it, she was exactly right. The children ran outside into the white sunlight and looked at the monkey in the lacy chinaberry tree. He was busy catching fleas on himself and biting each one carefully between his teeth as if it were a delicacy.

They drove off again into the hot afternoon. The 45 grandmother took cat naps and woke up every few minutes with her own snoring. Outside of Toombsboro she woke up and recalled an old plantation that she had visited in this neighborhood once when she was a young lady. She said the house had six white columns across the front and that there was an avenue of oaks leading up to it and two little wooden trellis arbors on either side in front where you sat down with your suitor after a stroll in the garden. She recalled exactly which road to turn off to get to it. She knew that Bailey would not be willing to lose any time looking at an old house, but the more she talked about it, the more she wanted to see it once again and find out if the little twin arbors were still standing. "There was a secret panel in this house," she said craftily, not telling the truth but wishing that she were, "and the story went that all the family silver was hidden in it when Sherman came through but it was never found . . ."

"Hey!" John Wesley said. "Let's go see it! We'll find it! We'll poke all the woodwork and find it! Who lives there? Where do you turn off at? Hey Pop, can't we turn off there?"

"We never have seen a house with a secret panel!" June Star shrieked. "Let's go to the house with the secret panel! Hey Pop, can't we go see the house with the secret panel!"

"It's not far from here, I know," the grandmother said. "It wouldn't take over twenty minutes."

Bailey was looking straight ahead. His jaw was as rigid as a horseshoe. "No," he said.

The children began to yell and scream that they 50 wanted to see the house with the secret panel. John Wesley kicked the back of the front seat and June Star hung over her mother's shoulder and whined desperately into her ear that they never had any fun even on their vacation, that they could never do what THEY wanted to do. The baby began to scream and John Wesley kicked the back of the seat so hard that his father could feel the blows in his kidney.

"All right!" he shouted and drew the car to a stop at the side of the road. "Will you all shut up? Will you all just shut up for one second? If you don't shut up, we won't go anywhere."

"It would be very educational for them," the grandmother murmured.

"All right," Bailey said, "but get this: this is the only time we're going to stop for anything like this. This is the one and only time."

"The dirt road that you have to turn down is about a mile back," the grandmother directed. "I marked it when we passed."

"A dirt road," Bailey groaned.   55

After they had turned around and were headed toward the dirt road, the grandmother recalled other points about the house, the beautiful glass over the front doorway and the candle-lamp in the hall. John Wesley said that the secret panel was probably in the fireplace.

"You can't go inside this house," Bailey said. "You don't know who lives there."

"While you all talk to the people in front, I'll run around behind and get in a window," John Wesley suggested.

"We'll all stay in the car," his mother said.

They turned onto the dirt road and the car raced 60 roughly along in a swirl of pink dust. The grandmother recalled the times when there were no paved roads and thirty miles was a day's journey. The dirt road was hilly and there were sudden washes in it and sharp curves on dangerous embankments. All at once they would be on a hill, looking down over the blue tops of trees for miles around, then the next minute, they would be in a red depression with the dust-coated trees looking down on them.

"This place had better turn up in a minute," Bailey said, "or I'm going to turn around."

The road looked as if no one had traveled on it in months.

"It's not much farther," the grandmother said and just as she said it, a horrible thought came to her. The thought was so embarrassing that she turned red in the face and her eyes dilated and her feet jumped up, upsetting her valise in the corner. The instant the valise moved, the newspaper top she had over the basket under it rose with a snarl and Pitty Sing, the cat, sprang onto Bailey's shoulder.

The children were thrown to the floor and their mother, clutching the baby, was thrown out the door onto the ground; the old lady was thrown into the front seat. The car turned over once and landed right-side-up in a gulch off the side of the road. Bailey remained in the driver's seat with the cat—gray-striped with a broad white face and an orange nose—clinging to his neck like a caterpillar.

As soon as the children saw they could move their 65 arms and legs, they scrambled out of the car, shouting, "We've had an ACCIDENT!" The grandmother was curled up under the dashboard, hoping she was injured so that Bailey's wrath would not come down on her all at once. The horrible thought she had had before the accident was that the house she had remembered so vividly was not in Georgia but in Tennessee.

Bailey removed the cat from his neck with both hands and flung it out the window against the side of a pine tree. Then he got out of the car and started looking for the children's mother. She was sitting against the side of the red gutted ditch, holding the screaming baby, but she only had a cut down her face and a broken shoulder. "We've had an ACCIDENT!" the children screamed in a frenzy of delight.

"But nobody's killed," June Star said with disappointment as the grandmother limped out of the car, her hat still pinned to her head but the broken front brim standing up at a jaunty angle and the violet spray hanging off the side. They all sat down in the ditch, except the children, to recover from the shock. They were all shaking.

"Maybe a car will come along," said the children's mother hoarsely.

"I believe I have injured an organ," said the grandmother, pressing her side, but no one answered her. Bailey's teeth were clattering. He had on a yellow sport shirt with bright blue parrots designed in it and his face was as yellow as the shirt. The grandmother decided that she would not mention that the house was in Tennessee.

The road was about ten feet above and they could see 70 only the tops of the trees on the other side of it. Behind the ditch they were sitting in there were more woods, tall and dark and deep. In a few minutes they saw a car some distance away on top of a hill, coming slowly as if the occupants were watching them. The grandmother stood up and waved both arms dramatically to attract their attention. The car continued to come on slowly, disappeared around a bend and appeared again, moving even slower, on top of the hill they had gone over. It was a big black battered hearse-like automobile. There were three men in it.

It came to a stop just over them and for some minutes, the driver looked down with a steady expressionless gaze to where they were sitting, and didn't speak. Then he turned his head and muttered something to the other two and they got out. One was a fat boy in black trousers and a red sweat shirt with a silver stallion embossed on the front of it. He moved around on the right side of them and stood staring, his mouth partly open in a kind of loose grin. The other had on khaki pants and a blue striped coat and a gray hat pulled down very low, hiding most of his face. He came around slowly on the left side. Neither spoke.

The driver got out of the car and stood by the side of it, looking down at them. He was an older man than the other two. His hair was just beginning to gray and he wore silver-rimmed spectacles that gave him a scholarly look. He had a long creased face and didn't have on any shirt or undershirt. He had on blue jeans that were too tight for him and was holding a black hat and a gun. The two boys also had guns.

"We've had an ACCIDENT!" the children screamed.

The grandmother had the peculiar feeling that the bespectacled man was someone she knew. His face was as familiar to her as if she had known him all her life but she could not recall who he was. He moved away from the car and began to come down the embankment, placing his feet carefully so that he wouldn't slip. He had on tan and white shoes and no socks, and his ankles were red and thin. "Good afternoon," he said. "I see you all had you a little spill."

"We turned over twice!" said the grandmother. 75

"Oncet," he corrected. "We seen it happen. Try their car and see will it run, Hiram," he said quietly to the boy with the gray hat.

"What you got that gun for?" John Wesley asked. "Watcha gonna do with that gun?"

"Lady," the man said to the children's mother, "would you mind calling them children to sit down by you? Children make me nervous. I want all you all to sit down right together there where you're at."

"What are you telling US what to do for?" June Star asked.

Behind them the line of woods gaped like a dark open 80 mouth. "Come here," said their mother.

"Look here now," Bailey began suddenly, "we're in a predicament! We're in . . ."

The grandmother shrieked. She scrambled to her feet and stood staring. "You're The Misfit!" she said. "I recognized you at once!"

"Yes'm," the man said, smiling slightly as if he were pleased in spite of himself to be known, "but it would have been better for all of you, lady, if you hadn't of reckernized me."

Bailey turned his head sharply and said something to his mother that shocked even the children. The old lady began to cry and The Misfit reddened.

"Lady," he said, "don't you get upset. Sometimes a 85 man says things he don't mean. I don't reckon he meant to talk to you thataway."

"You wouldn't shoot a lady, would you?" the grandmother said and removed a clean handkerchief from her cuff and began to slap at her eyes with it.

The Misfit pointed the toe of his shoe into the ground and made a little hole and then covered it up again. "I would hate to have to," he said.

"Listen," the grandmother almost screamed, "I know you're a good man. You don't look a bit like you have common blood. I know you must come from nice people!"

"Yes mam," he said, "finest people in the world." When he smiled he showed a row of strong white teeth. "God never made a finer woman than my mother and my daddy's heart was pure gold," he said. The boy with the red sweat shirt had come around behind them and was standing with his gun at his hip. The Misfit squatted down on the ground. "Watch them children, Bobby Lee," he said. "You know they make me nervous." He looked at the six of them huddled together in front of him and he seemed to be embarrassed as if he couldn't think of anything to say. "Ain't a cloud in the sky," he remarked, looking up at it. "Don't see no sun but don't see no cloud neither."

"Yes, it's a beautiful day," said the grandmother. "Lis- 90 ten," she said, "you shouldn't call yourself The Misfit because I know you're a good man at heart. I can just look at you and tell."

"Hush!" Bailey yelled. "Hush! Everybody shut up and let me handle this!" He was squatting in the position of a runner about to sprint forward but he didn't move.

"I pre-chate that, lady," The Misfit said and drew a little circle in the ground with the butt of his gun.

"It'll take a half a hour to fix this here car," Hiram called, looking over the raised hood of it.

"Well, first you and Bobby Lee get him and that little boy to step over yonder with you," The Misfit said, pointing to Bailey and John Wesley. "The boys want to ast you something," he said to Bailey. "Would you mind stepping back in them woods there with them?"

"Listen," Bailey began, "we're in a terrible predica- 95 ment! Nobody realizes what this is," and his voice cracked. His eyes were as blue and intense as the parrots in his shirt and he remained perfectly still.

The grandmother reached up to adjust her hat brim as if she were going to the woods with him but it came off in her hand. She stood staring at it and after a second she let

 EXPLORE ONLINE >

To listen to an instructor podcast of "A Good Man Is Hard to Find," visit your Literature CourseMate, accessed through www.cengagebrain.com.

it fall on the ground. Hiram pulled Bailey up by the arm as if he were assisting an old man. John Wesley caught hold of his father's hand and Bobby Lee followed. They went off toward the woods and just as they reached the dark edge, Bailey turned and supporting himself against a gray naked pine trunk, he shouted, "I'll be back in a minute, Mamma, wait on me!"

"Come back this instant!" his mother shrilled but they all disappeared into the woods.

"Bailey Boy!" the grandmother called in a tragic voice but she found she was looking at The Misfit squatting on the ground in front of her. "I just know you're a good man," she said desperately. "You're not a bit common!"

"Nome, I ain't a good man," The Misfit said after a second as if he had considered her statement carefully, "but I ain't the worst in the world neither. My daddy said I was a different breed of dog from my brothers and sisters. 'You know,' Daddy said, 'it's some that can live their whole life out without asking about it and it's others has to know why it is, and this boy is one of the latters. He's going to be into everything!'" He put on his black hat and looked up suddenly and then away deep into the woods as if he were embarrassed again. "I'm sorry I don't have on a shirt before you ladies," he said, hunching his shoulders slightly. "We buried our clothes that we had on when we escaped and we're just making do until we can get better. We borrowed these from some folks we met," he explained.

"That's perfectly all right," the grandmother said. 100 "Maybe Bailey has an extra shirt in his suitcase."

"I'll look and see terrectly," The Misfit said.

"Where are they taking him?" the children's mother screamed.

"Daddy was a card himself," The Misfit said. "You couldn't put anything over on him. He never got in trouble with the Authorities though. Just had the knack of handling them."

"You could be honest too if you'd only try," said the grandmother. "Think how wonderful it would be to settle down and live a comfortable life and not have to think about somebody chasing you all the time."

The Misfit kept scratching in the ground with the butt 105 of his gun as if he were thinking about it. "Yes'm, somebody is always after you," he murmured.

The grandmother noticed how thin his shoulder blades were just behind his hat because she was standing up looking down on him. "Do you ever pray?" she asked.

He shook his head. All she saw was the black hat wiggle between his shoulder blades. "Nome," he said.

There was a pistol shot from the woods, followed closely by another. Then silence. The old lady's head jerked around. She could hear the wind move through the tree tops like a long satisfied insuck of breath. "Bailey Boy!" she called.

"I was a gospel singer for a while," The Misfit said. "I been most everything. Been in the arm service, both land and sea, at home and abroad, been twict married, been an undertaker, been with the railroads, plowed Mother Earth, been in a tornado, seen a man burnt alive oncet," and he looked up at the children's mother and the little girl who were sitting close together, their faces white and their eyes glassy; "I even seen a woman flogged," he said.

"Pray, pray," the grandmother began, "pray, pray . . ." 110

"I never was a bad boy that I remember of," The Misfit said in an almost dreamy voice, "but somewheres along the line I done something wrong and got sent to the penitentiary. I was buried alive," and he looked up and held her attention to him by a steady stare.

"That's when you should have started to pray," she said. "What did you do to get sent to the penitentiary that first time?"

"Turn to the right, it was a wall," The Misfit said, looking up again at the cloudless sky. "Turn to the left, it was a wall. Look up it was a ceiling, look down it was a floor. I forget what I done, lady. I set there and set there, trying to remember what it was I done and I ain't recalled it to this day. Oncet in a while, I would think it was coming to me, but it never come."

"Maybe they put you in by mistake," the old lady said vaguely.

"Nome," he said. "It wasn't no mistake. They had the 115 papers on me."

"You must have stolen something," she said.

The Misfit sneered slightly. "Nobody had nothing I wanted," he said. "It was a head-doctor at the penitentiary said what I had done was kill my daddy but I known that for a lie. My daddy died in nineteen ought nineteen of the epidemic flu and I never had a thing to do with it. He was buried in the Mount Hopewell Baptist churchyard and you can go there and see for yourself."

"If you would pray," the old lady said, "Jesus would help you."

"That's right," The Misfit said.

"Well then, why don't you pray?" she asked trembling 120 with delight suddenly.

"I don't want no hep," he said. "I'm doing all right by myself."

Bobby Lee and Hiram came ambling back from the woods. Bobby Lee was dragging a yellow shirt with bright blue parrots in it.

"Thow me that shirt, Bobby Lee," The Misfit said. The shirt came flying at him and landed on his shoulder and he put it on. The grandmother couldn't name what the shirt reminded her of. "No, lady," The Misfit said while he was buttoning it up, "I found out the crime don't matter. You can do one thing or you can do another, kill a man or take a tire off his car, because sooner or later you're going to forget what it was you done and just be punished for it."

The children's mother had begun to make heaving noises as if she couldn't get her breath. "Lady," he asked, "would you and that little girl like to step off yonder with Bobby Lee and Hiram and join your husband?"

"Yes, thank you," the mother said faintly. Her left arm 125 dangled helplessly and she was holding the baby, who had gone to sleep, in the other. "Hep that lady up, Hiram," The Misfit said as she struggled to climb out of the ditch, "and Bobby Lee, you hold onto that little girl's hand."

"I don't want to hold hands with him," June Star said. "He reminds me of a pig."

The fat boy blushed and laughed and caught her by the arm and pulled her off into the woods after Hiram and her mother.

Alone with The Misfit, the grandmother found that she had lost her voice. There was not a cloud in the sky nor any sun. There was nothing around her but woods. She wanted to tell him that he must pray. She opened and closed her mouth several times before anything came out. Finally she found herself saying, "Jesus, Jesus," meaning, Jesus will help you, but the way she was saying it, it sounded as if she might be cursing.

"Yes'm," The Misfit said as if he agreed. "Jesus thown everything off balance. It was the same case with Him as with me except He hadn't committed any crime and they could prove I had committed one because they had the papers on me. Of course," he said, "they never shown me my papers. That's why I sign myself now. I said long ago, you get you a signature and sign everything you do and keep a copy of it. Then you'll know what you done and you can hold up the crime to the punishment and see do they match and in the end you'll have something to prove you ain't been treated right. I call myself The Misfit," he said, "because I can't make what all I done wrong fit what all I gone through in punishment."

There was a piercing scream from the woods, fol- 130 lowed closely by a pistol report. "Does it seem right to you, lady, that one is punished a heap and another ain't punished at all?"

"Jesus!" the old lady cried. "You've got good blood! I know you wouldn't shoot a lady! I know you come from nice people! Pray! Jesus, you ought not to shoot a lady. I'll give you all the money I've got!"

"Lady," The Misfit said, looking beyond her far into the woods, "there never was a body that give the undertaker a tip."

There were two more pistol reports and the grandmother raised her head like a parched old turkey hen crying for water and called, "Bailey Boy, Bailey Boy!" as if her heart would break.

"Jesus was the only One that ever raised the dead," The Misfit continued, "and He shouldn't have done it. He thown everything off balance. If He did what He said, then it's nothing for you to do but thow away everything and follow Him, and if He didn't, then it's nothing for you to do but enjoy the few minutes you got left the best way you can—by killing somebody or burning down his house or doing some other meanness to him. No pleasure but meanness," he said and his voice became almost a snarl.

"Maybe He didn't raise the dead," the old lady mum- 135 bled, not knowing what she was saying and feeling so dizzy that she sank down in the ditch with her legs twisted under her.

"I wasn't there so I can't say He didn't," The Misfit said. "I wisht I had of been there," he said, hitting the ground with his fist. "It ain't right I wasn't there because if I had of been there I would of known. Listen, lady," he said in a high voice, "if I had of been there I would of known and I wouldn't be like I am now." His voice seemed about to crack and the grandmother's head cleared for an instant. She saw the man's face twisted close to her own as if he were going to cry and she murmured, "Why you're one of my babies. You're one of my own children!" She reached out and touched him on the shoulder. The Misfit sprang back as if a snake had bitten him and shot her three times through the chest. Then he put his gun down on the ground and took off his glasses and began to clean them.

Hiram and Bobby Lee returned from the woods and stood over the ditch, looking down at the grandmother who half sat and half lay in a puddle of blood with her legs crossed under her like a child's and her face smiling up at the cloudless sky.

Without his glasses, The Misfit's eyes were red-rimmed and pale and defenseless-looking. "Take her off and thow her where you thown the others," he said, picking up the cat that was rubbing itself against his leg.

"She was a talker, wasn't she?" Bobby Lee said, sliding down the ditch with a yodel.

"She would of been a good woman," The Misfit said, 140 "if it had been somebody there to shoot her every minute of her life."

"Some fun!" Bobby Lee said.

"Shut up, Bobby Lee," The Misfit said. "It's no real pleasure in life."

Related Works

"Accident" (p. 102), "The Lottery" (p. 251), "Where Are You Going, Where Have You Been?" (p. 325), "The Tell-Tale Heart" (p. 331)

See Chapter 15 Review Card for Reading and Reacting questions about (Mary) Flannery O'Connor, "A Good Man Is Hard to Find."

© AP Photo/David Pickoff

Tim O'Brien (1946–   )

is sometimes described as a writer whose books are on the short list of essential fiction about the Vietnam War. After graduating *summa cum laude* from Macalester College in 1968, O'Brien was immediately drafted into the United States Army and sent to Vietnam, where he served with the 198th Infantry Brigade. He was promoted to sergeant and awarded a Purple Heart after receiving a shrapnel wound in a battle near My Lai. In 1970, after his discharge from the army, he attended Harvard graduate school to study government. He worked as a reporter for the *Washington Post* before pursuing a full-time career as a writer.

O'Brien's plots focus on danger, violence, courage, endurance, despair, and other topics often associated with war fiction, but he treats these topics with an emphasis on the contemporary dilemmas faced by those who may be unwilling participants in an unpopular war. O'Brien calls *If I Die in a Combat Zone, Box Me Up and Ship Me Home* (1979) a memoir because it relates his war experiences as a

naive young college graduate who suddenly finds himself facing bullets and land mines rather than sitting behind a desk. *Northern Lights* (1975) concentrates on the wilderness survival experiences of two brothers, one of whom has just returned from the Vietnam War. A fantastic daydream of an American soldier, *Going after Cacciato* (1978), won a National Book Award. *The Things They Carried* (1990) is a quasi-fictional collection of interrelated stories that deal with a single platoon. *The Vietnam in Me* (1994) emphasizes the destructive effects of war on a soldier, even after he has returned home, and *In the Lake of the Woods* (1994) tells a dramatic story of a couple missing in Minnesota. O'Brien's most recent books are *Tomcat in Love* (1998) and *July, July* (2002).

The Things They Carried (1986)

First Lieutenant Jimmy Cross carried letters from a girl named Martha, a junior at Mount Sebastian College in New Jersey. They were not love letters, but Lieutenant Cross was hoping, so he kept them folded in plastic at the bottom of his rucksack. In the late afternoon, after a day's march, he would dig his foxhole, wash his hands under a canteen, unwrap the letters, hold them with the tips of his fingers, and spend the last hour of light pretending. He would imagine romantic camping trips into the White Mountains in New Hampshire. He would sometimes taste the envelope flaps, knowing her tongue had been there. More than anything, he wanted Martha to love him as he loved her, but the letters were most-

> "The things they carried were largely determined by necessity. Among the necessities or near necessities were P-38 can openers, pocket knives ...."

ly chatty, elusive on the matter of love. She was a virgin, he was almost sure. She was an English major at Mount Sebastian, and she wrote beautifully about her professors and roommates and midterm exams, about her respect for Chaucer and her great affection for Virginia Woolf. She often quoted lines of poetry; she never mentioned the war, except to say, Jimmy, take care of yourself. The letters weighed ten ounces. They were signed "Love, Martha," but Lieutenant Cross understood that "Love" was only a way of signing and did not mean what he sometimes pretended it meant. At dusk, he would carefully return the letters to his rucksack. Slowly, a bit distracted, he would get up and move among his men, checking the perimeter, then at full dark he would return to his hole and watch the night and wonder if Martha was a virgin.

The things they carried were largely determined by necessity. Among the necessities or near necessities were P-38 can openers, pocket knives, heat tabs, wrist watches, dog tags, mosquito repellent, chewing gum, candy, cigarettes, salt tablets, packets of Kool-Aid, lighters, matches, sewing kits, Military Payment Certificates, C rations, and two or three canteens of water. Together, these items weighed between fifteen and twenty pounds, depending upon a man's habits or rate of metabolism. Henry Dobbins, who was a big man, carried extra rations; he was especially fond of canned peaches in heavy syrup over pound cake. Dave Jensen, who practiced field hygiene, carried a toothbrush, dental floss, and several hotel-size bars of soap he'd stolen on R&R in Sydney, Australia. Ted Lavender, who was scared, carried tranquilizers until he was shot in the head outside the village of Than Khe in mid-April. By necessity, and because it was SOP,° they all carried steel helmets that weighed five pounds including the liner and camouflage cover. They carried the standard fatigue jackets and trousers. Very few carried underwear. On their feet they carried jungle boots—2.1 pounds—and Dave Jensen carried three pairs of socks and a can of Dr. Scholl's foot powder as a precaution against trench foot. Until he was shot, Ted Lavender carried six or seven ounces of premium dope, which for him was a necessity. Mitchell Sanders, the RTO,° carried condoms. Norman Bowker carried a diary. Rat Kiley carried comic books. Kiowa, a devout Baptist, carried an illustrated New Testament that had been presented to him by his father, who taught Sunday school in Oklahoma City, Oklahoma. As a hedge against bad times, however, Kiowa also carried his grandmother's distrust of the white man, his grandfather's old hunting hatchet. Necessity dictated. Because the land was mined and booby-trapped, it was SOP for each man to carry a steel-centered, nylon-covered flak jacket, which weighed 6.7 pounds, but which on hot days seemed much heavier. Because you could die so quickly, each man carried at least one large compress bandage, usually in the helmet band for easy access. Because the nights were cold, and because the monsoons were wet, each carried a green plastic poncho that could be used as a raincoat or ground sheet or makeshift tent. With its quilted liner, the poncho weighed almost two pounds, but it was worth every ounce. In April, for instance, when Ted Lavender was shot, they used his poncho to wrap him up, then to carry him across the paddy, then to lift him into the chopper that took him away.

° **SOP** Standard operating procedure.

° **RTO** Radio telephone operator.

Cultural Context

United States involvement in the Vietnam War lasted from the early 1960s until the mid 1970s. By the war's end, more than 47,000 Americans had been killed in action, nearly 11,000 had died of other causes, and more than 303,000 had been wounded. Estimates of South Vietnamese army casualties range from 185,000 to 225,000 killed and 500,000 to 570,000 wounded. The North Vietnamese and the Viet Cong, the guerrilla force that fought against South Vietnam and the United States, lost about 900,000 troops. In addition, more than 1 million North and South Vietnamese civilians were killed during the war. In 1976, North and South Vietnam reunified to form the Socialist Republic of Vietnam, which, due in large part to the Vietnamese occupation of Cambodia, continued to face domestic and international struggles through the late 1980s. Vietnamese troops finally withdrew from Cambodia in 1989.

They were called legs or grunts.

To carry something was to "hump" it, as when Lieutenant Jimmy Cross humped his love for Martha up the hills and through the swamps. In its intransitive form, "to hump" meant "to walk," or "to march," but it implied burdens far beyond the intransitive.

Almost everyone humped photographs. In his wallet, 5 Lieutenant Cross carried two photographs of Martha. The first was a Kodachrome snapshot signed "Love," though he knew better. She stood against a brick wall. Her eyes were gray and neutral, her lips slightly open as she stared straight-on at the camera. At night, sometimes, Lieutenant Cross wondered who had taken the picture, because he knew she had boyfriends, because he loved her so much, and because he could see the shadow of the picture taker spreading out against the brick wall. The second photograph had been clipped from the 1968 Mount Sebastian yearbook. It was an action shot—women's volleyball— and Martha was bent horizontal to the floor, reaching, the palms of her hands in sharp focus, the tongue taut, the expression frank and competitive. There was no visible sweat. She wore white gym shorts. Her legs, he thought, were almost certainly the legs of a virgin, dry and without hair, the left knee cocked and carrying her entire weight, which was just over one hundred pounds. Lieutenant Cross remembered touching that left knee. A dark theater, he remembered, and the movie was *Bonnie and Clyde*, and Martha wore a tweed skirt, and during the final scene, when he touched her knee, she turned and looked at him in a sad, sober way that made him pull his hand back, but he would always remember the feel of the tweed skirt and the knee beneath it and the sound of the gunfire that killed Bonnie and Clyde, how embarrassing it was, how slow and oppressive. He remembered kissing her good night at the dorm door. Right then, he thought, he should've done something brave. He should've carried her up the stairs to her room and tied her to the bed and touched that left knee all night long. He should've risked it. Whenever he looked at the photographs, he thought of new things he should've done.

ranks of the men

What they carried was partly a function of rank, partly of field specialty.

As a first lieutenant and platoon leader, Jimmy Cross carried a compass, maps, code books, binoculars, and a .45-caliber pistol that weighed 2.9 pounds fully loaded. He carried a strobe light and the responsibility for the lives of his men.

As an RTO, Mitchell Sanders carried the PRC-25 radio, a killer, twenty-six pounds with its battery.

As a medic, Rat Kiley carried a canvas satchel filled with morphine and plasma and malaria tablets and surgical tape and comic books and all the things a medic must carry, including M&M's for especially bad wounds, for a total weight of nearly twenty pounds.

As a big man, therefore a machine gunner, Henry 10 Dobbins carried the M-60, which weighed twenty-three

>> American marines on patrol near Da Nang, Vietnam, 1968

pounds unloaded, but which was almost always loaded. In addition, Dobbins carried between ten and fifteen pounds of ammunition draped in belts across his chest and shoulders.

As PFCs or Spec 4s, most of them were common grunts and carried the standard M-16 gas-operated assault rifle. The weapon weighed 7.5 pounds unloaded, 8.2 pounds with its full twenty-round magazine. Depending on numerous factors, such as topography and psychology, the riflemen carried anywhere from twelve to twenty magazines, usually in cloth bandoliers, adding on another 8.4 pounds at minimum, fourteen pounds at maximum. When it was available, they also carried M-16 maintenance gear—rods and steel brushes and swabs and tubes of LSA oil—all of which weighed about a pound. Among the grunts, some carried the M-79 grenade launcher, 5.9 pounds unloaded, a reasonably light weapon except for the ammunition, which was heavy. A single round weighed ten ounces. The typical load was twenty-five rounds. But Ted Lavender, who was scared, carried thirty-four rounds when he was shot and killed outside Than Khe, and he went down under an exceptional burden, more than twenty pounds of ammunition, plus the flak jacket and helmet and rations and water and toilet paper and tranquilizers and all the rest, plus the unweighed fear. He was dead weight. There was no twitching or flopping. Kiowa, who saw it happen, said it was like watching a rock fall, or a big sandbag or something—just boom, then down—not like the movies where the dead guy rolls around and does fancy spins and goes ass over teakettle— not like that, Kiowa said, the poor bastard just flat-fuck fell. Boom. Down. Nothing else. It was a bright morning in mid-April. Lieutenant Cross felt the pain. He blamed himself. They stripped off Lavender's canteens and ammo, all the heavy things, and Rat Kiley said the obvious, the guy's dead, and Mitchell Sanders used his radio to report one U.S. KIA and to request a chopper. Then they wrapped Lavender in his poncho. They carried him out to a dry paddy, established

Popperfoto/Getty Images

>> American soldier carrying gear, Bong Son, Vietnam, 1966

black-market Uzis and .38-caliber Smith & Wesson hand-guns and 66 mm LAWs and shotguns and silencers and blackjacks and bayonets and C-4 plastic explosives. Lee Strunk carried a slingshot; a weapon of last resort, he called it. Mitchell Sanders carried brass knuckles. Kiowa carried his grandfather's feathered hatchet. Every third or fourth man carried a Claymore antipersonnel mine—3.5 pounds with its firing device. They all carried fragmentation gre-nades—fourteen ounces each. They all carried at least one M-18 colored smoke grenade—twenty-four ounces. Some carried CS or tear-gas grenades. Some carried white-phos-phorus grenades. They carried all they could bear, and then some, including a silent awe for the terrible power of the things they carried.

In the first week of April, before Lavender died, Lieutenant Jimmy Cross received a good-luck charm from Martha. It was a simple pebble, an ounce at most. Smooth to the touch, it was a milky-white color with flecks of or-ange and violet, oval-shaped, like a miniature egg. In the accompanying letter, Martha wrote that she had found the pebble on the Jersey shoreline, precisely where the land touched water at high tide, where things came together but also separated. It was this separate-but-together quality, she wrote, that had inspired her to pick up the pebble and to carry it in her breast pocket for several days, where it seemed weightless, and then to send it through the mail, by air, as a token of her truest feelings for him. Lieutenant Cross found this romantic. But he wondered what her tru-est feelings were, exactly, and what she meant by separate-but-together. He wondered how the tides and waves had come into play on that afternoon along the Jersey shoreline when Martha saw the pebble and bent down to rescue it from geology. He imagined bare feet. Martha was a poet, with the poet's sensibilities, and her feet would be brown and bare, the toenails unpainted, the eyes chilly and somber like the ocean in March, and though it was painful, he won-dered who had been with her that afternoon. He imagined a pair of shadows moving along the strip of sand where things came together but also separated. It was phantom jealousy, he knew, but he couldn't help himself. He loved her so much. On the march, through the hot days of early April, he carried the pebble in his mouth, turning it with his tongue, tasting sea salts and moisture. His mind wandered. He had difficulty keeping his attention on the war. On oc-casion he would yell at his men to spread out the column, to keep their eyes open, but then he would slip away into daydreams, just pretending, walking barefoot along the Jersey shore, with Martha, carrying nothing. He would feel himself rising. Sun and waves and gentle winds, all love and lightness.

What they carried varied by mission.

When a mission took them to the mountains, they car- 15 ried mosquito netting, machetes, canvas tarps, and extra bug juice.

If a mission seemed especially hazardous, or if it in-volved a place they knew to be bad, they carried every-thing they could. In certain heavily mined AOs,° where the

security, and sat smoking the dead man's dope until the chopper came. Lieutenant Cross kept to himself. He pic-tured Martha's smooth young face, thinking he loved her more than anything, more than his men, and now Ted Lav-ender was dead because he loved her so much and could not stop thinking about her. When the dust-off arrived, they car-ried Lavender aboard. Afterward they burned Than Khe. They marched until dusk, then dug their holes, and that night Kiowa kept explaining how you had to be there, how fast it was, how the poor guy just dropped like so much concrete. Boom-down, he said. Like cement.

*　　*　　*

In addition to the three standard weapons—the M-60, M-16, and M-79—they carried whatever presented itself, or whatever seemed appropriate as a means of killing or staying alive. They carried catch-as-catch-can. At various times, in various situations, they carried M-14s and CAR-15s and Swedish Ks and grease guns and captured AK-47s and Chi-Coms and RPGs and Simonov carbines and

° **AOs** Areas of operation.

land was dense with Toe Poppers and Bouncing Betties, they took turns humping a twenty-eight-pound mine detector. With its headphones and big sensing plate, the equipment was a stress on the lower back and shoulders, awkward to handle, often useless because of the shrapnel in the earth, but they carried it anyway, partly for safety, partly for the illusion of safety.

On ambush, or other night missions, they carried peculiar little odds and ends. Kiowa always took along his New Testament and a pair of moccasins for silence. Dave Jensen carried night-sight vitamins high in carotin. Lee Strunk carried his slingshot; ammo, he claimed, would never be a problem. Rat Kiley carried brandy and M&M's. Until he was shot, Ted Lavender carried the starlight scope, which weighed 6.3 pounds with its aluminum carrying case. Henry Dobbins carried his girlfriend's panty-hose wrapped around his neck as a comforter. They all carried ghosts. When dark came, they would move out single file across the meadows and paddies to their ambush coordinates, where they would quietly set up the Claymores and lie down and spend the night waiting.

Other missions were more complicated and required special equipment. In mid-April, it was their mission to search out and destroy the elaborate tunnel complexes in the Than Khe area south of Chu Lai. To blow the tunnels, they carried one-pound blocks of pentrite high explosives, four blocks to a man, sixty-eight pounds in all. They carried wiring, detonators, and battery-powered clackers. Dave Jensen carried earplugs. Most often, before blowing the tunnels, they were ordered by higher command to search them, which was considered bad news, but by and large they just shrugged and carried out orders. Because he was a big man, Henry Dobbins was excused from tunnel duty. The others would draw numbers. Before Lavender died there were seventeen men in the platoon, and whoever drew the number seventeen would strip off his gear and crawl in head first with a flashlight and Lieutenant Cross's .45-caliber pistol. The rest of them would fan out as security. They would sit down or kneel, not facing the hole, listening to the ground beneath them, imagining cobwebs and ghosts, whatever was down there—the tunnel walls squeezing in—how the flashlight seemed impossibly heavy in the hand and how it was tunnel vision in the very strictest sense, compression in all ways, even time, and how you had to wiggle in—ass and elbows—a swallowed-up feeling—and how you found yourself worrying about odd things—will your flashlight go dead? Do rats carry rabies? If you screamed, how far would the sound carry? Would your buddies hear it? Would they have the courage to drag you out? In some respects, though not many, the waiting was worse than the tunnel itself. Imagination was a killer.

On April 16, when Lee Strunk drew the number seventeen, he laughed and muttered something and went down quickly. The morning was hot and very still. Not good, Kiowa said. He looked at the tunnel opening, then out across a dry paddy toward the village of Than Khe. Nothing moved. No clouds or birds or people. As they

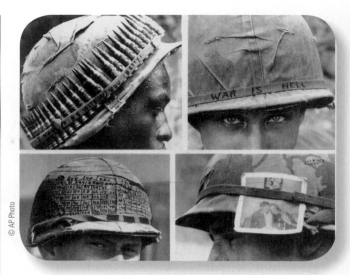

>> American soldiers' helmets, Vietnam, 1967

waited, the men smoked and drank Kool-Aid, not talking much, feeling sympathy for Lee Strunk but also feeling the luck of the draw. You win some, you lose some, said Mitchell Sanders, and sometimes you settle for a rain check. It was a tired line and no one laughed.

Henry Dobbins ate a tropical chocolate bar. Ted Lavender popped a tranquilizer and went off to pee. 20

After five minutes, Lieutenant Jimmy Cross moved to the tunnel, leaned down, and examined the darkness. Trouble, he thought—a cave-in maybe. And then suddenly, without willing it, he was thinking about Martha. The stresses and fractures, the quick collapse, the two of them buried alive under all that weight. Dense, crushing love. Kneeling, watching the hole, he tried to concentrate on Lee Strunk and the war, all the dangers, but his love was too much for him, he felt paralyzed, he wanted to sleep inside her lungs and breathe her blood and be smothered. He wanted her to be a virgin and not a virgin, all at once. He wanted to know her. Intimate secrets—why poetry? Why so sad? Why that grayness in her eyes? Why so alone? Not lonely, just alone—riding her bike across campus or sitting off by herself in the cafeteria. Even dancing, she danced alone—and it was the aloneness that filled him with love. He remembered telling her that one evening. How she nodded and looked away. And how, later, when he kissed her, she received the kiss without returning it, her eyes wide open, not afraid, not a virgin's eyes, just flat and uninvolved.

Lieutenant Cross gazed at the tunnel. But he was not there. He was buried with Martha under the white sand at the Jersey shore. They were pressed together, and the pebble in his mouth was her tongue. He was smiling. Vaguely, he was aware of how quiet the day was, the sullen paddies, yet he could not bring himself to worry about matters of security. He was beyond that. He was just a kid at war, in love. He was twenty-two years old. He couldn't help it.

A few moments later Lee Strunk crawled out of the tunnel. He came up grinning, filthy but alive. Lieutenant

Cross nodded and closed his eyes while the others clapped Strunk on the back and made jokes about rising from the dead.

Worms, Rat Kiley said. Right out of the grave. Fuckin' zombie.

The men laughed. They all felt great relief. 25

Spook City, said Mitchell Sanders.

Lee Strunk made a funny ghost sound, a kind of moaning, yet very happy, and right then, when Strunk made that high happy moaning sound, when he went *Ah-hooooo*, right then Ted Lavender was shot in the head on his way back from peeing. He lay with his mouth open. The teeth were broken. There was a swollen black bruise under his left eye. The cheekbone was gone. Oh shit, Rat Kiley said, the guy's dead. The guy's dead, he kept saying, which seemed profound—the guy's dead. I mean really.

The things they carried were determined to some extent by superstition. Lieutenant Cross carried his good-luck pebble. Dave Jensen carried a rabbit's foot. Norman Bowker, otherwise a very gentle person, carried a thumb that had been presented to him as a gift by Mitchell Sanders. The thumb was dark brown, rubbery to the touch, and weighed four ounces at most. It had been cut from a VC corpse, a boy of fifteen or sixteen. They'd found him at the bottom of an irrigation ditch, badly burned, flies in his mouth and eyes. The boy wore black shorts and sandals. At the time of his death he had been carrying a pouch of rice, a rifle, and three magazines of ammunition.

You want my opinion, Mitchell Sanders said, there's a definite moral here.

He put his hand on the dead boy's wrist. He was quiet 30 for a time, as if counting a pulse, then he patted the stomach, almost affectionately, and used Kiowa's hunting hatchet to remove the thumb.

Henry Dobbins asked what the moral was.

Moral?

You know. *Moral.*

Sanders wrapped the thumb in toilet paper and handed it across to Norman Bowker. There was no blood. Smiling, he kicked the boy's head, watched the flies scatter, and said, It's like with that old TV show—Paladin. Have gun, will travel.

Henry Dobbins thought about it. 35

Yeah, well, he finally said. I don't see no moral.

There it *is*, man.

Fuck off.

They carried USO stationery and pencils and pens. They carried Sterno, safety pins, trip flares, signal flares, spools of wire, razor blades, chewing tobacco, liberated joss sticks and statuettes of the smiling Buddha, candles, grease pencils, *The Stars and Stripes,* fingernail clippers, Psy Ops leaflets, bush hats, bolos, and much more. Twice a week, when the resupply choppers came in, they carried hot chow in green Mermite cans and large canvas bags filled with iced beer and soda pop. They carried plastic water containers, each with a two-gallon capacity. Mitchell Sanders carried a set of starched tiger fatigues for special occasions. Henry Dobbins carried Black Flag insecticide. Dave Jensen carried empty sandbags that could be filled at night for added protection. Lee Strunk carried tanning lotion. Some things they carried in common. Taking turns, they carried the big PRC-77 scrambler radio, which weighed thirty pounds with its battery. They shared the weight of memory. They took up what others could no longer bear. Often, they carried each other, the wounded or weak. They carried infections. They carried chess sets, basketballs, Vietnamese-English dictionaries, insignia of rank, Bronze Stars and Purple Hearts, plastic cards imprinted with the Code of Conduct. They carried diseases, among them malaria and dysentery. They carried lice and ringworm and leeches and paddy algae and various rots and molds. They carried the land itself—Vietnam, the place, the soil—a powdery orange-red dust that covered their boots and fatigues and faces. They carried the sky. The whole atmosphere, they carried it, the humidity, the monsoons, the stink of fungus and decay, all of it, they carried gravity. They moved like mules. By daylight they took sniper fire, at night they were mortared, but it was not battle, it was just the endless march, village to village, without purpose, nothing won or lost. They marched for the sake of the march. They plodded along slowly, dumbly, leaning forward against the heat, unthinking, all blood and bone, simple grunts, soldiering with their legs, toiling up the hills and down into the paddies and across the rivers and up again and down, just humping, one step and then the next and then another, but no volition, no will, because it was automatic, it was anatomy, and the war was entirely a matter of posture and carriage, the hump was everything, a kind of inertia, a kind of emptiness, a dullness of desire and intellect and conscience and hope and human sensibility. Their principles were in their feet. Their calculations were biological. They had no sense of strategy or mission. They searched the villages without knowing what to look for, not caring, kicking over jars of rice, frisking children and old men, blowing tunnels, sometimes setting fires and sometimes not, then forming up and moving on to the next village, then other villages, where it would always be the same. They carried their own lives. The pressures were enormous. In the heat of early afternoon, they would remove their helmets and flak jackets, walking bare, which was dangerous but which helped ease the strain. They would often discard things along the route of march. Purely for comfort, they would throw away rations, blow their Claymores and grenades, no matter, because by nightfall the resupply choppers would arrive with more of the same, then a day or two later still more, fresh watermelons and crates of ammunition and sunglasses and woolen sweaters—the resources were stunning—sparklers for the Fourth of July, colored eggs for Easter. It was the great American war chest—the fruits of science, the smokestacks, the canneries, the arsenals at Hartford, the Minnesota forests, the machine shops, the vast fields of corn and wheat—they carried like freight trains; they carried it on their backs and shoulders—and for all the ambiguities of Vietnam, all the mysteries and unknowns, there was at least the single abiding certainty that they would never be at a loss for things to carry.

*   *   *

After the chopper took Lavender away, Lieutenant Jim-40 my Cross led his men into the village of Than Khe. They burned everything. They shot chickens and dogs, they trashed the village well, they called in artillery and watched the wreckage, then they marched for several hours through the hot afternoon, and then at dusk, while Kiowa explained how Lavender died, Lieutenant Cross found himself trembling.

He tried not to cry. With his entrenching tool, which weighed five pounds, he began digging a hole in the earth.

He felt shame. He hated himself. He had loved Martha more than his men, and as a consequence Lavender was now dead, and this was something he would have to carry like a stone in his stomach for the rest of the war.

All he could do was dig. He used his entrenching tool like an ax, slashing, feeling both love and hate, and then later, when it was full dark, he sat at the bottom of his foxhole and wept. It went on for a long while. In part, he was grieving for Ted Lavender, but mostly it was for Martha, and for himself, because she belonged to another world, which was not quite real, and because she was a junior at Mount Sebastian College in New Jersey, a poet and a virgin and uninvolved, and because he realized she did not love him and never would.

Like cement, Kiowa whispered in the dark. I swear to God—boom-down. Not a word.

I've heard this, said Norman Bowker. 45

A pisser, you know? Still zipping himself up. Zapped while zipping.

All right, fine. That's enough.

Yeah, but you had to see it, the guy just—

I *heard*, man. Cement. So why not shut the fuck *up?*

Kiowa shook his head sadly and glanced over at the 50 hole where Lieutenant Jimmy Cross sat watching the night. The air was thick and wet. A warm, dense fog had settled over the paddies and there was the stillness that precedes rain.

After a time Kiowa sighed.

One thing for sure, he said. The Lieutenant's in some deep hurt. I mean that crying jag—the way he was carrying on—it wasn't fake or anything, it was real heavy-duty hurt. The man cares.

Sure, Norman Bowker said.

Say what you want, the man does care.

We all got problems. 55

Not Lavender.

No, I guess not, Bowker said. Do me a favor, though.

Shut up?

That's a smart Indian. Shut up.

Shrugging, Kiowa pulled off his boots. He wanted to 60 say more, just to lighten up his sleep, but instead he opened his New Testament and arranged it beneath his head as a pillow. The fog made things seem hollow and unattached. He tried not to think about Ted Lavender, but then he was thinking how fast it was, no drama, down and dead, and how it was hard to feel anything except surprise. It seemed un-Christian. He wished he could find some great sadness, or even anger, but the emotion wasn't there and he couldn't make it happen. Mostly he felt pleased to be alive. He liked the smell of the New Testament under his cheek, the leather and ink and paper and glue, whatever the chemicals were. He liked hearing the sounds of night. Even his fatigue, it felt fine, the stiff muscles and the prickly awareness of his own body, a floating feeling. He enjoyed not being dead. Lying there, Kiowa admired Lieutenant Jimmy Cross's capacity for grief. He wanted to share the man's pain, he wanted to care as Jimmy Cross cared. And yet when he closed his eyes, all he could think was Boom-down, and all he could feel was the pleasure of having his boots off and the fog curling in around him and the damp soil and the Bible smells and the plush comfort of night.

After a moment Norman Bowker sat up in the dark.

What the hell, he said. You want to talk, *talk*. Tell it to me.

Forget it.

No, man, go on. One thing I hate, it's a silent Indian.

For the most part they carried themselves with poise, a 65 kind of dignity. Now and then, however, there were times of panic, when they squealed or wanted to squeal but couldn't, when they twitched and made moaning sounds and covered their heads and said Dear Jesus and flopped around on the earth and fired their weapons blindly and cringed and sobbed and begged for the noise to stop and went wild and made stupid promises to themselves and to God and to their mothers and fathers, hoping not to die. In different ways, it happened to all of them. Afterward, when the firing ended, they would blink and peek up. They would touch their bodies, feeling shame, then quickly hiding it. They would force themselves to stand. As if in slow motion, frame by frame, the world would take on the old logic—absolute silence, then the wind, then sunlight, then voices. It was the burden of being alive. Awkwardly, the men would reassemble themselves, first in private, then in groups, becoming soldiers again. They would repair the leaks in their eyes. They would check for casualties, call in dust-offs, light cigarettes, try to smile, clear their throats and spit and begin cleaning their weapons. After a time someone would shake his head and say, No lie, I almost shit my pants, and someone else would laugh, which meant it was bad, yes, but the guy had obviously not shit his pants, it wasn't that bad, and in any case nobody would ever do such a thing and then go ahead and talk about it. They would squint into the dense, oppressive sunlight. For a few moments, perhaps, they would fall silent, lighting a joint and tracking its passage from man to man, inhaling, holding in the humiliation. Scary stuff, one of them might say. But then someone else would grin or flick his eyebrows and say, Roger-dodger, almost cut me a new asshole, *almost*.

There were numerous such poses. Some carried themselves with a sort of wistful resignation, others with pride or stiff soldierly discipline or good humor or macho zeal. They were afraid of dying but they were even more afraid to show it.

They found jokes to tell.

They used a hard vocabulary to contain the terrible softness. *Greased*, they'd say. *Offed, lit up,*° *zapped while zipping.*° It wasn't cruelty, just stage presence. They were actors and the war came at them in 3-D. When someone died, it wasn't quite dying, because in a curious way it seemed scripted, and because they had their lines mostly memorized, irony mixed with tragedy, and because they called it by other names, as if to encyst and destroy the reality of death itself. They kicked corpses. They cut off thumbs. They talked grunt lingo. They told stories about Ted Lavender's supply of tranquilizers, how the poor guy didn't feel a thing, how incredibly tranquil he was.

There's a moral here, said Mitchell Sanders.

They were waiting for Lavender's chopper, smoking 70 the dead man's dope.

The moral's pretty obvious, Sanders said, and winked. Stay away from drugs. No joke, they'll ruin your day every time.

Cute, said Henry Dobbins.

Mind-blower, get it? Talk about wiggy—nothing left, just blood and brains.

They made themselves laugh.

There it is, they'd say, over and over, as if the repeti- 75 tion itself were an act of poise, a balance between crazy and almost crazy, knowing without going. There it is, which meant be cool, let it ride, because oh yeah, man, you can't change what can't be changed, there it is, there it absolutely and positively and fucking well *is*.

They were tough.

They carried all the emotional baggage of men who might die. Grief, terror, love, longing—these were intangibles, but the intangibles had their own mass and specific gravity, they had tangible weight. They carried shameful memories. They carried the common secret of cowardice barely restrained, the instinct to run or freeze or hide, and in many respects this was the heaviest burden of all, for it could never be put down, it required perfect balance and perfect posture. They carried their reputations. They carried the soldier's greatest fear, which was the fear of blushing. Men killed, and died, because they were embarrassed not to. It was what had brought them to the war in the first place, nothing positive, no dreams of glory or honor, just to avoid the blush of dishonor. They died so as not to die of embarrassment. They crawled into tunnels and walked point and advanced under fire. Each morning, despite the unknowns, they made their legs move. They endured. They kept humping. They did not submit to the obvious alternative, which was simply to close the eyes and fall. So easy, really. Go limp and tumble to the ground and let the muscles unwind and not speak and not budge until your buddies picked you up and lifted you into the chopper that would roar and dip its nose and carry you off to the world. A mere matter of falling, yet no one ever fell. It was not courage, exactly; the object was not valor. Rather, they were too frightened to be cowards.

By and large they carried these things inside, maintaining the masks of composure. They sneered at sick call. They spoke bitterly about guys who had found release by shooting off their own toes or fingers. Pussies, they'd say. Candyasses. It was fierce, mocking talk, with only a trace of envy or awe, but even so, the image played itself out behind their eyes.

They imagined the muzzle against flesh. They imagined the quick, sweet pain, then the evacuation to Japan, then a hospital with warm beds and cute geisha nurses.

They dreamed of freedom birds.   80

At night, on guard, staring into the dark, they were carried away by jumbo jets. They felt the rush of takeoff. *Gone!* they yelled. And then velocity, wings and engines, a smiling stewardess—but it was more than a plane, it was a real bird, a big sleek silver bird with feathers and talons and high screeching. They were flying. The weights fell off, there was nothing to bear. They laughed and held on tight, feeling the cold slap of wind and altitude, soaring, thinking *It's over, I'm gone!*—they were naked, they were light and free—it was all lightness, bright and fast and buoyant, light as light, a helium buzz in the brain, a giddy bubbling in the lungs as they were taken up over the clouds and the war, beyond duty, beyond gravity and mortification and global entanglements—*Sin loi!* they yelled, *I'm sorry, motherfuckers, but I'm out of it, I'm goofed, I'm on a space cruise, I'm gone!*—and it was a restful, disencumbered sensation, just riding the light waves, sailing that big silver freedom bird over the mountains and oceans, over America, over the farms and great sleeping cities and cemeteries and highways and the golden arches of McDonald's. It was flight, a kind of fleeing, a kind of falling, falling higher and higher, spinning off the edge of the earth and beyond the sun and through the vast, silent vacuum where there were no burdens and where everything weighed exactly nothing. *Gone!* they screamed, *I'm sorry but I'm gone!* And so at night, not quite dreaming, they gave themselves over to lightness, they were carried, they were purely borne.

On the morning after Ted Lavender died, First Lieutenant Jimmy Cross crouched at the bottom of his foxhole and burned Martha's letters. Then he burned the two photographs. There was a steady rain falling, which made it difficult, but he used heat tabs and Sterno to build a small

---

° **Offed, lit up** Killed.

° **zapped while zipping** Killed while urinating.

fire, screening it with his body, holding the photographs over the tight blue flame with the tips of his fingers.

He realized it was only a gesture. Stupid, he thought. Sentimental, too, but mostly just stupid.

Lavender was dead. You couldn't burn the blame.

Besides, the letters were in his head. And even now, 85 without photographs, Lieutenant Cross could see Martha playing volleyball in her white gym shorts and yellow T-shirt. He could see her moving in the rain.

When the fire died out, Lieutenant Cross pulled his poncho over his shoulders and ate breakfast from a can.

There was no great mystery, he decided.

In those burned letters Martha had never mentioned the war, except to say, Jimmy, take care of yourself. She wasn't involved. She signed the letters "Love," but it wasn't love, and all the fine lines and technicalities did not matter.

The morning came up wet and blurry. Everything seemed part of everything else, the fog and Martha and the deepening rain.

It was a war, after all. 90

Half smiling, Lieutenant Jimmy Cross took out his maps. He shook his head hard, as if to clear it, then bent forward and began planning the day's march. In ten minutes, or maybe twenty, he would rouse the men and they would pack up and head west, where the maps showed the country to be green and inviting. They would do what they had always done. The rain might add some weight, but otherwise it would be one more day layered upon all the other days.

He was realistic about it. There was that new hardness in his stomach.

No more fantasies, he told himself.

Henceforth, when he thought about Martha, it would be only to think that she belonged elsewhere. He would shut down the daydreams. This was not Mount Sebastian, it was another world, where there were no pretty poems or midterm exams, a place where men died because of carelessness and gross stupidity. Kiowa was right. Boom-down, and you were dead, never partly dead.

Briefly, in the rain, Lieutenant Cross saw Martha's 95 gray eyes gazing back at him.

He understood.

It was very sad, he thought. The things men carried inside. The things men did or felt they had to do.

He almost nodded at her, but didn't.

Instead he went back to his maps. He was now determined to perform his duties firmly and without negligence.

It wouldn't help Lavender, he knew that, but from this point on he would comport himself as a soldier. He would dispose of his good-luck pebble. Swallow it, maybe, or use Lee Strunk's slingshot, or just drop it along the trail. On the march he would impose strict field discipline. He would be careful to send out flank security, to prevent straggling or bunching up, to keep his troops moving at the proper pace and at the proper interval. He would insist on clean weapons. He would confiscate the remainder of Lavender's dope. Later in the day, perhaps, he would call the men together and speak to them plainly. He would accept the blame for what had happened to Ted Lavender. He would be a man about it. He would look them in the eyes, keeping his chin level, and he would issue the new SOPs in a calm, impersonal tone of voice, an officer's voice, leaving no room for argument or discussion. Commencing immediately, he'd tell them, they would no longer abandon equipment along the route of march. They would police up their acts. They would get their shit together, and keep it together, and maintain it neatly and in good working order.

He would not tolerate laxity. He would show strength, 100 distancing himself.

Among the men there would be grumbling, of course, and maybe worse, because their days would seem longer and their loads heavier, but Lieutenant Cross reminded himself that his obligation was not to be loved but to lead. He would dispense with love; it was not now a factor. And if anyone quarreled or complained, he would simply tighten his lips and arrange his shoulders in the correct command posture. He might give a curt little nod. Or he might not. He might just shrug and say Carry on, then they would saddle up and form into a column and move out toward the villages west of Than Khe.

Related Works

"The Soldier" (p. 491), "Dulce et Decorum Est" (p. 492), "Facing It" (p. 495)

 See Chapter 15 Review Card for Reading and Reacting questions about Tim O'Brien, "The Things They Carried."

Writing Suggestions: Style, Tone, and Language

1. In "The Things They Carried," Tim O'Brien considers his characters' emotional and psychological burdens as well as the physical "things they carry." Applying O'Brien's criteria to "The Yellow Wallpaper" (p. 313), write an essay in which you consider what the narrator "carries" (and what her husband "carries") and why.

2. In several of this text's stories—for example, "The Hunger Artist" and "The Yellow Wallpaper"—characters are trapped. Whether trapped by social roles, by circumstance, or by their own limitations, they are unable to escape their destinies. Choose two or three such stories, and explain what factors imprison each character; then, consider whether—and how—each might escape.

3. Imagine The Misfit in a prison cell, relating the violent incident at the end of "A Good Man Is Hard to Find" to another prisoner—or to a member of the clergy. Would his tone be boastful? regretful? apologetic? defiant? Would he use the elaborate poetic style he sometimes uses in the story or more straightforward language? Tell his version of the incident in his own words.

4. Both "Araby" and "The Things They Carried" deal, at least in part, with infatuation. Compare and contrast the infatuations described in the two stories. How does the language used by the narrators in the two stories communicate the two characters' fascination and subsequent disillusionment?

 CHECKLIST

WRITING ABOUT STYLE, TONE, AND LANGUAGE

- [ ] Does the writer make any unusual creative use of word choice, word order, or sentence structure?
- [ ] Is the story's tone intimate? distant? ironic? How does the tone advance the writer's purpose?
- [ ] Does the style emphasize the sound and rhythm of language? For example, does the writer use alliteration and assonance? repetition and parallelism? What do such techniques add to the story?
- [ ] Is the level of diction generally formal, informal, or somewhere in between?
- [ ] Is there a difference between the style of the narrator and the style of the characters' speech? If so, what is the effect of this difference?
- [ ] Do any of the story's characters use regionalisms, colloquial language, or nonstandard speech? If so, what effect does this language have?
- [ ] What do different characters' levels of diction reveal about them?
- [ ] What kind of imagery predominates? Where, and why, is imagery used?
- [ ] Does the story develop a pattern of imagery? How does this pattern of imagery help to convey the story's themes?
- [ ] Does the story use simile and metaphor? personification? What is the effect of these figures of speech?
- [ ] Do figures of speech reinforce the story's themes? reveal information about characters?
- [ ] Does the story make any historical, literary, or biblical allusions? What do these allusions contribute to the story?
- [ ] Are any unfamiliar, obscure, or foreign words, phrases, or images used in the story? What do these words or expressions contribute to the story?

Glossary Terms

alliteration Repetition of consonant sounds (usually the initial sounds) in a series of words.

allusion Reference, often to literature, history, mythology, or the Bible, that is unacknowledged in the text but that the author expects a reader to recognize.

figures of speech Expressions that use words to achieve effects beyond ordinary language.

formal diction Diction that is lofty and elaborate, with a learned vocabulary and a detached tone.

hyperbole Figurative language that depends on intentional overstatement.

imagery Words and phrases that describe the five senses, most often sight.

informal diction Diction that is idiomatic, like everyday speech.

metaphor Comparison equating two things that may at first seem completely dissimilar.

personification A figure of speech that endows inanimate objects or abstract ideas with life or human characteristics.

simile Comparison of two seemingly unlike things using *like* or *as*.

stream of consciousness Form of narration controlled by the thoughts and subjective impressions of the narrator, commonly found in modern literature.

style How words are selected and arranged to express ideas.

tone Attitude of the speaker or narrator of a work toward the subject, the characters, or the audience, as determined by word choice, use of imagery, and so on.

understatement Intentional downplaying of a situation's significance, often for ironic or humorous effect.

16

Symbol, Allegory, and Myth

Learning Outcomes

After reading this chapter, you should be able to do the following:

LO1 Recognize symbols

LO2 Recognize allegory

LO3 Recognize myth

Timeline

Alison Bechdel, from *Fun Home* **2006**

Raymond Carver, "Cathedral" **1983**

Alice Walker, "Everyday Use" **1973**

Shirley Jackson, "The Lottery" **1948**

| 1830 | 1860 | 1890 | 1920 | 1950 | 1980 |

Nuremberg Trials of Nazi war criminals. **1945-46**

Architect and author Buckminster Fuller dies. **1983**

The system of Apartheid formally begins in South Africa. **1950**

1836 The Battle of the Alamo is fought.

Restoration of Dresden Frauenkirche ("Church of Our Lady"), which had been destroyed in World War II, is completed. **2005**

In *Brown vs. Board of Education,* Supreme Court finds segregated schools unconstitutional. **1954**

1835 Texas declares its independence from Mexico.

Arizona and California ban same-sex marriage. **2008**

1833 Slavery is abolished in the British Empire.

A federal judge declares California's law banning same-sex marriage unconstitutional. **2010**

EXPLORE ONLINE >

To complete a tutorial of "Symbol," visit your Literature CourseMate, accessed through www.cengagebrain.com.

LO1 Recognize Symbols

A **symbol** is a person, object, action, place, or event that, in addition to its literal meaning, suggests a more complex meaning or range of meanings. **Universal** or **archetypal symbols,** such as the Old Man, the Mother, or the Grim Reaper, are so much a part of human experience that they suggest the same thing to most people. **Conventional symbols** are also likely to suggest the same thing to most people (a rose suggests love, a skull and crossbones denotes poison), provided the people share cultural and social assumptions. For this reason, symbols are often used as a kind of shorthand in films, popular literature, and advertising, where they elicit predictable responses.

A conventional symbol, such as the stars and stripes of the American flag, can evoke powerful feelings of pride and patriotism in a group of people who share certain cultural assumptions, just as the maple leaf and the Union Jack can. Symbols used in works of literature can function in much the same way, enabling writers to convey particular emotions or messages with a high degree of predictability. Thus, spring can be expected to suggest rebirth and promise; autumn, declining years and powers; summer, youth and beauty. Because a writer expects a dark forest to evoke fear, or a rainbow to communicate hope, he or she can be quite confident in using such images to convey a particular idea or mood (provided the audience shares the writer's frame of reference).

Many symbols, however, suggest different things to different people, and different cultures may react differently to the same symbols. (In the United States, for example, an owl suggests wisdom; in India it suggests the opposite.) Thus, symbols enhance meaning, expanding the possibilities for interpretation and for readers' interaction with the text. Because they are so potentially rich, symbols have the power to open up a work of literature.

---

symbol/universal symbol/conventional symbol/ literary symbol Person, object, action, or idea whose meaning transcends its literal or denotative sense in a complex way. A symbol is invested with significance beyond what it could carry on its own. **Universal symbols,** such as the grim reaper, may be called **archetypes; conventional symbols,** such as national flags, evoke a general and agreed-upon response from most people.

LITERARY SYMBOLS

Both universal and conventional symbols can function as **literary symbols**—symbols that take on additional meanings in particular works. For instance, a watch or clock denotes time; as a conventional symbol, it suggests the passing of time; as a literary symbol in a particular work, it might also convey anything from a character's inability to recapture the past to the idea of time running out—or it might suggest something else.

Considering an object's symbolic significance can suggest a variety of ways to interpret a text. For instance, William Faulkner focuses attention on an unseen watch in a pivotal scene in "A Rose for Emily" (p. 121). The narrator first describes Emily Grierson as "a small, fat woman in black, with a thin gold chain descending to her waist and vanishing into her belt." Several sentences later, the narrator notes that Emily's visitors "could hear the invisible watch ticking at the end of the gold chain." Like these visitors, readers are drawn to the unseen watch as it ticks away. Because Emily is portrayed as a woman living in the past, readers can assume that the watch is intended to reinforce the impression that she cannot see that time (the watch) has moved on. The vivid picture of the pale, plump woman in the musty room with the watch invisibly ticking does indeed suggest both that she has been left back in time and that she remains unaware of the progress around her. Thus, the symbol of the watch enriches both the depiction of character and the story's theme.

In "Barn Burning" (p. 194), another Faulkner story, the clock is a more complex symbol. The itinerant Snopes family is without financial security and apparently without a future. The clock the mother carries from shack to shack—"The clock inlaid with mother-of-pearl, which would not run, stopped at some fourteen minutes past two o'clock of a dead and forgotten day and time, which had been [Sarty's] mother's dowry"—is their only possession of value. The fact that the clock no longer works seems at first to suggest that time has run out for the family. On another level, the clock stands in stark contrast to Major de Spain's grand home, with its gold and glitter and Oriental rugs. Knowing that the clock was part of the mother's dowry, and that a dowry suggests a promise, readers may decide that the broken clock symbolizes lost hope. The fact that the mother still clings to the clock, however, could suggest just the opposite: her refusal to give up.

As you read, you should not try to find one exact equivalent for each symbol; that kind of search is unproductive. Instead, consider the different meanings a symbol might suggest. Then, consider how these various interpretations enrich other elements of the story and the work as a whole.

RECOGNIZING SYMBOLS

When is a clock just a clock, and when is it also a symbol with a meaning (or meanings) beyond its literal significance?

If a character waiting for a friend glances once at a watch to check the time, there is probably nothing symbolic about the watch or about the act of looking at it. If, however, the watch keeps appearing again and again in the story, at key moments; if the narrator devotes a good deal of time to describing it; if it is placed in a conspicuous physical location; if characters keep noticing it and commenting on its presence; if it is lost (or found) at a critical moment; if its function in some way parallels the development of plot or character (for instance, if it stops as a relationship ends or when a character dies); if the story's opening or closing paragraph focuses on the timepiece; or if the story is called "The Watch"—the watch most likely has symbolic significance. In other words, considering how an image is used, how often it is used, and when it appears will help you to determine whether or not it functions as a symbol.

Symbols expand the possible meanings of a story, thereby heightening interest and actively involving readers in the text. In "The Lottery" (p. 251), for example, the mysterious black box has symbolic significance. It is mentioned prominently and repeatedly, and it plays a pivotal role in the story's action. Of course, the black box is important on a purely literal level: it functions as a key component of the lottery. But the box has other associations as well, and it is these associations that suggest what its symbolic significance might be.

The black wooden box is very old, a relic of many past lotteries; the narrator observes that it represents tradition. It is also closed and closely guarded, suggesting mystery and uncertainty. It is shabby, "splintered badly along one side . . . and in places faded or stained," and this state of disrepair could suggest that the ritual it is part of has also deteriorated or that tradition itself has deteriorated. The box is also simple in construction and design, suggesting the primitive (and therefore perhaps outdated) nature of the ritual. Thus, this symbol encourages readers to probe the story for values and ideas, to consider and weigh the suitability of a variety of interpretations. It serves as a "hot spot" that invites questions, and the answers to these questions reinforce and enrich the story's theme.

LO2 Recognize Allegory

An **allegory** communicates a doctrine, message, or moral principle by making it into a narrative in which the characters personify ideas, concepts, qualities, or other abstractions. Thus, an allegory is a story with two parallel and consistent levels of meaning—one literal and one figurative. The figurative level, which offers some moral or political lesson, is the story's main concern.

Whereas a symbol has multiple symbolic associations as well as a literal meaning, an **allegorical figure**—a character, object, place, or event in the allegory—has just one meaning within an **allegorical framework,** the set of ideas that conveys the allegory's message. (At the

---

allegory/allegorical figure/allegorical framework Story with two parallel and consistent levels of meaning, one literal and one figurative, in which the figurative level offers a moral or political lesson. An **allegorical figure** has only one meaning (for instance, it may represent good or evil). An **allegorical framework** is the system of ideas that conveys the allegory's message.

beast fable Short tale, usually including a moral, in which animals assume human characteristics—for example, Aesop's "The Tortoise and the Hare."

---

simplest level, for instance, one character can stand for good and another can stand for evil.) For this reason, allegorical figures do not open up a text to various interpretations the way symbols do. The allegorical figures are significant only because they represent something beyond their literal meaning in a fixed system. Because the purpose of allegory is to communicate a particular lesson, readers are not encouraged to speculate about the allegory's possible meanings; each element has only one equivalent, which readers must discover if they are to make sense of the story.

Naturally, the better a reader understands the political, religious, and literary assumptions of a writer, the easier it will be to recognize the allegorical significance of his or her work. John Bunyan's *The Pilgrim's Progress*, for example, is a famous seventeenth-century allegory based on the Christian doctrine of salvation. In order to appreciate the complexity of Bunyan's work, readers would have to familiarize themselves with this doctrine.

One type of allegory, called a **beast fable,** is a short tale, usually including a moral, in which animals assume human characteristics. Aesop's fables are the best-known examples of beast fables. More recently, contemporary writers have used beast fables to satirize the political and social conditions of our time. In one such tale, "The Gentlemen of the Jungle" by the Kenyan writer Jomo Kenyatta, an elephant is allowed to put his trunk inside a man's hut during a rainstorm. Not content with keeping his trunk dry, the elephant pushes his entire body inside the hut, displacing the man. When the man protests, the elephant takes the matter to the lion, who appoints a Commission of Enquiry to settle the matter. Eventually, the man is forced not only to abandon his hut to the elephant but also to build new huts for all the animals on the Commission. Even so, the jealous animals occupy the man's new hut and begin fighting for space; while they are arguing, the man burns down the hut, animals and all. Like the tales told by Aesop, "The Gentlemen of the Jungle" has a moral: "Peace is costly," says the man as he walks away happily, "but it's worth the expense."

myth Story reflecting the religious and social values of a culture or explaining natural phenomena, often involving gods and heroes.

The following passage from Kenyatta's tale reveals how the allegorical figures work within the framework of the allegory:

> The elephant, obeying the command of his master (the lion), got busy with the other ministers to appoint a Commission of Enquiry. The following elders of the jungle were appointed to sit in the Commission: (1) Mr. Rhinoceros; (2) Mr. Buffalo; (3) Mr. Alligator; (4) The Rt. Hon. Mr. Fox to act as chairman; and (5) Mr. Leopard to act as Secretary of the Commission. On seeing the personnel, the man protested and asked if it was not necessary to include in this Commission a member from his side. But he was told that it was impossible, since no one from his side was well enough educated to understand the intricacy of jungle law.

From this excerpt, we can see that each character represents a particular idea. For example, the members of the Commission stand for bureaucratic smugness and inequity, and the man stands for the citizens who are victimized by the government. In order to fully understand the allegorical significance of each figure in this story, of course, readers would have to know something about government bureaucracies, colonialism in Africa, and possibly a specific historical event in Kenya.

Some works contain both symbolic elements *and* allegorical elements, as Nathaniel Hawthorne's "Young Goodman Brown" (p. 320) does. The names of the story's two main characters, "Goodman" and "Faith," suggest that they fit within an allegorical system of some sort: Young Goodman Brown represents a good person who, despite his best efforts, strays from the path of righteousness; his wife, Faith, represents the quality he must hold on to in order to avoid temptation. As characters, they have no significance outside of their allegorical functions. Other elements of the story, however, are not so clear-cut. The older man whom Young Goodman Brown meets in the woods carries a staff that has carved on it "the likeness of a great black snake, so curiously wrought, that it might almost be seen to twist and wriggle itself like a living serpent." This staff, carried by a Satanic figure who represents evil and temptation, suggests the snake in the Garden of Eden, an association that neatly fits into the allegorical framework of the story. Alternatively, however, the staff could suggest the "slippery," ever-changing nature of sin, the difficulty people have in perceiving sin, or even sexuality (which may explain Young Goodman Brown's susceptibility to temptation). This range of possible meanings suggests that the staff functions as a symbol (not an allegorical figure) that enriches Hawthorne's allegory.

Other stories work entirely on a symbolic level and contain no allegorical figures. "The Lottery," despite its moral overtones, is not an allegory because its characters, events, and objects are not arranged to serve one rigid, didactic purpose. In fact, many different interpretations have been suggested for this story. When it was first published in June 1948 in the *New Yorker*, some readers believed it to be a story about an actual custom or ritual. As author Shirley Jackson reports in her essay "Biography of a Story," even those who recognized it as fiction speculated about its meaning, seeing it as (among other things) an attack on prejudice, a criticism of society's need for a scapegoat, or a treatise on witchcraft, Christian martyrdom, or village gossip. The fact is that an allegorical interpretation will not account for every major character, object, and event in the story.

LO3 Recognize Myth

Throughout history, human beings have been makers of myths. For the purpose of this discussion, a **myth** is a story that is central to a culture; it embodies the values on which a culture or society is built. Thus, myths are not synonymous with falsehoods or fairy tales. Rather, they are stories that contain ideas that inform a culture and that give that culture meaning. In this sense, then, both an ancient epic and a contemporary religious text can be considered myths.

Although many myths have to do with religion, myths are not limited to the theological. Myths explain everything from natural phenomena—such as the creation of the world—to the existence of human beings and the beginnings of agriculture. The importance of myths rests on their ability to embody a set of beliefs that unifies both individuals and the society in which they live. By examining myths, we can learn much about our own origins and about our most deeply held beliefs.

One of the most prevalent types of myth is the **creation myth.** Almost every culture has an explanation for how the earth, sun, and stars—not to mention people—came into being. According to the ancient Greeks, for example, the world began as an empty void from which Nyx, a bird with black wings, emerged. She laid a golden egg, and out of it arose Eros, the god of love. The two halves of the eggshell became the earth and the sky, who fell in love with each other and had many children and grandchildren. These offspring became the gods of the Greek pantheon, who eventually created human beings in their own likeness. Each of these gods had a role to play in the creation and maintenance of the world, and their actions—in particular, their constant meddling in the lives of people—comprise the myths of ancient Greece.

In various cultures all over the world, creation myths take different forms. According to the ancient Japanese, for example, the world emerged from a single seed, which grew to form a god who, in turn, created other gods and eventually the islands of Japan and their inhabitants. Several Native American tribes share common beliefs about "sky ancestors," who created the people on the planet.

In Western culture, the most recognizable creation myth appears in Genesis, the first book of the Old Testament. According to Genesis, God created the heavens and the earth as well as all living creatures—including Adam and Eve. Other stories are part of the oral tradition of Judaism and do not appear in Genesis. An example of such a story is the tale of Lilith, which emerged sometime between the eighth and eleventh centuries. According to this Hebrew myth, Lilith, who was created before Eve, was Adam's first wife. However, she refused to be subservient to Adam, and so she left Eden, eventually to be replaced by Eve. Talmudic tradition holds that she later mated with demons and gave birth to a legion of demonic offspring who inhabit the dark places of the earth.

The influence of mythology on literature is profound, and our contemporary understanding of narrative fiction owes a great deal to mythology. In fact, many of the short stories in this anthology contain allusions to myth. Consider, for example, the role of myth in "The Lottery," "Young Goodman Brown," and Raymond Carver's "Cathedral" (p. 261). In each of these short stories, myth is central to the characters' behavior, sensibility, and understanding of the world in which they live.

Alison Bechdel (1960–   )

Courtesy Alison Bechdel

was born in Loch Haven, Pennsylvania, where her parents, who were teachers, owned and operated a funeral home. After graduating from college, Bechdel created the comic strip *Dykes to Watch out For*, which appears on the author's Web site, http://dykestowatchoutfor.com/, and in numerous award-winning collections. Her illustrations have appeared in the publications *Slate, Ms.*, and the *Advocate*. Her graphic memoir *Fun Home* (2006), from which the following excerpt is taken, has been hailed as the Best Book of the Year by numerous publications.

from Fun Home   (2006)

This graphic story starts on the next page.

 See Chapter 16 Review Card for Reading and Reacting questions about Alison Bechdel, from *Fun Home*.

Related Works

"Gryphon" (p. 138), "I'm nobody! Who are you?" (p. 361), "Musée des Beaux Arts" (p. 475), "Those Winter Sundays" (p. 482)

Cultural Context

The following graphic story refers to the Greek myth of Icarus and Daedalus. According to the myth, Daedalus, a famous Greek architect, inventor, and craftsman, was imprisoned by King Minos of Crete. He devised an escape plan in which he and his son, Icarus, would fly to Sicily using wings he had made from feathers and wax. Daedalus warned Icarus not to fly too close to the hot sun, fearing that the wax would melt. The recklessly overconfident Icarus disobeyed his father, plummeting into the sea and drowning. This myth is often alluded to as a metaphor for the self-destructiveness caused by overly ambitious behavior.

LIKE MANY FATHERS, MINE COULD OCCASIONALLY BE PREVAILED ON FOR A SPOT OF "AIRPLANE."

AS HE LAUNCHED ME, MY FULL WEIGHT WOULD FALL ON THE PIVOT POINT BETWEEN HIS FEET AND MY STOMACH.

OOF!

IT WAS A DISCOMFORT WELL WORTH THE RARE PHYSICAL CONTACT, AND CERTAINLY WORTH THE MOMENT OF PERFECT BALANCE WHEN I SOARED ABOVE HIM.

IN THE CIRCUS, ACROBATICS WHERE ONE PERSON LIES ON THE FLOOR BALANCING ANOTHER ARE CALLED "ICARIAN GAMES."

CONSIDERING THE FATE OF ICARUS AFTER HE FLOUTED HIS FATHER'S ADVICE AND FLEW SO CLOSE TO THE SUN HIS WINGS MELTED, PERHAPS SOME DARK HUMOR IS INTENDED.

UH-OH!

IN OUR PARTICULAR REENACTMENT OF THIS MYTHIC RELATIONSHIP, IT WAS NOT ME BUT MY FATHER WHO WAS TO PLUMMET FROM THE SKY.

BUT BEFORE HE DID SO, HE MANAGED TO GET QUITE A LOT DONE.

AGAIN!

THIS RUG IS FILTHY. GO GET THE VACUUM CLEANER.

HIS GREATEST ACHIEVEMENT, ARGUABLY, WAS HIS MONOMANIACAL RESTORATION OF OUR OLD HOUSE.

AND THEN GET ME MY TACK HAMMER. THAT STRIP OF MOLDING IS LOOSE.

WHEN OTHER CHILDREN CALLED OUR HOUSE A MANSION, I WOULD DEMUR. I RESENTED THE IMPLICATION THAT MY FAMILY WAS RICH, OR UNUSUAL IN ANY WAY.

IN FACT, WE WERE UNUSUAL, THOUGH I WOULDN'T APPRECIATE EXACTLY HOW UNUSUAL UNTIL MUCH LATER. BUT WE WERE NOT RICH.

THE GILT CORNICES, THE MARBLE FIREPLACE, THE CRYSTAL CHANDELIERS, THE SHELVES OF CALF-BOUND BOOKS--THESE WERE NOT SO MUCH BOUGHT AS PRODUCED FROM THIN AIR BY MY FATHER'S REMARKABLE LEGERDEMAIN.

MY FATHER COULD SPIN GARBAGE...

...INTO GOLD.

HE COULD TRANSFIGURE A ROOM WITH THE SMALLEST OFFHAND FLOURISH.

HE COULD CONJURE AN ENTIRE, FINISHED PERIOD INTERIOR FROM A PAINT CHIP.

HE WAS AN ALCHEMIST OF APPEARANCE, A SAVANT OF SURFACE, A DAEDALUS OF DECOR.

FOR IF MY FATHER WAS ICARUS, HE WAS ALSO DAEDALUS--THAT SKILLFUL ARTIFICER, THAT MAD SCIENTIST WHO BUILT THE WINGS FOR HIS SON AND DESIGNED THE FAMOUS LABYRINTH...

...AND WHO ANSWERED NOT TO THE LAWS OF SOCIETY, BUT TO THOSE OF HIS CRAFT.

THIS IS THE WALLPAPER FOR MY ROOM?

BUT I **HATE** PINK! I **HATE** FLOWERS!

TOUGH TITTY.

HISTORICAL RESTORATION WASN'T HIS JOB.

(TWELFTH-GRADE ENGLISH)

ARCHI-TECTURAL DIGEST

IT WAS HIS PASSION. AND I MEAN PASSION IN EVERY SENSE OF THE WORD.

LIBIDINAL. MANIC. MARTYRED.

Shirley Jackson (1916–1965)

is best known for her restrained tales of horror and the supernatural, most notably her novel *The Haunting of Hill House* (1959) and the short story "The Lottery" (1948). Among her other works are two novels dealing with multiple personalities—*The Bird's Nest* (1954) and *We Have Always Lived in the Castle* (1962)—and two collections of comic tales about her children and family life, *Life among the Savages* (1953) and *Raising Demons* (1957). A posthumous collection of stories, *Just an Ordinary Day* (1997), was published after the discovery of a box of some of Jackson's unpublished papers in a Vermont barn and her heirs' subsequent search for her other uncollected works.

With her husband, literary critic Stanley Edgar Hyman, she settled in the small town of Bennington, Vermont, but was never accepted by

© AP Photo

the townspeople. "The Lottery" is set in much the same kind of small, parochial town. Despite the story's matter-of-fact tone and familiar setting, its publication in the *New Yorker* provoked a torrent of letters from enraged and shocked readers. In her quiet way, Jackson presented the underside of village life and revealed to readers the dark side of human nature. Future writers of gothic tales recognized their great debt to Jackson. Horror master Stephen King dedicated his book *Firestarter* "to Shirley Jackson, who never had to raise her voice."

The Lottery (1948)

The morning of June 27th was clear and sunny, with the fresh warmth of a full-summer day; the flowers were blossoming profusely and the grass was richly green. The people of the village began to gather in the square, between the post office and the bank, around ten o'clock; in some towns there were so many people that the lottery took two days and had to be started on June 26th, but in this village, where there were only about three hundred people, the whole lottery took less than two hours, so it could begin at ten o'clock in the morning and still be through in time to allow the villagers to get home for noon dinner.

The children assembled first, of course. School was recently over for the summer, and the feeling of liberty sat uneasily on most of them; they tended to gather together quietly for a while before they broke into boisterous play, and their talk was still of the classroom and the teacher, of books and reprimands. Bobby Martin had already stuffed his pockets full of stones, and the other boys soon followed his example, selecting the smoothest and roundest stones; Bobby and Harry Jones and Dickie Delacroix—the villagers pronounced this name "Dellacroy"—eventually made a great pile of stones in one corner of the square and guarded it against the raids of the other boys. The girls stood aside, talking among themselves, looking over their shoulders at the boys, and the very small children rolled in the dust or clung to the hands of their older brothers or sisters.

Soon the men began to gather, surveying their own children, speaking of planting and rain, tractors and taxes. They stood together, away from the pile of stones in the corner, and their jokes were quiet and they smiled rather than laughed. The women, wearing faded house dresses and sweaters, came shortly after their menfolk. They greeted one another and exchanged bits of gossip as they went to join their husbands. Soon the women, standing by their husbands, began to call to their children, and the children came reluctantly, having to be called four or five times. Bobby Martin ducked under his mother's grasping hand and ran, laughing, back to the pile of stones. His father spoke up sharply, and Bobby came quickly and took his place between his father and his oldest brother.

Collective Copies, Amherst, MA

June

Sunday	Monday	Tuesday	Wednesday	Thursday	Friday	Saturday
					1	2
4	5	6	7	8	9	10
11	12	13	14	15	16	17
18	19	20	21	22	23	24
25	26	27	28	29	30	

Summer Solstice

>> Calendar identifying date of annual lottery

Cultural Context

"The Lottery" is sometimes seen as a protest against totalitarianism, a form of authoritarian government that permits no individual freedom. In *Eichmann in Jerusalem* (1963), political scientist Hannah Arendt (1906–1975) wrote about totalitarianism as it pertained to Nazi Germany and the Holocaust. Here, she introduced the concept of "the banality of evil," the potential in ordinary people to do evil things. Americans of the post–World War II era saw themselves as "good guys" defending the world against foreign evils. Jackson's story, written scarcely three years after the liberation of Auschwitz, told Americans something they did not want to hear—that the face of human evil could look just like their next-door neighbor.

>> New England village

The lottery was conducted—as were the square dances, the teen-age club, the Halloween program—by Mr. Summers, who had time and energy to devote to civic activities. He was a round-faced, jovial man and he ran the coal business, and people were sorry for him, because he had no children and his wife was a scold. When he arrived in the square, carrying the black wooden box, there was a murmur of conversation among the villagers, and he waved and called, "Little late today, folks." The postmaster, Mr. Graves, followed him, carrying a three-legged stool, and the stool was put in the center of the square and Mr. Summers set the black box down on it. The villagers kept their distance, leaving a space between themselves and the stool, and when Mr. Summers said, "Some of you fellows want to give me a hand?" there was a hesitation before two men, Mr. Martin and his oldest son, Baxter, came forward to hold the box steady on the stool while Mr. Summers stirred up the papers inside it.

The original paraphernalia for the lottery had been lost 5 long ago, and the black box now resting on the stool had been put into use even before Old Man Warner, the oldest man in town, was born. Mr. Summers spoke frequently to the villagers about making a new box, but no one liked to upset even as much tradition as was represented by the black box. There was a story that the present box had been made

> "The original paraphernalia for the lottery had been lost long ago, and the black box now resting on the stool had been put into use even before Old Man Warner, the oldest man in town, was born."

with some pieces of the box that had preceded it, the one that had been constructed when the first people settled down to make a village here. Every year, after the lottery, Mr. Summers began talking again about a new box, but every year the subject was allowed to fade off without anything's being done. The black box grew shabbier each year; by now it was no longer completely black but splintered badly along one side to show the original wood color, and in some places faded or stained.

Mr. Martin and his oldest son, Baxter, held the black box securely on the stool until Mr. Summers had stirred the papers thoroughly with his hand. Because so much of the ritual had been forgotten or discarded, Mr. Summers had been successful in having slips of paper substituted for the chips of wood that had been used for generations. Chips of wood, Mr. Summers had argued, had been all very well when the village was tiny, but now that the population was more than three hundred and likely to keep on growing, it was necessary to use something that would fit more easily into the black box. The night before the lottery, Mr. Summers and Mr. Graves made up the slips of paper and put them in the box, and it was then taken to the safe of Mr. Summers's coal company and locked up until Mr. Summers was ready to take it to the square next morning. The rest of the year, the box was put away, sometimes one place, sometimes another; it had spent one year in Mr. Graves's barn and another year underfoot in the post office, and sometimes it was set on a shelf in the Martin grocery and left there.

There was a great deal of fussing to be done before Mr. Summers declared the lottery open. There were the lists to make up—of heads of families, heads of households in each family, members of each household in each family. There was the proper swearing-in of Mr. Summers by the postmaster, as the official of the lottery; at one time, some people remembered, there had been a recital of some sort, performed by the official of the lottery, a perfunctory, tuneless chant that had been rattled off duly each year; some people believed that the official of the lottery used to stand just so when he said or sang it, others believed that he was supposed to walk among the people, but years and years ago this part of the ritual had been allowed to lapse. There had been, also, a ritual salute, which the official of the lottery had had to use in addressing each person who came up to draw from the box, but this also had changed with time, until now it was felt necessary only for the official to speak to each person approaching. Mr. Summers was very good at all this; in his clean white shirt and blue jeans, with one hand resting carelessly on the black box, he seemed very proper and important as he talked interminably to Mr. Graves and the Martins.

Just as Mr. Summers finally left off talking and turned to the assembled villagers, Mrs. Hutchinson came hurriedly along the path to the square, her sweater thrown over her shoulders, and slid into place in the back of the crowd. "Clean forgot what day it was," she said to Mrs. Delacroix, who stood next to her, and they both laughed softly. "Thought my old man was out back stacking wood," Mrs. Hutchinson went on, "and then I looked out the window and the kids was gone, and then I remembered it was the twenty-seventh and came a-running." She dried her hands on her apron, and Mrs. Delacroix said, "You're in time, though. They're still talking away up there."

Mrs. Hutchinson craned her neck to see through the crowd and found her husband and children standing near the front. She tapped Mrs. Delacroix on the arm as a farewell and began to make her way through the crowd. The people separated good-humoredly to let her through; two or three people said, in voices just loud enough to be heard across the crowd, "Here comes your Missus, Hutchinson," and "Bill, she made it after all." Mrs. Hutchinson reached her husband, and Mr. Summers, who had been waiting, said cheerfully, "Thought we were going to have to get on without you, Tessie." Mrs. Hutchinson said, grinning, "Wouldn't have me leave m'dishes in the sink, now, would you, Joe?," and soft laughter ran through the crowd as the people stirred back into position after Mrs. Hutchinson's arrival.

"Well, now," Mr. Summers said soberly, "guess we better get started, get this over with, so's we can go back to work. Anybody ain't here?" 10

"Dunbar," several people said. "Dunbar, Dunbar."

Mr. Summers consulted his list. "Clyde Dunbar," he said. "That's right. He's broke his leg, hasn't he? Who's drawing for him?"

"Me, I guess," a woman said, and Mr. Summers turned to look at her. "Wife draws for her husband," Mr. Summers said. "Don't you have a grown boy to do it for you, Janey?" Although Mr. Summers and everyone else in the village knew the answer perfectly well, it was the business of the official of the lottery to ask such questions formally. Mr. Summers waited with an expression of polite interest while Mrs. Dunbar answered.

"Horace's not but sixteen yet," Mrs. Dunbar said regretfully. "Guess I gotta fill in for the old man this year."

"Right," Mr. Summers said. He made a note on the list 15 he was holding. Then he asked, "Watson boy drawing this year?"

A tall boy in the crowd raised his hand. "Here," he said. "I'm drawing for m'mother and me." He blinked his eyes nervously and ducked his head as several voices in the crowd said things like "Good fellow, Jack," and "Glad to see your mother's got a man to do it."

"Well," Mr. Summers said, "guess that's everyone. Old Man Warner make it?"

"Here," a voice said, and Mr. Summers nodded.

A sudden hush fell on the crowd as Mr. Summers cleared his throat and looked at the list. "All ready?" he called. "Now, I'll read the names—heads of families first—and the men come up and take a paper out of the box. Keep the paper folded in your hand without looking at it until everyone has had a turn. Everything clear?"

The people had done it so many times that they only 20 half listened to the directions; most of them were quiet, wetting their lips, not looking around. Then Mr. Summers raised one hand high and said, "Adams." A man disengaged himself from the crowd and came forward. "Hi, Steve," Mr. Summers said, and Mr. Adams said, "Hi, Joe." They grinned at one another humorlessly and nervously. Then Mr. Adams reached into the black box and took out a folded paper. He held it firmly by one corner as he turned and went hastily back to his place in the crowd, where he stood a little apart from his family, not looking down at his hand.

"Allen," Mr. Summers said. "Anderson. . . . Bentham."

"Seems like there's no time at all between lotteries any more," Mrs. Delacroix said to Mrs. Graves in the back row. "Seems like we got through with the last one only last week."

"Time sure goes fast," Mrs. Graves said.

"Clark. . . . Delacroix."

"There goes my old man," Mrs. Delacroix said. She 25 held her breath while her husband went forward.

"Dunbar," Mr. Summers said, and Mrs. Dunbar went steadily to the box while one of the women said, "Go on, Janey," and another said, "There she goes."

"We're next," Mrs. Graves said. She watched while Mr. Graves came around from the side of the box, greeted Mr. Summers gravely, and selected a slip of paper from the box. By now, all through the crowd there were men holding the small folded papers in their large hands, turning them over and over nervously. Mrs. Dunbar and her two sons stood together, Mrs. Dunbar holding the slip of paper.

"Harburt. . . . Hutchinson."

"Get up there, Bill," Mrs. Hutchinson said, and the people near her laughed.

"Jones." 30

"They do say," Mr. Adams said to Old Man Warner, who stood next to him, "that over in the north village they're talking of giving up the lottery."

Old Man Warner snorted. "Pack of crazy fools," he said. "Listening to the young folks, nothing's good enough for *them*. Next thing you know, they'll be wanting to go back to living in caves, nobody work any more, live *that* way for a while. Used to be a saying about 'Lottery in June, corn be heavy soon.' First thing you know, we'd all be eating stewed chickweed and acorns. There's *always* been a lottery," he added petulantly. "Bad enough to see young Joe Summers up there joking with everybody."

"Some places have already quit lotteries," Mrs. Adams said.

"Nothing but trouble in *that*," Old Man Warner said stoutly. "Pack of young fools."

"Martin." And Bobby Martin watched his father go 35 forward. "Overdyke. . . . Percy."

"I wish they'd hurry," Mrs. Dunbar said to her older son. "I wish they'd hurry."

"They're almost through," her son said.

"You get ready to run tell Dad," Mrs. Dunbar said.

Mr. Summers called his own name and then stepped forward precisely and selected a slip from the box. Then he called, "Warner."

"Seventy-seventh year I been in the lottery," Old Man 40 Warner said as he went through the crowd. "Seventy-seventh time."

"Watson." The tall boy came awkwardly through the crowd. Someone said, "Don't be nervous, Jack," and Mr. Summers said, "Take your time, son."

"Zanini."

After that, there was a long pause, a breathless pause, until Mr. Summers, holding his slip of paper in the air, said, "All right, fellows." For a minute, no one moved, and then all the slips of paper were opened. Suddenly, all the women began to speak at once, saying, "Who is it?," "Who's got it?," "Is it the Dunbars?," "Is it the Watsons?" Then the voices began to say, "It's Hutchinson. It's Bill," "Bill Hutchinson's got it."

"Go tell your father," Mrs. Dunbar said to her older son.

People began to look around to see the Hutchinsons. 45 Bill Hutchinson was standing quiet, staring down at the paper in his hand. Suddenly, Tessie Hutchinson shouted to Mr. Summers, "You didn't give him time enough to take any paper he wanted. I saw you. It wasn't fair!"

"Be a good sport, Tessie," Mrs. Delacroix called, and Mrs. Graves said, "All of us took the same chance."

"Shut up, Tessie," Bill Hutchinson said.

"Well, everyone," Mr. Summers said, "that was done pretty fast, and now we've got to be hurrying a little more to get done in time." He consulted his next list. "Bill," he said, "you draw for the Hutchinson family. You got any other households in the Hutchinsons?"

>> Statue of Ceres, goddess of agriculture

"There's Don and Eva," Mrs. Hutchinson yelled, "Make *them* take their chance!"

"Daughters draw with their husbands' families, Tes- 50 sie," Mr. Summers said gently. "You know that as well as anyone else."

"It wasn't *fair*," Tessie said.

"I guess not, Joe," Bill Hutchinson said regretfully. "My daughter draws with her husband's family, that's only fair. And I've got no other family except the kids."

"Then, as far as drawing for families is concerned, it's you," Mr. Summers said in explanation, "and as far as drawing for households is concerned, that's you, too. Right?"

"Right," Bill Hutchinson said.

"How many kids, Bill?" Mr. Summers asked formally. 55

"Three," Bill Hutchinson said. "There's Bill, Jr., and Nancy, and little Dave. And Tessie and me."

"All right, then," Mr. Summers said. "Harry, you got their tickets back?"

Mr. Graves nodded and held up the slips of paper. "Put them in the box, then," Mr. Summers directed. "Take Bill's and put it in."

"I think we ought to start over," Mrs. Hutchinson said, as quietly as she could. "I tell you it wasn't *fair*. You didn't give him time enough to choose. *Every*body saw that."

Mr. Graves had selected the five slips and put them in 60 the box, and he dropped all the papers but those onto the ground, where the breeze caught them and lifted them off.

"Listen, everybody," Mrs. Hutchinson was saying to the people around her.

"Ready, Bill?" Mr. Summers asked, and Bill Hutchinson, with one quick glance around at his wife and children, nodded.

"Remember," Mr. Summers said, "take the slips and keep them folded until each person has taken one. Harry, you help little Dave." Mr. Graves took the hand of the little boy, who came willingly with him up to the box. "Take a paper out of the box, Davy," Mr. Summers said. Davy put his hand into the box and laughed. "Take just *one* paper," Mr. Summers said. "Harry, you hold it for him." Mr. Graves took the child's hand and removed the folded paper from the tight fist and held it while little Dave stood next to him and looked at him wonderingly.

"Nancy next," Mr. Summers said. Nancy was twelve, and her school friends breathed heavily as she went forward, switching her skirt, and took a slip daintily from the box. "Bill, Jr.," Mr. Summers said, and Billy, his face red and his feet overlarge, nearly knocked the box over as he got a paper out. "Tessie," Mr. Summers said. She hesitated for a minute, looking around defiantly, and then set her lips and went up to the box. She snatched a paper out and held it behind her.

"Bill," Mr. Summers said, and Bill Hutchinson reached 65 into the box and felt around, bringing his hand out at last with the slip of paper in it.

The crowd was quiet. A girl whispered, "I hope it's not Nancy," and the sound of the whisper reached the edges of the crowd.

"It's not the way it used to be," Old Man Warner said clearly. "People ain't the way they used to be."

"All right," Mr. Summers said. "Open the papers. Harry, you open little Dave's."

Mr. Graves opened the slip of paper and there was a general sigh through the crowd as he held it up and everyone could see that it was blank. Nancy and Bill, Jr., opened theirs at the same time, and both beamed and laughed, turning around to the crowd and holding their slips of paper above their heads.

"Tessie," Mr. Summers said. There was a pause, and 70 then Mr. Summers looked at Bill Hutchinson, and Bill unfolded his paper and showed it. It was blank.

"It's Tessie," Mr. Summers said, and his voice was hushed. "Show us her paper, Bill."

Bill Hutchinson went over to his wife and forced the slip of paper out of her hand. It had a black spot on it, the black spot Mr. Summers had made the night before with the heavy pencil in the coal-company office. Bill Hutchinson held it up, and there was a stir in the crowd.

"All right, folks," Mr. Summers said. "Let's finish quickly."

Although the villagers had forgotten the ritual and lost the original black box, they still remembered to use stones. The pile of stones the boys had made earlier was ready; there were stones on the ground with the blowing scraps of paper that had come out of the box. Mrs. Delacroix selected a stone so large she had to pick it up with both hands and turned to Mrs. Dunbar. "Come on," she said. "Hurry up."

Mrs. Dunbar had small stones in both hands, and she 75 said, gasping for breath, "I can't run at all. You'll have to go ahead and I'll catch up with you."

The children had stones already, and someone gave little Davy Hutchinson a few pebbles.

Tessie Hutchinson was in the center of a cleared space by now, and she held her hands out desperately as the villagers moved in on her. "It isn't fair," she said. A stone hit her on the side of the head.

Old Man Warner was saying, "Come on, come on, everyone." Steve Adams was in the front of the crowd of villagers, with Mrs. Graves beside him.

"It isn't fair, it isn't right," Mrs. Hutchinson screamed, and then they were upon her.

Related Works

"Young Goodman Brown" (p. 320), "Where Are You Going, Where Have You Been?" (p. 325), "Patterns" (p. 370), *Nine Ten* (p. 553)

 See Chapter 16 Review Card for Reading and Reacting questions about Shirley Jackson, "The Lottery."

Alice Walker (1944–   )

was the youngest of eight children born to Willie Lee and Minnie Tallulah Grant Walker, sharecroppers who raised cotton. She left the rural South to attend Spelman College in Atlanta (1961–1963) and Sarah Lawrence College in Bronxville, New York (1963–1965).

In 1967, Walker moved to Mississippi, where she was supported in the writing of her first novel, *The Third Life of Grange Copeland* (1970), by a National Endowment for the Arts grant. Her short story "Everyday Use" was included in *Best American Short Stories 1973* and has been widely anthologized and studied. Other novels and collections of short stories followed, including *In Love & Trouble: Stories of Black Women* (1973), *Meridian* (1976), *You Can't Keep a Good Woman Down* (1981), *The Temple of My Familiar* (1989), *Possessing the Secret of Joy* (1993), *The Complete Stories* (1994), *By the Light of My Father's Smile* (1998), and *Now Is the Time to Open Your Heart* (2004). Her latest book is a collection of poems, *Hard Times Require Furious Dancing* (2010). Her third novel, *The Color Purple* (1982), won the American Book Award and a Pulitzer Prize and was made into an award-winning movie and a long-running Broadway play.

In the third year of her marriage, Walker took back her maiden name because she wanted to honor her great-great-great-grandmother who had walked, carrying her two children, from Virginia to Georgia. Walker's renaming is consistent with one of her goals in writing, which is to further the process of reconnecting people to their ancestors. She has said that "it is fatal to see yourself as separate" and that if people can reaffirm the past, they can "make a different future."

Everyday Use (1973)

For Your Grandmama

I will wait for her in the yard that Maggie and I made so clean and wavy yesterday afternoon. A yard like this is more comfortable than most people know. It is not just a yard. It is like an extended living room. When the hard clay is swept clean as a floor and the fine sand around the edges lined with tiny, irregular grooves, anyone can come and sit and look up into the elm tree and wait for the breezes that never come inside the house.

Maggie will be nervous until after her sister goes: she will stand hopelessly in corners, homely and ashamed of the burn scars down her arms and legs, eying her sister with a mixture of envy and awe. She thinks her sister has held life always in the palm of one hand, that "no" is a word the world never learned to say to her.

You've no doubt seen those TV shows where the child who has "made it" is confronted, as a surprise, by her own mother and father, tottering in weakly from backstage. (A pleasant surprise, of course: What would they do if parent and child came on the show only to curse out and insult each other?) On TV mother and child embrace and smile into each other's faces. Sometimes the mother and father weep, the child wraps them in her arms and leans across the table to tell how she would not have made it without their help. I have seen these programs.

Sometimes I dream a dream in which Dee and I are suddenly brought together on a TV program of this sort. Out of a dark and soft-seated limousine I am ushered into a bright room filled with many people. There I meet a smiling, gray, sporty man like Johnny Carson who shakes my hand and tells me what a fine girl I have. Then we are on the stage and Dee is embracing me with tears in her eyes. She pins on my dress a large orchid, even though she has told me once that she thinks orchids are tacky flowers.

In real life I am a large, big-boned woman with rough, 5 man-working hands. In the winter I wear flannel nightgowns to bed and overalls during the day. I can kill and clean a hog as mercilessly as a man. My fat keeps me hot in zero weather. I can work outside all day, breaking ice to get water for washing; I can eat pork liver cooked over the open fire minutes after it comes steaming from the hog. One winter I knocked a bull calf straight in the brain between the eyes with a sledge hammer and had the meat hung up to chill before nightfall. But of course all this does not show on television. I am the way my daughter would want me to be: a hundred pounds lighter, my skin like an uncooked barley pancake. My hair glistens in the hot bright lights. Johnny Carson has much to do to keep up with my quick and witty tongue.

But that is a mistake. I know even before I wake up. Who ever knew a Johnson with a quick tongue? Who can even imagine me looking a strange white man in the eye? It seems to me I have talked to them always with one foot raised in flight, with my head turned in whichever way is farthest from them. Dee, though. She would always look anyone in the eye. Hesitation was no part of her nature.

"How do I look, Mama?" Maggie says, showing just enough of her thin body enveloped in pink skirt and red blouse for me to know she's there, almost hidden by the door.

"Come out into the yard," I say.

Have you ever seen a lame animal, perhaps a dog run over by some careless person rich enough to own a car, sidle up to someone who is ignorant enough to be kind to him? That is the way my Maggie walks. She has been like this, chin on chest, eyes on ground, feet in shuffle, ever since the fire that burned the other house to the ground.

Dee is lighter than Maggie, with nicer hair and a fuller 10 figure. She's a woman now, though sometimes I forget. How long ago was it that the other house burned? Ten, twelve years? Sometimes I can still hear the flames and feel Maggie's arms sticking to me, her hair smoking and her

>> Johnny Carson (right), longtime *Tonight Show* host, with sidekick Ed McMahon

>> Detail of a quilt

dress falling off her in little black papery flakes. Her eyes seemed stretched open, blazed open by the flames reflected in them. And Dee. I see her standing off under the sweet gum tree she used to dig gum out of; a look of concentration on her face as she watched the last dingy gray board of the house fall in toward the red-hot brick chimney. Why don't you do a dance around the ashes? I'd wanted to ask her. She had hated the house that much.

I used to think she hated Maggie, too. But that was before we raised the money, the church and me, to send her to Augusta to school. She used to read to us without pity; forcing words, lies, other folks' habits, whole lives upon us two, sitting trapped and ignorant underneath her voice. She washed us in a river of make-believe, burned us with a lot of knowledge we didn't necessarily need to know. Pressed us to her with the serious way she read, to shove us away at just the moment, like dimwits, we seemed about to understand.

Dee wanted nice things. A yellow organdy dress to wear to her graduation from high school; black pumps to match a green suit she'd made from an old suit somebody gave me. She was determined to stare down any disaster in her efforts. Her eyelids would not flicker for minutes at a time. Often I fought off the temptation to shake her. At sixteen she had a style of her own, and knew what style was.

I never had an education myself. After second grade the school was closed down. Don't ask me why: in 1927 colored asked fewer questions than they do now. Sometimes Maggie reads to me. She stumbles along good-naturedly but can't see well. She knows she is not bright. Like good looks and money, quickness passed her by. She will marry John Thomas (who has mossy teeth in an earnest face) and then I'll be free to sit here and I guess just sing church songs to myself. Although I never was a good singer. Never could carry a tune. I was always better at a man's job. I used to love to milk till I was hooked in the side in

'49. Cows are soothing and slow and don't bother you, unless you try to milk them the wrong way.

I have deliberately turned my back on the house. It is three rooms, just like the one that burned, except the roof is tin; they don't make shingle roofs any more. There are no real windows, just some holes cut in the sides, like the portholes in a ship, but not round and not square, with rawhide holding the shutters up on the outside. This house is in a pasture, too, like the other one. No doubt when Dee sees it she will want to tear it down. She wrote me once that no matter where we "choose" to live, she will manage to come see us. But she will never bring her friends. Maggie and I thought about this and Maggie asked me, "Mama, when did Dee ever *have* any friends?"

She had a few. Furtive 15 boys in pink shirts hanging about on washday after school. Nervous girls who never laughed. Impressed with her they worshiped the well-turned phrase, the cute shape, the scalding humor that erupted like bubbles in lye. She read to them.

When she was courting Jimmy T she didn't have much time to pay to us, but turned all her faultfinding power on him. He *flew* to marry a cheap city girl from a family of ignorant flashy people. She hardly had time to recompose herself.

When she comes I will meet—but there they are!

Maggie attempts to make a dash for the house, in her shuffling way, but I stay her with my hand. "Come back here," I say. And she stops and tries to dig a well in the sand with her toe.

It is hard to see them clearly through the strong sun. But even the first glimpse of leg out of the car tells me it is Dee. Her feet were always neat-looking, as if God himself had shaped them with a certain style. From the other side of the car comes a short, stocky man. Hair is all over his head a foot long and hanging from his chin like a kinky mule tail. I hear Maggie suck in her breath. "Uhnnnh," is what it sounds like. Like when you see the wriggling end of a snake just in front of your foot on the road. "Uhnnnh."

Dee next. A dress down to the ground, in this hot 20 weather. A dress so loud it hurts my eyes. There are yellows and oranges enough to throw back the light of the sun. I feel my whole face warming from the heat waves it throws out. Earrings gold, too, and hanging down to her shoulders. Bracelets dangling and making noises when she moves her arm up to shake the folds of the dress out of her

> "Dee wanted nice things. A yellow organdy dress to wear to her graduation from high school; black pumps to match a green suit she'd made from an old suit somebody gave me."

armpits. The dress is loose and flows, and as she walks closer, I like it. I hear Maggie go "Uhnnnh" again. It is her sister's hair. It stands straight up like the wool on a sheep. It is black as night and around the edges are two long pigtails that rope about like small lizards disappearing behind her ears.

"Wa-su-zo-Tean-o!"° she says, coming on in that gliding way the dress makes her move. The short stocky fellow with the hair to his navel is all grinning and he follows up with "Asalamalakim,° my mother and sister!" He moves to hug Maggie but she falls back, right up against the back of my chair. I feel her trembling there and when I look up I see the perspiration falling off her chin.

"Don't get up," says Dee. Since I am stout it takes something of a push. You can see me trying to move a second or two before I make it. She turns, showing white heels through her sandals, and goes back to the car. Out she peeks next with a Polaroid. She stoops down quickly and lines up picture after picture of me sitting there in front of the house with Maggie cowering behind me. She never takes a shot without making sure the house is included. When a cow comes nibbling around the edge of the yard she snaps it and me and Maggie *and* the house. Then she puts the Polaroid in the back seat of the car, and comes up and kisses me on the forehead.

Meanwhile Asalamalakim is going through motions with Maggie's hand. Maggie's hand is as limp as a fish, and probably as cold, despite the sweat, and she keeps trying to pull it back. It looks like Asalamalakim wants to shake hands but wants to do it fancy. Or maybe he don't know how people shake hands. Anyhow, he soon gives up on Maggie.

"Well," I say. "Dee."

"No, Mama," she says. "Not 'Dee,' Wangero Leewan- 25 ika Kemanjo!"

"What happened to 'Dee'?" I wanted to know.

"She's dead," Wangero said. "I couldn't bear it any longer, being named after the people who oppress me."

"You know as well as me you was named after your aunt Dicie," I said. Dicie is my sister. She named Dee. We called her "Big Dee" after Dee was born.

"But who was *she* named after?" asked Wangero.

"I guess after Grandma Dee," I said.   30

"And who was she named after?" asked Wangero.

"Her mother," I said, and saw Wangero was getting tired. "That's about as far back as I can trace it," I said. Though, in fact, I probably could have carried it back beyond the Civil War through the branches.

"Well," said Asalamalakim, "there you are."

"Uhnnnh," I heard Maggie say.

"There I was not," I said, "before 'Dicie' cropped up in 35 our family, so why should I try to trace it that far back?"

He just stood there grinning, looking down on me like somebody inspecting a Model A car. Every once in a while he and Wangero sent eye signals over my head.

"How do you pronounce this name?" I asked.

"You don't have to call me by it if you don't want to," said Wangero.

"Why shouldn't I?" I asked. "If that's what you want us to call you, we'll call you."

"I know it might sound awkward at first," said 40 Wangero.

"I'll get used to it," I said. "Ream it out again."

Well, soon we got the name out of the way. Asalamalakim had a name twice as long and three times as hard. After I tripped over it two or three times he told me to just call him Hakim-a-barber. I wanted to ask him was he a barber, but I didn't really think he was, so I didn't ask.

"You must belong to those beef-cattle peoples down the road," I said. They said "Asalamalakim" when they met you, too, but they didn't shake hands. Always too busy: feeding the cattle, fixing the fences, putting up salt-lick shelters, throwing down hay. When the white folks poisoned some of the herd the men stayed up all night with rifles in their hands. I walked a mile and a half just to see the sight.

Hakim-a-barber said, "I accept some of their doctrines, but farming and raising cattle is not my style." (They didn't tell me, and I didn't ask, whether Wangero [Dee] had really gone and married him.)

We sat down to eat and right away he said he didn't eat 45 collards and pork was unclean. Wangero, though, went on through the chitlins and corn bread, the greens and everything else. She talked a blue streak over the sweet potatoes. Everything delighted her. Even the fact that we still used the benches her daddy made for the table when we couldn't afford to buy chairs.

"Oh, Mama!" she cried. Then turned to Hakim-a-barber. "I never knew how lovely these benches are. You can feel the rump prints," she said, running her hands underneath her and along the bench. Then she gave a sigh and her hand closed over Grandma Dee's butter dish. "That's it!" she said. "I knew there was something I wanted to ask you if I could have." She jumped up from the table and went over in the corner where the churn stood, the milk in it clabber by now. She looked at the churn and looked at it.

"This churn top is what I need," she said. "Didn't Uncle Buddy whittle it out of a tree you all used to have?"

"Yes," I said.

"Uh huh," she said happily. "And I want the dasher, too."

"Uncle Buddy whittle that, too?" asked the barber.   50

Dee (Wangero) looked up at me.

"Aunt Dee's first husband whittled the dash," said Maggie so low you almost couldn't hear her. "His name was Henry, but they called him Stash."

"Maggie's brain is like an elephant's," Wangero said, laughing. "I can use the churn top as a centerpiece for the alcove table," she said, sliding a plate over the churn, "and I'll think of something artistic to do with the dasher."

° **Wa-su-zo-Tean-o** A greeting in Swahili; Dee sounds it out one syllable at a time.

° **Asalamalakim** A greeting in Arabic: "Peace be upon you."

>> Butter churn

EXPLORE ONLINE >

To listen to an instructor podcast of "Everyday Use,"
visit your Literature CourseMate, accessed through
www.cengagebrain.com.

When she finished wrapping the dasher the handle stuck out. I took it for a moment in my hands. You didn't even have to look close to see where hands pushing the dasher up and down to make butter had left a kind of sink in the wood. In fact, there were a lot of small sinks; you could see where thumb and fingers had sunk into the wood. It was beautiful light yellow wood, from a tree that grew in the yard where Big Dee and Stash had lived.

After dinner Dee (Wangero) went to the trunk at the foot of my bed and started rifling through it. Maggie hung back in the kitchen over the dishpan. Out came Wangero with two quilts. They had been pieced by Grandma Dee and then Big Dee and me had hung them on the quilt frames on the front porch and quilted them. One was in the Lone Star pattern. The other was Walk Around the Mountain. In both of them were scraps of dresses Grandma Dee had worn fifty and more years ago. Bits and pieces of Grandpa Jarrell's Paisley shirts. And one teeny faded blue piece, about the size of a penny matchbox, that was from Great Grandpa Ezra's uniform that he wore in the Civil War.

"Mama," Wangero said sweet as a bird. "Can I have these old quilts?"

I heard something fall in the kitchen, and a minute later the kitchen door slammed.

"Why don't you take one or two of the others?" I asked. "These old things was just done by me and Big Dee from some tops your grandma pieced before she died."

"No," said Wangero. "I don't want those. They are stitched around the borders by machine."

"That'll make them last better," I said.

"That's not the point," said Wangero. "These are all pieces of dresses Grandma used to wear. She did all this stitching by hand. Imagine!" She held the quilts securely in her arms, stroking them.

"Some of the pieces, like those lavender ones, come from old clothes her mother handed down to her," I said, moving up to touch the quilts. Dee (Wangero) moved back just enough so that I couldn't reach the quilts. They already belonged to her.

"Imagine!" she breathed again, clutching them closely to her bosom.

"The truth is," I said, "I promised to give them quilts to Maggie, for when she marries John Thomas."

She gasped like a bee had stung her. "Maggie can't appreciate these quilts!" she said. "She'd probably be backward enough to put them to everyday use."

"I reckon she would," I said. "God knows I been saving 'em for long enough with nobody using 'em. I hope she will!" I didn't want to bring up how I had offered Dee (Wangero) a quilt when she went away to college. Then she had told me they were old-fashioned, out of style.

"But, they're *priceless!*" she was saying now, furiously; for she has a temper. "Maggie would put them on the bed and in five years they'd be in rags. Less than that!"

"She can always make some more," I said. "Maggie knows how to quilt."

>> Trunk with patchwork quilt

Dee (Wangero) looked at me with hatred. "You just will not understand. The point is these quilts, *these* quilts!"

"Well," I said, stumped. "What would *you* do with 70 them?"

"Hang them," she said. As if that was the only thing you *could* do with quilts.

Maggie by now was standing in the door. I could almost hear the sound her feet made as they scraped over each other.

"She can have them, Mama," she said, like somebody used to never winning anything, or having anything reserved for her. "I can 'member Grandma Dee without the quilts."

I looked at her hard. She had filled her bottom lip with checkerberry snuff and it gave her face a kind of dopey, hangdog look. It was Grandma Dee and Big Dee who taught her how to quilt herself. She stood there with her scarred hands hidden in the folds of her skirt. She looked at her sister with something like fear but she wasn't mad at her. This was Maggie's portion. This was the way she knew God to work.

When I looked at her like that something hit me in the 75 top of my head and ran down to the soles of my feet. Just like when I'm in church and the spirit of God touches me and I get happy and shout. I did something I never had done before: hugged Maggie to me, then dragged her on into the room, snatched the quilts out of Miss Wangero's hands and dumped them into Maggie's lap. Maggie just sat there on my bed with her mouth open.

"Take one or two of the others," I said to Dee.

But she turned without a word and went out to Ha- 70 kim-a-barber.

"You just don't understand," she said, as Maggie and I came out to the car.

"What don't I understand?" I wanted to know.

"Your heritage," she said. And then she turned to 80 Maggie, kissed her, and said, "You ought to try to make something of yourself, too, Maggie. It's really a new day for us. But from the way you and Mama still live you'd never know it."

She put on some sunglasses that hid everything above the tip of her nose and her chin.

Maggie smiled; maybe at the sunglasses. But a real smile, not scared. After we watched the car dust settle I asked Maggie to bring me a dip of snuff. And then the two of us sat there just enjoying, until it was time to go in the house and go to bed.

Related Works

"Two Kinds" (p. 336), "My Grandmother Would Rock Quietly and Hum" (p. 363), "Aunt Jennifer's Tigers" (p. 433), *Trifles* (p. 555), *Fences* (p. 724)

See Chapter 16 Review Card for Reading and Reacting questions about Alice Walker, "Everyday Use."

Raymond Carver (1938–1988)

was one of the most influential and widely read writers of our time. He fashioned his stories from the stuff of common life uncommonly perceived. He married at nineteen and fathered two children by the time he was twenty; during this period, he also began to write. He received a degree from Humboldt State University and later from the University of Iowa. His first collection of stories, *Will You Please Be Quiet, Please* (1976), was nominated for a National Book Award. Five more collections of stories followed, including *Cathedral* (1983) — nominated for both a Pulitzer Prize and a National Book Critics Circle Award — and *Where I'm Calling From: New and Selected Stories* (1988). Carver was also the author of five books of poetry. In his last years, Carver was praised as the best American short story writer since Ernest Hemingway; novelist Robert Stone called him "a hero of perception." He was made an Honorary Doctor of Letters at the University of Hartford and was inducted into the American Academy and Institute of Arts and Letters.

© Bob Adelman / Magnum Photos

Cathedral (1983)

This blind man, an old friend of my wife's, he was on his way to spend the night. His wife had died. So he was visiting the dead wife's relatives in Connecticut. He called my wife from his in-laws'. Arrangements were made. He would come by train, a five-hour trip, and my wife would meet him at the station. She hadn't seen him since she worked for him one summer in Seattle ten years ago. But she and the blind man had kept in touch. They made tapes and mailed them back and forth. I wasn't enthusiastic about his visit. He was no one I knew. And his being blind bothered me. My idea of blindness came from the movies. In the movies, the blind moved slowly and never laughed. Sometimes they were led by seeing-eye dogs. A blind man in my house was not something I looked forward to.

That summer in Seattle she had needed a job. She didn't have any money. The man she was going to marry at the end of the summer was in officers' training school. He didn't have any money, either. But she was in love with the guy, and he was in love with her, etc. She'd seen something in the paper: HELP WANTED—*Reading to Blind Man*, and a telephone number. She phoned and went over, was hired on the spot. She'd worked with this blind man all summer. She read stuff to him, case studies, reports, that sort of thing. She helped him organize his little office in the county social-service department. They'd become good friends, my wife and the blind man. How do I know these things? She told me. And she told me something else. On her last day in the office, the blind man asked if he could touch her face. She agreed to this. She told me he touched his fingers to every part of her face, her nose—even her neck! She never forgot it. She even tried to write a poem about it. She was always trying to write a poem. She wrote a poem or two every year, usually after something really important had happened to her.

When we first started going out together, she showed me the poem. In the poem, she recalled his fingers and the way they had moved around over her face. In the poem, she talked about what she had felt at the time, about what went through her mind when the blind man touched her nose and lips. I can remember I didn't think much of the poem. Of course, I didn't tell her that. Maybe I just don't understand poetry. I admit it's not the first thing I reach for when I pick up something to read.

Anyway, this man who'd first enjoyed her favors, the officer-to-be, he'd been her childhood sweetheart. So okay. I'm saying that at the end of the summer she let the blind man run his hands over her face, said goodbye to him, married her childhood etc., who was now a commissioned officer, and she moved away from Seattle. But they'd kept in touch, she and the blind man. She made the first contact after a year or so. She called him up one night from an Air Force base in Alabama. She wanted to talk. They talked. He asked her to send a tape and tell him about her life. She did this. She sent the tape. On the tape, she told the blind man about her husband and about their life together in the military. She told the blind man she loved her husband but she didn't like it where they lived and she didn't like it that he was part of the military-industrial thing. She told the blind man she'd written a poem and he was in it. She told him that she was writing a poem about what it was like to be an Air Force officer's wife. The poem wasn't finished yet. She was still writing it. The blind man made a tape. He sent her the tape. She made a tape. This went on for years. My wife's officer was posted to one base and then another. She sent tapes from Moody AFB, McGuire, McConnell, and finally Travis,° near Sacramento, where one night she got to feeling lonely and cut off from people she kept losing in that moving-around life. She got to feeling she couldn't go it another step. She went in and swallowed all the pills and capsules in the medicine chest and washed them down with a bottle of gin. Then she got into a hot bath and passed out.

But instead of dying, she got sick. She threw up. Her officer—why should he have a name? he was the childhood sweetheart, and what more does he want?—came home from somewhere, found her, and called the ambulance. In time, she put it all on a tape and sent the tape to the blind man. Over the years, she put all kinds of stuff on tapes and sent the tapes off lickety-split. Next to writing a poem every year, I think it was her chief means of recreation. On one tape, she told the blind man she'd decided to live away from her officer for a time. On another tape, she told him about her divorce. She and I began going out, and of course she told her blind man about it. She told him everything, or so it seemed to me. Once she asked me if I'd like to hear the latest tape from the blind man. This was a year ago. I was on the tape, she said. So I said okay, I'd listen to it. I got us drinks and we settled down in the living room. We made ready to listen. First she inserted the tape into the player and adjusted a couple of dials. Then she pushed a lever. The tape squeaked and someone began to talk in this loud voice. She lowered the volume. After a few minutes of harmless chitchat, I heard

> "My idea of blindness came from the movies. In the movies, the blind moved slowly and never laughed. Sometimes they were led by seeing-eye dogs. A blind man in my house was not something I looked forward to."

° **Moody . . . Travis** United States Air Force bases.

my own name in the mouth of this stranger, this blind man I didn't even know! And then this: "From all you've said about him, I can only conclude—" But we were interrupted, a knock at the door, something, and we didn't ever get back to the tape. Maybe it was just as well. I'd heard all I wanted to.

Now this same blind man was coming to sleep in my house.

"Maybe I could take him bowling," I said to my wife. She was at the draining board doing scalloped potatoes. She put down the knife she was using and turned around.

"If you love me," she said, "you can do this for me. If you don't love me, okay. But if you had a friend, any friend, and the friend came to visit, I'd make him feel comfortable." She wiped her hands with the dish towel.

"I don't have any blind friends," I said.

"You don't have *any* friends," she said. "Period. Be- 10 sides," she said, "goddamn it, his wife's just died! Don't you understand that? The man's lost his wife!"

I didn't answer. She'd told me a little about the blind man's wife. Her name was Beulah. Beulah! That's a name for a colored woman.

"Was his wife a Negro?" I asked.

"Are you crazy?" my wife said. "Have you just flipped or something?" She picked up a potato. I saw it hit the floor, then roll under the stove. "What's wrong with you?" she said. "Are you drunk?"

"I'm just asking," I said.

Right then my wife filled me in with more detail 15 than I cared to know. I made a drink and sat at the kitchen table to listen. Pieces of the story began to fall into place.

Beulah had gone to work for the blind man the summer after my wife had stopped working for him. Pretty soon Beulah and the blind man had themselves a church wedding. It was a little wedding—who'd want to go to such a wedding in the first place?—just the two of them, plus the minister and the minister's wife. But it was a church wedding just the same. It was what Beulah had wanted, he'd said. But even then Beulah must have been carrying the cancer in her glands. After they had been inseparable for eight years—my wife's word, *inseparable*—Beulah's health went into a rapid decline. She died in a Seattle hospital room, the blind man sitting beside the bed and holding on to her hand. They'd married, lived and worked together, slept together—had sex, sure—and then the blind man had to bury her. All this without his having ever seen what the goddamned woman looked like. It was beyond my understanding. Hearing this, I felt sorry for the blind man for a little bit. And then I found myself thinking what a pitiful life this woman must have led. Imagine a woman who could never see herself as she was seen in the eyes of her loved one. A woman who could go on day after day and never receive the smallest compliment from her beloved. A woman whose husband could never read the expression on her face, be it misery or something better. Someone who could wear makeup or not—what difference to him? She could, if she wanted, wear green eye-shadow around one eye, a straight pin in her nostril, yellow slacks, and purple shoes, no matter. And then to slip off into death, the blind man's hand on her hand, his blind eyes streaming tears—I'm imagining now—her last thought maybe this: that he never even knew what she looked like, and she on an express to the grave. Robert was left with a small insurance policy and a half of a twenty-peso Mexican coin. The other half of the coin went into the box with her. Pathetic.

So when the time rolled around, my wife went to the depot to pick him up. With nothing to do but wait—sure, I blamed him for that—I was having a drink and watching the TV when I heard the car pull into the drive. I got up from the sofa with my drink and went to the window to have a look.

I saw my wife laughing as she parked the car. I saw her get out of the car and shut the door. She was still wearing a smile. Just amazing. She went around to the other side of the car to where the blind man was already starting to get out. This blind man, feature this, he was wearing a full beard! A beard on a blind man! Too much, I say. The blind man reached into the backseat and dragged out a suitcase. My wife took his arm, shut the car door, and, talking all the way, moved him down the drive and then up the steps to the front porch. I turned off the TV. I finished my drink, rinsed the glass, dried my hands. Then I went to the door.

My wife said, "I want you to meet Robert. Robert, this is my husband. I've told you all about him." She was beaming. She had this blind man by his coat sleeve.

The blind man let go of his suitcase and up came his 20 hand.

I took it. He squeezed hard, held my hand, and then he let it go.

"I feel like we've already met," he boomed.

"Likewise," I said. I didn't know what else to say. Then I said, "Welcome. I've heard a lot about you." We began to move then, a little group, from the porch into the living room, my wife guiding him by the arm. The blind man was carrying his suitcase in his other hand. My wife said things like, "To your left here, Robert. That's right. Now watch it, there's a chair. That's it. Sit down right here. This is the sofa. We just bought this sofa two weeks ago."

I started to say something about the old sofa. I'd liked that old sofa. But I didn't say anything. Then I wanted to say something else, small-talk, about the scenic ride along the Hudson.° How going *to* New York, you should sit on the right-hand side of the train, and coming *from* New York, the left-hand side.

"Did you have a good train ride?" I said. "Which side of the train did you sit on, by the way?"

"What a question, which side!" my wife said. "What's it matter which side?" she said.

"I just asked," I said.

"Right side," the blind man said. "I hadn't been on a train in nearly forty years. Not since I was a kid. With my folks. That's been a long time. I'd nearly forgotten the sensation. I have winter in my beard now," he said. "So I've been told, anyway. Do I look distinguished, my dear?" the blind man said to my wife.

"You look distinguished, Robert," she said. "Robert," she said. "Robert, it's just so good to see you."

My wife finally took her eyes off the blind man and looked at me. I had the feeling she didn't like what she saw. I shrugged.

I've never met, or personally known, anyone who was blind. This blind man was late forties, a heavy-set, balding man with stooped shoulders, as if he carried a great weight there. He wore brown slacks, brown shoes, a light-brown shirt, a tie, a sports coat. Spiffy. He also had this full beard. But he didn't use a cane and he didn't wear dark glasses. I'd always thought dark glasses were a must for the blind. Fact was, I wished he had a pair. At first glance, his eyes looked like anyone else's eyes. But if you looked close, there was something different about them. Too much white in the iris, for one thing, and the pupils seemed to move around in the sockets without his knowing it or being able to stop it. Creepy. As I stared at his face, I saw the left pupil turn in toward his nose while the other made an effort to keep in one place. But it was only an effort, for that eye was on the roam without his knowing it or wanting it to be.

I said, "Let me get you a drink. What's your pleasure? We have a little of everything. It's one of our pastimes."

"Bub, I'm a Scotch man myself," he said fast enough in this big voice.

"Right," I said. Bub! "Sure you are. I knew it."

He let his fingers touch his suitcase, which was sitting alongside the sofa. He was taking his bearings. I didn't blame him for that.

"I'll move that up to your room," my wife said.

"No, that's fine," the blind man said loudly. "It can go up when I go up."

"A little water with the Scotch?" I said.

"Very little," he said.

"I knew it," I said.

He said, "Just a tad. The Irish actor, Barry Fitzgerald? I'm like that fellow. When I drink water, Fitzgerald said, I

>> Narrator, wife, and blind man in scene from DVD of "Cathedral"

drink water. When I drink whiskey, I drink whiskey." My wife laughed. The blind man brought his hand up under his beard. He lifted his beard slowly and let it drop.

I did the drinks, three big glasses of Scotch with a splash of water in each. Then we made ourselves comfortable and talked about Robert's travels. First the long flight from the West Coast to Connecticut, we covered that. Then from Connecticut up here by train. We had another drink concerning that leg of the trip.

I remembered having read somewhere that the blind didn't smoke because, as speculation had it, they couldn't see the smoke they exhaled. I thought I knew that much and that much only about blind people. But this blind man smoked his cigarette down to the nubbin and then lit another one. This blind man filled his ashtray and my wife emptied it.

When we sat down at the table for dinner, we had another drink. My wife heaped Robert's plate with cube steak, scalloped potatoes, green beans. I buttered him up two slices of bread. I said, "Here's bread and butter for you." I swallowed some of my drink. "Now let us pray," I said, and the blind man lowered his head. My wife looked at me, her mouth agape. "Pray the phone won't ring and the food doesn't get cold," I said.

We dug in. We ate everything there was to eat on the table. We ate like there was no tomorrow. We didn't talk. We ate. We scarfed. We grazed that table. We were into serious eating. The blind man had right away located his foods, he knew just where everything was on his plate. I watched with admiration as he used his knife and fork on the meat. He'd cut two pieces of meat, fork the meat into his mouth, and then go all out for the scalloped potatoes, the beans next, and then he'd tear off a hunk of buttered bread and eat that. He'd follow this up with a big drink of milk. It didn't seem to bother him to use his fingers once in a while, either.

We finished everything, including half a strawberry pie. For a few moments, we sat as if stunned. Sweat beaded on our faces. Finally, we got up from the table and left the dirty plates. We didn't look back. We took ourselves into the living room and sank into our places again. Robert and my wife sat on the sofa. I took the big chair. We had us two or

---

°**Hudson** A river in New York State.

EXPLORE ONLINE >

To watch a video interview with Tess Gallagher about
"Cathedral," visit your Literature CourseMate, accessed
through www.cengagebrain.com.

three more drinks while they talked about the major things
that had come to pass for them in the past ten years. For the
most part, I just listened. Now and then I joined in. I didn't
want him to think I'd left the room, and I didn't want her to
think I was feeling left out. They talked of things that had
happened to them—to them!—these past ten years. I waited
in vain to hear my name on my wife's sweet lips: "And then
my dear husband came into my life"—something like that.
But I heard nothing of the sort. More talk of Robert. Robert
had done a little of everything, it seemed, a regular blind
jack-of-all-trades. But most recently he and his wife had had
an Amway distributorship, from which, I gathered, they'd
earned their living, such as it was. The blind man was also a
ham radio operator.° He talked in his loud voice about con-
versations he'd had with fellow operators in Guam, in the
Philippines, in Alaska, and even in Tahiti. He said he'd have
a lot of friends there if he ever wanted to go visit those places. From time to time, he'd turn his blind face toward me,
put his hand under his beard, ask me something. How long
had I been in my present position? (Three years.) Did I like
my work? (I didn't.) Was I going to stay with it? (What were
the options?) Finally, when I thought he was beginning to
run down, I got up and turned on the TV.

My wife looked at me with irritation. She was heading
toward a boil. Then she looked at the blind man and said,
"Robert, do you have a TV?"

The blind man said, "My dear, I have two TVs. I have
a color set and a black-and-white thing, an old relic. It's
funny, but if I turn the TV on, and I'm always turning it on,
I turn on the color set. It's funny, don't you think?"

I didn't know what to say to that. I had absolutely nothing to say to that. No opinion. So I watched the news program and tried to listen to what the announcer was saying.

"This is a color TV," the blind man said. "Don't ask 50
me how, but I can tell."

"We traded up a while ago," I said.

The blind man had another taste of his drink. He lifted his beard, sniffed it, and let it fall. He leaned forward on
the sofa. He positioned his ashtray on the coffee table,
then put the lighter to his cigarette. He leaned back on the
sofa and crossed his legs at the ankles.

My wife covered her mouth, and then she yawned.
She stretched. She said, "I think I'll go upstairs and put on
my robe. I think I'll change into something else. Robert,
you make yourself comfortable," she said.

"I'm comfortable," the blind man said.

° **ham radio operator**   A licensed amateur radio operator.

° **toked**   Inhaled.

"I want you to feel comfortable in this house," she said. 55
"I am comfortable," the blind man said.

After she'd left the room, he and I listened to the
weather report and then to the sports roundup. By that
time, she'd been gone so long I didn't know if she was going to come back. I thought she might have gone to bed. I
wished she'd come back downstairs. I didn't want to be
left alone with a blind man. I asked him if he wanted another drink, and he said sure. Then I asked if he wanted to
smoke some dope with me. I said I'd just rolled a number. I
hadn't, but I planned to do so in about two shakes.

"I'll try some with you," he said.

"Damn right," I said. "That's the stuff."

I got our drinks and sat down on the sofa with him. 60
Then I rolled us two fat numbers. I lit one and passed it. I
brought it to his fingers. He took it and inhaled.

"Hold it as long as you can," I said. I could tell he
didn't know the first thing.

My wife came back downstairs wearing her pink robe
and her pink slippers.

"What do I smell?" she said.

"We thought we'd have us some cannabis," I said.

My wife gave me a savage look. Then she looked at 65
the blind man and said, "Robert, I didn't know you
smoked."

He said, "I do now, my dear. There's a first time for
everything. But I don't feel anything yet."

"This stuff is pretty mellow," I said. "This stuff is
mild. It's dope you can reason with," I said. "It doesn't
mess you up."

"Not much it doesn't, bub," he said, and laughed.

My wife sat on the sofa between the blind man and
me. I passed her the number. She took it and toked° and
then passed it back to me. "Which way is this going?" she
said. Then she said, "I shouldn't be smoking this. I can
hardly keep my eyes open as it is. That dinner did me in. I
shouldn't have eaten so much."

"It was the strawberry pie," the blind man said. 70
"That's what did it," he said, and he laughed his big laugh.
Then he shook his head.

"There's more strawberry pie," I said.

"Do you want some more, Robert?" my wife said.

"Maybe in a little while," he said.

We gave our attention to the TV. My wife yawned again.
She said, "Your bed is made up when you feel like going to bed,
Robert. I know you must have had a long day. When you're
ready to go to bed, say so." She pulled his arm. "Robert?"

He came to and said, "I've had a real nice time. This 75
beats tapes, doesn't it?"

I said, "Coming at you," and I put the number between
his fingers. He inhaled, held the smoke, and then let it go. It
was like he'd been doing it since he was nine years old.

"Thanks, bub," he said. "But I think this is all for me.
I think I'm beginning to feel it," he said. He held the burning roach out for my wife.

"Same here," she said. "Ditto. Me, too." She took the
roach and passed it to me. "I may just sit here for a while

between you two guys with my eyes closed. But don't let me bother you, okay? Either one of you. If it bothers you, say so. Otherwise, I may just sit here with my eyes closed until you're ready to go to bed," she said. "Your bed's made up, Robert, when you're ready. It's right next to our room at the top of the stairs. We'll show you up when you're ready. You wake me up now, you guys, if I fall asleep." She said that and then she closed her eyes and went to sleep.

The news program ended. I got up and changed the channel. I sat back down on the sofa. I wished my wife hadn't pooped out. Her head lay across the back of the sofa, her mouth open. She'd turned so that her robe slipped away from her legs, exposing a juicy thigh. I reached to draw her robe back over her, and it was then that I glanced at the blind man. What the hell! I flipped the robe open again.

"You say when you want some strawberry pie," I said. 80

"I will," he said.

I said, "Are you tired? Do you want me to take you up to your bed? Are you ready to hit the hay?"

"Not yet," he said. "No, I'll stay up with you, bub. If that's all right. I'll stay up until you're ready to turn in. We haven't had a chance to talk. Know what I mean? I feel like me and her monopolized the evening." He lifted his beard and he let it fall. He picked up his cigarettes and his lighter.

"That's all right," I said. Then I said, "I'm glad for the company."

And I guess I was. Every night I smoked dope and 85 stayed up as long as I could before I fell asleep. My wife and I hardly ever went to bed at the same time. When I did go to sleep, I had these dreams. Sometimes I'd wake up from one of them, my heart going crazy.

Something about the church and the Middle Ages was on the TV. Not your run-of-the-mill TV fare. I wanted to watch something else. I turned to the other channels. But there was nothing on them, either. So I turned back to the first channel and apologized.

"Bub, it's all right," the blind man said. "It's fine with me. Whatever you want to watch is okay. I'm always learning something. Learning never ends. It won't hurt me to learn something tonight. I got ears," he said.

>> Notre Dame Cathedral, Paris

We didn't say anything for a time. He was leaning forward with his head turned at me, his right ear aimed in the direction of the set. Very disconcerting. Now and then his eyelids drooped and then they snapped open again. Now and then he put his fingers into his beard and tugged, like he was thinking about something he was hearing on the television.

On the screen, a group of men wearing cowls was being set upon and tormented by men dressed in skeleton costumes and men dressed as devils. The men dressed as devils wore devil masks, horns, and long tails. This pageant was part of a procession. The Englishman who was narrating the thing said it took place in Spain once a year. I tried to explain to the blind man what was happening.

"Skeletons," he said. "I know about skeletons," he 90 said, and nodded.

The TV showed this one cathedral. Then there was a long, slow look at another one. Finally, the picture switched to the famous one in Paris, with its flying buttresses and its spires reaching up to the clouds. The camera pulled away to show the whole of the cathedral rising above the skyline.

There were times when the Englishman who was telling the thing would shut up, would simply let the camera move around the cathedrals. Or else the camera would tour the countryside, men in fields walking behind oxen. I waited as long as I could. Then I felt I had to say something. I said, "They're showing the outside of this cathedral now. Gargoyles. Little statues carved to look like monsters. Now I guess they're in Italy. Yeah, they're in Italy. There's paintings on the walls of this one church."

"Are those fresco° paintings, bub?" he asked, and he sipped from his drink.

I reached for my glass. But it was empty. I tried to remember what I could remember. "You're asking me are those frescoes?" I said. "That's a good question. I don't know."

The camera moved to a cathedral outside Lisbon.° The 95 differences in the Portuguese cathedral compared with the French and Italian were not that great. But they were there. Mostly the interior stuff. Then something occurred to me, and I said, "Something has occurred to me. Do you have any idea what a cathedral is? What they look like, that is? Do you follow me? If somebody says cathedral to you, do you have any notion what they're talking about? Do you know the difference between that and a Baptist church, say?"

He let the smoke dribble from his mouth. "I know they took hundreds of workers fifty or a hundred years to build," he said. "I just heard the man say that, of course. I know generations of the same families worked on a cathedral. I heard him say that, too. The men who began their life's work on them, they never lived to see the completion of their work. In that wise, bub, they're no different from the rest of us, right?" He laughed. Then his eyelids drooped again. His head nodded. He seemed to be snoozing. Maybe he was imagining himself in Portugal. The TV was showing another

---

° **fresco** Painted plaster.
°**Lisbon** The capital of Portugal.

EXPLORE ONLINE >

To complete a video activity of "Cathedral," visit
your Literature CourseMate, accessed through
www.cengagebrain.com.

cathedral now. This one was in Germany. The Englishman's
voice droned on. "Cathedrals," the blind man said. He sat up
and rolled his head back and forth. "If you want the truth,
bub, that's about all I know. What I just said. What I heard
him say. But maybe you could describe one to me? I wish
you'd do it. I'd like that. If you want to know, I really don't
have a good idea."

I stared hard at the shot of the cathedral on the TV.
How could I even begin to describe it? But say my life
depended on it. Say my life was being threatened by an
insane guy who said I had to do it or else.

I stared some more at the cathedral before the picture flipped off into the countryside. There was no use. I
turned to the blind man and said, "To begin with, they're
very tall." I was looking around the room for clues.
"They reach way up. Up and up. Toward the sky. They're
so big, some of them, they have to have these supports.
To help hold them up, so to speak. These supports are
called buttresses. They remind me of viaducts,° for some
reason. But maybe you don't know viaducts, either?

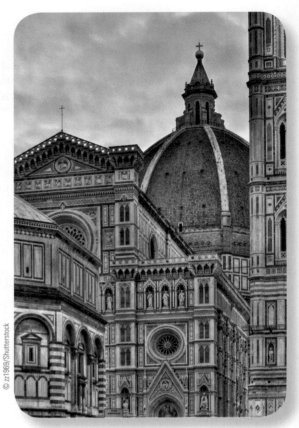

>> Santa Maria del fiore, Florence, Italy

>> Fresco in the interior of a cathedral, Spoleto, Italy

Sometimes the cathedrals have devils and such carved
into the front. Sometimes lords and ladies. Don't ask me
why this is," I said.

He was nodding. The whole upper part of his body
seemed to be moving back and forth.

"I'm not doing so good, am I?" I said.   100

He stopped nodding and leaned forward on the edge
of the sofa. As he listened to me, he was running his fingers
through his beard. I wasn't getting through to him, I could
see that. But he waited for me to go on just the same. He
nodded, like he was trying to encourage me. I tried to
think what else to say. "They're really big," I said. "They're
massive. They're built of stone. Marble, too, sometimes. In
those olden days, when they built cathedrals, men wanted
to be close to God. In those olden days, God was an important part of everyone's life. You could tell this from
their cathedral-building. I'm sorry," I said, "but it looks
like that's the best I can do for you. I'm just no good at it."

"That's all right, bub," the blind man said. "Hey, listen. I
hope you don't mind my asking you. Can I ask you something? Let me ask you a simple question, yes or no. I'm just
curious and there's no offense. You're my host. But let me ask
if you are in any way religious? You don't mind my asking?"

I shook my head. He couldn't see that, though. A
wink is the same as a nod to a blind man. "I guess I don't
believe in it. In anything. Sometimes it's hard. You know
what I'm saying?"

"Sure, I do," he said.

° **viaducts** Long, elevated roadways.

© Howard Ksia/Worm Path Productions

>> Blind man and narrator drawing Cathedral in scene from DVD of "Cathedral"

"Right," I said.

The Englishman was still holding forth. My wife sighed in her sleep. She drew a long breath and went on with her sleeping.

"You'll have to forgive me," I said. "But I can't tell you what a cathedral looks like. It just isn't in me to do it. I can't do any more than I've done."

The blind man sat very still, his head down, as he listened to me.

I said, "The truth is, cathedrals don't mean anything special to me. Nothing. Cathedrals. They're something to look at on late-night TV. That's all they are."

It was then that the blind man cleared his throat. He brought something up. He took a handkerchief from his back pocket. Then he said, "I get it, bub. It's okay. It happens. Don't worry about it," he said. "Hey, listen to me. Will you do me a favor? I got an idea. Why don't you find us some heavy paper? And a pen. We'll do something. We'll draw one together. Get us a pen and some heavy paper. Go on, bub, get the stuff," he said.

So I went upstairs. My legs felt like they didn't have any strength in them. They felt like they did after I'd done some running. In my wife's room, I looked around. I found some ballpoints in a little basket on her table. And then I tried to think where to look for the kind of paper he was talking about.

Downstairs, in the kitchen, I found a shopping bag with onion skins in the bottom of the bag. I emptied the bag and shook it. I brought it into the living room and sat down with it near his legs. I moved some things, smoothed the wrinkles from the bag, spread it out on the coffee table.

The blind man got down from the sofa and sat next to me on the carpet.

He ran his fingers over the paper. He went up and down the sides of the paper. The edges, even the edges. He fingered the corners.

"All right," he said. "All right, let's do her."

He found my hand, the hand with the pen. He closed his hand over my hand. "Go ahead, bub, draw," he said. "Draw. You'll see. I'll follow along with you. It'll be okay. Just begin now like I'm telling you. You'll see. Draw," the blind man said.

So I began. First I drew a box that looked like a house. It could have been the house I lived in. Then I put a roof on it. At either end of the roof, I drew spires. Crazy.

"Swell," he said. "Terrific. You're doing fine," he said.

"Never thought anything like this could happen in your lifetime, did you, bub? Well, it's a strange life, we all know that. Go on now. Keep it up."

I put in windows with arches. I drew flying buttresses. I hung great doors. I couldn't stop. The TV station went off the air. I put down the pen and closed and opened my fingers. The blind man felt around over the paper. He moved the tips of his fingers over the paper, all over what I had drawn, and he nodded.

"Doing fine," the blind man said.

I took up the pen again, and he found my hand. I kept at it. I'm no artist. But I kept drawing just the same.

My wife opened up her eyes and gazed at us. She sat up on the sofa, her robe hanging open. She said, "What are you doing? Tell me, I want to know."

I didn't answer her.

The blind man said, "We're drawing a cathedral. Me and him are working on it. Press hard," he said to me. "That's right. That's good," he said. "Sure. You got it, bub, I can tell. You didn't think you could. But you can, can't you? You're cooking with gas now. You know what I'm saying? We're going to really have us something here in a minute. How's the old arm?" he said. "Put some people in there now. What's a cathedral without people?"

My wife said, "What's going on? Robert, what are you doing? What's going on?"

"It's all right," he said to her. "Close your eyes now," the blind man said to me.

I did it. I closed them just like he said.

"Are they closed?" he said. "Don't fudge."

"They're closed," I said.

"Keep them that way," he said. He said, "Don't stop now. Draw."

So we kept on with it. His fingers rode my fingers as my hand went over the paper. It was like nothing else in my life up to now.

Then he said, "I think that's it. I think you got it," he said. "Take a look. What do you think?"

But I had my eyes closed. I thought I'd keep them that way for a little longer. I thought it was something I ought to do.

"Well?" he said. "Are you looking?"

My eyes were still closed. I was in my house. I knew that. But I didn't feel like I was inside anything.

"It's really something," I said.

Related Works

"Gryphon" (p. 138), "Doe Season" (p. 290), "When I Heard the Learn'd Astronomer" (p. 383), "The Value of Education" (p. 391), "On First Looking into Chapman's Homer" (p. 447)

 See Chapter 16 Review Card for Reading and Reacting questions about Raymond Carver, "Cathedral."

Writing Suggestions: Symbol, Allegory, and Myth

1. Strangers figure prominently in "Cathedral" and other stories included in this anthology, such as "Young Goodman Brown" (p. 320). Write an essay in which you discuss the possible symbolic significance of strangers in both of these stories.

2. Write an essay in which you discuss the use of myth in the excerpt from *Fun Home*.

3. If Shirley Jackson had wished to write "The Lottery" as an allegory whose purpose was to expose the evils of Nazi Germany, what revisions would she have had to make to convey the dangers of blind obedience to authority? Consider the story's symbols, the characters (and their names), and the setting.

4. In literary works, objects can function as symbols. In this chapter, for example, the quilt in "Everyday Use" and the box in "The Lottery" take on symbolic significance. Write an essay in which you analyze objects that have symbolic significance in two or three of the stories in this text and discuss how these objects help to convey the main themes of the stories in which they appear.

 CHECKLIST

WRITING ABOUT SYMBOL, ALLEGORY, AND MYTH

- ☐ Are any universal symbols used in the work? any conventional symbols? What is their function?
- ☐ Is any character, place, action, event, or object given unusual prominence or emphasis in the story? If so, does this element seem to have symbolic as well as literal significance?
- ☐ What possible meanings does each symbol suggest?
- ☐ How do symbols help to depict the story's characters?
- ☐ How do symbols help to characterize the story's setting?
- ☐ How do symbols help to advance the story's plot?
- ☐ Does the story have a moral or didactic purpose? What is the message, idea, or moral principle the story seeks to convey? Is the story an allegory?
- ☐ What equivalent may be assigned to each allegorical figure in the story?
- ☐ What is the allegorical framework of the story?
- ☐ Does the story combine allegorical figures and symbols? How do they work together in the story?
- ☐ Does the story have any references to myth? If so, what do these references contribute to the story's plot or theme?

Glossary Terms

allegory/allegorical figure/ allegorical framework Story with two parallel and consistent levels of meaning, one literal and one figurative, in which the figurative level offers a moral or political lesson. An **allegorical figure** has only one meaning (for instance, it may represent good or evil). An **allegorical framework** is the system of ideas that conveys the allegory's message.

beast fable Short tale, usually including a moral, in which animals assume human characteristics—for example, Aesop's "The Tortoise and the Hare."

myth Story reflecting the religious and social values of a culture or explaining natural phenomena, often involving gods and heroes.

symbol/universal symbol/ conventional symbol/literary symbol Person, object, action, or idea whose meaning transcends its literal or denotative sense in a complex way. A symbol is invested with significance beyond what it could carry on its own. **Universal symbols,** such as the grim reaper, may be called **archetypes; conventional symbols,** such as national flags, evoke a general and agreed-upon response from most people.

17

Theme

Learning Outcomes

After reading this chapter, you should be able to do the following:

LO1 Understand theme

LO2 Discover a story's theme

Timeline

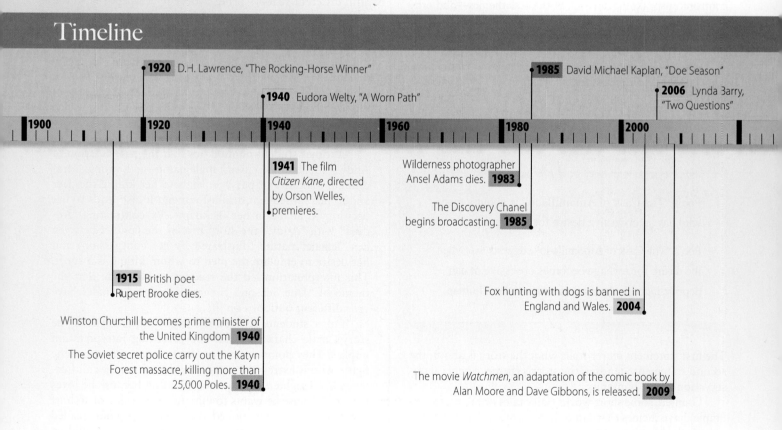

1920 D.H. Lawrence, "The Rocking-Horse Winner"

1940 Eudora Welty, "A Worn Path"

1985 David Michael Kaplan, "Doe Season"

2006 Lynda Barry, "Two Questions"

1900   1920   1940   1960   1980   2000

1941 The film *Citizen Kane*, directed by Orson Welles, premieres.

Wilderness photographer Ansel Adams dies. **1983**

The Discovery Chanel begins broadcasting. **1985**

1915 British poet Rupert Brooke dies.

Winston Churchill becomes prime minister of the United Kingdom **1940**

The Soviet secret police carry out the Katyn Forest massacre, killing more than 25,000 Poles. **1940**

Fox hunting with dogs is banned in England and Wales. **2004**

The movie *Watchmen*, an adaptation of the comic book by Alan Moore and Dave Gibbons, is released. **2009**

theme Central or dominant idea of a work of literature.

plot Way in which the events of the story are arranged. When there is more than one story but one string of events is clearly the most significant, the other stories are called **subplots**. Plot in fiction often follows the pattern of action in drama, rising toward a **climax** and then falling toward a **resolution**.

cliché Overused phrase or expression.

 EXPLORE ONLINE >

To complete a tutorial of "Theme," visit your Literature CourseMate, accessed through www.cengagebrain.com.

The **theme** of a work of literature is its central or dominant idea. *Theme* is not the same as *plot* or *subject*, two terms with which it is sometimes confused. A summary of the **plot** of Tadeusz Borowski's "Silence," a story about survivors of the Holocaust, could be, "Prisoners are liberated from a concentration camp, and, despite the warnings of the American officer, they kill a captured German guard." The statement "'Silence' is about freed prisoners and a guard" could define the **subject** of the story. A statement of the **theme** of "Silence," however, has to do more than summarize its plot or define its subject; it has to convey the values and ideas expressed by the story.

Many effective stories are complex, expressing more than one theme, and "Silence" is no exception. You could say that "Silence" suggests that human beings have a need for vengeance. You could also say the story demonstrates that silence is sometimes the only response possible when people confront unspeakable horrors. Both these themes—and others—are expressed in the story, yet one theme seems to dominate: the idea that under extreme conditions the oppressed can have the same capacity for evil as their oppressors.

When you write about theme, you need to do more than tell what happens in the story. The theme you identify should be a general idea that extends beyond the story and applies to the world outside fiction. Compare these two statements that a student wrote about Edgar Allan Poe's "The Cask of Amontillado" (p. 190):

> Poe's "The Cask of Amontillado" is about a man who has an obsessive desire for revenge.
>
> Poe's "The Cask of Amontillado" suggests that when the desire for revenge becomes obsessive, it can deprive individuals of all that makes them human.

The first statement merely tells what the story is about; the second statement identifies the story's theme, a general observation about humanity.

Granted, some short works (fairy tales or fables, for example) have themes that can only be expressed as **clichés**—overused phrases or expressions—or as **morals**—lessons dramatized by the work. The fairy tale "Cinderella," for example, expresses the clichéd theme that a virtuous girl who endures misfortune will eventually achieve her just reward; the fable "The Tortoise and the Hare" illustrates the moral "Slow and steady wins the race." Like "The Cask of Amontillado," however, the stories in this anthology have themes that are much more complex than clichés or morals.

LO1 Understand Theme

Contemporary critical theory holds that the theme of a work of fiction is as much a creation of readers as of the writer. Readers' backgrounds, knowledge, values, and beliefs all play a part in determining the theme (or themes) they will identify in a work. Many readers, for example, will realize that David Michael Kaplan's story "Doe Season" (p. 290)—in which the main character goes hunting, kills her first deer, and is forced to confront suffering and death—expresses a conventional **initiation theme**, revealing growing up to be a disillusioning and painful process. Still, different readers bring different perspectives to the story and, in some cases, see different themes.

During a classroom discussion of "Doe Season," a student familiar with hunting saw more than his classmates did in the story's conventional initiation theme. He knew that in many states there really is a doe season. Shorter than the ten-day buck season, it allows hunters to control the size of the deer herd by killing females. This knowledge enabled the student to conclude that by the end of the story the female child's innocence is destroyed, just as the doe is.

Another student pointed out that the participation of Andy—a female who uses a male name—in hunting, a traditional male rite of passage, leads to her killing the deer and to her subsequent disillusionment. It also leads to her decision to abandon her nickname. By contrasting "Andrea" with "Andy," the story reveals the conflict between her "female" nature (illustrated by her compassion) and her desire to emulate the men to whom killing is a sport. This interpretation led the student to conclude that the theme of "Doe Season" is that males and females have very different outlooks on life.

Other students rejected the negative portrayal of the story's male characters that the preceding interpretation implies. They pointed out that the father is a sympathetic figure who is extremely supportive; he encourages and defends his daughter. He takes her hunting because he loves her, not because he wants to initiate her into life or to hurt her. One student mentioned that Andy's reaction (called *buck fever*) when she sees the doe is common in children who kill their first deer. In light of this information, several students concluded that far from being about irreconcilable male and female differences, "Doe Season" makes a statement about a young girl who is hunting for her own identity and who in the process discovers her own mortality. Her father is therefore the agent who enables her to confront the inevitability of death, a fact she must accept if she is going to take her place in the adult world. In this sense, the theme of the story is the idea that in order to mature, a child must come to terms with the reality of death.

Different readers may see different themes in a story, but any interpretation of a theme must make sense in light of what is actually in the story. Evidence from the work, not just your own feelings or assumptions, must support your interpretation, and a single statement by a character is not enough in itself to reveal a story's theme. Therefore, you must present a cross-section of examples from the text to support your interpretation of the story's theme. If you say that the theme of James Joyce's "Araby" (p. 220) is that an innocent idealist is inevitably doomed to disillusionment, you have to find examples from the text to support this statement. You could begin with the title, concluding that the word *Araby* suggests idealistic dreams of exotic beauty that the boy tries to find when he goes to the bazaar. You could reinforce your interpretation by pointing out that the unattainable woman is a symbol of all that the boy wants so desperately to find. Finally, you could show how idealism is ultimately crushed by society: at the end of the story, the boy stands alone in the darkness and realizes that his dreams are childish fantasies. Although other readers may have different responses to "Araby," they should find your interpretation reasonable if you support it with enough examples.

LO2 Discover a Story's Theme

Every element of a story can shed light on its themes. As you analyze a short story, you should look for features that reveal and reinforce what you perceive to be the story's most important ideas.

- *The **title** can often provide insight into the theme or themes of a story.* The title of an F. Scott Fitzgerald story, "Babylon Revisited," emphasizes a major idea in the story—that Paris of the 1920s is like Babylon, the ancient city the Bible singles out as the epitome of evil and corruption. The story's protagonist, Charlie Wales, comes to realize that no matter how much money he lost after the 1929 stock market crash, he lost more— his wife and his daughter—during the boom, when he was in Paris. Charlie's search through his past—his return to "Babylon"—provides new meaning to his life and offers at least a small bit of hope for the future.
- *Sometimes a narrator's or character's statement can reveal a theme.* For example, at the beginning of Alberto Alvaro Ríos's "The Secret Lion" (p. 333), the first-person narrator says, "I was twelve and in junior high school and something happened that we didn't have a name for, but it was there nonetheless like a lion, and roaring, roaring that way the biggest

point of view Perspective from which a story is told. The storyteller may be a major character in the story or a character who witnesses the story's events (*first-person narrator*) or someone who does not figure in the action at all (*third-person narrator*), in which case he or she may know the actions and thoughts of everyone in the story (*omniscient narrator*) or just know some part of these (*limited omniscient narrator*).

things do. Everything changed." Although the narrator does not directly announce the story's theme, he suggests that the story will convey the idea that the price children pay for growing up is realizing that everything changes, that nothing stays the way it is.
- *The **arrangement of events** can suggest a story's theme*, as it does in an Ernest Hemingway story, "The Short Happy Life of Francis Macomber." At the beginning of the story, the title character is a coward who is stuck in an unhappy marriage. As the story progresses, he gradually learns the nature of courage and, finally, finds it in himself. At the moment of his triumph, however, Francis is shot by his wife; his "happy life" is short indeed. The way the events of the story are presented, through foreshadowing and flashbacks, reveals the connection between Macomber's marriage and his behavior as a hunter, and this connection in turn helps to reveal a possible theme: that sometimes courage can be more important than life itself.
- *A story's central **conflict** can offer clues to its theme.* For example, the main character in "The Yellow Wallpaper" (p. 313), a woman who has recently had a baby, is in conflict with the nineteenth-century society in which she lives. She is suffering from "temporary nervous depression," what doctors today recognize as postpartum depression. Following the practice of the time, her physician has ordered complete bed rest and has instructed her husband to deprive her of all mental and physical stimulation. This harsh treatment leads the narrator to lose her grasp on reality; eventually, she begins to hallucinate. The main conflict of the story is clearly between the woman and her society, controlled by men. This conflict communicates the central theme: that in nineteenth-century America, women are controlled not just by their husbands and the male medical establishment, but also by the society men have created.
- *The **point of view** of a story can shed light on its theme.* For instance, a writer's use of an unreliable first-person narrator can help to communicate the theme of a story. Thus, Montresor's self-serving first-person account of his crime in "The Cask of Amontillado"— along with his attempts to justify these actions— enable readers to understand the dangers of irrational anger and misplaced ideas about honor. The voice of a third-person narrator can also help to convey a story's theme. For example, the detachment of the narrator in Stephen Crane's Civil War novel *The Red Badge of Courage* reinforces the theme of the novel: that bravery,

cowardice, war, and even life itself are insignificant when set beside the indifference of the universe.

- *Quite often a story's **symbols**—names, places, and objects—can suggest its theme.* For example, the rocking horse in D. H. Lawrence's "The Rocking-Horse Winner" (p. 297) can be seen as a symbol of the boy's desperate desire to remain a child. Interpreted in this way, it reinforces the theme that innocence cannot survive when it confronts adult greed and selfishness. Similarly, Hawthorne's "Young Goodman Brown" (p. 320) uses symbols such as the walking stick, the woods, sunset and night, and the vague shadows to develop one of its central themes: that once a person strays from the path of faith, evil is everywhere.

- *Finally, **changes in a character** can shed light on the theme or themes of the story.* The main character in Charles Baxter's "Gryphon" (p. 138), for example, eventually comes to realize that the "lies" his substitute teacher tells may be closer to the truth than the "facts" his other teachers present, and his changing attitude toward her helps to communicate the story's central theme about the nature of truth.

Lynda Barry (1956–   )

© Lynda Barry/Lewis & Clark College, Portland, OR

is a widely published comic artist whose strips have appeared in numerous newspapers, magazines, and collections. According to Barry, she began compulsively drawing comic strips in college when her boyfriend left her for another girl. Her schoolmate, Matt Groening, the creator of *The Simpsons,* saw her comics and published them in the school paper. Since then, her comic strips have appeared in over fifty papers. She has also published the illustrated novels *The Good Times Are Killing Me* (1988), which she adapted into an off-Broadway play, and *Cruddy* (1999). Named Comics of the Year by the *Comics Journal,* her latest collections of work include *The Greatest of Marlys!* (2000), *One Hundred Demons* (2002), *What It Is* (2008), and *Picture This: The Near-Sighted Monkey Book* (2010).

Two Questions   (2006)

This graphic story starts on the next page.

Related Works

"Araby" (p. 220), "Cathedral" (p. 261), "Diving into the Wreck" (p. 469).

See Chapter 17 Review Card for Reading and Reacting questions about Lynda Barry, "Two Questions."

Cultural Context
This graphic story deals with writer's block, the inability to put words down on paper. Experts say that writer's block can have many causes. For example, the writer simply isn't ready to write, the writer is anxious about writing, or the writer is simply trying to do too much at once. Some anxiety-reduction strategies that can be used to overcome writer's block include brainstorming, writing in a journal, talking through the writing project with a friend or colleague, visualizing the project in manageable steps, repeating affirmations that stimulate creativity, dispelling unrealistic goals of perfection, or simply taking a break. The fact is that no two writers are the same; what works for one writer might not work for another. The only effective way to deal with writers' block is to experiment and to discover what works.

FROM *McSweeney's*

Eudora Welty (1909–2001)

© Bettmann / Corbis

was born and raised in Jackson, Mississippi. After attending the Mississippi College for Women, the University of Wisconsin, and Columbia University (where she studied advertising), she returned to Jackson to pursue her long career as a writer, beginning as a journalist. In 1936, she wrote the first of her many short stories, which are gathered in *Collected Stories* (1980). Welty also wrote several novels, including *Delta Wedding* (1946), *Losing Battles* (1970), and the Pulitzer Prize–winning *The Optimist's Daughter* (1972). Her volume of memoirs, *One Writer's Beginnings* (1934), was a best-seller.

One of America's most accomplished writers, Welty focused much of her fiction on life in southern towns and villages peopled with dreamers, eccentrics, and close-knit families. Her sharply observed characters are sometimes presented with great humor, sometimes with poignant lyricism, but always with clarity and sympathy. "Of course any writer is in part all of his characters," she observed. "How otherwise would they be known to him, occur to him, become what they are?" In "A Worn Path," Welty creates a particularly memorable character in the tenacious Phoenix Jackson, and through her she explores a theme that transcends race and region.

A Worn Path (1940)

It was December—a bright frozen day in the early morning. Far out in the country there was an old Negro woman with her head tied in a red rag, coming along a path through the pinewoods. Her name was Phoenix Jackson. She was very old and small and she walked slowly in the dark pine shadows, moving a little from side to side in her steps, with the balanced heaviness and lightness of a pendulum in a grandfather clock. She carried a thin, small cane made from an umbrella, and with this she kept tapping the frozen earth in front of her. This made a grave and persistent noise in the still air, that seemed meditative like the chirping of a solitary little bird.

She wore a dark striped dress reaching down to her shoe tops, and an equally long apron of bleached sugar sacks, with a full pocket: all neat and tidy, but every time she took a step she might have fallen over her shoelaces, which dragged from her unlaced shoes. She looked straight ahead. Her eyes were blue with age. Her skin had a pattern all its own of numberless branching wrinkles and as though a whole little tree stood in the middle of her forehead, but a golden color ran underneath, and the two knobs of her cheeks were illumined by a yellow burning under the dark. Under the red rag her hair came down on her neck in the frailest of ringlets, still black, and with an odor like copper.

> "Her name was Phoenix Jackson. She was very old and small and she walked slowly in the dark pine shadows . . ."

Now and then there was a quivering in the thicket. Old Phoenix said, "Out of my way, all you foxes, owls, beetles, jack rabbits, coons and wild animals! . . . Keep out from under these feet, little bob-whites. . . . Keep the big wild hogs out of my path. Don't let none of those come running my direction. I got a long way." Under her small black-freckled hand her cane, limber as a buggy whip, would switch at the brush as if to rouse up any hiding things.

On she went. The woods were deep and still. The sun made the pine needles almost too bright to look at, up where the wind rocked. The cones dropped as light as feathers. Down in the hollow was the mourning dove—it was not too late for him.

The path ran up a hill. "Seem like there is chains 5 about my feet, time I get this far," she said, in the voice of argument old people keep to use with themselves.

Cultural Context During the 1930s, the years of the Great Depression, poverty and unemployment were widespread but were especially severe in isolated rural areas of the South. For the black population living in this poor and undeveloped region, difficult economic conditions were made worse by the system of segregation that prevented them from voting, receiving a good education, or enjoying the same rights and privileges as their white counterparts. Hoping to improve their situation, many African-American families left the South and moved into northern and midwestern cities where there were better opportunities for education and employment. Others, like the protagonist of this story, remained in the South in an atmosphere of residual racism and oppression.

EXPLORE ONLINE >

To complete a video activity of "A Worn Path," visit
your Literature CourseMate, accessed through
www.cengagebrain.com.

"Something always take a hold of me on this hill—pleads I should stay."

After she got to the top she turned and gave a full, severe look behind her where she had come. "Up through pines," she said at length. "Now down through oaks."

Her eyes opened their widest, and she started down gently. But before she got to the bottom of the hill a bush caught her dress.

Her fingers were busy and intent, but her skirts were full and long, so that before she could pull them free in one place they were caught in another. It was not possible to allow the dress to tear. "I in the thorny bush," she said. "Thorns, you doing your appointed work. Never want to let folks pass, no sir. Old eyes thought you was a pretty little *green* bush."

Finally, trembling all over, she stood free, and after a moment dared to stoop for her cane.

"Sun so high!" she cried, leaning back and looking, 10 while the thick tears went over her eyes. "The time getting all gone here."

At the foot of this hill was a place where a log was laid across the creek.

"Now comes the trial," said Phoenix.

Putting her right foot out, she mounted the log and shut her eyes. Lifting her skirt, leveling her cane fiercely before her, like a festival figure in some parade, she began to march across. Then she opened her eyes and she was safe on the other side.

"I wasn't as old as I thought," she said.

But she sat down to rest. She spread her skirts on the 15 bank around her and folded her hands over her knees. Up above her was a tree in a pearly cloud of mistletoe. She did not dare to close her eyes, and when a little boy brought her a plate with a slice of marble-cake on it she spoke to him. "That would be acceptable," she said. But when she went to take it there was just her own hand in the air.

So she left that tree, and had to go through a barbed-wire fence. There she had to creep and crawl, spreading her knees and stretching her fingers like a baby trying to climb the steps. But she talked loudly to herself: she could not let her dress be torn now, so late in the day, and she could not pay for having her arm or her leg sawed off if she got caught fast where she was.

At last she was safe through the fence and risen up out in the clearing. Big dead trees, like black men with one arm, were standing in the purple stalks of the withered cotton field. There sat a buzzard.

"Who you watching?"

In the furrow she made her way along.

>> Buzzards in a tree

"Glad this not the season for bulls," she said, looking 20 sideways, "and the good Lord made his snakes to curl up and sleep in the winter. A pleasure I don't see no two-headed snake coming around that tree, where it come once. It took a while to get by him, back in the summer."

She passed through the old cotton and went into a field of dead corn. It whispered and shook and was taller than her head. "Through the maze now," she said, for there was no path.

>> Scarecrow in a field

Then there was something tall, black, and skinny there, moving before her.

At first she took it for a man. It could have been a man dancing in the field. But she stood still and listened, and it did not make a sound. It was as silent as a ghost.

"Ghost," she said sharply, "who be you the ghost of? For I have heard of nary death close by."

But there was no answer—only the ragged dancing in the wind. 25

She shut her eyes, reached out her hand, and touched a sleeve. She found a coat and inside that an emptiness, cold as ice.

"You scarecrow," she said. Her face lighted. "I ought to be shut up for good," she said with laughter. "My senses is gone. I too old. I the oldest people I ever know. Dance, old scarecrow," she said, "while I dancing with you."

She kicked her foot over the furrow, and with mouth drawn down, shook her head once or twice in a little strutting way. Some husks blew down and whirled in streamers about her skirts.

Then she went on, parting her way from side to side with the cane, through the whispering field. At last she came to the end, to a wagon track where the silver grass blew between the red ruts. The quail were walking around like pullets, seeming all dainty and unseen.

"Walk pretty," she said. "This is the easy place. This 30 the easy going."

She followed the track, swaying through the quiet bare fields, through the little strings of trees silver in their dead leaves, past cabins silver from weather, with the doors and windows boarded shut, all like old women under a spell sitting there. "I walking in their sleep," she said, nodding her head vigorously.

In a ravine she went where a spring was silently flowing through a hollow log. Old Phoenix bent and drank. "Sweet-gum makes the water sweet," she said, and drank more. "Nobody know who made this well, for it was here when I was born."

The track crossed a swampy part where the moss hung as white as lace from every limb. "Sleep on, alligators, and blow your bubbles." Then the track went into the road.

Deep, deep the road went down between the high green-colored banks. Overhead the live-oaks met, and it was as dark as a cave.

>> Phoenix Jackson with hunter in scene from DVD of "A Worn Path."

© Bruce Schwartz / Worn Path Productions

EXPLORE ONLINE >

To listen to an instructor podcast of "A Worn Path," visit your Literature CourseMate, accessed through www.cengagebrain.com.

A black dog with a lolling tongue came up out of the 35 weeds by the ditch. She was meditating, and not ready, and when he came at her she only hit him a little with her cane. Over she went in the ditch, like a little puff of milkweed.

Down there, her senses drifted away. A dream visited her, and she reached her hand up, but nothing reached down and gave her a pull. So she lay there and presently went to talking. "Old woman," she said to herself, "that black dog come up out of the weeds to stall you off, and now there he sitting on his fine tail, smiling at you."

A white man finally came along and found her—a hunter, a young man, with his dog on a chain.

"Well, Granny!" he laughed. "What are you doing there?"

"Lying on my back like a June-bug waiting to be turned over, mister," she said, reaching up her hand.

He lifted her up, gave her a swing in the air, and set 40 her down. "Anything broken, Granny?"

"No sir, them old dead weeds is springy enough," said Phoenix, when she had got her breath. "I thank you for your trouble."

"Where do you live, Granny?" he asked, while the two dogs were growling at each other.

"Away back yonder, sir, behind the ridge. You can't even see it from here."

"On your way home?"

"No sir, I going to town." 45

"Why, that's too far! That's as far as I walk when I come out myself, and I get something for my trouble." He patted the stuffed bag he carried, and there hung down a little closed claw. It was one of the bob-whites, with its beak hooked bitterly to show it was dead. "Now you go on home, Granny!"

"I bound to go to town, mister," said Phoenix. "The time come around."

He gave another laugh, filling the whole landscape. "I know you old colored people! Wouldn't miss going to town to see Santa Claus!"

But something held old Phoenix very still. The deep lines in her face went into a fierce and different radiation. Without warning, she had seen with her own eyes a flashing nickel fall out of the man's pocket onto the ground.

"How old are you, Granny?" he was saying. 50

"There is no telling, mister," she said, "no telling."

Then she gave a little cry and clapped her hands and said, "Git on away from here, dog! Look! Look at that dog!" She laughed as if in admiration. "He ain't scared of nobody. He a big black dog." She whispered. "Sic him!"

"Watch me get rid of that cur," said the man. "Sic him, Pete! Sic him!"

Phoenix heard the dogs fighting, and heard the man running and throwing sticks. She even heard a gunshot. But she was slowly bending forward by that time, further and further forward, the lid stretched down over her eyes, as if she were doing this in her sleep. Her chin was lowered almost to her knees. The yellow palm of her hand came out from the fold of her apron. Her fingers slid down and along the ground under the piece of money with the grace and care they would have in lifting an egg from under a setting hen. Then she slowly straightened up, she stood erect, and the nickel was in her apron pocket. A bird flew by. Her lips moved. "God watching me the whole time. I come to stealing."

The man came back, and his own dog panted about 55 them. "Well, I scared him off that time," he said, and then he laughed and lifted his gun and pointed it at Phoenix.

She stood straight and faced him.

"Doesn't the gun scare you?" he said, still pointing it.

"No, sir, I seen plenty go off closer by, in my day, and for less than what I done," she said, holding utterly still.

He smiled, and shouldered the gun. "Well, Granny," he said, "you must be a hundred years old, and scared of nothing. I'd give you a dime if I had any money with me. But you take my advice and stay home, and nothing will happen to you."

"I bound to go on my way, mister," said Phoenix. She 60 inclined her head in the red rag. Then they went in different directions, but she could hear the gun shooting again and again over the hill.

She walked on. The shadows hung from the oak trees to the road like curtains. Then she smelled wood-smoke, and smelled the river, and she saw a steeple and the cabins on their steep steps. Dozens of little black children whirled around her. There ahead was Natchez shining. Bells were ringing. She walked on.

In the paved city it was Christmas time. There were red and green electric lights strung and crisscrossed everywhere, and all turned on in the daytime. Old Phoenix would have been lost if she had not distrusted her eyesight and depended on her feet to know where to take her.

She paused quietly on the sidewalk where people were passing by. A lady came along in the crowd, carrying an armful of red-, green- and silver-wrapped presents; she

>> Phoenix Jackson asking woman to tie her shoe in a scene from DVD of "A Worn Path."

EXPLORE ONLINE >

To watch a video interview with Eudora Welty about "A Worn Path," visit your Literature CourseMate, accessed through www.cengagebrain.com.

gave off perfume like the red roses in hot summer, and Phoenix stopped her.

"Please, missy, will you lace up my shoe?" She held up her foot.

"What do you want, Grandma?" 65

"See my shoe," said Phoenix. "Do all right for out in the country, but wouldn't look right to go in a big building."

"Stand still then, Grandma," said the lady. She put her packages down on the sidewalk beside her and laced and tied both shoes tightly.

"Can't lace 'em with a cane," said Phoenix. "Thank you, missy. I doesn't mind asking a nice lady to tie up my shoe, when I gets out on the street."

Moving slowly and from side to side, she went into the big building, and into a tower of steps, where she walked up and around and around until her feet knew to stop.

She entered a door, and there she saw nailed up on the 70 wall the document that had been stamped with the gold seal and framed in the gold frame, which matched the dream that was hung up in her head.

"Here I be," she said. There was a fixed and ceremonial stiffness over her body.

"A charity case, I suppose," said an attendant who sat at the desk before her.

But Phoenix only looked above her head. There was sweat on her face, the wrinkles in her face shone like a bright net.

"Speak up, Grandma," the woman said. "What's your name? We must have your history, you know. Have you been here before? What seems to be the trouble with you?"

Old Phoenix only gave a twitch to her face as if a fly 75 were bothering her.

"Are you deaf?" cried the attendant.

But then the nurse came in.

"Oh, that's just old Aunt Phoenix," she said. "She doesn't come for herself—she has a little grandson. She makes these trips just as regular as clockwork. She lives away back off the Old Natchez Trace." She bent down. "Well, Aunt Phoenix, why don't you just take a seat? We won't keep you standing after your long trip." She pointed.

The old woman sat down, bolt upright in the chair.

"Now, how is the boy?" asked the nurse. 80

Old Phoenix did not speak.

"I said, how is the boy?"

But Phoenix only waited and stared straight ahead, her face very solemn and withdrawn into rigidity.

"Is his throat any better?" asked the nurse. "Aunt Phoenix, don't you hear me? Is your grandson's throat any better since the last time you came for the medicine?"

With her hands on her knees, the old woman waited, 85 silent, erect and motionless, just as if she were in armor.

>> Phoenix Jackson in doctor's office in scene from DVD of "A Worn Path"

>> Phoenix rising from its ashes, nineteenth-century woodcut

"You mustn't take up our time this way, Aunt Phoenix," the nurse said. "Tell us quickly about your grandson, and get it over. He isn't dead, is he?"

At last there came a flicker and then a flame of comprehension across her face, and she spoke.

"My grandson. It was my memory had left me. There I sat and forgot why I made my long trip."

"Forgot?" The nurse frowned. "After you came so far?"

Then Phoenix was like an old woman begging a 90 dignified forgiveness for waking up frightened in the night. "I never did go to school, I was too old at the Surrender,"° she said in a soft voice. "I'm an old woman without an education. It was my memory fail me. My little grandson, he is just the same, and I forgot it in the coming."

"Throat never heals, does it?" said the nurse, speaking in a loud, sure voice to old Phoenix. By now she had a card with something written on it, a little list. "Yes. Swallowed lye. When was it?—January—two-three years ago—"

Phoenix spoke unasked now. "No, missy, he not dead, he just the same. Every little while his throat begin to close up again, and he not able to swallow. He not get his breath. He not able to help himself. So the time come around, and I go on another trip for the soothing medicine."

"All right. The doctor said as long as you came to get it, you could have it," said the nurse. "But it's an obstinate case."

"My little grandson, he sit up there in the house all wrapped up, waiting by himself," Phoenix went on. "We is the only two left in the world. He suffer and it don't seem to put him back at all. He got a sweet look. He going to last. He wear a little patch quilt and peep out holding his mouth open like a little bird. I remembers so plain now. I not going to forget him again, no, the whole enduring time. I could tell him from all the others in creation."

"All right." The nurse was trying to hush her now. 95 She brought her a bottle of medicine. "Charity," she said, making a check mark in a book.

Old Phoenix held the bottle close to her eyes, and then carefully put it into her pocket.

"I thank you," she said.

"It's Christmas time, Grandma," said the attendant. "Could I give you a few pennies out of my purse?"

"Five pennies is a nickel," said Phoenix stiffly.

"Here's a nickel," said the attendant. 100

Phoenix rose carefully and held out her hand. She received the nickel and then fished the other nickel out of her pocket and laid it beside the new one. She stared at her palm closely, with her head on one side.

Then she gave a tap with her cane on the floor.

"This is what come to me to do," she said. "I going to the store and buy my child a little windmill they sells, made out of paper. He going to find it hard to believe there such a thing in the world. I'll march myself back where he waiting, holding it straight up in this hand."

She lifted her free hand, gave a little nod, turned around, and walked out of the doctor's office. Then her slow step began on the stairs, going down.

° **the Surrender** The surrender of General Robert E. Lee to General Ulysses S. Grant at the end of the Civil War, April 9, 1865.

Related Works

"Miss Brill" (p. 135), "Araby" (p. 220), "Everyday Use" (p. 256)

 See Chapter 17 Review Card for Reading and Reacting questions about Eudora Welty, "A Worn Path."

David Michael Kaplan (1946–)

is one of a group of American writers who, along with South American writers such as Gabriel García Márquez of Columbia, are called "magic realists." Magic realists work outside of the "hobbits and wizards" borders of traditional fantasy writing, seamlessly interweaving magical elements with detailed, realistically drawn "everyday" settings. These elements, says a reviewer of Kaplan's work, are invoked "to illuminate and underscore heightened moments of reality." The story "Doe Season," which appeared in Kaplan's debut collection, *Comfort* (1987), was included in *Best American Short Stories 1985*. Kaplan's first novel, *Skating in the Dark*, was published in 1991, and his writing text, *Revision: A Creative Approach to Writing and Re-writing Fiction*, was published in 1997. Kaplan teaches fiction writing at Loyola University Chicago, where he directs the

creative writing program. He is currently writing the novel *Luna Park*.

Interestingly, the stories in *Comfort* break from classic "first-time author" tradition by sidestepping the autobiographical, young-man-comes-of-age theme. Instead, these stories are about young girls—or young women—coming to grips with parents (present or absent) and with loss and searching for ways to resolve their ambivalence about becoming women. In "Doe Season," Andy's surreal encounter with the doe may be a dream, but the beauty and horror of their meeting will affect the rest of her life.

Doe Season (1985)

They were always the same woods, she thought sleepily as they drove through the early morning darkness—deep and immense, covered with yesterday's snowfall, which had frozen overnight. They were the same woods that lay behind her house, *and they stretch all the way to here*, she thought, *for miles and miles, longer than I could walk in a day, or a week even, but they are still the same woods*. The thought made her feel good: it was like thinking of God; it was like thinking of the space between here and the moon; it was like thinking of all the foreign countries from her geography book where even now, Andy knew, people were going to bed, while they—she and her father and Charlie Spoon and Mac, Charlie's eleven-year-old son—were driving deeper into the Pennsylvania countryside, to go hunting.

They had risen long before dawn. Her mother, yawning and not trying to hide her sleepiness, cooked them eggs and French toast. Her father smoked a cigarette and flicked ashes into his saucer while Andy listened, wondering *Why doesn't he come?* and *Won't he ever come?* until at last a car pulled into the graveled drive and honked. "That will be Charlie Spoon," her father said; he always said "Charlie Spoon," even though his real name was Spreun, because Charlie was, in a sense, shaped like a spoon, with a large head and a narrow waist and chest.

Andy's mother kissed her and her father and said, "Well, have a good time" and "Be careful." Soon they were outside in the bitter dark, loading gear by the back-porch light, their breath steaming. The woods behind the house were then only a black streak against the wash of night.

> "They were riding over gentle hills, the woods on both sides now—the same woods, she knew, because she had been watching the whole way, even while she slept."

Andy dozed in the car and woke to find that it was half light. Mac—also sleeping—had slid against her. She pushed him away and looked out the window. Her breath clouded the glass, and she was cold; the car's heater didn't work right. They were riding over gentle hills, the woods on both sides now—the same woods, she knew, because she had been watching the whole way, even while she slept. They had been in her dreams, and she had never lost sight of them.

Charlie Spoon was driving. "I don't understand why 5 she's coming," he said to her father. "How old is she anyway—eight?"

"Nine," her father replied. "She's small for her age."

"So—nine. What's the difference? She'll just add to the noise and get tired besides."

"No, she won't," her father said. "She can walk me to death. And she'll bring good luck, you'll see. Animals—I don't know how she does it, but they come right up to her. We go walking in the woods, and we'll spot more raccoons and possums and such than I ever see when I'm alone."

Charlie grunted.

"Besides, she's not a bad little shot, even if she doesn't 10 hunt yet. She shoots the .22 real good."

>> Silhouette of hunter at dawn

"Popgun," Charlie said, and snorted. "And target shooting ain't deer hunting."

"Well, she's not gonna be shooting anyway, Charlie," her father said. "Don't worry. She'll be no bother."

"I still don't know why she's coming," Charlie said.

"Because she wants to, and I want her to. Just like you and Mac. No difference."

Charlie turned onto a side road and after a mile or so 15 slowed down. "That's it!" he cried. He stopped, backed up, and entered a narrow dirt road almost hidden by trees. Five hundred yards down, the road ran parallel to a fenced-in field. Charlie parked in a cleared area deeply rutted by frozen tractor tracks. The gate was locked. *In the spring,* Andy thought, *there will be cows here, and a dog that chases them,* but now the field was unmarked and bare.

"This is it," Charlie Spoon declared. "Me and Mac was up here just two weeks ago, scouting it out, and there's deer. Mac saw the tracks."

"That's right," Mac said.

"Well, we'll just see about that," her father said, putting on his gloves. He turned to Andy. "How you doing, honeybun?"

"Just fine," she said.

Andy shivered and stamped as they unloaded: first 20 the rifles, which they unsheathed and checked, sliding the bolts, sighting through scopes, adjusting the slings; then the gear, their food and tents and sleeping bags and stove stored in four backpacks—three big ones for Charlie Spoon and her father and Mac, and a day pack for her.

"That's about your size," Mac said, to tease her.

She reddened and said, "Mac, I can carry a pack big as yours any day." He laughed and pressed his knee against the back of hers, so that her leg buckled. "Cut it out," she said. She wanted to make an iceball and throw it at him, but she knew that her father and Charlie were anxious to get going, and she didn't want to displease them.

Mac slid under the gate, and they handed the packs over to him. Then they slid under and began walking across the field toward the same woods that ran all the way back to her home, where even now her mother was probably rising again to wash their breakfast dishes and make herself a fresh pot of coffee. *She is there, and we are here:* the thought satisfied Andy. There was no place else she would rather be.

Mac came up beside her. "Over there's Canada," he said, nodding toward the woods.

"Huh!" she said. "Not likely." 25

"I don't mean *right* over there. I mean farther up north. You think I'm dumb?"

Dumb as your father, she thought.

"Look at that," Mac said, pointing to a piece of cow dung lying on a spot scraped bare of snow. "A frozen meadow muffin." He picked it up and sailed it at her. "Catch!"

"Mac!" she yelled. His laugh was as gawky as he was. She walked faster. He seemed different today somehow, bundled in his yellow-and-black-checkered coat, a rifle in hand, his silly floppy hat not quite covering his ears. They all seemed different as she watched them trudge through the snow—Mac and her father and Charlie Spoon—bigger, maybe, as if the cold landscape enlarged rather than diminished them, so that they, the only figures in that landscape, took on size and meaning just by being there. If they weren't there, everything would be quieter, and the woods would be the same as before. *But they are here,* Andy thought, looking behind her at the boot prints in the snow, *and I am too, and so it's all different.*

"We'll go down to the cut where we found those deer 30 tracks," Charlie said as they entered the woods. "Maybe we'll get lucky and get a late one coming through."

The woods descended into a gully. The snow was softer and deeper here, so that often Andy sank to her knees. Charlie and Mac worked the top of the gully while she and her father walked along the base some thirty yards behind them. "If they miss the first shot, we'll get the second," her father said, and she nodded as if she had known this all the time. She listened to the crunch of their boots, their breathing, and the drumming of a distant woodpecker. And the crackling. In winter the woods crackled as if everything were straining, ready to snap like dried chicken bones.

We are hunting, Andy thought. The cold air burned her nostrils.

They stopped to make lunch by a rock outcropping that protected them from the wind. Her father heated the bean soup her mother had made for them, and they ate it with bread already stiff from the cold. He and Charlie took a few pulls from a flask of Jim Beam while she scoured the plates with snow and repacked them. Then they all had coffee with sugar and powdered milk, and her father poured her a cup too. "We won't tell your momma," he said, and Mac laughed. Andy held the cup the way her father did, not by the handle but around the rim. The coffee tasted smoky. She felt a little queasy, but she drank it all.

Charlie Spoon picked his teeth with a fingernail. "Now, you might've noticed one thing," he said.

"What's that?" her father asked. 35

"You might've noticed you don't hear no rifles. That's because there ain't no other hunters here. We've got the whole damn woods to ourselves. Now, I ask you—do I know how to find 'em?"

"We haven't seen deer yet, neither."

"Oh, we will," Charlie said, "but not for a while now." He leaned back against the rock. "Deer're sleeping, resting up for the evening feed."

"I seen a deer behind our house once, and it was afternoon," Andy said.

"Yeah, honey, but that was *before* deer season," Char- 40 lie said, grinning. "They know something now. They're smart that way."

"That's right," Mac said.

Andy looked at her father—had she said something stupid?

"Well, Charlie," he said, "if they know so much, how come so many get themselves shot?"

"Them's the ones that don't *believe* what they know," Charlie replied. The men laughed. Andy hesitated, and then laughed with them.

They moved on, as much to keep warm as to find a 45 deer. The wind became even stronger. Blowing through the treetops, it sounded like the ocean, and once Andy thought she could smell salt air. But that was impossible; the ocean was *hundreds* of miles away, farther than Canada even. She and her parents had gone last summer to stay for a week at a motel on the New Jersey shore. That was the first time she'd seen the ocean, and it frightened her. It was huge and empty, yet always moving. Everything lay hidden. If you walked in it, you couldn't see how deep it was or what might be below; if you swam, something could pull you under and you'd never be seen again. Its musky, rank smell made her think of things dying. Her mother had floated beyond the breakers, calling to her to come in, but Andy wouldn't go farther than a few feet into the surf. Her mother swam and splashed with animal-like delight while her father, smiling shyly, held his white arms above the waist-deep water as if afraid to get them wet. Once a comber rolled over and sent them both tossing, and when her mother tried to stand up, the surf receding behind, Andy saw that her mother's swimsuit top had come off, so that her breasts swayed free, her nipples like two dark eyes. Embarrassed, Andy looked around: except for two women under a yellow umbrella farther up, the beach was empty. Her mother stood up unsteadily, regained her footing. Taking what seemed the longest time, she calmly refixed her top. Andy lay on the beach towel and closed her eyes. The sound of the surf made her head ache.

And now it was winter; the sky was already dimming, not just with the absence of light but with a mist that clung to the hunters' faces like cobwebs. They made camp early. Andy was chilled. When she stood still, she kept wiggling her toes to make sure they were there. Her father rubbed her arms and held her to him briefly, and that felt better. She unpacked the food while the others put up the tents.

"How about rounding us up some firewood, Mac?" Charlie asked.

"I'll do it," Andy said. Charlie looked at her thoughtfully and then handed her the canvas carrier.

There wasn't much wood on the ground, so it took her a while to get a good load. She was about a hundred yards from camp, near a cluster of high, lichen-covered boulders, when she saw through a crack in the rock a buck and two does walking gingerly, almost daintily, through the alder trees. She tried to hush her breathing as they passed not more than twenty yards away. There was nothing she could do. If she yelled, they'd be gone; by the time she got back to camp, they'd be gone. The buck stopped, nostrils quivering, tail up and alert. He looked directly at her. Still she didn't move, not one muscle. He was a beautiful buck, the color of late-turned maple leaves. Unafraid, he lowered his tail, and he and his does silently merged into the trees. Andy walked back to camp and dropped the firewood.

"I saw three deer," she said. "A buck and two does." 50

"Where?" Charlie Spoon cried, looking behind her as if they might have followed her into camp.

"In the woods yonder. They're gone now."

"Well, hell!" Charlie banged his coffee cup against his knee.

"Didn't I say she could find animals?" her father said, grinning.

"Too late to go after them," Charlie muttered. "It'll be 55 dark in a quarter hour. Damn!"

"Damn," Mac echoed.

"They just walk right up to her," her father said.

"Well, leastwise this proves there's deer here." Charlie began snapping long branches into shorter ones. "You know, I think I'll stick with you," he told Andy, "since you're so good at finding deer and all. How'd that be?"

"Okay, I guess," Andy murmured. She hoped he was kidding; no way did she want to hunt with Charlie Spoon. Still, she was pleased he had said it.

Her father and Charlie took one tent, she and Mac the 60 other. When they were in their sleeping bags, Mac said in the darkness, "I bet you really didn't see no deer, did you?"

She sighed. "I did, Mac. Why would I lie?"

"How big was the buck?"

>> Doe

>> Buck

"Four point. I counted."

Mac snorted.

"You just believe what you want, Mac," she said testily. 65

"Too bad it ain't buck season," he said. "Well, I got to go pee."

"So pee."

She heard him turn in his bag. "You ever see it?" he asked.

"It? What's 'it'?"

"It. A pecker." 70

"Sure," she lied.

"Whose? Your father's?"

She was uncomfortable. "No," she said.

"Well, whose then?"

"Oh I don't know! Leave me be, why don't you?" 75

"Didn't see a deer, didn't see a pecker," Mac said teasingly.

She didn't answer right away. Then she said, "My cousin Lewis. I saw his."

"Well, how old's he?"

"One and a half."

"Ha! A baby! A baby's is like a little worm. It ain't a 80 real one at all."

If he says he'll show me his, she thought, *I'll kick him. I'll just get out of my bag and kick him.*

"I went hunting with my daddy and Versh and Danny Simmons last year in buck season," Mac said, "and we got ourselves one. And we hog-dressed the thing. You know what that is, don't you?"

"No," she said. She was confused. What was he talking about now?

"That's when you cut him open and take out all his guts, so the meat don't spoil. Makes him lighter to pack out, too."

She tried to imagine what the deer's guts might look 85 like, pulled from the gaping hole. "What do you do with them?" she said. "The guts?"

"Oh, just leave 'em for the bears."

She ran her finger like a knife blade along her belly.

"When we left them on the ground," Mac said, "they smoked. Like they were cooking."

"Huh," she said.

"They cut off the deer's pecker, too, you know." 90

Andy imagined Lewis's pecker and shuddered. "Mac, you're disgusting."

He laughed. "Well, I gotta go pee." She heard him rustle out of his bag. "Broo!" he cried, flapping his arms. "It's cold!"

He makes so much noise, she thought, *just noise and more noise.*

Her father woke them before first light. He warned them to talk softly and said that they were going to the place where Andy had seen the deer, to try to cut them off on their way back from their night feeding. Andy couldn't shake off her sleep. Stuffing her sleeping bag into its sack seemed to take an hour, and tying her boots was the strangest thing she'd ever done. Charlie Spoon made hot chocolate and oatmeal with raisins. Andy closed her eyes and, between beats of her heart, listened to the breathing of the forest. *When I open my eyes, it will be lighter,* she decided. But when she did, it was still just as dark, except for the swaths of their flashlights and the hissing blue flame of the stove. *There has to be just one moment when it all changes from dark to light,* Andy thought. She had missed it yesterday, in the car; today she would watch more closely.

But when she remembered again, it was already first 95 light and they had moved to the rocks by the deer trail and had set up shooting positions—Mac and Charlie Spoon on the up-trail side, she and her father behind them, some six feet up on a ledge. The day became brighter, the sun piercing the tall pines, raking the hunters, yet providing little warmth. Andy now smelled alder and pine and the slightly rotten odor of rock lichen. She rubbed her hand over the stone and considered that it must be very old, had probably been here before the giant pines, *before anyone was in these woods at all.* A chipmunk sniffed on a nearby branch. She aimed an imaginary rifle and pressed the trigger. The chipmunk froze, then scurried away. Her legs were cramping on the narrow ledge. Her father seemed to doze, one hand in his parka, the other cupped lightly around the rifle. She could smell his scent of old wool and leather. His cheeks were speckled with gray-black whiskers, and he worked his jaws slightly, as if chewing a small piece of gum.

Please let us get a deer, she prayed.

A branch snapped on the other side of the rock face. Her father's hand stiffened on the rifle, startling her—*He hasn't been sleeping at all,* she marveled—and then his jaw relaxed, as did the lines around his eyes, and she heard Charlie Spoon call, "Yo, don't shoot, it's us." He and Mac appeared from around the rock. They stopped beneath the ledge. Charlie solemnly crossed his arms.

"I don't believe we're gonna get any deer here," he said drily.

Andy's father lowered his rifle to Charlie and jumped down from the ledge. Then he reached up for Andy. She dropped into his arms and he set her gently on the ground.

Mac sidled up to her. "I knew you didn't see no deer," [100] he said.

"Just because they don't come when you want 'em to don't mean she didn't see them," her father said.

Still, she felt bad. Her telling about the deer had caused them to spend the morning there, cold and expectant, with nothing to show for it.

They tramped through the woods for another two hours, not caring much about noise. Mac found some deer tracks, and they argued about how old they were. They split up for a while and then rejoined at an old logging road that deer might use, and followed it. The road crossed a stream, which had mostly frozen over but in a few spots still caught leaves and twigs in an icy swirl. They forded it by jumping from rock to rock. The road narrowed after that, and the woods thickened.

They stopped for lunch, heating up Charlie's wife's corn chowder. Andy's father cut squares of applesauce cake with his hunting knife and handed them to her and Mac, who ate his almost daintily. Andy could faintly taste knife oil on the cake. She was tired. She stretched her leg; the muscle that had cramped on the rock still ached.

"Might as well relax," her father said, as if reading her [105] thoughts. "We won't find deer till suppertime."

Charlie Spoon leaned back against his pack and folded his hands across his stomach. "Well, even if we don't get a deer," he said expansively, "it's still great to be out here, breathe some fresh air, clomp around a bit. Get away from the house and the old lady." He winked at Mac, who looked away.

"That's what the woods are all about, anyway," Charlie said. "It's where the women don't want to go." He bowed his head toward Andy. "With your exception, of course, little lady." He helped himself to another piece of applesauce cake.

"She ain't a woman," Mac said.

"Well, she damn well's gonna be," Charlie said. He grinned at her. "Or will you? You're half a boy anyway. You go by a boy's name. What's your real name? Andrea, ain't it?"

"That's right," she said. She hoped that if she didn't [110] look at him, Charlie would stop.

"Well, which do you like? Andy or Andrea?"

"Don't matter," she mumbled. "Either."

"She's always been Andy to me," her father said.

Charlie Spoon was still grinning. "So what are you gonna be, Andrea? A boy or a girl?"

"I'm a girl," she said. [115]

"But you want to go hunting and fishing and everything, huh?"

"She can do whatever she likes," her father said.

"Hell, you might as well have just had a boy and be done with it!" Charlie exclaimed.

"That's funny," her father said, and chuckled. "That's just what her momma tells me."

They were looking at her, and she wanted to get away [120] from them all, even from her father, who chose to joke with them.

"I'm going to walk a bit," she said.

She heard them laughing as she walked down the logging trail. She flapped her arms; she whistled. *I don't care how much noise I make,* she thought. Two grouse flew from the underbrush, startling her. A little farther down, the trail ended in a clearing that enlarged into a frozen meadow; beyond it the woods began again. A few moldering posts were all that was left of a fence that had once enclosed the field. The low afternoon sunlight reflected brightly off the snow, so that Andy's eyes hurt. She squinted hard. A gust of wind blew across the field, stinging her face. And then, as if it had been waiting for her, the doe emerged from the trees opposite and stepped cautiously into the field. Andy watched: it stopped and stood quietly for what seemed a long time and then ambled across. It stopped again about seventy yards away and began to browse in a patch of sugar grass uncovered by the wind. Carefully, slowly, never taking her eyes from the doe, Andy walked backward, trying to step into the boot prints she'd already made. When she was far enough back into the woods, she turned and walked faster, her heart racing. *Please let it stay,* she prayed.

"There's doe in the field yonder," she told them.

They got their rifles and hurried down the trail.

"No use," her father said. "We're making too much [125] noise any way you look at it."

"At least we got us the wind in our favor," Charlie Spoon said, breathing heavily.

But the doe was still there, grazing.

"Good Lord," Charlie whispered. He looked at her father. "Well, whose shot?"

"Andy spotted it," her father said in a low voice. "Let her shoot it."

"What!" Charlie's eyes widened. [130]

Andy couldn't believe what her father had just said. She'd only shot tin cans and targets; she'd never even fired her father's .30-.30, and she'd never killed anything.

"I can't," she whispered.

"That's right, she can't," Charlie Spoon insisted. "She's not old enough and she don't have a license even if she was!"

"Well, who's to tell?" her father said in a low voice. "Nobody's going to know but us." He looked at her. "Do you want to shoot it, punkin?"

Why doesn't it hear us? she wondered. *Why doesn't it* [135] *run away?* "I don't know," she said.

"Well, I'm sure as hell gonna shoot it," Charlie said. Her father grasped Charlie's rifle barrel and held it. His voice was steady.

"Andy's a good shot. It's her deer. She found it, not you. You'd still be sitting on your ass back in camp." He turned to her again. "Now—do you want to shoot it, Andy? Yes or no."

He was looking at her; they were all looking at her. Suddenly she was angry at the deer, who refused to hear them, who wouldn't run away even when it could. "I'll shoot it," she said. Charlie turned away in disgust.

She lay on the ground and pressed the rifle stock against her shoulder bone. The snow was cold through her parka; she smelled oil and wax and damp earth. She pulled off one glove with her teeth. "It sights just like the .22," her father said gently. "Cartridge's already chambered." As she had done so many times before, she sighted down the scope; now the doe was in the reticle. She moved the barrel until the cross hairs lined up. Her father was breathing beside her.

"Aim where the chest and legs meet, or a little above, punkin," he was saying calmly. "That's the killing shot."

But now, seeing it in the scope, Andy was hesitant. Her finger weakened on the trigger. Still, she nodded at what her father said and sighted again, the cross hairs lining up in exactly the same spot—the doe had hardly moved, its brownish-gray body outlined starkly against the blue-backed snow. *It doesn't know,* Andy thought. *It just doesn't know.* And as she looked, deer and snow and faraway trees flattened within the circular frame to become like a picture on a calendar, not real, and she felt calm, as if she had been dreaming everything—the day, the deer, the hunt itself. And she, finger on trigger, was only a part of that dream.

"Shoot!" Charlie hissed.

Through the scope she saw the deer look up, ears high and straining.

Charlie groaned, and just as he did, and just at the moment when Andy knew—*knew*—the doe would bound away, as if she could feel its haunches tensing and gathering power, she pulled the trigger. Later she would think, *I felt the recoil, I smelled the smoke, but I don't remember pulling the trigger.* Through the scope the deer seemed to shrink into itself, and then slowly knelt, hind legs first, head raised as if to cry out. It trembled, still straining to keep its head high, as if that alone would save it; failing, it collapsed, shuddered, and lay still.

"Whoee!" Mac cried.

"One shot! One shot!" her father yelled, clapping her on the back. Charlie Spoon was shaking his head and smiling dumbly.

"I told you she was a great little shot!" her father said. "I told you!" Mac danced and clapped his hands. She was dazed, not quite understanding what had happened. And then they were crossing the field toward the fallen doe, she walking dreamlike, the men laughing and joking, released now from the tension of silence and anticipation. Suddenly Mac pointed and cried out, "Look at that!"

The doe was rising, legs unsteady. They stared at it, unable to comprehend, and in that moment the doe regained its feet and looked at them, as if it too were trying to understand. Her father whistled softly. Charlie Spoon unslung his rifle and raised it to his shoulder, but the doe was already bounding away. His hurried shot missed, and the deer disappeared into the woods.

"Damn, damn, damn," he moaned.

"I don't believe it," her father said. "That deer was dead."

"Dead, hell!" Charlie yelled. "It was gutshot, that's all. Stunned and gutshot. Clean shot, my ass!"

What have I done? Andy thought.

Her father slung his rifle over his shoulder. "Well, let's go. It can't get too far."

"Hell, I've seen deer run ten miles gutshot," Charlie said. He waved his arms. "We may never find her!"

As they crossed the field, Mac came up to her and said in a low voice, "Gutshoot a deer, you'll go to hell."

"Shut up, Mac," she said, her voice cracking. It was a terrible thing she had done, she knew. She couldn't bear to think of the doe in pain and frightened. *Please let it die,* she prayed.

But though they searched all the last hour of daylight, so that they had to recross the field and go up the logging trail in a twilight made even deeper by thick, smoky clouds, they didn't find the doe. They lost its trail almost immediately in the dense stands of alderberry and larch.

"I am cold, and I am tired," Charlie Spoon declared. "And if you ask me, that deer's in another county already."

"No one's asking you, Charlie," her father said.

They had a supper of hard salami and ham, bread, and the rest of the applesauce cake. It seemed a bother to heat the coffee, so they had cold chocolate instead. Everyone turned in early.

"We'll find it in the morning, honeybun," her father said, as she went to her tent.

"I don't like to think of it suffering." She was almost in tears.

"It's dead already, punkin. Don't even think about it." He kissed her, his breath sour and his beard rough against her cheek.

Andy was sure she wouldn't get to sleep; the image of the doe falling, falling, then rising again, repeated itself whenever she closed her eyes. Then she heard an owl hoot and realized that it had awakened her, so she must have been asleep after all. She hoped the owl would hush, but instead it hooted louder. She wished her father or Charlie Spoon would wake up and do something about it, but no one moved in the other tent, and suddenly she was afraid that they had all decamped, wanting nothing more to do with her. She whispered, "Mac, Mac," to the sleeping bag where he should be, but no one answered. She tried to find the flashlight she always kept by her side, but couldn't, and she cried in panic, "Mac, are you there?" He mumbled something, and immediately she felt foolish and hoped he wouldn't reply.

When she awoke again, everything had changed. The owl was gone, the woods were still, and she sensed light, blue and pale, light where before there had been none. *The moon must have come out,* she thought. And it was warm, too, warmer than it should have been. She got out of her sleeping bag and took off her parka—it was that warm. Mac was asleep, wheezing like an old man. She unzipped the tent and stepped outside.

The woods were more beautiful than she had ever seen them. The moon made everything ice-rimmed glimmer with a crystallized, immanent light, while underneath that ice the branches of trees were as stark as skeletons. She heard a crunching in the snow, the one sound in all that silence, and there, walking down the logging trail into their camp, was the doe. Its body, like everything around her, was silvered with frost and moonlight. It walked past the tent where her father and Charlie Spoon were sleeping and stopped no more than six feet from her. Andy saw that she had shot it, yes, had shot it cleanly, just where she thought she had, the wound a jagged, bloody hole in the doe's chest.

A heart shot, she thought.

The doe stepped closer, so that Andy, if she wished, could have reached out and touched it. It looked at her as if expecting her to do this, and so she did, running her hand, slowly at first, along the rough, matted fur, then down to the edge of the wound, where she stopped. The doe stood still. Hesitantly, Andy felt the edge of the wound. The torn flesh was sticky and warm. The wound parted under her touch. And then, almost without her knowing it, her fingers were within, probing, yet still the doe didn't move. Andy pressed deeper, through flesh and muscle and sinew, until her whole hand and more was inside the wound and she had found the doe's heart, warm and beating. She cupped it gently in her hand. *Alive,* she marveled. *Alive.*

The heart quickened under her touch, becoming warmer and warmer until it was hot enough to burn. In pain, Andy tried to remove her hand, but the wound closed about it and held her fast. Her hand was burning. She cried out in agony, sure they would all hear and come help, but they didn't. And then her hand pulled free, followed by a steaming rush of blood, more blood than she ever could have imagined—it covered her hand and arm, and she saw to her horror that her hand was steaming. She moaned and fell to her knees and plunged her hand into the snow. The doe looked at her gently and then turned and walked back up the trail.

In the morning, when she woke, Andy could still smell 170 the blood, but she felt no pain. She looked at her hand. Even though it appeared unscathed, it felt weak and withered. She couldn't move it freely and was afraid the others would notice. *I will hide it in my jacket pocket,* she decided, *so nobody can see.* She ate the oatmeal that her father cooked and stayed apart from them all. No one spoke to her, and that suited her. A light snow began to fall. It was the last day of their hunting trip. She wanted to be home.

Her father dumped the dregs of his coffee. "Well, let's go look for her," he said.

Again they crossed the field. Andy lagged behind. She averted her eyes from the spot where the doe had fallen, already filling up with snow. Mac and Charlie entered the woods first, followed by her father. Andy remained in the field and considered the smear of gray sky, the nearby flock of crows pecking at unyielding stubble. *I will stay here,* she thought, *and not move for a long while.* But now someone—Mac—was yelling. Her father appeared at the woods' edge and waved for her to come. She ran and pushed through a brake of alderberry and larch. The thick underbrush scratched her face. For a moment she felt lost and looked wildly about. Then, where the brush thinned, she saw them standing quietly in the falling snow. They were staring down at the dead doe. A film covered its upturned eye, and its body was lightly dusted with snow.

"I told you she wouldn't get too far," Andy's father said triumphantly. "We must've just missed her yesterday. Too blind to see."

"We're just damn lucky no animal got to her last night," Charlie muttered.

Her father lifted the doe's foreleg. The wound was 175 blood-clotted, brown, and caked like frozen mud. "Clean shot," he said to Charlie. He grinned. "My little girl."

Then he pulled out his knife, the blade gray as the morning. Mac whispered to Andy, "Now watch this," while Charlie Spoon lifted the doe from behind by its forelegs so that its head rested between his knees, its underside exposed. Her father's knife sliced thickly from chest to belly to crotch, and Andy was running from them, back to the field and across, scattering the crows who cawed and circled angrily. And now they were all calling to her—Charlie Spoon and Mac and her father—crying *Andy, Andy* (but that wasn't her name, she would no longer be called that); yet louder than any of them was the wind blowing through the treetops, like the ocean where her mother floated in green water, also calling *Come in, come in,* while all around her roared the mocking of the terrible, now inevitable, sea.

Related Works

"A&P" (p. 131), "Greasy Lake" (p. 306), "Traveling through the Dark" (p. 488), "The Lamb" (p. 499)

 See Chapter 17 Review Card for Reading and Reacting questions about David Michael Kaplan, "Doe Season."

D(avid) H(erbert) Lawrence
(1885–1930)

was born in Nottinghamshire, England, the son of a coal miner and a schoolteacher. Determined to escape the harsh life of a miner, Lawrence taught for several years after graduating from high school. He soon began writing fiction and established himself in London literary circles.

During World War I, Lawrence and his wife were suspected of treason because of his pacifism and her connection to German aristocracy. Because Lawrence suffered from tuberculosis, he and his wife left England after the armistice in search of a healthier climate. They traveled in Australia, France, Italy, Mexico, and the United States throughout their lives.

Lawrence is recognized for his impassioned portrayal of our unconscious and instinctive natures. In his novel *Lady Chatterley's Lover* (1928), he attempted to incorporate explicit sexuality into English fiction, and the book was banned for years in Britain and the United States. His other novels include *Sons and Lovers* (1913), *The Rainbow* (1915), *Women in Love* (1921), and *The Plumed Serpent* (1926). Lawrence was also a gifted poet, essayist, travel writer, and short story writer, and his work had a strong influence on other writers.

Lawrence's fascination with the struggle between the unconscious and the intellect is revealed in his short story "The Rocking-Horse Winner" (1920). Lawrence sets his story in a house full of secrets and weaves symbolism with elements of the fairy tale and the gothic to produce a tale that has often been the subject of literary debate.

The Rocking-Horse Winner (1920)

There was a woman who was beautiful, who started with all the advantages, yet she had no luck. She married for love, and the love turned to dust. She had bonny children, yet she felt they had been thrust upon her, and she could not love them. They looked at her coldly, as if they were finding fault with her. And hurriedly she felt she must cover up some fault in herself. Yet what it was that she must cover up she never knew. Nevertheless, when her children were present, she always felt the centre of her heart go hard. This troubled her, and in her manner she was all the more gentle and anxious for her children, as if she loved them very much. Only she herself knew that at the centre of her heart was a hard little place that could not feel love, no, not for anybody. Everybody else said of her: "She is such a good mother. She adores her children." Only she herself, and her children themselves, knew it was not so. They read it in each other's eyes.

There were a boy and two little girls. They lived in a pleasant house, with a garden, and they had discreet servants, and felt themselves superior to anyone in the neighbourhood.

Although they lived in style, they felt always an anxiety in the house. There was never enough money. The mother had a small income, and the father had a small income, but not nearly enough for the social position which they had to keep up. The father went into town to some office. But though he had good prospects, these prospects never materialised. There was always the grinding sense of the shortage of money, though the style was always kept up.

At last the mother said: "I will see if *I* can't make something." But she did not know where to begin. She racked her brains, and tried this thing and the other, but could not find anything successful. The failure made deep lines come into her face. Her children were growing up, they would

> *"And so the house came to be haunted by the unspoken phrase: There must be more money! There must be more money!"*

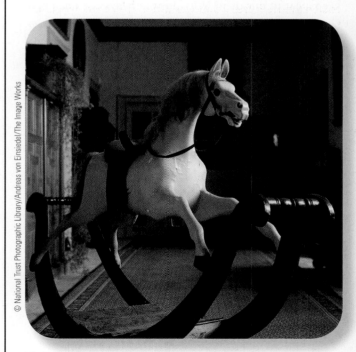

>> Wooden rocking horse, nineteenth century

have to go to school. There must be more money, there must be more money. The father, who was always very handsome and expensive in his tastes, seemed as if he never *would* be able to do anything worth doing. And the mother, who had a great belief in herself, did not succeed any better, and her tastes were just as expensive.

And so the house came to be haunted by the unspoken [5] phrase: *There must be more money! There must be more money!* The children could hear it all the time, though nobody said it aloud. They heard it at Christmas, when the expensive and splendid toys filled the nursery. Behind the shining modern rocking-horse, behind the smart doll's house, a voice would start whispering: "There *must* be more money! There *must* be more money!" And the children would stop playing, to listen for a moment. They would look into each other's eyes, to see if they had all heard. And each one saw in the eyes of the other two that they too had heard. "There *must* be more money! There *must* be more money!"

It came whispering from the springs of the still-swaying rocking-horse, and even the horse, bending his wooden, champing head, heard it. The big doll, sitting so pink and smirking in her new pram, could hear it quite plainly, and seemed to be smirking all the more self-consciously because of it. The foolish puppy, too, that took the place of the teddybear, he was looking so extraordinarily foolish for no other reason but that he heard the secret whisper all over the house: "There *must* be more money!"

Yet nobody ever said it aloud. The whisper was everywhere, and therefore no one spoke it. Just as no one ever says: "We are breathing!" in spite of the fact that breath is coming and going all the time.

"Mother," said the boy Paul one day, "why don't we keep a car of our own? Why do we always use uncle's, or else a taxi?"

"Because we're the poor members of the family," said the mother.

"But why *are* we, mother?" [10]

"Well—I suppose," she said slowly and bitterly, "it's because your father has no luck."

The boy was silent for some time.

"Is luck money, mother?" he asked, rather timidly.

"No, Paul. Not quite. It's what causes you to have money."

"Oh!" said Paul vaguely. "I thought when Uncle Oscar [15] said *filthy lucker,* it meant money."

"*Filthy lucre* does mean money," said the mother. "But it's lucre, not luck."

"Oh!" said the boy. "Then what *is* luck, mother?"

"It's what causes you to have money. If you're lucky you have money. That's why it's better to be born lucky than rich. If you're rich, you may lose your money. But if you're lucky, you will always get more money."

"Oh! Will you? And is father not lucky?"

"Very unlucky, I should say," she said bitterly. [20]

The boy watched her with unsure eyes.

"Why?" he asked.

"I don't know. Nobody ever knows why one person is lucky and another unlucky."

"Don't they? Nobody at all? Does *nobody* know?"

"Perhaps God. But He never tells." [25]

"He ought to, then. And aren't you lucky either, mother?"

"I can't be, if I married an unlucky husband."

"But by yourself, aren't you?"

"I used to think I was, before I married. Now I think I am very unlucky indeed."

"Why?" [30]

"Well—never mind! Perhaps I'm not really," she said.

The child looked at her to see if she meant it. But he saw, by the lines of her mouth, that she was only trying to hide something from him.

"Well, anyhow," he said stoutly, "I'm a lucky person."

"Why?" said his mother, with a sudden laugh.

He stared at her. He didn't even know why he had [35] said it.

"God told me," he asserted, brazening it out.

"I hope He did, dear!" she said, again with a laugh, but rather bitter.

"He did, mother!"

"Excellent!" said the mother, using one of her husband's exclamations.

The boy saw she did not believe him; or rather, that [40] she paid no attention to his assertion. This angered him somewhat, and made him want to compel her attention.

He went off by himself, vaguely, in a childish way, seeking for the clue to "luck." Absorbed, taking no heed of other people, he went about with a sort of stealth, seeking inwardly for luck. He wanted luck, he wanted it, he wanted it. When the two girls were playing dolls in the nursery, he would sit on his big rocking-horse, charging madly into space, with a frenzy that made the little girls peer at him uneasily. Wildly the horse careered, the waving dark hair of the boy tossed, his eyes had a strange glare in them. The little girls dared not speak to him.

When he had ridden to the end of his mad little journey, he climbed down and stood in front of his rocking-horse,

Cultural Context
Horse racing in England has a long history, beginning with casual competitions organized by Roman soldiers in Yorkshire in A.D. 200. The first recorded horse race was run during the reign of Henry II in 1174. Today, horses can be raced over fences or hurdles (National Hunt Racing) or over unobstructed distances (flat racing). There are also cross-country races from point to point, which are called steeplechases. A derby, like the one mentioned in this story, usually denotes a race in which three-year-old horses compete. The name *derby* is derived from the Epsom Derby, which is still run at the Epsom racecourse and is named for Edward Smith Stanley, the twelfth Earl of Derby.

>> Illustration of horse race in ad for 1898 play

staring fixedly into its lowered face. Its red mouth was slightly open, its big eye was wide and glassy-bright.

"Now!" he would silently command the snorting steed. "Now, take me to where there is luck! Now take me!"

And he would slash the horse on the neck with the little whip he had asked Uncle Oscar for. He *knew* the horse could take him to where there was luck, if only he forced it. So he would mount again and start on his furious ride, hoping at last to get there. He knew he could get there.

"You'll break your horse, Paul!" said the nurse.   45

"He's always riding like that! I wish he'd leave off!" said his elder sister Joan.

But he only glared down on them in silence. Nurse gave him up. She could make nothing of him. Anyhow, he was growing beyond her.

One day his mother and his Uncle Oscar came in when he was on one of his furious rides. He did not speak to them.

"Hallo, you young jockey! Riding a winner?" said his uncle.

"Aren't you growing too big for a rocking-horse? 50 You're not a very little boy any longer, you know," said his mother.

But Paul only gave a blue glare from his big, rather close-set eyes. He would speak to nobody when he was in full tilt. His mother watched him with an anxious expression on her face.

At last he suddenly stopped forcing his horse into the mechanical gallop and slid down.

"Well, I got there!" he announced fiercely, his blue eyes still flaring, and his sturdy long legs straddling apart.

"Where did you get to?" asked his mother.

"Where I wanted to go," he flared back at her.   55

"That's right, son!" said Uncle Oscar. "Don't you stop till you get there. What's the horse's name?"

"He doesn't have a name," said the boy.

"Gets on without all right?" asked the uncle.

"Well, he has different names. He was called Sansovino last week."

"Sansovino, eh? Won the Ascot.° How did you know 60 this name?"

"He always talks about horse-races with Bassett," said Joan.

The uncle was delighted to find that his small nephew was posted with all the racing news. Bassett, the young gardener, who had been wounded in the left foot in the war and had got his present job through Oscar Cresswell, whose batman° he had been, was a perfect blade of the "turf." He lived in the racing events, and the small boy lived with him.

Oscar Cresswell got it all from Bassett.

"Master Paul comes and asks me, so I can't do more than tell him, sir," said Bassett, his face terribly serious, as if he were speaking of religious matters.

"And does he ever put anything on a horse he fancies?" 65

"Well—I don't want to give him away—he's a young sport, a fine sport, sir. Would you mind asking him himself? He sort of takes a pleasure in it, and perhaps he'd feel I was giving him away, sir, if you don't mind."

Bassett was serious as a church.

The uncle went back to his nephew and took him off for a ride in the car.

"Say, Paul, old man, do you ever put anything on a horse?" the uncle asked.

The boy watched the handsome man closely.   70

"Why, do you think I oughtn't to?" he parried.

"Not a bit of it! I thought perhaps you might give me a tip for the Lincoln."°

The car sped on into the country, going down to Uncle Oscar's place in Hampshire.

"Honour bright?" said the nephew.

"Honour bright, son!" said the uncle.   75

"Well, then, Daffodil."

"Daffodil! I doubt it, sonny. What about Mirza?"

"I only know the winner," said the boy. "That's Daffodil."

"Daffodil, eh?"

There was a pause. Daffodil was an obscure horse 80 comparatively.

"Uncle!"

"Yes, son?"

"You won't let it go any further, will you? I promised Bassett."

"Bassett be damned, old man! What's he got to do with it?"

"We're partners. We've been partners from the first. 85 Uncle, he lent me my first five shillings, which I lost. I promised him, honour bright, it was only between me and him; only you gave me that ten-shilling note I started winning with, so I thought you were lucky. You won't let it go any further, will you?"

° **the Ascot** The annual horse race at Ascot Heath in England.

° **batman** A British military officer's personal assistant.

° **the Lincoln** The Lincolnshire Handicap, a horse race.

>> Crowds inspect their betting slips at Bournemouth (England) races, 1925

The boy gazed at his uncle from those big, hot, blue eyes, set rather close together. The uncle stirred and laughed uneasily.

"Right you are, son! I'll keep your tip private. Daffodil, eh? How much are you putting on him?"

"All except twenty pounds," said the boy. "I keep that in reserve."

The uncle thought it a good joke.

"You keep twenty pounds in reserve, do you, you 90 young romancer? What are you betting, then?"

"I'm betting three hundred," said the boy gravely. "But it's between you and me, Uncle Oscar! Honour bright?"

The uncle burst into a roar of laughter.

"It's between you and me all right, you young Nat Gould,"° he said, laughing. "But where's your three hundred?"

"Bassett keeps it for me. We're partners."

"You are, are you! And what is Bassett putting on 95 Daffodil?"

"He won't go quite as high as I do, I expect. Perhaps he'll go a hundred and fifty."

"What, pennies?" laughed the uncle.

"Pounds," said the child, with a surprised look at his uncle. "Bassett keeps a bigger reserve than I do."

Between wonder and amusement Uncle Oscar was silent. He pursued the matter no further, but he determined to take his nephew with him to the Lincoln races.

"Now, son," he said, "I'm putting twenty on Mirza, 100 and I'll put five on for you on any horse you fancy. What's your pick?"

"Daffodil, uncle."

"No, not the fiver on Daffodil!"

"I should if it was my own fiver," said the child.

"Good! Good! Right you are! A fiver for me and a fiver for you on Daffodil."

The child had never been to a race-meeting before, 105 and his eyes were blue fire. He pursed his mouth tight and watched. A Frenchman just in front had put his money on Lancelot. Wild with excitement, he flayed his arms up and down, yelling *"Lancelot! Lancelot!"* in his French accent.

Daffodil came in first, Lancelot second, Mirza third. The child, flushed and with eyes blazing, was curiously serene. His uncle brought him four five-pound notes, four to one.

"What am I to do with these?" he cried, waving them before the boy's eyes.

"I suppose we'll talk to Bassett," said the boy. "I expect I have fifteen hundred now; and twenty in reserve; and this twenty."

His uncle studied him for some moments.

"Look here, son!" he said. "You're not serious about 110 Bassett and that fifteen hundred, are you?"

"Yes, I am. But it's between you and me, uncle. Honour bright?"

"Honour bright all right, son! But I must talk to Bassett."

"If you'd like to be a partner, uncle, with Bassett and me, we could all be partners. Only, you'd have to promise, honour bright, uncle, not to let it go beyond us three. Bassett and I are lucky, and you must be lucky, because it was your ten shillings I started winning with. . . ."

Uncle Oscar took both Bassett and Paul into Richmond Park for an afternoon, and there they talked.

"It's like this, you see, sir," Bassett said. "Master Paul 115 would get me talking about racing events, spinning yarns, you know, sir. And he was always keen on knowing if I'd made or if I'd lost. It's about a year since, now, that I put five shillings on Blush of Dawn for him: and we lost. Then the luck turned, with that ten shillings he had from you: that we put on Singhalese. And since that time, it's been pretty steady, all things considering. What do you say, Master Paul?"

"We're all right when we're sure," said Paul. "It's when we're not quite sure that we go down."

"Oh, but we're careful then," said Bassett.

"But when are you *sure*?" smiled Uncle Oscar.

"It's Master Paul, sir," said Bassett in a secret, religious voice. "It's as if he had it from heaven. Like Daffodil, now, for the Lincoln. That was as sure as eggs."

"Did you put anything on Daffodil?" asked Oscar 120 Cresswell.

"Yes, sir. I made my bit."

"And my nephew?"

Bassett was obstinately silent, looking at Paul.

"I made twelve hundred, didn't I, Bassett? I told uncle I was putting three hundred on Daffodil."

"That's right," said Bassett, nodding.   125

"But where's the money?" asked the uncle.

"I keep it safe locked up, sir. Master Paul can have it any minute he likes to ask for it."

"What, fifteen hundred pounds?"

°**Nat Gould** Nathaniel Gould (1857–1919), British journalist and writer known for his stories about horse racing.

"And twenty! And *forty*, that is, with the twenty he made on the course."

"It's amazing!" said the uncle.   130

"If Master Paul offers you to be partners, sir, I would, if I were you: if you'll excuse me," said Bassett.

Oscar Cresswell thought about it.

"I'll see the money," he said.

They drove home again, and, sure enough, Bassett came round to the garden-house with fifteen hundred pounds in notes. The twenty pounds reserve was left with Joe Glee, in the Turf Commission deposit.

"You see, it's all right, uncle, when I'm *sure!* Then we 135 go strong, for all we're worth. Don't we, Bassett?"

"We do that, Master Paul."

"And when are you sure?" said the uncle, laughing.

"Oh, well, sometimes I'm *absolutely* sure, like about Daffodil," said the boy; "and sometimes I have an idea; and sometimes I haven't even an idea, have I, Bassett? Then we're careful, because we mostly go down."

"You do, do you! And when you're sure, like about Daffodil, what makes you sure, sonny?"

"Oh, well, I don't know," said the boy uneasily. "I'm 140 sure, you know, uncle; that's all."

"It's as if he had it from heaven, sir," Bassett reiterated.

"I should say so!" said the uncle.

But he became a partner. And when the Leger° was coming on Paul was "sure" about Lively Spark, which was a quite inconsiderable horse. The boy insisted on putting a thousand on the horse, Bassett went for five hundred, and Oscar Cresswell two hundred. Lively Spark came in first, and the betting had been ten to one against him. Paul had made ten thousand.

"You see," he said, "I was absolutely sure of him."

Even Oscar Cresswell had cleared two thousand.   145

"Look here, son," he said, "this sort of thing makes me nervous."

"It needn't, uncle! Perhaps I shan't be sure again for a long time."

"But what are you going to do with your money?" asked the uncle.

"Of course," said the boy, "I started it for mother. She said she had no luck, because father is unlucky, so I thought if *I* was lucky, it might stop whispering."

"What might stop whispering?"   150

"Our house. I *hate* our house for whispering."

"What does it whisper?"

"Why—why"—the boy fidgeted—"why, I don't know. But it's always short of money, you know, uncle."

"I know it, son, I know it."

"You know people send mother writs,° don't you, 155 uncle?"

"I'm afraid I do," said the uncle.

"And then the house whispers, like people laughing at you behind your back. It's awful, that is! I thought if I was lucky . . ."

"You might stop it," added the uncle.

The boy watched him with big blue eyes, that had an uncanny cold fire in them, and he said never a word.

"Well, then!" said the uncle. "What are we doing?"   160

"I shouldn't like mother to know I was lucky," said the boy.

"Why not, son?"

"She'd stop me."

"I don't think she would."

"Oh!"—and the boy writhed in an odd way—"I *don't* 165 want her to know, uncle."

"All right, son! We'll manage it without her knowing."

They managed it very easily. Paul, at the other's suggestion, handed over five thousand pounds to his uncle, who deposited it with the family lawyer, who was then to inform Paul's mother that a relative had put five thousand pounds into his hands, which sum was to be paid out a thousand pounds at a time, on the mother's birthday, for the next five years.

"So she'll have a birthday present of a thousand pounds for five successive years," said Uncle Oscar. "I hope it won't make it all the harder for her later."

Paul's mother had her birthday in November. The house had been "whispering" worse than ever lately, and, even in spite of his luck, Paul could not bear up against it. He was very anxious to see the effect of the birthday letter, telling his mother about the thousand pounds.

When there were no visitors, Paul now took his meals 170 with his parents, as he was beyond the nursery control. His mother went into town nearly every day. She had discovered that she had an odd knack of sketching furs and dress materials, so she worked secretly in the studio of a friend who was the chief "artist" for the leading drapers. She drew the figures of ladies in furs and ladies in silk and sequins for the newspaper advertisements. This young woman artist earned several thousand pounds a year, but Paul's mother only made several hundreds, and she was again dissatisfied. She so wanted to be first in something, and she did not succeed, even in making sketches for drapery advertisements.

She was down to breakfast on the morning of her birthday. Paul watched her face as she read her letters. He knew the lawyer's letter. As his mother read it, her face hardened and became more expressionless. Then a cold, determined look came on her mouth. She hid the letter under the pile of others, and said not a word about it.

"Didn't you have anything nice in the post for your birthday, mother?" said Paul.

"Quite moderately nice," she said, her voice cold and absent.

She went away to town without saying more.

But in the afternoon Uncle Oscar appeared. He said 175 Paul's mother had had a long interview with the lawyer, asking if the whole five thousand could not be advanced at once, as she was in debt.

"What do you think, uncle?" asked the boy.

"I leave it to you, son."

° **the Leger** The St. Leger Stakes, a horse race.
° **writs** Letters from creditors requesting payment.

"Oh, let her have it, then! We can get some more with the other," said the boy.

"A bird in the hand is worth two in the bush, laddie!" said Uncle Oscar.

"But I'm sure to *know* for the Grand National; or the Lincolnshire; or else the Derby.° I'm sure to know for *one* of them," said Paul.

So Uncle Oscar signed the agreement, and Paul's mother touched the whole five thousand. Then something very curious happened. The voices in the house suddenly went mad, like a chorus of frogs on a spring evening. There was certain new furnishings, and Paul had a tutor. He was *really* going to Eton, his father's school, in the following autumn. There were flowers in the winter, and a blossoming of the luxury Paul's mother had been used to. And yet the voices in the house, behind the sprays of mimosa and almond-blossom, and from under the piles of iridescent cushions, simply trilled and screamed in a sort of ecstasy: "There *must* be more money! Oh-h-h; there *must* be more money. Oh, now, now-w! Now-w-w—there *must* be more money!—more than ever! More than ever!"

It frightened Paul terribly. He studied away at his Latin and Greek with his tutor. But his intense hours were spent with Bassett. The Grand National had gone by: he had not "known," and had lost a hundred pounds. Summer was at hand. He was in agony for the Lincoln. But even for the Lincoln he didn't "know," and he lost fifty pounds. He became wild-eyed and strange, as if something were going to explode in him.

"Let it alone, son! Don't you bother about it!" urged Uncle Oscar. But it was as if the boy couldn't really hear what his uncle was saying.

"I've got to know for the Derby! I've got to know for the Derby!" the child reiterated, his big blue eyes blazing with a sort of madness.

His mother noticed how overwrought he was. 185

"You'd better go to the seaside. Wouldn't you like to go now to the seaside, instead of waiting? I think you'd better," she said, looking down at him anxiously, her heart curiously heavy because of him.

But the child lifted his uncanny blue eyes.

"I couldn't possibly go before the Derby, mother!" he said. "I couldn't possibly!"

"Why not?" she said, her voice becoming heavy when she was opposed. "Why not? You can still go from the seaside to see the Derby with your Uncle Oscar, if that's what you wish. No need for you to wait here. Besides, I think you care too much about these races. It's a bad sign. My family has been a gambling family, and you won't know till you grow up how much damage it has done. But it has done damage. I shall have to send Bassett away, and ask Uncle Oscar not to talk racing to you, unless you promise to be reasonable about it: go away to the seaside and forget it. You're all nerves!"

"I'll do what you like, mother, so long as you don't 190 send me away till after the Derby," the boy said.

"Send you away from where? Just from this house?"

"Yes," he said, gazing at her.

"Why, you curious child, what makes you care about this house so much, suddenly? I never knew you loved it."

He gazed at her without speaking. He had a secret within a secret, something he had not divulged, even to Bassett or to his Uncle Oscar.

But his mother, after standing undecided and a little 195 bit sullen for some moments, said:

"Very well, then! Don't go to the seaside till after the Derby, if you don't wish it. But promise me you won't let your nerves go to pieces. Promise you won't think so much about horse-racing and *events,* as you call them!"

"Oh no," said the boy casually. "I won't think much about them, mother. You needn't worry. I wouldn't worry, mother, if I were you."

"If you were me and I were you," said his mother, "I wonder what we *should* do!"

"But you know you needn't worry, mother, don't you?" the boy repeated.

"I should be awfully glad to know it," she said wearily. 200

"Oh, well, you *can,* you know. I mean, you *ought* to know you needn't worry," he insisted.

"Ought I? Then I'll see about it," she said.

Paul's secret of secrets was his wooden horse, that which had no name. Since he was emancipated from a nurse and a nursery-governess, he had had his rocking-horse removed to his own bedroom at the top of the house.

"Surely you're too big for a rocking-horse!" his mother had remonstrated.

"Well, you see, mother, till I can have a *real* horse, I 205 like to have *some* sort of animal about," had been his quaint answer.

"Do you feel he keeps you company?" she laughed.

"Oh yes! He's very good, he always keeps me company, when I'm there," said Paul.

So the horse, rather shabby, stood in an arrested prance in the boy's bedroom.

The Derby was drawing near, and the boy grew more and more tense. He hardly heard what was spoken to him, he was very frail, and his eyes were really uncanny. His mother had sudden strange seizures of uneasiness about him. Sometimes, for half an hour, she would feel a sudden anxiety about him that was almost anguish. She wanted to rush to him at once, and know he was safe.

Two nights before the Derby, she was at a big party 210 in town, when one of her rushes of anxiety about her boy, her firstborn, gripped her heart till she could hardly speak. She fought with the feeling, might and main, for she believed in common sense. But it was too strong. She had to leave the dance and go downstairs to telephone to the country. The children's nursery-governess was terribly surprised and startled at being rung up in the night.

"Are the children all right, Miss Wilmot?"

"Oh yes, they are quite all right."

° **Grand National . . . Derby** Famous British horse races. The Grand National is run at Aintree; the Derby, at Epsom Downs.

"Master Paul? Is he all right?"

"He went to bed as right as a trivet. Shall I run up and look at him?"

"No," said Paul's mother reluctantly. "No! Don't trou-215 ble. It's all right. Don't sit up. We shall be home fairly soon." She did not want her son's privacy intruded upon.

"Very good," said the governess.

It was about one o'clock when Paul's mother and father drove up to their house. All was still. Paul's mother went to her room and slipped off her white fur cloak. She had told her maid not to wait up for her. She heard her husband downstairs, mixing a whisky and soda.

And then, because of the strange anxiety at her heart, she stole upstairs to her son's room. Noiselessly she went along the upper corridor. Was there a faint noise? What was it?

She stood, with arrested muscles, outside his door, listening. There was a strange, heavy, and yet not loud noise. Her heart stood still. It was a soundless noise, yet rushing and powerful. Something huge, in violent, hushed motion. What was it? What in God's name was it? She ought to know. She felt that she knew the noise. She knew what it was.

Yet she could not place it. She couldn't say what it220 was. And on and on it went, like a madness.

Softly, frozen with anxiety and fear, she turned the door-handle.

The room was dark. Yet in the space near the window, she heard and saw something plunging to and fro. She gazed in fear and amazement.

Then suddenly she switched on the light, and saw her son, in his green pyjamas, madly surging on the rocking-horse. The blaze of light suddenly lit him up, as he urged the wooden horse, and lit her up, as she stood, blonde, in her dress of pale green and crystal, in the doorway.

"Paul!" she cried. "Whatever are you doing?"

"It's Malabar!" he screamed in a powerful, strange225 voice. "It's Malabar!"

His eyes blazed at her for one strange and senseless second, as he ceased urging his wooden horse. Then he fell with a crash to the ground, and she, all her tormented motherhood flooding upon her, rushed to gather him up.

But he was unconscious, and unconscious he remained, with some brain-fever. He talked and tossed, and his mother sat stonily by his side.

"Malabar! It's Malabar! Bassett, Bassett, I *know*! It's Malabar!"

So the child cried, trying to get up and urge the rocking-horse that gave him his inspiration.

"What does he mean by Malabar?" asked the heart-230 frozen mother.

"I don't know," said the father stonily.

"What does he mean by Malabar?" she asked her brother Oscar.

"It's one of the horses running for the Derby," was the answer.

And, in spite of himself, Oscar Cresswell spoke to Bassett, and himself put a thousand on Malabar: at fourteen to one.

The third day of the illness was critical: they were wait-235 ing for a change. The boy, with his rather long, curly hair, was tossing ceaselessly on the pillow. He neither slept nor regained consciousness, and his eyes were like blue stones. His mother sat, feeling her heart had gone, turned actually into a stone.

In the evening, Oscar Cresswell did not come, but Bassett sent a message, saying could he come up for one moment, just one moment? Paul's mother was very angry at the intrusion, but on second thought she agreed. The boy was the same. Perhaps Bassett might bring him to consciousness.

The gardener, a shortish fellow with a little brown moustache and sharp little brown eyes, tiptoed into the room, touched his imaginary cap to Paul's mother, and stole to the bedside, staring with glittering, smallish eyes at the tossing, dying child.

"Master Paul!" he whispered. "Master Paul! Malabar came in first all right, a clean win. I did as you told me. You've made over seventy thousand pounds, you have; you've got over eighty thousand. Malabar came in all right, Master Paul."

"Malabar! Malabar! Did I say Malabar, mother? Did I say Malabar? Do you think I'm lucky, mother? I knew Malabar, didn't I? Over eighty thousand pounds! I call that lucky, don't you, mother? Over eighty thousand pounds! I knew, didn't I know I knew? Malabar came in all right. If I ride my horse till I'm sure, then I tell you, Bassett, you can go as high as you like. Did you go for all you were worth, Bassett?"

"I went a thousand on it, Master Paul."   240

"I never told you, mother, that if I can ride my horse, and *get there,* then I'm absolutely sure—oh, absolutely! Mother, did I ever tell you? I *am* lucky!"

"No, you never did," said his mother.

But the boy died in the night.

And even as he lay dead, his mother heard her brother's voice saying to her: "My God, Hester, you're eighty-odd thousand to the good, and a poor devil of a son to the bad. But, poor devil, poor devil, he's best gone out of a life where he rides his rocking-horse to find a winner."

Related Works

"Gretel in Darkness" (p. 362), "Suicide Note" (p. 367), "Birches" (p. 487), *Death of a Salesman* (p. 605)

 See Chapter 17 Review Card for Reading and Reacting questions about D(avid) H(erbert) Lawrence, "The Rocking-Horse Winner."

Writing Suggestions: Theme

1. In a sense, all of the stories in this chapter deal with the importance of patience and persistence. Write an essay in which you examine the value of enduring despite difficulties, citing the experiences of the main characters in two of this chapter's stories—for example, "Two Questions" and "Doe Season."

2. Both "The Rocking-Horse Winner" and "A Worn Path" focus on characters who make journeys. What is the significance of each journey? How do the protagonists of these two stories overcome the obstacles they encounter? In what sense are these journeys symbolic as well as real?

 CHECKLIST

WRITING ABOUT THEME
☐ What is the central theme of the story?
☐ What other themes can you identify?
☐ Does the title of the story suggest a theme?
☐ Does the narrator, or any character, make statements that express or imply a theme?
☐ In what way does the arrangement of events in the story suggest a theme?
☐ In what way does the central conflict of the story suggest a theme?
☐ How does the point of view shed light on the story's central theme?
☐ Do any symbols suggest a theme?
☐ Do any characters in the story change in any significant way? Do these changes convey a particular theme?

Glossary Terms

cliché Overused phrase or expression.

plot Way in which the events of the story are arranged. When there is more than one story but one string of events is clearly the most significant, the other stories are called **subplots**. Plot in fiction often follows the pattern of action in drama, rising toward a **climax** and then falling toward a **resolution**.

point of view Perspective from which a story is told. The storyteller may be a major character in the story or a character who witnesses the story's events (*first-person narrator*) or someone who does not figure in the action at all (*third-person narrator*), in which case he or she may know the actions and thoughts of everyone in the story (*omniscient narrator*) or just know some part of these (*limited omniscient narrator*).

theme Central or dominant idea of a work of literature.

18

Fiction for Further Reading

Learning Outcomes

After reading this chapter, you should be able to do the following:

LO1 Appreciate different kinds of fiction

Timeline

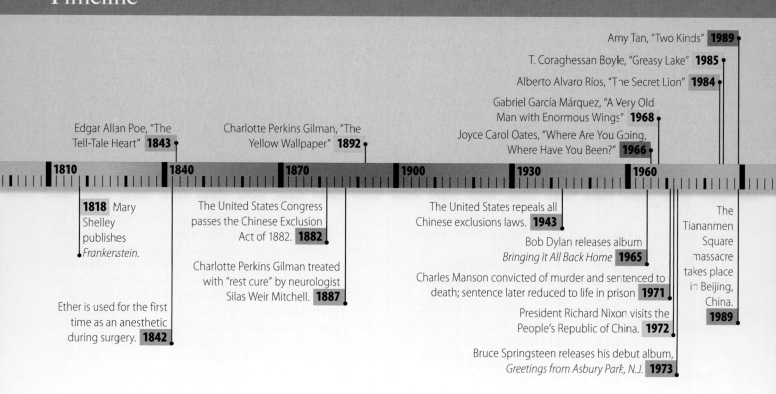

Edgar Allan Poe, "The Tell-Tale Heart" **1843**

Charlotte Perkins Gilman, "The Yellow Wallpaper" **1892**

Joyce Carol Oates, "Where Are You Going, Where Have You Been?" **1966**

Gabriel García Márquez, "A Very Old Man with Enormous Wings" **1968**

Alberto Alvaro Ríos, "The Secret Lion" **1984**

T. Coraghessan Boyle, "Greasy Lake" **1985**

Amy Tan, "Two Kinds" **1989**

1810 **1840** **1870** **1900** **1930** **1960**

1818 Mary Shelley publishes *Frankenstein.*

Ether is used for the first time as an anesthetic during surgery. **1842**

The United States Congress passes the Chinese Exclusion Act of 1882. **1882**

Charlotte Perkins Gilman treated with "rest cure" by neurologist Silas Weir Mitchell. **1887**

The United States repeals all Chinese exclusions laws. **1943**

Bob Dylan releases album *Bringing It All Back Home* **1965**

Charles Manson convicted of murder and sentenced to death; sentence later reduced to life in prison **1971**

President Richard Nixon visits the People's Republic of China. **1972**

Bruce Springsteen releases his debut album, *Greetings from Asbury Park, N.J.* **1973**

The Tiananmen Square massacre takes place in Beijing, China. **1989**

LO1 Appreciate Different Kinds of Fiction

T. Coraghessan Boyle (1948–)

Greasy Lake (1985)

It's about a mile down on the dark side of Route 88.
—*Bruce Springsteen*

There was a time when courtesy and winning ways went out of style, when it was good to be bad, when you cultivated decadence like a taste. We were all dangerous characters then. We wore torn-up leather jackets, slouched around with toothpicks in our mouths, sniffed glue and ether and what somebody claimed was cocaine. When we wheeled our parents' whining station wagons out into the street we left a patch of rubber half a block long. We drank gin and grape juice, Tango, Thunderbird, and Bali Hai. We were nineteen. We were bad. We read André Gide° and struck elaborate poses to show that we didn't give a shit about anything. At night, we went up to Greasy Lake.

Through the center of town, up the strip, past the housing developments and shopping malls, street lights giving way to the thin streaming illumination of the headlights, trees crowding the asphalt in a black unbroken wall: that was the way out to Greasy Lake. The Indians had called it Wakan, a reference to the clarity of its waters. Now it was fetid and murky, the mud banks glittering with broken glass and strewn with beer cans and the charred remains of bonfires. There was a single ravaged island a hundred yards from shore, so stripped of vegetation it looked as if the air force had strafed it. We went up to the lake because everyone went there, because we wanted to snuff the rich scent of possibility on the breeze, watch a girl take off her clothes and plunge into the festering murk, drink beer, smoke pot, howl at the stars, savor the incongruous full-throated roar of rock and roll against the primeval susurrus° of frogs and crickets. This was nature.

I was there one night, late, in the company of two dangerous characters. Digby wore a gold star in his right ear and allowed his father to pay his tuition at Cornell; Jeff was thinking of quitting school to become a painter/musician/head-shop proprietor. They were both expert in the social graces, quick with a sneer, able to manage a Ford with lousy shocks over a rutted and gutted blacktop road at eighty-five while rolling a joint as compact as a Tootsie Roll Pop stick. They could lounge against a bank of booming speakers and trade "man"s with the best of them or roll out across the dance floor as if their joints worked on bearings. They were slick and quick and they wore their mirror shades at breakfast and dinner, in the shower, in closets and caves. In short, they were bad.

I drove. Digby pounded the dashboard and shouted along with Toots & the Maytals while Jeff hung his head out the window and streaked the side of my mother's Bel Air with vomit. It was early June, the air soft as a hand on your cheek, the third night of summer vacation. The first two nights we'd been out till dawn, looking for something we never found. On this, the third night, we'd cruised the strip sixty-seven times, been in and out of every bar and club we could think of in a twenty-mile radius, stopped twice for bucket chicken and forty-cent hamburgers, debated going to a party at the house of a girl Jeff's sister knew, and chucked two dozen raw eggs at mailboxes and hitchhikers. It was 2:00 A.M.; the bars were closing. There was nothing to do but take a bottle of lemon-flavored gin up to Greasy Lake.

The taillights of a single car winked at us as we swung 5 into the dirt lot with its tufts of weed and washboard corrugations; '57 Chevy, mint, metallic blue. On the far side of the lot, like the exoskeleton of some gaunt chrome insect, a chopper leaned against its kickstand. And that was it for excitement: some junkie half-wit biker and a car freak pumping his girlfriend. Whatever it was we were looking for, we weren't about to find it at Greasy Lake. Not that night.

But then all of a sudden Digby was fighting for the wheel. "Hey, that's Tony Lovett's car! Hey!" he shouted, while I stabbed at the brake pedal and the Bel Air nosed up to the gleaming bumper of the parked Chevy. Digby leaned on the horn, laughing, and instructed me to put my brights on. I flicked on the brights. This was hilarious. A joke. Tony would experience premature withdrawal and expect to be confronted by grim-looking state troopers with flashlights. We hit the horn, strobed the lights, and then jumped out of the car to press our witty faces to Tony's windows; for all we knew we might even catch a glimpse

---

° **André Gide** French novelist and critic (1869–1951) whose work—much of it semiautobiographical—examines the conflict between desire and discipline and shows individuals battling conventional morality.

° **susurrus** A whispering or rustling sound.

> "I was terrified. Blood was beating in my ears, my hands were shaking, my heart turning over like a dirtbike in the wrong gear."

of some little fox's tit, and then we could slap backs with red-faced Tony, roughhouse a little, and go on to new heights of adventure and daring.

The first mistake, the one that opened the whole floodgate, was losing my grip on the keys. In the excitement, leaping from the car with the gin in one hand and a roach clip in the other, I spilled them in the grass—in the dark, rank, mysterious nighttime grass of Greasy Lake. This was a tactical error, as damaging and irreversible in its way as Westmoreland's decision to dig in at Khe Sanh.° I felt it like a jab of intuition, and I stopped there by the open door, peering vaguely into the night that puddled up round my feet.

The second mistake—and this was inextricably bound up with the first—was identifying the car as Tony Lovett's. Even before the very bad character in greasy jeans and engineer boots ripped out of the driver's door, I began to realize that this chrome blue was much lighter than the robin's-egg of Tony's car, and that Tony's car didn't have rear-mounted speakers. Judging from their expressions, Digby and Jeff were privately groping toward the same inevitable and unsettling conclusion as I was.

In any case, there was no reasoning with this bad greasy character—clearly he was a man of action. The first lusty Rockette° kick of his steel-toed boot caught me under the chin, chipped my favorite tooth, and left me sprawled in the dirt. Like a fool, I'd gone down on one knee to comb the stiff hacked grass for the keys, my mind making connections in the most dragged-out, testudineous° way, knowing that things had gone wrong, that I was in a lot of trouble, and that the lost ignition key was my grail and my salvation. The three or four succeeding blows were mainly absorbed by my right buttock and the tough piece of bone at the base of my spine.

Meanwhile, Digby vaulted the kissing bumpers and 10 delivered a savage kung-fu blow to the greasy character's collarbone. Digby had just finished a course in martial arts for phys-ed credit and had spent the better part of the past two nights telling us apocryphal tales of Bruce Lee types and of the raw power invested in lightning blows shot from coiled wrists, ankles, and elbows. The greasy character was unimpressed. He merely backed off a step, his face like a Toltec mask, and laid Digby out with a single whistling roundhouse blow. . . but by now Jeff had got into the act, and I was beginning to extricate myself from the dirt, a tinny compound of shock, rage, and impotence wadded in my throat.

Jeff was on the guy's back, biting at his ear. Digby was on the ground, cursing. I went for the tire iron I kept under the driver's seat. I kept it there because bad characters always keep tire irons under the driver's seat, for just such an occasion as this. Never mind that I hadn't been involved in a fight since sixth grade, when a kid with a sleepy eye and two streams of mucus depending from his nostrils hit me in the knee with a Louisville slugger,° never mind that I'd touched the tire iron exactly twice before, to change tires: it was there. And I went for it.

I was terrified. Blood was beating in my ears, my hands were shaking, my heart turning over like a dirtbike in the wrong gear. My antagonist was shirtless, and a single cord of muscle flashed across his chest as he bent forward to peel Jeff from his back like a wet overcoat. "Motherfucker," he spat, over and over, and I was aware in that instant that all four of us—Digby, Jeff, and myself included—were chanting "motherfucker, motherfucker," as if it were a battle cry. (What happened next? the detective asks the murderer from beneath the turned-down brim of his porkpie hat. I don't know, the murderer says, something came over me. Exactly.)

Digby poked the flat of his hand in the bad character's face and I came at him like a kamikaze, mindless, raging, stung with humiliation—the whole thing, from the initial boot in the chin to this murderous primal instant involving no more than sixty hyperventilating, gland-flooding seconds—I came at him and brought the tire iron down across his ear. The effect was instantaneous, astonishing. He was a stunt man and this was Hollywood, he was a big grimacing toothy balloon and I was a man with a straight pin. He collapsed. Wet his pants. Went loose in his boots.

A single second, big as a zeppelin, floated by. We were standing over him in a circle, gritting our teeth, jerking our necks, our limbs and hands and feet twitching with glandular discharges. No one said anything. We just stared down at the guy, the car freak, the lover, the bad greasy character laid low. Digby looked at me; so did Jeff. I was still holding the tire iron, a tuft of hair clinging to the crook like dandelion fluff, like down. Rattled, I dropped it in the dirt, already envisioning the headlines, the pitted faces of the police inquisitors, the gleam of handcuffs, clank of bars, the big black shadows rising from the back of the cell . . . when suddenly a raw torn

---

° **Khe Sanh** In late 1967, North Vietnamese and Viet Cong forces mounted a strong attack against American troops at Khe Sanh, thereby causing General William C. Westmoreland, commander of United States forces in Vietnam, to "dig in" to defend an area of relatively little tactical importance.

° **Rockette** The reference is to the Rockettes, a dance troupe at New York's Radio City Music Hall noted for precision and cancan-like high kicks.

° **testudineous** Slow, like the pace of a tortoise.

° **Louisville slugger** A popular brand of baseball bat.

shriek cut through me like all the juice in all the electric chairs in the country.

It was the fox. She was short, barefoot, dressed in panties and a man's shirt. "Animals!" she screamed, running at us with her fists clenched and wisps of blow-dried hair in her face. There was a silver chain round her ankle, and her toenails flashed in the glare of the headlights. I think it was the toenails that did it. Sure, the gin and the cannabis and even the Kentucky Fried may have had a hand in it, but it was the sight of those flaming toes that set us off—the toad emerging from the loaf in *Virgin Spring*,° lipstick smeared on a child: she was already tainted. We were on her like Bergman's deranged brothers—see no evil, hear none, speak none—panting, wheezing, tearing at her clothes, grabbing for flesh. We were bad characters, and we were scared and hot and three steps over the line—anything could have happened.

It didn't.

Before we could pin her to the hood of the car, our eyes masked with lust and greed and the purest primal badness, a pair of headlights swung into the lot. There we were, dirty, bloody, guilty, dissociated from humanity and civilization, the first of the Ur-crimes° behind us, the second in progress, shreds of nylon panty and spandex brassiere dangling from our fingers, our flies open, lips licked—there we were, caught in the spotlight. Nailed.

We bolted. First for the car, and then, realizing we had no way of starting it, for the woods. I thought nothing. I thought escape. The headlights came at me like accusing fingers. I was gone.

Ram-bam-bam, across the parking lot, past the chopper and into the feculent undergrowth at the lake's edge, insects flying up in my face, weeds whipping, frogs and snakes and red-eyed turtles splashing off into the night: I was already ankle-deep in muck and tepid water and still going strong. Behind me, the girl's screams rose in intensity, disconsolate, incriminating, the screams of the Sabine women,° the Christian martyrs, Anne Frank° dragged from the garret. I kept going, pursued by those cries, imagining cops and bloodhounds. The water was up to my knees when I realized what I was doing: I was going to swim for it. Swim the breadth of Greasy Lake and hide

myself in the thick clot of woods on the far side. They'd never find me there.

I was breathing in sobs, in gasps. The water lapped at my waist as I looked out over the moon-burnished ripples, the mats of algae that clung to the surface like scabs. Digby and Jeff had vanished. I paused. Listened. The girl was quieter now, screams tapering to sobs, but there were male voices, angry, excited, and the high-pitched ticking of the second car's engine. I waded deeper, stealthy, hunted, the ooze sucking at my sneakers. As I was about to take the plunge—at the very instant I dropped my shoulder for the first slashing stroke—I blundered into something. Something unspeakable, obscene, something soft, wet, moss-grown. A patch of weed? A log? When I reached out to touch it, it gave like a rubber duck, it gave like flesh.

In one of those nasty little epiphanies for which we are prepared by films and TV and childhood visits to the funeral home to ponder the shrunken painted forms of dead grandparents, I understood what it was that bobbed there so inadmissibly in the dark. Understood, and stumbled back in horror and revulsion, my mind yanked in six different directions (I was nineteen, a mere child, an infant, and here in the space of five minutes I'd struck down one greasy character and blundered into the water-logged carcass of a second), thinking, The keys, the keys, why did I have to go and lose the keys? I stumbled back, but the muck took hold of my feet—a sneaker snagged, balance lost—and suddenly I was pitching face forward into the buoyant black mass, throwing out my hands in desperation while simultaneously conjuring the image of reeking frogs and muskrats revolving in slicks of their own deliquescing° juices. AAAAArrrgh! I shot from the water like a torpedo, the dead man rotating to expose a mossy beard and eyes cold as the moon. I must have shouted out, thrashing around in the weeds, because the voices behind me suddenly became animated.

"What was that?"

"It's them, it's them: they tried to, tried to . . . *rape* me!" Sobs.

A man's voice, flat Midwestern accent. "You sons a bitches, we'll kill you!"

Frogs, crickets.

Then another voice, harsh, *r*-less, Lower East Side: "Motherfucker!" I recognized the verbal virtuosity of the bad greasy character in the engineer boots. Tooth chipped, sneakers gone, coated in mud and slime and worse, crouching breathless in the weeds waiting to have my ass thoroughly and definitively kicked and fresh from the hideous stinking embrace of a three-days-dead-corpse, I suddenly felt a rush of joy and vindication: the son of a bitch was alive! Just as quickly, my bowels turned to ice. "Come on out of there, you pansy mothers!" the bad greasy character was screaming. He shouted curses till he was out of breath.

The crickets started up again, then the frogs. I held my breath. All at once there was a sound in the reeds, a swishing, a splash: thunk-a-thunk. They were throwing rocks. The frogs fell silent. I cradled my head. Swish, swish,

---

° ***Virgin Spring*** A film by Swedish director Ingmar Bergman.

° **Ur-crimes** Primitive crimes.

° **Sabine women** According to legend, members of an ancient Italian tribe abducted by Romans who took them for wives. The "Rape of the Sabine Women" has been depicted by various artists, most notably by seventeenth-century French painter Nicolas Poussin.

° **Anne Frank** German Jewish girl (1929–1945) whose family hid in an attic in Amsterdam during the Nazi occupation of the Netherlands. Frank, who along with her family was eventually sent to die at the concentration camp at Belsen, is famous for her diary, which recounts her days in hiding. A new version of the diary containing five missing pages surfaced in 1998.

° **deliquescing** Melting.

thunk-a-thunk. A wedge of feldspar the size of a cue ball glanced off my knee. I bit my finger.

It was then that they turned to the car. I heard a door slam, a curse, and then the sound of the headlights shattering—almost a good-natured sound, celebratory, like corks popping from the necks of bottles. This was succeeded by the dull booming of the fenders, metal on metal, and then the icy crash of the windshield. I inched forward, elbows and knees, my belly pressed to the muck, thinking of guerrillas and commandos and *The Naked and the Dead.*° I parted the weeds and squinted the length of the parking lot.

The second car—it was a Trans-Am—was still running, its high beams washing the scene in a lurid stagy light. Tire iron flailing, the greasy bad character was laying into the side of my mother's Bel Air like an avenging demon, his shadow riding up the trunks of the trees. Whomp. Whomp. Whomp-whomp. The other two guys—blond types, in fraternity jackets—were helping out with tree branches and skull-sized boulders. One of them was gathering up bottles, rocks, muck, candy wrappers, used condoms, pop-tops, and other refuse and pitching it through the window on the driver's side. I could see the fox, a white bulb behind the windshield of the '57 Chevy. "Bobbie," she whined over the thumping, "come *on.*" The greasy character paused a moment, took one good swipe at the left taillight, and then heaved the tire iron halfway across the lake. Then he fired up the '57 and was gone.

Blond head nodded at blond head. One said some- 30 thing to the other, too low for me to catch. They were no doubt thinking that in helping to annihilate my mother's car they'd committed a fairly rash act, and thinking too that there were three bad characters connected with that very car watching them from the woods. Perhaps other possibilities occurred to them as well—police, jail cells, justices of the peace, reparations, lawyers, irate parents, fraternal censure. Whatever they were thinking, they suddenly dropped branches, bottles, and rocks and sprang for their car in unison, as if they'd choreographed it. Five seconds. That's all it took. The engine shrieked, the tires squealed, a cloud of dust rose from the rutted lot and then settled back on darkness.

I don't know how long I lay there, the bad breath of decay all around me, my jacket heavy as a bear, the primordial ooze subtly reconstituting itself to accommodate my upper thighs and testicles. My jaws ached, my knee throbbed, my coccyx° was on fire. I contemplated suicide, wondered if I'd need bridgework, scraped the recesses of my brain for some sort of excuse to give my parents—a tree had fallen on the car, I was blindsided by a bread truck, hit and run, vandals had got to it while we were playing chess at Digby's. Then I thought of the dead man. He was probably the only person on the planet worse off than I was. I thought about him, fog on the lake, insects chirring eerily, and felt the tug of fear, felt the darkness opening up inside me like a set of jaws. Who was he, I wondered, this victim of time and circumstance bobbing sorrowfully in the lake

at my back. The owner of the chopper, no doubt, a bad older character come to this. Shot during a murky drug deal, drowned while drunkenly frolicking in the lake. Another headline. My car was wrecked; he was dead.

When the eastern half of the sky went from black to cobalt and the trees began to separate themselves from the shadows, I pushed myself up from the mud and stepped out into the open. By now the birds had begun to take over for the crickets, and dew lay slick on the leaves. There was a smell in the air, raw and sweet at the same time, the smell of the sun firing buds and opening blossoms. I contemplated the car. It lay there like a wreck along the highway, like a steel sculpture left over from a vanished civilization. Everything was still. This was nature.

I was circling the car, as dazed and bedraggled as the sole survivor of an air blitz, when Digby and Jeff emerged from the trees behind me. Digby's face was crosshatched with smears of dirt; Jeff's jacket was gone and his shirt was torn across the shoulder. They slouched across the lot, looking sheepish, and silently came up beside me to gape at the ravaged automobile. No one said a word. After a while Jeff swung open the driver's door and began to scoop the broken glass and garbage off the seat. I looked at Digby. He shrugged. "At least they didn't slash the tires," he said.

It was true: the tires were intact. There was no windshield, the headlights were staved in, and the body looked as if it had been sledgehammered for a quarter a shot at the county fair, but the tires were inflated to regulation pressure. The car was drivable. In silence, all three of us bent to scrape the mud and shattered glass from the interior. I said nothing about the biker. When we were finished, I reached in my pocket for the keys, experienced a nasty stab of recollection, cursed myself, and turned to search the grass. I spotted them almost immediately, no more than five feet from the open door, glinting like jewels in the first tapering shaft of sunlight. There was no reason to get philosophical about it: I eased into the seat and turned the engine over.

It was at that precise moment that the silver Mustang 35 with the flame decals rumbled into the lot. All three of us froze; then Digby and Jeff slid into the car and slammed

---

° ***The Naked and the Dead*** A popular and critically praised 1948 novel by Norman Mailer depicting United States Army life during World War II.

° **coccyx** Tailbone.

> "Then I thought of the dead man. He was probably the only person on the planet worse off than I was."

the door. We watched as the Mustang rocked and bobbed across the ruts and finally jerked to a halt beside the forlorn chopper at the far end of the lot. "Let's go," Digby said. I hesitated, the Bel Air wheezing beneath me.

Two girls emerged from the Mustang. Tight jeans, stiletto heels, hair like frozen fur. They bent over the motorcycle, paced back and forth aimlessly, glanced once or twice at us, and then ambled over to where the reeds sprang up in a green fence round the perimeter of the lake. One of them cupped her hands to her mouth. "Al," she called, "Hey, Al!"

"Come on," Digby hissed. "Let's get out of here."

But it was too late. The second girl was picking her way across the lot, unsteady on her heels, looking up at us and then away. She was older—twenty-five or -six—and as she came closer we could see there was something wrong with her: she was stoned or drunk, lurching now and waving her arms for balance. I gripped the steering wheel as if it were the ejection lever of a flaming jet, and Digby spat out my name, twice, terse and impatient.

"Hi," the girl said.

We looked at her like zombies, like war veterans, like 40 deaf-and-dumb pencil peddlers.

She smiled, her lips cracked and dry. "Listen," she said, bending from the waist to look in the window, "you guys seen Al?" Her pupils were pinpoints, her eyes glass. She jerked her neck. "That's his bike over there—Al's. You seen him?"

Al. I didn't know what to say. I wanted to get out of the car and retch, I wanted to go home to my parents' house and crawl into bed. Digby poked me in the ribs. "We haven't seen anybody," I said.

The girl seemed to consider this, reaching out a slim veiny arm to brace herself against the car. "No matter," she said, slurring the *t*'s, "he'll turn up." And then, as if she'd just taken stock of the whole scene—the ravaged car and our battered faces, the desolation of the place— she said: "Hey, you guys look like some pretty bad characters—been fightin', huh?" We stared straight ahead, rigid as catatonics. She was fumbling in her pocket and muttering something. Finally she held out a handful of tablets in glassine wrappers: "Hey, you want to party, you want to do some of these with me and Sarah?"

I just looked at her. I thought I was going to cry. Digby broke the silence. "No, thanks," he said, leaning over me. "Some other time."

I put the car in gear and it inched forward with a 45 groan, shaking off pellets of glass like an old dog shedding water after a bath, heaving over the ruts on its worn springs, creeping toward the highway. There was a sheen of sun on the lake. I looked back. The girl was still standing there, watching us, her shoulders slumped, hand outstretched.

*　　*　　*

Gabriel García Márquez (1928–   )

A Very Old Man with Enormous Wings (1968)

A Tale for Children

Translated from the Spanish by Gregory Rabassa

On the third day of rain they had killed so many crabs inside the house that Pelayo had to cross his drenched courtyard and throw them into the sea, because the newborn child had a temperature all night and they thought it was due to the stench. The world had been sad since Tuesday. Sea and sky were a single ash-gray thing and the sands of the beach, which on March nights glimmered like powdered light, had become a stew of mud and rotten shellfish. The light was so weak at noon that when Pelayo was coming back to the house after throwing away the crabs, it was hard for him to see what it was that was moving and groaning in the rear of the courtyard. He had to go very close to see that it was an old man, a very old man, lying face down in the mud, who, in spite of his tremendous efforts, couldn't get up, impeded by his enormous wings.

Frightened by that nightmare, Pelayo ran to get Elisenda, his wife, who was putting compresses on the sick child, and he took her to the rear of the courtyard. They both looked at the fallen body with mute stupor. He was dressed like a ragpicker.° There were only a few faded hairs left on his bald skull and very few teeth in his mouth, and his pitiful condition of a drenched great-grandfather had taken away any sense of grandeur he might have had. His huge buzzard wings, dirty and half-plucked, were forever entangled in the mud. They looked at him so long and so closely that Pelayo and Elisenda very soon overcame their surprise and in the end found him familiar. Then they dared speak to him, and he answered in an incomprehensible dialect with a strong sailor's voice. That was how they skipped over the inconvenience of the wings and quite intelligently concluded that he was a lonely

---

° **ragpicker** Someone who makes a living collecting rags and other refuse.

> *"On the following day everyone knew that a flesh-and-blood angel was held captive in Pelayo's house."*

castaway from some foreign ship wrecked by the storm. And yet, they called in a neighbor woman who knew everything about life and death to see him, and all she needed was one look to show them their mistake.

"He's an angel," she told them. "He must have been coming for the child, but the poor fellow is so old that the rain knocked him down."

On the following day everyone knew that a flesh-and-blood angel was held captive in Pelayo's house. Against the judgment of the wise neighbor woman, for whom angels in those times were the fugitive survivors of a celestial conspiracy, they did not have the heart to club him to death. Pelayo watched over him all afternoon from the kitchen, armed with his bailiff's club, and before going to bed he dragged him out of the mud and locked him up with the hens in the wire chicken coop. In the middle of the night, when the rain stopped, Pelayo and Elisenda were still killing crabs. A short time afterward the child woke up without a fever and with a desire to eat. Then they felt magnanimous and decided to put the angel on a raft with fresh water and provisions for three days and leave him to his fate on the high seas. But when they went out into the courtyard with the first light of dawn, they found the whole neighborhood in front of the chicken coop having fun with the angel, without the slightest reverence, tossing him things to eat through the openings in the wire as if he weren't a supernatural creature but a circus animal.

Father Gonzaga arrived before seven o'clock, 5 alarmed by the strange news. By that time onlookers less frivolous than those at dawn had already arrived and they were making all kinds of conjectures concerning the captive's future. The simplest among them thought that he should be named mayor of the world. Others of sterner mind felt that he should be promoted to the rank of five-star general in order to win all wars. Some visionaries hoped that he could be put to stud in order to implant on earth a race of winged wise men who could take charge of the universe. But Father Gonzaga, before becoming a priest, had been a robust woodcutter. Standing by the wire, he reviewed his catechism° in an instant and asked them to open the door so that he could take a close look at that pitiful man who looked more like a huge decrepit hen among the fascinated chickens. He was lying in a corner drying his open wings in the sunlight among the fruit peels and breakfast leftovers that the early risers had thrown him. Alien to the impertinences of the world, he only lifted his antiquarian° eyes and murmured something in his dialect when Father Gonzaga went into the chicken coop and said good morning to him in Latin. The parish priest had his first suspicion of an imposter when he saw that he did not understand the language of God or know how to greet His ministers. Then he noticed that seen close up he was much too human; he had an unbearable smell of the outdoors, the back side of his wings was strewn with parasites and his main feathers had been mistreated by terrestrial winds, and nothing about him measured up to the proud dignity of angels. Then he came out of the chicken coop and in a brief sermon warned the curious against the risks of being ingenuous. He reminded them that the devil had the bad habit of making use of carnival tricks in order to confuse the unwary. He argued that if wings were not the essential element in determining the difference between a hawk and an airplane, they were even less so in the recognition of angels. Nevertheless, he promised to write a letter to his bishop so that the latter would write to his primate so that the latter would write to the Supreme Pontiff° in order to get the final verdict from the highest courts.

His prudence fell on sterile hearts. The news of the captive angel spread with such rapidity that after a few hours the courtyard had the bustle of a marketplace and they had to call in troops with fixed bayonets to disperse the mob that was about to knock the house down. Elisenda, her spine all twisted from sweeping up so much marketplace trash, then got the idea of fencing in the yard and charging five cents admission to see the angel.

The curious came from far away. A traveling carnival arrived with a flying acrobat who buzzed over the crowd several times, but no one paid any attention to him because his wings were not those of an angel but, rather, those of a sidereal° bat. The most unfortunate invalids on earth came in search of health: a poor woman who since childhood had been counting her heartbeats and had run out of numbers; a Portuguese man who couldn't sleep because the noise of the stars disturbed him; a sleepwalker who got up at night to undo the things he had done while awake; and many others with less serious ailments. In the midst of that shipwreck disorder that made the earth tremble, Pelayo and Elisenda were happy with fatigue, for in less than a week they had crammed their rooms with money and the line of pilgrims waiting their turn to enter still reached beyond the horizon.

The angel was the only one who took no part in his own act. He spent his time trying to get comfortable in his borrowed nest, befuddled by the hellish heat of the oil lamps and sacramental candles that had been placed along the wire. At first they tried to make him eat some mothballs,

---

° **catechism** A book that summarizes the doctrines of Roman Catholicism in question-and-answer form.

° **antiquarian** Ancient.

° **the Supreme Pontiff** The pope.

° **sidereal** Relating to the stars.

which, according to the wisdom of the wise neighbor woman, were the food prescribed for angels. But he turned them down, just as he turned down the papal lunches that the penitents brought him, and they never found out whether it was because he was an angel or because he was an old man that in the end he ate nothing but eggplant mush. His only supernatural virtue seemed to be patience. Especially during the first days, when the hens pecked at him, searching for the stellar parasites that proliferated in his wings, and the cripples pulled out feathers to touch their defective parts with, and even the most merciful threw stones at him, trying to get him to rise so they could see him standing. The only time they succeeded in arousing him was when they burned his side with an iron for branding steers, for he had been motionless for so many hours that they thought he was dead. He awoke with a start, ranting in his hermetic° language and with tears in his eyes, and he flapped his wings a couple of times, which brought on a whirlwind of chicken dung and lunar dust and a gale of panic that did not seem to be of this world. Although many thought that his reaction had been one not of rage but of pain, from then on they were careful not to annoy him, because the majority understood that his passivity was not that of a hero taking his ease but that of a cataclysm in repose.

Father Gonzaga held back the crowd's frivolity with formulas of maid-servant inspiration while awaiting the arrival of a final judgment on the nature of the captive. But the mail from Rome showed no sense of urgency. They spent their time finding out if the prisoner had a navel, if his dialect had any connection with Aramaic,° how many times he could fit on the head of a pin, or whether he wasn't just a Norwegian with wings. Those meager letters might have come and gone until the end of time if a providential event had not put an end to the priest's tribulations.

It so happened that during those days, among so many other carnival attractions, there arrived in town the traveling show of the woman who had been changed into a spider for having disobeyed her parents. The admission to see her was not only less than the admission to see the angel, but people were permitted to ask her all manner of questions about her absurd state and to examine her up and down so that no one would ever doubt the truth of her horror. She was a frightful tarantula the size of a ram and with the head of a sad maiden. What was most heart-rending, however, was not her outlandish shape but the sincere affliction with which she recounted the details of her misfortune. While still practically a child she had sneaked out of her parents' house to go to a dance, and while she was coming back through the woods after having danced all night without permission, a fearful thunderclap rent the sky in two and through the crack came the lightning bolt of brimstone that changed her into a spider. Her only nourishment came from the meatballs that charitable souls chose to toss into her mouth. A spectacle like that, full of so much human truth and with such a fearful lesson, was bound to defeat without even trying that of a haughty angel who scarcely deigned to look at mortals. Besides, the few miracles attributed to the angel showed a certain mental disorder, like the blind man who didn't recover his sight but grew three new teeth, or the paralytic who didn't get to walk but almost won the lottery, and the leper whose sores sprouted sunflowers. Those consolation miracles, which were more like mocking fun, had already ruined the angel's reputation when the woman who had been changed into a spider finally crushed him completely. That was how Father Gonzaga was cured forever of his insomnia and Pelayo's courtyard went back to being as empty as during the time it had rained for three days and crabs walked through the bedrooms.

The owners of the house had no reason to lament. With the money they saved they built a two-story mansion with balconies and gardens and high netting so that crabs wouldn't get in during the winter, and with iron bars on the windows so that angels wouldn't get in. Pelayo also set up a rabbit warren close to town and gave up his job as bailiff for good, and Elisenda bought some satin pumps with high heels and many dresses of iridescent silk, the kind worn on Sunday by the most desirable women in those times. The chicken coop was the only thing that didn't receive any attention. If they washed it down with creolin° and burned tears of myrrh° inside it every so often, it was not in homage to the angel but to drive away the dungheap stench that still hung everywhere like a ghost and was turning the new house into an old one. At first, when the child learned to walk, they were careful that he not get too close to the chicken coop. But then they began to lose their fears and got used to the smell, and before the child got his second teeth he'd gone inside the chicken coop to play, where the wires were falling apart. The angel was no less standoffish with him than with other mortals, but he tolerated the most ingenious infamies with the patience of a dog who had no illusions. They both came down with chicken pox at the same time. The doctor who took care of the child couldn't resist the temptation to listen to the angel's heart, and he found so much whistling in the heart and so many sounds in his kidneys that it seemed impossible for him to be alive. What surprised him most, however, was the logic of his wings. They seemed so natural on that completely human organism that he couldn't understand why other men didn't have them too.

When the child began school it had been some time since the sun and rain had caused the collapse of the

---

°**hermetic** Occult, magical.

°**Aramaic** An all-but-extinct ancient Middle Eastern language believed to have been the language spoken by Jesus.

°**creolin** A disinfectant.

°**myrrh** A type of incense.

chicken coop. The angel went dragging himself about here and there like a stray dying man. They would drive him out of the bedroom with a broom and a moment later find him in the kitchen. He seemed to be in so many places at the same time that they grew to think that he'd been duplicated, that he was reproducing himself all through the house, and the exasperated and unhinged Elisenda shouted that it was awful living in that hell full of angels. He could scarcely eat and his antiquarian eyes had also become so foggy that he went about bumping into posts. All he had left were the bare cannulae° of his last feathers. Pelayo threw a blanket over him and extended him the charity of letting him sleep in the shed, and only then did they notice that he had a temperature at night, and was delirious with the tongue twisters of an old Norwegian. That was one of the few times they became alarmed, for they thought he was going to die and not even the wise neighbor woman had been able to tell them what to do with dead angels.

And yet he not only survived his worst winter, but seemed improved with the first sunny days. He remained motionless for several days in the farthest corner of the courtyard, where no one would see him, and at the beginning of December some large, stiff feathers began to grow on his wings, the feathers of a scarecrow, which looked more like another misfortune of decrepitude. But he must

have known the reason for those changes, for he was quite careful that no one should notice them, that no one should hear the sea chanteys that he sometimes sang under the stars. One morning Elisenda was cutting some bunches of onions for lunch when a wind that seemed to come from the high seas blew into the kitchen. Then she went to the window and caught the angel in his first attempts at flight. They were so clumsy that his fingernails opened a furrow in the vegetable patch and he was on the point of knocking the shed down with the ungainly flapping that slipped on the light and couldn't get a grip on the air. But he did manage to gain altitude. Elisenda let out a sigh of relief, for herself and for him, when she saw him pass over the last houses, holding himself up in some way with the risky flapping of a senile vulture. She kept watching him even when she was through cutting the onions and she kept on watching until it was no longer possible for her to see him, because then he was no longer an annoyance in her life but an imaginary dot on the horizon of the sea.

*　　*　　*

°**cannulae** Quills.

Charlotte Perkins Gilman (1860–1935)

The Yellow Wallpaper (1892)

It is very seldom that mere ordinary people like John and myself secure ancestral halls for the summer.

A colonial mansion, a hereditary estate, I would say a haunted house, and reach the height of romantic felicity—but that would be asking too much of fate!

Still I will proudly declare that there is something queer about it.

Else, why should it be let so cheaply? And why have stood so long untenanted?

John laughs at me, of course, but one expects that in 5 marriage.

John is practical in the extreme. He has no patience with faith, an intense horror of superstition, and he scoffs openly at any talk of things not to be felt and seen and put down in figures.

John is a physician, and *perhaps*—(I would not say it to a living soul, of course, but this is dead paper and a great relief to my mind—) *perhaps* that is one reason I do not get well faster.

You see he does not believe I am sick!

And what can one do?

If a physician of high standing, and one's own husband, 10 assures friends and relatives that there is really nothing the matter with one but temporary nervous depression—a slight hysterical tendency—what is one to do?

My brother is also a physician, and also of high standing, and he says the same thing.

So I take phosphates or phosphites°—whichever it is, and tonics, and journeys, and air, and exercise, and am absolutely forbidden to "work" until I am well again.

Personally, I disagree with their ideas.

Personally, I believe that congenial work, with excitement and change, would do me good.

°**phosphates or phosphites** The narrator means "phosphate," a carbonated beverage of water, flavoring, and a small amount of phosphoric acid.

But what is one to do? 15

I did write for a while in spite of them; but it *does* exhaust me a good deal—having to be so sly about it, or else meet with heavy opposition.

I sometimes fancy that in my condition if I had less opposition and more society and stimulus—but John says the very worst thing I can do is to think about my condition, and I confess it always makes me feel bad.

So I will let it alone and talk about the house.

The most beautiful place! It is quite alone, standing well back from the road, quite three miles from the village. It makes me think of English places that you read about, for there are hedges and walls and gates that lock, and lots of separate little houses for the gardeners and people.

There is a *delicious* garden! I never saw such a gar- 20 den—large and shady, full of box-bordered paths, and lined with long grape-covered arbors with seats under them.

There were greenhouses, too, but they are all broken now.

There was some legal trouble, I believe, something about the heirs and co-heirs; anyhow, the place has been empty for years.

That spoils my ghostliness, I am afraid, but I don't care—there is something strange about the house—I can feel it.

I even said so to John one moonlight evening, but he said what I felt was a *draught,* and shut the window.

I get unreasonably angry with John sometimes. I'm 25 sure I never used to be so sensitive. I think it is due to this nervous condition.

But John says if I feel so, I shall neglect proper self-control; so I take pains to control myself—before him, at least, and that makes me very tired.

I don't like our room a bit. I wanted one downstairs that opened on the piazza and had roses all over the window, and such pretty old-fashioned chintz hangings! But John would not hear of it.

He said there was only one window and not room for two beds, and no near room for him if he took another.

He is very careful and loving, and hardly lets me stir without special direction.

I have a schedule prescription for each hour in the 30 day; he takes all care from me, and so I feel basely ungrateful not to value it more.

He said we came here solely on my account, that I was to have perfect rest and all the air I could get. "Your exercise depends on your strength, my dear," said he, "and your food somewhat on your appetite; but air you can absorb all the time." So we took the nursery at the top of the house.

It is a big, airy room, the whole floor nearly, with windows that look all ways, and air and sunshine galore. It was nursery first and then playroom and gymnasium, I should judge; for the windows are barred for little children, and there are rings and things in the walls.

The paint and paper look as if a boys' school had used it. It is stripped off—the paper—in great patches all around the head of my bed, about as far as I can reach, and in a great place on the other side of the room low down. I never saw a worse paper in my life.

One of those sprawling flamboyant patterns committing every artistic sin.

It is dull enough 35 to confuse the eye in following, pronounced enough to constantly irritate and provoke study, and when you follow the lame uncertain curves for a little distance they suddenly commit suicide—plunge off at outrageous angles, destroy themselves in unheard of contradictions.

The color is repellent, almost revolting; a smouldering unclean yellow, strangely faded by the slow-turning sunlight.

It is a dull yet lurid orange in some places, a sickly sulphur tint in others.

No wonder the children hated it! I should hate it myself if I had to live in this room long.

There comes John, and I must put this away,—he hates to have me write a word.

*   *   *

We have been here two weeks, and I haven't felt like writ- 40 ing before, since that first day.

I am sitting by the window now, up in this atrocious nursery, and there is nothing to hinder my writing as much as I please, save lack of strength.

John is away all day, and even some nights when his cases are serious.

I am glad my case is not serious!

But these nervous troubles are dreadfully depressing.

John does not know how much I really suffer. He knows 45 there is no *reason* to suffer, and that satisfies him.

Of course it is only nervousness. It does weigh on me so not to do my duty in any way!

I meant to be such a help to John, such a real rest and comfort, and here I am a comparative burden already!

Nobody would believe what an effort it is to do what little I am able,—to dress and entertain, and order things.

It is fortunate Mary is so good with the baby. Such a dear baby!

And yet I *cannot* be with him, it makes me so nervous. 50

I suppose John never was nervous in his life. He laughs at me so about this wallpaper!

At first he meant to repaper the room, but afterwards he said that I was letting it get the better of me, and that nothing was worse for a nervous patient than to give way to such fancies.

> "The color is repellent, almost revolting; a smouldering unclean yellow, strangely faded by the slow-turning sunlight."

He said that after the wallpaper was changed it would be the heavy bedstead, and then the barred windows, and then that gate at the head of the stairs, and so on.

"You know the place is doing you good," he said, "and really, dear, I don't care to renovate the house just for a three months' rental."

"Then do let us go downstairs," I said, "there are such pretty rooms there."

Then he took me in his arms and called me a blessed little goose, and said he would go down cellar, if I wished, and have it whitewashed into the bargain.

But he is right enough about the beds and windows and things.

It is an airy and comfortable room as any one need wish, and, of course, I would not be so silly as to make him uncomfortable just for a whim.

I'm really getting quite fond of the big room, all but that horrid paper.

Out of one window I can see the garden, those mysterious deep-shaded arbors, the riotous old-fashioned flowers, and bushes and gnarly trees.

Out of another I get a lovely view of the bay and a little private wharf belonging to the estate. There is a beautiful shaded lane that runs down there from the house. I always fancy I see people walking in these numerous paths and arbors, but John has cautioned me not to give way to fancy in the least. He says that with my imaginative power and habit of story-making, a nervous weakness like mine is sure to lead to all manner of excited fancies, and that I ought to use my will and good sense to check the tendency. So I try.

I think sometimes that if I were only well enough to write a little it would relieve the press of ideas and rest me.

But I find I get pretty tired when I try.

It is so discouraging not to have any advice and companionship about my work. When I get really well, John says we will ask Cousin Henry and Julia down for a long visit; but he says he would as soon put fireworks in my pillowcase as to let me have those stimulating people about now.

I wish I could get well faster.

But I must not think about that. This paper looks to me as if it _knew_ what a vicious influence it had!

There is a recurrent spot where the pattern lolls like a broken neck and two bulbous eyes stare at you upside down.

I get positively angry with the impertinence of it and the everlastingness. Up and down and sideways they crawl, and those absurd, unblinking eyes are everywhere. There is one place where two breadths didn't match, and the eyes go all up and down the line, one a little higher than the other.

I never saw so much expression in an inanimate thing before, and we all know how much expression they have! I used to lie awake as a child and get more entertainment and terror out of blank walls and plain furniture than most children could find in a toy-store.

I remember what a kindly wink the knobs of our big, old bureau used to have, and there was one chair that always seemed like a strong friend.

I used to feel that if any of the other things looked too fierce I could always hop into that chair and be safe.

The furniture in this room is no worse than inharmonious, however, for we had to bring it all from downstairs. I suppose when this was used as a playroom they had to take the nursery things out, and no wonder! I never saw such ravages as the children have made here.

The wallpaper, as I said before, is torn off in spots, and it sticketh closer than a brother—they must have had perseverance as well as hatred.

Then the floor is scratched and gouged and splintered, the plaster itself is dug out here and there, and this great heavy bed which is all we found in the room, looks as if it had been through the wars.

But I don't mind it a bit—only the paper.

There comes John's sister. Such a dear girl as she is, and so careful of me! I must not let her find me writing.

She is a perfect and enthusiastic housekeeper, and hopes for no better profession. I verily believe she thinks it is the writing which made me sick!

But I can write when she is out, and see her a long way off from these windows.

There is one that commands the road, a lovely shaded winding road, and one that just looks off over the country. A lovely country, too, full of great elms and velvet meadows.

This wallpaper has a kind of sub-pattern in a different shade, a particularly irritating one, for you can only see it in certain lights, and not clearly then.

But in the places where it isn't faded and where the sun is just so—I can see a strange, provoking, formless sort of figure, that seems to skulk about behind that silly and conspicuous front design.

There's sister on the stairs!

*   *   *

Well, the Fourth of July is over! The people are all gone and I am tired out. John thought it might do me good to see a little company, so we just had mother and Nellie and the children down for a week.

Of course I didn't do a thing. Jennie sees to everything now.

But it tired me all the same.

John says if I don't pick up faster he shall send me to Weir Mitchell° in the fall.

But I don't want to go there at all. I had a friend who was in his hands once, and she says he is just like John and my brother, only more so!

Besides, it is such an undertaking to go so far.

°**Weir Mitchell** Silas Weir Mitchell (1829–1914) a Philadelphia neurologist-psychologist who introduced the "rest cure" for nervous diseases.

I don't feel as if it was worth while to turn my hand over for anything, and I'm getting dreadfully fretful and querulous.

I cry at nothing, and cry most of the time. 90

Of course I don't when John is here, or anybody else, but when I am alone.

And I am alone a good deal just now. John is kept in town very often by serious cases, and Jennie is good and lets me alone when I want her to.

So I walk a little in the garden or down that lovely lane, sit on the porch under the roses, and lie down up here a good deal.

I'm getting really fond of the room in spite of the wall-paper. Perhaps *because* of the wallpaper.

It dwells in my mind so! 95

I lie here on this great immovable bed—it is nailed down, I believe—and follow that pattern about by the hour. It is as good as gymnastics, I assure you. I start, we'll say, at the bottom, down in the corner over there where it has not been touched, and I determine for the thousandth time that I *will* follow that pointless pattern to some sort of a conclusion.

I know a little of the principle of design, and I know this thing was not arranged on any laws of radiation, or alternation, or repetition, or symmetry, or anything else that I ever heard of.

It is repeated, of course, by the breadths, but not otherwise.

Looked at in one way each breadth stands alone, the bloated curves and flourishes—a kind of "debased Roman-esque" with *delirium tremens°* go waddling up and down in isolated columns of fatuity.

But, on the other hand, they connect diagonally, and 100 the sprawling outlines run off in great slanting waves of optic horror, like a lot of wallowing seaweeds in full chase.

The whole thing goes horizontally, too, at least it seems so, and I exhaust myself in trying to distinguish the order of its going in that direction.

They have used a horizontal breadth for a frieze, and that adds wonderfully to the confusion.

There is one end of the room where it is almost intact, and there, when the crosslights fade and the low sun shines directly upon it, I can almost fancy radiation after all,— the interminable grotesques seems to form around a com-mon center and rush off in headlong plunges of equal dis-traction.

It makes me tired to follow it. I will take a nap I guess.

I don't know why I should write this. 105

I don't want to.

I don't feel able.

And I know John would think it absurd. But I *must* say what I feel and think in some way—it is such a relief!

But the effort is getting to be greater than the relief.

Half the time now I am awfully lazy, and lie down 110 ever so much.

John says I mustn't lose my strength, and has me take cod liver oil and lots of tonics and things, to say nothing of ale and wine and rare meat.

Dear John! He loves me very dearly, and hates to have me sick. I tried to have a real earnest reasonable talk with him the other day, and tell him how I wish he would let me go and make a visit to Cousin Henry and Julia.

But he said I wasn't able to go, nor able to stand it after I got there; and I did not make out a very good case for myself, for I was crying before I had finished.

It is getting to be a great effort for me to think straight. Just this nervous weakness I suppose.

And dear John gathered me up in his arms, and just 115 carried me upstairs and laid me on the bed, and sat by me and read to me till it tired my head.

He said I was his darling and his comfort and all he had, and that I must take care of myself for his sake, and keep well.

He says no one but myself can help me out of it, that I must use my will and self-control and not let any silly fancies run away with me.

There's one comfort, the baby is well and happy, and does not have to occupy this nursery with the horrid wallpaper.

If we had not used it, that blessed child would have! What a fortunate escape! Why, I wouldn't have a child of mine, an impressionable little thing, live in such a room for worlds.

I never thought of it before, but it is lucky that John 120 kept me here after all, I can stand it so much easier than a baby, you see.

Of course I never mention it to them any more—I am too wise,—but I keep watch of it all the same.

There are things in that paper that nobody knows but me, or ever will.

Behind that outside pattern the dim shapes get clearer every day.

It is always the same shape, only very numerous.

And it is like a woman stooping down and creeping 125 about behind that pattern. I don't like it a bit. I wonder—I begin to think—I wish John would take me away from here!

It is so hard to talk with John about my case, because he is so wise, and because he loves me so.

But I tried it last night.

It was moonlight. The moon shines in all around just as the sun does.

I hate to see it sometimes, it creeps so slowly, and al-ways comes in by one window or another.

John was asleep and I hated to waken him, so I kept 130 still and watched the moonlight on that undulating wall-paper till I felt creepy.

The faint figure behind seemed to shake the pattern, just as if she wanted to get out.

I got up softly and went to feel and see if the paper *did* move, and when I came back John was awake.

° **delirium tremens** Mental confusion caused by alcohol poisoning and characterized by physical tremors and hallucinations.

"What is it, little girl?" he said. "Don't go walking about like that—you'll get cold."

I thought it was a good time to talk, so I told him that I really was not gaining here, and that I wished he would take me away.

"Why, darling!" said he, "our lease will be up in three weeks, and I can't see how to leave before. [135]

"The repairs are not done at home, and I cannot possibly leave town just now. Of course if you were in any danger, I could and would, but you really are better, dear, whether you can see it or not. I am a doctor, dear, and I know. You are gaining flesh and color, your appetite is better, I feel really much easier about you."

"I don't weigh a bit more," said I, "nor as much; and my appetite may be better in the evening when you are here, but it is worse in the morning when you are away!"

"Bless her little heart!" said he with a big hug, "she shall be as sick as she pleases! But now let's improve the shining hours by going to sleep, and talk about it in the morning!"

"And you won't go away?" I asked gloomily.

"Why, how can I, dear? It is only three weeks more and [140] then we will take a nice little trip of a few days while Jennie is getting the house ready. Really dear you are better!"

"Better in body perhaps—" I began, and stopped short, for he sat up straight and looked at me with such a stern, reproachful look that I could not say another word.

"My darling," said he, "I beg of you, for my sake and for our child's sake, as well as for your own, that you will never for one instant let that idea enter your mind! There is nothing so dangerous, so fascinating, to a temperament like yours. It is a false and foolish fancy. Can you not trust me as a physician when I tell you so?"

So of course I said no more on that score, and we went to sleep before long. He thought I was asleep first, but I wasn't, and lay there for hours trying to decide whether that front pattern and the back pattern really did move together or separately.

On a pattern like this, by daylight, there is a lack of sequence, a defiance of law, that is a constant irritant to a normal mind.

The color is hideous enough, and unreliable enough, [145] and infuriating enough, but the pattern is torturing.

You think you have mastered it, but just as you get well underway in following, it turns back-somersault and there you are. It slaps you in the face, knocks you down, and tramples upon you. It is like a bad dream.

The outside pattern is a florid arabesque, reminding one of a fungus. If you can imagine a toadstool in joints, an interminable string of toadstools, budding and sprouting in endless convolutions—why, that is something like it.

That is, sometimes!

There is one marked peculiarity about this paper, a thing nobody seems to notice but myself, and that is that it changes as the light changes.

When the sun shoots in through the east window— I [150] always watch for that first long, straight ray—it changes so quickly that I never can quite believe it.

That is why I watch it always.

By moonlight— the moon shines in all night when there is a moon—I wouldn't know it was the same paper.

At night in any kind of light, in twilight, candlelight, lamplight, and worst of all by moonlight, it becomes bars! The outside pattern I mean, and the woman behind it is as plain as can be.

I didn't realize for a long time what the thing was that showed behind, that dim sub-pattern, but now I am quite sure it is a woman.

By daylight she is subdued, quiet. I fancy it is the pat- [155] tern that keeps her so still. It is so puzzling. It keeps me quiet by the hour.

I lie down ever so much now. John says it is good for me, and to sleep all I can.

Indeed he started the habit by making me lie down for an hour after each meal.

It is a very bad habit I am convinced, for you see I don't sleep.

And that cultivates deceit, for I don't tell them I'm awake—O no!

The fact is I am getting a little afraid of John. [160]

He seems very queer sometimes, and even Jennie has an inexplicable look.

It strikes me occasionally, just as a scientific hypothesis,—that perhaps it is the paper!

I have watched John when he did not know I was looking, and come into the room suddenly on the most innocent excuses, and I've caught him several times *looking at the paper!* And Jennie too. I caught Jennie with her hand on it once.

She didn't know I was in the room, and when I asked her in a quiet, a very quiet voice, with the most restrained manner possible, what she was doing with the paper—she turned around as if she had been caught stealing, and looked quite angry—asked me why I should frighten her so!

Then she said that the paper stained everything it [165] touched, that she had found yellow smooches on all my clothes and John's, and she wished we would be more careful!

Did not that sound innocent? But I know she was studying that pattern, and I am determined that nobody shall find it out but myself!

Life is very much more exciting now than it used to be. You see I have something more to expect, to look forward

> *"The color is hideous enough, and unreliable enough, and infuriating enough, but the pattern is torturing."*

to, to watch. I really do eat better, and am more quiet than I was.

John is so pleased to see me improve! He laughed a little the other day, and said I seemed to be flourishing in spite of my wallpaper.

I turned it off with a laugh. I had no intention of telling him it was *because* of the wallpaper—he would make fun of me. He might even want to take me away.

I don't want to leave now until I have found it out. 170 There is a week more, and I think that will be enough.

I'm feeling ever so much better! I don't sleep much at night, for it is so interesting to watch developments; but I sleep a good deal in the daytime.

In the daytime it is tiresome and perplexing.

There are always new shoots on the fungus, and new shades of yellow all over it. I cannot keep count of them, though I have tried conscientiously.

It is the strangest yellow, that wallpaper! It makes me think of all the yellow things I ever saw—not beautiful ones like buttercups, but old foul, bad yellow things.

But there is something else about that paper—the 175 smell! I noticed it the moment we came into the room, but with so much air and sun it was not bad. Now we have had a week of fog and rain, and whether the windows are open or not, the smell is here.

It creeps all over the house.

I find it hovering in the dining-room, skulking in the parlor, hiding in the hall, lying in wait for me on the stairs.

It gets into my hair.

Even when I go to ride, if I turn my head suddenly and surprise it—there is that smell!

Such a peculiar odor, too! I have spent hours in trying 180 to analyze it, to find what it smelled like.

It is not bad—at first, and very gentle, but quite the subtlest, most enduring odor I ever met.

In this damp weather it is awful, I wake up in the night and find it hanging over me.

It used to disturb me at first. I thought seriously of burning the house—to reach the smell.

But now I am used to it. The only thing I can think of that it is like is the *color* of the paper! A yellow smell.

There is a very funny mark on this wall, low down, near 185 the mop-board. A streak that runs round the room. It goes behind every piece of furniture, except the bed, a long, straight, even *smooch*, as if it had been rubbed over and over.

I wonder how it was done and who did it, and what they did it for. Round and round and round—round and round and round!—it makes me dizzy!

I really have discovered something at last.

Through watching so much at night, when it changes so, I have finally found out.

The front pattern *does* move—and no wonder! The woman behind shakes it!

Sometimes I think there are a great many women be- 190 hind, and sometimes only one, and she crawls around fast, and her crawling shakes it all over.

Then in the very bright spots she keeps still, and in the very shady spots she just takes hold of the bars and shakes them hard.

And she is all the time trying to climb through. But nobody could climb through that pattern—it strangles so; I think that is why it has so many heads.

They get through, and then the pattern strangles them off and turns them upside down, and makes their eyes white!

If those heads were covered or taken off it would not be half so bad.

I think that woman gets out in the daytime! 195

And I'll tell you why—privately—I've seen her!

I can see her out of every one of my windows!

It is the same woman, I know, for she is always creeping, and most women do not creep by daylight.

I see her in that long shaded lane, creeping up and down. I see her in those dark grape arbors, creeping all around the garden.

I see her on that long road under the trees, creeping 200 along, and when a carriage comes she hides under the blackberry vines.

I don't blame her a bit. It must be very humiliating to be caught creeping by daylight!

I always lock the door when I creep by daylight. I can't do it at night, for I know John would suspect something at once.

And John is so queer now, that I don't want to irritate him. I wish he would take another room! Besides, I don't want anybody to get that woman out at night but myself.

I often wonder if I could see her out of all the windows at once.

But, turn as fast as I can, I can only see out of one at 205 one time.

And though I always see her, she *may* be able to creep faster than I can turn!

I have watched her sometimes away off in the open country, creeping as fast as a cloud shadow in a high wind.

If only that top pattern could be gotten off from the under one! I mean to try it, little by little.

I have found out another funny thing, but I shan't tell it this time! It does not do to trust people too much.

There are only two more days to get this paper off, 210 and I believe John is beginning to notice. I don't like the look in his eyes.

And I heard him ask Jennie a lot of professional questions about me. She had a very good report to give.

She said I slept a good deal in the daytime.

John knows I don't sleep very well at night, for all I'm so quiet!

He asked me all sorts of questions, too, and pretended to be very loving and kind.

As if I couldn't see through him! 215

Still, I don't wonder he acts so, sleeping under this paper for three months.

It only interests me, but I feel sure John and Jennie are secretly affected by it.

*   *   *

Hurrah! This is the last day, but it is enough. John is to stay in town over night, and won't be out until this evening.

Jennie wanted to sleep with me—the sly thing! But I told her I should undoubtedly rest better for a night all alone.

That was clever, for really I wasn't alone a bit! As soon as it was moon-light and that poor thing began to crawl and shake the pattern, I got up and ran to help her.

I pulled and she shook, I shook and she pulled, and before morning we had peeled off yards of that paper.

A strip about as high as my head and half around the room.

And then when the sun came and that awful pattern began to laugh at me, I declared I would finish it to-day!

We go away to-morrow, and they are moving all my furniture down again to leave things as they were before.

Jennie looked at the wall in amazement, but I told her merrily that I did it out of pure spite at the vicious thing.

She laughed and said she wouldn't mind doing it herself, but I must not get tired.

How she betrayed herself that time!

But I am here, and no person touches this paper but me,—not *alive!*

She tried to get me out of the room—it was too patent! But I said it was so quiet and empty and clean now that I believed I would lie down again and sleep all I could; and not to wake me even for dinner—I would call when I woke.

So now she is gone, and the servants are gone, and the things are gone, and there is nothing left but that great bedstead nailed down, with the canvas mattress we found on it.

We shall sleep downstairs to-night, and take the boat home tomorrow.

I quite enjoy the room, now it is bare again.

How those children did tear about here!

This bedstead is fairly gnawed!

But I must get to work.

I have locked the door and thrown the key down into the front path.

I don't want to go out, and I don't want to have anybody come in, till John comes.

I want to astonish him.

I've got a rope up here that even Jennie did not find. If that woman does get out, and tries to get away, I can tie her!

But I forgot I could not reach far without anything to stand on!

This bed will *not* move!

I tried to lift and push it until I was lame, and then I got so angry I bit off a little piece at one corner—but it hurt my teeth.

Then I peeled off all the paper I could reach standing on the floor. It sticks horribly and the pattern just enjoys it! All those strangled heads and bulbous eyes and waddling fungus growths just shriek with derision!

I am getting angry enough to do something desperate. To jump out of the window would be admirable exercise, but the bars are too strong even to try.

Besides I wouldn't do it. Of course not. I know well enough that a step like that is improper and might be misconstrued.

I don't like to *look* out of the windows even—there are so many of those creeping women, and they creep so fast.

I wonder if they come out of that wallpaper as I did?

But I am securely fastened now by my well-hidden rope—you don't get *me* out in the road there!

I suppose I shall have to get back behind the pattern when it comes night, and that is hard!

It is so pleasant to be out in this great room and creep around as I please!

I don't want to go outside. I won't, even if Jennie asks me to.

For outside you have to creep on the ground, and everything is green instead of yellow.

But here I can creep smoothly on the floor, and my shoulder just fits in that long smooch around the wall, so I cannot lose my way.

Why there's John at the door!

It is no use, young man, you can't open it!

How he does call and pound!

Now he's crying for an axe.

It would be a shame to break down that beautiful door!

"John dear!" said I in the gentlest voice, "the key is down by the front steps, under a plantain leaf!"

That silenced him for a few moments.

Then he said—very quietly indeed, "Open the door, my darling!"

"I can't," said I. "The key is down by the front door under a plantain leaf!"

And then I said it again, several times, very gently and slowly, and said it so often that he had to go and see, and he got it of course, and came in. He stopped short by the door.

"What is the matter?" he cried. "For God's sake, what are you doing!"

I kept on creeping just the same, but I looked at him over my shoulder.

"I've got out at last," said I, "in spite of you and Jane. And I've pulled off most of the paper, so you can't put me back!"

Now why should that man have fainted? But he did, and right across my path by the wall, so that I had to creep over him every time!

Nathaniel Hawthorne (1804–1864)

Young Goodman° Brown (1835)

Young Goodman Brown came forth at sunset, into the street of Salem village, but put his head back, after crossing the threshold, to exchange a parting kiss with his young wife. And Faith, as the wife was aptly named, thrust her own pretty head into the street, letting the wind play with the pink ribbons of her cap, while she called to Goodman Brown.

"Dearest heart," whispered she, softly and rather sadly, when her lips were close to his ear, "prithee, put off your journey until sunrise, and sleep in your own bed tonight. A lone woman is troubled with such dreams and such thoughts, that she's afeard of herself, sometimes. Pray, tarry with me this night, dear husband, of all nights in the year!"

"My love and my Faith," replied young Goodman Brown, "of all nights in the year, this one night must I tarry away from thee. My journey, as thou callest it, forth and back again, must needs be done 'twixt now and sunrise. What, my sweet, pretty wife, dost thou doubt me already, and we but three months married!"

"Then God bless you!" said Faith with the pink ribbons, "and may you find all well, when you come back."

"Amen!" cried Goodman Brown. "Say thy prayers, 5 dear Faith, and go to bed at dusk, and no harm will come to thee."

So they parted; and the young man pursued his way, until, being about to turn the corner by the meeting-house, he looked back and saw the head of Faith still peeping after him, with a melancholy air, in spite of her pink ribbons.

"Poor little Faith!" thought he, for his heart smote him. "What a wretch am I, to leave her on such an errand! She talks of dreams, too. Methought, as she spoke, there was trouble in her face, as if a dream had warned her what work is to be done to-night. But no, no! 't would kill her to think it. Well; she's a blessed angel on earth; and after this one night, I'll cling to her skirts and follow her to Heaven."

With this excellent resolve for the future, Goodman Brown felt himself justified in making more haste on his present evil purpose. He had taken a dreary road, darkened by all the gloomiest trees of the forest, which barely stood aside to let the narrow path creep through, and closed immediately behind. It was as lonely as could be; and there is this peculiarity in such a solitude, that the traveller knows not who may be concealed by the innumerable trunks and the thick boughs overhead; so that, with lonely footsteps, he may yet be passing through an unseen multitude.

"There may be a devilish Indian behind every tree," said Goodman Brown to himself; and he glanced fearfully behind him, as he added, "What if the devil himself should be at my very elbow!"

His head being turned back, he passed a crook of the 10 road, and looking forward again, beheld the figure of a man, in grave and decent attire, seated at the foot of an old tree. He arose at Goodman Brown's approach, and walked onward, side by side with him.

"You are late, Goodman Brown," said he. "The clock of the Old South° was striking, as I came through Boston; and that is full fifteen minutes agone."

"Faith kept me back awhile," replied the young man, with a tremor in his voice, caused by the sudden appearance of his companion, though not wholly unexpected.

It was now deep dusk in the forest, and deepest in that part of it where these two were journeying. As nearly as could be discerned, the second traveller was about fifty years old, apparently in the same rank of life as Goodman Brown, and bearing a considerable resemblance to him, though perhaps more in expression than features. Still, they might have been taken for father and son. And yet, though the elder person was as simply clad as the younger, and as simple in manner too, he had an indescribable air of one who knew the world, and would not have felt abashed at the governor's dinner-table, or in King William's court,° were it possible that his affairs should call him thither. But the only thing about him that could be fixed upon as remarkable, was his staff, which bore the likeness of a great black snake, so curiously wrought, that it might almost be seen to twist and wriggle itself like a living serpent. This, of course, must have been an ocular deception, assisted by the uncertain light.

"Come, Goodman Brown!" cried his fellow-traveller, "this is a dull pace for the beginning of a journey. Take my staff, if you are so soon weary."

"Friend," said the other, exchanging his slow pace for 15 a full stop, "having kept covenant by meeting thee here, it is my purpose now to return whence I came. I have scruples, touching the matter thou wot'st of°."

"Sayest thou so?" replied he of the serpent, smiling apart. "Let us walk on, nevertheless, reasoning as we go, and if I convince thee not, thou shalt turn back. We are but a little way in the forest, yet."

"Too far, too far!" exclaimed the goodman, unconsciously resuming his walk. "My father never went into the woods on such an errand, nor his father before him. We have been a race of honest men and good Christians, since the days of the martyrs. And shall I be the first of the name of Brown that ever took this path and kept—"

"Such company, thou wouldst say," observed the elder person, interrupting his pause. "Well said, Goodman Brown! I have been as well acquainted with your family as

---

° **Goodman** A form of address, similar to *Mr.*, meaning "husband."

° **Old South** Old South Church in Boston, renowned meeting place for American patriots during the Revolution.

° **King William** William III, king of England from 1689 to 1702.

° **wot'st of** Know of.

with ever a one among the Puritans; and that's no trifle to say. I helped your grandfather, the constable, when he lashed the Quaker woman so smartly through the streets of Salem. And it was I that brought your father a pitch-pine knot, kindled at my own hearth, to set fire to an Indian village, in King Philip's war.° They were my good friends, both; and many a pleasant walk have we had along this path, and returned merrily after midnight. I would fain be friends with you, for their sake."

"If it be as thou sayest," replied Goodman Brown, "I marvel they never spoke of these matters. Or, verily, I marvel not, seeing that the least rumor of the sort would have driven them from New England. We are a people of prayer, and good works to boot, and abide no such wickedness."

"Wickedness or not," said the traveller with the twist- 20 ed staff, "I have a very general acquaintance here in New England. The deacons of many a church have drunk the communion wine with me; the selectmen, of divers towns, make me their chairman; and a majority of the Great and General Court are firm supporters of my interest. The governor and I, too—but these are state secrets."

"Can this be so!" cried Goodman Brown, with a stare of amazement at his undisturbed companion. "Howbeit, I have nothing to do with the governor and council; they have their own ways, and are no rule for a simple husbandman like me. But, were I to go on with thee, how should I meet the eye of that good old man, our minister, at Salem village? Oh, his voice would make me tremble, both Sabbath-day and lecture-day!"°

Thus far, the elder traveller had listened with due gravity, but now burst into a fit of irrepressible mirth, shaking himself so violently, that his snakelike staff actually seemed to wriggle in sympathy.

"Ha, ha, ha!" shouted he, again and again; then composing himself, "Well, go on, Goodman Brown, go on; but, prithee, don't kill me with laughing!"

"Well, then, to end the matter at once," said Goodman Brown, considerably nettled, "there is my wife, Faith. It would break her dear little heart; and I'd rather break my own!"

"Nay, if that be the case," answered the other, "e'en go 25 thy ways, Goodman Brown. I would not, for twenty old women like the one hobbling before us, that Faith should come to any harm."

As he spoke, he pointed his staff at a female figure on the path, in whom Goodman Brown recognized a very pious and exemplary dame, who had taught him his catechism in youth, and was still his moral and spiritual adviser, jointly with the minister and Deacon Gookin.

"A marvel, truly, that Goody° Cloyse should be so far in the wilderness, at nightfall!" said he. "But, with your leave, friend, I shall take a cut through the woods, until we have left this Christian woman behind. Being a stranger to you, she might ask whom I was consorting with, and whither I was going."

"Be it so," said his fellow-traveller. "Betake you to the woods, and let me keep the path."

Accordingly, the young man turned aside, but took care to watch his companion, who advanced softly along the road, until he had come within a staff's length of the old dame. She, meanwhile, was making the best of her way, with singular speed for so aged a woman, and mumbling some indistinct words, a prayer, doubtless, as she went. The traveller put forth his staff, and touched her withered neck with what seemed the serpent's tail.

"The devil!" screamed the pious old lady. 30

"Then Goody Cloyse knows her old friend?" observed the traveller, confronting her, and leaning on his writhing stick.

"Ah, forsooth, and is it your worship, indeed?" cried the good dame. "Yea, truly is it, and in the very image of my old gossip, Goodman Brown, the grandfather of the silly fellow that now is. But, would your worship believe it? my broomstick hath strangely disappeared, stolen, as I suspect, by that unhanged witch, Goody Cory, and that, too, when I was all anointed with the juice of smallage and cinque-foil and wolf's bane—"°

"Mingled with fine wheat and the fat of a new-born babe," said the shape of old Goodman Brown.

"Ah, your worship knows the recipe," cried the old lady, cackling aloud. "So, as I was saying, being all ready for the meeting, and no horse to ride on, I made up my mind to foot it; for they tell me there is a nice young man to be taken into communion to-night. But now your good worship will lend me your arm, and we shall be there in a twinkling."

"That can hardly be," answered her friend. "I may not 35 spare you my arm, Goody Cloyse, but here is my staff, if you will."

So saying, he threw it down at her feet, where, perhaps, it assumed life, being one of the rods which its owner

"The traveller put forth his staff, and touched her withered neck with what seemed the serpent's tail. "The devil!" screamed the pious old lady."

° **King Philip's war** A war of Indian resistance led by Metacomet of the Wampanoags, known to the English as "King Philip." The war, intended to halt expansion of English settlers in Massachusetts, collapsed after Metacomet's death in August 1676.

° **lecture-day** The day of the midweek sermon, usually Thursday.

° **Goody** A contraction of "Goodwife," a term of politeness used in addressing a woman of humble station. Goody Cloyse, like Goody Cory and Martha Carrier, who appear later in the story, was one of the Salem "witches" sentenced in 1692.

° **smallage . . . wolf's bane** Plants believed to have magical powers. Smallage is wild celery.

had formerly lent to the Egyptian Magi. Of this fact, however, Goodman Brown could not take cognizance. He had cast his eyes in astonishment, and looking down again, beheld neither Goody Cloyse nor the serpentine staff, but his fellow-traveller alone, who waited for him as calmly as if nothing had happened.

"That old woman taught me my catechism!" said the young man; and there was a world of meaning in this simple comment.

They continued to walk onward, while the elder traveller exhorted his companion to make good speed and persevere in the path, discoursing so aptly, that his arguments seemed rather to spring up in the bosom of his auditor, than to be suggested by himself. As they went he plucked a branch of maple, to serve for a walking-stick, and began to strip it of the twigs and little boughs, which were wet with evening dew. The moment his fingers touched them, they became strangely withered and dried up, as with a week's sunshine. Thus the pair proceeded, at a good free pace, until suddenly, in a gloomy hollow of the road, Goodman Brown sat himself down on the stump of a tree, and refused to go any farther.

"Friend," said he, stubbornly, "my mind is made up. Not another step will I budge on this errand. What if a wretched old woman do choose to go to the devil, when I thought she was going to Heaven! Is that any reason why I should quit my dear Faith, and go after her?"

"You will think better of this by and by," said his acquaintance, composedly. "Sit here and rest yourself awhile; and when you feel like moving again, there is my staff to help you along."

Without more words, he threw his companion the maple stick, and was as speedily out of sight as if he had vanished into the deepening gloom. The young man sat a few moments by the roadside, applauding himself greatly, and thinking with how clear a conscience he should meet the minister, in his morning walk, nor shrink from the eye of good old Deacon Gookin. And what calm sleep would be his, that very night, which was to have been spent so wickedly, but purely and sweetly now, in the arms of Faith! Amidst these pleasant and praiseworthy meditations, Goodman Brown heard the tramp of horses along the road, and deemed it advisable to conceal himself within the verge of the forest, conscious of the guilty purpose that had brought him thither, though now so happily turned from it.

On came the hoof-tramps and the voices of the riders, two grave old voices, conversing soberly as they drew near. These mingled sounds appeared to pass along the road, within a few yards of the young man's hiding-place; but owing, doubtless, to the depth of the gloom, at that particular spot, neither the travellers nor their steeds were visible. Though their figures brushed the small boughs by the wayside, it could not be seen that they intercepted, even for a moment, the faint gleam from the strip of bright sky, athwart which they must have passed. Goodman Brown alternately crouched and stood on tiptoe, pulling aside the branches, and thrusting forth his head as far as he durst, without discerning so much as a shadow. It vexed him the more, because he could have sworn, were such a thing possible, that he recognized the voices of the minister and Deacon Gookin, jogging along quietly, as they were wont to do, when bound to some ordination or ecclesiastical council. While yet within hearing, one of the riders stopped to pluck a switch.

"Of the two, reverend Sir," said the voice like the deacon's, "I had rather miss an ordination dinner than to-night's meeting. They tell me that some of our community are to be here from Falmouth and beyond, and others from Connecticut and Rhode Island; besides several of the Indian powwows, who, after their fashion, know almost as much deviltry as the best of us. Moreover, there is a goodly young woman to be taken into communion."

"Mighty well, Deacon Gookin!" replied the solemn old tones of the minister. "Spur up, or we shall be late. Nothing can be done, you know, until I get on the ground."

The hoofs clattered again, and the voices, talking so strangely in the empty air, passed on through the forest, where no church had ever been gathered, nor solitary Christian prayed. Whither, then, could these holy men be journeying, so deep into the heathen wilderness? Young Goodman Brown caught hold of a tree, for support, being ready to sink down on the ground, faint and over-burthened with the heavy sickness of his heart. He looked up to the sky, doubting whether there really was a Heaven above him. Yet, there was the blue arch, and the stars brightening in it.

"With Heaven above, and Faith below, I will yet stand firm against the devil!" cried Goodman Brown.

While he still gazed upward, into the deep arch of the firmament, and had lifted his hands to pray, a cloud, though no wind was stirring, hurried across the zenith, and hid the brightening stars. The blue sky was still visible, except directly overhead, where this black mass of cloud was sweeping swiftly northward. Aloft in the air, as if from the depths of the cloud, came a confused and doubtful sound of voices. Once, the listener fancied that he could distinguish the accents of townspeople of his own, men and women, both pious and ungodly, many of whom he had met at the communion-table, and had seen others rioting at the tavern. The next moment, so indistinct were the sounds, he doubted whether he had heard aught but the murmur of the old forest, whispering without a wind. Then came a stronger swell of those familiar tones, heard daily in the sunshine, at Salem village, but never, until now, from a cloud at night. There was one voice, of a young woman, uttering lamentations, yet with an uncertain sorrow, and entreating for some favor, which, perhaps, it would grieve her to obtain. And all the unseen multitude, both saints and sinners, seemed to encourage her onward.

"Faith!" shouted Goodman Brown, in a voice of agony and desperation; and the echoes of the forest mocked him, crying—"Faith! Faith!" as if bewildered wretches were seeking her, all through the wilderness.

The cry of grief, rage, and terror was yet piercing the night, when the unhappy husband held his breath for a response. There was a scream, drowned immediately in a louder murmur of voices fading into far-off laughter, as the dark cloud swept away, leaving the clear and silent sky above Goodman Brown. But something fluttered lightly down through the air, and caught on the branch of a tree. The young man seized it and beheld a pink ribbon.

"My Faith is gone!" cried he, after one stupefied mo- 50 ment. "There is no good on earth, and sin is but a name. Come, devil! for to thee is this world given."

And maddened with despair, so that he laughed loud and long, did Goodman Brown grasp his staff and set forth again, at such a rate, that he seemed to fly along the forest path, rather than to walk or run. The road grew wilder and drearier, and more faintly traced, and vanished at length, leaving him in the heart of the dark wilderness, still rushing onward, with the instinct that guides mortal man to evil. The whole forest was peopled with frightful sounds: the creaking of the trees, the howling of wild beasts, and the yell of Indians; while, sometimes, the wind tolled like a distant church bell, and sometimes gave a broad roar around the traveller, as if all Nature was laughing him to scorn. But he was himself the chief horror of the scene, and shrank not from its other horrors.

"Ha! ha! ha!" roared Goodman Brown, when the wind laughed at him. "Let us hear which will laugh loudest! Think not to frighten me with your deviltry! Come witch, come wizard, come Indian powwow, come devil himself! and here comes Goodman Brown. You may as well fear him as he fear you!"

In truth, all through the haunted forest, there could be nothing more frightful than the figure of Goodman Brown. On he flew, among the black pines, brandishing his staff with frenzied gestures, now giving vent to an inspiration of horrid blasphemy, and now shouting forth such laughter, as set all the echoes of the forest laughing like demons around him. The fiend in his own shape is less hideous, than when he rages in the breast of man. Thus sped the demoniac on his course, until, quivering among the trees, he saw a red light before him, as when the felled trunks and branches of a clearing have been set on fire, and throw up their lurid blaze against the sky, at the hour of midnight. He paused, in a lull of the tempest that had driven him onward, and heard the swell of what seemed a hymn, rolling solemnly from a distance, with the weight of many voices. He knew the tune. It was a familiar one in the choir of the village meeting-house. The verse died heavily away, and was lengthened by a chorus, not of human voices, but of all the sounds of the benighted wilderness, pealing in awful harmony together. Goodman Brown cried out; and his cry was lost to his own ear, by its unison with the cry of the desert.

In the interval of silence, he stole forward, until the light glared full upon his eyes. At one extremity of an open space, hemmed in by the dark wall of the forest, arose a rock, bearing some rude, natural resemblance either to an altar or a pulpit, and surrounded by four blazing pines, their tops aflame, their stems untouched, like candles at an evening meeting. The mass of foliage, that had overgrown the summit of the rock, was all on fire, blazing high into the night, and fitfully illuminating the whole field. Each pendent twig and leafy festoon was in a blaze. As the red light arose and fell, a numerous congregation alternately shone forth, then disappeared in shadow, and again grew, as it were, out of the darkness, peopling the heart of the solitary woods at once.

"A grave and dark-clad company!" quoth Goodman 55 Brown.

In truth, they were such. Among them, quivering to-and-fro, between gloom and splendor, appeared faces that would be seen, next day, at the council-board of the province, and others which, Sabbath after Sabbath, looked devoutly heavenward, and benignantly over the crowded pews, from the holiest pulpits in the land. Some affirm, that the lady of the governor was there. At least, there were high dames well known to her, and wives of honored husbands, and widows a great multitude, and ancient maidens, all of excellent repute, and fair young girls, who trembled lest their mothers should espy them. Either the sudden gleams of light, flashing over the obscure field, bedazzled Goodman Brown, or he recognized a score of the church members of Salem village, famous for their especial sanctity. Good old Deacon Gookin had arrived, and waited at the skirts of that venerable saint, his reverend pastor. But, irreverently consorting with these grave, reputable, and pious people, these elders of the church, these chaste dames and dewy virgins, there were men of dissolute lives and women of spotted fame, wretches given over to all mean and filthy vice, and suspected even of horrid crimes. It was strange to see, that the good shrank not from the wicked, nor were the sinners abashed by the saints. Scattered, also, among their pale-faced enemies, were the Indian priests, or powwows, who had often scared their native forest with more hideous incantations than any known to English witchcraft.

"But, where is Faith?" thought Goodman Brown; and, as hope came into his heart, he trembled.

Another verse of the hymn arose, a slow and mournful strain, such as the pious love, but joined to words which expressed all that our nature can conceive of sin, and darkly hinted at far more. Unfathomable to mere mortals is the lore of fiends. Verse after verse was sung, and still the chorus of the desert swelled between, like the deepest tone of a mighty organ. And, with the final peal of that dreadful anthem, there came a sound, as if the roaring wind, the rushing streams, the howling beasts, and every other voice of the unconverted wilderness were mingling and according with the voice of guilty man, in homage to the prince of all. The four blazing pines threw up a loftier flame, and obscurely discovered shapes and visages of horror on the smoke-wreaths, above the impious assembly. At the same moment, the fire on the rock shot redly forth, and formed a glowing arch above its base, where now appeared a figure. With reverence be it spoken, the apparition bore no slight similitude, both in garb and manner, to some grave divine of the New England churches.

"Bring forth the converts!" cried a voice, that echoed through the field and rolled into the forest.

At the word, Goodman Brown stepped forth from the shadow of the trees, and approached the congregation, with whom he felt a loathful brotherhood, by the sympathy of all that was wicked in his heart. He could have well-nigh sworn, that the shape of his own dead father beckoned him to advance, looking downward from a smoke-wreath, while a woman, with dim features of despair, threw out her hand to warn him back. Was it his mother? But he had no power to retreat one step, nor to resist, even in thought, when the minister and good old Deacon Gookin seized his arms, and led him to the blazing rock. Thither came also the slender form of a veiled female, led between Goody Cloyse, that pious teacher of the catechism, and Martha Carrier, who had received the devil's promise to be queen of hell. A rampant hag was she! And there stood the proselytes, beneath the canopy of fire.

"Welcome, my children," said the dark figure, "to the communion of your race! Ye have found, thus young, your nature and your destiny. My children, look behind you!"

They turned; and flashing forth, as it were, in a sheet of flame, the fiend-worshippers were seen; the smile of welcome gleamed darkly on every visage.

"There," resumed the sable form, "are all whom ye have reverenced from youth. Ye deemed them holier than yourselves, and shrank from your own sin, contrasting it with their lives of righteousness and prayerful aspirations heavenward. Yet, here are they all, in my worshipping assembly! This night it shall be granted you to know their secret deeds; how hoary-bearded elders of the church have whispered wanton words to the young maids of their households; how many a woman, eager for widow's weeds, has given her husband a drink at bedtime, and let him sleep his last sleep in her bosom; how beardless youths have made haste to inherit their father's wealth; and how fair damsels—blush not, sweet ones!—have dug little graves in the garden, and bidden me, the sole guest, to an infant's funeral. By the sympathy of your human hearts for sin, ye shall scent out all the places—whether in church, bedchamber, street, field, or forest—where crime has been committed, and shall exult to behold the whole earth one stain of guilt, one mighty blood-spot. Far more than this! It shall be yours to penetrate, in every bosom, the deep mystery of sin, the fountain of all wicked arts, and which inexhaustibly supplies more evil impulses than human power—than my power, at its utmost!—can make manifest in deeds. And now, my children, look upon each other."

They did so; and, by the blaze of the hell-kindled torches, the wretched man beheld his Faith, and the wife her husband, trembling before that unhallowed altar.

"Lo! there ye stand, my children," said the figure, in a deep and solemn tone, almost sad, with its despairing awfulness, as if his once angelic nature could yet mourn for our miserable race. "Depending upon one another's hearts, ye had still hoped that virtue were not all a dream! Now are ye undeceived!—Evil is the nature of mankind. Evil must be your only happiness. Welcome, again, my children, to the communion of your race!"

"Welcome!" repeated the fiend-worshippers, in one cry of despair and triumph.

And there they stood, the only pair, as it seemed, who were yet hesitating on the verge of wickedness, in this dark world. A basin was hollowed, naturally, in the rock. Did it contain water, reddened by the lurid light? or was it blood? or, perchance, a liquid flame? Herein did the Shape of Evil dip his hand, and prepare to lay the mark of baptism upon their foreheads, that they might be partakers of the mystery of sin, more conscious of the secret guilt of others, both in deed and thought, than they could now be of their own. The husband cast one look at his pale wife, and Faith at him. What polluted wretches would the next glance show them to each other, shuddering alike at what they disclosed and what they saw!

"Faith! Faith!" cried the husband. "Look up to Heaven, and resist the Wicked One!"

Whether Faith obeyed, he knew not. Hardly had he spoken, when he found himself amid calm night and solitude, listening to a roar of the wind, which died heavily away through the forest. He staggered against the rock, and felt it chill and damp, while a hanging twig, that had been all on fire, besprinkled his cheek with the coldest dew.

The next morning, young Goodman Brown came slowly into the street of Salem village staring around him like a bewildered man. The good old minister was taking a walk along the grave-yard, to get an appetite for breakfast and meditate his sermon, and bestowed a blessing, as he passed, on Goodman Brown. He shrank from the venerable saint, as if to avoid an anathema. Old Deacon Gookin was at domestic worship, and the holy words of his prayer were heard through the open window. "What God doth the wizard pray to?" quoth Goodman Brown. Goody Cloyse, that excellent old Christian, stood in the early sunshine, at her own lattice, catechising a little girl, who had brought her a pint of morning's milk. Goodman Brown snatched away the child, as from the grasp of the fiend himself. Turning the corner by the meeting-house, he spied the head of Faith, with the pink ribbons, gazing anxiously forth, and bursting into such joy at sight of him that she skipt along the street, and almost kissed her husband before the whole village. But Goodman Brown looked sternly and sadly into her face, and passed on without a greeting.

Had Goodman Brown fallen asleep in the forest, and only dreamed a wild dream of a witch-meeting?

Be it so, if you will. But, alas! it was a dream of evil omen for young Goodman Brown. A stern, a sad, a darkly meditative, a distrustful, if not a desperate man did he become, from the night of that fearful dream. On the Sabbath day, when the congregation were singing a holy psalm, he could not listen, because an anthem of sin rushed loudly upon his ear, and drowned all the blessed strain. When the minister spoke from the pulpit, with power and fervid eloquence, and with his hand on the open Bible, of the sacred truths of our religion, and of saint-like lives and triumphant deaths, and of future bliss or misery unutterable, then did Goodman Brown turn pale, dreading lest the roof should thunder down upon the gray blasphemer and his hearers. Often, awaking suddenly at midnight, he shrank from the bosom of Faith, and at morning or eventide, when the family knelt down at prayer, he scowled, and muttered to himself, and gazed sternly at his wife, and turned away. And when he had lived long, and was borne to his grave, a hoary corpse, followed by Faith, an aged woman, and children and grand-children, a goodly procession, besides neighbors not a few, they carved no hopeful verse upon his tombstone; for his dying hour was gloom.

Joyce Carol Oates (1938–   )

Where Are You Going, Where Have You Been? (1966)

For Bob Dylan

Her name was Connie. She was fifteen and she had a quick nervous giggling habit of craning her neck to glance into mirrors, or checking other people's faces to make sure her own was all right. Her mother, who noticed everything and knew everything and who hadn't much reason any longer to look at her own face, always scolded Connie about it. "Stop gawking at yourself, who are you? You think you're so pretty?" she would say. Connie would raise her eye-brows at these familiar complaints and look right through her mother, into a shadowy vision of herself as she was right at that moment: she knew she was pretty and that was everything. Her mother had been pretty once too, if you could believe those old snapshots in the album, but now her looks were gone and that was why she was always after Connie.

"Why don't you keep your room clean like your sister? How've you got your hair fixed—what the hell stinks? Hair spray? You don't see your sister using that junk."

Her sister June was twenty-four and still lived at home. She was a secretary in the high school Connie attended, and if that wasn't bad enough—with her in the same building—she was so plain and chunky and steady that Connie had to hear her praised all the time by her mother and her mother's sisters. June did this, June did that, she saved money and helped clean the house and cooked and Connie couldn't do a thing, her mind was all filled with trashy daydreams. Their father was away at work most of the time and when he came home he wanted supper and he read the newspaper at supper and after supper he went to bed. He didn't bother talking much to them, but around his bent head Connie's mother kept picking at her until Connie wished her mother was dead and she herself was dead and it was all over. "She makes me want to throw up sometimes," she complained to her friends. She had a high, breathless, amused voice which made everything she said sound a little forced, whether it was sincere or not.

There was one good thing: June went places with girl friends of hers, girls who were just as plain and steady as she, and so when Connie wanted to do that her mother had no objections. The father of Connie's best girl friend drove the girls the three miles to town and left them off at a shopping plaza, so that they could walk through the stores or go to a movie, and when he came to pick them up again at eleven he never bothered to ask what they had done.

They must have 5 been familiar sights, walking around that shopping plaza in their shorts and flat ballerina slippers that always scuffed the sidewalk, with charm bracelets jingling on their thin wrists; they would lean together to whisper and laugh secretly if someone passed by who amused or interested them. Connie had long dark blond hair that drew anyone's eye to it, and she wore part of it pulled up on her head and puffed out and the rest of it she let fall down her back. She wore a pull-over jersey blouse that looked one way when she was at home and another way when she was away from home. Everything about her had two sides to it, one for home and one for anywhere that was not home: her walk that could be childlike and bobbing, or languid enough to make anyone think she was hearing music in her head, her mouth which was pale and smirking most of the time, but bright and pink on these evenings out, her laugh which was cynical and drawling at home—"Ha, ha, very funny"—but high-pitched and nervous anywhere else, like the jingling of the charms on her bracelet.

Sometimes they did go shopping or to a movie, but sometimes they went across the highway, ducking fast across the busy road, to a drive-in restaurant where older kids hung out. The restaurant was shaped like a big bottle, though squatter than a real bottle, and on its cap was a revolving figure of a grinning boy who held a hamburger aloft. One night in mid-summer they ran across, breathless

> *"She wore a pull-over jersey blouse that looked one way when she was at home and another way when she was away from home. Everything about her had two sides to it. . . ."*

with daring, and right away someone leaned out a car window and invited them over, but it was just a boy from high school they didn't like. It made them feel good to be able to ignore him. They went up through the maze of parked and cruising cars to the bright-lit, fly-infested restaurant, their faces pleased and expectant as if they were entering a sacred building that loomed out of the night to give them what haven and what blessing they yearned for. They sat at the counter and crossed their legs at the ankles, their thin shoulders rigid with excitement, and listened to the music that made everything so good: the music was always in the background like music at a church service, it was something to depend upon.

A boy named Eddie came in to talk with them. He sat backwards on his stool, turning himself jerkily around in semi-circles and then stopping and turning again, and after a while he asked Connie if she would like something to eat. She said she did and so she tapped her friend's arm on her way out—her friend pulled her face up into a brave droll look—and Connie said she would meet her at eleven, across the way. "I just hate to leave her like that," Connie said earnestly, but the boy said that she wouldn't be alone for long. So they went out to his car and on the way Connie couldn't help but let her eyes wander over the windshields and faces all around her, her face gleaming with a joy that had nothing to do with Eddie or even this place; it might have been the music. She drew her shoulders up and sucked in her breath with the pure pleasure of being alive, and just at that moment she happened to glance at a face just a few feet from hers. It was a boy with shaggy black hair, in a convertible jalopy painted gold. He stared at her and then his lips widened into a grin. Connie slit her eyes at him and turned away, but she couldn't help glancing back and there he was still watching her. He wagged a finger and laughed and said, "Gonna get you, baby," and Connie turned away again without Eddie noticing anything.

She spent three hours with him, at the restaurant where they ate hamburgers and drank Cokes in wax cups that were always sweating, and then down an alley a mile or so away, and when he left her off at five to eleven only the movie house was still open at the plaza. Her girl friend was there, talking with a boy. When Connie came up the two girls smiled at each other and Connie said, "How was the movie?" and the girl said, "*You* should know." They rode off with the girl's father, sleepy and pleased, and Connie couldn't help but look at the darkened shopping plaza with its big empty parking lot and its signs that were faded and ghostly now, and over at the drive-in restaurant where cars were still circling tirelessly. She couldn't hear the music at this distance.

Next morning June asked her how the movie was and Connie said, "So-so."

She and that girl and occasionally another girl went 10 out several times a week that way, and the rest of the time Connie spent around the house—it was summer vacation—getting in her mother's way and thinking, dreaming, about the boys she met. But all the boys fell back and dissolved into a single face that was not even a face, but an idea, a feeling, mixed up with the urgent insistent pounding of the music and the humid night air of July. Connie's mother kept dragging her back to the daylight by finding things for her to do or saying, suddenly, "What's this about the Pettinger girl?"

And Connie would say nervously, "Oh, her. That dope." She always drew thick clear lines between herself and such girls, and her mother was simple and kindly enough to believe her. Her mother was so simple, Connie thought, that it was maybe cruel to fool her so much. Her mother went scuffling around the house in old bedroom slippers and complained over the telephone to one sister about the other, then the other called up and the two of them complained about the third one. If June's name was mentioned her mother's tone was approving, and if Connie's name was mentioned it was disapproving. This did not really mean she disliked Connie and actually Connie thought that her mother preferred her to June because she was prettier, but the two of them kept up a pretense of exasperation, a sense that they were tugging and struggling over something of little value to either of them. Sometimes, over coffee, they were almost friends, but something would come up—some vexation that was like a fly buzzing suddenly around their heads—and their faces went hard with contempt.

One Sunday Connie got up at eleven—none of them bothered with church—and washed her hair so that it could dry all day long, in the sun. Her parents and sister were going to a barbecue at an aunt's house and Connie said no, she wasn't interested, rolling her eyes to let her mother know just what she thought of it. "Stay home alone then," her mother said sharply. Connie sat out back in a lawn chair and watched them drive away, her father quiet and bald, hunched around so that he could back the car out, her mother with a look that was still angry and not at all softened through the windshield, and in the back seat poor old June all dressed up as if she didn't know what a barbecue was, with all the running yelling kids and the flies. Connie sat with her eyes closed in the sun, dreaming and dazed with the warmth about her as if this were a kind of love, the caresses of love, and her mind slipped over onto thoughts of the boy she had been with the night before and how nice he had been, how sweet it always was, not the way someone like June would suppose but sweet, gentle, the way it was in movies and promised in songs; and when she opened her eyes she hardly knew where she was, the back yard ran off into weeds and a fence-line of trees and behind it the sky was perfectly blue and still. The asbestos "ranch house" that was now three years old startled her—it looked small. She shook her head as if to get awake.

It was too hot. She went inside the house and turned on the radio to drown out the quiet. She sat on the edge of her bed, barefoot, and listened for an hour and a half to a program called *XYZ Sunday Jamboree*, record after record of hard, fast, shrieking songs she sang along with, interspersed by exclamations from "Bobby King": "An' look here you girls at Napoleon's—Son and Charley want you to pay real close attention to this song coming up!"

[margin annotations: "On their way to the restaurant", "The night ending", "Scene Change", "Scene Change"]

And Connie paid close attention herself, bathed in a glow of slow-pulsed joy that seemed to rise mysteriously out of the music itself and lay languidly about the airless little room, breathed in and breathed out with each gentle rise and fall of her chest.

After a while she heard a car coming up the drive. She 15 sat up at once, startled, because it couldn't be her father so soon. The gravel kept crunching all the way in from the road—the driveway was long—and Connie ran to the window. It was a car she didn't know. It was an open jalopy, painted a bright gold that caught the sunlight opaquely. Her heart began to pound and her fingers snatched at her hair, checking it, and she whispered "Christ. Christ," wondering how bad she looked. The car came to a stop at the side door and the horn sounded four short taps as if this were a signal Connie knew.

She went into the kitchen and approached the door slowly, then hung out the screen door, her bare toes curling down off the step. There were two boys in the car and now she recognized the driver: he had shaggy, shabby black hair that looked crazy as a wig and he was grinning at her.

"I ain't late, am I?" he said.

"Who the hell do you think you are?" Connie said.

"Toldja I'd be out, didn't I?"

"I don't even know who you are." 20

She spoke sullenly, careful to show no interest or pleasure, and he spoke in a fast bright monotone. Connie looked past him to the other boy, taking her time. He had fair brown hair, with a lock that fell onto his forehead. His sideburns gave him a fierce, embarrassed look, but so far he hadn't even bothered to glance at her. Both boys wore sunglasses. The driver's glasses were metallic and mirrored everything in miniature.

"You wanta come for a ride?" he said.

Connie smirked and let her hair fall loose over one shoulder.

"Don'tcha like my car? New paint job," he said. "Hey."

"What?" 25

"You're cute."

She pretended to fidget, chasing flies away from the door.

"Don'tcha believe me, or what?" he said.

"Look, I don't even know who you are," Connie said in disgust.

"Hey, Ellie's got a radio, see. Mine's broke down." He 30 lifted his friend's arm and showed her the little transistor the boy was holding, and now Connie began to hear the music. It was the same program that was playing inside the house.

"Bobby King?" she said.

"I listen to him all the time. I think he's great."

"He's kind of great," Connie said reluctantly.

"Listen, that guy's *great*. He knows where the action is."

Connie blushed a little, because the glasses made it 35 impossible for her to see just what this boy was looking at. She couldn't decide if she liked him or if he was just a jerk,

and so she dawdled in the doorway and wouldn't come down or go back inside. She said, "What's all that stuff painted on your car?"

"Can'tcha read it?" He opened the door very carefully, as if he was afraid it might fall off. He slid out just as carefully, planting his feet firmly on the ground, the tiny metallic world in his glasses slowing down like gelatine hardening and in the midst of it Connie's bright green blouse. "This here is my name, to begin with," he said. ARNOLD FRIEND was written in tarlike black letters on the side, with a drawing of a round grinning face that reminded Connie of a pumpkin, except it wore sunglasses. "I wanta introduce myself, I'm Arnold Friend and that's my real name and I'm gonna be your friend, honey, and inside the car's Ellie Oscar, he's kinda shy." Ellie brought his transistor radio up to his shoulder and balanced it there. "Now these numbers are a secret code, honey," Arnold Friend explained. He read off the numbers 33, 19, 17 and raised his eyebrows at her to see what she thought of that, but she didn't think much of it. The left rear fender had been smashed and around it was written, on the gleaming gold background: DONE BY CRAZY WOMAN DRIVER. Connie had to laugh at that. Arnold Friend was pleased at her laughter and looked up at her. "Around the other side's a lot more—you wanta come and see them?"

"No."

"Why not?"

"Why should I?"

"Don'tcha wanta see what's on the car? Don'tcha 40 wanta go for a ride?"

"I don't know."

"Why not?"

"I got things to do."

"Like what?"

"Things." 45

He laughed as if she had said something funny. He slapped his thighs. He was standing in a strange way, leaning back against the car as if he were balancing himself. He wasn't tall, only an inch or so taller than she would be if she came down to him. Connie liked the way he was dressed, which was the way all of them dressed: tight faded jeans stuffed into black, scuffed boots, a belt that pulled his waist in and showed how lean he was, and a white pull-over shirt that was a little soiled and showed the hard small muscles of his arms and shoulders. He looked as if he probably did hard work, lifting and carrying things. Even his neck looked muscular. And his face was a familiar face, somehow: the jaw and chin and cheeks slightly darkened, because he hadn't shaved for a day or two, and the nose long and hawk-like, sniffing as if she were a treat he was going to gobble up and it was all a joke.

"Connie, you ain't telling the truth. This is your day set aside for a ride with me and you know it," he said, still laughing. The way he straightened and recovered from his fit of laughing showed that it had been all fake.

"How do you know what my name is?" she said suspiciously.

"It's Connie."

"Maybe and maybe not."

"I know my Connie," he said, wagging his finger. Now she remembered him even better, back at the restaurant, and her cheeks warmed at the thought of how she sucked in her breath just at the moment she passed him—how she must have looked to him. And he had remembered her. "Ellie and I come out here especially for you," he said. "Ellie can sit in back. How about it?"

"Where?"

"Where what?"

"Where're we going?"

He looked at her. He took off the sunglasses and she saw how pale the skin around his eyes was, like holes that were not in shadow but instead in light. His eyes were chips of broken glass that catch the light in an amiable way. He smiled. It was as if the idea of going for a ride somewhere, to some place, was a new idea to him.

"Just for a ride, Connie sweetheart."

"I never said my name was Connie," she said.

"But I know what it is. I know your name and all about you, lots of things," Arnold Friend said. He had not moved yet but stood still leaning back against the side of his jalopy. "I took a special interest in you, such a pretty girl, and found out all about you like I know your parents and sister are gone somewheres and I know where and how long they're going to be gone, and I know who you were with last night, and your best girl friend's name is Betty. Right?"

He spoke in a simple lilting voice, exactly as if he were reciting the words to a song. His smile assured her that everything was fine. In the car Ellie turned up the volume on his radio and did not bother to look around at them.

"Ellie can sit in the back seat," Arnold Friend said. He indicated his friend with a casual jerk of his chin, as if Ellie did not count and she should not bother with him.

"How'd you find out all that stuff?" Connie said.

"Listen: Betty Schultz and Tony Fitch and Jimmy Pettinger and Nancy Pettinger," he said, in a chant. "Raymond Stanley and Bob Hutter—"

"Do you know all those kids?"

"I know everybody."

"Look, you're kidding. You're not from around here."

"Sure."

"But—how come we never saw you before?"

"Sure you saw me before," he said. He looked down at his boots, as if he were a little offended. "You just don't remember."

"I guess I'd remember you," Connie said.

"Yeah?" He looked up at this, beaming. He was pleased. He began to mark time with the music from Ellie's radio, tapping his fists lightly together. Connie looked away from his smile to the car, which was painted so bright it almost hurt her eyes to look at it. She looked at that name, ARNOLD FRIEND. And up at the front fender was an expression that was familiar—MAN THE FLYING SAUCERS. It was an expression kids had used the year before, but didn't use this year. She looked at it for a while as if the

words meant something to her that she did not yet know.

"What're you thinking about? Huh?" Arnold Friend demanded. "Not worried about your hair blowing around in the car, are you?"

"No."

"Think I maybe can't drive good?"

"How do I know?"

"You're a hard girl to handle. How come?" he said. "Don't you know I'm your friend? Didn't you see me put my sign in the air when you walked by?"

"What sign?"

"My sign." And he drew an X in the air, leaning out toward her. They were maybe ten feet apart. After his hand fell back to his side the X was still in the air, almost visible. Connie let the screen door close and stood perfectly still inside it, listening to the music from her radio and the boy's blend together. She stared at Arnold Friend. He stood there so stiffly relaxed, pretending to be relaxed, with one hand idly on the door handle as if he were keeping himself up that way and had no intention of ever moving again. She recognized most things about him, the tight jeans that showed his thighs and buttocks and the greasy leather boots and the tight shirt, and even that slippery friendly smile of his, that sleepy dreamy smile that all the boys used to get across ideas they didn't want to put into words. She recognized all this and also the singsong way he talked, slightly mocking, kidding, but serious and a little melancholy, and she recognized the way he tapped one fist against the other in homage to the perpetual music behind him. But all these things did not come together.

She said suddenly, "Hey, how old are you?"

His smile faded. She could see then that he wasn't a kid, he was much older—thirty, maybe more. At this knowledge her heart began to pound faster.

"That's a crazy thing to ask. Can'tcha see I'm your own age?"

"Like hell you are."

"Or maybe a coupla years older, I'm eighteen."

"Eighteen?" she said doubtfully.

He grinned to reassure her and lines appeared at the corners of his mouth. His teeth were big and white. He grinned so broadly his eyes became slits and she saw how thick the lashes were, thick and black as if painted with a black tarlike material. Then he seemed to become embarrassed, abruptly, and looked over his shoulder at Ellie. "*Him*, he's crazy," he said. "Ain't he a riot, he's a nut, a real character." Ellie was still listening to the music. His sunglasses told nothing about what he was thinking. He wore a bright orange shirt unbuttoned halfway to show his chest, which was a pale, bluish chest and not muscular like Arnold Friend's. His shirt collar was turned up all around and the very tips of the collar pointed out past his chin as if they were protecting him. He was pressing the transistor radio up against his ear and sat there in a kind of daze, right in the sun.

"He's kinda strange," Connie said.

"Hey, she says you're kinda strange! Kinda strange!" Arnold Friend cried. He pounded on the car to get Ellie's attention. Ellie turned for the first time and Connie saw with shock that he wasn't a kid either—he had a fair, hairless face, cheeks reddened slightly as if the veins grew too close to the surface of his skin, the face of a forty-year-old baby. Connie felt a wave of dizziness rise in her at this sight and she stared at him as if waiting for something to change the shock of the moment, make it all right again. Ellie's lips kept shaping words, mumbling along with the words blasting in his ear.

"Maybe you two better go away," Connie said faintly.

"What? How come?" Arnold Friend cried. "We come out here to take you for a ride. It's Sunday." He had the voice of the man on the radio now. It was the same voice, Connie thought. "Don'tcha know it's Sunday all day and honey, no matter who you were with last night today you're with Arnold Friend and don't you forget it!—Maybe you better step out here," he said, and this last was in a different voice. It was a little flatter, as if the heat was finally getting to him.

"No. I got things to do."

"Hey." 90

"You two better leave."

"We ain't leaving until you come with us."

"Like hell I am—"

"Connie, don't fool around with me. I mean, I mean, don't fool *around*," he said, shaking his head. He laughed incredulously. He placed his sunglasses on top of his head, carefully, as if he were indeed wearing a wig, and brought the stems down behind his ears. Connie stared at him, another wave of dizziness and fear rising in her so that for a moment he wasn't even in focus but was just a blur, standing there against his gold car, and she had the idea that he had driven up the driveway all right but had come from nowhere before that and belonged nowhere and that everything about him and even about the music that was so familiar to her was only half real.

"If my father comes and sees you—" 95

"He ain't coming. He's at a barbecue."

"How do you know that?"

"Aunt Tillie's. Right now they're—uh—they're drinking. Sitting around," he said vaguely, squinting as if he were staring all the way to town and over to Aunt Tillie's backyard. Then the vision seemed to get clear and he nodded energetically. "Yeah. Sitting around. There's your sister in a blue dress, huh? And high heels, the poor sad bitch—nothing like you sweetheart! And your mother's helping some fat woman with the corn, they're cleaning the corn—husking the corn—"

"What fat woman?" Connie cried.

"How do I know what fat woman. I don't know every 100 goddam fat woman in the world!" Arnold Friend laughed.

"Oh, that's Mrs. Hornby.... Who invited her?" Connie said. She felt a little light-headed. Her breath was coming quickly.

"She's too fat. I don't like them fat. I like them the way you are, honey," he said, smiling sleepily at her. They stared at each other for a while, through the screen door. He said softly, "Now what you're going to do is this: you're going to come out that door. You're going to sit up front with me and Ellie's going to sit in the back, the hell with Ellie, right? This isn't Ellie's date. You're my date. I'm your lover, honey."

"What? You're crazy—"

"Yes, I'm your lover. You don't know what that is but you will," he said. "I know that too. I know all about you. But look: it's real nice and you couldn't ask for nobody better than me, or more polite. I always keep my word. I'll tell you how it is, I'm always nice at first, the first time. I'll hold you so tight you won't think you have to try to get away or pretend anything because you'll know you can't. And I'll come inside you where it's all secret and you'll give in to me and you'll love me—"

"Shut up! You're crazy!" Connie said. She backed 105 away from the door. She put her hands against her ears as if she'd heard something terrible, something not meant for her. "People don't talk like that, you're crazy," she muttered. Her heart was almost too big now for her chest and its pumping made sweat break out all over her. She looked out to see Arnold Friend pause and then take a step toward the porch lurching. He almost fell. But, like a clever drunken man, he managed to catch his balance. He wobbled in his high boots and grabbed hold of one of the porch posts.

"Honey?" he said. "You still listening?"

"Get the hell out of here!"

"Be nice, honey. Listen."

"I'm going to call the police—"

He wobbled again and out of the side of his mouth 110 came a fast spat curse, an aside not meant for her to hear. But even this "Christ!" sounded forced. Then he began to smile again. She watched this smile come, awkward as if he were smiling from inside a mask. His whole face was a mask, she thought wildly, tanned down onto his throat but then running out as if he had plastered makeup on his face but had forgotten about his throat.

"Honey—? Listen, here's how it is. I always tell the truth and I promise you this: I ain't coming in that house after you."

"You better not! I'm going to call the police if you—if you don't—"

"Honey," he said, talking right through her voice, "honey, I'm not coming in there but you are coming out here. You know why?"

She was panting. The kitchen looked like a place she had never seen before, some room she had run inside but which wasn't good enough, wasn't going to help her. The kitchen window had never had a curtain, after three years, and there were dishes in the sink for her to do—probably—and if you ran your hand across the table you'd probably feel something sticky there.

"You listening, honey? Hey?" 115

"—going to call the police—"

"Soon as you touch the phone I don't need to keep my promise and can come inside. You won't want that."

She rushed forward and tried to lock the door. Her fingers were shaking. "But why lock it," Arnold Friend said gently, talking right into her face. "It's just a screen door. It's just nothing." One of his boots was at a strange angle, as if his foot wasn't in it. It pointed out to the left, bent at the ankle. "I mean, anybody can break through a screen door and glass and wood and iron or anything else if he needs to, anybody at all and specially Arnold Friend. If the place got lit up with a fire honey you'd come running out into my arms, right into my arms and safe at home—like you knew I was your lover and'd stopped fooling around. I don't mind a nice shy girl but I don't like no fooling around." Part of those words were spoken with a slight rhythmic lilt, and Connie somehow recognized them—the echo of a song from last year, about a girl rushing into her boy friend's arms and coming home again—

Connie stood barefoot on the linoleum floor, staring at him. "What do you want?" she whispered.

"I want you," he said.   120

"What?"

"Seen you that night and thought, that's the one, yes sir. I never needed to look any more."

"But my father's coming back. He's coming to get me. I had to wash my hair first—" She spoke in a dry, rapid voice, hardly raising it for him to hear.

"No, your daddy is not coming and yes, you had to wash your hair and you washed it for me. It's nice and shining and all for me, I thank you, sweetheart," he said, with a mock bow, but again he almost lost his balance. He had to bend and adjust his boots. Evidently his feet did not go all the way down; the boots must have been stuffed with something so that he would seem taller. Connie stared out at him and behind him Ellie in the car, who seemed to be looking off toward Connie's right, into nothing. This Ellie said, pulling the words out of the air one after another as if he were just discovering them, "You want me to pull out the phone?"

"Shut your mouth and keep it shut," Arnold Friend   125
said, his face red from bending over or maybe from embarrassment because Connie had seen his boots. "This ain't none of your business."

"What—what are you doing? What do you want?" Connie said. "If I call the police they'll get you, they'll arrest you—"

"Promise was not to come in unless you touch that phone, and I'll keep that promise," he said. He resumed his erect position and tried to force his shoulders back. He sounded like a hero in a movie, declaring something important. He spoke too loudly and it was as if he were speaking to someone behind Connie. "I ain't made plans for coming in that house where I don't belong but just for you to come out to me, the way you should. Don't you know who I am?"

"You're crazy," she whispered. She backed away from the door but did not want to go into another part of the house, as if this would give him permission to come through the door. "What do you. . . . You're crazy, you . . ."

"Huh? What're you saying, honey?"

Her eyes darted everywhere in the kitchen. She could   130
not remember what it was, this room.

"This is how it is, honey: you come out and we'll drive away, have a nice ride. But if you don't come out we're gonna wait till your people come home and then they're all going to get it."

"You want that telephone pulled out?" Ellie said. He held the radio away from his ear and grimaced, as if without the radio the air was too much for him.

"I toldja shut up, Ellie," Arnold Friend said, "you're deaf, get a hearing aid, right? Fix yourself up. This little girl's no trouble and's gonna be nice to me, so Ellie keep to yourself, this ain't your date—right? Don't hem in on me. Don't hog. Don't crush. Don't bird dog. Don't trail me," he said in a rapid meaningless voice, as if he were running through all the expressions he'd learned but was no longer sure which one of them was in style, then rushing on to new ones, making them up with his eyes closed, "Don't crawl under my fence, don't squeeze in my chipmunk hole, don't sniff my glue, suck my popsicle, keep your own greasy fingers on yourself!" He shaded his eyes and peered in at Connie, who was backed against the kitchen table. "Don't mind him honey he's just a creep. He's a dope. Right? I'm the boy for you and like I said you come out here nice like a lady and give me your hand, and nobody else gets hurt, I mean, your nice old bald-headed daddy and your mummy and your sister in her high heels. Because listen: why bring them in this?"

"Leave me alone," Connie whispered.

"Hey, you know that old woman down the road, the   135
one with the chickens and stuff—you know her?"

"She's dead!"

"Dead? What? You know her?" Arnold Friend said.

"She's dead—"

"Don't you like her?"

"She's dead—she's—she isn't here any more—"   140

"But don't you like her, I mean, you got something against her? Some grudge or something?" Then his voice dipped as if he were conscious of a rudeness. He touched the sunglasses perched on top of his head as if to make sure they were still there. "Now you be a good girl."

"What are you going to do?"

"Just two things, or maybe three," Arnold Friend said. "But I promise it won't last long and you'll like me that way you get to like people you're close to. You will. It's all over for you here, so come on out. You don't want your people in any trouble, do you?"

She turned and bumped against a chair or something, hurting her leg, but she ran into the back room and picked up the telephone. Something roared in her ear, a tiny roaring, and she was so sick with fear that she could do nothing but listen to it—the telephone was clammy and very heavy and her fingers groped down to the dial but were too weak to touch it. She began to scream into the phone, into the roaring. She cried out, she cried for her mother, she felt her breath start jerking back and forth in her lungs as if it were something Arnold Friend were stabbing her with again and again with no tenderness. A noisy sorrowful wailing rose all about her and she was locked inside it the way she was locked inside the house.

After a while she could hear again. She was sitting on the floor with her wet back against the wall. 145

Arnold Friend was saying from the door, "That's a good girl. Put the phone back."

She kicked the phone away from her.

"No, honey. Pick it up. Put it back right."

She picked it up and put it back. The dial tone stopped.

"That's a good girl. Now you come outside." 150

She was hollow with what had been fear, but what was now just an emptiness. All that screaming had blasted it out of her. She sat, one leg cramped under her, and deep inside her brain was something like a pinpoint of light that kept going and would not let her relax. She thought, I'm not going to see my mother again. She thought, I'm not going to sleep in my bed again. Her bright green blouse was all wet.

Arnold Friend said, in a gentle-loud voice that was like a stage voice, "The place where you came from ain't there any more, and where you had in mind to go is cancelled out. This place you are now—inside your daddy's house—is nothing but a cardboard box I can knock down any time. You know that and always did know it. You hear me?"

She thought, I have got to think. I have to know what to do.

"We'll go out to a nice field, out in the country here where it smells so nice and it's sunny," Arnold Friend said. "I'll have my arms around you so you won't need to try to get away and I'll show you what love is like, what it does. The hell with this house! It looks solid all right," he said. He ran a fingernail down the screen and the noise did not make Connie shiver, as it would have the day before. "Now put your hand on your heart, honey. Feel that? That feels solid too but we know better, be nice to me, be sweet like you can because what else is there for a girl like you but to be sweet and pretty and give in?—and get away before her people come back?"

She felt her pounding heart. Her hand seemed to en- 155 close it. She thought for the first time in her life that it was nothing that was hers, that belonged to her, but just a pounding, living thing inside this body that wasn't really hers either.

"You don't want them to get hurt," Arnold Friend went on. "Now get up, honey. Get up all by yourself."

She stood.

"Now turn this way. That's right. Come over here to me—Ellie, put that away, didn't I tell you? You dope. You miserable creepy dope," Arnold Friend said. His words were not angry but only part of an incantation. The incantation was kindly. "Now come out through the kitchen to me honey and let's see a smile, try it, you're a brave sweet little girl and now they're eating corn and hotdogs cooked to bursting over an outdoor fire, and they don't know one thing about you and never did and honey you're better than them because not a one of them would have done this for you."

Connie felt the linoleum under her feet; it was cool. She brushed her hair back out of her eyes. Arnold Friend let go of the post tentatively and opened his arms for her, his elbows pointing in toward each other and his wrists limp, to show that this was an embarrassed embrace and a little mocking, he didn't want to make her self-conscious.

She put out her hand against the screen. She watched 160 herself push the door slowly open as if she were safe back somewhere in the other doorway, watching this body and this head of long hair moving out into the sunlight where Arnold Friend waited.

"My sweet little blue-eyed girl," he said, in a half-sung sigh that had nothing to do with her brown eyes but was taken up just the same by the vast sunlit reaches of the land behind him and on all sides of him, so much land that Connie had never seen before and did not recognize except to know that she was going to it.

Edgar Allan Poe (1809–1849)

The Tell-Tale Heart (1843)

True!—nervous—very, very dreadfully nervous I had been and am; but why *will* you say that I am mad? The disease had sharpened my senses—not destroyed—not dulled them. Above all was the sense of hearing acute. I heard all things in the heaven and in the earth. I heard many things in hell. How, then, am I mad? Hearken! and observe how healthily—how calmly I can tell you the whole story.

It is impossible to say how first the idea entered my brain; but once conceived, it haunted me day and night. Object there was none. Passion there was none. I loved the old man. He had never wronged me. He had never given me insult. For his gold I had no desire. I think it was his eye! yes, it was this! One of his eyes resembled that of a vulture—a pale eye, with a film over it. Whenever it fell upon me, my blood ran cold; and so by degrees—very gradually—I made up my mind to take the life of the old man, and thus rid myself of the eye forever.

Now this is the point. You fancy me mad. Madmen know nothing. But you should have seen *me*. You should

> *"He shrieked once—once only. In an instant I dragged him to the floor, and pulled the heavy bed over him. I then smiled gaily, to find the deed so far done."*

have seen how wisely I proceeded—with what caution—with what foresight—with what dissimulation I went to work! I was never kinder to the old man than during the whole week before I killed him. And every night, about midnight, I turned the latch of his door and opened it—oh, so gently! And then, when I had made an opening sufficient for my head, I put in a dark lantern, all closed, closed, so that no light shone out, and then I thrust in my head. Oh, you would have laughed to see how cunningly I thrust it in! I moved it slowly—very, very slowly, so that I might not disturb the old man's sleep. It took me an hour to place my whole head within the opening so far that I could see him as he lay upon his bed. Ha!—would a madman have been so wise as this? And then, when my head was well in the room, I undid the lantern cautiously—oh, so cautiously—cautiously (for the hinges creaked)—I undid it just so much that a single thin ray fell upon the vulture eye. And this I did for seven long nights—every night just at midnight—but I found the eye always closed; and so it was impossible to do the work; for it was not the old man who vexed me, but his Evil Eye. And every morning, when the day broke, I went boldly into the chamber, and spoke courageously to him, calling him by name in a hearty tone, and inquiring how he had passed the night. So you see he would have been a very profound old man, indeed, to suspect that every night, just at twelve, I looked in upon him while he slept.

Upon the eighth night I was more than usually cautious in opening the door. A watch's minute hand moves more quickly than did mine. Never before that night had I *felt* the extent of my own powers—of my sagacity. I could scarcely contain my feelings of triumph. To think that there I was, opening the door little by little, and he not even to dream of my secret deeds or thoughts. I fairly chuckled at the idea; and perhaps he heard me; for he moved on the bed suddenly, as if startled. Now you may think that I drew back—but no. His room was as black as pitch with the thick darkness (for the shutters were close fastened through fear of robbers), and so I knew that he could not see the opening of the door, and I kept pushing it on steadily, steadily.

I had my head in, and was about to open the lantern, 5 when my thumb slipped upon the tin fastening, and the old man sprang up in the bed, crying out—"Who's there?"

° **death watches** Wood-burrowing beetles. Their clicking sound was superstitiously thought of as an omen of death.

I kept quite still and said nothing. For a whole hour I did not move a muscle, and in the meantime I did not hear him lie down. He was still sitting up in the bed listening;—just as I have done, night after night, hearkening to the death watches° in the wall.

Presently I heard a slight groan, and I knew it was the groan of mortal terror. It was not a groan of pain or of grief—oh, no!—it was the low stifled sound that arises from the bottom of the soul when overcharged with awe. I knew the sound very well. Many a night, just at midnight, when all the world slept, it has welled up from my own bosom, deepening, with its dreadful echo, the terrors that distracted me. I say I knew it well. I knew what the old man felt, and pitied him, although I chuckled at heart. I knew that he had been lying awake ever since the first slight noise, when he had turned in the bed. His fears had been ever since growing upon him. He had been trying to fancy them causeless, but could not. He had been saying to himself—"It is nothing but the wind in the chimney—it is only a mouse crossing the floor," or "it is merely a cricket which has made a single chirp." Yes, he had been trying to comfort himself with these suppositions; but he had found all in vain. *All in vain*; because Death, in approaching him, had stalked with his black shadow before him, and enveloped the victim. And it was the mournful influence of the unperceived shadow that caused him to feel—although he neither saw nor heard—to *feel* the presence of my head within the room.

When I had waited a long time, very patiently, without hearing him lie down, I resolved to open a little—a very, very little crevice in the lantern. So I opened it—you cannot imagine how stealthily, stealthily—until, at length, a single dim ray, like the thread of the spider, shot from out of the crevice and fell upon the vulture eye.

It was open—wide, wide open—and I grew furious as I gazed upon it. I saw it with perfect distinctness—all a dull blue, with a hideous veil over it that chilled the very marrow in my bones; but I could see nothing else of the old man's face or person: for I had directed the ray as if by instinct, precisely upon the damned spot.

And now have I not told you that what you mistake for 10 madness is but over-acuteness of the senses?—now, I say, there came to my ears a low, dull, quick sound, such as a watch makes when enveloped in cotton. I knew *that* sound well, too. It was the beating of the old man's heart. It increased my fury, as the beating of a drum stimulates the soldier into courage.

But even yet I refrained and kept still. I scarcely breathed. I held the lantern motionless. I tried how steadily I could maintain the ray upon the eye. Meantime the hellish tattoo of the heart increased. It grew quicker and quicker, and louder and louder every instant. The old man's terror *must* have been extreme! It grew louder, I say, louder every moment!—do you mark me well? I have told you that I am nervous: so I am. And now at the dead hour of the night, amid the dreadful silence of that old house, so strange a noise as this excited me to uncontrollable terror. Yet, for some minutes longer I refrained and stood still. But the beating grew louder, louder! I thought the heart must burst. And now a new anxiety seized me—the sound would be heard by a neighbor! The old man's hour had come! With a loud yell, I threw open the lantern and leaped into the room. He shrieked once—once only. In an instant I dragged him to the floor, and pulled the heavy bed over him. I then smiled gaily, to find the deed so far done. But, for many minutes, the heart beat on with a muffled sound. This, however, did not vex me; it would not be heard through the wall. At length it ceased. The old man was dead. I removed the bed and examined the corpse. Yes, he was stone, stone dead. I placed my hand upon the heart and held it there many minutes.

If still you think me mad, you will think so no longer when I describe the wise precautions I took for the concealment of the body. The night waned, and I worked hastily, but in silence. First of all I dismembered the corpse. I cut off the head and the arms and the legs.

I then took up three planks from the flooring of the chamber, and deposited all between the scantlings. I then replaced the boards so cleverly, so cunningly, that no human eye—not even *his*—could have detected anything wrong. There was nothing to wash out—no stain of any kind—no bloodspot whatever. I had been too wary for that. A tub had caught all—ha! ha!

When I had made an end of these labors, it was four o'clock—still dark as midnight. As the bell sounded the hour, there came a knocking at the street door. I went down to open it with a light heart,—for what had I *now* to fear? There entered three men, who introduced themselves, with perfect suavity, as officers of the police. A shriek had been heard by a neighbor during the night; suspicion of foul play had been aroused, information had been lodged at the police office, and they (the officers) had been deputed to search the premises.

I smiled,—for *what* had I to fear? I bade the gentlemen welcome. The shriek, I said, was my own in a dream. The old man, I mentioned, was absent in the country. I took my visitors all over the house. I bade them search—search *well*. I led them, at length, to *his* chamber. I showed them his treasures, secure, undisturbed. In the enthusiasm of my confidence, I brought chairs into the room, and desired them *here* to rest from their fatigues, while I myself, in the wild audacity of my perfect triumph, placed my own seat upon the very spot beneath which reposed the corpse of the victim.

The officers were satisfied. My *manner* had convinced them. I was singularly at ease. They sat, and while I answered cheerily, they chatted of familiar things. But, ere long, I felt myself getting pale and wished them gone. My head ached, and I fancied a ringing in my ears: but still they sat and still chatted. The ringing became more distinct:—it continued and became more distinct: I talked more freely to get rid of the feeling: but it continued and gained definitiveness—until, at length, I found that the noise was *not* within my ears.

No doubt I now grew *very* pale:—but I talked more fluently, and with a heightened voice. Yet the sound increased—and what could I do? It was a *low, dull, quick sound—much such a sound as a watch makes when enveloped in cotton.* I gasped for breath—and yet the officers heard it not. I talked more quickly—more vehemently; but the noise steadily increased. I arose and argued about trifles, in a high key and with violent gesticulations; but the noise steadily increased. Why *would* they not be gone? I paced the floor to and fro with heavy strides, as if excited to fury by the observations of the men—but the noise steadily increased. Oh God! what *could* I do? I foamed—I raved—I swore! I swung the chair upon which I had been sitting, and grated it upon the boards, but the noise arose over all and continually increased. It grew louder—louder—*louder!* And still the men chatted pleasantly, and smiled. Was it possible they heard not? Almighty God!—no, no! They heard!—they suspected!—they *knew!*—they were making a mockery of my horror!—this I thought, and this I think. But anything was better than this agony! Anything was more tolerable than this derision! I could bear those hypocritical smiles no longer! I felt that I must scream or die!—and now—again!—hark! louder! louder! louder! *louder!—*

"Villains!" I shrieked, "dissemble no more! I admit the deed!—tear up the planks!—here, here!—it is the beating of his hideous heart!"

*　　*　　*

Alberto Alvaro Ríos (1957–   )

The Secret Lion (1984)

I was twelve and in junior high school and something happened that we didn't have a name for, but it was there nonetheless like a lion, and roaring, roaring that way the biggest things do. Everything changed. Just that. Like the rug, the one that gets pulled—or better, like the tablecloth those magicians pull where the stuff on the table stays the same but the gasp! from the audience makes the staying-the-same part not matter. Like that.

What happened was there were teachers now, not just one teacher, teach-erz, and we felt personally abandoned somehow. When a person had all these teachers now, he didn't get taken care of the same way, even though six was more than one. Arithmetic went out the door when we walked in. And we saw girls now, but they weren't the same girls we used to know because we couldn't talk to them anymore, not the same way we used to, certainly not to Sandy, even though she was my neighbor, too. Not even to her. She just played the piano all the time. And there were words, oh there were words in junior high school, and we wanted to know what they were, and how a person did them—that's what school was supposed to be for. Only, in junior high school, school wasn't school, everything was backward-like. If you went up to a teacher and said the word to try and find out what it meant you got in trouble for saying it. So we didn't. And we figured it must have been that way about other stuff, too, so we never said anything about anything—we weren't stupid.

But my friend Sergio and I, we solved junior high school. We would come home from school on the bus, put our books away, change shoes, and go across the highway to the arroyo°. It was the one place we were not supposed to go. So we did. This was, after all, what junior high had at least shown us. It was our river, though, our personal Mississippi, our friend from long back, and it was full of stories and all the branch forts we had built in it when we were still the Vikings of America, with our own symbol, which we had carved everywhere, even in the sand, which let the water take it. That was good, we had decided; whoever was at the end of this river would know about us.

At the very very top of our growing lungs, what we would do down there was shout every dirty word we could think of, in every combination we could come up with, and we would yell about girls, and all the things we wanted to do with them, as loud as we could—we didn't know what we wanted to do with them, just things—and we would yell about teachers, and how we loved some of them, like Miss Crevelone, and how we wanted to dissect some of them, making signs of the cross, like priests, and we would yell this stuff over and over because it felt good, we couldn't explain why, it just felt good and for the first time in our lives there was nobody to tell us we couldn't. So we did.

One Thursday we were walking along shouting this 5 way, and the railroad, the Southern Pacific, which ran above and along the far side of the arroyo, had dropped a grinding ball down there, which was, we found out later, a cannonball thing used in mining. A bunch of them were put in a big vat which turned around and crushed the ore. One had been dropped, or thrown—what do caboose men do when they get bored—but it got down there regardless and as we were walking along yelling about one girl or another, a particular Claudia, we found it, one of these things, looked at it, picked it up, and got very very excited, and held it and passed it back and forth, and we were saying "Guythisis, this is, gee-Guythis . . .": we had this perception about nature then, that

° **arroyo** Water-carved gulch or channel in an arid region.

nature is imperfect and that round things are perfect: we said "Guy-Godthis is perfect, this-isthis is perfect, it's round, round and heavy, it'sit's the best thing we'veeverseen. Whatisit?" We didn't know. We just knew it was great. We just, whatever, we played with it, held it some more.

And then we had to decide what to do with it. We knew, because of a lot of things, that if we were going to take this and show it to anybody, this discovery, this best thing, was going to be taken away from us. That's the way it works with little kids, like all the polished quartz, the tons of it we had collected piece by piece over the years. Junior high kids too. If we took it home, my mother, we knew, was going to look at it and say "throw that dirty thing in the, get rid of it." Simple like, like that. "But ma it's the best thing I" "Getridofit." Simple.

So we didn't. Take it home. Instead, we came up with the answer. We dug a hole and buried it. And we marked it secretly. Lots of secret signs. And came back the next week to dig it up and, we didn't know, pass it around some more or something, but we didn't find it. We dug up that whole bank, and we never found it again. We tried.

Sergio and I talked about that ball or whatever it was when we couldn't find it. All we used were small words, neat, good. Kid words. What we were really saying, but didn't know the words, was how much that ball was like that place, that whole arroyo: couldn't tell anybody about it, didn't understand what it was, didn't have a name for it. It just felt good. It was just perfect in the way it was that place, that whole going to that place, that whole junior high school lion. It was just iron-heavy, it had no name, it felt good or not, we couldn't take it home to show our mothers, and once we buried it, it was gone forever.

The ball was gone, like the first reasons we had come to that arroyo years earlier, like the first time we had seen the arroyo, it was gone like everything else that had been taken away. This was not our first lesson. We stopped going to the arroyo after not finding the thing, the same way we had stopped going there years earlier and headed for the mountains. Nature seemed to keep pushing us around one way or another, teaching us the same thing every place we ended up. Nature's gang was tough that way, teaching us stuff.

When we were young we moved away from town, me 10 and my family. Sergio's was already out there. Out in the wilds. Or at least the new place seemed like the wilds since everything looks bigger the smaller a man is. I was five, I guess, and we had moved three miles north of Nogales

> "The ball was gone, like the first reasons we had come to that arroyo years earlier, like the first time we had seen the arroyo, it was gone like everything else that had been taken away."

where we had lived, three miles north of the Mexican border. We looked across the highway in one direction and there was the arroyo; hills stood up in the other direction. Mountains, for a small man.

When the first summer came the very first place we went to was of course the one place we weren't supposed to go, the arroyo. We went down in there and found water running, summer rain water mostly, and we went swimming. But every third or fourth or fifth day, the sewage treatment plant that was, we found out, upstream, would release whatever it was that it released, and we would never know exactly what day that was, and a person really couldn't tell right off by looking at the water, not every time, not so a person could get out in time. So, we went swimming that summer and some days we had a lot of fun. Some days we didn't. We found a thousand ways to explain what happened on those other days, constructing elaborate stories about the neighborhood dogs, and hadn't she, my mother, miscalculated her step before, too? But she knew something was up because we'd come running into the house those days, wanting to take a shower, even—if this can be imagined—in the middle of the day.

That was the first time we stopped going to the arroyo. It taught us to look the other way. We decided, as the second side of summer came, we wanted to go into the mountains. They were still mountains then. We went running in one summer Thursday morning, my friend Sergio and I, into my mother's kitchen, and said, well, what'zin, what'zin those hills over there—we used her word so she'd understand us—and she said nothingdon'tworryaboutit. So we went out, and we weren't dumb, we thought with our eyes to each other, ohhoshe'stryingtokeepsomethingfromus. We knew adults.

We had read the books, after all; we knew about bridges and castles and wildtreacherousraging alligatormouth rivers. We wanted them. So we were going to go out and get them. We went back that morning into that kitchen and we said, "We're going out there, we're going into the hills, we're going away for three days, don't worry." She said, "All right."

"You know," I said to Sergio, "if we're going to go away for three days, well, we ought to at least pack a lunch."

But we were two young boys with no patience for [15] what we thought at the time was mom-stuff: making sa-and-wiches. My mother didn't offer. So we got out little kid knapsacks that my mother had sewn for us, and into them we put the jar of mustard. A loaf of bread. Knivesforksplates, bottles of Coke, a can opener. This was lunch for the two of us. And we were weighed down, humped over to be strong enough to carry this stuff. But we started walking anyway, into the hills. We were going to eat berries and stuff otherwise. "Goodbye." My mom said that.

After the first hill we were dead. But we walked. My mother could still see us. And we kept walking. We walked until we got to where the sun is straight overhead, noon. That place. Where that is doesn't matter; it's time to eat. The truth is we weren't anywhere close to that place. We just

agreed that the sun was overhead and that it was time to eat, and by tilting our heads a little we could make that the truth.

"We really ought to start looking for a place to eat."

"Yeah. Let's look for a good place to eat." We went back and forth saying that for fifteen minutes, making it lunchtime because that's what we always said back and forth before lunchtimes at home. "Yeah, I'm hungry all right." I nodded my head. "Yeah, I'm hungry all right too. I'm hungry." He nodded his head. I nodded my head back. After a good deal more nodding, we were ready, just as we came over a little hill. We hadn't found the mountains yet. This was a little hill.

And on the other side of this hill we found heaven.

It was just what we thought it would be. [20]

Perfect. Heaven was green, like nothing else in Arizona. And it wasn't a cemetery or like that because we had seen cemeteries and they had gravestones and stuff and this didn't. This was perfect, had trees, lots of trees, had birds, like we had never seen before. It was like "The Wizard of Oz," like when they got to Oz and everything was so green, so emerald, they had to wear those glasses, and we ran just like them, laughing, laughing that way we did that moment, and we went running down to this clearing in it all, hitting each other that good way we did.

We got down there, we kept laughing, we kept hitting each other, we unpacked our stuff, and we started acting "rich." We knew all about how to do that, like blowing on our nails, then rubbing them on our chests for the shine. We made our sandwiches, opened our Cokes, got out the rest of the stuff, the salt and pepper shakers. I found this particular hole and I put my Coke right into it, a perfect fit, and I called it my Coke-holder. I got down next to it on my back, because everyone knows that rich people eat lying down, and I got my sandwich in one hand and put my other arm around the Coke in its holder. When I wanted a drink, I lifted my neck a little, put out my lips, and tipped my Coke a little with the crook of my elbow. Ah.

We were there, lying down, eating our sandwiches, laughing, throwing bread at each other and out for the birds. This was heaven. We were laughing and we couldn't believe it. My mother was keeping something from us, ah ha, but we had found her out. We even found water over at the side of the clearing to wash our plates with—we had brought plates. Sergio started washing his plates when he was done, and I was being rich with my Coke, and this day in summer was right.

When suddenly these two men came, from around a corner of trees and the tallest grass we had ever seen. They had bags on their backs, leather bags, bags and sticks.

We didn't know what clubs were, but I learned later, [25] like I learned about the grinding balls. The two men yelled at us. Most specifically, one wanted me to take my Coke out of my Coke-holder so he could sink his golf ball into it.

Something got taken away from us that moment. Heaven. We grew up a little bit, and couldn't go backward. We learned. No one had ever told us about golf. They had told us about heaven. And it went away. We got golf in exchange.

We went back to the arroyo for the rest of that summer, and tried to have fun the best we could. We learned to be ready for finding the grinding ball. We loved it, and when we buried it we knew what would happen. The truth is, we didn't look so hard for it. We were two boys and twelve summers then, and not stupid. Things get taken away.

We buried it because it was perfect. We didn't tell my mother, but together it was all we talked about, till we forgot. It was the lion.

*   *   *

Amy Tan (1952–   )

Two Kinds (1989)

My mother believed you could be anything you wanted to be in America. You could open a restaurant. You could work for the government and get good retirement. You could buy a house with almost no money down. You could become rich. You could become instantly famous.

"Of course you can be prodigy, too," my mother told me when I was nine. "You can be best anything. What does Auntie Lindo know? Her daughter, she is only best tricky."

America was where all my mother's hopes lay. She had come here in 1949 after losing everything in China: her mother and father, her family home, her first husband, and two daughters, twin baby girls. But she never looked back with regret. There were so many ways for things to get better.

> "In all of my imaginings, I was filled with a sense that I would soon become perfect. My mother and father would adore me. I would be beyond reproach. I would never feel the need to sulk for anything."

We didn't immediately pick the right kind of prodigy. At first my mother thought I could be a Chinese Shirley Temple. We'd watch Shirley's old movies on TV as though they were training films. My mother would poke my arm and say, *"Ni kan"*—You watch. And I would see Shirley tapping her feet, or singing a sailor song, or pursing her lips into a very round O while saying, "Oh my goodness."

"Ni kan," said my mother as Shirley's eyes flooded with 5 tears. "You already know how. Don't need talent for crying!"

Soon after my mother got this idea about Shirley Temple, she took me to a beauty training school in the Mission district and put me in the hands of a student who could barely hold the scissors without shaking. Instead of getting big fat curls, I emerged with an uneven mass of crinkly black fuzz. My mother dragged me off to the bathroom and tried to wet down my hair.

"You look like Negro Chinese," she lamented, as if I had done this on purpose.

The instructor of the beauty training school had to lop off these soggy clumps to make my hair even again. "Peter Pan is very popular these days," the instructor assured my mother. I now had hair the length of a boy's, with straight-across bangs that hung at a slant two inches above my eyebrows. I liked the haircut and it made me actually look forward to my future fame.

In fact, in the beginning, I was just as excited as my mother, maybe even more so. I pictured this prodigy part of me as many different images, trying each one on for size. I was a dainty ballerina girl standing by the curtains, waiting to hear the right music that would send me floating on my tiptoes. I was like the Christ child lifted out of the straw manger, crying with holy indignity. I was Cinderella stepping from her pumpkin carriage with sparkly cartoon music filling the air.

In all of my imaginings, I was filled with a sense that I 10 would soon become *perfect*. My mother and father would adore me. I would be beyond reproach. I would never feel the need to sulk for anything.

But sometimes the prodigy in me became impatient. "If you don't hurry up and get me out of here, I'm disappearing for good," it warned. "And then you'll always be nothing."

Every night after dinner, my mother and I would sit at the Formica kitchen table. She would present new tests, taking her examples from stories of amazing children she had read in *Ripley's Believe It or Not*, or *Good Housekeeping, Reader's Digest*, and a dozen other magazines she kept in a pile in our bathroom. My mother got these magazines from people whose houses she cleaned. And since she cleaned many houses each week, we had a great assortment. She would look through them all, searching for stories about remarkable children.

The first night she brought out a story about a three-year-old boy who knew the capitals of all the states and even most of the European countries. A teacher was quoted as saying the little boy could also pronounce the names of the foreign cities correctly.

"What's the capital of Finland?" my mother asked me, looking at the magazine story.

All I knew was the capital of California, because Sacra- 15 mento was the name of the street we lived on in Chinatown. "Nairobi!" I guessed, saying the most foreign word I could think of. She checked to see if that was possibly one way to pronounce "Helsinki" before showing me the answer.

The tests got harder—multiplying numbers in my head, finding the queen of hearts in a deck of cards, trying to stand on my head without using my hands, predicting the daily temperatures in Los Angeles, New York, and London.

One night I had to look at a page from the Bible for three minutes and then report everything I could remember. "Now Jehoshaphat had riches and honor in abundance and . . . that's all I remember, Ma," I said.

And after seeing my mother's disappointed face once again, something inside of me began to die. I hated the tests, the raised hopes and failed expectations. Before going to bed that night, I looked in the mirror above the bathroom sink and when I saw only my face staring back—and that it would always be this ordinary face—I began to cry. Such a sad, ugly girl! I made high-pitched noises like a crazed animal, trying to scratch out the face in the mirror.

And then I saw what seemed to be the prodigy side of me—because I had never seen that face before. I looked at my reflection, blinking so I could see more clearly. The girl staring back at me was angry, powerful. This girl and I were the same. I had new thoughts, willful thoughts, or rather thoughts filled with lots of won'ts. I won't let her change me, I promised myself. I won't be what I'm not.

So now on nights when my mother presented her 20 tests, I performed listlessly, my head propped on one arm. I pretended to be bored. And I was. I got so bored I started counting the bellows of the foghorns out on the bay while my mother drilled me in other areas. The sound was comforting and reminded me of the cow jumping over the moon. And the next day, I played a game with myself, seeing if my mother would give up on me before eight bellows. After a while I usually counted only one, maybe two bellows at most. At last she was beginning to give up hope.

Two or three months had gone by without any mention of my being a prodigy again. And then one day my mother was watching *The Ed Sullivan Show* on TV. The TV was old and the sound kept shorting out. Every time my mother got halfway up from the sofa to adjust the set, the sound would go back on and Ed would be talking. As soon as she sat down, Ed would go silent again. She got up, the TV broke into loud piano music. She sat down. Silence. Up and down, back and forth, quiet and loud. It was like a stiff embraceless dance between her and the TV set. Finally she stood by the set with her hand on the sound dial.

She seemed entranced by the music, a little frenzied piano piece with this mesmerizing quality, sort of quick passages and then teasing lilting ones before it returned to the quick playful parts.

"*Ni kan,*" my mother said, calling me over with hurried hand gestures, "Look here."

I could see why my mother was fascinated by the music. It was being pounded out by a little Chinese girl, about nine years old, with a Peter Pan haircut. The girl had the sauciness of a Shirley Temple. She was proudly modest like a proper Chinese child. And she also did this fancy sweep of a curtsy, so that the fluffy skirt of her white dress cascaded slowly to the floor like the petals of a large carnation.

In spite of these warning signs, I wasn't worried. Our 25 family had no piano and we couldn't afford to buy one, let alone reams of sheet music and piano lessons. So I could be generous in my comments when my mother badmouthed the little girl on TV.

"Play note right, but doesn't sound good! No singing sound," complained my mother.

"What are you picking on her for?" I said carelessly. "She's pretty good. Maybe she's not the best, but she's trying hard." I knew almost immediately I would be sorry I said that.

"Just like you," she said. "Not the best. Because you not trying." She gave a little huff as she let go of the sound dial and sat down on the sofa.

The little Chinese girl sat down also to play an encore of "Anitra's Dance" by Grieg. I remember the song, because later on I had to learn how to play it.

Three days after watching *The Ed Sullivan Show,* my 30 mother told me what my schedule would be for piano lessons and piano practice. She had talked to Mr. Chong, who lived on the first floor of our apartment building. Mr. Chong was a retired piano teacher and my mother had traded housecleaning services for weekly lessons and a piano for me to practice on every day, two hours a day, from four until six.

When my mother told me this, I felt as though I had been sent to hell. I whined and then kicked my foot a little when I couldn't stand it anymore.

"Why don't you like me the way I am? I'm *not* a genius! I can't play the piano. And even if I could, I wouldn't go on TV if you paid me a million dollars!" I cried.

My mother slapped me. "Who ask you be genius?" she shouted. "Only ask you be your best. For you sake. You think I want you be genius? Hnnh! What for! Who ask you!"

"So ungrateful," I heard her mutter in Chinese. "If she had as much talent as she has temper, she would be famous now."

Mr. Chong, whom I secretly nicknamed Old Chong, 35 was very strange, always tapping his fingers to the silent music of an invisible orchestra. He looked ancient in my eyes. He had lost most of the hair on top of his head and he wore thick glasses and had eyes that always looked tired and sleepy. But he must have been younger than I thought, since he lived with his mother and was not yet married.

I met Old Lady Chong once and that was enough. She had this peculiar smell like a baby that had done something in its pants. And her fingers felt like a dead person's, like an old peach I once found in the back of the refrigerator; the skin just slid off the meat when I picked it up.

I soon found out why Old Chong had retired from teaching piano. He was deaf. "Like Beethoven!" he shouted to me. "We're both listening only in our head!" And he would start to conduct his frantic silent sonatas.

Our lessons went like this. He would open the book and point to different things, explaining their purpose: "Key! Treble! Bass! No sharps or flats! So this is C major! Listen now and play after me!"

And then he would play the C scale a few times, a simple chord, and then, as if inspired by an old, unreachable itch, he gradually added more notes and running trills and a pounding bass until the music was really something quite grand.

I would play after him, the simple scale, the simple chord, 40 and then I just played some nonsense that sounded like a cat running up and down on top of garbage cans. Old Chong smiled and applauded and then said, "Very good! But now you must learn to keep time!"

So that's how I discovered that Old Chong's eyes were too slow to keep up with the wrong notes I was playing. He went through the motions in half-time. To help me keep rhythm, he stood behind me, pushing down on my right shoulder for every beat. He balanced pennies on top of my wrists so I would keep them still as I slowly played scales and arpeggios. He had me curve my hand around an apple and keep that shape when playing chords. He marched stiffly to show me how to make each finger dance up and down, staccato like an obedient little soldier.

He taught me all these things, and that was how I also learned I could be lazy and get away with mistakes, lots of mistakes. If I hit the wrong notes because I hadn't practiced enough, I never corrected myself. I just kept playing in rhythm. And Old Chong kept conducting his own private reverie.

So maybe I never really gave myself a fair chance. I did pick up the basics pretty quickly, and I might have become a good pianist at that young age. But I was so determined not to try, not to be anybody different that I learned to play only the most ear-splitting preludes, the most discordant hymns.

Over the next year, I practiced like this, dutifully in my own way. And then one day I heard my mother and her friend Lindo Jong both talking in a loud bragging tone of voice so others could hear. It was after church, and I was leaning against the brick wall wearing a dress with stiff white petticoats. Auntie Lindo's daughter, Waverly, who was about my age, was standing farther down the wall about five feet away. We had grown up together and shared all the closeness of two sisters squabbling over crayons and dolls. In other words, for the most part, we hated each other. I thought she was snotty. Waverly Jong had gained a certain amount of fame as "Chinatown's Littlest Chinese Chess Champion."

"She bring home too many trophy," lamented Auntie 45 Lindo that Sunday. "All day she play chess. All day I have no time do nothing but dust off her winnings." She threw a scolding look at Waverly, who pretended not to see her.

"You lucky you don't have this problem," said Auntie Lindo with a sigh to my mother.

And my mother squared her shoulders and bragged: "Our problem worser than yours. If we ask Jing-mei wash dish, she hear nothing but music. It's like you can't stop this natural talent."

And right then, I was determined to put a stop to her foolish pride.

A few weeks later, Old Chong and my mother conspired to have me play in a talent show which would be held in the church hall. By then, my parents had saved up enough to buy me a secondhand piano, a black Wurlitzer spinet with a scarred bench. It was the showpiece of our living room.

For the talent show, I was to play a piece called "Plead- 50 ing Child" from Schumann's *Scenes from Childhood*. It was a simple, moody piece that sounded more difficult than it was. I was supposed to memorize the whole thing, playing the repeat parts twice to make the piece sound longer. But I dawdled over it, playing a few bars and then cheating, looking up to see what notes followed. I never really listened to what I was playing. I daydreamed about being somewhere else, about being someone else.

The part I liked to practice best was the fancy curtsy: right foot out, touch the rose on the carpet with a pointed foot, sweep to the side, left leg bends, look up and smile.

My parents invited all the couples from the Joy Luck Club° to witness my debut. Auntie Lindo and Uncle Tin were there. Waverly and her two older brothers had also come. The first two rows were filled with children both younger and older than I was. The littlest ones got to go first. They recited simple nursery rhymes, squawked out tunes on miniature violins, twirled Hula Hoops, pranced in pink ballet tutus, and when they bowed or curtsied, the audience would sigh in unison, "Awww," and then clap enthusiastically.

When my turn came, I was very confident. I remember my childish excitement. It was as if I knew, without a doubt, that the prodigy side of me really did exist. I had no fear whatsoever, no nervousness. I remember thinking to myself, This is it! This is it! I looked out over the audience, at my mother's blank face, my father's yawn, Auntie Lindo's stiff-lipped smile, Waverly's sulky expression. I had on a white dress layered with sheets of lace, and a pink bow in my Peter Pan haircut. As I sat down I envisioned people jumping to their feet and Ed Sullivan rushing up to introduce me to everyone on TV.

And I started to play. It was so beautiful. I was so caught up in how lovely I looked that at first I didn't worry how I would sound. So it was a surprise to me when I hit the first wrong note and I realized something didn't sound quite right. And then I hit another and another followed that. A chill started at the top of my head and began to trickle down. Yet I couldn't stop playing, as though my hands were bewitched. I kept thinking my fingers would adjust themselves back, like a train switching to the right track. I played this strange jumble through

° **Joy Luck Club** A name denoting the mother's circle of friends, all of whom were Chinese immigrants to the United States.

two repeats, the sour notes staying with me all the way to the end.

When I stood up, I discovered my legs were shaking. Maybe I had just been nervous and the audience, like Old Chong, had seen me go through the right motions and had not heard anything wrong at all. I swept my right foot out, went down on my knee, looked up and smiled. The room was quiet, except for Old Chong, who was beaming and shouting, "Bravo! Bravo! Well done!" But then I saw my mother's face, her stricken face. The audience clapped weakly, and as I walked back to my chair, with my whole face quivering as I tried not to cry, I heard a little boy whisper loudly to his mother, "That was awful," and the mother whispered back, "Well, she certainly tried."

And now I realized how many people were in the audience, the whole world it seemed. I was aware of eyes burning into my back. I felt the shame of my mother and father as they sat stiffly throughout the rest of the show.

We could have escaped during intermission. Pride and some strange sense of honor must have anchored my parents to their chairs. And so we watched it all: the eighteen-year-old boy with a fake mustache who did a magic show and juggled flaming hoops while riding a unicycle. The breasted girl with white makeup who sang from *Madama Butterfly* and got honorable mention. And the eleven-year-old boy who won first prize playing a tricky violin song that sounded like a busy bee.

After the show, the Hsus, the Jongs, and the St. Clairs from the Joy Luck Club came up to my mother and father.

"Lots of talented kids," Auntie Lindo said vaguely, smiling broadly.

"That was somethin' else," said my father, and I wondered if he was referring to me in a humorous way, or whether he even remembered what I had done.

Waverly looked at me and shrugged her shoulders. "You aren't a genius like me," she said matter-of-factly. And if I hadn't felt so bad, I would have pulled her braids and punched her stomach.

But my mother's expression was what devastated me: a quiet, blank look that said she had lost everything. I felt the same way, and it seemed as if everybody were now coming up, like gawkers at the scene of an accident, to see what parts were actually missing. When we got on the bus to go home, my father was humming the busy-bee tune and my mother was silent. I kept thinking she wanted to wait until we got home before shouting at me. But when my father unlocked the door to our apartment, my mother walked in and then went to the back, into the bedroom. No accusations. No blame. And in a way, I felt disappointed. I had been waiting for her to start shouting, so I could shout back and cry and blame her for all my misery.

I assumed my talent-show fiasco meant I never had to play the piano again. But two days later, after school, my mother came out of the kitchen and saw me watching TV.

"Four clock," she reminded me as if it were any other day. I was stunned, as though she were asking me to go through the talent-show torture again. I wedged myself more tightly in front of the TV.

"Turn off TV," she called from the kitchen five minutes later.

I didn't budge. And then I decided. I didn't have to do what my mother said anymore. I wasn't her slave. This wasn't China. I had listened to her before and look what happened. She was the stupid one.

She came out from the kitchen and stood in the arched entryway of the living room. "Four clock," she said once again, louder.

"I'm not going to play anymore," I said nonchalantly. "Why should I? I'm not a genius."

She walked over and stood in front of the TV. I saw her chest was heaving up and down in an angry way.

"No!" I said, and I now felt stronger, as if my true self had finally emerged. So this was what had been inside me all along.

"No! I won't!" I screamed.

She yanked me by the arm, pulled me off the floor, snapped off the TV. She was frighteningly strong, half pulling, half carrying me toward the piano as I kicked the throw rugs under my feet. She lifted me up and onto the hard bench. I was sobbing by now, looking at her bitterly. Her chest was heaving even more and her mouth was open, smiling crazily as if she were pleased I was crying.

"You want me to be someone that I'm not!" I sobbed. "I'll never be the kind of daughter you want me to be!"

"Only two kinds of daughters," she shouted in Chinese. "Those who are obedient and those who follow their own mind! Only one kind of daughter can live in this house. Obedient daughter!"

"Then I wish I wasn't your daughter. I wish you weren't my mother," I shouted. As I said these things I got scared. It felt like worms and toads and slimy things crawling out of my chest, but it also felt good, as if this awful side of me had surfaced, at last.

"Too late change this," said my mother shrilly.

And I could sense her anger rising to its breaking point. I wanted to see it spill over. And that's when I remembered the babies she had lost in China, the ones we never talked about. "Then I wish I'd never been born!" I shouted. "I wish I were dead! Like them."

It was as if I had said the magic words. Alakazam!— and her face went blank, her mouth closed, her arms went slack, and she backed out of the room, stunned, as if she were blowing away like a small brown leaf, thin, brittle, lifeless.

It was not the only disappointment my mother felt in me. In the years that followed, I failed her so many times, each time asserting my own will, my right to fall short of expectations. I didn't get straight As. I didn't become class president. I didn't get into Stanford. I dropped out of college.

For unlike my mother, I did not believe I could be anything I wanted to be. I could only be me.

And for all those years, we never talked about the disaster at the recital or my terrible accusations afterward at the piano bench. All that remained unchecked, like a betrayal that was now unspeakable. So I never found a way to ask her why she had hoped for something so large that failure was inevitable.

And even worse, I never asked her what frightened me the most: Why had she given up hope?

For after our struggle at the piano, she never mentioned my playing again. The lessons stopped. The lid to the piano was closed, shutting out the dust, my misery, and her dreams.

So she surprised me. A few years ago, she offered to give me the piano, for my thirtieth birthday. I had not played in all those years. I saw the offer as a sign of forgiveness, a tremendous burden removed.

"Are you sure?" I asked shyly. "I mean, won't you and 85 Dad miss it?"

"No, this your piano," she said firmly. "Always your piano. You only one can play."

"Well, I probably can't play anymore," I said. "It's been years."

"You pick up fast," said my mother, as if she knew this was certain. "You have natural talent. You could been genius if you want to."

"No I couldn't."

"You just not trying," said my mother. And she was 90 neither angry nor sad. She said it as if to announce a fact that could never be disproved. "Take it," she said.

But I didn't at first. It was enough that she had offered it to me. And after that, every time I saw it in my parents' living room, standing in front of the bay windows, it made me feel proud, as if it were a shiny trophy I had won back.

Last week I sent a tuner over to my parents' apartment and had the piano reconditioned, for purely sentimental reasons. My mother had died a few months before and I had been getting things in order for my father, a little bit at a time. I put the jewelry in special silk pouches. The sweaters she had knitted in yellow, pink, bright orange—all the colors I hated—I put those in moth-proof boxes. I found some old Chinese silk dresses, the kind with little slits up the sides. I rubbed the old silk against my skin, then wrapped them in tissue and decided to take them home with me.

After I had the piano tuned, I opened the lid and touched the keys. It sounded even richer than I remembered. Really, it was a very good piano. Inside the bench were the same exercise notes with handwritten scales, the same secondhand music books with their covers held together with yellow tape.

I opened up the Schumann book to the dark little piece I had played at the recital. It was on the left-hand side of the page, "Pleading Child." It looked more difficult than I remembered. I played a few bars, surprised at how easily the notes came back to me.

And for the first time, or so it seemed, I noticed the 95 piece on the right-hand side. It was called "Perfectly Contented." I tried to play this one as well. It had a lighter melody but the same flowing rhythm and turned out to be quite easy. "Pleading Child" was shorter but slower; "Perfectly Contented" was longer, but faster. And after I played them both a few times, I realized they were two halves of the same song.

*   *   *

81% of students surveyed find that 4LTR Press Solutions help them prepare better for their exams

REVIEW

HE DID

LIT puts a multitude of study aids at your fingertips. After reading the chapters, check out these resources for further help:

- **Chapter-In-Review Cards**, found at the ends of chapters, include writing suggestions, checklists, glossary terms, and other resources to help you review chapter material.

- **Reading and Reacting Cards** at the back of the book offer a detachable study tool containing useful resources for reading selections in the anthology.

Other great ways to help students study include **online tutorials and quizzes, flashcards, video activities, podcasts, and more!**

You can find it all at **the Premium Website.** Login at **www.cengagebrain.com.**

PART 3
POETRY

Anne Sexton (1928–1974)

The Starry Night (1962)

That does not keep me from having a terrible need of—shall I say the
word—religion. Then I go out at night to paint the stars. Vincent Van Gogh in a
letter to his brother

The town does not exist
except where one black-haired tree slips
up like a drowned woman into the hot sky.
The town is silent. The night boils with eleven stars.
Oh starry starry night! This is how
I want to die.

It moves. They are all alive.
Even the moon bulges in its orange irons
to push children, like a god, from its eye.
The old unseen serpent swallows up the stars.
Oh starry starry night! This is how
I want to die:

into that rushing beast of the night,
sucked up by that great dragon, to split
from my life with no flag,
no belly,
no cry.

19
Understanding Poetry

Learning Outcomes

After reading this chapter, you should be able to do the following:

LO1 Identify the origins of modern poetry

LO2 Define poetry

LO3 Recognize kinds of poetry

Timeline

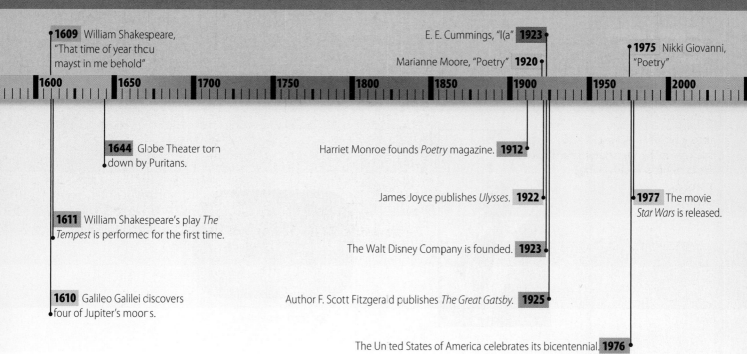

1609 William Shakespeare, "That time of year thou mayst in me behold"

1644 Globe Theater torn down by Puritans.

1611 William Shakespeare's play *The Tempest* is performed for the first time.

1610 Galileo Galilei discovers four of Jupiter's moons.

Harriet Monroe founds *Poetry* magazine. **1912**

James Joyce publishes *Ulysses*. **1922**

The Walt Disney Company is founded. **1923**

Author F. Scott Fitzgerald publishes *The Great Gatsby*. **1925**

The United States of America celebrates its bicentennial. **1976**

Marianne Moore, "Poetry" **1920**

E. E. Cummings, "l(a" **1923**

1975 Nikki Giovanni, "Poetry"

1977 The movie *Star Wars* is released.

1600 1650 1700 1750 1800 1850 1900 1950 2000

Marianne Moore (1887–1972)

Poetry (1921)

I, too, dislike it: there are things that are important beyond all this fiddle.
    Reading it, however, with a perfect contempt for it, one discovers in
       it after all, a place for the genuine.
           Hands that can grasp, eyes
           that can dilate, hair that can rise   5
               if it must, these things are important not because a

high-sounding interpretation can be put upon them but because they are
    useful. When they become so derivative as to become unintelligible,
      the same thing may be said for all of us, that we
        do not admire what   10
          we cannot understand: the bat
             holding on upside down or in quest of something to

eat, elephants pushing, a wild horse taking a roll, a tireless wolf under
    a tree, the immovable critic twitching his skin like a horse that feels a flea,
                            the base-
      ball fan, the statistician—   15
        nor is it valid
          to discriminate against "business documents and

school-books";° all these phenomena are important. One must make a
                   distinction
    however: when dragged into prominence by half poets, the result is not
                 poetry,
    nor till the poets among us can be   20
      "literalists of
        the imagination"°—above
           insolence and triviality and can present

for inspection, "imaginary gardens with real toads in them,"° shall we have
    it. In the meantime, if you demand on the one hand,   25
      the raw material of poetry in
        all its rawness and
        that which is on the other hand
           genuine, you are interested in poetry.

° **"business documents and school-books"** Moore quotes the *Diaries of Tolstoy* (New York, 1917): "Where the boundary between prose and poetry lies, I shall never be able to understand. . . . Poetry is verse; prose is not verse. Or else poetry is everything with the exception of business documents and school books."

° **"literalists of the imagination"** A reference (given by Moore) to W. B. Yeats's "William Blake and His Illustrations" (in *Ideas of Good and Evil*, 1903): "The imitation of his view was from the very intensity of his vision; he was a too literal realist of the imagination as others are of nature; and because he believed that the figures seen by the mind's eye, when exalted by inspiration, were 'external existences,' symbols of divine essences, he hated every grace of style that might obscure their lineaments."

° **"imaginary gardens with real toads in them"** Moore places these words in quotations, but the source is unknown.

>> Toad in garden

Nikki Giovanni (1943–   )

Poetry (1975)

poetry is motion graceful
as a fawn
gentle as a teardrop
strong like the eye
finding peace in a crowded room   5
we poets tend to think
our words are golden
though emotion speaks too
loudly to be defined
by silence   10

sometimes after midnight or just before
the dawn
we sit typewriter in hand
pulling loneliness around us
forgetting our lovers or children   15
who are sleeping
ignoring the weary wariness
of our own logic
to compose a poem
no one understands it   20
it never says "love me" for poets are
beyond love
it never says "accept me" for poems seek not
acceptance but controversy
it only says "i am" and therefore   25
i concede that you are too
a poem is pure energy
horizontally contained
between the mind
of the poet and the ear of the reader   30
if it does not sing discard the ear
for poetry is song
if it does not delight discard
the heart for poetry is joy
if it does not inform then close   35
off the brain for it is dead
if it cannot heed the insistent message
that life is precious

which is all we poets
wrapped in our loneliness   40
are trying to say

>> Typewriter

LO1 Identify the Origins of Modern Poetry

The history of poetry begins where the history of all literature begins—with the **oral tradition.** In a time before literacy and the printing press, the oral tradition was relied on as a way of preserving stories, histories, values, and beliefs. These stories were usually put into the form of rhyming poems, with repeated words and sounds used to make the poems easier to memorize and remember.

These extended narratives were eventually transcribed as **epics**—long poems depicting the actions of heroic figures who determine the fate of a nation or of an entire race. Early epics include Homer's *Iliad* and *Odyssey,* the *Epic of Gilgamesh,* the *Bhagavad Gita,* and Virgil's *Aeneid.* Early poetry can also be found in various religious texts, including ancient Hindu holy books like the Upanishads; sections of the Bible, including the Song of Solomon; and the Koran.

During the **Anglo-Saxon era** (late sixth to mid-eleventh centuries), poetry flourished as a literary form. Unfortunately, only about 30,000 lines of poetry survive from this period. Those poems that did survive are marked by heroic deeds and the absence of romantic love. The major texts of this time include *Beowulf, The Battle of Maldon,* and *The Dream of the Rood,* which is one of the earliest Christian poems. The theme of Christian morality in poetry continued into the Middle Ages with poems such as William Langland's *Piers Plowman,* which consists of three religious dream visions, and Chaucer's *Canterbury Tales,* a collection of narrative poems told by pilgrims as they travel to Canterbury, England. Using a slightly different approach to similar subject matter, Dante Alighieri wrote the Italian epic poem *The Divine Comedy,* which depicts an imaginary journey through hell, purgatory, and heaven. In France, the **troubadours,** poets of the Provençal region, wrote complex lyric poems about courtly love.

The next major literary period, the **Renaissance** (late fourteenth to mid-sixteenth centuries), witnessed the rebirth of science, philosophy, and the classical arts. Perhaps the most important writer of this period was William Shakespeare. A prolific poet, Shakespeare also wrote plays in verse, continuing in the tradition of the ancient Greek tragedian Sophocles and the ancient Roman playwright Seneca. Other notable writers of the Renaissance included Sir Philip Sidney, Christopher Marlowe, and Edmund Spenser.

During the seventeenth century, several literary movements emerged that contributed to poetry's growing prevalence and influence. John Milton continued the tradition of Christian poetry with his epic *Paradise Lost,* which told the tale of Adam and Eve's exile from the Garden of Eden. The **metaphysical poets** (John Donne, Andrew Marvell, and George Herbert) used elaborate figures of speech and favored intellect over emotions in their writing. Their poems were characterized by reason, complex comparisons and allusions, and paradoxes, and they introduced the **meditative poem** (a poem that abstractly ponders a concept or idea) into the literary world.

In the early eighteenth century, British poets (such as Alexander Pope and Samuel Johnson) wrote poems, biographies, and literary criticism. Toward the end of the

>> Image depicting the pilgrims from Geoffrey Chaucer's *The Canterbury Tales*

>> Illuminated manuscript (fifteenth century) from Dante's *Divine Comedy* depicting Dante and Virgil in Hell

The Bard, c. 1817 (oil on canvas). John Martin (1789-1854) / Yale Center for British Art, Paul Mellon Collection, USA / Paul Mellon Collection / The Bridgeman Art Library International.

>> John Martin's painting *The Bard* (1817) illustrating the mystical view of nature characteristic of Romanticism

>> Undated engraving of Edgar Allan Poe's "The Raven"

Romanticism Eighteenth- and nineteenth-century literary movement that valued subjectivity, individuality, the imagination, nature, excess, the exotic, and the mysterious.

The twentieth century had perhaps the largest number of literary movements to date, with each one reflecting its predecessors and influencing future generations of poets. In the early twentieth century, a literary movement that became known as **modernism** developed. As writers responded to the increasing complexity of a changing world, the overarching sentiment of modernism was that the "old ways" would no longer suffice in a world that had changed almost overnight as a result of the rise of industrialization and urbanization, as well as the devastation of World War I. Key modernist poets included W. H. Auden, William Butler Yeats, Ezra Pound, and T. S. Eliot, whose epic poem *The Waste Land* expressed the fragmentation of consciousness in the modern world.

The Tyger, plate 36 (Bentley 42) from Songs of Innocence and Experience (Bentley Copy L) 1789-94 (relief etching with pen and watercolor), William Blake (1757-1827) / Yale Center for British Art, Paul Mellon Collection, USA / The Bridgeman Art Library International.

>> Illuminated manuscript from William Blake's "The Tyger."

eighteenth century, the movement known as **Romanticism** began. Romantic poetry was marked by heightened emotion and sentiment; a strong sense of individualism; a respect for nature, history, and mysticism; and a return to first-person lyric poems. The early British Romantics included Samuel Taylor Coleridge, William Wordsworth, and William Blake. This generation was followed by the later Romantics, including Percy Bysshe Shelley, John Keats, and George Gordon, Lord Byron. American Romantics included Henry David Thoreau, Ralph Waldo Emerson, and Walt Whitman.

The nineteenth century was marked by yet another shift in poetic consciousness. This time, poets moved away from the contemplation of the self within nature that characterized Romanticism and returned to a more elevated sense of rhetoric and subject matter. Notable British poets included Matthew Arnold, Robert Browning, Elizabeth Barrett Browning, and Alfred, Lord Tennyson. American poets of the this period included Edgar Allan Poe, Henry Wadsworth Longfellow, Emily Dickinson, and Phillis Wheatley, a slave who became the first African-American poet.

After World War I, poets began to challenge the prevailing ideas of subject matter and form. Ezra Pound, along with Amy Lowell and other poets, founded **imagism,** a poetic movement that experimented with free verse and emphasized the writer's response to a visual scene or an object. William Carlos Williams wrote poems that were often deceptively simple, while the poetry of Wallace Stevens was often opaque and difficult to grasp. Dylan Thomas and E. E. Cummings also experimented with form, with Cummings intentionally manipulating the accepted constructs of grammar, syntax, and punctuation.

In the 1920s, the United States experienced the **Harlem Renaissance.** This rebirth of arts and culture was centered in Harlem, an area in New York City where, by the mid-1920s, the African-American population had reached 150,000. Harlem was teeming with creativity, especially in music (jazz and blues), literature, art, and drama. The poets who were part of the Harlem Renaissance—including Langston Hughes, Countee Cullen, James Weldon Johnson, and Jean Toomer—chose diverse subject matter and styles, but they were united in their celebration of African-American culture.

In the early 1930s, a group of poets gathered at a college in Black Mountain, North Carolina, with the aim of teaching and writing about poetry in a new way. The **Black Mountain poets,** as they were called, stressed the process of writing poetry rather than the finished poem. Notable poets in this group included Robert Creeley, Denise Levertov, and Charles Olson. Meanwhile, in Latin America, poetry was growing in importance, with poets such as Pablo Neruda experimenting with subject matter, language, form, and imagery.

In the late 1940s, in the aftermath of World War II, a group of disillusioned American poets turned to eastern mysticism and newly available hallucinogenic drugs to achieve higher consciousness. They became known as the **Beat poets,** and their work was known for social and political criticism that challenged the established norms of the time. These poets included Allen Ginsberg, whose long poem "Howl" became an unofficial anthem of the revolutionary 1960s, and Lawrence Ferlinghetti.

Up until the late 1950s, subject matter in American poetry was largely impersonal, concentrating chiefly on symbols, ideas, and politics. This changed when a group of poets—including Robert Lowell, Anne Sexton, W. D. Snodgrass, and Sylvia Plath—began to write **confessional poems** about their own personal experiences, emotions, triumphs, and tragedies (including mental illness and attempted suicide). Although there was considerable backlash against these poets from writers who thought that such highly personal subjects were not suitable for poetry, contemporary poets such as Sharon Olds continue to write confessional poetry.

The early 1960s witnessed the rise of the **Black Arts Movement,** which had its roots in the ideas of the civil rights struggle, Malcolm X and the Nation of Islam, and the Black Power Movement. The Black Arts poets wrote political works that addressed the sociopolitical and cultural context of African-American life. Notable authors in this group included Amiri Baraka, Gwendolyn Brooks, Jayne Cortez, and Etheridge Knight.

The next major literary movement in poetry had its beginnings in the mid to late 1980s with slam poetry. **Slam poetry,** with origins in the oral tradition, was influenced by the Beat poets, who stressed the live performance of poems. In a **slam,** poets compete either individually or in teams before an audience, which serves as the judge. (The structure of a traditional poetry slam was created by Marc Smith, a poet and construction worker, in 1986.) Slam poetry is concerned with current events and social and political themes, and often the winning poet is the one who best combines enthusiasm, presentation, and attitude with contemporary subject matter. A home base for slam poetry is the Nyuorican Poets Café in New York City, which has become a forum for poetry, music, video, and theater. Notable slam poets past and present include Miguel Piñero, Maggie Estep, and Jeffrey McDaniel.

A spinoff of slam poetry is the **spoken word** movement, which, unlike slam poetry, is a rehearsed performance. Spoken word performances have captivated a broad audience due in part to television shows such as HBO's *Def Poetry Jam*. **Hip-hop** and **rap,** musical forms whose lyrics rely heavily on rhyme, alliteration, assonance, consonance, and other poetic devices, also owe a debt to slam poetry and the spoken word movement.

Contemporary poetry is an extremely diverse genre whose practitioners have been influenced by many of the

AP Photo / In the Life TV, Pat Johnson.

>> Staceyann Chin, acclaimed slam poet and the star of *Def Poetry Jam on Broadway*

> *"Throughout history and across national and cultural boundaries, poetry has occupied an important place."*

literary movements discussed above. Some contemporary poets embrace narrative poetry; others favor the lyric. Some write free verse; others experiment with traditional forms like the **sonnet** or the **villanelle.** Still others write **concrete poetry,** which uses words as well as varying type sizes and type fonts to form pictures on a page, or other forms of visual poetry. The types of poetry being written today vary greatly, and this diversity is part of the appeal for those who read and write it.

LO2 Define Poetry

Throughout history and across national and cultural boundaries, poetry has occupied an important place. In ancient China and Japan, for example, poetry was prized above all else. One story tells of a samurai warrior who, when defeated, asked for a pen and paper. Thinking that he wanted to write a will before being executed, his captor granted his wish. Instead of writing a will, however, the warrior wrote a farewell poem that so moved his captor that he immediately released him.

To the ancient Greeks and Romans, poetry was the medium of spiritual and philosophical expression. Today, throughout the world, poetry continues to delight and to inspire. For many people in countless places, poetry is the language of the emotions, the medium of expression they use when they speak from the heart.

But what exactly *is* poetry? Is a poem "pure energy / horizontally contained / between the mind / of the poet and the readers," as Nikki Giovanni (page 345) describes it? Or is a poem simply what Marianne Moore (page 344) calls "all this fiddle"?

One way of defining poetry is to examine how it is different from other forms of literature, such as fiction or drama. The first and most important element of poetry that distinguishes it from other genres is its **form.** Unlike prose, which is written from margin to margin, poetry is made up of individual **lines.** A poetic line begins and ends where the poet chooses: it can start at the left margin or halfway across the page, and it can end at the right margin or after only a word or two. A poet chooses when to stop, or break, the line according to his or her sense of rhythm and meter.

Poets also use the **sound** of the words themselves, alone and in conjunction with the other words of the poem, to create a sense of rhythm and melody. **Alliteration** (the repetition of initial consonant sounds in consecutive or neighboring words), **assonance** (the repetition of vowel sounds), and **consonance** (the repetition of consonant

sonnet Fourteen-line poem, usually a **lyric** in *iambic pentameter.* It has a strict rhyme scheme in one of two forms: the *Italian,* or **Petrarchan sonnet** (an eight-line **octave** rhymed *abba/abba* with a six-line **sestet** rhymed *cdc/cdc* or a variation) and the *English,* or **Shakespearean sonnet** (three quatrains rhymed *abab/cdcd/efef* with a concluding couplet rhymed *gg*).

villanelle A nineteen-line poem composed of five tercets and a concluding quatrain; its rhyme scheme is *aba aba aba aba aba abaa.* Two different lines are systematically repeated in the poem: line 1 appears again in lines 6, 12, and 18, and line 3 reappears as lines 9, 15, and 19. Thus, each tercet concludes with an exact (or close) duplication of either line 1 or line 3, and the final quatrain concludes by repeating both line 1 and line 3.

form Structure or shape of a literary work; the way a work's parts fit together to form a whole. In poetry, form is described in terms of the presence (or absence) of elements like rhyme, meter, and stanzaic pattern.

alliteration Repetition of consonant sounds (usually the initial sounds) in a series of words, as in Blake's "The Chimney Sweeper": "So your chimneys I sweep, and in soot I sleep." Alliteration may be reinforced by repeated sounds within and at the ends of words.

assonance Repetition of the same or similar vowel sounds in a series of words: "creep three feet."

rhyme Repetition of concluding sounds in different words, often intentionally used at the ends of poetic lines.

imagery Words and phrases that describe the concrete experience of the five senses, most often sight. A **pattern of imagery** is a group of related images developed throughout a work.

sounds within words) are three devices commonly used by poets to help create the music of a poem. Poets can also use **rhyme** (either at the ends of lines or within the lines themselves), which contributes to the pattern of sounds in a poem.

In addition, poets are more likely than writers of other kinds of literature to rely on **imagery,** words or phrases that describe the senses. These vivid descriptions or details help the reader to connect with the poet's ideas in a tangible way. Poets also make extensive use of **figurative language,** including metaphors and similes, to convey their ideas and to help their readers access these ideas.

Another way of defining poetry is to examine our assumptions about it. Different readers, different poets, different generations of readers and poets, and different cultures often have different expectations about poetry. As a result, they have varying assumptions about what poetry should be, and these assumptions raise questions. Must poetry be written to delight or inspire, or can a poem have a political or social message? Must a poem's theme be conveyed subtly, embellished with imaginatively chosen sounds and words, or can it be explicit and straightforward? Such questions, which have been debated by literary critics as well as by poets for many years, have no easy answers—and perhaps no answers at all. A **haiku**—a short poem, rich in imagery, adhering to a rigid formal structure—is certainly poetry, and so is a **prose poem** like Carolyn Forché's "The Colonel" (p. 458). To some Western readers, however, a haiku might seem too plain or understated to be "poetic," and Forché's poem might seem to be a political tract masquerading as poetry. Still, most of these readers would agree that the following lines qualify as poetry.

William Shakespeare (1564–1616)

That time of year thou mayst in me behold (1609)

That time of year thou mayst in me behold
When yellow leaves, or none, or few, do hang
Upon those boughs which shake against the cold,
Bare ruined choirs, where late the sweet birds sang.
In me thou see'st the twilight of such day   5
As after sunset fadeth in the west;
Which by and by black night doth take away,
Death's second self that seals up all in rest.
In me thou see'st the glowing of such fire,
That on the ashes of his youth doth lie,   10
As the deathbed whereon it must expire,
Consumed with that which it was nourished by,
   This thou perceiv'st, which makes thy love more strong,
   To love that well which thou must leave ere long.

>> Bare branches against winter sky

This poem includes many of the characteristics that Western readers commonly associate with poetry. For instance, its lines have a regular pattern of rhyme and meter that identifies it as a **sonnet**. The poem also develops a complex network of related images and figures of speech that compare the lost youth of the aging speaker to the sunset and to autumn. Finally, the pair of rhyming lines at the end of the poem expresses a familiar poetic theme: the lovers' realization that they must eventually die makes their love stronger.

Although most readers would classify Shakespeare's sonnet as a poem, they might be less certain about the following lines.

E. E. Cummings (1894–1962)

l(a (1923)

l(a

le

af

fa

ll

s)

one

l

iness

5

>> Falling leaves

Unlike Shakespeare's poem, "l(a" does not seem to have any of the characteristics normally associated with poetry. It has no meter, rhyme, or imagery. It has no repeated sounds and no figures of speech. It cannot even be read aloud because its "lines" are fragments of words. In spite of its odd appearance, however, "l(a" does communicate a conventional poetic theme.

When reconstructed, the words Cummings broke apart have the following appearance: "l (a leaf falls) one l iness." In a sense, this poem is a complex visual and verbal pun. If the parenthetical insertion "(a leaf falls)" is removed, the remaining letters spell "loneliness." Moreover, the form of the letter *l* in loneliness suggests the number *1*—which, in turn, suggests the loneliness and isolation of the individual, as reflected in nature (the single leaf). Like Shakespeare, Cummings uses an image of a leaf to express his ideas about life and human experience. At the same time, by breaking words into bits and pieces, Cummings suggests the flexibility of language and conveys the need to break out of customary ways of using words to define experience.

As these two poems illustrate, defining what a poem is (and what it is not) can be difficult. Poems can rhyme or not rhyme. They can be divided into stanzas and have a distinct form, or they can flow freely and have no discernable form. These and other choices are what many poets find alluring about the process of writing poetry. As a form, poetry is compact and concise, and choosing the right words to convey ideas is a challenge. As a literary genre, it offers room for experimentation while at the same time remaining firmly grounded in a literary tradition that stretches back through time to antiquity.

LO3 Recognize Kinds of Poetry

Most poems are either **narrative** poems, which recount a story, or **lyric** poems, which communicate a speaker's mood, feelings, or state of mind.

NARRATIVE POETRY

Although any brief poem that tells a story, such as Edwin Arlington Robinson's "Richard Cory" (p. 516), may be considered a narrative poem, the two most familiar forms of narrative poetry are the *epic* and the *ballad*.

Epics are narrative poems that recount the accomplishments of heroic figures, typically including expansive settings, superhuman feats, and gods and supernatural beings. The language of epic poems tends to be formal, even elevated, and often quite elaborate. In ancient times, epics were handed down orally; more recently, poets have written literary epics, such as John Milton's *Paradise Lost* (1667) and Nobel Prize–winning poet Derek Walcott's *Omeros* (1990), that follow many of the same conventions.

The **ballad** is another type of narrative poetry with roots in an oral tradition. Originally intended to be sung, a ballad uses repeated words and phrases, including a refrain, to advance its story. Some—but not all—ballads use the **ballad stanza.** Dudley Randall's "Ballad of Birmingham" (p. 378) is an example of a contemporary ballad.

---

narrative The "storytelling" of a piece of literature; the forward-moving recounting of episode and description.

lyric Form of poetry, usually brief and intense, that expresses a poet's subjective response to the world. In classical times, lyrics were set to music. The Romantic poets, particularly Keats, often wrote lyrics about love, death, and nature.

ballad Narrative poem, rooted in an oral tradition, usually arranged in quatrains rhyming *abcb* and containing a refrain.

ballad stanza Stanza that alternates lines of eight and six syllables. Typically, only the second and fourth lines rhyme.

elegy Poem commemorating someone's death, usually in a reflective or mournful tone.

ode Relatively long lyric poem, common in antiquity and adapted by the Romantic poets, for whom it was a serious poem of formal diction, often addressed to some significant object (such as a nightingale or the west wind) that has stimulated the poet's imagination.

terza rima Form used by Dante that has a rhyme scheme (*aba, bcb, ded*) that creates an interlocking series of stanzas.

aubade Poem about morning, usually celebrating the dawn.

meditation Lyric poem that focuses on a physical object using this object as a vehicle for considering larger issues.

pastoral Literary work that deals nostalgically and usually unrealistically with a simple, preindustrial rural life; the name comes from the fact that pastorals traditionally feature shepherds.

dramatic monologue Type of poem perfected by Robert Browning that consists of a single speaker talking to one or more listeners and often revealing much more about the speaker than he or she seems to intend.

LYRIC POETRY

Like narrative poems, lyric poems take various forms.

An **elegy** is a poem in which a poet mourns the death of a specific person, as in A. E. Housman's "To an Athlete Dying Young" (p. 395).

An **ode** is a long lyric poem, formal and serious in style, tone, and subject matter. An ode typically has a fairly complex stanzaic pattern, such as the **terza rima** used by Percy Bysshe Shelley in "Ode to the West Wind" (p. 518). Another ode in this text is John Keats's "Ode on a Grecian Urn" (p. 511).

An **aubade** is a poem about morning, usually celebrating the coming of dawn. An example is Philip Larkin's 1977 poem "Aubade."

An **occasional poem** is written to celebrate a particular event or occasion. An example is Billy Collins's poem "The Names," read before a joint session of Congress to commemorate the first anniversary of the terrorist attacks on the World Trade Center.

A **meditation** is a lyric poem that focuses on a physical object, using this object as a vehicle for considering larger issues. Edmund Waller's seventeenth-century poem "Go, lovely rose" is a meditation.

A **pastoral**—for example, Christopher Marlowe's "The Passionate Shepherd to His Love" (p. 513)—is a lyric poem that celebrates the simple, idyllic pleasures of country life.

A **dramatic monologue** is a poem whose speaker addresses one or more silent listeners, often revealing much more than he or she intends. Robert Browning's "My Last Duchess" (p. 365) and "Porphyria's Lover" (p. 375) are dramatic monologues.

As you read the poems in this text, you will encounter works with a wide variety of forms, styles, and themes. Some you will find appealing, amusing, uplifting, or moving; others may strike you as puzzling, intimidating, or depressing. But regardless of your critical reaction to the poems, one thing is certain: if you take the time to connect with the lines you are reading, you will come away from them thinking not just about the images and ideas they express but also about yourself and your world.

20

Poetry Sampler: Poetry and Art

Learning Outcomes

After reading this chapter, you should be able to do the following:

LO1 Appreciate poems about art

Timeline

Cathy Song, "Girl Powdering Her Neck" **1983**

Robert Hayden, "Monet's Waterlilies" **1966**

May Swenson, "The Tall Figures of Giacometti" **1966**

1995 Rita Dove, "Sonnet in Primary Colors"

Allen Ginsberg, "Cezanne's Ports" **1961**

2001 Kevin Young, "The Fun Gallery"

1800 1820 1840 1860 1880 1900 1920 1940 1960 1980 2000 2020

1806 Artist Kitagawa Utamaro dies.

Painter Paul Cezanne dies. **1906**

Painter Claude Monet dies. **1926**

Painter Frida Kahlo dies. **1954**

1993 Rita Dove begins a two-year term as Poet Laureate of the United States.

Alberto Giacometti is awarded the Grand Prize for sculpture at the Venice Bienalle. **1962**

Three Civil Rights marches take place, each beginning in Selma, Alabama. **1965**

Sculptor Alberto Giacometti dies. **1966**

The Civil Liberties Act, which ncludes an official apology for internment of Japanese Americans during World War II, becomes law. **1988**

Painter Jean-Michel Basquiat dies. **1988**

LO1 Appreciate Poems about Art

Many poets have found visual art to be a source of inspiration for their poems. In fact, the ancient Greeks used the word *ekphrasis* to denote poetry that focused on paintings, artistic objects, and highly visual scenes. In the *Illiad,* for example, Homer vividly describes the shield of Achilles. The ancient Romans also saw the connection between art and poetry. The Roman poet Horace made this point in *Ars Poetica* when he observed, "as in painting, so in poetry." Other more contemporary examples of *ekphrasis* occur in John Keats's "Ode on a Grecian Urn" (p. 511) and W. H. Auden's "Musée des Beaux Arts" (p. 475).

A poem about a work of art often expresses a poet's deep emotional response to it. Sometimes the poet not only gives voice to his or her reactions but also gives voice to the work of art itself. This is true of Keats when he writes about a Grecian urn (which he probably saw in the British Museum in London). Keats attempts to come to terms not only with the static images he sees on the urn but also with the effect it has on him. For Keats, the quiet majesty of the urn reflects a basic principle of art: "Heard melodies are sweet, but those unheard / Are sweeter; therefore, ye soft pipes, play on" (lines 11–12). For Keats, the message of the urn is simple and very direct: " 'Beauty is truth, truth beauty,'—that is all / Ye know on earth, and all ye need to know" (lines 49–50).

A poem about a work of art can also try convey its essence to readers. Auden attempts to achieve this in his "Musée des Beaux Arts." By pointing out the inherent contradictions in the Brueghel painting his poem describes, Auden seeks to penetrate the painting and to interpret it for readers. As Icarus plunges to his death into the sea, "dogs go on with their doggy life" (line 12) and the ploughman goes on plowing, never having heard "the splash, the forsaken cry" (line 16). For Auden, Brueghel's painting expresses a basic truth that the old masters knew: that no matter how momentous an occurrence, life goes on. While someone is suffering—whether it be Christ or Icarus—"someone else is eating or opening a window or just walking dully along" (line 4).

Each of the poems in this sampler is accompanied by the art that inspired it. In "Sonnet in Primary Colors," Rita Dove explores her reactions to paintings by the artist Frida Kahlo. In "Cézanne's Ports," Alan Ginsberg uses a painting by a well-known impressionist as inspiration just as Robert Hayden does in "Monet's 'Waterlilies' " In "Girl Powdering Her Neck," Cathy Song contemplates a portrait by Kitagawa Ultamaro of a geisha preparing herself for her next assignation. In "Tall Figures," May Swenson explores the meaning of a sculpture by Alberto Giacometti. Finally, in "Fun Gallery," Kevin Young reacts to the work of graffiti artist and painter Jean-Michel Basquiat.

Rita Dove (1952–   )

Sonnet in Primary Colors (1995)

This is for the woman with one black wing
perched over her eyes: lovely Frida,° erect
among parrots, in the stern petticoats
   of the peasant,
who painted herself a present—
wildflowers entwining the plaster corset   5
her spine resides in the romance of mirrors.

Each night she lay down in pain and rose
to her celluloid butterflies of her Beloved Dead,
Lenin° and Marx° and Stalin° arrayed at
   the footstead.
And rose to her easel, the hundred dogs panting   10
like children along the graveled walks
   of the garden, Diego's°
love a skull in the circular window
of the thumbprint searing her immutable brow.

° **Frida** Frida Kahlo (1907–1954), Mexican painter, feminist and Communist.

° **Lenin** Vladimir Ilyich Lenin (1870–1924), Communist revolutionary and first leader of the Soviet Union.

° **Marx** Karl Marx (1818–1883), political theorist and author of *The Communist Manifesto.*

° **Stalin** Joseph Stalin (1878–1953), second leader of the Soviet Union.

° **Diego's** Diego Rivera (1886–1957), Communist Mexican artist, husband of Frida Kahlo.

© 2010 Banco de Mexico Diego Rivera Frida Kahlo Museums Trust, Mexico, D.F./Artists Rights Society (ARS), New York

>> Self Portrait with Monkey and Parrot (1938) by Frida Kahlo

Allen Ginsberg (1926–1997)

Cézanne's° Ports (1961)

In the foreground we see time and life
swept in a race
toward the left hand side of the picture
where shore meets shore.

But that meeting place   5
isn't represented;
it doesn't occur on the canvas.

For the other side of the bay
is Heaven and Eternity,
with a bleak white haze over
   its mountains.   10

And the immense water of L'Estaque°
   is a go-between
for minute rowboats.

» *The Gulf of Marseilles Seen from L'Estaque (ca. 1885) by Paul Cezanne*

° **Cézanne's** Paul Cézanne (1839–1906), French postimpressionist painter.

° **L'Estaque** Fishing village in France where Cézanne painted many views of the sea.

Robert Hayden (1913–1980)

Monet's "Waterlilies"° (1966)

Today as the news from Selma° and Saigon°
poisons the air like fallout,
I come again to see
the serene, great picture that I love.

Here space and time exist in light   5
the eye like the eye of faith believes.
The seen, the known
dissolve in iridescence, become
illusive flesh of light
that was not, was, forever is.   10

O light beheld as through refracting tears.
Here is the aura of that world
each of us has lost.
Here is the shadow of its joy.

» *Waterlilies (1914–1917) oil on canvas by Claude Monet*

° **"Waterlilies"** A series of paintings by Claude Monet (1840–1926), a French impressionist painter.

° **Selma** Selma, Alabama. The site of civil rights marches in the mid 1960s, one of which was ended by police violence.

° **Saigon** Capital of South Vietnam from 1954 to 1975; now know as Ho Chi Mihn City.

Cathy Song (1955–)

Girl Powdering Her Neck (1983)

from a ukiyo-e° print by Utamaro°

The light is the inside
sheen of an oyster shell,
sponged with talc and vapor,
moisture from a bath.

A pair of slippers   5
are placed outside
the rice-paper doors.
She kneels at a low table
in the room,
her legs folded beneath her   10
as she sits on a buckwheat pillow.

Her hair is black
with hints of red,
the color of seaweed
spread over rocks.   15

Morning begins the ritual
wheel of the body,
the application of translucent skins.
She practices pleasure:
the pressure of three fingertips   20
applying powder.
Fingerprints of pollen
some other hand will trace.

The peach-dyed kimono
patterned with maple leaves   25
drifting across the silk,
falls from right to left
in a diagonal, revealing
the nape of her neck
and the curve of a shoulder   30
like the slope of a hill
set deep in snow in a country
of huge white solemn birds.
Her face appears in the mirror,
a reflection in a winter pond,   35
rising to meet itself.
She dips a corner of her sleeve
like a brush into water
to wipe the mirror;
she is about to paint herself.   40
The eyes narrow
in a moment of self-scrutiny.
The mouth parts
as if desiring to disturb
the placid plum face;   45
break the symmetry of silence.
But the berry-stained lips,
stenciled into the mask of beauty,
do not speak.

° **ukiyo-e** A type of Japanese woodblock print.

° **Utamaro** Kitagawa Utamaro (1754–1806), Japanese printmaker.

>> *Geisha of the House of Sumiyoshi before a Mirror* (1790) by Kitagawa Utamaro

Two chrysanthemums
touch in the middle of the lake
and drift apart.

50

May Swenson (1919–1989)

The Tall Figures of Giacometti° (1966)

We move by means of our mud bumps.
We bubble as do the dead but more slowly.

The products of excruciating purges
we are squeezed out thin hard and dry.

If we exude a stench it is petrified sainthood.   5
Our feet are large crude fused together

solid like anvils. Ugly as truth is ugly
we are meant to stand upright a long time

and shudder without motion
under the scintillating pins of light   10

that dart between our bodies
of pimpled mud and your eyes.

>> *City Square (La Place)* (1948) bronze by Alberto Giacometti

° **Giacometti** Alberto
Giacometti (1901–1966),
Swiss sculptor, painter, and
printmaker.

Kevin Young (1970–   )

The Fun Gallery° (2001)

A buzz in the air
already, Basquiat°
beaming. RAY GUN

set to stun—
—maximum—a hold   5
up in this hole

in the wall,
a billion
paintings pinned

to dry wall   10
like butterflies,
stomachs. He's made it

all from scratch
& paint.
The work's too low   15

° **Fun Gallery** Art gallery
founded in New York City's
East Village in 1981, which
introduced graffiti as an art
form to the mainstream art
world.
° **Basquiat** Jean-Michel
Basquiat (1960–1988) a
graffiti and neo-expressionist
artist of Puerto Rican and
Haitian heritage. He died of a
drug overdose at age
twenty-eight.

his dealer warned—
everything should be higher
to keep up

your prices,
speed. All night   20
the crowds line

outside like Disneyland
& love it. Taken
over Manhattan

he's King   25
Kong or Mighty Joe
Young, social

climbing—gone
from trains
to scale the Empire   30

State. Keeping most
of the show
for hisself, hitches

a limo to Bklyn
by dawn—the armored   35
car hour—up

early—or late—
as if to his own
funeral—

"Papa I've made it"   40

hugs & hands
him a blooming
bouquet.

>> Untitled (1981) acrylic and pencil on canvas by Jean-Michel Basquiat

Writing Suggestions: Poetry and Art

1. Look at one of the pieces of visual art that appears in this sampler. Then, write a poem about it. Before you write your poem, consider whether you want to try to describe the piece of visual art or whether you want to use it as inspiration for your own ideas. (You could, of course, do both.)

2. Write an essay in which you compare the poem you wrote to the one in the sampler that accompanies the work of visual art. What details about the piece of visual art did you choose to emphasize? What details does the poet emphasize? How do you account for the differences?

3. Select one of the poems in this sampler and write an **explication** (see Chapter 3).

Reading and Reacting to Poetry and Art

1. What particular aspects of the work of art does the poet focus on? Which aspects does he or she ignore?

2. What purpose is the poet trying to achieve? For example, is he or she expressing emotion, offering an analysis, or attempting to shed light on a particular aspect of the art?

3. What insight into the art do you gain from reading the poem? Do you think the poet is missing anything?

4. Compare the poem to the artwork that inspired it. How are the two alike? How are they different?

5. What questions about the art does the poem raise?

6. Do you disagree with the speaker's interpretation of the work of art? With what do you disagree?

21

Voice

Learning Outcomes

After reading this chapter, you should be able to do the following:

LO1 Identify the speaker in the poem

LO2 Identify the tone of the poem

LO3 Recognize irony

Timeline

1646 Robert Herrick, "To the Virgins, to Make Much of Time"

Robert Browning, "My Last Duchess" **1842**

Robert Browning, "Porphyria's Lover" **1836**

Percy Bysshe Shelley, "Ozymandias" **1818**

William Wordsworth, "The World Is Too Much with Us" **1807**

Thomas Hardy, "The Man He Killed" **1902**

Amy Lowell, "Patterns" **1915**

Robert Frost, "Fire and Ice" **1923**

Emily Dickinson, "I'm nobody! Who are you?" **1891**

1926 Langston Hughes, "Negro"

1939 W. H. Auden, "The Unknown Citizen"

1969 Dudley Randall, "Ballad of Birmingham"

1971 Louise Glück, "Gretel in Darkness"

1973 Leonard Adamé, "My Grandmother Would Rock Quietly and Hum"

1973 Leslie Marmon Silko, "Where Mountain Lion Lay Down with Deer"

1987 Janice Mirikitani, "Suicide Note"

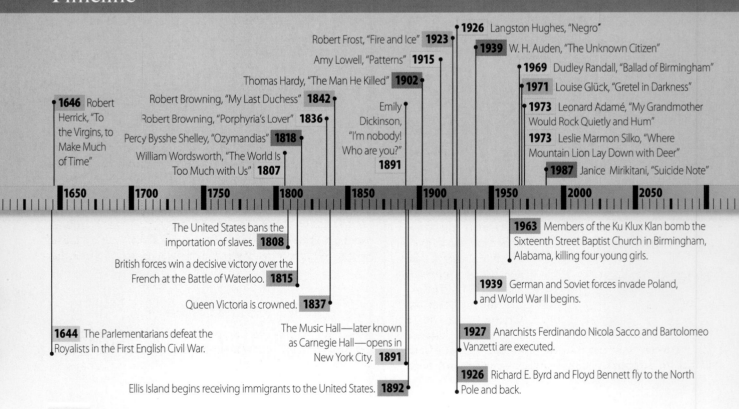

The United States bans the importation of slaves. **1808**

British forces win a decisive victory over the French at the Battle of Waterloo. **1815**

Queen Victoria is crowned. **1837**

1644 The Parlementarians defeat the Royalists in the First English Civil War.

The Music Hall—later known as Carnegie Hall—opens in New York City. **1891**

Ellis Island begins receiving immigrants to the United States. **1892**

1963 Members of the Ku Klux Klan bomb the Sixteenth Street Baptist Church in Birmingham, Alabama, killing four young girls.

1939 German and Soviet forces invade Poland, and World War II begins.

1927 Anarchists Ferdinando Nicola Sacco and Bartolomeo Vanzetti are executed.

1926 Richard E. Byrd and Floyd Bennett fly to the North Pole and back.

Emily Dickinson (1830–1886)

I'm nobody! Who are you? (1891)

© Bettmann/Corbis

I'm nobody! Who are you?
Are you—Nobody—Too?
Then there's a pair of us?
Don't tell! they'd advertise—you know!

How dreary—to be—Somebody!   5
How public—like a Frog—
To tell one's name—the livelong June—
To an admiring Bog!

LO1 Identify the Speaker in the Poem

When they read a work of fiction, readers decide whether the narrator is sophisticated or unsophisticated, trustworthy or untrustworthy, innocent or experienced. Just as fiction depends on a narrator, poetry depends on a **speaker** who describes events, feelings, and ideas to readers. Finding out as much as possible about this speaker can help readers to interpret a poem. For example, the speaker in Emily Dickinson's "I'm nobody! Who are you?" seems at first to be playful, even flirtatious. As the poem continues, however, the speaker becomes a more complex persona. In the first stanza, the speaker reveals her private self—internal, isolated, with little desire to be well known; in the second stanza, she expresses disdain for those who seek to become "somebody," whom she sees as self-centered, self-promoting, and inevitably superficial. Far from being defeated by her isolation, the speaker rejects fame and celebrates her status as a "nobody."

One question readers might ask about "I'm nobody! Who are you?" is how close the speaker's voice is to the poet's. Readers who conclude that the poem is about the conflict between a poet's public and private selves may be tempted to see the speaker and the poet as one. But this is not necessarily the case. Like the narrator of a short story, the speaker of a poem is a **persona**, or mask, that the poet puts on. Granted, in some poems little distance exists between the poet and the speaker. Without hard evidence to support a link between speaker and poet,

> *"Just as fiction depends on a narrator, poetry depends on a speaker who describes events, feelings, and ideas to readers."*

EXPLORE ONLINE >

To complete a tutorial of "Voice," visit your Literature CourseMate, accessed through www.cengagebrain.com.

however, readers should not simply assume they are one and the same.

In many cases, the speaker is quite different from the poet—even when the speaker's voice conveys the attitude of the poet, either directly or indirectly. In his 1758 poem "The Chimney Sweeper," for example, William Blake assumes the voice of a child to criticize the system of child labor that existed in eighteenth-century England. Even though the child speaker does not understand the economic and social forces that cause his misery, readers sense the poet's anger as the trusting speaker describes the appalling conditions under which he works. The poet's indignation is especially apparent in the biting irony of the last line, in which the victimized speaker innocently assures readers that if all people do their duty, "they need not fear harm."

Sometimes the poem's speaker is anonymous. In such cases—as in William Carlos Williams's "Red Wheelbarrow" (p. 401), for instance—the first-person voice is absent, and the speaker remains outside the poem. At other times, the speaker has a set identity—a king, a beggar, a highwayman, a sheriff, a husband, a wife, a rich man, a murderer, a child, a mythical figure, an explorer, a teacher, a faithless lover, a saint—or even a flower, an animal, or a clod of earth. Whatever the case, the speaker is not the poet but

speaker The narrative voice the poet uses.

persona An identity the poet assumes; in Greek tragedy, a persona was a mask worn by an actor.

rather a creation that the poet uses to convey his or her ideas. (For this reason, poems by a single poet may have very different voices. Compare Sylvia Plath's bitter and sardonic poem "Daddy" [p. 416] with the very different voice of her poem "Metaphors" [p. 413], for example.)

Sometimes a poem's title tells readers that the poet is assuming a particular persona. In the following poem, for example, the title identifies the speaker as a fictional character, Gretel from the fairy tale "Hansel and Gretel."

Louise Glück (1943–)

Gretel in Darkness (1971)

This is the world we wanted.
All who would have seen us dead
are dead. I hear the witch's cry
break in the moonlight through a sheet
of sugar: God rewards.   5
Her tongue shrivels into gas. . . .
     Now, far from women's arms
And memory of women, in our father's hut
we sleep, are never hungry.
Why do I not forget?   10
My father bars the door, bars harm
from this house, and it is years.

No one remembers. Even you, my brother,
summer afternoons you look at me as though
you meant to leave,   15
as though it never happened.
But I killed for you. I see armed firs,
the spires of that gleaming kiln—

Nights I turn to you to hold me
but you are not there.   20
Am I alone? Spies
hiss in the stillness, Hansel
we are there still, and it is real, real,
that black forest, and the fire in earnest.

>> Gretel pushing witch into oven (illustration for 1930 children's book)

The speaker in this poem comments on her life after her encounter with the witch in the forest. Speaking to her brother, Gretel observes that they now live in the world they wanted: they live with their father in his hut, and the witch and the wicked stepmother are dead. Even so, the memory of the events in the forest haunts Gretel and makes it impossible for her to live "happily ever after."

By assuming the persona of Gretel, the poet is able to convey some interesting and complex ideas. On one level, Gretel represents any person who has lived through a traumatic experience. Memories of the event keep breaking through into the present, frustrating her attempts to reestablish her belief in the goodness of the world. The voice we hear is sad, alone, and frightened: "Nights I turn to you to hold me," she says, "but you are not there." Although the murder Gretel committed for her brother was justified, it

seems to haunt her. "No one remembers," laments Gretel, not even her brother. At some level, she realizes that by killing the witch she has killed a part of herself, perhaps the part of women that men fear and consequently transform into witches and wicked stepmothers. The world that is left after the killing is her father's and her brother's, not her own, and she is now alone in a dark world haunted by the memories of the black forest. In this sense, Gretel—"Now, far from women's arms / And memory of women"—may be the voice of all victimized women who, because of men, act against their own best interests—and regret it.

As "Gretel in Darkness" illustrates, a title can identify a poem's speaker, but the speaker's own words can provide much more information. This is also the case in the following poem, where Spanish words help to characterize the speaker.

Leonard Adamé (1947–   )

My Grandmother Would Rock Quietly and Hum (1973)

in her house
she would rock quietly and hum
until her swelled hands
calmed

in summer   5
she wore thick stockings
sweaters
and grey braids

(when "el cheque"° came
we went to Payless   10
and I laughed greedily
when given a quarter)

mornings,
sunlight barely lit
the kitchen   15
and where
there were shadows
it was not cold

she quietly rolled
flour tortillas—   20
the "papas"°
cracking in hot lard
would wake me

she had lost her teeth
and when we ate   25
she had bread
soaked in "café"°

always her eyes
were clear
and she could see   30
as I cannot yet see—
through her eyes
she gave me herself
she would sit
and talk   35
of her girlhood—
of things strange to me:
    México
    epidemics
    relatives shot   40
    her father's hopes
    of this country—
how they sank
with cement dust
to his insides   45
now

>> Mexican woman making tortillas

° **el cheque** The check.
° **papas** Potatoes.
° **café** Coffee.

when I go
to the old house
the worn spots
by the stove   50
echo of her shuffling
and
México
still hangs in her
fading   55
calendar pictures

In Adamé's poem, the speaker is an adult recalling childhood memories of his grandmother. Spanish words—*el cheque, tortillas, papas,* and *café*—identify the speaker as Latino. His easy use of English, his comment that Mexico is strange to him, and his observation that he cannot yet see through his grandmother's eyes suggest, however, that he is not in touch with his Mexican identity. At one level, the grandmother evokes nostalgic memories of the speaker's youth. At another level, she is a living symbol of his ties with Mexico, connecting him to the ethnic culture he is trying to recover. The poem ends on an ambivalent note: even though the speaker is able to return to "the old house," the pictures of Mexico are fading, perhaps suggesting the speaker's inevitable assimilation into mainstream American culture.

Direct statements by speakers can also help to characterize them. In the next poem, the first line of each stanza establishes the identity of the speaker—and defines his perspective.

Langston Hughes (1902–1967)

© AP Photo

Negro (1926)

I am a Negro:
   Black as the night is black,
   Black like the depths of my Africa.

I've been a slave:
   Caesar told me to keep his door-steps clean.   5
   I brushed the boots of Washington.

I've been a worker:
   Under my hand the pyramids arose.
   I made mortar for the Woolworth Building.

I've been a singer: 10
   All the way from Africa to Georgia
   I carried my sorrow songs.
I made ragtime.

I've been a victim:
   The Belgians cut off my hands in the Congo.   15
   They lynch me still in Mississippi.

I am a Negro:
   Black as the night is black,
   Black like the depths of my Africa.

>> Pyramids in Egypt

soulpies/Shutterstock.com

Here the speaker, identifying himself as "a Negro," assumes each of the roles African Americans have historically played in Western society—slave, worker, singer, and victim. By so doing, he gives voice to his ancestors who, by being forced to serve others, were deprived of their identities. By presenting not only their suffering but also their accomplishments, the speaker asserts his pride in being black. The speaker also implies that the suffering of black people has been caused by economic exploitation: Romans, Egyptians, Belgians, and Americans all used black labor to help build their societies. In this context, the speaker's implied warning is clear: except for the United States, all the societies that have exploited blacks have declined, and long after the fall of those empires, black people still endure.

dramatic monologue Type of poem that consists of a single speaker talking to one or more listeners—often revealing much more than he or she seems to intend.

In each of the preceding poems, the speaker is alone. The following poem, a **dramatic monologue**, presents a more complex situation in which the poet creates a complete dramatic scene. The speaker is developed as a character whose distinctive personality is revealed through his words as he addresses a silent listener.

Robert Browning (1812–1889)

My Last Duchess (1842)

Ferrara

That's my last Duchess painted on the wall,
Looking as if she were alive. I call
That piece a wonder, now: Frà Pandolf's° hands
Worked busily a day, and there she stands.
Will't please you sit and look at her? I said   5
"Frà Pandolf" by design, for never read
Strangers like you that pictured countenance,
The depth and passion of its earnest glance,
But to myself they turned (since none puts by
The curtain I have drawn for you, but I)   10
And seemed as they would ask me, if they durst,
How such a glance came there; so, not the first
Are you to turn and ask thus. Sir, 'twas not
Her husband's presence only, called that spot
Of joy into the Duchess' cheek: perhaps   15
Frà Pandolf chanced to say "Her mantle laps
Over my lady's wrist too much," or "Paint
Must never hope to reproduce the faint
Half-flush that dies along her throat": such stuff
Was courtesy, she thought, and cause enough   20
For calling up that spot of joy. She had
A heart—how shall I say?—too soon made glad,
Too easily impressed; she liked whate'er
She looked on, and her looks went everywhere.
Sir, 'twas all one! My favor at her breast,   25
The dropping of the daylight in the West,
The bough of cherries some officious fool
Broke in the orchard for her, the white mule
She rode with round the terrace—all and each
Would draw from her alike the approving speech,   30
Or blush, at least. She thanked men—good! but thanked
Somehow—I know not how—as if she ranked
My gift of a nine-hundred-years-old name
With anybody's gift. Who'd stoop to blame
This sort of trifling? Even had you skill   35
In speech—(which I have not)—to make your will
Quite clear to such an one, and say, "Just this

>> The King's Closet, Windsor Castle, from 'Royal Residences', engraved by William James Bennett (1769–1844)

° **Frà Pandolf** "Brother" Pandolf, a fictive painter.

Or that in you disgusts me; here you miss,
Or there exceed the mark"—and if she let
Herself be lessoned so, nor plainly set   40
Her wits to yours, forsooth, and made excuse
—E'en then would be some stooping; and I choose
Never to stoop. Oh sir, she smiled, no doubt,
Whene'er I passed her; but who passed without
Much the same smile? This grew; I gave commands;   45
Then all smiles stopped together. There she stands
As if alive. Will't please you rise? We'll meet
The company below, then. I repeat,
The Count your master's known munificence
Is ample warrant that no just pretense   50
Of mine for dowry will be disallowed;
Though his fair daughter's self, as I avowed
At starting, is my object. Nay, we'll go
Together down, sir. Notice Neptune,° though,
Taming a sea horse, thought a rarity,   55
Which Claus of Innsbruck° cast in bronze for me!

° **Neptune** In Roman mythology, the god of the sea.

° **Claus of Innsbruck** A fictive—or unidentified—sculptor. The count of Tyrol's capital was at Innsbrück, Austria.

EXPLORE ONLINE >

To listen to audio of "My Last Duchess," visit your Literature CourseMate, accessed through www.cengagebrain.com.

The speaker is probably Alfonso II, duke of Ferrara, Italy, whose young wife, Lucrezia, died in 1561 after only three years of marriage. Shortly after her death, the duke began negotiations to marry again. When the poem opens, the duke is showing a portrait of his late wife to an emissary of an unnamed count who is there to arrange a marriage between the duke and the count's daughter. The duke remarks that the artist, Frà Pandolf, has caught a certain look on the duchess's face. This look aroused the jealousy of the duke, who thought that it should have been for him alone. Eventually, the duke could tolerate the situation no longer; he "gave commands," and "all smiles stopped together."

Though silent, the listener plays a subtle but important role in the poem: his presence establishes the dramatic situation that allows the character of the duke to be revealed. The purpose of the story is to communicate to the emissary exactly what the duke expects from his prospective bride and from her father. As he speaks, the duke provides only the information that he wants the emissary to take back to his master, the count. Although the duke appears vain and superficial, he is actually extraordinarily shrewd. Throughout the poem, he turns the conversation to his own ends and gains the advantage through flattery and false modesty. The success of the poem lies in the poet's ability to develop the voice of this complex character, who embodies both superficial elegance and shocking cruelty.

FURTHER READING: The Speaker in the Poem

Leslie Marmon Silko (1948–   )

Where Mountain Lion Lay Down with Deer (1973)

I climb the black rock mountain
    stepping from day to day
                    silently.
I smell the wind for my ancestors
    pale blue leaves   5
    crushed wild mountain smell.

>> Mountain lion

Returning
   up the gray stone cliff
   where I descended
         a thousand years ago.   10
Returning to faded black stone.
   where mountain lion lay down with deer.
It is better to stay up here
               watching wind's reflection
               in tall yellow flowers.   15
The old ones who remember me are gone
        the old songs are all forgotten
and the story of my birth.
How I danced in snow-frost moonlight
        distant stars to the end of the Earth,   20
How I swam away
       in freezing mountain water
       narrow mossy canyon tumbling down
         out of the mountain
           out of the deep canyon stone   25
        down
          the memory
           spilling out
           into the world.

Related Works

"This Is What It Means to Say Phoenix, Arizona" (p. 157), "Simile" (p. 412), "Sleeping in the Forest" (p. 486)

Janice Mirikitani (1942–   )

Suicide Note (1987)

. . . An Asian-American college student was reported to have jumped to her death from her dormitory window. Her body was found two days later under a deep cover of snow. Her suicide note contained an apology to her parents for having received less than a perfect four point grade average. . . .

How many notes written . . .
ink smeared like birdprints in snow.
  not good enough   not pretty enough   not smart enough
dear mother and father.
I apologize   5
for disappointing you.
I've worked very hard,
       not good enough
harder, perhaps to please you.
If only I were a son, shoulders broad   10
as the sunset threading through pine,
I would see the light in my mother's
eyes, or the golden pride reflected
in my father's dream
of my wide, male hands worthy of work   15
and comfort.
I would swagger through life
muscled and bold and assured,

>> College campus after snowfall

drawing praises to me
like currents in the bed of wind, virile   20
with confidence.
   not good enough   not strong enough   not good enough

I apologize.
Tasks do not come easily.
Each failure, a glacier.   25
Each disapproval, a bootprint.
Each disappointment,
ice above my river.
So I have worked hard.
        not good enough   30
My sacrifice I will drop
bone by bone, perched
on the ledge of my womanhood,
fragile as wings.
       not strong enough   35
It is snowing steadily
surely not good weather
for flying—this sparrow
sillied and dizzied by the wind
on the edge.   40
       not smart enough
I make this ledge my altar
to offer penance.
This air will not hold me,
the snow burdens my crippled wings,   45
my tears drop like bitter cloth
softly into the gutter below.
  not good enough   not strong enough   not smart enough
      Choices thin as shaved
      ice. Notes shredded   50
      drift like snow
on my broken body,
cover me like whispers
of sorries
sorries.   55
Perhaps when they find me
they will bury
my bird bones beneath
a sturdy pine
and scatter my feathers like   60
unspoken song
over this white and cold and silent
breast of earth.

Related Works

"Eye Ball" (p. 130), "The Rocking-Horse Winner" (p. 297), "The Value of
Education" (p. 391), "Dreams of Suicide" (p. 472), "Death Be Not Proud"
(p. 503)

 See Chapter 21 Review Card for Reading and Reacting questions
about Janice Mirikitani, "Suicide Note."

LO2 Identify the Tone of the Poem

The **tone** of a poem conveys the speaker's attitude toward his or her subject or audience. In speech, this attitude can be conveyed easily: stressing a word in a sentence can modify or color a statement. For example, the statement "Of course, you would want to go to that restaurant" is quite straightforward, but changing the emphasis to "Of course *you* would want to go to *that* restaurant" transforms a neutral statement into a sarcastic one. For poets, however, conveying a particular tone to readers poses a challenge because readers rarely hear poets' spoken voices. Instead, poets indicate tone by using rhyme, meter, word choice, sentence structure, figures of speech, and imagery.

The range of possible tones is wide. For example, a poem's speaker may be joyful, sad, playful, serious, comic, intimate, formal, relaxed, condescending, or ironic. In the following poem, notice how the tone conveys the speaker's attitude toward his subject.

> **tone** Attitude of speaker or author of a work toward the subject, characters, and audience, as determined by word choice, use of imagery, and so on.
>
> **understatement** Intentional downplaying of a situation's significance, often for ironic or humorous effect.
>
> **epigram** Short pithy poem or statement — for example, Dorothy Parker's comment on an actress's performance, "She runs the gamut of emotions from A to B."

⊕ EXPLORE ONLINE >

To complete a tutorial of "Tone," visit your Literature CourseMate, accessed through www.cengagebrain .com.

Robert Frost (1874–1963)

Fire and Ice (1923)

Some say the world will end in fire,
Some say in ice.
From what I've tasted of desire
I hold with those who favor fire.
But if it had to perish twice,   5
I think I know enough of hate
To say that for destruction ice
Is also great
And would suffice.

>> Mushroom cloud from atomic bomb test

Here the speaker uses word choice, rhyme, and especially **understatement** to comment on the human condition. The conciseness as well as the simple, regular meter and rhyme suggest an **epigram**—a short poem that makes a pointed comment in an unusually clear, and often witty, manner. This pointedness is consistent with the speaker's glib, unemotional tone, as is the last line's wry understatement that ice "would suffice." The contrast between the poem's serious message—that hatred and indifference are equally destructive—and its informal style and offhand tone complement the speaker's detached, almost smug, posture.

Sometimes shifts in tone reveal changes in the speaker's attitude. In the next poem, subtle shifts in tone reveal a change in the speaker's attitude toward war.

Thomas Hardy (1840–1928)

The Man He Killed (1902)

"Had he and I but met
    By some old ancient inn,
We should have sat us down to wet
    Right many a nipperkin!°

"But ranged as infantry,   5
    And staring face to face,
I shot at him as he at me,
    And killed him in his place.

"I shot him dead because—
    Because he was my foe,   10
Just so: my foe of course he was;
    That's clear enough; although

"He thought he'd 'list,° perhaps,
    Off-hand-like—just as I—
Was out of work—had sold his traps—   15
    No other reason why.

"Yes; quaint and curious war is!
    You shoot a fellow down
You'd treat if met where any bar is,
    Or help to half-a-crown."   20

°**nipperkin** A small
    container of liquor.
°**'list** Enlist.

>> English and French troops waiting for
German attack, 1918

The speaker in this poem is a soldier relating a wartime experience. Quotation marks indicate that he is engaged in conversation—perhaps in a pub—and his dialect indicates that he is a member of the English working class. For him, at least at first, the object of war is simple: kill or be killed. To Hardy, this speaker represents all men who are thrust into a war without understanding its underlying social, economic, or ideological causes. In this sense, the speaker and his enemy are both victims of forces beyond their comprehension or control.

The tone of "The Man He Killed" changes as the speaker tells his story. In the first two stanzas, sentences are smooth and unbroken, establishing the speaker's matter-of-fact tone and reflecting his confidence that he has done what he had to do. In the third and fourth stanzas, broken syntax reflects the narrator's increasingly disturbed state of mind as he tells about the man he killed. The poem's singsong meter and regular rhyme scheme (*met/wet, inn/nipperkin*) suggest that the speaker is struggling to maintain his composure; the smooth sentence structure of the last stanza and the use of a cliché ("Yes; quaint and curious war is!") indicate that the speaker is trying to trivialize an incident that has seriously traumatized him.

Sometimes a poem's tone can establish an ironic contrast between the speaker and his or her subject. The speaker's abrupt change of tone at the end of the next poem establishes such a contrast.

Amy Lowell (1874–1925)

Patterns (1915)

I walk down the garden-paths,
And all the daffodils
Are blowing, and the bright blue squills.
I walk down the patterned garden-paths
In my stiff, brocaded gown.   5

With my powdered hair and jewelled fan,
I too am a rare
Pattern. As I wander down
The garden-paths.

My dress is richly figured, 10
And the train
Makes a pink and silver stain
On the gravel, and the thrift
Of the borders.
Just a plate of current fashion 15
Tripping by in high-heeled, ribboned shoes.
Not a softness anywhere about me,
Only whalebone° and brocade.
And I sink on a seat in the shade
Of a lime tree. For my passion 20
Wars against the stiff brocade.
The daffodils and squills
Flutter in the breeze
As they please.
And I weep; 25
For the lime-tree is in blossom
And one small flower has dropped upon my bosom.

And the plashing of waterdrops
In the marble fountain
Comes down the garden-paths. 30
The dripping never stops.
Underneath my stiffened gown
Is the softness of a woman bathing in a marble basin,
A basin in the midst of hedges grown
So thick, she cannot see her lover hiding, 35
But she guesses he is near,
And the sliding of the water
Seems the stroking of a dear
Hand upon her.
What is Summer in a fine brocaded gown! 40
I should like to see it lying in a heap upon the ground.
All the pink and silver crumpled up on the ground.

I would be the pink and silver as I ran along the paths,
And he would stumble after,
Bewildered by my laughter. 45
I should see the sun flashing from his sword-hilt
    and buckles on his shoes.
I would choose
To lead him in a maze along the patterned paths,
A bright and laughing maze for my heavy-booted
    lover.
Till he caught me in the shade, 50
And the buttons of his waistcoat bruised my body
    as he clasped me,
Aching, melting, unafraid.
With the shadows of the leaves and the sundrops,
And the plopping of the waterdrops,
All about us in the open afternoon— 55
I am very like to swoon
With the weight of this brocade,
For the sun sifts through the shade.

>> Detail of brocade gown

° **whalebone** The type of
bone used to stiffen corsets.

Underneath the fallen blossom
In my bosom,   60
Is a letter I have hid.
It was brought to me this morning by a rider
    from the Duke.
Madam, we regret to inform you that
    Lord Hartwell
Died in action Thursday se'nnight.°
As I read it in the white, morning sunlight,   65
The letters squirmed like snakes.
"Any answer, Madam," said my footman.
"No," I told him.
"See that the messenger takes some refreshment.
No, no answer."   70
And I walked into the garden,
Up and down the patterned paths,
In my stiff, correct brocade.
The blue and yellow flowers stood up proudly
    in the sun,
Each one.   75
I stood upright too,
Held rigid to the pattern
By the stiffness of my gown.
Up and down I walked.
Up and down.   80

In a month he would have been my husband.
In a month, here, underneath this lime,
We would have broken the pattern;
He for me, and I for him,
He as Colonel, I as Lady,   85
On this shady seat.
He had a whim
That sunlight carried blessing.
And I answered, "It shall be as you have said."
Now he is dead.   90

In Summer and in Winter I shall walk
Up and down
The patterned garden-paths
In my stiff, brocaded gown.
The squills and daffodils   95
Will give place to pillared roses, and to asters,
    and to snow.
I shall go
Up and down,
In my gown.
Gorgeously arrayed,   100
Boned and stayed.
And the softness of my body will be guarded
    from embrace
By each button, hook, and lace.
For the man who should loose me is dead,
Fighting with the Duke in Flanders,°   105
In a pattern called a war.
Christ! What are patterns for?

° **Flanders** A region in
northwestern Europe,
including part of northern
France and western Belgium.
Flanders was a site of fighting
during World War I.

The speaker in Lowell's poem begins by describing herself walking down garden paths. She wears a stiff brocaded gown, has powdered hair, and carries a jeweled fan. By her own admission, she is "a plate of current fashion." Although her tone is controlled, she is preoccupied by sensual thoughts. Beneath her "stiffened gown / Is the softness of a woman bathing in a marble basin," and the "sliding of the water" in a fountain reminds the speaker of the stroking of her lover's hand. She imagines herself shedding her brocaded gown and running with her lover along the maze of "patterned paths." The sensuality of the speaker's thoughts stands in ironic contrast to the images of stiffness and control that dominate the poem: her passion "Wars against the stiff brocade." She is also full of repressed rage. She knows that her lover has been killed, and she realizes the meaninglessness of the patterns of her life, patterns to which she has conformed, just as her lover conformed by going to war. Throughout the poem, the speaker's tone reflects her barely contained anger and frustration. In the last line, when she finally lets out her rage, the poem's point about the senselessness of conformity and war becomes apparent.

FURTHER READING: The Tone of the Poem

William Wordsworth (1770–1850)

The World Is Too Much with Us (1807)

The world is too much with us; late and soon,
Getting and spending, we lay waste our powers;
Little we see in Nature that is ours;
We have given our hearts away, a sordid boon!
This Sea that bares her bosom to the moon;   5
The winds that will be howling at all hours,
And are up-gathered now like sleeping flowers;
For this, for everything, we are out of tune;
It moves us not. Great God! I'd rather be
A Pagan suckled in a creed outworn;   10
So might I, standing on this pleasant lea,
Have glimpses that would make me less forlorn;
Have sight of Proteus° rising from the sea;
Or hear old Triton° blow his wreathèd horn.

>> Statue of Triton blowing conch shell

° **Proteus** Sometimes said to be Poseidon's son, this Greek sea-god had the ability to change shape at will and to tell the future.

° **Triton** The trumpeter of the sea, this sea-god is usually pictured blowing on a conch shell. Triton was the son of Poseidon, ruler of the sea.

Related Works

"The Rocking-Horse Winner" (p. 297), "Dover Beach" (p. 498), "The Lake Isle of Innisfree" (p. 522)

 See Chapter 21 Review Card for Reading and Reacting questions about William Wordsworth, "The World Is Too Much with Us."

Robert Herrick (1591–1674)

To the Virgins, to Make Much of Time (1646)

Gather ye rosebuds while ye may,
Old Time is still a-flying;
And this same flower that smiles today,
Tomorrow will be dying.

The glorious lamp of heaven, the sun,   5
The higher he's a-getting,
The sooner will his race be run,
And nearer he's to setting.

That age is best which is the first,
When youth and blood are warmer;   10
But being spent, the worse, and worst
Times still succeed the former.

Then be not coy, but use your time,
And while ye may, go marry;
For having lost but once your prime,   15
You may forever tarry.

>> *Gather Ye Rosebuds While Ye May,* 1909 (oil on canvas); John William Waterhouse (1849–1917)

Related Works

"The Passionate Shepherd to His Love" (p. 513), *The Brute* (p. 532)

 See Chapter 21 Review Card for Reading and Reacting questions about Robert Herrick, "To the Virgins, to Make Much of Time."

EXPLORE ONLINE >

To complete a tutorial of "Irony," visit your Literature CourseMate, accessed through www.cengagebrain.com.

irony Literary device or situation that depends on the existence of at least two separate and contrasting levels of meaning or experience. **Dramatic irony** occurs when the speaker believes one thing and readers realize something else. **Situational irony** exists when what happens is at odds with what readers are led to expect will happen. **Verbal irony** occurs when what is said is in contrast with what is meant.

LO3 Recognize Irony

Just as in fiction and drama, **irony** occurs in poetry when a discrepancy exists between two levels of meaning or experience. Consider the tone of the following lines by Stephen Crane:

Do not weep, maiden, for war is kind.
Because your lover threw wild hands toward the sky
And the afrightened steed ran on alone,
Do not weep.
War is kind.

Surely the speaker in this poem does not intend his words to be taken literally. How can war be "kind"? Isn't war exactly the opposite of "kind"? By making this ironic statement, the speaker actually conveys the opposite idea: war is a cruel, mindless exercise of violence.

Skillfully used, irony enables a poet to make a pointed comment about a situation or to manipulate a reader's emotions. Implicit in irony is the writer's assumption that readers will not be misled by the literal meaning of a statement. In order for irony to work, readers must recognize the disparity between what is said and what is meant, or between what a speaker thinks is occurring and what readers know to be occurring.

One kind of irony that appears in poetry is **dramatic irony,** which occurs when a speaker believes one thing and readers realize something else. In the following poem, the poet uses a deranged speaker to tell a story that is filled with irony.

Robert Browning (1812–1889)

Porphyria's Lover (1836)

The rain set early in to-night,
  The sullen wind was soon awake,
It tore the elm-tops down for spite,
  And did its worst to vex the lake:
  I listened with heart fit to break.   5
When glided in Porphyria; straight
  She shut the cold out and the storm,
And kneeled and made the cheerless grate
  Blaze up, and all the cottage warm;
  Which done, she rose, and from her form   10
Withdrew the dripping cloak and shawl,
  And laid her soiled gloves by, untied
Her hat and let the damp hair fall,
  And, last, she sat down by my side
  And called me. When no voice replied,   15
She put my arm about her waist,
  And made her smooth white shoulder bare,
And all her yellow hair displaced,
  And, stooping, made my cheek lie there,
  And spread, o'er all, her yellow hair,   20
Murmuring how she loved me—she
  Too weak, for all her heart's endeavour,
To set its struggling passion free
  From pride, and vainer ties dissever,
  And give herself to me for ever.   25
But passion sometimes would prevail,
  Nor could to-night's gay feast restrain
A sudden thought of one so pale
  For love of her, and all in vain:
  So, she was come through wind and rain.   30
Be sure I looked up at her eyes
  Happy and proud; at last I knew
Porphyria worshipped me; surprise
  Made my heart swell, and still it grew
  While I debated what to do.   35
That moment she was mine, mine, fair,
  Perfectly pure and good: I found
A thing to do, and all her hair
  In one long yellow string I wound
  Three times her little throat around,   40
And strangled her. No pain felt she;
  I am quite sure she felt no pain.

>> Untitled (Woman with Flowers in Hair) by Odilon Redon

The Art Archive/Superstock Image #AA546066

As a shut bud that holds a bee,
  I warily oped her lids: again
    Laughed the blue eyes without a stain.   45
And I untightened next the tress
  About her neck; her cheek once more
Blushed bright beneath my burning kiss:
  I propped her head up as before,
    Only, this time my shoulder bore   50
Her head, which droops upon it still:
  The smiling rosy little head,
So glad it has its utmost will,
  That all it scorned at once is fled,
    And I, its love, am gained instead!   55
Porphyria's love: she guessed not how
  Her darling one wish would be heard.
And thus we sit together now,
  And all night long we have not stirred,
    And yet God has not said a word!   60

Like Browning's "My Last Duchess" (p. 365), this poem is a dramatic monologue, a poem that assumes an implied listener as well as a speaker. The speaker recounts his story in a straightforward manner, seemingly unaware of the horror of his tale. In fact, much of the effect of this poem comes from the speaker's telling his tale of murder in a flat, unemotional tone—and from readers' gradual realization that the speaker is mad.

The irony of the poem, as well as its title, becomes apparent as the monologue progresses. At first, the speaker fears that Porphyria is too weak to free herself from pride and vanity to love him. As he looks into her eyes, however, he comes to believe that she worships him. The moment the speaker realizes that Porphyria loves him, he feels compelled to kill her and keep her his forever. According to him, she is at this point "mine, mine, fair, / Perfectly pure and good," and he believes that by murdering her, he actually fulfills "Her darling one wish"—to stay with him forever. As he attempts to justify his actions, the speaker reveals himself to be a deluded psychopathic killer.

Another kind of irony is **situational irony,** which occurs when the situation itself contradicts readers' expectations. For example, in "Porphyria's Lover" the meeting of two lovers ironically results not in joy and passion but in murder.

In the next poem, the situation also creates irony.

Percy Bysshe Shelley (1792–1822)

Ozymandias° (1818)

I met a traveler from an antique land
Who said: Two vast and trunkless legs of stone
Stand in the desert. Near them, on the sand,
Half sunk, a shattered visage lies, whose frown,
And wrinkled lip, and sneer of cold command,   5
Tell that its sculptor well those passions read
Which yet survive, stamped on these lifeless things,
The hand that mocked them, and the heart that fed;
And on the pedestal these words appear:
"My name is Ozymandias, king of kings: 10
Look on my works, ye Mighty, and despair!"
Nothing beside remains. Round the decay
Of that colossal wreck, boundless and bare
The lone and level sands stretch far away.

° **Ozymandias** The Greek name for Ramses II, ruler of Egypt in the thirteenth century B.C.

>> Massive granite head of statue of Ramses II (Egypt)

The speaker recounts a tale about a colossal statue that lies shattered in the desert. Its head lies separated from the trunk, and the face has a wrinkled lip and a "sneer of cold command." On the pedestal of the monument are words exhorting all those who pass: "Look on my works, ye Mighty, and despair!" The situational irony of the poem has its source in the contrast between the "colossal wreck" and the boastful inscription on its base: Ozymandias is a monument to the vanity of those who mistakenly think they can withstand the ravages of time.

Perhaps the most common kind of irony found in poetry is **verbal irony,** which is created when words say one thing but mean another, often exactly the opposite. When verbal irony is particularly biting, it is called **sarcasm**—for

> **sarcasm** Form of irony in which apparent praise is used to convey strong, bitter criticism.

example, Stephen Crane's use of the word *kind* in his anti-war poem "War Is Kind." In speech, verbal irony is easy to detect through the speaker's change in tone or emphasis. In writing, when these signals are absent, verbal irony becomes more difficult to convey. Poets must depend on the context of a remark or on the contrast between a word and other images in the poem to create irony.

Consider how verbal irony is communicated in the following poem.

FURTHER READING: Irony

W. H. Auden (1907–1973)

The Unknown Citizen (1939)

(To JS/07/M/378 This Marble Monument Is Erected by the State)

He was found by the Bureau of Statistics to be
One against whom there was no official complaint,
And all the reports on his conduct agree
That, in the modern sense of an old-fashioned word,
   he was a saint,
For in everything he did he served the
   Greater Community.   5
Except for the War till the day he retired
He worked in a factory and never got fired,
But satisfied his employers, Fudge Motors Inc.
Yet he wasn't a scab or odd in his views,
For his Union reports that he paid his dues,   10
(Our report on his Union shows it was sound)
And our Social Psychology workers found
That he was popular with his mates and liked a drink.
The Press are convinced that he bought a paper every day
And that his reactions to advertisements were normal
   in every way.   15
Policies taken out in his name prove that he was fully insured,
And his Health-card shows he was once in hospital but
   left it cured.
Both Producers Research and High-Grade Living declare
He was fully sensible to the advantages of the Installment Plan
And had everything necessary to the Modern Man,   20
A phonograph, a radio, a car and a frigidaire.
Our researchers into Public Opinion are content
That he held the proper opinions for the time of year;
When there was peace, he was for peace; when there was war,
   he went.
He was married and added five children to the population,   25

>> Accountant's balance sheet

° **Eugenist** A person who
studies eugenics, the science
of human improvement
through genetic manipulation.

Which our Eugenist° says was the right number for a parent of his
   generation,
And our teachers report that he never interfered with their
   education.
Was he free? Was he happy? The question is absurd:
Had anything been wrong, we should certainly have heard.

Related Works

"A&P" (p. 131), "The Man He Killed" (p. 370), "The Love Song of J. Alfred
Prufrock" (p. 504), *A Doll House* (p. 562)

Dudley Randall (1914–2000)

Ballad of Birmingham (1969)

(On the bombing of a church in Birmingham, Alabama, 1963)

"Mother dear, may I go downtown
Instead of out to play,
And march the streets of Birmingham
In a Freedom March today?"

"No, baby, no, you may not go,   5
For the dogs are fierce and wild,
And clubs and hoses, guns and jails
Aren't good for a little child."

"But, mother, I won't be alone.
Other children will go with me,   10
And march the streets of Birmingham
To make our country free."

>> Four young girls killed in bombing of Birmingham, Alabama, church in 1963 (left to right): Denise McNair (11), Carole Robinson (14), Addie Mae Collins (14), and Cynthia Wesley (14)

"No, baby, no, you may not go,
For I fear those guns will fire.
But you may go to church instead   15
And sing in the children's choir."

She has combed and brushed her night-dark hair,
And bathed rose petal sweet,
And drawn white gloves on her small brown hands,
And white shoes on her feet.   20

The mother smiled to know her child
Was in the sacred place,
But that smile was the last smile
To come upon her face.

For when she heard the explosion,   25
Her eyes grew wet and wild.
She raced through the streets of Birmingham
Calling for her child.

She clawed through bits of glass and brick,
Then lifted out a shoe.   30
"O, here's the shoe my baby wore,
But, baby, where are you?"

Related Works

"If We Must Die" (p. 514), *Fences* (p. 724)

>> 16th Street Baptist Church, Birmingham, Alabama

 See Chapter 21 Review Card for Reading and Reacting questions about Dudley Randall, "Ballad of Birmingham."

Writing Suggestions: Voice

1. The poet Robert Frost once said that he wanted to write "poetry that talked." According to Frost, "whenever I write a line it is because that line has already been spoken clearly by a voice within my mind, an audible voice." Choose some poems in this chapter (or from elsewhere in the book) that you consider "poetry that talks." Then, write an essay about how successful they are in communicating "an audible voice."

2. Compare the speakers' voices in "Barbie doll" (p. 515) and "Gretel in Darkness" (p. 362). How are their attitudes toward men similar? How are they different?

3. The theme of Herrick's poem "To the Virgins, to Make Much of Time" (p. 374) is known as **carpe diem,** or "seize the day." Read Andrew Marvell's "To His Coy Mistress" (p. 419), which has the same theme, and compare its tone with that of "To the Virgins, to Make Much of Time."

4. Because the speaker and the poet are not the same, poems by the same author can have different voices. Compare the voices of several poems by one poet—for example, Sylvia Plath, W. H. Auden, or William Blake, whose works are included in this anthology.

 CHECKLIST

WRITING ABOUT VOICE

The Speaker in the Poem
- [ ] What do we know about the speaker?
- [ ] Is the speaker anonymous, or does he or she have a particular identity?
- [ ] How does assuming a particular persona help the poet to convey his or her ideas?
- [ ] Does the title give readers any information about the speaker's identity?
- [ ] How does word choice provide information about the speaker?
- [ ] Does the speaker make any direct statements to readers that help establish his or her identity or character?
- [ ] Does the speaker address anyone? How can you tell? How does the presence of a listener affect the speaker?

The Tone of the Poem
- [ ] What is the speaker's attitude toward his or her subject?
- [ ] How do word choice, rhyme, meter, sentence structure, figures of speech, and imagery help to convey the attitude of the speaker?
- [ ] Is the poem's tone consistent? How do shifts in tone reveal the changing mood or attitude of the speaker?

Irony
- [ ] Does the poem include dramatic irony? situational irony? verbal irony?

Glossary Terms

dramatic monologue Type of poem that consists of a single speaker talking to one or more listeners and often revealing much more about the speaker than he or she seems to intend.

epigram Short pithy poem or statement—for example, Dorothy Parker's comment on an actress's performance, "She runs the gamut of emotions from A to B."

irony Literary device or situation that depends on the existence of at least two separate and contrasting levels of meaning or experience. **Dramatic irony** occurs when the speaker believes one thing and readers realize something else. **Situational irony** exists when what happens is at odds with what readers are led to expect will happen. **Verbal irony** occurs when what is said is in contrast with what is meant.

persona An identity the poet assumes; in Greek tragedy, a persona was a mask worn by an actor.

sarcasm Form of irony in which apparent praise is used to convey strong, bitter criticism.

speaker The narrative voice the poet uses.

tone Attitude of the speaker or author of a work toward the subject, characters, and audience, as determined by word choice, use of imagery, and so on.

understatement Intentional downplaying of a situation's significance, often for ironic or humorous effect.

22

Word Choice, Word Order

Learning Outcomes

After reading this chapter, you should be able to do the following:

LO1 Evaluate word choice

LO2 Recognize levels of diction

LO3 Evaluate word order

Timeline

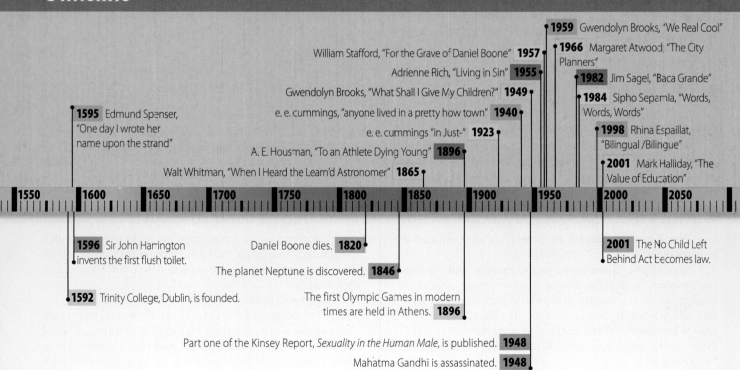

1959 Gwendolyn Brooks, "We Real Cool"

1966 Margaret Atwood, "The City Planners"

William Stafford, "For the Grave of Daniel Boone" 1957

1982 Jim Sagel, "Baca Grande"

Adrienne Rich, "Living in Sin" 1955

Gwendolyn Brooks, "What Shall I Give My Children?" 1949

1984 Sipho Sepamla, "Words, Words, Words"

1595 Edmund Spenser, "One day I wrote her name upon the strand"

e. e. cummings, "anyone lived in a pretty how town" 1940

e. e. cummings "in Just-" 1923

1998 Rhina Espaillat, "Bilingual /Bilingue"

A. E. Housman, "To an Athlete Dying Young" 1896

2001 Mark Halliday, "The Value of Education"

Walt Whitman, "When I Heard the Learn'd Astronomer" 1865

1550 1600 1650 1700 1750 1800 1850 1900 1950 2000 2050

1596 Sir John Harington invents the first flush toilet.

Daniel Boone dies. 1820

2001 The No Child Left Behind Act becomes law.

The planet Neptune is discovered. 1846

1592 Trinity College, Dublin, is founded.

The first Olympic Games in modern times are held in Athens. 1896

Part one of the Kinsey Report, *Sexuality in the Human Male*, is published. 1948

Mahatma Gandhi is assassinated. 1948

Sipho Sepamla (1932–   )

Words, Words, Words (1984)

Courtesy, Estate of Sipho Sepamla

We don't speak of tribal wars anymore
we say simple faction fights
there are no tribes around here
only nations
it makes sense you see   5
'cause from there
one moves to multinational
it makes sense you get me
'cause from there
one gets one's homeland   10
which is a reasonable idea
'cause from there
one can dabble with independence
which deserves warm applause
—the bloodless revolution   15

we are talking of words
words tossed around as if
denied location by the wind
we mean those words some spit
others grab   20
dress them up for the occasion
fling them on the lap of an audience
we are talking of those words
that stalk our lives like policemen
words no dictionary can embrace   25
words that change sooner than seasons
we mean words
that spell out our lives
words, words, words
for there's a kind of poetic licence   30
doing the rounds in these parts

Words identify and name, characterize and distinguish, compare and contrast. Words describe, limit, and embellish; words locate and measure. Even though words may be elusive and uncertain and changeable, "tossed around as if / denied location by the wind" and "can change sooner than seasons," they still can "stalk our lives like policemen." In poetry, as in love and in politics, words matter.

Beyond the quantitative—how many words, how many letters and syllables—is a much more important consideration: the *quality* of words. Which words are chosen, and why? Why are certain words placed next to others? What does a word suggest in a particular context? How are the words arranged? What exactly constitutes the "right word"?

LO1 Evaluate Word Choice

In poetry, even more than in fiction or drama, words are the focus—sometimes even the true subject—of a work. For this reason, the choice of one word over another can be crucial. Because poems are brief, they must compress many ideas into just a few lines; poets know how much weight each individual word carries, so they choose with great care, trying to select words that imply more than they state.

In general, poets (like prose writers) select words because they communicate their ideas. However, poets may also choose words for their sound. For instance, a word may echo another word's sound, and such repetition may place emphasis on both words; a word may rhyme with

> *"Sometimes a poet wants a precise word, one that is both specific and concrete. At other times, a poet might prefer general or abstract language, which may allow for more subtlety—or even for intentional ambiguity."*

another word and therefore be needed to preserve the poem's rhyme scheme; or a word may have a certain combination of stressed and unstressed syllables needed to maintain the poem's metrical pattern. Occasionally, a poet may even choose a word because of how it looks on the page.

At the same time, poets may choose words for their degree of concreteness or abstraction, specificity or generality. A **concrete** word refers to an item that is a perceivable, tangible entity—for example, a kiss or a flag. An **abstract** word refers to an intangible idea, condition, or quality, something that cannot be perceived by the senses—love or patriotism, for instance. **Specific** words refer to particular items; **general** words refer to entire classes or groups of items. As the following sequence illustrates, whether a word is specific or general is relative; its degree of specificity or generality depends on its relationship to other words.

> Poem → closed form poem → sonnet → seventeenth-century sonnet → Elizabethan sonnet → sonnet by Shakespeare → "My mistress' eyes are nothing like the sun"

> **connotation** Meaning that a word suggests beyond its literal, dictionary meaning; its emotional associations, judgments, or opinions. Connotations can be positive, neutral, or negative.

Sometimes a poet wants a precise word, one that is both specific and concrete. At other times, a poet might prefer general or abstract language, which may allow for more subtlety—or even for intentional ambiguity.

Finally, a word may be chosen for its **connotation**—what it suggests. Every word has one or more **denotations**—what it signifies without emotional associations, judgments, or opinions. The word *family*, for example, denotes "a group of related things or people." Connotation is a more complex matter; after all, a single word may have many different associations. In general terms, a word may have a connotation that is positive, neutral, or negative. Thus, *family* may have a positive connotation when it describes a group of loving relatives, a neutral connotation when it describes a biological category, and an ironically negative connotation when it describes an organized crime family. Beyond this distinction, *family*, like any other word, may have a variety of emotional and social associations, suggesting loyalty, warmth, home, security, or duty. In fact, many words have somewhat different meanings in different contexts. When poets choose words, then, they must consider what a particular word may suggest to readers as well as what it denotes.

In the poem that follows, the poet chooses words for their sounds and for their relationships to other words as well as for their connotations.

Walt Whitman (1819–1892)

When I Heard the Learn'd Astronomer (1865)

When I heard the learn'd astronomer,
When the proofs, the figures, were ranged in columns before me,
When I was shown the charts and diagrams, to add, divide, and measure them,
When I sitting heard the astronomer where he lectured with much applause
   in the lecture-room,
How soon unaccountable I became tired and sick,   5
Till rising and gliding out I wander'd off by myself,
In the mystical moist night-air, and from time to time,
Look'd up in perfect silence at the stars.

>> Nineteenth-century astronomer

 The Granger Collection, New York Image #0000112

Whitman's poem might be paraphrased as follows: "When I grew restless listening to an astronomy lecture, I went outside, where I found I learned more just by looking at the stars than I had learned inside." However, the paraphrase is obviously neither as rich nor as complex as the poem. Through careful use of diction, Whitman establishes a dichotomy that supports the poem's central theme about the relative merits of two ways of learning.

The poem can be divided into two groups of four lines each. The first four lines, unified by the repetition of "When," introduce the astronomer and his tools: "proofs," "figures," and "charts and diagrams" to be added, divided, or measured. In this section of the poem, the speaker is passive: he sits and listens ("I heard"; "I was shown"; "I sitting heard"). The repetition of "When" reinforces the dry monotony of the lecture. In the next four lines, the choice of words signals the change in the speaker's actions and reactions. The confined lecture hall is replaced by "the mystical moist night-air," and the dry lecture and the applause give way to "perfect silence"; instead of sitting passively, the speaker becomes active (he rises, glides, wanders); instead of listening, he looks. The mood of the first half of the poem is restrained: the language is concrete and physical, and the speaker is passively receiving information from a "learn'd" authority. The rest of the poem, celebrating intuitive knowledge and feelings, is more abstract, freer. Throughout the poem, the lecture hall is set in sharp contrast to the natural world outside its walls.

After considering the poem as a whole, readers should not find it hard to understand why the poet selected certain words. Whitman's use of "lectured" in line 4 rather than a more neutral word like "spoke" is appropriate both because it suggests formality and distance and because it echoes "lecture-room" in the same line. The word "sick" in line 5 is striking because it connotes physical as well as emotional distress, more effectively conveying the extent of the speaker's discomfort than "bored" or "restless" would. "Rising" and "gliding" (line 6) are used rather than "standing" and "walking out" both because of the way their stressed vowel sounds echo each other (and echo "time to time" in the next line) and because of their connotation of dreaminess, which is consistent with "wander'd" (line 6) and "mystical" (line 7). The word "moist" (line 7) is chosen not only because its consonant sounds echo the *m* and *st* sounds in "mystical," but also because it establishes a contrast with the dry, airless lecture hall. Finally, line 8's "perfect silence" is a better choice than a reasonable substitute like "complete silence" or "total silence," either of which would suggest the degree of the silence but not its quality.

In the next poem, the poet also pays careful attention to word choice.

William Stafford (1914–1993)

For the Grave of Daniel Boone (1957)

The farther he went the farther home grew.
Kentucky became another room;
the mansion arched over the Mississippi;
flowers were spread all over the floor.
He traced ahead a deepening home,   5
and better, with goldenrod:

Leaving the snakeskin of place after place,
going on—after the trees
the grass, a bird flying after a song.
Rifle so level, sighting so well   10
his picture freezes down to now,
a story-picture for children.

>> Daniel Boone

They go over the velvet falls
into the tapestry of his time,
heirs to the landscape, feeling no jar: 15
it is like evening; they are the quail
surrounding his fire, coming in for the kill;
their little feet move sacred sand.

Children, we live in a barbwire time
but like to follow the old hands back—   20
the ring in the light, the knuckle, the palm,
all the way to Daniel Boone,
hunting our own kind of deepening home.
From the land that was his I heft this rock.

Here on his grave I put it down.   25

A number of words in "For the Grave of Daniel Boone" are noteworthy for their multiple denotations and connotations. In the first stanza, for example, "home" does not simply mean Boone's residence; it connotes an abstract state, a dynamic concept that grows and deepens, encompassing states and rivers while becoming paradoxically more and more elusive. In literal terms, Boone's "home" at the poem's end is a narrow, confined space: his grave. In a wider sense, his home is the United States, particularly the natural landscape he explored. Thus, the word "home" comes to have a variety of associations for readers beyond its denotative meaning, suggesting both the infinite possibilities beyond the frontier and the realities of civilization's walls and fences.

The word "snakeskin" denotes "the skin of a snake"; its most obvious connotations are smoothness and slipperiness. In this poem, however, the snakeskin signifies more, because it is Daniel Boone who is "Leaving the snakeskin of place after place." Like a snake, Boone belongs to the natural world—and, like a snake, he wanders from place to place, shedding his skin as he goes. Thus, the word "snakeskin," with its connotation of rebirth and its links to nature, passing time, and the inevitability of change, is consistent with the image of Boone as both a man of nature and a restless wanderer, "a bird flying after a song."

In the poem's third stanza, the phrases "velvet falls" and "tapestry of . . . time" seem at first to have been selected solely for their pleasing repetition of sounds ("velvet falls"; "tapestry of time"). However, both of these paradoxical phrases also support the poem's theme. Alive, Boone was in constant movement; he was also larger than life. Now, in death, he has been diminished; "his picture freezes down to . . . / a story-picture for children" (lines 11–12), and he is as static and inorganic as velvet or tapestry—no longer dynamic, like "falls" and "time."

The word "barbwire" (line 19) is another word whose multiple meanings enrich the poem's theme. In the simplest terms, "barbwire" denotes a metal fencing material. In light of the poem's concern with space and distance, however, "barbwire" (with its connotations of sharpness, danger, and confinement) is also the antithesis of Boone's free and peaceful wilderness, evoking images of enclosure and imprisonment and reinforcing the poem's central dichotomy between past freedom and present restriction.

The phrase "old hands" (line 20) might also have multiple meanings in the context of the poem. On one level, the hands could belong to an elderly person holding a storybook; on another level, "old hands" could refer to people with considerable life experience—like Boone, who was an "old hand" at scouting. On still another level, given the poem's concern with time, "old hands" could even suggest the hands of a clock.

Through what it says literally and through what its words suggest, "For the Grave of Daniel Boone" communicates a good deal about the speaker's identification with Daniel Boone and with the nation he called home. Boone's horizons, his concept of "home," expanded as he wandered. Now, when he is frozen in time and space, a character in a child's picture book, a body in a grave, we are still "hunting our own kind of deepening home," but our horizons, like Boone's, have narrowed in this "barbwire time."

FURTHER READING: Word Choice

Rhina Espaillat (1932–   )

Bilingual/Bilingue (1998)

My father liked them separate, one there, one
here (allá y aquí), as if aware

that words might cut in two his daughter's heart
(el corazón) and lock the alien part

to what he was—his memory, his name   5
(su nombre)—with a key he could not claim.

"English outside this door, Spanish inside,"
he said, "y basta."° But who can divide

the world, the word (mundo y palabra) from
any child? I knew how to be dumb   10

and stubborn (testaruda); late, in bed,
I hoarded secret syllables I read

until my tongue (mi lengua) learned to run
where his stumbled. And still the heart was one.

I like to think he knew that, even when,   15
proud (orgulloso) of his daughter's pen,

he stood outside mis versos,° half in fear of words
he loved but wanted not to hear.

° **"y basta."** and enough.
° **mis versos** my poems.

>> Bilingual sign

Dogs Must Be On Leash
Los Perros Deben Estar A Marrados
S.B.M.C. 6.08.020

Stock Connection Blue / Alamy Image #AFXXM

Related Works

"Two Questions" (p. 273), "Two Kinds" (p. 336), "Baca Grande"
(p. 389)

Adrienne Rich (1929–2012)

Living in Sin (1995)

She had thought the studio would keep itself,
no dust upon the furniture of love.
Half heresy, to wish the taps less vocal,
the panes relieved of grime. A plate of pears,
a piano with a Persian shawl, a cat   5
stalking the picturesque amusing mouse
had risen at his urging.
Not that at five each separate stair would writhe
under the milkman's tramp; that morning light
so coldly would delineate the scraps   10
of last night's cheese and three sepulchral bottles;
that on the kitchen shelf among the saucers
a pair of beetle-eyes would fix her own—
envoy from some black village in the mouldings . . .
Meanwhile, he, with a yawn,   15
sounded a dozen notes upon the keyboard,
declared it out of tune, shrugged at the mirror,

>> Milkman making morning
delivery, 1950s

© Bettmann/CORBIS Image #BE047884

rubbed at his beard, went out for cigarettes;
while she, jeered by the minor demons,
pulled back the sheets and made the bed and found   20
a towel to dust the table-top,
and let the coffee-pot boil over on the stove.
By evening she was back in love again,
though not so wholly but throughout the night
she woke sometimes to feel the daylight coming   25
like a relentless milkman up the stairs.

Related Works

"Hills Like White Elephants" (p. 96), "Love and Other Catastrophes:
A Mix Tape" (p. 103), "The Storm" (p. 154), "What Lips My Lips Have Kissed"
(p. 490), *The Stronger* (p. 602)

E. E. Cummings (1894–1962)

in Just-° (1923)

in Just-
spring when the world is mud-
luscious the little
lame balloonman
whistles   far   and wee   5

and eddieandbill come
running from marbles and
piracies and it's
spring

when the world is puddle-wonderful   10
the queer
old balloonman whistles
far   and   wee
and bettyandisbel come dancing

from hop-scotch and jump-rope and   15
it's
spring
and

    the

        goat-footed   20

balloonMan whistles
far
and
wee

>> Balloon man

° **in Just-** This poem is also
known as "Chansons
Innocentes I."

Related Works

"The Secret Lion" (p. 333), "anyone lived in a pretty how town" (p. 394),
"Constantly Risking Absurdity" (p. 410), "Jabberwocky" (p. 440), "the sky
was can dy" (p. 455), *Words, Words, Words* (p. 697)

See Chapter 22 Review Card for Reading and Reacting questions
about E. E. Cummings, "in Just-."

LO2 Recognize Levels of Diction

The diction of a poem may be formal or informal or fall anywhere in between, depending on the identity of the speaker and on the speaker's attitude toward the reader and toward his or her subject. At one extreme, very formal poems can seem lofty and dignified, far removed in style and vocabulary from everyday speech. At the other extreme, highly informal poems can be full of jargon, regionalisms, and slang. Many poems, of course, use language that falls somewhere between formal and informal diction.

Formal diction is characterized by a learned vocabulary and grammatically correct forms. In general, formal diction does not include colloquialisms, such as contractions and shortened word forms (*phone* for *telephone*). As the following poem illustrates, a speaker who uses formal diction can sound aloof and impersonal.

Margaret Atwood (1939–   )

The City Planners (1966)

Cruising these residential Sunday
streets in dry August sunlight:
what offends us is
the sanities:
the houses in pedantic rows, the planted   5
sanitary trees, assert
levelness of surface like a rebuke
to the dent in our car door.
No shouting here, or
shatter of glass; nothing more abrupt   10
than the rational whine of a power mower
cutting a straight swath in the discouraged grass.

But though the driveways neatly
sidestep hysteria
by being even, the roofs all display   15
the same slant of avoidance to the hot sky,
certain things:
the smell of spilled oil a faint

sickness lingering in the garages,
a splash of paint on brick surprising as a bruise,   20
a plastic hose poised in a vicious

>> Aerial view of suburban housing development, 1950s

coil; even the too-fixed stare of the wide windows
give momentary access to
the landscape behind or under
the future cracks in the plaster   25

when the houses, capsized, will slide
obliquely into the clay seas, gradual as glaciers
that right now nobody notices.

That is where the City Planners
with the insane faces of political conspirators   30
are scattered over unsurveyed
territories, concealed from each other,
each in his own private blizzard;

guessing directions, they sketch
transitory lines rigid as wooden borders   35
on a wall in the white vanishing air

tracing the panic of suburb
order in a bland madness of snows.

Atwood's speaker is clearly concerned about the poem's central issue, but rather than use *I*, the poem uses the first-person plural (*us*) to convey some degree of emotional detachment. Although phrases such as "sickness lingering in the garages" and "insane faces of political conspirators" subjectively communicate the speaker's disapproval, formal words— "pedantic," "rebuke," "display," "poised," "obliquely," "conspirators," "transitory"—help her to maintain her distance. Both the speaker herself and her attack on the misguided city planners gain credibility through her balanced, measured tone and through her use of language that is as formal and "professional" as theirs.

Informal diction is the language closest to everyday conversation. It includes **colloquialisms**—contractions,

shortened word forms, and the like—and may also include slang, regional expressions, and even nonstandard words.

In the poem that follows, the speaker uses informal diction to highlight the contrast between James Baca, a law student speaking to the graduating class of his old high school, and the graduating seniors.

Jim Sagel (1947–1998)

Baca Grande° (1982)

> *Una vaca se topó con un ratón y le dice:*
> *"Tú—¿tan chiquito y con bigote?" Y le responde el ratón:*
> *"Y tú tan grandota—¿y sin brassiere?"°*

It was nearly a miracle
James Baca remembered anyone at all
from the old hometown gang
having been two years at Yale
    no less   5
and halfway through law school
at the University of California at Irvine
They hardly recognized him either
in his three-piece grey business suit
and surfer-swirl haircut   10
with just the menacing hint
of a tightly trimmed Zapata moustache
    for cultural balance
and relevance

He had come to deliver the keynote address   15
to the graduating class of 80
at his old alma mater
and show off his well-trained lips
which laboriously parted
    each Kennedyish "R"   20
and drilled the first person pronoun
through the microphone

° **Baca Grande** *Baca* is both a phonetic spelling of the Spanish word *vaca* (cow) and the last name of one of the poem's characters. *Grande* means "large."

° **Una . . . brassiere?** A cow ran into a rat and said: "You—so small and with a moustache?" The rat responded: "And you—so big and without a bra?"

like an oil bit
with the slick, elegantly honed phrases
that slid so smoothly   25
off his meticulously bleached
    tongue
He talked Big Bucks
with astronautish fervor and if he
    the former bootstrapless James A. Baca   30
could dazzle the ass
off the universe
then even you
    yes you

Joey Martinez toying with your yellow   35
    tassel
and staring dumbly into space
could emulate Mr. Baca someday
    possibly
well   40
there was of course
such a thing
as being an outrageously successful
gas station attendant too
    let us never forget   45
it doesn't really matter what you do
so long as you excel
    James said
never believing a word
of it   50
for he had already risen
    as high as they go

Wasn't nobody else
from this deprived environment
who'd ever jumped   55
        straight out of college
into the Governor's office
and maybe one day
he'd sit in that big chair
    himself   60
and when he did
he'd forget this damned town
and all the petty little people
in it
once and for all   65

That much he promised himself

>> Mortarboards with yellow tassels

"Baca Grande" uses numerous colloquialisms, including contractions; conversational placeholders, such as "no less" and "well"; shortened word forms, such as "gas"; slang terms, such as "Big Bucks"; whimsical coinages ("Kennedyish," "astronautish," "bootstrapless"); nonstandard grammatical constructions, such as "Wasn't nobody else"; and even profanity. The level of language is perfectly appropriate for the poem's speaker, one of the students Baca addresses—suspicious, streetwise, and unimpressed by Baca's "three-piece grey business suit" and "surfer-swirl haircut." In fact, the informal diction is a key element in the poem, expressing the gap between the slick James Baca, with "his well-trained lips / which laboriously parted / each Kennedyish 'R'" and members of his audience, with their unpretentious, forthright speech—and also the gap between Baca as he is today and the student he once was. In this sense, "Baca Grande" is as much a linguistic commentary as a social one.

FURTHER READING: Levels of Diction

Mark Halliday (1949–   )

The Value of Education (2000)

I go now to the library. When I sit in the library
I am not illegally dumping bags of kitchen garbage
in the dumpster behind Clippinger Laboratory,
and a very pissed-off worker at Facilities Management
is not picking through my garbage and finding   5
several yogurt-stained and tomato-sauce-stained envelopes
with my name and address on them.
When I sit in the library,
I might doze off a little,
and what I read might not penetrate my head   10
which is mostly porridge in a bowl of bone.
However, when I sit there trying to read
I am not, you see, somewhere else being a hapless ass.
I am not leaning on the refrigerator
in the apartment of a young female colleague   15
chatting with oily pep
because I imagine she may suddenly decide to
do sex with me while her boyfriend is on a trip.
Instead I am in the library! Sitting still!
No one in town is approaching my chair   20
with a summons, or a bill, or a huge fist.
This is good. You may say,
"But this is merely a negative definition of
the value of education." Maybe so,
but would you be able to say that   25
if you hadn't been to the library?

>> Student in college library

Related Works

"Gryphon" (p. 138), "When I Heard the Learn'd Astronomer" (p. 383), "Why I Went to College" (p. 452)

Gwendolyn Brooks (1917–2000)

We Real Cool (1959)

The Pool Players.
Seven at the Golden Shovel.

We real cool. We
Left School. We

Lurk late. We
Strike straight. We

Sing sin. We   5
Thin gin. We

Jazz June. We
Die soon.

>> Pool players, 1955

Related Works

"Greasy Lake" (p. 306), "Where Are You Going,
Where Have You Been?" (p. 325), *Tape* (p. 543),
Poker! (p. 546)

See Chapter 22 Review Card for Reading and Reacting questions
about Gwendolyn Brooks, "We Real Cool."

EXPLORE ONLINE >

To listen to audio of "We Real Cool," visit your
Literature CourseMate, accessed through
www.cengagebrain.com.

Gwendolyn Brooks (1917–2000)

What Shall I Give My Children? (1949)

What shall I give my children? who are poor,
Who are adjudged the leastwise of the land,
Who are my sweetest lepers, who demand
No velvet and no velvety velour;
But who have begged me for a brisk contour,   5
Crying that they are quasi, contraband
Because unfinished, graven by a hand
Less than angelic, admirable or sure.
My hand is stuffed with mode, design, device.
But I lack access to my proper stone.   10
And plenitude of plan shall not suffice
Nor grief nor love shall be enough alone
To ratify my little halves who bear
Across an autumn freezing everywhere.

Related Work

"We Real Cool" (p. 392)

See Chapter 22 Review Card for Reading and Reacting questions
about Gwendolyn Brooks, "What Shall I Give My Children?"

LO3 Evaluate Word Order

The order in which words are arranged in a poem is as important as the choice of words. Because English sentences nearly always have a subject-verb-object sequence, with adjectives preceding the nouns they modify, a departure from this order calls attention to itself. Thus, poets can use readers' expectations about word order to their advantage.

For example, poets often manipulate word order to place emphasis on a word. Sometimes they achieve this emphasis by using a very unconventional sequence; sometimes they simply place the word first or last in a line or place it in a stressed position in the line. Poets may also choose a particular word order to make two related—or startlingly unrelated—words fall in adjacent or parallel positions, calling attention to the similarity (or the difference) between them. In other cases, poets may manipulate syntax to preserve a poem's rhyme or meter or to highlight sound correspondences that might otherwise not be noticeable. Finally, irregular syntax may be used throughout a poem to reveal a speaker's mood—for example, to give a playful quality to a poem or to suggest a speaker's disoriented state.

In the poem that follows, word order frequently departs from conventional English syntax.

Edmund Spenser (1552–1599)

One day I wrote her name upon the strand (1595)

One day I wrote her name upon the strand,°
But came the waves and washed it away:
Again I wrote it with a second hand,
But came the tide and made my pains his prey.
"Vain man," said she, "that doest in vain assay,   5
A mortal thing so to immortalize,
For I myself shall like to this decay,
And eek° my name be wiped out likewise."
"Not so," quod° I, "let baser things devise,
To die in dust, but you shall live by fame: 10
My verse your virtues rare shall eternize,
And in the heavens write your glorious name.
Where whenas death shall all the world subdue,
Our love shall live, and later life renew."

>> Tide coming in at shoreline

° **strand** Beach.
° **eek** Also, indeed.
° **quod** Said.

"One day I wrote her name upon the strand," a sonnet, has a fixed metrical pattern and rhyme scheme. To accommodate the sonnet's rhyme and meter, Spenser makes a number of adjustments in syntax. For example, to make sure certain rhyming words fall at the ends of lines, the poet sometimes moves words out of their conventional order, as the following three comparisons illustrate.

Conventional Word Order	Inverted Sequence
"'Vain man,' she said, 'that doest *assay in vain.*'"	"'Vain man,' said she, 'that doest *in vain assay.*'" ("Assay" appears at end of line 5, to rhyme with line 7's "decay.")
"My verse shall *eternize your rare virtues.*"	"My verse *your virtues rare shall eternize.*" ("Eternize" appears at end of line 11 to rhyme with line 9's "devise.")
"Where whenas death shall *subdue all the world,* / Our love shall live, and *later renew life.*"	"Where whenas death shall *all the world subdue,* / Our love shall live, and *later life renew.*" (Rhyming words "subdue" and "renew" are placed at ends of lines.)

To make sure the metrical pattern stresses certain words, the poet occasionally moves a word out of conventional order and places it in a stressed position. The following comparison illustrates this technique.

Conventional Word Order	Inverted Sequence
"But *the waves came* and washed it away."	"But *came the waves* and washed it away." (Stress in line 2 falls on "waves" rather than on "the.") and washed it away."

As the above comparisons show, Spenser's adjustments in syntax are motivated at least in part by a desire to preserve his sonnet's rhyme and meter.

The next poem does more than simply invert word order; it presents an intentionally disordered syntax.

E. E. Cummings (1894–1962)

anyone lived in a pretty how town (1940)

anyone lived in a pretty how town
(with up so floating many bells down)
spring summer autumn winter
he sang his didn't he danced his did.

Women and men (both little and small)   5
cared for anyone not at all
they sowed their isn't they reaped their same
sun moon stars rain

children guessed (but only a few
and down they forgot as up they grew   10
autumn winter spring summer)
that noone loved him more by more

when by now and tree by leaf
she laughed his joy she cried his grief
bird by snow and stir by still   15
anyone's any was all to her

someones married their everyones
laughed their cryings and did their dance
(sleep wake hope and then) they
said their nevers they slept their dream   20

stars rain sun moon
(and only the snow can begin to explain
how children are apt to forget to remember
with up so floating many bells down)

>> Pictures illustrating four seasons

one day anyone died i guess   25
(and noone stooped to kiss his face)
busy folk buried them side by side
little by little and was by was

all by all and deep by deep
and more by more they dream their sleep   30
noone and anyone earth by april
wish by spirit and if by yes.

Women and men (both dong and ding)
summer autumn winter spring
reaped their sowing and went their came   35
sun moon stars rain

Cummings, like Spenser, sometimes manipulates syntax in response to the demands of rhyme and meter—for example, in line 10. But Cummings goes much further, using unconventional syntax as part of a scheme that includes other unusual elements of the poem, such as its unexpected departures from the musical metrical pattern (for example, in lines 3 and 8) and from the rhyme scheme (for example, in lines 3 and 4) and its use of various parts of speech in unfamiliar contexts. Together, these techniques give the poem a playful quality. The refreshing disorder of the syntax (for instance, in lines 1–2, 10, and 24) adds to the poem's whimsical effect.

FURTHER READING: Word Order

A. E. Housman (1859–1936)

To an Athlete Dying Young (1896)

The time you won your town the race
We chaired you through the market-place;
Man and boy stood cheering by,
And home we brought you shoulder-high.

Today, the road all runners come,   5
Shoulder-high we bring you home,
And set you at your threshold down,
Townsman of a stiller town.

Smart lad, to slip betimes away
From fields where glory does not stay,   10
And early though the laurel grows
It withers quicker than the rose.

Eyes the shady night has shut
Cannot see the record cut,
And silence sounds no worse than cheers   15
After earth has stopped the ears.

Now you will not swell the rout
Of lads that wore their honors out,
Runners whom renown outran
And the name died before the man.   20

Steven Sutton/Duomo/Corbis

>> Athlete being crowned with laurel wreath

So set, before its echoes fade,
The fleet foot on the sill of shade,
And hold to the low lintel up
The still-defended challenge-cup.

And round that early-laureled head   25
Will flock to gaze the strengthless dead,
And find unwithered on its curls
The garland briefer than a girl's.

Related Work

"Nothing Gold Can Stay" (p. 403)

 See Chapter 22 Review Card for Reading and Reacting questions about A. E. Housman, "To an Athlete Dying Young."

Writing Suggestions: Word Choice, Word Order

1. Reread the two poems in this chapter by E. E. Cummings—"in Just-" (p. 387) and "anyone lived in a pretty how town" (p. 394). If you like, you may also read one or two additional poems in this book by Cummings. Do you believe Cummings chose words primarily for their sound? for their appearance on the page? What other factors might have influenced his choices?

2. The tone of "We Real Cool" (p. 392) is flat and unemotional; the problem on which it focuses, however, is serious. Expand this concise poem into a few paragraphs that retain the poem's informal, colloquial tone but use more detailed, more emotional language to communicate the hopeless situation of the speaker and his friends. Include dialogue as well as narrative.

3. Reread "For the Grave of Daniel Boone" (p. 384) alongside another poem about a historical figure or event—for example, "For the Union Dead" (p. 492). What does each poem's choice of words reveal about the speaker's attitude toward his subject?

4. Analyze the choice of words and the level of diction in several poems in this book that use language to express social or political criticism. Some poems that might work well include, Claude McKay's "If We Must Die" (p. 514) and Marge Piercy's "Barbie doll" (p. 515).

 CHECKLIST

WRITING ABOUT WORD CHOICE AND WORD ORDER

Word Choice

☐ Which words are of key importance in the poem? What is the denotative meaning of each of these key words?

☐ Which key words have neutral connotations? Which have negative connotations? Which have positive connotations? Beyond its literal meaning, what does each word suggest?

☐ Why is each word chosen instead of a synonym? (For example, is the word chosen for its sound? its connotation? its relationship to other words in the poem? its contribution to the poem's metrical pattern?)

☐ What other words could be effectively used in place of words now in the poem? How would substitutions change the poem's meaning?

☐ Are any words repeated? Why?

Levels of Diction

☐ How would you characterize the poem's level of diction? Why is this level of diction used? Is it appropriate?

☐ Does the poem mix different levels of diction? If so, why?

Word Order

☐ Is the poem's word order conventional, or are words arranged in unexpected order?

☐ What is the purpose of the unusual word order? (For example, does it preserve the poem's meter or rhyme scheme? Does it highlight particular sound correspondences? Does it place emphasis on a particular word or phrase? Does it reflect the speaker's mood?)

☐ How would the poem's impact change if conventional syntax were used?

Glossary Terms

connotation Meaning that a word suggests beyond its literal, dictionary meaning; its emotional associations, judgments, or opinions. Connotations can be positive, neutral, or negative.

formal diction Diction that is lofty and elaborate, with a learned vocabulary and a detached tone.

informal diction Diction that is idiomatic and relaxed, like everyday speech.

23
Imagery

Learning Outcomes

After reading this chapter, you should be able to do the following:

LO1 Recognize and interpret imagery

Timeline

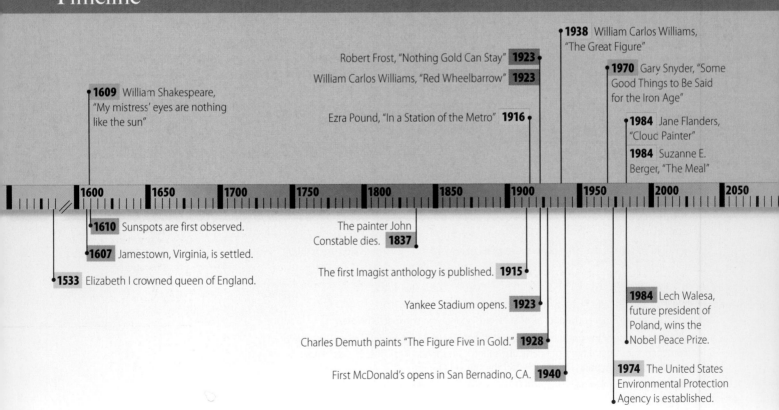

1938 William Carlos Williams, "The Great Figure"

Robert Frost, "Nothing Gold Can Stay" **1923**

William Carlos Williams, "Red Wheelbarrow" **1923**

1970 Gary Snyder, "Some Good Things to Be Said for the Iron Age"

1609 William Shakespeare, "My mistress' eyes are nothing like the sun"

Ezra Pound, "In a Station of the Metro" **1916**

1984 Jane Flanders, "Cloud Painter"

1984 Suzanne E. Berger, "The Meal"

1610 Sunspots are first observed.

The painter John Constable dies. **1837**

1607 Jamestown, Virginia, is settled.

The first Imagist anthology is published. **1915**

1533 Elizabeth I crowned queen of England.

Yankee Stadium opens. **1923**

1984 Lech Walesa, future president of Poland, wins the Nobel Peace Prize.

Charles Demuth paints "The Figure Five in Gold." **1928**

First McDonald's opens in San Bernadino, CA. **1940**

1974 The United States Environmental Protection Agency is established.

Jane Flanders (1940–2001)

Cloud Painter (1984)

Suggested by the life and art of John Constable°

©Steven Flanders

At first, as you know, the sky is incidental—
a drape, a backdrop for trees and steeples.
Here an oak clutches a rock (already he
   works outdoors),
a wall buckles but does not break,
water pearls through a lock, a haywain° trembles.   5

The pleasures of landscape are endless.
   What we see
around us should be enough.
Horizons are typically high and far away.

Still, clouds let us drift and remember.
   He is, after all,
a miller's son, used to trying   10
to read the future in the sky, seeing instead
ships, horses, instruments of flight.
Is that his mother's wash flapping on the line?
His schoolbook, smudged, illegible?

In this period the sky becomes significant.   15
Cloud forms are technically correct—mares' tails,
sheep-in-the-meadow, thunderheads.
You can almost tell which scenes have
   been interrupted
by summer showers.

Now his young wife dies.   20
His landscapes achieve belated success.
He is invited to join the Academy. I forget
whether he accepts or not.

In any case, the literal forms give way
to something spectral, nameless.
   His palette shrinks   25
to gray, blue, white—the colors of charity.
Horizons sink and fade,
trees draw back till they are little more than frames,
then they too disappear.

Finally the canvas itself begins to vibrate   30
with waning light,
as if the wind could paint.
And we too, at last, stare into a space
which tells us nothing,
except that the world can vanish along with
   our need for it.   35

° **John Constable** British
painter (1776–1837) noted for
his landscapes.

° **haywain** An open
horse-drawn wagon for
carrying hay.

imagery Words and phrases that describe the concrete experience of the five senses, most often sight. A **pattern of imagery** is a group of related images developed throughout a work. **Synesthesia** is a form of imagery that mixes the experience of the senses (hearing something visual, smelling something audible, and so on). **Static imagery** freezes the moment to give it the timeless quality of a painting or sculpture. **Kinetic imagery** attempts to show motion or change.

connotation Meaning that a word suggests beyond its literal, dictionary meaning; its emotional associations, judgments, or opinions. Connotations can be positive, neutral, or negative.

atmosphere Tone or mood of a literary work, often established by the setting and language. Atmosphere is the emotional aura that determines readers' expectations about a work.

mood Atmosphere created by the elements of a literary work (setting, characterization, imagery, tone, and so on).

LO1 Recognize and Interpret Imagery

Because the purpose of poetry—and, for that matter, of all literature—is to expand the perception of readers, poets appeal to the senses. In "Cloud Painter," Jane Flanders uses **images**, such as the mother's wash on the line and the smudged school-book, to enable readers to visualize particular scenes in John Constable's early paintings. (For additional poems written in response to works of art, see Chapter 20, "Poetry Sampler: Poetry and Art," p. 353). Clouds are described so readers can picture them—"mares' tails, / sheep-in-the-meadow, thunderheads." Thus, "Cloud Painter" is not only about the work of John Constable but also about the ability of an artist—poet or painter—to call up images in the minds of an audience. To achieve this end, a poet uses **imagery,** language

> *"Readers come to a poem with their own unique experiences, so an image in a poem does not suggest exactly the same thing to all readers."*

that evokes a physical sensation produced by one or more of the five senses—sight, hearing, taste, touch, smell.

Although the effect can be complex, the way images work is simple: when you read the word *red*, your memory of the various red things that you have seen determines how you picture the image. In addition, the word *red* may have **connotations**—emotional associations that define your response. A red sunset, for example, can have a positive connotation or a negative one, depending on whether it is associated with the end of a perfect day or with air pollution. By choosing images carefully, poets not only create pictures in a reader's mind but also create a great number of imaginative associations. These associations help poets to establish the **atmosphere** or **mood** of the poem. The image of softly falling snow in "Stopping by Woods on a Snowy Evening" (p. 509), for example, creates a quiet, almost mystical mood.

Readers come to a poem with their own unique experiences, so an image in a poem does not suggest exactly the same thing to all readers. In "Cloud Painter," for example, the poet presents the image of an oak tree clutching a rock. Although most readers will probably see a picture that is generally consistent with the one the poet sees, no two images will be identical. Every reader will have his or her own distinct mental image of a tree clinging to a rock; some images will be remembered experiences, whereas others will be imaginative creations. Some readers may even be familiar enough with the work of the painter John Constable to visualize a particular tree clinging to a particular rock in one of his paintings. By conveying what the poet imagines, images open readers' minds to perceptions and associations different

The Hay Wain, 1821 (oil on canvas), John Constable (1776-1837) / National Gallery, London, UK / The Bridgeman Art Library International

>> John Constable (1776–1837). *The Hay Wain*, 1821 (oil on canvas), National Gallery, London.

from—and possibly more original and complex than—their own.

One advantage of imagery is its extreme economy. A few carefully chosen words enable poets to evoke a range of emotions and reactions. In the following poem, William Carlos Williams uses simple visual images to create a rich and compelling picture.

⊕ EXPLORE ONLINE >

To complete a tutorial of "Imagery," visit your Literature CourseMate, accessed through www.cengagebrain.com.

William Carlos Williams (1883–1963)

Red Wheelbarrow (1923)

so much depends
upon

a red wheel
barrow

glazed with rain   5
water

beside the white
chickens

>> Painting of red wheelbarrow and chickens

What is immediately apparent in this poem is its verbal economy. The poet does not tell readers what the barnyard smells like or what sounds the animals make. In fact, he does not even present a detailed picture of the scene. How large is the wheelbarrow? What is its condition? How many chickens are in the barnyard? In this poem, the answers to these questions are not important.

Even without answering these questions, the poet is able to use simple imagery to create a scene on which, he says, "so much depends." The wheelbarrow establishes a momentary connection between the poet and his world. Like a still-life painting, the red wheelbarrow beside the white chickens gives order to a world that is full of

seemingly unrelated objects. In this poem, the poet suggests that our ability to perceive the objects of this world gives our lives meaning and that our ability to convey our perceptions to others is central to our lives as well as to poetry.

Images enable poets to present ideas that would be difficult to convey in any other way. One look at a dictionary will illustrate that concepts such as *beauty* and *mystery* are so abstract that they are difficult to define, let alone to discuss in specific terms. However, by choosing an image or a series of images to embody these ideas, poets can effectively make their feelings known, as Ezra Pound does in the two-line poem that follows.

Ezra Pound (1885–1972)

In a Station
of the Metro (1916)

The apparition of these faces in the crowd;
Petals on a wet, black bough.

>> Paris Metro station, early twentieth century

EXPLORE ONLINE >

To listen to an instructor podcast of "In a Station of the Metro," visit your Literature CourseMate, accessed through www.cengagebrain.com.

Pound's poem is almost impossible to paraphrase because the information it communicates is less important than the feelings associated with this information. The poem's title indicates that the first line is meant to suggest a group of people standing in a station of the Paris subway. The scene, however, is presented not as a clear picture but as an "apparition," suggesting that it is unexpected or even dreamlike. In contrast with the image of the subway platform is the image of the people's faces as flower petals on the dark branch of a tree. Thus, the subway platform—dark, cold, wet, subterranean (associated with baseness, death, and hell)—is juxtaposed with flower petals—delicate, pale, radiant, lovely (associated with the ideal, life, and heaven). These contrasting images, presented without comment, bear the entire weight of the poem.

Although images can be strikingly visual, they can also appeal to the senses of hearing, smell, taste, and touch. The following poem uses images of sound and taste as well as sight.

Gary Snyder (1930–   )

Some Good Things to Be Said for the Iron Age (1970)

A ringing tire iron
   dropped on the pavement
Whang of a saw
brusht on limbs
the taste   5
of rust

>> Tire iron

© Tina Rencelj / Shutterstock

Here Snyder presents two commonplace aural images: the ringing of a tire iron and the sound of a saw. These somewhat ordinary images gain power, however, through their visual isolation on separate lines in the poem. Together they produce a harsh and jarring chord that creates a sense of uneasiness in the reader. This poem does more than present sensory images, though; it also conveys the speaker's interpretations of these images. The last two lines imply not only that the time in which we live (the Iron Age) is base and mundane, but also that it is declining, decaying into an age of rust. The title of the poem makes an ironic comment, suggesting that compared to the time that is approaching, the age of iron may be "good." Thus, in the mind of the poet, ordinary events gain added significance, and images that spring from everyday experience become sources of insight.

In short poems, such as most of those discussed above, one or two images may serve as focal points. A longer poem may introduce a cluster of images, creating a more complex tapestry of sensory impressions—as in the following poem, where a number of related images are woven together.

Suzanne E. Berger (1944–   )

The Meal (1984)

They have washed their faces until they are pale,
their homework is beautifully complete.
They wait for the adults to lean towards each other.
The hands of the children are oval
and smooth as pine-nuts.   5

The girls have braided and rebraided their hair,
and tied ribbons without a single mistake.
The boy has put away his coin collection.
They are waiting for the mother to straighten
    her lipstick,
and for the father to speak.   10

They gather around the table, carefully
as constellations waiting to be named.
Their minds shift and ready, like dunes.
It is so quiet, all waiting stars and dunes.

Their forks move across their plates without scraping,   15
they wait for the milk and the gravy
at the table with its forgotten spices.
They are waiting for a happiness to lift their eyes,
like sudden light flaring in the trees outside.

The white miles of the meal continue,   20
the figures still travel across a screen:
the father carving the Sunday roast,
her mouth uneven as a torn hibiscus,
their braids still gleaming in the silence.

V.I. Shamanov (20th century), Picnic Supper in the Country (The Family), Russian State Museum, St. Petersburg / Scala / Art Resource, NY

>> Painting of a family meal

"The Meal" begins with the image of faces washed "until they are pale" and goes on to describe the children's oval hands as "smooth as pine-nuts." Forks move across plates "without scraping," and the table hints at the memory of "forgotten spices." Despite the poem's title, these children are emotionally starved. The attentive, well-scrubbed children sit at a table where, neither eating nor speaking, they wait for "the milk and the gravy" and for happiness that never comes. The "white miles of the meal" seem to go on forever, reinforcing the sterility and emptiness of the Sunday ritual. Suggesting an absence of sensation or feeling, a kind of paralysis, the poem's images challenge conventional assumptions about the family and its rituals.

Much visual imagery is **static,** freezing the moment and thereby giving it the timeless quality of a painting or sculpture. ("The Meal" presents such a tableau, and so do "Red Wheelbarrow" and "In a Station of the Metro.") Some imagery, however, is **kinetic,** conveying a sense of motion or change.

William Carlos Williams (1883–1963)

The Great Figure (1938)

Among the rain
and lights
I saw the figure 5
in gold
on a red   5
firetruck
moving
tense
unheeded
to gong clangs   10
siren howls
and wheels rumbling
through the dark city.

©Bettmann/Corbis

Commenting on "The Great Figure" in his autobiography, Williams explained that while walking in New York, he heard the sound of a fire engine. As he turned the corner, he saw a golden figure 5 on a red background speed by. The impression was so forceful that he immediately jotted down a poem about it. In the poem, Williams attempts to recreate the sensation the figure 5 made as it moved into his consciousness. The poet presents images in the order in which he perceived them: first the 5, and then the red fire truck howling and clanging into the darkness. Thus, "The Great Figure" uses images of sight, sound, and movement to convey the poet's experience. The American painter Charles Demuth was fascinated by the poem. Working closely with Williams, he attempted to capture the poem's kinetic energy in a painting.

Note

A special use of imagery, called **synesthesia**, occurs when one sense is described in a way that is more appropriate for another sense—for instance, when a sound is described with color. When people say they are feeling *blue* or describe music as *hot*, they are using synesthesia.

>> Charles Henry Demuth (1883–1935). *The Figure 5 in Gold*. Oil on composition board, 36 × 29¾ in.

The Figure 5 in Gold. 1928. Oil on cardboard. H. 35-1/2. W. 30 in. (90.2 x 76.2 cm). Alfred Stieglitz Collection, 1949 (49.59.1). The Metropolitan Museum of Art, New York, NY, U.S.A. Image copyright © The Metropolitan Museum of Art/Art Resource, NY

Further Reading: Imagery

Robert Frost (1874–1963)

Nothing Gold Can Stay (1923)

Nature's first green is gold,
Her hardest hue to hold.
Her early leaf's a flower;
But only so an hour.
Then leaf subsides to leaf.   5
So Eden sank to grief.
So dawn goes down to day.
Nothing gold can stay.

>> *The Garden of Eden*, 1860 painting

Erastus Salisbury Field (1805–1900). *The Garden of Eden*, oil on canvas; The Art Archive / Superstock

Related Works

"Araby" (p. 220), "Greasy Lake" (p. 306), "Shall I compare thee to a summer's day?" (p. 408)

See Chapter 23 Review Card for Reading and Reacting questions about Robert Frost, "Nothing Gold Can Stay."

William Shakespeare (1564–1616)

My mistress' eyes are nothing like the sun (1609)

My mistress' eyes are nothing like the sun;
Coral is far more red than her lips' red;
If snow be white, why then her breasts are dun;
If hairs be wires, black wires grow on her head.
I have seen roses damasked red and white,   5
But no such roses see I in her cheeks;
And in some perfumes is there more delight
Than in the breath that from my mistress reeks.
I love to hear her speak, yet well I know
That music hath a far more pleasing sound;   10
I grant I never saw a goddess go:
My mistress, when she walks, treads on the ground.
   And yet, by heaven, I think my love as rare
   As any she, belied with false compare.

>> Nineteenth-century image of damask rose

Related Works

"A&P" (p. 131), "The Storm" (p. 154), "How Do I Love Thee?" (p. 490), *The Brute* (p. 532)

See Chapter 23 Review Card for Reading and Reacting questions about William Shakespeare, "My mistress' eyes are nothing like the sun."

Writing Suggestions: Imagery

1. Read "Four Haiku" (p. 453), focusing on its use of imagery. How are short poems such as "Some Good Things to Be Said for the Iron Age" (p. 402) and "In a Station of the Metro" (p. 401) like and unlike **haiku**?

2. After rereading "Cloud Painter" (p. 399) and "The Great Figure" (p. 403), read "Musée des Beaux Arts" (p. 475) and study the corresponding paintings *The Hay Wain* (p. 400), *The Figure 5 in Gold* (p. 404), and *Landscape with the Fall of Icarus* (p. 476). Then, write an essay in which you draw some conclusions about the differences between artistic and poetic images. If you like, you may also consider the pictures and poems in Chapter 20, "Poetry Sampler: Poetry and Art" (p. 353).

3. Reread "The Meal" (p. 402) and the discussion that accompanies it. Then, analyze the role of imagery in the depiction of the parent/child relationships in "Daddy" (p. 416) and "My Papa's Waltz" (p. 481). How does each poem's imagery convey the nature of the relationship it describes?

4. Write an essay in which you discuss the color imagery in "Nothing Gold Can Stay" (p. 403) and "Spring and All" (p. 457). In what way does color reinforce the themes of these poems?

5. Sometimes imagery can be used to make a comment about the society in which a scene takes place. Choose two poems in which imagery functions in this way—"For the Union Dead" (p. 492) or "right on: white america" (p. 517), for example—and discuss how the images chosen reinforce the social comment each poem makes.

✔ CHECKLIST

WRITING ABOUT IMAGERY

- ☐ Do the images in the poem appeal to the sense of sight? hearing? taste? touch? smell?
- ☐ Does the poem depend on a single image or on several different images?
- ☐ Does the poem depend on a cluster of related images?
- ☐ What details make the images memorable?
- ☐ What mood do the images create?
- ☐ Are the images static or kinetic?
- ☐ How do the poem's images help to convey its theme?
- ☐ How effective are the images? How do they enhance your enjoyment of the poem?

Glossary Terms

atmosphere Tone or mood of a literary work, often established by the setting and language. Atmosphere is the emotional aura that determines readers' expectations about a work.

connotation Meaning that a word suggests beyond its literal, dictionary meaning; its emotional associations, judgments, or opinions. Connotations can be positive, neutral, or negative.

imagery Words and phrases that describe the concrete experience of the five senses, most often sight. A **pattern of imagery** is a group of related images developed throughout a work. **Synesthesia** is a form of imagery that mixes the experience of the senses (hearing something visual, smelling something audible, and so on). **Static imagery** freezes the moment to give it the timeless quality of a painting or sculpture. **Kinetic imagery** attempts to show motion or change.

mood Atmosphere created by the elements of a literary work (setting, characterization, imagery, tone, and so on).

24
Figures of Speech

Learning Outcomes
After reading this chapter, you should be able to do the following:

LO1 Recognize simile, metaphor, and personification

LO2 Recognize hyperbole and understatement

LO3 Recognize metonymy and synecdoche

LO4 Recognize apostrophe

Timeline

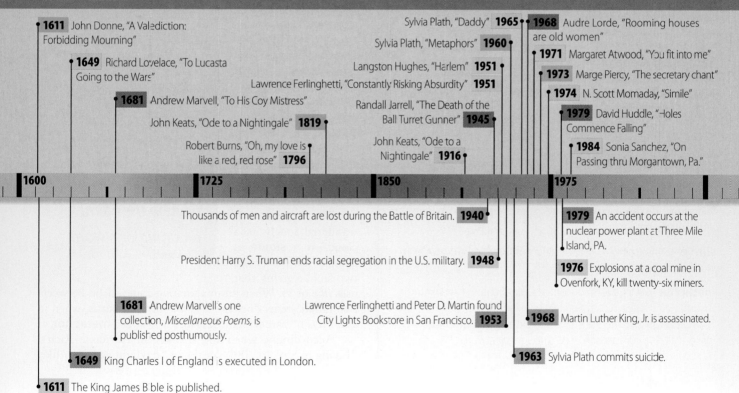

1611 John Donne, "A Valediction: Forbidding Mourning"

1649 Richard Lovelace, "To Lucasta Going to the Wars"

1681 Andrew Marvell, "To His Coy Mistress"

John Keats, "Ode to a Nightingale" **1819**

Robert Burns, "Oh, my love is like a red, red rose" **1796**

Sylvia Plath, "Daddy" **1965**

Sylvia Plath, "Metaphors" **1960**

Langston Hughes, "Harlem" **1951**

Lawrence Ferlinghetti, "Constantly Risking Absurdity" **1951**

Randall Jarrell, "The Death of the Ball Turret Gunner" **1945**

John Keats, "Ode to a Nightingale" **1916**

1968 Audre Lorde, "Rooming houses are old women"

1971 Margaret Atwood, "You fit into me"

1973 Marge Piercy, "The secretary chant"

1974 N. Scott Momaday, "Simile"

1979 David Huddle, "Holes Commence Falling"

1984 Sonia Sanchez, "On Passing thru Morgantown, Pa."

1600   1725   1850   1975

Thousands of men and aircraft are lost during the Battle of Britain. **1940**

President Harry S. Truman ends racial segregation in the U.S. military. **1948**

1681 Andrew Marvell's one collection, *Miscellaneous Poems,* is published posthumously.

Lawrence Ferlinghetti and Peter D. Martin found City Lights Bookstore in San Francisco. **1953**

1649 King Charles I of England is executed in London.

1611 The King James Bible is published.

1979 An accident occurs at the nuclear power plant at Three Mile Island, PA.

1976 Explosions at a coal mine in Ovenfork, KY, kill twenty-six miners.

1968 Martin Luther King, Jr. is assassinated.

1963 Sylvia Plath commits suicide.

William Shakespeare (1564–1616)

Shall I compare thee to a summer's day? (1609)

©Bettmann/Corbis

Shall I compare thee to a summer's day?
Thou art more lovely and more temperate.
Rough winds do shake the darling buds of May,
And summer's lease hath all too short a date.
Sometime too hot the eye of heaven shines,   5
And often is his gold complexion dimmed;
And every fair from fair sometimes declines,
By chance, or nature's changing course, untrimmed.
But thy eternal summer shall not fade,
Nor lose possession of that fair thou ow'st;°   10
Nor shall death brag thou wand'rest in his shade,
When in eternal lines to time thou grow'st.
     So long as men can breathe or eyes can see,
     So long lives this, and this gives life to thee.

° **that fair thou ow'st** That beauty you possess.

Although writers experiment with language in all kinds of literary works, poets in particular recognize the power of a figure of speech to take readers beyond the literal meaning of a word. For this reason, **figures of speech**—expressions that use words to achieve effects beyond the power of ordinary language—are more prominent in poetry than in other kinds of writing. For example, the sonnet above compares a loved one to a summer's day in order to make the point that, unlike the fleeting summer, the loved one will—within the poem—remain forever young. But this sonnet goes beyond the obvious equation (loved one = summer's day): the speaker's assertion that his loved one will live forever in his poem actually says more about his confidence in his own talent and reputation (and about the power of language) than about the loved one's beauty.

figures of speech Expressions—such as simile, metaphor, personification, hyperbole, understatement, metonymy, and synechdoche—that use words to achieve effects beyond ordinary language.

simile Comparison of two seemingly unlike things using the words *like* or *as*.

metaphor Concise form of comparison equating two things that may at first seem completely dissimilar, often an abstraction and a concrete image. An **extended metaphor** (or conceit) is a comparison used throughout a work.

LO1 Recognize Simile, Metaphor, and Personification

When William Wordsworth opens a poem with "I wandered lonely as a cloud" (p. 486), he conveys a good deal more than he would if he simply began, "I wandered, lonely." By comparing himself in his loneliness to a cloud, the speaker suggests that like the cloud he is a part of nature and that he too is drifting, passive, blown by winds, and lacking will or substance. Thus, by using a figure of speech, the poet can suggest a wide variety of feelings and associations in very few words.

The phrase "I wandered lonely as a cloud" is a **simile**, a comparison between two unlike items that uses *like* or *as*. When an imaginative comparison between two unlike items does not use *like* or *as*—that is, when it says "a *is* b" rather than "a is *like* b"—it is a **metaphor**.

Accordingly, when the speaker in Adrienne Rich's "Living in Sin" (p. 386) speaks of "daylight coming / like

> *"Although writers experiment with language in all kinds of literary works, poets in particular recognize the power of a figure of speech to take readers beyond the literal meaning of a word."*

EXPLORE ONLINE >

To complete a tutcrial of "Metaphor and Simile," visit
your Literature CourseMate, accessed through
www.cengagebraih.com.

personification A figure of speech that endows
inanimate objects or abstract ideas with life or human
characteristics: "the river wept."

a relentless milkman up the stairs," she is using a strikingly original simile to suggest that daylight brings not
the conventional associations of promise and awakening
but rather a stale, never-ending routine that is greeted
without enthusiasm. This idea is consistent with the rest
of the poem, an account of an unfulfilling relationship.
However, when the speaker in the Audre Lorde poem on
page 411 says, "Rooming houses are old women," she
uses a metaphor, equating two elements to stress their
common associations with emptiness, transience, and
hopelessness. At the same time, by identifying rooming
houses as old women, Lorde is using **personification,** a

special kind of comparison, closely related to metaphor,
that gives life or human characteristics to inanimate objects or abstract ideas.

Sometimes, as in Wordsworth's "I wandered lonely as
a cloud," a single brief simile or metaphor can be appreci-
ated for what it communicates on its own. At other times,
however, a simile or metaphor may be one of several related figures of speech that work together to convey a poem's meaning. The following poem, for example, presents
a series of related similes. Together, they suggest the depth
of the problem the poem explores in a manner that each
individual simile could not do on its own.

Langston Hughes (1902–1967)

Harlem (1951)

What happens to a dream deferred?

    Does it dry up
    like a raisin in the sun?
    Or fester like a sore—
    And then run?
    Does it stink like rotten meat?   5
    Or crust and sugar over—
    like a syrupy sweet?

    Maybe it just sags
    like a heavy load.   10

Or does it explode?

>> Harlem street scene, 1957

EXPLORE ONLINE >

To listen to an instructor podcast of "Harlem," visit
your Literature CourseMate, accessed through
www.cengagebrain.com.

The dream to which Hughes alludes in this poem is the
dream of racial equality. It is also the American Dream—
or, by extension, any important unrealized dream. His
speaker offers six tentative answers to the question asked
in the poem's first line, and five of the six are presented as

similes. As the poem unfolds, the speaker considers different alternatives: the dream can shrivel up and die, fester,
decay, crust over—or sag under the weight of the burden
those who hold the dream must carry. In each case, the
speaker transforms an abstract entity—a dream—into a

concrete item—a raisin in the sun, a sore, rotten meat, syrupy candy, a heavy load. The final line, italicized for emphasis, gains power less from what it says than from what it leaves unsaid. Unlike the other alternatives explored in the poem, *"Or does it explode?"* is not presented as a simile. Nevertheless, because of the pattern of figurative language the poem has established, readers can supply the other, unspoken half of the comparison: ". . . like a bomb."

Sometimes a single extended simile or extended metaphor is developed throughout a poem. The following poem develops an **extended simile,** comparing a poet to an acrobat.

Lawrence Ferlinghetti (1919–   )

Constantly Risking Absurdity (1958)

Constantly risking absurdity
                and death
      whenever he performs
            above the heads
                of his audience   5
the poet like an acrobat
            climbs on rime
              to a high wire of his own making
and balancing on eyebeams
            above a sea of faces   10
    paces his way
          to the other side of day
    performing entrechats
           and sleight-of-foot tricks
and other high theatrics   15
        and all without mistaking
    any thing
        for what it may not be

    For he's the super realist
           who must perforce perceive   20
     taut truth
        before the taking of each stance or step
in his supposed advance
        toward that still higher perch
where Beauty stands and waits   25
      with gravity
        to start her death-defying leap

And he
    a little charleychaplin man
        who may or may not catch   30
her fair eternal form
      spreadeagled in the empty air
  of existence

>> Charlie Chaplin balancing on high wire in *The Circus*, 1928

© Bettmann/Corbis

In his extended comparison of a poet and an acrobat, Ferlinghetti characterizes the poet as a circus performer, at once swinging recklessly on a trapeze and balancing carefully on a tightrope.

What the poem suggests is that the poet, like an acrobat, works hard at his craft but manages to make it all look easy. Something of an exhibitionist, the poet is innovative and creative, taking impossible chances yet also building on traditional skills in his quest for truth and beauty. Moreover, like an acrobat, the poet is balanced "on eyebeams / above a sea of faces," for he too depends on audience reaction to help him keep his performance focused. The poet may be "the super realist," but he also has plenty of playful tricks up his sleeve: "entrechats / and sleight-of-foot tricks / and other high theatrics," including puns ("above the heads / of his audience"), unexpected rhyme ("climbs on rime"), alliteration ("taut truth"), coinages ("a little charleychaplin man"), and all the other linguistic acrobatics available to poets. (Even the arrangement of the poem's lines on the page suggests the acrobatics

it describes.) Like these tricks, the poem's central simile is a whimsical one, perhaps suggesting that Ferlinghetti is poking fun at poets who take their craft too seriously. In any case, the simile helps him to illustrate the acrobatic possibilities of language in a fresh and original manner.

The following poem develops an **extended metaphor,** personifying rooming houses as old women.

Audre Lorde (1934–1992)

Rooming houses are old women (1968)

Rooming houses are old women
rocking dark windows into their whens
waiting incomplete circles
rocking
rent office to stoop to   5
community bathrooms to gas rings and
under-bed boxes of once useful garbage
city issued with a twice monthly check
and the young men next door
with their loud midnight parties   10
and fishy rings left in the bathtub
no longer arouse them
from midnight to mealtime no stops inbetween
light breaking to pass through jumbled up windows
and who was it who married the widow that Buzzie's   15
    son messed with?

To Welfare and insult form the slow shuffle
from dayswork to shopping bags
heavy with leftovers
Rooming houses
are old women waiting   20
searching
through darkening windows
the end or beginning of agony
old women seen through half-ajar doors
hoping   25
they are not waiting
but being
the entrance to somewhere
unknown and desired
but not new.   30

>> Elderly woman at window in rooming house

So closely does Lorde equate rooming houses and old women in this poem that at times it is difficult to tell which of the two is actually the poem's subject. Despite the poem's assertion, rooming houses are *not* old women; however, they are *comparable to* the old women who live there because their walls enclose a lifetime of disappointments as well as the physical detritus of life. Like the old women, rooming houses are in decline, rocking away their remaining years. And, like the houses they inhabit, these women's boundaries are fixed—"rent office to stoop to / community bathrooms to gas rings"—and their hopes and expectations are few. They are surrounded by other people's loud parties, but their own lives have been reduced to a "slow shuffle" to nowhere, a hopeless, frightened—and perhaps pointless—"waiting / searching." Over time, the women and the places in which they live have become one. By using an unexpected comparison between two seemingly unrelated entities, the poem illuminates both the essence of the rooming houses and the essence of their elderly occupants.

FURTHER READING: Simile, Metaphor, and Personification

Robert Burns (1759–1796)

Oh, my love is like a red, red rose (1796)

>> Hourglass

Oh, my love is like a red, red rose
   That's newly sprung in June;
My love is like the melody
   That's sweetly played in tune.

So fair art thou, my bonny lass,   5
   So deep in love am I;
And I will love thee still, my dear,
   Till a' the seas gang° dry.

Till a' the seas gang dry, my dear,
   And the rocks melt wi' the sun;   10
And I will love thee still, my dear,
   While the sands o' life shall run.

And fare thee weel, my only love!
   And fare thee weel awhile!
And I will come again, my love   15
   Though it were ten thousand mile.

° **gang** Go.

Related Works

"Araby" (p. 220), "Baca Grande" (p. 389), "My mistress' eyes are nothing like the sun" (p. 405), "To His Coy Mistress" (p. 419), "How Do I Love Thee?" (p. 490), *The Brute* (p. 532)

N. Scott Momaday (1934–   )

Simile (1974)

What did we say to each other
that now we are as the deer
who walk in single file
with heads high
with ears forward   5
with eyes watchful
with hooves always placed on firm ground
in whose limbs there is latent flight

>> Deer

Related Work

"Let me not to the marriage of true minds" (p. 517)

Sylvia Plath (1932–1963)

Metaphors (1960)

I'm a riddle in nine syllables,
An elephant, a ponderous house,
A melon strolling on two tendrils.
O red fruit, ivory, fine timbers!
This loaf's big with its yeasty rising.   5
Money's new-minted in this fat purse.
I'm a means, a stage, a cow in calf.
I've eaten a bag of green apples,
Boarded the train there's no getting off.

Related Work

"I Stand Here Ironing" (p. 162)

 See Chapter 24 Review Card for Reading and Reacting questions about Sylvia Plath, "Metaphors."

Randall Jarrell (1914–1965)

The Death of the Ball Turret Gunner° (1945)

From my mother's sleep I fell into the State
And I hunched in its belly till my wet fur froze.
Six miles from earth, loosed from its dream of life,
I woke to black flak and the nightmare fighters.
When I died they washed me out of the turret with a hose.   5

©Cape Canaveral Hangar, United States Air Force

° **Ball turret gunner** World War II machine gunner positioned upside-down in a plexiglass sphere in the belly of a bomber.

Related Works

"Buffalo Soldiers" (p. 105), "The Things They Carried" (p. 232), "The Soldier" (p. 491)

 See Chapter 24 Review Card for Reading and Reacting questions about Randall Jarrell "The Death of the Ball Turret Gunner."

Marge Piercy (1936–   )

The secretary chant (1973)

My hips are a desk.
From my ears hang
chains of paper clips.
Rubber bands form my hair.
My breasts are wells of mimeograph ink.   5
My feet bear casters.
Buzz. Click.
My head is a badly organized file.
My head is a switchboard
where crossed lines crackle.   10
Press my fingers
and in my eyes appear
credit and debit.
Zing. Tinkle.
My navel is a reject button.   15
From my mouth issue canceled reams.
Swollen, heavy, rectangular
I am about to be delivered
of a baby
Xerox machine.   20
File me under W
because I wonce
was

a woman.

>> Secretaries in typing pool, 1956

Related Works

"Girl" (p. 104), "Buffalo Soldiers" (p. 105), "A&P"
(p. 131)

John Donne (1572–1631)

A Valediction: Forbidding Mourning (1611)

As virtuous men pass mildly away,
    And whisper to their souls to go,
Whilst some of their sad friends do say
    The breath goes now, and some say no:

So let us melt, and make no noise,   5
    No tear-floods, nor sigh-tempests move;
'Twere profanation of our joys
    To tell the laity° our love.

Moving of th' earth brings harms and fears;
    Men reckon what it did and meant;   10
But trepidation of the spheres,
    Though greater far, is innocent.

°**laity** Here, "common
people."

Dull sublunary lovers' love
    (Whose soul is sense) cannot admit
Absence, because it doth remove
    Those things which elemented it.   15

But we, by a love so much refined
    That ourselves know not what it is,
Inter-assurèd of the mind,
    Care less, eyes, lips, and hands to miss.   20

Our two souls, therefore, which are one,
    Though I must go, endure not yet
A breach, but an expansion,
    Like gold to airy thinness beat.

If they be two, they are two so   25
    As stiff twin compasses° are two:
Thy soul, the fixed foot, makes no show
    To move, but doth, if th' other do.

And though it in the center sit,
    Yet when the other far doth roam,   30
It leans and harkens after it,
    And grows erect as that comes home.

Such wilt thou be to me, who must,
    Like th' other foot, obliquely run;
Thy firmness makes my circle just,°   35
    And makes me end where I begun.

The Granger Collection, New York

>> Engraving of compass

° **compasses** V-shaped
instruments used for drawing
circles.
° **just** Perfect.

Related Works

"How Do I Love Thee?" (p. 490), *A Doll House*
(p. 562)

LO2 Recognize Hyperbole and Understatement

Two additional kinds of figurative language, *hyperbole* and *understatement*, also give poets opportunities to suggest meaning beyond the literal level of language.

Hyperbole is intentional exaggeration—saying more than is actually meant. In the poem "Oh, my love is like a red, red rose" (p. 412), when the speaker says that he will love his lady until all the seas go dry, he is using hyperbole.

Understatement is the opposite—saying less than is meant. When the speaker in the poem "Fire and Ice" (p. 369), weighing two equally grim alternatives for the end of the world, says that "for destruction ice / Is also great / And would suffice," he is using understatement. In both cases, poets expect their readers to understand that their words are not to be taken literally.

By using hyperbole and understatement, poets enhance the impact of their poems. For example, poets can use hyperbole to convey exaggerated anger or graphic images of horror—and to ridicule and satirize as well as to inflame and shock. With understatement, poets can convey the same kind of powerful emotions subtly, without artifice or embellishment, thereby leading readers to read more closely than they might otherwise.

The emotionally charged poem that follows uses hyperbole to convey anger and bitterness that seem almost beyond the power of words.

hyperbole Figurative language that depends on intentional overstatement.

understatement Intentional downplaying of a situation's significance, often for ironic or humorous effect.

Sylvia Plath (1932–1963)

Daddy (1965)

You do not do, you do not do
Any more, black shoe
In which I have lived like a foot
For thirty years, poor and white,
Barely daring to breathe or Achoo.   5

Daddy, I have had to kill you.
You died before I had time—
Marble-heavy, a bag full of God,
Ghastly statue with one grey toe
Big as a Frisco seal   10

And a head in the freakish Atlantic
Where it pours bean green over blue
In the waters off beautiful Nauset.
I used to pray to recover you.
Ach, du.°   15

In the German tongue, in the Polish town°
Scraped flat by the roller
Of wars, wars, wars.
But the name of the town is common.
My Polack friend   20

Says there are a dozen or two.
So I never could tell where you
Put your foot, your root,
I never could talk to you.
The tongue stuck in my jaw.   25

It stuck in a barb wire snare.
Ich, ich, ich, ich,°
I could hardly speak.
I thought every German was you.
And the language obscene   30

An engine, an engine
Chuffing me off like a Jew.
A Jew to Dachau, Auschwitz, Belsen.°
I began to talk like a Jew.
I think I may well be a Jew.   35

The snows of the Tyrol, the clear beer of Vienna
Are not very pure or true.
With my gypsy ancestress and my weird luck
And my Taroc pack and my Taroc pack
I may be a bit of a Jew.   40

I have always been scared of you,
With your Luftwaffe,° your gobbledygoo.
And your neat moustache
And your Aryan eye, bright blue.
Panzer°-man, panzer-man, O You—   45

>> Nazi poster, 1941

° **Ach, du** "Ah, you" (German).

° **Polish town** Grabôw, where Plath's father was born.

° **ich** "I" (German).

° **Dachau, Auschwitz, Belsen** Nazi concentration camps.

° **Luftwaffe** The German air force.

° **Panzer** The Panzer division was the German armored division.

Not God but a swastika
So black no sky could squeak through.
Every woman adores a Fascist,
The boot in the face, the brute
Brute heart of a brute like you.   50

You stand at the blackboard, daddy,
In the picture I have of you,
A cleft in your chin instead of your foot
But no less a devil for that, no not
Any less the black man who   55

Bit my pretty red heart in two.
I was ten when they buried you.
At twenty I tried to die
And get back, back, back to you.
I thought even the bones would do.   60

But they pulled me out of the sack,
And they stuck me together with glue.
And then I knew what to do.
I made a model of you,
A man in black with a Meinkampf° look   65

And a love of the rack and the screw.
And I said I do, I do.
So daddy, I'm finally through.
The black telephone's off at the root,
The voices just can't worm through.   70

If I've killed one man, I've killed two—
The vampire who said he was you
And drank my blood for a year,
Seven years, if you want to know.
Daddy, you can lie back now.   75

There's a stake in your fat black heart
And the villagers never liked you.
They are dancing and stamping on you.
They always *knew* it was you.
Daddy, daddy, you bastard, I'm through.   80

°**Meinkampf** *Mein Kampf* (My Struggle) is Adolf Hitler's autobiography.

In her anger and frustration, the speaker sees herself as a helpless victim—a foot entrapped in a shoe, a Jew in a concentration camp—of her father's (and, later, her husband's) absolute tyranny. Thus, her hated father is characterized as a "black shoe," "a bag full of God," a "Ghastly statue," and, eventually, a Nazi, a torturer, the devil, a vampire. The poem "Daddy" is widely accepted by scholars as autobiographical, and the fact that Plath's own father was actually neither a Nazi nor a sadist (nor, obviously, the devil or a vampire) makes it clear that the figures of speech in the poem are wildly exaggerated.

Even so, they may convey the poet's true feelings toward her father—and, perhaps, toward the patriarchal society in which she lived.

Plath uses hyperbole to communicate these emotions to readers who she knows cannot possibly feel the way she does. Her purpose, therefore, is not only to shock but also to enlighten, to persuade, and perhaps even to empower her readers. Throughout the poem, the inflammatory language is set in ironic opposition to the childish, affectionate term "Daddy"—most strikingly in the last line's choked out "Daddy, daddy, you bastard, I'm through." The result of the exaggerated rhetoric is a poem that is vivid and shocking. And, although some might believe that Plath's almost wild exaggeration undermines the poem's impact, others would argue that the powerful language is necessary to convey the extent of the speaker's rage.

Like "Daddy," the following poem presents a situation whose emotional impact is devastating. In this case, however, the poet does not use highly charged language; instead, he uses understatement, presenting events without embellishment.

David Huddle (1942–   )

Holes Commence Falling (1979)

The lead & zinc company
owned the mineral rights
to the whole town anyway,
and after drilling holes
for 3 or 4 years,   5
they finally found the right
place and sunk a mine shaft.
We were proud
of all that digging,
even though nobody from   10
town got hired. They
were going to dig right
under New River and hook up
with the mine at Austinville.
Then people's wells   15
started drying up just like
somebody'd shut off a faucet,
and holes commenced falling,
big chunks of people's yards
would drop 5 or 6 feet,   20
houses would shift and crack.
Now and then the company'd
pay out a little money
in damages; they got a truck
to haul water and sell it   25
to the people whose wells
had dried up, but most
everybody agreed the
situation wasn't
serious.   30

>> Sinkhole

Although "Holes Commence Falling" relates a tragic sequence of events, the tone of the poem is matter-of-fact, and the language is understated. The speaker could have overdramatized the events, using inflated rhetoric to denounce big business and to predict disastrous events for the future. At the very least, he could have colored the facts with realistic emotions, assigning blame to the lead and zinc company with justifiable anger. Instead, the speaker is so restrained, so nonchalant, so passive that readers must supply the missing emotions themselves—realizing, for example, that when the speaker concludes "everybody agreed the / situation wasn't / serious," he means exactly the opposite.

Throughout the poem, unpleasant information is presented without comment or emotion. As it proceeds, the poem traces the high and low points in the town's fortunes, but for every hope ("We were proud / of all that digging"), there is a disappointment ("even though nobody from / town got hired"). The lead and zinc company offers some compensation for the damage it does, but it is never enough. The present tense verb of the poem's title indicates that the problems the town faces—wells drying up, yards dropping, houses shifting and cracking—are regular occurrences. Eventually, readers come to see that what is not expressed, what lurks just below the surface—anger, powerlessness, resentment, hopelessness—is the poem's real subject.

Andrew Marvell (1621–1678)

To His Coy Mistress (1681)

Had we but world enough and time,
This coyness, lady, were no crime.
We would sit down and think which way
To walk, and pass our long love's day.
Thou by the Indian Ganges' side   5
Should'st rubies find; I by the tide
Of Humber° would complain. I would
Love you ten years before the Flood,
And you should, if you please, refuse
Till the conversion of the Jews.   10
My vegetable love should grow
Vaster than empires, and more slow.
An hundred years should go to praise
Thine eyes, and on thy forehead gaze,
Two hundred to adore each breast,   15
But thirty thousand to the rest.
An age at least to every part,
And the last age should show your heart.
For, lady, you deserve this state,
Nor would I love at lower rate.   20
　But at my back I always hear
Time's wingèd chariot hurrying near,
And yonder all before us lie
Deserts of vast eternity.
Thy beauty shall no more be found,   25
Nor in thy marble vault shall sound
My echoing song; then worms shall try
That long preserved virginity,
And your quaint honor turn to dust,
And into ashes all my lust.   30
The grave's a fine and private place,
But none, I think, do there embrace.
　Now therefore, while the youthful hue
Sits on thy skin like morning glew°
And while thy willing soul transpires   35
At every pore with instant fires,
Now let us sport us while we may;
And now, like amorous birds of prey,
Rather at once our time devour
Than languish in his slow-chapped° power.   40
Let us roll all our strength and all
Our sweetness up into one ball
And tear our pleasures with rough strife
Thorough the iron gates of life.
Thus, though we cannot make our sun   45
Stand still, yet we will make him run.

>> Winged horses pulling chariot

°**Humber** An estuary on the east coast of England.

°**glew** Dew.

°**slow-chapped** Slowly crushing.

Related Works

"Where Are You Going, Where Have You Been?" (p. 325), "To the Virgins, to Make Much of Time" (p. 374), "The Passionate Shepherd to His Love" (p. 513), *The Brute* (p. 532)

 See Chapter 24 Review Card for Reading and Reacting questions about Andrew Marvell, "To His Coy Mistress."

Robert Frost (1874–1963)

"Out, Out—" (1916)

The buzz saw snarled and rattled in the yard
And made dust and dropped stove-length sticks
   of wood,
Sweet-scented stuff when the breeze drew across it.
And from there those that lifted eyes could count
Five mountain ranges one behind the other   5
Under the sunset far into Vermont.
And the saw snarled and rattled, snarled and rattled,
As it ran light, or had to bear a load.
And nothing happened: day was all but done.
Call it a day, I wish they might have said   10
To please the boy by giving him the half hour
That a boy counts so much when saved from work.
His sister stood beside them in her apron
To tell them "Supper." At the word, the saw,
As if to prove saws knew what supper meant,   15
Leaped out at the boy's hand, or seemed to leap—
He must have given the hand. However it was,
Neither refused the meeting. But the hand!
The boy's first outcry was a rueful laugh,
As he swung toward them holding up the hand   20
Half in appeal, but half as if to keep
The life from spilling. Then the boy saw all—
Since he was old enough to know, big boy
Doing a man's work, though a child at heart—
He saw all spoiled. "Don't let him cut my hand off—   25
The doctor, when he comes. Don't let him, sister!"
So. But the hand was gone already.
The doctor put him in the dark of ether.
He lay and puffed his lips out with his breath.
And then—the watcher at his pulse took fright.   30
No one believed. They listened at his heart.
Little—less—nothing!—and that ended it.
No more to build on there. And they, since they
Were not the one dead, turned to their affairs.

>> Buzz saw

Related Works

"Accident" (p. 103), "Kansas" (p. 117), "The Lottery" (p. 251), "The Death of the Ball Turret Gunner" (p. 413), "What Were They Like?" (p. 494)

See Chapter 24 Review Card for Reading and Reacting questions about Robert Frost, "Out, Out—."

Margaret Atwood (1939–)

You fit into me (1971)

you fit into me
like a hook into an eye

a fish hook
an open eye

Related Works

"Hills Like White Elephants" (p. 96), "Love and Other Catastrophes: A
Mix Tape" (p. 103), "Daddy" (p. 416), *A Doll House* (p. 562)

LO3 Recognize Metonymy and Synecdoche

Metonymy and synecdoche are two related figures of
speech. **Metonymy** is the substitution of the name of one
thing for the name of another thing that most readers associate with the first—for example, using *hired gun* to
mean "paid assassin" or *suits* to mean "business executives." A specific kind of metonymy, called **synecdoche,** is
the substitution of a part for the whole (for example, using *bread*—as in "Give us this day our daily bread"—to
mean "food") or the whole for a part (for example, using
the law to refer to a police officer.)

> **metonymy** Figure of speech in which the term for one thing
> can be applied to another with which it is closely associated.
>
> **synecdoche** Figure of speech in which a part of something
> is used to represent the whole.

With metonymy and synecdoche, instead of describing something by saying it is like something else (as in
simile) or by equating it with something else (as in metaphor), writers can characterize an object or concept by using a term that evokes it. The following poem illustrates
the use of synecdoche.

Richard Lovelace (1618–1658)

To Lucasta Going to the Wars (1649)

Tell me not, Sweet, I am unkind
   That from the nunnery
Of thy chaste breast and quiet mind,
   To war and arms I fly.

True, a new mistress now I chase,   5
   The first foe in the field;
And with a stronger faith embrace
   A sword, a horse, a shield.

Yet this inconstancy is such
   As you too shall adore;   10
I could not love thee, Dear, so much,
   Loved I not Honor more.

>> Prince Rupert's Cavalry
charging at Edgehill in 1642

Here, Lovelace's use of synecdoche allows him to condense a number of complex ideas into a very few words. In line 3, when the speaker says that he is flying from his loved one's "chaste breast and quiet mind," he is using "breast" and "mind" to stand for all his loved one's physical and intellectual attributes. In line 8, when he says that he is embracing "A sword, a horse, a shield," he is using these three items to represent the trappings of war—and, thus, to represent war itself.

LO4 Recognize Apostrophe

With **apostrophe,** a poem's speaker addresses an absent person or thing—for example, a historical or literary figure or even an inanimate object or an abstract concept.

In the following poem, the speaker addresses Vincent Van Gogh.

Sonia Sanchez (1934–   )

On Passing thru Morgantown, Pa. (1984)

i saw you
vincent van
gogh perched
on those pennsylvania
cornfields communing   5
amid secret black
bird societies. yes.
i'm sure that was
you exploding your
fantastic delirium   10
while in the
distance
red indian
hills beckoned.

>> (Detail) *Wheatfield with Crows*, 1890 (oil on canvas), Vincent van Gogh (1853–90)

Expecting her readers to be aware that Van Gogh, a nineteenth-century Dutch postimpressionist painter, is known for his mental instability as well as for his art, Sanchez is able to give added meaning to a phrase such as "fantastic delirium" as well as to the poem's visual images. Perhaps picturing his 1890 painting *Wheatfield with Crows*, the speaker sees Van Gogh perched like a black bird on a fence, and at the same time she also sees what he sees. Like Van Gogh, then, the speaker sees the Pennsylvania cornfields as both a natural landscape and an "exploding" work of art.

° **hemlock** A medicinal plant used as a sedative or, in higher doses, a deadly poison.

° **opiate** A medicine containing opium, a substance derived from poppies, which aids sleep and relieves pain.

° **Lethe** In Greek mythology, a river in Hades, the land of the dead. Those who drank its water lost all memory of the past.

FURTHER READING: Apostrophe

John Keats (1795–1821)

Ode to a Nightingale (1819)

My heart aches, and a drowsy numbness pains
    My sense, as though of hemlock° I had drunk,
Or emptied some dull opiate° to the drains
    One minute past, and Lethe°–wards had sunk:
'Tis not through envy of thy happy lot.   5

>> Lithograph of nightingale, c. 1830

But being too happy in thine happiness,—
   That thou, light-wingèd Dryad° of the trees,
     In some melodious plot
Of beechen° green, and shadows numberless,
   Singest of summer in full-throated ease.   10

O for a draught° of vintage! that hath been
   Cool'd a long age in the deep-delvèd° earth,
Tasting of Flora° and the country-green,
   Dance, and Provençal° song, and sunburnt mirth!
O for a beaker full of the warm South!   15
   Full of the true, the blushful Hippocrene,°
     With beaded bubbles winking at the brim,
       And purple-stainèd mouth;
That I might drink, and leave the world unseen,
   And with thee fade away into the forest dim: 20

Fade far away, dissolve, and quite forget
   What thou among the leaves hast never known,
The weariness, the fever, and the fret
   Here, where men sit and hear each other groan;
Where palsy shakes a few, sad, last grey hairs,   25
   Where youth grows pale, and spectre-thin, and dies;
     Where but to think is to be full of sorrow
       And leaden-eyed despairs,
Where beauty cannot keep her lustrous eyes,
   Or new Love pine at them beyond to-morrow.   30

Away! away! for I will fly to thee,
   Not charioted by Bacchus° and his pards,°
But on the viewless wings of Poesy,
   Though the dull brain perplexes and retards:
Already with thee! tender is the night,   35
   And haply the Queen-Moon is on her throne,
     Cluster'd around by all her starry Fays;°
       But here there is no light,
Save what from heaven is with the breezes blown
   Through verdurous° glooms and winding mossy ways.   40

I cannot see what flowers are at my feet,
   Nor what soft incense hangs upon the boughs,
But, in embalmèd darkness, guess each sweet
   Wherewith the seasonable month endows
The grass, the thicket, and the fruit-tree wild;   45
   White hawthorn, and the pastoral eglantine;°
     Fast-fading violets cover'd up in leaves;
       And mid-May's eldest child,
The coming musk-rose, full of dewy wine,
   The murmurous haunt of flies on summer eves.   50

Darkling I listen; and, for many a time
   I have been half in love with easeful Death,
Call'd him soft names in many a musèd rhyme,
   To take into the air my quiet breath;
Now more than ever seems it rich to die,   55
   To cease upon the midnight with no pain,

°**Dryad** A spirit believed to inhabit trees.

°**beechen** Of or relating to a beech tree.

°**draught** A large sip of liquid.

°**deep-delvèd** Excavated.

°**Flora** In Roman mythology, the goddess of flowers.

°**Provençal** From Provence, a region of southern France.

°**Hippocrene** A fountain on Mt. Helicon, in Greece, considered sacred to the Muses.

°**Bacchus** The god of wine.

°**pards** Leopards or panthers.

°**Fays** Fairies.

°**verdurous** Green with vegetation.

°**eglantine** A plant also known as the sweet-briar.

While thou art pouring forth the soul abroad
    In such an ecstasy!
Still wouldst thou sing, and I have ears in vain—
    To thy high requiem become a sod.   60

Thou wast not born for death, immortal Bird!
    No hungry generations tread thee down;
The voice I hear this passing night was heard
    In ancient days by emperor and clown:
Perhaps the self-same song that found a path   65
    Through the sad heart of Ruth, when, sick for home,
        She stood in tears amid the alien corn;°
            The same that ofttimes hath
Charm'd magic casements,° opening on the foam
    Of perilous seas, in faery lands forlorn.°   70

Forlorn! the very word is like a bell
    To toll me back from thee to my sole self!
Adieu! the fancy cannot cheat so well
    As she is famed to do, deceiving elf.
Adieu!° adieu! the plaintive anthem fades   75
    Past the near meadows, over the still stream,
    Up the hill-side; and now 'tis buried deep
        In the next valley-glades:
Was it a vision, or a waking dream?
    Fled is that music:—Do I wake or sleep?

° **corn** Grain.
° **casements** Windows.
° **forlorn** Lost.
° **Adieu** Farewell.

Related Works

"Young Goodman Brown" (p. 320), "The World Is Too Much with Us"
(p. 373), "Death Be Not Proud" (p. 503)

Writing Suggestions: Figures of Speech

1. Various figures of speech are often used to describe characters in literary works. Choose two or three works that focus on a single character—for example, "A Rose for Emily" (p. 121), "Miss Brill" (p. 135), "Gryphon" (p. 138), or "Richard Cory" (p. 516) —and explain how figures of speech are used to characterize each work's central figure. If you like, you may write about works that focus on real (rather than fictional) people.

2. Write an essay in which you discuss the different ways poets use figures of speech to examine the nature of poetry itself. What kinds of figures of speech do poets use to describe their craft? (You might begin by reading the two poems about poetry that open Chapter 19.)

3. Write a letter replying to the speaker in the poem by Marvell, Donne, or Burns that appears in this chapter. Use figures of speech to express the depth of your love and the extent of your devotion.

4. Choose three or four poems that have a common subject—for example, love or nature—and write an essay in which you draw some general conclusions about the relative effectiveness of the poems' use of figures of speech to examine that subject. (If you like, you may focus on the poems clustered under the heads "Poems about Parents," "Poems about Nature," "Poems about Love," and "Poems about War" in Chapter 28.)

5. Select a poem and a short story that deal with the same subject, and write an essay in which you compare their use of figures of speech.

 CHECKLIST

WRITING ABOUT FIGURES OF SPEECH

- [ ] What figures of speech are present in the poem? Identify any examples of simile, metaphor, personification, hyperbole, understatement, metonymy, synecdoche, and apostrophe.
- [ ] What two elements are being compared in each use of simile, metaphor, and personification? What characteristics are shared by the two items being compared?
- [ ] Does the poet use hyperbole? Why? For example, is it used to move or to shock readers, or is its use intended to produce a humorous or satirical effect? Would more understated language be more effective?
- [ ] Does the poet use understatement? For what purpose? Would more emotionally charged language be more effective?
- [ ] In metonymy and synecdoche, what item is being substituted for another? What purpose does the substitution serve?
- [ ] If the poem includes apostrophe, whom or what does the speaker address? What does the use of apostrophe accomplish?
- [ ] How do figures of speech contribute to the impact of the poem as a whole?

Glossary Terms

apostrophe Figure of speech in which an absent character or a personified force or object is addressed directly, as if it were present or could comprehend.

extended metaphor Metaphor used throughout a work.

extended simile Simile used throughout a work.

figures of speech Expressions— such as **simile, metaphor, personification, hyperbole, understatement, metonymy, and synechdoche**—that use words to achieve effects beyond ordinary language.

hyperbole Figurative language that depends on intentional overstatement.

metaphor Concise form of comparison equating two things that may at first seem completely dissimilar, often an abstraction and a concrete image.

metonymy Figure of speech in which the term for one thing can be applied to another with which it is closely associated.

personification A figure of speech that endows inanimate objects or abstract ideas with life or human characteristics: "the river wept."

simile Comparison of two seemingly unlike things using the words *like* or *as*.

synecdoche Figure of speech in which a part of something is used to represent the whole.

understatement Intentional downplaying of a situation's significance, often for ironic or humorous effect.

25

Sound

Learning Outcomes

After reading this chapter, you should be able to do the following:

LO1 Recognize rhythm

LO2 Recognize meter

LO3 Recognize alliteration and assonance

LO4 Recognize rhyme

Timeline

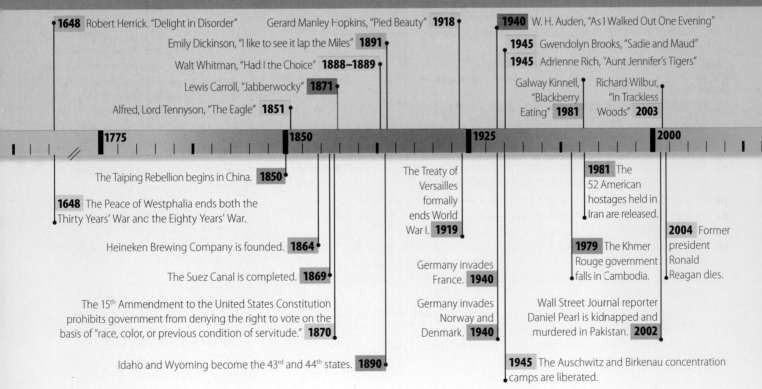

1648 Robert Herrick. "Delight in Disorder"

Emily Dickinson, "I like to see it lap the Miles" **1891**

Walt Whitman, "Had I the Choice" **1888–1889**

Lewis Carroll, "Jabberwocky" **1871**

Alfred, Lord Tennyson, "The Eagle" **1851**

Gerard Manley Hopkins, "Pied Beauty" **1918**

1940 W. H. Auden, "As I Walked Out One Evening"

1945 Gwendolyn Brooks, "Sadie and Maud"

1945 Adrienne Rich, "Aunt Jennifer's Tigers"

Galway Kinnell, "Blackberry Eating" **1981**

Richard Wilbur, "In Trackless Woods" **2003**

1775 | **1850** | **1925** | **2000**

The Taiping Rebellion begins in China. **1850**

1648 The Peace of Westphalia ends both the Thirty Years' War and the Eighty Years' War.

Heineken Brewing Company is founded. **1864**

The Suez Canal is completed. **1869**

The 15th Ammendment to the United States Constitution prohibits government from denying the right to vote on the basis of "race, color, or previous condition of servitude." **1870**

Idaho and Wyoming become the 43rd and 44th states. **1890**

The Treaty of Versailles formally ends World War I. **1919**

Germany invades France. **1940**

Germany invades Norway and Denmark. **1940**

1981 The 52 American hostages held in Iran are released.

1979 The Khmer Rouge government falls in Cambodia.

Wall Street Journal reporter Daniel Pearl is kidnapped and murdered in Pakistan. **2002**

2004 Former president Ronald Reagan dies.

1945 The Auschwitz and Birkenau concentration camps are liberated.

Walt Whitman (1819–1892)

Had I the Choice*

Had I the choice to tally greatest bards,
To limn° their portraits, stately, beautiful,
  and emulate at will,
Homer with all his wars and warriors—Hector,
  Achilles, Ajax,
Or Shakespeare's woe-entangled Hamlet, Lear,
  Othello—Tennyson's fair ladies,
Meter or wit the best, or choice conceit to
  wield in perfect rhyme, delight of singers;   5
These, these, O sea, all these I'd gladly barter,
Would you the undulation of one wave, its
  trick to me transfer,
Or breathe one breath of yours upon my verse,
And leave its odor there.

>> Detail of vase showing
Achilles killing Hector

*Publication date is not available.

° **limn** To describe, depict.

LO1 Recognize Rhythm

Rhythm—the regular recurrence of sounds—is at the center of all natural phenomena: the beating of a heart, the lapping of waves against the shore, the croaking of frogs on a summer's night, the whispering of wheat swaying in the wind. Even mechanical phenomena, such as the movement of rush-hour traffic through a city's streets, have a kind of rhythm. Poetry, which explores these phenomena, often tries to reflect the same rhythms. Walt Whitman expresses this idea in "Had I the Choice" when he says that he would gladly trade the "perfect rhyme" of Shakespeare for the ability to reproduce "the undulation of one wave" in his verse.

> "Rhythm—the regular recurrence of sounds—is at the center of all natural phenomena ...."

Public speakers frequently repeat key words and phrases to create rhythm. In his "I have a dream" speech, for example, Martin Luther King Jr. repeats the phrase "I have a dream" to create a rhythm that ties the central section of the speech together:

I say to you today, my friends, even though we face the difficulties of today and tomorrow, I still have a dream. It is a dream deeply rooted in the American dream. I have a dream that one day this nation will rise up and live out the true meaning of its creed: "We hold these truths to be self-evident, that all men are created equal." I have a dream that one day, on the red hills of Georgia, sons of former slaves and the sons of former slave owners will be able to sit down together at the table of brotherhood. I have a dream that one day even the state of Mississippi, a state sweltering with the heat of injustice, sweltering with the heat of oppression, will be transformed into an oasis of freedom and justice. I have a dream that my four little children will one day live in a nation where they will not be judged by the color of their skin, but by the content of their character.

Poets too create rhythm by using repeated words and phrases, as Gwendolyn Brooks does in the poem on the following page.

> **rhythm** Regular recurrence of sounds in a poem.

Gwendolyn Brooks (1917–2000)

Sadie and Maud (1945)

Maud went to college.
Sadie stayed at home.
Sadie scraped life
With a fine-tooth comb.

She didn't leave a tangle in.   5
Her comb found every strand.
Sadie was one of the livingest chits
In all the land.

Sadie bore two babies
Under her maiden name.   10
Maud and Ma and Papa
Nearly died of shame.

When Sadie said her last so-long
Her girls struck out from home.
(Sadie had left as heritage   15
Her fine-tooth comb.)

Maud, who went to college,
Is a thin brown mouse.
She is living all alone
In this old house.   20

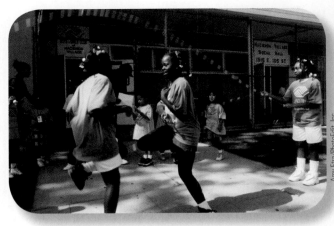

>> Girls jumping rope

Much of the force of this poem comes from the repeated words "Sadie" and "Maud," which shift the focus from one subject to the other and back again ("<u>Maud</u> went to college / <u>Sadie</u> stayed home"). The poem's singsong rhythm recalls the rhymes children recite when jumping rope. This evocation of carefree childhood is ironically contrasted with the adult realities that both Sadie and Maud face as they grow up: Sadie stays at home and has two children out of wedlock; Maud goes to college and ends up "a thin brown mouse." The speaker implies that the alternatives Sadie and Maud represent are both undesirable. Although Sadie "scraped life / with a fine-tooth comb," she dies young and leaves nothing to her girls but her desire to experience life. Maud, who graduated from college, shuts out life and cuts herself off from her roots.

Just as the repetition of words and phrases can create rhythm, so can the appearance of words on the printed page. How a poem looks is especially important in **open form poetry** (see p. 454), which dispenses with traditional patterns of versification. In the following excerpt from a poem by E. E. Cummings, for example, an unusual arrangement of words forces readers to slow down and then to speed up, creating a rhythm that emphasizes a key phrase—"The/lily":

the moon is hiding
in her hair.
The
lily
of heaven
full of all dreams,
draws down.

LO2 Recognize Meter

Although rhythm can be affected by the regular repetition of words and phrases or by the arrangement of words into

EXPLORE ONLINE >

To complete a tutorial of "Meter," visit your Literature CourseMate, accessed through www.cengagebrain.com.

lines, poetic rhythm is largely created by **meter,** the recurrence of regular units of stressed and unstressed syllables. A **stress** (or accent) occurs when one syllable is emphasized more than another, unstressed, syllable: *fór • ceps, bá • sic, il • lú • sion, ma • lár • i • a.* In a poem, even one-syllable words can be stressed to create a particular effect. For example, in Elizabeth Barrett Browning's line "How do I love thee? Let me count the ways," the metrical pattern that places stress on "love" creates one meaning; stressing "I" would create another.

Scansion is the analysis of patterns of stressed and unstressed syllables within a line. The most common method of poetic notation indicates stressed syllables with *a* and unstressed syllables with *a*. Although scanning lines gives readers the "beat" of the poem, scansion only generally suggests the sound of spoken language, which contains an infinite variety of stresses. By providing a graphic representation of the stressed and unstressed syllables of a poem, scansion aids understanding, but it is no substitute for reading the poem aloud and experimenting with various patterns of emphasis.

The basic unit of meter is a **foot**—a group of syllables with a fixed pattern of stressed and unstressed syllables. The chart that follows illustrates the most common types of metrical feet in English and American verse.

Foot	Stress Pattern	Example
Iamb	˘′	They pace | in sleek | chi val | ric cer | tain ty (Adrienne Rich)
Trochee	′˘	Thou, when | thou re | turn'st, wilt | tell me. (John Donne)
Anapest	˘˘′	With a hey, | and a ho, | and a hey | no ni no (William Shakespeare)

meter Regular pattern of stressed and unstressed syllables, each repeated unit of which is called a **foot.** A poem's meter is described in terms of the kind of foot and the number of feet found in each line. The most common meter in English is *iambic pentameter.*

stress Accent or emphasis, either strong or weak, given to each syllable in a poem.

scansion Process of determining the meter of a poem by analyzing the strong and weak stresses in a line.

rising meter Iambic and anapestic meters, so called because they move from unstressed to stressed syllables.

falling meter Trochaic and dactylic meters, so called because they move from stressed to unstressed syllables.

Foot	Stress Pattern	Example
Dactyl	′˘˘	Constantly | risking ab | surdity (Lawrence Ferlinghetti)

Iambic and *anapestic* meters are called **rising meters** because they progress from unstressed to stressed syllables. *Trochaic* and *dactylic* meters are called **falling meters** because they progress from stressed to unstressed syllables.

The following types of metrical feet, less common than those listed above, are used to add emphasis or to provide variety rather than to create the dominant meter of a poem.

Foot	Stress Pattern	Example
Spondee	′′	Pomp, pride | and circumstance of glorious war! (William Shakespeare)
Pyrrhic	˘˘	A horse! a horse! My king | dom for | a horse! (William Shakespeare)

A metric line of poetry is measured by the number of feet it contains.

Monometer	one foot	**Pentameter**	five feet
Dimeter	two feet	**Hexameter**	six feet
Trimeter	three feet	**Heptameter**	seven feet
Tetrameter	four feet	**Octameter**	eight feet

The name for a metrical pattern of a line of verse identifies the name of the foot used and the number of feet the line contains. For example, the most common foot in English poetry is the **iamb,** most often occurring in lines of three or five feet.

Metrical Pattern	Example
Iambic trimeter	Eight hun | dred of | the brave (William Cowper)
Iambic pentameter	O, how | much more | doth beau | ty beau | tous sem (William Shakespeare)

Because **iambic pentameter** is so well suited to the rhythms of English speech, writers frequently use it in plays and poems. Shakespeare's plays, for example, are written in unrhymed lines of iambic pentameter called **blank verse** (see p. 445).

Many other metrical combinations are also possible; following are a few examples.

Metrical Pattern	Example
Trochaic trimeter	Like a | high-born | maiden (Percy Bysshe Shelley)
Anapestic tetrameter	The As sy | rian came down | like the wolf | on the fold (Lord Byron)
Dactylic hexameter	Maid en most | beau ti ful | moth er most | boun ti ful, | la dy of | lands, (A. C. Swinburne)
Iambic heptameter	The yel | low fog | that rubs | its back | up on | the win | dow-panes (T. S. Eliot)

Scansion can be an extremely technical process, and when readers become bogged down with anapests and dactyls, they can easily forget that poetic scansion is not an end in itself. Meter should be appropriate for the ideas expressed by the poem, and it should help to create a suitable tone. A light, skipping rhythm, for example, would be inappropriate for an **elegy,** and a slow, heavy rhythm would surely be out of place in an **epigram** or a limerick. The following lines of a poem by Samuel Taylor Coleridge illustrate the uses of different types of metrical feet:

> *"Meter should be appropriate for the ideas expressed by the poem, and it should help to create a suitable tone."*

Trochee trips from long to short;
From long to long in solemn sort
Slow Spondee stalks; strong foot! yet ill able
Ever to come up with Dactyl trisyllable.
Iambics march from short to long—
With a leap and a bound the swift Anapests throng;

One syllable long, with one short at each side,
Amphibrachys hastes with a stately stride—
First and last being long, middle short, Amphimacer
Strikes his thundering hoofs like a proud high-bred Racer.

5

10

A poet may use one kind of meter—iambic meter, for example—throughout a poem, but may vary line length to relieve monotony or to accommodate the poem's meaning or emphasis. In the following poem, the poet uses iambic lines of different lengths.

Emily Dickinson (1830–1886)

I like to see it lap the Miles— (1891)

I like to see it lap the Miles—
And lick the Valleys up—
And stop to feed itself at Tanks—
And then—prodigious step

Around a Pile of Mountains—
And supercilious peer
In Shanties—by the sides of Roads—
And then a Quarry pare

5

To fit its Ribs
And crawl between
Complaining all the while
In horrid—hooting stanza—

10

Then chase itself down Hill—
And neigh like Boanerges°—
Then—punctual as a Star
Stop—docile and omnipotent
At its own stable door—

15

>> Vintage train going through mountains

° **Boanerges** A vociferous preacher and orator. Also, the name, meaning "son of thunder," Jesus gave to apostles John and James because of their fiery zeal.

Dickinson's poem is a single sentence that, except for some pauses, stretches unbroken from beginning to end. Iambic lines of varying lengths actually suggest the movements of the train that the poet describes. Lines of iambic tetrameter, such as the first, give readers a sense of the train's steady, rhythmic movement across a flat landscape, and shorter lines ("To fit its Ribs / And crawl between") suggest the train's slowing motion. Beginning with two iambic dimeter lines and progressing to iambic trimeter lines, the third stanza increases in speed just like the train that is racing downhill "In horrid—hooting stanza—."

When a poet uses more than one type of metrical foot, any variation in a metrical pattern—the substitution of a trochee for an iamb, for instance—immediately calls attention to itself. For example, in line 16 of "I like to see it lap the Miles," the poet departs from iambic meter by placing unexpected stress on the first word, *stop*. By emphasizing this word, the poet brings the flow of the poem to an abrupt halt, suggesting the jolt riders experience when a train comes to a stop.

Another way of varying the meter of a poem is to introduce a pause known as a **caesura**—a Latin word meaning "a cutting"—within a line. When scanning a poem, you indicate a caesura with two parallel lines: ‖. Unless a line of poetry is extremely short, it probably will contain a caesura.

A caesura occurs after a punctuation mark or at a natural break in phrasing:

How do I love thee? ‖ Let me count the ways.

Elizabeth Barrett Browning

Two loves I have ‖ of comfort and despair.

William Shakespeare

High on a throne of royal state, ‖ which far
Outshone the wealth of Ormus ‖ and of Ind

John Milton

Sometimes more than one caesura occurs in a single line:

'Tis good. ‖ Go to the gate. ‖ Somebody knocks.

William Shakespeare

Although the end of a line may mark the end of a metrical unit, it does not always coincide with the end of a sentence. Lines that have distinct pauses at the end—usually signaled by punctuation—are called **end-stopped lines.** Lines that do not end with strong pauses are called **run-on lines.** (Sometimes the term **enjambment** is used to describe run-on lines.) End-stopped lines can sometimes seem formal, or even forced, because their length is rigidly dictated by the poem's meter, rhythm, and rhyme scheme. In the following excerpt from John Keats's "La Belle Dame sans Merci," for example, rhythm, meter, and rhyme dictate the pauses that occur at the ends of the lines:

O, what can ail thee, knight-at-arms,
    Alone and palely loitering?
The sedge has wither'd from the lake,
    And no birds sing.

In contrast to end-stopped lines, run-on lines often seem more natural. Because their ending points are determined by the rhythms of speech and by the meaning and emphasis the poet wishes to convey rather than by meter and rhyme, run-on lines are suited to the open form of much modern poetry. In the following lines from the poem "We Have Come Home," by Lenrie Peters, run-on lines give readers the sense of spoken language:

We have come home
From the bloodless war
With sunken hearts
Our boots full of pride—
From the true massacre of the soul
When we have asked
"What does it cost
To be loved and left alone?"

Rather than relying exclusively on end-stopped or run-on lines, poets often use a combination of the two to produce the effects they want. For example, the following lines from "Pot Roast," by Mark Strand, juxtapose end-stopped and run-on lines:

I gaze upon the roast,
that is sliced and laid out
on my plate
and over it
I spoon the juices
of carrot and onion.
And for once I do not regret
the passage of time.

Adrienne Rich (1929–2012)

Aunt Jennifer's Tigers (1951)

Aunt Jennifer's tigers prance across a screen,
Bright topaz denizens of a world of green.
They do not fear the men beneath the tree;
They pace in sleek chivalric certainty.

Aunt Jennifer's fingers fluttering through her wool   5
Find even the ivory needle hard to pull.
The massive weight of Uncle's wedding band
Sits heavily upon Aunt Jennifer's hand.

When Aunt is dead, her terrified hands will lie
Still ringed with ordeals she was mastered by.   10
The tigers in the panel that she made
Will go on prancing, proud and unafraid.

>> Detail of tiger on embroidered mat

Related Works

"Miss Brill" (p. 135), "Everyday Use" (p. 256), "Rooming houses are old women" (p. 411)

 See Chapter 25 Review Card for Reading and Reacting questions about Adrienne Rich, "Aunt Jennifer's Tigers."

LO3 Recognize Alliteration and Assonance

Just as poetry depends on rhythm, it also depends on the sounds of individual words. An effect pleasing to the ear, such as "Did he who made the Lamb make thee?" from William Blake's "The Tyger" (p. 499), is called **euphony.** A jarring or discordant effect, such as "The vorpal blade went snicker-snack!" from Lewis Carroll's "Jabberwocky" (p. 440), is called **cacophony.**

One of the earliest, and perhaps the most primitive, methods of enhancing sound is **onomatopoeia,** which occurs when the sound of a word echoes its meaning, as it does in common words such as *bang, crash,* and *hiss.* Poets make broad application of this technique by using combinations of words that suggest a correspondence between sound and meaning, as Edgar Allan Poe does in these lines from his poem "The Bells":

> Yet the ear, it fully knows,
> By the twanging
> And the clanging,
> How the danger ebbs and flows;
> Yet the ear distinctly tells,
> In the jangling
> And the wrangling
> How the danger sinks and swells
> By the sinking or the swelling in the anger of the bells—
> Of the bells,—
> Of the bells, bells, bells, bells. . . .

Poe's primary objective in this poem is to re-create the sound of ringing bells. Although he succeeds, the poem

euphony Pleasant spoken sound.

cacophony Harsh or unpleasant spoken sound.

onomatopoeia Word whose sound resembles what it describes: "snap, crackle, pop." Lewis Carroll's "Jabberwocky" uses onomatopoeia.

🌐 EXPLORE ONLINE >

To complete a tutorial of "Alliteration," visit your Literature CourseMate, accessed through www.cengagebrain.com.

(113 lines long in its entirety) is extremely tedious. A more subtle use of onomatopoetic words appears in the following passage from *An Essay on Criticism* by Alexander Pope:

> Soft is the strain when Zephyr gently blows,
> And the smooth stream in smoother numbers flows;
> But when the loud surges lash the sounding shore,
> The hoarse, rough verse should like the torrent roar:
> When Ajax strives some rock's vast weight to throw,
> The line too Labors, and the words move slow.

After earlier admonishing readers that sound must echo sense, Pope uses onomatopoetic words such as *lash* and *roar* to convey the fury of the sea, and he uses repeated consonants to echo the sounds these words suggest. Notice, for example, how the *s* and *m* sounds suggest the gently blowing Zephyr and the flowing of the smooth stream and how the series of *r* sounds echoes the torrent's roar.

Alliteration—the repetition of consonant sounds in consecutive or neighboring words, usually at the beginning of words—is another device used to enhance sound in a poem. Both Poe ("<u>s</u>inks and <u>s</u>wells") and Pope ("<u>s</u>mooth <u>s</u>tream") make use of alliteration in the preceding excerpts, and so does Tennyson in the following poem.

Alfred, Lord Tennyson (1809–1892)

The Eagle (1851)

He clasps the crag with crooked hands;
Close to the sun in lonely lands,
Ringed with the azure world, he stands.

The wrinkled sea beneath him crawls:
He watches from his mountain walls,
And like a thunderbolt he falls.

5

>> Bald eagle

Throughout the poem, *c*, *l*, and *w* sounds occur repeatedly. The poem is drawn together by the recurrence of these sounds and, as a result, it flows smoothly from beginning to end.

Assonance—the repetition of the same or similar vowel sounds, especially in stressed syllables—can also enrich a poem. When used effectively, assonance can create both mood and tone in a subtle, musical way.

Consider, for example, the use of assonance in the following lines from Dylan Thomas's "Do not go gentle into that good night": "Old age should burn and rave at close of day; / Rage, rage, against the dying of the light."

Sometimes assonance unifies an entire poem. In the following poem, assonance emphasizes the thematic connections among words and thus links the poem's ideas.

Robert Herrick (1591–1674)

Delight in Disorder (1648)

A sweet disorder in the dress
Kindles in clothes a wantonness.
A lawn° about the shoulders thrown
Into a fine distraction;
An erring lace, which here and there   5
Enthralls the crimson stomacher;°
A cuff neglectful, and thereby
Ribbons to flow confusedly;
A winning wave, deserving note,
In the tempestuous petticoat;   10
A careless shoestring, in whose tie
I see a wild civility;
Do more bewitch me than when art
Is too precise in every part.

>> *Portrait of a Lady* 17th century oil on canvas by Sir Peter Lely

° **lawn** A shawl made of fine fabric.

° **stomacher** A heavily embroidered garment worn by females over the chest and stomach.

Repeated vowel sounds extend throughout this poem—for instance, "sh<u>ou</u>lders" and "thr<u>ow</u>n" in line 3; and "t<u>ie</u>," "w<u>i</u>ld," and "prec<u>i</u>se" in lines 11, 12, and 14. Using alliteration as well as assonance, Herrick subtly links certain words—"<u>te</u>mpes<u>t</u>uous <u>pe</u>t<u>t</u>icoat," for example. By connecting these words, he calls attention to the pattern of imagery that helps to convey the poem's theme.

LO4 Recognize Rhyme

In addition to alliteration and assonance, poets create sound patterns with **rhyme**—the use of matching sounds in two or more words: "tight" and "might"; "born" and "horn"; "sleep" and "deep." For a rhyme to be **perfect**, final vowel and consonant sounds must be the same, as they are in each of the preceding examples. **Imperfect rhyme** (also called *near rhyme, slant rhyme, approximate rhyme,* or **consonance**) occurs when the final consonant sounds in two words are the same but intervening vowel sounds are different—"learn" / "barn" or "pads" / "lids," for example. William Stafford uses imperfect rhyme in "Traveling through the Dark" (p. 488) when he rhymes "road" with "dead." Finally, **eye rhyme** occurs when two words look as if they should rhyme but do not—for example, "watch" and "catch."

Rhyme can also be classified according to the position of the rhyming syllables in a line of verse. The most common type of rhyme is **end rhyme,** which occurs at the end of a line:

Tyger! Tyger! burning <u>bright</u>
In the forests of the <u>night</u>

William Blake, "The Tyger"

Internal rhyme occurs within a line:

The Sun came up upon the left,
Out of the <u>sea</u> came <u>he</u>!
And he shone <u>bright</u> and on the <u>right</u>
Went down into the sea.
Samuel Taylor Coleridge, "The Rime of the Ancient Mariner"

Beginning rhyme occurs in the first syllable or syllables of a line:

Red river, red river,
<u>Slow</u> flow heat is silence
<u>No</u> will is still as a river
T. S. Eliot, "Virginia"

> **rhyme** Repetition of concluding sounds in different words, often intentionally used at the ends of poetic lines.

Rhyme can also be classified according to the number of syllables that correspond. **Masculine rhyme** (also called **rising rhyme**) occurs when single syllables correspond ("can" / "ran"; "descend" / "contend"). **Feminine rhyme** (also called **double rhyme** or **falling rhyme**) occurs when two syllables, a stressed one followed by an unstressed one, correspond ("ocean" / "motion"; "leaping" / "sleeping"). **Triple rhyme** occurs when three syllables correspond. Less common than the other two, triple rhyme is often used for humorous or satiric purposes, as in the following lines from the long poem *Don Juan* by Lord Byron:

> Sagest of women, even of widows, she
>   Resolved that Juan should be quite a <u>paragon</u>,
> And worthy of the noblest pedigree:
>   (His sire of Castile, his dam from <u>Aragon</u>).

In some cases—for example, when it is overused or when it is used in unexpected places—rhyme can create unusual and even comic effects. In the following poem, humor

EXPLORE ONLINE >

To complete a tutorial of "Rhyme," visit your Literature CourseMate, accessed through www.cengagebrain.com.

is created by the incongruous connections established by rhymes such as "priest" / "beast" and "pajama" / "lllama."

The conventional way to describe a poem's rhyme scheme is to chart rhyming sounds that appear at the ends of lines. The sound that ends the first line is designated *a*, and all subsequent lines that end in that sound are also labeled *a*. The next sound to appear at the end of a line is designated *b*, and all other lines whose last sounds rhyme with it are also designated *b*—and so on through the alphabet. The lines of the poem that follows are labeled in this manner.

RICHARD WILBUR (1921–   )

In Trackless Woods (2003)

In trackless woods, it puzzled me to find	a
Four great rock maples seemingly aligned,	a
As if they had been set out in a row	b
Before some house a century ago,	b
To edge the property and lend some shade.	c 5
I looked to see if ancient wheels had made	c
Old ruts to which these trees can parallel,	d
But there were none, so far as I could tell—	d
There'd been no roadway. Nor could I find the square	e
Depression of a cellar anywhere,	e 10
And so I tramped on further, to survey	f
Amazing patterns in a hornbeam spray	f
Or spirals in a pinecone, under trees	g
Not subject to our stiff geometries.	g

>> Trees planted in a row

"In Trackless Woods" has a simple rhyme scheme (*aa, bb, cc,* and so on). In a sense, this fourteen-line poem is a sonnet—but one that that rejects the fixed rhyme scheme of the traditional sonnet. Despite its simplicity, the rhyme scheme of the poem is important. It reinforces the central point of the poem: that the four maples standing in a row—perhaps planted by someone one hundred years ago—are standing in opposition to the "amazing patterns" in nature. The poem suggests that the "stiff geometries" imposed by human beings (in formal gardens and possibly even in the rigid forms of some poetry) do not reflect the more subtle

and organic patterns that the speaker perceives in the natural world.

Other poems have a more complicated rhyme scheme. Notice in the following excerpt from "The Road Not Taken" (p. 509) how Robert Frost uses rhyme:

Two roads diverged in a yellow wood,	*a*
And sorry I could not travel both	*b*
And be one traveler, long I stood,	*a*
And looked down one as far as I could	*a*
To where it bent in the undergrowth;	*b*

This rhyme scheme of Frost's five-line stanza (and indeed of the whole poem) is *abaab*. In addition, there are four stressed syllables per line, mostly in iambic tetrameter. Despite its rather complex rhyme and metrical scheme, the poem sounds conversational, as if someone just spoke it without any effort or planning. The beauty of this poem comes from Frost's subtle use of rhyme and rhythm to create a musical effect that makes the lines flow together. In addition, the alternating *a* and *b* rhymes suggest the divergent roads that the speaker is forced to choose between.

FURTHER READING: Alliteration, Assonance, and Rhyme

Gerard Manley Hopkins (1844–1889)

Pied Beauty (1918)

Glory be to God for dappled things—
    For skies of couple-color as a brinded° cow;
      For rose-moles all in stipple upon trout that swim;
Fresh-firecoal chestnut-falls; finches' wings;
    Landscape plotted and pieced—fold, fallow,
      and plow;   5
      And áll trádes, their gear and tackle and trim.°

All things counter, original, spare, strange;
    Whatever is fickle, freckled (who knows how?)
      With swift, slow; sweet, sour; adazzle, dim;
He fathers-forth whose beauty is past change: 10
        Praise him.

\>\> John Constable, *Summer Evening near East Bergholt, Suffolk* (1806–1809)

° **brinded** Brindled (streaked).

° **trim** Equipment.

Related Work

"Cathedral" (p. 261)

 See Chapter 25 Review Card for Reading and Reacting questions about Gerard Manley Hopkins, "Pied Beauty."

EXPLORE ONLINE >

To listen to audio of "Pied Beauty," visit your Literature CourseMate, accessed through www.cengagebrain.com.

W. H. Auden (1907–1973)

As I Walked Out
One Evening (1940)

As I walked out one evening,
　　Walking down Bristol Street,
The crowds upon the pavement
　　Were fields of harvest wheat.

And down by the brimming river 　　　　　　　5
　　I heard a lover sing
Under an arch of the railway:
　　"Love has no ending.

"I'll love you, dear, I'll love you
　　Till China and Africa meet, 　　　　　　　10
And the river jumps over the mountain
　　And the salmon sing in the street,

"I'll love you till the ocean
　　Is folded and hung up to dry,
And the seven stars go squawking 　　　　　　15
　　Like geese about the sky.

"The years shall run like rabbits,
　　For in my arms I hold
The Flower of the Ages,
　　And the first love of the world." 　　　　　20

But all the clocks in the city
　　Began to whirr and chime:
"O let not Time deceive you,
　　You cannot conquer Time.

"In the burrows of the Nightmare 　　　　　　25
　　Where Justice naked is,
Time watches from the shadow
　　And coughs when you would kiss.

"In headaches and in worry
　　Vaguely life leaks away, 　　　　　　　　30
And Time will have his fancy
　　Tomorrow or today.

"Into many a green valley
　　Drifts the appalling snow;
Time breaks the threaded dances 　　　　　　35
　　And the diver's brilliant bow.

"O plunge your hands in water,
　　Plunge them in up to the wrist;
Stare, stare in the basin
　　And wonder what you've missed. 　　　　　40

>> Antique clocks

"The glacier knocks in the cupboard,
    The desert sighs in the bed,
And the crack in the teacup opens
    A lane to the land of the dead.

"Where the beggars raffle the banknotes   45
    And the Giant is enchanting to Jack,
And the Lily-white Boy is a Roarer,
    And Jill goes down on her back.

"O look, look in the mirror,
    O look in your distress;   50
Life remains a blessing
    Although you cannot bless.

"O stand, stand at the window
    As the tears scald and start;
You shall love your crooked neighbor   55
    With your crooked heart."

It was late, late in the evening,
    The lovers they were gone;
The clocks had ceased their chiming,
    And the deep river ran on.   60

Related Works

"The Story of an Hour" (p. 115), "The World Is Too Much with Us"
(p. 373), "Oh, my love is like a red, red rose" (p. 412), "To His Coy
Mistress" (p. 419), "Not marble, nor the gilded monuments" (p. 518)

Galway Kinnell (1927–   )

Blackberry Eating (1980)

I love to go out in late September
among the fat, overripe, icy, black blackberries
to eat blackberries for breakfast,
the stalks very prickly, a penalty
they earn for knowing the black art   5
of blackberry-making; and as I stand among them
lifting the stalks to my mouth, the ripest berries
fall almost unbidden to my tongue,
as words sometimes do, certain peculiar words
like *strengths* or *squinched*,   10
many-lettered, one-syllabled lumps,
which I squeeze, squinch open, and splurge well
in the silent, startled, icy, black language
of blackberry-eating in late September.

>> Blackberries

© Josef Mohyla/iStockphoto.com

Related Works

"Snow" (p. 102), "Cathedral" (p. 261), "Two Questions" (p. 273),
"Words, Words, Words" (p. 382), "Introduction to Poetry" (p. 502)

See Chapter 25 Review Card for Reading and Reacting questions about Galway Kinnell, "Blackberry Eating."

Lewis Carroll (1832–1898)

Jabberwocky (1871)

'Twas brillig, and the slithy toves
    Did gyre and gimble in the wabe:
All mimsy were the borogoves,
    And the mome raths outgrabe.

"Beware the Jabberwock, my son!   5
    The jaws that bite, the claws that catch!
Beware the Jubjub bird, and shun
    The frumious Bandersnatch!"

He took his vorpal sword in hand;
    Long time the manxome foe he sought—   10
So rested he by the Tumtum tree
    And stood awhile in thought.

And, as in uffish thought he stood,
    The Jabberwock, with eyes of flame,
Came whiffling through the tulgey wood,   15
    And burbled as it came!

One, two! One, two! And through and through
    The vorpal blade went snicker-snack!
He left it dead, and with its head
    He went galumphing back.   20

"And hast thou slain the Jabberwock?
    Come to my arms, my beamish boy!
O frabjous day! Callooh, Callay!"
    He chortled in his joy.

'Twas brillig, and the slithy toves   25
    Did gyre and gimble in the wabe:
All mimsy were the borogoves,
    And the mome raths outgrabe.

Mary Evans Picture Library/Alamy

>> Illustration of Jabberwock from
Alice in Wonderland

See Chapter 25 Review Card for Reading and Reacting
questions about Lewis Carroll, "Jabberwocky."

Writing Suggestions: Sound

1. William Blake's "The Tyger" appeared in a collection entitled *Songs of Experience*. Compare this poem (p. 499) to "The Lamb" (p. 499), which appeared in a collection called *Songs of Innocence*. In what sense are the speakers in these two poems either "innocent" or "experienced"? How does sound help to convey the voice of the speakers in these two poems?

2. "Sadie and Maud" (p. 428), like "My Papa's Waltz" (p. 481), and "Daddy" (p. 416), communicate the speakers' attitudes toward home and family. How does the presence or absence of rhyme in these poems help to convey the speakers' attitudes?

3. Robert Frost once said that writing **free verse** poems, which have no fixed metrical pattern, is like playing tennis without a net. What do you think he meant? Do you agree? After reading "Out, Out—" (p. 420), "Stopping by Woods on a Snowy Evening" (p. 509), and "The Road Not Taken" (p. 509), write an essay in which you discuss Frost's use of meter.

4. Select two or three contemporary poems that have no end rhyme. Write an essay in which you discuss what these poets gain and lose by not using end rhyme.

5. Prose writers as well as poets use assonance and alliteration. Choose two or three passages of prose—from "Araby" (p. 220), "Barn Burning" (p. 194), or "The Things They Carried" (p. 232), for example—and discuss their use of assonance and alliteration. Where are these techniques used? How do they help the writer create a mood?

 CHECKLIST

WRITING ABOUT SOUND

Rhythm and Meter

☐ Does the poem contain repeated words and phrases? If so, how do they help to create rhythm?

☐ Does the poem use one kind of meter throughout, or does the meter vary from line to line?

☐ How does the meter contribute to the overall effect of the poem?

☐ Where do caesuras appear? What effect do they have?

☐ Are the lines of the poem end-stopped, run-on, or a combination of the two? What effects are created by the presence or absence of pauses at the ends of lines?

Alliteration, Assonance, and Rhyme

☐ Does the poem include alliteration or assonance?

☐ Does the poem have a regular rhyme scheme?

☐ Does the poem use internal rhyme? beginning rhyme?

☐ Does the poem include examples of masculine, feminine, or triple rhyme?

☐ How does rhyme unify the poem?

☐ How does rhyme reinforce the poem's ideas?

Glossary Terms

alliteration Repetition of consonant sounds in a series of words.

assonance Repetition of the same or similar vowel sounds.

blank verse Lines of unrhymed iambic pentameter.

cacophony Harsh spoken sound created by clashing consonants.

caesura Strong or long pause in the middle of a poetic line.

elegy Poem commemorating someone's death.

end-stopped line Line of poetry that has a full pause at the end.

epigram Short pithy poem.

euphony Pleasant spoken sound created by smooth consonants such as "ripple" or "pleasure."

falling meter Trochaic and dactylic meters, so called because they move from stressed to unstressed syllables.

meter Regular pattern of stressed and unstressed syllables.

onomatopoeia Word whose sound resembles what it describes.

rhyme Repetition of concluding sounds in different words

rhythm Regular recurrence of sounds in a poem.

rising meter Iambic and anapestic meters, so called because they move from unstressed to stressed syllables.

run-on line/enjambment Line of poetry with no punctuation that runs over into the next line.

scansion Determining the meter of a poem by analyzing the stresses in a line.

stress Accent or emphasis.

26
Form

Learning Outcomes

After reading this chapter, you should be able to do the following:

LO1 Recognize closed form

LO2 Recognize open form

Timeline

1609 William Shakespeare, "When, in disgrace with Fortune and men's eyes"

1793–1811 William Blake, "Her Whole Life Is an Epigram"

1802 Samuel Taylor Coleridge, "What Is an Epigram?"

1816 John Keats, "On First Looking into Chapman's Homer"

1819 John Keats, "On the Sonnet"

Walt Whitman, from "Out of the Cradle Endlessly Rocking" **1881**

Theodore Roethke, "The Waking" **1953**

e. e. cummings, "the sky was can dy" **1925**

William Carlos Williams, "Spring and All" **1923**

Carl Sandburg, "Chicago" **1914**

Gwendolyn Brooks, "First Fight. Then Fiddle" **1949**

1965 Elizabeth Bishop, "Sestina"

1978 Carolyn Forché, "The Colonel"

1982 Alberto Alvaro Ríos, "Nani"

1986 Pat Mora, "Immigrants"

1999 Billy Collins, "Sonnet"

2000 Martin Espada, "Why I Went to College"

1800 **1870** **1940** **2010**

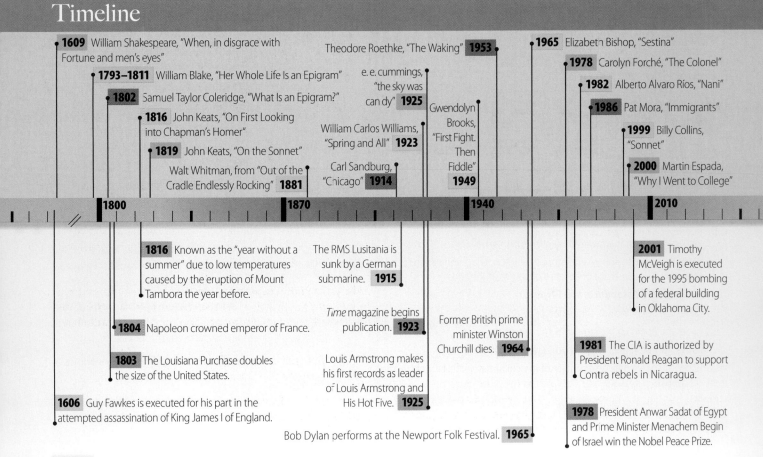

1816 Known as the "year without a summer" due to low temperatures caused by the eruption of Mount Tambora the year before.

The RMS Lusitania is sunk by a German submarine. **1915**

1804 Napoleon crowned emperor of France.

Time magazine begins publication. **1923**

Former British prime minister Winston Churchill dies. **1964**

1803 The Louisiana Purchase doubles the size of the United States.

Louis Armstrong makes his first records as leader of Louis Armstrong and His Hot Five. **1925**

1606 Guy Fawkes is executed for his part in the attempted assassination of King James I of England.

Bob Dylan performs at the Newport Folk Festival. **1965**

2001 Timothy McVeigh is executed for the 1995 bombing of a federal building in Oklahoma City.

1981 The CIA is authorized by President Ronald Reagan to support Contra rebels in Nicaragua.

1978 President Anwar Sadat of Egypt and Prime Minister Menachem Begin of Israel win the Nobel Peace Prize.

John Keats (1795–1821)

On the Sonnet (1819)

If by dull rhymes our English must be chained,
And like Andromeda,° the sonnet sweet
Fettered, in spite of painéd loveliness,
Let us find, if we must be constrained,
Sandals more interwoven and complete   5
To fit the naked foot of Poesy:
Let us inspect the lyre, and weigh the stress
Of every chord, and see what may be gained
By ear industrious, and attention meet;
Misers of sound and syllable, no less   10
Than Midas° of his coinage, let us be
Jealous of dead leaves in the bay-wreath crown;
So, if we may not let the Muse be free,
She will be bound with garlands of her own.

>> Andromeda in chains

° **Andromeda** In Greek mythology, an Ethiopian princess chained to a rock to appease a sea monster.

° **Midas** A legendary king of Phrygia; everything he touched turned to gold.

EXPLORE ONLINE >

To complete a tutorial of "On the Sonnet," visit your Literature CourseMate, accessed through www.cengagebrain.com.

Billy Collins (1941–   )

Sonnet (1999)

All we need is fourteen lines, well, thirteen now,
and after this one just a dozen
to launch a little ship on love's storm chased seas,
then only ten more left like rows of beans.
How easily it goes unless you get Elizabethan   5
and insist the iambic bongos must be played
and rhymes positioned at the ends of lines,
one for every station of the cross.
But hang on here while we make the turn
into the final six where all will be resolved,   10
where longing and heartache will find an end,
where Laura will tell Petrarch to put down his pen,
take off those crazy medieval tights,
blow out the lights, and come at last to bed.

>> Young man in Elizabethan dress

The **form** of a literary work is its structure or shape, the way its elements fit together to form a whole; **poetic form** is the design of a poem described in terms of rhyme, meter, and stanzaic pattern.

Until the twentieth century, most poetry was written in **closed form** (sometimes called **fixed form**), characterized by regular patterns of meter, rhyme, line length, and stanzaic divisions. Early poems that were passed down orally—epics and ballads, for example—relied on regular form to facilitate memorization. Even after poems began to be written down, poets tended to favor regular patterns. In fact, until relatively recently, regular form was what distinguished poetry from prose. Of course, strict adherence

form Structure or shape of a literary work; the way a work's parts fit together to form a whole.

closed form Type of poetic structure that has a recognizable rhyme scheme, meter, or stanzaic pattern; also called *fixed form*.

villanelle A nineteen-line poem composed of five tercets and a concluding quatrain; its rhyme scheme is *aba aba aba aba aba abaa*.

sestina Poem composed of six six-line stanzas and a three-line conclusion called an **envoi**.

open form/free verse (vers libre) Form of poetry that makes use of varying line lengths, abandoning stanzaic divisions, breaking lines in unexpected places, and even dispensing with any pretense of formal structure.

prose poem Open form poem whose long lines appear to be prose set in paragraphs.

imagism Movement in modern poetry, stressing terseness and concrete imagery. **Imagists** were a group of early twentieth-century American poets, including Ezra Pound, William Carlos Williams, and Amy Lowell, who focused on visual images and created new rhythms and meters.

to regular patterns sometimes produced poems that were, in John Keats's words, "chained" by "dull rhymes" and "fettered" by the rules governing a particular form. But rather than feeling "constrained" by form, many poets—like Billy Collins in the playful sonnet above— have experimented with imagery, figures of speech, allusion, and other techniques, moving away from rigid patterns of rhyme and meter and thus stretching closed form to its limits.

As they sought new ways in which to express themselves, poets also borrowed forms from other cultures, adapting them to the demands of their own languages. English and American poets, for example, adopted (and still use) early French forms, such as the **villanelle** and the **sestina,** and early Italian forms, such as the **Petrarchan sonnet** and **terza rima.** The nineteenth-century American poet Henry Wadsworth Longfellow studied Icelandic epics; the twentieth-century poet Ezra Pound studied the works of French troubadours; and Pound and other twentieth-century American poets, such as Richard Wright and Carolyn Kizer, were inspired by Japanese haiku. Other American poets, such as Vachel Lindsay, Langston Hughes, and Maya Angelou, looked closer to home—to the rhythms of blues, jazz, and spirituals—for inspiration.

As time went on, more and more poets moved away from closed form to experiment with **open form** poetry (sometimes called **free verse** or *vers libre*), varying line length within a poem, dispensing with meter and stanzaic divisions, breaking lines in unexpected places, and even abandoning any semblance of formal structure. In English, nineteenth-century poets—such as William Blake and Matthew Arnold—experimented with lines of irregular meter and length, and Walt Whitman wrote **prose poems,** open form poems whose long lines made them look like prose. (Well before this time, Asian poetry and some biblical passages had used a type of free verse.) In nineteenth-century

France, symbolist poets, such as Baudelaire, Rimbaud, Verlaine, and Mallarmé, also used free verse. In the early twentieth century, a group of American poets—including Ezra Pound, William Carlos Williams, and Amy Lowell—who were associated with a movement known as **imagism** wrote poetry that dispensed with traditional principles of English versification, creating new rhythms and meters.

Although much contemporary English and American poetry is composed in open form, many poets also continue to write in closed form—even in very traditional, highly structured patterns. Still, new forms, and new variations of old forms, are being created all the time. And, because contemporary poets do not necessarily feel bound by rules or restrictions about what constitutes "acceptable" poetic form, they experiment freely, trying to discover the form that best suits the poem's purpose, subject, language, and theme.

> *"Although much contemporary English and American poetry is composed in open form, many poets also continue to write in closed form"*

LO1 Recognize Closed Form

A **closed form** (or *fixed form*) poem looks symmetrical; it has an identifiable, repeated pattern, with lines of similar length arranged in groups of two, three, four, or more. A closed form poem also tends to rely on regular metrical patterns and rhyme schemes.

Despite what its name suggests, closed form poetry does not have to be confining or conservative. In fact, contemporary poets often experiment with closed form—for example, by using characteristics of open form poetry (such as lines of varying length) within a closed form. Sometimes poets move back and forth within a single poem from open to closed to open form; sometimes (like their eighteenth-century counterparts) they combine different stanzaic forms (stanzas of two and three lines, for example) within a single poem.

Even when poets work within a traditional closed form, such as a sonnet, sestina, or villanelle, they can break new ground. For example, they can write a sonnet with an unexpected meter or rhyme scheme (or with no consistent pattern of rhyme or meter at all), add an extra line or even extra stanzas to a traditional sonnet form, combine two different traditional sonnet forms in a single poem, or write an abbreviated version of a sestina or villanelle. In other words, poets can use traditional forms as building blocks, combining them in innovative ways to create new patterns and new forms.

Sometimes a pattern (such as **blank verse**) simply determines the meter of a poem's individual lines. At other times, the pattern extends to the level of the stanza, with lines arranged into groups (**couplets, quatrains,** and so on). At still other times, as in the case of traditional closed forms like sonnets, a poetic pattern gives shape to an entire poem.

BLANK VERSE

Blank verse is unrhymed poetry with each line written in a pattern of five stressed and five unstressed syllables called **iambic pentameter** (see p. 430). Many passages from Shakespeare's plays, such as the following lines from *Hamlet,* are written in blank verse:

> To sleep! perchance to dream:—ay, there's the rub;
> For in that sleep of death what dreams may come,
> When we have shuffled off this mortal coil,
> Must give us pause: there's the respect
> That makes calamity of so long life

STANZA

A **stanza** is a group of two or more lines with the same metrical pattern—and often with a regular rhyme scheme as well—separated by blank space from other such groups of lines. Stanzas in poetry are like paragraphs in prose: they group related ideas into units.

A two-line stanza with rhyming lines of similar length and meter is called a **couplet.** The **heroic couplet,** first used by Chaucer and later very popular throughout the eighteenth century, consists of two rhymed lines of iambic pentameter, with a weak pause after the first line and a strong pause after the second. The following example, from Alexander Pope's *An Essay on Criticism,* is a heroic couplet:

> True ease in writing comes from art, not chance,
> As those move easiest who have learned to dance.

A three-line stanza with lines of similar length and a set rhyme scheme is called a **tercet.** Percy Bysshe Shelley's "Ode to the West Wind" (p. 518) is built largely of tercets:

> O wild West Wind, thou breath of Autumn's being,
> Thou, from whose unseen presence the leaves dead
> Are driven, like ghosts from an enchanter fleeing,
>
> Yellow, and black, and pale, and hectic red,
> Pestilence-stricken multitudes: O Thou,
> Who chariotest to their dark wintry bed

Although in many tercets all three lines rhyme, "Ode to the West Wind" uses a special rhyme scheme, also used by Dante, called **terza rima.** This rhyme scheme (*aba, bcb, cdc, ded,* and so on) creates an interlocking series of stanzas: line 2's *dead* looks ahead to the rhyming words *red* and *bed,* which close lines 4 and 6, and the pattern

blank verse Lines of unrhymed iambic pentameter in no particular stanzaic form.

stanza Group of lines in a poem that forms a metrical or thematic unit. Each stanza is usually separated from others by a blank space on the page.

continues throughout the poem.

A four-line stanza with lines of similar length and a set rhyme scheme is called a **quatrain.** The quatrain, the most widely used and versatile unit in English and American poetry, is used by William Wordsworth in the following excerpt from his 1800 poem "She dwelt among the untrodden ways":

> A violet by a mossy stone
>   Half hidden from the eye!
> —Fair as a star, when only one
>   Is shining in the sky.

"A stanza is a group of two or more lines with the same metrical pattern—and often with a regular rhyme scheme as well—separated by blank space from other such groups of lines."

Quatrains are frequently used by contemporary poets as well—for instance, in Theodore Roethke's "My Papa's Waltz" (p. 481), Adrienne Rich's "Aunt Jennifer's Tigers" (p. 433), and William Stafford's "Traveling through the Dark" (p. 488).

One special kind of quatrain, called the **ballad stanza,** alternates lines of eight and six syllables; typically, only the second and fourth lines rhyme. The following lines from the traditional Scottish ballad "Sir Patrick Spence" illustrate the ballad stanza:

> The king sits in Dumferling toune,
>   Drinking the blude-reid wine:
> "O whar will I get guid sailor
>   To sail this schip of mine?"

Common measure, a four-line stanzaic pattern closely related to the ballad stanza, is used in hymns as well as in poetry. It differs from the ballad stanza in that its rhyme scheme is *abab* rather than *abcb.*

Other stanzaic forms include **rhyme royal,** a seven-line stanza (*ababbcc*) set in iambic pentameter, used in Sir Thomas Wyatt's sixteenth-century poem "They Flee from Me That Sometimes Did Me Seke" as well as in Theodore Roethke's twentieth-century "I Knew a Woman"; **ottava rima,** an eight-line stanza (*abababcc*) set in iambic

EXPLORE ONLINE >

To complete a tutorial of "Stanza," visit your
Literature CourseMate, accessed through
www.cengagebrain.com.

sonnet Fourteen-line poem, usually a **lyric** in *iambic pentameter*. It has a strict rhyme scheme in one of two forms: the *Italian*, or **Petrarchan sonnet** (an eight-line **octave** rhymed *abba/abba* with a six-line **sestet** rhymed *cdc/cdc* or a variation) and the *English*, or **Shakespearean sonnet** (three quatrains rhymed *abab/cdcd/efef* with a concluding couplet rhymed *gg*).

pentameter; and the **Spenserian stanza,** a nine-line form (*ababbcbcc*) whose first eight lines are set in iambic pentameter and whose last line is in iambic hexameter. The Romantic poets John Keats and Percy Bysshe Shelley were among those who used the Spenserian stanza. (See Chapter 25 for definitions and examples of various metrical patterns.)

THE SONNET

Perhaps the most familiar kind of traditional closed form poem written in English is the **sonnet,** a fourteen-line poem with a distinctive rhyme scheme and metrical pattern. The English or **Shakespearean sonnet,** which consists of fourteen lines divided into three quatrains and a concluding couplet, is written in iambic pentameter and follows the rhyme scheme *abab cdcd efef gg*. The **Petrarchan sonnet,** popularized in the fourteenth century by the Italian poet Francesco Petrarch, also consists of fourteen lines of iambic pentameter, but these lines are divided into an eight-line unit called an **octave** and a six-line unit (composed of two tercets) called a **sestet.** The rhyme scheme of the octave is *abba abba*; the rhyme scheme of the sestet is *cde cde*.

The conventional structures of these sonnet forms reflect the arrangement of ideas within the poem. In the Shakespearean sonnet, the poet typically presents three "paragraphs" of related thoughts, introducing an idea in the first quatrain, developing it in the two remaining quatrains, and summing up in a succinct closing couplet. In the Petrarchan sonnet, the octave introduces a problem that is resolved in the sestet. (Many Shakespearean sonnets also have a problem-solution structure.) Some poets vary the traditional patterns somewhat to suit the poem's language or ideas. For example, they may depart from the pattern to sidestep a forced rhyme or unnatural stress on a syllable, or they may shift from problem to solution in a place other than between octave and sestet.

The following poem has the form of a traditional English sonnet.

William Shakespeare (1564–1616)

When, in disgrace with Fortune and men's eyes (1609)

When, in disgrace with Fortune and men's eyes,
I all alone beweep my outcast state,
And trouble deaf heaven with my bootless° cries,
And look upon myself and curse my fate,
Wishing me like to one more rich in hope,   5
Featured like him, like him with friends possessed,
Desiring this man's art, and that man's scope,
With what I most enjoy contented least,
Yet in these thoughts myself almost despising,
Haply° I think on thee, and then my state,   10
Like to the lark at break of day arising
From sullen earth, sings hymns at heaven's gate;
    For thy sweet love rememb'red such wealth brings
    That then I scorn to change my state with kings.

°**bootless** Futile.
°**Haply** Luckily.

>> Goddess of fortune turning wheel

Shakespeare's sonnet is written in iambic pentameter and has a conventional rhyme scheme: *abab* (eyes-state-cries-fate), *cdcd* (hope-possessed-scope-least), *efef* (despising-state-arising-gate), *gg* (brings-kings). In this poem, in which the speaker explains how thoughts of his loved one can rescue him from despair, each quatrain is unified by subject matter as well as by rhyme.

In the first quatrain, the speaker presents his problem: he is down on his luck and out of favor with his peers, isolated in self-pity and cursing his fate. In the second quatrain, he develops this idea further: he is envious of others and dissatisfied with things that usually please him. In the third quatrain, the focus shifts. After the first two quatrains develop a dependent clause ("When . . ."), that introduces a problem, line 9 begins to present the resolution. In the third quatrain, the speaker explains how, in the midst of his despair and self-hatred, he thinks of his loved one, and his spirits soar. The closing couplet sums up the mood transformation the poem describes and explains its significance: when the speaker realizes the emotional riches his loved one gives him, he is no longer envious of others.

FURTHER READING: The Sonnet

John Keats (1795–1821)

On First Looking into Chapman's Homer° (1816)

Much have I traveled in the realms of gold,
    And many goodly states and kingdoms seen;
    Round many western islands have I been
Which bards in fealty to Apollo° hold.
Oft of one wide expanse had I been told   5
    That deep-browed Homer ruled as his demesne,°
    Yet did I never breathe its pure serene°
Till I heard Chapman speak out loud and bold.
Then felt I like some watcher of the skies
    When a new planet swims into his ken;   10
Or like stout Cortez° when with eagle eyes
    He stared at the Pacific—and all his men
Looked at each other with a wild surmise—
    Silent, upon a peak in Darien.°

>> Bust of Homer

° **Chapman's Homer** The translation of Homer's works by Elizabethan poet George Chapman.

° **Apollo** Greek god of light, truth, reason, male beauty; associated with music and poetry.

° **demesne** Realm, domain.

° **serene** Air, atmosphere.

° **Cortez** It was Vasco de Balboa (not Hernando Cortez as Keats suggests) who first saw the Pacific Ocean, from "a peak in Darien."

° **Darien** Former name of the Isthmus of Panama.

Related Works

"Snow" (p. 102), "Gryphon" (p. 138), "Araby" (p. 220), "When I Heard the Learn'd Astronomer" (p. 383), *Trifles* (p. 555)

Gwendolyn Brooks (1917–2000)

First Fight. Then Fiddle (1949)

First fight. Then fiddle. Ply the slipping string
With feathery sorcery; muzzle the note
With hurting love; the music that they wrote
Bewitch, bewilder. Qualify to sing
Threadwise. Devise no salt, no hempen thing   5
For the dear instrument to bear. Devote
The bow to silks and honey. Be remote
A while from malice and from murdering.
But first to arms, to armor. Carry hate
In front of you and harmony behind.   10
Be deaf to music and to beauty blind.
Win war. Rise bloody, maybe not too late
For having first to civilize a space
Wherein to play your violin with grace.

>> Violin

Perkus/Shutterstock.com

Related Works

"Buffalo Soldiers" (p. 105), "The Soldier" (p. 491)

 See Chapter 26 Review Card for Reading and Reacting questions about Gwendolyn Brooks, "First Fight. Then Fiddle."

THE SESTINA

The sestina, introduced in thirteenth-century France, is composed of six six-line stanzas and a three-line conclusion called an **envoi**. The sestina does not require end rhyme; however, it requires that each line end with one of six key words, which are repeated throughout the poem in a fixed order. The alternation of these six words in different positions—but always at the ends of lines—in each of the poem's six stanzas creates a rhythmic verbal pattern that unifies the poem, as the key words do in the poem that follows.

Alberto Alvaro Ríos (1952–   )

Nani (1982)

Sitting at her table, she serves
the sopa de arroz° to me
instinctively, and I watch her,
the absolute mamá, and eat words
I might have had to say more   5
out of embarrassment. To speak,
now-foreign words I used to speak,
too, dribble down her mouth as she serves
me albóndigas.° No more
than a third are easy to me.   10
By the stove she does something with words
and looks at me only with her
back. I am full. I tell her
I taste the mint, and watch her speak
smiles at the stove. All my words   15
make her smile. Nani never serves
herself, she only watches me
with her skin, her hair. I ask for more.

I watch the mamá warming more
tortillas for me. I watch her   20
fingers in the flame for me.
Near her mouth, I see a wrinkle speak
of a man whose body serves
the ants like she serves me, then more words
from more wrinkles about children, words   25
about this and that, flowing more
easily from these other mouths. Each serves
as a tremendous string around her,
holding her together. They speak
nani was this and that to me   30
and I wonder just how much of me
will die with her, what were the words
I could have been, was. Her insides speak
through a hundred wrinkles, now, more
than she can bear, steel around her,   35
shouting, then, What is this thing she serves?

She asks me if I want more.
I own no words to stop her.
Even before I speak, she serves.

>> Latina grandmother at stove

° **sopa de arroz** Rice soup.
° **albóndigas** Meatballs.

In many respects, Ríos's poem closely follows the form of the traditional sestina. For instance, it interweaves six key words—"serves," "me," "her," "words," "more," and "speak"—through six groups of six lines each, rearranging the order in which the words appear so that the first line of each group of six lines ends with the same key word that also ended the preceding group of lines. The poem repeats the key words in exactly the order prescribed: *abcdef, faeb-dc, cfdabe,* and so on. In addition, the sestina closes with a three-line envoi that includes all six of the poem's key words, three at the ends of lines and three within the lines.

Despite this generally strict adherence to the sestina form, Ríos departs from the form by grouping his six sets of six lines not into six separate stanzas but rather into two eighteen-line stanzas.

The sestina form suits Ríos's subject matter. The focus of the poem, on the verbal and nonverbal interaction between the poem's "me" and "her," is reinforced by each of the related words. "Nani" is a poem about communication, and the key words return to probe this theme again and again. Throughout the poem, these repeated words help to create a fluid, melodic, and tightly woven work.

FURTHER READING: The Sestina

Elizabeth Bishop (1911–1979)

Sestina (1965)

September rain falls on the house.
In the failing light, the old grandmother
sits in the kitchen with the child
beside the Little Marvel Stove,
reading the jokes from the almanac,   5
laughing and talking to hide her tears.

She thinks that her equinoctial tears
and the rain that beats on the roof of the house
were both foretold by the almanac,
but only known to a grandmother.   10
The iron kettle sings on the stove.
She cuts some bread and says to the child,

It's time for tea now; but the child
is watching the teakettle's small hard tears
dance like mad on the hot black stove,   15
the way the rain must dance on the house.
Tidying up, the old grandmother
hangs up the clever almanac

on its string. Birdlike, the almanac
hovers half open above the child,   20
hovers above the old grandmother
and her teacup full of dark brown tears.
She shivers and says she thinks the house
feels chilly, and puts more wood in the stove.

It was to be, says the Marvel Stove.   25
I know what I know, says the almanac.
With crayons the child draws a rigid house
and a winding pathway. Then the child
puts in a man with buttons like tears
and shows it proudly to the grandmother.   30

But secretly, while the grandmother
busies herself about the stove,
the little moons fall down like tears
from between the pages of the almanac
into the flower bed the child   35
has carefully placed in the front of the house.

Time to plant tears, says the almanac.
The grandmother sings to the marvellous stove
and the child draws another inscrutable house.

>> Cast iron stove similar
to Little Marvel Stove

Related Works

"The Meal" (p. 402), "Nani" (p. 449), "My Papa's Waltz" (p. 481)

EXPLORE ONLINE >

To complete a tutorial of "Sestina," visit your
Literature CourseMate, accessed through
www.cengagebrain.com.

THE VILLANELLE

The villanelle, first introduced in France during the Middle Ages, is a nineteen-line poem composed of five tercets and a concluding quatrain; its rhyme scheme is *aba aba aba aba aba abaa*. Two different lines are systematically repeated in the poem: line 1 appears again in lines 6, 12, and 18, and line 3 reappears as lines 9, 15, and 19. Thus, each tercet concludes with an exact (or close) duplication of either line 1 or line 3, and the final quatrain concludes by repeating both line 1 and line 3.

Theodore Roethke (1908–1963)

The Waking (1953)

I wake to sleep, and take my waking slow.
I feel my fate in what I cannot fear.
I learn by going where I have to go.

We think by feeling. What is there to know?
I hear my being dance from ear to ear.   5
I wake to sleep, and take my waking slow.

Of those so close beside me, which are you?
God bless the Ground! I shall walk softly there,
And learn by going where I have to go.

Light takes the Tree; but who can tell us how?   10
The lowly worm climbs up a winding stair;
I wake to sleep, and take my waking slow.

Great Nature has another thing to do
To you and me; so take the lively air,
And, lovely, learn by going where to go.   15

This shaking keeps me steady. I should know.
What falls away is always. And is near.
I wake to sleep, and take my waking slow.
I learn by going where I have to go.

>> *Earth Mother*, painting of Mother Nature by Sir Edward Burne-Jones, 1882

"The Waking," like all villanelles, closely intertwines threads of sounds and words. The repeated lines and the very regular rhyme and meter give the poem a monotonous, almost hypnotic, rhythm. This poem uses end rhyme and repeats entire lines. It also makes extensive use of alliteration ("I <u>f</u>eel my <u>f</u>ate in what I cannot <u>f</u>ear") and internal rhyme ("I <u>hear</u> my being dance from <u>ear</u> to <u>ear</u>"; "I <u>wake</u> to sleep and <u>take</u> my <u>wak</u>ing slow"). The result is a tightly constructed poem of overlapping sounds and images.

THE EPIGRAM

Originally, an epigram was an inscription carved in stone on a monument or statue. As a literary form, an **epigram** is a very brief poem that makes a pointed, often sarcastic, comment in a surprising twist at the end. In a sense, it is a poem with a punch line. Although some epigrams rhyme, others do not. Many are only two lines long, but others are somewhat longer.

What they have in common is their economy of language and their tone. One of the briefest of epigrams, written by Ogden Nash, appeared in the *New Yorker* magazine in 1931:

> The Bronx?
> No thonx.

Here, in four words, Nash manages to convey the unexpected, using rhyme and creative spelling to convey his assessment of one of New York City's five boroughs. The poem's two lines are perfectly balanced, making the contrast between the noncommittal tone of the first and the negative tone of the second quite striking.

FURTHER READING: The Epigram

Samuel Taylor Coleridge (1772–1834)

What Is an Epigram? (1802)

What is an epigram? a dwarfish whole,
Its body brevity, and wit its soul.

William Blake (1757–1827)

Her Whole Life Is an Epigram (c. 1793–1811)

° Platted Braided.

Her whole life is an epigram: smack, smooth & neatly penned,
Platted° quite neat to catch applause, with a sliding noose at the end.

Related Works

"55 Miles to the Gas Pump" (p. 107), "Fire and Ice" (p. 369), "You fit into me" (p. 421), "General Review of the Sex Situation" (p. 490), *Nine Ten* (p. 553)

Martin Espada (1957–   )

Why I Went to College (2000)

If you don't,
my father said,
you better learn
to eat soup
through a straw,   5
'cause I'm gonna
break your jaw

Related Works

"Baca Grande" (p. 389), "My Papa's Waltz" (p. 481), "'Faith' is a fine invention" (p. 503)

>> Mortarboard and college diploma

 See Chapter 26 Review Card for Reading and Reacting questions about Martin Espada, "Why I Went to College."

haiku Seventeen-syllable, three-line form of Japanese verse that almost always uses concrete imagery and deals with the natural world.

HAIKU

Like an epigram, a haiku compresses words into a very small package. Unlike an epigram, however, a haiku focuses on an image, not an idea. A traditional Japanese form, the **haiku** is a brief unrhymed poem that presents the essence of some aspect of nature, concentrating a vivid image in three lines. Although in the strictest sense a haiku consists of seventeen syllables divided into lines of five, seven, and five syllables, respectively, not all poets conform to this rigid structure.

The following poem is a translation of a classic Japanese haiku by Matsuo Bashō:

> Silent and still: then
> Even sinking into the rocks,
> The cicada's screech.

Notice that this poem conforms to the haiku's three-line structure and traditional subject matter, vividly depicting a natural scene without comment or analysis.

FURTHER READING: Haiku

Matsuo Bashō (1644–1694)

Four Haiku*

Translated by Geoffrey Bownas and Anthony Thwaite

Spring:
A hill without a name
Veiled in morning mist.

The beginning of autumn:
Sea and emerald paddy   5
Both the same green.

The winds of autumn
Blow: yet still green
The chestnut husks.

A flash of lightning: 10
Into the gloom
Goes the heron's cry.

Related Works

"Where Mountain Lion Lay Down with Deer"
(p. 366), "the sky was can dy" (p. 455), "Birches"
(p. 487)

>> *Plum Garden, Kamata* by Ando
Hiroshige, 1857

© Anita Cruz-Eberhard/Brooklyn Museum/Corbis

*Publication date is not available.

 See Chapter 26 Review Card for Reading and Reacting
questions about Matsuo Bashō, "Four Haiku."

L02 Recognize Open Form

An **open form poem** may make occasional use of rhyme and meter, but it has no easily identifiable pattern or design: no conventional stanzaic divisions, no consistent metrical pattern or line length, no repeated rhyme scheme. Still, open form poetry is not necessarily shapeless, untidy, or randomly ordered. All poems have form, and the form of a poem may be determined by factors such as repeated sounds, the appearance of words on the printed page, or pauses in natural speech as well as by a conventional metrical pattern or rhyme scheme.

Open form poetry invites readers to participate in the creative process, to discover the relationship between form and meaning. In fact, some modern poets believe that only open form offers them freedom to express their ideas or that the subject matter or mood of their poetry demands a relaxed, experimental approach to form. For example, when Lawrence Ferlinghetti portrays the poet as an acrobat who "climbs on rime" (p. 410), he constructs his poem in a way that is consistent with the poet/acrobat's willingness to take risks. Thus, the poem's idiosyncratic form supports its ideas about the limitless possibilities of poetry and the poet as experimenter.

Without a predetermined pattern, however, poets must create forms that suit their needs, and they must continue to shape and reshape the look of the poem on the page as they revise its words. Thus, open form is a challenge, but it is also a way for poets to experiment with fresh arrangements of words and new juxtapositions of ideas.

For some poets, such as Carl Sandburg, open form provides an opportunity to create prose poems, poems that look like prose.

> "Open form poetry invites readers to participate in the creative process, to discover the relationship between form and meaning."

Carl Sandburg (1878–1967)

Chicago (1914)

©Bettmann/Corbis

Hog Butcher for the World,
Tool Maker, Stacker of Wheat,
Player with Railroads and the Nation's Freight Handler;
Stormy, husky, brawling,
City of the Big Shoulders: 5

They tell me you are wicked and I believe them, for I have seen
   your painted women under the gas lamps luring the farm boys.
And they tell me you are crooked and I answer: Yes, it is true
   I have seen the gunman kill and go free to kill again.
And they tell me you are brutal and my reply is: On the faces of
   women and children I have seen the marks of wanton hunger.
And having answered so I turn once more to those who sneer at
   this my city, and I give them back the sneer and say to them:
Come and show me another city with lifted head singing so
   proud to be alive and coarse and strong and cunning.   10
Flinging magnetic curses amid the toil of piling job on job,
   here is a tall bold slugger set vivid against the little soft cities;
Fierce as a dog with tongue lapping for action, cunning as a
   savage pitted against the wilderness,
      Bareheaded,
        Shoveling,
        Wrecking,   15
        Planning,
        Building, breaking, rebuilding,
Under the smoke, dust all over his mouth, laughing
   with white teeth,

Under the terrible burden of destiny laughing as a
   young man laughs,
Laughing even as an ignorant fighter laughs who
   has never lost a battle,
Bragging and laughing that under his wrist is the pulse,   20
   and under his ribs the heart of the people,
                Laughing!
Laughing the stormy, husky, brawling laughter of Youth,
   half-naked, sweating, proud to be Hog Butcher,
   Tool Maker, Stacker of Wheat, Player with Railroads
   and Freight Handler to the Nation.

<< Chicago street scene, 1925

"Chicago" uses capitalization and punctuation conventionally, and it generally (though not always) arranges words in lines in a way that is consistent with the natural divisions of phrases and sentences. However, the poem is not divided into stanzas, and its lines vary widely in length—from a single word isolated on a line to a line crowded with words—and follow no particular metrical pattern. Instead, its form is created through its pattern of alternating sections of long and short lines; through its repeated words and phrases ("They tell me" in lines 6–8, "under" in lines 18–19, and "laughing" in lines 18–23, for example); through alliteration (for instance, "slugger set vivid against the little soft cities" in line 11); and, most of all, through the piling up of words and images into catalogs in lines 1–5, 13–17, and 22.

In order to understand Sandburg's reasons for choosing such a form, readers need to consider the poem's subject matter and theme. "Chicago" celebrates the scope and power of a "Stormy, husky, brawling" city, one that is exuberant and outgoing, not sedate and civilized. Chicago is a city that does not follow anyone else's rules; it is, after all, "Bareheaded, / Shoveling, / Wrecking, / Planning, / Building, breaking, rebuilding," constantly active, in flux, on the move, "proud to be alive." "Fierce as a dog . . . cunning as a savage," the city is characterized as, among other things, a worker, a fighter, and a harborer of "painted women" and killers and hungry women and children. Just as Chicago itself does not conform to the rules, the poem departs from the orderly confines of stanzaic form and measured rhyme and meter, a kind of form that is, after all, better suited to "the little soft cities" than to the "tall bold slugger" that is Chicago.

Of course, open form poetry does not have to look like Sandburg's prose poem. The following poem, an extreme example of open form, looks almost as if it has spilled out of a box of words.

E. E. Cummings (1894–1962)

the sky was can dy (1925)

the
    sky
        was
can   dy lu
minous   5
      edible
spry
      pinks shy
lemons
greens   coo   l choc   10
olate
s.
     un   der,
     a   lo
co   15
mo
    tive   s pout
           ing
             vi
             o   20
            lets

Like many of Cummings's poems, the one on the preceding page seems ready to skip off the page. Its irregular line length and its unconventional capitalization, punctuation, and word divisions immediately draw readers' attention to its form. Despite these oddities, and despite the absence of orderly rhyme and meter, the poem does have its conventional elements.

A closer examination reveals that the poem's theme—the beauty of the sky—is quite conventional; that the poem is divided, though somewhat crudely, into two sections; and that the poet does use some rhyme—"spry" and "shy," for example. However, Cummings's sky is described not in traditional terms but rather as something "edible," not only in terms of color but of flavor as well. The breaks within words ("can dy lu / minous"; "coo l choc / olate / s") seem to expand the words' possibilities, visually stretching them to the limit, extending their taste and visual image over several lines and, in the case of the poem's last two words, visually reinforcing the picture the words describe. In addition, the isolation of syllables exposes hidden rhyme, as in "lo / co / mo" and "lu" / "coo." Thus, by using open form, Cummings illustrates the capacity of a poem to move beyond the traditional boundaries set by words and lines.

FURTHER READING: Open Form

Walt Whitman (1819–1892)

from "Out of the Cradle Endlessly Rocking" (1881)

Out of the cradle endlessly rocking,
Out of the mocking-bird's throat, the musical shuttle,
Out of the Ninth-month° midnight,
Over the sterile sands and the fields beyond, where the child
    leaving his bed wander'd alone, bareheaded, barefoot,
Down from the shower'd halo,   5
Up from the mystic play of shadows twining and twisting as if they were alive,
Out from the patches of briers and blackberries,
From the memories of the bird that chanted to me,
From your memories sad brother, from the fitful risings and fallings I heard,
From under that yellow half-moon late-risen and swollen as if with tears,   10
From those beginning notes of yearning and love there in the mist,
From the thousand responses of my heart never to cease,
From the myriad thence-arous'd words,
From the word stronger and more delicious than any,
From such as now they start the scene revisiting,   15
As a flock, twittering, rising, or overhead passing,
Borne hither, ere all eludes me, hurriedly,
A man, yet by these tears a little boy again,
Throwing myself on the sand, confronting the waves,
I, chanter of pains and joys, uniter of here and hereafter,   20
Taking all hints to use them, but swiftly leaping beyond them,
A reminiscence sing.

°**Ninth-month** The Quaker designation for September; in context, an allusion to the human birth cycle.

Related Works

"Chicago" (p. 454), *from* "Song of Myself" (p. 520)

 See Chapter 26 Review Card for Reading and Reacting questions about Walt Whitman, from "Out of the Cradle Endlessly Rocking."

William Carlos Williams (1883–1963)

Spring and All (1923)

By the road to the contagious hospital
under the surge of the blue
mottled clouds driven from the
northeast—a cold wind. Beyond, the
waste of broad, muddy fields   5
brown with dried weeds, standing and fallen

patches of standing water
the scattering of tall trees

All along the road the reddish
purplish, forked, upstanding, twiggy   10
stuff of bushes and small trees
with dead, brown leaves under them
leafless vines—

Lifeless in appearance, sluggish
dazed spring approaches—   15

They enter the new world naked,
cold, uncertain of all
save that they enter. All about them
the cold, familiar wind—

Now the grass, tomorrow   20
the stiff curl of wildcarrot leaf
One by one objects are defined—
It quickens: clarity, outline of leaf

But now the stark dignity of
entrance—Still, the profound change   25
has come upon them: rooted, they
grip down and begin to awaken

Related Work

"Pied Beauty" (p. 437)

>> Contagious Hospital, Brookline, MA, 1909

Carolyn Forché (1950–   )

The Colonel (1978)

What you have heard is true. I was in his house. His wife carried a tray of coffee and sugar. His daughter filed her nails, his son went out for the night. There were daily papers, pet dogs, a pistol on the cushion beside him. The moon swung bare on its black cord over the house. On the television was a cop show. It was in English. Broken bottles were embedded in the walls around the house to scoop the kneecaps from a man's legs or cut his hands to lace. On the windows there were gratings like those in liquor stores. We had dinner, rack of lamb, good wine, a gold bell was on the table for calling the maid. The maid brought green mangoes, salt, a type of bread. I was asked how I enjoyed the country. There was a brief commercial in Spanish. His wife took everything away. There was some talk then of how difficult it had become to govern. The parrot said hello on the terrace. The colonel told it to shut up, and pushed himself from the table. My friend said to me with his eyes: say nothing. The colonel returned with a sack used to bring groceries home. He spilled many human ears on the table. They were like dried peach halves. There is no other way to say this. He took one of them in his hands, shook it in our faces, dropped it into a water glass. It came alive there. I am tired of fooling around he said. As for the rights of anyone, tell your people they can go fuck themselves. He swept the ears to the floor with his arm and held the last of his wine in the air. Something for your poetry, no? he said. Some of the ears on the floor caught this scrap of his voice. Some of the ears on the floor were pressed to the ground.

Pat Mora (1942–)

Immigrants (1986)

wrap their babies in the American flag,
feed them mashed hot dogs and apple pie,
name them Bill and Daisy,
buy them blonde dolls that blink blue
eyes or a football and tiny cleats   5
before the baby can even walk,
speak to them in thick English,
   hallo, babee, hallo.
whisper in Spanish or Polish
when the babies sleep, whisper   10
in a dark parent bed, that dark
parent fear, "Will they like
our boy, our girl, our fine american
boy, our fine american girl?"

>> Naturalization ceremony, Seattle, WA, 1994

Writing Suggestions: Form

1. Some poets—for example, Emily Dickinson and Robert Frost—write both open and closed form poems. Choose one open and one closed form poem by a single poet and analyze the two poems, explaining the poet's possible reasons for choosing each type of form.

2. Do you see complex forms, such as the villanelle and the sestina, as exercises or even merely as opportunities for poets to show off their skills—or do you believe the special demands of the forms add something valuable to a poem? To help you answer this question, read Dylan Thomas's "Do not go gentle into that good night" (p. 484), and Elizabeth Bishop's "Sestina" (p. 450).

3. Look through Chapter 29, "Poetry for Further Reading," and identify one or two **prose poems.** Write an essay in which you consider why the form seems suitable for the poem or poems you have chosen. Is there a particular kind of subject matter that seems especially appropriate for a prose poem?

 CHECKLIST

WRITING ABOUT FORM

- ☐ Is the poem written in open or closed form? On what characteristics do you base your conclusion?
- ☐ Why did the poet choose open or closed form? For example, is the poem's form consistent with its subject matter, tone, or theme? Is it determined by the conventions of the historical period in which it was written?
- ☐ If the poem is arranged in closed form, does the pattern apply to single lines, to groups of lines, or to the entire poem? What factors determine the breaks between groups of lines?
- ☐ Is the poem a sonnet? a sestina? a villanelle? an epigram? a haiku? How do the traditional form's conventions suit the poet's language and theme? Does the poem follow the rules of the form at all times, or does it break any new ground?
- ☐ If the poem is arranged in open form, what determines the breaks at the ends of lines?
- ☐ Are certain words or phrases isolated on lines? Why?
- ☐ How do elements such as assonance, alliteration, rhyme, and repetition of words give the poem form?
- ☐ What use does the poet make of punctuation and capitalization? of white space on the page?
- ☐ Is the poem a prose poem? How does this form support the poem's subject matter?
- ☐ Is the poem a concrete poem? How does the poet use the visual shape of the poem to convey meaning?

Glossary Terms

blank verse Lines of unrhymed iambic pentameter.

closed form Type of poetic structure that has a recognizable rhyme scheme, meter, or stanzaic pattern; also called *fixed form.*

epigram Short pithy poem or statement.

form Structure or shape of a literary work; the way a work's parts fit together to form a whole. In poetry, form is described in terms of the presence (or absence) of elements like rhyme, meter, and stanzaic pattern.

haiku Seventeen-syllable, three-line form of Japanese verse that almost always uses concrete imagery and deals with the natural world.

imagism Movement in modern poetry stressing terseness and concrete imagery.

open form/free verse *(vers libre)* Form of poetry that makes use of varying line lengths, abandoning stanzaic divisions, breaking lines in unexpected places, and even dispensing with any pretense of formal structure.

prose poem Open form poem whose long lines appear to be prose set in paragraphs.

sestina Poem composed of six six-line stanzas and a three-line conclusion called an **envoi.**

sonnet Fourteen-line poem, usually a **lyric** in *iambic pentameter.*

stanza Group of lines in a poem that forms a metrical or thematic unit. Each stanza is usually separated from others by a blank space on the page.

villanelle A nineteen-line poem composed of five tercets and a concluding quatrain; its rhyme scheme is *aba aba aba aba aba abaa.*

27

Symbol, Allegory, Allusion, Myth

Learning Outcomes

After reading this chapter, you should be able to do the following:

LO1 Recognize symbol

LO2 Recognize allegory

LO3 Recognize allusion

LO4 Recognize myth

Timeline

1794 William Blake, "The Sick Rose"

Christina Rossetti, "Uphill" **1861**

Edgar Allan Poe, "The Raven" **1844**

Countee Cullen, "Yet Do I Marvel" **1925**

William Butler Yeats, "Leda and the Swan" **1924**

Robert Frost, "For Once, Then, Something" **1923**

Emily Dickinson, "Volcanoes be in Sicily" **1914**

1927 T. S. Eliot, "Journey of the Magi"

1940 W. H. Auden, "Musée des Beaux Arts"

Adrienne Rich, "Diving into the Wreck" **1973**

Wole Soyinka, "Future Plans" **1972**

1980 William Meredith, "Dreams of Suicide"

Bill Coyle, 'Post-Colonial Studies" **2006**

1800   **1860**   **1920**   **1980**

Artist and ornithologist John James Audubon dies. **1851**

The American Civil War begins. **1861**

The first issue of the *New Yorker* is published. **1925**

Idi Amin becomes president of Uganda. **1971**

Charles Lindbergh receives the Medal of Honor for his solo transatlantic flight. **1928**

1793 Marie Antoinette, queen of France, is executed.

The Swiss painter Paul Klee dies. **1940**

President Ronald Reagan is shot during an assassination attempt. **1981**

1791 Wolfgang Amadeus Mozart dies.

William Blake (1757–1827)

The Sick Rose (1794)

O Rose thou art sick.
The invisible worm
That flies in the night,
In the howling storm:

Has found out thy bed
Of crimson joy:
And his dark secret love
Does thy life destroy.

5

>> Sick rose

LO1 Recognize Symbol

A **symbol** is an idea or image that suggests something else—but not in the simple way that a dollar sign stands for money or a flag represents a country. A symbol is an image that transcends its literal, or denotative, meaning in a complex way. For instance, if someone gives a rose to a loved one, it could simply be a sign of love. But in the poem "The Sick Rose," the rose has a range of contradictory and complementary meanings. What does the rose represent? Beauty? Perfection? Passion? Something else? As this poem illustrates, the distinctive trait of a symbol is that its meaning cannot easily be pinned down or defined.

Such ambiguity can be frustrating, but it is precisely this characteristic of a symbol that enriches a poem by giving it additional layers of meaning. As Robert Frost has said, a symbol is a little thing that touches a larger thing. In the poem of his that follows, the central symbol does just this.

symbol/conventional symbol/universal symbol Person, object, action, or idea whose meaning transcends its literal or denotative sense in a complex way. A symbol is invested with significance beyond what it could carry on its own. **Universal symbols,** such as the grim reaper, may be called **archetypes; conventional symbols,** such as national flags, evoke a general and agreed-upon response from most people.

⊕ EXPLORE ONLINE >

To complete a tutorial of "Symbol," visit your Literature CourseMate, accessed through www.cengagebrain.com.

"A symbol is an image that transcends its literal, or denotative, meaning in a complex way."

Robert Frost (1874–1963)

For Once, Then, Something (1923)

Others taunt me with having knelt at well-curbs
Always wrong to the light, so never seeing
Deeper down in the well than where the water
Gives me back in a shining surface picture
Me myself in the summer heaven, godlike,   5
Looking out of a wreath of fern and cloud puffs.
Once, when trying with chin against a well-curb,
I discerned, as I thought, beyond the picture,
Through the picture, a something white, uncertain,
Something more of the depths—and then I lost it.   10
Water came to rebuke the too clear water.
One drop fell from a fern, and lo, a ripple
Shook whatever it was lay there at bottom,
Blurred it, blotted it out. What was that whiteness?
Truth? A pebble of quartz? For once, then, something. 15

>> Water at the bottom of a well

The central symbol in this poem is the "something" that the speaker thinks he sees at the bottom of a well. Traditionally, the act of looking down a well suggests a search for truth. In this poem, the speaker says that he always seems to look down the well at the wrong angle, so that all he can see is his own reflection—the surface, not the depths. Once, however, the speaker thought he saw something "beyond the picture," something "white, uncertain," but the image remained indistinct, disappearing when a drop of water from a fern caused the water to ripple. The poem ends with the speaker questioning the significance of what he saw. Like a reader encountering a symbol, the speaker is left trying to come to terms with images that cannot be clearly perceived and associations that cannot be readily understood. In light of the elusive nature of truth, all the speaker can do is ask questions that have no definite answers.

Symbols that appear in poetic works can be *conventional* or *universal*. **Conventional symbols** are those recognized by people who share certain cultural and social assumptions. For example, national flags evoke a general and agreed-upon response in most people of a particular country and—for better or for worse—American children have for years perceived the golden arches of McDonald's as a symbol of food and fun. **Universal symbols** are those likely to be recognized by people regardless of their culture. In 1890, the noted Scottish anthropologist Sir James George Frazer wrote the first version of his work *The Golden Bough,* in which he identified parallels between the rites and beliefs of early pagan cultures and those of Christianity. Fascinated by Frazer's work, the psychologist Carl Jung sought to explain these parallels by formulating a theory of **archetypes,** which held that certain images or ideas reside in the subconscious of all people. According to Jung, archetypal symbols include water, symbolizing rebirth; spring, symbolizing growth; and winter, symbolizing death.

Sometimes symbols that appear in poems can be obscure or highly idiosyncratic. William Blake is one of many poets (William Butler Yeats is another) whose works combine symbols from different cultural, theological, and philosophical sources to form complex networks of personal symbolic associations. To Blake, for example, the scientist Isaac Newton represents the tendency of scientists to quantify experience while ignoring the beauty and mystery of nature. Readers cannot begin to understand his use of Newton as a symbol until they have read a number of Blake's more difficult poems.

How do you know when an idea or image in a poem is a symbol? At what point do you decide that a particular

archetype Image or symbol that is so common or important that it seems to have universal significance. Many archetypes appear in classical myths (for example, a journey to the underworld).

object or idea goes beyond the literal level and takes on symbolic significance? When is a rose more than a rose or a well more than a well? Frequently you can recognize a symbol by its prominence or repetition. In "For Once, Then, Something," for example, the well is introduced in the first line of the poem, and it is the poem's focal point; in "The Sick Rose," the importance of the rose is emphasized by the title.

It is not enough, however, to identify an image or idea that seems to suggest something else. Your decision that a particular item has symbolic significance must be supported by the details of the poem and make sense in light of the ideas the poem develops. In the following poem, the symbolic significance of the volcano helps readers to understand the poem's central theme.

Emily Dickinson (1830–1886)

Volcanoes be in Sicily (1914)

Volcanoes be in Sicily
And South America
I judge from my Geography—
Volcanoes nearer here
A Lava step at any time   5
Am I inclined to climb—
A Crater I may contemplate
Vesuvius at Home.

>> Eruption of Mt. Etna (Sicily), 2001

This poem opens with a statement of fact: volcanoes are located in Sicily and South America. In line 3, however, the speaker introduces the improbable idea that volcanoes are located near where she is at the moment. Readers familiar with Dickinson know that her poems are highly autobiographical and that she lived in Massachusetts, where there are no volcanoes. This information leads readers to suspect that they should not take the speaker's observation literally and that in the context of the poem volcanoes may have symbolic significance. But what do volcanoes suggest here?

On the one hand, volcanoes represent the awesome creative power of nature; on the other hand, they suggest its destructiveness. The speaker's contemplation of the crater of Vesuvius—the volcano that buried the ancient Roman city of Pompeii in A.D. 79—is therefore filled with contradictory associations. Because Dickinson was a recluse, volcanoes—active, destructive, unpredictable, and dangerous—may be

seen as symbolic of everything she fears in the outside world—and, perhaps, within herself. Volcanoes may even suggest her own creative power, which, like a volcano, is something to be feared as well as contemplated. Dickinson seems to have a voyeur's attraction to danger and power, but she is also afraid of them. For this reason, she (and her speaker) may feel safer contemplating Vesuvius at home—not traveling to exotic lands but simply reading a geography book.

> "On the one hand, volcanoes represent the awesome creative power of nature; on the other hand, they suggest its destructiveness."

FURTHER READING: Symbol

Edgar Allan Poe (1809–1849)

© AP Photo

The Raven (1844)

© Ivan Bliznetsov | Dreamstime.com

>> Raven

Once upon a midnight dreary, while I pondered, weak and weary,
Over many a quaint and curious volume of forgotten lore,
While I nodded, nearly napping, suddenly there came a tapping,
As of some one gently rapping, rapping at my chamber door.
" 'Tis some visitor," I muttered, "tapping at my chamber door—   5
               Only this, and nothing more."

Ah, distinctly I remember it was in the bleak December,
And each separate dying ember wrought its ghost upon the floor.
Eagerly I wished the morrow;—vainly I had sought to borrow
From my books surcease of sorrow—sorrow for the lost Lenore—   10
For the rare and radiant maiden whom the angels name Lenore—
               Nameless here for evermore.

And the silken sad uncertain rustling of each purple curtain
Thrilled me—filled me with fantastic terrors never felt before;
so that now, to still the beating of my heart, I stood repeating   15
" 'Tis some visitor entreating entrance at my chamber door;—
Some late visitor entreating entrance at my chamber door;—
               This it is, and nothing more."

Presently my soul grew stronger; hesitating then no longer,
"Sir," said I, "or Madam, truly your forgiveness I implore;   20
But the fact is I was napping, and so gently you came rapping,
And so faintly you came tapping, tapping at my chamber door,
That I scarce was sure I heard you"—here I opened wide the door;—
               Darkness there, and nothing more.

Deep into that darkness peering, long I stood there wondering, fearing,   25
Doubting, dreaming dreams no mortal ever dared to dream before;
But the silence was unbroken, and the darkness gave no token,
And the only word there spoken was the whispered word, "Lenore!"
This I whispered, and an echo murmured back the word, "Lenore!"—
                        Merely this, and nothing more.   30

Back into the chamber turning, all my soul within me burning,
Soon I heard again a tapping somewhat louder than before.
"Surely," said I, "surely that is something at my window lattice;
Let me see, then, what thereat is, and this mystery explore—
Let my heart be still a moment and this mystery explore;—   35
                        'Tis the wind and nothing more!"

Open here I flung the shutter, when, with many a flirt and flutter,
In there stepped a stately raven of the saintly days of yore;
Not the least obeisance made he; not an instant stopped or stayed he;
But, with mien of lord or lady, perched above my chamber door—   40
Perched upon a bust of Pallas° just above my chamber door—
                        Perched, and sat, and nothing more.

Then this ebony bird beguiling my sad fancy into smiling,
By the grave and stern decorum of the countenance it wore,
"Though thy crest be shorn and shaven, thou," I said, "art sure no craven,   45
Ghastly grim and ancient raven wandering from the Nightly shore—
Tell me what thy lordly name is on the Night's Plutonian° shore!"
                        Quoth the raven, "Nevermore."

Much I marvelled this ungainly fowl to hear discourse so plainly,
Though its answer little meaning—little relevancy bore,   50
For we cannot help agreeing that no living human being
Ever yet was blessed with seeing bird above his chamber door—
Bird or beat upon the sculptured bust above his chamber door,
                        With such name as "Nevermore."

But the raven, sitting lonely on the placid bust, spoke only   55
That one word, as if his soul in that one word he did outpour.
Nothing farther then he uttered—not a feather then he fluttered—
Till I scarcely more than muttered "Other friends have flown before—
On the morrow *he* will leave me, as my hopes have flown before."
                        Then the bird said "Nevermore."   60

Startled at the stillness broken by reply so aptly spoken,
"Doubtless," said I, "what it utters is its only stock and store
Caught from some unhappy master whom unmerciful Disaster
Followed fast and followed faster till his songs one burden bore—
Till the dirges of his Hope that melancholy burden bore   65
                        Of 'Never—nevermore.'"

But the raven still beguiling all my sad soul into smiling,
Straight I wheeled a cushioned seat in front of bird and bust and door;
Then, upon the velvet sinking, I betook myself to linking
Fancy unto fancy, thinking what this ominous bird of yore—   70
What this grim, ungainly, ghastly, gaunt, and ominous bird of yore
                        Meant in croaking "Nevermore."

° **Pallas** Athena, Greek goddess of wisdom.

° **Plutonian** Dark; Pluto was the Greek god of the dead and ruler of the underworld.

This I sat engaged in guessing, but no syllable expressing
To the fowl whose fiery eyes now burned into my bosom's core;
This and more I sat divining, with my head at ease reclining   75
On the cushion's velvet lining that the lamplight gloated o'er,
But whose velvet violet lining with the lamplight gloating o'er,
                          she shall press, ah, nevermore!

Then, methought, the air grew denser, perfumed from an unseen censer
Swung by angels whose faint foot-falls tinkled on the tufted floor.   80
"Wretch," I cried, "thy God hath lent thee—by these angels he
   hath sent thee
Respite—respite and nepenthe° from thy memories of Lenore!
Quaff, oh quaff this kind nepenthe and forget this lost Lenore!"
                          Quoth the raven, "Nevermore."

"Prophet!" said I, "thing of evil!—prophet still, if bird or devil!—   85
Whether Tempter sent, or whether tempest tossed thee here
   ashore,
Desolate, yet all undaunted, on this desert land enchanted—
On this home by Horror haunted—tell me truly, I implore—
Is there—*is* there balm in Gilead?°—tell me—tell me, I implore!"
                          Quoth the raven, "Nevermore."   90

"Prophet!" said I, "thing of evil—prophet still, if bird or devil!
By that Heaven that bends above us—by that God we both adore—
Tell this soul with sorrow laden if, within the distant Aidenn,
It shall clasp a sainted maiden whom the angels name Lenore—
Clasp a rare and radiant maiden whom the angels name Lenore."   95
                          Quoth the raven, "Nevermore."

"Be that word our sign of parting, bird or fiend!" I shrieked upstarting—
"Get thee back into the tempest and the Night's Plutonian shore!
Leave no black plume as a token of that lie thy soul hath spoken!
Leave my loneliness unbroken!—quit the bust above my door!   100
Take thy beak from out my heart, and take thy form from off my
   door!"
                          Quoth the raven, "Nevermore."

And the raven, never flitting, still is sitting, still is sitting
On the pallid bust of Pallas just above my chamber door;
And his eyes have all the seeming of a demon's that is dreaming,   105
And the lamp-light o'er him streaming throws his shadow on the floor;
And my soul from out that shadow that lies floating on the floor
                    Shall be lifted—nevermore!

° **nepenthe** A drug
mentioned in the *Odessy* as a
remedy for grief

° **Gilead** A region mentioned
in the Bible; noted for its
soothing ointments.

Related Works

"A Hunger Artist" (p. 210), "Rooming houses are old women" (p. 411), "The Eagle" (p. 434), "The Tyger" (p. 499), *Hamlet* (p. 644)

 See Chapter 27 Review Card for Reading and Reacting questions about Edgar Allan Poe, "The Raven."

LO2 Recognize Allegory

Allegory is a form of narrative that conveys a message or doctrine by using people, places, or things to stand for abstract ideas. **Allegorical figures,** each with a strict equivalent, form an **allegorical framework,** a set of ideas that conveys the allegory's message or lesson. Thus, the allegory takes place on two levels: a **literal level** that tells a story and a **figurative level** on which the allegorical figures in the story stand for ideas, concepts, and other qualities.

Like symbols, allegorical figures suggest other things. But unlike symbols, which have a range of possible meanings, allegorical figures can always be assigned specific meanings. (Because writers use allegory to instruct, they gain nothing by hiding its significance.) Thus, symbols open up possibilities for interpretation, whereas allegories tend to restrict possibilities.

Quite often an allegory involves a journey or an adventure, as in the case of Dante's *Divine Comedy,* which traces a journey through Hell, Purgatory, and Heaven. Within an allegory, everything can have meaning: the road on which the characters walk, the people they encounter, or a phrase that one of them repeats throughout the journey. Once you understand the allegorical framework, your main task is to see how the various elements fit within this system. Some allegorical poems can be relatively straightforward, but others can be so complicated that it takes a great deal of effort to unlock their meaning. In the following poem, a journey is central to the allegory.

Christina Rossetti (1830–1894)

Uphill (1861)

Does the road wind uphill all the way?
   Yes, to the very end.
Will the day's journey take the whole long day?
   From morn to night, my friend.

But is there for the night a resting-place?   5
   A roof for when the slow dark hours begin.
May not the darkness hide it from my face?
   You cannot miss that inn.

Shall I meet other wayfarers at night?
   Those who have gone before.   10
Then must I knock, or call when just in sight?
   They will not keep you standing at that door.

Shall I find comfort, travel-sore and weak?
   Of labor you shall find the sum.
Will there be beds for me and all who seek?   15
   Yea, beds for all who come.

>> Illustration from 1776 printing of *The Pilgrim's Progress*

"Uphill" uses a question-and-answer structure to describe a journey along an uphill road. Like the one described in John Bunyan's seventeenth-century allegory *The Pilgrim's Progress,* this is a spiritual journey, one that suggests the challenges a person faces throughout life. The day-and-night duration of the journey stands for life and death, and the inn at the end of the road stands for the grave, the final resting place.

Adrienne Rich (1929–2012)

Diving into the Wreck (1973)

>> Underwater shipwreck

First having read the book of myths,
and loaded the camera,
and checked the edge of the knife-blade,
I put on
the body-armor of black rubber   5
the absurd flippers
the grave and awkward mask.
I am having to do this
not like Cousteau with his
assiduous team   10
aboard the sun-flooded schooner
but here alone.

There is a ladder.
The ladder is always there
hanging innocently   15
close to the side of the schooner.
We know what it is for,
we who have used it.
Otherwise
it's a piece of maritime floss   20
some sundry equipment.

I go down.
Rung after rung and still
the oxygen immerses me
the blue light   25
the clear atoms
of our human air.
I go down.
My flippers cripple me,
I crawl like an insect down the ladder   30
and there is no one
to tell me when the ocean
will begin.

First the air is blue and then
it is bluer and then green and then   35
black I am blacking out and yet
my mask is powerful
it pumps my blood with power
the sea is another story
the sea is not a question of power   40
I have to learn alone
to turn my body without force
in the deep element.

And now: it is easy to forget
what I came for   45
among so many who have always
lived here

swaying their crenellated fans
between the reefs
and besides   50
you breathe differently down here.

I came to explore the wreck.
The words are purposes.
The words are maps.
I came to see the damage that was done   55
and the treasures that prevail.
I stroke the beam of my lamp
slowly along the flank
of something more permanent
than fish or weed   60

the thing I came for:
the wreck and not the story of the wreck
the thing itself and not the myth
the drowned face always staring
toward the sun   65
the evidence of damage
worn by salt and sway into this threadbare beauty
the ribs of the disaster
curving their assertion
among the tentative haunters.   70

This is the place.
And I am here, the mermaid whose dark hair
streams black, the merman in his armored body
We circle silently
about the wreck   75
we dive into the hold.
I am she: I am he
whose drowned face sleeps with open eyes
whose breasts still bear the stress
whose silver, copper, vermeil cargo lies   80
obscurely inside barrels
half-wedged and left to rot
we are the half-destroyed instruments
that once held to a course
the water-eaten log   85
the fouled compass

We are, I am, you are
by cowardice or courage
the one who finds our way
back to this scene   90
carrying a knife, a camera
a book of myths
in which
our names do not appear.

Related Works

"Two Questions" (p. 273), "Young Goodman Brown" (p. 320),
"The Love Song of J. Alfred Prufrock" (p. 504)

 See Chapter 27 Review Card for Reading and Reacting
questions about Adrienne Rich, "Diving into the Wreck."

EXPLORE ONLINE >

To complete a tutorial of "Allusion," visit your
Literature CourseMate, accessed through
www.cengagebrain.com.

allusion Reference, often to literature, history, mythology, or the Bible, that the author expects a reader to recognize.

may depend on your ability to interpret an unfamiliar reference.

Although most poets expect readers to recognize their references, some use allusions to exclude certain readers from their work. In his 1922 poem "The Waste Land," for example, T. S. Eliot alludes to historical events, ancient languages, and obscure literary works. He even includes a set of notes to accompany his poem, but they do little more than complicate an already difficult text. (As you might expect, initial critical response to this poem was mixed: some critics said that it was a work of genius, while others thought that it was arcane and pretentious.)

Allusions can come from any source: history, the arts, other works of literature, the Bible, current events, or even the personal life of the poet. In the following poem, the Nigerian poet and playwright Wole Soyinka alludes to several political figures.

LO3 Recognize Allusion

An **allusion** is a brief reference to a person, place, or event (fictional or actual) that readers are expected to recognize. Like symbols and allegories, allusions enrich a work by introducing associations from another context.

When poets use allusions, they assume that they and their readers have a common body of knowledge. If, when reading a poem, you come across a reference with which you are not familiar, take the time to look it up online or in a dictionary or an encyclopedia. As you have probably realized by now, your understanding of a poem

Wole Soyinka (1934–   )

Future Plans (1972)

The meeting is called
To odium: Forgers, framers
Fabricators Inter-
national. Chairman,
A dark horse, a circus nag turned blinkered sprinter   5

Mach Three
We rate him—one for the Knife
Two for 'iavelli, Three—
Breaking speed
Of the truth barrier by a swooping detention decree   10

Projects in view:
Mao Tse Tung in league
With Chiang Kai. Nkrumah
Makes a secret
Pact with Verwood, sworn by Hastings Banda.   15
Proven: Arafat
In flagrante cum
Golda Meir. Castro drunk
With Richard Nixon
Contraceptives stacked beneath the papal bunk . . .   20
                              . . . and more to come

>> Richard Nixon meeting
   Mao Tse Tung, 1972

© AP Photo

This poem is structured like an agenda for a meeting. From the moment it announces that a meeting has been called "To odium" (a pun on "to order"), it is clear that the poem will be a bitter political satire. Those in attendance are "Forgers, framers/Fabricators." The second stanza contains three allusions that shed light on the character of the chairman. The first is to Mack the Knife, a petty criminal in Bertolt Brecht and Kurt Weill's *Three-penny Opera* (1933). The second is to Niccolò Machiavelli, whose book *The Prince* (1532) advocates the use of unscrupulous means to strengthen the state. The last is to the term *mach,* which denotes the speed of an airplane in relation to the speed of sound—mach one, two, three, and so on. By means of these allusions, the poem implies that the meeting's chairman has been chosen for his ability to engage in violence, to be ruthless, and to break the "truth barrier"—that is, to lie.

The rest of the poem alludes to individuals involved in global politics around the time it was written, in 1972—specifically, the politics of developing nations. According to the speaker, instead of fighting for the rights of the oppressed, these people consolidate their own political power by collaborating with those who oppose their positions. Thus, Mao Tse-tung, the communist leader of China, is "in league / With" Chiang Kai-shek, his old Nationalist Chinese enemy; Yassir Arafat, the leader of the Palestine Liberation Organization, is linked with Golda Meir, the prime minister of Israel; Kwame Nkrumah, the first president of Ghana, conspires with Hendrick Verwoerd, the prime minister of South Africa, assassinated in 1966; and United States president Richard Nixon gets drunk with Cuba's communist leader, Fidel Castro. These allusions suggest the self-serving nature of political alliances and the extreme disorder of world politics. Whether the poem is satirizing the United Nations and its agenda, criticizing the tendency of politics to make strange bedfellows, or showing how corrupt politicians are, its allusions enable the poet to broaden his frame of reference and thus make the poem more meaningful to readers.

The next poem uses allusions to prominent literary figures, as well as to myth, to develop its theme.

William Meredith (1919–)

Dreams of Suicide (1980)

(in sorrowful memory of Ernest Hemingway, Sylvia Plath, and John Berryman)

>> Ernest Hemingway at his writing desk, 1945

I

I reach for the awkward shotgun not to disarm
you, but to feel the metal horn,
furred with the downy membrane of dream.
More surely than the unicorn,
you are the mythical beast.   5

II

Or I am sniffing an oven. On all fours
I am imitating a totemic animal
but she is not my totem or the totem
of my people, this is not my magic oven.

III

If I hold you tight by the ankles,   10
still you fly upward from the iron railing.
Your father made these wings,
after he made his own, and now from beyond
he tells you *fly down,* in the voice
my own father might say *walk, boy.*   15

"Dreams of Suicide" is dedicated to the memory of three writers who committed suicide. In each stanza, the speaker envisions in a dream the death of one of the writers. In the first stanza, he dreams of Ernest Hemingway, who killed himself with a shotgun. The speaker grasps the "metal horn" of Hemingway's shotgun and transforms Hemingway into a mythical beast who, like a unicorn, represents the rare, unique talent of the artist. In the second stanza, the speaker dreams of Sylvia Plath, who asphyxiated herself in a gas oven. He sees himself, like Plath, on his knees imitating an animal sniffing an oven. In the third stanza, the speaker dreams of John Berryman, who leaped to his death. Berryman is characterized as Icarus, a mythological figure who, along with his father Daedalus, fled Crete by building wings made of feathers and wax. Together they flew away; however, ignoring his father's warning, Icarus flew so close to the sun that the wax melted, and he fell to his death in the sea. In this poem, then, the speaker uses allusions to make a point about the difficult lives of writers—and, perhaps, to convey his own empathy for those who could not survive the struggle to reconcile art and life.

FURTHER READING: Allusion

Bill Coyle (1968–   )

Post-Colonial Studies° (2006)

Australia
The two surviving
speakers of Mati Ke,° ancient
sister and brother,
honor a tribal taboo°   5
and do not speak to each other.

Fiji
On an island bought
for him by a worthy follower,
Adi da Samraj,°   10
long awaited avatar,°
native New Yorker, holds sway.

Laos
In the country, homes
are often set on stilts. Some   15
of the stilts are bombs,
ordnance left from the war.°
Some of the bombs are still live.

° **post-colonial studies** A school of literary criticism that examines literature written in and about the former colonies of Western powers.

° **Mati Ke** An indigenous language of Australia.

° **taboo** A prohibition against a certain action.

° **Adi Da Samraj** Literally, "the radiant avatar, primordial giver, universal ruler."

° **avatar** The embodiment of a divinity.

° **the war** The Laotian Civil War (1962–1975).

Related Works

"Love and Other Catastrophes: A Mix Tape" (p. 103), "The Things They Carried" (p. 232), "B lingual/Bilingüe" (p. 386)

LO4 Recognize Myth

A **myth** is a narrative that embodies—and in some cases helps to explain—the religious, philosophical, moral, and political values of a culture. Using gods and supernatural beings, myths try to make sense of occurrences in the natural world. (The term *myth* can also refer to a private belief system devised by an individual poet as well as to any fully realized fictitious setting in which a literary work takes place, such as the myths of William Faulkner's Yoknapatawpha County or of novelist Lawrence Durrell's Alexandria.) Contrary to popular usage, *myth* does not mean "falsehood."

> **myth** Story reflecting the religious and social values of a culture or explaining natural phenomena, often involving gods and heroes.

In the broadest sense, myths are stories—usually whole groups of stories—that can be true or partly true as well as false; regardless of their degree of accuracy, however, myths frequently express the deepest beliefs of a culture. According to this definition, the *Iliad* and the *Odyssey*, the Koran, and the Old and New Testaments can all be referred to as myths.

The mythologist Joseph Campbell wrote that myths contain truths that link people together, whether they live today or lived 2,500 years ago. Myths attempt to explain phenomena that human beings care about, regardless of when and where they live. It is not surprising, then, that myths frequently contain **archetypal images**—images that cut across cultural and racial boundaries and touch us at a very deep level. Many Greek myths illustrate this power. For example, when Orpheus descends into Hades to rescue his wife, Eurydice, he acts out the universal human desire to transcend death; and when Telemachus sets out in search of his father, Odysseus, he reminds readers that we are all lost children searching for parents. When Icarus ignores his father and flies too near the sun and when Pandora cannot resist looking into a box that she has been told not to open, we are reminded of the human weaknesses we all share.

When poets use myths, they are actually making allusions. They expect readers to bring to the poem the cultural, emotional, and ethical context of the myths to which they are alluding. At one time, when all educated individuals studied the Greek and Latin classics as well as the Bible and other religious texts, poets could safely assume that readers would recognize the mythological allusions they made. Today, many readers are unable to understand the full significance of an allusion or its application within a poem. Many of the poems in this anthology are accompanied by notes, but these may not provide all the information you will need to understand the full significance of each mythological allusion. Occasionally, you may have to look elsewhere for answers, turning to dictionaries, encyclopedias, online information sites such as <http://www.answers.com>, or collections of myths such as the *New Larousse Encyclopedia of Mythology* or *Bulfinch's Mythology*.

Sometimes a poet alludes to a myth in a title; sometimes references to various myths appear throughout a poem; at other times, an entire poem focuses on a single myth. In each case, as in the following poem, the use of myth helps to develop the poem's theme.

Countee Cullen (1903–1946)

Yet Do I Marvel (1925)

I doubt not God is good, well-meaning, kind,
And did He stoop to quibble could tell why
The little buried mole continues blind,
Why flesh that mirrors Him must some day die,
Make plain the reason tortured Tantalus   5
Is baited by the fickle fruit, declare
If merely brute caprice dooms Sisyphus
To struggle up a never-ending stair.
Inscrutable His ways are, and immune
To catechism by a mind too strewn   10
With petty cares to slightly understand
What awful brain compels His awful hand.
Yet do I marvel at this curious thing:
To make a poet black, and bid him sing!

>> Engraving of Tantalus reaching for fruit

The speaker begins by affirming his belief in the benevolence of God but then questions why God engages in what appear to be capricious acts. As part of his catalog of questions, the speaker alludes to Tantalus and Sisyphus, two figures from Greek mythology. Tantalus was a king who was condemned to Hades for his crimes. There, he was forced to stand in a pool of water up to his chin. Overhead hung a tree branch laden with fruit. When Tantalus got thirsty and tried to drink, the level of the water dropped, and when he got hungry and reached for fruit, it moved just out of reach. Thus, Tantalus was doomed to be near what he most desired but forever unable to obtain it.

Sisyphus also was condemned to Hades. For his disrespect to Zeus, he was sentenced to endless toil. Every day, Sisyphus pushed a boulder up a steep hill. Every time he neared the top, the boulder rolled back down the hill, and Sisyphus had to begin again. Like Tantalus, the speaker in "Yet Do I Marvel" cannot have what he wants; like Sisyphus, he is forced to toil in vain. He wonders why a well-meaning God would "make a poet black, and bid him sing" in a racist society that does not listen to his voice. Thus, the poet's two allusions to Greek mythology enrich the poem by connecting the suffering of the speaker to a universal drama that has been acted out again and again.

EXPLORE ONLINE >

To listen to audio of "Leda and the Swan," visit
your Literature CourseMate, accessed through
www.cengagebrain.com.

FURTHER READING: Myth

William Butler Yeats (1865–1939)

Leda and the Swan (1924)

A sudden blow: the great wings beating still
Above the staggering girl, her thighs caressed
By the dark webs, her nape caught in his bill,
He holds her helpless breast upon his breast.

How can those terrified vague fingers push   5
The feathered glory from her loosening thighs?
And how can body, laid in that white rush,
But feel the strange heart beating where it lies?

A shudder in the loins engenders there
The broken wall, the burning roof and tower   10
And Agamemnon dead.
                                    Being so caught up,
So mastered by the brute blood of the air,
Did she put on his knowledge with his power
Before the indifferent beak could let her drop?   15

>> Peter Paul Rubens, *Leda and the Swan*, 1598

Related Works

"Greasy Lake" (p. 306), "Where Are You Going, Where Have You Been?"
(p. 325), "The Second Coming" (p. 523)

See Chapter 27 Review Card for Reading and Reacting
questions about William Butler Yeats, "Leda and the Swan."

W. H. Auden (1907–1973)

Musée des Beaux Arts (1940)

About suffering they were never wrong,
The Old Masters: how well they understood
Its human position; how it takes place
While someone else is eating or opening a window or just
    walking dully along
How, when the aged are reverently, passionately waiting   5

EXPLORE ONLINE >

To listen to audio of "Musée des Beaux Arts," visit
your Literature CourseMate, accessed through
www.cengagebrain.com.

For the miraculous birth, there always must be
Children who did not specially want it to happen, skating
On a pond at the edge of the wood:
They never forgot
That even the dreadful martyrdom must run its course   10
Anyhow in a corner, some untidy spot
Where the dogs go on with their doggy life and the torturer's
   horse
Scratches its innocent behind on a tree.
In Brueghel's *Icarus*, for instance: how everything turns away
Quite leisurely from the disaster; the ploughman may   15
Have heard the splash, the forsaken cry,
But for him it was not an important failure; the sun shone
As it had to on the white legs disappearing into the green
Water; and the expensive delicate ship that must have seen
Something amazing, a boy falling out of the sky,   20
Had somewhere to get to and sailed calmly on.

>> Peter Breugel, *Landscape with the Fall of Icarus*, 1558

Related Works

"The Lottery" (p. 251), "One day I wrote her name upon the strand"
(p. 393), "Shall I compare thee to a summer's day?" (p. 408), "The Second
Coming" (p. 523)

 See Chapter 27 Review Card for Reading and Reacting
questions about W. H. Auden, "Musée des Beaux Arts."

T. S. Eliot (1888–1965)

Journey of the Magi° (1927)

"A cold coming we had of it,
Just the worst time of the year
For a journey, and such a long journey:
The ways deep and the weather sharp,
The very dead of winter."*   5
And the camels galled, sore-footed, refractory,
Lying down in the melting snow.
There were times we regretted
The summer palaces on slopes, the terraces,
And the silken girls bringing sherbet.   10
Then the camel men cursing and grumbling
And running away, and wanting their liquor and women,
And the night-fires going out, and the lack of shelters,
And the cities hostile and the towns unfriendly
And the villages dirty and charging high prices: 15
A hard time we had of it.
At the end we preferred to travel all night,
Sleeping in snatches,
With the voices singing in our ears, saying
That this was all folly.   20

Then at dawn we came down to a temperate valley,
Wet, below the snow line, smelling of vegetation;
With a running stream and a water-mill beating the darkness,
And three trees° on the low sky,
And an old white horse° galloped away in the meadow.   25
Then we came to a tavern with vine-leaves over the lintel,
Six hands at an open door dicing for pieces of silver,°
And feet kicking the empty wine-skins.
But there was no information, and so we continued
And arrived at evening, not a moment too soon   30
Finding the place; it was (you may say) satisfactory.
All this was a long time ago, I remember,
And I would do it again, but set down
This set down
This: were we led all that way for   35
Birth or Death? There was a Birth, certainly,
We had evidence and no doubt. I had seen birth and death,
But had thought they were different; this Birth was
Hard and bitter agony for us, like Death, our death.
We returned to our places, these Kingdoms,   40
But no longer at ease here, in the old dispensation,
With an alien people clutching their gods.
I should be glad of another death.

>> *Adoration of the Magi* by Lavinia Hamer

° **Magi** The three wise men who traveled east to pay tribute to the infant Jesus (see Matthew 12.1–12)

* The five quoted lines are adapted from a passage in a 1622 Christmas Day sermon by Bishop Lancelot Andrewes.

° **three trees** The three crosses at Calvary (see Luke 23.32–33).

° **white horse** The horse ridden by the conquering Christ in Revelation 19.11–16.

° **dicing . . . silver** Echoes the soldiers gambling for Christ's garments, as well as his betrayal by Judas Iscariot for thirty pieces of silver (see Matthew 27.35 and 26.14–16).

Related Works

"Araby" (p. 220), "The World Is Too Much with Us" (p. 373), "On First Looking into Chapman's Homer" (p. 447), "Do not go gentle into that good night" (p. 484), "The Love Song of J. Alfred Prufrock" (p. 504)

Writing Suggestions: Symbol, Allegory, Allusion, Myth

1. Read "Aunt Jennifer's Tigers" (p. 433) and "Diving into the Wreck" (p. 469) by Adrienne Rich. Then, write an essay in which you discuss the similarities and differences in Rich's use of symbols in the two poems.

2. Many popular songs make use of allusion. Choose one or two popular songs that you know well, and analyze their use of allusion, paying particular attention to whether the allusions expand the impact and meaning of the song or create barriers to listeners' understanding.

3. Read the Emily Dickinson poem "Because I could not stop for Death—" (p. 502), and then write an interpretation of the poem, identifying its allegorical figures.

4. What applications do the lessons of myth have for life today? Analyze a poem in which myth is central, and then discuss how you might use myth to make generalizations about your own life.

 CHECKLIST

SYMBOL, ALLEGORY, ALLUSION, MYTH

Symbol
- [ ] Are there any symbols in the poem? What leads you to believe they are symbols?
- [ ] Are these symbols conventional?
- [ ] Are they universal or archetypal?
- [ ] Are any symbols obscure or highly idiosyncratic?
- [ ] What is the literal meaning of each symbol in the context of the poem?
- [ ] Beyond its literal meaning, what else could each symbol suggest?
- [ ] How does your interpretation of each symbol enhance your understanding of the poem?

Allegory
- [ ] Is the poem an allegory?
- [ ] Are there any allegorical figures within the poem? How can you tell?
- [ ] What do the allegorical figures signify on a literal level?
- [ ] What lesson does the allegory illustrate?

Allusion
- [ ] Are there any allusions in the poem?
- [ ] Do you recognize the names, places, historical events, or literary works to which the poet alludes?
- [ ] In what way does each allusion deepen the poem's meaning? Does any allusion interfere with your understanding or enjoyment of the poem? If so, how?
- [ ] Would the poem be more effective without a particular allusion?

Myth
- [ ] What myths or mythological figures are alluded to?
- [ ] How does the poem use myth to convey its meaning?
- [ ] How faithful is the poem to the myth? Does the poet add material to the myth? Are any details from the original myth omitted? Is any information distorted? Why?

Glossary Terms

allegory Story with two parallel and consistent levels of meaning, one literal and one figurative, in which the figurative level offers a moral or political lesson. An **allegorical figure** has only one meaning (for instance, it may represent good or evil). An **allegorical framework** is the system of ideas that conveys the allegory's message.

allusion Reference, often to literature, history, mythology, or the Bible that the author expects a reader to recognize. An example of allusion in a title is Charles Baxter's "Gryphon" (a mythical beast).

archetype Image or symbol that is so common or important that it seems to have universal significance. Many archetypes appear in classical myths (for example, a journey to the underworld).

myth Story reflecting the religious and social values of a culture or explaining natural phenomena, often involving gods and heroes.

symbol Person, object, action, or idea whose meaning transcends its literal or denotative sense in a complex way. A symbol is invested with significance beyond what it could carry on its own. **Universal symbols**, such as the grim reaper, may be called **archetypes**; **conventional symbols**, such as national flags, evoke a general and agreed-upon response from most people.

28
Discovering Themes in Poetry

Learning Outcomes

After reading this chapter, you should be able to do the following:

LO1 Evaluate poems about parents

LO2 Evaluate poems about nature

LO3 Evaluate poems about love

LO4 Evaluate poems about war

Timeline

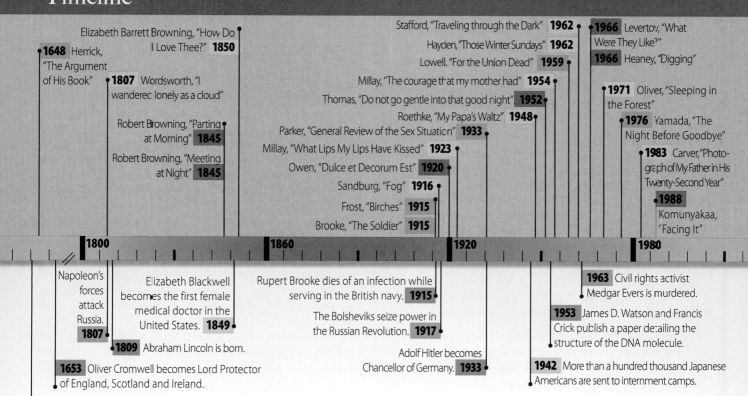

Elizabeth Barrett Browning, "How Do I Love Thee?" **1850**

1648 Herrick, "The Argument of His Book"

1807 Wordsworth, "I wandered lonely as a cloud"

Robert Browning, "Parting at Morning" **1845**

Robert Browning, "Meeting at Night" **1845**

Stafford, "Traveling through the Dark" **1962**

Hayden, "Those Winter Sundays" **1962**

Lowell. "For the Union Dead" **1959**

Millay, "The courage that my mother had" **1954**

Thomas, "Do not go gentle into that good night" **1952**

Roethke, "My Papa's Waltz" **1948**

Parker, "General Review of the Sex Situation" **1933**

Millay, "What Lips My Lips Have Kissed" **1923**

Owen, "Dulce et Decorum Est" **1920**

Sandburg, "Fog" **1916**

Frost, "Birches" **1915**

Brooke, "The Soldier" **1915**

1966 Levertov, "What Were They Like?"

1966 Heaney, "Digging"

1971 Oliver, "Sleeping in the Forest"

1976 Yamada, "The Night Before Goodbye"

1983 Carver, "Photograph of My Father in His Twenty-Second Year"

1988 Komunyakaa, "Facing It"

1800 **1860** **1920** **1980**

Napoleon's forces attack Russia. **1807**

Elizabeth Blackwell becomes the first female medical doctor in the United States. **1849**

1809 Abraham Lincoln is born.

1653 Oliver Cromwell becomes Lord Protector of England, Scotland and Ireland.

1647 Christmas is banned by England's Puritan rulers.

Rupert Brooke dies of an infection while serving in the British navy. **1915**

The Bolsheviks seize power in the Russian Revolution. **1917**

Adolf Hitler becomes Chancellor of Germany. **1933**

1963 Civil rights activist Medgar Evers is murdered.

1953 James D. Watson and Francis Crick publish a paper detailing the structure of the DNA molecule.

1942 More than a hundred thousand Japanese Americans are sent to internment camps.

© Hulton-Deutsch Collection / Corbis

Robert Herrick (1591–1674)

The Argument of His Book (1648)

I sing of brooks, of blossoms, birds, and bowers,
Of April, May, of June, and July-flowers;
I sing of May-poles, hock-carts, wassails, wakes,
Of bridegrooms, brides and of their bridal-cakes;
I write of youth, of love, and have access   5
By these to sing of cleanly wantonness;
I sing of dews, of rains, and piece by piece
Of balm, of oil, of spice and ambergris;
I sing of times trans-shifting, and I write
How roses first came red and lilies white;   10
I write of groves, of twilights, and I sing
The court of Mab,° and of the fairy king;
I write of Hell; I sing (and ever shall)
Of Heaven, and hope to have it after all.

° **Mab** Queen of the fairies.

Hulton Archive/Getty Images

>> Dance around maypole

> *"In general terms,* theme *refers to the ideas that the poet explores, the concerns that the poem examines. More specifically, a poem's theme is its main point or idea."*

As the poem above makes clear, a poem can be about anything, from the mysteries of the universe to poetry itself. Although no subject is really inappropriate for poetic treatment, certain conventional subjects—family, nature, love, war, death, the folly of human desires, and the inevitability of growing old—recur frequently.

A poem's *theme*, however, is more than its *subject*. In general terms, *theme* refers to the ideas that the poet explores, the concerns that the poem examines. More specifically, a poem's **theme** is its main point or idea. Poems "about death," for example, may examine the difficulty of facing one's own mortality, eulogize a friend, assert the need for the acceptance of life's cycles, or cry out against death's inevitability. Or, such poems may explore the *carpe diem* theme—the belief that life is brief, so we must "seize the day."

In order to understand the theme of a poem, readers should consider its form, voice, tone, language, images, allusions, sound—all of its individual elements. Together, these elements communicate the ideas that are important in the poem. Keep in mind, however, that a poem may not mean the same thing to every reader. Different readers will bring different backgrounds, attitudes, and experiences to a poem and will therefore see things in various ways. Moreover, poets may approach the same subject in drastically different ways, emphasizing different elements as they view the subject matter from their own unique perspectives. Ultimately, there are as many different themes, and ways to approach these themes, as there are writers (and readers) of poetry.

LO1 Evaluate Poems about Parents

Although a poet's individual experience may be vastly different from the experiences of his or her readers, certain ideas seem universal in poems about parents. On the one hand, such poems can express positive sentiments: love, joy, wistfulness, nostalgia, and gratitude for childhood's happy memories and a parent's unconditional love. On the other hand, they may express negative emotions: anger, detachment, frustration, resentment, or regret. When they write about parents, poets may be emotionally engaged or distant, curious or apathetic, remorseful or grateful; they may idealize parents or despise them. Regardless of the particulars of the poem's specific theme, however, virtually all poems about parents address one general concept—the influence of a parent over his or her child.

For as long as poets have been writing poetry, their personal experiences (and childhoods) have influenced their subject matter and their poems. In American poetry,

theme Central or dominant idea of a work of literature.

carpe diem Latin for "seize the day"; the philosophy arguing that one should enjoy life today before it passes by.

poems about parents became more common with the advent of **confessionalism,** a movement in the mid 1950s in which poets began to write subjective verse about their personal experiences. Poems in Robert Lowell's *Life Studies* and W. D. Snodgrass's *Heart's Needle* both addressed the positive and negative aspects of the poets' families (including their parents and children), thus opening the door for an influx of poems about similar themes. Poems by Sylvia Plath and Anne Sexton dealt with previously taboo subjects such as abortion, suicide, and mental illness. Though confessional poets often adapted or fictionalized their experiences when putting them into verse, the line between art and life could be thin, sometimes dangerously so: both Plath and Sexton committed suicide.

The poems in this section all deal with issues related to parents and family, but their styles, voices, and focuses are very different. Sometimes the speakers' voices express ambivalence, communicating conventional sentiments of love and admiration alongside perplexity, frustration, and even anger. This ambivalence is apparent in Theodore Roethke's "My Papa's Waltz" and Robert Hayden's "Those Winter Sundays," as adult speakers struggle to understand their fathers' long-ago behavior. In Edna St. Vincent Millay's "The courage that my mother had," Seamus Heaney's "Digging," and Louis Simpson's "Working Late," the speakers are more positive, finding traits in their parents that they would like to emulate. Raymond Carver's "Photograph of My Father in His Twenty-Second Year," and Sharon Olds's " I Go Back to May 1937" are meditations on visual images of the speakers' parents in their younger years, while Mitsuye Yamada's "The Night Before Goodbye" focuses on a mother's quiet sacrifice. Finally, Dylan Thomas's "Do not go gentle into that good night" confronts the death of a parent.

EXPLORE ONLINE >

To listen to audio of "My Papa's Waltz," visit your Literature CourseMate, accessed through www.cengagebrain.com.

Theodore Roethke (1908–1963)

My Papa's Waltz (1948)

© Bettmann/Corbis

The whiskey on your breath
Could make a small boy dizzy;
But I hung on like death:
Such waltzing was not easy.

We romped until the pans   5
Slid from the kitchen shelf;
My mother's countenance
Could not unfrown itself.

The hand that held my wrist
Was battered on one knuckle;   10
At every step you missed
My right ear scraped a buckle.

You beat time on my head
With a palm caked hard by dirt,
Then waltzed me off to bed   15
Still clinging to your shirt.

EXPLORE ONLINE >

To listen to audio of "Those Winter Sundays," visit
your Literature CourseMate, accessed through
www.cengagebrain.com.

Robert Hayden (1913–1980)

Those Winter Sundays (1962)

Sundays too my father got up early
and put his clothes on in the blueblack cold,
then with cracked hands that ached
from labor in the weekday weather made
banked fires blaze. No one ever thanked him.   5

I'd wake and hear the cold splintering, breaking.
When the rooms were warm, he'd call,
and slowly I would rise and dress,
fearing the chronic angers of that house,

Speaking indifferently to him,   10
who had driven out the cold
and polished my good shoes as well.
What did I know, what did I know
of love's austere and lonely offices?

Edna St. Vincent Millay (1892–1950)

The courage that my mother had (1954)

The courage that my mother had
Went with her, and is with her still:
Rock from New England quarried;
New granite in a granite hill.

The golden brooch my mother wore   5
She left behind for me to wear;
I have no thing I treasure more:
Yet, it is something I could spare.

Oh, if instead she'd left to me
The thing she took into the grave!—   10
That courage like a rock, which she
Has no more need of, and I have.

Seamus Heaney (1939–   )

Digging (1966)

Between my finger and my thumb
The squat pen rests; snug as a gun.

Under my window, a clean rasping sound
When the spade sinks into gravelly ground:
My father, digging. I look down   5

Till his straining rump among the flowerbeds
Bends low, comes up twenty years away
Stooping in rhythm through potato drills
Where he was digging.

The coarse boot nestled on the lug, the shaft   10
Against the inside knee was levered firmly.
He rooted out tall tops, buried the bright edge deep
To scatter new potatoes that we picked
Loving their cool hardness in our hands.

By God, the old man could handle a spade.   15
Just like his old man.

>> Potatoes and spade

My grandfather cut more turf in a day
Than any other man on Toner's bog.
Once I carried him milk in a bottle
Corked sloppily with paper. He straightened up   20
To drink it, then fell to right away

Nicking and slicing neatly, heaving sods
Over his shoulder, going down and down
For the good turf. Digging.

The cold smell of potato mould, the squelch and slap   25
Of soggy peat, the curt cuts of an edge
Through living roots awaken in my head.
But I've no spade to follow men like them.

Between my finger and my thumb
The squat pen rests.   30
I'll dig with it.

Raymond Carver (1938–1988)

Photograph of My Father in His Twenty-Second Year (1983)

October. Here in this dank, unfamiliar kitchen
I study my father's embarrassed young man's face.
Sheepish grin, he holds in one hand a string
of spiny yellow perch, in the other
a bottle of Carlsbad beer.   5

In jeans and denim shirt, he leans
against the front fender of a 1934 Ford.
He would like to pose bluff and hearty for his posterity,
wear his old hat cocked over his ear.
All his life my father wanted to be bold.   10

But the eyes give him away, and the hands
that limply offer the string of dead perch
and the bottle of beer. Father, I love you,
yet how can I say thank you, I who can't hold my liquor either,
and don't even know the places to fish?   15

Mitsuye Yamada (1923–   )

The Night Before Goodbye (1976)

Mama is mending
my underwear
while my brothers sleep.
Her husband taken away by the FBI
one son lured away by the Army   5
now another son and daughter
lusting for the free world outside.
She must let go.
The war goes on.
She will take one still small son   10
and join Papa in internment°
to make a family.
Still sewing
squinting in the dim light
in room C barrack 4 block 4   15
she whispers
Remember
keep your underwear
in good repair
in case of accident   20
don't bring shame
on us.

>> Manzanar Relocation Center,
1943

internment Shortly after
the attack on Pearl Harbor,
President Roosevelt ordered
that all people of Japanese
ancestry—even American
citizens—be removed from
the West Coast. About
112,000 people were
relocated to "internment
camps," relocation centers
where they remained until
after the war's end.

🌐 EXPLORE ONLINE >

To listen to an instructor podcast of "Do not go gentle into
that good night," visit your Literature CourseMate, accessed
through www.cengagebrain.com.

Dylan Thomas (1914–1953)

Do not go gentle into that good night* (1952)

Do not go gentle into that good night,
Old age should burn and rave at close of day;
Rage, rage against the dying of the light.

Though wise men at their end know dark is right,
Because their words had forked no lightning they   5
Do not go gentle into that good night.

Good men, the last wave by, crying how bright
Their frail deeds might have danced in a green bay,
Rage, rage against the dying of the light.

Wild men who caught and sang the sun in flight,   10
And learn, too late, they grieved it on its way,
Do not go gentle into that good night.

*This poem was written during
the last illness of the poet's
father.

Grave men, near death, who see with blinding sight
Blind eyes could blaze like meteors and be gay,
Rage, rage against the dying of the light.

15

And you, my father, there on the sad height,
Curse, bless, me now with your fierce tears, I pray,
Do not go gentle into that good night.
Rage, rage against the dying of the light.

Related Works

"I Stand Here Ironing" (p. 162), from *Fun Home* (p. 246), "Two Kinds" (p. 336), "Daddy" (p. 416), *Fences* (p. 724)

LO2 Evaluate Poems about Nature

In his 1913 poem "Trees," the American poet Joyce Kilmer neatly summarized the symbiotic relationship that exists between poetry and nature: "I think that I shall never see / A poem lovely as a tree." Poets have always found inspiration in the beauty, majesty, and grandeur of the natural world; in fact, some forms of poetry are dedicated solely to the subject of nature. For example, a **pastoral** is a literary form that deals nostalgically with a simple rural life. Many of the early Greek and Roman pastorals were about shepherds who passed the time writing about love while watching their flocks. In these poems, the shepherd's life is idealized; thus, the pastoral tradition celebrates simple times and the beauty of the rural life. Similarly, an **idyll**, a short work in verse or prose (or a painting or a piece of music), depicts simple pastoral or rural scenes, often in idealized terms.

> *"Poets have always found inspiration in the beauty, majesty, and grandeur of the natural world…"*

Certain literary movements also focused on the subject of nature. For the **romantic** poets, nature was a source of inspiration, authenticity, and spiritual refreshment, elements they by and large saw as lacking in the lives of Europeans—both the educated classes and those working in the mills and factories that came with industrialization. Later, the American **transcendentalists,** including Ralph Waldo Emerson and Henry David Thoreau, examined the relationships between philosophy, religion, and nature. In

Walden, for example, Thoreau wrote about the pleasures and rewards of withdrawing from mainstream life in order to live simply in the woods.

While all poems about nature deal with the same general subject, their approaches, and their focuses, can differ greatly. Poems "about nature" may focus on the seasons, the weather, mountains or the sea, birds or animals, or trees and flowers. They may praise the beauty of nature, assert the superiority of its simplest creatures, consider its evanescence, or mourn its destruction. In this section, romantic poet William Wordsworth's "I wandered lonely as a cloud" extols the virtue of nature and the value of immersing oneself in its beauty, while in Carl Sandburg's "Fog," the speaker focuses on a single image of a natural phenomenon. In Robert Frost's "Birches," the speaker recalls the childhood enjoyment of climbing trees, and he longs for the simplicity of those times; Mary Oliver's "Sleeping in the Forest" expresses a oneness with nature and its creatures. Finally, in William Stafford's "Traveling through the Dark," the speaker presents human beings as adversaries of nature and its other creatures.

pastoral Literary work that deals nostalgically (and usually unrealistically) with a simple, preindustrial rural life; the name comes from the fact that traditionally pastorals feature shepherds.

romanticism Eighteenth- and nineteenth-century literary movement that valued subjectivity, individuality, the imagination, nature, excess, the exotic, and the mysterious.

William Wordsworth (1770–1850)

I wandered lonely
as a cloud (1807)

I wandered lonely as a cloud
   That floats on high o'er vales and hills,
When all at once I saw a crowd,
   A host, of golden daffodils,
Beside the lake, beneath the trees,   5
Fluttering and dancing in the breeze.

Continuous as the stars that shine
   And twinkle on the milky way,
They stretched in never-ending line
   Along the margin of a bay: 10
Ten thousand saw I at a glance,
Tossing their heads in sprightly dance.

The waves beside them danced; but they
   Out-did the sparkling waves in glee;
A poet could not but be gay,   15
   In such a jocund company;
I gazed—and gazed—but little thought
What wealth the show to me had brought:

For oft, when on my couch I lie
   In vacant or in pensive mood,   20
They flash upon that inward eye
   Which is the bliss of solitude;
And then my heart with pleasure fills,
And dances with the daffodils.

>> Field of daffodils

Mary Oliver (1935–   )

Sleeping in the Forest (1979)

I thought the earth remembered me,
she took me back so tenderly,
arranging her dark skirts, her pockets
full of lichens and seeds.
I slept as never before, a stone on the river bed,   5
nothing between me and the white fire of the stars
but my thoughts, and they floated light as moths
among the branches of the perfect trees.
All night I heard the small kingdoms
breathing around me, the insects,   10
and the birds who do their work in the darkness.
All night I rose and fell, as if in water,
grappling with a luminous doom. By morning
I had vanished at least a dozen times
into something better.   15

Robert Frost (1874–1963)

Birches (1915)

When I see birches bend to left and right
Across the lines of straighter darker trees,
I like to think some boy's been swinging them.
But swinging doesn't bend them down to stay
As ice-storms do. Often you must have seen them   5
Loaded with ice a sunny winter morning
After a rain. They click upon themselves
As the breeze rises, and turn many-colored
As the stir cracks and crazes their enamel.
Soon the sun's warmth makes them shed crystal shells   10
Shattering and avalanching on the snow-crust—
Such heaps of broken glass to sweep away
You'd think the inner dome of heaven had fallen.
They are dragged to the withered bracken by the load,
And they seem not to break; though once they are bowed   15
So low for long, they never right themselves:
You may see their trunks arching in the woods
Years afterwards, trailing their leaves on the ground
Like girls on hands and knees that throw their hair
Before them over their heads to dry in the sun.   20
But I was going to say when Truth broke in
With all her matter-of-fact about the ice-storm
I should prefer to have some boy bend them
As he went out and in to fetch the cows—
Some boy too far from town to learn baseball,   25
Whose only play was what he found himself,
Summer or winter, and could play alone.
One by one he subdued his father's trees
By riding them down over and over again
Until he took the stiffness out of them,   30
And not one but hung limp, not one was left
For him to conquer. He learned all there was
To learn about not launching out too soon
And so not carrying the tree away
Clear to the ground. He always kept his poise   35
To the top branches, climbing carefully
With the same pains you use to fill a cup
Up to the brim, and even above the brim.
Then he flung outward, feet first, with a swish,
Kicking his way down through the air to the ground.   40
So was I once myself a swinger of birches.
And so I dream of going back to be.
It's when I'm weary of considerations,
And life is too much like a pathless wood
Where your face burns and tickles with the cobwebs   45
Broken across it, and one eye is weeping
From a twig's having lashed across it open.
I'd like to get away from earth awhile
And then come back to it and begin over.
May no fate willfully misunderstand me   50
And half grant what I wish and snatch me away
Not to return. Earth's the right place for love:
I don't know where it's likely to go better.
I'd like to go by climbing a birch tree,

>> Birches heavy with snow

And climb black branches up a snow-white trunk   55
Toward Heaven, till the tree could bear no more,
But dipped its top and set me down again.
That would be good both going and coming back.
One could do worse than be a swinger of birches.

EXPLORE ONLINE >

To listen to audio of "Traveling through the Dark,"
visit your Literature CourseMate, accessed through
www.cengagebrain.com.

William Stafford (1914–1993)

Traveling through the Dark (1962)

Traveling through the dark I found a deer
dead on the edge of the Wilson River road.
It is usually best to roll them into the canyon:
that road is narrow; to swerve might make more dead.

By glow of the tail-light I stumbled back of the car   5
and stood by the heap, a doe, a recent killing;
she had stiffened already, almost cold.
I dragged her off; she was large in the belly.

My fingers touching her side brought me the reason—
her side was warm; her fawn lay there waiting,   10
alive, still, never to be born.
Beside that mountain road I hesitated.

The car aimed ahead its lowered parking lights;
under the hood purred the steady engine.
I stood in the glare of the warm exhaust turning red;   15
around our group I could hear the wilderness listen.

I thought hard for us all—my only swerving—
then pushed her over the edge into the river.

>> Dead deer at side of road

Carl Sandburg (1878–1967)

Fog (1916)

The fog comes
on little cat feet.
It sits looking
over harbor and city
on silent haunches   5
and then moves on.

Related Works

"Snow" (p. 101), "Doe Season" (p. 290), "Greasy Lake" (p. 306), "Nothing
Gold Can Stay" (p. 404), "Blackberry Eating" (p. 439), "Four Haiku" (p. 453)

LO3 Evaluate Poems about Love

Since the earliest times, romantic love has been one of the great themes of poetry. In the European tradition, Sappho, whose works exist largely in fragments, is one of the early classic Greek poets. Even more influential, in part because most of their works survived, were the Romans Catullus and Ovid. Although the Bible may strike some as an unlikely place to find love poetry, the *Song of Songs* is just that (although it is also commonly interpreted as an allegory of the love between God and his people). In *La Vita Nuova* (*The New Life*), Dante wrote about the life-changing effect of his meeting with Beatrice, a beautiful young woman who was to die young. It is this same Beatrice with whose help Dante embarks on his journey from hell to heaven in *The Divine Comedy*.

Love has played an equally important part in English poetry. During the Middle Ages, poems such as *Sir Gawain and the Green Knight* and *Le Morte d'Arthur* employed the conventions of "courtly love," in which a protagonist performs gallant deeds to win the hand of a fair maiden. Examples of Renaissance love poems include many of the sonnets of William Shakespeare and Edmund Spenser. Christopher Marlowe's "The Passionate Shepherd to His Love" (p. 513) was answered by Sir Walter Raleigh's "The Nymph's Reply to the Shepherd" (p. 516). Andrew Marvel produced a seduction poem on much the same theme with "To His Coy Mistress" (p. 419).

Although the Renaissance may arguably be considered the high point of love poetry in English, the tradition has continued to the present day. Increased opportunities for women to read, write, and publish poetry have brought new perspectives to what was once a male-dominated field. Confessional poetry has allowed a more direct, frank discussion of love. And, of course, love songs today are as much in fashion as they were in the time of Shakespeare, Dante, or Sappho—and heard by more people than ever.

In each of the poems in this section, the poets address the subject of love in their own styles and voices. Robert Browning and Elizabeth Barrett Browning (who were married to each other) are represented with traditional love poems, including "Meeting at Night," "Parting at Morning," and "How Do I Love Thee?" (which is one of the most often quoted poems in the English language). In Edna St. Vincent Millay's "What Lips My Lips Have Kissed," the speaker reminisces about her past lovers with a mixture of nostalgia and wistfulness. On a lighter note, Dorothy Parker's "General Review of the Sex Situation" is a tongue-in-cheek explanation of the differences between the sexes.

Robert Browning (1812–1889)

Meeting at Night (1845)

The gray sea and the long black land;
And the yellow half-moon large and low;
And the startled little waves that leap
In fiery ringlets from their sleep,
As I gain the cove with pushing prow,   5
And quench its speed i' the slushy sand.

Then a mile of warm sea-scented beach;
Three fields to cross till a farm appears;
A tap at the pane, the quick sharp scratch
And blue spurt of a lighted match,   10
And a voice less loud, through its joys and fears,
Than the two hearts beating each to each!

Parting at Morning (1845)

Round the cape of a sudden came the sea,
And the sun looked over the mountain's rim:
And straight was a path of gold for him,
And the need of a world of men for me.

>> Twelfth-century tapestry illustrating courtly love

Prisma Archive/Alamy

Elizabeth Barrett Browning (1806–1861)

How Do I Love Thee? (1850)

How do I love thee? Let me count the ways.
I love thee to the depth and breadth and height
My soul can reach, when feeling out of sight
For the ends of being and ideal grace.
I love thee to the level of every day's   5
Most quiet need, by sun and candle-light.
I love thee freely, as men strive for right.
I love thee purely, as they turn from praise.
I love thee with the passion put to use
In my old griefs, and with my childhood's faith.   10
I love thee with a love I seemed to lose
With my lost saints. I love thee with the breath,
Smiles, tears, of all my life; and, if God choose,
I shall but love thee better after death.

Edna St. Vincent Millay (1892–1950)

What Lips My Lips Have Kissed (1923)

What lips my lips have kissed, and where, and why,
I have forgotten, and what arms have lain
Under my head till morning; but the rain
Is full of ghosts tonight, that tap and sigh
Upon the glass and listen for reply,   5
And in my heart there stirs a quiet pain
For unremembered lads that not again
Will turn to me at midnight with a cry.
Thus in the winter stands the lonely tree,
Nor knows what birds have vanished one by one,   10
Yet knows its boughs more silent than before:
I cannot say what loves have come and gone,
I only know that summer sang in me
A little while, that in me sings no more.

Dorothy Parker (1893–1967)

General Review of the Sex Situation (1933)

Woman wants monogamy;
Man delights in novelty.
Love is woman's moon and sun;
Man has other forms of fun.

Woman lives but in her lord;   5
Count to ten, and man is bored.
With this the gist and sum of it,
What earthly good can come of it?

Related Works

"Hills Like White Elephants" (p. 96), "Love and Other Catastrophes: A Mix Tape" (p. 103), "The Storm" (p. 154), "Living in Sin" (p. 386), "My mistress' eyes are nothing like the sun" (p. 405), "Shall I compare thee to a summer's day?" (p. 408), "A Valediction: Forbidding Mourning" (p. 414), "You fit into me" (p. 421), *The Brute* (p. 532)

LO4 Evaluate Poems about War

In poetry, war is as ancient a theme as love and nature. In fact, the earliest poems, including Homer's *Iliad* and *Odyssey* and Virgil's *Aeneid*, have at their centers epic battles and struggles. These poems were created in metered verse so they could be remembered and passed down from one generation to the next. Portions of them would be recited at public gatherings and festivals, making them analogous to the war movies of today. Epic poems reflected the belief that war could be a noble and glorious endeavor, and they often glorified the heroes of the wars and battles they described. Even in the earliest of these poems, however, there is a sense of the futility and devastation that war brings with it; for example, in the *Iliad,* many of the Greeks laying siege to the city of Troy are sick of the war and want to go home. In the *Aeneid,* the scene where Aeneas witnesses the destruction of his native Troy by the Greeks, and by the gods aiding them, is one of the most moving in literature.

In modern times, poets have tended to concentrate on the horrors of war, no doubt in part because technology has allowed armies to do more damage more quickly than ever before. World War I, which saw the first widespread use of aircraft, poison gas, and machine guns in warfare, marked a turning point in war and in poetic responses to it. One of the best-known poems to come out of this war is "Dulce et Decorum Est," written toward the end of the war by Wilfred Owen, a soldier who was killed on the Western Front in 1918. The poem, which includes graphic images of war, ends with a bitterly ironic quotation that summarizes the mentality that fuels war: "It is sweet and fitting to die for one's country."

Of course, not all modern poems about war are poems of protest. Robert Lowell's "For the Union Dead," written in 1959, is an elegy for Colonel Robert Gould Shaw, the leader of a regiment of African-American soldiers who fought and died for the Union Army during the Civil War. And "The Soldier," by Rupert Brooke (a contemporary of Wilfred Owen), celebrates the nobility of fighting for the sake of one's beloved country.

Although war poems tend to focus on death and destruction, in modern poems, the victims of war are not always soldiers. In the post–World War II years, enemies (like victims) were not as clearly defined as they had been in the past. The war in Vietnam unfolded before the American people on their television screens, and as a result, many Americans questioned the war and its goals. This skepticism carried over into poems about the war, as seen in Denise Levertov's "What Were They Like?" (a call and response poem that asks questions about the people in Vietnam in an effort to heighten their humanity and diminish their identity as "the enemy") and in Yusef Komunyakaa's "Facing It," in which a Vietnam veteran visits the Vietnam War Memorial in Washington.

Rupert Brooke (1887–1915)

The Soldier (1915)

If I should die, think only this of me;
  That there's some corner of a foreign field
That is forever England. There shall be
  In that rich earth a richer dust concealed;
A dust whom England bore, shaped, made aware,   5
  Gave, once, her flowers to love, her ways to roam,
A body of England's breathing English air,

  Washed by the rivers, blest by suns of home.
And think, this heart, all evil shed away,
   A pulse in the eternal mind, no less   10
    Gives somewhere back the thoughts by England given;
Her sights and sounds; dreams happy as her day;
  And laughter, learnt of friends; and gentleness,
    In hearts at peace, under an English heaven.

>> British soldier, World War I

Wilfred Owen (1893–1918)

Dulce et Decorum Est° (1920)

Bent double, like old beggars under sacks,
Knock-kneed, coughing like hags, we cursed through sludge,
Till on the haunting flares we turned our backs
And towards our distant rest began to trudge.
Men marched asleep. Many had lost their boots   5
But limped on, blood-shod. All went lame; all blind;
Drunk with fatigue; deaf even to the hoots
Of tired, outstripped Five-Nines° that dropped behind.

Gas! GAS Quick, boys!—An ecstasy of fumbling,
Fitting the clumsy helmets just in time;   10
But someone still was yelling out and stumbling
And flound'ring like a man in fire or lime . . .
Dim, through the misty panes and thick green light,

As under a green sea, I saw him drowning.
In all my dreams, before my helpless sight,   15
He plunges at me, guttering, choking, drowning.

If in some smothering dreams you too could pace
Behind the wagon that we flung him in,
And watch the white eyes writhing in his face,
His hanging face, like a devil's sick of sin;   20
If you could hear, at every jolt, the blood
Come gargling from the froth-corrupted lungs,
Obscene as cancer, bitter as the cud
Of vile, incurable sores on innocent tongues,—
My friend, you would not tell with such high zest   25
To children ardent for some desperate glory,
The old Lie: Dulce et decorum est
Pro patria mori.

>> Gas attack, 1918

° **Dulce et Decorum Est** The title and last two lines are from Horace, *Odes* 3.2: "Sweet and fitting it is to die for one's country."

° **Five-Nines** Shells that explode on impact and release poison gas.

Robert Lowell (1917–1977)

For the Union Dead (1959)

"Relinquunt omnia servare rem publicam."°

The old South Boston Aquarium stands
in a Sahara of snow now. Its broken windows are boarded.
The bronze weathervane cod has lost half its scales.
The airy tanks are dry.

Once my nose crawled like a snail on the glass;   5
my hand tingled
to burst the bubbles
drifting from the noses of the cowed, compliant fish.

My hand draws back. I often sigh still
for the dark downward and vegetating kingdom   10
of the fish and reptile. One morning last March,
I pressed against the new barbed and galvanized

° *Relinquunt omnia servare rem publicam* "They gave up everything to preserve the Republic" (Latin). A monument in Boston Common bears a similar form of this quotation. Designed by Augustus Saint-Gaudens, the monument is dedicated to Colonel Robert Gould Shaw, a white officer, and the African-American troops he commanded during a Civil War battle at Fort Wagner, South Carolina, on July 18, 1863.

fence on the Boston Common. Behind their cage,
yellow dinosaur steamshovels were grunting
as they cropped up tons of mush and grass   15
to gouge their underworld garage.

Parking spaces luxuriate like civic
sandpiles in the heart of Boston.
A girdle of orange, Puritan-pumpkin colored girders
braces the tingling Statehouse,   20

shaking over the excavations, as it faces Colonel Shaw
and his bell-cheeked Negro infantry
on St. Gauden's shaking Civil War relief,
propped by a plant splint against the garage's earthquake.

Two months after marching through Boston,   25
half the regiment was dead;
at the dedication,
William James° could almost hear the bronze Negroes breathe.

Their monument sticks like a fishbone
in the city's throat.   30
Its Colonel is as lean
as a compass-needle.

He has an angry wrenlike vigilance,
a greyhound's gentle tautness;
he seems to wince at pleasure,   35
and suffocate for privacy.

He is out of bounds now. He rejoices in man's lovely,
peculiar power to choose life and die—
when he leads his black soldiers to death,
he cannot bend his back.   40

On a thousand small town New England greens,
the old white churches hold their air
of sparse, sincere rebellion; frayed flags
quilt the graveyards of the Grand Army of the
    Republic.

The stone statues of the abstract Union Soldier   45
grow slimmer and younger each year—
wasp-waisted, they doze over muskets
and muse through their sideburns . . .

Shaw's father wanted no monument
except the ditch,   50
where his son's body was thrown
and lost with his "niggers."

The ditch is nearer.
There are no statues for the last war here;
on Boylston Street, a commercial photograph   55
shows Hiroshima boiling

>> Detail of Robert Gould Shaw memorial,
Boston, MA

° **William James** Harvard
psychologist and philosopher
(1842–1910), often called the
father of modern psychology.

over a Mosler Safe,° the "Rock of Ages"
that survived the blast. Space is nearer.
When I crouch to my television set,
the drained faces of Negro school-children rise like balloons.   60

Colonel Shaw
is riding on his bubble,
he waits
for the blessed break.

The Aquarium is gone. Everywhere,   65
giant finned cars nose forward like fish;
a savage servility
slides by on grease.

° **Mosler Safe** A brand of
safe known for being
especially strong.

Denise Levertov (1923–1997)

What Were They Like? (1966)

1)   Did the people of Viet Nam
      use lanterns of stone?
2)   Did they hold ceremonies
      to reverence the opening of buds?
3)   Were they inclined to rippling laughter?   5
4)   Did they use bone and ivory,
      jade and silver, for ornament?
5)   Had they an epic poem?
6)   Did they distinguish between speech and singing?

1)   Sir, their light hearts turned to stone.   10
      It is not remembered whether in gardens
      stone lanterns illumined pleasant ways.
2)   Perhaps they gathered once to delight in blossom,
      but after the children were killed
      there were no more buds.   15
3)   Sir, laughter is bitter to the burned mouth.
4)   A dream ago, perhaps. Ornament is for joy.
      All the bones were charred.
5)   It is not remembered. Remember,
      most were peasants; their life   20
      was in rice and bamboo.
      When peaceful clouds were reflected in the paddies
      and the water buffalo stepped surely along terraces,
      maybe fathers told their sons old tales.
      When bombs smashed the mirrors   25
      there was time only to scream.
6)   There is an echo yet, it is said,
      of their speech which was like a song.
      It is reported their singing resembled
      the flight of moths in moonlight.   30
      Who can say? It is silent now.

>> Peasants harvesting
rice, Vietnam

Yusef Komunyakaa (1947–   )

Facing It (1988)

© Dan Getsug

My black face fades,
hiding inside the black granite.
I said I wouldn't,
dammit: No tears.
I'm stone. I'm flesh.   5
My clouded reflection eyes me
like a bird of prey, the profile of night
slanted against morning. I turn
this way—the stone lets me go.
I turn that way—I'm inside   10
the Vietnam Veterans Memorial
again, depending on the light
to make a difference.
I go down the 58,022 names,
half-expecting to find   15
my own in letters like smoke.
I touch the name Andrew Johnson;
I see the booby trap's white flash.
Names shimmer on a woman's blouse
but when she walks away   20
the names stay on the wall.
Brushstrokes flash, a red bird's
wings cutting across my stare.
The sky. A plane in the sky.
A white vet's image floats   25
closer to me, then his pale eyes
look through mine. I'm a window.
He's lost his right arm
inside the stone. In the black mirror
a woman's trying to erase names: 30
No, she's brushing a boy's hair.

© AP Photo/Dennis Cook

>> Hand tracing names of
dead on the Vietnam
War Memorial

Related Works

"Buffalo Soldiers" (p. 105), "The Things They Carried" (p. 232),
"The Man He Killed" (p. 370), "Patterns" (p. 370), "The Death of
the Ball Turret Gunner" (p. 413), *Nine Ten* (p. 553)

Writing Suggestions: Discovering Themes in Poetry

1. Compare any two poems in this chapter about parents, nature, love, or war.

2. Write an **explication** of one of the poems in this chapter.

3. Write an essay in which you compare one of the poems in this chapter to a short story or play on the same general subject. (For possible topics, consult the Related Works list that follows each group of poems.)

4. Some poets write multiple poems on the same general subject. For example, Shakespeare wrote many love poems, and Robert Frost wrote a number of poems about nature. Choose two poems by a single poet that explore the same subject, and compare and contrast the themes of the two poems.

5. A number of poems in this book focus on the theme of poetry itself. Choose three poems on this theme, and write an essay that compares the poems' ideas about reading and writing poetry

Glossary Terms

carpe diem "Seize the day"; the philosophy arguing that one should enjoy life today before it passes by.

pastoral Literary work that deals nostalgically (and usually unrealistically) with a simple, preindustrial rural life; the name comes from the fact that traditionally pastorals feature shepherds.

romanticism Eighteenth- and nineteenth-century literary movement that valued subjectivity, individuality, the imagination, nature, excess, the exotic, and the mysterious.

theme Central or dominant idea of a work of literature.

29

Poetry for Further Reading

Learning Outcomes

After reading this chapter, you should be able to do the following:

LO1 Appreciate different kinds of poetry

Timeline

1600 Marlowe, "The Passionate Shepherd to His Love"

1600 Raleigh, "The Nymph's Reply to the Shepherd"

1609 Shakespeare, "Not marble, nor the gilded monuments"

c. 1610 Donne, "Death Be Not Proud"

Wordsworth, "London, 1802" **1802**

Coleridge, "Kubla Khan" **1797–98**

Blake, "The Lamb" **1789**

Wheatley, "On Being Brought from Africa to America" **1773**

1815 Gordon, Lord Byron, "She Walks in Beauty"

1819 Keats, "Ode on a Grecian Urn"

1820 Shelley, "Ode to the West Wind"

Whitman from "Song of Myself" **1855**

1863 Dickinson, "Because I could not stop for Death—"

1867 Arnold, "Dover Beach"

Eliot, "The Love Song of J. Alfred Prufrock" **1917**

Robinson, "Richard Cory" **1897**

Frost "Mend-ing Wall" **1914**

Butler Yeats, "The Lake Isle of Innisfree" **1892**

1922 McKay, "If We Must Die"

1923 Stevens, "The Emperor of Ice-Cream"

1926 MacLeish, "Ars Poetica"

Sanchez, "right on: white america" **1970**

Plath, "Mirror" **1963**

Hughes, "Theme for English B" **1949**

1973 Piercy, "Barbie doll"

1983 Olds, "The One Girl at the Boys' Party"

1984 Erdrich, "Indian Boarding School: The Runaways"

1988 Collins, "Introduction to Poetry"

1600

1800

1880

1960

Massachusetts declares slavery illegal. **1783**

The poet Anne Bradstreet arrives in New England. **1630**

1633 Galileo Galilei is tried by the Inquisition.

The Elgin Marbles are first displayed in the British Museum. **1817**

1593 Christopher Marlowe is stabbed to death.

Psychiatrist Sigmund Freud is born. **1856**

President Lincoln issues the Emancipation Proclamation, freeing all slaves in the Confederate states. **1862**

The Klondike Bar is introduced. **1922**

Adolf Hitler publishes *Mein Kampf* (*My Struggle*). **1925**

President Harry S. Truman announces that the Soviet Union has developed an atomic bomb. **1949**

The Samaritans are founded to provide help to those contemplating suicide. **1953**

Betty Friedan publishes *The Feminine Mystique*. **1963**

1983 Martin Luther King Jr. Day becomes a federal holiday.

1972 Title IX of the Educational Amendments of 1972 bans sex discrimination in public higher education

1971 Malibu Barbie is introduced.

EXPLORE ONLINE >

To listen to audio, or an instructor podcast of "Dover Beach,"
visit your Literature CourseMate, accessed through
www.cengagebrain.com.

Matthew Arnold (1822–1888)

Dover Beach (1867)

The sea is calm tonight.
The tide is full, the moon lies fair
Upon the straits;—on the French coast the light
Gleams and is gone; the cliffs of England stand,
Glimmering and vast, out in the tranquil bay.   5
Come to the window, sweet is the night-air!
Only, from the long line of spray
Where the sea meets the moon-blanched° land,
Listen! you hear the grating roar
Of pebbles which the waves draw back, and fling,   10
At their return, up the high strand,°
Begin, and cease, and then again begin,
With tremulous cadence slow, and bring
The eternal note of sadness in.

Sophocles° long ago   15
Heard it on the Aegean,° and it brought
Into his mind the turbid ebb and flow
Of human misery; we
Find also in the sound a thought,
Hearing it by this distant northern sea.   20

The Sea of Faith
Was once, too, at the full, and round earth's shore
Lay like the folds of a bright girdle furled.
But now I only hear
Its melancholy, long, withdrawing roar,   25
Retreating, to the breath
Of the night-wind, down the vast edges drear
And naked shingles° of the world.

Ah, love, let us be true
To one another! for the world, which seems   30
To lie before us like a land of dreams,
So various, so beautiful, so new,
Hath really neither joy, nor love, nor light,
Nor certitude, nor peace, nor help for pain;
And we are here as on a darkling° plain   35
Swept with confused alarms of struggle and flight,
Where ignorant armies clash by night.

°**moon-blanched** Whitened
by moonlight.

°**strand** Beach

°**Sophocles** Greek
playwright (496–406 B.C.),
author of tragedies such as
Oedipus the King and
Antigone.

°**Aegean** Sea between
Greece and Turkey.

°**shingles** Gravel beaches.

°**darkling** Darkening.

William Blake (1757–1827)

The Lamb (1789)

Little Lamb, who made thee?
  Dost thou know who made thee?
Gave thee life & bid thee feed,
By the stream & o'er the mead;
Gave thee clothing of delight,   5
Softest clothing wooly bright;
Gave thee such a tender voice,
Making all the vales rejoice!
  Little Lamb who made thee?
  Dost thou know who made thee?   10

  Little Lamb I'll tell thee,
  Little Lamb I'll tell thee!
He is calléd by thy name,
For he calls himself a Lamb:
He is meek & he is mild,   15
He became a little child:
I a child & thou a lamb,
We are calléd by his name.
  Little Lamb God bless thee.
  Little Lamb God bless thee.   20

William Blake (1757–1827)

To see a World in a Grain of Sand (1803)

To see a World in a Grain of Sand
And a Heaven in a Wild Flower,
Hold Infinity in the palm of your hand
And Eternity in an hour.

William Blake (1757–1827)

The Tyger (1794)

Tyger! Tyger! burning bright
In the forests of the night,
What immortal hand or eye
Could frame thy fearful symmetry?

In what distant deeps or skies   5
Burnt the fire of thine eyes?
On what wings dare he aspire?
What the hand dare seize the fire?

And what shoulder, and what art,
Could twist the sinews of thy heart?   10
And when thy heart began to beat,
What dread hand? and what dread feet?

What the hammer? what the chain?
In what furnace was thy brain?
What the anvil? what dread grasp   15
Dare its deadly terrors clasp?

When the stars threw down their spears,
And watered heaven with their tears,
Did he smile his work to see?
Did he who made the Lamb make thee?   20

Tyger! Tyger! burning bright
In the forests of the night,
What immortal hand or eye
Dare frame thy fearful symmetry?

George Gordon, Lord Byron (1788–1824)

She Walks in Beauty (1815)

1

She walks in beauty, like the night
   Of cloudless climes and starry skies;
And all that's best of dark and bright
   Meet in her aspect and her eyes:
Thus mellowed to that tender light   5
   Which heaven to gaudy day denies.

2

One shade the more, one ray the less,
   Had half impaired the nameless grace
Which waves in every raven tress,
   Or softly lightens o'er her face;   10
Where thoughts serenely sweet express
   How pure, how dear their dwelling place.

3

And on that cheek, and o'er that brow,
   So soft, so calm, yet eloquent,
The smiles that win, the tints that glow,   15
   But tell of days in goodness spent,
A mind at peace with all below,
   A heart whose love is innocent!

Samuel Taylor Coleridge (1772–1834)

Kubla Khan° (1797, 1798)

Or, a Vision in a Dream. A Fragment.

In Xanadu did Kubla Khan
A stately pleasure-dome decree:
Where Alph,° the sacred river, ran
Through caverns measureless to man
Down to a sunless sea.   5

° **Kubla Khan** Coleridge mythologizes the actual Kublai Khan, a thirteenth-century Mongol emperor, as well as the Chinese city of Xanadu.

° **Alph** Probably derived from the Greek river Alpheus, whose waters, according to legend, rose from the Ionian Sea in Sicily as the fountain of Arethusa.

EXPLORE ONLINE >

To listen to audio of "Kubla Kahn," visit your
Literature CourseMate, accessed through
www.cengagebrain.com.

So twice five miles of fertile ground
With walls and towers were girdled round;
And there were gardens bright with sinuous rills,
Where blossomed many an incense-bearing tree;
And here were forests ancient as the hills,   10
Enfolding sunny spots of greenery.

But oh! that deep romantic chasm which slanted
Down the green hill athwart a cedarn cover!
A savage place! as holy and enchanted
As e'er beneath a waning moon was haunted   15
By woman wailing for her demon-lover!
And from this chasm, with ceaseless turmoil seething,
As if this earth in fast thick pants were breathing,
A mighty fountain momently was forced:
Amid whose swift half-intermitted burst   20
Huge fragments vaulted like rebounding hail,
Or chaffy grain beneath the thresher's flail:
And 'mid these dancing rocks at once and ever
It flung up momently the sacred river.
Five miles meandering with a mazy motion   25
Through wood and dale the sacred river ran,
Then reached the caverns measureless to man,
And sank in tumult to a lifeless ocean:
And 'mid this tumult Kubla heard from far
Ancestral voices prophesying war!   30

   The shadow of the dome of pleasure
   Floated midway on the waves;
   Where was heard the mingled measure
   From the fountain and the caves.
It was a miracle of rare device,   35
A sunny pleasure-dome with caves of ice!

   A damsel with a dulcimer
   In a vision once I saw:
   It was an Abyssinian maid,
   And on her dulcimer she played,   40
   Singing of Mount Abora.°
   Could I revive within me
   Her symphony and song,
   To such a deep delight 'twould win me,
That with music loud and long,   45
I would build that dome in air,
That sunny dome! those caves of ice!
And all who heard should see them there,
And all should cry, Beware! Beware!
His flashing eyes, his floating hair!   50
Weave a circle round him thrice,°
And close your eyes with holy dread,
For he on honey-dew hath fed,
And drunk the milk of Paradise.

° **Mount Abora** Some
scholars see a reminiscence
here of John Milton's *Paradise
Lost* 4.280–82: "where
Abassin kings their issue
guard / Mount Amara,
though this by some
supposed / True Paradise
under the Ethiop Line."

° **Weave . . . thrice** A magic
ritual to keep away intruding
spirits.

Billy Collins (1941–   )

Introduction to Poetry (1988)

I ask them to take a poem
and hold it up to the light
like a color slide

or press an ear against its hive.

I say drop a mouse into a poem   5
and watch him probe his way out,

or walk inside the poem's room
and feel the walls for a light switch.

I want them to waterski
across the surface of a poem   10
waving at the author's name on the shore.

But all they want to do
is tie the poem to a chair with rope
and torture a confession out of it.

They begin beating it with a hose   15
to find out what it really means.

Emily Dickinson (1830–1886)

Because I could not stop for Death— (1863)

Because I could not stop for Death—
He kindly stopped for me—
The Carriage held but just Ourselves—
And Immortality.

We slowly drove—He knew no haste   5
And I had put away
My labor and my leisure too,
For His Civility—

We passed the School, where Children strove
At Recess—in the Ring—   10
We passed the Fields of Gazing Grain—
We passed the Setting Sun—

Or rather—He passed Us—
The Dews drew quivering and chill—
For only Gossamer, my Gown—   15
My Tippet°—only Tulle—

We passed before a House that seemed
A Swelling of the Ground—
The Roof was scarcely visible—
The Cornice—in the Ground—   20

Since then—'tis Centuries—and yet
Feels shorter than the Day
I first surmised the Horses' Heads
Were toward Eternity—

° **Tippet** A short cape or
scarf.

Emily Dickinson (1830–1886)

"Faith" is a fine invention (1860)

"Faith" is a fine invention
When Gentlemen can see—
But *Microscopes* are prudent
In an Emergency.

Emily Dickinson (1830–1886)

I heard a Fly buzz—when I died— (1862)

I heard a Fly buzz—when I died—
The Stillness in the Room
Was like the Stillness in the Air—
Between the Heaves of Storm—

The Eyes around—had wrung them dry—   5
And Breaths were gathering firm
For that last Onset—when the King
Be witnessed—in the Room—

I willed my Keepsakes—Signed away
What portion of me be   10
Assignable—and then it was
There interposed a Fly—

With Blue—uncertain stumbling Buzz—
Between the light—and me—
And then the Windows failed—and then   15
I could not see to see—

John Donne (1572–1631)

Death Be Not Proud (c. 1610)

Death be not proud, though some have callèd thee
Mighty and dreadful, for thou art not so;
For those whom thou think'st thou dost overthrow
Die not, poor death, nor yet canst thou kill me.
From rest and sleep, which but thy pictures be,   5
Much pleasure, then from thee much more must flow,
And soonest our best men with thee do go,
Rest of their bones, and soul's delivery.
Thou art slave to fate, chance, kings, and desperate men,
And dost with poison, war, and sickness dwell,   10
And poppy, or charms can make us sleep as well,
And better than thy stroke; why swell'st thou then?
One short sleep past, we wake eternally,
And death shall be no more; death, thou shalt die.

EXPLORE ONLINE >
To listen to audio of "Death Be Not Proud," visit your Literature CourseMate, accessed through www.cengagebrain.com.

John Donne (1572–1631)

The Flea (1633)

Mark but this flea, and mark in this°
How little that which thou deny'st me is;
It sucked me first, and now sucks thee,
And in this flea our two bloods mingled be;
Thou know'st that this cannot be said   5
A sin, nor shame, nor loss of maidenhead,
    Yet this enjoys before it woo,
    And pampered swells with one blood made of two,
    And this, alas, is more than we would do.°

Oh stay, three lives in one flea spare,   10
Where we almost, yea more than, married are.
This flea is you and I, and this
Our marriage bed, and marriage temple is;
Though parents grudge, and you, we're met
And cloistered in these living walls of jet.   15
    Though use make you apt to kill me,
    Let not to that, self-murder added be,
    And sacrilege, three sins in killing three.

Cruel and sudden, hast thou since
Purpled thy nail in blood of innocence?   20
Wherein could this flea guilty be,
Except in that drop which it sucked from thee?
Yet thou triumph'st, and say'st that thou
Find'st not thyself, nor me, the weaker now;   25
    'Tis true; then learn how false, fears be;
    Just so much honor, when thou yield'st to me,
    Will waste, as this flea's death took life from thee.

° **mark in this** Note the moral lesson in it.

° **more than we would do** If we do not join our blood.

T. S. Eliot (1888–1965)

The Love Song of J. Alfred Prufrock (1917)

S'io credessi che mia risposta fosse
A persona che mai tornasse al mondo,
Questa fiamma staria senza piu scosse.
Ma perciocche giammai di questo fondo
Non torno vivo alcun, s'i'odo il vero,
Senza tema d'infamia ti rispondo.°

° **S'io ... rispondo** The epigraph is from Dante's *Inferno*, Canto 27. In response to the poet's question about his identity, Guido da Montefelto, who for his sin of fraud must spend eternity wrapped in flames, replies: "If I thought that I was speaking to someone who could go back to the world, this flame would shake me no more. But since from this place nobody ever returns alive, if what I hear is true, I answer you without fear of infamy."

Let us go then, you and I,
When the evening is spread out against the sky
Like a patient etherized upon a table;
Let us go, through certain half-deserted streets,
The muttering retreats   5
Of restless nights in one-night cheap hotels
And sawdust restaurants with oyster-shells:
Streets that follow like a tedious argument
Of insidious intent
To lead you to an overwhelming question . . .   10
Oh, do not ask, "What is it?"
Let us go and make our visit.

In the room the women come and go
Talking of Michelangelo.

The yellow fog that rubs its back upon the window-panes,   15
The yellow smoke that rubs its muzzle on the window-panes
Licked its tongue into the corners of the evening,
Lingered upon the pools that stand in drains,
Let fall upon its back the soot that falls from chimneys,
Slipped by the terrace, made a sudden leap,   20
And seeing that it was a soft October night,
Curled once about the house, and fell asleep.

And indeed there will be time
For the yellow smoke that slides along the street,
Rubbing its back upon the window-panes;   25
There will be time, there will be time
To prepare a face to meet the faces that you meet;
There will be time to murder and create,
And time for all the works and days° of hands
That lift and drop a question on your plate;   30
Time for you and time for me,
And time yet for a hundred indecisions,
And for a hundred visions and revisions,
Before the taking of a toast and tea.

In the room the women come and go   35
Talking of Michelangelo.

And indeed there will be time
To wonder, "Do I dare?" and, "Do I dare?"
Time to turn back and descend the stair,
With a bald spot in the middle of my hair—   40
(They will say: "How his hair is growing thin!")
My morning coat, my collar mounting firmly to the chin,
My necktie rich and modest, but asserted by a simple pin—
(They will say: "But how his arms and legs are thin!")
Do I dare   45
Disturb the universe?
In a minute there is time
For decisions and revisions which a minute will reverse.

For I have known them all already, known them all—
Have known the evenings, mornings, afternoons,   50
I have measured out my life with coffee spoons;
I know the voices dying with a dying fall°
Beneath the music from a farther room.
    So how should I presume?

And I have known the eyes already, known them all—   55
The eyes that fix you in a formulated phrase,
And when I am formulated, sprawling on a pin,
When I am pinned and wriggling on the wall,

° **works and days:** *Works
and Days*, by the eighth-
century B.C. Greek poet
Hesiod, is a poem that
celebrates farm life.

° **dying fall** An allusion to
Orsino's speech in *Twelfth
Night* (1.1): "That strain again!
It had a dying fall."

Then how should I begin
To spit out all the butt-ends of my days and ways?   60
  And how should I presume?

And I have known the arms already, known them all—
Arms that are braceleted and white and bare
(But in the lamplight, downed with light brown hair!)
Is it perfume from a dress   65
That makes me so digress?
Arms that lie along a table, or wrap about a shawl.
  And should I then presume?
  And how should I begin?

                         *   *   *

Shall I say, I have gone at dusk through narrow streets   70
And watched the smoke that rises from the pipes
Of lonely men in shirt-sleeves, leaning out of windows? . . .

I should have been a pair of ragged claws
Scuttling across the floors of silent seas.

                         *   *   *

And the afternoon, the evening, sleeps so peacefully!   75
Smoothed by long fingers,
Asleep . . . tired . . . or it malingers,
Stretched on the floor, here beside you and me.
Should I, after tea and cakes and ices,
Have the strength to force the moment to its crisis?   80
But though I have wept and fasted, wept and prayed,
Though I have seen my head (grown slightly bald) brought in
  upon a platter,°
I am no prophet—and here's no great matter;
I have seen the moment of my greatness flicker,
And I have seen the eternal Footman° hold my coat, and snicker,   85
And in short, I was afraid.

And would it have been worth it, after all,
After the cups, the marmalade, the tea,
Among the porcelain, among some talk of you and me,
Would it have been worth while,   90
To have bitten off the matter with a smile,
To have squeezed the universe into a ball
To roll it toward some overwhelming question,
To say: "I am Lazarus,° come from the dead,
Come back to tell you all, I shall tell you all"—   95
If one, settling a pillow by her head,
          Should say: "That is not what I meant at all.
          That is not it, at all."

And would it have been worth it, after all,
Would it have been worth while,   100
After the sunsets and the dooryards and the sprinkled streets,
After the novels, after the teacups, after the skirts that trail
  along the floor—
And this, and so much more?—
It is impossible to say just what I mean!

But as if a magic lantern threw the nerves in patterns on a screen: 105
Would it have been worth while
If one, settling a pillow or throwing off a shawl,
And turning toward the window, should say:
    "That is not it at all,
    That is not what I meant, at all."   110

                    *   *   *

No! I am not Prince Hamlet, nor was meant to be;
Am an attendant lord, one that will do
To swell a progress,° start a scene or two,
Advise the prince; no doubt, an easy tool,
Deferential, glad to be of use,   115
Politic, cautious, and meticulous;
Full of high sentence,° but a bit obtuse;
At times, indeed, almost ridiculous—
Almost, at times, the Fool.

I grow old . . . I grow old . . .   120
I shall wear the bottoms of my trousers rolled.

Shall I part my hair behind? Do I dare to eat a peach?
I shall wear white flannel trousers, and walk upon the beach.
I have heard the mermaids singing, each to each.

I do not think that they will sing to me.   125

I have seen them riding seaward on the waves
Combing the white hair of the waves blown back
When the wind blows the water white and black.

We have lingered in the chambers of the sea
By sea-girls wreathed with seaweed red and brown   130
Till human voices wake us, and we drown.

° **a progress** Here, in the Elizabethan sense of a royal journey.

° **sentence** Opinions.

Louise Erdrich (1954–   )

Indian Boarding School:
The Runaways (1984)

Home's the place we head for in our sleep.
Boxcars stumbling north in dreams
don't wait for us. We catch them on the run.
The rails, old lacerations that we love,
shoot parallel across the face and break   5
just under Turtle Mountains.° Riding scars
you can't get lost. Home is the place they cross.

The lame guard strikes a match and makes the dark
less tolerant. We watch through cracks in boards
as the land starts rolling, rolling till it hurts   10
to be here, cold in regulation clothes.
We know the sheriff's waiting at midrun
to take us back. His car is dumb and warm.

° **Turtle Mountains** Erdrich is a descendant of the Turtle Mountain band of the Chippewa.

The highway doesn't rock, it only hums
like a wing of long insults. The worn-down welts   15
of ancient punishments lead back and forth.

All runaways wear dresses, long green ones,
the color you would think shame was. We scrub
the sidewalks down because it's shameful work.
Our brushes cut the stone in watered arcs   20
and in the soak frail outlines shiver clear
a moment, things us kids pressed on the dark
face before it hardened, pale, remembering
delicate old injuries, the spines of names and leaves.

Robert Frost (1874–1963)

Mending Wall (1914)

Something there is that doesn't love a wall,
That sends the frozen-ground-swell under it,
And spills the upper boulders in the sun;
And makes gaps even two can pass abreast.
The work of hunters is another thing: 5
I have come after them and made repair
Where they have left not one stone on a stone,
But they would have the rabbit out of hiding,
To please the yelping dogs. The gaps I mean,
No one has seen them made or heard them made,   10
But at spring mending-time we find them there.
I let my neighbor know beyond the hill;
And on a day we meet to walk the line
And set the wall between us once again.
We keep the wall between us as we go.   15
To each the boulders that have fallen to each.
And some are loaves and some so nearly balls
We have to use a spell to make them balance:
"Stay where you are until our backs are turned!"
We wear our fingers rough with handling them.   20
Oh, just another kind of outdoor game,
One on a side. It comes to little more:
There where it is we do not need the wall:
He is all pine and I am apple orchard.
My apple trees will never get across   25
And eat the cones under his pines, I tell him.
He only says, "Good fences make good neighbors."
Spring is the mischief in me, and I wonder
If I could put a notion in his head:
"Why do they make good neighbors? Isn't it   30
Where there are cows? But here there are no cows.
Before I built a wall I'd ask to know
What I was walling in or walling out,
And to whom I was like to give offense.
Something there is that doesn't love a wall,   35
That wants it down." I could say "Elves" to him,
But it's not elves exactly, and I'd rather
He said it for himself. I see him there

Bringing a stone grasped firmly by the top
In each hand, like an old-stone savage armed.   40
He moves in darkness as it seems to me,
Not of woods only and the shade of trees.
He will not go behind his father's saying,
And he likes having thought of it so well
He says again, "Good fences make good neighbors."   45

Robert Frost (1874–1963)

The Road Not Taken (1915)

Two roads diverged in a yellow wood,
And sorry I could not travel both
And be one traveler, long I stood
And looked down one as far as I could
To where it bent in the undergrowth;   5

Then took the other, as just as fair,
And having perhaps the better claim,
Because it was grassy and wanted wear;
Though as for that the passing there
Had worn them really about the same,   10

And both that morning equally lay
In leaves no step had trodden black.
Oh, I kept the first for another day!
Yet knowing how way leads on to way,
I doubted if I should ever come back.   15

I shall be telling this with a sigh
Somewhere ages and ages hence:
Two roads diverged in a wood, and I—
I took the one less traveled by,
And that has made all the difference.   20

Robert Frost (1874–1963)

Stopping by Woods on a Snowy Evening (1923)

Whose woods these are I think I know.
His house is in the village though;
He will not see me stopping here
To watch his woods fill up with snow.

My little horse must think it queer   5
To stop without a farmhouse near
Between the woods and frozen lake
The darkest evening of the year.

He gives his harness bells a shake
To ask if there is some mistake.   10
The only other sound's the sweep
Of easy wind and downy flake.

The woods are lovely, dark and deep,
But I have promises to keep,
And miles to go before I sleep, 15
And miles to go before I sleep.

Langston Hughes (1902–1967)

Theme for English B (1949)

The instructor said,

> *Go home and write*
> *a page tonight.*
> *And let that page come out of you—*
> *Then, it will be true.* 5

I wonder if it's that simple?
I am twenty-two, colored, born in Winston-Salem.
I went to school there, then Durham, then here
to this college on the hill above Harlem.
I am the only colored student in my class. 10
The steps from the hill lead down into Harlem,
through a park, then I cross St. Nicholas,
Eighth Avenue, Seventh, and I come to the Y,
the Harlem Branch Y, where I take the elevator
up to my room, sit down and write this page: 15

It's not easy to know what is true for you or me
at twenty-two, my age. But I guess I'm what
I feel and see and hear, Harlem, I hear you:
hear you, hear me—we two—you, me, talk on this page.
(I hear New York, too) Me—who? 20
Well, I like to eat, sleep, drink, and be in love.
I like to work, read, learn, and understand life.
I like a pipe for a Christmas present,
or records—Bessie,° bop,° or Bach.
I guess being colored doesn't make me not like 25
the same things other folks like who are other races.
So will my page be colored that I write?
Being me, it will not be white.
But it will be
a part of you, instructor. 30
You are white—
yet a part of me, as I am a part of you.
That's American.
Sometimes perhaps you don't want to be a part of me.
Nor do I often want to be a part of you. 35
But we are, that's true!
As I learn from you,
I guess you learn from me—
although you're older—and white—
and somewhat more free. 40

This is my page for English B.

EXPLORE ONLINE >

To listen to audio for "Theme f[or]
English B," visit your Literature
CourseMate, accessed through
www.cengagebrain.com.

° **Bessie** Bessie Smith
(1894–1937), blues singer.

° **bop** Short for "bebop," a
jazz style developed in the
early 1940s by Charlie Parker,
Dizzy Gillespie, and others.

Langston Hughes (1902–1967)

The Negro Speaks of Rivers (1921)

I've known rivers:
I've known rivers ancient as the world and old as the flow of
    human blood in human veins.

My soul has grown deep like the rivers.

I bathed in the Euphrates° when dawns were young.   5
I built my hut near the Congo° and it lulled me to sleep.
I looked upon the Nile and raised the pyramids above it.
I heard the singing of the Mississippi when Abe Lincoln went
    down to New Orleans, and I've seen its muddy bosom turn
    all golden in the sunset.

I've known rivers:
Ancient, dusky rivers.

My soul has grown deep like the rivers.   10

° **Euphrates** Major river of southwest Asia; with the Tigris, the Euphrates forms a valley sometimes referred to as the "cradle of civilization."

° **Congo** River in equatorial Africa, the continent's second longest.

John Keats 1795–1821)

Ode on a Grecian Urn (1819)

1

Thou still unravish'd bride of quietness,
    Thou foster-child of silence and slow time,
Sylvan° historian, who canst thus express
A flowery tale more sweetly than our rhyme:
What leaf-fring'd legend haunts about thy shape   5
    Of deities or mortals, or of both,
        In Tempe° or the dales of Arcady?°
    What men or gods are these? What maidens loth?
What mad pursuit? What struggle to escape?
What pipes and timbrels? What wild ecstasy?   10

2

Heard melodies are sweet, but those unheard
    Are sweeter; therefore, ye soft pipes, play on;
Not to the sensual ear, but, more endear'd,
    Pipe to the spirit ditties of no tone:
Fair youth, beneath the trees, thou canst not leave   15
    Thy song, nor ever can those trees be bare;
        Bold lover, never, never canst thou kiss,
Though winning near the goal—yet, do not grieve;
    She cannot fade, though thou hast not thy bliss,
    For ever wilt thou love, and she be fair!   20

➤➤ Sketch by John Keats of the Sosibios Vase that may have inspired "Ode on a Grecian Urn."

° **Sylvan** Pertaining to woods or forests.

° **Tempe** A beautiful valley in Greece.

° **Arcady** The valleys of Arcadia, a mountainous region on the Greek peninsula. Like Tempe, they represent a rustic pastoral ideal.

3

Ah, happy, happy boughs! that cannot shed
   Your leaves, nor ever bid the spring adieu;
And, happy melodist, unwearied,
   For ever piping songs for ever new;
More happy love! more happy, happy love!   25
   For ever warm and still to be enjoy'd,
     For ever panting, and for ever young;
All breathing human passion far above,
   That leaves a heart high-sorrowful and cloy'd,
A burning forehead, and a parching tongue.   30

4

Who are these coming to the sacrifice?
   To what green altar, O mysterious priest,
Lead'st thou that heifer lowing at the skies,
   And all her silken flanks with garlands drest?
What little town by river or sea shore,   35
   Or mountain-built with peaceful citadel,
     Is emptied of this folk, this pious morn?
And, little town, thy streets for evermore
   Will silent be; and not a soul to tell
     Why thou art desolate, can e'er return   40

5

O Attic° shape! Fair attitude! with brede°
   Of marble men and maidens overwrought,°
With forest branches and the trodden weed;
   Thou, silent form, dost tease us out of thought
As doth eternity: Cold Pastoral!   45
   When old age shall this generation waste,
     Thou shalt remain, in midst of other woe
Than ours, a friend to man, to whom thou say'st,
"Beauty is truth, truth beauty,"—that is all
   Ye know on earth, and all ye need to know.   50

° **Attic** Characteristic of Athens or Athenians.

° **brede** Braid.

° **overwrought** Elaborately ornamented.

John Keats (1795–1821)

When I Have Fears (1818)

When I have fears that I may cease to be
   Before my pen has gleaned my teeming brain,
Before high-piléd books, in charact'ry,°
   Hold like rich garners the full-ripened grain;
When I behold, upon the night's starred face,   5
   Huge cloudy symbols of a high romance,
And think that I may never live to trace
   Their shadows, with the magic hand of chance;
And when I feel, fair creature of an hour,
   That I shall never look upon thee more,   10
Never have relish in the faery power
   Of unreflecting love!—then on the shore
Of the wide world I stand alone, and think
Till Love and Fame to nothingness do sink.

° **charact'ry** Print.

Archibald MacLeish (1892–1982)

Ars Poetica° (1926)

A poem should be palpable and mute
As a globed fruit,

Dumb
As old medallions to the thumb,

Silent as the sleeve-worn stone   5
Of casement ledges where the moss has grown—

A poem should be wordless
As the flight of birds.

A poem should be motionless in time
As the moon climbs,   10

Leaving, as the moon releases
Twig by twig the night-entangled trees,

Leaving, as the moon behind the winter leaves,
Memory by memory the mind—

A poem should be motionless in time   15
As the moon climbs.

A poem should be equal to:
Not true.

For all the history of grief
An empty doorway and a maple leaf.   20

For love
The leaning grasses and two lights above the sea—

A poem should not mean
But be.

° **Ars Poetica** "The Art of Poetry" (Latin).

Christopher Marlowe (1564–1593)

The Passionate Shepherd to His Love (1600)

Come live with me and be my love,
And we will all the pleasures prove
That valleys, groves, hills, and fields,
Woods, or steepy mountain yields.

And we will sit upon the rocks,   5
Seeing the shepherds feed their flocks
By shallow rivers, to whose falls
Melodious birds sing madrigals.

And I will make thee beds of roses
And a thousand fragrant posies,   10
A cap of flowers and a kirtle°
Embroidered all with leaves of myrtle;

A gown made of the finest wool
Which from our pretty lambs we pull;
Fair-linèd slippers for the cold,   15
With buckles of the purest gold;

° **kirtle** Skirt.

A belt of straw and ivy buds,
With coral clasps and amber studs.
And if these pleasures may thee move,
Come live with me and be my love.   20

The shepherds' swains shall dance and sing
For thy delight each May morning.
If these delights thy mind may move,
Then live with me and be my love.

Claude McKay (1890–1948)

If We Must Die (1922)

If we must die, let it not be like hogs
Hunted and penned in an inglorious spot,
While round us bark the mad and hungry dogs,
Making their mock at our accursed lot.
If we must die, O let us nobly die,   5
So that our precious blood may not be shed
In vain; then even the monsters we defy
Shall be constrained to honor us though dead!
O kinsmen! we must meet the common foe!
Though far outnumbered let us show us brave,   10
And for their thousand blows deal one deathblow!
What though before us lies the open grave?
Like men we'll face the murderous, cowardly pack,
Pressed to the wall, dying, but fighting back!

Sharon Olds (1942–   )

The One Girl at the Boys' Party (1983)

When I take my girl to the swimming party
I set her down among the boys. They tower and
bristle, she stands there smooth and sleek,
her math scores unfolding in the air around her.
They will strip to their suits, her body hard and   5
indivisible as a prime number,
they'll plunge in the deep end, she'll subtract
her height from ten feet, divide it into
hundreds of gallons of water, the numbers
bouncing in her mind like molecules of chlorine   10
in the bright blue pool. When they climb out,
her ponytail will hang its pencil lead
down her back, her narrow silk suit
with hamburgers and french fries printed on it
will glisten in the brilliant air, and they will   15
see her sweet face, solemn and
sealed, a factor of one, and she will
see their eyes, two each,
their legs, two each, and the curves of their sexes,
one each, and in her head she'll be doing her   20
wild multiplying, as the drops
sparkle and fall to the power of a thousand from her body.

Marge Piercy (1936–   )

Barbie doll (1973)

This girlchild was born as usual
and presented dolls that did pee-pee
and miniature GE stoves and irons
and wee lipsticks the color of cherry candy.
Then in the magic of puberty, a classmate said: 5
You have a great big nose and fat legs.

She was healthy, tested intelligent,
possessed strong arms and back,
abundant sexual drive and manual dexterity.
She went to and fro apologizing.   10
Everyone saw a fat nose on thick legs.

She was advised to play coy,
exhorted to come on hearty,
exercise, diet, smile and wheedle.
Her good nature wore out   15
like a fan belt.
So she cut off her nose and her legs
and offered them up.
In the casket displayed on satin she lay
with the undertaker's cosmetics painted on,   20
a turned-up putty nose,
dressed in a pink and white nightie.
Doesn't she look pretty? everyone said.
Consummation at last.
To every woman a happy ending.   25

Sylvia Plath (1932–1963)

Mirror (1963)

I am silver and exact. I have no preconceptions.
Whatever I see I swallow immediately
Just as it is, unmisted by love or dislike.
I am not cruel, only truthful—
The eye of a little god, four-cornered.   5
Most of the time I meditate on the opposite wall.
It is pink, with speckles. I have looked at it so long
I think it is a part of my heart. But it flickers.
Faces and darkness separate us over and over.

Now I am a lake. A woman bends over me,   10
Searching my reaches for what she really is.
Then she turns to those liars, the candles or the moon.
I see her back, and reflect it faithfully.
She rewards me with tears and an agitation of hands.
I am important to her. She comes and goes.   15
Each morning it is her face that replaces the darkness.
In me she has drowned a young girl, and in me an old woman
Rises toward her day after day, like a terrible fish.

Sir Walter Raleigh (1552–1618)

The Nymph's Reply to the Shepherd (1600)

If all the world and love were young,
And truth in every shepherd's tongue,
These pretty pleasures might me move
To live with thee and be thy love.

Time drives the flocks from field to fold,   5
When rivers rage and rocks grow cold;
And Philomel° becometh dumb;
The rest complains of cares to come.

The flowers do fade, and wanton fields
To wayward winter reckoning yields: 10
A honey tongue, a heart of gall,
Is fancy's spring, but sorrow's fall.

Thy gowns, thy shoes, thy beds of roses,
Thy cap, thy kirtle, and thy posies
Soon break, soon wither, soon forgotten,   15
In folly ripe, in reason rotten.

Thy belt of straw and ivy buds,
Thy coral clasps and amber studs.
All these in me no means can move
To come to thee and be thy love.   20

But could youth last, and love still breed,
Had joys no date, nor age no need,
Then these delights my mind might move
To live with thee and be thy love.

° Philomel The nightingale.

Edwin Arlington Robinson (1869–1935)

Richard Cory (1897)

Whenever Richard Cory went down town,
We people on the pavement looked at him:
He was a gentleman from sole to crown,
Clean favored, and imperially slim.

And he was always quietly arrayed,   5
And he was always human when he talked;
But still he fluttered pulses when he said,
"Good-morning," and he glittered when he walked.

And he was rich—yes, richer than a king—
And admirably schooled in every grace: 10
In fine, we thought that he was everything
To make us wish that we were in his place.

So on we worked, and waited for the light,
And went without the meat, and cursed the bread;
And Richard Cory, one calm summer night,   15
Went home and put a bullet through his head.

Sonia Sanchez (1934–   )

right on: white america (1970)

```
this country might have
been a pio
    neer land
once.
    but.        there ain't                         5
no mo
    indians         blowing
custer's° mind
            with a different
image of america.                                   10
            this country
might have
        needed shoot/
outs/ daily/
        once.                                        15
            but. there ain't
no mo real/ white/   allamerican
                bad/guys.
just.
    u & me.                                          20
        blk/ and un/armed.
this country might have
been a pion
        eer land.        once.
                    and it still is.                 25
check out
        the falling
gun/shells        on our blk/tomorrows.
```

° **custer** General George Armstrong Custer (1839–1876) was killed by Sioux in his "last stand" at the Little Bighorn in Montana.

William Shakespeare (1564–1616)

Let me not to the marriage of true minds (1609)

```
Let me not to the marriage of true minds
Admit impediments.° Love is not love
Which alters when it alteration finds,
Or bends with the remover to remove:
Oh, no! it is an ever-fixéd mark,                    5
That looks on tempests and is never shaken;
It is the star to every wandering bark,
Whose worth's unknown, although his height be taken.°
Love's not Time's fool,° though rosy lips and cheeks
Within his bending sickle's compass come;            10
Love alters not with his brief hours and weeks,
But bears it out even to the edge of doom.°
    If this be error and upon me proved,
    I never writ, nor no man ever loved.
```

° **Admit impediments** A reference to "The Order of Solemnization of Matrimony" in the Anglican Book of Common Prayer: "I require that if either of you know any impediments why ye may not be lawfully joined together in Matrimony, ye do now confess it."

° **Whose worth's . . . taken** Although the altitude of a star may be measured, its worth is unknowable.

° **Love's not Time's fool** Love is not mocked by Time.

° **doom** Doomsday.

William Shakespeare (1564–1616)

Not marble, nor the gilded monuments (1609)

Not marble, nor the gilded monuments
Of princes, shall outlive this powerful rhyme;
But you shall shine more bright in these contents
Than unswept stone, besmeared with sluttish time.
When wasteful war shall statues overturn,   5
And broils root out the work of masonry,
Nor Mars° his sword nor war's quick fire shall burn
The living record of your memory.
'Gainst death and all-oblivious enmity
Shall you pace forth; your praise shall still find room   10
Even in the eyes of all posterity
That wear this world out to the ending doom.
   So, till the judgment that yourself arise,
   You live in this, and dwell in lovers' eyes.

Percy Bysshe Shelley (1792–1822)

Ode to the West Wind (1820)

I

O wild West Wind, thou breath of Autumn's being,
Thou, from whose unseen presence the leaves dead
Are driven, like ghosts from an enchanter fleeing,

Yellow, and black, and pale, and hectic red,°
Pestilence-stricken multitudes: O Thou,   5
Who chariotest to their dark wintry bed

The winged seeds, where they lie cold and low,
Each like a corpse within its grave, until
Thine azure sister of the Spring° shall blow

Her clarion o'er the dreaming earth, and fill   10
(Driving sweet buds like flocks to feed in air)
With living hues and odours plain and hill:

Wild Spirit, which art moving everywhere;
Destroyer and Preserver; hear, O hear!

II

Thou on whose stream, mid the steep sky's commotion,   15
Loose clouds like Earth's decaying leaves are shed,
Shook from the tangled boughs of Heaven and Ocean,

Angels of rain and lightning: there are spread
On the blue surface of thine aery surge,
Like the bright hair uplifted from the head   20

Of some fierce Maenad,° even from the dim verge
Of the horizon to the zenith's height,
The locks of the approaching storm. Thou Dirge

Of the dying year, to which this closing night
Will be the dome of a vast sepulchre,   25
Vaulted with all thy congregated might

Of vapours, from whose solid atmosphere
Black rain and fire and hail will burst: O hear!

° **Yellow . . . hectic red** A reference to a tubercular fever that produces flushed cheeks.

° **azure . . . Spring** The west wind of the spring.

° **Maenad** A female votary who danced wildly in ceremonies for Diorysus (or Bacchus), Greek god of wine and vegetation, who according to legend died in the fall and was reborn in the spring.

III

Thou who didst waken from his summer dreams
The blue Mediterranean, where he lay,   30
Lulled by the coil of his crystalline streams,

Beside a pumice isle in Baiae's bay,°
And saw in sleep old palaces and towers
Quivering within the wave's intenser day,

All overgrown with azure moss and flowers   35
So sweet, the sense faints picturing them! Thou
For whose path the Atlantic's level powers

Cleave themselves into chasms, while far below
The sea-blooms and the oozy woods which wear
The sapless foliage of the ocean, know   40

Thy voice, and suddenly grow grey with fear,
And tremble and despoil themselves: O hear!

IV

If I were a dead leaf thou mightest bear;
If I were a swift cloud to fly with thee;
A wave to pant beneath thy power, and share   45

The impulse of thy strength, only less free
Than thou, O Uncontrollable! If even
I were as in my boyhood, and could be

The comrade of thy wanderings over Heaven,
As then, when to outstrip thy skiey speed   50
Scarce seemed a vision; I would ne'er have striven

As thus with thee in prayer in my sore need,
Oh! lift me as a wave, a leaf, a cloud!
I fall upon the thorns of life! I bleed!

A heavy weight of hours has chained and bowed   55
One too like thee: tameless, and swift, and proud.

V

Make me thy lyre,° even as the forest is:
What if my leaves are falling like its own!
The tumult of thy mighty harmonies

Will take from both a deep, autumnal tone,   60
Sweet though in sadness. Be thou, Spirit fierce,
My spirit! Be thou me, impetuous one!

Drive my dead thoughts over the universe
Like withered leaves to quicken a new birth!
And, by the incantation of this verse,   65

Scatter, as from an unextinguished hearth
Ashes and sparks, my words among mankind!
Be through my lips to unawakened Earth

The trumpet of a prophecy! O Wind,
If Winter comes, can Spring be far behind?   70

° **Baiae's bay** A bay in the Mediterranean Sea, west of Naples. It was known for the opulent villas built by Roman emperors along its shores.

° **lyre** An Aeolian harp, a stringed instrument that produces musical sounds when exposed to the wind.

Wallace Stevens (1879–1955)

The Emperor of Ice-Cream (1923)

Call the roller of big cigars,
The muscular one, and bid him whip
In kitchen cups concupiscent curds.
Let the wenches dawdle in such dress
As they are used to wear, and let the boys   5
Bring flowers in last month's newspapers.
Let be be finale of seem.
The only emperor is the emperor of ice-cream.

Take from the dresser of deal,°
Lacking the three glass knobs, that sheet   10
On which she embroidered fantails° once
And spread it so as to cover her face.
If her horny feet protrude, they come
To show how cold she is, and dumb.
Let the lamp affix its beam.   15
The only emperor is the emperor of ice-cream.

° **deal** Fir or pine wood.

° **fantails** According to Stevens, "the word fantails does not mean fans, but fantail pigeons."

Phillis Wheatley (1753–1784)

On Being Brought from Africa to America (1773)

'Twas mercy brought me from my *Pagan* land,
Taught my benighted soul to understand
That there's a God, that there's a *Saviour* too:
Once I redemption neither sought nor knew.
Some view our sable race with scornful eye,   5
"Their colour is a diabolic die."
Remember, *Christians*, *Negroes*, black as *Cain*,
May be refin'd, and join th' angelic train.

Walt Whitman (1819–1892)

from "Song of Myself" (1855)

1

I celebrate myself, and sing myself,
And what I assume you shall assume,
For every atom belonging to me as good belongs to you.

I loafe and invite my soul,
I lean and loafe at my ease observing a spear of summer grass.   5

My tongue, every atom of my blood, form'd from this soil, this air,
Born here of parents born here from parents the same, and their
     parents the same,
I, now thirty-seven years old in perfect health begin,
Hoping to cease not till death.

Creeds and schools in abeyance,   10
Retiring back a while sufficed at what they are, but never forgotten,

I harbor for good or bad, I permit to speak at every hazard,
Nature without check with original energy.

2

Houses and rooms are full of perfumes, the shelves are crowded with perfumes,
I breathe the fragrance myself and know it and like it,   15
The distillation would intoxicate me also, but I shall not let it.

The atmosphere is not a perfume, it has no taste of the distillation, it is odorless,
It is for my mouth forever, I am in love with it,
I will go to the bank by the wood and become undisguised and naked,
I am mad for it to be in contact with me.   20

The smoke of my own breath,
Echoes, ripples, buzz'd whispers, love-root, silk-thread, crotch and vine,
My respiration and inspiration, the beating of my heart, the passing of blood
    and air through my lungs,
The sniff of green leaves and dry leaves, and of the shore and dark-color'd
    sea-rocks, and of hay in the barn,
The sound of the belch'd words of my voice loos'd to the eddies of the wind,   25
A few light kisses, a few embraces, a reaching around of arms,
The play of shine and shade on the trees as the supple boughs wag,
The delight alone or in the rush of the streets, or along the fields and hill-sides,
The feeling of health, the full-noon trill, the song of me rising from bed
    and meeting the sun.

Have you reckon'd a thousand acres much? have you reckon'd the earth much?   30
Have you practis'd so long to learn to read?
Have you felt so proud to get at the meaning of poems?

Stop this day and night with me and you shall possess the origin of all poems,
You shall possess the good of the earth and sun, (there are millions of suns left,)
You shall no longer take things at second or third hand, nor look
    through the eyes of the dead, nor feed on the spectres in books,   35
You shall not look through my eyes either, nor take things from me,
You shall listen to all sides and filter them from your self.

William Wordsworth (1770–1850)

London, 1802 (1802)

Milton!° thou should'st be living at this hour:
England hath need of thee: she is a fen
Of stagnant waters: altar, sword and pen,
Fireside, the heroic wealth of hall and bower,
Have forfeited their ancient English dower   5
Of inward happiness. We are selfish men;
Oh! raise us up, return to us again;
And give us manners, virtue, freedom, power.
Thy soul was like a star, and dwelt apart:
Thou hadst a voice whose sound was like the sea: 10
Pure as the naked heavens, majestic, free,
So didst thou travel on life's common way,
In cheerful godliness; and yet thy heart
The lowliest duties on herself did lay.

° **Milton** John Milton
(1608–1674), poet, best
known for *Paradise Lost*.

William Wordsworth (1770–1850)

My heart leaps up when I behold (1807)

My heart leaps up when I behold
  A rainbow in the sky:
So was it when my life began;
So is it now I am a man;
So be it when I shall grow old,   5
  Or let me die!
The Child is father of the Man;
And I could wish my days to be
Bound each to each by natural piety.

William Butler Yeats (1865–1939)

The Lake Isle of Innisfree (1892)

I will arise and go now, and go to Innisfree,°
And a small cabin build there, of clay and wattles° made:
Nine bean-rows will I have there, a hive for the honey-bee,
And live alone in the bee-loud glade.

And I shall have some peace there, for peace comes
  dropping slow,   5
Dropping from the veils of the morning to where the
  cricket sings;
There midnight's all a glimmer, and noon a purple glow,
And evening full of the linnet's wings.

I will arise and go now, for always night and day
I hear lake water lapping with low sounds by the shore;   10
While I stand on the roadway, or on the pavements grey,
I hear it in the deep heart's core.

° **Innisfree** An island in Lough (Lake) Gill, County Sligo, in Ireland.

° **wattles** Stakes interwoven with twigs or branches, used for walls and roofing.

William Butler Yeats (1865–1939)

Sailing to Byzantium° (1927)

That is no country for old men. The young
In one another's arms, birds in the trees
—Those dying generations—at their song,
The salmon-falls, the mackerel-crowded seas,
Fish, flesh, or fowl, commend all summer long   5
Whatever is begotten, born, and dies.
Caught in that sensual music all neglect
Monuments of unaging intellect.

An aged man is but a paltry thing,
A tattered coat upon a stick, unless   10
Soul clap its hands and sing, and louder sing
For every tatter in its mortal dress,
Nor is there singing school but studying
Monuments of its own magnificence;

° **Byzantium** Ancient Greek city later rebuilt as Constantinople (now Istanbul).

And therefore I have sailed the seas and come   15
To the holy city of Byzantium.

O sages standing in God's holy fire
As in the gold mosaic of a wall,
Come from the holy fire, perne in a gyre,
And be the singing-masters of my soul.   20
Consume my heart away; sick with desire
And fastened to a dying animal
It knows not what it is; and gather me
Into the artifice of eternity.

Once out of nature I shall never take   25
My bodily form from any natural thing,
But such a form as Grecian goldsmiths make
Of hammered gold and gold enameling
To keep a drowsy Emperor awake;
Or set upon a golden bough to sing   30
To lords and ladies of Byzantium
Of what is past, or passing, or to come.

William Butler Yeats (1865–1939)

The Second Coming° (1921)

Turning and turning in the widening gyre°
The falcon cannot hear the falconer;
Things fall apart; the center cannot hold;
Mere anarchy is loosed upon the world,
The blood-dimmed tide is loosed, and everywhere   5
The ceremony of innocence is drowned;
The best lack all conviction, while the worst
Are full of passionate intensity.°

Surely some revelation is at hand;
Surely the Second Coming is at hand;   10
The Second Coming! Hardly are those words out
When a vast image out of *Spiritus Mundi*°
Troubles my sight: somewhere in sands of the desert
A shape with lion body and the head of a man,
A gaze blank and pitiless as the sun,   15
Is moving its slow thighs, while all about it
Reel shadows of the indignant desert birds.
The darkness drops again; but now I know
That twenty centuries° of stony sleep
Were vexed to nightmare by a rocking cradle,   20
And what rough beast, its hour come round at last,
Slouches towards Bethlehem to be born?

° **The Second Coming** The phrase usually refers to the return of Christ. Yeats theorized cycles of history, much like the turning of a wheel. Here he offers a poetic comment on his view of the dissolution of civilization at the end of one such cycle.

° **gyre** Spiral.

° **Mere . . . intensity** Lines 4–8 refer to the Russian Revolution of 1917.

° *Spiritus Mundi* Literally, "Spirit of the World" (Latin). Yeats believed all souls to be connected by a "Great Memory."

° **twenty centuries** The centuries between the birth of Christ and the twentieth century, in which Yeats was writing.

PART 4
DRAMA

© The New York Times / Redux Pictures

© Robbie Jack / Corbis

© Sara Krulwich / The New York Times / Redux Pictures

30
Understanding Drama

Learning Outcomes

After reading this chapter, you should be able to do the following:

LO1 Identify the origins of modern drama

LO2 Understand the nuances of translations

LO3 Read drama

LO1 Identify the Origins of Modern Drama

THE ANCIENT GREEK THEATER

The dramatic presentations of ancient Greece developed out of religious rites performed to honor gods or to mark the coming of spring. Playwrights such as Aeschylus (525–456 B.C.), Sophocles (496–406 B.C.), and Euripides (480?–406 B.C.) wrote plays to be performed and judged at competitions held during the yearly Dionysian festivals. Works were chosen by a selection board and evaluated by a panel of judges. To compete in the contest, writers had to submit three tragedies, which could be either based on a common theme or unrelated, and one comedy. Unfortunately, relatively few of these ancient Greek plays survive today.

The open-air, semicircular ancient Greek theater, built into the side of a hill, looked much like a primitive version of a modern sports stadium. Some Greek theaters, such as the Athenian theater, could seat almost seventeen thousand spectators. Sitting in tiered seats, the audience would look down on the **orchestra,** or "dancing place," occupied by the **chorus**—originally a group of men (led by an individual called the **choragos**) who danced and chanted and later a group of onlookers who commented on the drama. Raised a few steps above the orchestra was a platform on which the actors performed. Behind this platform was a **skene,** or building, that originally served as a resting place or dressing room. (The modern word *scene* is derived from the Greek *skene.*) Behind the skene was a line of pillars called a **colonnade,** which was covered by a roof. Actors used the skene for entrances and exits; beginning with the plays of Sophocles, painted backdrops were hung there. These backdrops, however, were most likely more decorative than

> **chorus** Group of actors in classical Greek drama who comment in unison on the action and the hero; they are led by the **choragos.**

realistic. Historians believe that realistic props and scenery were probably absent from the ancient Greek theater. Instead, the setting was suggested by the play's dialogue, and the audience had to imagine the physical details of a scene.

Two mechanical devices were used. One, a rolling cart or platform, was sometimes employed to introduce action that had occurred offstage. For example, actors frozen in position could be rolled onto the roof of the skene to illustrate an event such as the killing of Oedipus's father, which occurred before the play began. Another mechanical device, a small crane, was used to show gods ascending to or descending from heaven. Such devices enabled playwrights to dramatize the myths that were celebrated at the Dionysian festivals.

The ancient Greek theater was designed to enhance acoustics. The flat stone wall of the skene reflected the sound from the orchestra and the stage, and the curved shape of the amphitheater captured the sound, enabling the audience to hear the lines spoken by the actors. Each actor wore a stylized mask, or **persona,** to convey to the audience the personality traits of the particular character being portrayed—a king, a soldier, a wise old man, a young girl (female roles were played by men). The mouths of these masks were probably constructed so they amplified the voice and projected it into the audience. In addition, the actors wore *kothorni,* high shoes that elevated them above the stage, perhaps also helping to project their voices. Due to the excellent acoustics, audiences who see plays performed in these ancient theaters today can hear clearly without microphones or speaker systems.

Because actors wore masks and because males played the parts of women and gods as well as men, acting methods in the ancient Greek theater were probably not realistic. In their masks, high shoes, and full-length tunics (called *chiton*), actors could not hope to appear natural or to mimic the attitudes of everyday life. Instead, they probably recited their lines while standing in stylized poses, with emotions conveyed more by gesture and tone than by action. Typically, three actors had all the speaking roles. One actor—the **protagonist**—would play the central role and have the largest speaking part. Two other actors would divide the remaining lines between them. Although other characters would come on and off the stage, they would usually not have speaking roles.

Ancient Greek tragedies were typically divided into five parts. The first part was the **prologos,** or prologue, in which an actor gave the background or explanations that the audience needed to follow the rest of the drama. Then came the **párodos,** in which the chorus entered and commented on the events presented in the prologue. Following this were several **episodia,** or episodes, in which characters spoke to one another on the stage and developed the central conflict of the play. Alternating with episodes were **stasimon** (choral odes), in which the chorus commented on the exchanges that had taken place during the preceding episode. Frequently, the choral odes were divided into *strophes,* or stanzas, which were recited or sung as the chorus moved across the orchestra in one direction, and *antistrophes,* which were recited as it moved in the opposite direction. (Interestingly, the chorus stood between the audience and the actors, often functioning as an additional audience, expressing the political, social, and moral views of the community.) The fifth part was the **exodos,** the last scene of the play, during which the conflict was resolved and the actors left the stage.

Using music, dance, and verse—as well as a variety of architectural and technical innovations—the ancient Greek theater was able to convey the traditional themes of tragedy. Thus, the Greek theater powerfully expressed ideas that were central to the religious festivals in which they first appeared: the reverence for the cycles of life and death, the unavoidable dictates of the gods, and the inscrutable workings of fate.

THE ELIZABETHAN THEATER

The Elizabethan theater, influenced by the classical traditions of Roman and Greek dramatists, traces its roots back to local religious pageants performed at medieval festivals during the twelfth and thirteenth centuries. Town guilds—organizations of craftsmen who worked in the same profession—reenacted Old and New Testament stories: the fall of man, Noah and the flood, David and Goliath, and the crucifixion of Christ, for example. Church fathers encouraged these plays because they brought the Bible to a largely illiterate audience. Sometimes

>> Grand Theater at Ephesus (3rd century B.C.), a Greek settlement in what is now Turkey.

these spectacles, called **mystery plays,** were presented in the market square or on the church steps, and at other times actors appeared on movable stages or wagons called **pageants,** which could be wheeled to a given location. (Some of these wagons were quite elaborate, with trapdoors and pulleys and an upper tier that simulated heaven.) As mystery plays became more popular, they were performed in series over several days, presenting an entire cycle of a holiday—the crucifixion and resurrection of Christ during Easter, for example.

Related to mystery plays are **morality plays,** which developed in the fourteenth and fifteenth centuries. Unlike mystery plays, which depict stories from the Bible, morality plays allegorize the Christian way of life. Typically, characters representing various virtues and vices struggle or debate over the soul of man. *Everyman* (1500), the best known of these plays, dramatizes the good and bad qualities of Everyman and shows his struggle to determine what is of value to him as he journeys toward death.

By the middle of the sixteenth century, mystery and morality plays had lost ground to a new secular drama. One reason for this decline was that mystery and morality plays were associated with Catholicism and consequently discouraged by the Protestant clergy. In addition, newly discovered plays of ancient Greece and Rome introduced a dramatic tradition that supplanted the traditions of religious drama. English plays that followed the classic model were sensational and bombastic, often dealing with murder, revenge, and blood retribution. Appealing to privileged classes and commoners alike, these plays were extremely popular. (One source estimates that in London, between 20,000 and 25,000 people attended performances each week.)

In spite of the popularity of the theater, actors and playwrights encountered a number of difficulties. First, they faced opposition from city officials who were averse to theatrical presentations because they thought that the crowds attending these performances spread disease. Puritans opposed the theater because they thought plays were immoral and sinful. Finally, some people attached to the royal court opposed the theater because they thought that the playwrights undermined the authority of Queen Elizabeth by spreading seditious ideas. As a result, during Elizabeth's reign, performances were placed under the strict control of the **Master of Revels,** a public official who had the power to censor plays (and did so with great regularity) and to grant licenses for performances.

Acting companies that wanted to put on a performance had to obtain a license— possible only with the patronage of a powerful

C. Walter Hodges, The Globe Restored: A Study of the Elizabethan Theatre. New York: Norton, 1973.

> **mystery play** Medieval play depicting biblical stories.
>
> **morality play** Medieval Christian allegory in which personified abstractions, such as Selfishness and Pride, struggle for a character's soul.

nobleman—and to perform the play in an area designated by the queen. Despite these difficulties, a number of actors and playwrights gained a measure of financial independence by joining together and forming acting companies. These companies of professional actors performed works such as Christopher Marlowe's *Tamburlaine* and Thomas Kyd's *The Spanish Tragedy* in tavern courtyards and then eventually in permanent theaters. According to scholars,

The Globe Playhouse, 1599–1613

A CONJECTURAL RECONSTRUCTION

KEY
AA Main entrance
B   The Yard
CC Entrances to lowest gallery
D   Entrances to staircase and upper galleries
E   Corridor serving the different sections of the whole gallery
F   Middle gallery ('Twopenny Rooms')
G   'Gentlemen's Rooms' or 'Lords' Rooms'
H   The stage
J   The hanging being put up round the stage
K   The 'Hell' under the stage
L   The stage trap, leading down to the Hell
MM Stage doors
N   Curtained 'place behind the stage'
O   Gallery above the stage, used as required sometimes by musicians, sometimes by spectators, and often as part of the play
P   Back-stage area (the tiring-house)
Q   Tiring-house door
R   Dressing-rooms
S   Wardrobe and storage
T   The hut housing the machine for lowering enthroned gods, etc., to the stage
U   The 'Heavens'
W   Hoisting the playhouse flag

The Globe Playhouse, 1599–1613; A Conjectural Reconstruction. From C. Walter Hodges, *The Global Restored.*

>> The Globe Playhouse, 1599–1613; a conjectural reconstruction. From C. Walter Hodges *The Globe Restored: A Study of the Elizabethan Theatre.* New York: Norton, 1973.

the structures of the Elizabethan theater evolved from these tavern courtyards.

William Shakespeare's plays were performed at the Globe Theatre (a corner of which was unearthed in December 1988). Although scholars do not know the exact design of the original Globe, drawings from the period provide a good idea of its physical features. The major difference between the Globe and today's theaters is the multiple stages on which action could be performed. The Globe consisted of a large main **stage** that extended out into the open-air **yard** where the **groundlings,** or common people, stood. Spectators who paid more sat on small stools in two or three levels of galleries that extended in front of and around the stage. (The theater could probably seat almost two thousand people at a performance.) Most of the play's action occurred on the stage, which had no curtain and could be seen from three sides. Beneath the stage was a space called the **hell,** which could be reached when the floorboards were removed. This space enabled actors to "disappear" or descend into a hole or grave when the play called for such action. Above the stage was a roof called the **heavens,** which protected the actors from the weather and contained ropes and pulleys used to lower props or to create special effects.

At the rear of the stage was a narrow **alcove** covered by a curtain that could be open or closed. This curtain, often painted, functioned as a decorative rather than a realistic backdrop. The main function of this alcove was to enable actors to hide or disappear when the script called for them to do so. Some Elizabethan theaters contained a **rear stage** instead of an alcove. Because the rear stage was concealed by a curtain, props could be arranged on it ahead of time. When the action on the rear stage was finished, the curtain would be closed and the action would continue on the front stage.

On either side of the rear stage was a door through which the actors could enter and exit the front stage. Above the rear stage was a curtained stage called the **chamber,** which functioned as a balcony or as any other setting located above the action taking place on the stage

EXPLORE ONLINE >

To watch video on "The Globe Theatre," visit your Literature CourseMate, accessed through www.cengagebrain.com.

below. On either side of the chamber were casement windows, which actors could use when a play called for a conversation with someone leaning out a window or standing on a balcony. Above the chamber was the **music gallery,** a balcony that housed the musicians who provided musical interludes throughout the play (and that doubled as a stage if the play required it). The **huts,** windows located above the music gallery, could be used by characters playing lookouts or sentries. Because of the many acting sites, more than one action could take place simultaneously. For example, lookouts could stand in the towers of Hamlet's castle while Hamlet and Horatio walked the walls below.

During Shakespeare's time, the theater had many limitations that challenged the audience's imagination. First, young boys—usually between the ages of ten and twelve—played all the women's parts. In addition, there was no artificial lighting, so plays had to be performed in daylight. Rain, wind, or clouds could disrupt a performance or ruin an image—such as "the morn in russet mantle clad"—that the audience was asked to imagine. Finally, because few sets and props were used, the audience often had to visualize the high walls of a castle or the trees of a forest. The plays were performed without intermission, except for musical interludes that occurred at various points. Thus, the experience of seeing one of Shakespeare's plays staged in the Elizabethan theater was different from seeing it staged today in a modern theater.

Today, a reconstruction of the Globe Theatre stands on the south bank of the Thames River in London. In the 1940s, the American actor Sam Wanamaker visited London and was shocked to find nothing that commemorated the site of the original Globe. He eventually decided to try to raise enough money to reconstruct the Globe in its original location. The Globe Playhouse Trust was founded in the 1970s, but the actual construction of the new theater did not begin until the 1980s. After a number of setbacks—for example, the Trust ran out of funds after the construction of a large underground "diaphragm" wall needed to keep out the river water—the project was finally completed. The first performance at the reconstructed Globe was given on June 14, 1996, which would have been the late Sam Wanamaker's 77th birthday.

THE MODERN THEATER

Unlike the theaters of ancient Greece and Elizabethan England, seventeenth- and eighteenth-century theaters—such as the Palais Royal, where the great French playwright Molière presented many of his plays—were covered by a roof, beautifully decorated, and illuminated by candles so

©Jason Hawkes/Corbis

>> Aerial view of the reconstructed Globe Theatre in London.

that plays could be performed at night. The theater remained brightly lit even during performances, partly because there was no easy way to extinguish hundreds of candles and partly because people went to the theater as much to see each other as to see the play. A curtain opened and closed between acts. The audience of about five hundred spectators sat in a long room and viewed the play on a **picture-frame stage.** This type of stage, which resembles the stages on which plays are performed today, contained the action within a **proscenium arch** that surrounded the opening through which the audience viewed the performance. Thus, the action seemed to take place in an adjoining room with one of its walls cut away. Painted scenery (some of it quite elaborate), intricately detailed costumes, and stage makeup were commonplace, and for the first time women performed female roles. In addition, a complicated series of ropes, pulleys, and cranks enabled stagehands to change scenery quickly, and sound-effects machines could give audiences the impression that they were hearing a galloping horse or a raging thunderstorm. Because the theaters were small, audiences were relatively close to the stage, so actors could use subtle movements and facial expressions to enhance their performances.

Many of the first innovations in the theater were quite basic. For example, the first stage lighting was produced by candles lining the front of the stage. This method of lighting was not only ineffective—actors were lit from below and had to step forward to be fully illuminated—but also dangerous. Costumes and even entire theaters could (and did) catch fire. Later, covered lanterns with reflectors provided better and safer lighting. In the nineteenth century, a device that used an oxyhydrogen flame directed on a cylinder of lime created extremely bright illumination that could, with the aid of a lens, be concentrated into a spotlight. (It is from this method of stage lighting that we get the expression *to be in the limelight.*)

Eventually, in the twentieth century, electric lights provided a dependable and safe way of lighting the stage. Electric spotlights, footlights, and ceiling light bars made the actors clearly visible and enabled playwrights to create special effects. In Arthur Miller's *Death of a Salesman* (p. 605), for example, lighting focuses attention on action in certain areas of the stage while other areas are left in complete darkness.

Along with electric lighting came other innovations, such as electronic amplification. Microphones made it possible for actors to speak conversationally and to avoid using unnaturally loud "stage diction" to project their voices to the rear of the theater. Microphones placed at various points around the stage enabled actors and actresses to interact naturally and to deliver their lines audibly even without facing the audience. More recently, small wireless microphones have eliminated the unwieldy wires and the "dead spaces" left between upright or hanging microphones, allowing characters to move freely around the stage.

The true revolutions in staging came with the advent of **realism** in the middle of the nineteenth century. Until this time, scenery had been painted on canvas backdrops

Alvis Upitis / Getty Images

>> **Thrust-Stage Theater.** Rendering of the thrust stage at the Guthrie Theatre in Minneapolis. With seats on three sides of the stage area, the thrust stage and its background can assume many forms. Entrances can be made from the aisles, from the sides, through the stage floor, and from the back.

that trembled visibly, especially when they were intersected by doors through which actors and actresses entered. With realism came settings that were accurate down to the smallest detail. (Improved lighting, which revealed the inadequacies of painted backdrops, made such realistic stage settings necessary.) Backdrops were replaced by the **box set,** three flat panels arranged to form connected walls, with the fourth wall removed to give the audience the illusion of looking into a room. The room itself was decorated with real furniture, plants, and pictures on the walls; the door of one room might connect to another completely furnished room, or a window might open to a garden filled with realistic foliage. In addition, new methods of changing scenery were employed. Elevator stages, hydraulic lifts, and moving platforms enabled directors to make complicated changes in scenery out of the audience's view.

picture-frame stage Stage that looks like a room with a missing fourth wall through which the audience views the play.

proscenium arch Arch that surrounds the opening in a **picture-frame stage;** through this arch the audience views the performances.

realism Writing that stresses life as it really is. Realism relies on careful description of setting and the details of daily life, psychological probability, and the lives of ordinary people.

box set Stage setting that gives the audience the illusion of looking into a room.

During the late nineteenth and early twentieth centuries, however, some playwrights reacted against what they saw as the excesses of realism. They introduced **surrealistic** stage settings, in which color and scenery mirrored the uncontrolled images of dreams, and **expressionistic** stage settings, in which costumes and scenery were exaggerated and distorted to reflect the workings of a troubled, even unbalanced mind. In addition, playwrights used lighting to create areas of light, shadow, and color that reinforced the themes of the play or reflected the emotions of the protagonist. Eugene O'Neill's 1933 play *The Emperor Jones,* for example, used a series of expressionistic scenes to show the mental state of the terrified protagonist.

Sets in contemporary plays run the gamut from realistic to fantastic, from a detailed re-creation of a room in a production of Tennessee Williams's *The Glass Menagerie* to a dreamlike set for *The Emperor Jones* and Edward Albee's *The Sandbox* (1959). Motorized devices, such as revolving turntables, and *wagons*—scenery mounted on wheels—make possible rapid changes of scenery. The Broadway musical *Les Misérables,* for example, required scores of elaborate sets—Parisian slums, barricades, walled gardens—to be shifted as the audience watched. A gigantic barricade constructed on stage at one point in the play was later rotated to show the carnage that had taken place on both sides of a battle. Light, sound, and smoke were used to heighten the impact of the scene.

Photo by Dennis Taylor, courtesy of Riverside Community Players, Riverside, CA.

>> **Arena Theater.** The arena theater at the Riverside Community Players in Riverside, California. The audience surrounds the stage area, which may or may not be raised. Use of scenery is limited—perhaps to a single piece of scenery standing alone in the middle of the stage.

Today, as dramatists attempt to break down the barriers that separate audiences from the action they are viewing, plays are not limited to the picture-frame stage; in fact, they are performed on many different kinds of stages. Some plays take place on a **thrust stage,** (pictured on the previous page), which has an area that projects out into the audience. Other plays are performed on an **arena stage,** with the audience surrounding the actors. (This kind of performance is often called **theater in the round.**) In addition, experiments have been done with **environmental staging,** in which the stage surrounds the audience or several stages are situated at various locations throughout the audience. Plays may also be performed outdoors, in settings ranging from parks to city streets.

Some playwrights even try to blur the line that divides the audience from the stage by having actors move through or sit in the audience—or even by eliminating the stage entirely. For example, *Tony 'n Tina's Wedding,* a **participatory drama** created in 1988 by the theater group Artificial Intelligence, takes place not in a theater but at a church where a wedding is performed and then at a catering hall where the wedding reception is held. Throughout the play, the members of the audience function as guests, joining in the wedding celebration and mingling with the actors, who improvise freely. Recent examples of such interactive drama include *Grandma Sylvia's Funeral* and *Off the Wall,* in which audiences "attend" an art auction. Today, no single architectural form defines the theater. The modern stage is a flexible space suited to the many varieties of contemporary theatrical production.

LO2 Understand the Nuances of Translations

Many dramatic works that we read or see are translations from other languages. For example, Ibsen wrote in Norwegian, Sophocles in Greek, Molière in French, and Chekhov in Russian. Before English-speaking viewers or readers can evaluate the language of a translated play, they must understand that the language they hear or read is the translator's interpretation of what the playwright intended to communicate. Translation is interpretation, not just a search for literal equivalents; as a result, a translation is always different from the original. Moreover, because translators make different choices, two translations of the same work into English can vary considerably.

Compare these two versions of an exchange of dialogue from two translations of the same Chekhov play, called *The Brute* in the translation that begins on page 532 and *The Bear* in the alternate version.

From *The Brute*

SMIRNOV: You'd like me to come simpering to you in French, I suppose. "*Enchanté, madame! Merci beaucoup* for not paying zee money, *madame! Pardonnez-moi* if I 'ave disturbed you, *madame!* How *charmante* you look in mourning, *madame!*"

MRS. POPOV: Now you're being silly, Mr. Smirnov.

SMIRNOV: *(mimicking)* "Now you're being silly, Mr. Smirnov." "You don't know how to talk to a lady, Mr. Smirnov." Look here, Mrs. Popov. I've known more women than you've known pussy cats. I've fought three duels on their account. I've jilted twelve, and been jilted by nine others. Oh, yes, Mrs. Popov, I've played the fool in my time, whispered sweet nothings, bowed and scraped and endeavored to please. Don't tell me I don't know what it is to love, to pine away with longing, to have the blues, to melt like butter, to be weak as water. I was full of tender emotion. I was carried away with passion. I squandered half my fortune on the sex. I chattered about women's emancipation. But there's an end to everything, dear madam. . . . (1.71–73)

From *The Bear*

SMIRNOV: Ach, it's astonishing! How would you like me to talk to you? In French, perhaps? *(Lisps in anger.) Madame, je vous prie. . . . how happy I am that you're not paying me the money. . . . Ah, pardon, I've made you uneasy! Such lovely weather we're having today! And you look so becoming in your mourning dress. (Bows and scrapes.)*

MRS. POPOV: That's rude and not very clever!

SMIRNOV: *(teasing)* Rude and not very clever! I don't know how to behave in the company of ladies. Madam, in my time I've seen far more women than you've seen sparrows. Three times I've fought duels over women; I've jilted twelve women, nine have jilted me! Yes! There was a time when I played the fool; I became sentimental over women, used honeyed words, fawned on them, bowed and scraped. . . . I loved, suffered, sighed at the moon; I became limp, melted, shivered . . . I loved passionately, madly, every which way, devil take me, I chattered away like a magpie about the emancipation of women, ran through half my fortune as a result of my tender feelings; but now, if you will excuse me, I'm on to your ways! I've had enough!

Although both translations convey Smirnov's anger and frustration, they use different words (with different connotations), different phrasing, and even different stage directions. In *The Bear*, for instance, only one French phrase is used, whereas *The Brute* uses several and specifies a French accent as well; other differences between the two translations include *The Bear's* use of "teasing," "sparrows," and "I've had enough!" where *The Brute* uses "mimicking," "pussy cats," and "But there's an end to everything, dear madam." (Elsewhere in the play, *The Bear* uses profanity while *The Brute* uses more polite language.) Many words and idiomatic expressions used in daily speech cannot be translated exactly from one language to another; as a result, the two translators make different choices to try to convey a sense of the original.

stage directions Words in a play that describe an actor's movements, attitudes, and so on.

dialogue Conversation between two or more characters.

monologue Extended speech by one character.

soliloquy Convention of drama in which a character speaks directly to the audience, revealing thoughts and feelings that other characters present on stage are assumed not to hear.

farce Comedy in which stereotypical characters engage in boisterous horseplay and slapstick humor.

LO3 Read Drama

Dramatic works differ from other prose works in a number of fairly obvious ways. For one thing, plays look different on the page: generally, they are divided into **acts** and **scenes;** they include **stage directions** that specify characters' entrances and exits and describe what settings look like and how characters look and act; and they consist primarily of **dialogue,** lines spoken by the characters. And, of course, plays are different from other prose works in that they are written not to be read but to be performed in front of an audience.

Unlike novels and short stories, plays do not usually have narrators to tell the audience what a character is thinking or what happened in the past; for the most part, the audience knows only what characters reveal. To compensate for the absence of a narrator, playwrights can use **monologues** (extended speeches by one character), **soliloquies** (monologues in which a character expresses private thoughts while alone on stage), or **asides** (brief comments by a character who reveals thoughts by speaking directly to the audience without being heard by the other characters). In addition to these dramatic techniques, a play can also use costumes, scenery, props, music, lighting, and other techniques to enhance its impact on the audience.

The play that follows, Anton Chekhov's *The Brute* (1888), is typical of modern drama in many respects. A one-act play translated from Russian, it is essentially a struggle of wills between two headstrong characters, a man and a woman, with action escalating through the characters' increasingly heated exchanges of dialogue. Stage directions briefly describe the setting—"*the drawing room of a country house*"—and announce the appearance of various props. They also describe the major characters' appearances as well as their actions, gestures, and emotions. Because the play is a **farce,** it features broad physical comedy, asides, wild dramatic gestures, and elaborate figures of speech, all designed to enhance its comic effect.

Anton Chekhov (1860–1904)

is an important nineteenth-century Russian playwright and short story writer. He became a doctor and, as a young adult, supported the rest of his family after his father's bankruptcy. After his early adult years in Moscow, Chekhov spent the rest of his life in the country, moving to Yalta, a resort town in Crimea, for his health (he suffered from tuberculosis). He continued to write plays, mostly for the Moscow Art Theatre, although he could not supervise their production as he would have wished. His plays include *The Seagull* (1896), *Uncle Vanya* (1898), *The Three Sisters* (1901), and *The Cherry Orchard* (1904).

©Bettmann/Corbis

The Brute, or *The Bear* (1888), is one of a number of one-act farces Chekhov wrote just before his major plays. It is based on a French farce (*Les Jurons de Cadillac* by Pierre Breton) about a man who cannot refrain from swearing. The woman he loves offers to marry him if he can avoid swearing for one hour; he is unable to do it, but he fails so charmingly that she agrees to marry him anyway.

The Brute

A Joke in One Act (1888)

Translated by Eric Bentley

CHARACTERS

Mrs. Popov, *widow and landowner, small, with dimpled cheeks*
Mr. Grigory S. Smirnov, *gentleman farmer, middle-aged*
Luka, *Mrs. Popov's footman, an old man*

Gardener
Coachman
Hired Men

SCENE

The drawing room of a country house. Mrs. Popov, in deep mourning, is staring hard at a photograph. Luka is with her.

Luka: It's not right, ma'am, you're killing yourself. The cook has gone off with the maid to pick berries. The cat's having a high old time in the yard catching birds. Every living thing is happy. But you stay moping here in the house like it was a convent, taking no pleasure in nothing. I mean it, ma'am! It must be a full year since you set foot out of doors.

Mrs. Popov: I must never set foot out of doors again, Luka. Never! I have nothing to set foot out of doors *for*. My life is done. *He* is in his grave. I have buried myself alive in this house. We are *both* in our graves.

Luka: You're off again, ma'am. I just won't listen to you no more. Mr. Popov is dead, but what can we do about that? It's God's doing. God's will be done. You've cried over him, you've done your share of mourning, haven't you? There's a limit to everything. You can't go on weeping and wailing forever. My old lady died, for that matter, and I wept and wailed over her a whole month long. Well, that was it. I couldn't weep and wail all my life. She just wasn't worth it. *(He sighs.)* As for the neighbors, you've forgotten all about them, ma'am. You don't visit them and you don't let them visit you. You and I are like a pair of spiders—excuse the expression, ma'am—here we are in this house like a pair of spiders, we never see the light of day. And it isn't like there was no nice people around either. The whole county's swarming with 'em. There's a regiment quartered at Riblov, and the officers are so good-looking! The girls can't take their eyes off them—There's a ball at the camp every Friday—The military band plays most every day of the week—What do you say, ma'am? You're young, you're pretty, you could enjoy yourself! Ten years from now you may want to strut and show your feathers to the officers, and it'll be too late.

Mrs. Popov: *(firmly)* You must never bring this subject up again, Luka. Since Popov died, life has been an empty dream to me, you know that. *You* may think I am alive. Poor ignorant Luka! You are wrong. I am dead. I'm in my grave. Never more shall I see the light of day, never strip from my body this . . . raiment of death! Are you listening, Luka? Let his ghost learn how I love him! Yes, *I* know, and *you* know, he was often unfair to me, he was cruel to me, and he was unfaithful to me. What of it? *I* shall be faithful to *him*, that's all. I will show him how *I* can love. Hereafter, in a better world than this, he will welcome me back, the same loyal girl I always was—

Luka: Instead of carrying on this way, ma'am, you should 5 go out in the garden and take a bit of a walk, ma'am. Or why not harness Toby and take a drive? Call on a couple of the neighbours, ma'am?

Mrs. Popov: *(breaking down)* Oh, Luka!

Luka: Yes, ma'am? What have I said, ma'am? Oh, dear!

Mrs. Popov: Toby! You said Toby! He adored that horse. When he drove me out to the Korchagins and the Vlasovs, it was always with Toby! He was a wonderful driver, do you remember, Luka? So graceful! So strong! I can see him now, pulling at those reins with all his might and main! Toby! Luka, tell them to give Toby an extra portion of oats today.

Luka: Yes, ma'am.

A bell rings.

Mrs. Popov: Who is that? Tell them I'm not at home. 10

Luka: Very good, ma'am. *(Exit.)*

Mrs. Popov: *(gazing again at the photograph)* You shall see, my Popov, how a wife can love and forgive. Till death do us part. Longer than that. Till death re-unite us forever! *(Suddenly a titter breaks through her tears.)* Aren't you ashamed of yourself, Popov? Here's your little wife, being good, being faithful, so faithful she's locked up here waiting for her own funeral, while you—doesn't it make you ashamed, you naughty boy? You were terrible, you know. You were unfaithful, and you made those awful scenes about it, you stormed out and left me alone for weeks—

Enter Luka.

Luka: *(upset)* There's someone asking for you, ma'am. Says he must—

Mrs. Popov: I suppose you told him that since my husband's death I see no one?

Luka: Yes, ma'am. I did, ma'am. But he wouldn't listen, 15 ma'am. He says it's urgent.

Mrs. Popov: *(shrilly)* I see no one!!

Luka: He won't take no for an answer, ma'am. He just curses and swears and comes in anyway. He's a perfect monster, ma'am. He's in the dining room right now.

Mrs. Popov: In the dining room, is he? I'll give him his come-uppance. Bring him in here this minute.

Exit Luka.

(Suddenly sad again.) Why do they do this to me? Why? Insulting my grief, intruding on my solitude? *(She sighs.)* I'm afraid I'll have to enter a convent. I will, I *must* enter a convent!

Enter Mr. Smirnov and Luka.

Smirnov: *(to Luka)* Dolt! Idiot! You talk too much! *(Seeing Mrs. Popov. With dignity.)* May I have the honor of introducing myself, madam? Grigory S. Smirnov, landowner and lieutenant of artillery, retired. Forgive me, madam, if I disturb your peace and quiet, but my business is both urgent and weighty.

Mrs. Popov: *(declining to offer him her hand)* What is it 20 you wish, sir?

Smirnov: At the time of his death, your late husband—with whom I had the honor to be acquainted, ma'am—was in my debt to the tune of twelve hundred rubles. I have two notes to prove it. Tomorrow, ma'am, I must pay the interest on a bank loan. I have therefore no alternative, ma'am, but to ask you to pay me the money today.

Mrs. Popov: Twelve hundred rubles? But what did my husband owe it to you for?

Smirnov: He used to buy his oats from me, madam.

Mrs. Popov: *(to Luka, with a sigh)* Remember what I said, Luka: tell them to give Toby an extra portion of oats today!

Exit Luka.

My dear Mr.—what was the name again?

Smirnov: Smirnov, ma'am. 25

Mrs. Popov: My dear Mr. Smirnov, if Mr. Popov owed you money, you shall be paid—to the last ruble, to the last kopeck. But today—you must excuse me, Mr.—what was it?

> *"Since Popov died, life has been an empty dream to me, you know that. You may think I am alive. Poor ignorant Luka! You are wrong. I am dead. I'm in my grave."*

Smirnov: Smirnov, ma'am.

Mrs. Popov: Today, Mr. Smirnov, I have no ready cash in the house. *(Smirnov starts to speak.)* Tomorrow, Mr. Smirnov, no, the day after tomorrow, all will be well. My steward will be back from town. I shall see that he pays what is owing. Today, no. In any case, today is exactly seven months from Mr. Popov's death. On such a day you will understand that I am in no mood to think of money.

Smirnov: Madam, if you don't pay up now, you can carry me out feet foremost. They'll seize my estate.

Mrs. Popov: You can have your money. *(He starts to thank her.)* Tomorrow. *(He again starts to speak.)* That is: the day after tomorrow.

Smirnov: I don't need the money the day after tomorrow. I need it today.

Mrs. Popov: I'm sorry, Mr.—

Smirnov: *(shouting)* Smirnov!

Mrs. Popov: *(sweetly)* Yes, of course. But you can't have it today.

Smirnov: But I can't wait for it any longer!

Mrs. Popov: Be sensible, Mr. Smirnov. How can I pay you if I don't have it?

Smirnov: You don't have it?

Mrs. Popov: I don't have it.

Smirnov: Sure?

Mrs. Popov: Positive.

Smirnov: Very well. I'll make a note to that effect. *(Shrugging.)* And then they want me to keep cool. I meet the tax commissioner on the street, and he says, "Why are you always in such a bad humor, Smirnov?" Bad humor! How can I help it, in God's name? I need money, I need it desperately. Take yesterday: I leave home at the crack of dawn, I call on all my debtors. Not a one of them pays up. Footsore and weary. I creep at midnight into some little dive, and try to snatch a few winks of sleep on the floor by the vodka barrel. Then today, I come here, fifty miles from home, saying to myself, "At last, at last, I can be sure of something," and you're not in the mood! You give me a mood! Christ, how can I help getting all worked up?

Mrs. Popov: I thought I'd made it clear, Mr. Smirnov, that you'll get your money the minute my steward is back from town.

Smirnov: What the hell do I care about your steward? Pardon the expression, ma'am. But it was you I came to see.

Mrs. Popov: What language! What a tone to take to a lady! I refuse to hear another word. *(Quickly, exit.)*

Smirnov: Not in the mood, huh? "Exactly seven months since Popov's death," huh? How about me? *(Shouting after her.)* Is there this interest to pay, or isn't there? I'm asking you a question: is there this interest to pay, or isn't there? So your husband died, and you're not in the mood, and your steward's gone off some place, and so forth and so on, but what can *I* do about all that, huh? What do *you* think I should

do? Take a running jump and shove my head through the wall? Take off in a balloon? You don't know my *other* debtors. I call on Gruzdeff. Not at home. I look for Yaroshevitch. He's hiding out. I find Kooritsin. He kicks up a row, and I have to throw him through the window. I work my way right down the list. Not a kopeck. Then I come to you, and God damn it to hell, if you'll pardon the expression, you're not in the mood! *(Quietly, as he realizes he's talking to air.)* I've spoiled them all, that's what, I've let them play me for a sucker. Well, I'll show them. I'll show this one. I'll stay right here till she pays up. Ugh! *(He shudders with rage.)* I'm in a rage! I'm in a positively towering rage! Every nerve in my body is trembling at forty to the dozen! I can't breathe, I feel ill, I think I'm going to faint, hey, you there!

Enter Luka.

Luka: Yes, sir? Is there anything you wish, sir?

Smirnov: Water! Water! No, make it vodka.

Exit Luka.

Consider the logic of it. A fellow creature is desperately in need of cash, so desperately in need that he has to seriously contemplate hanging himself, and this woman, this mere chit of a girl, won't pay up, and why not? Because, forsooth, she isn't in the mood! Oh, the logic of women! Come to that, I never have liked them, I could do without the whole sex. Talk to a woman? I'd rather sit on a barrel of dynamite, the very thought gives me gooseflesh. Women! Creatures of poetry and romance! Just to see one in the distance gets me mad. My legs start twitching with rage. I feel like yelling for help.

Enter Luka, handing Smirnov a glass of water.

Luka: Mrs. Popov is indisposed, sir. She is seeing no one.

Smirnov: Get out.

Exit Luka.

Indisposed, is she? Seeing no one, huh? Well, she can see me or not, but I'll be here, I'll be right here till she pays up. If you're sick for a week, I'll be here for a week. If you're sick for a year, I'll be here for a year. You won't get around *me* with your widow's weeds and your schoolgirl dimples. I know all about dimples. *(Shouting through the window.)* Semyon, let the horses out of those shafts, we're not leaving, we're staying, and tell them to give the horses some oats, yes, oats, you fool, what do you think? *(Walking away from the window.)* What a mess, what an unholy mess! I didn't sleep last night, the heat is terrific today, not a damn one of 'em has paid up, and here's this—this skirt in mourning that's not in the mood! My head aches, where's that—*(He drinks from the glass.)* Water, ugh! You there!

30

35

40

45

Enter Luka.

Luka: Yes, sir. You wish for something, sir? 50

Smirnov: Where's that confounded vodka I asked for?

Exit Luka.

(*Smirnov sits and looks himself over.*) Oof! A fine figure of a man *I* am! Unwashed, uncombed, unshaven, straw on my vest, dust all over me. The little woman must've taken me for a highwayman. (*Yawns.*) I suppose it wouldn't be considered polite to barge into a drawing room in this state, but who cares? I'm not a visitor, I'm a creditor—most unwelcome of guests, second only to Death.

Enter Luka.

Luka: (*handing him the vodka*) If I may say so, sir, you take too many liberties, sir.

Smirnov: What?!

Luka: Oh, nothing, sir, nothing.

Smirnov: Who in hell do you think you're talking to? 55
Shut your mouth!

Luka: (*aside*) There's an evil spirit abroad. The Devil must have sent him. Oh! (*Exit Luka.*)

Smirnov: What a rage I'm in! I'll grind the whole world to powder. Oh, I feel ill again. You there!

Enter Mrs. Popov.

Mrs. Popov: (*looking at the floor*) In the solitude of my rural retreat, Mr. Smirnov, I've long since grown unaccustomed to the sound of the human voice. Above all, I cannot bear shouting. I must beg you not to break the silence.

Smirnov: Very well. Pay me my money and I'll go.

Mrs. Popov: I told you before, and I tell you again, Mr. 60
Smirnov. I have no cash, you'll have to wait till the day after tomorrow. Can I express myself more plainly?

Smirnov: And *I* told *you* before, and *I* tell *you* again, that I need the money today, that the day after tomorrow is too late, and that if you don't pay, and pay now, I'll have to hang myself in the morning!

Mrs. Popov: But I have no cash. This is quite a puzzle.

Smirnov: You won't pay, huh?

Mrs. Popov: I *can't* pay, Mr. Smirnov.

Smirnov: In that case, I'm going to sit here and wait. (*Sits* 65
down.) You'll pay up the day after tomorrow? Very good. Till the day after tomorrow, here I sit. (*Pause. He jumps up.*) Now look, do I have to pay that interest tomorrow, or don't I? Or do you think I'm joking?

Mrs. Popov: I must ask you not to raise your voice, Mr. Smirnov. This is not a stable.

Smirnov: Who said it was? Do I have to pay the interest tomorrow or not?

Mrs. Popov: Mr. Smirnov, do you know how to behave in the presence of a lady?

Smirnov: No, madam, I do not know how to behave in the presence of a lady.

Mrs. Popov: Just what I thought. I look at you, and I say: 70
ugh! I hear you talk, and I say to myself: "That man doesn't know how to talk to a lady."

Smirnov: You'd like me to come simpering to you in French, I suppose. "*Enchanté, madame! Merci beaucoup* for not paying zee money, *madame! Pardonnez-moi* if I 'ave disturbed you, *madame!* How *charmante* you look in mourning, *madame!*"

Mrs. Popov: Now you're being silly, Mr. Smirnov.

Smirnov: (*mimicking*) "Now you're being silly, Mr. Smirnov." "You don't know how to talk to a lady, Mr. Smirnov." Look here, Mrs. Popov, I've known more women than you've known pussy cats. I've fought three duels on their account. I've jilted twelve, and been jilted by nine others. Oh, yes, Mrs. Popov, I've played the fool in my time, whispered sweet nothings, bowed and scraped and endeavored to please. Don't tell me I don't know what it is to love, to pine away with longing, to have the blues, to melt like butter, to be weak as water. I was full of tender emotion. I was carried away with passion. I squandered half my fortune on the sex. I chattered about women's emancipation. But there's an end to everything, dear madam. Burning eyes, dark eyelashes, ripe, red lips, dimpled cheeks, heaving bosoms, soft whisperings, the moon above; the lake below—I don't give a rap for that sort of nonsense any more, Mrs. Popov. I've found out about women. Present company excepted, they're liars. Their behavior is mere play acting; their conversation is sheer gossip. Yes, dear lady, women, young or old, are false, petty, vain, cruel, malicious, unreasonable. As for intelligence, any sparrow could give them points. Appearances, I admit, can be deceptive. In appearance, a woman may be all poetry and romance, goddess and angel, muslin and fluff. To look at her exterior is to be transported to heaven. But I have looked at her interior, Mrs. Popov, and what did I find there—in her very soul? A crocodile. (*He has gripped the back of the chair so firmly that it snaps.*) And, what is more revolting, a crocodile with an illusion, a crocodile that imagines tender sentiments are its own special province, a crocodile that thinks itself queen of the realm of love! Whereas, in sober fact, dear madam, if a woman can love anything except a lapdog you can hang me by the feet on that nail. For a man, love is suffering, love is sacrifice. A woman just swishes her train around and tightens her grip on your nose. Now, you're a woman, aren't you, Mrs. Popov? You must be an expert on some of this. Tell me, quite frankly, did you ever know a woman to be—faithful, for instance? Or even sincere? Only old hags, huh? Though some women are old hags from birth. But as for the others? You're right: a faithful woman is a freak of nature—like a cat with horns.

Mrs. Popov: Who *is* faithful, then? Who *have* you cast for the faithful lover? Not man?

Smirnov: Right first time, Mrs. Popov: man. 75

Mrs. Popov: (going off into a peal of bitter laughter) Man! Man is faithful! that's a new one! (Fiercely.) What right do you have to say this, Mr. Smirnov? Men faithful? Let me tell you something. Of all the men I have ever known my late husband Popov was the best. I loved him, and there are women who know how to love, Mr. Smirnov. I gave him my youth, my happiness, my life, my fortune. I worshipped the ground he trod on—and what happened? The best of men was unfaithful to me, Mr. Smirnov. Not once in a while. All the time. After he died, I found his desk drawer full of love letters. While he was alive, he was always going away for the week-end. He squandered my money. He made love to other women before my very eyes. But, in spite of all, Mr. Smirnov, *I* was faithful. Unto death. And beyond. I am *still* faithful, Mr. Smirnov! Buried alive in this house, I shall wear mourning till the day I, too, am called to my eternal rest.

> "Trying to scare me again? Just because you have big fists and a voice like a bull? You're a brute."

Smirnov: (laughing scornfully) Expect me to believe that? As if I couldn't see through all this hocus-pocus. Buried alive! Till you're called to your eternal rest! Till when? Till some little poet—or some little subaltern with his first moustache—comes riding by and asks: "Can that be the house of the mysterious Tamara who for love of her late husband has buried herself alive, vowing to see no man?" Ha!

Mrs. Popov: (flaring up) How dare you? How dare you insinuate—?

Smirnov: You may have buried yourself alive, Mrs. Popov, but you haven't forgotten to powder your nose.

Mrs. Popov: (incoherent) How dare you? How—? 80

Smirnov: Who's raising his voice now? Just because I call a spade a spade. Because I shoot straight from the shoulder. Well, don't shout at me, I'm not your steward.

Mrs. Popov: I'm not shouting, you're shouting! Oh, leave me alone!

Smirnov: Pay me the money, and I will.

Mrs. Popov: You'll get no money out of me!

Smirnov: Oh, so that's it! 85

Mrs. Popov: Not a ruble, not a kopeck. Get out! Leave me alone!

Smirnov: Not being your husband, I must ask you not to make scenes with me. (He sits.) I don't like scenes.

Mrs. Popov: (choking with rage) You're sitting down?

Smirnov: Correct, I'm sitting down.

Mrs. Popov: I asked you to leave! 90

Smirnov: Then give me the money. (Aside.) Oh, what a rage I'm in, what a rage!

Mrs. Popov: The impudence of the man! I won't talk to you a moment longer. Get out. (Pause.) Are you going?

Smirnov: No.

Mrs. Popov: No?!

Smirnov: No. 95

Mrs. Popov: On your head be it. Luka!

Enter Luka.

Show the gentleman out, Luka.

Luka: (approaching) I'm afraid, sir, I'll have to ask you, um, to leave, sir, now, um—

Smirnov: (jumping up) Shut your mouth, you old idiot! Who do you think you're talking to? I'll make mince-meat of you.

Luka: (clutching his heart) Mercy on us! Holy saints above! (He falls into an armchair.) I'm taken sick! I can't breathe!!

Mrs. Popov: Then where's Dasha? Dasha! Dasha! Come here at once! (She rings.) 100

Luka: They gone picking berries, ma'am, I'm alone here—Water, water, I'm taken sick!

Mrs. Popov: (to Smirnov) Get out, you!

Smirnov: Can't you even be polite with me, Mrs. Popov?

Mrs. Popov: (clenching her fists and stamping her feet) With you? You're a wild animal, you were never house-broken!

Smirnov: What? What did you say? 105

Mrs. Popov: I said you were a wild animal, you were never house-broken.

Smirnov: (advancing upon her) And what right do you have to talk to me like that?

Mrs. Popov: Like what?

Smirnov: You have insulted me, madam.

Mrs. Popov: What of it? Do you think I'm scared of you? 110

Smirnov: So you think you can get away with it because you're a woman. A creature of poetry and romance, huh? Well, it doesn't go down with me. I hereby challenge you to a duel.

Luka: Mercy on us! Holy saints alive! Water!

Smirnov: I propose we shoot it out.

Mrs. Popov: Trying to scare me again? Just because you have big fists and a voice like a bull? You're a brute.

Smirnov: No one insults Grigory S. Smirnov with impunity! And I don't care if you *are* a female. 115

Mrs. Popov: (trying to outshout him) Brute, brute, brute!

Smirnov: The sexes are equal, are they? Fine: then it's just prejudice to expect men alone to pay for insults. I hereby challenge—

Mrs. Popov: (screaming) All right! You want to shoot it out? All right! Let's shoot it out!

Smirnov: And let it be here and now!

Mrs. Popov: Here and now! All right! I'll have Popov's   120
pistols here in one minute! *(Walks away, then turns.)*
Putting one of Popov's bullets through your silly
head will be a pleasure! Au revoir. *(Exit.)*

Smirnov: I'll bring her down like a duck, a sitting duck.
I'm not one of your little poets, I'm no little subaltern with his first moustache. No, sir, there's no
weaker sex where I'm concerned!

Luka: Sir! Master! *(He goes down on his knees.)* Take
pity on a poor old man, and do me a favor: go away.
It was bad enough before, you nearly scared me to
death. But a duel—!

Smirnov: *(ignoring him)* A duel! That's equality of the
sexes for you! That's women's emancipation! Just
as a matter of principle I'll bring her down like a
duck. But what a woman! "Putting one of Popov's
bullets through your silly head . . ." Her cheeks
were flushed, her eyes were gleaming! And, by God,
she's accepted the challenge! I never knew a woman
like this before!

Luka: Sir! Master! Please go away! I'll always pray for
you!

Smirnov: *(again ignoring him)* What a woman! Phew!!   125
She's no sour puss, she's no cry baby. She's fire and
brimstone. She's a human cannon ball. What a shame
I have to kill her!

Luka: *(weeping)* Please, kind sir, please, go away!

Smirnov: *(as before)* I like her, isn't that funny? With
those dimples and all? I like her. I'm even prepared to
consider letting her off that debt. And where's my
rage? It's gone. I never knew a woman like this
before.

Enter Mrs. Popov with pistols.

Mrs. Popov: *(boldly)* Pistols, Mr. Smirnov! *(Matter of
fact.)* But before we start, you'd better show me how
it's done. I'm not too familiar with these things. In
fact I never gave a pistol a second look.

Luka: Lord, have mercy on us, I must go hunt up the
gardener and the coachman. Why has this catastro-
phe fallen upon us, O Lord? *(Exit.)*

Smirnov: *(examining the pistols)* Well, it's like this. There   130
are several makes: one is the Mortimer, with cap-
sules, especially constructed for dueling. What you
have here are Smith and Wesson triple-action
revolvers, with extractor, first-rate job, worth ninety
rubles at the very least. You hold it this way. *(Aside.)*
My God, what eyes she has! They're setting me on
fire.

Mrs. Popov: This way?

Smirnov: Yes, that's right. You cock the trigger, take aim
like this, head up, arm out like this. Then you just
press with this finger here, and it's all over. The main
thing is, keep cool, take slow aim, and don't let your
arm jump.

Mrs. Popov: I see. And if it's inconvenient to do the job
here, we can go out in the garden.

Smirnov: Very good. Of course, I should warn you: I'll be
firing in the air.

Mrs. Popov: What? This is the end. Why?   135

Smirnov: Oh, well—because—for private reasons.

Mrs. Popov: Scared, huh? *(She laughs heartily.)* Now
don't you try to get out of it, Mr. Smirnov. My blood
is up. I won't be happy till I've drilled a hole through
that skull of yours. Follow me. What's the matter?
Scared?

Smirnov: That's right. I'm scared.

Mrs. Popov: Oh, come on, what's the matter with you?

Smirnov: Well, um, Mrs. Popov, I, um, I like you.   140

Mrs. Popov: *(laughing bitterly)* Good God! He likes me,
does he? The gall of the man. *(Showing him the
door.)* You may leave, Mr. Smirnov.

Smirnov: *(Quietly puts the gun down, takes his hat, and
walks to the door. Then he stops and the pair look at
each other without a word. Then, approaching
gingerly.)* Listen, Mrs. Popov. Are you still mad at
me? I'm in the devil of a temper myself, of course.
But then, you see—what I mean is—it's this way—
the fact is—(Roaring.)* Well, is it my fault, damn it, if
I like you? *(Clutches the back of a chair. It breaks.)*
Christ, what fragile furniture you have here. I like
you. Know what I mean? I could fall in love with
you.

Mrs. Popov: I hate you. Get out!

Smirnov: What a woman! I never saw anything like it.
Oh, I'm lost, I'm done for, I'm a mouse in a trap.

Mrs. Popov: Leave this house, or I shoot!   145

Smirnov: Shoot away! What bliss to die of a shot that
was fired by that little velvet hand! To die gazing into
those enchanting eyes. I'm out of my mind. I know:
you must decide at once. Think for one second, then
decide. Because if I leave now, I'll never be back.
Decide! I'm a pretty decent chap. Landed gentleman,
I should say. Ten thousand a year. Good stable.
Throw a kopeck up in the air, and I'll put a bullet
through it. Will you marry me?

Mrs. Popov: *(indignant, brandishing the gun)* We'll shoot
it out! Get going! Take your pistol!

Smirnov: I'm out of my mind. I don't understand anything
any more. *(Shouting.)* You there! That vodka!

Mrs. Popov: No excuses! No delays! We'll shoot it out!

Smirnov: I'm out of my mind. I'm falling in love. I *have*   150
fallen in love. *(He takes her hand vigorously; she
squeals.)* I love you. *(He goes down on his knees.)* I
love you as I've never loved before. I jilted twelve, and
was jilted by nine others. But I didn't love a one of
them as I love you. I'm full of tender emotion. I'm
melting like butter. I'm weak as water. I'm on my knees
like a fool, and I offer you my hand. It's a shame, it's a
disgrace. I haven't been in love in five years. I took a
vow against it. And now, all of a sudden, to be swept
off my feet, it's a scandal. I offer you my hand, dear
lady. Will you or won't you? You won't? Then don't!
(He rises and walks toward the door.)

Mrs. Popov: I didn't say anything.

Smirnov: *(stopping)* What?

Mrs. Popov: Oh, nothing, you can go. Well, no, just a minute. No, you can go. Go! I detest you! But, just a moment. Oh, if you knew how furious I feel! *(Throws the gun on the table.)* My fingers have gone to sleep holding that horrid thing. *(She is tearing her handkerchief to shreds.)* And what are you standing around for? Get out of here!

Smirnov: Goodbye.

Mrs. Popov: Go, go, go! *(Shouting.)* Where are you going? Wait a minute! No, no, it's all right, just go. I'm fighting mad. Don't come near me, don't come near me!

Smirnov: *(who is coming near her)* I'm pretty disgusted with myself—falling in love like a kid, going down on my knees like some moongazing whippersnapper, the very thought gives me gooseflesh. *(Rudely.)* I love you. But it doesn't make sense. Tomorrow, I have to pay that interest, and we've already started mowing. *(He puts his arm about her waist.)* I shall never forgive myself for this.

Mrs. Popov: Take your hands off me, I hate you! Let's shoot it out!

A long kiss. Enter Luka with an axe, the Gardener with a rake, the coachman with a pitchfork, hired men with sticks.

Luka: *(seeing the kiss)* Mercy on us! Holy saints above!

Mrs. Popov: *(dropping her eyes)* Luka, tell them in the stable that Toby is *not* to have any oats today.

*   *   *

31 |

Drama Sampler: Ten-Minute Plays

Learning Outcomes

After reading this chapter, you should be able to do the following:

LO1 Define the ten-minute play

Timeline

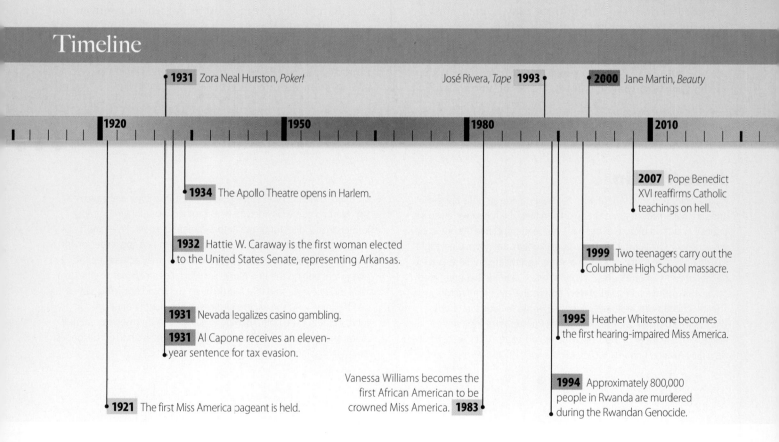

1931 Zora Neal Hurston, *Poker!*

José Rivera, *Tape* **1993**

2000 Jane Martin, *Beauty*

1920   1950   1980   2010

2007 Pope Benedict XVI reaffirms Catholic teachings on hell.

1934 The Apollo Theatre opens in Harlem.

1932 Hattie W. Caraway is the first woman elected to the United States Senate, representing Arkansas.

1999 Two teenagers carry out the Columbine High School massacre.

1931 Nevada legalizes casino gambling.

1931 Al Capone receives an eleven-year sentence for tax evasion.

1995 Heather Whitestone becomes the first hearing-impaired Miss America.

Vanessa Williams becomes the first African American to be crowned Miss America. **1983**

1994 Approximately 800,000 people in Rwanda are murdered during the Rwandan Genocide.

1921 The first Miss America pageant is held.

ten-minute play Short play that can be performed in ten minutes or less.

haiku Seventeen-syllable, three-line form of Japanese verse that almost always uses concrete imagery and deals with the natural world.

exposition First stage of a plot, where the author presents the information about characters or setting that a reader or viewer will need to understand the subsequent action.

conflict Struggle between opposing forces (protagonist and antagonist) in a work of literature.

resolution Also called the **denouement,** final stage in the plot. Here the action comes to an end and remaining loose ends are tied up.

LO1 Define the Ten-Minute Play

Throughout the long history of playwriting, many types and forms of drama have emerged. In recent years, theater has become more experimental, as evidenced by the proliferation of one-act and ten-minute plays, which strive to convey complex ideas in a short amount of time. While traditional one-act plays such as Anton Chekhov's *The Brute* (p. 532) and Susan Glaspell's *Trifles* (p. 555) may have the luxury of unfolding in a more extended period, the **ten-minute play,** which must be performed in ten minutes or less, offers a very small window of opportunity in which the playwright can create meaning. In fact, as director Jon Jory has noted, the ten-minute play is in a sense the dramatic equivalent of the **haiku** in that it is intended to be taken in all at once, and thus to have a particularly intense effect on the audience. According to Jory, considered to be the father of the ten-minute play genre, these plays "must, by nature, imply rather than explain. They often depend on metaphor to extend their reach. They stick like glue in the mind because the viewer remembers the *whole* play."

Since a page of script roughly translates into a minute of time onstage, a ten-minute play is generally limited to about ten pages. Despite its brevity, however, a ten-minute play is more than just a scene or an excerpt from a longer play: it is written to stand alone as a complete dramatic work. Although its brief length means it has little or no room for **exposition,** it must introduce a **conflict** (usually relatively early in the play), and it must provide a **resolution,** just as any other play does.

Ten-minute plays are generally staged in groups, allowing the audience to watch several plays in sequence. Casts are usually small; often, the same actors appear in a number of different plays. For this reason, elaborate costumes and staging are impractical (and therefore rare). The most popular venue for a ten-minute play is a drama festival, and numerous competitions offer prizes that include the staging of the winning play. The most prominent contest is sponsored by the Actors Theatre of Louisville, which stages the annual Humana Festival of New American Plays.

The ten-minute plays in this sampler treat a variety of topics. In Jane Martin's *Beauty,* the two protagonists trade lives, with unexpected consequences; in *Tape,* by José Rivera, the protagonist is forced to confront his entire life and face up to his own truths; and in Zora Neale Hurston's *Poker!* a group of men gather for a card game that threatens to escalate into a different kind of contest. (Warren Leight's *Nine Ten* on page 553 is also a ten-minute play.)

Jane Martin

is a prize-winning playwright who has never made a public appearance or spoken about any of her works. In fact, she has never given an interview, and no picture of her has ever been published. As one critic wryly observed, Martin is "America's best known, unknown playwright." Martin first came to the attention of American theater audiences with her collection of monologues, *Talking With . . . ,* a work that premiered at the 1981 Humana Festival of New American Plays at the Actors Theatre of Louisville, Kentucky. Her other works include *Vital Signs; What Mama Don't Know; Cementville;* the Pulitzer Prize–nominated *Keely and Du* (winner of the 1994 American Theatre Critics Association New Play Award); *Criminal Hearts; Middle Aged White Guys; Jack and Jill;*

Mr. Bundy; Flaming Guns of the Purple Sage; Good Boys; Flags; and *Sez She.* Martin's name is widely believed to be a pseudonym. Jon Jory, former artistic director of the Actors Theatre of Louisville — and director of the premieres of all of Martin's plays — is spokesperson for the playwright and, according to some people, may actually be the playwright behind the pen name. Jory has repeatedly denied this; in a 1994 interview, he said that Martin "feels she could not write plays if people knew who she was, regardless of her identity or gender." In Jory's opinion, "The point in the end is the plays themselves. . . . But if Jane's anonymity is a P. T. Barnum publicity stunt, it's one of the longest circus acts going."

Beauty (2000)

CHARACTERS

Carla   *Bethany*

An apartment. Minimalist set. A young woman, Carla, on the phone.

Carla: In love with me? You're in love with me? Could you describe yourself again? Uh-huh. Uh-huh. And you spoke to me? *(A knock at the door.)* Listen, I always hate to interrupt a marriage proposal, but . . . could you possibly hold that thought? *(Puts phone down and goes to door. Bethany, the same age as Carla and a friend, is there. She carries the sort of Mideastern lamp we know of from Aladdin.)*

Bethany: Thank God you were home. I mean, you're not going to believe this!

Carla: Somebody on the phone. *(Goes back to it.)*

Bethany: I mean, I just had a beach urge, so I told them at work my uncle was dying . . .

Carla: *(motions to Bethany for quiet)* And you were the one in the leather jacket with the tattoo? What was the tattoo? *(Carla again asks Bethany, who is gesturing wildly that she should hang up, to cool it.)* Look, a screaming eagle from shoulder to shoulder, maybe. There were a lot of people in the bar.

Bethany: *(gesturing and mouthing)* I have to get back to work.

Carla: *(on phone)* See, the thing is, I'm probably not going to marry someone I can't remember . . . particularly when I don't drink. Sorry. Sorry. Sorry. *(She hangs up.)* Madness.

Bethany: So I ran out to the beach . . .

Carla: This was some guy I never met who apparently offered me a beer . . .

Bethany: . . . low tide and this . . . *(The lamp.)* . . . was just sitting there, lying there . . .

Carla: . . . and he tracks me down . . .

Bethany: . . . on the beach, and I lift this lid thing . . .

Carla: . . . and seriously proposes marriage.

Bethany: . . . and a genie comes out.

Carla: I mean, that's twice in a . . . what?

Bethany: A genie comes out of this thing.

Carla: A genie?

Bethany: I'm not kidding, the whole Disney kind of thing, swirling smoke, and then this twenty-foot-high, see-through guy in like an Arabian outfit.

Carla: Very funny.

Bethany: Yes, funny, but twenty feet high! I look up and down the beach, I'm alone. I don't have my pepper spray or my hand alarm. You know me, when I'm petrified I joke. I say his voice is too high for Robin Williams, and he says he's a castrati. Naturally. Who else would I meet?

Carla: What's a castrati?

Bethany: You know . . .

The appropriate gesture.

Carla: Bethany, dear one, I have three modeling calls. I am meeting Ralph Lauren!

Bethany: Okay, good. Ralph Lauren. Look, I am not kidding!

Carla: You're not kidding what?!

Bethany: There is a genie in this thingamajig.

Carla: Uh-huh. I'll be back around eight.

Bethany: And he offered me *wishes!*

Carla: Is this some elaborate practical joke because it's my birthday?

Bethany: No, happy birthday, but I'm like crazed because I'm on this deserted beach with a twenty-foot-high, see-through genie, so like sarcastically . . . you know how I need a new car . . . I said fine, gimme 25,000 dollars . . .

Carla: On the beach with the genie?

Bethany: Yeah, right, exactly, and it rains down out of the sky.

Carla: Oh sure.

Bethany: *(pulling a wad out of her purse)* Count it, those are thousands. I lost one in the surf.

Carla sees the top bill. Looks at Bethany, who nods encouragement. Carla thumbs through them.

Carla: These look real.

Bethany: Yeah.

Carla: And they rained down out of the sky?

Bethany: Yeah.

Carla: You've been really strange lately, are you dealing?

Bethany: Dealing what, I've even given up chocolate.

Carla: Let me see the genie.

Bethany: Wait, wait.

Carla: Bethany, I don't have time to screw around. Let me see the genie or let me go on my appointments.

Bethany: Wait! So I pick up the money . . . see, there's sand on the money . . . and I'm like nuts so I say, you know, "Okay, look, ummm, big guy, my uncle is in the hospital" . . . because as you know when I said to the people at work my uncle was dying, I was on one level telling the truth although it had nothing to do with the beach, but he was in Intensive Care after the accident, and that's on my mind, so I say, okay, Genie, heal my uncle . . . which is like impossible given he was hit by two trucks, and the genie says, "Yes, Master" . . . like they're supposed to say, and he goes into this like kind of whirlwind, kicking up sand and stuff, and I'm like, "Oh my God!" and the air clears, and he bows, you know, and says, "It is done, Master," and I say, "Okay, whatever-you-are, I'm calling on my cell phone," and I get it out and I get this doctor who is like dumbstruck who says my uncle came to, walked out of Intensive Care and left the hospital! I'm not kidding, Carla.

Carla: On your mother's grave?   45

Bethany: On my mother's grave.

They look at each other.

Carla: Let me see the genie.

Bethany: No, no, look, that's the whole thing . . . I was just, like, reacting, you know, responding, and that's already two wishes . . . although I'm really pleased about my uncle, the $25,000 thing, I could have asked for $10 million, and there is only one wish left.

Carla: So ask for $10 million.

Bethany: I don't think so. I don't think so. I mean, I gotta   50 focus in here. Do you have a sparkling water?

Carla: No. Bethany, I'm missing Ralph Lauren now. Very possibly my one chance to go from catalogue model to the very, very big time, so, if you are joking, stop joking.

Bethany: Not joking. See, see, the thing is, I know what I want. In my guts. Yes. Underneath my entire bitch of a life is this unspoken, ferocious, all-consuming urge . . .

Carla: *(trying to get her to move this along)* Ferocious, all-consuming urge . . .

Bethany: I want to be like you.

Carla: Me?   55

Bethany: Yes.

Carla: Half the time you don't even like me.

Bethany: Jealous. The ogre of jealousy.

Carla: You're the one with the $40,000 job straight out of school. You're the one who has published short stories. I'm the one hanging on by her fingernails in modeling. The one who has creeps calling her on the phone. The one who had to have a nose job.

Bethany: I want to be beautiful.   60

Carla: You are beautiful.

Bethany: Carla, I'm not beautiful.

Carla: You have charm. You have personality. You know perfectly well you're pretty.

Bethany: "Pretty," see, that's it. Pretty is the minor leagues of beautiful. Pretty is what people discover about you after they know you. Beautiful is what knocks them out across the room. Pretty, you get called a couple of times a year; *beautiful* is twenty-four hours a day.

Carla: Yeah? So?   65

Bethany: So?! We're talking *beauty* here. Don't say "So?" Beauty is the real deal. You are the center of any moment of your life. People stare. Men flock.

I've seen you get offered discounts on makeup for no reason. Parents treat beautiful children better. Studies show your income goes up. You can have sex anytime you want it. Men have to know me. That takes up to a year. I'm continually horny.

Carla: Bethany, I don't even like sex. I can't have a conversation without men coming on to me. I have no privacy. I get hassled on the street. They start pressuring me from the beginning. Half the time, it never occurs to them to start with a conversation. Smart guys like you. You've had three long-term relationships, and you're only twenty-three. I haven't had one. The good guys, the smart guys are scared to death of me. I'm surrounded by male bimbos who think a preposition is when you go to school away from home. I have no woman friends except you. I don't even want to talk about this!

Bethany: I knew you'd say something like this. See, you're "in the club" so you can say this. It's the way beauty functions as an elite. You're trying to keep it all for yourself.

Carla: I'm trying to tell you it's no picnic.

Bethany: But it's what everybody wants. It's the nasty   70 secret at large in the world. It's the unspoken tidal desire in every room and on every street. It's the unspoken, the soundless whisper . . . millions upon millions of people longing hopelessly and forever to stop being whatever they are and be beautiful, but the difference between those ardent multitudes and me is that I have a goddamn genie and one more wish!

Carla: Well, it's not what I want. This is me, Carla. I have never read a whole book. Page six, I can't remember page four. The last thing I read was *The Complete Idiot's Guide to WordPerfect.* I leave dinner parties right after the dessert because I'm out of conversation. You know the dumb blond joke about the application where it says, "Sign here," she put Sagittarius? I've done that. Only beautiful guys approach me, and that's because they want to borrow my eye shadow. I barely exist outside a mirror! You don't want to *be me.*

Bethany: None of you tell the truth. That's why you have no friends. We can all see you're just trying to make us feel better because we aren't in your league. This only proves to me it should be my third wish. Money can only buy things. Beauty makes you the center of the universe.

Bethany picks up the lamp.

Carla: Don't do it. Bethany, don't wish it! I am telling you you'll regret it.

Bethany lifts the lid. There is a tremendous crash, and the lights go out. Then they flicker and come back up, revealing Bethany and Carla on the floor where they have been thrown by the explosion. We don't realize it at first, but they have exchanged places.

Carla/Bethany: Oh God.

Bethany/Carla: Oh God. 75

Carla/Bethany: Am I bleeding? Am I dying?

Bethany/Carla: I'm so dizzy. You're not bleeding.

Carla/Bethany: Neither are you.

Bethany/Carla: I feel so weird.

Carla/Bethany: Me too. I feel . . . *(Looking at her hands.)* 80 Oh, my God, I'm wearing your jewelry. I'm wearing your nail polish.

Bethany/Carla: I know I'm over here, but I can see myself over there.

Carla/Bethany: I'm wearing your dress. I have your legs!!

Bethany/Carla: These aren't my shoes. I can't meet Ralph Lauren wearing these shoes!

Carla/Bethany: I wanted to be beautiful, but I didn't want to be you.

Bethany/Carla: Thanks a lot!! 85

Carla/Bethany: I've got to go. I want to pick someone out and get laid.

Bethany/Carla: You can't just walk out of here in my body!

Carla/Bethany: Wait a minute. Wait a minute. What's eleven eighteenths of 1,726?

Bethany/Carla: Why?

Carla/Bethany: I'm a public accountant. I want to know 90 if you have my brain.

Bethany/Carla: One hundred thirty-two and a half.

Carla/Bethany: You have my brain.

Bethany/Carla: What shade of Rubenstein lipstick does Cindy Crawford wear with teal blue?

Carla/Bethany: Raging Storm.

Bethany/Carla: You have my brain. You poor bastard. 95

Carla/Bethany: I don't care. Don't you see?

Bethany/Carla: See what?

Carla/Bethany: We both have the one thing, the one and only thing everybody wants.

Bethany/Carla: What is that?

Carla/Bethany: It's better than beauty for me; it's better 100 than brains for you.

Bethany/Carla: What? What?!

Carla/Bethany: Different problems.

Blackout.

*   *   *

José Rivera (1955–   )

was born in San Juan, Puerto Rico, and grew up in a household where the only book was a Bible. When he was four years old, his family moved to New York. Early in his life, he saw a staged version of the play *Rumpelstiltskin* and decided to become a playwright. He has written numerous plays and won several awards, including two Obie Awards, a Fulbright Fellowship, and the Whiting Foundation Writing Award. In 2002, Rivera wrote the screenplay for *The Motorcycle Diaries*, a movie based on a motorcycle trip that Cuban revolutionary Che Guevara took as a young man. In 2005, Rivera became the first Puerto Rican to be nominated for an Academy Award for best adapted screenplay.

Tape (1993)

CHARACTERS

Person   Attendant

A small dark room. No windows. One door. A Person is being led in by an Attendant. In the room is a simple wooden table and chair. On the table is a large reel-to-reel tape recorder, a glass of water, and a pitcher of water.

Person: Dark in here.

Attendant: I'm sorry.

Person: No, I know it's not your fault.

Attendant: I'm afraid of those lights . . .

Person: I guess, what does it matter now? 5

Attendant: . . . not very bright.

Person: Who cares, really?

Attendant: We don't want to cause you any undue suffering. If it's too dark in here, I'll make sure one of the other attendants replaces the light bulb.

(The Person looks at the Attendant.)

Person: Any "undue suffering"?

Attendant: That's right. *(The Person looks at the room.)* 10

Person: Is this where I'll be?

Attendant: That's right.

Person: Will you be outside?

Attendant: Yes.

Person: The entire time? 15

Attendant: The entire time.

Person: Is it boring?

Attendant: I'm sorry?

Person: Is it boring? You know. Waiting outside all the time.

Attendant: *(Soft smile.)* It's my job. It's what I do. 20

Person: Of course. *(Beat.)* Will I get anything to eat or drink?

Attendant: Well, we're not really set up for that. We don't have what you'd call a kitchen. But we can send out for things. Little things. Cold food.

Person: I understand.

Attendant: Soft drinks.

Person: *(Hopefully.)* Beer? 25

Attendant: I'm afraid not.

Person: Not even on special occasions like my birthdays?

Attendant: *(Thinking.)* I guess maybe on your birthday.

Person: *(Truly appreciative.)* Great, thanks. *(Beat.)*

Attendant: Do you have any more questions before we 30 start? Because if you do, that's okay. It's okay to ask as many questions as you want. I'm sure you're very curious. I'm sure you'd like to know as much as possible, so you can figure out how it all fits together and what it all means. So please ask. That's why I'm here. Don't worry about the time. We have a lot of time. *(Beat.)*

Person: I don't have any questions.

Attendant: *(Disappointed.)* Are you sure?

Person: There's not much I really have to know is there? Really?

Attendant: No, I guess not. I just thought . . .

Person: It's okay. I appreciate it. I guess I really want 35 to sit.

Attendant: Sit. *(The person sits on the chair and faces the tape recorder.)*

Person: Okay, I'm sitting.

Attendant: Is it . . . comfortable?

Person: Does it matter? Does it really fucking matter?

Attendant: No. I suppose not. *(The Attendant looks 40 sad. The Person looks at the Attendant and feels bad.)*

Person: Hey I'm sorry. I know it's not your fault. I know you didn't mean it. I'm sorry.

Attendant: It's all right.

Person: What's your name anyway? Do you have a name?

Attendant: Not really. It's not allowed.

Person: Really? Not allowed? Who says? 45

Attendant: The rules say.

Person: Have you actually seen these rules? Are they in writing?

Attendant: Oh yes. There's a long and extensive training course.

Person: *(Surprised.)* There is?

Attendant: Oh yes. It's quite rigorous. 50

Person: Imagine that.

Attendant: You have to be a little bit of everything. Confidant, confessor, friend, stern taskmaster. Guide.

Person: I guess that would take time.

Attendant: My teachers were all quite strong and capable. They really pushed me. I was grateful. I knew I had been chosen for something unique and exciting. Something significant. Didn't mind the hard work and sleepless nights.

Person: *(Surprised.)* Oh? You sleep? 55

Attendant: *(Smiles.)* When I can. *(Beat.)*

Person: Do you dream? *(Beat.)*

Attendant: No. *(Beat.)* That's not allowed. *(Beat.)*

Person: I'm sorry.

Attendant: No. It's something you get used to. 60

Person: *(Trying to be chummy.)* I know. I went years and years without being able to remember one single dream I had. It really scared the shit out of me when I was ten and . . .

Attendant: I know.

Person: I'm sorry.

Attendant: I said I know. I know that story. When you were ten.

Person: Oh. Yeah. I guess you would know everything. 65 Every story.

Attendant: *(Apologetic.)* It's part of the training.

Person: I figured. *(A long uncomfortable silence.)*

Attendant: *(Softly.)* Have you ever operated a reel-to-reel tape recorder before?

Person: No I haven't. I mean—no.

Attendant: It's not hard. 70

Person: I, uhm, these things were pretty obsolete by the time I was old enough to afford stereo equipment, you know, I got into cassettes, and, later, CDs, but never one of these jobbies.

Attendant: It's not hard. *(Demonstrates.)* On here. Off here. Play. Pause. Rewind.

Person: *(Surprised.)* Rewind?

Attendant: In some cases the quality of the recording is so poor . . . you'll want to rewind it until you understand.

Person: No fast forward? 75

Attendant: No.

Person: It looks like a pretty good one. Sturdy. Very strong.

Attendant: They get a lot of use.

Person: I bet. *(Beat.)* Is this the only tape? *(The Attendant laughs out loud—then quickly stops.)*

Attendant: No.

Person: I didn't think so.

Attendant: There are many more.

Person: How many? A lot?

Attendant: There are ten thousand boxes.

Person: *Ten* thousand?

Attendant: I'm afraid so.

Person: Did I really . . .

Attendant: I'm afraid you did.

Person: So . . . everyone goes into a room like this?

Attendant: Exactly like this. There's no differentiation. Everyone's equal.

Person: For once.

Attendant: What isn't equal, of course, is the . . . amount of time you spend here listening.

Person: Oh God.

Attendant: *(Part of the training.)* Listening, just to yourself. To your voice.

Person: I know.

Attendant: Listening, word by word, to every lie you ever told while you were alive.

Person: Oh God!

Attendant: Every ugly lie to every person, every single time, every betrayal, every lying thought, every time you lied to yourself, deep in your mind, we were listening, we were recording, and it's all in these tapes, ten thousand boxes of them, in your own words, one lie after the next, over and over, until we're finished. So the amount of time varies. The amount of time you spend here all depends on how many lies you told. How many boxes of tape we have to get through together.

Person: *(Almost in tears.)* I'm sorry . . .

Attendant: Too late.

Person: I said I'm sorry! I said I'm sorry! I said it a million times! What happened to forgiveness? I don't want to be here! I don't want this! I don't want to listen! I don't want to hear myself! I didn't mean to say the things that I said! I don't want to listen!

Attendant: Yes, well. Neither did we. Neither did we. *(The Attendant looks sadly at the Person. The Attendant turns on the tape recorder. The Attendant hits the Play button, the reels spin slowly, and the tape starts snaking its way through the machine. Silence. The Attendant leaves the room, leaving the Person all alone. The Person nervously pours a glass of water, accidentally spilling water on the floor. From the depths of the machine comes a long-forgotten voice.)*

Woman's Voice: "Where have you been? Do you know I've been looking all over? Jesus Christ! I went to Manny's! I went to the pharmacy! The school! I even called the police! Look at me, Jesus Christ, I'm shaking! Now look at me—look at me and tell me where the hell you were! Tell me right now!" *(Silence. As the Person waits for the lying response, the lights fade to black.)*

*   *   *

Zora Neale Hurston (1891–1960)

was born in Notasulga, Alabama, and grew up in Eatonville, Florida, the first incorporated African American town in the United States and the subject of much of her literary work. After overcoming various personal setbacks that uprooted her from one home to another, she attended Howard University, where she published her work in the school's journals and where she joined the theater group the Howard Players. After winning second prize in the *Opportunity* literary contest for her short story "Drenched in Light," Hurston moved to New York City in 1925. There, she attended Barnard College and met Langston Hughes, Countee Cullen, and other preeminent African American writers who came to be known as the Harlem renaissance writers. Despite continued personal setbacks, she went on to publish various plays, poems, short stories, folk tales, and the novels *Jonah's Gourd Vine* (1934); *Their Eyes Were Watching God* (1937); *Moses, Man of the Mountain* (1939); and *Seraph on the Suwannee* (1948). The following play was one of several unpublished dramatic works written by Hurston that surfaced in 1997 at the Library of Congress.

Poker! (1931)

Time—Present

Place—New York

CHARACTERS

Nunkie Too-Sweet
Peckerwood* Black Baby
Sack Daddy Tush Hawg
Aunt Dilsey

SCENE

A shabby front room in a shotgun house.°

A door covered by dingy portieres° upstage C. Small panel window in side Wall L. Plain centre table with chairs drawn up about it. Gaudy calendars on wall. Battered piano against wall R. Kerosene lamp with reflector against wall on either side of room.

At rise of curtain Nunkie is at piano playing. . . . Others at table with small stacks of chips before each man. Tush Hawg is seated at table so that he faces audience. He is expertly riffing° the cards. . . looks over his shoulder and speaks to Nunkie.

Tush Hawg: Come on here, Nunkie—and take a hand! You're holding up the game. You been woofin' round here about the poker you can play—now do it!

Nunkie: Yeah, I plays poker. I plays the piano and Gawd knows I plays the devil.

Black Baby: Aw, you can be had! Come on and get in the game! My britches is cryin' for your money!

Nunkie: Soon as I play the deck I'm comin' and take you alls money! Don' rush me.

Ace means the first time that I met you
Duece means there was nobody there but us two
Trey means the third party—Charlie was his name
Four spot means the fourth time you tried that same old game—
Five spot means five years you played me for a clown
Six spot means six feet of earth when the deal goes down
Now I'm holding the seven spot for each day of the week

---

* "Peckerwood" and "Beckerwood" are used interchangeably in the original manuscript.

° **shotgun house** Narrow rectangular house most common in the South.

° **portieres** Curtains.

° **riffing** Skimming.

° **John Henry** Hero of a popular African-American folk ballad who competes against a steam drill and breaks more rock with his hammer but who consequently dies.

Eight means eight hours that she Sheba-ed with your Sheik—
Nine spot means nine hours that I work hard every day—
Ten spot means tenth of every month I brought you home my pay—
The Jack is three-card Charlie who played me for a goat
The Queen, that's my pretty Mama, also trying to cut my throat—
The King stands for Sweet Papa Nunkie and he's goin' to wear the crown,
So be careful you all ain't broke when the deal goes down!

He laughs—X'es to table, bringing piano stool for seat.

Tush Hawg: Aw now, brother, two dollars for your seat before you try to sit in this game. 5

Nunkie: *Laughs sheepishly—puts money down—Tush Hawg pushes stack of chips toward him. Bus.*

I didn't put it down because I knew you all goin' to be puttin' it right back in my pocket.

Peckerwood: Aw, Y'all go ahead and play. (*to Tush Hawg*) Deal!

Tush Hawg beings to deal for draw poker. The game gets tense. Sack Daddy is first man at Tush's left—he throws back three cards and is dealt three more.

Sack Daddy: My luck sure is rotten! My gal must be cheatin' on me. I ain't had a pair since John Henry° had a hammer!

Black Baby: (*drawing three new cards*) You might be fooling the rest with the cryin' you're doin' but I'm squattin' for you! You're cryin' worse than cryin' Emma!

Too-Sweet: (*studying his three new cards—Sings*) 10
When yo' cards gets lucky, oh Partner, you oughter be in a rollin' game. Get you foot offa my chair.

Aunt Dilsey: (*enters through portieres—stands and looks disapprovingly*) You all oughter be ashamed of yourself, gamblin' and carryin' on like this!

Black Baby: Aw, this ain't no harm, Aunt Dilsey! You go on back to bed and git your night's rest.

Aunt Dilsey: No harm! I know all about these no-harm sins! If you don't stop this card playin', all of you all goin' to die and go to Hell.

Shakes warning finger—exits through portieres. While she is talking the men have been hiding cards out of their hands and pulling aces out of sleeves and vest pockets and shoes. It is done quickly. One does not see the other do it.

Nunkie: (*shoving a chip forward*) A dollar!

Sack daddy: Raise you two! 15

Black Baby: I don't like to strain with nobody but it's goin' to cost you five. Come on, you shag-nags!

Too-Sweet: You all act like you're spuddin'!° Bet some money! Put your money where your mouth is els my fist where yo mouf is.

Tush Hawg: Twenty-five dollars to keep my company! Dog-gone, I'm spreadin' my knots!

Sack Daddy: And I bet you a fat man I'll take your money—I call you.

Turns up his cards—he has four aces and king.

Tush Hawg: (*showing his cards*) 20

Youse a liar! I ain't dealt you no aces. Don't try to carry the Pam-Pam to me 'cause I'll gently chain-gang° for you!

Sack Daddy: Oh yeah! I ain't goin' to fit no jail for you and nobody else. I'm to get me a green club and season it over your head. Then I'll give my case to Miss Bush and let Mother Green stand my bond! I got deal them aces!

Nunkie: That's a lie! Both of you is lyin'! Lyin' like the cross-ties° from New York to Key West! How can you all hold aces when I got *four*? Somebody is goin' to West hell before midnight!

Peckerwood: Don't you woof at Tush Hawg. If you do I'm goin' to bust hell wide open with a man!

Black Baby: (*pulls out razor—bus.*) My chop-axe tells me I got the only clean aces they is on this table! Before I'll leave you all rob me outa my money, I'm goin' to die it off!

Too-Sweet: I promised the devil one man and I'm goin' to give him five! 25

Draws gun.

Tush Hawg: Don't draw your bosom on me! God sent me a pistol and I'm goin' to send him a man!

Fires. Bus. for all.

Aunt Dilsey: (*enters after shooting bus. Stands. Bus. Drops to chair.*)
They wouldn't lissen—(*looks men over—bus.*) It sure is goin' to be a whole lot tougher in hell now!

CURTAIN

° **spuddin'** Betting with small change.

° **chain-gang** Group of convicts chained together to perform outside work.

° **cross-ties:** beams connecting the rails of a railroad.

Writing Suggestions: Ten-Minute Plays

1. Assume you are a director writing notes for an actor who is to play a role in one of this chapter's plays. Write a character sketch in which you outline the character's background and explain his or her emotions, actions, conflicts, and motivation.

2. Choose a scene from one of the longer plays in this text that has a definite beginning, middle, and end. Rewrite this scene as a self-contained ten-minute play. (If you like, you can update the scene to the present time, change the characters' names or genders, and make other changes you see as necessary.)

3. Write an original ten-minute play for two characters.

Reading and Reacting to Ten-Minute Plays

1. Do you think any of the characters in the three plays in this chapter are fully developed, or do you see most (or all) of them as stereotypes? Given the limits of its form, can a ten-minute play ever really develop a character?

2. Both *Beauty* and *Tape* have only two characters. Should any additional parts have been written for these plays?

3. The play *Tape* was written for two actors of either gender. Could the roles in the other plays in this chapter also be portrayed by actors of either gender? By actors of any age? Of any race?

4. Identify the central conflict in each play. What do you see as the **climax,** or highest point of tension, in each? Where does the climax generally occur in these plays?

5. Each play in this chapter has a single setting, and each of these settings is described only minimally. Do any settings seem to require more detailed descriptions? If you were going to expand each play, what additional settings might you show?

6. Considering the subject matter of each of the plays in this chapter, what kinds of topics seem to be most appropriate for ten-minute plays? Why do you think this is so? What kinds of topics would *not* be suitable for ten-minute plays?

7. The Web site *10-Minute-Plays.com,* whose slogan is "High-octane drama for a fast-food nation," summarizes the structure of a ten-minute play as follows:

   Pages 1 to 2: Set up the world of your main character.
   Pages 2 to 3: Something happens to throw your character's world out of balance.
   Pages 4 to 7: Your character struggles to restore order to his world.
   Page 8: Just when your character is about to restore order, something happens to complicate matters.
   Pages 9 to 10: Your character either succeeds or fails in his attempt to restore order.

   Although the plays in this chapter are not all ten pages long, do they nevertheless conform to the general structure outlined above?

Glossary Terms

conflict Struggle between opposing forces (protagonist and antagonist) in a work of literature.

exposition First stage of a plot, where the author presents the information about characters or setting that a reader or viewer will need to understand the subsequent action.

haiku Seventeen-syllable, three-line form of Japanese verse that almost always uses concrete imagery and deals with the natural world.

resolution Also called the **denouement,** this is the final stage in the plot. Here the action comes to an end, and remaining loose ends are tied up.

ten-minute play Short play that can be performed in ten minutes or less.

32

Plot

Learning Outcomes

After reading this chapter, you should be able to do the following:

LO1 Understand plot structure

LO2 Understand plot development

Timeline

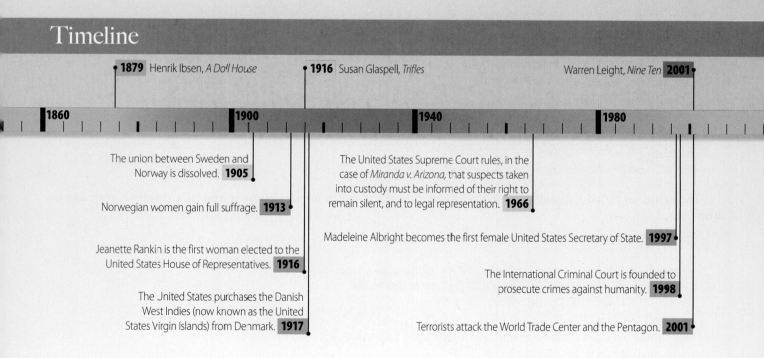

1879 Henrik Ibsen, *A Doll House*

1916 Susan Glaspell, *Trifles*

Warren Leight, *Nine Ten* **2001**

1860   1900   1940   1980

The union between Sweden and Norway is dissolved. **1905**

Norwegian women gain full suffrage. **1913**

Jeanette Rankin is the first woman elected to the United States House of Representatives. **1916**

The United States purchases the Danish West Indies (now known as the United States Virgin Islands) from Denmark. **1917**

The United States Supreme Court rules, in the case of *Miranda v. Arizona*, that suspects taken into custody must be informed of their right to remain silent, and to legal representation. **1966**

Madeleine Albright becomes the first female United States Secretary of State. **1997**

The International Criminal Court is founded to prosecute crimes against humanity. **1998**

Terrorists attack the World Trade Center and the Pentagon. **2001**

plot Way in which the events of the story are arranged. When there are two stories of more or less equal importance, the work has a **double plot**; when there is more than one story but one string of events is clearly the most significant, the other stories are called **subplots**.

exposition First stage of a plot, where the author presents the information about characters or setting that a reader or viewer will need to understand the subsequent action.

rising action Stage in a play's plot during which the action builds in intensity.

climax Point of greatest tension or importance, where the decisive action of a play takes place.

falling action Stage in a play's plot during which the intensity of the climax subsides.

resolution (also called **denouement**) Final stage in the plot of a drama or work of fiction, where the action comes to an end and remaining loose ends are tied up.

Plot denotes the way events are arranged in a work of literature. Although the conventions of drama require that the plot of a play be presented somewhat differently from the plot of a short story, the same components of plot are present in both. Plot in a dramatic work, like plot in a short story, is shaped by conflicts that are revealed, intensified, and resolved through the characters' actions. (See Chapter 11 for a discussion of conflict.)

LO1 Understand Plot Structure

In 1863, the German critic Gustav Freytag devised a pyramid (see below) to represent a prototype for the plot of a dramatic work. According to Freytag, a play typically begins with **exposition,** which presents characters and setting and introduces the basic situation in which the characters are involved. Then, during the **rising action,** complications develop, conflicts emerge, suspense builds, and crises occur. The rising action culminates in a **climax,** a point at which the plot's tension peaks. Finally, during the **falling action,** the intensity subsides, eventually winding down to a **resolution,** or **denouement,** in which all loose ends are tied up.

The familiar plot of a detective story follows Freytag's concept of plot: the exposition section includes the introduction of the detective and the explanation of the crime; the rising action develops as the investigation of the crime proceeds, with suspense increasing as the solution approaches; the high point of the action, the climax, comes with the revelation of the crime's solution; and the falling action presents the detective's explanation of the solution. The story concludes with a resolution that typically includes the capture of the criminal and the restoration of order.

>> **FREYTAG'S PYRAMID**

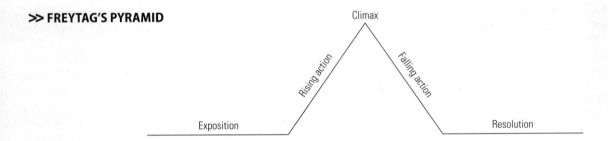

The action of Susan Glaspell's one-act play *Trifles* (p. 555), which in many ways resembles a detective story, can be diagrammed like this.

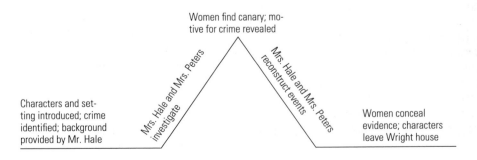

Of course, the plot of a complex dramatic work rarely conforms to the neat pattern represented by Freytag's pyramid. For example, a play can lack exposition entirely. Because long stretches of exposition can be dull, a playwright may decide to arouse audience interest by moving directly into conflict, as Sophocles does in *Oedipus the King* (p. 701). Similarly, because audiences tend to lose interest after the play's climax is reached, a playwright may choose to dispense with extended falling action. Thus, after Hamlet's death, the play ends quite abruptly, with no real resolution.

PLOT AND SUBPLOT

While the main plot is developing, a parallel plot, called a **subplot,** may be developing alongside it. This structural device is common in the works of Shakespeare and in many other plays as well. The subplot's function may not immediately be clear, so at first it may seem to draw attention away from the main plot. Ultimately, however, the subplot reinforces elements of the primary plot. In Henrik Ibsen's *A Doll House* (p. 562), for example, the threat of Dr. Rank's impending death parallels the threat of Nora's approaching exposure; for both of them, time is running out.

In Shakespeare's *King Lear,* a more elaborate subplot involves the Earl of Gloucester, who, like Lear, misjudges his children, favoring a deceitful son who does not deserve his support and overlooking a more deserving one. Both families suffer greatly as a result of the fathers' misplaced loyalties. Thus, the parallel plot places additional emphasis on Lear's poor judgment and magnifies the consequences of his misguided acts: both fathers, and all but one of the five children, are dead by the play's end. A subplot can also set up a contrast with the main plot—as it does in *Hamlet* (p. 644), where Fortinbras acts decisively to avenge his father, an action that underscores Hamlet's hesitation and procrastination when faced with a similar challenge.

LO2 Understand Plot Development

In a dramatic work, plot unfolds through **action:** what characters say and do. Generally, a play does not include a narrator. Instead, dialogue, stage directions, and various staging techniques work together to move the play's action along.

Exchanges of **dialogue** reveal what is happening—and, sometimes, indicate what happened in the past or suggest what will happen in the future. Characters can recount past events to other characters, announce an intention to take some action in the future, or summarize events that are occurring offstage. Thus, dialogue takes the place of formal narrative.

On the printed page, **stage directions** efficiently move readers from one location and time period to another by specifying entrances and exits and identifying the play's structural divisions—acts and scenes—and their accompanying changes of setting.

action What happens in a drama.

dialogue Conversation between two or more characters.

stage directions Words in a play that describe an actor's movements, attitudes, and so on.

props (short for **properties**) Pictures, furnishings, and the like that decorate the stage for a play.

flashback Departure from chronological order that presents an event or situation that occurred before the time in which the action of a play takes place.

Staging techniques can also advance a play's action. For example, a change in **lighting** can shift the focus to another part of the stage—and thus to another place and time. An adjustment of **scenery** or **props**—for instance, a breakfast table, complete with morning paper, replacing a bedtime setting—can indicate that the action has moved forward in time, as can a change of costumes. **Music** can also move a play's action along, predicting excitement or doom or a romantic interlude—or a particular character's entrance.

In Tennessee Williams's classic 1945 play *The Glass Menagerie,* unusual staging devices—such as words projected on a screen that preview words to be spoken by a character and visual images on screen that predict scenes to follow—were designed to help keep the action moving. For example, a screen image of blue roses leads into a scene in which the shy, fragile Laura tells her mother how she was given the nickname "Blue Roses." Other unconventional staging techniques are also used to advance the plot. For example, toward the end of scene 5, stage directions announce, *"The Dance-Hall Music Changes To A Tango That Has A Minor and Somewhat Ominous Tone,"* and a "music legend" repeated throughout the play serves as a signature in scenes focusing on Laura.

Occasionally, a play does have a formal narrator. In Thornton Wilder's play *Our Town* (1938), a character known as the Stage Manager functions as a narrator, not only describing the play's setting and introducing the characters to the audience but also soliciting questions from characters scattered around the audience, prompting characters, and interrupting dialogue. In *The Glass Menagerie,* the protagonist, Tom Wingfield, also serves as a narrator, summarizing what has happened and moving the audience on to the next scene, as in these lines that introduce scene 3: "After the fiasco at Rubicam's Business College, the idea of getting a gentleman caller for Laura began to play a more important part in Mother's calculations."

FLASHBACKS

Many plays—such as Arthur Miller's *Death of a Salesman* (p. 605)—include **flashbacks,** which depict events that

FORESHADOWING

In addition to revealing past events, dialogue can **foreshadow,** or look ahead to, future action. In many cases, seemingly unimportant comments have significance that becomes clear as the play develops. For example, in act 3 of *A Doll House*, Torvald Helmer says to Kristine, "An exit should always be effective, Mrs. Linde, but that's what I can't get Nora to grasp." At the end of the play, Nora's exit is not only effective but also memorable.

Elements of staging can also suggest events to come. In *The Glass Menagerie*, the ever-present photograph of the absent father—who, the audience is told in scene 1, may be seen as a symbol of "the long delayed but always expected something that we live for"—foreshadows the eventual escape of Tom, the protagonist. Finally, various bits of **stage business**—gestures or movements designed to attract the audience's attention—may also foreshadow future events. In *A Doll House*, Nora's sneaking forbidden macaroons seems at first to suggest her fear of her husband, but her actions actually foreshadow her eventual defiance of his authority.

occurred before the play's main action. Dialogue can also summarize events that occurred earlier, thereby overcoming the limitations set by the time frame in which the play's action unfolds. Thus, Mr. Hale in *Trifles* tells the other characters how he discovered John Wright's murder, and Nora in *A Doll House* confides her secret past to her friend Kristine. As characters on stage are brought up to date, the audience is also given necessary information—facts that are essential to an understanding of the characters' motivation. (In less realistic dramas, characters can interrupt the action to deliver long monologues or soliloquies that fill in background details—or even address the audience directly.)

Warren Leight (1957–)

is a widely acclaimed writer and director and was a writer/producer for the television series *Law and Order: Criminal Intent*. His play *Side Man* (1998) was nominated for a Pulitzer Prize and won Broadway's 1999 Tony Award for Best Play. His other plays include *Glimmer, Glimmer and Shine* (2001)

and *No Foreigners Beyond This Point* (2006). His screen credits include *The Night We Never Met* (1993) and *Dear God* (1996).

© Scott Gries/Getty Images

Cultural Context

The right of the accused to a trial by jury is stated in the Sixth Amendment to the United States Constitution as well as in the constitutions of individual states. However, even though it is a civic duty and an important cultural mainstay, many Americans see jury duty as a burden because it requires them to take time off from their work and family responsibilities to serve. Although failing to appear for jury service is a crime, a study conducted by the American Judicature Society reported that, on any given day, an average of twenty percent of Americans summoned for jury duty do not appear. (That number drops to fewer than ten percent in some urban areas.) Some common excuses people use to try to get out of serving include obligations at school, work, or home; child or elder care; illness or disability; and bias (which may result from prior knowledge of the case or having a previous or ongoing relationship with someone involved in the case). In one 2007 criminal case in Miami, Florida, a prospective juror was dismissed after she told the judge that, if she served, her pet ferret would be left home alone.

Nine Ten (2001)

Leslie
John
Kearrie
Nick
Lyris

Jury Duty Grand Hall. Morning.

John, a slightly awkward bond trader, sits on a bench. Very neat, buttoned down. He reads a perfectly folded Wall Street Journal. *Lyris Touzet, a dancer, enters, almost spills her coffee on him.*

Lyris: Is this Part B?
John: What?
Lyris: Part B, or not part B?
John: Ah . . . that is the question.
Lyris: Are you making fun of me? 5
John: No no. Um, let me look at your . . . (*She hands him a slip of paper, he reads it.*) Where you are is where you're supposed to be.

She sits next to him. He needs a little more personal space than she does.

Lyris: Why do they call us at eight-thirty? It's like, nine already, and they haven't said anything.
John: They build in a grace period.
Lyris: They what?
John: They say eight-thirty so that most people get here 10 by nine. And around nine ten they start calling names.
Lyris: You knew this, and you came at eight-thirty?
John: Eight actually.
Lyris: Eight A.M.? You must hate your wife.
John: I don't see her much. We both have to be at work at six.
Lyris: You punch in at six? 15
John: Well, I don't . . . punch in exactly. But, the desk opens at six so . . . .
Lyris: Your desk opens?
John: Sorry. Trading desk. Bonds. Euros, mostly. From my desk, I'm up so high, on a clear day, you can see Europe.

At a bench opposite, Nick Theron works the Times *crossword puzzle as Leslie Rudin arrives, pissed off and hyper.*

Leslie: Part B?
Nick: Must be. 20
Lyris: Have they called any—
Nick: Does it look like it? (*She looks to the court officer's desk, downstage left.*) Every once in a while this guy comes out and says we should wait. Which is . . . helpful.
Leslie: I tried to get out of it on the phone and they said it was my third postponement and I had to come down here in person on the day of and that I wasn't going to get out anyway. And I finally get here— do they just change the names of the subway lines for spite lately?—and there's a line a mile long to get through security and they go through my purse like I'm a serial killer and it turns out if I want to smoke I'm going to have to go down and outside, and then wait on line again for them to check my bag. This just sucks.
Nick: I'm going to tell the judge that I'm a felon. He won't even question it. And he'll tell me felons can't serve. I'll act offended at this. And then he'll just let me go back to my life.
Leslie: (*impressed*) That's good. 25
Nick: Racial profiling. A two-way street.

Over to John and Lyris.

Lyris: My brother's in the same building. Security guard. You probably don't know him.

Kearrie, a tough businesswoman, enters, rushed.

Kearrie: Part B?
lyris and John: Or not part B?
Kearrie: It's too early for cute. (*They look at her, she* 30 *means it.*) Have they started to give out postponements yet?
Lyris: No one gets postponement.
Kearrie: I'm on a flight tomorrow. (*Pulls something out of her bag.*) I've got a ticket.

John takes another look at her.

John: Kearrie?
Kearrie: What?
John: It's me, John. . . . 35
Kearrie: Right. John. That narrows it down.
John: John McCormack. From Wharton.

Kearrie still doesn't place him.

Lyris: (*to John*) You sure leave an impression.

John: Story of my life. (*To Kearrie.*) Case study. Euro-economic unity.

Kearrie: You got an A, I got a B plus. Even though we worked together. 40

John: (*to Lyris*) You know about Irish Alzheimer's . . . you forget everything except your grudges.

Kearrie: You went to Gold and Strauss when we graduated, right?

John: Still there.

Kearrie: (*grades him a loser*) You're kidding. You are not still at—

John: Just the last ten years. Kearrie this is— 45

Lyris: Lyris Touzet. Spiritual dancer. And healer.

John: Lyris this is Kearrie Whitman. We went to Wharton together. Classof 91.

Lyris: I must have missed you two by like . . . one year.

Leslie and Nick. He has no hope of attending to his crossword puzzle. Leslie must talk or die.

Leslie: I'm out in the Hamptons. One week after Labor Day. Paradise found. The assholes are gone. The beaches are empty. The water is warm.

Nick: Sharks are hungry. 50

Leslie: No sharks in the Hamptons. Professional courtesy.

Nick: Touché.

Leslie: I think I'll stay another day. Then I remember . . . fuck me—eightthirty summons. Drive in at midnight. Get stuck in traffic. The L.I.E. has got to be the only road in the world that has traffic jams at two A.M. By the time I get to my garage it's locked for the night. You ever try to find a space on the right side of the street at two A.M.?

Back to John and Lyris chatting. Kearrie plays with her Palm Pilot.

John: It's funny, I always wanted to be a spiritual dancer.

Lyris: You're making fun of me. 55

John: I'm not. . . . swear to god. But what is a—

Lyris: I heal people, through movement. Rhythm. Every person has theirown . . . pulse. Below the surface, that—

Kearrie: Fuck me!

Lyris: I help them to get in touch with their inner—

Kearrie: (*Turns to them.*) Fuck me fuck me fuck . . . 60

John: What's hers?

Kearrie now rants in their direction, about her Palm Pilot.

Kearrie: Money on the table. I've got a watch list. It's programmed to signal me when there's a discrepancy between euro prices and ADRs. The spread is sitting there. Sitting there. It's blinking—buy me. Buy me. I try to buy and my damn signal fades. What's the point of fucking having a watch list if you can't follow up on it. This whole building should be wired. This city is . . . in the stone ages.

Lyris: (*to John*) Some people are harder cases than others.

Over to Nick and Leslie.

Nick: My neighborhood, downtown, they're *always* filming. Some sequel to a sequel to a disaster flick. *Mortal Danger Times Four*. Whatever. Which means like—

Leslie: They take every parking place. Big lights up— 65

Nick: —all night long.

Leslie: Idiots in walkie-talkies saying don't walk there. On your own street. Call the cops to complain, they don't care. No one in this city cares. The film crew can be, like, setting off concussion bombs, and nobody does anything.

Back to John and Lyris.

John: (*to Lyris*) I can't.

Lyris: Everybody can move. Even you . . . Stand up.

He doesn't.

Lyris: (*loud*) STAND UP! 70

Nick and Leslie hear this. Look over to John and Lyris. John doesn't want to attract attention, so he stands. John and Lyris now overlap with Nick and Leslie. Kearrie is in her own world.

Lyris: (*to John*) Just start to, sway a little . . . from your hips.

Leslie: (*to Nick*) That is sick the way he's flirting with her.

John sits back down.

John: I can't.

Lyris: Yes you can.

Nick: (*to Leslie*) How do you know it's his fault? 75

Leslie: (*to Nick*) It's always the guy's fault. I date cops. Believe me. I know.

John: (*to Lyris*) I don't like to. Move. I like things as they are. I've had the same job for ten years.

Kearrie: (*on her cell phone, to her office*) Here? It's a fucking hellhole. What do you think? Ah-huh. Ah-huh. Ah-huh. Look—keep that on hold.

John: (*to Lyris, oblivious to Kearrie*) Same office, same view. Married my junior high school sweetheart. We take the same train to work. We have the same lunch. Tuna. On rye. No mayo.

Lyris: No mayo? 80

John: It's not so bad, once you get used to it.

Kearrie: (*into phone*) Yeah as soon as they call roll, I show my plane ticket . . . and I'm out of here.

Now, from downstage left, a court officer enters.

Court Officer: Hello folks. Welcome to New York County Jury Duty. Before you all come up to me . . .

Kearrie: Excuse me, I have a flight to—

Nick: I have a record—   85

Court Officer: (*He drowns her out.*)—with your reasons for why you shouldn't be here, let me tell you: I've heard them all. On the bright side, most of you will get to go back to your life in two or three days.

Leslie, Nick, Kearrie, John, and Lyris all groan. Two days is eternity.

Court Officer: And we are as happy to have you, as you are happy to be here. First things first. Check your summons, and be sure you're in the right place. This is Civil Court. Part B. 60 Centre Street. Today is Monday, September 10th . . . Two thousand and one.

Blackout.

Related Works

"55 Miles to the Gas Pump" (p. 107), *Trifles* (p. 555)

Susan Glaspell (1882–1948)

was born in Davenport, Iowa, and graduated from Drake University in 1899. First a reporter and then a freelance writer, she lived in Chicago (where she was part of the Chicago renaissance that included poet Carl Sandburg and novelist Theodore Dreiser) and later in Greenwich Village. Her works include two plays in addition to *Trifles*, *The Verge* (1921) and *Alison's House* (1930), and several novels, including *Fidelity* (1915) and *The Morning Is Near Us* (1939). With her husband, George Cram Cook, she founded the Provincetown Players, which became the staging ground for innovative plays by Eugene O'Neill, among others.

Glaspell herself wrote plays for the Provincetown Players, beginning with *Trifles*, which she created for the 1916 season although she had never previously written a drama. The play opened on August 8, 1916, with Glaspell and her husband in the cast. Glaspell said she wrote *Trifles* in one afternoon, sitting in the empty theater and looking at the bare stage: "After a time, the stage became a kitchen—a kitchen there all by itself." She remembered a murder trial she had covered in Iowa in her days as a reporter, and the story began to play itself out on the stage as she gazed. Throughout her revisions, she said, she returned to look at the stage to see whether the events she was recording came to life on it. Although Glaspell later rewrote *Trifles* as a short story called "A Jury of Her Peers," the play remains her most successful and memorable work.

Trifles (1916)

CHARACTERS

George Henderson, *county attorney*

Henry Peters, *sheriff*

Lewis Hale, *a neighboring farmer*

Mrs. Peters

Mrs. Hale

SCENE

The kitchen in the now abandoned farmhouse of John Wright, a gloomy kitchen, and left without having been put in order—unwashed pans under the sink, a loaf of bread outside the breadbox, a dish towel on the table—other signs of incompleted work. At the rear the outer door opens and the Sheriff comes in followed by the County Attorney and Hale. The Sheriff and Hale are men in middle life, the County

Cultural Context One of the main themes of this play is the contrast between the sexes in terms of their roles, rights, and responsibilities. In 1916, when *Trifles* was first produced, women were not allowed to serve on juries in most states. This circumstance was in accordance with other rights denied to women, including the right to vote, which was not ratified in all states until 1920. Unable to participate in the most basic civic functions, women largely discussed politics only among themselves and were relegated to positions of lesser status in their personal and professional lives.

Attorney is a young man; all are much bundled up and go at once to the stove. They are followed by two women—the Sheriff's wife first; she is a slight wiry woman, a thin nervous face. Mrs. Hale is larger and would ordinarily be called more comfortable looking, but she is disturbed now and looks fearfully about as she enters. The women have come in slowly, and stand close together near the door.

County Attorney: *(rubbing his hands)* This feels good. Come up to the fire, ladies.

Mrs. Peters: *(after taking a step forward)* I'm not—cold.

Sheriff: *(unbuttoning his overcoat and stepping away from the stove as if to mark the beginning of official business)* Now, Mr. Hale, before we move things about, you explain to Mr. Henderson just what you saw when you came here yesterday morning.

County Attorney: By the way, has anything been moved? Are things just as you left them yesterday?

Sheriff: *(looking about)* It's just the same. When it 5 dropped below zero last night I thought I'd better send Frank out this morning to make a fire for us—no use getting pneumonia with a big case on, but I told him not to touch anything except the stove—and you know Frank.

County Attorney: Somebody should have been left here yesterday.

Sheriff: Oh—yesterday. When I had to send Frank to Morris Center for that man who went crazy—I want you to know I had my hands full yesterday. I knew you could get back from Omaha by today and as long as I went over everything here myself—

County Attorney: Well, Mr. Hale, tell just what happened when you came here yesterday morning.

Hale: Harry and I had started to town with a load of potatoes. We came along the road from my place and as I got here I said, "I'm going to see if I can't get John Wright to go in with me on a party

>> In this scene from the Provincetown Players' 1917 production of *Trifles,* the three men discuss the crime while Mrs. Peters and Mrs. Hale look on.

EXPLORE ONLINE >

To listen to an instructor podcast of *Trifles,* visit your Literature CourseMate, accessed through www.cengagebrain.com.

telephone." I spoke to Wright about it once before and he put me off, saying folks talked too much anyway, and all he asked was peace and quiet—I guess you know about how much he talked himself; but I thought maybe if I went to the house and talked about it before his wife, though I said to Harry that I didn't know as what his wife wanted made much difference to John—

County Attorney: Let's talk about that later, Mr. Hale. I do 10 want to talk about that, but tell now just what happened when you got to the house.

Hale: I didn't hear or see anything; I knocked at the door, and still it was all quiet inside. I knew they must be up, it was past eight o'clock. So I knocked again, and I thought I heard somebody say, "Come in." I wasn't sure, I'm not sure yet, but I opened the door—this door *(indicating the door by which the two women are still standing)* and there in that rocker—*(pointing to it)* sat Mrs. Wright.

They all look at the rocker.

County Attorney: What—was she doing?

Hale: She was rockin' back and forth. She had her apron in her hand and was kind of—pleating it.

County Attorney: And how did she—look?

Hale: Well, she looked queer. 15

County Attorney: How do you mean—queer?

Hale: Well, as if she didn't know what she was going to do next. And kind of done up.

County Attorney: How did she seem to feel about your coming?

Hale: Why, I don't think she minded—one way or other. She didn't pay much attention. I said, "How do, Mrs. Wright, it's cold, ain't it?" And she said, "Is it?"—and went on kind of pleating at her apron. Well, I was surprised; she didn't ask me to come up to the stove, or to set down, but just sat there, not even looking at me, so I said, "I want to see John." And then she—laughed. I guess you would call it a laugh. I thought of Harry and the team outside, so I said a little sharp: "Can't I see John?" "No," she says,

> "I said to Harry that I didn't know as what his wife wanted made much difference to John—"

kind o' dull like. "Ain't he home?" says I. "Yes," says she, "he's home." "Then why can't I see him?" I asked her, out of patience. "'Cause he's dead," says she. *"Dead?"* says I. She just nodded her head, not getting a bit excited, but rockin' back and forth. "Why—where is he?" says I, not knowing what to say. She just pointed upstairs—like that. *(Himself pointing to the room above.)* I got up, with the idea of going up there. I walked from there to here—then I says, "Why, what did he die of?" "He died of a rope round his neck," says she, and just went on pleatin' at her apron. Well, I went out and called Harry. I thought I might—need help. We went upstairs and there he was lyin'—

> "Why, what did he die of?" 'He died of a rope round his neck,' says she . . . ."

County Attorney: I think I'd rather have you go into that upstairs, where you can point it all out. Just go on now with the rest of the story. 20

Hale: Well, my first thought was to get that rope off. It looked . . . *(stops, his face twitches)* . . . but Harry, he went up to him, and he said, "No, he's dead all right, and we'd better not touch anything." So we went back down stairs. She was still sitting that same way. "Has anybody been notified?" I asked. "No," says she, unconcerned. "Who did this, Mrs. Wright?" said Harry. He said it businesslike—and she stopped pleatin' of her apron. "I don't know," she says. "You don't *know?*" says Harry. "No," says she. "Weren't you sleepin' in the bed with him?" says Harry. "Yes," says she, "but I was on the inside." "Somebody slipped a rope round his neck and strangled him and you didn't wake up?" says Harry. "I didn't wake up," she said after him. We must 'a looked as if we didn't see how that could be, for after a minute she said, "I sleep sound." Harry was going to ask her more questions but I said maybe we ought to let her tell her story first to the coroner, or the sheriff, so Harry went fast as he could to Rivers' place, where there's a telephone.

County Attorney: And what did Mrs. Wright do when she knew that you had gone for the coroner?

Hale: She moved from that chair to this one over here *(pointing to a small chair in the corner)* and just sat there with her hands held together and looking down. I got a feeling that I ought to make some conversation, so I said I had come in to see if John wanted to put in a telephone, and at that she started to laugh, and then she stopped and looked at me—scared. *(The County Attorney, who has had his notebook out, makes a note.)* I dunno, maybe it wasn't scared. I wouldn't like to say it was. Soon Harry got back, and then Dr. Lloyd came, and you, Mr. Peters, and so I guess that's all I know that you don't.

County Attorney: *(looking around)* I guess we'll go upstairs first—and then out to the barn and around there. *(To the Sheriff.)* You're convinced that there was nothing important here—nothing that would point to any motive.

Sheriff: Nothing here but kitchen things. 25

The County Attorney, after again looking around the kitchen, opens the door of a cupboard closet. He gets up on a chair and looks on a shelf. Pulls his hand away, sticky.

County Attorney: Here's a nice mess.

The women draw nearer.

Mrs. Peters: *(to the other woman)* Oh, her fruit; it did freeze. *(To the County Attorney.)* She worried about that when it turned so cold. She said the fire'd go out and her jars would break.

Sheriff: Well, can you beat the women! Held for murder and worryin' about her preserves.

County Attorney: I guess before we're through she may have something more serious than preserves to worry about.

Hale: Well, women are used to worrying over trifles. 30

The two women move a little closer together.

County Attorney: *(with the gallantry of a young politician)* And yet, for all their worries, what would we do without the ladies? *(The women do not unbend. He goes to the sink, takes a dipperful of water from the pail and pouring it into a basin, washes his hands. Starts to wipe them on the roller towel, turns it for a cleaner place.)* Dirty towels! *(Kicks his foot against the pans under the sink.)* Not much of a housekeeper, would you say, ladies?

Mrs. Hale: *(stiffly)* There's a great deal of work to be done on a farm.

County Attorney: To be sure. And yet *(with a little bow to her)* I know there are some Dickson county farmhouses which do not have such roller towels.

He gives it a pull to expose its full length again.

Mrs. Hale: Those towels get dirty awful quick. Men's hands aren't always as clean as they might be.

County Attorney: Ah, loyal to your sex, I see. But you and Mrs. Wright were neighbors. I suppose you were friends, too. 35

Mrs. Hale: *(shaking her head)* I've not seen much of her of late years. I've not been in this house—it's more than a year.

County Attorney: And why was that? You didn't like her?

Mrs. Hale: I liked her all well enough. Farmers' wives have their hands full, Mr. Henderson. And then—

County Attorney: Yes—?

Mrs. Hale: (looking about) It never seemed a very cheerful place. 40

County Attorney: No—it's not cheerful. I shouldn't say she had the homemaking instinct.

Mrs. Hale: Well, I don't know as Wright had, either.

County Attorney: You mean that they didn't get on very well?

Mrs. Hale: No, I don't mean anything. But I don't think a place'd be any cheerfuller for John Wright's being in it.

County Attorney: I'd like to talk more of that a little 45 later. I want to get the lay of things upstairs now.

He goes to the left, where three steps lead to a stair door.

Sheriff: I suppose anything Mrs. Peters does'll be all right. She was to take in some clothes for her, you know, and a few little things. We left in such a hurry yesterday.

County Attorney: Yes, but I would like to see what you take, Mrs. Peters, and keep an eye out for anything that might be of use to us.

Mrs. Peters: Yes, Mr. Henderson.

The women listen to the men's steps on the stairs, then look about the kitchen.

Mrs. Hale: I'd hate to have men coming into my kitchen, snooping around and criticizing.

She arranges the pans under sink which the County Attorney had shoved out of place.

Mrs. Peters: Of course it's no more than their duty. 50

Mrs. Hale: Duty's all right, but I guess that deputy sheriff that came out to make the fire might have got a little of this on. (Gives the roller towel a pull.) Wish I'd thought of that sooner. Seems mean to talk about her for not having things slicked up when she had to come away in such a hurry.

Mrs. Peters: (who has gone to a small table in the left rear corner of the room, and lifted one end of a towel that covers a pan) She had bread set.

Stands still.

Mrs. Hale: (eyes fixed on a loaf of bread beside the breadbox, which is on a low shelf at the other side of the room. Moves slowly toward it.) She was going to put this in there. (Picks up loaf, then abruptly drops it. In a manner of returning to familiar things.) It's a shame about her fruit. I wonder if it's all gone. (Gets up on the chair and looks.) I think there's some here that's all right, Mrs. Peters. Yes—here; (holding it toward the window) this is cherries, too. (Looking again.) I declare I believe that's the only one. (Gets down, bottle in her hand. Goes to the sink and wipes it off on the outside.) She'll feel awful bad after all her hard work in the hot weather. I remember the afternoon I put up my cherries last summer.

She puts the bottle on the big kitchen table, center of the room. With a sigh, is about to sit down in the rocking-chair. Before she is seated realizes what chair it is; with a slow look at it, steps back. The chair which she has touched rocks back and forth.

Mrs. Peters: Well, I must get those things from the front room closet. (She goes to the door at the right, but after looking into the other room, steps back.) You coming with me, Mrs. Hale? You could help me carry them.

They go in the other room; reappear, Mrs. Peters carrying a dress and skirt, Mrs. Hale following with a pair of shoes.

Mrs. Peters: My, it's cold in there. 55

She puts the clothes on the big table, and hurries to the stove.

Mrs. Hale: (examining her skirt) Wright was close. I think maybe that's why she kept so much to herself. She didn't even belong to the Ladies Aid. I suppose she felt she couldn't do her part, and then you don't enjoy things when you feel shabby. She used to wear pretty clothes and be lively, when she was Minnie Foster, one of the town girls singing in the choir. But that—oh, that was thirty years ago. This all you was to take in?

Mrs. Peters: She said she wanted an apron. Funny thing to want, for there isn't much to get you dirty in jail, goodness knows. But I suppose just to make her feel more natural. She said they was in the top drawer in this cupboard. Yes, here. And then her little shawl that always hung behind the door. (Opens stair door and looks.) Yes, here it is.

Quickly shuts door leading upstairs.

Mrs. Hale: (abruptly moving toward her) Mrs. Peters?

Mrs. Peters: Yes, Mrs. Hale?

Mrs. Hale: Do you think she did it? 60

Mrs. Peters: (in a frightened voice) Oh, I don't know.

Mrs. Hale: Well, I don't think she did. Asking for an apron and her little shawl. Worrying about her fruit.

Mrs. Peters: (starts to speak, glances up, where footsteps are heard in the room above. In a low voice.) Mr. Peters says it looks bad for her. Mr. Henderson is awful sarcastic in a speech and he'll make fun of her sayin' she didn't wake up.

Mrs. Hale: Well, I guess John Wright didn't wake when they was slipping that rope under his neck.

Mrs. Peters: No, it's strange. It must have been done 65 awful crafty and still. They say it was such a—funny way to kill a man, rigging it all up like that.

Mrs. Hale: That's just what Mr. Hale said. There was a gun in the house. He says that's what he can't understand.

Mrs. Peters: Mr. Henderson said coming out that what was needed for the case was a motive; something to show anger, or—sudden feeling.

Mrs. Hale: *(who is standing by the table)* Well, I don't see any signs of anger around here. *(She puts her hand on the dish towel which lies on the table, stands looking down at table, one half of which is clean, the other half messy.)* It's wiped to here. *(Makes a move as if to finish work, then turns and looks at loaf of bread outside the breadbox. Drops towel. In that voice of coming back to familiar things.)* Wonder how they are finding things upstairs. I hope she had it a little more red-up° up there. You know, it seems kind of *sneaking*. Locking her up in town and then coming out here and trying to get her own house to turn against her!

Mrs. Peters: But Mrs. Hale, the law is the law.

Mrs. Hale: I s'pose 'tis. *(Unbuttoning her coat.)* Better   70 loosen up your things, Mrs. Peters. You won't feel them when you go out.

Mrs. Peters takes off her fur tippet, goes to hang it on hook at back of room, stands looking at the under part of the small corner table.

Mrs. Peters: She was piecing a quilt.

She brings the large sewing basket and they look at the bright pieces.

Mrs. Hale: It's log cabin pattern. Pretty, isn't it? I wonder if she was goin' to quilt it or just knot it?

Footsteps have been heard coming down the stairs. The Sheriff enters followed by Hale and the County Attorney.

Sheriff: They wonder if she was going to quilt it or just knot it!

The men laugh; the women look abashed.

County Attorney: *(rubbing his hands over the stove)* Frank's fire didn't do much up there, did it? Well, let's go out to the barn and get that cleared up.

The men go outside.

Mrs. Hale: *(resentfully)* I don't know as there's anything so   75 strange, our takin' up our time with little things while we're waiting for them to get the evidence. *(She sits down at the big table smoothing out a block with decision.)* I don't see as it's anything to laugh about.

Mrs. Peters: *(apologetically)* Of course they've got awful important things on their minds.

Pulls up a chair and joins Mrs. Hale at the table.

Mrs. Hale: *(examining another block)* Mrs. Peters, look at this one. Here, this is the one she was working on, and look at the sewing! All the rest of it has been so nice and even. And look at this! It's all over the place! Why, it looks as if she didn't know what she was about!

After she has said this they look at each other, then start to glance back at the door. After an instant Mrs. Hale has pulled at a knot and ripped the sewing.

Mrs. Peters: Oh, what are you doing, Mrs. Hale?

Mrs. Hale: *(mildly)* Just pulling out a stitch or two that's not sewed very good. *(Threading a needle.)* Bad sewing always made me fidgety.

Mrs. Peters: *(nervously)* I don't think we ought to touch   80 things.

Mrs. Hale: I'll just finish up this end. *(Suddenly stopping and leaning forward.)* Mrs. Peters?

Mrs. Peters: Yes, Mrs. Hale?

Mrs. Hale: What do you suppose she was so nervous about?

Mrs. Peters: Oh—I don't know. I don't know as she was nervous. I sometimes sew awful queer when I'm just tired. *(Mrs. Hale starts to say something, looks at Mrs. Peters, then goes on sewing.)* Well, I must get these things wrapped up. They may be through sooner than we think. *(Putting apron and other things together.)* I wonder where I can find a piece of paper, and string.

Mrs. Hale: In that cupboard, maybe.   85

Mrs. Peters: *(looking in cupboard)* Why, here's a birdcage. *(Holds it up.)* Did she have a bird, Mrs. Hale?

Mrs. Hale: Why, I don't know whether she did or not—I've not been here for so long. There was a man around last year selling canaries cheap, but I don't know as she took one; maybe she did. She used to sing real pretty herself.

Mrs. Peters: *(glancing around)* Seems funny to think of a bird here. But she must have had one, or why would she have a cage? I wonder what happened to it.

Mrs. Hale: I s'pose maybe the cat got it.

Mrs. Peters: No, she didn't have a cat. She's got that   90 feeling some people have about cats—being afraid of them. My cat got in her room and she was real upset and asked me to take it out.

Mrs. Hale: My sister Bessie was like that. Queer, ain't it?

Mrs. Peters: *(examining the cage)* Why, look at this door. It's broke. One hinge is pulled apart.

Mrs. Hale: *(looking too)* Looks as if someone must have been rough with it.

Mrs. Peters: Why, yes.

She brings the cage forward and puts it on the table.

Mrs. Hale: I wish if they're going to find any evidence   95 they'd be about it. I don't like this place.

Mrs. Peters: But I'm awful glad you came with me, Mrs. Hale. It would be lonesome for me sitting here alone.

Mrs. Hale: It would, wouldn't it? *(Dropping her sewing.)* But I tell you what I do wish, Mrs. Peters. I wish I had come over sometimes when *she* was here. I—*(looking around the room)*—wish I had.

Mrs. Peters: But of course you were awful busy, Mrs. Hale—your house and your children.

° **red-up** Spruced-up (slang).

Mrs. Hale: I could've come. I stayed away because it weren't cheerful—and that's why I ought to have come. I—I've never liked this place. Maybe because it's down in a hollow and you don't see the road. I dunno what it is but it's a lonesome place and always was. I wish I had come over to see Minnie Foster sometimes. I can see now—

Shakes her head.

Mrs. Peters: Well, you mustn't reproach yourself, Mrs. 100 Hale. Somehow we just don't see how it is with other folks until—something comes up.

Mrs. Hale: Not having children makes less work—but it makes a quiet house, and Wright out to work all day, and no company when he did come in. Did you know John Wright, Mrs. Peters?

Mrs. Peters: Not to know him; I've seen him in town. They say he was a good man.

Mrs. Hale: Yes—good; he didn't drink, and kept his word as well as most, I guess, and paid his debts. But he was a hard man, Mrs. Peters. Just to pass the time of day with him—(*Shivers.*) Like a raw wind that gets to the bone. (*Pauses, her eye falling on the cage.*) I should think she would 'a wanted a bird. But what do you suppose went with it?

Mrs. Peters: I don't know, unless it got sick and died.

She reaches over and swings the broken door, swings it again. Both women watch it.

Mrs. Hale: You weren't raised round here, were you? 105 (*Mrs. Peters shakes her head.*) You didn't know—her?

Mrs. Peters: Not till they brought her yesterday.

Mrs. Hale: She—come to think of it, she was kind of like a bird herself—real sweet and pretty, but kind of timid and—fluttery. How—she—did—change. (*Silence; then as if struck by a happy thought and relieved to get back to everyday things.*) Tell you what, Mrs. Peters, why don't you take the quilt in with you? It might take up her mind.

Mrs. Peters: Why, I think that's a real nice idea, Mrs. Hale. There couldn't possibly be any objection to it, could there? Now, just what would I take? I wonder if her patches are in here—and her things.

They look in the sewing basket.

Mrs. Hale: Here's some red. I expect this has got sewing things in it. (*Brings out a fancy box.*) What a pretty box. Looks like something somebody would give you. Maybe her scissors are in here. (*Opens box. Suddenly puts her hand to her nose.*) Why—(*Mrs. Peters bends nearer, then turns her face away.*) There's something wrapped up in this piece of silk.

Mrs. Peters: Why, this isn't her scissors. 110

Mrs. Hale: (*lifting the silk*) Oh, Mrs. Peters—it's—

Mrs. Peters bends closer.

Mrs. Peters: It's the bird.

Mrs. Hale: (*jumping up*) But, Mrs. Peters—look at it! Its neck! Look at its neck! It's all—other side *to*.

Mrs. Peters: Somebody—wrung—its—neck.

Their eyes meet. A look of growing comprehension, of horror. Steps are heard outside. Mrs. Hale slips box under quilt pieces, and sinks into her chair. Enter Sheriff and County Attorney. Mrs. Peters rises.

County Attorney: (*as one turning from serious things to* 115 *little pleasantries*) Well, ladies, have you decided whether she was going to quilt it or knot it?

Mrs. Peters: We think she was going to—knot it.

County Attorney: Well, that's interesting, I'm sure. (*Seeing the birdcage.*) Has the bird flown?

Mrs. Hale: (*putting more quilt pieces over the box*) We think the—cat got it.

County Attorney: (*preoccupied*) Is there a cat?

Mrs. Hale glances in a quick covert way at Mrs. Peters.

Mrs. Peters: Well, not *now*. They're superstitious, you 120 know. They leave.

County Attorney: (*to Sheriff Peters, continuing an interrupted conversation*) No sign at all of anyone having come from the outside. Their own rope. Now let's go up again and go over it piece by piece. (*They start upstairs.*) It would have to have been someone who knew just the—

Mrs. Peters sits down. The two women sit there not looking at one another, but as if peering into something and at the same time holding back. When they talk now it is in the manner of feeling their way over strange ground, as if afraid of what they are saying, but as if they can not help saying it.

Mrs. Hale: She liked the bird. She was going to bury it in that pretty box.

Mrs. Peters: (*in a whisper*) When I was a girl—my kitten—there was a boy took a hatchet, and before my eyes—and before I could get there—(*Covers her face an instant.*) If they hadn't held me back I would have—(*catches herself, looks upstairs where steps are heard, falters weakly*)—hurt him.

Mrs. Hale: (*with a slow look around her*) I wonder how it would seem never to have had any children around. (*Pause.*) No, Wright wouldn't like the bird—a thing that sang. She used to sing. He killed that, too.

Mrs. Peters: (*moving uneasily*) We don't know who killed 125 the bird.

Mrs. Hale: I knew John Wright.

Mrs. Peters: It was an awful thing was done in this house that night, Mrs. Hale. Killing a man while he slept, slipping a rope around his neck that choked the life out of him.

Mrs. Hale: His neck. Choked the life out of him.

Her hand goes out and rests on the birdcage.

Mrs. Peters: *(with rising voice)* We don't know who killed him. We don't know.

Mrs. Hale: *(her own feeling not interrupted)* If there'd 130 been years and years of nothing, then a bird to sing to you, it would be awful—still, after the bird was still.

Mrs. Peters: *(something within her speaking)* I know what stillness is. When we homesteaded in Dakota, and my first baby died—after he was two years old, and me with no other then—

Mrs. Hale: *(moving)* How soon do you suppose they'll be through, looking for the evidence?

Mrs. Peters: I know what stillness is. *(Pulling herself back.)* The law has got to punish crime, Mrs. Hale.

Mrs. Hale: *(not as if answering that)* I wish you'd seen Minnie Foster when she wore a white dress with blue ribbons and stood up there in the choir and sang. *(A look around the room.)* Oh, I *wish* I'd come over here once in a while! That was a crime! That was a crime! Who's going to punish that?

Mrs. Peters: *(looking upstairs)* We mustn't—take on. 135

Mrs. Hale: I might have known she needed help! I know how things can be—for women. I tell you, it's queer, Mrs. Peters. We live close together and we live far apart. We all go through the same things—it's all just a different kind of the same thing. *(Brushes her eyes; noticing the bottle of fruit, reaches out for it.)* If I was you I wouldn't tell her her fruit was gone. Tell her it *ain't.* Tell her it's all right. Take this in to prove it to her. She—she may never know whether it was broke or not.

Mrs. Peters: *(takes the bottle, looks about for something to wrap it in; takes petticoat from the clothes brought from the other room, very nervously begins winding this around the bottle. In a false voice)* My, it's a good thing the men couldn't hear us. Wouldn't they just laugh! Getting all stirred up over a little thing like a—dead canary. As if that could have anything to do with—with—wouldn't they *laugh!*

The men are heard coming down stairs.

Mrs. Hale: *(under her breath)* Maybe they would—maybe they wouldn't.

County Attorney: No, Peters, it's all perfectly clear except a reason for doing it. But you know juries when it comes to women. If there was some definite thing. Something to show—something to make a story about—a thing that would connect up with this strange way of doing it—

The women's eyes meet for an instant. Enter Hale from outer door.

Hale: Well, I've got the team around. Pretty cold out 140 there.

County Attorney: I'm going to stay here a while by myself. *(To the Sheriff.)* You can send Frank out for me, can't you? I want to go over everything. I'm not satisfied that we can't do better.

Sheriff: Do you want to see what Mrs. Peters is going to take in?

The County Attorney goes to the table, picks up the apron, laughs.

County Attorney: Oh, I guess they're not very dangerous things the ladies have picked out. *(Moves a few things about, disturbing the quilt pieces which cover the box. Steps back.)* No, Mrs. Peters doesn't need supervising. For that matter, a sheriff's wife is married to the law. Ever think of it that way, Mrs. Peters?

Mrs. Peters: Not—just that way.

Sheriff: *(chuckling)* Married to the law. *(Moves toward* 145 *the other room.)* I just want you to come in here a minute, George. We ought to take a look at these windows.

County Attorney: *(scoffingly)* Oh, windows!

Sheriff: We'll be right out, Mr. Hale.

Hale goes outside. The Sheriff follows the County Attorney into the other room. Then Mrs. Hale rises, hands tight together, looking intensely at Mrs. Peters, whose eyes make a slow turn, finally meeting Mrs. Hale's. A moment Mrs. Hale holds her, then her own eyes point the way to where the box is concealed. Suddenly Mrs. Peters throws back quilt pieces and tries to put the box in the bag she is wearing. It is too big. She opens box, starts to take bird out, cannot touch it, goes to pieces, stands there helpless. Sound of a knob turning in the other room. Mrs. Hale snatches the box and puts it in the pocket of her big coat. Enter County Attorney and Sheriff.

County Attorney: *(facetiously)* Well, Henry, at least we found out that she was not going to quilt it. She was going to—what is it you call it, ladies?

Mrs. Hale: *(her hand against her pocket)* We call it—knot it, Mr. Henderson.

Related Works

from *Persepolis* (p. 151), "The Yellow Wallpaper" (p. 313), "I Stand Here Ironing" (p. 162), "Everyday Use" (p. 256), "Harlem" (p. 409), "Daddy" (p. 416), *A Doll House* (p. 562), *The Stronger* (p. 602)

See Chapter 32 Review Card for Reading and Reacting questions about Susan Glaspell, *Trifles.*

Henrik Ibsen (1828–1906)

© Hulton Archive/Getty Images

was Norway's foremost dramatist. He was born into a prosperous family; however, his father lost his fortune when Ibsen was six. When Ibsen was fifteen, he was apprenticed to an apothecary away from home and was permanently estranged from his family. During his apprenticeship, he studied to enter the university and wrote plays. Although he did not pass the university entrance exam, his second play, *The Warrior's Barrow* (1850), was produced by the Christiania Theatre in 1850. He began a life in the theater, writing plays and serving as artistic director of a theatrical company. Disillusioned by the public's lack of interest in theater, he left Norway, living with his wife and son in Italy and Germany between 1864 and 1891. By the time he returned to Norway, he was famous and revered. Ibsen's most notable plays include *Brand* (1865), *Peer Gynt* (1867), *A Doll House* (1879), *Ghosts* (1881), *An Enemy of the People* (1882), *The Wild Duck* (1884), *Hedda Gabler* (1890), and *When We Dead Awaken* (1899).

   A Doll House marks the beginning of Ibsen's successful realist period, during which he explored the ordinary lives of small-town people—in this case, writing what he called "a modern tragedy." Ibsen based the play on a true story, which closely paralleled the main events of the play: a wife borrows money to finance a trip for an ailing husband, repayment is demanded, she forges a check and is discovered. (In the real-life story, however, the husband demanded a divorce, and the wife had a nervous breakdown and was committed to a mental institution.) The issue in *A Doll House*, he said, is that there are "two kinds of moral law, . . . one in man and a completely different one in woman. They do not understand each other. . . ." Nora and Helmer's marriage is destroyed because they cannot comprehend or accept their differences. The play begins conventionally but does not fulfill the audience's expectations for a tidy resolution; as a result, it was not a success when it was first performed. Nevertheless, the publication of *A Doll House* made Ibsen internationally famous.

A Doll House (1879)

Translated by Rolf Fjelde

CHARACTERS

Torvald Helmer, *a lawyer*
Nora, *his wife*
Dr. Rank
Mrs. Linde
A Delivery Boy

Nils Krogstad, *a bank clerk*
The Helmers' three small children
Anne-Marie, *their nurse*
Helene, *a maid*

The action takes place in Helmer's residence.

ACT I

A comfortable room, tastefully but not expensively furnished. A door to the right in the back wall leads to the entryway; another to the left leads to Helmer's study. Between these doors, a piano. Midway in the left-hand wall a door, and further back a window. Near the window a round table with an armchair and a small sofa. In the right-hand wall, toward the rear, a door, and nearer the foreground a porcelain stove with two armchairs and a rocking chair beside it. Between the stove and the side door, a small table. Engravings on the walls. An étagère with china figures and other small art objects; a small bookcase with richly bound books; the floor carpeted; a fire burning in the stove. It is a winter day.

Cultural Context

During the nineteenth century, the law treated women only a little better than it did children. Women could not vote, and they were not considered able to handle their own financial affairs. A woman could not borrow money in her own name, and when she married, her finances were placed under the control of her husband. Moreover, working outside the home was out of the question for a middle-class woman. So, if a woman were to leave her husband, she was not likely to have any way of supporting herself, and she would lose the custody of her children. At the time when *A Doll House* was first performed, most viewers were offended by the way Nora spoke to her husband, and Ibsen was considered an anarchist for suggesting that a woman could leave her family in search of herself. However, Ibsen argued that he was merely asking people to look at, and think about, the social structure they supported.

A bell rings in the entryway; shortly after we hear the door being unlocked. Nora comes into the room, humming happily to herself; she is wearing street clothes and carries an armload of packages, which she puts down on the table to the right. She has left the hall door open; and through it a Delivery Boy is seen, holding a Christmas tree and a basket, which he gives to the Maid who let them in.

Nora: Hide the tree well, Helene. The children mustn't get a glimpse of it till this evening, after it's trimmed. *(To the Delivery Boy, taking out her purse.)* How much?

Delivery Boy: Fifty, ma'am.

Nora: There's a crown. No, keep the change. *(The Boy thanks her and leaves. Nora shuts the door. She laughs softly to herself while taking off her street things. Drawing a bag of macaroons from her pocket, she eats a couple, then steals over and listens at her husband's study door.)* Yes, he's home. *(Hums again as she moves to the table right.)*

Helmer: *(from the study)* Is that my little lark twittering out there?

Nora: *(busy opening some packages)* Yes, it is.   5

Helmer: Is that my squirrel rummaging around?

Nora: Yes!

Helmer: When did my squirrel get in?

Nora: Just now. *(Putting the macaroon bag in her pocket and wiping her mouth.)* Do come in, Torvald, and see what I've bought.

Helmer: Can't be disturbed. *(After a moment he opens the door and peers in, pen in hand.)* Bought, you say? All that there? Has the little spendthrift been out throwing money around again?   10

Nora: Oh, but Torvald, this year we really should let ourselves go a bit. It's the first Christmas we haven't had to economize.

Helmer: But you know we can't go squandering.

Nora: Oh yes, Torvald, we can squander a little now. Can't we? Just a tiny, wee bit. Now that you've got a big salary and are going to make piles and piles of money.

Helmer: Yes—starting New Year's. But then it's a full three months till the raise comes through.

Nora: Pooh! We can borrow that long.   15

Helmer: Nora! *(Goes over and playfully takes her by the ear.)* Are your scatterbrains off again? What if today

> "No debts! Never borrow! Something of freedom's lost—and something of beauty, too—from a home that's founded on borrowing and debt."

EXPLORE ONLINE >

To listen to an instructor podcast of *A Doll House*, visit your Literature CourseMate, accessed through www.cengagebrain.com.

I borrowed a thousand crowns, and you squandered them over Christmas week, and then on New Year's Eve a roof tile fell on my head, and I lay there—

Nora: *(putting her hand on his mouth)* Oh! Don't say such things!

Helmer: Yes, but what if it happened—then what?

Nora: If anything so awful happened, then it just wouldn't matter if I had debts or not.

Helmer: Well, but the people I'd borrowed from?   20

Nora: Them? Who cares about them! They're strangers.

Helmer: Nora, Nora, how like a woman! No, but seriously, Nora, you know what I think about that. No debts! Never borrow! Something of freedom's lost—and something of beauty, too—from a home that's founded on borrowing and debt. We've made a brave stand up to now, the two of us; and we'll go right on like that the little while we have to.

Nora: *(going toward the stove)* Yes, whatever you say, Torvald.

Helmer: *(following her)* Now, now, the little lark's wings mustn't droop. Come on, don't be a sulky squirrel. *(Taking out his wallet.)* Nora, guess what I have here.

Nora: *(turning quickly)* Money!   25

Helmer: There, see. *(Hands her some notes.)* Good grief, I know how costs go up in a house at Christmastime.

Nora: Ten—twenty—thirty—forty. Oh, thank you, Torvald; I can manage no end on this.

Helmer: You really will have to.

Nora: Oh yes, I promise I will! But come here so I can show you everything I bought. And so cheap! Look, new clothes for Ivar here—and a sword. Here a horse and a trumpet for Bob. And a doll and a doll's bed here for Emmy; they're nothing much, but she'll tear them to bits in no time anyway. And here I have dress material and handkerchiefs for the maids. Old Anne-Marie really deserves something more.

Helmer: And what's in that package there?   30

Nora: *(with a cry)* Torvald, no! You can't see that till tonight!

Helmer: I see. But tell me now, you little prodigal, what have you thought of for yourself?

Nora: For myself? Oh, I don't want anything at all.

Helmer: Of course you do. Tell me just what—within reason—you'd most like to have.

Nora: I honestly don't know. Oh, listen, Torvald— 35

Helmer: Well?

Nora: *(fumbling at his coat buttons, without looking at him)* If you want to give me something, then maybe you could—you could—

Helmer: Come on, out with it.

Nora: *(hurriedly)* You could give me money, Torvald. No more than you think you can spare; then one of these days I'll buy something with it.

Helmer: But Nora— 40

Nora: Oh, please, Torvald darling, do that! I beg you, please. Then I could hang the bills in pretty gilt paper on the Christmas tree. Wouldn't that be fun?

Helmer: What are those little birds called that always fly through their fortunes?

Nora: Oh yes, spendthrifts; I know all that. But let's do as I say, Torvald; then I'll have time to decide what I really need most. That's very sensible, isn't it?

Helmer: *(smiling)* Yes, very—that is, if you actually hung onto the money I give you, and you actually used it to buy yourself something. But it goes for the house and for all sorts of foolish things, and then I only have to lay out some more.

Nora: Oh, but Torvald— 45

Helmer: Don't deny it, my dear little Nora. *(Putting his arm around her waist.)* Spendthrifts are sweet, but they use up a frightful amount of money. It's incredible what it costs a man to feed such birds.

Nora: Oh, how can you say that! Really, I save everything I can.

Helmer: *(laughing)* Yes, that's the truth. Everything you can. But that's nothing at all.

Nora: *(humming, with a smile of quiet satisfaction)* Hm, if you only knew what expenses we larks and squirrels have, Torvald.

Helmer: You're an odd little one. Exactly the way your 50 father was. You're never at a loss for scaring up money; but the moment you have it, it runs right out through your fingers; you never know what you've done with it. Well, one takes you as you are. It's deep in your blood. Yes, these things are hereditary, Nora.

Nora: Ah, I could wish I'd inherited many of Papa's qualities.

Helmer: And I couldn't wish you

> "You're never at a loss for scaring up money; but the moment you have it, it runs right out through your fingers; you never know what you've done with it."

anything but just what you are, my sweet little lark. But wait; it seems to me you have a very—what should I call it?—a very suspicious look today—

Nora: I do?

Helmer: You certainly do. Look me straight in the eye.

Nora: *(looking at him)* Well? 55

Helmer: *(shaking an admonitory finger)* Surely my sweet tooth hasn't been running riot in town today, has she?

Nora: No. Why do you imagine that?

Helmer: My sweet tooth really didn't make a little detour through the confectioner's?

Nora: No, I assure you, Torvald—

Helmer: Hasn't nibbled some pastry? 60

Nora: No, not at all.

Helmer: Nor even munched a macaroon or two?

Nora: No, Torvald, I assure you, really—

Helmer: There, there now. Of course I'm only joking.

Nora: *(going to the table, right)* You know I could never 65 think of going against you.

Helmer: No, I understand that; and you *have* given me your word. *(Going over to her.)* Well, you keep your little Christmas secrets to yourself, Nora darling. I expect they'll come to light this evening, when the tree is lit.

Nora: Did you remember to ask Dr. Rank?

Helmer: No. But there's no need for that; it's assumed he'll be dining with us. All the same, I'll ask him when he stops by here this morning. I've ordered some fine wine. Nora, you can't imagine how I'm looking forward to this evening.

Nora: So am I. And what fun for the children, Torvald!

Helmer: Ah, it's so gratifying to know that one's gotten a 70 safe, secure job, and with a comfortable salary. It's a great satisfaction, isn't it?

Nora: Oh, it's wonderful!

Helmer: Remember last Christmas? Three whole weeks before, you shut yourself in every evening till long after midnight, making flowers for the Christmas tree, and all the other decorations to surprise us. Ugh, that was the dullest time I've ever lived through.

Nora: It wasn't at all dull for me.

Helmer: *(smiling)* But the outcome *was* pretty sorry, Nora.

Nora: Oh, don't tease me with that again. How could I 75 help it that the cat came in and tore everything to shreds.

Helmer: No, poor thing, you certainly couldn't. You wanted so much to please us all, and that's what counts. But it's just as well that the hard times are past.

Nora: Yes, it's really wonderful.

Helmer: Now I don't have to sit here alone, boring myself, and you don't have to tire your precious eyes and your fair little delicate hands—

Nora: (*clapping her hands*) No, is it really true, Torvald, I don't have to? Oh, how wonderfully lovely to hear! (*Taking his arm.*) Now I'll tell you just how I've thought we should plan things. Right after Christmas—(*The doorbell rings.*) Oh, the bell. (*Straightening the room up a bit.*) Somebody would have to come. What a bore!

Helmer: I'm not at home to visitors, don't forget. 80

Maid: (*from the hall doorway*) Ma'am, a lady to see you—

Nora: All right, let her come in.

Maid: (*to Helmer*) And the doctor's just come too.

Helmer: Did he go right to my study?

Maid: Yes, he did. 85

Helmer goes into his room. The Maid shows in Mrs. Linde, dressed in traveling clothes, and shuts the door after her.

Mrs. Linde: (*in a dispirited and somewhat hesitant voice*) Hello, Nora.

Nora: (*uncertain*) Hello—

Mrs. Linde: You don't recognize me.

Nora: No, I don't know—but wait, I think—(*Exclaiming.*) What! Kristine! Is it really you?

Mrs. Linde: Yes, it's me. 90

Nora: Kristine! To think I didn't recognize you. But then, how could I? (*More quietly.*) How you've changed, Kristine!

Mrs. Linde: Yes, no doubt I have. In nine—ten long years.

Nora: Is it so long since we met! Yes, it's all of that. Oh, these last eight years have been a happy time, believe me. And so now you've come in to town, too. Made the long trip in the winter. That took courage.

Mrs. Linde: I just got here by ship this morning.

Nora: To enjoy yourself over Christmas, of course. Oh, 95 how lovely! Yes, enjoy ourselves, we'll do that. But take your coat off. You're not still cold? (*Helping her.*) There now, let's get cozy here by the stove. No, the easy chair there! I'll take the rocker here. (*Seizing her hands.*) Yes, now you have your old look again; it was only in that first moment. You're a bit more pale, Kristine—and maybe a bit thinner.

Mrs. Linde: And much, much older, Nora.

Nora: Yes, perhaps a bit older; a tiny, tiny bit; not much at all. (*Stopping short; suddenly serious.*) Oh, but thoughtless me, to sit here, chattering away. Sweet, good Kristine, can you forgive me?

Mrs. Linde: What do you mean, Nora?

Nora: (*softly*) Poor Kristine, you've become a widow.

Mrs. Linde: Yes, three years ago. 100

Nora: Oh, I knew it, of course; I read it in the papers. Oh, Kristine, you must believe me; I often thought of writing you then, but I kept postponing it, and something always interfered.

Mrs. Linde: Nora dear, I understand completely.

Nora: No, it was awful of me, Kristine. You poor thing, how much you must have gone through. And he left you nothing?

Mrs. Linde: No.

Nora: And no children? 105

Mrs. Linde: No.

Nora: Nothing at all, then?

Mrs. Linde: Not even a sense of loss to feed on.

Nora: (*looking incredulously at her*) But Kristine, how could that be?

Mrs. Linde: (*smiling wearily and smoothing her hair*) Oh, 110 sometimes it happens, Nora.

Nora: So completely alone. How terribly hard that must be for you. I have three lovely children. You can't see them now; they're out with the maid. But now you must tell me everything—

Mrs. Linde: No, no, no, tell me about yourself.

Nora: No, you begin. Today I don't want to be selfish. I want to think only of you today. But there *is* something I must tell you. Did you hear of the wonderful luck we had recently?

Mrs. Linde: No, what's that?

Nora: My husband's been made manager in the bank, 115 just think!

Mrs. Linde: Your husband? How marvelous!

Nora: Isn't it? Being a lawyer is such an uncertain living, you know, especially if one won't touch any cases that aren't clean and decent. And of course Torvald would never do that, and I'm with him completely there. Oh, we're simply delighted, believe me! He'll join the bank right after New Year's and start getting a huge salary and lots of commissions. From now on we can live quite differently—just as we want. Oh, Kristine, I feel so light and happy! Won't it be lovely to have stacks of money and not a care in the world?

Mrs. Linde: Well, anyway, it would be lovely to have enough for necessities.

Nora: No, not just for necessities, but stacks and stacks of money!

Mrs. Linde: (*smiling*) Nora, Nora, aren't you sensible yet? 120 Back in school you were such a free spender.

Nora: (*with a quiet laugh*) Yes, that's what Torvald still says. (*Shaking her finger.*) But "Nora, Nora" isn't as silly as you all think. Really, we've been in no position for me to go squandering. We've had to work, both of us.

Mrs. Linde: You too?

Nora: Yes, at odd jobs—needlework, crocheting, embroidery, and such—(*casually*) and other things too. You remember that Torvald left the department when we were married? There was no chance of promotion in his office, and of course he needed to earn more money. But that first year he drove himself terribly. He took on all kinds of extra work that kept him going morning and night. It wore him down, and then he fell deathly ill. The doctors said it was essential for him to travel south.

Mrs. Linde: Yes, didn't you spend a whole year in Italy?

Nora: That's right. It wasn't easy to get away, you know. Ivar had just been born. But of course we had to go. Oh, that was a beautiful trip, and it saved Torvald's life. But it cost a frightful sum, Kristine.

Mrs. Linde: I can well imagine.

Nora: Four thousand, eight hundred crowns it cost. That's really a lot of money.

Mrs. Linde: But it's lucky you had it when you needed it.

Nora: Well, as it was, we got it from Papa.

Mrs. Linde: I see. It was just about the time your father died.

Nora: Yes, just about then. And, you know, I couldn't make that trip out to nurse him. I had to stay here, expecting Ivar any moment, and with my poor sick Torvald to care for. Dearest Papa, I never saw him again, Kristine. Oh, that was the worst time I've known in all my marriage.

Mrs. Linde: I know how you loved him. And then you went off to Italy?

Nora: Yes. We had the means now, and the doctors urged us. So we left a month after.

Mrs. Linde: And your husband came back completely cured?

Nora: Sound as a drum!

Mrs. Linde: But—the doctor?

Nora: Who?

Mrs. Linde: I thought the maid said he was a doctor, the man who came in with me.

Nora: Yes, that was Dr. Rank—but he's not making a sick call. He's our closest friend, and he stops by at least once a day. No, Torvald hasn't had a sick moment since, and the children are fit and strong, and I am, too. *(Jumping up and clapping her hands.)* Oh, dear God, Kristine, what a lovely thing to live and be happy! But how disgusting of me—I'm talking of nothing but my own affairs. *(Sits on a stool close by Kristine, arms resting across her knees.)* Oh, don't be angry with me! Tell me, is it really true that you weren't in love with your husband? Why did you marry him, then?

Mrs. Linde: My mother was still alive, but bedridden and helpless—and I had my two younger brothers to look after. In all conscience, I didn't think I could turn him down.

Nora: No, you were right there. But was he rich at the time?

Mrs. Linde: He was very well off, I'd say. But the business was shaky, Nora. When he died, it all fell apart, and nothing was left.

Nora: And then—?

Mrs. Linde: Yes, so I had to scrape up a living with a little shop and a little teaching and whatever else I could find. The last three years have been like one endless workday without a rest for me. Now it's over, Nora. My poor mother doesn't need me, for she's passed on. Nor the boys, either; they're working now and can take care of themselves.

Nora: How free you must feel—

Mrs. Linde: No—only unspeakably empty. Nothing to live for now. *(Standing up anxiously.)* That's why I couldn't take it any longer out in that desolate hole. Maybe here it'll be easier to find something to do and keep my mind occupied. If I could only be lucky enough to get a steady job, some office work—

Nora: Oh, but Kristine, that's so dreadfully tiring, and you already look so tired. It would be much better for you if you could go off to a bathing resort.

Mrs. Linde: *(going toward the window)* I have no father to give me travel money, Nora.

Nora: *(rising)* Oh, don't be angry with me.

Mrs. Linde: *(going to her)* Nora dear, don't you be angry with me. The worst of my kind of situation is all the bitterness that's stored away. No one to work for, and yet you're always having to snap up your opportunities. You have to live; and so you grow selfish. When you told me the happy change in your lot, do you know I was delighted less for your sakes than for mine?

Nora: How so? Oh, I see. You think Torvald could do something for you.

Mrs. Linde: Yes, that's what I thought.

Nora: And he will, Kristine! Just leave it to me; I'll bring it up so delicately—find something attractive to humor him with. Oh, I'm so eager to help you.

Mrs. Linde: How very kind of you, Nora, to be so concerned over me—doubly kind, considering you really know so little of life's burdens yourself.

Nora: I—? I know so little—?

Mrs. Linde: *(smiling)* Well my heavens—a little needlework and such—Nora, you're just a child.

Nora: *(tossing her head and pacing the floor)* You don't have to act so superior.

Mrs. Linde: Oh?

Nora: You're just like the others. You all think I'm incapable of anything serious—

Mrs. Linde: Come now—

Nora: That I've never had to face the raw world.

Mrs. Linde: Nora dear, you've just been telling me all your troubles.

Nora: Hm! Trivial! *(Quietly.)* I haven't told you the big thing.

Mrs. Linde: Big thing? What do you mean?

Nora: You look down on me so, Kristine, but you   165
shouldn't. You're proud that you worked so long and hard for your mother.

Mrs. Linde: I don't look down on a soul. But it *is* true: I'm proud—and happy, too—to think it was given to me to make my mother's last days almost free of care.

Nora: And you're also proud thinking of what you've done for your brothers.

Mrs. Linde: I feel I've a right to be.

Nora: I agree. But listen to this, Kristine—I've also got something to be proud and happy for.

Mrs. Linde: I don't doubt it. But whatever do you mean?   170

Nora: Not so loud. What if Torvald heard! He mustn't, not for anything in the world. Nobody must know, Kristine. No one but you.

Mrs. Linde: But what is it, then?

Nora: Come here. *(Drawing her down beside her on the sofa.)* It's true—I've also got something to be proud and happy for. I'm the one who saved Torvald's life.

Mrs. Linde: Saved—? Saved how?

Nora: I told you about the trip to Italy. Torvald never   175
would have lived if he hadn't gone south—

Mrs. Linde: Of course; your father gave you the means—

Nora: *(smiling)* That's what Torvald and all the rest think, but—

Mrs. Linde: But—?

Nora: Papa didn't give us a pin. I was the one who raised the money.

Mrs. Linde: You? That whole amount?   180

Nora: Four thousand, eight hundred crowns. What do you say to that?

Mrs. Linde: But Nora, how was it possible? Did you win the lottery?

Nora: *(disdainfully)* The lottery? Pooh! No art to that.

Mrs. Linde: But where did you get it from then?

Nora: *(humming, with a mysterious smile)* Hmm,   185
tra-la-la-la.

Mrs. Linde: Because you couldn't have borrowed it.

Nora: No? Why not?

Mrs. Linde: A wife can't borrow without her husband's consent.

Nora: *(tossing her head)* Oh, but a wife with a little business sense, a wife who knows how to manage—

Mrs. Linde: Nora, I simply don't understand—   190

Nora: You don't have to. Whoever said I *borrowed* the money? I could have gotten it other ways. *(Throwing herself back on the sofa.)* I could have gotten it from some admirer or other. After all, a girl with my ravishing appeal—

Mrs. Linde: You lunatic.

Nora: I'll bet you're eaten up with curiosity, Kristine.

Mrs. Linde: Now listen here, Nora—you haven't done something indiscreet?

Nora: *(sitting up again)* Is it indiscreet to save your   195
husband's life?

Mrs. Linde: I think it's indiscreet that without his knowledge you—

Nora: But that's the point: he mustn't know! My Lord, can't you understand? He mustn't ever know the close call he had. It was to *me* the doctors came to say his life was in danger—that nothing could save him but a stay in the south. Didn't I try strategy then! I began talking about how lovely it would be for me to travel abroad like other young wives; I begged and I cried; I told him please to remember my condition, to be kind and indulge me; and then I dropped a hint that he could easily take out a loan. But at that, Kristine, he nearly exploded. He said I was frivolous, and it was his duty as man of the house not to indulge me in whims and fancies—as I think he called them. Aha, I thought, now you'll just have to be saved—and that's when I saw my chance.

Mrs. Linde: And your father never told Torvald the money wasn't from him?

Nora: No, never. Papa died right about then. I'd considered bringing him into my secret and begging him never to tell. But he was too sick at the time—and then, sadly, it didn't matter.

Mrs. Linde: And you've never confided in your husband   200
since?

Nora: For heaven's sake, no! Are you serious? He's so strict on that subject. Besides—Torvald, with all his masculine pride—how painfully humiliating for him if he ever found out he was in debt to me. That would just ruin our relationship. Our beautiful, happy home would never be the same.

Mrs. Linde: Won't you ever tell him?

Nora: *(thoughtfully, half smiling)* Yes—maybe sometime, years from now, when I'm no longer so attractive. Don't laugh! I only mean when Torvald loves me less than now, when he stops enjoying my dancing and dressing up and reciting for him. Then it might be wise to have something in reserve—*(Breaking off.)* How ridiculous! That'll never happen—Well, Kristine, what do you think of my big secret? I'm capable of something too, hm? You can imagine, of course, how this thing hangs over me. It really hasn't been easy meeting the payments on time. In the business world there's what they call quarterly interest and what they call amortization, and these are always so terribly hard to manage. I've had to skimp a little here and there, wherever I could, you know. I could hardly spare anything from my house allowance, because Torvald has to live well. I couldn't let the children go poorly dressed; whatever I got for them, I felt I had to use up completely—the darlings!

Mrs. Linde: Poor Nora, so it had to come out of your own budget, then?

Nora: Yes, of course. But I was the one most responsible, too. Every time Torvald gave me money for new clothes and such, I never used more than half; always bought the simplest, cheapest outfits. It was a godsend that everything looks so well on me that Torvald never noticed. But it did weigh me down at times, Kristine. It *is* such a joy to wear fine things. You understand.

Mrs. Linde: Oh, of course.

Nora: And then I found other ways of making money. Last winter I was lucky enough to get a lot of copying to do. I locked myself in and sat writing every evening till late in the night. Ah, I was tired so often, dead tired. But still it was wonderful fun, sitting and working like that, earning money. It was almost like being a man.

Mrs. Linde: But how much have you paid off this way so far?

Nora: That's hard to say, exactly. These accounts, you know, aren't easy to figure. I only know that I've paid out all I could scrape together. Time and again I haven't known where to turn. *(Smiling.)* Then I'd sit here dreaming of a rich old gentleman who had fallen in love with me—

Mrs. Linde: What! Who is he?

Nora: Oh, really! And that he'd died, and when his will was opened, there in big letters it said, "All my fortune shall be paid over in cash, immediately, to that enchanting Mrs. Nora Helmer."

Mrs. Linde: But Nora dear—who *was* this gentleman?

Nora: Good grief, can't you understand? The old man never existed; that was only something I'd dream up time and again whenever I was at my wits' end for money. But it makes no difference now; the old fossil can go where he pleases for all I care; I don't need him or his will—because now I'm free. *(Jumping up.)* Oh, how lovely to think of that, Kristine! Carefree! To know you're carefree, utterly carefree; to be able to romp and play with the children, and to keep up a beautiful, charming home—everything just the way Torvald likes it! And think, spring is coming, with big blue skies. Maybe we can travel a little then. Maybe I'll see the ocean again. Oh yes, it *is* so marvelous to live and be happy!

The front doorbell rings.

Mrs. Linde: *(rising)* There's the bell. It's probably best that I go.

Nora: No, stay. No one's expected. It must be for Torvald.

Maid: *(from the hall doorway)* Excuse me, ma'am—there's a gentleman here to see Mr. Helmer, but I didn't know—since the doctor's with him—

Nora: Who is the gentleman?

Krogstad: *(from the doorway)* It's me, Mrs. Helmer.

Mrs. Linde starts and turns away toward the window.

Nora: *(stepping toward him, tense, her voice a whisper)* You? What is it? Why do you want to speak to my husband?

Krogstad: Bank business—after a fashion. I have a small job in the investment bank, and I hear now your husband is going to be our chief—

Nora: In other words, it's—

Krogstad: Just dry business, Mrs. Helmer. Nothing but that.

Nora: Yes, then please be good enough to step into the study. *(She nods indifferently as she sees him out by the hall door, then returns and begins stirring up the stove.)*

Mrs. Linde: Nora—who was that man?

Nora: That was a Mr. Krogstad—a lawyer.

Mrs. Linde: Then it really was him.

Nora: Do you know that person?

Mrs. Linde: I did once—many years ago. For a time he was a law clerk in our town.

Nora: Yes, he's been that.

Mrs. Linde: How he's changed.

Nora: I understand he had a very unhappy marriage.

Mrs. Linde: He's a widower now.

Nora: With a number of children. There now, it's burning. *(She closes the stove door and moves the rocker a bit to one side.)*

Mrs. Linde: They say he has a hand in all kinds of business.

Nora: Oh? That may be true: I wouldn't know. But let's not think about business. It's so dull.

Dr. Rank enters from Helmer's study.

Rank: *(still in the doorway)* No, no, really—I don't want to intrude, I'd just as soon talk a little while with your wife. *(Shuts the door, then notices Mrs. Linde.)* Oh, beg pardon. I'm intruding here too.

Nora: No, not at all. *(Introducing him.)* Dr. Rank, Mrs. Linde.

Rank: Well now, that's a name much heard in this house. I believe I passed the lady on the stairs as I came.

Mrs. Linde: Yes, I take the stairs very slowly. They're rather hard on me.

Rank: Uh-hm, some touch of internal weakness? 240

Mrs. Linde: More overexertion, I'd say.

Rank: Nothing else? Then you're probably here in town to rest up in a round of parties?

Mrs. Linde: I'm here to look for work.

Rank: Is that the best cure for overexertion?

Mrs. Linde: One has to live, Doctor. 245

Rank: Yes, there's a common prejudice to that effect.

Nora: Oh, come on, Dr. Rank—you really do want to live yourself.

Rank: Yes, I really do. Wretched as I am, I'll gladly prolong my torment indefinitely. All my patients feel like that. And it's quite the same, too, with the morally sick. Right at this moment there's one of those moral invalids in there with Helmer—

Mrs. Linde: *(softly)* Ah!

Nora: Who do you mean? 250

Rank: Oh, it's a lawyer, Krogstad, a type you wouldn't know. His character is rotten to the root—but even he began chattering all-importantly about how he had to *live*.

Nora: Oh? What did he want to talk to Torvald about?

Rank: I really don't know. I only heard something about the bank.

Nora: I didn't know that Krog—that this man Krogstad had anything to do with the bank.

Rank: Yes, he's gotten some kind of berth down there. 255 *(To Mrs. Linde.)* I don't know if you also have, in your neck of the woods, a type of person who scuttles about breathlessly, sniffing out hints of moral corruption, and then maneuvers his victim into some sort of key position where he can keep an eye on him. It's the healthy these days that are out in the cold.

Mrs. Linde: All the same, it's the sick who most need to be taken in.

Rank: *(with a shrug)* Yes, there we have it. That's the concept that's turning society into a sanatorium.

Nora, lost in her thoughts, breaks out into quiet laughter and claps her hands.

Rank: Why do you laugh at that? Do you have any real idea of what society is?

Nora: What do I care about dreary old society? I was laughing at something quite different—something terribly funny. Tell me, Doctor—is everyone who works in the bank dependent now on Torvald?

Rank: Is that what you find so terribly funny? 260

Nora: *(smiling and humming)* Never mind, never mind! *(Pacing the floor.)* Yes, that's really immensely amusing: that we—that Torvald has so much power now over all those people. *(Taking the bag out of her pocket.)* Dr. Rank, a little macaroon on that?

Rank: See here, macaroons! I thought they were contraband here.

Nora: Yes, but these are some that Kristine gave me.

Mrs. Linde: What? I—?

Nora: Now, now, don't be afraid. You couldn't possibly 265 know that Torvald had forbidden them. You see, he's worried they'll ruin my teeth. But hmp! Just this once! Isn't that so, Dr. Rank? Help yourself! *(Puts a macaroon in his mouth.)* And you too, Kristine. And I'll also have one, only a little one—or two, at the most. *(Walking about again.)* Now I'm really tremendously happy. Now there's just one last thing in the world that I have an enormous desire to do.

Rank: Well! And what's that?

Nora: It's something I have such a consuming desire to say so Torvald could hear.

Rank: And why can't you say it?

Nora: I don't dare. It's quite shocking.

Mrs. Linde: Shocking? 270

Rank: Well, then it isn't advisable. But in front of us you certainly can. What do you have such a desire to say so Torvald could hear?

Nora: I have such a huge desire to say—to hell and be damned!

Rank: Are you crazy?

Mrs. Linde: My goodness, Nora!

Rank: Go on, say it. Here he is. 275

Nora: *(hiding the macaroon bag)* Shh, shh, shh!

Helmer comes in from his study, hat in hand, overcoat over his arm.

Nora: *(going toward him)* Well, Torvald dear, are you through with him?

Helmer: Yes, he just left.

Nora: Let me introduce you—this is Kristine, who's arrived here in town.

Helmer: Kristine—? I'm sorry, but I don't know— 280

Nora: Mrs. Linde, Torvald dear. Mrs. Kristine Linde.

Helmer: Of course. A childhood friend of my wife's, no doubt?

Mrs. Linde: Yes, we knew each other in those days.

Nora: And just think, she made the long trip down here in order to talk with you.

Helmer: What's this? 285

Mrs. Linde: Well, not exactly—

Nora: You see, Kristine is remarkably clever in office work, and so she's terribly eager to come under a capable man's supervision and add more to what she already knows—

Helmer: Very wise, Mrs. Linde.

Nora: And then when she heard that you'd become a bank manager—the story was wired out to the papers—then she came in as fast as she could and—Really, Torvald, for my sake you can do a little something for Kristine, can't you?

Helmer: Yes, it's not at all impossible. Mrs. Linde, I suppose you're a widow?   290

Mrs. Linde: Yes.

Helmer: Any experience in office work?

Mrs. Linde: Yes, a good deal.

Helmer: Well, it's quite likely that I can make an opening for you—

Nora: *(clapping her hands)* You see, you see!   295

Helmer: You've come at a lucky moment, Mrs. Linde.

Mrs. Linde: Oh, how can I thank you?

Helmer: Not necessary. *(Putting his overcoat on.)* But today you'll have to excuse me—

Rank: Wait, I'll go with you. *(He fetches his coat from the hall and warms it at the stove.)*

Nora: Don't stay out long, dear.   300

Helmer: An hour; no more.

Nora: Are you going too, Kristine?

Mrs. Linde: *(putting on her winter garments)* Yes, I have to see about a room now.

Helmer: Then perhaps we can all walk together.

Nora: *(helping her)* What a shame we're so cramped here, but it's quite impossible for us to—   305

Mrs. Linde: Oh, don't even think of it! Good-bye, Nora dear, and thanks for everything.

Nora: Good-bye for now. Of course you'll be back this evening. And you too, Dr. Rank. What? If you're well enough? Oh, you've got to be! Wrap up tight now.

In a ripple of small talk the company moves out into the hall; children's voices are heard outside on the steps.

Nora: There they are! There they are! *(She runs to open the door. The children come in with their nurse, Anne-Marie.)* Come in, come in! *(Bends down and kisses them.)* Oh, you darlings—! Look at them, Kristine. Aren't they lovely!

Rank: No loitering in the draft here.

Helmer: Come, Mrs. Linde—this place is unbearable now for anyone but mothers.   310

Dr. Rank, Helmer, and Mrs. Linde go down the stairs. Anne-Marie goes into the living room with the children. Nora follows, after closing the hall door.

Nora: How fresh and strong you look. Oh, such red cheeks you have! Like apples and roses. *(The children interrupt her throughout the following.)* And it was so much fun? That's wonderful. Really? You pulled both

>> Jennifer Hennessey as Mrs. Linde and Kananu Kirimi as Nora at Southwark Playhouse (2003)

Emmy and Bob on the sled? Imagine, all together! Yes, you're a clever boy, Ivar. Oh, let me hold her a bit, Anne-Marie. My sweet little doll baby! *(Takes the smallest from the nurse and dances with her.)* Yes, yes, Mama will dance with Bob as well. What? Did you throw snowballs? Oh, if I'd only been there! No, don't bother, Anne-Marie—I'll undress them myself. Oh yes, let me. It's such fun. Go in and rest; you look half frozen. There's hot coffee waiting for you on the stove. *(The nurse goes into the room to the left. Nora takes the children's winter things off, throwing them about, while the children talk to her all at once.)* Is that so? A big dog chased you? But it didn't bite? No, dogs never bite little, lovely doll babies. Don't peek in the packages, Ivar! What is it? Yes, wouldn't you like to know. No, no, it's an ugly something. Well? Shall we play? What shall we play? Hide-and-seek? Yes, let's play hide-and-seek. Bob must hide first. I must? Yes, let me hide first. *(Laughing and shouting, she and the children play in and out of the living room and the adjoining room to the right. At last Nora hides under the table. The children come storming in, search, but cannot find her, then hear her muffled laughter, dash over to the table, lift the cloth up and find her. Wild shouting. She creeps forward as if to scare them. More shouts. Meanwhile, a knock at the hall door; no one has noticed it. Now the door half opens, and Krogstad appears. He waits a moment; the game goes on.)*

Krogstad: Beg pardon, Mrs. Helmer—

Nora: *(with a strangled cry, turning and scrambling to her knees)* Oh! What do you want?

Krogstad: Excuse me. The outer door was ajar; it must be someone forgot to shut it—

Nora: *(rising)* My husband isn't home, Mr. Krogstad.   315

Krogstad: I know that.

Nora: Yes—then what do you want here?

Krogstad: A word with you.

Nora: With—? *(To the children, quietly.)* Go in to Anne-Marie. What? No, the strange man won't hurt Mama. When he's gone, we'll play some more. *(She leads the children into the room to the left and shuts the door after them. Then, tense and nervous.)* You want to speak to me?

Krogstad: Yes, I want to. 320

Nora: Today? But it's not yet the first of the month—

Krogstad: No, it's Christmas Eve. It's going to be up to you how merry a Christmas you have.

Nora: What is it you want? Today I absolutely can't—

Krogstad: We won't talk about that till later. This is something else. You do have a moment to spare, I suppose?

Nora: Oh yes, of course—I do, except— 325

Krogstad: Good. I was sitting over at Olsen's Restaurant when I saw your husband go down the street—

Nora: Yes?

Krogstad: With a lady.

Nora: Yes. So?

Krogstad: If you'll pardon my asking: wasn't that lady a Mrs. Linde? 330

Nora: Yes.

Krogstad: Just now come into town?

Nora: Yes, today.

Krogstad: She's a good friend of yours?

Nora: Yes, she is. But I don't see— 335

Krogstad: I also knew her once.

Nora: I'm aware of that.

Krogstad: Oh? You know all about it. I thought so. Well, then let me ask you short and sweet: is Mrs. Linde getting a job in the bank?

Nora: What makes you think you can cross-examine me, Mr. Krogstad—you, one of my husband's employees? But since you ask, you might as well know—yes, Mrs. Linde's going to be taken on at the bank. And I'm the one who spoke for her, Mr. Krogstad. Now you know.

Krogstad: So I guessed right. 340

Nora: *(pacing up and down)* Oh, one does have a tiny bit of influence, I should hope. Just because I am a woman, don't think it means that—When one has a subordinate position, Mr. Krogstad, one really ought to be careful about pushing somebody who—hm—

Krogstad: Who has influence?

Nora: That's right.

Krogstad: *(in a different tone)* Mrs. Helmer, would you be good enough to use your influence on my behalf?

Nora: What? What do you mean? 345

Krogstad: Would you please make sure that I keep my subordinate position in the bank?

Nora: What does that mean? Who's thinking of taking away your position?

Krogstad: Oh, don't play the innocent with me. I'm quite aware that your friend would hardly relish the chance of running into me again; and I'm also aware now whom I can thank for being turned out.

Nora: But I promise you—

Krogstad: Yes, yes, yes, to the point: there's still time, and 350 I'm advising you to use your influence to prevent it.

Nora: But Mr. Krogstad, I have absolutely no influence.

Krogstad: You haven't? I thought you were just saying—

Nora: You shouldn't take me so literally. I! How can you believe that I have any such influence over my husband?

Krogstad: Oh, I've known your husband from our student days. I don't think the great bank manager's more steadfast than any other married man.

Nora: You speak insolently about my husband, and I'll 355 show you the door.

Krogstad: The lady has spirit.

Nora: I'm not afraid of you any longer. After New Year's, I'll soon be done with the whole business.

Krogstad: *(restraining himself)* Now listen to me, Mrs. Helmer. If necessary, I'll fight for my little job in the bank as if it were life itself.

Nora: Yes, so it seems.

Krogstad: It's not just a matter of income; that's the 360 least of it. It's something else—All right, out with it! Look, this is the thing. You know, just like all the others, of course, that once, a good many years ago, I did something rather rash.

Nora: I've heard rumors to that effect.

Krogstad: The case never got into court; but all the same, every door was closed in my face from then on. So I took up those various activities you know about. I had to grab hold somewhere; and I dare say I haven't been among the worst. But now I want to drop all that. My boys are growing up. For their sakes, I'll have to win back as much respect as possible here in town. That job in the bank was like the first rung in my ladder. And now your husband wants to kick me right back down in the mud again.

Nora: But for heaven's sake, Mr. Krogstad, it's simply not in my power to help you.

Krogstad: That's because you haven't the will to—but I have the means to make you.

Nora: You certainly won't tell my husband that I owe 365 you money?

Krogstad: Hm—what if I told him that?

Nora: That would be shameful of you. *(Nearly in tears.)* This secret—my joy and my pride—that he should learn it in such a crude and disgusting way—learn it from you. You'd expose me to the most horrible unpleasantness—

Krogstad: Only unpleasantness?

Nora: *(vehemently)* But go on and try. It'll turn out the worse for you, because then my husband will really see what a crook you are, and then you'll *never* be able to hold your job.

Krogstad: I asked if it was just domestic unpleasantness you were afraid of.   370

Nora: If my husband finds out, then of course he'll pay what I owe at once, and then we'd be through with you for good.

Krogstad: *(a step closer)* Listen, Mrs. Helmer—you've either got a very bad memory, or else no head at all for business. I'd better put you a little more in touch with the facts.

Nora: What do you mean?

Krogstad: When your husband was sick, you came to me for a loan of four thousand, eight hundred crowns.

Nora: Where else could I go?   375

Krogstad: I promised to get you that sum—

Nora: And you got it.

Krogstad: I promised to get you that sum, on certain conditions. You were so involved in your husband's illness, and so eager to finance your trip, that I guess you didn't think out all the details. It might just be a good idea to remind you. I promised you the money on the strength of a note I drew up.

Nora: Yes, and that I signed.

Krogstad: Right. But at the bottom I added some lines   380
for your father to guarantee the loan. He was supposed to sign down there.

Nora: Supposed to? He did sign.

Krogstad: I left the date blank. In other words, your father would have dated his signature himself. Do you remember that?

Nora: Yes, I think—

Krogstad: Then I gave you the note for you to mail to your father. Isn't that so?

Nora: Yes.   385

Krogstad: And naturally you sent it at once—because only some five, six days later you brought me the note, properly signed. And with that, the money was yours.

Nora: Well, then; I've made my payments regularly, haven't I?

Krogstad: More or less. But—getting back to the point—those were hard times for you then, Mrs. Helmer.

Nora: Yes, they were.

Krogstad: Your father was very ill, I believe.   390

Nora: He was near the end.

Krogstad: He died soon after?

Nora: Yes.

Krogstad: Tell me, Mrs. Helmer, do you happen to recall the date of your father's death? The day of the month, I mean.

Nora: Papa died the twenty-ninth of September.   395

Krogstad: That's quite correct; I've already looked into that. And now we come to a curious thing—*(taking out a paper)* which I simply cannot comprehend.

Nora: Curious thing? I don't know—

Krogstad: This is the curious thing: that your father co-signed the note for your loan three days after his death.

Nora: How—? I don't understand.

Krogstad: Your father died the twenty-ninth of September. 400
But look. Here your father dated his signature October second. Isn't that curious, Mrs. Helmer? *(Nora is silent.)* Can you explain it to me? *(Nora remains silent.)* It's also remarkable that the words "October second" and the year aren't written in your father's hand, but rather in one that I think I know. Well, it's easy to understand. Your father forgot perhaps to date his signature, and then someone or other added it, a bit sloppily, before anyone knew of his death. There's nothing wrong in that. It all comes down to the signature. And there's no question about *that*, Mrs. Helmer. It really *was* your father who signed his own name here, wasn't it?

Nora: *(after a short silence, throwing her head back and looking squarely at him)* No, it wasn't. I signed Papa's name.

Krogstad: Wait, now—are you fully aware that this is a dangerous confession?

Nora: Why? You'll soon get your money.

Krogstad: Let me ask you a question—why didn't you send the paper to your father?

Nora: That was impossible. Papa was so sick. If I'd asked 405
him for his signature, I also would have had to tell him what the money was for. But I couldn't tell him, sick as he was, that my husband's life was in danger. That was just impossible.

Krogstad: Then it would have been better if you'd given up the trip abroad.

Nora: I couldn't possibly. The trip was to save my husband's life. I couldn't give that up.

Krogstad: But didn't you ever consider that this was a fraud against me?

Nora: I couldn't let myself be bothered by that. You weren't any concern of mine. I couldn't stand you, with all those cold complications you made, even though you knew how badly off my husband was.

Krogstad: Mrs. Helmer, obviously you haven't the vaguest idea of what you've involved yourself in. But I can tell you this: it was nothing more and nothing worse than I once did—and it wrecked my whole reputation.

Nora: You? Do you expect me to believe that you ever acted bravely to save your wife's life?

Krogstad: Laws don't inquire into motives.

Nora: Then they must be very poor laws.

Krogstad: Poor or not—if I introduce this paper in court, you'll be judged according to law.

Nora: This I refuse to believe. A daughter hasn't a right to protect her dying father from anxiety and care? A wife hasn't a right to save her husband's life? I don't know much about laws, but I'm sure that somewhere in the books these things are allowed. And you don't know anything about it—you who practice the law? You must be an awful lawyer, Mr. Krogstad.

Krogstad: Could be. But business—the kind of business we two mixed up in—don't you think I know about that? All right. Do what you want now. But I'm telling you *this*: if I get shoved down a second time, you're going to keep me company. (*He bows and goes out through the hall.*)

Nora: (*pensive for a moment, then tossing her head*) Oh, really! Trying to frighten me! I'm not so silly as all that. (*Begins gathering up the children's clothes, but soon stops.*) But—? No, but that's impossible! I did it out of love.

The Children: (*in the doorway, left*) Mama, that strange man's gone out the door.

Nora: Yes, yes, I know it. But don't tell anyone about the strange man. Do you hear? Not even Papa!

The Children: No, Mama. But now will you play again?

Nora: No, not now.

The Children: Oh, but Mama, you promised.

Nora: Yes, but I can't now. Go inside; I have too much to do. Go in, go in, my sweet darlings. (*She herds them gently back in the room and shuts the door after them. Settling on the sofa, she takes up a piece of embroidery and makes some stitches, but soon stops abruptly.*) No! (*Throws the work aside, rises, goes to the hall door and calls out.*) Helene! Let me have the tree in here. (*Goes to the table, left, opens the table drawer, and stops again.*) No, but that's utterly impossible!

Maid: (*with the Christmas tree*) Where should I put it, ma'am?

Nora: There. The middle of the floor.

Maid: Should I bring anything else?

Nora: No, thanks. I have what I need.

The Maid, who has set the tree down, goes out.

Nora: (*absorbed in trimming the tree*) Candles here—and flowers here. That terrible creature! Talk, talk, talk! There's nothing to it at all. The tree's going to be lovely. I'll do anything to please you, Torvald. I'll sing for you, dance for you—

Helmer comes in from the hall, with a sheaf of papers under his arm.

Nora: Oh! You're back so soon?

Helmer: Yes. Has anyone been here?

Nora: Here? No.

Helmer: That's odd. I saw Krogstad leaving the front door.

Nora: So? Oh yes, that's true. Krogstad was here a moment.

Helmer: Nora, I can see by your face that he's been here, begging you to put in a good word for him.

Nora: Yes.

Helmer: And it was supposed to seem like your own idea? You were to hide it from me that he'd been here. He asked you that, too, didn't he?

Nora: Yes, Torvald, but—

Helmer: Nora, Nora, and you could fall for that? Talk with that sort of person and promise him anything? And then in the bargain, tell me an untruth.

Nora: An untruth—?

Helmer: Didn't you say that no one had been here? (*Wagging his finger.*) My little songbird must never do that again. A songbird needs a clean beak to warble with. No false notes. (*Putting his arm about her waist.*) That's the way it should be, isn't it? Yes, I'm sure of it. (*Releasing her.*) And so, enough of that. (*Sitting by the stove.*) Ah, how snug and cozy it is here. (*Leafing among his papers.*)

Nora: (*busy with the tree, after a short pause*) Torvald!

Helmer: Yes.

Nora: I'm so much looking forward to the Stenborgs' costume party, day after tomorrow.

Helmer: And I can't wait to see what you'll surprise me with.

Nora: Oh, that stupid business!

Helmer: What?

Nora: I can't find anything that's right. Everything seems so ridiculous, so inane.

Helmer: So my little Nora's come to *that* recognition?

Nora: (*going behind his chair, her arms resting on its back*) Are you very busy, Torvald?

Helmer: Oh—

Nora: What papers are those?

Helmer: Bank matters.

Nora: Already?

Helmer: I've gotten full authority from the retiring management to make all necessary changes in personnel and procedure. I'll need Christmas week for that. I want to have everything in order by New Year's.

Nora: So that was the reason this poor Krogstad— 455

Helmer: Hm.

Nora: *(still leaning on the chair and slowly stroking the nape of his neck)* If you weren't so very busy, I would have asked you an enormous favor, Torvald.

Helmer: Let's hear. What is it?

Nora: You know, there isn't anyone who has your good taste—and I want so much to look well at the costume party. Torvald, couldn't you take over and decide what I should be and plan my costume?

Helmer: Ah, is my stubborn little creature calling for a 460 lifeguard?

Nora: Yes, Torvald, I can't get anywhere without your help.

Helmer: All right—I'll think it over. We'll hit on something.

Nora: Oh, how sweet of you. *(Goes to the tree again. Pause.)* Aren't the red flowers pretty—? But tell me, was it really such a crime that this Krogstad committed?

Helmer: Forgery. Do you have any idea what that means?

Nora: Couldn't he have done it out of need? 465

Helmer: Yes, or thoughtlessness, like so many others. I'm not so heartless that I'd condemn a man categorically for just one mistake.

Nora: No, of course not, Torvald!

Helmer: Plenty of men have redeemed themselves by openly confessing their crimes and taking their punishment.

Nora: Punishment—?

Helmer: But now Krogstad didn't go that way. He got 470 himself out by sharp practices, and that's the real cause of his moral breakdown.

Nora: Do you really think that would—?

Helmer: Just imagine how a man with that sort of guilt in him has to lie and cheat and deceive on all sides, has to wear a mask even with the nearest and dearest he has, even with his own wife and children. And with the children, Nora—that's where it's most horrible.

Nora: Why?

Helmer: Because that kind of atmosphere of lies infects the whole life of a home. Every breath the children take in is filled with the germs of something degenerate.

Nora: *(coming closer behind him)* Are you sure of that? 475

Helmer: Oh, I've seen it often enough as a lawyer. Almost everyone who goes bad early in life has a mother who's a chronic liar.

Nora: Why just—the mother?

Helmer: It's usually the mother's influence that's dominant, but the father's works in the same way, of course. Every lawyer is quite familiar with it. And still this Krogstad's been going home year in, year out, poisoning his own children with lies and pretense; that's why I call him morally lost. *(Reaching his hands out toward her.)* So my sweet little Nora must promise me never to plead his cause. Your hand on it. Come, come, what's this? Give me your hand. There, now. All settled. I can tell you it'd be impossible for me to work alongside of him. I literally feel physically revolted when I'm anywhere near such a person.

Nora: *(withdraws her hand and goes to the other side of the Christmas tree)* How hot it is here! And I've got so much to do.

Helmer: *(getting up and gathering his papers)* Yes, and I 480 have to think about getting some of these read through before dinner. I'll think about your costume, too. And something to hang on the tree in gilt paper, I may even see about that. *(Putting his hand on her head.)* Oh you, my darling little songbird. *(He goes into his study and closes the door after him.)*

Nora: *(softly, after a silence)* Oh, really! It isn't so. It's impossible. It must be impossible.

Anne-Marie: *(in the doorway, left)* The children are begging so hard to come in to Mama.

Nora: No, no, no, don't let them in to me! You stay with them, Anne-Marie.

Anne-Marie: Of course, ma'am. *(Closes the door.)*

Nora: *(pale with terror)* Hurt my children—! Poison my 485 home? *(A moment's pause; then she tosses her head.)* That's not true. Never. Never in all the world.

Act 2

Same room. Beside the piano the Christmas tree now stands stripped of ornaments, burned-down candle stubs on its ragged branches. Nora's street clothes lie on the sofa. Nora, alone in the room, moves restlessly about; at last she stops at the sofa and picks up her coat.

Nora: *(dropping the coat again)* Someone's coming! *(Goes toward the door, listens.)* No—there's no one. Of course—nobody's coming today, Christmas Day—or tomorrow, either. But maybe—*(Opens the door and looks out.)* No, nothing in the mailbox. Quite empty. *(Coming forward.)* What nonsense! He won't do anything serious. Nothing terrible could happen. It's impossible. Why, I have three small children.

Anne-Marie, with a large carton, comes in from the room to the left.

Anne-Marie: Well, at last I found the box with the masquerade clothes.

Nora: Thanks. Put it on the table.

Anne-Marie: *(does so)* But they're all pretty much of a mess.

Nora: Ahh! I'd love to rip them in a million pieces! 5

Anne-Marie: Oh, mercy, they can be fixed right up. Just a little patience.

Nora: Yes, I'll go get Mrs. Linde to help me.

Anne-Marie: Out again now? In this nasty weather? Miss Nora will catch cold—get sick.

Nora: Oh, worse things could happen—How are the children?

Anne-Marie: The poor mites are playing with their Christmas presents, but— 10

Nora: Do they ask for me much?

Anne-Marie: They're so used to having Mama around, you know.

Nora: Yes. But Anne-Marie, I *can't* be together with them as much as I was.

Anne-Marie: Well, small children get used to anything.

Nora: You think so? Do you think they'd forget their mother if she was gone for good? 15

Anne-Marie: Oh, mercy—gone for good!

Nora: Wait, tell me, Anne-Marie—I've wondered so often—how could you ever have the heart to give your child over to strangers?

Anne-Marie: But I had to, you know, to become little Nora's nurse.

Nora: Yes, but how could you *do* it?

Anne-Marie: When I could get such a good place? A girl 20 who's poor and who's gotten in trouble is glad enough for that. Because that slippery fish, he didn't do a thing for me, you know.

Nora: But your daughter's surely forgotten you.

Anne-Marie: Oh, she certainly has not. She's written to me, both when she was confirmed and when she was married.

Nora: *(clasping her about the neck)* You old Anne-Marie, you were a good mother for me when I was little.

Anne-Marie: Poor little Nora, with no other mother but me.

Nora: And if the babies didn't have one, then I know that 25 you'd—What silly talk! *(Opening the carton.)* Go in to them. Now I'll have to—Tomorrow you can see how lovely I'll look.

Anne-Marie: Oh, there won't be anyone at the party as lovely as Miss Nora. *(She goes off into the room, left.)*

Nora: *(begins unpacking the box, but soon throws it aside)* Oh, if I dared to go out. If only nobody would come. If only nothing would happen here while I'm out. What craziness—nobody's coming. Just don't think. This muff—needs a brushing. Beautiful gloves, beautiful gloves. Let it go. Let it go! One, two, three, four, five, six—*(With a cry.)* Oh, there they are! *(Poises to move toward the door, but remains irresolutely standing. Mrs. Linde enters from the hall, where she has removed her street clothes.)*

Nora: Oh, it's you, Kristine. There's no one else out there? How good that you've come.

Mrs. Linde: I hear you were up asking for me.

Nora: Yes, I just stopped by. There's something you 30 really can help me with. Let's get settled on the sofa. Look, there's going to be a costume party tomorrow evening at the Stenborgs' right above us, and now Torvald wants me to go as a Neapolitan peasant girl and dance the tarantella that I learned in Capri.

Mrs. Linde: Really, are you giving a whole performance?

Nora: Torvald says yes, I should. See, here's the dress. Torvald had it made for me down there; but now it's all so tattered that I just don't know—

Mrs. Linde: Oh, we'll fix that up in no time. It's nothing more than the trimmings—they're a bit loose here and there. Needle and thread? Good, now we have what we need.

Nora: Oh, how sweet of you!

Mrs. Linde: *(sewing)* So you'll be in disguise tomorrow, 35 Nora. You know what? I'll stop by then for a moment and have a look at you all dressed up. But listen, I've absolutely forgotten to thank you for that pleasant evening yesterday.

Nora: *(getting up and walking about)* I don't think it was as pleasant as usual yesterday. You should have come to town a bit sooner, Kristine—Yes, Torvald really knows how to give a home elegance and charm.

Mrs. Linde: And you do, too, if you ask me. You're not your father's daughter for nothing. But tell me, is Dr. Rank always so down in the mouth as yesterday?

Nora: No, that was quite an exception. But he goes around critically ill all the time—tuberculosis of the spine, poor man. You know, his father was a disgusting thing who kept mistresses and so on—and that's why the son's been sickly from birth.

Mrs. Linde: *(lets her sewing fall to her lap)* But my dearest Nora, how do you know about such things?

Nora: *(walking more jauntily)* Hmp! When you've had 40 three children, then you've had a few visits from—from women who know something of medicine, and they tell you this and that.

>> Anthony Hopkins as Torvald and Claire Bloom as Nora in 1973 film version of *A Doll House*

Mrs. Linde: *(resumes sewing; a short pause)* Does Dr. Rank come here every day?

Nora: Every blessed day. He's Torvald's best friend from childhood, and *my* good friend, too. Dr. Rank almost belongs to this house.

Mrs. Linde: But tell me—is he quite sincere? I mean, doesn't he rather enjoy flattering people?

Nora: Just the opposite. Why do you think that?

Mrs. Linde: When you introduced us yesterday, he was proclaiming that he'd often heard my name in this house; but later I noticed that your husband hadn't the slightest idea who I really was. So how could Dr. Rank—? 45

Nora: But it's all true, Kristine. You see, Torvald loves me beyond words, and, as he puts it, he'd like to keep me all to himself. For a long time he'd almost be jealous if I even mentioned any of my old friends back home. So of course I dropped that. But with Dr. Rank I talk a lot about such things, because he likes hearing about them.

Mrs. Linde: Now listen, Nora; in many ways you're still like a child. I'm a good deal older than you, with a little more experience. I'll tell you something: you ought to put an end to all this with Dr. Rank.

Nora: What should I put an end to?

Mrs. Linde: Both parts of it, I think. Yesterday you said something about a rich admirer who'd provide you with money—

Nora: Yes, one who doesn't exist—worse luck. So? 50

Mrs. Linde: Is Dr. Rank well off?

Nora: Yes, he is.

Mrs. Linde: With no dependents?

Nora: No, no one. But—

Mrs. Linde: And he's over here every day? 55

Nora: Yes, I told you that.

Mrs. Linde: How can a man of such refinement be so grasping?

Nora: I don't follow you at all.

Mrs. Linde: Now don't try to hide it, Nora. You think I can't guess who loaned you the forty-eight hundred crowns?

Nora: Are you out of your mind? How could you think such a thing! A friend of ours, who comes here every single day. What an intolerable situation that would have been! 60

Mrs. Linde: Then it really wasn't him.

Nora: No, absolutely not. It never even crossed my mind for a moment—And he had nothing to lend in those days; his inheritance came later.

Mrs. Linde: Well, I think that was a stroke of luck for you, Nora dear.

Nora: No, it never would have occurred to me to ask Dr. Rank—Still, I'm quite sure that if I had asked him—

Mrs. Linde: Which you won't, of course. 65

Nora: No, of course not. I can't see that I'd ever need to. But I'm quite positive that if I talked to Dr. Rank—

Mrs. Linde: Behind your husband's back?

Nora: I've got to clear up this other thing; *that's* also behind his back. I've *got* to clear it all up.

Mrs. Linde: Yes, I was saying that yesterday, but—

Nora: *(pacing up and down)* A man handles these problems so much better than a woman— 70

Mrs. Linde: One's husband does, yes.

Nora: Nonsense. *(Stopping.)* When you pay everything you owe, then you get your note back, right?

Mrs. Linde: Yes, naturally.

Nora: And can rip it into a million pieces and burn it up—that filthy scrap of paper!

Mrs. Linde: *(looking hard at her, laying her sewing aside, and rising slowly)* Nora, you're hiding something from me. 75

Nora: You can see it in my face?

Mrs. Linde: Something's happened to you since yesterday morning. Nora, what is it?

Nora: *(hurrying toward her)* Kristine! *(Listening.)* Shh! Torvald's home. Look, go in with the children a while. Torvald can't bear all this snipping and stitching. Let Anne-Marie help you.

Mrs. Linde: *(gathering up some of the things)* All right, but I'm not leaving here until we've talked this out. *(She disappears into the room, left, as Torvald enters from the hall.)*

Nora: Oh, how I've been waiting for you, Torvald dear. 80

Helmer: Was that the dressmaker?

Nora: No, that was Kristine. She's helping me fix up my costume. You know, it's going to be quite attractive.

Helmer: Yes, wasn't that a bright idea I had?

Nora: Brilliant! But then wasn't I good as well to give in to you?

Helmer: Good—because you give in to your husband's 85 judgment? All right, you little goose, I know you didn't mean it like that. But I won't disturb you. You'll want to have a fitting, I suppose.

Nora: And you'll be working?

Helmer: Yes. *(Indicating a bundle of papers.)* See. I've been down to the bank. *(Starts toward his study.)*

Nora: Torvald.

Helmer: *(stops)* Yes.

Nora: If your little squirrel begged you, with all her heart 90 and soul, for something—?

Helmer: What's that?

Nora: Then would you do it?

Helmer: First, naturally, I'd have to know what it was.

Nora: Your squirrel would scamper about and do tricks, if you'd only be sweet and give in.

Helmer: Out with it. 95

Nora: Your lark would be singing high and low in every room—

Helmer: Come on, she does that anyway.

Nora: I'd be a wood nymph and dance for you in the moonlight.

Helmer: Nora—don't tell me it's that same business from this morning?

Nora: *(coming closer)* Yes, Torvald, I beg you, please! 100

Helmer: And you actually have the nerve to drag that up again?

Nora: Yes, yes, you've got to give in to me; you *have* to let Krogstad keep his job in the bank.

Helmer: My dear Nora, I've slated his job for Mrs. Linde.

Nora: That's awfully kind of you. But you could just fire another clerk instead of Krogstad.

Helmer: This is the most incredible stubbornness! 105 Because you go and give an impulsive promise to speak up for him, I'm expected to—

Nora: That's not the reason, Torvald. It's for your own sake. That man does writing for the worst papers; you said it yourself. He could do you any amount of harm. I'm scared to death of him—

Helmer: Ah, I understand. It's the old memories haunting you.

Nora: What do you mean by that?

Helmer: Of course, you're thinking about your father.

Nora: Yes, all right. Just remember how those nasty 110 gossips wrote in the papers about Papa and slandered him so cruelly. I think they'd have had him dismissed if the department hadn't sent you up to investigate, and if you hadn't been so kind and open-minded toward him.

Helmer: My dear Nora, there's a notable difference between your father and me. Your father's official career was hardly above reproach. But mine is; and I hope it'll stay that way as long as I hold my position.

Nora: Oh, who can ever tell what vicious minds can invent? We could be so snug and happy now in our quiet, carefree home—you and I and the children, Torvald! That's why I'm pleading with you so—

Helmer: And just by pleading for him you make it impossible for me to keep him on. It's already known at the bank that I'm firing Krogstad. What if it's rumored around now that the new bank manager was vetoed by his wife—

Nora: Yes, what then—?

Helmer: Oh yes—as long as our little bundle of stub- 115 bornness gets her way—! I should go and make myself ridiculous in front of the whole office—give people the idea I can be swayed by all kinds of outside pressure. Oh, you can bet I'd feel the effects of that soon enough! Besides—there's something that rules Krogstad right out at the bank as long as I'm the manager.

Nora: What's that?

Helmer: His moral failings I could maybe overlook if I had to—

Nora: Yes, Torvald, why not?

Helmer: And I hear he's quite efficient on the job. But he was a crony of mine back in my teens—one of those rash friendships that crop up again and again to embarrass you later in life. Well, I might as well say it straight out: we're on a first-name basis. And that tactless fool makes no effort at all to hide it in front of others. Quite the contrary—he thinks that entitles him to take a familiar air around me, and so every other second he comes booming out with his "Yes, Torvald!" and "Sure thing, Torvald!" I tell you, it's been excruciating for me. He's out to make my place in the bank unbearable.

Nora: Torvald, you can't be serious about all this. 120

Helmer: Oh no? Why not?

Nora: Because these are such petty considerations.

Helmer: What are you saying? Petty? You think I'm petty!

Nora: No, just the opposite, Torvald dear. That's exactly why—

Helmer: Never mind. You call my motives petty; then I might as well be just that. Petty! All right! We'll put a stop to this for good. *(Goes to the hall door and calls.)* Helene!

Nora: What do you want?

Helmer: *(searching among his papers)* A decision. *(The Maid comes in.)* Look here; take this letter; go out with it at once. Get hold of a messenger and have him deliver it. Quick now. It's already addressed. Wait, here's some money.

Maid: Yes, sir. *(She leaves with the letter.)*

Helmer: *(straightening his papers)* There, now, little Miss Willful.

Nora: *(breathlessly)* Torvald, what was that letter?

Helmer: Krogstad's notice.

Nora: Call it back, Torvald! There's still time. Oh, Torvald, call it back! Do it for my sake—for your sake, for the children's sake! Do you hear, Torvald; do it! You don't know how this can harm us.

Helmer: Too late.

Nora: Yes, too late.

Helmer: Nora dear, I can forgive you this panic, even though basically you're insulting me. Yes, you are! Or isn't it an insult to think that *I* should be afraid of a courtroom hack's revenge? But I forgive you anyway, because this shows so beautifully how much you love me. *(Takes her in his arms.)* This is the way it should be, my darling Nora. Whatever comes, you'll see: when it really counts, I have strength and courage enough as a man to take on the whole weight myself.

Nora: *(terrified)* What do you mean by that?

Helmer: The whole weight, I said.

Nora: *(resolutely)* No, never in all the world.

Helmer: Good. So we'll share it, Nora, as man and wife. That's as it should be. *(Fondling her.)* Are you happy now? There, there, there—not these frightened dove's eyes. It's nothing at all but empty fantasies—Now you should run through your tarantella and practice your tambourine. I'll go to the inner office and shut both doors, so I won't hear a thing; you can make all the noise you like. *(Turning in the doorway.)* And when Rank comes, just tell him where he can find me. *(He nods to her and goes with his papers into the study, closing the door.)*

Nora: *(standing as though rooted, dazed with fright, in a whisper)* He really could do it. He will do it. He'll do it in spite of everything. No, not that, never, never! Anything but that! Escape! A way out—*(The doorbell rings.)* Dr. Rank! Anything but that! *Anything*, whatever it is! *(Her hands pass over her face, smoothing it; she pulls herself together, goes over and opens the hall door. Dr. Rank stands outside, hanging his fur coat up. During the following scene, it begins getting dark.)*

Nora: Hello, Dr. Rank. I recognized your ring. But you mustn't go in to Torvald yet; I believe he's working.

Rank: And you?

Nora: For you, I always have an hour to spare—you know that. *(He has entered, and she shuts the door after him.)*

Rank: Many thanks. I'll make use of these hours while I can.

Nora: What do you mean by that? While you can?

Rank: Does that disturb you?

Nora: Well, it's such an odd phrase. Is anything going to happen?

Rank: What's going to happen is what I've been expecting so long—but I honestly didn't think it would come so soon.

Nora: *(gripping his arm)* What is it you've found out? Dr. Rank, you have to tell me!

Rank: *(sitting by the stove)* It's all over with me. There's nothing to be done about it.

Nora: *(breathing easier)* Is it you—then—?

Rank: Who else? There's no point in lying to one's self. I'm the most miserable of all my patients, Mrs. Helmer. These past few days I've been auditing my internal accounts. Bankrupt! Within a month I'll probably be laid out and rotting in the churchyard.

Nora: Oh, what a horrible thing to say.

Rank: The thing itself is horrible. But the worst of it is all the other horror before it's over. There's only one final examination left; when I'm finished with that, I'll know about when my disintegration will begin. There's something I want to say. Helmer with his sensitivity has such a sharp distaste for anything ugly. I don't want him near my sickroom.

Nora: Oh, but Dr. Rank—

Rank: I won't have him in there. Under no condition. I'll lock my door to him—As soon as I'm completely sure of the worst, I'll send you my calling card marked with a black cross, and you'll know then the wreck has started to come apart.

Nora: No, today you're completely unreasonable. And I wanted you so much to be in a really good humor.

Rank: With death up my sleeve? And then to suffer this way for somebody else's sins. Is there any justice in that? And in every single family, in some way or another, this inevitable retribution of nature goes on—

Nora: *(her hands pressed over her ears)* Oh, stuff! Cheer up! Please—be gay!

Rank: Yes, I'd just as soon laugh at it all. My poor, innocent spine, serving time for my father's gay army days.

Nora: *(by the table, left)* He was so infatuated with asparagus tips and *pâté de foie gras*, wasn't that it?

Rank: Yes—and with truffles.

Nora: Truffles, yes. And then with oysters, I suppose?

Rank: Yes, tons of oysters, naturally.

Nora: And then the port and champagne to go with it. 165
It's so sad that all these delectable things have to
strike at our bones.

Rank: Especially when they strike at the unhappy bones
that never shared in the fun.

Nora: Ah, that's the saddest of all.

Rank: (looks searchingly at her) Hm.

Nora: (after a moment) Why did you smile?

Rank: No, it was you who laughed. 170

Nora: No, it was you who smiled, Dr. Rank!

Rank: (getting up) You're even a bigger tease than I'd
thought.

Nora: I'm full of wild ideas today.

Rank: That's obvious.

Nora: (putting both hands on his shoulders) Dear, dear 175
Dr. Rank, you'll never die for Torvald and me.

Rank: Oh, that loss you'll easily get over. Those who go
away are soon forgotten.

Nora: (looks fearfully at him) You believe that?

Rank: One makes new connections, and then—

Nora: Who makes new connections?

Rank: Both you and Torvald will when I'm gone. I'd say 180
you're well under way already. What was that Mrs.
Linde doing here last evening?

Nora: Oh, come—you can't be jealous of poor Kristine?

Rank: Oh yes, I am. She'll be my successor here in the
house. When I'm down under, that woman will
probably—

Nora: Shh! Not so loud. She's right in there.

Rank: Today as well. So you see.

Nora: Only to sew on my dress. Good gracious, how 185
unreasonable you are. (Sitting on the sofa.) Be nice
now, Dr. Rank. Tomorrow you'll see how beautifully
I'll dance; and you can imagine then that I'm
dancing only for you—yes, and of course for
Torvald, too—that's understood. (Takes various
items out of the carton.) Dr. Rank, sit over here and
I'll show you something.

Rank: (sitting) What's that?

Nora: Look here. Look.

Rank: Silk stockings.

Nora: Flesh-colored. Aren't they lovely? Now it's so dark
here, but tomorrow—No, no, no, just look at the
feet. Oh well, you might as well look at the rest.

Rank: Hm— 190

Nora: Why do you look so critical? Don't you believe
they'll fit?

Rank: I've never had any chance to form an opinion on
that.

Nora: (glancing at him a moment) Shame on you. (Hits
him lightly on the ear with the stockings.) That's for
you. (Puts them away again.)

Rank: And what other splendors am I going to see now?

Nora: Not the least bit more, because you've been 195
naughty. (She hums a little and rummages among her
things.)

Rank: (after a short silence) When I sit here together with
you like this, completely easy and open, then I don't
know—I simply can't imagine—whatever would
have become of me if I'd never come into this house.

Nora: (smiling) Yes, I really think you feel completely at
ease with us.

Rank: (more quietly, staring straight ahead) And then to
have to go away from it all—

Nora: Nonsense, you're not going away.

Rank: (his voice unchanged)—and not even be able to 200
leave some poor show of gratitude behind, scarcely a
fleeting regret—no more than a vacant place that
anyone can fill.

Nora: And if I asked you now for—? No—

Rank: For what?

Nora: For a great proof of your friendship—

Rank: Yes, yes?

Nora: No, I mean—for an exceptionally big favor— 205

Rank: Would you really, for once, make me so happy?

Nora: Oh, you haven't the vaguest idea what it is.

Rank: All right, then tell me.

Nora: No, but I can't, Dr. Rank—it's all out of reason.
It's advice and help, too—and a favor—

Rank: So much the better. I can't fathom what you're 210
hinting at. Just speak out. Don't you trust me?

Nora: Of course. More than anyone else. You're my best
and truest friend, I'm sure. That's why I want to talk
to you. All right, then, Dr. Rank: there's something
you can help me prevent. You know how deeply, how
inexpressibly dearly Torvald loves me; he'd never
hesitate a second to give up his life for me.

Rank: (leaning close to her) Nora—do you think he's the
only one—

Nora: (with a slight start) Who—?

Rank: Who'd gladly give up his life for you.

Nora: (heavily) I see. 215

Rank: I swore to myself you should know this before I'm
gone. I'll never find a better chance. Yes, Nora, now
you know. And also you know now that you can
trust me beyond anyone else.

Nora: (rising, natural and calm) Let me by.

Rank: (making room for her, but still sitting) Nora—

Nora: *(in the hall doorway)* Helene, bring the lamp in. *(Goes over to the stove.)* Ah, dear Dr. Rank, that was really mean of you.

Rank: *(getting up)* That I've loved you just as deeply as 220 somebody else? Was *that* mean?

Nora: No, but that you came out and told me. That was quite unnecessary—

Rank: What do you mean? Have you known—?

The Maid comes in with the lamp, sets it on the table, and goes out again.

Rank: Nora—Mrs. Helmer—I'm asking you: have you known about it?

Nora: Oh, how can I tell what I know or don't know? Really, I don't know what to say—Why did you have to be so clumsy, Dr. Rank! Everything was so good.

Rank: Well, in any case, you now have the knowledge 225 that my body and soul are at your command. So won't you speak out?

Nora: *(looking at him)* After that?

Rank: Please, just let me know what it is.

Nora: You can't know anything now.

Rank: I have to. You mustn't punish me like this. Give me the chance to do whatever is humanly possible for you.

Nora: Now there's nothing you can do for me. Besides, 230 actually, I don't need any help. You'll see—it's only my fantasies. That's what it is. Of course! *(Sits in the rocker, looks at him, and smiles.)* What a nice one you are, Dr. Rank. Aren't you a little bit ashamed, now that the lamp is here?

Rank: No, not exactly. But perhaps I'd better go—for good?

Nora: No, you certainly can't do that. You must come here just as you always have. You know Torvald can't do without you.

Rank: Yes, but *you*?

Nora: You know how much I enjoy it when you're here.

Rank: That's precisely what threw me off. You're a 235 mystery to me. So many times I've felt you'd almost rather be with me than with Helmer.

Nora: Yes—you see, there are some people that one loves most and other people that one would almost prefer being with.

Rank: Yes, there's something to that.

Nora: When I was back home, of course I loved Papa most. But I always thought it was so much fun when I could sneak down to the maids' quarters, because they never tried to improve me, and it was always so amusing, the way they talked to each other.

Rank: Aha, so it's *their* place that I've filled.

Nora: *(jumping up and going to him)* Oh, dear, sweet 240 Dr. Rank, that's not what I mean at all. But you can

understand that with Torvald it's just the same as with Papa—

The Maid enters from the hall.

Maid: Ma'am—please! *(She whispers to Nora and hands her a calling card.)*

Nora: *(glancing at the card)* Ah! *(Slips it into her pocket.)*

Rank: Anything wrong?

Nora: No, no, not at all. It's only some—it's my new dress—

Rank: Really? But—there's your dress. 245

Nora: Oh, that. But this is another one—I ordered it— Torvald mustn't know—

Rank: Ah, now we have the big secret.

Nora: That's right. Just go in with him—he's back in the inner study. Keep him there as long as—

Rank: Don't worry. He won't get away. *(Goes into the study.)*

Nora: *(to the Maid)* And he's standing waiting in the 250 kitchen?

Maid: Yes, he came up by the back stairs.

Nora: But didn't you tell him somebody was here?

Maid: Yes, but that didn't do any good.

Nora: He won't leave?

Maid: No, he won't go till he's talked with you, ma'am. 255

Nora: Let him come in, then—but quietly. Helene, don't breathe a word about this. It's a surprise for my husband.

Maid: Yes, yes, I understand—*(Goes out.)*

Nora: This horror—it's going to happen. No, no, no, it can't happen, it mustn't. *(She goes and bolts Helmer's door. The Maid opens the hall door for Krogstad and shuts it behind him. He is dressed for travel in a fur coat, boots, and a fur cap.)*

Nora: *(going toward him)* Talk softly. My husband's home.

Krogstad: Well, good for him. 260

Nora: What do you want?

Krogstad: Some information.

Nora: Hurry up, then. What is it?

Krogstad: You know, of course, that I got my notice.

Nora: I couldn't prevent it, Mr. Krogstad. I fought for 265 you to the bitter end, but nothing worked.

Krogstad: Does your husband's love for you run so thin? He knows everything I can expose you to, and all the same he dares to—

Nora: How can you imagine he knows anything about this?

Krogstad: Ah, no—I can't imagine it either, now. It's not at all like my fine Torvald Helmer to have so much guts—

Nora: Mr. Krogstad, I demand respect for my husband!

Krogstad: Why, of course—all due respect. But since the 270
lady's keeping it so carefully hidden, may I presume
to ask if you're also a bit better informed than yesterday about what you've actually done?

Nora: More than you ever could teach me.

Krogstad: Yes, I *am* such an awful lawyer.

Nora: What is it you want from me?

Krogstad: Just a glimpse of how you are, Mrs. Helmer.
I've been thinking about you all day long. A cashier,
a night-court scribbler, a—well, a type like me also
has a little of what they call a heart, you know.

Nora: Then show it. Think of my children. 275

Krogstad: Did you or your husband ever think of mine?
But never mind. I simply wanted to tell you that you
don't need to take this thing too seriously. For the
present, I'm not proceeding with any action.

Nora: Oh no, really! Well—I knew that.

Krogstad: Everything can be settled in a friendly spirit. It
doesn't have to get around town at all; it can stay
just among us three.

Nora: My husband must never know anything of this.

Krogstad: How can you manage that? Perhaps you can 280
pay me the balance?

Nora: No, not right now.

Krogstad: Or you know some way of raising the money
in a day or two?

Nora: No way that I'm willing to use.

Krogstad: Well, it wouldn't have done you any good,
anyway. If you stood in front of me with a fistful of
bills, you still couldn't buy your signature back.

Nora: Then tell me what you're going to do with it. 285

Krogstad: I'll just hold onto it—keep it on file. There's
no outsider who'll even get wind of it. So if you've
been thinking of taking some desperate step—

Nora: I have.

Krogstad: Been thinking of running away from home—

Nora: I have!

Krogstad: Or even of something worse— 290

Nora: How could you guess that?

Krogstad: You can drop those thoughts.

Nora: How could you guess I was thinking of *that*?

Krogstad: Most of us think about *that* at first. I thought
about it too, but I discovered I hadn't the courage—

Nora: *(lifelessly)* I don't either. 295

Krogstad: *(relieved)* That's true, you haven't the courage?
You too?

Nora: I don't have it—I don't have it.

Krogstad: It would be terribly stupid, anyway. After that
first storm at home blows out, why, then—I have
here in my pocket a letter for your husband—

>> Palestinian actors perform in *A Doll House* on International
Women's Day, March 9, 2008

Nora: Telling everything?

Krogstad: As charitably as possible. 300

Nora: *(quickly)* He mustn't ever get that letter. Tear it up.
I'll find some way to get money.

Krogstad: Beg pardon, Mrs. Helmer, but I think I just
told you—

Nora: Oh, I don't mean the money I owe you. Let me
know how much you want from my husband, and
I'll manage it.

Krogstad: I don't want any money from your husband.

Nora: What do you want, then? 305

Krogstad: I'll tell you what. I want to recoup, Mrs.
Helmer; I want to get on in the world—and there's
where your husband can help me. For a year and a
half I've kept myself clean of anything disreputable—
all that time struggling with the worst conditions;
but I was satisfied, working my way up step by step.
Now I've been written right off, and I'm just not in
the mood to come crawling back. I tell you, I want
to move on. I want to get back in the bank—in a
better position. Your husband can set up a job for
me—

Nora: He'll never do that!

Krogstad: He'll do it. I know him. He won't dare
breathe a word of protest. And once I'm in there
together with him, you just wait and see! Inside of
a year, I'll be the manager's right-hand man. It'll
be Nils Krogstad, not Torvald Helmer, who runs
the bank.

Nora: You'll never see the day!

Krogstad: Maybe you think you can— 310

Nora: I have the courage now—for *that*.

Krogstad: Oh, you don't scare me. A smart, spoiled lady like you—

Nora: You'll see; you'll see!

Krogstad: Under the ice, maybe? Down in the freezing, coal-black water? There, till you float up in the spring, ugly, unrecognizable, with your hair falling out—

Nora: You don't frighten me.   315

Krogstad: Nor do you frighten me. One doesn't do these things, Mrs. Helmer. Besides, what good would it be? I'd still have him safe in my pocket.

Nora: Afterwards? When I'm no longer—?

Krogstad: Are you forgetting that *I'll* be in control then over your final reputation? *(Nora stands speechless, staring at him.)* Good; now I've warned you. Don't do anything stupid. When Helmer's read my letter, I'll be waiting for his reply. And bear in mind that it's your husband himself who's forced me back to my old ways. I'll never forgive him for that. Good-bye, Mrs. Helmer. *(He goes out through the hall.)*

Nora: *(goes to the hall door, opens it a crack, and listens)* He's gone. Didn't leave the letter. Oh no, no, that's impossible too! *(Opening the door more and more.)* What's that? He's standing outside—not going downstairs. He's thinking it over? Maybe he'll—? *(A letter falls in the mailbox; then Krogstad's footsteps are heard, dying away down a flight of stairs. Nora gives a muffled cry and runs over toward the sofa table. A short pause.)* In the mailbox. *(Slips warily over to the hall door.)* It's lying there. Torvald, Torvald—now we're lost!

Mrs. Linde: *(entering with the costume from the room,*   320
left) There now, I can't see anything else to mend. Perhaps you'd like to try—

Nora: *(in a hoarse whisper)* Kristine, come here.

Mrs. Linde: *(tossing the dress on the sofa)* What's wrong? You look upset.

Nora: Come here. See that letter? *There!* Look—through the glass in the mailbox.

Mrs. Linde: Yes, yes, I see it.

Nora: That letter's from Krogstad—   325

Mrs. Linde: Nora—it's Krogstad who loaned you the money!

Nora: Yes, and now Torvald will find out everything.

Mrs. Linde: Believe me, Nora, it's best for both of you.

Nora: There's more you don't know. I forged a name.

Mrs. Linde: But for heaven's sake—?   330

Nora: I only want to tell you that, Kristine, so that you can be my witness.

Mrs. Linde: Witness? Why should I—?

Nora: If I should go out of my mind—it could easily happen—

Mrs. Linde: Nora!

Nora: Or anything else occurred—so I couldn't be   335
present here—

Mrs. Linde: Nora, Nora, you aren't yourself at all!

Nora: And someone should try to take on the whole weight, all of the guilt, you follow me—

Mrs. Linde: Yes, of course, but why do you think—?

Nora: Then you're the witness that it isn't true, Kristine. I'm very much myself; my mind right now is perfectly clear; and I'm telling you: nobody else has known about this; I alone did everything. Remember that.

Mrs. Linde: I will. But I don't understand all this.   340

Nora: Oh, how could you ever understand it? It's the miracle now that's going to take place.

Mrs. Linde: The miracle?

Nora: Yes, the miracle. But it's so awful, Kristine. It mustn't take place, not for anything in the world.

Mrs. Linde: I'm going right over and talk with Krogstad.

Nora: Don't go near him; he'll do you some terrible   345
harm!

Mrs. Linde: There was a time once when he'd gladly have done anything for me.

Nora: He?

Mrs. Linde: Where does he live?

Nora: Oh, how do I know? Yes. *(Searches in her pocket.)* Here's his card. But the letter, the letter—!

Helmer: *(from the study, knocking on the door)* Nora!   350

Nora: *(with a cry of fear)* Oh! What is it? What do you want?

Helmer: Now, now, don't be so frightened. We're not coming in. You locked the door—are you trying on the dress?

Nora: Yes, I'm trying it. I'll look just beautiful, Torvald.

Mrs. Linde: *(who has read the card)* He's living right around the corner.

Nora: Yes, but what's the use? We're lost. The letter's in   355
the box.

Mrs. Linde: And your husband has the key?

Nora: Yes, always.

Mrs. Linde: Krogstad can ask for his letter back unread; he can find some excuse—

Nora: But it's just this time that Torvald usually—

Mrs. Linde: Stall him. Keep him in there. I'll be back   360
as quick as I can. *(She hurries out through the hall entrance.)*

Nora: *(goes to Helmer's door, opens it, and peers in)* Torvald!

Helmer: *(from the inner study)* Well—does one dare set foot in one's own living room at last? Come on,

Rank, now we'll get a look—(*In the doorway.*) But what's this?

Nora: What, Torvald dear?

Helmer: Rank had me expecting some grand masquerade.

Rank: (*in the doorway*) That was my impression, but I 365 must have been wrong.

Nora: No one can admire me in my splendor—not till tomorrow.

Helmer: But Nora dear, you look so exhausted. Have you practiced too hard?

Nora: No, I haven't practiced at all yet.

Helmer: You know, it's necessary—

Nora: Oh, it's absolutely necessary, Torvald. But I can't 370 get anywhere without your help. I've forgotten the whole thing completely.

Helmer: Ah, we'll soon take care of that.

Nora: Yes, take care of me, Torvald, please! Promise me that? Oh, I'm so nervous. That big party—You must give up everything this evening for me. No business—don't even touch your pen. Yes? Dear Torvald, promise?

Helmer: It's a promise. Tonight I'm totally at your service—you little helpless thing. Hm—but first there's one thing I want to—(*Goes toward the hall door.*)

Nora: What are you looking for?

Helmer: Just to see if there's any mail. 375

Nora: No, no, don't do that, Torvald!

Helmer: Now what?

Nora: Torvald, please. There isn't any.

Helmer: Let me look, though. (*Starts out. Nora, at the piano, strikes the first notes of the tarantella. Helmer, at the door, stops.*) Aha!

Nora: I can't dance tomorrow if I don't practice with you. 380

Helmer: (*going over to her*) Nora dear, are you really so frightened?

Nora: Yes, so terribly frightened. Let me practice right now; there's still time before dinner. Oh, sit down and play for me, Torvald. Direct me. Teach me, the way you always have.

Helmer: Gladly, if it's what you want. (*Sits at the piano.*)

Nora: (*snatches the tambourine up from the box, then a long, varicolored shawl, which she throws around herself, whereupon she springs forward and cries out*) Play for me now! Now I'll dance!

Helmer plays and Nora dances. Rank stands behind Helmer at the piano and looks on.

Helmer: (*as he plays*) Slower. Slow down. 385

Nora: Can't change it.

Helmer: Not so violent, Nora!

Nora: Has to be just like this.

Helmer: (*stopping*) No, no, that won't do at all.

Nora: (*laughing and swinging her tambourine*) Isn't that 390 what I told you?

Rank: Let me play for her.

Helmer: (*getting up*) Yes, go on. I can teach her more easily then.

Rank sits at the piano and plays; Nora dances more and more wildly. Helmer has stationed himself by the stove and repeatedly gives her directions; she seems not to hear them; her hair loosens and falls over her shoulders; she does not notice, but goes on dancing. Mrs. Linde enters.

Mrs. Linde: (*standing dumbfounded at the door*) Ah—!

Nora: (*still dancing*) See what fun, Kristine!

Helmer: But Nora darling, you dance as if your life were 395 at stake.

Nora: And it is.

Helmer: Rank, stop! This is pure madness. Stop it, I say!

Rank breaks off playing, and Nora halts abruptly.

Helmer: (*going over to her*) I never would have believed it. You've forgotten everything I taught you.

Nora: (*throwing away the tambourine*) You see for yourself.

Helmer: Well, there's certainly room for instruction here. 400

Nora: Yes, you see how important it is. You've got to teach me to the very last minute. Promise me that, Torvald?

Helmer: You can bet on it.

Nora: You mustn't, either today or tomorrow, think about anything else but me; you mustn't open any letters—or the mailbox—

Helmer: Ah, it's still the fear of that man—

Nora: Oh yes, yes, that too. 405

Helmer: Nora, it's written all over you—there's already a letter from him out there.

Nora: I don't know. I guess so. But you mustn't read such things now; there mustn't be anything ugly between us before it's all over.

Rank: (*quietly to Helmer*) You shouldn't deny her.

Helmer: (*putting his arm around her*) The child can have her way. But tomorrow night, after you've danced—

Nora: Then you'll be free. 410

Maid: (*in the doorway, right*) Ma'am, dinner is served.

Nora: We'll be wanting champagne, Helene.

Maid: Very good, ma'am. (*Goes out.*)

Helmer: So—a regular banquet, hm?

Nora: Yes, a banquet—champagne till daybreak! *(Calling* 415 *out.)* And some macaroons, Helene. Heaps of them—just this once.

Helmer: *(taking her hands)* Now, now, now—no hysterics. Be my own little lark again.

Nora: Oh, I will soon enough. But go on in—and you, Dr. Rank. Kristine, help me put up my hair.

Rank: *(whispering, as they go)* There's nothing wrong—really wrong, is there?

Helmer: Oh, of course not. It's nothing more than this childish anxiety I was telling you about. *(They go out, right.)*

Nora: Well? 420

Mrs. Linde: Left town.

Nora: I could see by your face.

Mrs. Linde: He'll be home tomorrow evening. I wrote him a note.

Nora: You shouldn't have. Don't try to stop anything now. After all, it's a wonderful joy, this waiting here for the miracle.

Mrs. Linde: What is it you're waiting for? 425

Nora: Oh, you can't understand that. Go in to them: I'll be along in a moment.

Mrs. Linde goes into the dining room. Nora stands a short while as if composing herself; then she looks at her watch.

Nora: Five. Seven hours to midnight. Twenty-four hours to the midnight after, and then the tarantella's done. Seven and twenty-four? Thirty-one hours to live.

Helmer: *(in the doorway, right)* What's become of the little lark?

Nora: *(going toward him with open arms)* Here's your lark!

ACT 3

Same scene. The table, with chairs around it, has been moved to the center of the room. A lamp on the table is lit. The hall door stands open. Dance music drifts down from the floor above. Mrs. Linde sits at the table, absently paging through a book, trying to read, but apparently unable to focus her thoughts. Once or twice she pauses, tensely listening for a sound at the outer entrance.

Mrs. Linde: *(glancing at her watch)* Not yet—and there's hardly any time left. If only he's not—*(Listening again.)* Ah, there he is. *(She goes out in the hall and cautiously opens the outer door. Quiet footsteps are heard on the stairs. She whispers:)* Come in. Nobody's here.

Krogstad: *(in the doorway)* I found a note from you at home. What's back of all this?

Mrs. Linde: I just *had* to talk to you.

Krogstad: Oh? And it just *had* to be here in this house?

Mrs. Linde: At my place it was impossible; my room 5 hasn't a private entrance. Come in; we're all alone. The maid's asleep, and the Helmers are at the dance upstairs.

Krogstad: *(entering the room)* Well, well, the Helmers are dancing tonight? Really?

Mrs. Linde: Yes, why not?

Krogstad: How true—why not?

Mrs. Linde: All right, Krogstad, let's talk.

Krogstad: Do we two have anything more to talk about? 10

Mrs. Linde: We have a great deal to talk about.

Krogstad: I wouldn't have thought so.

Mrs. Linde: No, because you've never understood me, really.

Krogstad: Was there anything more to understand—except what's all too common in life? A calculating woman throws over a man the moment a better catch comes by.

Mrs. Linde: You think I'm so thoroughly calculating? 15 You think I broke it off lightly?

Krogstad: Didn't you?

Mrs. Linde: Nils—is that what you really thought?

Krogstad: If you cared, then why did you write me the way you did?

Mrs. Linde: What else could I do? If I had to break off with you, then it was my job as well to root out everything you felt for me.

Krogstad: *(wringing his hands)* So that was it. And 20 this—all this, simply for money!

Mrs. Linde: Don't forget I had a helpless mother and two small brothers. We couldn't wait for you, Nils; you had such a long road ahead of you then.

Krogstad: That may be; but you still hadn't the right to abandon me for somebody else's sake.

Mrs. Linde: Yes—I don't know. So many, many times I've asked myself if I did have that right.

Krogstad: *(more softly)* When I lost you, it was as if all the solid ground dissolved from under my feet. Look at me; I'm a half-drowned man now, hanging onto a wreck.

Mrs. Linde: Help may be near. 25

Krogstad: It was near—but then you came and blocked it off.

Mrs. Linde: Without my knowing it, Nils. Today for the first time I learned that it's you I'm replacing at the bank.

Krogstad: All right—I believe you. But now that you know, will you step aside?

Mrs. Linde: No, because that wouldn't benefit you in the slightest.

Krogstad: Not "benefit" me, hm! I'd step aside anyway. 30

Mrs. Linde: I've learned to be realistic. Life and hard, bitter necessity have taught me that.

Krogstad: And life's taught me never to trust fine phrases.

Mrs. Linde: Then life's taught you a very sound thing. But you do have to trust in actions, don't you?

Krogstad: What does that mean?

Mrs. Linde: You said you were hanging on like a half-drowned man to a wreck. 35

Krogstad: I've good reason to say that.

Mrs. Linde: I'm also like a half-drowned woman on a wreck. No one to suffer with; no one to care for.

Krogstad: You made your choice.

Mrs. Linde: There wasn't any choice then.

Krogstad: So—what of it? 40

Mrs. Linde: Nils, if only we two shipwrecked people could reach across to each other.

Krogstad: What are you saying?

Mrs. Linde: Two on one wreck are at least better off than each on his own.

Krogstad: Kristine!

Mrs. Linde: Why do you think I came into town? 45

Krogstad: Did you really have some thought of me?

Mrs. Linde: I have to work to go on living. All my born days, as long as I can remember, I've worked, and it's been my best and my only joy. But now I'm completely alone in the world; it frightens me to be so empty and lost. To work for yourself—there's no joy in that. Nils, give me something—someone to work for.

Krogstad: I don't believe all this. It's just some hysterical feminine urge to go out and make a noble sacrifice.

Mrs. Linde: Have you ever found me to be hysterical?

Krogstad: Can you honestly mean this? Tell me—do you know everything about my past? 50

Mrs. Linde: Yes.

Krogstad: And you know what they think I'm worth around here.

Mrs. Linde: From what you were saying before, it would seem that with me you could have been another person.

Krogstad: I'm positive of that.

Mrs. Linde: Couldn't it happen still? 55

Krogstad: Kristine—you're saying this in all seriousness? Yes, you are! I can see it in you. And do you really have the courage, then—?

Mrs. Linde: I need to have someone to care for; and your children need a mother. We both need each other. Nils, I have faith that you're good at heart—I'll risk everything together with you.

Krogstad: (gripping her hands) Kristine, thank you, thank you—Now I know I can win back a place in their eyes. Yes—but I forgot—

Mrs. Linde: (listening) Shh! The tarantella. Go now! Go on!

Krogstad: Why? What is it? 60

Mrs. Linde: Hear the dance up there? When that's over, they'll be coming down.

Krogstad: Oh, then I'll go. But—it's all pointless. Of course, you don't know the move I made against the Helmers.

Mrs. Linde: Yes, Nils, I know.

Krogstad: And all the same, you have the courage to—?

Mrs. Linde: I know how far despair can drive a man like you. 65

Krogstad: Oh, if I only could take it all back.

Mrs. Linde: You easily could—your letter's still lying in the mailbox.

Krogstad: Are you sure of that?

Mrs. Linde: Positive. But—

Krogstad: (looks at her searchingly) Is that the meaning of it, then? You'll save your friend at any price. Tell me straight out. Is that it? 70

Mrs. Linde: Nils—anyone who's sold herself for somebody else once isn't going to do it again.

Krogstad: I'll demand my letter back.

Mrs. Linde: No, no.

Krogstad: Yes, of course. I'll stay here till Helmer comes down; I'll tell him to give me my letter again—that it only involves my dismissal—that he shouldn't read it—

Mrs. Linde: No, Nils, don't call the letter back. 75

Krogstad: But wasn't that exactly why you wrote me to come here?

Mrs. Linde: Yes, in that first panic. But it's been a whole day and night since then, and in that time I've seen such incredible things in this house. Helmer's got to learn everything; this dreadful secret has to be aired; those two have to come to a full understanding; all these lies and evasions can't go on.

Krogstad: Well, then, if you want to chance it. But at least there's one thing I can do, and do right away—

Mrs. Linde: (listening) Go now, go, quick! The dance is over. We're not safe another second.

Krogstad: I'll wait for you downstairs. 80

Mrs. Linde: Yes, please do; take me home.

Krogstad: I can't believe it; I've never been so happy. (He leaves by way of the outer door; the door between the room and the hall stays open.)

Mrs. Linde: (straightening up a bit and getting together her street clothes) How different now! How different!

Someone to work for, to live for—a home to build. Well, it is worth the try! Oh, if they'd only come! *(Listening.)* Ah, there they are. Bundle up. *(She picks up her hat and coat. Nora's and Helmer's voices can be heard outside; a key turns in the lock, and Helmer brings Nora into the hall almost by force. She is wearing the Italian costume with a large black shawl about her; he has on evening dress, with a black domino open over it.)*

Nora: *(struggling in the doorway)* No, no, no, not inside! I'm going up again. I don't want to leave so soon.

Helmer: But Nora dear—   85

Nora: Oh, I beg you, please, Torvald. From the bottom of my heart, *please*—only an hour more!

Helmer: Not a single minute, Nora darling. You know our agreement. Come on, in we go; you'll catch cold out here. *(In spite of her resistance, he gently draws her into the room.)*

Mrs. Linde: Good evening.

Nora: Kristine!

Helmer: Why, Mrs. Linde—are you here so late?   90

Mrs. Linde: Yes, I'm sorry, but I did want to see Nora in costume.

Nora: Have you been sitting here, waiting for me?

Mrs. Linde: Yes. I didn't come early enough; you were all upstairs; and then I thought I really couldn't leave without seeing you.

Helmer: *(removing Nora's shawl)* Yes, take a good look. She's worth looking at, I can tell you that, Mrs. Linde. Isn't she lovely?

Mrs. Linde: Yes, I should say—   95

Helmer: A dream of loveliness, isn't she? That's what everyone thought at the party, too. But she's horribly stubborn—this sweet little thing. What's to be done with her? Can you imagine, I almost had to use force to pry her away.

Nora: Oh, Torvald, you're going to regret you didn't indulge me, even for just a half hour more.

Helmer: There, you see. She danced her tarantella and got a tumultuous hand—which was well earned, although the performance may have been a bit too naturalistic—I mean it rather overstepped the proprieties of art. But never mind—what's important is, she made a success, an overwhelming success. You think I could let her stay on after that and spoil the effect? Oh no; I took my lovely little Capri girl—my capricious little Capri girl, I should say—took her under my arm; one quick tour of the ballroom, a curtsy to every side, and then—as they say in novels—the beautiful vision disappeared. An exit should always be effective, Mrs. Linde, but that's what I can't get Nora to grasp. Phew, it's hot in here. *(Flings the domino on a chair and opens the*

>> Janet McTeer as Nora and Owen Teale as Torvald in the 1997 Broadway production of *A Doll House*

door to his room.) Why's it dark in here? Oh yes, of course. Excuse me. *(He goes in and lights a couple of candles.)*

Nora: *(in a sharp, breathless whisper)* So?

Mrs. Linde: *(quietly)* I talked with him.   100

Nora: And—?

Mrs. Linde: Nora—you must tell your husband everything.

Nora: *(dully)* I knew it.

Mrs. Linde: You've got nothing to fear from Krogstad, but you have to speak out.

Nora: I won't tell.   105

Mrs. Linde: Then the letter will.

Nora: Thanks, Kristine. I know now what's to be done. Shh!

Helmer: *(reentering)* Well, then, Mrs. Linde—have you admired her?

Mrs. Linde: Yes, and now I'll say good night.

Helmer: Oh, come, so soon? Is this yours, this knitting?   110

Mrs. Linde: Yes, thanks. I nearly forgot it.

Helmer: Do you knit, then?

Mrs. Linde: Oh yes.

Helmer: You know what? You should embroider instead.

Mrs. Linde: Really? Why? 115

Helmer: Yes, because it's a lot prettier. See here, one holds the embroidery so, in the left hand, and then one guides the needle with the right—so—in an easy, sweeping curve—right?

Mrs. Linde: Yes, I guess that's—

Helmer: But, on the other hand, knitting—it can never be anything but ugly. Look, see here, the arms tucked in, the knitting needles going up and down—there's something Chinese about it. Ah, that was really a glorious champagne they served.

Mrs. Linde: Yes, good night, Nora, and don't be stubborn any more.

Helmer: Well put, Mrs. Linde! 120

Mrs. Linde: Good night, Mr. Helmer.

Helmer: *(accompanying her to the door)* Good night, good night. I hope you get home all right. I'd be very happy to—but you don't have far to go. Good night, good night. *(She leaves. He shuts the door after her and returns.)* There, now, at last we got her out the door. She's a deadly bore, that creature.

Nora: Aren't you pretty tired, Torvald?

Helmer: No, not a bit.

Nora: You're not sleepy? 125

Helmer: Not at all. On the contrary, I'm feeling quite exhilarated. But you? Yes, you really look tired and sleepy.

Nora: Yes, I'm very tired. Soon now I'll sleep.

Helmer: See! You see! I was right all along that we shouldn't stay longer.

Nora: Whatever you do is always right.

Helmer: *(kissing her brow)* Now my little lark talks 130 sense. Say, did you notice what a time Rank was having tonight?

Nora: Oh, was he? I didn't get to speak with him.

Helmer: I scarcely did either, but it's a long time since I've seen him in such high spirits. *(Gazes at her a moment, then comes nearer her.)* Hm—it's marvelous, though, to be back home again—to be completely alone with you. Oh, you bewitchingly lovely young woman!

Nora: Torvald, don't look at me like that!

Helmer: Can't I look at my richest treasure? At all that beauty that's mine, mine alone—completely and utterly.

Nora: *(moving around to the other side of the table)* You 135 mustn't talk to me that way tonight.

Helmer: *(following her)* The tarantella is still in your blood, I can see—and it makes you even more enticing. Listen. The guests are beginning to go.

(Dropping his voice.) Nora—it'll soon be quiet through this whole house.

Nora: Yes, I hope so.

Helmer: You do, don't you, my love? Do you realize—when I'm out at a party like this with you—do you know why I talk to you so little, and keep such a distance away; just send you a stolen look now and then—you know why I do it? It's because I'm imagining then that you're my secret darling, my secret young bride-to-be, and that no one suspects there's anything between us.

Nora: Yes, yes; oh, yes, I know you're always thinking of me.

Helmer: And then when we leave and I place the shawl 140 over those fine young rounded shoulders—over that wonderful curving neck—then I pretend that you're my young bride, that we're just coming from the wedding, that for the first time I'm bringing you into my house—that for the first time I'm alone with you—completely alone with you, your trembling young beauty! All this evening I've longed for nothing but you. When I saw you turn and sway in the tarantella—my blood was pounding till I couldn't stand it—that's why I brought you down here so early—

Nora: Go away, Torvald! Leave me alone. I don't want all this.

Helmer: What do you mean? Nora, you're teasing me. You will, won't you? Aren't I your husband—?

A knock at the outside door.

Nora: *(startled)* What's that?

Helmer: *(going toward the hall)* Who is it?

Rank: *(outside)* It's me. May I come in a moment? 145

Helmer: *(with quiet irritation)* Oh, what does he want now? *(Aloud.)* Hold on. *(Goes and opens the door.)* Oh, how nice that you didn't just pass us by!

Rank: I thought I heard your voice, and then I wanted so badly to have a look in. *(Lightly glancing about.)* Ah, me, these old familiar haunts. You have it snug and cozy in here, you two.

Helmer: You seemed to be having it pretty cozy upstairs, too.

Rank: Absolutely. Why shouldn't I? Why not take in everything in life? As much as you can, anyway, and as long as you can. The wine was superb—

Helmer: The champagne especially. 150

Rank: You noticed that too? It's amazing how much I could guzzle down.

Nora: Torvald also drank a lot of champagne this evening.

Rank: Oh?

Nora: Yes, and that always makes him so entertaining.

Rank: Well, why shouldn't one have a pleasant evening after a well spent day? 155

Helmer: Well spent? I'm afraid I can't claim that.

Rank: *(slapping him on the back)* But I can, you see!

Nora: Dr. Rank, you must have done some scientific research today.

Rank: Quite so.

Helmer: Come now—little Nora talking about scientific research! 160

Nora: And can I congratulate you on the results?

Rank: Indeed you may.

Nora: Then they were good?

Rank: The best possible for both doctor and patient—certainty.

Nora: *(quickly and searchingly)* Certainty? 165

Rank: Complete certainty. So don't I owe myself a gay evening afterwards?

Nora: Yes, you're right, Dr. Rank.

Helmer: I'm with you—just so long as you don't have to suffer for it in the morning.

Rank: Well, one never gets something for nothing in life.

Nora: Dr. Rank—are you very fond of masquerade parties? 170

Rank: Yes, if there's a good array of odd disguises—

Nora: Tell me, what should we two go as at the next masquerade?

Helmer: You little featherhead—already thinking of the next!

Rank: We two? I'll tell you what: you must go as Charmed Life—

Helmer: Yes, but find a costume for *that!* 175

Rank: Your wife can appear just as she looks every day.

Helmer: That was nicely put. But don't you know what you're going to be?

Rank: Yes, Helmer, I've made up my mind.

Helmer: Well?

Rank: At the next masquerade I'm going to be invisible. 180

Helmer: That's a funny idea.

Rank: They say there's a hat—black, huge—have you never heard of the hat that makes you invisible? You put it on, and then no one on earth can see you.

Helmer: *(suppressing a smile)* Ah, of course.

Rank: But I'm quite forgetting what I came for. Helmer, give me a cigar, one of the dark Havanas.

Helmer: With the greatest of pleasure. *(Holds out his case.)* 185

Rank: Thanks. *(Takes one and cuts off the tip.)*

Nora: *(striking a match)* Let me give you a light.

Rank: Thank you. *(She holds the match for him; he lights the cigar.)* And now good-bye.

>> Toby Stephens as Torvald and Gillian Anderson as Nora (in her tarantella costume) in the 2009 London production of *A Doll House*

Helmer: Good-bye, good-bye, old friend.

Nora: Sleep well, Doctor. 190

Rank: Thanks for that wish.

Nora: Wish me the same.

Rank: You? All right, if you like—Sleep well. And thanks for the light. *(He nods to them both and leaves.)*

Helmer: *(his voice subdued)* He's been drinking heavily.

Nora: *(absently)* Could be. *(Helmer takes his keys from his pocket and goes out in the hall.)* Torvald—what are you after? 195

Helmer: Got to empty the mailbox; it's nearly full. There won't be room for the morning papers.

Nora: Are you working tonight?

Helmer: You know I'm not. Why—what's this? Someone's been at the lock.

Nora: At the lock—?

Helmer: Yes, I'm positive. What do you suppose—? I can't imagine one of the maids—? Here's a broken hairpin. Nora, it's yours— 200

Nora: *(quickly)* Then it must be the children—

Helmer: You'd better break them of that. Hm, hm—well, opened it after all. *(Takes the contents out and calls into the kitchen.)* Helene! Helene, would you put out the lamp in the hall. *(He returns to the room, shutting* *the hall door, then displays the handful of mail.)* Look how it's piled up. *(Sorting through them.)* Now what's this?

Nora: *(at the window)* The letter! Oh, Torvald, no!

Helmer: Two calling cards—from Rank.

Nora: From Dr. Rank? 205

Helmer: *(examining them)* "Dr. Rank, Consulting Physician." They were on top. He must have dropped them in as he left.

Nora: Is there anything on them?

Helmer: There's a black cross over the name. See? That's a gruesome notion. He could almost be announcing his own death.

Nora: That's just what he's doing.

Helmer: What! You've heard something? Something 210 he's told you?

Nora: Yes. That when those cards came, he'd be taking his leave of us. He'll shut himself in now and die.

Helmer: Ah, my poor friend! Of course I knew he wouldn't be here much longer. But so soon—And then to hide himself away like a wounded animal.

Nora: If it has to happen, then it's best it happens in silence—don't you think so, Torvald?

Helmer: *(pacing up and down)* He'd grown right into our lives. I simply can't imagine him gone. He with his suffering and loneliness—like a dark cloud setting off our sunlit happiness. Well, maybe it's best this way. For him, at least. *(Standing still.)* And maybe for us too, Nora. Now we're thrown back on each other, completely. *(Embracing her.)* Oh you, my darling wife, how can I hold you close enough? You know what, Nora—time and again I've wished you were in some terrible danger, just so I could stake my life and soul and everything, for your sake.

Nora: *(tearing herself away, her voice firm and decisive)* 215 Now you must read your mail, Torvald.

Helmer: No, no, not tonight. I want to stay with you, dearest.

Nora: With a dying friend on your mind?

Helmer: You're right. We've both had a shock. There's ugliness between us—these thoughts of death and corruption. We'll have to get free of them first. Until then—we'll stay apart.

Nora: *(clinging about his neck)* Torvald—good night! Good night!

Helmer: *(kissing her on the cheek)* Good night, little 220 songbird. Sleep well, Nora. I'll be reading my mail now. *(He takes the letters into his room and shuts the door after him.)*

Nora: *(with bewildered glances, groping about, seizing Helmer's domino, throwing it around her, and speaking in short, hoarse, broken whispers)* Never see him again. Never, never. *(Putting her shawl over her*

head.) Never see the children either—them, too. Never, never. Oh, the freezing black water! The depths—down—Oh, I wish it were over—He has it now; he's reading it—now. Oh no, no, not yet. Torvald, good-bye, you and the children—*(She starts for the hall; as she does, Helmer throws open his door and stands with an open letter in his hand.)*

Helmer: Nora!

Nora: *(screams)* Oh—!

Helmer: What is this? You know what's in this letter?

Nora: Yes, I know. Let me go! Let me out! 225

Helmer: *(holding her back)* Where are you going?

Nora: *(struggling to break loose)* You can't save me, Torvald!

Helmer: *(slumping back)* True! Then it's true what he writes? How horrible! No, no, it's impossible—it can't be true.

Nora: It *is* true. I've loved you more than all this world.

Helmer: Ah, none of your slippery tricks. 230

Nora: *(taking one step toward him)* Torvald—!

Helmer: What *is* this you've blundered into!

Nora: Just let me loose. You're not going to suffer for my sake. You're not going to take on my guilt.

Helmer: No more playacting. *(Locks the hall door.)* You stay right here and give me a reckoning. You understand what you've done? Answer! You understand?

Nora: *(looking squarely at him, her face hardening)* Yes. 235 I'm beginning to understand everything now.

Helmer: *(striding about)* Oh, what an awful awakening! In all these eight years—she who was my pride and joy—a hypocrite, a liar—worse, worse—a criminal! How infinitely disgusting it all is! The shame! *(Nora says nothing and goes on looking straight at him. He stops in front of her.)* I should have suspected something of the kind. I should have known. All your father's flimsy values—Be still! All your father's flimsy values have come out in you. No religion, no morals, no sense of duty—Oh, how I'm punished for letting him off! I did it for your sake, and you repay me like this.

Nora: Yes, like this.

Helmer: Now you've wrecked all my happiness—ruined my whole future. Oh, it's awful to think of. I'm in a cheap little grafter's hands; he can do anything he wants with me, ask for anything, play with me like a puppet—and I can't breathe a word. I'll be swept down miserably into the depths on account of a featherbrained woman.

Nora: When I'm gone from this world, you'll be free.

Helmer: Oh, quit posing. Your father had a mess of those 240 speeches too. What good would that ever do me if you were gone from this world, as you say? Not the slightest. He can still make the whole thing known;

and if he does, I could be falsely suspected as your accomplice. They might even think that I was behind it—that I put you up to it. And all that I can thank you for—you that I've coddled the whole of our marriage. Can you see now what you've done to me?

Nora: *(icily calm)* Yes.

Helmer: It's so incredible, I just can't grasp it. But we'll have to patch up whatever we can. Take off the shawl. I said, take it off! I've got to appease him somehow or other. The thing has to be hushed up at any cost. And as for you and me, it's got to seem like everything between us is just as it was—to the outside world, that is. You'll go right on living in this house, of course. But you can't be allowed to bring up the children; I don't dare trust you with them— Oh, to have to say this to someone I've loved so much! Well, that's done with. From now on happiness doesn't matter; all that matters is saving the bits and pieces, the appearance—*(The doorbell rings. Helmer starts.)* What's that? And so late. Maybe the worst—? You think he'd—? Hide, Nora! Say you're sick. *(Nora remains standing motionless. Helmer goes and opens the door.)*

Maid: *(half dressed, in the hall)* A letter for Mrs. Helmer.

Helmer: I'll take it. *(Snatches the letter and shuts the door.)* Yes, it's from him. You don't get it; I'm reading it myself.

Nora: Then read it.   245

Helmer: *(by the lamp)* I hardly dare. We may be ruined, you and I. But—I've got to know. *(Rips open the letter, skims through a few lines, glances at an enclosure, then cries out joyfully.)* Nora! *(Nora looks inquiringly at him.)* Nora! Wait—better check it again—Yes, yes, it's true. I'm saved. Nora, I'm saved!

Nora: And I?

Helmer: You too, of course. We're both saved, both of us. Look. He's sent back your note. He says he's sorry and ashamed—that a happy development in his life—oh, who cares what he says! Nora, we're saved! No one can hurt you. Oh, Nora, Nora—but first, this ugliness all has to go. Let me see—*(Takes a look at the note.)* No, I don't want to see it; I want the whole thing to fade like a dream. *(Tears the note and both letters to pieces, throws them into the stove and watches them burn.)* There—now there's nothing left—He wrote that since Christmas Eve you—Oh, they must have been three terrible days for you, Nora.

Nora: I fought a hard fight.

Helmer: And suffered pain and saw no escape but—No,   250 we're not going to dwell on anything unpleasant. We'll just be grateful and keep on repeating: it's over now, it's over! You hear me, Nora? You don't seem to realize—it's over. What's it mean—that frozen look? Oh, poor little Nora, I understand. You can't believe I've forgiven you. But I have, Nora; I swear I have. I know that what you did, you did out of love for me.

Nora: That's true.

Helmer: You loved me the way a wife ought to love her husband. It's simply the means that you couldn't judge. But you think I love you any the less for not knowing how to handle your affairs? No, no—just lean on me; I'll guide you and teach you. I wouldn't be a man if this feminine helplessness didn't make you twice as attractive to me. You mustn't mind those sharp words I said—that was all in the first confusion of thinking my world had collapsed. I've forgiven you, Nora; I swear I've forgiven you.

Nora: My thanks for your forgiveness. *(She goes out through the door, right.)*

Helmer: No, wait—*(Peers in.)* What are you doing in there?

Nora: *(inside)* Getting out of my costume.   255

Helmer: *(by the open door)* Yes, do that. Try to calm yourself and collect your thoughts again, my frightened little songbird. You can rest easy now; I've got wide wings to shelter you with. *(Walking about close by the door.)* How snug and nice our home is, Nora. You're safe here; I'll keep you like a hunted dove I've rescued out of a hawk's claws. I'll bring peace to your poor, shuddering heart. Gradually it'll happen, Nora; you'll see. Tomorrow all this will look different to you; then everything will be as it was. I won't have to go on repeating I forgive you; you'll feel it for yourself. How can you imagine I'd ever conceivably want to disown you—or even blame you in any way? Ah, you don't know a man's heart, Nora. For a man there's something indescribably sweet and satisfying in knowing he's forgiven his wife—and forgiven her out of a full and open heart. It's as if she belongs to him in two ways now: in a sense he's given her fresh into the world again, and she's become his wife and his child as well. From now on that's what you'll be to me—you little, bewildered, helpless thing. Don't be afraid of anything, Nora; just open your heart to me, and I'll be conscience and will to you both—*(Nora enters in her regular clothes.)* What's this? Not in bed? You've changed your dress?

Nora: Yes, Torvald, I've changed my dress.

Helmer: But why now, so late?

Nora: Tonight I'm not sleeping.

Helmer: But Nora dear—   260

Nora: *(looking at her watch)* It's still not so very late. Sit down, Torvald; we have a lot to talk over. *(She sits at one side of the table.)*

Helmer: Nora—what is this? That hard expression—

Nora: Sit down. This'll take some time. I have a lot to say.

Helmer: *(sitting at the table directly opposite her)* You worry me, Nora. And I don't understand you.

Nora: No, that's exactly it. You don't understand me. 265
And I've never understood you either—until tonight.
No, don't interrupt. You can just listen to what I say.
We're closing out accounts, Torvald.

Helmer: How do you mean that?

Nora: *(after a short pause)* Doesn't anything strike you
about our sitting here like this?

Helmer: What's that?

Nora: We've been married now eight years. Doesn't it
occur to you that this is the first time we two, you
and I, man and wife, have ever talked seriously
together?

Helmer: What do you mean—seriously? 270

Nora: In eight whole years—longer even—right from our
first acquaintance, we've never exchanged a serious
word on any serious thing.

Helmer: You mean I should constantly go and involve
you in problems you couldn't possibly help me with?

Nora: I'm not talking of problems. I'm saying that we've
never sat down seriously together and tried to get to
the bottom of anything.

Helmer: But dearest, what good would that ever do you?

Nora: That's the point right there: you've never under- 275
stood me. I've been wronged greatly, Torvald—first
by Papa, and then by you.

Helmer: What! By us—the two people who've loved you
more than anyone else?

Nora: *(shaking her head)* You never loved me. You've
thought it fun to be in love with me, that's all.

Helmer: Nora, what a thing to say!

Nora: Yes, it's true now, Torvald. When I lived at home
with Papa, he told me all his opinions, so I had the
same ones too; or if they were different I hid them,
since he wouldn't have cared for that. He used to call
me his doll-child, and he played with me the way I
played with my dolls. Then I came into your house—

Helmer: How can you speak of our marriage like that? 280

Nora: *(unperturbed)* I mean, then I went from Papa's
hands into yours. You arranged everything to your
own taste, and so I got the same taste as you—or I
pretended to; I can't remember. I guess a little of
both, first one, then the other. Now when I look
back, it seems as if I'd lived here like a beggar—just
from hand to mouth. I've lived by doing tricks for
you, Torvald. But that's the way you wanted it. It's a
great sin what you and Papa did to me. You're to
blame that nothing's become of me.

Helmer: Nora, how unfair and ungrateful you are!
Haven't you been happy here?

Nora: No, never. I thought so—but I never have.

Helmer: Not—not happy!

Nora: No, only lighthearted. And you've always been 285
so kind to me. But our home's been nothing but a
playpen. I've been your doll-wife here, just as at
home I was Papa's doll-child. And in turn the
children have been my dolls. I thought it was fun
when you played with me, just as they thought it fun
when I played with them. That's been our marriage,
Torvald.

Helmer: There's some truth in what you're saying—
under all the raving exaggeration. But it'll all be
different after this. Playtime's over; now for the
schooling.

Nora: Whose schooling—mine or the children's?

Helmer: Both yours and the children's, dearest.

Nora: Oh, Torvald, you're not the man to teach me to be
a good wife to you.

Helmer: And you can say that? 290

Nora: And I—how am I equipped to bring up children?

Helmer: Nora!

Nora: Didn't you say a moment ago that that was no job
to trust me with?

Helmer: In a flare of temper! Why fasten on that?

Nora: Yes, but you were so very right. I'm not up to the 295
job. There's another job I have to do first. I have to
try to educate myself. You can't help me with that.
I've got to do it alone. And that's why I'm leaving
you now.

Helmer: *(jumping up)* What's that?

Nora: I have to stand completely alone, if I'm ever going
to discover myself and the world out there. So I can't
go on living with you.

Helmer: Nora, Nora!

Nora: I want to leave right away. Kristine should put me
up for the night—

Helmer: You're insane! You've no right! I forbid you! 300

Nora: From here on, there's no use forbidding me
anything. I'll take with me whatever is mine. I don't
want a thing from you, either now or later.

Helmer: What kind of madness is this!

Nora: Tomorrow I'm going home—I mean, home where
I came from. It'll be easier up there to find something
to do.

Helmer: Oh, you blind, incompetent child!

Nora: I must learn to be competent, Torvald. 305

Helmer: Abandon your home, your husband, your
children! And you're not even thinking what people
will say.

Nora: I can't be concerned about that. I only know how
essential this is.

Helmer: Oh, it's outrageous. So you'll run out like this
on your most sacred vows.

Nora: What do you think are my most sacred vows?

Helmer: And I have to tell you that! Aren't they your 310
duties to your husband and children?

Nora: I have other duties equally sacred.

Helmer: That isn't true. What duties are they?

Nora: Duties to myself.

Helmer: Before all else, you're a wife and a mother.

Nora: I don't believe in that any more. I believe that, before all else, I'm a human being, no less than you—or anyway, I ought to try to become one. I know the majority thinks you're right, Torvald, and plenty of books agree with you, too. But I can't go on believing what the majority says, or what's written in books. I have to think over these things myself and try to understand them. 315

Helmer: Why can't you understand your place in your own home? On a point like that, isn't there one everlasting guide you can turn to? Where's your religion?

Nora: Oh, Torvald, I'm really not sure what religion is.

Helmer: What—?

Nora: I only know what the minister said when I was confirmed. He told me religion was this thing and that. When I get clear and away by myself, I'll go into that problem too. I'll see if what the minister said was right, or, in any case, if it's right for me.

Helmer: A young woman your age shouldn't talk like that. If religion can't move you, I can try to rouse your conscience. You do have some moral feeling? Or, tell me—has that gone too? 320

Nora: It's not easy to answer that, Torvald. I simply don't know. I'm all confused about these things. I just know I see them so differently from you. I find out, for one thing, that the law's not at all what I'd thought—but I can't get it through my head that the law is fair. A woman hasn't a right to protect her dying father or save her husband's life! I can't believe that.

Helmer: You talk like a child. You don't know anything of the world you live in.

Nora: No, I don't. But now I'll begin to learn for myself. I'll try to discover who's right, the world or I.

Helmer: Nora, you're sick; you've got a fever. I almost think you're out of your head.

Nora: I've never felt more clearheaded and sure in my life. 325

Helmer: And—clearheaded and sure—you're leaving your husband and children?

Nora: Yes.

Helmer: Then there's only one possible reason.

Nora: What?

Helmer: You no longer love me. 330

Nora: No. That's exactly it.

Helmer: Nora! You can't be serious!

Nora: Oh, this is so hard, Torvald—you've been so kind to me always. But I can't help it. I don't love you any more.

Helmer: (struggling for composure) Are you also clearheaded and sure about that?

Nora: Yes, completely. That's why I can't go on staying here. 335

Helmer: Can you tell me what I did to lose your love?

Nora: Yes, I can tell you. It was this evening when the miraculous thing didn't come—then I knew you weren't the man I'd imagined.

Helmer: Be more explicit; I don't follow you.

Nora: I've waited now so patiently eight long years—for, my Lord, I know miracles don't come every day. Then this crisis broke over me, and such a certainty filled me: *now* the miraculous event would occur. While Krogstad's letter was lying out there, I never for an instant dreamed that you could give in to his terms. I was so utterly sure you'd say to him: go on, tell your tale to the whole wide world. And when he'd done that—

Helmer: Yes, what then? When I'd delivered my own wife into shame and disgrace—! 340

Nora: When he'd done that, I was so utterly sure that you'd step forward, take the blame on yourself and say: I am the guilty one.

Helmer: Nora—!

Nora: You're thinking I'd never accept such a sacrifice from you? No, of course not. But what good would my protests be against you? That was the miracle I was waiting for, in terror and hope. And to stave that off, I would have taken my life.

Helmer: I'd gladly work for you day and night, Nora—and take on pain and deprivation. But there's no one who gives up honor for love.

Nora: Millions of women have done just that. 345

Helmer: Oh, you think and talk like a silly child.

Nora: Perhaps. But you neither think nor talk like the man I could join myself to. When your big fright was over—and it wasn't from any threat against me, only for what might damage you—when all the danger was past, for you it was just as if nothing had happened. I was exactly the same, your little lark, your doll, that you'd have to handle with double care now that I'd turned out so brittle and frail. (Gets up.) Torvald—in that instant it dawned on me that for eight years I've been living here with a stranger, and that I'd even conceived three children—oh, I can't stand the thought of it! I could tear myself to bits.

Helmer: (heavily) I see. There's a gulf that's opened between us—that's clear. Oh, but Nora, can't we bridge it somehow?

Nora: The way I am now, I'm no wife for you.

Helmer: I have the strength to make myself over. 350

Nora: Maybe—if your doll gets taken away.

Helmer: But to part! To part from you! No, Nora, no—I can't imagine it.

Nora: *(going out, right)* All the more reason why it has to be. *(She reenters with her coat and a small overnight bag, which she puts on a chair by the table.)*

Helmer: Nora, Nora, not now! Wait till tomorrow.

Nora: I can't spend the night in a strange man's room. 355

Helmer: But couldn't we live here like brother and sister—

Nora: You know very well how long that would last. *(Throws her shawl about her.)* Good-bye, Torvald. I won't look in on the children. I know they're in better hands than mine. The way I am now, I'm no use to them.

Helmer: But someday, Nora—someday—?

Nora: How can I tell? I haven't the least idea what'll become of me.

Helmer: But you're my wife, now and wherever you go. 360

Nora: Listen, Torvald—I've heard that when a wife deserts her husband's house just as I'm doing, then the law frees him from all responsibility. In any case, I'm freeing you from being responsible. Don't feel yourself bound, any more than I will. There has to be absolute freedom for us both. Here, take your ring back. Give me mine.

Helmer: That too?

Nora: That too.

Helmer: There it is.

Nora: Good. Well, now it's all over. I'm putting the keys 365 here. The maids know all about keeping up the house—better than I do. Tomorrow, after I've left town, Kristine will stop by to pack up everything that's mine from home. I'd like those things shipped up to me.

Helmer: Over! All over! Nora, won't you ever think about me?

Nora: I'm sure I'll think of you often, and about the children and the house here.

Helmer: May I write you?

Nora: No—never. You're not to do that.

Helmer: Oh, but let me send you— 370

Nora: Nothing. Nothing.

Helmer: Or help you if you need it.

Nora: No. I accept nothing from strangers.

Helmer: Nora—can I never be more than a stranger to you?

Nora: *(picking up the overnight bag)* Ah, Torvald—it 375 would take the greatest miracle of all—

Helmer: Tell me the greatest miracle!

Nora: You and I both would have to transform ourselves to the point that—Oh, Torvald, I've stopped believing in miracles.

Helmer: But I'll believe. Tell me! Transform ourselves to the point that—?

Nora: That our living together could be a true marriage. *(She goes out down the hall.)*

Helmer: *(sinks down on a chair by the door, face buried in* 380 *his hands)* Nora! Nora! *(Looking about and rising.)* Empty. She's gone. *(A sudden hope leaps in him.)* The greatest miracle—?

From below, the sound of a door slamming shut.

Related Works

"The Story of an Hour" (p. 115), "The Rocking-Horse Winner" (p. 297), "The Yellow Wallpaper" (p. 363), "Barbie doll" (p. 515), *The Stronger* (p. 602)

 See Chapter 32 Review Card for Reading and Reacting questions about Henrik Ibsen, *A Doll House*.

Writing Suggestions: Plot

1. Central to the plots of both *Trifles* and *A Doll House* is a woman who commits a crime. Compare and contrast the desperate situations that motivate the two women. Then, consider the reactions of other characters in the two plays to each woman's crime. If you like, you may also discuss the crime committed by Emily Grierson in "A Rose for Emily" (p. 121).

2. Write an essay in which you discuss the influence of Nora's father on the plot of *A Doll House*.

3. Write a monologue for Nora in *A Doll House*, including everything you think she would like to tell her children. Or, write a monologue for Mrs. Wright in *Trifles* in which she describes her marriage and explains the motivation for her crime.

4. Write a play called *Nine Twelve*. Keep all the major characters of *Nine Ten*, but put them together on September 12 in another setting, where they discuss what happened to them since they last met and how their attitudes toward jury duty, work, and life in general have changed as a result.

✓ CHECKLIST

WRITING ABOUT PLOT

- ☐ What happens in the play?
- ☐ What is the play's central conflict? How is it resolved? What other conflicts are present?
- ☐ What section of the play constitutes its rising action?
- ☐ Where does the play's climax occur?
- ☐ What crises can you identify?
- ☐ How is suspense created?
- ☐ What section of the play constitutes its falling action?
- ☐ Does the play contain a subplot? What is its purpose? How is it related to the main plot?
- ☐ How do characters' actions advance the play's plot?
- ☐ How does dialogue advance the play's plot?
- ☐ How do stage directions advance the play's plot?
- ☐ How do staging techniques advance the play's plot?
- ☐ Does the play include a narrator?
- ☐ Does the play include flashbacks? foreshadowing? Does the play's dialogue contain summaries of past events or references to events in the future? How does the use of flashbacks or foreshadowing advance the play's plot?

Glossary Terms

action What happens in a drama.

climax Point of greatest tension or importance, where the decisive action of a play takes place.

dialogue Conversation between two or more characters.

exposition First stage of a plot, where information about characters or setting is presented.

falling action Stage in a play's plot during which the intensity of the climax subsides.

flashback Departure from chronological order that presents an event or situation that occurred before the time in which the action of a play takes place.

foreshadowing Presentation early in a story or play of situations, characters, or objects that seem to have no special importance but in fact are later revealed to have great significance.

plot Way in which the events of the story are arranged.

props (short for **properties**) Pictures, furnishings, and the like that decorate the stage for a play.

resolution (**also called denouement**) Final stage in the plot of a drama.

rising action Stage in a play's plot during which the action builds in intensity.

stage directions Words in a play that describe an actor's role, movements, attitudes, and so on.

33
Character

Learning Outcomes

After reading this chapter, you should be able to do the following:

LO1 Consider characters' words

LO2 Consider characters' actions

LO3 Consider stage directions

LO4 Consider actors' interpretations

Timeline

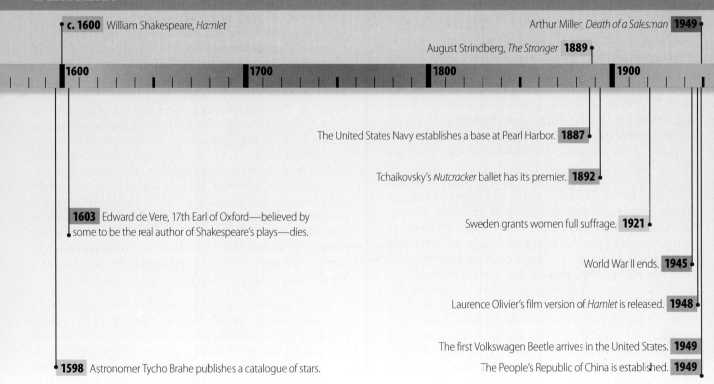

c. 1600 William Shakespeare, *Hamlet*

Arthur Miller, *Death of a Salesman* **1949**

August Strindberg, *The Stronger* **1889**

1600   **1700**   **1800**   **1900**

The United States Navy establishes a base at Pearl Harbor. **1887**

Tchaikovsky's *Nutcracker* ballet has its premier. **1892**

1603 Edward de Vere, 17th Earl of Oxford—believed by some to be the real author of Shakespeare's plays—dies.

Sweden grants women full suffrage. **1921**

World War II ends. **1945**

Laurence Olivier's film version of *Hamlet* is released. **1948**

The first Volkswagen Beetle arrives in the United States. **1949**

1598 Astronomer Tycho Brahe publishes a catalogue of stars.

The People's Republic of China is established. **1949**

monologue Extended speech by one character.

soliloquy Convention of drama in which a character speaks directly to the audience, revealing thoughts and feelings that other characters present on stage are assumed not to hear.

dialogue Conversation between two or more characters.

In Tennessee Williams's 1945 play *The Glass Menagerie*, the protagonist, Tom Wingfield, functions as the play's narrator. Stepping out of his role as a character and speaking directly to the audience, he directs the play's action, music, lighting, and other elements. In addition, he summarizes characters' actions, explains what motivates them, and discusses the significance of their behavior in the context of the play—commenting on his own character's actions as well. As narrator, Tom also presents useful background information about the characters. For instance, when he introduces his coworker, Jim, he prepares the audience for Jim's entrance and helps them to understand his subsequent actions:

> In high school Jim was a hero. He had tremendous Irish good nature and vitality with the scrubbed and polished look of white chinaware. He seemed to move in a continual spotlight. . . . But Jim apparently ran into more interference after his graduation. . . . His speed had definitely slowed. Six years after he left high school he was holding a job that wasn't much better than mine. (scene 6)

Most plays, however, do not include narrators who present background. Instead, the audience learns about characters from their own words and from comments by others about them, as well as from the characters' actions. When reading a play, we learn about the characters from the playwright's stage directions; when watching a performance, we gain insight into characters from the way actors interpret them.

Characters in plays, like characters in novels and short stories, may be *round* or *flat, static,* or *dynamic.* Generally speaking, major characters are likely to be round, whereas minor characters are likely to be flat. Through the language and the actions of the characters, audiences learn whether the characters are multidimensional, skimpily developed, or perhaps merely **foils,** players whose main purpose is to shed light on more important characters. Audiences also learn about the emotions, attitudes, and values that help to shape the characters—their hopes and fears, their strengths and weaknesses. In addition, by comparing characters' early words and actions with later ones, audiences learn from the play whether or not characters grow and change emotionally.

LO1 Consider Characters' Words

Characters' words reveal the most about their attitudes, feelings, beliefs, and values. Sometimes information is communicated (to other characters as well as to the audience) in a **monologue**—an extended speech by one character. This device is used throughout August Strindberg's *The Stronger* (p. 602). A **soliloquy**—a monologue revealing a character's thoughts and feelings, directed at the audience and presumed not to be heard by other characters—can also convey information about a character. For example, Hamlet's well-known soliloquy that begins "To be or not to be" eloquently communicates his distraught mental state—his resentment of his mother and uncle, his confusion about what course of action to take, and his suicidal thoughts. Finally, **dialogue**—an exchange of words between two characters—can reveal misunderstanding or conflict between them, or it can show their agreement, mutual support, or similar beliefs.

In Henrik Ibsen's *A Doll House* (p. 562), dialogue reveals a good deal about the characters. Nora Helmer, the spoiled young wife, has broken the law and kept her crime secret from her husband. Through her words, we learn about her motivation, her values, her emotions, and her reactions to other characters and to her potentially dangerous situation. We learn that she is flirtatious—"If your little squirrel begged you, with all her heart and soul . . ."—and that she is childishly unrealistic about the consequences of her actions. When her husband, Torvald, asks what she would do if he was seriously injured, leaving her in debt, she says, "If anything so awful happened, then it just wouldn't matter if I had debts or not." When Torvald presses, "Well, but the people I'd borrowed from?" she dismisses them: "Them? Who cares about them! They're strangers." As the play progresses, Nora's lack of understanding of the power of the law becomes more and more significant as she struggles with her moral and ethical dilemma.

The inability of both Nora and Torvald to confront ugly truths is also revealed through their words. When, in act 1, Nora tells Krogstad, her blackmailer, that his revealing her secret could expose her to "the most horrible unpleasantness," he responds, "Only unpleasantness?" Yet later on, in act 3, Torvald echoes her language, fastidiously dismissing the horror with, "No, we're not going to dwell on anything unpleasant."

The ease with which Torvald is able to dismiss his dying friend Dr. Rank in act 3 ("He with his suffering and loneliness—like a dark cloud setting off our sunlit happiness. Well, maybe it's best this way.") foreshadows the lack of support he will give Nora immediately thereafter. Especially revealing is his use of *I* and *my* and *me,* which convey his self-centeredness:

> Now you've wrecked all my happiness—ruined my whole future. Oh, it's awful to think of. I'm in a cheap little grafter's hands; he can do anything he wants with me, ask for anything, play with me like a puppet—and I can't breathe a word. I'll be swept down miserably into the depths on account of a featherbrained woman.

Just as Torvald's words reveal that he has not been changed by the play's events, Nora's words show that she has changed significantly. Her dialogue near the end of act 3 shows that she has become a responsible, determined woman—one who understands her situation and her options and is no longer blithely oblivious to her duties. When she says, "I've never felt more clearheaded and sure in my life," she is calm and decisive. When she says, "Our home's been nothing but a playpen. I've been your doll-wife here, just as at home I was Papa's doll-child," she reveals a new self-awareness. And, when she confronts her husband, she displays —perhaps for the first time in their relationship—complete honesty.

Sometimes what other characters say to (or about) a character can reveal more to an audience than the character's own words. For instance, in *A Doll House,* when the dying Dr. Rank says, apparently without malice, "[Torvald] Helmer with his sensitivity has such a sharp distaste for anything ugly," the audience not only thinks ill of the man who is too "sensitive" to visit his sick friend but also questions his ability to withstand situations that may be emotionally or morally "ugly" as well.

When a character is offstage for much (or even all) of the action, the audience must rely on other characters' assessments of the absent character. In Susan Glaspell's *Trifles* (p. 555), the play's focus is on an absent character, Minnie Wright, who is described solely through other characters' remarks. The evidence suggests that Mrs. Wright killed her husband, and only Mrs. Hale's and Mrs. Peters's comments about Mrs. Wright's dreary life can delineate her character and suggest a likely motive for the murder. Although Mrs. Wright never appears on stage, we learn essential information from the other women about her: that as a young girl she liked to sing and that more recently she was so distraught about the lack of beauty in her life that even her sewing revealed her distress. Similarly, the father in *The Glass Menagerie* never appears (and therefore never speaks), but the play's other characters describe him as "A telephone man who—fell in love with long-distance!"—the absent husband and father who symbolizes abandonment and instability to his wife and daughter and the possibility of freedom and escape to his son Tom.

Whether a character's words are in the form of a monologue, a soliloquy, or dialogue, and whether they reveal information about the character who is speaking or about someone else, such words are always revealing. Explicitly or implicitly, they convey a character's nature, attitudes, and relationships with other characters.

The language characters use can vary widely. A character may, for instance, use learned words, foreign words, elaborate figures of speech, irony or sarcasm, regionalisms, slang, jargon, clichés, or profanity. Words can also be used to indicate tone—for example, to express irony. Any of these uses of language may communicate vital information to the audience about a character's background, attitudes, and motivation. And, of course, a character's language may change as a play progresses, and this change too may be revealing.

figures of speech Expressions—such as **simile, metaphor, personification, hyperbole, understatement, metonymy,** and **synechdoche**—that use words to achieve effects beyond ordinary language.

FORMAL AND INFORMAL LANGUAGE

One character in a dramatic work may speak very formally, using absolutely correct grammar, a learned vocabulary, and long, complex sentences; another may speak in an informal style, using conversational speech, colloquialisms, and slang. At times, two characters with different levels of language may be set in opposition for dramatic effect, as they are in Irish playwright George Bernard Shaw's classic play *Pygmalion* (1912), which updates the ancient Greek myth of a sculptor who creates (and falls in love with) a statue of a woman. In Shaw's version, a linguistics professor sets out to teach "proper" speech and manners to a woman who sells flowers on the street. Throughout the play, the contrasting language of Henry Higgins, the professor, and Eliza Doolittle, the flower seller, reveals their differing social standing. The following exchange illustrates this contrast:

LIZA: I ain't got no mother. Her that turned me out was my sixth stepmother. But I done without them. And I'm a good girl, I am.

HIGGINS: Very well, then, what on earth is all this fuss about?

A character's accent or dialect may also be significant. In **comedies of manners,** for instance, rustic or provincial characters, identified by their speech, are often objects of humor. In *Pygmalion,* Eliza Doolittle uses cockney dialect, the dialect spoken in the East End of London. At first, her colorful, distinctive language (complete with expressions like *Nah-ow, garn,* and *ah-ah-ah-ow-ow-ow-oo*) and her nonstandard grammatical constructions make her an object of ridicule; later, the transformation of her speech reveals the dramatic changes in her character.

PLAIN AND ELABORATE LANGUAGE

A character's speech may be simple and straightforward or complex and convoluted; it may be plain and unadorned or embellished with elaborate **figures of speech.** The relative complexity or lack of complexity of a character's speech may have different effects on the audience. For example, a character whose language is simple and unsophisticated may seem to be unintelligent, unenlightened, gullible, or naive—especially if he or she also uses slang, dialect, or colloquial expressions. Conversely, a character's plain, down-to-earth language may convey common sense or intelligence. Plain language may also be quite emotionally powerful. Thus, Willy Loman's speech in act 2 of *Death of a Salesman* (p. 605), about an eighty-four-year-old salesman named Dave Singleman, moves the audience with its sincerity and directness:

tone Attitude of the speaker or author toward a work's subject or audience, as determined by word choice and arrangement of ideas.

irony Literary device or situation that depends on the existence of at least two separate and contrasting levels of meaning or experience. **Dramatic** or **tragic irony,** such as that found in *Oedipus the King,* depends on the audience's knowing something the protagonist has not yet realized. **Situational irony** exists when what happens is at odds with what the story's situation leads readers to expect will happen. **Cosmic irony** (or irony of fate) exists when fate frustrates any effort a character might make to control or reverse his or her destiny. **Verbal irony** occurs when what is said is in contrast with what is meant. Verbal irony can be expressed as **understatement, hyperbole,** or **sarcasm.**

Do you know? When he died—and by the way he died the death of a salesman, in his green velvet slippers in the smoker of the New York, New Haven and Hartford, going into Boston—when he died, hundreds of salesmen and buyers were at his funeral. Things were sad on a lotta trains for months after that.

Like plain speech, elaborate language may have different effects in different contexts. Sometimes, use of figures of speech can make a character seem to have depth and insight and analytical skills absent in other characters. In the following excerpt from a soliloquy in act 1 scene 2 of *Hamlet,* for example, complex language reveals the depth of Hamlet's anguished self-analysis:

HAMLET: O, that this too too solid flesh would melt,
    Thaw, and resolve itself into a dew!
    Or that the Everlasting had not fix'd
    His canon 'gainst self-slaughter! O God! O God!
    How weary, stale, flat, and unprofitable
    Seem to me all the uses of this world!
    Fie on't, O fie, 'tis an unweeded garden,
    That grows to seed. . . .

In these lines, Hamlet compares the world to a garden gone to seed. His use of imagery and figures of speech vividly communicates his feelings about the world and his internal struggle against the temptation to commit suicide.

Sometimes, however, elaborate language may make a character seem aloof, pompous, or even untrustworthy. In the following passages from Shakespeare's *King Lear,* Goneril and Regan, the deceitful daughters, use complicated verbal constructions to conceal their true feelings from their father, King Lear. In contrast, Cordelia—the loyal, loving daughter—uses simple, straightforward language that suggests her sincerity and lack of artifice. Compare the three speeches:

GONERIL: Sir, I love you more than words can wield the
    matter;

    Dearer than eyesight, space, and liberty;
    Beyond what can be valued, rich or rare;
    No less than life, with grace, health, beauty, honour;
    As much as child e'er lov'd, or father found;
    A love that makes breath poor, and speech unable.
    Beyond all manner of so much I love you. . . .
REGAN: Sir, I am made
    Of the selfsame metal that my sister is,
    And prize me at her worth. In my true heart
    I find she names my very deed of love;
    Only she comes too short, that I profess
    Myself an enemy to all other joys
    Which the most precious square of sense possesses,
    And find I am alone felicitate
    In your dear Highness' love. . . .
CORDELIA: Unhappy that I am, I cannot heave
    My heart into my mouth. I love your Majesty
    According to my bond; no more no less. . . .

Cordelia's unwillingness, even when she is prodded by Lear, to exaggerate her feelings or misrepresent her love through inflated language shows the audience her honesty and nobility. The contrast between her language and that of her sisters makes their very different motives clear.

TONE

Tone reveals a character's mood or attitude. Tone can be flat or emotional, bitter or accepting, affectionate or aloof, anxious or calm. Contrasts in tone can indicate differences in outlook or emotional state between two characters; changes in tone from one point in a play to another can suggest corresponding changes within a character. At the end of *A Doll House,* for instance, Nora is resigned to what she must do, and her language is appropriately controlled. Her husband, however, is desperate to change her mind, and his language reflects this desperation. The following exchanges of dialogue from the end of act 3 illustrate the two characters contrasting emotional states:

HELMER: But to part! To part from you! No, Nora, no—I
    can't imagine it.
NORA: *(going out, right)* All the more reason why it has
    to be.
HELMER: Over! All over! Nora, won't you ever think
    about me?
NORA: I'm sure I'll think of you often, and about the
    children and the house here.

In earlier scenes between the two characters, Nora is emotional—at times, hysterical—and her husband is considerably more controlled. As the above exchanges indicate, both Nora and Torvald Helmer change drastically during the course of the play.

IRONY

Irony, a contradiction or discrepancy between two levels of meaning, can reveal a great deal about character.

Verbal irony—a contradiction between what a character says and what he or she means—is very important in drama, where the verbal interplay between characters may carry the weight of the play. For example, when Nora and Dr. Rank discuss the latest news about his health in *A Doll House*, there is deep irony in his use of the phrase "complete certainty." Although the phrase usually suggests reassuring news, here it is meant to suggest death, and both Nora and Dr. Rank understand this.

Dramatic irony depends on the audience's knowing something that a character has not yet realized, or on one character's knowing something that other characters do not know. In some cases, dramatic irony is created by an audience's awareness of historical background or events of which characters are unaware. Familiar with the story of Oedipus, for instance, the audience knows that the man who has caused all the problems in Thebes—the man Oedipus vows to find and take revenge on—is Oedipus himself. In other cases, dramatic irony emerges when the audience learns something—something the characters do not yet know or comprehend—from a play's unfolding action. The central irony in *A Doll House*, for example, is that the family's "happy home" rests on a foundation of secrets, lies, and deception. Torvald does not know about the secrets, and Nora does not understand how they have poisoned her marriage. The audience, however, quickly becomes aware of the atmosphere of deceit—and aware of how it threatens the family's happiness.

Dramatic irony may also be conveyed through dialogue. Typically, dramatic irony is revealed when a character says something that gives the audience information that other characters, offstage at the time, do not know. In *A Doll House*, the audience knows—because Nora has explained her situation to Kristine—that Nora spent the previous Christmas season hard at work, earning money to pay her secret debt. Torvald, however, remains unaware of her activities and believes her story that she was using the time to make holiday decorations, which the cat destroyed. This belief is consistent with his impression of Nora as an irresponsible child, yet the audience has quite a different impression of her. This discrepancy, one of many contradictions between the audience's view of Nora and Torvald's view of her, helps to create dramatic tension in the play.

Finally, **asides** (comments to the audience that other characters do not hear) can create dramatic irony by undercutting dialogue, providing ironic contrast between what the characters on stage know and what the audience knows. In Anton Chekhov's *The Brute* (p. 532), for example, the audience knows that Mr. Smirnov is succumbing to Mrs. Popov's charms because he says, in an aside, "My God, what eyes she has! They're setting me on fire." Mrs. Popov, however, is not yet aware of his infatuation. The discrepancy between the audience's awareness and the character's adds to the play's humor.

LO2 Consider Characters' Actions

Through their actions, characters convey their values and attitudes to the audience. Actions also reveal aspects of a

aside Brief comment spoken by an actor to the audience (such as, "*Here she comes. I'll play a fine trick on her now!*") and assumed not to be heard by the other characters.

stage directions Words in a play that describe an actor's role apart from the dialogue, dealing with movements, attitudes, and so on.

staging Overall production of a play in performance: the sets, costumes, lighting, sound, music, and so on.

character's personality. When Laura Wingfield, a character in *The Glass Menagerie*, hides rather than face the "gentleman caller," the audience sees how shy she is; when Nora in *A Doll House* plays hide-and-seek with her children, eats forbidden macaroons, and takes childish joy in Christmas, her immaturity is apparent.

Audiences also learn about characters from what they do *not* do. Thus, Nora's failure to remain in touch with her friend Kristine, who has had a hard life, reveals her selfishness, and the failure of Mrs. Peters and Mrs. Hale in *Trifles* to give their evidence to the sheriff indicates their defiant support for Mrs. Wright and their understanding of what motivated her to take such drastic action.

Audiences also learn a good deal about characters by observing how they interact with other characters. In William Shakespeare's *Othello*, Iago is the embodiment of evil, and as the play's action unfolds, we discover his true nature. He reveals the secret marriage of Othello and Desdemona to her father; he schemes to arouse Othello's jealousy, making him believe Desdemona has been unfaithful with his lieutenant, Cassio; he persuades Cassio to ask Desdemona to plead his case with Othello, knowing this act will further arouse Othello's suspicions; he encourages Othello to be suspicious of Desdemona's defense of Cassio; he plants Desdemona's handkerchief in Cassio's room; and, finally, he persuades Othello to kill Desdemona and then kills his own wife, Emilia, to prevent her from exposing his role in the intrigue. As the play progresses, then, Iago's dealings with others consistently reveal him to be evil and corrupt.

LO3 Consider Stage Directions

When we read a play, we also read the playwright's italicized **stage directions,** the notes that concern **staging**—the scenery, props, lighting, music, sound effects, costumes, and other elements that contribute to the way the play looks and sounds to an audience (see Chapter 34). In addition to commenting on staging, stage directions may supply physical details about the characters, suggesting their age, appearance, movements, gestures, and facial expressions. These details may in turn convey additional information about characters: appearance may reveal social position or economic status, expressions may reveal attitudes, and so on. Stage directions may also indicate the manner in which a line of dialogue is to be delivered—*confidently* or *hesitantly,* for instance. The way a line is spoken may reveal a character to be excited, upset, angry, shy, or disappointed. Finally, stage directions may indicate *changes* in characters—for instance, a character whose speech is described as timid in early scenes may deliver lines emphatically and forcefully later on in the play.

Some stage directions provide a good deal of detail about character; others do little more than list characters' names. Arthur Miller is one playwright who often provides detailed information about character through stage directions. In *Death of a Salesman,* for instance, Miller's stage directions at the beginning of act 1 characterize Willy Loman immediately and specifically:

> *He is past sixty years of age, dressed quietly. Even as he crosses the stage to the doorway of the house, his exhaustion is apparent. He unlocks the door, comes into the kitchen, and thankfully lets his burden down, feeling the soreness of his palms. A word-sigh escapes his lips. . . .*

Subsequent stage directions indicate how lines are to be spoken. For example, in the play's opening lines, Willy's wife Linda calls out to him *"with some trepidation"*; Linda speaks *"very carefully, delicately,"* and Willy speaks *"with casual irritation."* These instructions to readers (and actors) are meant to suggest the strained relationship between the two characters.

George Bernard Shaw is notorious for the full character description in his stage directions. In these directions—seen by readers of the play but of course not heard by audiences—he communicates complex information about characters' attitudes and values, motivation and reactions, and relationships with other characters. In doing so, Shaw functions as a narrator, explicitly communicating his own attitudes toward various characters. (Unlike the voice of Tom Wingfield in *The Glass Menagerie,* however, the voice in Shaw's stage directions is not also the voice of a character in the play; it is the voice of the playwright.) Shaw's stage directions for *Pygmalion* initially describe Eliza Doolittle as follows:

> *She is not at all an attractive person. She is perhaps eighteen, perhaps twenty, hardly older. She wears a little sailor hat of black straw that has long been exposed to the dust and soot of London and has seldom if ever been brushed. Her hair needs washing rather badly; its mousy color can hardly be natural. She wears a shoddy black coat that reaches nearly to her knees and is shaped to her waist. She has a brown skirt with a coarse apron. Her boots are much the worse for wear. She is no doubt as clean as she can afford to be; but compared to the ladies she is very dirty. Her features are no worse than theirs; but their condition leaves something to be desired; and she needs the services of a dentist.*

Rather than providing an objective summary of the character's most notable physical attributes, Shaw injects subjective comments (*"seldom if ever brushed"*; *"color can hardly be natural"*; *"no doubt as clean as she can afford to be"*) that reveal his attitude toward Eliza. This initially supercilious attitude, which he has in common with Professor Higgins, is tempered considerably by the end of the play, helping to make Eliza's transformation more obvious to readers than it would be if measured by her words and actions alone. By act 5, the tone of the stage directions characterizing Eliza has changed to admiration: *"Eliza enters, sunny, self-possessed, and giving a staggeringly convincing exhibition of ease of manner."*

Stage directions in other plays are not nearly as comprehensive. In *Hamlet,* for example, characters are introduced with only the barest identifying tags: "Claudius, *King of Denmark*"; "Hamlet, *Son to the former, and nephew to the present King*"; "Gertrude, *Queen of Denmark, mother to Hamlet.*" Most stage directions do little more than chronicle the various characters' entrances and exits or specify particular physical actions: *"Enter Ghost"*; *"Spreads his arms"*; *"Ghost beckons Hamlet"*; *"He kneels"*; *"Sheathes his sword"*; *"Leaps in the grave."* Occasionally, stage directions specify a prop (*"Puts down the skull"*); a sound effect (*"A noise within"*); or a costume (*"Enter the ghost in his nightgown"*). Such brevity is typical of Shakespeare's plays, in which characters are delineated almost solely by their words—and, not incidentally, by the way actors have interpreted the characters over the years. In fact, because Shakespeare's stage directions only suggest characters' gestures, physical reactions, movements, and facial expressions, actors have been left quite free to experiment, reading various interpretations into Shakespeare's characters.

LO4 Consider Actors' Interpretations

When we watch a play, we gain insight into a character not merely through what the character says and does or how other characters react, but also through the way an actor interprets the role. If a playwright does not specify a character's mannerisms, gestures, or movements, or does not indicate how a line is to be delivered (and sometimes even if he or she does), an actor is free to interpret the role as he or she believes it should be played. Even when a playwright *does* specify such actions, the actor has a good deal of freedom to decide which gestures or expressions will convey a particular emotion.

In "Some Thoughts on Playwriting," American dramatist Thornton Wilder argues that "the theatre is an art which reposes upon the work of many collaborators" rather than on "one governing selecting will." Citing examples from Shakespeare and Ibsen, Wilder illustrates the great degree of "intervention" that may occur in dramatic productions. For instance, Wilder observes, Shakespeare's Shylock has been portrayed by two different actors as "noble, wronged and indignant" and as "a vengeful and hysterical buffoon"—and both performances were considered plausible interpretations. As noted earlier, the absence of detailed stage directions in Shakespeare's plays makes possible (and perhaps even encourages) such widely divergent interpretations. However, as Wilder points out, even when playing roles created by a dramatist such as Ibsen, whose stage directions are typically quite specific, actors and directors have a good deal of leeway. Thus, actress Janet McTeer, who played the part of Ibsen's Nora in the 1997 London production of *A Doll House*, saw Nora and Torvald, despite their many problems, as "the perfect couple," deeply in love and involved in a passionate marriage. "You have to make that marriage sexually credible," McTeer told the *New York Times*, "to imagine they have a wonderful time in bed, so there becomes something to lose. If you play them as already past it or no longer attracted to each other, then there is no play." This interpretation is not inconsistent with the play, but it does go beyond what Ibsen actually wrote.

Similarly, the role of Catherine in David Auburn's Pulitzer Prize-winning play *Proof* (2001) has been played by several actresses—among them Mary-Louise Parker, Jennifer Jason Leigh, Anne Heche, Gwyneth Paltrow, and Lea Salonga—and each actress has interpreted this complex character in a different way. As *New York Times* theater critic John Rockwell observes, "Catherine can be loopy-ethereal-sexy (Ms. Parker), earthy and even a little bitter (Ms. Leigh), or adorable-needy-fragile (Ms. Heche), and Mr. Auburn's structure and characters and ideas still work."

Irish playwright Samuel Beckett devotes a good deal of attention to indicating actors' movements and gestures and their physical reactions to one another. In his 1952 play *Waiting for Godot*, for example, Beckett's stage directions seem to choreograph every gesture, every emotion, every intention:

- *(he looks at them ostentatiously in turn to make it clear they are both meant)*
- *Vladimir seizes Lucky's hat. Silence of Lucky. He falls. Silence. Panting of the victors.*
- *Estragon hands him the boot. Vladimir inspects it, throws it down angrily.*
- *Estragon pulls, stumbles, falls. Long silence.*
- *He goes feverishly to and fro, halts finally at extreme left, broods.*

Beckett provides full and obviously carefully thought-out stage directions and, in so doing, attempts to retain a good deal of control over his characters. Still, in a 1988 production of *Godot*, director Mike Nichols and comic actors Robin Williams and Steve Martin felt free to improvise, adding gestures and movements not specified or even hinted at—and most critics believed that this production remained true to the tragicomic spirit of Beckett's existentialist play. In a sense, then, the playwright's words on the page are just the beginning of the characters' lives on the stage.

August Strindberg (1849–1912)

was born in Stockholm, Sweden, the child of a shipping merchant and his former maid. He studied at Uppsala University but left the university without a degree. By 1872, he had moved into the artistic circles in Stockholm and had begun work as a journalist.

In 1874, Strindberg was appointed assistant librarian at the Royal Library in Stockholm. Beginning the first of several stormy marriages, he struggled over the next few years; in 1879, he declared bankruptcy. During the same period, he wrote *The Red Room* (1879), the novel that marked his breakthrough as a writer. In 1881, he left the Royal Library to devote himself to writing, and in 1883, he left Sweden to join an artists' colony near Paris. His restlessness continued, however, and he soon moved to Switzerland, later living in Denmark, Germany, and Austria before returning at last to Stockholm.

Strindberg was a prolific artist, and his work includes novels, plays, poetry, and paintings. He is considered one of the most influential dramatists in literature.

The Stronger has been called a monodrama, a dramatic monologue, and a battle of brains in one scene. This play was the kind of experimental work being encouraged in the late nineteenth century at the Théâtre Libre in Paris, for which Strindberg wrote several plays while hoping to form his own experimental theater in Stockholm. Though written in 1889, *The Stronger* did not premiere on stage until 1907.

The Stronger (1889)

Translated by Elizabeth Sprigge

CHARACTERS

Mrs. X.,   actress, married
Miss Y.,   actress, unmarried
A Waitress

SCENE

A corner of a ladies' café [in Stockholm in the eighteen eighties].° Two small wrought-iron tables, a red plush settee and a few chairs.

Miss Y. is sitting with a half-empty bottle of beer on the table before her, reading an illustrated weekly which from time to time she exchanges for another.

Mrs. X. enters, wearing a winter hat and coat and carrying a decorative Japanese basket.

Mrs. X: Why, Millie, my dear, how are you? Sitting here all alone on Christmas Eve like some poor bachelor.

Miss Y. looks up from her magazine, nods, and continues to read.

Mrs. X: You know it makes me feel really sad to see you. Alone. Alone in a café and on Christmas Eve of all times. It makes me feel as sad as when once in Paris I saw a wedding party at a restaurant. The bride was reading a comic paper and the bridegroom playing billiards with the witnesses. Ah me, I said to myself, with such a beginning how will it go, and how will it end? He was playing billiards on his wedding day! And she, you were going to say, was reading a comic paper on hers. But that's not quite the same.

A waitress brings a cup of chocolate to Mrs. X. and goes out.

Mrs. X: Do you know, Amelia, I really believe now you would have done better to stick to him. Don't forget I was the first who told you to forgive him. Do you remember? Then you would be married now and have a home. Think how happy you were that Christmas when you stayed with your financé's people in the country. How warmly you spoke of domestic happiness! You really quite longed to be out of the theatre. Yes, Amelia dear, home is best—next best to the stage, and as for children—but you couldn't know anything about that.

Miss Y.'s expression is disdainful. Mrs. X. sips a few spoonfuls of chocolate, then opens her basket and displays some Christmas presents.

Mrs. X: Now you must see what I have bought for my little chicks. *(Takes out a doll.)* Look at this. That's for Lisa. Do you see how she can roll her eyes and turn her head. Isn't she lovely? And here's a toy pistol for Maja.° *(She loads the pistol and shoots it at Miss Y. who appears frightened.)*

> "Do you know, Amelia, I really believe now you would have done better to stick to him. Don't forget I was the first who told you to forgive him. Do you remember?"

Mrs. X: Were you scared? Did you think I was going to   5 shoot you? Really, I didn't think you'd believe that of me. Now if *you* were to shoot *me* it wouldn't be so surprising, for after all I did get in your way, and I know you never forget it—although I was entirely innocent. You still think I intrigued to get you out of the Grand Theatre, but I didn't. I didn't, however much you think I did. Well, it's no good talking, you will believe it was me . . . *(Takes out a pair of embroidered slippers.)* And these are for my old man, with tulips on them that I embroidered myself. As a matter of fact I hate tulips, but he has to have tulips on everything.

Miss Y. looks up, irony and curiosity in her face.

Mrs. X: *(putting one hand in each slipper)* Look what small feet Bob has, hasn't he? And you ought to see the charming way he walks—you've never seen him in slippers, have you?

Miss Y. laughs.

Mrs. X: Look, I'll show you. *(She makes the slippers walk across the table, and Miss Y. laughs again.)*

Mrs. X: But when he gets angry, look, he stamps his foot like this. "Those damn girls who can never learn how to make coffee! Blast! That silly idiot hasn't trimmed the lamp properly!" Then there's a draught under the door and his feet get cold. "Hell, it's freezing, and the damn fools can't even keep the stove going!" *(She rubs the sole of one slipper against the instep of the other. Miss Y roars with laughter.)*

° [*In Stockholm in the eighteen eighties*] Brackets indicate translator's addition to scene.

° **Maja** Pronounced "Maya."

Mrs. X: And then he comes home and has to hunt for his slippers, which Mary has pushed under the bureau . . . Well, perhaps it's not right to make fun of one's husband like this. He's sweet anyhow, and a good, dear husband. You ought to have had a husband like him, Amelia. What are you laughing at? What is it? Eh? And, you see, I know he is faithful to me. Yes, I know it. He told me himself—what *are* you giggling at?—that while I was on tour in Norway that horrible Frederica came and tried to seduce him. Can you imagine anything more abominable? *(Pause.)* I'd have scratched her eyes out if she had come around while I was at home. *(Pause.)* I'm glad Bob told me about it himself, so I didn't just hear it from gossip. *(Pause.)* And, as a matter of fact, Frederica wasn't the only one. I can't think why, but all the women in the Company° seem to be crazy about my husband. They must think his position gives him some say in who is engaged at the Theatre. Perhaps you have run after him yourself? I don't trust you very far, but I know he has never been attracted by you, and you always seemed to have some sort of grudge against him, or so I felt. *(Pause. They look at one another guardedly.)*

Mrs. X: Do come and spend Christmas Eve with us   10
tonight, Amelia—just to show that you're not offended with us, or anyhow not with me. I don't know why, but it seems specially unpleasant not to be friends with you. Perhaps it's because I did get in your way that time . . . *(slowly)* or—I don't know—really, I don't know at all why it is.

Pause. Miss Y. gazes curiously at Mrs. X.

Mrs. X: *(thoughtfully)* It was so strange when we were getting to know one another. Do you know, when we first met, I was frightened of you, so frightened I didn't dare let you out of my sight. I arranged all my goings and comings to be near you. I dared not be your enemy, so I became your friend. But when you came to our home, I always had an uneasy feeling, because I saw my husband didn't like you, and that irritated me—like when a dress doesn't fit. I did all I could to make him be nice to you, but it was no good—until you went and got engaged. Then you became such tremendous friends that at first it looked as if you only dared show your real feelings then—when you were safe. And then, let me see, how was it after that? I wasn't jealous—that's queer. And I remember at the christening, when you were the godmother, I told him to kiss you. He did, and you were so upset . . . As a matter of fact I didn't notice that then . . . I didn't think about it afterwards either . . . I've never thought about it—until *now! (Rises abruptly.)* Why don't you say something? You haven't said a word all this time. You've just let me go on talking. You have sat there with your eyes drawing all these thoughts out of me—they were there in me like silk in a cocoon—thoughts. . . Mistaken thoughts? Let me think. Why did you break off your engagement? Why did you never come to our house after that? Why don't you want to come to us tonight?

Miss Y. makes a motion, as if about to speak.

Mrs. X: No. You don't need to say anything, for now I see it all. That was why—and why—and why. Yes. Yes, that's why it was. Yes, yes, all the pieces fit together now. That's it. I won't sit at the same table as you. *(Moves her things to the other table.)* That's why I have to embroider tulips, which I loathe, on his slippers—because you liked tulips. *(Throws the slippers on the floor.)* That's why we have to spend the summer on the lake—because you couldn't bear the seaside. That's why my son had to be called Eskil—because it was your father's name. That's why I had to wear your colours, read your books, eat the dishes you liked, drink your drinks—your chocolate, for instance. That's why—oh my God, it's terrible to think of, terrible! Everything, everything came to me from you—even your passions. Your soul bored into mine like a worm into an apple, and ate and ate and burrowed and burrowed, till nothing was left but the skin and a little black mould. I wanted to fly from you, but I couldn't. You were there like a snake, your black eyes fascinating me. When I spread my wings, they only dragged me down. I lay in the water with my feet tied together, and the harder I worked my arms, the deeper I sank—down, down, till I reached the bottom, where you lay in waiting like a giant crab to catch me in your claws—and now here I am. Oh how I hate you! I hate you, I hate you! And you just go on sitting there, silent, calm, indifferent, not caring whether the moon is new or full, if it's Christmas or New Year, if other people are happy or unhappy. You don't know how to hate or to love. You just sit there without moving—like a cat° at a mouse-hole. You can't drag your prey out, you can't chase it, but

---

° **in the Company** Translator's addition.

° **cat** In Swedish, "stork."

> "Perhaps, my dear, taking everything into consideration, at this moment it is I who am the stronger."

you can out-stay it. Here you sit in your corner—you know they call it the rat-trap after you—reading the papers to see if anyone's ruined or wretched or been thrown out of the Company. Here you sit sizing up your victims and weighing your chances—like a pilot his shipwrecks for the salvage. *(Pause.)* Poor Amelia! Do you know, I couldn't be more sorry for you. I know you are miserable, miserable like some wounded creature, and vicious because you are wounded. I can't be angry with you. I should like to be, but after all you are the small one—and as for your affair with Bob, that doesn't worry me in the least. Why should it matter to me? And if you, or somebody else taught me to drink chocolate, what's the difference? *(Drinks a spoonful. Smugly.)* Chocolate is very wholesome anyhow. And if I learnt from you how to dress, *tant mieux!*—that only gave me a stronger hold over my husband, and you have lost what I gained. Yes, to judge from various signs, I think you have now lost him. Of course, you meant me to walk out, as you once did, and which you're now regretting. But I won't do that, you may be sure. One shouldn't be narrow-minded, you know. And why should

nobody else want what I have? *(Pause.)* Perhaps, my dear, taking everything into consideration, at this moment it is I who am the stronger. You never got anything from me, you just gave away—from yourself. And now, like the thief in the night, when you woke up I had what you had lost. Why was it then that everything you touched became worthless and sterile? You couldn't keep a man's love—for all your tulips and your passions—but I could. You couldn't learn the art of living from your books—but I learnt it. You bore no little Eskil, although that was your father's name. *(Pause.)* And why is it you are silent—everywhere, always silent? Yes, I used to think this was strength, but perhaps it was because you hadn't anything to say, because you couldn't think of anything. *(Rises and picks up the slippers.)* Now I am going home, taking the tulips with me—*your* tulips. You couldn't learn from others, you couldn't bend, and so you broke like a dry stick. I did not. Thank you, Amelia, for all your good lessons. Thank you for teaching my husband how to love. Now I am going home—to love him.

Exit.

Related Works

"Hills Like White Elephants" (p. 96), "The Storm" (p. 154), "Big Black Good Man" (p. 184), "General Review of the Sex Situation" (p. 490)

Arthur Miller (1915–2005)

was born in New York City and graduated in 1938 from the University of Michigan, where he began to write plays. His first big success, which won the New York Drama Critics Circle Award, was *All My Sons* (1947), about a man who has knowingly manufactured faulty airplane parts during World War II. Other significant plays are *The Crucible* (1953), based on the Salem witch trials of 1692, which Miller saw as parallel to contemporary investigations of suspected Communists by the House Un-American Activities Committee; *A View from the Bridge* (1955); and *After the Fall* (1955). He was married for a time to actress Marilyn Monroe and wrote the screenplay for her movie *The Misfits* (1961). His play *The Last Yankee* opened off-Broadway in 1993, *Broken Glass* was both published and performed in 1994, and *Mr. Peter's Connection* was published in 1998. In 2001, Miller was awarded an NEH fellowship and the John H. Finney Award for Exemplary Service to New York City.

Death of a Salesman is Miller's most significant work, a play that quickly became an American classic. Miller said he was very much influenced by the structure of Greek tragedy, and in his play he shows that a tragedy can also be the story of an ordinary person told in realistic terms. The play is frequently produced, and each production interprets it a bit differently. When Miller directed *Death of a Salesman* in China in 1983, audiences perceived it as primarily the story of the mother. In the 1983 Broadway production, Miller himself realized "at a certain point that it was far more the story of Biff, the son, than it was of Willy Loman, the salesman of the title."

Death of a Salesman (1949)

Certain Private Conversations in Two Acts and a Requiem

CHARACTERS

Willy Loman	The Woman
Linda, *his wife*	Howard Wagner
Biff } *his sons*	Jenny
Happy }	Stanley
Uncle Ben	Miss Forsythe
Charley	Letta
Bernard	

The action takes place in Willy Loman's house and yard and in various places he visits in the New York and Boston of today.

Throughout the play, in the stage directions, left and right mean stage left and stage right.

ACT I

A melody is heard, played upon a flute. It is small and fine, telling of grass and trees and the horizon. The curtain rises.

Before us is the Salesman's house. We are aware of towering, angular shapes behind it, surrounding it on all sides. Only the blue light of the sky falls upon the house and forestage; the surrounding area shows an angry glow of orange. As more light appears, we see a solid vault of apartment houses around the small, fragile-seeming home. An air of the dream clings to the place, a dream rising out of reality. The kitchen at center seems actual enough, for there is a kitchen table with three chairs, and a refrigerator. But no other fixtures are seen. At the back of the kitchen there is a draped entrance, which leads to the living room. To the right of the kitchen, on a level raised two feet, is a bedroom furnished only with a brass bedstead and a straight chair. On a shelf over the bed a silver athletic trophy stands. A window opens onto the apartment house at the side.

Behind the kitchen, on a level raised six and a half feet, is the boys' bedroom, at present barely visible. Two beds are dimly seen, and at the back of the room a dormer window. (This bedroom is above the unseen living room.) At the left a stairway curves up to it from the kitchen. The entire setting is wholly or, in some places, partially transparent. The roofline of the house is one-dimensional; under and over it we see the apartment buildings. Before the house lies an apron, curving beyond the forestage into the orchestra. This forward area serves as the back yard as well as the locale of all Willy's imaginings and of his city scenes. Whenever the action is in the present the actors observe the imaginary wall-lines, entering the house only through the door at the left. But in the scenes of the past these boundaries are broken, and characters enter or leave a room by stepping "through" a wall onto the forestage.

From the right, Willy Loman, the Salesman, enters, carrying two large sample cases. The flute plays on. He hears but is not aware of it. He is past sixty years of age, dressed quietly. Even as he crosses the stage to the doorway of the house, his exhaustion is apparent. He unlocks the door, comes into the kitchen, and thankfully lets his burden down, feeling the soreness of his palms. A word-sigh escapes his lips—it might be "Oh, boy, oh, boy." He closes the door, then carries his cases out into the living room, through the draped kitchen doorway.

Linda, his wife, has stirred in her bed at the right. She gets out and puts on a robe, listening. Most often jovial, she has developed an iron repression of her exceptions to Willy's behavior—she more than loves him, she admires him, as though his mercurial nature, his temper, his massive dreams and little cruelties, served her only as sharp reminders of the turbulent longings within him, longings which she shares but lacks the temperament to utter and follow to their end.

Linda: *(hearing Willy outside the bedroom, calls with some trepidation)* Willy!

Willy: It's all right. I came back.

Linda: Why? What happened? *(Slight pause.)* Did something happen, Willy?

Willy: No, nothing happened.

Linda: You didn't smash the car, did you? 5

Willy: *(with casual irritation)* I said nothing happened. Didn't you hear me?

Linda: Don't you feel well?

Willy: I am tired to the death. *(The flute has faded away. He sits on the bed beside her, a little numb.)* I couldn't make it. I just couldn't make it, Linda.

Linda: *(very carefully, delicately)* Where were you all day? You look terrible.

Willy: I got as far as a little above Yonkers. I stopped for 10 a cup of coffee. Maybe it was the coffee.

Linda: What?

Willy: *(after a pause)* I suddenly couldn't drive any more. The car kept going onto the shoulder, y'know?

Linda: *(helpfully)* Oh. Maybe it was the steering again. I don't think Angelo knows the Studebaker.

Willy: No, it's me, it's me. Suddenly I realize I'm goin' sixty miles an hour and I don't remember the last five minutes. I'm—I can't seem to—keep my mind to it.

Linda: Maybe it's your glasses. You never went for your new glasses. 15

Willy: No, I see everything. I came back ten miles an hour. It took me nearly four hours from Yonkers.

Linda: *(resigned)* Well, you'll just have to take a rest, Willy, you can't continue this way.

Willy: I just got back from Florida.

Linda: But you didn't rest your mind. Your mind is overactive, and the mind is what counts, dear.

Willy: I'll start out in the morning. Maybe I'll feel better in the morning. *(She is taking off his shoes.)* These 20 goddam arch supports are killing me.

> "If old man Wagner was alive I'd a been in charge of New York now!"

Linda: Take an aspirin. Should I get you an aspirin? It'll soothe you.

Willy: *(with wonder)* I was driving along, you understand? And I was fine. I was even observing the scenery. You can imagine, me looking at scenery, on the road every week of my life. But it's so beautiful up there, Linda, the trees are so thick, and the sun is warm. I opened the windshield and just let the warm air bathe over me. And then all of a sudden I'm goin' off the road! I'm tellin' ya, I absolutely forgot I was driving. If I'd've gone the other way over the white line I might've killed somebody. So I went on again—and five minutes later I'm dreamin' again, and I nearly—*(He presses two fingers against his eyes.)* I have such thoughts, I have such strange thoughts.

Linda: Willy, dear. Talk to them again. There's no reason why you can't work in New York.

>> Ron Eldard, Brian Dennehy, and Ted Koch in 2000 TV film of *Death of a Salesman*

Cultural Context

At the t me *Death of a Salesman* was written in 1949, the United States was experiencing the largest economic expansion in its history. After World War II, soldiers returned home, women left the factory jobs they had held while men were at war, and more and more consumer goods were developed and manufactured. As companies expanded and were consolidated, large, impersonal corporations began to replace the mom-and-pop businesses that had dominated the American scene. The foot soldiers of these corporations were the traveling salesmen (today called *manufacturers' representatives*) who moved from town to town and covered large territories in a relentless effort to sign up clients and generate sales. During the same period, the American suburbs began to appear, with a mass movement of population from older urban neighborhoods to massive housing developments such as those constructed in Levittown, Long Island, in 1946. It is against this background that the events of *Death of a Salesman* unfold.

Willy: They don't need me in New York. I'm the New England man. I'm vital in New England.

Linda: But you're sixty years old. They can't expect you to keep traveling every week. 25

Willy: I'll have to send a wire to Portland. I'm supposed to see Brown and Morrison tomorrow morning at ten o'clock to show the line. Goddammit, I could sell them! *(He starts putting on his jacket.)*

Linda: *(taking the jacket from him)* Why don't you go down to the place tomorrow and tell Howard you've simply got to work in New York? You're too accommodating, dear.

Willy: If old man Wagner was alive I'd a been in charge of New York now! That man was a prince, he was a masterful man. But that boy of his, that Howard, he don't appreciate. When I went north the first time, the Wagner Company didn't know where New England was!

Linda: Why don't you tell those things to Howard, dear?

Willy: *(encouraged)* I will, I definitely will. Is there any cheese? 30

Linda: I'll make you a sandwich.

Willy: No, go to sleep. I'll take some milk. I'll be up right away. The boys in?

Linda: They're sleeping. Happy took Biff on a date tonight.

Willy: *(interested)* That so?

Linda: It was so nice to see them shaving together, one behind the other, in the bathroom. And going out together. You notice? The whole house smells of shaving lotion. 35

Willy: Figure it out. Work a lifetime to pay off a house. You finally own it, and there's nobody to live in it.

> "The street is lined with cars. There's not a breath of fresh air in the neighborhood. The grass don't grow any more, you can't raise a carrot in the back yard. They should've had a law against apartment houses".

Linda: Well, dear, life is a casting off. It's always that way.

Willy: No, no, some people—some people accomplish something. Did Biff say anything after I went this morning?

Linda: You shouldn't have criticized him, Willy, especially after he just got off the train. You mustn't lose your temper with him.

Willy: When the hell 40 did I lose my temper? I simply asked him if he was making any money. Is that a criticism?

Linda: But, dear, how could he make any money?

Willy: *(worried and angered)* There's such an undercurrent in him. He became a moody man. Did he apologize when I left this morning?

Linda: He was crestfallen, Willy. You know how he admires you. I think if he finds himself, then you'll both be happier and not fight any more.

Willy: How can he find himself on a farm? Is that a life? A farmhand? In the beginning, when he was young, I thought, well, a young man, it's good for him to tramp around, take a lot of different jobs. But it's more than ten years now and he has yet to make thirty-five dollars a week!

Linda: He's finding himself, Willy. 45

Willy: Not finding yourself at the age of thirty-four is a disgrace!

Linda: Shh!

Willy: The trouble is he's lazy, goddammit!

Linda: Willy, please!

Willy: Biff is a lazy bum! 50

Linda: They're sleeping. Get something to eat. Go on down.

Willy: Why did he come home? I would like to know what brought him home.

Linda: I don't know. I think he's still lost, Willy. I think he's very lost.

Willy: Biff Loman is lost. In the greatest country in the world a young man with such—personal attractiveness, gets lost. And such a hard worker. There's one thing about Biff—he's not lazy.

Linda: Never. 55

Willy: *(with pity and resolve)* I'll see him in the morning; I'll have a nice talk with him. I'll get him a job selling. He could be big in no time. My God! Remember how they used to follow him around in high school? When he smiled at one of them their faces lit up. When he walked down the street . . . *(He loses himself in reminiscences.)*

Linda: *(trying to bring him out of it)* Willy, dear, I got a new kind of American-type cheese today. It's whipped.

Willy: Why do you get American when I like Swiss?

Linda: I just thought you'd like a change—

Willy: I don't want a change! I want Swiss cheese. Why 60 am I always being contradicted?

Linda: *(with a covering laugh)* I thought it would be a surprise.

Willy: Why don't you open a window in here, for God's sake?

Linda: *(with infinite patience)* They're all open, dear.

Willy: The way they boxed us in here. Bricks and windows, windows and bricks.

Linda: We should've bought the land next door. 65

Willy: The street is lined with cars. There's not a breath of fresh air in the neighborhood. The grass don't grow any more, you can't raise a carrot in the back yard. They should've had a law against apartment houses. Remember those two beautiful elm trees out there? When I and Biff hung the swing between them?

Linda: Yeah, like being a million miles from the city.

Willy: They should've arrested the builder for cutting those down. They massacred the neighborhood. *(Lost.)* More and more I think of those days, Linda. This time of year it was lilac and wisteria. And then the peonies would come out, and the daffodils. What fragrance in this room!

Linda: Well, after all, people had to move somewhere.

Willy: No, there's more people now. 70

Linda: I don't think there's more people. I think—

Willy: There's more people! That's what's ruining this country! Population is getting out of control. The competition is maddening! Smell the stink from that apartment house! And another on the other side . . . How can they whip cheese?

On Willy's last line, Biff and Happy raise themselves up in their beds, listening.

Linda: Go down, try it. And be quiet.

Willy: *(turning to Linda, guiltily)* You're not worried about me, are you, sweetheart?

Biff: What's the matter? 75

Happy: Listen!

Linda: You've got too much on the ball to worry about.

Willy: You're my foundation and my support, Linda.

Linda: Just try to relax, dear. You make mountains out of molehills.

Willy: I won't fight with him any more. If he wants to go 80 back to Texas, let him go.

Linda: He'll find his way.

Willy: Sure. Certain men just don't get started till later in life. Like Thomas Edison, I think. Or B. F. Goodrich. One of them was deaf. *(He starts for the bedroom doorway.)* I'll put my money on Biff.

>> Dustin Hoffman as Willy, John Malkovich as Biff, Stephen Lang as Happy, and Kate Reid as Linda in 1984 TV movie

Linda: And Willy—if it's warm Sunday we'll drive in the country. And we'll open the windshield, and take lunch.

Willy: No, the windshields don't open on the new cars.

Linda: But you opened it today. 85

Willy: Me? I didn't. *(He stops.)* Now isn't that peculiar! Isn't that remarkable—*(He breaks off in amazement and fright as the flute is heard distantly.)*

Linda: What, darling?

Willy: That is the most remarkable thing.

Linda: What, dear?

Willy: I was thinking of the Chevvy. *(Slight pause.)* 90
Nineteen twenty-eight . . . when I had that red Chevvy—*(Breaks off.)* That funny? I coulda sworn I was driving that Chevvy today.

Linda: Well, that's nothing. Something must've reminded you.

Willy: Remarkable. Ts. Remember those days? The way Biff used to simonize that car? The dealer refused to believe there was eighty thousand miles on it. *(He shakes his head.)* Heh! *(To Linda.)* Close your eyes, I'll be right up. *(He walks out of the bedroom.)*

Happy: *(to Biff)* Jesus, maybe he smashed up the car again!

Linda: *(calling after Willy)* Be careful on the stairs, dear! The cheese is on the middle shelf! *(She turns, goes over to the bed, takes his jacket, and goes out of the bedroom.)*

Light has risen on the boys' room. Unseen, Willy is heard talking to himself, "Eighty thousand miles," and a little laugh. Biff gets out of bed, comes downstage a bit, and stands attentively. Biff is two years older than his brother Happy, well built, but in these days bears a worn air and seems less self-assured. He has succeeded less, and his dreams are stronger and less acceptable than Happy's. Happy is tall, powerfully made. Sexuality is like a visible color on him, or a scent that many women have discovered. He, like his brother, is lost, but in a different way, for he has never allowed himself to turn his face toward defeat and is thus more confused and hard-skinned, although seemingly more content.

Happy: *(getting out of bed)* He's going to get his license 95
taken away if he keeps that up. I'm getting nervous about him, y'know, Biff?

Biff: His eyes are going.

Happy: No, I've driven with him. He sees all right. He just doesn't keep his mind on it. I drove into the city with him last week. He stops at a green light and then it turns red and he goes. *(He laughs.)*

Biff: Maybe he's color-blind.

Happy: Pop? Why he's got the finest eye for color in the business. You know that.

Biff: *(sitting down on his bed)* I'm going to sleep. 100

Happy: You're not still sour on Dad, are you, Biff?

Biff: He's all right, I guess.

Willy: *(underneath them, in the living room)* Yes, sir, eighty thousand miles—eighty-two thousand!

Biff: You smoking?

Happy: *(holding out a pack of cigarettes)* Want one? 105

Biff: *(taking a cigarette)* I can never sleep when I smell it.

Willy: What a simonizing job, heh!

Happy: *(with deep sentiment)* Funny, Biff, y'know? Us sleeping in here again? The old beds. *(He pats his bed affectionately.)* All the talk that went across those two beds, huh? Our whole lives.

Biff: Yeah. Lotta dreams and plans.

Happy: *(with a deep and masculine laugh)* About five 110
hundred women would like to know what was said in this room.

They share a soft laugh.

Biff: Remember that big Betsy something—what the hell was her name—over on Bushwick Avenue?

Happy: *(combing his hair)* With the collie dog!

Biff: That's the one. I got you in there, remember?

Happy: Yeah, that was my first time—I think. Boy, there was a pig! *(They laugh, almost crudely.)* You taught me everything I know about women. Don't forget that.

Biff: I bet you forgot how bashful you used to be. 115
Especially with girls.

Happy: Oh, I still am, Biff.

Biff: Oh, go on.

>> Lee J. Cobb, Mildred Dunnock, Arthur Kennedy, and Cameron Michael in original Broadway production directed by Elia Kazan (1949–50)

Happy: I just control it, that's all. I think I got less bashful and you got more so. What happened, Biff? Where's the old humor, the old confidence? *(He shakes Biff's knee. Biff gets up and moves restlessly about the room.)* What's the matter?

Biff: Why does Dad mock me all the time?

Happy: He's not mocking you, he— 120

Biff: Everything I say there's a twist of mockery on his face. I can't get near him.

Happy: He just wants you to make good, that's all. I wanted to talk to you about Dad for a long time, Biff. Something's—happening to him. He—talks to himself.

Biff: I noticed that this morning. But he always mumbled.

Happy: But not so noticeable. It got so embarrassing I sent him to Florida. And you know something? Most of the time he's talking to you.

Biff: What's he say about me? 125

Happy: I can't make it out.

Biff: What's he say about me?

Happy: I think the fact that you're not settled, that you're still kind of up in the air . . .

Biff: There's one or two other things depressing him, Happy.

Happy: What do you mean? 130

Biff: Never mind. Just don't lay it all to me.

Happy: But I think if you just got started—I mean—is there any future for you out there?

Biff: I tell ya, Hap, I don't know what the future is. I don't know—what I'm supposed to want.

Happy: What do you mean?

Biff: Well, I spent six or seven years after high school 135 trying to work myself up. Shipping clerk, salesman, business of one kind or another. And it's a measly manner of existence. To get on that subway on the hot mornings in summer. To devote your whole life to keeping stock, or making phone calls, or selling or buying. To suffer fifty weeks of the year for the sake of a two-week vacation, when all you really desire is to be outdoors, with your shirt off. And always to have to get ahead of the next fella. And still—that's how you build a future.

Happy: Well, you really enjoy it on a farm? Are you content out there?

Biff: *(with rising agitation)* Hap, I've had twenty or thirty different kinds of jobs since I left home before the war, and it always turns out the same. I just realized it lately. In Nebraska when I herded cattle, and the Dakotas, and Arizona, and now in Texas. It's why I came home now, I guess, because I realized it. This farm I work on, it's spring there now, see? And they've got about fifteen new colts. There's nothing more inspiring or—beautiful than the sight of a mare and a new colt. And it's cool there now, see? Texas is cool now, and it's spring. And whenever spring comes to where I am, I suddenly get the feeling, my God, I'm not gettin' anywhere! What the hell am I doing, playing around with horses, twenty-eight dollars a week! I'm thirty-four years old, I oughta be makin' my future. That's when I come running home. And now, I get here, and I don't know what to do with myself. *(After a pause.)* I've always made a point of not wasting my life, and every time I come back here I know that all I've done is to waste my life.

Happy: You're a poet, you know that, Biff? You're a— you're an idealist!

Biff: No, I'm mixed up very bad. Maybe I oughta get married. Maybe I oughta get stuck into something. Maybe that's my trouble. I'm like a boy. I'm not married, I'm not in business, I just—I'm like a boy. Are you content, Hap? You're a success, aren't you? Are you content?

Happy: Hell, no! 140

Biff: Why? You're making money, aren't you?

Happy: *(moving about with energy, expressiveness)* All I can do now is wait for the merchandise manager to die. And suppose I get to be merchandise manager? He's a good friend of mine, and he just built a terrific estate on Long Island. And he lived there about two months and sold it, and now he's building another one. He can't enjoy it once it's finished. And I know that's just what I would do. I don't know what the hell I'm workin' for. Sometimes I sit in my apartment—all alone. And I think of the rent I'm paying. And it's crazy. But then, it's what I always wanted.

>> Mildred Dunnock and Fredric March in a 1952 production

My own apartment, a car, and plenty of women. And still, goddammit, I'm lonely.

Biff: *(with enthusiasm)* Listen, why don't you come out West with me?

Happy: You and I, heh?

Biff: Sure, maybe we could buy a ranch. Raise cattle, use our muscles. Men built like we are should be working out in the open. 145

Happy: *(avidly)* The Loman Brothers, heh?

Biff: *(with vast affection)* Sure, we'd be known all over the counties!

Happy: *(enthralled)* That's what I dream about, Biff. Sometimes I want to just rip my clothes off in the middle of the store and outbox that goddam merchandise manager. I mean I can outbox, outrun, and outlift anybody in that store, and I have to take orders from those common, petty sons-of-bitches till I can't stand it any more.

Biff: I'm telln' you, kid, if you were with me I'd be happy out there.

Happy: *(enthused)* See, Biff, everybody around me is so false that I'm constantly lowering my ideals . . . 150

Biff: Baby, together we'd stand up for one another, we'd have someone to trust.

Happy: If I were around you—

Biff: Hap, the trouble is we weren't brought up to grub for money. I don't know how to do it.

Happy: Neither can I!

Biff: Then let's go! 155

Happy: The only thing is—what can you make out there?

Biff: But look at your friend. Builds an estate and then hasn't the peace of mind to live in it.

Happy: Yeah, but when he walks into the store the waves part in front of him. That's fifty-two thousand dollars a year coming through the revolving door, and I got more in my pinky finger than he's got in his head.

Biff: Yeah, but you just said—

Happy: I gotta show some of those pompous, self-impor- 160 tant executives over there that Hap Loman can make the grade. I want to walk into the store the way he walks in. Then I'll go with you, Biff. We'll be together yet, I swear. But take those two we had tonight. Now weren't they gorgeous creatures?

Biff: Yeah, yeah, most gorgeous I've had in years.

Happy: I get that any time I want, Biff. Whenever I feel disgusted. The only trouble is, it gets like bowling or something. I just keep knockin' them over and it doesn't mean anything. You still run around a lot?

Biff: Naa. I'd like to find a girl—steady, somebody with substance.

Happy: That's what I long for.

Biff: Go on! You'd never come home. 165

Happy: I would! Somebody with character, with resistance! Like Mom, y'know? You're gonna call me a bastard when I tell you this. That girl Charlotte I was with tonight is engaged to be married in five weeks. *(He tries on his new hat.)*

Biff: No kiddin'!

Happy: Sure, the guy's in line for the vice-presidency of the store. I don't know what gets into me, maybe I just have an overdeveloped sense of competition or something, but I went and ruined her, and furthermore I can't get rid of her. And he's the third executive I've done that to. Isn't that a crummy characteristic? And to top it all, I go to their weddings! *(Indignantly, but laughing.)* Like I'm not supposed to take bribes. Manufacturers offer me a hundred-dollar bill now and then to throw an order their way. You know how honest I am, but it's like this girl, see. I hate myself for it. Because I don't want the girl, and, still, I take it and—I love it!

Biff: Let's go to sleep.

Happy: I guess we didn't settle anything, heh? 170

Biff: I just got one idea that I think I'm going to try.

Happy: What's that?

Biff: Remember Bill Oliver?

Happy: Sure, Oliver is very big now. You want to work for him again?

Biff: No, but when I quit he said something to me. He 175 put his arm on my shoulder, and he said, "Biff, if you ever need anything, come to me."

Happy: I remember that. That sounds good.

Biff: I think I'll go to see him. If I could get ten thousand or even seven or eight thousand dollars I could buy a beautiful ranch.

Happy: I bet he'd back you. 'Cause he thought highly of you, Biff, I mean, they all do. You're well liked, Biff. That's why I say to come back here, and we both have the apartment. And I'm telln' you, Biff, any babe you want . . .

Biff: No, with a ranch I could do the work I like and still be something. I just wonder though. I wonder if Oliver still thinks I stole that carton of basketballs.

Happy: Oh, he probably forgot that long ago. It's almost ten years. You're too sensitive. Anyway, he didn't really fire you. 180

Biff: Well, I think he was going to. I think that's why I quit. I was never sure whether he knew or not. I know he thought the world of me, though. I was the only one he'd let lock up the place.

Willy: *(below)* You gonna wash the engine, Biff?

Happy: Shh!

Biff looks at Happy, who is gazing down, listening. Willy is mumbling in the parlor.

Happy: You hear that?

They listen. Willy laughs warmly.

Biff: *(growing angry)* Doesn't he know Mom can hear that? 185

Willy: Don't get your sweater dirty, Biff!

A look of pain crosses Biff's face.

Happy: Isn't that terrible? Don't leave again, will you? You'll find a job here. You gotta stick around. I don't know what to do about him, it's getting embarrassing.

Willy: What a simonizing job!

Biff: Mom's hearing that!

Willy: No kiddin', Biff, you got a date? Wonderful! 190

Happy: Go on to sleep. But talk to him in the morning, will you?

Biff: *(reluctantly getting into bed)* With her in the house. Brother!

Happy: *(getting into bed)* I wish you'd have a good talk with him.

The light on their room begins to fade.

Biff: *(to himself in bed)* That selfish, stupid . . .

Happy: Sh . . . Sleep, Biff. 195

Their light is out. Well before they have finished speaking, Willy's form is dimly seen below in the darkened kitchen. He opens the refrigerator, searches in there, and takes out a bottle of milk. The apartment houses are fading out, and the entire house and surroundings become covered with leaves. Music insinuates itself as the leaves appear.

Willy: Just wanna be careful with those girls, Biff, that's all. Don't make any promises. No promises of any kind. Because a girl, y'know, they always believe what you tell'em, and you're very young, Biff, you're too young to be talking seriously to girls.

Light rises on the kitchen. Willy, talking, shuts the refrigerator door and comes downstage to the kitchen table. He pours milk into a glass. He is totally immersed in himself, smiling faintly.

Willy: Too young entirely, Biff. You want to watch your schooling first. Then when you're all set, there'll be plenty of girls for a boy like you. *(He smiles broadly at a kitchen chair.)* That so? The girls pay for you? *(He laughs.)* Boy, you must really be makin' a hit.

Willy is gradually addressing—physically—a point offstage, speaking through the wall of the kitchen, and his voice has been rising in volume to that of a normal conversation.

Willy: I been wondering why you polish the car so careful. Ha! Don't leave the hubcaps, boys. Get the chamois to the hubcaps. Happy, use newspaper on the windows, it's the easiest thing. Show him how to do it, Biff! You see, Happy? Pad it up, use it like a pad. That's it, that's it, good work. You're doin' all right, Hap. *(He pauses, then nods in approbation for a few seconds, then looks upward.)* Biff, first thing we gotta do when we get time is clip that big branch over the house. Afraid it's gonna fall in a storm and hit the roof. Tell you what. We get a rope and sling her around, and then we climb up there with a couple of saws and take her down. Soon as you finish the car, boys, I wanna see ya. I got a surprise for you, boys.

Biff: *(offstage)* Whatta ya got, Dad?

Willy: No, you finish first. Never leave a job till you're finished—remember that. *(Looking toward the "big trees.")* Biff, up in Albany I saw a beautiful hammock. I think I'll buy it next trip, and we'll hang it right between those two elms. Wouldn't that be something? Just swingin' there under those branches. Boy, that would be . . . 200

Young Biff and Young Happy appear from the direction Willy was addressing. Happy carries rags and a pail of water. Biff, wearing a sweater with a block "S," carries a football.

Biff: *(pointing in the direction of the car offstage)* How's that, Pop, professional?

Willy: Terrific. Terrific job, boys. Good work, Biff.

Happy: Where's the surprise, Pop?

Willy: In the back seat of the car.

Happy: Boy! *(He runs off.)* 205

Biff: What is it, Dad? Tell me, what'd you buy?

Willy: *(laughing, cuffs him)* Never mind, something I want you to have.

Biff: *(turns and starts off)* What is it, Hap?

Happy: *(offstage)* It's a punching bag!

Biff: Oh, Pop! 210

Willy: It's got Gene Tunney's° signature on it!

Happy runs onstage with a punching bag.

Biff: Gee, how'd you know we wanted a punching bag?

Willy: Well, it's the finest thing for the timing.

° **Gene Tunney's** James Joseph ("Gene") Tunney (1897–1978)— American boxer, world heavyweight champion from his defeat of Jack Dempsey in 1926 until his retirement in 1928.

Happy: *(lies down on his back and pedals with his feet)* I'm losing weight, you notice, Pop?

Willy: *(to Happy)* Jumping rope is good too.   215

Biff: Did you see the new football I got?

Willy: *(examining the ball)* Where'd you get a new ball?

Biff: The coach told me to practice my passing.

Willy: That so? And he gave you the ball, heh?

Biff: Well, I borrowed it from the locker room. *(He* 220 *laughs confidentially.)*

Willy: *(laughing with him at the theft)* I want you to return that.

Happy: I told you he wouldn't like it!

Biff: *(angrily)* Well, I'm bringing it back!

Willy: *(stopping the incipient argument, to Happy)* Sure, he's gotta practice with a regulation ball, doesn't he? *(To Biff.)* Coach'll probably congratulate you on your initiative!

Biff: Oh, he keeps congratulating my initiative all the 225 time, Pop.

Willy: That's because he likes you. If somebody else took that ball there'd be an uproar. So what's the report, boys, what's the report?

Biff: Where'd you go this time, Dad? Gee we were lonesome for you.

Willy: *(pleased, puts an arm around each boy and they come down to the apron)* Lonesome, heh?

Biff: Missed you every minute.

Willy: Don't say? Tell you a secret, boys. Don't breathe it 230 to a soul. Someday I'll have my own business, and I'll never have to leave home any more.

Happy: Like Uncle Charley, heh?

Willy: Bigger than Uncle Charley! Because Charley is not—liked. He's liked, but he's not—well liked.

Biff: Where'd you go this time, Dad?

Willy: Well, I got on the road, and I went north to Providence. Met the Mayor.

Biff: The Mayor of Providence!   235

Willy: He was sitting in the hotel lobby.

Biff: What'd he say?

Willy: He said, "Morning!" And I said, "You've got a fine city here, Mayor." And then he had coffee with me. And then I went to Waterbury. Waterbury is a fine city. Big clock city, the famous Waterbury clock. Sold a nice bill there. And then Boston—Boston is the cradle of the Revolution. A fine city. And a couple of other towns in Mass., and on to Portland and Bangor and straight home!

Biff: Gee, I'd love to go with you sometime, Dad.

Willy: Soon as summer comes.   240

Happy: Promise?

Willy: You and Hap and I, and I'll show you all the towns. America is full of beautiful towns and fine, upstanding people. And they know me, boys, they know me up and down New England. The finest people. And when I bring you fellas up, there'll be open sesame for all of us, 'cause one thing, boys: I have friends. I can park my car in any street in New England, and the cops protect it like their own. This summer, heh?

Biff and Happy: *(together)* Yeah! You bet!

Willy: We'll take our bathing suits.

Happy: We'll carry your bags, Pop!   245

Willy: Oh, won't that be something! Me comin' into the Boston store with you boys carryin' my bags. What a sensation!

Biff is prancing around, practicing passing the ball.

Willy: You nervous, Biff, about the game?

Biff: Not if you're gonna be there.

Willy: What do they say about you in school, now that they made you captain?

Happy: There's a crowd of girls behind him everytime 250 the classes change.

Biff: *(taking Willy's hand)* This Saturday, Pop, this Saturday—just for you, I'm going to break through for a touchdown.

Happy: You're supposed to pass.

Biff: I'm takin' one play for Pop. You watch me, Pop, and when I take off my helmet, that means I'm breakin' out. Then you watch me crash through that line!

Willy: *(kisses Biff)* Oh, wait'll I tell this in Boston!

Bernard enters in knickers. He is younger than Biff, earnest and loyal, a worried boy.

Bernard: Biff, where are you? You're supposed to study 255 with me today.

Willy: Hey, looka Bernard. What're you lookin' so anemic about, Bernard?

Bernard: He's gotta study, Uncle Willy. He's got Regents next week.

Happy: *(tauntingly, spinning Bernard around)* Let's box, Bernard!

Bernard: Biff! *(He gets away from Happy.)* Listen, Biff, I heard Mr. Birnbaum say that if you don't start studyin' math he's gonna flunk you, and you won't graduate. I heard him!

Willy: You better study with him, Biff. Go ahead now.   260

Bernard: I heard him!

Biff: Oh, Pop, you didn't see my sneakers! *(He holds up a foot for Willy to look at.)*

Willy: Hey, that's a beautiful job of printing!

Bernard: *(wiping his glasses)* Just because he printed University of Virginia on his sneakers doesn't mean they've got to graduate him, Uncle Willy!

Willy: *(angrily)* What're you talking about? With scholar- 265 ships to three universities they're gonna flunk him?

Bernard: But I heard Mr. Birnbaum say—

Willy: Don't be a pest, Bernard! *(To his boys.)* What an anemic!

Bernard: Okay, I'm waiting for you in my house, Biff.

Bernard goes off. The Lomans laugh.

Willy: Bernard is not well liked, is he?

Biff: He's liked, but he's not well liked.   270

Happy: That's right, Pop.

Willy: That's just what I mean. Bernard can get the best marks in school, y'understand, but when he gets out in the business world, y'understand, you are going to be five times ahead of him. That's why I thank Almighty God you're both built like Adonises. Because the man who makes an appearance in the business world, the man who creates personal interest, is the man who gets ahead. Be liked and you will never want. You take me, for instance. I never have to wait in line to see a buyer. "Willy Loman is here!" That's all they have to know, and I go right through.

Biff: Did you knock them dead, Pop?

Willy: Knocked 'em cold in Providence, slaughtered 'em in Boston.

Happy: *(on his back, pedaling again)* I'm losing weight, 275
you notice, Pop?

Linda enters, as of old, a ribbon in her hair, carrying a basket of washing.

Linda: *(with youthful energy)* Hello, dear!

Willy: Sweetheart!

Linda: How'd the Chevvy run?

Willy: Chevrolet, Linda, is the greatest car ever built. *(To the boys.)* Since when do you let your mother carry wash up the stairs?

Biff: Grab hold there, boy! 280

Happy: Where to, Mom?

Linda: Hang them up on the line. And you better go down to your friends, Biff. The cellar is full of boys. They don't know what to do with themselves.

Biff: Ah, when Pop comes home they can wait!

Willy: *(laughs appreciatively)* You better go down and tell them what to do, Biff.

Biff: I think I'll have them sweep out the furnace room. 285

Willy: Good work, Biff.

Biff: *(goes through wall-line of kitchen to doorway at back and calls down)* Fellas! Everybody sweep out the furnace room! I'll be right down!

Voices: All right! Okay, Biff.

Biff: George and Sam and Frank, come out back! We're hangin' up the wash! Come on, Hap, on the double! *(He and Happy carry out the basket.)*

Linda: The way they obey him! 290

Willy: Well, that's training, the training. I'm tellin' you, I was sellin' thousands and thousands, but I had to come home.

Linda: Oh, the whole block'll be at that game. Did you sell anything?

Willy: I did five hundred gross in Providence and seven hundred gross in Boston.

Linda: No! Wait a minute, I've got a pencil. *(She pulls pencil and paper out of her apron pocket.)* That makes your commission . . . Two hundred—my God! Two hundred and twelve dollars!

Willy: Well, I didn't figure it yet, but . . . 295

Linda: How much did you do?

Willy: Well, I—I did—about a hundred and eighty gross in Providence. Well, no—it came to—roughly two hundred gross on the whole trip.

Linda: *(without hesitation)* Two hundred gross. That's . . . *(She figures.)*

Willy: The trouble was that three of the stores were half closed for inventory in Boston. Otherwise I woulda broke records.

Linda: Well, it makes seventy dollars and some pennies. 300
That's very good.

Willy: What do we owe?

Linda: Well, on the first there's sixteen dollars on the refrigerator—

Willy: Why sixteen?

Linda: Well, the fan belt broke, so it was a dollar eighty.

Willy: But it's brand new. 305

Linda: Well, the man said that's the way it is. Till they work themselves in, y'know.

They move through the wall-line into the kitchen.

Willy: I hope we didn't get stuck on that machine.

Linda: They got the biggest ads of any of them!

Willy: I know, it's a fine machine. What else?

Linda: Well, there's nine-sixty for the washing machine. 310
And for the vacuum cleaner there's three and a half due on the fifteenth. Then the roof, you got twenty-one dollars remaining.

Willy: It don't leak, does it?

Linda: No, they did a wonderful job. Then you owe Frank for the carburetor.

Willy: I'm not going to pay that man! That goddam Chevrolet, they ought to prohibit the manufacture of that car!

Linda: Well, you owe him three and a half. And odds and ends, comes to around a hundred and twenty dollars by the fifteenth.

Willy: A hundred and twenty dollars! My God, if 315
business don't pick up I don't know what I'm gonna do!

Linda: Well, next week you'll do better.

Willy: Oh, I'll knock them dead next week. I'll go to Hartford. I'm very well liked in Hartford. You know, the trouble is, Linda, people don't seem to take to me.

They move onto the forestage.

Linda: Oh, don't be foolish.

Willy: I know it when I walk in. They seem to laugh at me.

Linda: Why? Why would they laugh at you? Don't talk 320
that way, Willy.

Willy moves to the edge of the stage. Linda goes into the kitchen and starts to darnstockings.

Willy: I don't know the reason for it, but they just pass me by. I'm not noticed.

Linda: But you're doing wonderful, dear. You're making seventy to a hundred dollars a week.

Willy: But I gotta be at it ten, twelve hours a day. Other men—I don't know—they do it easier. I don't know why—I can't stop myself—I talk too much. A man oughta come in with a few words. One thing about Charley. He's a man of few words, and they respect him.

Linda: You don't talk too much, you're just lively.

Willy: *(smiling)* Well, I figure, what the hell, life is short, a 325 couple of jokes. *(To himself.)* I joke too much! *(The smile goes.)*

Linda: Why? You're—

Willy: I'm fat. I'm very—foolish to look at, Linda. I didn't tell you, but Christmas time I happened to be calling on F. H. Stewarts, and a salesman I know, as I was going in to see the buyer, I heard him say something about—walrus. And I—I cracked him right across the face. I won't take that. I simply will not take that. But they do laugh at me. I know that.

Linda: Darling . . .

Willy: I gotta overcome it. I know I gotta overcome it. I'm not dressing to advantage, maybe.

Linda: Willy, darling, you're the handsomest man in the 330 world—

Willy: Oh, no, Linda.

Linda: To me you are. *(Slight pause.)* The handsomest.

From the darkness is heard the laughter of a woman. Willy doesn't turn to it, but it continues through Linda's lines.

Linda: And the boys, Willy. Few men are idolized by their children the way you are.

>> Brian Dennehy as Willy Loman and Abigail McKern as The Woman in 2005 Lyric Theater production

Music is heard as behind a scrim, to the left of the house, The Woman, dimly seen, is dressing.

Willy: *(with great feeling)* You're the best there is, Linda, you're a pal, you know that? On the road—on the road I want to grab you sometimes and just kiss the life outa you.

The laughter is loud now, and he moves into a brightening area at the left, where The Woman has come from behind the scrim and is standing, putting on her hat, looking into a "mirror" and laughing.

Willy: 'Cause I get so lonely—especially when business 335 is bad and there's nobody to talk to. I get the feeling that I'll never sell anything again, that I won't make a living for you, or a business, a business for the boys. *(He talks through The Woman's subsiding laughter; The Woman primps at the "mirror.")* There's so much I want to make for—

The Woman: Me? You didn't make me, Willy. I picked you.

Willy: *(pleased)* You picked me?

The Woman: *(who is quite proper-looking, Willy's age)* I did. I've been sitting at that desk watching all the salesmen go by, day in, day out. But you've got such a sense of humor, and we do have such a good time together, don't we?

Willy: Sure, sure. *(He takes her in his arms.)* Why do you have to go now?

The Woman: It's two o'clock . . . 340

Willy: No, come on in! *(He pulls her.)*

The Woman: . . . my sisters'll be scandalized. When'll you be back?

Willy: Oh, two weeks about. Will you come up again?

The Woman: Sure thing. You do make me laugh. It's good for me. *(She squeezes his arm, kisses him.)* And I think you're a wonderful man.

Willy: You picked me, heh? 345

The Woman: Sure. Because you're so sweet. And such a kidder.

Willy: Well, I'll see you next time I'm in Boston.

The Woman: I'll put you right through to the buyers.

Willy: *(slapping her bottom)* Right. Well, bottoms up!

The Woman: *(slaps him gently and laughs)* You just kill 350 me, Willy. *(He suddenly grabs her and kisses her roughly.)* You kill me. And thanks for the stockings. I love a lot of stockings. Well, good night.

Willy: Good night. And keep your pores open!

The Woman: Oh, Willy!

The Woman bursts out laughing, and Linda's laughter blends in. The Woman disappears into the dark. Now the area at the kitchen table brightens. Linda is sitting where she was at the kitchen table, but now is mending a pair of silk stockings.

Linda: You are, Willy. The handsomest man. You've got no reason to feel that—

Willy: (coming out of The Woman's dimming area and going over to Linda) I'll make it all up to you, Linda, I'll—

Linda: There's nothing to make up, dear. You're doing fine, better than— 355

Willy: (noticing her mending) What's that?

Linda: Just mending my stockings. They're so expensive—

Willy: (angrily, taking them from her) I won't have you mending stockings in this house! Now throw them out!

Linda puts the stockings in her pocket.

Bernard: (entering on the run) Where is he? If he doesn't study!

Willy: (moving to the forestage, with great agitation) 360 You'll give him the answers!

Bernard: I do, but I can't on a Regents! That's a state exam! They're liable to arrest me!

Willy: Where is he? I'll whip him, I'll whip him!

Linda: And he'd better give back that football, Willy, it's not nice.

Willy: Biff! Where is he? Why is he taking everything?

Linda: He's too tough with the girls, Willy. All the 365 mothers are afraid of him!

Willy: I'll whip him!

Bernard: He's driving the car without a license!

The Woman's laugh is heard.

Willy: Shut up!

Linda: All the mothers—

Willy: Shut up! 370

Bernard: (backing quietly away and out) Mr. Birnbaum says he's stuck up.

Willy: Get outa here!

Bernard: If he doesn't buckle down he'll flunk math! (He goes off.)

Linda: He's right, Willy, you've gotta—

Willy: (exploding at her) There's nothing the matter with 375 him! You want him to be a worm like Bernard? He's got spirit, personality . . .

As he speaks, Linda, almost in tears, exits into the living room. Willy is alone in the kitchen, wilting and staring. The leaves are gone. It is night again, and the apartment houses look down from behind.

Willy: Loaded with it. Loaded! What is he stealing? He's giving it back, isn't he? Why is he stealing? What did I tell him? I never in my life told him anything but decent things.

Happy in pajamas has come down the stairs; Willy suddenly becomes aware of Happy's presence.

Happy: Let's go now, come on.

Willy: (sitting down at the kitchen table) Huh! Why did she have to wax the floors herself? Everytime she waxes the floors she keels over. She knows that!

Happy: Shh! Take it easy. What brought you back tonight?

Willy: I got an awful scare. Nearly hit a kid in Yonkers. 380 God! Why didn't I go to Alaska with my brother Ben that time! Ben! That man was a genius, that man was success incarnate! What a mistake! He begged me to go.

Happy: Well, there's no use in—

Willy: You guys! There was a man started with the clothes on his back and ended up with diamond mines!

Happy: Boy, someday I'd like to know how he did it.

Willy: What's the mystery? The man knew what he wanted and went out and got it! Walked into a jungle, and comes out, the age of twenty-one, and he's rich! The world is an oyster, but you don't crack it open on a mattress!

Happy: Pop, I told you I'm gonna retire you for life. 385

Willy: You'll retire me for life on seventy goddam dollars a week? And your women and your car and your apartment, and you'll retire me for life! Christ's sake, I couldn't get past Yonkers today! Where are you guys, where are you? The woods are burning! I can't drive a car!

Charley has appeared in the doorway. He is a large man, slow of speech, laconic, immovable. In all he says, despite what he says, there is pity, and now trepidation. He has a robe over his pajamas, slippers on his feet. He enters the kitchen.

Charley: Everything all right?

Happy: Yeah, Charley, everything's . . .

Willy: What's the matter?

Charley: I heard some noise. I thought something hap- 390 pened. Can't we do something about the walls? You sneeze in here, and in my house hats blow off.

Happy: Let's go to bed, Dad. Come on.

Charley signals to Happy to go.

Willy: You go ahead, I'm not tired at the moment.

Happy: (to Willy) Take it easy, huh? (He exits.)

Willy: What're you doin' up?

Charley: (sitting down at the kitchen table opposite Willy) 395 Couldn't sleep good. I had a heartburn.

Willy: Well, you don't know how to eat.

Charley: I eat with my mouth.

Willy: No, you're ignorant. You gotta know about vitamins and things like that.

Charley: Come on, let's shoot. Tire you out a little.

Willy: (hesitantly) All right. You got cards? 400

Charley: (taking a deck from his pocket) Yeah. I got them. Someplace. What is it with those vitamins?

Willy: (dealing) They build up your bones. Chemistry.

Charley: Yeah, but there's no bones in a heartburn.

Willy: What are you talkin' about? Do you know the first thing about it?

Charley: Don't get insulted. 405

Willy: Don't talk about something you don't know anything about.

They are playing. Pause.

Charley: What're you doin' home?
Willy: A little trouble with the car.
Charley: Oh. *(Pause.)* I'd like to take a trip to California.
Willy: Don't say.   410
Charley: You want a job?
Willy: I got a job, I told you that. *(After a slight pause.)* What the hell are you offering me a job for?
Charley: Don't get insulted.
Willy: Don't insult me.
Charley: I don't see no sense in it. You don't have to go   415
on this way.
Willy: I got a good job. *(Slight pause.)* What do you keep comin' in here for?
Charley: You want me to go?
Willy: *(after a pause, withering)* I can't understand it. He's going back to Texas again. What the hell is that?
Charley: Let him go.
Willy: I got nothin' to give him, Charley, I'm clean, I'm   420
clean.
Charley: He won't starve. None a them starve. Forget about him.
Willy: Then what have I got to remember?
Charley: You take it too hard. To hell with it. When a deposit bottle is broken you don't get your nickel back.
Willy: That's easy enough for you to say.
Charley: That ain't easy for me to say.   425
Willy: Did you see the ceiling I put up in the living room?
Charley: Yeah, that's a piece of work. To put up a ceiling is a mystery to me. How do you do it?
Willy: What's the difference?
Charley: Well, talk about it.
Willy: You gonna put up a ceiling?   430
Charley: How could I put up a ceiling?
Willy: Then what the hell are you bothering me for?
Charley: You're insulted again.
Willy: A man who can't handle tools is not a man. You're disgusting.
Charley: Don't call me disgusting, Willy.   435

Uncle Ben, carrying a valise and an umbrella, enters the forestage from around the right corner of the house. He is a stolid man, in his sixties, with a mustache and an authoritative air. He is utterly certain of his destiny, and there is an aura of far places about him. He enters exactly as Willy speaks.

Willy: I'm getting awfully tired, Ben.

Ben's music is heard. Ben looks around at everything.

Charley: Good, keep playing; you'll sleep better. Did you call me Ben?

Ben looks at his watch.

Willy: That's funny. For a second there you reminded me of my brother Ben.
Ben: I have only a few minutes. *(He strolls, inspecting the place. Willy and Charley continue playing.)*
Charley: You never heard from him again, heh? Since   440
that time?
Willy: Didn't Linda tell you? Couple of weeks ago we got a letter from his wife in Africa. He died.
Charley: That so.
Ben: *(chuckling)* So this is Brooklyn, eh?
Charley: Maybe you're in for some of his money.
Willy: Naa, he had seven sons. There's just one opportu-   445
nity I had with that man . . .
Ben: I must make a train, William. There are several properties I'm looking at in Alaska.
Willy: Sure, sure! If I'd gone with him to Alaska that time, everything would've been totally different.
Charley: Go on, you'd froze to death up there.
Willy: What're you talking about?
Ben: Opportunity is tremendous in Alaska, William.   450
Surprised you're not up there.
Willy: Sure, tremendous.
Charley: Heh?
Willy: There was the only man I ever met who knew the answers.
Charley: Who?
Ben: How are you all?   455
Willy: *(taking a pot, smiling)* Fine, fine.
Charley: Pretty sharp tonight.
Ben: Is Mother living with you?
Willy: No, she died a long time ago.
Charley: Who?   460
Ben: That's too bad. Fine specimen of a lady, Mother.
Willy: *(to Charley)* Heh?
Ben: I'd hoped to see the old girl.
Charley: Who died?
Ben: Heard anything from Father, have you?   465
Willy: *(unnerved)* What do you mean, who died?
Charley: *(taking a pot)* What're you talkin' about?
Ben: *(looking at his watch)* William, it's half-past eight!
Willy: *(as though to dispel his confusion he angrily stops Charley's hand)* That's my build!
Charley: I put the ace—   470
Willy: If you don't know how to play the game I'm not gonna throw my money away on you!
Charley: *(rising)* It was my ace, for God's sake!
Willy: I'm through, I'm through!
Ben: When did Mother die?
Willy: Long ago. Since the beginning you never knew   475
how to play cards.
Charley: *(picks up the cards and goes to the door)* All right! Next time I'll bring a deck with five aces.
Willy: I don't play that kind of game!

Charley: *(turning to him)* You should be ashamed of yourself!

Willy: Yeah?

Charley: Yeah! *(He goes out.)* 480

Willy: *(slamming the door after him)* Ignoramus!

Ben: *(as Willy comes toward him through the wall-line of the kitchen)* So you're William.

Willy: *(shaking Ben's hand)* Ben! I've been waiting for you so long! What's the answer? How did you do it?

Ben: Oh, there's a story in that.

Linda enters the forestage, as of old, carrying the wash basket.

Linda: Is this Ben? 485

Ben: *(gallantly)* How do you do, my dear.

Linda: Where've you been all these years? Willy's always wondered why you—

Willy: *(pulling Ben away from her impatiently)* Where is Dad? Didn't you follow him? How did you get started?

Ben: Well, I don't know how much you remember.

Willy: Well, I was just a baby, of course, only three or four years old— 490

Ben: Three years and eleven months.

Willy: What a memory, Ben!

Ben: I have many enterprises, William, and I have never kept books.

Willy: I remember I was sitting under the wagon in—was it Nebraska?

Ben: It was South Dakota, and I gave you a bunch of wild flowers. 495

Willy: I remember you walking away down some open road.

Ben: *(laughing)* I was going to find Father in Alaska.

Willy: Where is he?

Ben: At that age I had a very faulty view of geography, William. I discovered after a few days that I was heading due south, so instead of Alaska, I ended up in Africa.

Linda: Africa! 500

Willy: The Gold Coast!

Ben: Principally, diamond mines.

Linda: Diamond mines!

Ben: Yes, my dear. But I've only a few minutes—

Willy: No! Boys! Boys! *(Young Biff and Happy appear.)* 505 Listen to this. This is your Uncle Ben, a great man! Tell my boys, Ben!

Ben: Why, boys, when I was seventeen I walked into the jungle, and when I was twenty-one I walked out. *(He laughs.)* And by God I was rich.

Willy: *(to the boys)* You see what I been talking about? The greatest things can happen!

Ben: *(glancing at his watch)* I have an appointment in Ketchikan Tuesday week.

Willy: No, Ben! Please tell about Dad. I want my boys to hear. I want them to know the kind of stock they

spring from. All I remember is a man with a big beard, and I was in Mamma's lap, sitting around a fire, and some kind of high music.

Ben: His flute. He played the flute. 510

Willy: Sure, the flute, that's right!

New music is heard, a high, rollicking tune.

Ben: Father was a very great and a very wild-hearted man. We would start in Boston, and he'd toss the whole family into the wagon, and then he'd drive the team right across the country; through Ohio, and Indiana, Michigan, Illinois, and all the Western states. And we'd stop in the towns and sell the flutes that he'd made on the way. Great inventor, Father. With one gadget he made more in a week than a man like you could make in a lifetime.

Willy: That's just the way I'm bringing them up. Ben— rugged, well liked, all-around.

Ben: Yeah? *(To Biff.)* Hit that, boy—hard as you can. *(He pounds his stomach.)*

Biff: Oh, no, sir! 515

Ben: *(taking boxing stance)* Come on, get to me! *(He laughs.)*

Willy: Go to it, Biff! Go ahead, show him!

Biff: Okay! *(He cocks his fist and starts in.)*

Linda: *(to Willy)* Why must he fight, dear?

Ben: *(sparring with Biff)* Good boy! Good boy! 520

Willy: How's that, Ben, heh?

Happy: Give him the left, Biff!

Linda: Why are you fighting?

Ben: Good boy! *(Suddenly comes in, trips Biff, and stands over him, the point of his umbrella poised over Biff's eye.)*

Linda: Look out, Biff! 525

Biff: Gee!

Ben: *(patting Biff's knee)* Never fight fair with a stranger, boy. You'll never get out of the jungle that way. *(Taking Linda's hand and bowing.)* It was an honor and a pleasure to meet you, Linda.

Linda: *(withdrawing her hand coldly, frightened)* Have a nice—trip.

Ben: *(to Willy)* And good luck with your—what do you do?

Willy: Selling. 530

Ben: Yes. Well . . . *(He raises his hand in farewell to all.)*

Willy: No, Ben, I don't want you to think . . . *(He takes Ben's arm to show him.)* It's Brooklyn, I know, but we hunt too.

Ben: Really, now.

Willy: Oh, sure, there's snakes and rabbits and—that's why I moved out here. Why, Biff can fell any one of these trees in no time! Boys! Go right over to where they're building the apartment house and get some sand. We're gonna rebuild the entire front stoop right now! Watch this, Ben!

Biff: Yes, sir! On the double, Hap! 535

Happy: *(as he and Biff run off)* I lost weight, Pop, you notice?

Charley enters in knickers, even before the boys are gone.

Charley: Listen, if they steal any more from that building the watchman'll put the cops on them!

Linda: *(to Willy)* Don't let Biff . . .

Ben laughs lustily.

Willy: You shoulda seen the lumber they brought home last week. At least a dozen six-by-tens worth all kinds of money.

Charley: Listen, if that watchman— 540

Willy: I gave them hell, understand. But I got a couple of fearless characters there.

Charley: Willy, the jails are full of fearless characters.

Ben: *(clapping Willy on the back, with a laugh at Charley)* And the stock exchange, friend!

Willy: *(joining in Ben's laughter)* Where are the rest of your pants?

Charley: My wife bought them. 545

Willy: Now all you need is a golf club and you can go upstairs and go to sleep. *(To Ben.)* Great athlete! Between him and his son Bernard they can't hammer a nail!

Bernard: *(rushing in)* The watchman's chasing Biff!

Willy: *(angrily)* Shut up! He's not stealing anything!

Linda: *(alarmed, hurrying off left)* Where is he? Biff, dear! *(She exits.)*

Willy: *(moving toward the left, away from Ben)* There's 550 nothing wrong. What's the matter with you?

Ben: Nervy boy. Good!

Willy: *(laughing)* Oh, nerves of iron, that Biff!

Charley: Don't know what it is. My New England man comes back and he's bleedin', they murdered him up there.

Willy: It's contacts, Charley, I got important contacts!

Charley: *(sarcastically)* Glad to hear it, Willy. Come in 555 later, we'll shoot a little casino. I'll take some of your Portland money. *(He laughs at Willy and exits.)*

Willy: *(turning to Ben)* Business is bad, it's murderous. But not for me, of course.

Ben: I'll stop by on my way back to Africa.

Willy: *(longingly)* Can't you stay a few days? You're just what I need, Ben, because I—I have a fine position here, but I—well, Dad left when I was such a baby and I never had a chance to talk to him and I still feel—kind of temporary about myself.

Ben: I'll be late for my train.

They are at opposite ends of the stage.

Willy: Ben, my boys—can't we talk? They'd go into the 560 jaws of hell for me, see, but I—

Ben: William, you're being first-rate with your boys. Outstanding, manly chaps!

Willy: *(hanging on to his words)* Oh, Ben, that's good to hear! Because sometimes I'm afraid that I'm not teaching them the right kind of—Ben, how should I teach them?

Ben: *(giving great weight to each word, and with a certain vicious audacity)* William, when I walked into the jungle, I was seventeen. When I walked out I was twenty-one. And, by God, I was rich! *(He goes off into darkness around the right corner of the house.)*

Willy: . . . was rich! That's just the spirit I want to imbue them with! To walk into a jungle! I was right! I was right! I was right!

Ben is gone, but Willy is still speaking to him as Linda, in nightgown and robe, enters the kitchen, glances around for Willy, then goes to the door of the house, looks out and sees him. Comes down to his left. He looks at her.

Linda: Willy, dear? Willy? 565

Willy: I was right!

Linda: Did you have some cheese? *(He can't answer.)* It's very late, darling. Come to bed, heh?

Willy: *(looking straight up)* Gotta break your neck to see a star in this yard.

Linda: You coming in?

Willy: What ever happened to that diamond watch fob? 570 Remember? When Ben came from Africa that time? Didn't he give me a watch fob with a diamond in it?

Linda: You pawned it, dear. Twelve, thirteen years ago. For Biff's radio correspondence course.

Willy: Gee, that was a beautiful thing. I'll take a walk.

Linda: But you're in your slippers.

Willy: *(starting to go around the house at the left)* I was right! I was! *(Half to Linda, as he goes, shaking his head.)* What a man! There was a man worth talking to. I was right!

Linda: *(calling after Willy)* But in your slippers, Willy! 575

Willy is almost gone when Biff, in his pajamas, comes down the stairs and enters the kitchen.

Biff: What is he doing out there?

Linda: Sh!

Biff: God Almighty, Mom, how long has he been doing this?

Linda: Don't, he'll hear you.

Biff: What the hell is the matter with him? 580

Linda: It'll pass by morning.

Biff: Shouldn't we do anything?

Linda: Oh, my dear, you should do a lot of things, but there's nothing to do, so go to sleep.

Happy comes down the stairs and sits on the steps.

Happy: I never heard him so loud, Mom.

Linda: Well, come around more often; you'll hear him. 585 *(She sits down at the table and mends the lining of Willy's jacket.)*

Biff: Why didn't you ever write me about this, Mom?

Linda: How would I write to you? For over three months you had no address.

Biff: I was on the move. But you know I thought of you all the time. You know that, don't you, pal?

Linda: I know, dear, I know. But he likes to have a letter. Just to know that there's still a possibility for better things.

Biff: He's not like this all the time, is he? 590

Linda: It's when you come home he's always the worst.

Biff: When I come home?

Linda: When you write you're coming, he's all smiles, and talks about the future, and—he's just wonderful. And then the closer you seem to come, the more shaky he gets, and then, by the time you get here, he's arguing, and he seems angry at you. I think it's just that maybe he can't bring himself to—to open up to you. Why are you so hateful to each other? Why is that?

Biff: *(evasively)* I'm not hateful, Mom.

Linda: But you no sooner come in the door than you're 595 fighting!

Biff: I don't know why. I mean to change. I'm tryin', Mom, you understand?

Linda: Are you home to stay now?

Biff: I don't know. I want to look around, see what's doin'.

Linda: Biff, you can't look around all your life, can you?

Biff: I just can't take hold, Mom. I can't take hold of 600 some kind of a life.

Linda: Biff, a man is not a bird, to come and go with the springtime.

Biff: Your hair . . . *(He touches her hair.)* Your hair got so gray.

Linda: Oh, it's been gray since you were in high school. I just stopped dyeing it, that's all.

Biff: Dye it again, will ya? I don't want my pal looking old. *(He smiles.)*

Linda: You're such a boy! You think you can go away 605 for a year and . . . You've got to get it into your head now that one day you'll knock on this door and there'll be strange people here—

Biff: What are you talking about? You're not even sixty, Mom.

Linda: But what about your father?

Biff: *(lamely)* Well, I meant him too.

Happy: He admires Pop.

Linda: Biff, dear, if you don't have any feeling for him, 610 then you can't have any feeling for me.

Biff: Sure I can, Mom.

Linda: No. You can't just come to see me, because I love him. *(With a threat, but only a threat, of tears.)* He's the dearest man in the world to me, and I won't have anyone making him feel unwanted and low and blue. You've got to make up your mind now, darling, there's no leeway any more. Either he's your father and you pay him that respect, or else you're not to come here. I know he's not easy to get along with—nobody knows that better than me—but . . .

Willy: *(from the left, with a laugh)* Hey, hey, Biffo!

Biff: *(starting to go out after Willy)* What the hell is the matter with him? *(Happy stops him.)*

Linda: Don't—don't go near him! 615

Biff: Stop making excuses for him! He always, always wiped the floor with you. Never had an ounce of respect for you.

Happy: He's always had respect for—

Biff: What the hell do you know about it?

Happy: *(surlily)* Just don't call him crazy!

Biff: He's got no character—Charley wouldn't do this. 620 Not in his own house—spewing out that vomit from his mind.

Happy: Charley never had to cope with what he's got to.

Biff: People are worse off than Willy Loman. Believe me, I've seen them!

Linda: Then make Charley your father, Biff. You can't do that, can you? I don't say he's a great man. Willy Loman never made a lot of money. His name was never in the paper. He's not the finest character that ever lived. But he's a human being, and a terrible thing is happening to him. So attention must be paid. He's not to be allowed to fall into his grave like an old dog. Attention, attention must be finally paid to such a person. You called him crazy—

Biff: I didn't mean—

Linda: No, a lot of people think he's lost his—balance. 625 But you don't have to be very smart to know what his trouble is. The man is exhausted.

Happy: Sure!

Linda: A small man can be just as exhausted as a great man. He works for a company thirty-six years this March, opens up unheard-of territories to their trademark, and now in his old age they take his salary away.

Happy: *(indignantly)* I didn't know that, Mom.

Linda: You never asked, my dear! Now that you get your spending money someplace else you don't trouble your mind with him.

Happy: But I gave you money last— 630

Linda: Christmas time, fifty dollars! To fix the hot water it cost ninety-seven fifty! For five weeks he's been on straight commission, like a beginner, an unknown!

Biff: Those ungrateful bastards!

Linda: Are they any worse than his sons? When he brought them business, when he was young, they were glad to see him. But now his old friends, the old buyers that loved him so and always found some order to hand him in a pinch—they're all dead, retired. He used to be able to make six, seven calls a day in Boston. Now he takes his valises out of the car and puts them back and takes them out again and he's exhausted. Instead of walking he talks now. He drives seven hundred miles, and when he gets there no one knows him any more, no one welcomes him. And what goes through a man's mind, driving seven hundred miles home without having earned a cent? Why shouldn't he talk to himself? Why? When he has to go to Charley and borrow fifty dollars a week and pretend to me that it's his pay? How long can that go on? How long? You see what I'm sitting here and waiting for? And you tell me he has no character? The man who never worked a day but for your benefit? When does he get the medal for that? Is this his reward—to turn around at the age of sixty-three and find his sons, who he loved better than his life, one a philandering bum—

Happy: Mom!

Linda: That's all you are, my baby! *(To Biff.)* And you!   635
What happened to the love you had for him? You were such pals! How you used to talk to him on the phone every night! How lonely he was till he could come home to you!

Biff: All right, Mom. I'll live here in my room, and I'll get a job. I'll keep away from him, that's all.

Linda: No, Biff. You can't stay here and fight all the time.

Biff: He threw me out of this house, remember that.

Linda: Why did he do that? I never knew why.

Biff: Because I know he's a fake and he doesn't like   640
anybody around who knows!

Linda: Why a fake? In what way? What do you mean?

Biff: Just don't lay it all at my feet. It's between me and him—that's all I have to say. I'll chip in from now on. He'll settle for half my pay check. He'll be all right. I'm going to bed. *(He starts for the stairs.)*

Linda: He won't be all right.

Biff: *(turning on the stairs, furiously)* I hate this city and I'll stay here. Now what do you want?

Linda: He's dying, Biff.   645

Happy turns quickly to her, shocked.

Biff: *(after a pause)* Why is he dying?

Linda: He's been trying to kill himself.

Biff: *(with great horror)* How?

Linda: I live from day to day.

Biff: What're you talking about?   650

Linda: Remember I wrote you that he smashed up the car again? In February?

Biff: Well?

Linda: The insurance inspector came. He said that they have evidence. That all these accidents in the last year—weren't—weren't—accidents.

Happy: How can they tell that? That's a lie.

Linda: It seems there's a woman . . . *(She takes a breath*   655
as—)

Biff: *(sharply but contained)* What woman?

Linda: *(simultaneously)* . . . and this woman . . .

Linda: What?

Biff: Nothing. Go ahead.

Linda: What did you say?   660

Biff: Nothing. I just said what woman?

Happy: What about her?

Linda: Well, it seems she was walking down the road and saw his car. She says that he wasn't driving fast at all, and that he didn't skid. She says he came to that little bridge, and then deliberately smashed into the railing, and it was only the shallowness of the water that saved him.

Biff: Oh, no, he probably just fell asleep again.

Linda: I don't think he fell asleep.   665

Biff: Why not?

Linda: Last month . . . *(With great difficulty.)* Oh, boys, it's so hard to say a thing like this! He's just a big stupid man to you, but I tell you there's more good in him than in many other people. *(She chokes, wipes her eyes.)* I was looking for a fuse. The lights blew out, and I went down the cellar. And behind the fuse box—it happened to fall out—was a length of rubber pipe—just short.

Happy: No kidding?

Linda: There's a little attachment on the end of it. I knew right away. And sure enough, on the bottom of the water heater there's a new little nipple on the gas pipe.

Happy: *(angrily)* That—jerk.   670

Biff: Did you have it taken off?

Linda: I'm—I'm ashamed to. How can I mention it to him? Every day I go down and take away that little rubber pipe. But, when he comes home, I put it back where it was. How can I insult him that way? I don't know what to do. I live from day to day, boys. I tell you, I know every thought in his mind. It sounds so old-fashioned and silly, but I tell you he put his whole life into you and you've turned your backs on him. *(She is bent over in the chair, weeping, her face in her hands.)* Biff, I swear to God! Biff, his life is in your hands!

Happy: *(to Biff)* How do you like that damned fool!

Biff: *(kissing her)* All right, pal, all right. It's all settled now. I've been remiss. I know that, Mom, but now I'll stay, and I swear to you, I'll apply myself. *(Kneeling in front of her, in a fever of self-reproach.)* It's just—you see, Mom, I don't fit in business. Not that I won't try. I'll try, and I'll make good.

Happy: Sure you will. The trouble with you in business   675
was you never tried to please people.

Biff: I know, I—

Happy: Like when you worked for Harrison's. Bob Harrison said you were tops, and then you go and do some damn fool thing like whistling whole songs in the elevator like a comedian.

Biff: *(against Happy)* So what? I like to whistle sometimes.

Happy: You don't raise a guy to a responsible job who whistles in the elevator!

Linda: Well, don't argue about it now.   680

Happy: Like when you'd go off and swim in the middle of the day instead of taking the line around.

Biff: *(his resentment rising)* Well, don't you run off? You take off sometimes, don't you? On a nice summer day?

Happy: Yeah, but I cover myself!

Linda: Boys!

Happy: If I'm going to take a fade the boss can call any 685
number where I'm supposed to be and they'll swear
to him that I just left. I'll tell you something that I
hate to say, Biff, but in the business world some of
them think you're crazy.

Biff: *(angered)* Screw the business world!

Happy: All right, screw it! Great, but cover yourself!

Linda: Hap, Hap!

Biff: I don't care what they think! They've laughed at Dad
for years, and you know why? Because we don't belong
in this nut-house of a city! We should be mixing cement
on some open plain, or—or carpenters. A carpenter is
allowed to whistle!

Willy walks in from the entrance of the house, at left.

Willy: Even your grandfather was better than a 690
carpenter. *(Pause. They watch him.)* You never
grew up. Bernard does not whistle in the elevator,
I assure you.

Biff: *(as though to laugh Willy out of it)* Yeah, but you
do, Pop.

Willy: I never in my life whistled in an elevator! And who
in the business world thinks I'm crazy?

Biff: I didn't mean it like that, Pop. Now don't make a
whole thing out of it, will ya?

Willy: Go back to the West! Be a carpenter, a cowboy,
enjoy yourself!

Linda: Willy, he was just saying— 695

Willy: I heard what he said!

Happy: *(trying to quiet Willy)* Hey, Pop, come on now . . .

Willy: *(continuing over Happy's line)* They laugh at me,
heh? Go to Filene's, go to the Hub, go to Slattery's,
Boston. Call out the name Willy Loman and see what
happens! Big shot!

Biff: All right, Pop.

Willy: Big! 700

Biff: All right!

Willy: Why do you always insult me?

Biff: I didn't say a word. *(To Linda.)* Did I say a word?

Linda: He didn't say anything, Willy.

Willy: *(going to the doorway of the living room)* All right, 705
good night, good night.

Linda: Willy, dear, he just decided . . .

Willy: *(to Biff)* If you get tired hanging around tomorrow,
paint the ceiling I put up in the living room.

Biff: I'm leaving early tomorrow.

Happy: He's going to see Bill Oliver, Pop.

Willy: *(interestedly)* Oliver? For what? 710

Biff: *(with reserve, but trying, trying)* He always said he'd
stake me. I'd like to go into business, so maybe I can
take him up on it.

Linda: Isn't that wonderful?

Willy: Don't interrupt. What's wonderful about it?
There's fifty men in the City of New York who'd
stake him. *(To Biff.)* Sporting goods?

Biff: I guess so. I know something about it and—

Willy: He knows something about it! You know sporting 715
goods better than Spalding, for God's sake! How
much is he giving you?

Biff: I don't know, I didn't even see him yet, but—

Willy: Then what're you talkin' about?

Biff: *(getting angry)* Well, all I said was I'm gonna see
him, that's all!

Willy: *(turning away)* Ah, you're counting your chickens
again.

Biff: *(starting left for the stairs)* Oh, Jesus, I'm going to 720
sleep!

Willy: *(calling after him)* Don't curse in this house!

Biff: *(turning)* Since when did you get so clean!

Happy: *(trying to stop them)* Wait a . . .

Willy: Don't use that language to me! I won't have it!

Happy: *(grabbing Biff, shouts)* Wait a minute! I got an 725
idea. I got a feasible idea. Come here, Biff, let's talk
this over now, let's talk some sense here. When I
was down in Florida last time, I thought of a great
idea to sell sporting goods. It just came back to me.
You and I, Biff—we have a line, the Loman Line.
We train a couple of weeks, and put on a couple of
exhibitions, see?

Willy: That's an idea!

Happy: Wait! We form two basketball teams, see? Two
water-polo teams. We play each other. It's a million
dollars' worth of publicity. Two brothers, see? The
Loman Brothers. Displays in the Royal Palms—all
the hotels. And banners over the ring and the
basketball court: "Loman Brothers." Baby, we could
sell sporting goods!

Willy: That is a one-million-dollar idea.

Linda: Marvelous!

Biff: I'm in great shape as far as that's concerned. 730

Happy: And the beauty of it is, Biff, it wouldn't be like a
business. We'd be out playin' ball again . . .

Biff: *(enthused)* Yeah, that's . . .

Willy: Million-dollar . . .

Happy: And you wouldn't get fed up with it, Biff. It'd be
the family again. There'd be the old honor, and
comradeship, and if you wanted to go off for a swim
or somethin'—well, you'd do it! Without some smart
cooky gettin' up ahead of you!

Willy: Lick the world! You guys together could absolutely 735
lick the civilized world.

Biff: I'll see Oliver tomorrow. Hap, if we could work that
out . . .

Linda: Maybe things are beginning to—

Willy: *(wildly enthused, to Linda)* Stop interrupting! *(To
Biff.)* But don't wear sport jacket and slacks when
you see Oliver.

Biff: No, I'll—

Willy: A business suit, and talk as little as possible, and 740
don't crack any jokes.

Biff: He did like me. Always liked me.

Linda: He loved you!

Willy: *(to Linda)* Will you stop! *(To Biff.)* Walk in very
serious. You are not applying for a boy's job. Money

is to pass. Be quiet, fine, and serious. Everybody likes a kidder, but nobody lends him money.

Happy: I'll try to get some myself, Biff. I'm sure I can.

Willy: I can see great things for you, kids, I think your troubles are over. But remember, start big and you'll end big. Ask for fifteen. How much you gonna ask for? 745

Biff: Gee, I don't know—

Willy: And don't say "Gee." "Gee" is a boy's word. A man walking in for fifteen thousand dollars does not say "Gee!"

Biff: Ten, I think, would be top though.

Willy: Don't be so modest. You always started too low. Walk in with a big laugh. Don't look worried. Start off with a couple of your good stories to lighten things up. It's not what you say, it's how you say it—because personality always wins the day.

Linda: Oliver always thought the highest of him— 750

Willy: Will you let me talk?

Biff: Don't yell at her, Pop, will ya?

Willy: (angrily) I was talking, wasn't I!

Biff: I don't like you yelling at her all the time, and I'm tellin' you, that's all.

Willy: What're you, takin' over this house? 755

Linda: Willy—

Willy: (turning on her) Don't take his side all the time, goddammit!

Biff: (furiously) Stop yelling at her!

Willy: (suddenly pulling on his cheek, beaten down, guilt ridden) Give my best to Bill Oliver—he may remember me. (He exits through the living room doorway.)

Linda: (her voice subdued) What'd you have to start that for? (Biff turns away.) You see how sweet he was as soon as you talked hopefully? (She goes over to Biff.) Come up and say good night to him. Don't let him go to bed that way. 760

Happy: Come on, Biff, let's buck him up.

Linda: Please, dear. Just say good night. It takes so little to make him happy. Come. (She goes through the living room doorway, calling upstairs from within the living room.) Your pajamas are hanging in the bathroom, Willy!

Happy: (looking toward where Linda went out) What a woman! They broke the mold when they made her. You know that, Biff?

Biff: He's off salary. My God, working on commission!

Happy: Well, let's face it: he's no hot-shot selling man. Except that sometimes, you have to admit, he's a sweet personality. 765

Biff: (deciding) Lend me ten bucks, will ya? I want to buy some new ties.

Happy: I'll take you to a place I know. Beautiful stuff. Wear one of my striped shirts tomorrow.

Biff: She got gray. Mom got awful old. Gee, I'm gonna go in to Oliver tomorrow and knock him for a—

Happy: Come on up. Tell that to Dad. Let's give him a whirl. Come on.

Biff: (steamed up) You know, with ten thousand bucks, boy! 770

Happy: (as they go into the living room) That's the talk, Biff, that's the first time I've heard the old confidence out of you! (From within the living room, fading off.) You're gonna live with me, kid, and any babe you want you just say the word . . . (The last lines are hardly heard. They are mounting the stairs to their parents' bedroom.)

Linda: (entering her bedroom and addressing Willy, who is in the bathroom. She is straightening the bed for him) Can you do anything about the shower? It drips.

Willy: (from the bathroom) All of a sudden everything falls to pieces! Goddam plumbing, oughta be sued, those people. I hardly finished putting it in and the thing . . . (His words rumble off.)

Linda: I'm just wondering if Oliver will remember him. You think he might?

Willy: (coming out of the bathroom in his pajamas) Remember him? What's the matter with you, you crazy? If he'd've stayed with Oliver he'd be on top by now! Wait'll Oliver gets a look at him. You don't know the average caliber any more. The average young man today—(he is getting into bed)—is got a caliber of zero. Greatest thing in the world for him was to bum around. 775

Biff and Happy enter the bedroom. Slight pause.

Willy: (stops short, looking at Biff) Glad to hear it, boy.

Happy: He wanted to say good night to you, sport.

Willy: (to Biff) Yeah. Knock him dead, boy. What'd you want to tell me?

Biff: Just take it easy, Pop. Good night. (He turns to go.)

Willy: (unable to resist) And if anything falls off the desk while you're talking to him—like a package or something—don't you pick it up. They have office boys for that. 780

Linda: I'll make a big breakfast—

Willy: Will you let me finish? (To Biff.) Tell him you were in the business in the West. Not farm work.

Biff: All right, Dad.

Linda: I think everything—

Willy: (going right through her speech) And don't under-sell yourself. No less than fifteen thousand dollars. 785

Biff: (unable to bear him) Okay. Good night, Mom. (He starts moving.)

Willy: Because you got a greatness in you, Biff, remember that. You got all kinds a greatness . . . (He lies back, exhausted. Biff walks out.)

Linda: (calling after Biff) Sleep well, darling!

Happy: I'm gonna get married, Mom. I wanted to tell you.

Linda: Go to sleep, dear. 790

Happy: (going) I just wanted to tell you.

Willy: Keep up the good work. (Happy exits.) God . . . remember that Ebbets Field game? The championship of the city?

Linda: Just rest. Should I sing to you?

Willy: Yeah. Sing to me. *(Linda hums a soft lullaby.)* When that team came out—he was the tallest, remember?

Linda: Oh, yes. And in gold. 795

Biff enters the darkened kitchen, takes a cigarette, and leaves the house. He comes downstage into a golden pool of light. He smokes, staring at the night.

Willy: Like a young god. Hercules—something like that. And the sun, the sun all around him. Remember how he waved to me? Right up from the field, with the representatives of three colleges standing by? And the buyers I brought, and the cheers when he came out—Loman, Loman, Loman! God Almighty, he'll be great yet. A star like that, magnificent, can never really fade away!

The light on Willy is fading. The gas heater begins to glow through the kitchen wall, near the stairs, a blue flame beneath red coils.

Linda: *(timidly)* Willy, dear, what has he got against you?

Willy: I'm so tired. Don't talk any more.

Biff slowly returns to the kitchen. He stops, stares toward the heater.

Linda: Will you ask Howard to let you work in New York?

Willy: First thing in the morning. Everything'll be all 800 right.

Biff reaches behind the heater and draws out a length of rubber tubing. He is horrified and turns his head toward Willy's room, still dimly lit, from which the strains of Linda's desperate but monotonous humming rise.

Willy: *(staring through the window into the moonlight)* Gee, look at the moon moving between the buildings!

Biff wraps the tubing around his hand and quickly goes up the stairs. Curtain.

ACT 2

Music is heard, gay and bright. The curtain rises as the music fades away. Willy, in shirt sleeves, is sitting at the kitchen table, sipping coffee, his hat in his lap. Linda is filling his cup when she can.

Willy: Wonderful coffee. Meal in itself.

Linda: Can I make you some eggs?

Willy: No. Take a breath.

Linda: You look so rested, dear.

Willy: I slept like a dead one. First time in months. 5 Imagine, sleeping till ten on a Tuesday morning. Boys left nice and early, heh?

Linda: They were out of here by eight o'clock.

Willy: Good work!

Linda: It was so thrilling to see them leaving together. I can't get over the shaving lotion in this house.

Willy: *(smiling)* Mmm—

Linda: Biff was very changed this morning. His whole 10 attitude seemed to be hopeful. He couldn't wait to get downtown to see Oliver.

Willy: He's heading for a change. There's no question, there simply are certain men that take longer to get—solidified. How did he dress?

Linda: His blue suit. He's so handsome in that suit. He could be a—anything in that suit!

Willy gets up from the table. Linda holds his jacket for him.

Willy: There's no question, no question at all. Gee, on the way home tonight I'd like to buy some seeds.

Linda: *(laughing)* That'd be wonderful. But not enough sun gets back there. Nothing'll grow any more.

Willy: You wait, kid, before it's all over we're gonna get a 15 little place out in the country, and I'll raise some vegetables, a couple of chickens . . .

Linda: You'll do it yet, dear.

Willy walks out of his jacket. Linda follows him.

Willy: And they'll get married, and come for a weekend. I'd build a little guest house. 'Cause I got so many fine tools, all I'd need would be a little lumber and some peace of mind.

Linda: *(joyfully)* I sewed the lining . . .

Willy: I could build two guest houses, so they'd both come. Did he decide how much he's going to ask Oliver for?

Linda: *(getting him into the jacket)* He didn't mention it, 20 but I imagine ten or fifteen thousand. You going to talk to Howard today?

Willy: Yeah. I'll put it to him straight and simple. He'll just have to take me off the road.

Linda: And Willy, don't forget to ask for a little advance, because we've got the insurance premium. It's the grace period now.

Willy: That's a hundred . . .?

Linda: A hundred and eight, sixty-eight. Because we're a little short again.

Willy: Why are we short? 25

Linda: Well, you had the motor job on the car . . .

Willy: That goddam Studebaker!

Linda: And you got one more payment on the refrigerator . . .

Willy: But it just broke again!

Linda: Well, it's old, dear. 30

Willy: I told you we should've bought a well-advertised machine. Charley bought a General Electric and it's twenty years old and it's still good, that son-of-a-bitch.

Linda: But, Willy—

Willy: Whoever heard of a Hastings refrigerator? Once in my life I would like to own something outright before it's broken! I'm always in a race with the junkyard! I just finished paying for the car and it's on its last legs. The refrigerator consumes belts like a goddam maniac. They time those things. They time them so when you finally paid for them, they're used up.

Linda: (buttoning up his jacket as he unbuttons it) All told, about two hundred dollars would carry us, dear. But that includes the last payment on the mortgage. After this payment, Willy, the house belongs to us.

Willy: It's twenty-five years! 35

Linda: Biff was nine years old when we bought it.

Willy: Well, that's a great thing. To weather a twenty-five year mortgage is—

Linda: It's an accomplishment.

Willy: All the cement, the lumber, the reconstruction I put in this house! There ain't a crack to be found in it any more.

Linda: Well, it served its purpose. 40

Willy: What purpose? Some stranger'll come along, move in, and that's that. If only Biff would take this house, and raise a family . . . (He starts to go.) Good-by, I'm late.

Linda: (suddenly remembering) Oh, I forgot! You're supposed to meet them for dinner.

Willy: Me?

Linda: At Frank's Chop House on Forty-eighth near Sixth Avenue.

Willy: Is that so! How about you? 45

Linda: No, just the three of you. They're gonna blow you to a big meal!

Willy: Don't say! Who thought of that?

Linda: Biff came to me this morning, Willy, and he said, "Tell Dad, we want to blow him to a big meal." Be there six o'clock. You and your two boys are going to have dinner.

Willy: Gee whiz! That's really somethin'. I'm gonna knock Howard for a loop, kid. I'll get an advance, and I'll come home with a New York job. Goddammit, now I'm gonna do it!

Linda: Oh, that's the spirit, Willy! 50

Willy: I will never get behind a wheel the rest of my life!

Linda: It's changing, Willy, I can feel it changing!

Willy: Beyond a question. G'by, I'm late. (He starts to go again.)

Linda: (calling after him as she runs to the kitchen table for a handkerchief) You got your glasses?

Willy: (feels for them, then comes back in) Yeah, yeah, got 55 my glasses.

Linda: (giving him the handkerchief) And a handkerchief.

Willy: Yeah, handkerchief.

Linda: And your saccharine?

Willy: Yeah, my saccharine.

Linda: Be careful on the subway stairs. 60

She kisses him, and a silk stocking is seen hanging from her hand. Willy notices it.

Willy: Will you stop mending stockings? At least while I'm in the house. It gets me nervous. I can't tell you. Please.

Linda hides the stocking in her hand as she follows Willy across the forestage in front of the house.

Linda: Remember, Frank's Chop House.

Willy: (passing the apron) Maybe beets would grow out there.

Linda: (laughing) But you tried so many times.

Willy: Yeah. Well, don't work hard today. (He disappears 65 around the right corner of the house.)

Linda: Be careful!

As Willy vanishes, Linda waves to him. Suddenly the phone rings. She runs across the stage and into the kitchen and lifts it.

Linda: Hello? Oh, Biff! I'm so glad you called, I just . . . Yes, sure, I just told him. Yes, he'll be there for dinner at six o'clock, I didn't forget. Listen, I was just dying to tell you. You know that little rubber pipe I told you about? That he connected to the gas heater? I finally decided to go down the cellar this morning and take it away and destroy it. But it's gone! Imagine? He took it away himself, it isn't there! (She listens.) When? Oh, then you took it. Oh—nothing, it's just that I'd hoped he'd taken it away himself. Oh, I'm not worried, darling, because this morning he left in such high spirits, it was like the old days! I'm not afraid any more. Did Mr. Oliver see you? . . . Well, you wait there then. And make a nice impression on him, darling. Just don't perspire too much before you see him. And have a nice time with Dad. He may have big news too! . . . That's right, a New York job. And be sweet to him tonight, dear. Be loving to him. Because he's only a little boat looking for a harbor. (She is trembling with sorrow and joy.) Oh, that's wonderful, Biff, you'll save his life. Thanks, darling. Just put your arm around him when he comes into the restaurant. Give him a smile. That's the boy . . . Good-by, dear. . . . You got your comb? . . . That's fine. Good-by, Biff dear.

In the middle of her speech, Howard Wagner, thirty-six, wheels in a small typewriter table on which is a wire-recording machine and proceeds to plug it in. This is on the left forestage. Light slowly fades on Linda as it rises on Howard. Howard is intent on threading the machine and only glances over his shoulder as Willy appears.

Willy: Pst! Pst!

Howard: Hello, Willy, come in.

Willy: Like to have a little talk with you, Howard. 70

Howard: Sorry to keep you waiting. I'll be with you in a minute.

Willy: What's that, Howard?

Howard: Didn't you ever see one of these? Wire recorder.

Willy: Oh. Can we talk a minute?

Howard: Records things. Just got delivery yesterday. Been 75 driving me crazy, the most terrific machine I ever saw in my life. I was up all night with it.

Willy: What do you do with it?

Howard: I bought it for dictation, but you can do anything with it. Listen to this. I had it home last night. Listen to what I picked up. The first one is my daughter. Get this. *(He flicks the switch and "Roll out the Barrel" is heard being whistled.)* Listen to that kid whistle.

Willy: That is lifelike, isn't it?

Howard: Seven years old. Get that tone.

Willy: Ts, ts. Like to ask a little favor if you . . . 80

The whistling breaks off, and the voice of Howard's Daughter is heard.

His Daughter: "Now you, Daddy."

Howard: She's crazy for me! *(Again the same song is whistled.)* That's me! Ha! *(He winks.)*

Willy: You're very good!

The whistling breaks off again. The machine runs silent for a moment.

Howard: Sh! Get this now, this is my son.

His Son: "The capital of Alabama is Montgomery; the 85 capital of Arizona is Phoenix; the capital of Arkansas is Little Rock; the capital of California is Sacramento . . ." *(And on, and on.)*

Howard: *(holding up five fingers)* Five years old, Willy!

Willy: He'll make an announcer some day!

His Son: *(continuing)* "The capital . . ."

Howard: Get that—alphabetical order! *(The machine breaks off suddenly.)* Wait a minute. The maid kicked the plug out.

Willy: It certainly is a— 90

Howard: Sh, for God's sake!

His Son: "It's nine o'clock, Bulova watch time. So I have to go to sleep."

Willy: That really is—

Howard: Wait a minute! The next is my wife.

They wait.

Howard's Voice: "Go on, say something." *(Pause.)* "Well, 95 you gonna talk?"

His Wife: "I can't think of anything."

Howard's Voice: "Well, talk—it's turning."

His Wife: *(shyly, beaten)* "Hello." *(Silence.)* "Oh, Howard, I can't talk into this . . ."

Howard: *(snapping the machine off)* That was my wife.

Willy: That is a wonderful machine. Can we— 100

Howard: I tell you, Willy, I'm gonna take my camera, and my bandsaw, and all my hobbies, and out they go. This is the most fascinating relaxation I ever found.

Willy: I think I'll get one myself.

Howard: Sure, they're only a hundred and a half. You can't do without it. Supposing you wanna hear Jack Benny, see? But you can't be at home at that hour. So you tell the maid to turn the radio on when Jack Benny comes on, and this automatically goes on with the radio . . .

Willy: And when you come home you . . .

Howard: You can come home twelve o'clock, one 105 o'clock, any time you like, and you get yourself a Coke and sit yourself down, throw the switch, and there's Jack Benny's program in the middle of the night!

Willy: I'm definitely going to get one. Because lots of time I'm on the road, and I think to myself, what I must be missing on the radio!

Howard: Don't you have a radio in the car?

Willy: Well, yeah, but who ever thinks of turning it on?

Howard: Say, aren't you supposed to be in Boston?

Willy: That's what I want to talk to you about, Howard. 110 You got a minute?

He draws a chair in from the wing.

Howard: What happened? What're you doing here?

Willy: Well . . .

Howard: You didn't crack up again, did you?

Willy: Oh, no. No . . .

Howard: Geez, you had me worried there for a minute. 115 What's the trouble?

Willy: Well, to tell you the truth, Howard, I've come to the decision that I'd rather not travel any more.

Howard: Not travel! Well, what'll you do?

Willy: Remember, Christmas time, when you had the party here? You said you'd try to think of some spot for me here in town.

Howard: With us?

Willy: Well, sure.

Howard: Oh, yeah, yeah. I remember. Well, I couldn't 120 think of anything for you, Willy.

Willy: I tell ya, Howard. The kids are all grown up, y'know. I don't need much any more. If I could take home—well, sixty-five dollars a week, I could swing it.

Howard: Yeah, but Willy, see I—

Willy: I tell ya why, Howard. Speaking frankly and between the two of us, y'know—I'm just a little tired.

Howard: Oh, I could understand that, Willy. But you're a 125 road man, Willy, and we do a road business. We've only got a half-dozen salesmen on the floor here.

Willy: God knows, Howard, I never asked a favor of any man. But I was with the firm when your father used to carry you in here in his arms.

Howard: I know that, Willy, but—

Willy: Your father came to me the day you were born and asked me what I thought of the name of Howard, may he rest in peace.

Howard: I appreciate that, Willy, but there just is no spot here for you. If I had a spot I'd slam you right in, but I just don't have a single, solitary spot.

He looks for his lighter. Willy has picked it up and gives it to him. Pause.

Willy: *(with increasing anger)* Howard, all I need to set my table is fifty dollars a week.

Howard: But where am I going to put you, kid?

Willy: Look, it isn't a question of whether I can sell merchandise, is it?

Howard: No, but it's a business, kid, and everybody's gotta pull his own weight.

Willy: *(desperately)* Just let me tell you a story, Howard—

Howard: 'Cause you gotta admit, business is business.

Willy: *(angrily)* Business is definitely business, but just listen for a minute. You don't understand this. When I was a boy—eighteen, nineteen—I was already on the road. And there was a question in my mind as to whether selling had a future for me. Because in those days I had a yearning to go to Alaska. See, there were three gold strikes in one month in Alaska, and I felt like going out. Just for the ride, you might say.

Howard: *(barely interested)* Don't say.

Willy: Oh, yeah, my father lived many years in Alaska. He was an adventurous man. We've got quite a little streak of self-reliance in our family. I thought I'd go out with my older brother and try to locate him, and maybe settle in the North with the old man. And I was almost decided to go, when I met a salesman in the Parker House. His name was Dave Singleman. And he was eighty-four years old, and he'd drummed merchandise in thirty-one states. And old Dave, he'd go up to his room, y'understand, put on his green velvet slippers—I'll never forget—and pick up his phone and call the buyers, and without ever leaving his room, at the age of eighty-four, he made his living. And when I saw that, I realized that selling was the greatest career a man could want. 'Cause what could be more satisfying than to be able to go, at the age of eighty-four, into twenty or thirty different cities, and pick up a phone, and be remembered and loved and helped by so many different people? Do you know? when he died—and by the way he died the death of a salesman, in his green velvet slippers in the smoker of the New York, New Haven and Hartford, going into Boston—when he died, hundreds of salesmen and buyers were at his funeral. Things were sad on a lotta trains for months after that. *(He stands up. Howard has not looked at him.)* In those days there was personality in it, Howard. There was respect, and comradeship, and gratitude in it. Today, it's all cut and dried, and there's no chance for bringing friendship to bear—or personality. You see what I mean? They don't know me any more.

Howard: *(moving away, to the right)* That's just the thing, Willy.

Willy: If I had forty dollars a week—that's all I'd need. Forty dollars, Howard.

Howard: Kid, I can't take blood from a stone, I—

Willy: *(desperation is on him now)* Howard, the year Al Smith was nominated, your father came to me and—

Howard: *(starting to go off)* I've got to see some people, kid.

Willy: *(stopping him)* I'm talking about your father! There were promises made across this desk! You mustn't tell me you've got people to see—I put thirty-four years into this firm, Howard, and now I can't pay my insurance! You can't eat the orange and throw the peel away—a man is not a piece of fruit! *(After a pause.)* Now pay attention. Your father—in 1928 I had a big year. I averaged a hundred and seventy dollars a week in commissions.

Howard: *(impatiently)* Now, Willy, you never averaged—

Willy: *(banging his hand on the desk)* I averaged a hundred and seventy dollars a week in the year of 1928! And your father came to me—or rather, I was in the office here—it was right over this desk—and he put his hand on my shoulder—

Howard: *(getting up)* You'll have to excuse me, Willy, I gotta see some people. Pull yourself together. *(Going out.)* I'll be back in a little while.

On Howard's exit, the light on his chair grows very bright and strange.

Willy: Pull myself together! What the hell did I say to him? My God, I was yelling at him! How could I! *(Willy breaks off, staring at the light, which occupies the chair, animating it. He approaches this chair, standing across the desk from it.)* Frank, Frank, don't you remember what you told me that time? How you put your hand on my shoulder, and Frank . . . *(He leans on the desk and as he speaks the dead man's name he accidentally switches on the recorder, and instantly—)*

Howard's Son: ". . . of New York is Albany. The capital of Ohio is Cincinnati, the capital of Rhode Island is . . ." *(The recitation continues.)*

Willy: *(leaping away with fright, shouting)* Ha! Howard! Howard! Howard!

Howard: *(rushing in)* What happened?

Willy: *(pointing at the machine, which continues nasally, childishly, with the capital cities)* Shut it off! Shut it off!

Howard: *(pulling the plug out)* Look, Willy . . .

Willy: *(pressing his hands to his eyes)* I gotta get myself some coffee. I'll get some coffee . . .

Willy starts to walk out. Howard stops him.

Howard: *(rolling up the cord)* Willy, look . . .

Willy: I'll go to Boston.

Howard: Willy, you can't go to Boston for us.

Willy: Why can't I go?

Howard: I don't want you to represent us. I've been meaning to tell you for a long time now.

Willy: Howard, are you firing me? 160

Howard: I think you need a good long rest, Willy.

Willy: Howard—

Howard: And when you feel better, come back, and we'll see if we can work something out.

Willy: But I gotta earn money, Howard. I'm in no position—

Howard: Where are your sons? Why don't your sons give 165 you a hand?

Willy: They're working on a very big deal.

Howard: This is no time for false pride, Willy. You go to your sons and tell them that you're tired. You've got two great boys, haven't you?

Willy: Oh, no question, no question, but in the meantime . . .

Howard: Then that's that, heh?

Willy: All right, I'll go to Boston tomorrow. 170

Howard: No, no.

Willy: I can't throw myself on my sons. I'm not a cripple!

Howard: Look, kid, I'm busy this morning.

Willy: (grasping Howard's arm) Howard, you've got to let me go to Boston!

Howard: (hard, keeping himself under control) I've got a 175 line of people to see this morning. Sit down, take five minutes, and pull yourself together, and then go home, will ya? I need the office, Willy. (He starts to go, turns, remembering the recorder, starts to push off the table holding the recorder.) Oh, yeah. Whenever you can this week, stop by and drop off the samples. You'll feel better, Willy, and then come back and we'll talk. Pull yourself together, kid, there's people outside.

Howard exits, pushing the table off left. Willy stares into space, exhausted. Now the music is heard—Ben's music—first distantly, then closer, closer. As Willy speaks, Ben enters from the right. He carries valise and umbrella.

Willy: Oh, Ben, how did you do it? What is the answer? Did you wind up the Alaska deal already?

Ben: Doesn't take much time if you know what you're doing. Just a short business trip. Boarding ship in an hour. Wanted to say good-by.

Willy: Ben, I've got to talk to you.

Ben: (glancing at his watch) Haven't the time, William.

Willy: (crossing the apron to Ben) Ben, nothing's working 180 out. I don't know what to do.

Ben: Now, look here, William. I've bought timberland in Alaska and I need a man to look after things for me.

Willy: God, timberland! Me and my boys in those grand outdoors!

Ben: You've a new continent at your doorstep, William. Get out of these cities, they're full of talk and time

payments and courts of law. Screw on your fists and you can fight for a fortune up there.

Willy: Yes, yes! Linda! Linda!

Linda enters as of old, with the wash.

Linda: Oh, you're back? 185

Ben: I haven't much time.

Willy: No, wait! Linda, he's got a proposition for me in Alaska.

Linda: But you've got—(To Ben.) He's got a beautiful job here.

Willy: But in Alaska, kid, I could—

Linda: You're doing well enough, Willy! 190

Ben: (to Linda) Enough for what, my dear?

Linda: (frightened of Ben and angry at him) Don't say those things to him! Enough to be happy right here, right now. (To Willy, while Ben laughs.) Why must everybody conquer the world? You're well liked, and the boys love you, and someday—(to Ben)—why, old man Wagner told him just the other day that if he keeps it up he'll be a member of the firm, didn't he, Willy?

Willy: Sure, sure. I am building something with this firm, Ben, and if a man is building something he must be on the right track, mustn't he?

Ben: What are you building? Lay your hand on it. Where is it?

Willy: (hesitantly) That's true, Linda, there's nothing. 195

Linda: Why? (To Ben.) There's a man eighty-four years old—

Willy: That's right, Ben, that's right. When I look at that man I say, what is there to worry about?

Ben: Bah!

Willy: It's true, Ben. All he has to do is go into any city, pick up the phone, and he's making his living and you know why?

Ben: (picking up his valise) I've got to go. 200

Willy: (holding Ben back) Look at this boy!

Biff, in his high school sweater, enters carrying suitcase. Happy carries Biff's shoulder guards, gold helmet, and football pants.

Willy: Without a penny to his name, three great universities are begging for him, and from there the sky's the limit, because it's not what you do, Ben. It's who you know and the smile on your face! It's contacts, Ben, contacts! The whole wealth of Alaska passes over the lunch table at the Commodore Hotel, and that's the wonder, the wonder of this country, that a man can end with diamonds here on the basis of being liked! (He turns to Biff.) And that's why when you get out on that field today it's important. Because thousands of people will be rooting for you and loving you. (To Ben, who has again begun to leave.) And Ben! when he walks into a business office his name will sound out like a bell and all the doors will open to him! I've seen it, Ben, I've seen it a thousand times! You can't feel it with your hand like timber, but it's there!

Ben: Good-by, William.

Willy: Ben, am I right? Don't you think I'm right? I value your advice.

Ben: There's a new continent at your doorstep, William. 205 You could walk out rich. Rich. *(He is gone.)*

Willy: We'll do it here, Ben! You hear me? We're gonna do it here!

Young Bernard rushes in. The gay music of the boys is heard.

Bernard: Oh, gee, I was afraid you left already!

Willy: Why? What time is it?

Bernard: It's half-past one!

Willy: Well, come on, everybody! Ebbets Field° next stop! 210 Where's the pennants? *(He rushes through the wall-line of the kitchen and out into the living room.)*

Linda: *(to Biff)* Did you pack fresh underwear?

Biff: *(who has been limbering up)* I want to go!

Bernard: Biff, I'm carrying your helmet, ain't I?

Happy: No, I'm carrying the helmet.

Bernard: Oh, Biff, you promised me. 215

Happy: I'm carrying the helmet.

Bernard: How am I going to get in the locker room?

Linda: Let him carry the shoulder guards. *(She puts her coat and hat on in the kitchen.)*

Bernard: Can I, Biff? 'Cause I told everybody I'm going to be in the locker room.

Happy: In Ebbets Field it's the clubhouse. 220

Bernard: I meant the clubhouse. Biff!

Happy: Biff!

Biff: *(grandly, after a slight pause)* Let him carry the shoulder guards.

Happy: *(as he gives Bernard the shoulder guards)* Stay close to us now.

Willy rushes in with the pennants.

Willy: *(handing them out)* Everybody wave when Biff 225 comes out on the field. *(Happy and Bernard run off.)* You set now, boy?

The music has died away.

Biff: Ready to go, Pop. Every muscle is ready.

Willy: *(at the edge of the apron)* You realize what this means?

Biff: That's right, Pop.

Willy: *(feeling Biff's muscles)* You're comin' home this afternoon captain of the All-Scholastic Championship Team of the City of New York.

° **Ebbets Field** The home park of the Brooklyn Dodgers.

° **Red Grange** Harold Edward ("Red") Grange (1903–1991) — American football player. A running back for the New York Giants football team and the Chicago Bears, Grange was elected to the Football Hall of Fame in 1963.

Biff: I got it, Pop. And remember, pal, when I take off my 230 helmet, that touchdown is for you.

Willy: Let's go! *(He is starting out, with his arm around Biff, when Charley enters, as of old, in knickers.)* I got no room for you, Charley.

Charley: Room? For what?

Willy: In the car.

Charley: You goin' for a ride? I wanted to shoot some casino.

Willy: *(furiously)* Casino! *(Incredulously.)* Don't you 235 realize what today is?

Linda: Oh, he knows, Willy. He's just kidding you.

Willy: That's nothing to kid about!

Charley: No, Linda, what's goin' on?

Linda: He's playing in Ebbets Field.

Charley: Baseball in this weather? 240

Willy: Don't talk to him. Come on, come on! *(He is pushing them out.)*

Charley: Wait a minute, didn't you hear the news?

Willy: What?

Charley: Don't you listen to the radio? Ebbets Field just blew up.

Willy: You go to hell! *(Charley laughs. Pushing them out.)* 245 Come on, come on! We're late.

Charley: *(as they go)* Knock a homer, Biff, knock a homer!

Willy: *(the last to leave, turning to Charley)* I don't think that was funny, Charley. This is the greatest day of his life.

Charley: Willy, when are you going to grow up?

Willy: Yeah, heh? When this game is over, Charley, you'll be laughing out of the other side of your face. They'll be calling him another Red Grange.° Twenty-five thousand a year.

Charley: *(kidding)* Is that so? 250

Willy: Yeah, that's so.

Charley: Well, then, I'm sorry, Willy. But tell me something.

Willy: What?

Charley: Who is Red Grange?

Willy: Put up your hands. Goddam you, put up your 255 hands!

Charley, chuckling, shakes his head and walks away, around the left corner of the stage. Willy follows him. The music rises to a mocking frenzy.

Willy: Who the hell do you think you are, better than everybody else? You don't know everything, you big, ignorant, stupid . . . Put up your hands!

Light rises, on the right side of the forestage, on a small table in the reception room of Charley's office. Traffic sounds are heard. Bernard, now mature, sits whistling to himself. A pair of tennis rackets and an overnight bag are on the floor beside him.

Willy: *(offstage)* What are you walking away for? Don't walk away! If you're going to say something say it to my face! I know you laugh at me behind my back. You'll laugh out of the other side of your goddam face after this game. Touchdown! Touchdown! Eighty thousand people! Touchdown! Right between the goal posts.

Bernard is a quiet, earnest, but self-assured young man. Willy's voice is coming from right upstage now. Bernard lowers his feet off the table and listens. Jenny, his father's secretary, enters.

Jenny: *(distressed)* Say, Bernard, will you go out in the hall?

Bernard: What is that noise? Who is it?

Jenny: Mr. Loman. He just got off the elevator. 260

Bernard: *(getting up)* Who's he arguing with?

Jenny: Nobody. There's nobody with him. I can't deal with him any more, and your father gets all upset everytime he comes. I've got a lot of typing to do, and your father's waiting to sign it. Will you see him?

Willy: *(entering)* Touchdown! Touch— *(He sees Jenny.)* Jenny, Jenny, good to see you. How're ya? Workin'? Or still honest?

Jenny: Fine. How've you been feeling?

Willy: Not much any more, Jenny. Ha, ha! *(He is surprised to see the rackets.)* 265

Bernard: Hello, Uncle Willy.

Willy: *(almost shocked)* Bernard! Well, look who's here! *(He comes quickly, guiltily, to Bernard and warmly shakes his hand.)*

Bernard: How are you? Good to see you.

Willy: What are you doing here?

Bernard: Oh, just stopped by to see Pop. Get off my feet 270 till my train leaves. I'm going to Washington in a few minutes.

Willy: Is he in?

Bernard: Yes, he's in his office with the accountant. Sit down.

Willy: *(sitting down)* What're you going to do in Washington?

Bernard: Oh, just a case I've got there, Willy.

Willy: That so? *(indicating the rackets)* You going to play 275 tennis there?

Bernard: I'm staying with a friend who's got a court.

Willy: Don't say. His own tennis court. Must be fine people, I bet.

Bernard: They are, very nice. Dad tells me Biff's in town.

Willy: *(with a big smile)* Yeah, Biff's in. Working on a very big deal, Bernard.

Bernard: What's Biff doing? 280

Willy: Well, he's been doing very big things in the West. But he decided to establish himself here. Very big. We're having dinner. Did I hear your wife had a boy?

Bernard: That's right. Our second.

Willy: Two boys! What do you know!

Bernard: What kind of a deal has Biff got?

Willy: Well, Bill Oliver—very big sporting-goods man— 285 he wants Biff very badly. Called him in from the West. Long distance, carte blanche, special deliveries. Your friends have their own private tennis court?

Bernard: You still with the old firm, Willy?

Willy: *(after a pause)* I'm—I'm overjoyed to see how you made the grade, Bernard, overjoyed. It's an encouraging thing to see a young man really—really—Looks very good for Biff—very— *(He breaks off, then.)* Bernard— *(He is so full of emotion, he breaks off again.)*

Bernard: What is it, Willy?

Willy: *(small and alone)* What—what's the secret?

Bernard: What secret? 290

Willy: How—how did you? Why didn't he ever catch on?

Bernard: I wouldn't know that, Willy.

Willy: *(confidentially, desperately)* You were his friend, his boyhood friend. There's something I don't understand about it. His life ended after that Ebbets Field game. From the age of seventeen nothing good ever happened to him.

Bernard: He never trained himself for anything.

Willy: But he did, he did. After high school he took so 295 many correspondence courses. Radio mechanics; television; God knows what, and never made the slightest mark.

Bernard: *(taking off his glasses)* Willy, do you want to talk candidly?

Willy: *(rising, faces Bernard)* I regard you as a very brilliant man, Bernard. I value your advice.

Bernard: Oh, the hell with the advice, Willy. I couldn't advise you. There's just one thing I've always wanted to ask you. When he was supposed to graduate, and the math teacher flunked him—

Willy: Oh, that son-of-a-bitch ruined his life.

Bernard: Yeah, but, Willy, all he had to do was go to 300 summer school and make up that subject.

Willy: That's right, that's right.

Bernard: Did you tell him not to go to summer school?

Willy: Me? I begged him to go. I ordered him to go!

Bernard: Then why wouldn't he go?

Willy: Why? Why! Bernard, that question has been 305 trailing me like a ghost for the last fifteen years. He flunked the subject, and laid down and died like a hammer hit him!

Bernard: Take it easy, kid.

Willy: Let me talk to you—I got nobody to talk to. Bernard, Bernard, was it my fault? Y'see? It keeps going around in my mind, maybe I did something to him. I got nothing to give him.

Bernard: Don't take it so hard.

Willy: Why did he lay down? What is the story there? You were his friend!

Bernard: Willy, I remember, it was June, and our grades 310 came out. And he'd flunked math.

Willy: That son-of-a-bitch!

Bernard: No, it wasn't right then. Biff just got very angry, I remember, and he was ready to enroll in summer school.

Willy: *(surprised)* He was?

Bernard: He wasn't beaten by it at all. But then, Willy, he disappeared from the block for almost a month. And

I got the idea that he'd gone up to New England to see you. Did he have a talk with you then?

Willy stares in silence.

Bernard: Willy? 315

Willy: *(with a strong edge of resentment in his voice)* Yeah, he came to Boston. What about it?

Bernard: Well, just that when he came back—I'll never forget this, it always mystifies me. Because I'd thought so well of Biff, even though he'd always taken advantage of me. I loved him, Willy, y'know? And he came back after that month and took his sneakers—remember those sneakers with "University of Virginia" printed on them? He was so proud of those, wore them every day. And he took them down in the cellar, and burned them up in the furnace. We had a fist fight. It lasted at least half an hour. Just the two of us, punching each other down the cellar, and crying right through it. I've often thought of how strange it was that I knew he'd given up his life. What happened in Boston, Willy?

Willy looks at him as at an intruder.

Bernard: I just bring it up because you asked me.

Willy: *(angrily)* Nothing. What do you mean, "What happened?" What's that got to do with anything?

Bernard: Well, don't get sore. 320

Willy: What are you trying to do, blame it on me? If a boy lays down is that my fault?

Bernard: Now, Willy, don't get—

Willy: Well, don't—don't talk to me that way! What does that mean, "What happened?"

Charley enters. He is in his vest, and he carries a bottle of bourbon.

Charley: Hey, you're going to miss that train. *(He waves the bottle.)*

Bernard: Yeah, I'm going. *(He takes the bottle.)* Thanks, 325
Pop. *(He picks up his rackets and bag.)* Good-by, Willy, and don't worry about it. You know, "If at first you don't succeed . . ."

Willy: Yes, I believe in that.

Bernard: But sometimes, Willy, it's better for a man just to walk away.

Willy: Walk away?

Bernard: That's right.

Willy: But if you can't walk away? 330

Bernard: *(after a slight pause)* I guess that's when it's tough. *(Extending his hand.)* Good-by, Willy.

Willy: *(shaking Bernard's hand)* Good-by, boy.

Charley: *(an arm on Bernard's shoulder)* How do you like this kid? Gonna argue a case in front of the Supreme Court.

Bernard: *(protesting)* Pop!

Willy: *(genuinely shocked, pained, and happy)* No! The 335
Supreme Court!

Bernard: I gotta run, 'By, Dad!

Charley: Knock 'em dead, Bernard!

Bernard goes off.

Willy: *(as Charley takes out his wallet)* The Supreme Court! And he didn't even mention it!

Charley: *(counting out money on the desk)* He don't have to—he's gonna do it.

Willy: And you never told him what to do, did you? You 340
never took any interest in him.

Charley: My salvation is that I never took any interest in anything. There's some money—fifty dollars. I got an accountant inside.

Willy: Charley, look . . . *(With difficulty.)* I got my insurance to pay. If you can manage it—I need a hundred and ten dollars.

Charley doesn't reply for a moment; merely stops moving.

Willy: I'd draw it from my bank but Linda would know, and I . . .

Charley: Sit down, Willy.

Willy: *(moving toward the chair)* I'm keeping an account 345
of everything, remember. I'll pay every penny back. *(He sits.)*

Charley: Now listen to me, Willy.

Willy: I want you to know I appreciate . . .

Charley: *(sitting down on the table)* Willy, what're you doin'? What the hell is goin' on in your head?

Willy: Why? I'm simply . . .

Charley: I offered you a job. You can make fifty dollars a 350
week. And I won't send you on the road.

Willy: I've got a job.

Charley: Without pay? What kind of a job is a job without pay? *(He rises.)* Now, look, kid, enough is enough. I'm no genius but I know when I'm being insulted.

Willy: Insulted!

Charley: Why don't you want to work for me?

Willy: What's the matter with you? I've got a job. 355

Charley: Then what're you walkin' in here every week for?

Willy: *(getting up)* Well, if you don't want me to walk in here—

Charley: I am offering you a job.

Willy: I don't want your goddam job!

Charley: When the hell are you going to grow up? 360

Willy: *(furiously)* You big ignoramus, if you say that to me again I'll rap you one! I don't care how big you are! *(He's ready to fight.)*

Pause.

Charley: *(kindly, going to him)* How much do you need, Willy?

Willy: Charley, I'm strapped. I'm strapped. I don't know what to do. I was just fired.

Charley: Howard fired you?

Willy: That snotnose. Imagine that? I named him. I named him Howard. 365

Charley: Willy, when're you gonna realize that them things don't mean anything? You named him Howard, but you can't sell that. The only thing you got in this world is what you can sell. And the funny thing is that you're a salesman, and you don't know that.

Willy: I've always tried to think otherwise, I guess. I always felt that if a man was impressive, and well liked, that nothing—

Charley: Why must everybody like you? Who liked J. P. Morgan?° Was he impressive? In a Turkish bath he'd look like a butcher. But with his pockets on he was very well liked. Now listen, Willy, I know you don't like me, and nobody can say I'm in love with you, but I'll give you a job because—just for the hell of it, put it that way. Now what do you say?

Willy: I—I just can't work for you, Charley.

Charley: What're you, jealous of me? 370

Willy: I can't work for you, that's all, don't ask me why.

Charley: (angered, takes out more bills) You been jealous of me all your life, you damned fool! Here, pay your insurance. (He puts the money in Willy's hand.)

Willy: I'm keeping strict accounts.

Charley: I've got some work to do. Take care of yourself. And pay your insurance.

Willy: (moving to the right) Funny, y'know? After all the highways, and the trains, and the appointments, and the years, you end up worth more dead than alive. 375

Charley: Willy, nobody's worth nothin' dead. (After a slight pause.) Did you hear what I said?

Willy stands still, dreaming.

Charley: Willy!

Willy: Apologize to Bernard for me when you see him. I didn't mean to argue with him. He's a fine boy. They're all fine boys, and they'll end up big—all of them. Someday they'll all play tennis together. Wish me luck, Charley. He saw Bill Oliver today.

Charley: Good luck.

Willy: (on the verge of tears) Charley, you're the only friend I got. Isn't that a remarkable thing? (He goes out.) 380

Charley: Jesus!

Charley stares after him a moment and follows. All light blacks out. Suddenly raucous music is heard, and a red glow rises behind the screen at right. Stanley, a young waiter, appears, carrying a table, followed by Happy, who is carrying two chairs.

Stanley: (putting the table down) That's all right, Mr. Loman, I can handle it myself. (He turns and takes the chairs from Happy and places them at the table.)

Happy: (glancing around) Oh, this is better.

Stanley: Sure, in the front there you're in the middle of all kinds a noise. Whenever you got a party, Mr. Loman, you just tell me and I'll put you back here. Y'know, there's a lotta people they don't like it private, because when they go out they like to see a lotta action around them because they're sick and tired to stay in the house by theirself. But I know you, you ain't from Hackensack. You know what I mean?

Happy: (sitting down) So, how's it coming, Stanley? 385

Stanley: Ah, it's a dog's life. I only wish during the war they'd a took me in the Army. I coulda been dead by now.

Happy: My brother's back, Stanley.

Stanley: Oh, he come back, heh? From the Far West.

Happy: Yeah, big cattle man, my brother, so treat him right. And my father's coming too.

Stanley: Oh, your father too! 390

Happy: You got a couple of nice lobsters?

Stanley: Hundred per cent, big.

Happy: I want them with the claws.

Stanley: Don't worry, I don't give you no mice. (Happy laughs.) How about some wine? It'll put a head on the meal.

Happy: No. You remember, Stanley, that recipe I brought you from overseas? With the champagne in it? 395

Stanley: Oh, yeah, sure. I still got it tacked up yet in the kitchen. But that'll have to cost a buck apiece anyways.

Happy: That's all right.

Stanley: What'd you, hit a number or somethin'?

Happy: No, it's a little celebration. My brother is—I think he pulled off a big deal today. I think we're going into business together.

Stanley: Great! That's the best for you. Because a family business, you know what I mean?—that's the best. 400

Happy: That's what I think.

Stanley: 'Cause what's the difference? Somebody steals? It's in the family. Know what I mean? (Sotto voce.) Like this bartender here. The boss is goin' crazy what kinda leak he's got in the cash register. You put it in but it don't come out.

Happy: (raising his head) Sh!

Stanley: What?

Happy: You notice I wasn't lookin' right or left, was I? 405

Stanley: No.

Happy: And my eyes are closed.

Stanley: So what's the—

Happy: Strudel's comin'.

Stanley: (catching on, looks around) Ah, no, there's no— 410

° **J. P. Morgan** John Pierpont Morgan (1837–1913) — American financier.

He breaks off as a furred, lavishly dressed Girl enters and sits at the next table. Both follow her with their eyes.

Stanley: Geez, how'd ya know?

Happy: I got radar or something. *(Staring directly at her profile.)* Oooooooo . . . Stanley.

Stanley: I think that's for you, Mr. Loman.

Happy: Look at that mouth. Oh, God. And the binoculars.

Stanley: Geez, you got a life, Mr. Loman.   415

Happy: Wait on her.

Stanley: *(going to The Girl's table)* Would you like a menu, ma'am?

Girl: I'm expecting someone, but I'd like a—

Happy: Why don't you bring her—excuse me, miss, do you mind? I sell champagne, and I'd like you to try my brand. Bring her a champagne, Stanley.

Girl: That's awfully nice of you.   420

Happy: Don't mention it. It's all company money. *(He laughs.)*

Girl: That's a charming product to be selling, isn't it?

Happy: Oh, gets to be like everything else. Selling is selling, y'know.

Girl: I suppose.

Happy: You don't happen to sell, do you?   425

Girl: No, I don't sell.

Happy: Would you object to a compliment from a stranger? You ought to be on a magazine cover.

Girl: *(looking at him a little archly)* I have been.

Stanley comes in with a glass of champagne.

Happy: What'd I say before, Stanley? You see? She's a cover girl.

Stanley: Oh, I could see, I could see.   430

Happy: *(to The Girl)* What magazine?

Girl: Oh, a lot of them. *(She takes the drink.)* Thank you.

Happy: You know what they say in France, don't you? "Champagne is the drink of the complexion"—Hya, Biff!

Biff has entered and sits with Happy.

Biff: Hello, kid. Sorry I'm late.

Happy: I just got here. Uh, Miss—?   435

Girl: Forsythe.

Happy: Miss Forsythe, this is my brother.

Biff: Is Dad here?

Happy: His name is Biff. You might've heard of him. Great football player.

Girl: Really? What team?   440

Happy: Are you familiar with football?

Girl: No, I'm afraid I'm not.

Happy: Biff is quarterback with the New York Giants.

Girl: Well, that is nice, isn't it? *(She drinks.)*

Happy: Good health.   445

Girl: I'm happy to meet you.

Happy: That's my name. Hap. It's really Harold, but at West Point they called me Happy.

Girl: *(now really impressed)* Oh, I see. How do you do? *(She turns her profile.)*

Biff: Isn't Dad coming?

Happy: You want her?   450

Biff: Oh, I could never make that.

Happy: I remember the time that idea would never come into your head. Where's the old confidence, Biff?

Biff: I just saw Oliver—

Happy: Wait a minute. I've got to see that old confidence again. Do you want her? She's on call.

Biff: Oh, no. *(He turns to look at The Girl.)*   455

Happy: I'm telling you. Watch this. *(Turning to The Girl.)* Honey? *(She turns to him.)* Are you busy?

Girl: Well, I am . . . but I could make a phone call.

Happy: Do that, will you, honey? And see if you can get a friend. We'll be here for a while. Biff is one of the greatest football players in the country.

Girl: *(standing up)* Well, I'm certainly happy to meet you.

Happy: Come back soon.   460

Girl: I'll try.

Happy: Don't try, honey, try hard.

The Girl exits. Stanley follows, shaking his head in bewildered admiration.

Happy: Isn't that a shame now? A beautiful girl like that? That's why I can't get married. There's not a good woman in a thousand. New York is loaded with them, kid!

Biff: Hap, look—

Happy: I told you she was on call!   465

Biff: *(strangely unnerved)* Cut it out, will ya? I want to say something to you.

Happy: Did you see Oliver?

Biff: I saw him all right. Now look, I want to tell Dad a couple of things and I want you to help me.

Happy: What? Is he going to back you?

Biff: Are you crazy? You're out of your goddam head,   470 you know that?

Happy: Why? What happened?

Biff: *(breathlessly)* I did a terrible thing today, Hap. It's been the strangest day I ever went through. I'm all numb, I swear.

Happy: You mean he wouldn't see you?

Biff: Well, I waited six hours for him, see? All day. Kept sending my name in. Even tried to date his secretary so she'd get me to him, but no soap.

Happy: Because you're not showin' the old confidence,   475 Biff. He remembered you, didn't he?

Biff: *(stopping Happy with a gesture)* Finally, about five o'clock, he comes out. Didn't remember who I was or anything. I felt like such an idiot, Hap.

Happy: Did you tell him my Florida idea?

Biff: He walked away. I saw him for one minute. I got so mad I could've torn the walls down! How the hell did I ever get the idea I was a salesman there? I even believed myself that I'd been a salesman for him! And then he gave me one look and—I realized what a ridiculous lie my whole life has been! We've been talking in a dream for fifteen years. I was a shipping clerk.

Happy: What'd you do?

Biff: *(with great tension and wonder)* Well, he left, see. 480 And the secretary went out. I was all alone in the waiting-room. I don't know what came over me, Hap. The next thing I know I'm in his office—paneled walls, everything. I can't explain it. I—Hap, I took his fountain pen.

Happy: Geez, did he catch you?

Biff: I ran out. I ran down all eleven flights. I ran and ran and ran.

Happy: That was an awful dumb—what'd you do that for?

Biff: *(agonized)* I don't know, I just—wanted to take something, I don't know. You gotta help me, Hap. I'm gonna tell Pop.

Happy: You crazy? What for? 485

Biff: Hap, he's got to understand that I'm not the man somebody lends that kind of money to. He thinks I've been spiting him all these years and it's eating him up.

Happy: That's just it. You tell him something nice.

Biff: I can't.

Happy: Say you got a lunch date with Oliver tomorrow.

Biff: So what do I do tomorrow? 490

Happy: You leave the house tomorrow and come back at night and say Oliver is thinking it over. And he thinks it over for a couple of weeks, and gradually it fades away and nobody's the worse.

Biff: But it'll go on forever!

Happy: Dad is never so happy as when he's looking forward to something!

Willy enters.

Happy: Hello, scout!

Willy: Gee, I haven't been here in years! 495

Stanley has followed Willy in and sets a chair for him. Stanley starts off but Happy stops him.

Happy: Stanley!

Stanley stands by, waiting for an order.

Biff: *(going to Willy with guilt, as to an invalid)* Sit down, Pop. You want a drink?

Willy: Sure, I don't mind.

Biff: Let's get a load on.

Willy: You look worried. 500

Biff: N-no. *(To Stanley.)* Scotch all around. Make it doubles.

Stanley: Doubles, right. *(He goes.)*

Willy: You had a couple already, didn't you?

Biff: Just a couple, yeah.

Willy: Well, what happened, boy? *(Nodding affirmatively,* 505 *with a smile.)* Everything go all right?

Biff: *(takes a breath, then reaches out and grasps Willy's hand)* Pal . . . *(He is smiling bravely, and Willy is smiling too.)* I had an experience today.

Happy: Terrific, Pop.

Willy: That so? What happened?

Biff: *(high, slightly alcoholic, above the earth)* I'm going to tell you everything from first to last. It's been a strange day. *(Silence. He looks around, composes himself as best he can, but his breath keeps breaking the rhythm of his voice.)* I had to wait quite a while for him, and—

Willy: Oliver? 510

Biff: Yeah, Oliver. All day, as a matter of cold fact. And a lot of—instances—facts, Pop, facts about my life came back to me. Who was it, Pop? Who ever said I was a salesman with Oliver?

Willy: Well, you were.

Biff: No, Dad, I was a shipping clerk.

Willy: But you were practically—

Biff: *(with determination)* Dad, I don't know who said it 515 first, but I was never a salesman for Bill Oliver.

Willy: What're you talking about?

Biff: Let's hold on to the facts tonight, Pop. We're not going to get anywhere bullin' around. I was a shipping clerk.

Willy: *(angrily)* All right, now listen to me—

Biff: Why don't you let me finish?

Willy: I'm not interested in stories about the past or any 520 crap of that kind because the woods are burning, boys, you understand? There's a big blaze going on all around. I was fired today.

Biff: *(shocked)* How could you be?

Willy: I was fired, and I'm looking for a little good news to tell your mother, because the woman has waited and the woman has suffered. The gist of it is that I haven't got a story left in my head, Biff. So don't give me a lecture about facts and aspects. I am not interested. Now what've you got to say to me?

Stanley enters with three drinks. They wait until he leaves.

Willy: Did you see Oliver?

Biff: Jesus, Dad!

Willy: You mean you didn't go up there? 525

Happy: Sure he went up there.

Biff: I did. I—saw him. How could they fire you?

Willy: *(on the edge of his chair)* What kind of a welcome did he give you?

Biff: He won't even let you work on commission?

Willy: I'm out! *(Driving.)* So tell me, he gave you a warm 530 welcome?

Happy: Sure, Pop, sure!

Biff: *(driven)* Well, it was kind of—

Willy: I was wondering if he'd remember you. *(To Happy.)* Imagine, man doesn't see him for ten, twelve years and gives him that kind of a welcome!

Happy: Damn right!

Biff: *(trying to return to the offensive)* Pop, look— 535

Willy: You know why he remembered you, don't you? Because you impressed him in those days.

Biff: Let's talk quietly and get this down to the facts, huh?

Willy: *(as though Biff had been interrupting)* Well, what happened? It's great news, Biff. Did he take you into his office or'd you talk in the waiting-room?

Biff: Well, he came in, see, and—

Willy: *(with a big smile)* What'd he say? Betcha he threw 540 his arm around you.

Biff: Well, he kinda—

Willy: He's a fine man. *(To Happy.)* Very hard man to see, y'know.

Happy: *(agreeing)* Oh, I know.

Willy: *(to Biff)* Is that where you had the drinks?

Biff: Yeah, he gave me a couple of—no, no! 545

Happy: *(cutting in)* He told him my Florida idea.

Willy: Don't interrupt. *(To Biff.)* How'd he react to the Florida idea?

Biff: Dad, will you give me a minute to explain?

Willy: I've been waiting for you to explain since I sat down here! What happened? He took you into his office and what?

Biff: Well—I talked. And—and he listened, see. 550

Willy: Famous for the way he listens, y'know. What was his answer?

Biff: His answer was—*(He breaks off, suddenly angry.)* Dad, you're not letting me tell you what I want to tell you!

Willy: *(accusing, angered)* You didn't see him, did you?

Biff: I did see him!

Willy: What'd you insult him or something? You insulted 555 him, didn't you?

Biff: Listen, will you let me out of it, will you just let me out of it!

Happy: What the hell!

Willy: Tell me what happened!

Biff: *(to Happy)* I can't talk to him!

A single trumpet note jars the ear. The light of green leaves stains the house, which holds the air of night and a dream. Young Bernard enters and knocks on the door of the house.

Young Bernard: *(frantically)* Mrs. Loman, Mrs. Loman! 560

Happy: Tell him what happened!

Biff: *(to Happy)* Shut up and leave me alone!

Willy: No, no! You had to go and flunk math!

Biff: What math? What're you talking about?

Young Bernard: Mrs. Loman, Mrs. Loman! 565

Linda appears in the house, as of old.

Willy: *(wildly)* Math, math, math!

Biff: Take it easy, Pop!

Young Bernard: Mrs. Loman!

Willy: *(furiously)* If you hadn't flunked you'd've been set by now!

Biff: Now, look, I'm gonna tell you what happened, and 570 you're going to listen to me.

Young Bernard: Mrs. Loman!

Biff: I waited six hours—

Happy: What the hell are you saying?

Biff: I kept sending in my name but he wouldn't see me. So finally he . . . *(He continues unheard as light fades low on the restaurant.)*

Young Bernard: Biff flunked math! 575

Linda: No!

Young Bernard: Birnbaum flunked him! They won't graduate him!

Linda: But they have to. He's gotta go to the university. Where is he? Biff! Biff!

Young Bernard: No, he left. He went to Grand Central.

Linda: Grand—You mean he went to Boston! 580

Young Bernard: Is Uncle Willy in Boston?

Linda: Oh, maybe Willy can talk to the teacher. Oh, the poor, poor boy!

Light on house area snaps out.

Biff: *(at the table, now audible, holding up a gold fountain pen)* . . . so I'm washed up with Oliver, you understand? Are you listening to me?

Willy: *(at a loss)* Yeah, sure. If you hadn't flunked—

Biff: Flunked what? What're you talking about? 585

Willy: Don't blame everything on me! I didn't flunk math— you did! What pen?

Happy: That was awful dumb, Biff, a pen like that is worth—

Willy: *(seeing the pen for the first time)* You took Oliver's pen?

Biff: *(weakening)* Dad, I just explained it to you.

Willy: You stole Bill Oliver's fountain pen! 590

Biff: I didn't exactly steal it! That's just what I've been explaining to you!

Happy: He had it in his hand and just then Oliver walked in, so he got nervous and stuck it in his pocket!

Willy: My God, Biff!

Biff: I never intended to do it, Dad!

Operator's Voice: Standish Arms, good evening! 595

Willy: *(shouting)* I'm not in my room!

Biff: *(frightened)* Dad, what's the matter? *(He and Happy stand up.)*

Operator: Ringing Mr. Loman for you!

Willy: I'm not there, stop it!

Biff: *(horrified, gets down on one knee before Willy)* Dad, 600 I'll make good, I'll make good. *(Willy tries to get to his feet. Biff holds him down.)* Sit down now.

Willy: No, you're no good, you're no good for anything.

Biff: I am, Dad, I'll find something else, you understand? Now don't worry about anything. *(He holds up Willy's face.)* Talk to me, Dad.

Operator: Mr. Loman does not answer. Shall I page him?

Willy: *(attempting to stand, as though to rush and silence the Operator)* No, no, no!

Happy: He'll strike something, Pop. 605

Willy: No, no . . .

Biff: *(desperately, standing over Willy)* Pop, listen! Listen to me! I'm telling you something good. Oliver talked to his partner about the Florida idea. You listening? He—he talked to his partner, and he came to me . . . I'm going to be all right, you hear? Dad, listen to me, he said it was just a question of the amount!

Willy: Then you . . . got it?

Happy: He's gonna be terrific, Pop!

Willy: *(trying to stand)* Then you got it, haven't you? You 610 got it! You got it!

Biff: *(agonized, holds Willy down)* No, no. Look, Pop. I'm supposed to have lunch with them tomorrow. I'm just telling you this so you'll know that I can still make an impression, Pop. And I'll make good somewhere, but I can't go tomorrow, see?

Willy: Why not? You simply—

Biff: But the pen, Pop!

Willy: You give it to him and tell him it was an oversight!

Happy: Sure, have lunch tomorrow! 615

Biff: I can't say that—

Willy: You were doing a crossword puzzle and accidentally used his pen!

Biff: Listen, kid, I took those balls years ago, now I walk in with his fountain pen? That clinches it, don't you see? I can't face him like that! I'll try elsewhere.

Page's Voice: Paging Mr. Loman!

Willy: Don't you want to be anything? 620

Biff: Pop, how can I go back?

Willy: You don't want to be anything, is that what's behind it?

Biff: *(now angry at Willy for not crediting his sympathy)* Don't take it that way! You think it was easy walking into that office after what I'd done to him? A team of horses couldn't have dragged me back to Bill Oliver!

Willy: Then why'd you go?

Biff: Why did I go? Why did I go? Look at you! Look at 625 what's become of you!

Off left, The Woman laughs.

Willy: Biff, you're going to go to that lunch tomorrow, or—

Biff: I can't go. I've got no appointment!

Happy: Biff, for . . .!

Willy: Are you spiting me?

Biff: Don't take it that way! Goddammit! 630

Willy: *(strikes Biff and falters away from the table)* You rotten little louse! Are you spiting me?

The Woman: Someone's at the door, Willy!

Biff: I'm no good, can't you see what I am?

Happy: *(separating them)* Hey, you're in a restaurant! Now cut it out, both of you! *(The Girls enter.)* Hello, girls, sit down.

The Woman laughs, off left.

Miss Forsythe: I guess we might as well. This is Letta. 635

The Woman: Willy, are you going to wake up?

Biff: *(ignoring Willy)* How're ya, miss, sit down. What do you drink?

Miss Forsythe: Letta might not be able to stay long.

Letta: I gotta get up very early tomorrow. I got jury duty. I'm so excited! Were you fellows ever on a jury?

Biff: No, but I been in front of them! *(The Girls laugh.)* 640 This is my father.

Letta: Isn't he cute? Sit down with us, Pop.

Happy: Sit him down, Biff!

Biff: *(going to him)* Come on, slugger, drink us under the table. To hell with it! Come on, sit down, pal.

On Biff's last insistence, Willy is about to sit.

The Woman: *(now urgently)* Willy, are you going to answer the door!

The Woman's call pulls Willy back. He starts right, befuddled.

Biff: Hey, where are you going? 645

Willy: Open the door.

Biff: The door?

Willy: The washroom . . . the door . . . where's the door?

Biff: *(leading Willy to the left)* Just go straight down.

Willy moves left.

The Woman: Willy, Willy, are you going to get up, get up, 650 get up, get up?

Willy exits left.

Letta: I think it's sweet you bring your daddy along.

Miss Forsythe: Oh, he isn't really your father!

Biff: *(at left, turning to her resentfully)* Miss Forsythe, you've just seen a prince walk by. A fine, troubled prince. A hard-working, unappreciated prince. A pal, you understand? A good companion. Always for his boys.

Letta: That's so sweet.

Happy: Well, girls, what's the program? We're wasting 655 time. Come on, Biff. Gather round. Where would you like to go?

Biff: Why don't you do something for him?

Happy: Me!

Biff: Don't you give a damn for him, Hap?

Happy: What're you talking about? I'm the one who—

Biff: I sense it, you don't give a good goddam about him. 660 *(He takes the rolled-up hose from his pocket and puts it on the table in front of Happy.)* Look what I found in the cellar, for Christ's sake. How can you bear to let it go on?

Happy: Me? Who goes away? Who runs off and—

Biff: Yeah, but he doesn't mean anything to you. You could help him—I can't! Don't you understand what I'm talking about? He's going to kill himself, don't you know that?

Happy: Don't I know it! Me!

Biff: Hap, help him! Jesus . . . help him . . . Help me, help me, I can't bear to look at his face! *(Ready to weep, he hurries out, up right.)*

Happy: *(starting after him)* Where are you going? 665

Miss Forsythe: What's he so mad about?

Happy: Come on, girls, we'll catch up with him.

Miss Forsythe: *(as Happy pushes her out)* Say, I don't like that temper of his!

Happy: He's just a little overstrung, he'll be all right!

Willy: *(off left, as The Woman laughs)* Don't answer! 670 Don't answer!

Letta: Don't you want to tell your father—

Happy: No, that's not my father. He's just a guy. Come on, we'll catch Biff, and, honey, we're going to paint this town! Stanley, where's the check! Hey, Stanley!

They exit. Stanley looks toward left.

Stanley: *(calling to Happy indignantly)* Mr. Loman! Mr. Loman!

Stanley picks up a chair and follows them off. Knocking is heard off left. The Woman enters, laughing. Willy follows her. She is in a black slip; he is buttoning his shirt. Raw, sensuous music accompanies their speech.

Willy: Will you stop laughing? Will you stop?

The Woman: Aren't you going to answer the door? He'll 675 wake the whole hotel.

Willy: I'm not expecting anybody.

The Woman: Whyn't you have another drink, honey, and stop being so damn self-centered?

Willy: I'm so lonely.

The Woman: You know you ruined me, Willy? From now on, whenever you come to the office, I'll see that you go right through to the buyers. No waiting at my desk any more, Willy. You ruined me.

Willy: That's nice of you to say that. 680

The Woman: Gee, you are self-centered! Why so sad? You are the saddest self-centeredest soul I ever did see-saw. *(She laughs. He kisses her.)* Come on inside, drummer boy. It's silly to be dressing in the middle of the night. *(As knocking is heard.)* Aren't you going to answer the door?

Willy: They're knocking on the wrong door.

The Woman: But I felt the knocking. And he heard us talking in here. Maybe the hotel's on fire!

Willy: *(his terror rising)* It's a mistake.

The Woman: Then tell him to go away! 685

Willy: There's nobody there.

The Woman: It's getting on my nerves, Willy. There's somebody standing out there and it's getting on my nerves!

Willy: *(pushing her away from him)* All right, stay in the bathroom here, and don't come out. I think there's a law in Massachusetts about it, so don't come out. It may be that new room clerk. He looked very mean. So don't come out. It's a mistake, there's no fire.

The knocking is heard again. He takes a few steps away from her, and she vanishes into the wing. The light follows him, and now he is facing Young Biff, who carries a suitcase. Biff steps toward him. The music is gone.

Biff: Why didn't you answer?

Willy: Biff! What are you doing in Boston? 690

Biff: Why didn't you answer? I've been knocking for five minutes, I called you on the phone—

Willy: I just heard you. I was in the bathroom and had the door shut. Did anything happen home?

Biff: Dad—I let you down.

Willy: What do you mean?

Biff: Dad . . . 695

Willy: Biffo, what's this about? *(Putting his arm around Biff.)* Come on, let's go downstairs and get you a malted.

Biff: Dad, I flunked math.

Willy: Not for the term?

Biff: The term. I haven't got enough credits to graduate.

Willy: You mean to say Bernard wouldn't give you the 700 answers?

Biff: He did, he tried, but I only got a sixty-one.

Willy: And they wouldn't give you four points?

Biff: Birnbaum refused absolutely. I begged him, Pop, but he won't give me those points. You gotta talk to him before they close the school. Because if he saw the kind of man you are, and you just talked to him in your way, I'm sure he'd come through for me. The class came right before practice, see, and I didn't go enough. Would you talk to him? He'd like you, Pop. You know the way you could talk.

Willy: You're on. We'll drive right back.

Biff: Oh, Dad, good work! I'm sure he'll change it for 705 you!

Willy: Go downstairs and tell the clerk I'm checkin' out. Go right down.

Biff: Yes, Sir! See, the reason he hates me, Pop—one day he was late for class so I got up at the blackboard and imitated him. I crossed my eyes and talked with a lithp.

Willy: *(laughing)* You did? The kids like it?

Biff: They nearly died laughing!

Willy: Yeah? What'd you do? 710

Biff: The thquare root of thixthy twee is . . . *(Willy bursts out laughing; Biff joins him.)* And in the middle of it he walked in!

Willy laughs and The Woman joins in offstage.

Willy: *(without hesitating)* Hurry downstairs and—

Biff: Somebody in there?

Willy: No, that was next door.

The Woman laughs offstage.

Biff: Somebody got in your bathroom! 715

Willy: No, it's the next room, there's a party—

The Woman: *(enters, laughing. She lisps this)* Can I come in? There's something in the bathtub, Willy, and it's moving!

Willy looks at Biff, who is staring open-mouthed and horrified at The Woman.

Willy: Ah—you better go back to your room. They must be finished painting by now. They're painting her room so I let her take a shower here. Go back, go back . . . *(He pushes her.)*

The Woman: *(resisting)* But I've got to get dressed, Willy, I can't—

Willy: Get out of here! Go back, go back . . . *(Suddenly* 720 *striving for the ordinary.)* This is Miss Francis, Biff, she's a buyer. They're painting her room. Go back, Miss Francis, go back . . .

The Woman: But my clothes, I can't go out naked in the hall!

Willy: *(pushing her offstage)* Get outa here! Go back, go back!

Biff slowly sits down on his suitcase as the argument continues offstage.

The Woman: Where's my stockings? You promised me stockings, Willy!

Willy: I have no stockings here!

The Woman: You had two boxes of size nine sheers for 725 me, and I want them!

Willy: Here, for God's sake, will you get outa here!

The Woman: *(enters holding a box of stockings)* I just hope there's nobody in the hall. That's all I hope. *(To Biff.)* Are you football or baseball?

Biff: Football.

The Woman: *(angry, humiliated)* That's me too. G'night. *(She snatches her clothes from Willy, and walks out.)*

Willy: *(after a pause)* Well, better get going. I want to get 730 to the school first thing in the morning. Get my suits out of the closet. I'll get my valise. *(Biff doesn't move.)* What's the matter? *(Biff remains motionless, tears falling.)* She's a buyer. Buys for J. H. Simmons. She lives down the hall—they're painting. You don't imagine—*(He breaks off. After a pause.)* Now listen, pal, she's just a buyer. She sees merchandise in her room and they have to keep it looking just so . . . *(Pause. Assuming command.)* All right, get my suits. *(Biff doesn't move.)* Now stop crying and do as I say. I gave you an order. Biff, I gave you an order! Is that what you do when I give you an order? How dare you cry! *(Putting his arm around Biff.)* Now look, Biff, when you grow up you'll understand about these things. You mustn't—you mustn't overemphasize a thing like this. I'll see Birnbaum first thing in the morning.

Biff: Never mind.

Willy: *(getting down beside Biff)* Never mind! He's going to give you those points. I'll see to it.

Biff: He wouldn't listen to you.

Willy: He certainly will listen to me. You need those points for the U. of Virginia.

Biff: I'm not going there. 735

Willy: Heh? If I can't get him to change that mark you'll make it up in summer school. You've got all summer to—

Biff: *(his weeping breaking from him)* Dad . . .

Willy: *(infected by it)* Oh, my boy . . .

Biff: Dad . . .

Willy: She's nothing to me, Biff. I was lonely, I was 740 terribly lonely.

Biff: You—you gave her Mama's stockings! *(His tears break through and he rises to go.)*

Willy: *(grabbing for Biff)* I gave you an order!

Biff: Don't touch me, you—liar!

Willy: Apologize for that!

Biff: You fake! You phony little fake! You fake! *(Over-* 745 *come, he turns quickly and weeping fully goes out with his suitcase. Willy is left on the floor on his knees.)*

Willy: I gave you an order! Biff, come back here or I'll beat you! Come back here! I'll whip you!

Stanley comes quickly in from the right and stands in front of Willy.

Willy: *(shouts at Stanley)* I gave you an order . . .

Stanley: Hey, let's pick it up, pick it up, Mr. Loman. *(He helps Willy to his feet.)* Your boys left with the chippies. They said they'll see you home.

A second waiter watches some distance away.

Willy: But we were supposed to have dinner together.

Music is heard, Willy's theme.

Stanley: Can you make it? 750

Willy: I'll—sure, I can make it. *(Suddenly concerned about his clothes.)* Do I—I look all right?

Stanley: Sure, you look all right. *(He flicks a speck off Willy's lapel.)*

Willy: Here—here's a dollar.

Stanley: Oh, your son paid me. It's all right.

Willy: *(putting it in Stanley's hand)* No, take it. You're a 755 good boy.

Stanley: Oh, no, you don't have to . . .

Willy: Here—here's some more, I don't need it any more. *(After a slight pause.)* Tell me—is there a seed store in the neighborhood?

Stanley: Seeds? You mean like to plant?

As Willy turns, Stanley slips the money back into his jacket pocket.

Willy: Yes. Carrots, peas . . .

Stanley: Well, there's hardware stores on Sixth Avenue, 760
but it may be too late now.

Willy: *(anxiously)* Oh, I'd better hurry. I've got to get
some seeds. *(He starts off to the right.)* I've got to get
some seeds, right away. Nothing's planted. I don't
have a thing in the ground.

*Willy hurries out as the light goes down. Stanley moves
over to the right after him, watches him off. The other
waiter has been staring at Willy.*

Stanley: *(to the waiter)* Well, whatta you looking at?

*The waiter picks up the chairs and moves off right. Stanley
takes the table and follows him. The light fades on this
area. There is a long pause, the sound of the flute
coming over. The light gradually rises on the kitchen,
which is empty. Happy appears at the door of the
house, followed by Biff. Happy is carrying a large
bunch of long-stemmed roses. He enters the kitchen,
looks around for Linda. Not seeing her, he turns to
Biff, who is just outside the house door, and makes a
gesture with his hands, indicating "Not here, I guess."
He looks into the living room and freezes. Inside,
Linda, unseen, is seated, Willy's coat on her lap. She
rises ominously and quietly and moves toward Happy,
who backs up into the kitchen, afraid.*

Happy: Hey, what're you doing up? *(Linda says nothing
but moves toward him implacably.)* Where's Pop? *(He
keeps backing to the right, and now Linda is in full
view in the doorway to the living room.)* Is he sleeping?

Linda: Where were you?

Happy: *(trying to laugh it off)* We met two girls, Mom, 765
very fine types. Here, we brought you some flowers.
(Offering them to her.) Put them in your room, Ma.

*She knocks them to the floor at Biff's feet. He has now
come inside and closed the door behind him. She
stares at Biff, silent.*

Happy: Now what'd you do that for? Mom, I want you
to have some flowers—

Linda: *(cutting Happy off, violently to Biff)* Don't you
care whether he lives or dies?

Happy: *(going to the stairs)* Come upstairs, Biff.

Biff: *(with a flare of disgust, to Happy)* Go away from me!
(To Linda.) What do you mean, lives or dies?
Nobody's dying around here, pal.

Linda: Get out of my sight! Get out of here! 770

Biff: I wanna see the boss.

Linda: You're not going near him!

Biff: Where is he? *(He moves into the living room and
Linda follows.)*

Linda: *(shouting after Biff)* You invite him for dinner. He
looks forward to it all day—*(Biff appears in his
parents' bedroom, looks around, and exits)*—and
then you desert him there. There's no stranger you'd
do that to!

Happy: Why? He had a swell time with us. Listen, when 775
I—*(Linda comes back into the kitchen)*—desert him I
hope I don't outlive the day!

Linda: Get out of here!

Happy: Now look, Mom . . .

Linda: Did you have to go to women tonight? You and
your lousy rotten whores!

Biff re-enters the kitchen.

Happy: Mom, all we did was follow Biff around trying
to cheer him up! *(To Biff.)* Boy, what a night you
gave me!

Linda: Get out of here, both of you, and don't come 780
back! I don't want you tormenting him any more. Go
on now, get your things together! *(To Biff.)* You can
sleep in his apartment. *(She starts to pick up the
flowers and stops herself.)* Pick up this stuff, I'm not
your maid any more. Pick it up, you bum, you!

*Happy turns his back to her in refusal. Biff slowly moves
over and gets down on his knees, picking up the flowers.*

Linda: You're a pair of animals! Not one, not another
living soul would have had the cruelty to walk out
on that man in a restaurant!

Biff: *(not looking at her)* Is that what he said?

Linda: He didn't have to say anything. He was so
humiliated he nearly limped when he came in.

Happy: But, Mom he had a great time with us—

Biff: *(cutting him off violently)* Shut up! 785

Without another word, Happy goes upstairs.

Linda: You! You didn't even go in to see if he was all right!

Biff: *(still on the floor in front of Linda, the flowers in his
hand; with self-loathing)* No. Didn't. Didn't do a
damned thing. How do you like that, heh? Left him
babbling in a toilet.

Linda: You louse. You . . .

Biff: Now you hit it on the nose! *(He gets up, throws the
flowers in the wastebasket.)* The scum of the earth,
and you're looking at him!

Linda: Get out of here! 790

Biff: I gotta talk to the boss, Mom. Where is he?

Linda: You're not going near him. Get out of this house!

Biff: *(with absolute assurance, determination)* No. We're
gonna have an abrupt conversation, him and me.

Linda: You're not talking to him!

*Hammering is heard from outside the house, off right. Biff
turns toward the noise.*

Linda: *(suddenly pleading)* Will you please leave him 795
alone?

Biff: What's he doing out there?

Linda: He's planting the garden!

Biff: *(quietly)* Now? Oh, my God!

*Biff moves outside, Linda following. The light dies down
on them and comes up on the center of the apron as*

Willy walks into it. He is carrying a flashlight, a hoe and a handful of seed packets. He raps the top of the hoe sharply to fix it firmly, and then moves to the left, measuring off the distance with his foot. He holds the flashlight to look at the seed packets, reading off the instructions. He is in the blue of night.

Willy: Carrots . . . quarter-inch apart. Rows . . . one-foot rows. *(He measures it off.)* One foot. *(He puts down a package and measures off.)* Beets. *(He puts down another package and measures again.)* Lettuce. *(He reads the package, puts it down.)* One foot— *(He breaks off as Ben appears at the right and moves slowly down to him.)* What a proposition, ts, ts. Terrific, terrific. 'Cause she's suffered, Ben, the woman has suffered. You understand me? A man can't go out the way he came in, Ben, a man has got to add up to something. You can't, you can't— *(Ben moves toward him as though to interrupt.)* You gotta consider, now. Don't answer so quick. Remember, it's a guaranteed twenty-thousand-dollar proposition. Now look, Ben, I want you to go through the ins and outs of this thing with me. I've got nobody to talk to, Ben, and the woman has suffered, you hear me?

Ben: *(standing still, considering)* What's the proposition? 800

Willy: It's twenty thousand dollars on the barrelhead. Guaranteed, gilt-edged, you understand?

Ben: You don't want to make a fool of yourself. They might not honor the policy.

Willy: How can they dare refuse? Didn't I work like a coolie to meet every premium on the nose? And now they don't pay off? Impossible!

Ben: It's called a cowardly thing, William.

Willy: Why? Does it take more guts to stand here the rest 805 of my life ringing up a zero?

Ben: *(yielding)* That's a point, William. *(He moves, thinking, turns.)* And twenty thousand—that *is* something one can feel with the hand, it is there.

Willy: *(now assured, with rising power)* Oh, Ben, that's the whole beauty of it! I see it like a diamond, shining in the dark, hard and rough, that I can pick up and touch in my hand. Not like—like an appointment! This would not be another damned-fool appointment, Ben, and it changes all the aspects. Because he thinks I'm nothing, see, and so he spites me. But the funeral— *(Straightening up.)* Ben, that funeral will be massive! They'll come from Maine, Massachusetts, Vermont, New Hampshire! All the old-timers with the strange license plates—that boy will be thunder-struck, Ben, because he never realized—I am known! Rhode Island, New York, New Jersey—I am known, Ben, and he'll see it with his eyes once and for all. He'll see what I am, Ben! He's in for a shock, that boy!

Ben: *(coming down to the edge of the garden)* He'll call you a coward.

Willy: *(suddenly fearful)* No, that would be terrible.

Ben: Yes. And a damned fool. 810

Willy: No, no, he mustn't, I won't have that! *(He is broken and desperate.)*

Ben: He'll hate you, William.

The gay music of the boys is heard.

Willy: Oh, Ben, how do we get back to all the great times? Used to be so full of light, and comradeship, the sleigh-riding in winter, and the ruddiness on his cheeks. And always some kind of good news coming up, always something nice coming up ahead. And never even let me carry the valises in the house, and simonizing, simonizing that little red car! Why, why can't I give him something and not have him hate me?

Ben: Let me think about it. *(He glances at his watch.)* I still have a little time. Remarkable proposition, but you've got to be sure you're not making a fool of yourself.

Ben drifts off upstage and goes out of sight. Biff comes down from the left.

Willy: *(suddenly conscious of Biff, turns and looks up at* 815 *him, then begins picking up the packages of seeds in confusion)* Where the hell is that seed? *(Indignantly.)* You can't see nothing out here! They boxed in the whole goddam neighborhood!

Biff: There are people all around here. Don't you realize that?

Willy: I'm busy. Don't bother me.

Biff: *(taking the hoe from Willy)* I'm saying good-by to you, Pop. *(Willy looks at him, silent, unable to move.)* I'm not coming back any more.

Willy: You're not going to see Oliver tomorrow?

Biff: I've got no appointment, Dad. 820

Willy: He put his arm around you, and you've got no appointment?

Biff: Pop, get this now, will you? Everytime I've left it's been a fight that sent me out of here. Today I realized something about myself and I tried to explain it to you and I—I think I'm just not smart enough to make any sense out of it for you. To hell with whose fault it is or anything like that. *(He takes Willy's arm.)* Let's just wrap it up, heh? Come on in, we'll tell Mom. *(He gently tries to pull Willy to the left.)*

Willy: *(frozen, immobile, with guilt in his voice)* No, I don't want to see her.

Biff: Come on! *(He pulls again, and Willy tries to pull away.)*

Willy: *(highly nervous)* No, no, I don't want to see her. 825

Biff: *(tries to look into Willy's face, as if to find the answer there)* Why don't you want to see her?

Willy: *(more harshly now)* Don't bother me, will you?

Biff: What do you mean, you don't want to see her? You don't want them calling you yellow, do you? This isn't your fault; it's me, I'm a bum. Now come inside! *(Willy strains to get away.)* Did you hear what I said to you?

Willy pulls away and quickly goes by himself into the house. Biff follows.

Linda: *(to Willy)* Did you plant, dear?

Biff: *(at the door, to Linda)* All right, we had it out. I'm going and I'm not writing any more. 830

Linda: *(going to Willy in the kitchen)* I think that's the best way, dear. 'Cause there's no use drawing it out, you'll just never get along.

Willy doesn't respond.

Biff: People ask where I am and what I'm doing, you don't know, and you don't care. That way it'll be off your mind and you can start brightening up again. All right? That clears it, doesn't it? *(Willy is silent, and Biff goes to him.)* You gonna wish me luck, scout? *(He extends his hand.)* What do you say?

Linda: Shake his hand, Willy.

Willy: *(turning to her, seething with hurt)* There's no necessity to mention the pen at all, y'know.

Biff: *(gently)* I've got no appointment, Dad. 835

Willy: *(erupting fiercely)* He put his arm around . . .?

Biff: Dad, you're never going to see what I am, so what's the use of arguing? If I strike oil I'll send you a check. Meantime forget I'm alive.

Willy: *(to Linda)* Spite, see?

Biff: Shake hands, Dad.

Willy: Not my hand. 840

Biff: I was hoping not to go this way.

Willy: Well, this is the way you're going. Good-by.

Biff looks at him a moment, then turns sharply and goes to the stairs.

Willy: *(stops him with)* May you rot in hell if you leave this house!

Biff: *(turning)* Exactly what is it that you want from me?

Willy: I want you to know, on the train, in the mountains, 845 in the valleys, wherever you go, that you cut down your life for spite!

Biff: No, no.

Willy: Spite, spite, is the word of your undoing! And when you're down and out, remember what did it. When you're rotting somewhere beside the railroad tracks, remember, and don't you dare blame it on me!

Biff: I'm not blaming it on you!

Willy: I won't take the rap for this, you hear?

Happy comes down the stairs and stands on the bottom step, watching.

Biff: That's just what I'm telling you! 850

Willy: *(sinking into a chair at the table, with full accusation)* You're trying to put a knife in me—don't think I don't know what you're doing!

Biff: All right, phony! Then let's lay it on the line. *(He whips the rubber tube out of his pocket and puts it on the table.)*

Happy: You crazy—

Linda: Biff! *(She moves to grab the hose, but Biff holds it down with his hand.)*

Biff: Leave it there! Don't move it! 855

Willy: *(not looking at it)* What is that?

Biff: You know goddam well what that is.

Willy: *(caged, wanting to escape)* I never saw that.

Biff: You saw it. The mice didn't bring it into the cellar! What is this supposed to do, make a hero out of you? This supposed to make me sorry for you?

Willy: Never heard of it. 860

Biff: There'll be no pity for you, you hear it? No pity!

Willy: *(to Linda)* You hear the spite!

Biff: No, you're going to hear the truth—what you are and what I am!

Linda: Stop it!

Willy: Spite! 865

Happy: *(coming down toward Biff)* You cut it now!

Biff: *(to Happy)* The man don't know who we are! The man is gonna know! *(To Willy.)* We never told the truth for ten minutes in this house!

Happy: We always told the truth!

Biff: *(turning on him)* You big blow, are you the assistant buyer? You're one of the two assistants to the assistant, aren't you?

Happy: Well, I'm practically— 870

Biff: You're practically full of it! We all are! And I'm through with it. *(To Willy.)* Now hear this, Willy, this is me.

Willy: I know you!

Biff: You know why I had no address for three months? I stole a suit in Kansas City and I was in jail. *(To Linda, who is sobbing.)* Stop crying. I'm through with it.

Linda turns away from them, her hands covering her face.

Willy: I suppose that's my fault!

Biff: I stole myself out of every good job since high school! 875

Willy: And whose fault is that?

Biff: And I never got anywhere because you blew me so full of hot air I could never stand taking orders from anybody! That's whose fault it is!

Willy: I hear that!

Linda: Don't, Biff!

Biff: It's goddam time you heard that! I had to be boss 880 big shot in two weeks, and I'm through with it!

Willy: Then hang yourself! For spite, hang yourself!

Biff: No! Nobody's hanging himself, Willy! I ran down eleven flights with a pen in my hand today. And suddenly I stopped, you hear me? And in the middle of that office building, do you hear this? I stopped in the middle of that building and I saw—the sky. I saw the things that I love in this world. The work and the food and time to sit and smoke. And I looked at the pen and said to myself, what the hell am I grabbing this for? Why am I trying to become what I don't want to be? What am I doing in an office, making a contemptuous, begging fool of myself, when all I want is out there, waiting for me the minute I say I know who I am! Why can't I say that, Willy? *(He tries to make Willy face him, but Willy pulls away and moves to the left.)*

Willy: (*with hatred, threateningly*) The door of your life is wide open!

Biff: Pop! I'm a dime a dozen, and so are you!

Willy: (*turning on him now in an uncontrolled outburst*) I am not a dime a dozen! I am Willy Loman, and you are Biff Loman!

Biff starts for Willy, but is blocked by Happy. In his fury, Biff seems on the verge of attacking his father.

Biff: I am not a leader of men, Willy, and neither are you. You were never anything but a hard-working drummer who landed in the ash can like all the rest of them! I'm one dollar an hour, Willy! I tried seven states and couldn't raise it. A buck an hour! Do you gather my meaning? I'm not bringing home any prizes any more, and you're going to stop waiting for me to bring them home!

Willy: (*directly to Biff*) You vengeful, spiteful mutt!

Biff breaks from Happy. Willy, in fright, starts up the stairs. Biff grabs him.

Biff: (*at the peak of his fury*) Pop, I'm nothing! I'm nothing, Pop. Can't you understand that? There's no spite in it any more. I'm just what I am, that's all.

Biff's fury has spent itself, and he breaks down, sobbing, holding on to Willy, who dumbly fumbles for Biff's face.

Willy: (*astonished*) What're you doing? What're you doing? (*To Linda.*) Why is he crying?

Biff: (*crying, broken*) Will you let me go, for Christ's sake? Will you take that phony dream and burn it before something happens? (*Struggling to contain himself, he pulls away and moves to the stairs.*) I'll go in the morning. Put him—put him to bed. (*Exhausted, Biff moves up the stairs to his room.*)

Willy: (*after a long pause, astonished, elevated*) Isn't that remarkable? Biff—he likes me!

Linda: He loves you, Willy!

Happy: (*deeply moved*) Always did, Pop.

Willy: Oh, Biff! (*Staring wildly.*) He cried! Cried to me! (*He is choking with his love, and now cries out his promise.*) That boy—that boy is going to be magnificent!

Ben appears in the light just outside the kitchen.

Ben: Yes, outstanding, with twenty thousand behind him.

Linda: (*sensing the racing of his mind, fearfully, carefully*) Now come to bed, Willy. It's all settled now.

Willy: (*finding it difficult not to rush out of the house*) Yes, we'll sleep. Come on. Go to sleep, Hap.

Ben: And it does take a great kind of man to crack the jungle.

In accents of dread, Ben's idyllic music starts up.

Happy: (*his arm around Linda*) I'm getting married, Pop, don't forget it. I'm changing everything. I'm gonna run that department before the year is up. You'll see, Mom. (*He kisses her.*)

Ben: The jungle is dark but full of diamonds, Willy.

Willy turns, moves, listening to Ben.

Linda: Be good. You're both good boys, just act that way, that's all.

Happy: 'Night, Pop. (*He goes upstairs.*)

Linda: (*to Willy*) Come, dear.

Ben: (*with greater force*) One must go in to fetch a diamond out.

Willy: (*to Linda, as he moves slowly along the edge of the kitchen, toward the door*) I just want to get settled down, Linda. Let me sit alone for a little.

Linda: (*almost uttering her fear*) I want you upstairs.

Willy: (*taking her in his arms*) In a few minutes, Linda. I couldn't sleep right now. Go on, you look awful tired. (*He kisses her.*)

Ben: Not like an appointment at all. A diamond is rough and hard to the touch.

Willy: Go on now. I'll be right up.

Linda: I think this is the only way, Willy.

Willy: Sure, it's the best thing.

Ben: Best thing!

Willy: The only way. Everything is gonna be—go on, kid, get to bed. You look so tired.

Linda: Come right up.

Willy: Two minutes.

Linda goes into the living room, then reappears in her bedroom. Willy moves just outside the kitchen door.

Willy: Loves me. (*Wonderingly.*) Always loved me. Isn't that a remarkable thing? Ben, he'll worship me for it!

Ben: (*with promise*) It's dark there, but full of diamonds.

Willy: Can you imagine that magnificence with twenty thousand dollars in his pocket?

Linda: (*calling from her room*) Willy! Come up!

Willy: (*calling from the kitchen*) Yes! Yes! Coming! It's very smart, you realize that, don't you, sweetheart? Even Ben sees it. I gotta go, baby. 'By! By! (*Going over to Ben, almost dancing.*) Imagine? When the mail comes he'll be ahead of Bernard again!

Ben: A perfect proposition all around.

Willy: Did you see how he cried to me? Oh, if I could kiss him, Ben!

Ben: Time, William, time!

Willy: Oh, Ben, I always knew one way or another we were gonna make it, Biff and I!

Ben: (*looking at his watch*) The boat. We'll be late. (*He moves slowly off into the darkness.*)

Willy: (*elegiacally, turning to the house*) Now when you kick off, boy, I want a seventy-yard boot, and get right down the field under the ball, and when you hit, hit low and hit hard, because it's important, boy. (*He swings around and faces the audience.*) There's all kinds of important people in the stands, and the first thing you know . . . (*Suddenly realizing he is alone.*) Ben! Ben, where do I . . . ? (*He makes a sudden movement of search.*) Ben, how do I . . . ?

Linda: *(calling)* Willy, you coming up?

Willy: *(uttering a gasp of fear, whirling about as if to quiet her)* Sh! *(He turns around as if to find his way; sounds, faces, voices, seem to be swarming in upon him and he flicks at them, crying.)* Sh! Sh! *(Suddenly music, faint and high, stops him. It rises in intensity, almost to an unbearable scream. He goes up and down on his toes, and rushes off around the house.)* Shhh!

Linda: Willy?

There is no answer. Linda waits. Biff gets up off his bed. He is still in his clothes. Happy sits up. Biff stands listening.

Linda: *(with real fear)* Willy, answer me! Willy! 930

There is the sound of a car starting and moving away at full speed.

Linda: No!

Biff: *(rushing down the stairs)* Pop!

As the car speeds off, the music crashes down in a frenzy of sound, which becomes the soft pulsation of a single cello string. Biff slowly returns to his bedroom. He and Happy gravely don their jackets. Linda slowly walks out of her room. The music has developed into a dead march. The leaves of day are appearing over everything. Charley and Bernard, somberly dressed, appear and knock on the kitchen door. Biff and Happy slowly descend the stairs to the kitchen as Charley and Bernard enter. All stop a moment when Linda, in clothes of mourning, bearing a little bunch of roses, comes through the draped doorway into the kitchen. She goes to Charley and takes his arm. Now all move toward the audience, through the wall-line of the kitchen. At the limit of the apron, Linda lays down the flowers, kneels, and sits back on her heels. All stare down at the grave.

REQUIEM

Charley: It's getting dark, Linda.

Linda doesn't react. She stares at the grave.

Biff: How about it, Mom? Better get some rest, heh? They'll be closing the gate soon.

Linda makes no move. Pause.

Happy: *(deeply angered)* He had no right to do that! There was no necessity for it. We would've helped him.

Charley: *(grunting)* Hmmm.

Biff: Come along, Mom. 5

Linda: Why didn't anybody come?

Charley: It was a very nice funeral.

Linda: But where are all the people he knew? Maybe they blame him.

Charley: Naa. It's a rough world, Linda. They wouldn't blame him.

Linda: I can't understand it. At this time especially. First 10 time in thirty-five years we were just about free and clear. He only needed a little salary. He was even finished with the dentist.

Charley: No man only needs a little salary.

Linda: I can't understand it.

Biff: There were a lot of nice days. When he'd come home from a trip; or on Sundays, making the stoop; finishing the cellar; putting on the new porch; when he built the extra bathroom; and put up the garage. You know something, Charley, there's more of him in that front stoop than in all the sales he ever made.

Charley: Yeah. He was a happy man with a batch of cement.

Linda: He was so wonderful with his hands. 15

Biff: He had the wrong dreams. All, all, wrong.

Happy: *(almost ready to fight Biff)* Don't say that!

Biff: He never knew who he was.

Charley: *(stopping Happy's movement and reply. To Biff.)* Nobody dast blame this man. You don't understand: Willy was a salesman. And for a salesman, there is no rock bottom to the life. He don't put a bolt to a nut, he don't tell you the law or give you medicine. He's a man out there in the blue, riding on a smile and a shoeshine. And when they start not smiling back—that's an earthquake. And then you get yourself a couple of spots on your hat, and you're finished. Nobody dast blame this man. A salesman is got to dream, boy. It comes with the territory.

Biff: Charley, the man didn't know who he was. 20

Happy: *(infuriated)* Don't say that!

Biff: Why don't you come with me, Happy?

Happy: I'm not licked that easily. I'm staying right in this city, and I'm gonna beat this racket! *(He looks at Biff, his chin set.)* The Loman Brothers!

Biff: I know who I am, kid.

Happy: All right, boy. I'm gonna show you and 25 everybody else that Willy Loman did not die in vain. He had a good dream. It's the only dream you can have—to come out number-one man. He fought it out here, and this is where I'm gonna win it for him.

Biff: *(with a hopeless glance at Happy, bends toward his mother)* Let's go, Mom.

Linda: I'll be with you in a minute. Go on, Charley. *(He hesitates.)* I want to, just for a minute. I never had a chance to say good-by.

Charley moves away, followed by Happy. Biff remains a slight distance up and left of Linda. She sits there, summoning herself. The flute begins, not far away, playing behind her speech.

Linda: Forgive me, dear. I can't cry. I don't know what it is, but I can't cry. I don't understand it. Why did you ever do that? Help me, Willy, I can't cry. It seems to me that you're just on another trip. I keep expecting you. Willy, dear, I can't cry. Why did you do it? I search and search and I search, and I can't understand it, Willy. I made the last payment on the house today. Today, dear. And there'll be nobody home. *(A sob rises in her throat.)* We're free and clear. *(Sobbing more fully, released.)* We're free. *(Biff comes slowly toward her.)* We're free . . . We're free . . .

Biff lifts her to her feet and moves out up right with her in his arms. Linda sobs quietly. Bernard and Charley come together and follow them, followed by Happy. Only the music of the flute is left on the darkening stage as over the house the hard towers of the apartment buildings rise into sharp focus, and—

The Curtain Falls

Related Works

"Those Winter Sundays" (p. 482), "Do not go gentle into that good night" (p. 484), "The Love Song of J. Alfred Prufrock" (p. 504), *Oedipus the King* (p. 701), *Fences* (p. 724)

 See Chapter 33 Review Card for Reading and Reacting questions about Arthur Miller, *Death of a Salesman*.

William Shakespeare (1564–1616)

© Bettmann / Corbis

is recognized as the greatest of English writers, but many details about his life are based on conjecture or tradition. The earliest dependable information concerning Shakespeare is found in the parish registers of Stratford-upon-Avon's Holy Trinity Church, where his baptism was recorded on April 26, 1564. Although his date of birth cannot be determined with certainty, tradition has assigned it to April 23, 1564. Little is known about his early life, but reliable information about significant events is available in church documents. For example, he married Ann Hathaway in 1582 and had three children—Susanna in 1583 and the twins Judith and Hamnet in 1585.

Soon after the birth of his children, Shakespeare left Stratford for London. Upon his arrival in the capital, he set out to establish himself in London's literary world. His first step toward achieving this goal occurred in 1592, when he published his narrative poem *Venus and Adonis;* the following year, he published a second poem, *The Rape of Lucrece.*

By 1594, Shakespeare had become quite involved with the London stage. For approximately twenty years, he enjoyed a successful professional career in London—as actor, playwright, shareholder in the Lord Chamberlain's Men (an acting company), part owner of the Globe Theatre (from 1599), and author of at least thirty-six plays. The income derived from these activities brought him significant wealth and enabled him, sometime between 1610 and 1613, to retire from the theater and to return to Stratford-upon-Avon, where he owned considerable property. On April 23, 1616, Shakespeare died at age fifty-two in Stratford and was buried two days later in Holy Trinity Church.

It is difficult to date many of Shakespeare's plays exactly because they must be dated by records of their first performance (often hard to come by) and by topical references in the text. Shakespeare's company probably first staged *Hamlet* at the Globe Theatre in 1600 or 1601, but some scholars believe the play was composed as early as 1598.

Hamlet has been called Shakespeare's most complex and most confusing play, yet it is also the play most frequently performed, read, and written about. Shakespeare's audience would have recognized *Hamlet* as a **revenge tragedy**—a play in which the hero discovers that a close relative has been murdered, experiences considerable trouble in identifying the murderer, and, after overcoming numerous obstacles, avenges the death by killing the murderer. Frequently, revenge tragedies featured murders, physical mutilations, and ghosts, all enacted with grand style and bold rhetoric. These plays were extremely popular productions that were the action movies of their day.

Hamlet, however, is different from the typical revenge tragedy. Because the ghost gives him the necessary information, Hamlet has no need to search for the cause of his father's death or find the murderer. In fact, the only impediments to Hamlet's revenge are those he himself creates. And, by the time the delay ends and Hamlet avenges his father's death, the loss is immense: his mother, the woman he loves, her father and brother, and Hamlet himself are all dead. Although the argument that there would be no play if Hamlet had immediately avenged his father may be valid, it fails to satisfy those who ponder the tragic cost of Hamlet's inaction.

Cultural Context

The appearance of a ghost was a long-standing tradition in Renaissance drama. The ghost appeared in Elizabethan revenge tragedies as a plot device to help further the action and prompt a reaction from the hero. For a Renaissance audience, the dramatic representation of a ghost from purgatory would evoke a rich context of legends and lore derived from paintings, illuminated manuscript, prints, and narratives. Moreover, stories involving ghosts were a frequent element of medieval sermons. However, the ghost in *Hamlet* transcends the traditions of the revenge tragedy. Here, Shakespeare's use of the ghost not only as a plot device but also as a character who may or may not be telling the truth adds depth and complexity to the play.

Hamlet

Prince of Denmark* (c. 1600)

CHARACTERS

Claudius, *King of Denmark*
Hamlet, *son to the late King Hamlet,*
and nephew to the present King
Polonius, *Lord Chamberlain*
Horatio, *friend to Hamlet*
Laertes, *son to Polonius*

Norwegian Captain
Doctor of Divinity
Players
Two Clowns, *grave-diggers*
English Ambassadors
Gertrude, *Queen of Denmark, and*
mother to Hamlet
Ophelia, *daughter to Polonius*
Ghost *of Hamlet's Father*
Lords, Ladies, Officers, Soldiers, Sailors,
Messengers, and Attendants

Voltemand
Cornelius
Rosencrantz   } *courtiers*
Guildenstern
Osric
Gentleman
Marcellus   } *officers*
Barnardo
Francisco, *a soldier*
Reynaldo, *servant to Polonius*
Fortinbras, *Prince of Norway*

Scene: *Denmark*

ACT I

SCENE 1°

Enter Barnardo and Francisco, two sentinels [meeting].°

Barnardo: Who's there?
Francisco: Nay, answer me.° Stand and unfold yourself.°
Barnardo: Long live the King!°
Francisco: Barnardo.
Barnardo: He.   5
Francisco: You come most carefully upon your hour.
Barnardo: 'Tis now strook twelf.° Get thee to bed, Francisco.
Francisco: For this relief much thanks. 'Tis bitter cold,
   And I am sick at heart.°
Barnardo: Have you had quiet guard?
Francisco: Not a mouse stirring.   10
Barnardo: Well, goodnight.
   If you do meet Horatio and Marcellus,
   The rivals° of my watch, bid them make haste.

Enter Horatio and Marcellus.

Francisco: I think I hear them. Stand ho! Who is there?

Horatio: Friends to this ground.
Marcellus: And liegemen° to the Dane.   15
Francisco: Give° you good night.
Marcellus: O, farewell, honest [soldier].
   Who hath reliev'd you?
Francisco: Barnardo hath my place.
   Give you goodnight.   *(Exit Francisco.)*
Marcellus: Holla, Barnardo!
Barnardo: Say—
   What, is Horatio there?
Horatio: A piece of him.
Barnardo: Welcome, Horatio, welcome, good Marcellus.   20
Horatio: What, has this thing appear'd again to-night?
Barnardo: I have seen nothing.
Marcellus: Horatio says 'tis but our fantasy,°
   And will not let belief take hold of him   25
   Touching this dreaded sight twice seen of us;

---

*Words and passages enclosed in square brackets in the text are either emendations of the copy-text or additions to it.
°**Location** Elsinore; a guard-platform of the castle. °**answer me** *You* answer *me.* Francisco is on watch; Barnardo has come to relieve him. °**unfold yourself** Make known who you are

°**Long . . . King** Perhaps a password, perhaps simply an utterance to allow the voice to be recognized. °**strook twelf** Struck twelve. °**sick at heart** In low spirits. °**rivals** Partners. °**liegemen . . . Dane** Loyal subjects to the king of Denmark. °**Give** God give. °**fantasy** Imagination.

Therefore I have entreated him along,
With us to watch the minutes of this night,
That if again this apparition come,
He may approve° our eyes and speak to it.

Horatio: Tush, tush, 'twill not appear. 30

Barnardo: Sit down a while,
And let us once again assail your ears,
That are so fortified against our story,
What we have two nights seen.

Horatio: Well, sit we down,
And let us hear Barnardo speak of this.

Barnardo: Last night of all, 35
When yond same star that's westward from the pole,°
Had made his° course t' illume that part of heaven
Where now it burns, Marcellus and myself,
The bell then beating one —

Enter Ghost.

Marcellus: Peace, break thee off! Look where it comes again! 40

Barnardo: In the same figure like° the King that's dead.

Marcellus: Thou art a scholar,° speak to it, Horatio.

Barnardo: Looks 'a° not like the King? Mark it, Horatio.

Horatio: Most like; it [harrows] me with fear and wonder.

Barnardo: It would be spoke to.° 45

Marcellus: Speak to it, Horatio.

Horatio: What art thou that usurp'st° this time of night,
Together with that fair and warlike form
In which the majesty of buried Denmark°
Did sometimes° march? By heaven I charge thee speak!

Marcellus: It is offended.

Barnardo: See, it stalks away! 50

Horatio: Stay! Speak, speak, I charge thee speak!

Exit Ghost.

Marcellus: 'Tis gone, and will not answer.

Barnardo: How now, Horatio, you tremble and look pale.
Is not this something more than fantasy? 55
What think you on't?

Horatio: Before my God, I might not this believe
Without the sensible° and true avouch°
Of mine own eyes.

Marcellus: Is it not like the King?

Horatio: As thou art to thyself.
Such was the very armor he had on 60
When he the ambitious Norway° combated.
So frown'd he once when in an angry parle°

He smote the sledded° [Polacks]° on the ice.
'Tis strange.

Marcellus: Thus twice before, and jump° at this dead hour, 65
With martial stalk hath he gone by our watch.

Horatio: In what particular thought to work I know not,
But in the gross and scope of mine opinion,°
This bodes some strange eruption° to our state.

Marcellus: Good now, sit down, and tell me, he that knows, 70
Why this same strict and most observant watch
So nightly toils° the subject° of the land,
And [why] such daily [cast] of brazen cannon,
And foreign mart° for implements of war,
Why such impress° of shipwrights, whose sore task 75
Does not divide the Sunday from the week,
What might be toward,° that this sweaty haste
Doth make the night joint-laborer with the day:
Who is't that can inform me?

Horatio: That can I,
At least the whisper goes so: our last king, 80
Whose image even but now appear'd to us,
Was, as you know, by Fortinbras of Norway,
Thereto prick'd on by a most emulate° pride,
Dar'd to the combat; in which our valiant Hamlet
(For so this side of our known world esteem'd him) 85
Did slay this Fortinbras, who, by a seal'd compact
Well ratified by law and heraldry,°
Did forfeit (with his life) all [those] his lands
Which he stood seiz'd of,° to the conqueror;
Against the which a moi'ty° competent° 90
Was gaged° by our king, which had° [return'd]
To the inheritance° of Fortinbras,
Had he been vanquisher; as by the same comart°
And carriage° of the article [design'd],°
His fell to Hamlet. Now, sir, young Fortinbras, 95
Of unimproved° mettle hot and full,
Hath in the skirts° of Norway here and there
Shark'd up° a list of lawless resolutes
For food and diet to some enterprise
That hath a stomach° in't, which is no other, 100
As it doth well appear unto our state,
But to recover of us, by strong hand
And terms compulsatory, those foresaid lands
So by his father lost; and this, I take it,
Is the main motive of our preparations, 105
The source of this our watch, and the chief head°
Of this post-haste and romage° in the land.

°**approve** Corroborate °**pole** Pole star. °**his** Its (the commonest form of the neuter possessive singular in Shakespeare's day) °**like** In the likeness of. °**a scholar** One who knows how best to address it. °**'a** He. °**It . . . to** A ghost had to be spoken to before it could speak. °**usurp'st** The ghost, a supernatural being, has invaded the realm of nature. °**majesty . . . Denmark** Late king of Denmark. °**sometimes** formerly. °**sensible** Relating to the senses °**avouch** Guarantee. °**Norway** King of Norway. °**parle** Parley °**sledded** Using sleds or sledges. °**Polacks** Poles. °**jump** Precisely. °**In . . . opinion** While I have no precise theory about it, my general feeling is that; *gross* = wholeness, totality; *scope* = range. °**eruption** Upheaval. °**toils** Causes to

work. °**subject** Subjects. °**foreign mart** Dealing with foreign markets. °**impress** Forced service. °**toward** In preparation. °**emulate** Emulous, proceeding from rivalry. °**law and heraldy** Heraldic law (governing combat). *Heraldy* is a variant of *heraldry*. °**seiz'd of** Possessed of. °**moi'ty** Portion. °**competent** Adequate, equivalent. °**gaged** Pledged. °**had** Would have. °**inheritance** Possession °**comart** Bargain. °**carriage** Tenor. °**design'd** Drawn up. °**unimproved** Untried (?) or not directed to any useful end (?). °**skirts** Outlying territories. °**Shark'd up** Gathered up hastily and indiscriminately. °**stomach** Relish of danger (?) or demand for courage (?) °**head** Source. °**romage** Rummage, bustling activity.

Barnardo: I think it be no other but e'en so.
    Well may it sort° that this portentous° figure
    Comes armed through our watch so like the King   110
    That was and is the question of these wars.
Horatio: A mote it is to trouble the mind's eye.
    In the most high and palmy state of Rome,
    A little ere the mightiest Julius fell,°
    The graves stood [tenantless] and the sheeted dead   115
    Did squeak and gibber in the Roman streets.
    As stars with trains of fire, and dews of blood,
    Disasters° in the sun; and the moist star°
    Upon whose influence Neptune's empire stands°   120
    Was sick almost to doomsday° with eclipse.°
    And even the like precurse° of [fear'd] events,
    As harbingers° preceding still° the fates
    And prologue to the omen° coming on,
    Have heaven and earth together demonstrated
    Unto our climatures° and countrymen.   125

Enter Ghost.

    But, soft, behold! lo where it comes again!

It spreads his° arms.

    I'll cross it° though it blast° me. Stay, illusion!
    If thou hast any sound or use of voice,
    Speak to me.
    If there be any good thing to be done   130
    That may to thee do ease, and grace to me,
    Speak to me.
    If thou art privy to thy country's fate,
    Which happily° foreknowing may avoid,
    O speak!   135
    Or if thou has uphoarded in thy life
    Extorted treasure in the womb of earth,

EXPLORE ONLINE >

To watch a video of "Being Hamlet," visit your
Literature CourseMate, accessed through
www.cengagebrain.com.

    For which, they say, your° spirits oft walk in death,
    Speak of it, stay and speak! *(The cock crows.)* Stop it, Marcellus.
Marcellus: Shall I strike it with my partisan?°   140
Horatio: Do, if it will not stand.
Barnardo: 'Tis here!
Horatio: 'Tis here!

Exit Ghost.

Marcellus: 'Tis gone!
    We do it wrong, being so majestical,
    To offer it the show of violence,
    For it is as the air, invulnerable,   145
    And our vain blows malicious mockery.°
Barnardo: It was about to speak when the cock crew.
Horatio: And then it started like a guilty thing
    Upon a fearful summons. I have heard
    The cock, that is the trumpet° to the morn,   150
    Doth with his lofty and shrill-sounding throat
    Awake the god of day, and at his warning,
    Whether in sea or fire, in earth or air,
    Th' extravagant° and erring° spirit hies°
    To his confine; and of the truth herein   155
    This present object° made probation.°
Marcellus: It faded on the crowing of the cock.
    Some say that ever 'gainst° that season comes

>> Richard Burton (left), Laurence Olivier (middle), and Mel Gibson (right) have all played the role of Hamlet.

°**sort** Fit. °**portentous** Ominous. °**fell** One or more lines may
have been lost between this line and the next. °**Disasters** Ominous
signs. °**moist star** Moon. °**Neptune's empire stands** The seas are
dependent. °**sick...doomsday** Almost totally darkened. When the
Day of Judgment is imminent, says Matthew 24:29, "the moon shall not
give her light." °**eclipse** There were a solar and two total lunar eclipses
visible in England in 1598; they caused gloomy speculation. °**precurse**
Foreshadowing. °**harbingers** Advance messengers. °**still** Always.
°**omen** The events portended. °**climatures** Regions.

°**s.d.** (stage direction) *his* Its. °**cross it** Cross its path, confront it
directly. °**blast** Wither (by supernatural means). °**happily** Haply,
perhaps. °**your** Colloquial and impersonal; cf. 1. 5. 186, 4. 3. 23–25.
Most editors adopt *you* from F1. °**partisan** Long-handled spear.
°**malicious mockery** Mockery of malice, empty pretenses
of harming it. °**trumpet** Trumpeter. °**extravagant** Wandering
outside its proper bounds. °**erring** Wandering abroad. °**hies**
Hastens. °**object** Sight. °**probation** Proof. °**gainst** Just before.

Wherein our Saviour's birth is celebrated,
This bird of dawning singeth all night long, 160
And then they say no spirit dare stir abroad,
The nights are wholesome, then no planets strike,°
No fairy takes,° nor witch hath power to charm,
So hallowed, and so gracious,° is that time.

Horatio: So have I heard and do in part believe it. 165
But look, the morn in russet° mantle clad
Walks o'er the dew of yon high eastward hill.
Break we our watch up, and by my advice
Let us impart what we have seen to-night
Unto young Hamlet, for, upon my life, 170
This spirit, dumb to us, will speak to him.
Do you consent we shall acquaint him with it,
As needful in our loves, fitting our duty?

Marcellus: Let's do't, I pray, and I this morning know
Where we shall find him most convenient. 175

Exeunt.

SCENE 2°

Flourish.° Enter Claudius, King of Denmark, Gertrude the Queen, Council: as Polonius; and his son Laertes, Hamlet, cum aliis° [including Voltemand and Cornelius].

King: Though yet of Hamlet our dear brother's death
The memory be green, and that it us befitted°
To bear our hearts in grief, and our whole kingdom
To be contracted in° one brow of woe,°
Yet so far hath discretion fought with nature 5
That we with wisest sorrow think on him
Together with remembrance of ourselves.
Therefore our sometime sister, now our queen,
Th' imperial jointress° of this warlike state,
Have we, as 'twere with defeated° joy, 10
With an auspicious, and a dropping° eye,
With mirth in funeral, and with dirge in marriage,
In equal scale weighing delight and dole,
Taken to wife; nor have we herein barr'd
Your better wisdoms, which have freely° gone 15
With this affair along. For all, our thanks.
Now follows that you know° young Fortinbras,
Holding a weak supposal° of our worth,
Or thinking by our late dear brother's death
Our state to be disjoint and out of frame, 20
Co-leagued° with this dream of his advantage,
He hath not fail'd to pester us with message°

Importing° the surrender of those lands
Lost by his father, with all bands° of law,
To our most valiant brother. So much for him. 25
Now for ourself, and for this time of meeting,
Thus much the business is: we have here writ
To Norway, uncle of young Fortinbras—
Who, impotent and bedred,° scarcely hears
Of this his nephew's purpose—to suppress 30
His further gait° herein, in that the levies,
The lists, and full proportions are all made
Out of his subject;° and we here dispatch
You, good Cornelius, and you, Voltemand,
For bearers of this greeting to old Norway, 35
Giving to you no further personal power
To business with the King, more than the scope
Of these delated° articles allow. [*Giving a paper.*]
Farewell, and let your haste commend your duty.

Cornelius, Voltemand: In that and all things, will we show our duty. 40
King: We doubt it nothing;° heartily farewell.

Exeunt Voltemand and Cornelius.

And now, Laertes, what's the news with you?
You told us of some suit, what is't, Laertes?
You cannot speak of reason to the Dane
And lose° your voice. What wouldst thou beg, Laertes, 45
That shall not be my offer, not thy asking?
The head is not more native° to the heart,
The hand more instrumental° to the mouth,
Than is the throne of Denmark to thy father.
What wouldst thou have, Laertes? 50

Laertes: My dread lord,
Your leave and favor° to return to France,
From whence though willingly I came to Denmark
To show my duty in your coronation,
Yet now I must confess, that duty done,
My thoughts and wishes bend again toward France, 55
And bow them to your gracious leave and pardon.°

King: Have you your father's leave? What says Polonius?
Polonius: H'ath,° my lord, wrung from me my slow leave
By laborsome petition, and at last
Upon his will I seal'd my hard° consent 60
I do beseech you give him leave to go.

King: Take thy fair hour, Laertes, time be thine,
And thy best graces spend it at thy will!
But now, my cousin° Hamlet, and my son—

Hamlet [*Aside.*]: A little more than kin, and less than kind.° 65
King: How is it that the clouds still hang on you?

°**strike** Exert malevolent influence. °**takes** Bewitches, charms.
°**gracious** Blessed. °**russet** Coarse greyish-brown cloth.
°**1.2. Location** The castle. o.s.d. (opening-stage direction).
°**Flourish** Trumpet fanfare. °**cum aliis** With others. °**befitted**
Would befit. °**contracted in** (1) Reduced to; (2) knit or wrinkled in.
°**brow of woe** Mournful brow. °**jointress** Joint holder.
°**defeated** Impaired. °**auspicious . . . dropping** Cheerful . . .
weeping. °**freely** Fully, without reservation. °**know** Be informed,
learn. °**supposal** Conjecture, estimate. °**Co-leagued** Joined.
°**pester . . . message** Trouble me with persistent messages (the
original sense of *pester* is overcrowd." °**Importing** Having as import.

°**bands** Bonds, binding terms. °**impotent and bedred** Feeble and
bedridden. °**gait** Proceeding. °**in . . . subject** Since the troops are
all drawn from his subjects. °**delated** Extended, detailed (a variant
of *dilated*). °**nothing** Not at all. °**lose** Waste. °**native** Closely
related. °**instrumental** Serviceable. °**leave and favor** Gracious
permission. °**pardon** Permission to depart. °**H'ath** He hath.
°**hard** Reluctant. °**cousin** Kinsman (used in familiar address to any
collateral relative more distant than a brother or sister; here to a
nephew.) °**A little . . . kind** Closer than a nephew, since you are my
mother's husband; yet more distant than a son, too (and not well
disposed to you).

> "O that this too
> too sallied flesh
> would melt, /
> Thaw, and
> resolve itself into
> a dew!"

Hamlet: Not so, my lord, I am
too much in the sun.°
Queen: Good Hamlet, cast thy
nighted color off,
And let thine eye look like a
friend on Denmark.
Do not for ever with thy vailed° lids 70
Seek for thy noble father in the dust.
Thou know'st 'tis common,° all
that lives must die,
Passing through nature to
eternity.
Hamlet: Ay, madam, it is
common.
Queen: If it be,
Why seems it so particular° with thee? 75
Hamlet: Seems, madam? nay, it is, I know not "seems."
'Tis not alone my inky cloak, [good] mother,
Nor customary suits of solemn black,
Nor windy suspiration of forc'd breath,
No, nor the fruitful° river in the eye, 80
Nor the dejected havior of the visage,
Together with all forms, moods, [shapes] of grief,
That can [denote] me truly. These indeed seem,
For they are actions that a man might play,
But I have that within which passes show, 85
These but the trappings and the suits of woe.
King: 'Tis sweet and commendable in your nature, Hamlet,
To give these mourning duties to your father.
But you must know your father lost a father,
That father lost, lost his, and the survivor bound 90
In filial obligation for some term
To do obsequious° sorrow. But to persever
In obstinate condolement° is a course
Of impious stubbornness, 'tis unmanly grief,
It shows a will most incorrect° to heaven, 95
A heart unfortified, a mind impatient,
An understanding simple and unschool'd:
For what we know must be, and is as common
As any the most vulgar thing to sense,°
Why should we in our peevish opposition 100
Take it to° heart? Fie, 'tis a fault to heaven,
A fault against the dead, a fault to nature,
To reason most absurd,° whose common theme
Is death of fathers, and who still hath cried,
From the first corse till he that died to-day, 105
"This must be so." We pray you throw to earth
This unprevailing° woe, and think of us
As of a father, for let the world take note
You are the most immediate to our throne,

>> David Tennant as Hamlet and Patrick Stewart as Claudius in 2008 Royal Shakespeare Company production

And with no less nobility of love 110
Than that which dearest° father bears his son
Do I impart° toward you. For your intent
In going back to school in Wittenberg,
It is most retrograde to our desire,
And we beseech you bend you to remain 115
Here in the cheer and comfort of our eye,
Our chiefest courtier, cousin, and our son.
Queen: Let not thy mother lose her prayers, Hamlet,
I pray thee stay with us, go not to Wittenberg.
Hamlet: I shall in all my best obey you, madam. 120
King: Why, 'tis a loving and a fair reply:
Be as ourself in Denmark. Madam, come.
This gentle and unforc'd accord of Hamlet
Sits smiling to my heart, in grace whereof,
No jocund health that Denmark drinks to-day, 125
But the great cannon to the clouds shall tell,
And the King's rouse° the heaven shall bruit° again,
Respeaking earthly thunder. Come away.

Flourish. Exeunt all but Hamlet.

Hamlet: O that this too too sallied° flesh would melt,
Thaw, and resolve itself into a dew! 130
Or that the Everlasting had not fix'd
His canon° 'gainst [self-]slaughter! O God, God,
How [weary], stale, flat, and unprofitable
Seem to me all the uses° of this world!
Fie on't, ah fie! 'tis an unweeded garden 135
That grows to seed, things rank and gross in nature

°**sun** With obvious quibble on *son.* °**vailed** Downcast.
°**common** General, universal. °**particular** Individual, personal.
°**fruitful** Copious. °**obsequious** Proper to obsequies.
°**condolement** Grief. °**incorrect** Unsubmissive. °**any . . .
sense** What is perceived to be commonest. °**to** Against.

°**absurd** Contrary. °**unprevailing** Unavailing. °**dearest** Most
loving. °**impart** Impart love. °**rouse** Bumper, drink. °**bruit**
Loudly declare. °**sallied** Sullied. Many editors prefer the F1 reading,
solid. °**canon** Law. °**uses** Customs.

Possess it merely.° That it should come [to° this]!
But two months dead, nay, not so much, not two.
So excellent a king, that was to this
Hyperion° to a satyr, so loving to my mother   140
That he might not beteem° the winds of heaven
Visit her face too roughly. Heaven and earth,
Must I remember? Why, she should hang on him
As if increase of appetite had grown
By what it fed on, and yet, within a month—   145
Let me not think on't! Frailty, thy name is woman!—
A little month, or ere° those shoes were old
With which she followed my poor father's body,
Like Niobe,° all tears, why, she, [even she]—
O God, a beast that wants discourse of reason°   150
Would have mourn'd longer—married with my uncle,
My father's brother, but no more like my father
Than I to Hercules. Within a month,
Ere yet the salt of most unrighteous° tears
Had left the flushing° in her galled° eyes,   155
She married—O most wicked speed: to post
With such dexterity to incestious° sheets,
It is not, nor it cannot come to good,
But break my heart, for I must hold my tongue.

Enter Horatio, Marcellus and Barnardo.

Horatio: Hail to your lordship!
Hamlet: I am glad to see you well.   160
    Horatio—or I do forget myself.
Horatio: The same, my lord, and your poor servant ever.
Hamlet: Sir, my good friend— I'll change° that name with you.
    And what make you from° Wittenberg, Horatio?
    Marcellus.   165
Marcellus: My good lord.
Hamlet: I am very glad to see you. [*to Barnardo*] Good even,
    sir.—But what, in faith, make you from Wittenberg?
Horatio: A truant disposition,° good my lord.
Hamlet: I would not hear your enemy say so,   170
    Nor shall you do my ear that violence
    To make it truster of your own report
    Against yourself. I know you are no truant.
    But what is your affair in Elsinore?
    We'll teach you to drink [deep] ere you depart.   175
Horatio: My lord, I came to see your father's funeral.
Hamlet: I prithee do not mock me, fellow-student,°
    I think it was to [see] my mother's wedding.

Horatio: Indeed, my lord, it followed hard upon.
Hamlet: Thrift, thrift, Horatio, the funeral bak'd-meats   180
    Did coldly° furnish forth the marriage tables.
    Would I had met my dearest° foe in heaven
    Or° ever I had seen that day, Horatio!
    My father—methinks I see my father.
Horatio: Where, my lord?
Hamlet: In my mind's eye, Horatio.   185
Horatio: I saw him once, 'a was a goodly king.
Hamlet: 'A was a man, take him for all in all,
    I shall not look upon his like again.
Horatio: My lord, I think I saw him yesternight.
Hamlet: Saw, who?   190
Horatio: My lord, the King your father.
Hamlet: The King my father?
Horatio: Season° your admiration° for a while
    With an attent ear, till I may deliver,°
    Upon the witness of these gentlemen,
    This marvel to you.
Hamlet: For   195
    God's love let me hear!
Horatio: Two nights together
    had these gentlemen,
    Marcellus and Barnardo,
    on their watch,
    In the dead waste° and
    middle of the night,
    Been thus encount'red: a
    figure like your father,
    Armed at point exactly,°   200
    cap-a-pe,°
    Appears before them, and
    with solemn march
    Goes slow and stately by them; thrice he walk'd
    By their oppress'd and fear-surprised° eyes
    Within his truncheon's° length, whilst they, distill'd
    Almost to jelly with the act° of fear,   205
    Stand dumb, and speak not to him. This to me
    In dreadful° secrecy impart they did,
    And I with them the third night kept the watch,
    Where, as they had delivered, both in time,
    Form of the thing, each word made true and good,   210
    The apparition comes. I knew your father,
    These hands are not more like.°
Hamlet: But where was this?

> "Thrift, thrift, Horatio, the funeral bak'd-meats Did coldly furnish forth the marriage tables."

°**merely** Utterly. °**to** In comparison with. °**Hyperion** The sun-god. °**beteem** Allow. °**or ere** Before. °**Niobe** She wept endlessly for her children, whom Apollo and Artemis had killed. °**wants . . . reason** Lacks the power of reason (which distinguishes men from beasts). °**unrighteous** Hypocritical. °**flushing** Redness. °**galled** Inflamed. °**incestious** Incestuous. The marriage of a man to his brother's widow was so regarded until long after Shakespeare's day. °**change** Exchange. °**what . . . from** What are you doing away from. °**truant disposition** Inclination to play truant.

°**student** Student. °**coldly** When cold. °**dearest** Most intensely hated. °**Or** Ere, before. °**Season** Temper. °**admiration** Wonder. °**deliver** Report. °**waste** Empty expanse. °**at point exactly** In every particular. °**cap-a-pe** From head to foot. °**fear-surprised** Overwhelmed by fear. °**truncheon's** Short staff carried as a symbol of military command. °**act** Action, operation. °**dreadful** Held in awe, solemnly sworn. °**are . . . like** Do not resemble each other more closely than the apparition resembled him.

>> Kenneth Branagh as Hamlet and Julie Christie as Gertrude in 1996 film version of *Hamlet*

Marcellus: My lord, upon the platform where we watch.
Hamlet: Did you not speak to it?
Horatio: My lord, I did,
    But answer made it none. Yet once methought   215
    It lifted up it° head and did address
    Itself to motion° like as it would speak;
    But even then the morning cock crew loud,
    And at the sound it shrunk in haste away
    And vanish'd from our sight.
Hamlet: 'Tis very strange.   220
Horatio: As I do live, my honor'd lord, 'tis true,
    And we did think it writ down in our duty
    To let you know of it.
Hamlet: Indeed, [indeed,] sirs. But this troubles me.
    Hold you the watch to-night?
[Marcellus, Barnardo]:   We do, my lord.   225
Hamlet: Arm'd, say you?
[Marcellus, Barnardo]: Arm'd, my lord.
Hamlet: From top to toe?
[Marcellus, Barnardo]: My lord, from head to foot.
Hamlet: Then saw you not his face.
Horatio: O yes, my lord, he wore his beaver° up.
Hamlet: What, look'd he frowningly?
Horatio: A countenance more   230
    In sorrow than in anger.
Hamlet: Pale, or red?
Horatio: Nay, very pale.
Hamlet: And fix'd his eyes upon you?
Horatio: Most constantly.
Hamlet: I would I had been there.
Horatio: It would have much amaz'd you.

Hamlet: Very like, [very like]. Stay'd it long?   235
Horatio: While one with moderate haste might tell a hundredth.°
Both [Marcellus, Barnardo]: Longer, longer.
Horatio: Not when I saw't.
Hamlet: His beard was grisl'd,° no?
Horatio: It was, as I have seen it in his life,
    A sable silver'd.
Hamlet: I will watch to-night,   240
    Perchance 'twill walk again.
Horatio: I warr'nt it will.
Hamlet: If it assume my noble father's person,
    I'll speak to it though hell itself should gape
    And bid me hold my peace. I pray you all,
    If you have hitherto conceal'd this sight,   245
    Let it be tenable° in your silence still,
    And whatsomever else shall hap to-night,
    Give it an understanding but no tongue.
    I will requite your loves. So fare you well.
    Upon the platform 'twixt aleven° and twelf   250
    I'll visit you.
All: Our duty to your honor.
Hamlet: Your loves, as mine to you; farewell.

Exeunt [all but Hamlet].

    My father's spirit—in arms! All is not well,
    I doubt° some foul play. Would the night were come!
    Till then sit still, my soul. [Foul] deeds will rise,   255
    Though all the earth o'erwhelm them, to men's eyes.

Exit.

SCENE 3°

Enter Laertes and Ophelia, his sister.

Laertes: My necessaries are inbark'd.° Farewell.
    And, sister, as the winds give benefit
    And convey [is] assistant,° do not sleep,
    But let me hear from you.
Ophelia: Do you doubt that?
Laertes: For Hamlet, and the trifling of his favor,   5
    Hold it a fashion° and a toy in blood,°
    A violet in the youth of primy° nature,
    Forward,° not permanent, sweet, not lasting,
    The perfume and suppliance° of a minute—
    No more.   10
Ophelia: No more but so?
Laertes: Think it no more:
    For nature crescent° does not grow alone
    In thews° and [bulk], but as this temple waxes,
    The inward service of the mind and soul

°**it** Its. °**address ... motion** Begin to make a gesture. °**beaver** visor. °**tell a hundreth** Count a hundred. °**grisl'd** Grizzled, mixed with grey. °**tenable** Held close. °**aleven** Eleven. °**doubt** Suspect. °**1.3. Location** Polonius's quarters in the castle. °**inbark'd** Embarked, abroad. °**convey is assistant** Means of transport is available. °**a fashion** Standard behavior for a young man. °**toy in blood** Idle fancy of youthful passion. °**primy** Springlike. °**Forward** Early of growth. °**suppliance** Pastime. °**crescent** Growing, increasing. °**thews** Muscles, sinews.

Grows wide withal.° Perhaps he loves you now,   15
And now no soil° nor cautel° doth besmirch
The virtue of his will,° but you must fear,
His greatness weigh'd,° his will is not his own,
[For he himself is subject to his birth:]
He may not, as unvalued° persons do,   20
Carve for himself,° for on his choice depends
The safety and health of this whole state,
And therefore must his choice be circumscrib'd
Unto the voice° and yielding° of that body°
Whereof he is the head. Then if he says he loves you,   25
It fits your wisdom so far to believe it
As he in his particular act and place°
May give his saying deed, which is no further
Than the main° voice of Denmark goes withal.°
Then weigh what loss your honor may sustain   30
If with too credent° ear you list his songs,
Or lose your heart, or your chaste treasure open
To his unmast'red importunity.
Fear it, Ophelia, fear it, my dear sister,
And keep you in the rear of your affection,   35
Out of the shot° and danger of desire.
The chariest maid is prodigal enough
If she unmask her beauty to the moon.
Virtue itself scapes not calumnious strokes.
The canker° galls the infants of the spring   40
Too oft before their buttons° be disclos'd,°
And in the morn and liquid dew of youth
Contagious blastments° are most imminent.
Be wary then, best safety lies in fear:
Youth to itself rebels, though none else near.   45
Ophelia: I shall the effect of this good lesson keep
As watchman to° my heart. But, good my brother,
Do not, as some ungracious° pastors do,
Show me the steep and thorny way to heaven,
Whiles, [like] a puff'd° and reckless libertine,   50
Himself the primrose path of dalliance treads,
And reaks° not his own rede.°
Laertes: O, fear me not.°

Enter Polonius.

I stay too long—but here my father comes.
A double blessing is a double grace,
Occasion° smiles upon° a second leave.   55

Polonius: Yet here, Laertes? Aboard, aboard, for shame!
The wind sits in the shoulder of your sail,
And you are stay'd for. There—[*Laying his hand on
Laertes' head*] my blessing with thee!
And these few precepts in thy memory   60
Look thou character.° Give thy thoughts no tongue,
Nor any unproportion'd° thought his act.
Be thou familiar,° but by no means vulgar.°
Those friends thou hast, and their adoption tried,°
Grapple them unto thy soul with hoops of steel,   65
But do not dull thy palm with entertainment
Of each new-hatch'd, unfledg'd courage.° Beware
Of entrance to a quarrel, but being in,
Bear't that° th' opposed may beware of thee.
Give every man thy ear, but few thy voice,   70
Take° each man's censure,° but reserve thy judgment.
Costly thy habit as thy purse can buy,
But not express'd in fancy, rich, not gaudy,
For the apparel oft proclaims the man,
And they in France of the best rank and station   75
[Are] of a most select and generous° chief° in that.
Neither a borrower nor a lender [be],
For a [loan] oft loses both itself and friend,
And borrowing dulleth [th'] edge of husbandry.°
This above all: to thine own self be true,   80
And it must follow, as the night the day,
Thou canst not then be false to any man.
Farewell, my blessing season° this in thee!
Laertes: Most humbly do I take my leave, my lord.
Polonius: The time invests° you, go, your servants tend.°   85
Laertes: Farewell, Ophelia, and remember well
What I have said to you.
Ophelia: 'Tis in my memory lock'd,
And you yourself shall keep the key of it.
Laertes: Farewell. (*Exit Laertes.*)
Polonius: What is't, Ophelia, he hath said to you?   90
Ophelia: So please you, something touching the Lord Hamlet.
Polonius: Marry,° well bethought.
'Tis told me, he hath very oft of late
Given private time to you, and you yourself
Have of your audience been most free and bounteous.   95
If it be so—as so 'tis put on° me,
And that in way of caution—I must tell you,
You do not understand yourself so clearly

°**as ... withal** As the body develops, the powers of mind and spirit grow along with it. °**soil** Stain. °**cautel** Deceit. °**will** Desire. °**His greatness weigh'd** Considering his princely status. °**unvalued** Of low rank. °**Carve for himself** Indulge his own wishes. °**voice** Vote, approval. °**yielding** Consent. °**that body** The state. °**in ... place** Acting as he must act in the position he occupies. °**main** General. °**goes withal** Accord with. °**credent** Credulous. °**shot** Range. °**canker** Canker-worm. °**buttons** Buds. °**disclos'd** Opened. °**blastments** Withering blights. °**to** Of. °**ungracious** Graceless. °**puff'd** Bloated. °**reaks** Recks, heeds. °**rede** Advice. °**fear me not** Don't worry about me. °**Occasion** Opportunity (here personified, as often).

°**smiles upon** Graciously bestows. °**character** Inscribe. °**unproportion'd** Unfitting. °**familiar** Affable, sociable. °**vulgar** Friendly with everybody. °**their adoption tried** Their association with you tested and proved. °**courage** Spirited, young blood. °**Bear't that** Manage it in such a way that. °**Take** Listen to. °**censure** Opinion. °**generous** Noble °**chief** Eminence (?). But the line is probably corrupt. Perhaps *of a* is intrusive, in which case **chief** = chiefly. °**husbandry** thrift. °**season** preserve (?) or ripen, make fruitful (?). °**invests** Besieges. °**tend** Wait. °**Marry** Indeed (originally the name of the Virgin Mary used as an oath). °**put on** Told to.

>> An audience at the reconstructed Globe Theatre in London

As it behooves my daughter and your honor.
What is between you? Give me up the truth.   100
Ophelia: He hath, my lord, of late made many tenders°
Of his affection to me.
Polonius: Affection, puh! You speak like a green girl,
Unsifted° in such perilous circumstance.
Do you believe his tenders, as you call them?
Ophelia: I do not know, my lord, what I should think.   105
Polonius: Marry, I will teach you: think yourself a baby
That you have ta'en these tenders° for true pay,
Which are not sterling. Tender° yourself more dearly,
Or (not to crack the wind of the poor phrase,
[Wringing]° it thus) you'll tender me a fool.°   110
Ophelia: My lord, he hath importun'd me with love
In honorable fashion.°
Polonius: Ay, fashion you may call it. Go to, go to.
Ophelia: And hath given countenance° to his speech, my lord,   115
With almost all the holy vows of heaven.
Polonius: Ay, springes° to catch woodcocks.° I do know,
When the blood burns, how prodigal the soul
Lends the tongue vows. These blazes, daughter,
Giving more light than heat, extinct in both   120
Even in their promise, as it is a-making,
You must not take for fire. From this time

Be something scanter of your maiden presence,
Set your entreatments at a higher rate
Than a command to parle.° For Lord Hamlet,   125
Believe so much in him,° that he is young,
And with a larger teder° may he walk
Than may be given you. In few, Ophelia,
Do not believe his vows, for they are brokers,°
Not of that dye which their investments show,°   130
But mere° [implorators] of unholy suits,
Breathing like sanctified and pious bonds,°
The better to [beguile]. This is for all:
I would not, in plain terms, from this time forth,
Have you so slander° any moment° leisure   135
As to give words or talk with the Lord Hamlet.
Look to't, I charge you. Come your ways.°
Ophelia: I shall obey, my lord.

Exeunt.

SCENE 4°

Enter Hamlet, Horatio, and Marcellus.

Hamlet: The air bites shrowdly,° it is very cold.
Horatio: It is [a] nipping and an eager° air.
Hamlet: What hour now?
Horatio: I think it lacks of twelf.
Marcellus: No, it is strook.
Horatio: Indeed? I heard it not: It then draws near the season   5
Wherein the spirit held his wont to walk.

A flourish of trumpets, and two pieces° goes off [within].

What does this mean, my lord?
Hamlet: The King doth wake to-night and takes his rouse,°
Keeps wassail,° and the swagg'ring up-spring° reels;
And as he drains his draughts of Rhenish° down,   10
The kettle-drum and trumpet thus bray out
The triumph of his pledge.°
Horatio: Is it a custom?
Hamlet: Ay, marry, is't,
But to my mind, though I am native here
And to the manner° born, it is a custom   15
More honor'd in the breach than the observance.°
This heavy-headed revel east and west
Makes us traduc'd and tax'd of° other nations.

°**tenders** Offers. °**Unsifted** Untried. °**tenders** With play on the sense "money offered in payment" (as in *legal tender*). °**Tender** Hold, value. °**Wringing** Straining, forcing to the limit. °**tender . . . fool** (1) Show me that you are a fool; (2) make me look like a fool; (3) present me with a (bastard) grandchild. °**fashion** See note on line 7. °**countenance** Authority. °**springes** Snares. °**woodcocks** Proverbially gullible birds. °**Set . . . parle** Place a higher value on your favors; do not grant interviews simply because he asks for them. Polonius uses a military figure **entreatments** = negotiations for surrender; **parle** = parley, discuss terms. °**so . . . him** No more than this with respect to him. °**larger teder** Longer tether. °**brokers** Procurers. °**Not . . . show** Not of

the color that their garments (*investments*) exhibit; not what they seem. °**mere** Out-and-out. °**bonds** (Lover's) vows or assurances. Many editors follow Theobald in reading *bawds*. °**slander** Disgrace. °**moment** Momentary. °**Come your ways** Come along. °**1.4 Location** The guard-platform of the castle. °**shrowdly** Shrewdly, wickedly. °**eager** Sharp. °**pieces** cannon. °**doth . . . rouse** Holds revels far into the night. °**wassail** Carousal. °**up-spring** Wild dance. °**Rhenish** Rhine wine. °**triumph . . . pledge** Accomplishment of his toast (by draining his cup at a single draught.) °**manner** Custom (of carousing). °**More . . . observance** Which it is more honorable to break than to observe. °**tax'd of** Censured by.

They clip° us drunkards, and with swinish phrase
Soil our addition,° and indeed it takes   20
From our achievements, though perform'd at height,°
The pith and marrow of our attribute.°
So, oft it chances in particular° men,
That for some vicious mole of nature° in them,
As in their birth, wherein they are not guilty   25
(Since nature cannot choose his° origin),
By their o'ergrowth of some complexion°
Oft breaking down the pales° and forts of reason,
Or by some habit that too much o'er-leavens°
The form of plausive° manners—that these men,   30
Carrying, I say, the stamp of one defect,
Being nature's livery, or fortune's star,°
His virtues else, be they as pure as grace,
As infinite as man may undergo,°
Shall in the general censure° take corruption   35
From that particular fault: the dram° of [ev'l]°
Doth all the noble substance of a doubt°
To his own scandal.°

Enter Ghost.

Horatio: Look, my lord, it comes!
Hamlet: Angels and ministers of grace defend us!
Be thou a spirit of health,° or goblin damn'd,   40
Bring with thee airs from heaven, or blasts from hell,
Be thy intents wicked, or charitable,
Thou com'st in such a questionable° shape
That I will speak to thee. I'll call thee Hamlet,
King, father, royal Dane. O, answer me!   45
Let me not burst in ignorance, but tell
Why thy canoniz'd° bones, hearsed in death,
Have burst their cerements;° why the sepulchre,
Wherein we saw thee quietly [inurn'd,]
Hath op'd his ponderous and marble jaws   50
To cast thee up again. What may this mean,
That thou, dead corpse, again in complete steel°
Revisits° thus the glimpses of the moon,
Making night hideous, and we fools of nature°
So horridly to shake our disposition°   55
With thoughts beyond the reaches of our souls?
Say why is this? wherefore? what should we do?

[*Ghost*] *beckons* [*Hamlet*].

Horatio: It beckons you to go away with it,
As if it some impartment° did desire
To you alone.
Marcellus: Look with what courteous action   60
It waves you to a more removed ground,
But do not go with it.
Horatio: No, by no means.
Hamlet: It will not speak, then I will follow it.
Horatio: Do not, my lord.
Hamlet: Why, what should be the fear?
I do not set my life at a pin's fee,°   65
And for my soul, what can it do to that,
Being a thing immortal as itself?
It waves me forth again, I'll follow it.
Horatio: What if it tempt you toward the flood, my lord,
Or to the dreadful summit of the cliff   70
That beetles o'er his base into the sea,
And there assume some other horrible form
Which might deprive your sovereignty of reason,°
And draw you into madness? Think of it.
The very place puts toys of desperation,°   75
Without more motive, into every brain
That looks so many fadoms° to the sea
And hears it roar beneath.
Hamlet: It waves me still.—
Go on, I'll follow thee.
Marcellus: You shall not go, my lord.
Hamlet: Hold off your hands.   80
Horatio: Be rul'd, you shall not go.
Hamlet: My fate cries out,
And makes each petty artere° in this body
As hardy as the Nemean lion's° nerve.°
Still am I call'd. Unhand me, gentlemen.
By heaven, I'll make a ghost of him that lets° me!   85
I say away!—Go on, I'll follow thee.

Exeunt Ghost and Hamlet.

Horatio: He waxes desperate with [imagination].
Marcellus: Let's follow. 'Tis not fit thus to obey him.
Horatio: Have after. To what issue will this come?
Marcellus: Something is rotten in the state of Denmark. 90
Horatio: Heaven will direct it.°
Marcellus: Nay, let's follow him.

Exeunt.

°**clip** Clepe, call. °**addition** Titles of honor. °**at height** Most excellently. °**attribute** Reputation. °**particular** Individual. °**vicious. . . nature** Small natural blemish. °**his** Its. °**By . . . complexion** By the excess of some one of the humors (which were thought to govern the disposition). °**pales** Fences. °**o'er-leavens** Makes itself felt throughout (as leaven works in the whole mass of dough). °**plausive** Pleasing. °**Being. . . star** Whether they were born with it, or got it by misfortune. **Star** means "blemish." °**undergo** Carry the weight of, sustain. °**general censure** Popular opinion. °**dram** Minute amount. °**ev'l** Evil, with a pun on *eale*, "yeast" (cf. **o'er-leavens** in line 29). °**of a doubt** A famous crux, for which many emendations have been suggested, the most widely accepted being Steevens' *often dout* (extinguish). °**To . . . scandal** So that it all shares in the disgrace. °**of health** Wholesome, good. °**questionable** Inviting talk. °**canoniz'd** Buried with the prescribed rites. °**cerements** Grave-clothes. °**complete steel** Full armor. °**Revisits** The *-s* ending in the second-person singular is common. °**fools of nature** The children (or the dupes) of a purely natural order, baffled by the supernatural. °**disposition** Nature. °**impartment** Communication. °**fee** Worth. °**deprive . . . reason** Unseat reason from the rule of your mind. °**toys of desperation** Fancies of desperate action, inclinations to jump off. °**fadoms** Fathoms. °**artere** Variant spelling of **artery;** here, ligament, sinew. °**Nemean lion** Slain by Hercules as one of his twelve labors. °**nerve** Sinew. °**lets** Hinders. °**it** The issue.

SCENE 5°

Enter Ghost and Hamlet.

Hamlet: Whither wilt thou lead me? Speak, I'll go no further.
Ghost: Mark me.
Hamlet: I will.
Ghost: My hour is almost come
   When I to sulph'rous and tormenting flames
   Must render up myself.
Hamlet: Alas, poor ghost!
Ghost: Pity me not, but lend thy serious hearing   5
   To what I shall unfold.
Hamlet: Speak, I am bound to hear.
Ghost: So art thou to revenge, when thou shalt hear.
Hamlet: What?
Ghost: I am thy father's spirit,
   Doom'd for a certain term to walk the night,   10
   And for the day confin'd to fast° in fires,
   Till the foul crimes° done in my days of nature
   Are burnt and purg'd away. But that I am forbid
   To tell the secrets of my prison-house,
   I could a tale unfold whose lightest word   15
   Would harrow up thy soul, freeze thy young blood,
   Make thy two eyes like stars start from their spheres,°
   Thy knotted and combined locks to part,
   And each particular hair to stand an end,°   20
   Like quills upon the fearful porpentine.°
   But this eternal blazon° must not be
   To ears of flesh and blood. List, list, O, list!
   If thou didst ever thy dear father love—
Hamlet: O God!
Ghost: Revenge his foul and most unnatural murther.   25
Hamlet: Murther!
Ghost: Murther most foul, as in the best it is,
   But this most foul, strange, and unnatural.
Hamlet: Haste me to know't, that I with wings as swift
   As meditation,° or the thoughts of love,   30
   May sweep to my revenge.
Ghost: I find thee apt,
   And duller shouldst thou be than the fat weed
   That roots itself in ease on Lethe° wharf,°
   Wouldst thou not stir in this. Now, Hamlet, hear:
   'Tis given out that, sleeping in my orchard,°   35
   A serpent stung me, so the whole ear of Denmark
   Is by a forged process° of my death
   Rankly abus'd:° but know, thou noble youth,

The serpent that did sting thy father's life
   Now wears his crown.
Hamlet: O my prophetic soul!   40
   My uncle?
Ghost: Ay, that incestuous, that adulterate° beast,
   With witchcraft of his wit, with traitorous gifts—
   O wicked wit and gifts that have the power
   So to seduce!—won to his shameful lust   45
   The will of my most seeming virtuous queen.
   O Hamlet, what [a] falling-off was there
   From me, whose love was of that dignity
   That it went hand in hand even with the vow
   I made to her in marriage, and to decline   50
   Upon a wretch whose natural gifts were poor
   To those of mine!
   But virtue, as it never will be moved,
   Though lewdness court it in a shape of heaven,°
   So [lust], though to a radiant angel link'd,   55
   Will [sate] itself in a celestial bed
   And prey on garbage.
   But soft, methinks I scent the morning air,
   Brief let me be. Sleeping within my orchard,
   My custom always of the afternoon,   60
   Upon my secure° hour thy uncle stole,
   With juice of cursed hebona° in a vial,
   And in the porches of my ears did pour
   The leprous distillment, whose effect
   Holds such an enmity with blood of man   65
   That, swift as quicksilver it courses through
   The natural gates and alleys of the body,
   And with a sudden vigor it doth [posset°]
   And curd, like eager° droppings into milk,
   The thin and wholesome blood. So did it mine,   70
   And a most instant tetter° bark'd° about,
   Most lazar-like,° with vile and loathsome crust
   All my smooth body.
   Thus was I, sleeping, by a brother's hand,
   Of life, of crown, of queen, at once° dispatch'd,°   75
   Cut off even in the blossoms of my sin,
   Unhous'led,° disappointed,° unanel'd,°
   No reck'ning made, but sent to my account
   With all my imperfections on my head.
   O, horrible, O, horrible, most horrible!   80
   If thou hast nature° in thee, bear it not,
   Let not the royal bed of Denmark be
   A couch for luxury° and damned incest.

°**1.5. Location** On the battlements of the castle. °**fast** Do penance.
°**crimes** Sins. °**spheres** Eye-sockets; with allusion to the revolving
spheres in which, according to the Ptolemaic astronomy, the stars
were fixed. °**an end** On end °**fearful porpentine** Frightened
porcupine. °**eternal blazon** Revelation of eternal things.
°**meditation** Thought. °**Lethe** River of Hades, the water of which
made the drinker forget the past. °**wharf** Bank. °**orchard**
Garden. °**forged process** False account. °**abus'd** Deceived.
°**adulterate** Adulterous. °**shape of heaven** Angelic form.
°**secure** Carefree. °**hebona** Ebony (which Shakespeare,

following a literary tradition, and perhaps also associating
the word with *henbane*, thought the name of a poison).
°**posset** Curdle. °**eager** Sour. °**tetter** Scabby eruption.
°**bark'd** Formed a hard covering, like bark on a tree.
°**lazar-like** Leperlike. °**at once** All at the same time.
°**dispatch'd** Deprived. °**Unhous'led** Without the Eucharist.
°**disappointed** Without (spiritual) preparation. °**unanel'd**
Unanointed, without extreme unction. °**nature** Natural
feeling. °**luxury** Lust.

But howsomever thou pursues this act,
Taint not thy mind, nor let thy soul contrive   85
Against thy mother aught. Leave her to heaven,
And to those thorns that in her bosom lodge
To prick and sting her. Fare thee well at once!
The glow-worm shows the matin° to be near,
And gins° to pale his uneffectual fire.
Adieu, adieu, adieu! remember me.   90

Exit.

Hamlet: O all you host of heaven! O earth! What else?
   And shall I couple hell? O fie, hold, hold, my heart,
   And you, my sinows,° grow not instant old,
   But bear me [stiffly] up. Remember thee!   95
   Ay, thou poor ghost, whiles memory holds a seat
   In this distracted globe.° Remember thee!
   Yea, from the table° of my memory
   I'll wipe away all trivial fond° records,
   All saws° of books, all forms,° all pressures° past   100
   That youth and observation copied there,
   And thy commandement all alone shall live
   Within the book and volume of my brain,
   Unmix'd with baser matter. Yes, by heaven!
   O most pernicious woman!   105
   O villain, villain, smiling, damned villain!
   My tables—meet it is I set it down
   That one may smile, and smile, and be a villain!
   At least I am sure it may be so in Denmark. [*He writes.*]
   So, uncle, there you are. Now to my word:°   110
   It is, "Adieu, adieu! remember me."
   I have sworn't.
Horatio [*Within.*]: My lord, my lord!
Marcellus [*Within.*]:   Lord Hamlet!

Enter Horatio and Marcellus.

Horatio: Heavens secure him!
Hamlet: So be it!
Marcellus: Illo, ho, ho, my lord!
Hamlet: Hillo, ho, ho, boy! Come,° [bird], come.   115
Marcellus: How is't, my noble lord?
Horatio: What news, my lord?
Hamlet: O, wonderful!
Horatio: Good my lord, tell it.
Hamlet: No, you will reveal it.   120
Horatio: Not I, my lord, by heaven.
Marcellus: Nor I, my lord.
Hamlet: How say you then, would heart of man once think it?—
   But you'll be secret?

Both [Horatio, Marcellus]: Ay, by heaven, [my lord].
Hamlet: There's never a villain dwelling in all Denmark   125
   But he's an arrant knave.
Horatio: There needs no ghost, my lord, come from the grave
   To tell us this.
Hamlet: Why, right, you are in the right,
   And so, without more circumstance° at all,
   I hold it fit that we shake hands and part,   130
   You, as your business and desire shall point you,
   For every man hath business and desire,
   Such as it is, and for my own poor part,
   I will go pray.
Horatio: These are but wild and whirling words, my lord.   135
Hamlet: I am sorry they offend you, heartily,
   Yes, faith, heartily.
Horatio: There's no offense, my lord.
Hamlet: Yes, by Saint Patrick, but there is, Horatio,
   And much offense too. Touching this vision here,   140
   It is an honest° ghost, that let me tell you.
   For your desire to know what is between us,
   O'ermaster't as you may. And now, good friends,
   As you are friends, scholars, and soldiers,
   Give me one poor request.
Horatio: What is't,° my lord, we will.
Hamlet: Never make known what you have seen tonight.   145
Both [Horatio, Marcellus]: My lord, we will not.
Hamlet: Nay, but swear't.
Horatio: In faith,
   My lord, not I.
Marcellus: Nor I, my lord, in faith.
Hamlet: Upon my sword.
Marcellus: We have sworn, my lord, already.
Hamlet: Indeed, upon my sword,° indeed.

Ghost cries under the stage.

Ghost: Swear.   150
Hamlet: Ha, ha, boy, say'st thou so? Art thou there, truepenny?°
   Come on, you hear this fellow in the cellarage,
   Consent to swear.
Horatio: Propose the oath, my lord.
Hamlet: Never to speak of this that you have seen,   155
   Swear by my sword.
Ghost [*beneath*]: Swear.
Hamlet *Hic et ubique?*° Then we'll shift our ground.
   Come hither, gentlemen,
   And lay your hands again upon my sword.   160
   Swear by my sword
   Never to speak of this that you have heard.
Ghost [*beneath*]: Swear by his sword.

°**matin** Morning. °**gins** Begins. °**sinows** Sinews. °**globe**
Head. °**table** Writing tablet. °**fond** Foolish. °**saws** Wise
sayings. °**forms** Shapes, images. °**pressures** Impressions.
°**word** Word of command from the Ghost °**Hillo . . . come**
Hamlet answers Marcellus' halloo with a falconer's cry.
°**circumstance** Ceremony. °**honest** True, genuine. °**What is't**
Whatever it is. °**upon my sword** On the cross formed by the hilt.
°**truepenny** Trusty fellow. °*Hic et ubique* Here and everywhere.

Hamlet: Well said, old mole, canst work i' th' earth so fast?
    A worthy pioner!° Once more remove, good friends. 165
Horatio: O day and night, but this is wondrous strange!
Hamlet: And therefore as a stranger give it welcome.°
    There are more things in heaven and earth, Horatio,
    Than are dreamt of in your° philosophy.°
    But come— 170
    Here, as before, never, so help you mercy,
    How strange or odd some'er I bear myself—
    As I perchance hereafter shall think meet
    To put an antic disposition on°—
    That you, at such times seeing me, never shall, 175
    With arms encumb'red° thus, or this headshake,
    Or by pronouncing of some doubtful phrase,
    As "Well, well, we know," or "We could, and if° we would,"
    Or "If we list° to speak," or "There be, and if they might,"
    Or such ambiguous giving out, to note°
    That you know aught of me—this do swear, 180
    So grace and mercy at your most need help you,
Ghost [*beneath*]: Swear. [*They swear.*]
Hamlet: Rest, rest, perturbed spirit! So, gentlemen,
    With all my love I do commend to you,
    And what so poor a man as Hamlet is 185
    May do t' express his love and friending to you,
    God willing, shall not lack. Let us go in together,
    And still° your fingers on your lips, I pray.
    The time is out of joint—O cursed spite,
    That ever I was born to set it right! 190
    Nay, come, let's go together.°

Exeunt.

ACT 2
SCENE 1°

Enter old Polonius with his man [Reynaldo].

Polonius: Give him this money and these notes, Reynaldo.
Reynaldo: I will, my lord.
Polonius: You shall do marvell's° wisely, good Reynaldo,
    Before you visit him, to make inquire
    On his behavior.
Reynaldo: My lord, I did intend it. 5
Polonius: Marry, well said, very well said. Look you, sir,
    Inquire me first what Danskers° are in Paris,
    And how, and who, what means, and where they keep,°
    What company, at what expense; and finding

    By this encompassment° and drift of question° 10
    That they do know my son, come you more nearer
    Than your particular demands° will touch it.
    Take you as 'twere some distant knowledge of him,
    As thus, "I know his father and his friends,
    And in part him." Do you mark this, Reynaldo? 15
Reynaldo: Ay, very well, my lord.
Polonius: "And in part him—but," you may say, "not well.
    But if't be he I mean, he's very wild,
    Addicted so and so," and there put on him
    What forgeries° you please: marry, none so rank 20
    As may dishonor him, take heed of that,
    But, sir, such wanton,° wild, and usual slips
    As are companions and most known
    To youth and liberty.
Reynaldo: As gaming, my lord.
Polonius: Ay, or drinking, fencing, swearing, quarreling, 25
    Drabbing°—you may go so far.
Reynaldo: My lord, that would dishonor him.
Polonius: Faith,° as you may season° it in the charge:
    You must not put another scandal on him,
    That he is open to incontinency°— 30
    That's not my meaning. But breathe his faults so quaintly°
    That they may seem the taints of liberty,
    The flash and outbreak of a fiery mind,
    A savageness in unreclaimed° blood,
    Of general assault.°
Reynaldo: But, my good lord— 35
Polonius: Wherefore should you do this?
Reynaldo: Ay, my lord,
    I would know that.
Polonius: Marry, sir, here's my drift,
    And I believe it is a fetch of wit:°
    You laying these slight sallies° on my son,
    As 'twere a thing a little soil'd [wi' th'] working,° 40
    Mark you,
    Your party in converse, him you would sound,
    Having° ever seen in the prenominate crimes°
    The youth you breathe of guilty, be assur'd
    He closes° with you in this consequence:° 45
    "Good sir," or so, or "friend," or "gentleman,"
    According to the phrase or the addition°
    Of man and country.
Reynaldo: Very good, my lord.
Polonius: And then, sir, does 'a this—'a does—what was I about
    to say? By the mass, I was about to say something. 50
    Where did I leave?

°**pioner** Digger, miner (variant of *pioneer*). °**as . . . welcome** Give it the welcome due in courtesy to strangers. °**your** See note on. 1. 1. 151. °**philosophy** Natural philosophy, science. °**put . . . on** Behave in some fantastic manner, act like a madman. °**encumb'red** Folded. °**and if** If. °**list** Cared, had a mind. °**note** Indicate. °**still** Always. °**Nay . . . together** They are holding back to let him go first. °**2. 1. Location** Polonius's quarters in the castle. °**marvell's** Marvellous(ly). °**Danskers** Danes. °**keep** Lodge. °**encompassment** Circuitousness. °**drift of question** Directing of the conversation. °**particular demands** Direct questions.

°**forgeries** Invented charges. °**wanton** Sportive. °**Drabbing** Whoring. °**Faith** Most editors read *Faith, no,* following F1; this makes easier sense. °**season** Qualify, temper. °**open to incontinency** Habitually profligate. °**quaintly** Artfully. °**unreclaimed** Untamed. °**Of general assault** To which young men are generally subject. °**fetch of wit** Ingenious device. °**sallies** Sullies, blemishes. °**soil'd . . . working** Shopworn. °**Having** If he has. °**prenominate crimes** Aforementioned faults. °**closes** Falls in. °**in this consequence** As follows. °**addition** Style of address.

Reynaldo: At "closes in the consequence."

Polonius: At "closes in the consequence," ay, marry.
He closes thus: "I know the gentleman.
"I saw him yesterday, or th' other day,
Or then, or then, with such or such, and as you say,   55
There was 'a gaming, there o'ertook in 's rouse,°
There falling out at tennis" or, perchance,
I saw him enter such a house of sale,"
Videlicet, a brothel, or so forth. See you now,
Your bait of falsehood take this carp of truth,   60
And thus do we of wisdom and of reach,°
With windlasses° and with assays of bias,°
By indirections find directions° out;
So by my former lecture and advice
Shall you my son. You have me,° have you not?   65

Reynaldo: My lord, I have.

Polonius: God buy ye,° fare ye well.

Reynaldo: Good my lord.

Polonius: Observe his inclination in° yourself.

Reynaldo: I shall, my lord.

Polonius: And let him ply° his music.

Reynaldo: Well, my lord.

Polonius: Farewell.   70

Exit Reynaldo.

Enter Ophelia.

How now, Ophelia, what's the matter?

Ophelia: O my lord, I have been so affrighted!

Polonius: With what, i' th' name of God?

Ophelia: My lord, as I was sewing in my closet,°   75
Lord Hamlet, with his doublet all unbrac'd,°
No hat upon his head, his stockins fouled,°
Ungart'red, and down-gyved° to his ankle,
Pale as his shirt, his knees knocking each other,
And with a look so piteous in purport   80
As if he had been loosed out of hell
To speak of horrors—he comes before me.

Polonius: Mad for thy love?

Ophelia: My lord, I do not know,
But truly I do fear it.

Polonius: What said he?

Ophelia: He took me by the wrist, and held me hard,   85
Then goes he to the length of all his arm,
And with his other hand thus o'er his brow,
He falls to such perusal of my face
As 'a would draw it. Long stay'd he so.
At last, a little shaking of mine arm,   90
And thrice his head thus waving up and down,
He rais'd a sigh so piteous and profound
As it did seem to shatter all his bulk°
And end his being. That done, he lets me go,
And with his head over his shoulder turn'd,   95
He seem'd to find his way without his eyes,
For out a' doors he went without their helps,
And to the last bended their light on me.

Polonius: Come, go with me. I will go seek the King.
This is the very ecstasy° of love,   100
Whose violent property° fordoes° itself,
And leads the will to desperate undertakings,
As oft as any passions under heaven
That does afflict our natures. I am sorry—
What, have you given him any hard words of late?   105

Ophelia: No, my good lord, but as you did command
I did repel his letters, and denied
His access to me.

Polonius: That hath made him mad.
I am sorry that with better heed and judgment
I had not coted° him. I fear'd he did but trifle   110
And meant to wreck thee, but, beshrow° my jealousy!°
By heaven, it is as proper to our age°
To cast beyond ourselves° in our opinions,
As it is common for the younger sort
To lack discretion. Come, go we to the King.   115
This must be known, which, being kept close,° might move
More grief to hide, than hate to utter love.°
Come

Exeunt.

SCENE 2°

Flourish. Enter King and Queen, Rosencrantz and Guildenstern [cum aliis].

King: Welcome, dear Rosencrantz and Guildenstern!
Moreover that we much did long to see you,°
The need we have to use you did provoke
Our hasty sending. Something have you heard
Of Hamlet's transformation; so call it,   5
Sith° nor th' exterior nor the inward man
Resembles that it was. What it should be,
More than his father's death, that thus hath put him

°**o'ertook in 's rouse** Overcome by drink. °**reach** Capacity, understanding. °**windlasses** Roundabout methods. °**assays of bias** Indirect attempts (a figure from the game of bowls in which the player must make allowance for the curving course his bowl will take toward its mark. °**directions** The way things are going. °**have me** Understand me. °**God buy ye** Good-bye (a contraction of *God be with you*). °**in** By; Polonius asks him to observe Laertes directly as well as making inquiries. °**let him ply** See that he goes on with. °**closet** Private room. °**unbrac'd** Unlaced. °**stockins fouled** Stockings dirty. °**down-gyved** Hanging down like fetters on a prisoner's legs. °**bulk** Body. °**ecstasy** Madness. °**property** Quality. °**fordoes** Destroys. °**coted** Observed. °**beshrow** Beshrew, plague take. °**jealousy** Suspicious mind. °**proper . . . age** Characteristic of men of my age. °**cast beyond ourselves** Overshoot, go too far (by way of caution). °**close** Secret. °**move . . . love** Cause more grievous consequences by its concealment than we shall incur displeasure by making it known. °**2.2. Location** The castle. °**Moreover . . . you** Besides the fact that we wanted to see you for your own sakes. °**Sith** Since.

So much from th' understanding of himself,
I cannot dream of. I entreat you both   10
That, being of° so young days brought up with him,
And sith so neighbored to his youth and havior,
That you voutsafe your rest° here in our court
Some little time, so by your companies
To draw him on to pleasures, and to gather   15
So much as from occasion you may glean,
Whether aught to us unknown afflicts him thus,
That, open'd, lies within our remedy.

Queen: Good gentlemen, he hath much talk'd of you,
And sure I am two men there is not living   20
To whom he more adheres.° If it will please you
To show us so much gentry° and good will
As to expend your time with us a while,
For the supply and profit° of our hope,
Your visitation shall receive such thanks   25
As fits a king's remembrance.

Rosencrantz: Both your Majesties
Might, by the sovereign power you have of us,
Put your dread pleasures more into command
Than to entreaty.

Guildenstern: But we both obey,
And here give up ourselves, in the full bent,°   30
To lay our service freely at your feet,
To be commanded.

King: Thanks, Rosencrantz and gentle Guildenstern.

Queen: Thanks, Guildenstern and gentle Rosencrantz.
And I beseech you instantly to visit   35
My too much changed son. Go some of you
And bring these gentlemen where Hamlet is.

Guildenstern: Heavens make our presence and our practices
Pleasant and helpful to him!

Queen: Ay, amen!

Exeunt Rosencrantz and Guildenstern [with some Attendants].

Enter Polonius.

Polonius: Th' embassadors° from Norway, my good lord,   40
Are joyfully return'd.

King: Thou still° has been the father of good news.

Polonius: Have I, my lord? Issure my good liege°
I hold my duty as I hold my soul,
Both to my God and to my gracious king;   45
And I do think, or else this brain of mine
Hunts not the trail of policy° so sure
As it hath us'd to do, that I have found
The very cause of Hamlet's lunacy.

King: O, speak of that, that do I long to hear.   50

Polonius: Give first admittance to th' ambassadors;
My news shall be the fruit° to that great feast.

King: Thyself do grace to them, and bring them in. *Exit Polonius.*
He tells me, my dear Gertrude, he hath found
The head° and source of all your son's distemper.°   55

Queen: I doubt° it is no other but the main,°
His father's death and our [o'erhasty] marriage.

Enter [Polonius, with Voltemand and Cornelius, the] Embassadors.

King: Well, we shall sift him.— Welcome, my good friends!
Say, Voltemand, what from our brother Norway?

Voltemand: Most fair return of greetings and desires.   60
Upon our first,° he sent out to suppress
His nephew's levies, which to him appear'd
To be a preparation 'gainst the Polack;
But better look'd into, he truly found
It was against your Highness. Whereat griev'd,°   65
That so his sickness, age, and impotence
Was falsely borne in hand,° sends out arrests
On Fortinbras, which he, in brief, obeys,
Receives rebuke from Norway, and in fine,°
Makes vows before his uncle never more   70
To give th' assay° of arms against your majesty.
Whereon old Norway, overcome with joy,
Gives him three score thousand crowns in annual fee,
And his commission to employ those soldiers,
So levied, as before, against the Polack,   75
With an entreaty, herein further shown,   [*giving a paper*]
That it might please you to give quiet pass
Through your dominions for this enterprise,
On such regards of safety and allowance°
As therein are set down.

King: It likes° us well,   80
And at our more consider'd° time we'll read,
Answer, and think upon this business.
Mean time, we thank you for your well-took labor.
Go to your rest, at night we'll feast together.
Most welcome home!

Exeunt Embassadors [and Attendants].

Polonius: This business is well ended.   85
My liege, and madam, to expostulate°
What majesty should be, what duty is,
Why day is day, night night, and time is time,
Were nothing but to waste night, day, and time;
Therefore, [since] brevity is the soul of wit,°   90
And tediousness the limbs and outward flourishes,
I will be brief. Your noble son is mad:
Mad call I it, for to define true madness,
What is't but to be nothing else but mad?
But let that go.

Queen: More matter with less art.°   95

°**of** From. °**voutsafe your rest** Vouchsafe to remain. °**more
adheres** Is more attached. °**gentry** Courtesy. °**supply and
profit** Support and advancement. °**in ... bent** To our utmost.
°**embassadors** Ambassadors. °**still** Always. °**liege** Sovereign.
°**policy** Statecraft. °**fruit** Dessert. °**head** Synonymous with
source. °**distemper** (Mental) illness. °**doubt** Suspect.

°**main** Main cause. °**Upon our first** At our first representation.
°**griev'd** Aggrieved, offended. °**borne in hand** Taken advantage of.
°**in fine** In the end. °**assay** Trial. °**On ... allowance** With such
safeguards and provisos. °**likes** Pleases. °**consider'd** Suitable for
consideration. °**expostulate** Expound. °**wit** Understanding,
wisdom. °**art** Rhetorical art.

Polonius: Madam, I swear I use no art at all.
That he's mad, 'tis true, 'tis true 'tis pity,
And pity 'tis 'tis true—a foolish figure,°
But farewell it, for I will use no art.   100
Mad let us grant him then, and now remains
That we find out the cause of this effect,
Or rather say, the cause of this defect,
For this effect defective comes by cause:°
Thus it remains, and the remainder thus.   105
Perpend.°
I have a daughter—have while she is mine—
Who in her duty and obedience, mark,
Hath given me this. Now gather, and surmise.

[reads the salutation of the letter]

"To the celestial, and my soul's idol, the most beautified
Ophelia"—
That's an ill phrase, a vile phrase, "beautified"° is a vile   110
phrase. But you shall hear. Thus:
In her excellent white bosom, these, etc.

Queen: Came this from Hamlet to her?
Polonius: Good madam, stay awhile. I will be faithful.

([reads the] letter)

"Doubt° thou the stars are fire,   115
Doubt that the sun doth move,
Doubt truth to be a liar,
But never doubt I love.

O dear Ophelia, I am ill at these numbers.° I have not
art to reckon° my groans, but that I love thee best, O   120
most best, believe it. Adieu.
Thine evermore, most dear lady,
whilst this machine° is to him, Hamlet"
This in obedience hath my daughter shown me,
And more [above],° hath his solicitings,
As they fell out by time, by means, and place,   125
All given to mine ear.
King: But how hath she
Receiv'd his love?
Polonius: What do you think of me?
King: As of a man faithful and honorable.
Polonius: I would fain° prove so. But what might you think,
When I had seen this hot love on the wing—   130
As I perceiv'd it (I must tell you that)
Before my daughter told me—what might you,
Or my dear Majesty your queen here, think,
If I had play'd the desk or table-book,°
Or given my heart a [winking,°] mute and dumb,   135

Or look'd upon this love with idle sight,°
What might you think? No, I went round° to work,
And my young mistress thus I did bespeak:°
"Lord Hamlet is a prince out of thy star;°
This must not be"; and then I prescripts gave her,   140
That she should lock herself from [his] resort,
Admit no messengers, receive no tokens.
Which done, she took the fruits of° my advice;
And he repell'd,° a short tale to make,
Fell into a sadness, then into a fast,   145
Thence to a watch,° thence into a weakness,
Thence to [a] lightness,° and by this declension,
Into the madness wherein now he raves,
And all we mourn for.
King: Do you think ['tis] this?
Queen: It may be, very like.   150
Polonius: Hath there been such a time—I would fain know that—
That I have positively said, " 'Tis so,"
When it prov'd otherwise?
King: Not that I know.
Polonius [points to his head and shoulder]: Take this from this,
if this be otherwise.   155
If circumstances lead me, I will find
Where truth is hid, though it were hid indeed
Within the centre.°
King: How may we try it further?
Polonius: You know sometimes he walks four hours together
Here in the lobby.
Queen: So he does indeed.   160
Polonius: At such a time I'll loose my daughter to him.
Be you and I behind an arras° then,
Mark the encounter: if he love her not,
And be not from his reason fall'n thereon,°
Let me be no assistant for a state,   165
But keep a farm and carters.
King: We will try it.

Enter Hamlet, [reading on a book].

Queen: But look where sadly the poor wretch comes reading.
Polonius: Away, I do beseech you, both away.
I'll board° him presently,°

Exeunt King, and Queen.

                                    O, give me leave,
How does my good Lord Hamlet?   170
Hamlet: Well, God-a-mercy.°
Polonius: Do you know me, my lord?
Hamlet: Excellent well, you are a fishmonger.°
Polonius: Not I, my lord.

°**figure** Figure of speech. °**For . . . cause** for this effect (which
shows as a defect in Hamlet's reason) is not merely accidental, and has
a cause we may trace. °**Perpend** Consider. °**beautified** Beautiful
(not an uncommon usage). °**Doubt** Suspect. °**ill . . . numbers**
Bad at versifying. °**reckon** count (with a quibble on *numbers*).
°**machine** Body. °**more above** Furthermore. °**fain** Willingly,
gladly. °**play'd . . . table-book** Noted the matter secretly.
°**winking** Closing of the eyes. °**idle sight** Noncomprehending

eyes. °**round** Straightforwardly. °**bespeak** Address. °**star**
Sphere, lot in life. °**took . . . of** Profited by, carried out. °**repell'd**
Repulsed. °**watch** Sleeplessness. °**lightness** Lightheadedness.
°**centre** Of the earth (which in the Ptolemaic system is also the centre
of the universe). °**arras** Hanging tapestry. °**thereon** Because of
that. °**board** Accost. °**presently** At once. °**God-a-mercy** Thank
you. °**fishmonger** Usually explained as slang for "bawd," but no
evidence has been produced for such a usage in Shakespeare's day.

Hamlet: Then I would you were so honest a man. 175

Polonius: Honest, my lord!

Hamlet: Ay, sir, to be honest, as this world goes, is to be one man pick'd out of ten thousand.

Polonius: That's very true, my lord.

Hamlet: For if the sun breed maggots in a dead dog, being a 180
good kissing carrion°—Have you a daughter?

Polonius: I have, my lord.

Hamlet: Let her not walk i' th' sun. Conception° is a blessing,
but as your daughter may conceive friend, look to't.

Polonius [aside]: How say you by that? still harping on my 185
daughter. Yet he knew me not at first, 'a said I was a
fishmonger. 'A is far gone. And truly in my youth I suff'red
much extremity for love—very near this. I'll speak to him
again.—What do you read, my lord?

Hamlet: Words, words, words.

Polonius: What is the matter,° my lord? 190

Hamlet: Between who?

Polonius: I mean, the matter that you read, my lord.

Hamlet: Slanders, sir; for the satirical rogue says here that old
men have grey beards, that their faces are wrinkled, their
eyes purging thick amber and plumtree gum, and that they
have a plentiful lack of wit, together with most weak hams; 195
all which, sir, though I most powerfully and potently
believe, yet I hold it not honesty° to have it thus set down,
for yourself, sir, shall grow old as I am, if like a crab you
could go backward.

Polonius [aside]: Though this be madness, yet there is method°
in't.—Will you walk out of the air, my lord? 200

Hamlet: Into my grave?

Polonius: Indeed, that's out of the air.° [aside] How pregnant°
sometimes his replies are! a happiness that often madness
hits on, which reason and [sanity] could not so prosper-
ously be deliver'd of. I will leave him, [and suddenly°
contrive the means of meeting between him] and my
daughter.—My lord, I will take my leave of you. 205

Hamlet: You cannot, take from me any thing that I will not
more willingly part withal—except my life, except my life,
except my life.

Polonius: Fare you well, my lord.

Hamlet: These tedious old fools! 210

Enter Guildenstern and Rosencrantz.

Polonius: You go to seek the Lord Hamlet, there he is.

Rosencrantz [to Polonius]: God save you, sir!

Exit Polonius.

Guildenstern: My honor'd lord!

Rosencrantz: My most dear lord!

Hamlet: My [excellent] good friends! How dost thou, Guilden- 215
stern? Ah, Rosencrantz? Good lads, how do you both?

Rosencrantz: As the indifferent° children of the earth.

Guildenstern: Happy, in that we are not [over-]happy; on
Fortune's [cap] we are not the very button.

Hamlet: Nor the soles of her shoe? 220

Rosencrantz: Neither, my lord.

Hamlet: Then you live about her waist, or in the middle of her
favors?

Guildenstern: Faith, her privates° we.

Hamlet: In the secret parts of Fortune? O, most true, she is a
strumpet.° What's the news? 225

Rosencrantz: None, my lord, but that the world's grown honest.

Hamlet: Then is doomsday near. But your news is not true. Let
me question more in particular. What have you, my good
friends, deserv'd at the hands of Fortune, that she sends
you to prison hither?

Guildenstern: Prison, my lord? 230

Hamlet: Denmark's a prison.

Rosencrantz: Then is the world one.

Hamlet: A goodly one, in which there are many confines,
wards,° and dungeons, Denmark being one o' th' worst.

Rosencrantz: We think not so, my lord. 235

Hamlet: Why, then 'tis none to you; for there is nothing either
good or bad, but thinking makes it so. To me it is a prison.

Rosencrantz: Why then your ambition makes it one. 'Tis too
narrow for your mind.

Hamlet: O God, I could be bounded in a nutshell, and count 240
myself a king of infinite space—were it not that I have bad
dreams.

Guildenstern: Which dreams indeed are ambition, for the very
substance of the ambitious is merely the shadow of a dream.

Hamlet: A dream itself is but a shadow.

Rosencrantz: Truly, and I hold ambition of so airy and light a 245
quality that it is but a shadow's shadow.

Hamlet: Then are our beggars bodies,° and our monarchs and
outstretch'd° heroes the beggars' shadows. Shall we to th'
court? for, by my fay,° I cannot reason.

Both [Rosencrantz Guildenstern]: We'll wait upon you.° 250

Hamlet: No such matter. I will not sort° you with the rest of my
servants; for to speak to you like an honest man, I am most
dreadfully° attended. But in the beaten way of friendship,
what make you at Elsinore?

Rosencrantz: To visit you, my lord, no other occasion.

Hamlet: Beggar that I am, I am [even] poor in thanks— but I 255
thank you, and sure, dear friends, my thanks are too dear a
halfpenny.° Were you not sent for? is it your own inclining?

°**good kissing carrion** Flesh good enough for the sun to kiss.
°**Conception** Understanding (with following play on the sense
"conceiving a child"). °**matter** Subject; but Hamlet replies as if he
had understood Polonius to mean "cause for a quarrel." °**honesty**
A fitting thing. °**method** Orderly arrangement, sequence of
ideas. °**out . . . air** Outdoor air was thought to be bad for
invalids. °**pregnant** Apt. °**suddenly** At once.
°**indifferent** Average. °**privates** (1) Intimate friends; (2)

genitalia. °**strumpet** A common epithet for Fortune, because
she grants favors to all men. °**wards** Cells. °**bodies** Not
shadows (since they lack ambition). °**outstretch'd** With their
ambition extended to the utmost (and hence producing stretched-
out or elongated shadows). °**fay** Faith. °**wait upon you**
Attend you thither. °**sort** Associate. °**dreadfully** Execrably.
°**too . . . halfpenny** Too expensive priced at a halfpenny; not
worth much.

Hamlet: is it a free visitation? Come, come, deal justly° with me. Come, come, nay, speak.

Guildenstern: What should we say, my lord?

Hamlet: Anything but° to th' purpose. You were sent for, and there is a kind of confession in your looks, which your modesties° have not craft enough to color: I know the good King and Queen have sent for you.   260

Rosencrantz: To what end, my lord?

Hamlet: That you must teach me. But let me conjure you, by the rights of our fellowship, by the consonancy of our youth,° by the obligation of our ever-preserv'd love, and by what more dear a better proposer could charge° you withal, be even° and direct with me, whether you were sent for or no?   265

Rosencrantz *[aside to Guildenstern]*: What say you?

Hamlet *[aside]*: Nay then I have an eye of° you!—If you love me, hold not off.

Guildenstern: My lord, we were sent for.   270

Hamlet: I will tell you why, so shall my anticipation prevent your discovery,° and your secrecy to the King and Queen moult no feather.° I have of late—but wherefore I know not—lost all my mirth, forgone all custom of exercises;° and indeed it goes so heavily with my disposition, that this goodly frame, the earth, seems to me a sterile promontory;   275 this most excellent canopy, the air, look you, this brave° o'erhanging firmament, this majestical roof fretted° with golden fire, why, it appeareth nothing to me but a foul and pestilent congregation of vapors. What [a] piece of work° is a man, how noble in reason, how infinite in faculties, in form and moving, how express° and admirable in action, how like an angel in apprehension, how like a god! the   280 beauty of the world; the paragon of animals; and yet to me what is this quintessence° of dust? Man delights not me—nor woman neither, though by your smiling you seem to say so.

Rosencrantz: My lord, there was no such stuff in my thoughts.

Hamlet: Why did you laugh then, when I said, "Man delights   285 not me"?

Rosencrantz: To think, my lord, if you delight not in man, what lenten entertainment° the players shall receive from you. We coted° them on the way, and hither are they coming to offer you service.

Hamlet: He that plays the king shall be welcome—his Majesty shall have tribute on° me, the adventerous° knight shall use his foil and target,° the lover shall not   290 sigh gratis,° the humorous° man shall end his part in peace, [the clown shall make those laugh whose lungs are [tickle a' th' sere,]° and the lady shall say her mind freely, or the [blank] verse shall halt° for't. What players are they?

Rosencrantz: Even those you were wont to take such delight in,   295 the tragedians of the city.

Hamlet: How chances it they travel? Their residence, both in reputation and profit, was better both ways.

Rosencrantz: I think their inhibition° comes by the means of the late innovation.°

Hamlet: Do they hold the same estimation they did when I was in the city? Are they so follow'd?   300

Rosencrantz: No indeed are they not.

Hamlet: How °comes it? do they grow rusty?

Rosencrantz: Nay, their endeavor keeps in the wonted pace; but there is, sir, an aery° of children, little eyases,° that cry out on the top of question,° and are most tyrannically° clapp'd   305 for't. These are now the fashion, and so—[berattle°] the common stages° so they call them—that many wearing rapiers are afraid of goose-quills° and dare scarce come thither.

Hamlet: What, are they children? Who maintains 'em? How are they escoted?° Will they pursue the quality° no longer than   310 they can sing?° Will they not say afterwards, if they should grow themselves to common players (as it is [most like], if

---

°**justly** Honestly. °**but** Ordinarily punctuated with a comma preceding, to give the sense "provided that it is"; but Q2 has no comma, and Hamlet may intend, or include, the sense "except." °**modesties** Sense of shame. °**consonancy . . . youth** Similarity of our ages. °**charge** Urge, adjure. °**even** Frank, honest (cf. modern "level with me"). °**of** On. °**prevent your discovery** Forestall your disclosure (of what the king and queen have said to you in confidence). °**moult no feather** Not be impaired in the least. °**custom of exercises** My usual athletic activities. °**brave** Splendid. °**fretted** Ornamented as with fretwork. °**piece of work** Masterpiece. °**express** Exact. °**quintessence** Finest and purest extract. °**lenten entertainment** Meagre reception. °**coted** Outstripped. °**on** Of, from. °**adventerous** Adventurous, wandering in search of adventure. °**foil and target** Light fencing sword and small shield. °**gratis** Without reward. °**humorous** Dominated by some eccentric trait (like the melancholy Jaques in *As You Like It*). °**tickle . . . sere** Easily made to laugh (literally, describing a gun that goes off easily; *sere* = a catch in the gunlock; *tickle* = easily affected, highly sensitive to stimulus. °**halt** Limp, come off lamely (the verse will not scan if she omits indecent words). °**inhibition** Hindrance (to playing in the city). The word could be used of an official prohibition. See next note. °**innovation** Shakespeare elsewhere uses

this word of a political uprising or revolt, and lines 332–33 are often explained as meaning that the company had been forbidden to play in the city as the result of some disturbance. It is commonly conjectured that the allusion is to the Essex rebellion of 1601, but it is known that Shakespeare's company, though to some extent involved on account of the special performance of *Richard II* they were commissioned to give on the eve of the rising, were not in fact punished by inhibition. A second interpretation explains *innovation* as referring to the new theatrical vogue described in lines 320 ff., and conjectures that *inhibition* may allude to a Privy Council order of 1600 restricting the number of London playhouses to two and the number of performances to two a week. °**How . . . too** This passage refers topically to the "War of the Theatres" between the child actors and their poet Jonson on the one side, and on the other the adults, with Dekker, Marston, and possibly Shakespeare as spokesmen, in 1600–1601. °**aery** Nest. °**eyases** Unfledged hawks. °**cry . . . question** Cry shrilly above others in controversy. °**tyrannically** Outrageously. °**berattle** Cry down, satirize. °**common stages** Public theatres (the children played at the Blackfriars, a private theatre). °**goose-quills** Pens (of satirical playwrights). °**escoted** Supported. °**quality** Profession (of acting). °**no . . . sing** Only until their voices change.

their means are [no] better), their writers do them wrong, to make them exclaim against their own succession?°

Rosencrantz: Faith, there has been much to do° on both sides, and the nation holds it no sin to tarre° them to controversy. There was for awhile no money bid for argument,° unless the poet and the player went to cuffs in the question.°

Hamlet: Is't possible?

Guildenstern: O, there has been much throwing about of brains.

Hamlet: Do the boys carry it away?°

Rosencrantz: Ay, that they do, my lord, Hercules and his load too.°

Hamlet: It is not strange, for my uncle is King of Denmark, and those that would make mouths° at him while my father liv'd, give twenty, forty, fifty, hundred ducats a-piece for his picture in little. 'Sblood,° there is something in this more than natural, if philosophy could find it out.

(a flourish [for the Players])

Guildenstern: There are the players.

Hamlet: Gentlemen, you are welcome to Elsinore. Your hands, come then: th' appurtenance of welcome is fashion and ceremony. Let me comply° with you in this garb,° [lest my] extent° to the players, which, I tell you, must show fairly outwards, should more appear like entertainment than yours.° You are welcome; but my uncle-father and aunt-mother are deceiv'd.

Guildenstern: In what, my dear lord?

Hamlet: I am but mad north-north-west. When the wind is southerly I know a hawk from a hand-saw.°

Enter Polonius.

Polonius: Well be with you, gentlemen!

Hamlet [*aside to them*]: Hark you, Guildenstern, and you too—at each ear a hearer—that great baby you see there is not yet out of his swaddling-clouts.°

Rosencrantz: Happily° he is the second time come to them, for they say an old man is twice° a child.

Hamlet: I will prophesy, he comes to tell me of the players, mark it. [*aloud*] You say right, sir, a' Monday morning, 'twas then indeed.

Polonius: My lord, I have news to tell you.

Hamlet: My lord, I have news to tell you. When Roscius° was an actor in Rome—

Polonius: The actors are come hither, my lord.

Hamlet: Buzz,° buzz!

Polonius: Upon my honor—

Hamlet: "Then came each actor on his ass"—

Polonius: The best actors in the world, either for tragedy, comedy, history, pastoral, pastoral-comical, historical-pastoral, [tragical-historical, tragical-comical-historical-pastoral,] scene individable,° or poem unlimited;° Seneca° cannot be too heavy, nor Plautus° too light, for the law of writ and the liberty:° these are the only° men.

Hamlet: O Jephthah, judge of Israel,° what a treasure hadst thou!

Polonius: What a treasure had he, my lord?

Hamlet: Why—

"One fair daughter, and no more,
The which he loved passing well."

Polonius [*aside*]: Still on my daughter.

Hamlet: Am I not i' th' right, old Jephthah?

Polonius: If you call me Jephthah, my lord, I have a daughter that I love passing well.

Hamlet: Nay, that follows not.

Polonius: What follows, then, my lord?

Hamlet: Why—

"As by lot, God wot,"
and then, you know,
"It came to pass, as most like it was,"—

the first row° of the pious chanson° will show you more, for look where my abridgment° comes.

Enter the Players, [four or five].

You are welcome, masters, welcome, all. I am glad to see thee well. Welcome, good friends. O, why old friend! thy face is valanc'd° since I saw thee last; com'st thou to beard° me in Denmark? What, my young lady and mistress! by' lady,° your ladyship is nearer to heaven than when I saw you last, by the altitude of a chopine.° Pray God your voice, like a piece of

---

°**succession** Future. °**to do** Ado. °**tarre** Incite. °**argument** Plot of a play. °**in the question** As part of the script °**carry it away** Win. °**Hercules . . . too** Hercules in the course of one of his twelve labors supported the world for Atlas; the children do better, for they carry away the world and Hercules as well. There is an allusion to the Globe playhouse, which reportedly had for its sign the figure of Hercules upholding the world. °**mouths** Derisive faces. °**Sblood** By God's (Christ's) blood. °**comply** Observe the formalities. °**garb** Fashion, manner. °**my extent** The degree of courtesy I show. °**more . . . yours** Seem to be a warmer reception than I have given you. °**hawk**, **hand-saw** both cutting tools; but also both birds, if *hand-saw* quibbles on *hernshaw*, "heron," a bird preyed upon by the hawk. °**swaddling-clouts** Swaddling clothes. °**Happily** Haply, perhaps. °**twice** For the second time. °**Roscius** The most famous of Roman actors (died 62 B.C.). News about him would be stale news

indeed. °**Buzz** Exclamation of impatience at someone who tells news already known. °**scene individable** Play observing the unity of place. °**poem unlimited** Play ignoring rules such as the three unities. °**Seneca** Roman writer of tragedies. °**Plautus** Roman writer of comedies. °**for . . . liberty** For strict observance of the rules, or for freedom from them (with possible allusion to the location of playhouses, which were not built in properties under city jurisdiction, but in the "liberties"—land once monastic and now outside the jurisdiction of the city authorities). °**only** very best (a frequent use). °**Jephthah . . . Israel** Title of a ballad, from which Hamlet goes on to quote. For the story of Jephthah and his daughter, see Judges 11. °**row** Stanza. °**chanson** Song, ballad. °**abridgment** (1) Interruption; (2) pastime. °**valanc'd** Fringed, bearded. °**beard** Confront boldly (with obvious pun). °**by' lady** By Our Lady. °**chopine** Thick-soled shoe.

---

uncurrent gold, be not crack'd within the ring.° Masters, you
are all welcome. We'll e'en to't like [French] falc'ners—fly at
any thing we see: we'll have a speech straight.° Come give us
a taste of your quality,° come, a passionate speech.   380
[1.] Player: What speech, my good lord?
Hamlet: I heard thee speak me a speech once, but it was never
acted, or if it was, not above once; for the play, I remember,
pleas'd not the million, 'twas caviarey to the general,° but it
was—as I receiv'd it, and others, whose judgments in such
matters cried in the top of° mine—an excellent play, well 385
digested in the scenes, set down with as much modesty as
cunning. I remember one said there were no sallets° in the
lines to make the matter savory,° nor no matter in the phrase
that might indict the author of affection,° but call'd it an
honest method, as wholesome as sweet, and by very much 390
more handsome than fine.° One speech in't I chiefly lov'd,
'twas Aeneas' [tale] to Dido, and thereabout of it especially
where he speaks of Priam's slaughter.° If it live in your memory, begin at this line—let me see, let me see:
    "The rugged Pyrrhus,° like th' Hyrcanian beast,°—"
'Tis not so it begins with Pyrrhus: 395
    "The rugged Pyrrhus, he whose sable arms,°
Black as his purpose, did the night resemble
When he lay couched in th' ominous horse,
Hath now this dread and black complexion smear'd
With heraldy° more dismal:° head to foot   400
Now is he total gules,° horridly trick'd°
With blood of fathers, mothers, daughters, sons,
Bak'd° and impasted° with the parching streets,°
That lend a tyrannous and a damned light
To their lord's murther. Roasted in wrath and fire,   405
And thus o'er-sized° with coagulate gore,
With eyes like carbuncles,° the hellish Pyrrhus
Old grandsire Priam seeks."
So proceed you.
Polonius: 'Fore God, my lord, well spoken, with good accent 410
and good discretion.
[1.] Player: "Anon he finds him
Striking too short at Greeks. His antique sword,
Rebellious to his arm, lies where it falls,
Repugnant° to command. Unequal match'd,   415

Pyrrhus at Priam drives, in rage strikes wide,
But with the whiff and wind of his fell° sword
Th' unnerved° father falls. [Then senseless° Ilium,°]
Seeming to feel this blow, with flaming top
Stoops to his base, and with a hideous crash   420
Takes prisoner Pyrrhus' ear; for lo his sword,
Which was declining on the milky head
Of reverent° Priam, seem'd i' th' air to stick.
So as a painted tyrant. Pyrrhus stood,
[And,] like a neutral to his will and matter,°   425
Did nothing.
But as we often see, against° some storm,
A silence in the heavens, the rack° stand still,
The bold winds speechless, and the orb below
As hush as death, anon the dreadful thunder   430
Doth rend the region;° so after Pyrrhus' pause,
A roused vengeance sets him new a-work,
And never did the Cyclops° hammers fall
On Mar's his armor forg'd for proof eterne°
With less remorse° than Pyrrhus' bleeding sword   435
Now falls on Priam.
Out, out, thou strumpet. Fortune! All you gods,
In general synod take away her power!
Break all the spokes and [fellies°] from her wheel,
And bowl the round nave° down the hill of heaven   440
As low as to the fiends!
Polonius: This is too long.
Hamlet: It shall to the barber's with your beard. Preythee, say
on, he's for a jig° or a tale of bawdry, or he sleeps. Say on,
come to Hecuba.
[1.] Player: "But who, ah woe," had seen the mobled° queen"— 445
Hamlet: "The mobled queen?"
Polonius: That's good [mobled] queen [is good.]
[1.] Player: "Run barefoot up and down, threatening the flames"
With bissom rheum,° a clout° upon that head
Where late the diadem stood, and for a robe,   450
About her lank and all o'er-teemed° loins,
A blanket, in the alarm of fear caught up—
Who this had seen, with tongue in venom steep'd,
'Gainst Fortune's state° would treason have pronounc'd.
But if the gods themselves did see her then,   455

When she saw Pyrrhus make malicious sport
In mincing with his sword her [husband's] limbs,
The instant burst of clamor that she made,
Unless things mortal move them not at all,
Would have made milch° the burning eyes of heaven,   460
And passion° in the gods."

Polonius: Look whe'er he has not° turn'd his color and has
tears in 's eyes.
Prithee no more.

Hamlet: 'Tis well, I'll have thee speak out the rest of this soon.
Good my lord, will you see the players well bestow'd?°   465
Do you hear, let them be well us'd,° for they are the
abstracts and brief chronicles of the time. After your
death you were better have a bad epitaph than their ill
report while you live.

Polonius: My lord, I will use them according to their desert.

Hamlet: God's bodkin,° man, much better: use every man after   470
his desert, and who shall scape whipping? Use them after
your own honor and dignity—the less they deserve, the
more merit is in your bounty. Take them in.

Polonius: Come, sirs.

Exit.

Hamlet: Follow him, friends, we'll hear a play tomorrow.   475

Exeunt all the Players but the First.

Dost thou hear me, old friend? Can you play "The Murther
of Gonzago"?

[1.] Player: Ay, my lord.

Hamlet: We'll ha't to-morrow night. You could for a need° study
a speech of some dozen lines, or sixteen lines, which I would
set down and insert in't, could you not?   480

[1.] Player: Ay, my lord.

Hamlet: Very well. Follow that lord, and look you mock him not.

Exit First Player.

My good friends, I'll leave you [till] night. You are welcome
to Elsinore.

Rosencrantz: Good my lord!

Hamlet: Ay, so, God buy to you.

Exeunt [Rosencrantz and Guildenstern.]

Now I am alone   485
O, what a rogue and peasant slave am I!
Is it not monstrous that this player here,
But in a fiction, in a dream of passion,
Could force his soul so to his own conceit°
That from her working all his visage wann'd,   490

Tears in his eyes, distraction in his aspect,
A broken voice, an' his whole function° suiting
With forms° to his conceit? And all for nothing,
For Hecuba?
What's Hecuba to him, or he to [Hecuba],   495
That he should weep for her? What would he do
Had he the motive and [the cue] for passion
That I have? He would drown the stage with tears,
And cleave the general ear with horrid speech,
Make mad the guilty, and appall the free,°   500
Confound the ignorant, and amaze,° indeed
The very faculties of eyes and ears. Yet I,
A dull and muddy-mettled° rascal, peak°
Like John-a-dreams,° unpregnant of° my cause,
And can say nothing; no, not for a king,   505
Upon whose property and most dear life
A damn'd defeat° was made. Am I a coward?
Who calls me villain, breaks my pate across,
Plucks off my beard and blows it in my face,
Tweaks me by the nose, gives me the lie i' th' throat,   510
As deep as to the lungs.° Who does me this?
Hah, 'swounds,° I should° take it: for it cannot be
But I am pigeon-liver'd, and lack gall°
To make oppression bitter, or ere this
I should 'a' fatted all the region kites   515
With this slave's offal.° Bloody, bawdy villain!
Remorseless, treacherous, lecherous, kindless° villain!
Why, what an ass am I! This is most brave,
That I, the son of a dear [father] murthered,
Prompted to my revenge by heaven and hell,   520
Must like a whore unpack my heart with words,
And fall a-cursing like a very drab,
A stallion.° Fie upon't, foh!
About,° my brains! Hum—I have heard
That guilty creatures sitting at a play   525
Have by the very cunning of the scene
Been strook so to the soul, that presently°
They have proclaim'd their malefactions:
For murther, though it have no tongue, will speak
With most miraculous organ. I'll have these players   530
Play something like the murther of my father
Before mine uncle: I'll observe his looks,
I'll tent° him to the quick. If 'a do blench,°
I know my course. The spirit° that I have seen
May be a [dev'l], and the [dev'l] hath power   535
T' assume a pleasing shape, yea, and perhaps,

°**milch** Moist (literally, milky). °**passion** Grief. °**Look...not**
Note how he has. °**bestow'd** Lodged. °**us'd** Treated. °**God's
bodkin** By God's (Christ's) little body. °**for need** If necessary.
°**conceit** Imaginative conception. °**his whole function** The
operation of his whole body. °**forms** Actions, expressions.
°**free** Innocent. °**amaze** Confound. °**muddy-mettled**
Dull-spirited. °**peak** Mope. °**John-a-dreams** A sleepy fellow.
°**unpregnant of** Unquickened by. °**defeat** Destruction.

°**gives...lungs** Calls me a liar in the extremest degree. °**swounds**
By God's (Christ's) wounds. °**should** Would certainly °**am...gall**
Am constitutionally incapable of resentment That doves were
mild because they had no gall was a popular belief. °**offal** Entrails.
°**kindless** Unnatural. °**stallion** Male whore. Most editors adopt the
F1 reading *scullion*, "kitchen menial." °**About** To work. °**presently**
At once, then and there. °**tent** Probe. °**blench** Flinch. °**spirit**
States of temperament.

Out of my weakness and my melancholy,
As he is very potent with such spirits,
Abuses° me to damn me. I'll have grounds
More relative° than this—the play's the thing   540
Wherein I'll catch the conscience of the King.

[*Exit.*]

ACT 3
SCENE 1°

*Enter King, Queen, Polonius, Ophelia, Rosencrantz, Guilden-
stern, Lords.*

King: An'° can you by no drift of conference°
    Get from him why he puts on this confusion,
    Grating so harshly all his days of quiet
    With turbulent and dangerous lunacy?
Rosencrantz: He does confess he feels himself distracted,   5
    But from what cause 'a will by no means speak.
Guildenstern: Nor do we find him forward° to be sounded°
    But with a crafty madness° keeps aloof
    When we would bring him on to some confession
    Of his true state.
Queen: Did he receive you well?   10
Rosencrantz: Most like a gentleman.
Guildenstern: But with much forcing of his disposition.°
Rosencrantz: Niggard of question,° but of our demands°
    Most free in his reply.
Queen: Did you assay° him
    To any pastime?   15
Rosencrantz: Madam, it so fell out that certain players
    We o'erraught° on the way; of these we told him,
    And there did seem in him a kind of joy
    To hear of it: They are here about the court,
    And as I think, they have already order   20
    This night to play before him.
Polonius: 'Tis most true,
    And he beseech'd me to entreat your Majesties
    To hear and see the matter.
King: With all my heart, and it doth much content me
    To hear him so inclin'd.   25
    Good gentlemen, give him a further edge,°
    And drive his purpose into° these delights.
Rosencrantz: We shall, my lord.

Exeunt Rosencrantz and Guildenstern.

King: Sweet Gertrude, leave us too,
    For we have closely° sent for Hamlet hither,
    That he, as 'twere by accident, may here   30
    Affront° Ophelia. Her father and myself,
    We'll so bestow ourselves that, seeing unseen,
    We may of their encounter frankly° judge,
    And gather by him, as he is behav'd,
    If't be th' affliction of his love or no   35
    That thus he suffers for.
Queen: I shall obey you.
    And for your part, Ophelia, I do wish
    That your good beauties be the happy cause
    Of Hamlet's wildness: So shall I hope your virtues
    Will bring him to his wonted way again,   40
    To both your honors.
Ophelia: Madam, I wish it may. *Exit Queen.*
Polonius: Ophelia, walk you here.—Gracious, so please you,
    We will bestow ourselves. [*to Ophelia*] Read on this book,
    That show of such an exercise° may color
    Your [loneliness].° We are oft to blame in this—   45
    'Tis too much prov'd° —that with devotion's visage
    And pious action° we do sugar o'er
    The devil himself.
King: [*aside*]   O, 'tis too true!
    How smart a lash that speech doth give my conscience!
    The harlot's cheek, beautied with plast'ring art,   50
    Is not more ugly to the thing that helps it°
    Than is my deed to my most painted word.
    O heavy burthen!
Polonius: I hear him coming. Withdraw, my lord.

Exeunt King and Polonius.

Enter Hamlet.

Hamlet: To be, or not to be, that is the question: 55
    Whether 'tis nobler in the mind to suffer°
    The slings and arrows of outrageous fortune,
    Or to take arms against a sea of troubles,
    And by opposing, end them. To die, to sleep—
    No more, and by a sleep to say we end   60
    The heart-ache and the thousand natural shocks
    That flesh is heir to; 'tis a consummation°
    Devoutly to be wish'd. To die, to sleep—
    To sleep, perchance to dream—ay, there's the rub,°
    For in that sleep of death what dreams may come,   65

°**Abuses** Deludes. °**relative** Closely related (to fact), conclusive.
°**3.1. Location** The castle. °**An'** And. °**drift of conference** Leading
on of conversation. °**forward** Readily willing. °**sounded** Plumbed,
probed. °**crafty madness** Mad craftiness, the shrewdness that mad
people sometimes exhibit. °**disposition** Inclination. °**question**
Conversation. °**demands** Questions. °**assay** Attempt to win.
°**o'erraught** Passed (literally, overreached). °**edge** Stimulus.

°**into** On to. °**closely** Privately. °**Affront** Meet. °**frankly** Freely.
°**exercise** Religious exercise (as the next sentence makes clear).
°**color Your loneliness** Make your solitude seem natural. °**too
much prov'd** Too often proved true. °**action** Demeanor. °**to . . . it**
In comparison with the paint that makes it look beautiful. °**suffer**
Submit to, endure patiently. °**consummation** Completion, end. °**rub**
Obstacle (a term from the game of bowls).

When we have shuffled off° this mortal coil,°
Must give us pause; there's the respect°
That makes calamity of so long life:°
For who would bear the whips and scorns of time,°
Th' oppressor's wrong, the proud man's contumely,   70
The pangs of despis'd love, the law's delay,
The insolence of office, and the spurns
That patient merit of th' unworthy takes,
When he himself might his quietus make°
With a bare bodkin;° who would fardels° bear,   75
To grunt and sweat under a weary life,
But that the dread of something after death,
The undiscover'd° country, from whose bourn°
No traveller returns, puzzles° the will,
And makes us rather bear those ills we have,   80
Than fly to others that we know not of?
Thus conscience° does make cowards [of us all],
And thus the native hue° of resolution
Is sicklied o'er with the pale cast° of thought,°
And enterprises of great pitch° and moments   85
With this regard their currents turn awry,
And lose the name of action.—Soft you now,
The fair Ophelia. Nymph, in thy orisons°
Be all my sins rememb'red.

Ophelia: Good my lord,
How does your honor for this many a day?   90

Hamlet: I humbly thank you, well, [well, well].

Ophelia: My lord, I have remembrances of yours
That I have longed long to redeliver.
I pray you now receive them.

Hamlet: No, not I,
I never gave you aught.   95

Ophelia: My honor'd lord, you know right well you did,
And with them words of so sweet breath compos'd
As made these things more rich. Their perfume lost,
Take these again, for to the noble mind
Rich gifts wax poor when givers prove unkind.   100
There, my lord.

Hamlet: Ha, ha! are you honest?°

Ophelia: My lord?

Hamlet: Are you fair?

Ophelia: What means your lordship?   105

Hamlet: That if you be honest and fair, [your honesty] should
admit no discourse to your beauty.

Ophelia: Could beauty, my lord, have better commerce than
with honesty?

Hamlet: Ay, truly, for the power of beauty will sooner transform
honesty from what it is to a bawd than the force of honesty 110
can translate beauty into his likeness. This was sometime° a
paradox,° but now the time gives it proof. I did love you
once.

Ophelia: Indeed, my lord, you made me believe so.

Hamlet: You should not have believ'd me, for virtue cannot so
[inoculate] our old stock but we shall relish of it.° I lov'd   115
you not.

Ophelia: I was the more deceiv'd.

Hamlet: Get thee [to] a nunn'ry, why wouldst thou be a breeder
of sinners? I am myself indifferent honest,° but yet I could
accuse me of such things that it were better my mother had
not borne me: I am very proud, revengeful, ambitious, with   120
more offenses at my beck than I have thoughts to put them
in, imagination to give them shape, or time to act them in.
What should such fellows as I do crawling between earth
and heaven? We are arrant knaves, believe none of us. Go
thy ways to a nunn'ry. Where's your father?

Ophelia: At home, my lord.   125

Hamlet: Let the doors be shut upon him, that he may play the
fool no where but in 's own house. Farewell.

Ophelia: O, help him, you sweet heavens!

Hamlet: If thou dost marry, I'll give thee this plague for thy dowry: be thou as chaste as ice, as pure as snow, thou shalt not 130
escape calumny. Get thee to a nunn'ry, farewell. Or if thou
wilt needs marry, marry a fool, for wise men know well
enough what monsters° you° make of them. To a nunn'ry,
go, and quickly too. Farewell.

Ophelia: Heavenly powers, restore him!

Hamlet: I have heard of your paintings, well enough. God hath   135
given you one face, and you make yourselves another. You
jig you amble, and you [lisp,] you nickname God's
creatures° and make your wantonness [your] ignorance.°
Go to, I'll no more on't, it hath made me mad. I say we will
have no moe° marriage. Those that are married already (all
but one) shall live, the rest shall keep as they are. To a
nunn'ry, go.   140

[*Exit.*]

Ophelia: O, what a noble mind is here o'erthrown!
The courtier's, soldier's, scholar's, eye, tongue, sword,
Th' expectation° and rose° of the fair° state,
The glass° of fashion and the mould of form,°
Th' observ'd of all observers,° quite, quite down!   145
And I, of ladies most deject and wretched,

°**shuffled off** Freed ourselves from. °**this mortal coil** The
turmoil of this mortal life. °**respect** Consideration. °**of . . . life**
So long-lived. °**time** The world. °**his quietus make** Write paid
to his account. °**bare bodkin** Mere dagger. °**fardels** Burdens.
°**undiscover'd** Not disclosed to knowledge; about which men have
no information. °**bourn** Boundary, region. °**puzzles** Paralyzes.
°**conscience** Reflection (but with some of the modern sense, too).
°**native hue** natural (ruddy) complexion. °**pale cast** Pallor.
°**thought** Melancholy thought, brooding. °**pitch** Loftiness
(a term from falconry, signifying the highest point of a hawk's flight).
°**orisons** Prayers. °**honest** Chaste. °**sometime** Formerly

°**paradox** Tenet contrary to accepted belief. °**virtue . . . it** Virtue,
engrafted on our old stock (of viciousness), cannot so change the nature
of the plant that no trace of the original will remain. °**indifferent
honest** Tolerably virtuous. °**monsters** Alluding to the notion that the
husbands of unfaithful wives grew horns. °**you** You women. °**you . . .
creatures** You walk and talk affectedly. °**make . . . ignorance** Excuse
your affectation as ignorance. °**moe** More. °**expectation** Hope.
°**rose** Ornament. °**fair** Probably proleptic "(the kingdom) made fair
by his presence." °**glass** Mirror. °**mould of form** Pattern of (courtly)
behavior. °**observ'd . . . observers** Shakespeare uses *observe* to mean
not only "behold, mark attentively" but also "pay honor to."

That suck'd the honey of his [music] vows,
Now see [that] noble and most sovereign reason
Like sweet bells jangled out of tune, and harsh;
That unmatch'd form and stature of blown° youth   150
Blasted° with ecstasy.° O, woe is me
T' have seen what I have seen, see what I see!

Ophelia withdraws.

Enter King and Polonius.

King: Love? his affections° do not that way tend,
Nor what he spake, though it lack'd form a little,
Was not like madness. There's something in his soul   155
O'er which his melancholy sits on brood,
And I do doubt° the hatch and the disclose°
Will be some danger; which for to prevent,
I have in quick determination
Thus set it down: he shall with speed to England   160
For the demand of our neglected tribute.
Haply the seas, and countries different,
With variable objects, shall expel
This something-settled matter in his heart,
Whereon his brains still beating puts him thus   165
From fashion of himself. What think you on't?

Polonius: It shall do well; but yet do I believe
The origin and commencement of his grief
Sprung from neglected° love. [*Ophelia comes forward.*]
    How now, Ophelia?   170
You need not tell us what Lord Hamlet said,
We heard it all. My lord, do as you please,
But if you hold it fit, after the play
Let his queen-mother all alone entreat him
To show his grief.° Let her be round° with him,   175
And I'll be plac'd (so please you) in the ear
Of all their conference. If she find him° not,
To England send him, or confine him where
Your wisdom best shall think.

King: It shall be so.
Madness in great ones must not [unwatch'd] go.   180

Exeunt.

SCENE 2°

Enter Hamlet and three of the Players.

Hamlet: Speak the speech, I pray you, as I pronounc'd it to you,
trippingly on the tongue, but if you mouth° it, as many of
your players do, I had as live° the town-crier spoke my lines.

Nor do not saw the air too much with your hand, thus, but
use all gently, for in the very torrent, tempest, and, as I may
say, whirlwind of your passion, you must acquire and beget   5
a temperance that may give it smoothness. O, it offends me
to the soul to hear a robustious periwig-pated fellow tear a
passion to totters,° to very rags, to spleet° the ears of the
groundlings,° who for the most part are capable° of nothing
but inexplicable dumb shows and noise. I would have such a
fellow whipt for o'erdoing Termagant,° it out-Herods
Herod, pray you avoid it.   10

[1.] Player: I warrant your honor.

Hamlet: Be not too tame neither, but let your own discretion be
your tutor. Suit the action to the word, the word to the action, with this special observance, that you o'erstep not the
modesty° of nature: for any thing so o'erdone is from° the   15
purpose of playing, whose end, both at the first and now,
was and is, to hold, as 'twere the mirror up to nature: to
show virtue her feature, scorn° her own image, and the very
age and body of the time his form and pressure.° Now this
overdone, or come tardy° off, though it makes the unskillful
laugh, cannot but make the judicious grieve; the censure° of
which one° must in your allowance° o'erweigh a whole theatre of others. O, there be players that I have seen play—and   20
heard others [praise], and that highly—not to speak it profanely,° that, neither having th' accent of Christians nor the
gait of Christian, pagan, nor man, have so strutted and
bellow'd that I have thought some of Nature's journeymen
had made men, and not made them well, they imitated hu-   25
manity so abominably.°

[1.] Player: I hope we have reform'd that indifferently° with us, [sir].

Hamlet: O, reform it altogether. And let those that play your
clowns speak no more than is set down for them, for there
be of them° that will themselves laugh to set on some quan-   30
tity of barren spectators to laugh too, though in the mean
time some necessary question of the play be then to be
consider'd. That's villainous, and shows a most pitiful ambition in the fool° that uses it. Go make you ready.

Exeunt Players.

Enter Polonius, Guildenstern, and Rosencrantz.

    How now, my lord! Will the King hear this piece of work?°   35
Polonius: And the Queen too, and that presently.°
Hamlet: Bid the players make haste. [*Exit Polonius.*]
    Will you two help to hasten them?
Rosencrantz: Ay, my lord.   [*Exeunt they two.*]
Hamlet: What, ho, Horatio!   40

°**blown** In full bloom. °**Blasted** Withered. °**ecstasy** Madness.
°**affections** Inclinations, feelings. °**doubt** fear. °**disclose**
Synonymous with *hatch*; see also 5.1.247. °**neglected** Unrequited.
°**his grief** What is troubling him. °**round** Blunt, outspoken.
°**find him** Learn the truth about him. °**3.2. Location** The castle.
°**mouth** Pronounce with exaggerated distinctness or declamatory
effect. °**live** Lief, willingly. °**totters** Tatters. °**spleet** Split.
°**groundlings** Those who paid the lowest admission price and
stood on the ground in the "yard" or pit of the theatre. °**capable
of** Able to take in. °**Termagant** A supposed god of the Saracens,

whose role in medieval drama, like that of Herod (line 10), was noisy
and violent. °**modesty** Moderation. °**from** Contrary to. °**scorn**
That which is worthy of scorn. °**pressure** Impression (as of a seal),
exact image. °**tardy** Inadequately. °**censure** Judgment. °**which
one** (Even) one of whom. °**allowance** Estimation. °**profanely**
Irreverently. °**some . . . abominably** They were so unlike men that
it seemed Nature had not made them herself, but had delegated the
task to mediocre assistants. °**indifferently** Pretty well. °**of them**
Some of them. °**fool** (1) Stupid person; (2) actor playing a fool's role.
°**piece of work** Masterpiece (said jocularly). °**presently** At once.

Enter Horatio.

Horatio: Here, sweet lord, at your service.

Hamlet: Horatio, thou art e'en as just a man°
  As e'er my conversation cop'd withal.°

Horatio: O my dear lord—

Hamlet: Nay, do not think I flatter,
  For what advancement may I hope from thee   45
  That no revenue hast but thy good spirits
  To feed and clothe thee? Why should the poor be flatter'd?
  No, let the candied° tongue lick absurd° pomp,
  And crook the pregnant° hinges of the knee
  Where thrift° may follow fawning. Dost thou hear?   50
  Since my dear soul was mistress of her choice
  And could of men distinguish her election,
  Sh' hath seal'd thee for herself, for thou hast been
  As one in suff'ring all that suffers nothing,
  A man that Fortune's buffets and rewards   55
  Hast ta'en with equal thanks; and blest are those
  Whose blood° and judgment are so well co-meddled,°
  That they are not a pipe for Fortune's finger
  To sound what stop she please. Give me that man
  That is not passion's slave, and I will wear him   60
  In my heart's core, ay, in my heart of heart,°
  As I do thee. Something too much of this.
  There is a play to-night before the King,
  One scene of it comes near the circumstance
  Which I have told thee of my father's death.   65
  I prithee, when thou seest that act afoot,
  Even with the very comment of thy soul°
  Observe my uncle. If his occulted° guilt
  Do not itself unkennel° in one speech,
  It is a damned ghost° that we have seen,   70
  And my imaginations are as foul
  As Vulcan's stithy.° Give him heedful note,
  For I mine eyes will rivet to his face,
  And after we will both our judgments join
  In censure of his seeming.°

Horatio: Well, my lord.   75
  If 'a steal aught the whilst this play is playing,
  And scape [detecting], I will pay the theft.

*[Sound a flourish. Danish march.] Enter Trumpets and Kettle-
drums, King, Queen, Polonius, Ophelia, [Rosencrantz,
Guildenstern, and other Lords, attendant, with his Guard
carrying torches].*

Hamlet: They are coming to the play. I must be idle;° Get you a place.

King: How fares° our cousin Hamlet?

Hamlet: Excellent, i' faith, of the chameleon's dish:° I eat the   80
  air,° promisecramm'd— you cannot feed capons so.

King: I have nothing with° this answer, Hamlet, these words are
  not mine.°

Hamlet: No, nor mine now. [*to Polonius*] My lord, you play'd
  once i' th' university, you say?

Polonius: That did I, my lord, and was accounted a good actor.   85

Hamlet: What did you enact?

Polonius: I did enact Julius Caesar: I was kill'd i' th' Capitol; Brutus
  kill'd me.

Hamlet: It was a brute part° of him to kill so capital a calf there.
  Be the players ready?

Rosencrantz: Ay, my lord, they stay upon your patience.   90

Queen: Come hither, my dear Hamlet, sit by me.

Hamlet: No, good mother, here's metal more attractive. [*lying
  down at Ophelia's feet*]

Polonius: [*to the King*] O ho, do you mark that?

Hamlet: Lady, shall I lie in your lap?   95

Ophelia: No, my lord.

[**Hamlet:** I mean, my head upon your lap?

Ophelia: Ay, my lord.

Hamlet: Do you think I meant country matters?°

Ophelia: I think nothing, my lord.   100

Hamlet: That's a fair thought to lie between maids' legs.

Ophelia: What is, my lord?

Hamlet: Nothing.

Ophelia: You are merry, my lord.

Hamlet: Who, I?   105

Ophelia: Ay, my lord.

Hamlet: O God, your only° jig-maker.° What should a man do
  but be merry,? for look you how cheerfully my mother
  looks, and my father died within 's° two hours.

Ophelia: Nay, 'tis twice two months, my lord.   110

Hamlet: So long? Nay then let the dev'l wear black, for I'll have a
  suit of sables.° O heavens, die two months ago, and not forgotten yet? Then there's hope a great man's memory may outlive
  his life half a year, but, by'r lady, 'a must build churches then,
  or else shall 'a suffer not thinking on,° with the hobby-horse,   115
  whose epitaph is, "For O, for O, the hobby-horse is forgot."°

The trumpets sound. Dumb show follows.

*Enter a King and a Queen [very lovingly], the Queen embracing
  him and he her. [She kneels and makes show of protestation*

°**thou...man** You come as close to being what a man should be (*just* = exact, precise). °**my...withal** My association with people has brought me into contact with. °**candied** Sugared, flattering. °**absurd** Tasteless (Latin sense). °**pregnant** Moving readily. °**thrift** Thriving, profit. °**blood** Passions. °**co-meddled** Mixed, blended. °**my heart of heart** The heart of my heart. °**very...soul** Your most intense critical observation. °**occulted** Hidden. °**unkennel** Bring into the open. °**damned ghost** Evil spirit, devil. °**stithy** Forge. °**censure...seeming** Reaching a verdict on his behavior. °**be idle** Act foolish, pretend to be crazy. °**fares** Hamlet takes up this word in another sense. °**chameleon's dish** Chameleons were thought to feed on air. Hamlet says that he

subsists on an equally nourishing diet, the promise of succession. There is probably a pun on *air/heir*. °**have nothing with** Do not understand. °**mine** An answer to my question. °**part** Action. °**country matters** Indecency. °**only** Very best. °**jig-maker** One who composed or played in the farcical song-and-dance entertainments that followed plays. °**'s** This. °**let...sables** To the devil with my garments; after so long a time I am ready for the old man's garb of sables (fine fur). °**not thinking on** Not being thought of, being forgotten. °**For...forgot** Line from a popular ballad lamenting puritanical suppression of such country sports as the May-games, in which the hobby-horse, a character costumed to resemble a horse, traditionally appeared.

unto him.] He takes her up and declines his head upon her neck. He lies him down upon a bank of flowers. She, seeing him asleep, leaves him. Anon comes in another man, takes off his crown, kisses it, pours poison in the sleeper's ears, and leaves him. The Queen returns, finds the King dead, makes passionate action. The pois'ner with some three or four [mutes] come in again, seem to condole with her. The dead body is carried away. The pois'ner woos the Queen with gifts; she seems harsh [and unwilling] awhile, but in the end accepts love. [Exeunt.]

Ophelia: What means this, my lord?

Hamlet: Marry, this' [miching] mallecho,° it means mischief.

Ophelia: Belike this show imports the argument° of the play.

Enter Prologue.

Hamlet: We shall know by this fellow. The players cannot keep 120 [counsel°], they'll tell all.

Ophelia: Will 'a tell us what this show meant?

Hamlet: Ay, or any show that you will show him. Be not you° asham'd to show, he'll not shame to tell you what it means.

Ophelia: You are naught, you are naught.° I'll mark the play. 125

Prologue: For us, and for our tragedy,
    Here stooping to your clemency,
    We beg your hearing patiently. [*Exit.*]

Hamlet: Is this a prologue, or the posy of a ring?°

Ophelia: 'Tis brief, my lord. 130

Hamlet: As woman's love.

Enter [two Players,] King and Queen.

[P.] King: Full thirty times hath Phoebus' cart° gone round
Neptune's salt wash and Tellus° orbed ground,
And thirty dozen moons with borrowed sheen
About the world have times twelve thirties been, 135
Since love our hearts and Hymen° did our hands
Unite comutual in most sacred bands.°

[P.] Queen: So many journeys may the sun and moon
Make us again count o'er ere love be done!
But woe is me, you are so sick of late, 140
So far from cheer and from [your] former state,
That I distrust° you. Yet though I distrust,
Discomfort you, my lord, it nothing must,
[For] women's fear and love hold quantity,°
In neither aught, or in extremity. 145
Now what my [love] is, proof°
hath made you know,
And as my love is siz'd, my fear is so.

Where love is great, the littlest doubts are fear;
Where little fears grow great, great love grows there.

[P.] King: Faith, I must leave thee, love, and shortly too; 150
My operant° powers their functions leave to do,°
And thou shalt live in this fair world behind,
Honor'd, belov'd, and haply one as kind
For husband shalt thou—

[P.] Queen: O, confound the rest!°
Such love must needs be treason in my breast. 155
In second husband let me be accurs'd!
None wed the second but who kill'd the first.

Hamlet [*aside*]: That's wormwood!

[P.] Queen: The instances° that second marriage move°
Are base respects of thrift,° but none of love. 160
A second time I kill my husband dead,
When second husband kisses me in bed.

[P.] King: I do believe you think what now you speak,
But what we do determine, oft we break.
Purpose is but the slave to memory, 165
Of violent birth, but poor validity,°
Which now, the fruit unripe, sticks on the tree,
But fall unshaken when they mellow be.
Most necessary 'tis that we forget
To pay ourselves what to ourselves is debt.° 170
What to ourselves in passion° we propose,
The passion ending, doth the purpose lose.
The violence of either grief or joy
Their own enactures with themselves destroy.°
Where joy most revels, grief doth most lament; 175
Grief [joys], joy grieves, on slender accident.°
This world is not for aye, nor 'tis not strange
That even our loves should with our fortunes change:
For 'tis a question left us yet to prove,
Whether love lead fortune, or else fortune love. 180
The great man down, you mark his favorite flies,
The poor advanc'd makes friends of enemies.
And hitherto doth love on fortune tend,
For who not needs shall never lack a friend,
And who in want a hollow friend doth try, 185
Directly seasons° him his enemy.
But orderly to end where I begun,
Our wills and fates do so contrary run
That our devices° still° are overthrown,
Our thoughts are ours, their ends none of our own: 190
So think thou wilt no second husband wed,
But die thy thoughts when thy first lord is dead.

[P.] Queen: Nor earth to me give food, nor heaven light,
Sport and repose lock from me day and night,

°**this' [miching] mallecho** This is sneaking mischief. °**argument** Subject, plot. °**counsel** Secrets. °**Be not you** If you are not. °**naught** Wicked. °**posy . . . ring** Verse motto inscribed in a ring (necessarily short). °**Phoebus' cart** The sun-god's chariot. °**Tellus** Goddess of the earth. °**Hymen** God of marriage. °**bands** Bonds. °**distrust** Fear for. °**hold quantity** Are related in direct proportion. °**proof** Experience. °**operant** Active, vital. °**leave to do** Cease to perform °**confound the rest** May destruction befall what you are about to speak of—a second marriage on my part.

°**instances** Motives. °**move** Give rise to. °**respects of thrift** Considerations of advantage. °**validity** Strength, power to last. °**Most . . . debt** Such resolutions are debts we owe to ourselves, and it would be foolish to pay such debts. °**passion** Violent emotion. °**The violence . . . destroy** Both violent grief and violent joy fail of their intended acts because they destroy themselves by their very violence. °**slender accident** Slight occasion. °**seasons** Ripens, converts into. °**devices** Devisings, intentions. °**still** Always.

To desperation turn my trust and hope,   195
[An] anchor's cheer° in prison be my scope!°
Each opposite that blanks° the face of joy
Meet what I would have well and it destroy!
Both here and hence pursue me lasting strife,
If once I be a widow, ever I be a wife!   200

Hamlet: If she should break it now!

[P.] King: 'Tis deeply sworn. Sweet, leave me here a while,
My spirits grow dull, and fain I would beguile
The tedious day with sleep. [*sleeps*]

[P.] Queen: Sleep rock thy brain,
And never come mischance between us twain! [*Exit.*]   205

Hamlet: Madam, how like you this play?

Queen: The lady doth protest too much, methinks.

Hamlet: O but she'll keep her word.

King: Have you heard the argument? is there no offense° in't?

Hamlet: No, no, they do but jest, poison in jest°—no offense i'
th' world.   210

King: What do you call the play?

Hamlet: "The Mouse-trap." Marry, how? tropically:° this play is
the image° of a murther done in Vienna; Gonzago is the
duke's name, his wife, Baptista. You shall see anon. 'Tis a
knavish piece of work, but what of that? Your Majesty, and
we that have free souls,° it touches us not. Let the gall'd 215
jade° winch,° our withers° are unwrung.°

Enter Lucianus.

This is one Lucianus, nephew to the king.

Ophelia: You are as good as a chorus,° my lord.

Hamlet: I could interpret between you and your love, if I could
see the puppets dallying.°   220

Ophelia: You are keen,° my lord, you are keen.

Hamlet: It would cost you a groaning to take off mine edge.

Ophelia: Still better, and worse.°

Hamlet: So° you mistake° your husbands. Begin, murtherer, leave
thy damnable faces° and begin. Come, the croaking raven 225
doth bellow for revenge.°

Lucianus: Thoughts black, hands apt, drugs fit, and time agreeing,
[Confederate] season,° else no creature seeing,
Thou mixture rank, of midnight weeds collected,
With Hecat's ban° thrice blasted, thrice [infected],   230
Thy natural magic and dire property
On wholesome life usurps immediately.

[*pours the poison into his ears.*]

Hamlet: 'A poisons him i' th' garden for his estate. His name's
Gonzago, the story is extant, and written in very choice Ital-
ian. You shall see anon how the murtherer gets the love of
Gonzago's wife.   235

Ophelia: The King rises.

[Hamlet: What, frighted with false fire?]°

Queen: How fares my lord?

Polonius: Give o'er the play.

King: Give me some light. Away!   240

Polonius: Lights, lights, lights!

Exeunt all but Hamlet and Horatio.

Hamlet: "Why, let the strooken° deer go weep,
The hart ungalled° play,
For some must watch° while some
must sleep,   245
Thus runs the world away."
Would not this, sir, and a forest of feathers°— if the rest
of my fortunes turn Turk° with me—with [two] Provincial
roses° on my raz'd° shoes, get me a fellowship° in a cry° of
players?

Horatio: Half a share.   250

Hamlet: A whole one, I.
"For thou dost know, O Damon dear,
This realm dismantled° was
Of Jove himself, and now reigns here
A very, very"—pajock.°   255

Horatio: You might have rhym'd.

Hamlet: O good Horatio, I'll take the ghost's word for a
thousand pound. Didst perceive?

Horatio: Very well, my lord.

Hamlet: Upon the talk of the pois'ning?   260

Horatio: I did very well note him.

Hamlet: Ah, ha! Come, some music! Come, the recorders!
For if the King like not the comedy,
Why then belike he likes it not, perdy.°
Come, some music!   265

Enter Rosencrantz and Guildenstern.

Guildenstern: Good my lord, voutsafe me a word with you.

Hamlet: Sir, a whole history.

°**anchor's cheer** Hermit's fare. °**my scope** The extent of my
comforts. °**blanks** Blanches, makes pale (a symptom of grief).
°**offense** Offensive matter (but Hamlet quibbles on the sense
"crime"). °**jest** pretend. °**tropically** Figuratively (with play on
trapically—which is the reading of Q1—and probably with allusion
to the children's saying *marry trap*, meaning "now you're caught").
°**image** Representation. °**free souls** Clear consciences. °**gall'd
jade** Chafed horse. °**winch** Wince. °**withers** Ridge between a
horse's shoulders. °**unwrung** Not rubbed sore. °**chorus** One who
explains the forthcoming action. °**I . . . dallying** I could speak the
dialogue between you and your lover like a puppet-master (with an
indecent jest). °**keen** Bitter, sharp. °**better, and worse** More
pointed and less decent. °**So** "For better, for worse," in the words of
the marriage service. °**mistake** Mistake, take, take wrongly. Their
vows, Hamlet suggests, prove false. °**faces** Facial expressions. °**the
croaking . . . revenge** Misquoted from an old play, *The True Tragedy of
Richard III*. °**Confederate season** The time being my ally. °**Hecat's
ban** The curse of Hecate, goddess of witchcraft. °**false fire** A blank
cartridge. °**strooken** Struck, wounded. °**ungalled** Unwounded.
°**watch** Stay awake. °**feathers** The plumes worn by tragic actors.
°**turn Turk** Go to the bad. °**Provincial roses** Rosettes designed to
look like a variety of French rose. °**raz'd** With decorating slashing.
°**fellowship** Partnership. °**cry** Company. °**dismantled** Divested,
deprived. °**pajock** Peacock (substituting for the rhyme-word *ass*). The
natural history of the time attributed many vicious qualities to the
peacock. °**perdy** Assuredly (French *pardieu*, "by God.").

Guildenstern: The King, sir—

Hamlet: Ay, sir, what of him?

Guildenstern: Is in his retirement marvellous distemp'red. 270

Hamlet: With drink, sir?

Guildenstern: No, my lord, with choler.°

Hamlet: Your wisdom should show itself more richer to signify this to the doctor, for for me to put him to his purgation° would perhaps plunge him into more choler. 275

Guildenstern: Good my lord, put your discourse into some frame,° and [start] not so wildly from my affair.

Hamlet: I am tame, sir. Pronounce.

Guildenstern: The Queen, your mother, in most great affliction of spirit, hath sent me to you. 280

Hamlet: You are welcome.

Guildenstern: Nay, good my lord, this courtesy is not of the right breed. If it shall please you to make me a wholesome° answer, I will do your mother's commandement; if not, your pardon° and my return shall be the end of [my] business. 285

Hamlet: Sir, I cannot.

Rosencrantz: What, my lord?

Hamlet: Make you a wholesome answer—my wit's diseas'd. But, sir, such answer as I can make, you shall command, or rather, as you say, my mother. Therefore no more, but to the matter: my mother, you say— 290

Rosencrantz: Then thus she says: your behavior hath strook her into amazement and admiration.°

Hamlet: O wonderful son, that can so stonish° a mother! But is there no sequel at the heels of this mother's admiration? Impart.

Rosencrantz: She desires to speak with you in her closet° ere you go to bed. 295

Hamlet: We shall obey, were she ten times our mother. Have you any further trade with us?

Rosencrantz: My lord, you once did love me.

Hamlet: And do still, by these pickers and stealers.°

Rosencrantz: Good my lord, what is your cause of distemper? 300 You do surely bar the door upon your own liberty if you deny your griefs to your friend.

Hamlet: Sir, I lack advancement.

Rosencrantz: How can that be, when you have the voice of the King himself for your succession in Denmark?

Hamlet: Ay, sir, but "While the grass grows"—the proverb° is 305 something musty.°

Enter the Players with recorders.

O, the recorders! Let me see one.—To withdraw with you—why do you go about to recover the wind° of me, as if you would drive me into a toil?°

Guildenstern: O my lord, if my duty be too bold, my love is too 310 unmannerly.

Hamlet: I do not well understand that. Will you play upon this pipe?

Guildenstern: My lord, I cannot.

Hamlet: I pray you.

Guildenstern: Believe me, I cannot.

Hamlet: I do beseech you.

Guildenstern: I know no touch of it, my lord.

Hamlet: It is as easy as lying. Govern these ventages° with your fingers and [thumbs], give it breath with your mouth, and it will discourse most eloquent music. Look you, these are the 315 stops.

Guildenstern: But these cannot I command to any utt'rance of harmony. I have not the skill.

Hamlet: Why, look you now, how unworthy a thing you make of me! You would play upon me, you would seem to know my 320 stops, you would pluck out the heart of my mystery; you would sound me from my lowest note to [the top of] my compass; and there is much music, excellent voice, in this little organ,° yet cannot you make it speak. 'Sblood, do you think I am easier to be play'd on than a pipe? Call me what instrument you will, though you fret° me, [yet] you cannot play upon me.

Enter Polonius.

God bless you, sir. 325

Polonius: My lord, the Queen would speak with you, and presently.°

Hamlet: Do you see yonder cloud that's almost in shape of a camel?

Polonius: By th' mass and 'tis, like a camel indeed.

Hamlet: Methinks it is like a weasel.

Polonius: It is back'd like a weasel. 330

Hamlet: Or like a whale.

Polonius: Very like a whale.

Hamlet: Then I will come to my mother by and by. [*aside*] They fool me to the top of my bent.°—I will come by and by.°

Polonius: I will say so. [*Exit.*] 335

Hamlet: "By and by" is easily said. Leave me, friends.

[*Exeunt all but Hamlet.*]

'Tis now the very witching° time of night,
When churchyards yawn and hell itself [breathes] out
Contagion to this world. Now could I drink hot blood,
And do such [bitter business as the] day 340
Would quake to look on. Soft, now to my mother.
O heart, lose not thy nature!° let not ever
The soul of Nero° enter this firm bosom,
Let me be cruel, not unnatural;

°**choler** Anger (but Hamlet willfully takes up the word in the sense "biliousness"). °**put . . . purgation** Prescribe for what's wrong with him. °**frame** Logical structure. °**wholesome** Sensible, rational. °**pardon** Permission for departure. °**amazement and admiration** Bewilderment and wonder. °**stonish** Astound. °**closet** Private room. °**pickers and stealers** Hands, which, as the Catechism says, we must keep "from picking and stealing."

°**proverb** While the grass grows, the steed starves." °**something musty** Somewhat stale. °**recover the wind** Get to windward. °**toil** Snare. °**ventages** Stops. °**organ** Instrument. °**fret** (1) Finger (an instrument); (2) vex. °**presently** At once. °**They . . . bent** They make me play the fool to the limit of my ability. °**by and by** At once. °**witching** When the powers of evil are at large. °**nature** Natural affection, filial feeling. °**Nero** Murderer of his mother.

I will speak [daggers] to her, but use none.   345
My tongue and soul in this be hypocrites—
How in my words someever she be shent,°
To give them seals° never my soul consent!

Exit.

SCENE 3°

Enter King, Rosencrantz, and Guildenstern.

King: I like him° not, nor stands it safe with us
    To let his madness range. Therefore prepare you.
    I your commission with forthwith dispatch,°
    And he to England shall along with you.
    The terms° of our estate° may not endure   5
    Hazard so near's as doth hourly grow
    Out of his brows.°

Guildenstern: We will ourselves provide.
    Most holy and religious fear° it is
    To keep those many many bodies safe
    That live and feed upon your Majesty.   10

Rosencrantz: The single and peculiar° life is bound
    With all the strength and armor of the mind
    To keep itself from noyance,° but much more,
    That spirit upon whose weal depends and rests
    The lives of many. The cess° of majesty   15
    Dies not alone, but like a gulf° doth draw
    What's near it with it. Or it is a massy wheel
    Fix'd on the summit of the highest mount,
    To whose [huge] spokes ten thousand lesser things
    Are mortis'd° and adjoin'd, which when it falls,   20
    Each small annexment, petty consequence,
    Attends° the boist'rous [ruin].° Never alone
    Did the King sigh, but [with] a general groan.

King: Arm° you, I pray you, to this speedy voyage,°
    For we will fetters put about this fear,°   25
    Which now goes too free-footed.

Rosencrantz: We will haste us.

Exeunt Gentleman [Rosencrantz and Guildenstern].

Enter Polonius.

Polonius: My lord, he's going to his mother's closet.
    Behind the arras I'll convey myself
    To hear the process.° I'll warrant she'll tax him home.°   30
    And as you said, and wisely was it said,
    'Tis meet that some more audience than a mother,

Since nature makes them partial, should o'erhear
The speech, of vantage.° Fare you well, my liege,
I'll call upon you ere you go to bed,   35
And tell you what I know.

King: Thanks, dear my lord.

Exit [Polonius].

O, my offense is rank, it smells to heavens,
It hath the primal eldest curse° upon't,
A brother's murther. Pray can I not,
Though inclination be as sharp as will.°   40
My stronger guilt defeats my strong intent,
And, like a man to double business bound,°
I stand in pause where I shall first begin,
And both neglect.° What if this cursed hand
Were thicker than itself with brother's blood,   45
Is there not rain enough in the sweet heavens
To wash it white as snow? Whereto serves mercy
But to confront the visage of offense?°
And what's in prayer but this twofold force,
To be forestalled ere we come to fall,   50
Or [pardon'd] being down? then I'll look up.
My fault is past, but, O, what form of prayer
Can serve my turn? "Forgive me my foul murther"?
That cannot be, since I am still possess'd
Of those effects for which I did the murther: 55
My crown, mine own ambition, and my queen.
May one be pardon'd and retain th' offense?°
In the corrupted currents° of this world
Offense's gilded° hand may [shove] by justice,
And oft 'tis seen the wicked prize° itself   60
Buys out the law, but 'tis not so above:
There is no shuffling,° there the action lies°
In his true nature, and we ourselves compell'd,
Even to the teeth and forehead° of our faults,
To give in evidence. What then? What rests?°   65
Try what repentance can. What can it not?
Yet what can it, when one can not repent?
O wretched state! O bosom black as death!
O limed° soul, that struggling to be free
Art more engag'd! Help, angels! Make assay,   70
Bow, stubborn knees, and heart, with strings of steel,
Be soft as sinews of the new-born babe!
All may be well. [*He kneels.*]

Enter Hamlet.

°**shent** Rebuked. °**give them seals** Confirm them by deeds.
°**3.3. Location** The castle. °**him** His state of mind, his behavior.
°**dispatch** Have drawn up. °**terms** Conditions, nature. °**our
estate** My position (as king). °**his brows** The madness visible
in his face (?). °**fear** Concern. °**single and peculiar** Individual
and private. °**noyance** Injury. °**cess** Cessation, death. °**gulf**
Whirlpool. °**mortis'd** Fixed. °**Attends** Accompanies. °**ruin**
Fall. °**Arm** Prepare. °**viage** Voyage. °**fear** Object of fear.
°**process** Course of the talk. °**tax him home** Take him severely to
task. °**of vantage** From an advantageous position (?) or in addition (?).

°**primal eldest curse** God's curse on Cain, who also slew his
brother. °**Though . . . will** Though my desire is as strong as
my resolve to do so. °**bound** Committed. °**neglect** Omit.
°**Whereto . . . offense** What function has mercy except when
there has been sin. °**th' offense** The "effects" or fruits of the
offense. °**currents** Courses. °**gilded** Bribing. °**wicked prize**
Rewards of vice. °**shuffling** Evasion. °**the action lies** The charge
comes for legal consideration. °**Even . . . forehead** Fully recognizing
their features, extenuating nothing. °**rests** Remains. °**limed**
Caught (as in birdlime, a sticky substance used for catching birds).

Hamlet: Now might I do it [pat], now 'a is a-praying;
And now I'll do't—and so 'a goes to heaven, 75
And so am I [reveng'd]. That would be scann'd:°
A villain kills my father, and for that
I, his sole son, do this same villain send
To heaven.
Why, this is [hire and salary], not revenge. 80
'A took my father grossly,° full of bread,
With all his crimes° broad blown,° as flush° as May,
And how his audit° stands who knows save heaven?
But in our circumstance and course of thought°
'Tis heavy with him. And am I then revenged, 85
To take him in the purging of his soul,
When he is fit and season'd for his passage?
No!
Up,° sword, and know thou a more horrid hent:°
When he is drunk asleep, or in his rage, 90
Or in th' incestuous pleasure of his bed,
At game a-swearing, or about some act
That has no relish° of salvation in't—
Then trip him, that his heels may kick at heaven,
And that his soul may be as damn'd and black 95
As hell, whereto it goes. My mother stays,
This physic° but prolongs thy sickly days.   *Exit.*
King [*rising*]: My words fly up, my thoughts remain below:
Words without thoughts never to heaven go.

Exit.

SCENE 4°

Enter [Queen] Gertrude and Polonius.

Polonius: 'A will come straight. Look you lay home to him.°
Tell him his pranks have been too broad° to bear with,
And that your Grace hath screen'd and stood between
Much heat and him. I'll silence me even here;
Pray you be round° [with him]. 5
Queen: I'll [warr'nt] you, fear me not.° Withdraw,
I hear him coming. [*Polonius hides behind the arras.*]

Enter Hamlet.

Hamlet: Now, mother, what's the matter?
Queen: Hamlet, thou hast thy father much offended.
Hamlet: Mother, you have my father much offended. 10
Queen: Come, come, you answer with an idle° tongue.
Hamlet: Go, go, you question with a wicked tongue.
Queen: Why, how now, Hamlet?

Hamlet: What's the matter now
Queen: Have you forgot me?
Hamlet: No, by the rood,° not so:
You are the Queen, your husband's brother's wife, 15
And would it were not so, you are my mother.
Queen: Nay, then I'll set those to you that can speak.
Hamlet: Come, come, and sit you down, you shall not boudge;°
You go not till I set you up a glass
Where you may see the [inmost] part of you. 20
Queen: What wilt thou do? Thou wilt not murther me?
Help ho!
Polonius [*behind*]: What ho, help!
Hamlet [*drawing*]: How now! A rat? Dead, for a ducat,° dead!
[*Kills Polonius through the arras.*] 25
Polonius [*behind*]: O, I am slain.
Queen: O me, what hast thou done?
Hamlet: Nay, I know not, is it the King?
Queen: O, what a rash and bloody deed is this!
Hamlet: A bloody deed! almost as bad, good mother, 30
As kill a king, and marry with his brother.
Queen: As kill a king!
Hamlet: Ay, lady, it was my word.

[parts the arras and discovers Polonius]

Thou wretched, rash, intruding fool, farewell!
I took thee for thy better. Take thy fortune;
Thou find'st to be too busy° is some danger.—
Leave wringing of your hands. Peace, sit you down, 35
And let me wring your heart, for so I shall
If it be made of penetrable stuff,
If damned custom° have not brass'd° it so
That it be proof° and bulwark against sense.°
Queen: What have I done, that thou dar'st wag thy tongue 40
In noise so rude against me?
Hamlet: Such an act
That blurs the grace and blush of modesty,
Calls virtue hypocrite, takes off the rose
From the fair forehead of an innocent love
And sets a blister° there, makes marriage vows 45
As false as dicers' oaths, O, such a deed
As from the body of contraction° plucks
The very soul, and sweet religion° makes
A rhapsody° of words. Heaven's face does glow°
O'er this solidity and compound mass° 50
With heated visage, as against the doom;°
Is thought-sick at the act.

°**engag'd** Entangled. °**would be scann'd** Must be carefully considered. °**grossly** In a gross state; not spiritually prepared. °**crimes** Sins. °**broad blown** In full bloom. °**flush** Lusty, vigorous. °**audit** Account. °**in . . . thought** To the best of our knowledge and belief. °**Up** into the sheath. °**know . . . hent** Be grasped at a more dreadful time. °**relish** Trace. °**physic** (Attempted) remedy, prayer. °**3. 4. Location** The queen's closet in the castle. °**lay . . . him** Reprove him severely. °**broad** Unrestrained. °**round** Plainspoken. °**fear me not** Have no fears about my handling of the

situation °**idle** foolish. °**rood** Cross. °**boudge** Budge. °**for a ducat** I'll wager a ducat. °**busy** Officious, meddlesome. °**damned custom** The habit of ill-doing. °**brass'd** Hardened, literally, plated with brass. °**proof** Armor. °**sense** Feeling. °**blister** Brand of shame. °**contraction** The making of contracts, the assuming of solemn obligation. °**religion** Sacred vows. °**rhapsody** Miscellaneous collection, jumble. °**glow** With anger. °**this . . . mass** The earth; *compound* = compounded of the four elements. °**as . . . doom** As if for Judgment Day.

Queen: Ay me, what act,
    That roars so loud and thunders in the index?°

Hamlet: Look here upon this picture, and on this,
    The counterfeit presentment° of two brothers.   55
    See what a grace was seated on this brow:
    Hyperion's° curls, the front° of Jove himself,
    An eye like Mars, to threaten and command,
    A station° like the herald Mercury
    New lighted on a [heaven-]kissing hill,   60
    A combination and a form indeed,
    Where every god did seem to set his seal
    To give the world assurance of a man.
    This was your husband. Look you now what follows:
    Here is your husband, like a mildewed ear,°   65
    Blasting his wholesome brother. Have you eyes?
    Could you not on this fair mountain leave to feed,
    And batten° on this moor? ha, have you eyes?
    You cannot call it love, for at your age
    The heyday° in the blood is tame, it's humble,   70
    And waits upon the judgment, and what judgment
    Would step from this to this? Sense° sure you have,
    Else could you not have motion, but sure that sense
    Is apoplex'd° for madness would not err,
    Nor sense to ecstasy was ne'er so thrall'd   75
    But it reserv'd some quantity of choice
    To serve in such a difference.° What devil was't
    That thus hath cozen'd° you at hoodman-blind?°
    Eyes without feeling, feeling without sight,
    Ears without hands or eyes, smelling sans° all,   80
    Or but a sickly part of one true sense
    Could not so mope.° O shame, where is thy blush?
    Rebellious hell,
    If thou canst mutine° in a matron's bones,
    To flaming youth let virtue be as wax   85
    And melt in her own fire. Proclaim no shame
    When the compulsive ardure gives the charge,
    Since frost itself as actively doth burn,
    And reason [panders] will.°

Queen: O Hamlet, speak no more!
    Thou turn'st my [eyes into my very] soul,   90
    And there I see such black and [grained°] spots
    As will [not] leave their tinct.°

Hamlet: Nay, but to live
    In the rank sweat of an enseamed° bed,

Stew'd in corruption, honeying and making love   95
    Over the nasty sty!

Queen: O, speak to me no more!
    These words like daggers enter in my ears.
    No more, sweet Hamlet!

Hamlet: A murtherer and a villain!
    A slave that is not twentith° part the [tithe]
    Of your precedent° lord, a Vice° of kings,
    A cutpurse of the empire and the rule,   100
    That from a shelf the precious diadem stole,
    And put it in his pocket—

Queen: No more!

Enter Ghost. [in his night-gown°].

Hamlet: A king of shreds and patches°—
    Save me, and hover o'er me with your wings,
    You heavenly guards! What would your gracious figure?   105

Queen: Alas, he's mad!

Hamlet: Do you not come your tardy son to chide,
    That, laps'd in time and passion,° lets go by
    Th' important° acting of your dread command?
    O, say!   110

Ghost: Do not forget! This visitation
    Is but to whet thy almost blunted purpose.
    But look, amazement° on thy mother sits,
    O, step between her and her fighting soul.
    Conceit° in weakest bodies strongest works,   115
    Speak to her, Hamlet.

Hamlet: How is it with you, lady?

Queen: Alas, how is't with you,
    That you do bend your eye on vacancy,
    And with th' incorporal air do hold discourse?
    Forth at your eyes your spirits wildly peep,   120
    And as the sleeping soldiers in th' alarm,°
    Your bedded hair, like life in excrements,°
    Start up and stand an end.° O gentle son,
    Upon the heat and flame of thy distemper
    Sprinkle cool patience.° Whereon do you look?   125

Hamlet: On him, on him! look you how pale he glares!
    His form and cause° conjoin'd, preaching to stones,
    Would make them capable.°—Do not look upon me,
    Lest with this piteous action you convert°
    My stern effects,° then what I have to do   130
    Will want true color°—tears perchance for blood.

°**index** Table of contents. The index was formerly placed at the beginning of a book. °**counterfeit presentment** Painted likenesses. °**Hyperion's** The sun-god's. °**front** Forehead. °**station** Bearing. °**ear** Of grain. °**batten** Gorge. °**heyday** Excitement. °**Sense** Sense perception, the five senses. °**apoplex'd** Paralyzed. °**madness...difference** Madness itself could not go so far astray, nor were the senses ever so enslaved by lunacy that they did not retain the power to make so obvious a distinction. °**cozen'd** Cheated °**hoodman-blind** Blindman's bluff. °**sans** Without. °**mope** Be dazed. °**mutine** Rebel. °**Proclaim...will** Do not call it sin when the hot blood of youth is responsible for lechery, since here we see people of calmer age on fire for it; and reason acts as procurer for desire, instead of restraining it. °**Ardure** = ardor.

°**grained** Fast-dyed, indelible. °**leave their tinct** Lose their color. °**enseamed** Greasy. °**twentith** Twentieth. °**precedent** Former. °**Vice** Buffoon (like the Vice of the morality plays). °**night-gown** Dressing gown. °**of...patches** Clownish (alluding to the motley worn by jesters) (?) or patched-up, beggarly (?). °**laps'd...passion** "Having suffered time to slip and passion to cool" (Johnson). °**important** Urgent. °**amazement** Utter bewilderment. °**Conceit** Imagination. °**in th' alarm** When the call to arms is sounded. °**excrements** Outgrowths; here, hair (also used of nails). °**an end** On end. °**patience** Self-control. °**His...cause** His appearance and what he has to say. °**capable** Sensitive, receptive. °**convert** Alter. °**effects** (Purposed) actions. °**want true color** Lack its proper appearance.

Queen: To whom do you speak this?
Hamlet: Do you see nothing there?
Queen: Nothing at all, yet all that is I see.
Hamlet: Nor did you nothing hear?
Queen: No, nothing but ourselves.
Hamlet: Why, look you there, look how it steals away! 135
    My father, in his habit° as he lived!
    Look where he goes, even now, out at the portal!

Exit Ghost.

Queen: This is the very coinage of your brain,
    This bodiless creation ecstasy°
    Is very cunning in.
Hamlet: [Ecstasy!] 140
    My pulse as yours doth temperately keep time,
    And makes as healthful music. It is not madness
    That I have utt'red. Bring me to the test,
    And [I] the matter will reword, which madness
    Would gambol° from. Mother, for love of grace, 145
    Lay not that flattering unction° to your soul,
    That not your trespass but my madness speaks;
    It will but skin and film the ulcerous place,
    Whiles rank corruption, mining all within,
    Infects unseen. Confess yourself to heaven, 150
    Repent what's past, avoid what is to come,
    And do not spread the compost° on the weeds
    To make them ranker. Forgive me this my virtue,
    For in the fatness of these pursy° times
    Virtue itself of vice must pardon beg, 155
    Yea, curb and woo° for leave to do him good.
Queen: O Hamlet, thou hast cleft my heart in twain.
Hamlet: O, throw away the worser part of it,
    And [live] the purer with the other half.
    Good night, but go not to my uncle's bed— 160
    Assume a virtue, if you have it not.
    That monster custom, who all sense doth eat,°
    Of habits devil,° is angel yet in this,
    That to the use of actions fair and good
    He likewise gives a frock or livery 165
    That aptly is put on.° Refrain [to-]night,
    And that shall lend a kind of easiness
    To the next abstinence, the next more easy;
    For use° almost can change the stamp of nature,
    And either [. . .]° the devil or throw him out 170
    With wondrous potency. Once more good night,

And when you are desirous to be blest,°
I'll blessing beg of you. For this same lord,

[*pointing to Polonius*]

    I do repent; but heaven hath pleas'd it so,
    To punish me with this, and this with me, 175
    That I must be their scourge and minister.°
    I will bestow° him, and will answer° well
    The death I gave him. So again good night.
    I must be cruel only to be kind.
    This bad begins and worse remains behind.° 180
    One word more, good lady.
Queen: What shall I do?
Hamlet: Not this, by no means, that I bid you do:
    Let the bloat king tempt you again to bed,
    Pinch wanton on your cheek, call you his mouse,
    And let him, for a pair of reechy° kisses, 185
    Or paddling in your neck with his damn'd fingers,
    Make you to ravel all this matter out,
    That I essentially am not in madness,
    But mad in craft. 'Twere good you let him know,
    For who that's but a queen, fair, sober, wise, 190
    Would from a paddock,° from a bat, a gib,°
    Such dear concernings° hide? Who would do so?
    No, in despite of sense and secrecy,
    Unpeg the basket° on the house's top,
    Let the birds fly, and like the famous ape,° 195
    To try conclusions° in the basket creep,
    And break your own neck down.°
Queen: Be thou assur'd, if words be made of breath,
    And breath of life, I have not life to breathe
    What thou hast said to me. 200
Hamlet: I must to England, you know that?
Queen: Alack,
    I had forgot: 'Tis so concluded on.
Hamlet: There's letters seal'd, and my two schoolfellows,
    Whom I will trust as I will adders fang'd,
    They bear the mandate, they must sweep my way 205
    And marshal me to knavery.° Let it work,
    For 'tis the sport to have the enginer°
    Hoist with° his own petar,° an't shall go hard
    But I will delve one yard below their mines,
    And blow them at the moon: O, 'tis most sweet 210
    When in one line two crafts° directly meet.
    This man shall set me packing;°

°**habit** Dress. °**ecstasy** Madness. °**gambol** Start, jerk away.
°**flattering unction** Soothing ointment. °**compost** Manure.
°**pursy** Puffy, out of condition. °**curb and woo** Bow and entreat.
°**all . . . eat** Wears away all natural feeling. °**Of habits devil** Though
it acts like a devil in establishing bad habits. Most editors read (in lines
175–76) eat / Of habits evil, following Theobald. °**frock . . . on** A "habit"
or customary garment, readily put on without need of any
decision. °**use** Habit. °**[. . .]** A word seems to be wanting after
either. °**desirous . . . blest** Repentant. °**scourge and minister**
The agent of heavenly justice against human crime. *Scourge* suggests a
permissive cruelty (Tamburlaine was the "scourge of God"), but "woe to

him by whom the offense cometh"; the scourge must suffer for the evil it
performs. °**bestow** Dispose of. °**answer** Answer for. °**behind**
To come. °**reechy** Filthy. °**paddock** Toad. °**gib** Tomcat. °**dear
concernings** Matters of intense concern. °**Unpeg the basket** Open
the door of the cage. °**famous ape** The actual story has been lost.
°**conclusions** Experiments (to see whether he too can fly if he enters
the cage and then leaps out). °**down** By the fall. °**knavery** Some
knavish scheme against me. °**enginer** Deviser of military "engines"
or contrivances. °**Hoist with** Blown up by. °**petar** Petard,
bomb. °**crafts** Plots. °**packing** (1) Taking on a load; (2) leaving
in a hurry.

I'll lug the guts into the neighbor room.
Mother, good night indeed. This counsellor
Is now most still, most secret, and most grave, 215
Who was in life a foolish prating knave.
Come, sir, to draw toward an end° with you.
Good night, mother.

Exeunt [severally, Hamlet tugging in Polonius].

ACT 4
SCENE 1°

Enter King and Queen with Rosencrantz and Guildenstern.

King: There's matter in these sighs, these profound heaves—
You must translate, 'tis fit we understand them.
Where is your son?
Queen: Bestow this place on us a little while.

Exeunt Rosencrantz and Guildenstern.

Ah, mine own lord, what have I seen to-night! 5
King: What, Gertrude? How does Hamlet?
Queen: Mad as the sea and wind, when both contend
Which is the mightier. In his lawless fit,
Behind the arras hearing something stir,
Whips out his rapier cries, "A rat, a rat!" 10
And in this brainish apprehension° kills
The unseen good old man.
King: O heavy deed!
It had been so with us had we been there.
His liberty is full of threats to all,
To you yourself, to us, to every one. 15
Alas, how shall this bloody deed be answer'd?°
It will be laid to us, whose providence°
Should have kept short,° restrain'd, and out of haunt°
This mad young man; but so much was our love,
We would not understand what was most fit, 20
But, like the owner of a foul disease,
To keep it from divulging,° let it feed
Even on the pith of life. Where is he gone?
Queen: To draw apart the body he hath kill'd,
O'er whom his very madness, like some ore° 25
Among a mineral° of metals base,
Shows itself pure: 'a weeps for what is done.
King: O Gertrude, come away!
The sun no sooner shall the mountains touch,
But we will ship him hence, and this vile deed, 30
We must, with all our majesty and skill
Both countenance and excuse. Ho, Guildenstern!

Enter Rosencrantz and Guildenstern.

Friends both, go join you with some further aid:
Hamlet in madness hath Polonius slain,
And from his mother's closet hath he dragg'd him. 35
Go seek him out, speak fair, and bring the body
Into the chapel. I pray you, haste in this.

Exeunt Rosencrantz and Guildenstern.

Come, Gertrude, we'll call up our wisest friends
And let them know both what we mean to do
And what's untimely done, [. . .]° 40
Whose whisper o'er the world's diameter,
As level° as the cannon to his blank,°
Transports his pois'ned shot, may amiss our name,
And hit the woundless° air. O, come away!
My soul is full of discord and dismay. 45

Exeunt.

SCENE 2°

Enter Hamlet.

Hamlet: Safely stow'd.
[Gentlemen (*Within.*): Hamlet! Lord Hamlet!]
Hamlet: But soft, what noise? Who calls on Hamlet? O, here
they come.

Enter Rosencrantz and [Guildenstern].

Rosencrantz: What have you done, my lord, with the dead body?
Hamlet: [Compounded] it with dust, whereto 'tis kin. 5
Rosencrantz: Tell us where 'tis, that we may take it thence,
And bear it to the chapel.
Hamlet: Do not believe it.
Rosencrantz: Believe what?
Hamlet: That I can keep your counsel and not mine own. Besides, 10
to be demanded of° a spunge,° what replication° should be
made by the son of a king?
Rosencrantz: Take you me for a spunge, my lord?
Hamlet: Ay, sir, that soaks up the King's countenance,° his re-
wards, his authorities. But such officers do the King best ser- 15
vice in the end: he keeps them, like [an ape] an apple in the
corner of his jaw, first mouth'd, to be last swallow'd. When
he needs what you have glean'd, it is but squeezing you, and,
spunge, you shall be dry again.
Rosencrantz: I understand you not, my lord.
Hamlet: I am glad of it a knavish speech sleeps° in a foolish ear. 20
Rosencrantz: My lord, you must tell us where the body is, and
go with us to the King.
Hamlet: The body is with the King, but the King is not with the
body.° The King is a thing—

°**draw . . . end** Finish my conversation. °**4.1. Location** The castle. °**brainish apprehension** Crazy notion. °**answer'd** Satisfactorily accounted for to the public. °**providence** Foresight. °**short** On a short leash. °**out of haunt** Away from other people. °**divulging** Being revealed. °**ore** Vein of gold. °**mineral** Mine. °Some words are wanting at the end of the line Capell's conjecture, *so, haply, slander,* probably indicates the intended sense of the passage. °**As level** With aim as good. °**blank** Target. °**woundless** Incapable of being hurt. °**4.2. Location** The castle. °**demanded of** Questioned by. °**spunge** Sponge. °**replication** Reply. °**countenance** Favor. °**sleeps** Is meaningless. °**The body . . . the body** Possibly alluding to the legal fiction that the king's dignity is separate from his mortal body.

Guildenstern: A thing, my lord!   25

Hamlet: Of nothing,° bring me to him. [Hide fox, and all after.°]

Exeunt.

SCENE 3°

Enter King and two or three.

King: I have sent to seek him, and to find the body.
How dangerous is it that this man goes loose!
Yet must not we put the strong law on him.
He's lov'd of the distracted° multitude,
Who like not in their judgment, but their eyes,   5
And where 'tis so, th' offender's scourge° is weigh'd,
But never the offense. To bear° all smooth and even,
This sudden sending him away must seem
Deliberate pause.° Diseases desperate grown
By desperate appliance are reliev'd,   10
Or not at all.

Enter Rosencrantz.

How now! what hath befall'n!

Rosencrantz: Where the dead body is bestow'd, my lord,
We cannot get from him.

King: But where is he?

Rosencrantz: Without, my lord, guarded, to know your   15
pleasure.

King: Bring him before us.

Rosencrantz: Ho, bring in my lord.

They [Hamlet and Guildenstern] enter.

King: Now, Hamlet, where's Polonius?

Hamlet: At supper.

King: At supper? where?

Hamlet: Not where he eats, but where 'a is eaten; a certain con-   20
vocation of politic° worms are e'en° at him. Your worm is
your only emperor for diet:° we fat all creatures else to fat
us, and we fat ourselves for maggots; your fat king and your
lean beggar is but variable service,° two dishes, but to one
table— that's the end.

King: Alas, alas!   25

Hamlet: A man may fish with the worm that hath eat of a king,
and eat of the fish that hath fed of that worm.

King: What does thou mean by this?

Hamlet: Nothing but to show you how a king may go a
progress° through the guts of a beggar.   30

King: Where is Polonius?

Hamlet: In heaven, send thither to see; if your messenger find him
not there, seek him i' th' other place yourself. But if, indeed,
if you find him not within this month, you shall nose him as
you go up the stairs into the lobby.

King [to Attendants]: Go seek him there.   35

Hamlet: 'A will stay till you come.

Exeunt Attendants.

King: Hamlet, this deed, for thine especial safety—
Which we do tender,° as we dearly° grieve
For that which thou hast done—must send thee hence
[With fiery quickness]; therefore prepare thyself,   40
The bark is ready, and the wind at help,°
Th'° associates tend,° and every thing is bent°
For England.

Hamlet: For England.

King: Ay, Hamlet.

Hamlet: Good.

King: So is it, if thou knew'st our purposes.

Hamlet: I see a cherub that sees them.° But come, for England!   45
Farewell, dear mother.

King: Thy loving father, Hamlet.

Hamlet: My mother: father and mother is man and wife,
man and wife is one flesh—so, my mother. Come, for
England!   (*Exit.*)

King: Follow him at foot,° tempt him with speed aboard.   50
Delay it not I'll have him hence to-night.
Away, for every thing is seal'd and done
That else leans on° th' affair. Pray you, make haste.

Exeunt Rosencrantz and Guildenstern.

And, England,° if my love thou hold'st at aught—
As my great power thereof may give thee sense,   55
Since yet thy cicatrice° looks raw and red
After the Danish sword, and thy free awe
Pays° homage to us—thou mayst not coldly set°
Our sovereign process,° which imports at full,
By letters to congruing to° that effect,   60
The present° death of Hamlet. Do it, England,
For like the hectic° in my blood he rages,
And thou must cure me. Till I know 'tis done,
How e'er my haps,° my joys [were] ne'er [begun].

Exit.

°**Of nothing** Of no account Cf. "Man is like a thing of nought, his time passeth away like a shadow" (Psalm 14:4 in the Prayer Book version) "Hamlet at once insults the King and hints that his days are numbered" (Dover Wilson). °**Hide ... after** Probably a cry in some game resembling hide-and-seek. °**4.3. Location** The castle. °**distracted** Unstable. °**scourge** Punishment. °**bear** Manage. °**must ... pause** Must be represented as a maturely considered decision. °**politic** Crafty, prying; "such worms as might breed in a politician's corpse" (Dowden). °**e'en** even now. °**for diet** with respect to what it eats. °**variable**

service Different courses of a meal. °**progress** Royal journey of state. °**tender** Regard with tenderness, hold dear. °**dearly** With intense feeling. °**at help** Favorable. °**Th'** Thy. °**tend** Await. °**bent** Made ready. °**I ... them** Heaven sees them. °**at foot** At his heels, close behind. °**leans on** Relates to. °**England** King of England. °**cicatrice** Scar. °**thy ... Pays** Your fear makes you pay voluntarily. °**coldly set** Undervalue, disregard. °**process** Command. °**congruing to** In accord with. °**present** Immediate. °**hectic** Continuous fever. °**haps** Fortunes.

SCENE 4°

Enter Fortinbras with his army over the stage.

Fortinbras: Go, captain, from me greet the Danish king.
    Tell him that by his license Fortinbras
    Craves the conveyance° of a promis'd march
    Over his kingdom. You know the rendezvous
    If that his Majesty would aught with us,   5
    We shall express our duty in his eye,°
    And let him know so.
Captain: I will do't, my lord.
Fortinbras: Go softly° on. [*Exeunt all but the Captain.*]

Enter Hamlet, Rosencrantz, [Guildenstern,] etc.

Hamlet: Good sir, whose powers° are these?
Captain: They are of Norway, sir.   10
Hamlet: How purpos'd, sir, I pray you?
Captain: Against some part of Poland.
Hamlet: Who commands them, sir?
Captain: The nephew to old Norway, Fortinbras.
Hamlet: Goes it against the main° of Poland, sir,   15
    Or for some frontier?
Captain: Truly to speak, and with no addition,
    We go to gain a little patch of ground
    That hath in it no profit but the name.
    To pay° five ducats, five, I would not farm° it;   20
    Nor will it yield to Norway or the Pole
    A ranker° rate, should it be sold in fee.°
Hamlet: Why, then the Polack never will defend it.
Captain: Yes, it is already garrison'd.
Hamlet: Two thousand souls and twenty thousand ducats   25
    Will not debate° the question of this straw.
    This is th' imposthume° of much wealth and peace,
    That inward breaks, and shows no cause without
    Why the man dies. I humbly thank you, sir.
Captain: God buy you, sir.   [*Exit.*]
Rosencrantz: Will't please you go, my lord?   30
Hamlet: I'll be with you straight—go a little before.

[*Exeunt all but Hamlet.*]

    How all occasions do inform against° me,
    And spur my dull revenge! What is a man,
    If his chief good and market° of his time
    Be but to sleep and feed? a beast, no more.   35
    Sure He that made us with such large discourse,°
    Looking before and after, gave us not
    That capability and godlike reason

To fust° in us unus'd. Now, whether it be
Bestial oblivion,° or some craven scruple   40
Of thinking too precisely on th' event°—
A thought which quarter'd hath but one part wisdom
And ever three parts coward—I do not know
Why yet I live to say, "This thing's to do,"
Sith I have cause, and will, and strength, and means   45
To do't. Examples, gross° as earth exhort me:
Witness this army of such mass and charge,°
Led by a delicate and tender prince,
Whose spirit with divine ambition puff'd
Makes mouths at° the invisible° event,   50
Exposing what is mortal and unsure
To all that fortune, death, and danger dare,
Even for an egg-shell. Rightly to be great
Is not to° stir without great argument,°
But greatly° to find quarrel in a straw   55
When honor's at the stake. How stand I then,
That have a father kill'd, a mother stain'd,
Excitements° of my reason and my blood,
And let all sleep, while to my shame I see
The imminent death of twenty thousand men,   60
That, for a fantasy° and trick° of fame
Go to their graves like beds, fight for a plot
Whereon the numbers cannot try the cause,°
Which is not tomb enough and continent°
To hide the slain? O, from this time forth,   65
My thoughts be bloody, or be nothing worth!

Exit.

SCENE 5°

Enter Horatio, [Queen] Gertrude, and a Gentlemen.

Queen: I will not speak with her.
Gentlemen: She is importunate, indeed distract.
    Her mood will needs be pitied.
Queen: What would she have?
Gentleman: She speaks much of her father, says she hears
    There's tricks i' th' world, and hems, and beats her heart,   5
    Spurns enviously at straws,° speaks things in doubt°
    That carry but half sense. Her speech° is nothing,
    Yet the unshaped use° of it doth move
    The hearers to collection;° they yawn at° it,
    And botch° the words up fit to their own thoughts,   10
    Which° as her winks and nods and gestures yield them,
    Indeed would make one think there might be thought,°
    Though nothing sure, yet much unhappily.

°**4.4. Location** The Danish coast, near the castle. °**conveyance of** Escort for. °**eye** Presence. °**softly** Slowly. °**powers** Forces. °**main** Main territory. °**To pay** For an annual rent of. °**farm** Lease. °**ranker** Higher. °**in fee** Outright. °**Will not debate** Will scarcely be enough to fight out. °**imposthume** Abscess. °**inform against** Denounce, accuse. °**market** Purchase, profit. °**discourse** Reasoning power. °**fust** Grow mouldy. °**oblivion** Forgetfulness. °**event** Outcome. °**gross** Large, obvious. °**mass and charge** Size and expense. °**Makes mouths at** Treats scornfully. °**invisible** Unforeseeable. °**Is not to** Is *not* not to. °**argument** Cause. °**greatly** Nobly. °**Excitements of** Urgings by. °**fantasy** Caprice. °**trick** Trifle. °**Whereon . . . cause** Which isn't large enough to let the opposing armies engage upon it. °**continent** Container. °**5.5. Location** The castle. °**Spurns . . . straws** Spitefully takes offense at trifles. °**in doubt** Obscurely. °**Her speech** What she says. °**unshaped use** Distracted manner. °**collection** Attempts to gather the meaning. °**yawn at** Gape eagerly (as if to swallow). Most editors adopt the F1 reading *aim at.* °**botch** Patch. °**Which** The words. °**thought** Inferred, conjectured.

Horatio: 'Twere good she were spoken with, for she may strew
Dangerous conjectures in ill-breeding° minds.   15
[Queen]: Let her come in. [*Exit Gentleman.*]
   [*aside*] To my sick soul, as sin's true nature is,
   Each toy° seems prologue to some great amiss,°
   So full of artless jealousy° is guilt,
   It spills° itself in fearing to be spilt.   20

Enter Ophelia [distracted, with her hair down, playing on a lute].

Ophelia: Where is the beauteous majesty of Denmark?
Queen: How now, Ophelia?
Ophelia: "How should I your true-love°
                 know   *She sings.*
              From another one?   25
           By his cockle hat° and staff,°
              And his sandal shoon.°"

Queen: Alas, sweet lady, what imports this song?
Ophelia: Say you? Nay, pray you mark.
              "He is dead and gone, lady,   *Song.* 30
                 He is dead and gone,
              At his head a grass-green turf,
                 At his heels a stone."
           O ho!
Queen: Nay, but, Ophelia—   35
Ophelia: Pray you, mark.   [*Sings.*]
"White his shroud as the mountain snow"—

Enter King.

Queen: Alas, look here, my lord.
Ophelia: "Larded° with sweet flowers, *Song.*
              Which bewept to the ground did not° go   40
                 With true-love showers."
King: How do you, pretty lady?
Ophelia: Well, God dild° you! They say the owl° was a baker's
   daughter. Lord, we know what we are, but know not what
   we may be. God be at your table!
King: Conceit° upon her father.   45
Ophelia: Pray let's have no words of this, but when they ask you
   what it means, say you this: *Song.*
              "To-morrow is Saint Valentine's day,
                 All in the morning betime,   50
              And I a maid at your window,
                 To be your Valentine.
              "Then up he rose and donn'd his clo'es,

And dupp'd° the chamber-door,
   Let in the maid, that out a maid   55
      Never departed more."
King: Pretty Ophelia!
Ophelia: Indeed without an oath, I'll make
   an end on't.   [*Sings.*]
      "By Gis,° and by Saint Charity,
         Alack, and fie for shame!   60
      Young men will do't if they come to't,
         By Cock,° they are to blame.
      "Quoth she, 'Before you tumbled me,
         You promis'd me to wed.'"
                                                 He answers.
      So would I 'a'done, by yonder sun,   65
         And° thou hadst not come to my bed.'"
King: How long hath she been thus?
Ophelia: I hope all will be well. We must be patient, but I cannot
   choose but weep to think they would lay him i' th' cold
   ground. My brother shall know of it, and so I thank you for
   your good counsel. Come, my coach! Good night, ladies, 70
   good night. Sweet ladies, good night, good night. [*Exit.*]
King: Follow her close, give her good watch, I pray you. [*Exit
   Horatio.*]
   O, this is the poison of deep grief, it springs
   All from her father's death—and now behold!
   O Gertrude, Gertrude,   75
   When sorrows come, they come not single spies,°
   But in battalions: first, her father slain;
   Next, your son gone, and he most violent author
   Of his own just remove; the people muddied,°
   Thick and unwholesome in [their] thoughts and whispers 80
   For good Polonius' death; and we have done but greenly°
   In hugger-mugger° to inter him; poor Ophelia
   Divided from herself and her fair judgment,
   Without the which we are pictures, or mere beasts;
   Last, and as much containing as all these,   85
   Her brother is in secret come from France,
   Feeds on his wonder, keeps himself in clouds,°
   And wants° not buzzers° to infect his ear
   With pestilent speeches of his father's death,
   Wherein necessity, of matter beggar'd,°   90
   Will nothing stick our person to arraign°
   In ear and ear. O my dear Gertrude, this,
   Like to a murd'ring-piece,° in many places
   Gives me superfluous death. *(a noise within)*

°**ill-breeding** Conceiving ill thoughts, prone to think the worst.
°**toy** Trifle. °**amiss** Calamity. °**artless jealousy** Uncontrolled
suspicion. °**spills** Destroys. °**23–27** These lines resemble a
passage in an earlier ballad beginning "As you came from the holy
land / Of Walsingham." Probably all the song fragments sung by
Ophelia were familiar to the Globe audience, but only one other line
(187) is from a ballad still extant. °**cockle hat** Hat bearing a cockle
shell, the badge of a pilgrim to the shrine of St. James of Compostela
in Spain. °**staff** Another mark of a pilgrim. °**shoon** Shoes (already
an archaic form in Shakespeare's day). °**Larded** Adorned. °**not**
Contrary to the expected sense, and unmetrical; explained as Ophelia's
alteration of the line to accord with the facts of Polonius' burial (see

line 83). °**dild** Yield, reward. °**owl** Alluding to the legend of a
baker's daughter whom Jesus turned into an owl because she did not
respond generously to his request for bread. °**Conceit** Fanciful
brooding °**dupp'd** Opened. °**Gis** Contraction of *Jesus.* °**Cock**
Corruption of *God.* °**And** If. °**spies** Soldiers sent ahead of the main
force to reconnoiter; scouts. °**muddied** Confused. °**greenly**
Unwisely. °**In hugger-mugger** Secretly and hastily. °**in clouds**
In cloudy surmise and suspicion (rather than the light of fact). °**wants**
Lacks. °**buzzers** Whispering informers. °**of matter beggar'd**
Destitute of facts. °**nothing...arraign** Scruple not at all to charge
me with the crime. °**murd'ring-piece** Cannon firing a scattering
charge.

[Queen: Alack, what noise is this?]
King: Attend!   95
    Where is my Swissers?° Let them guard the door.

Enter a Messenger.

    What is the matter?
Messenger: Save yourself, my lord!
    The ocean, overpeering of his list,°
    Eats not the flats with more impiteous haste
    Than young Laertes, in a riotous head,°   100
    O'erbears your officers. The rabble call him lord,
    And as° the world were now but to begin,
    Antiquity forgot, custom not known,
    The ratifiers and props of every word,°
    [They] cry, "Choose we, Laertes shall be king!"   105
    Caps, hands, and tongues applaud it to the clouds,
    "Laertes shall be king, Laertes king!" *(a noise within)*
Queen: How cheerfully on the false trail they cry!
    O, this is counter,° you false Danish dogs!

Enter Laertes with others.

King: The doors are broke.   110
Laertes: Where is this king? Sirs, stand you all without.
All: No, let's come in.
Laertes: I pray you give me leave.
All: We will, we will.
Laertes: I thank you keep the door. [*Exeunt Laertes' followers.*]
    O thou vile king,   115
    Give me my father!
Queen: Calmly, good Laertes.
Laertes: That drop of blood that's calm proclaims me bastard,
    Cries cuckold, to my father, brands the harlot
    Even here between the chaste unsmirched brow
    Of my true mother.
King: What is the cause, Laertes,   120
    That thy rebellion looks so giant-like?
    Let him go, Gertrude, do not fear° our person:
    There's such divinity doth hedge a king
    That treason can but peep to what it would,°
    Acts little of his will. Tell me, Laertes,   125
    Why thou art thus incens'd. Let him go, Gertrude.
    Speak, man.
Laertes: Where is my father?
King: Dead.
Queen: But not by him.
King: Let him demand his fill.
Laertes: How came he dead? I'll not be juggled with.   130
    To hell, allegiance! vows, to the blackest devil!
    Conscience and grace, to the profoundest pit!

    I dare damnation. To this point I stand,
    That both the worlds I give to negligence,°
    Let come what comes, only I'll be reveng'd   135
    Most throughly° for my father.
King: Who shall stay you?
Laertes: My will, not all the world's:°
    And for my means, I'll husband them so well,
    They shall go far with little.
King: Good Laertes,
    If you desire to know the certainty   140
    Of your dear father, is't writ in your revenge
    That, swoopstake,° you will draw both friend and foe,
    Winner or loser?
Laertes: None but his enemies.
King: Will you know them then?
Laertes: To his good friends thus wide I'll ope my arms,   145
    And like the kind life-rendoring pelican,°
    Repast them with my blood.
King: Why, now you speak
    Like a good child° and a true gentleman.
    That I am guiltless of your father's death,
    And am most sensibly° in grief for it,   150
    It shall as level° to your judgment 'pear
    As day does to your eye.
                (a noise within:) "Let her come in!"
Laertes: How now, what noise is that?

Enter Ophelia.

    O heat, dry up my brains! tears seven times salt
    Burn out the sense and virtue° of mine eye!   155
    By heaven, thy madness shall be paid by weight
    [Till] our scale turn the beam. O rose of May!
    Dear maid, kind sister, sweet Ophelia!
    O heavens, is't possible a young maid's wits
    Should be as mortal as [an old] man's life?   160
    [Nature is fine in° love, and where 'tis fine,
    It sends some precious instance° of itself
    After the thing it loves.]
Ophelia: "They bore him barefac'd on the   *Song.*
    bier,   165
      [Hey nor nonny, nonny, hey nonny,]
      And in his grave rain'd many a tear"—
    Fare you well, my dove!

Laertes: Hadst thou thy wits and didst persuade° revenge,
    It could not move thus.   170
Ophelia: You must sing, "A down-a-down," and you call him
    a-down-a.° O, how the wheel° becomes it! It is the false
    steward, that stole his master's daughter.

°**Swissers** Swiss guards. °**overpeering . . . list** Rising higher than its shores. °**in . . . head** With a rebellious force. °**as** As if. °**word** Pledge, promise. °**counter** On the wrong scent (literally, following the scent backward). °**fear** Fear for. °**would** Would like to do. °**both . . . negligence** I don't care what the consequences are in this world or in the next. °**thoroughly** Thoroughly. °**world's** World's will. °**swoopstake** Sweeping up everything without discrimination (modern *sweepstake*). °**pelican** The female pelican was believed to draw blood from her own breast to nourish her young. °**good child** Faithful son. °**sensibly** Feelingly. °**level** Plain. °**virtue** Faculty. °**fine in** Refined or spiritualized by. °**instance** Proof, token. So delicate is Ophelia's love for her father that her sanity has pursued him into the grave. °**persuade** Argue logically for. °**and . . . a-down-a** "If he indeed agrees that Polonius is 'a-down,' fallen low" (Dover Wilson). °**wheel** Refrain (?) or spinning-wheel, at which women sang ballads (?).

Laertes: This nothing's more than matter.°
Ophelia: There's rosemary, that's for remembrance; pray you, 175
love, remember. And there is pansies, that's for thoughts.
Laertes: A document in madness,° thoughts and remembrance
fitted.
Ophelia [*to Claudius*]: There's fennel for you, and columbines.°
[*to Gertrude*] There's rue° for you, and here's some of me of 180
we may call it herb-grace a' Sundays. You may wear your
rue with a difference.° There's a daisy.° I would give you
some violets, but they wither'd all when my father died.
They say, 'a made a good end— [*Sings*]
"For bonny sweet Robin is all my joy."
Laertes: Thought° and afflictions, passion, hell itself,
She turns to favor° and to prettiness. 185
Ophelia: And will 'a not come again? *Song.*
And will 'a not come again?
No, no, he is dead,
Go to thy death-bed,
He never will come again. 190
"His beard was as white as snow,
[*All*] flaxen° was his pole,°
He is gone, he is gone,
And we cast away moan,
God 'a' mercy on his soul!" 195

And of all Christian's souls, [I pray God]. God buy you. [*Exit.*]

Laertes: Do you [see] this, O God?
King: Laertes, I must commune with your grief,
Or you deny me right. Go but apart,
Make choice of whom your wisest friends you will, 200
And they shall hear and judge 'twixt you and me.
If by direct or by collateral° hand
They find us touch'd,° we will our kingdom give,
Our crown, our life, and all that we call ours,
To you in satisfaction; but if not, 205
Be you content to lend your patience to us,
And we shall jointly labor with your soul
To give it due content.
Laertes: Let this be so.
His means of death, his obscure funeral—
No trophy,° sword, nor hatchment° o'er his bones, 210
No noble rite nor formal ostentation°—
Cry to be heard, as 'twere from heaven to earth,
That° I must call't in question.
King: So you shall,
And where th' offense is, let the great axe fall.
I pray you, go with me. 215

Exeunt.

SCENE 6°

Enter Horatio and others.

Horatio: What are they that would speak with me?
Gentleman: Sea-faring men, sir. They say they have letters for
you.
Horatio: Let them come in. [*Exit Gentleman.*]
I do not know from what part of the world
I should be greeted, if not from Lord Hamlet. 5

Enter Sailors.

[1.] Sailor: God bless you, sir.
Horatio: Let him bless thee too.
[1.] Sailor: 'A shall, sir, and['t] please him. There's a letter for
you, sir—it came from th' embassador that was bound for
England—if your name be Horatio, as I am let to know it is. 10
Horatio [*reads*]: "Horatio, when thou shalt have overlook'd this,
give these fellows some means to the King, they have letters
for him. Ere we were two days old at sea, a pirate of very
warlike appointment gave us chase. Finding ourselves too
slow of sail, we put on a compell'd valor, and in the grapple
I boarded them. On the instant they got clear of our ship, so 15
I alone became their prisoner. They have dealt with me like
thieves of mercy,° but they knew what they did: I am to do a
[good] turn for them. Let the King have the letters I have
sent, and repair thou to me with as much speed as thou
wouldst fly death. I have words to speak in thine ear will
make thee dumb, yet are they much too light for the [bore°]
of the matter. These good fellows will bring thee where I am. 20
Rosencrantz and Guildenstern hold their course for England, of them I have much to tell thee. Farewell.
[He] that thou knowest thine,
Hamlet."
Come, I will [give] you way for these your letters,
And do't the speedier that you may direct me 25
To him from whom you brought them.

Exeunt.

SCENE 7°

Enter King and Laertes.

King: Now must your conscience my acquittance° seal,
And you must put me in your heart for friend,
Sith you have heard, and with a knowing ear,
That he which hath your noble father slain
Pursued my life. 5
Laertes: It well appears. But tell me
Why you [proceeded] not against these feats°

°**matter** Lucid speech. °**A document in madness** A lesson
contained in mad talk. °**fennel, columbines** Symbols respectively
of flattery and ingratitude. °**rue** Symbolic of sorrow and repentance.
°**with a difference** To represent a different cause of sorrow. *Difference*
is a term from heraldry, meaning a variation in a coat of arms made to
distinguish different members of a family. °**daisy, violets** Symbolic
respectively of dissembling and faithfulness. It is not clear who are the
recipients of these. °**Thought** Melancholy. °**favor** Grace; charm.

°**flaxen** White. °**pole** Poll, head. °**collateral** Indirect.
°**touch'd** Guilty. °**trophy** Memorial. °**hatchment** Heraldic
memorial tablet. °**formal ostentation** Fitting and customary
ceremony. °**That** So that. °**4. 6. Location** The castle °**thieves
of mercy** Merciful thieves. °**bore** Calibre, size (gunnery term).
°**4.7. Location** The castle. °**my acquittance seal** ratify my
acquittal; i.e.. acknowledge my innocence in Polonius's death.
°**feats** Acts.

So criminal and so capital in nature,
As by your safety,° greatness, wisdom, all things else
You mainly° were stirr'd up.

King: O, for two special reasons,
Which may to you perhaps seem much unsinow'd,°   10
But yet to me th' are strong. The Queen his mother
Lives almost by his looks, and for myself—
My virtue or my plague, be it either which°—
She is so [conjunctive°]—to my life and soul,
That, as the star moves not but in his sphere,°   15
I could not but by her. The other motive,
Why to a public count° I might not go,
Is the great love the general gender° bear him,
Who, dipping all his faults in their affection,
Work like the spring that turneth wood to stone,
Convert his gyves° to graces, so that my arrows,   20
Too slightly timber'd for so [loud a wind],
Would have reverted to my bow again,
But not where I have aim'd them.

Laertes: And so have I a noble father lost,   25
A sister driven into desp'rate terms,°
Whose worth, if praises may go back again,°
Stood challenger on mount° of all the age
For her perfections—but my revenge will come.

King: Break not your sleeps for that.° You must not think   30
That we are made of stuff so flat° and dull
That we can let our beard be shook° with° danger,
And think it pastime. You shortly shall hear more.
I lov'd your father, and we love ourself,
And that, I hope, will teach you to imagine—   35

Enter a Messenger with letters.

[How now! what news?

Messenger: Letters, my lord, from Hamlet:]
These to your Majesty, this to the Queen.

King: From Hamlet! Who brought them?

Messenger: Sailors, my lord, they say, I saw them not,
They were given me by Claudio. He receiv'd them   40
Of him that brought them.

King: Laertes, you shall hear them.
—Leave us. [*Exit Messenger.*]
[reads] "High and mighty, You shall know I am set naked°
on your kingdom. To-morrow shall I beg leave to see
your kingly eyes, when I shall, first asking you pardon

thereunto,° recount the occasion of my sudden [and more   45
strange] return.
                                   [*Hamlet*]"

What should this mean? Are all the rest come back?
Or is it some abuse,° and no such thing?

Laertes: Know you the hand?

King: 'Tis Hamlet's character.° Naked"!   50
And in a postscript here he says, "alone."
Can you devise me?°

Laertes: I am lost in it, my lord. But let him come,
It warms the very sickness in my heart
That I [shall] live and tell him to his teeth,   55
"Thus diddest thou."

King: If it be so, Laertes—
As how should it be so? how otherwise?°—
Will you be rul'd by me?

Laertes: Ay, my lord,
So° you will not o'errule me to a peace.

King: To thine own peace. If he be now returned,   60
As [checking] at° his voyage, and that he means
No more to undertake it. I will work him
To an exploit, now ripe in my device,
Under the which he shall not choose but fall;
And for his death no wind of blame shall breathe,   65
But even his mother shall uncharge the practice,°
And call it accident.

Laertes: My lord, I will be rul'd,
The rather if you could devise it so
That I might be the organ.°

King: It falls right.
You have been talk'd of since your travel much,   70
And that in Hamlet's hearing, for a quality°
Wherein they say you shine. Your sum of parts°
Did not together pluck such envy from him
As did that one, and that, in my regard,
Of the unworthiest° siege.°   75

Laertes: What part is that, my lord?

King: A very riband in the cap of youth,
Yet needful too, for youth no less becomes
The light and careless livery that it wears
Than settled age his sables and his weeds,°
Importing health and graveness.° Two months since   80
Here was a gentleman of Normandy:
I have seen myself, and serv'd against, the French,
And they can well on horseback,° but this gallant

°**safety** Regard for your own safety. °**mainly** Powerfully.
°**unsinow'd** Unsinewed, weak. °**either which** One or the
other. °**conjunctive** Closely joined. °**in his sphere** By the
movement of the sphere in which it is fixed (as the Ptolemaic
astronomy taught). °**count** Reckoning. °**the general gender**
Everybody. °**gyves** Fetters. °**terms** Condition. °**go back again**
Refer to what she was before she went mad. °**on mount** Preeminent.
°**for that** For fear of losing your revenge. °**flat** Spiritless. °**let . . .
shook** To ruffle or tweak a man's beard was an act of insolent defiance
that he could not disregard without loss of honor. Cf. 2.2. 521. °**with**
By. °**naked** Destitute. °**pardon thereunto** Permission to do so.

°**abuse** Deceit. °**character** Handwriting. °**devise me** Explain
it to me. °**As . . . otherwise** How can he have come back? Yet he
obviously has. °**So** Provided that. °**checking at** Turning from
(like a falcon diverted from its quarry by other prey). °**uncharge
the practice** Adjudge the plot no plot, fail to see the plot. °**organ**
Instrument, agent. °**quality** Skill. °**Your . . . parts** All your (other)
accomplishments put together. °**unworthiest** Least important
(with no implication of unsuitableness). °**siege** Status, position.
°**weeds** Characteristic) garb. °**Importing . . . graveness**
Signifying prosperity and dignity. °**can . . . horseback** Are excellent
riders.

Had witchcraft in't, he grew unto his seat,
And to such wondrous doing brought his horse, 85
As had he been incorps'd° and demi-natur'd°
With the brave beast. So far he topp'd [my] thought,
That I in forgery° of shapes and tricks
Come short of what he did.

Laertes: A Norman was't?

King: A Norman. 90

Laertes: Upon my life, Lamord.

King: The very same.

Laertes: I know him well. He is the brooch° indeed
And gem of all the nation.

King: He made confession of you,°
And gave you such a masterly report 95
For art and exercise in your defense,
And for your rapier most especial,
That he cried out 'twould be a sight indeed
If one could match you. The scrimers° of their nation
He swore had neither motion, guard, nor eye, 100
If you oppos'd them. Sir, this report of his
Did Hamlet so envenom with his envy
That he could nothing do but wish and beg
Your sudden° coming o'er to play with you.
Now, out of this— 105

Laertes: What out of this, my lord?

King: Laertes, was your father dear to you?
Or are you like the painting of a sorrow,
A face without a heart?

Laertes: Why ask you this?

King: Not that I think you did not love your father,
But that I know love is begun by time,° 110
And that I see, in passages of proof,°
Time qualifies° the spark and fire of it.
There lives within the very flame of love
A kind of week° or snuff that will abate it,
And nothing is at a like goodness still,° 115
For goodness, growing to a plurisy,°
Dies in his own too much.° That we would do,
We should do when we would; for this "would" changes,
And hath abatements and delays as many
As there are tongues, are hands, are accidents, 120
And then this "should" is like a spendthrift's sigh,°
That hurts by easing.° But to the quick of th' ulcer:

Hamlet comes back. What would you undertake
To show yourself in deed your father's son
More than in words?

Laertes: To cut his throat i' th' church. 125

King: No place indeed should murder sanctuarize,°
Revenge should have no bounds. But, good Laertes,
Will you do this,° keep close within your chamber.
Hamlet return'd shall know you are come home,
We'll put on those° shall praise your excellence, 130
And set a double varnish° on the fame
The Frenchman gave you, bring you in fine° together,
And wager o'er yours heads. He, being remiss,°
Most generous,° and free from all contriving,°
Will not peruse° the foils so that with ease, 135
Or with a little shuffling,° you may choose
A sword unbated,° and, in a [pass] of practice°
Requite him for your father.

Laertes: I will do't
And for [that] purpose I'll anoint my sword.
I bought an unction° of a mountebank,° 140
So mortal° that, but dip a knife in it,
Where it draws blood, no cataplasm° so rare,
Collected from all simples° that have virtue°
Under the moon, can save the thing from death
That is but scratch'd withal. I'll touch my point 145
With this contagion, that if I gall° him slightly,
It may be death.

King: Let's further think of this,
Weigh what convenience both of time and means
May fit us to our shape.° If this should fail,
And that our drift° look through° our bad performance, 150
'Twere better not assay'd; therefore this project
Should have a back or second,° that might hold
If this did blast in proof.° Soft, let me see.
We'll make a solemn wager on your cunnings—
I ha't! 155
When in your motion you are hot and dry—
As° make your bouts more violent to that end—
And that he calls for drink, I'll have preferr'd° him
A chalice for the nonce,° whereon but sipping,
If he by chance escape your venom'd stuck,° 160
Our purpose may hold there. But stay, what noise?

Enter Queen.

°**incorps'd** Made one body. °**demi-natur'd** Become half of a composite animal. °**forgery** Mere imagining. °**brooch** Ornament (worn in the hat). °**made . . . you** Acknowledged your excellence. °**scrimers** Fencers. °**sudden** Speedy. °**time** A particular set of circumstances. °**in . . . proof** By the test of experience, by actual examples. °**qualifies** Moderates. °**week** Wick. °**nothing . . . still** Nothing remains forever at the same pitch of perfection. °**plurisy** Plethora (a variant spelling of *pleurisy*, which was erroneously related to *plus*, stem *plur*, "more, overmuch"). °**too much** Excess. °**spendthrift's sigh** A sigh was supposed to draw blood from the heart. °**hurts by easing** Injures us at the same time that it gives us relief. °**sanctuarize** Offer asylum to. °**Will . . . this** If you want to undertake this. °**put on those** Incite those who.

°**double varnish** Second coat of varnish. °**in fine** Finally. °**remiss** Careless, overtrustful. °**generous** Noble-minded. °**free . . . contriving** Innocent of sharp practices. °**peruse** Examine. °**shuffling** Cunning exchange. °**unbated** Not blunted. °**pass of practice** Tricky thrust. °**unction** Ointment. °**mountebank** Traveling quack-doctor. °**mortal** Deadly. °**cataplasm** Poultice. °**simples** Medicinal herbs. °**virtue** Curative power. °**gall** Graze. °**fit . . . shape** Suit our purposes best. °**drift** purpose. °**look through** Become visible, be detected. °**back or second** A second plot in reserve for emergency. °**blast in proof** Blow up while being tried (an image from gunnery). °**As** And you should. °**preferr'd** Offered to. Most editors adopt the F1 reading *prepar'd*. °**nonce** Occasion. °**stuck** Thrust (from *stoccado*, a fencing term).

Queen: One woe doth tread upon another's heel,
So fast they follow. Your sister's drown'd, Laertes.

Laertes: Drown'd! O, where?

Queen: There is a willow grows askaunt° the brook,   165
That shows his hoary° leaves in the glassy stream,
Therewith° fantastic garlands did she make
Of crow-flowers, nettles, daisies, and long purples°
That liberal° shepherds give a grosser name,
But our cull-cold° maids do dead men's fingers call them.   170
There on the pendant boughs her cownet° weeds
Clamb'ring to hang, an envious sliver° broke,
When down her weedy trophies and herself
Fell in the weeping brook. Her clothes spread wide,
And mermaid-like awhile they bore her up,   175
Which time she chaunted snatches of old lauds,°
As one incapable° of her own distress,
Or like a creature native and indued°
Unto that element. But long it could not be
Till that her garments, heavy with their drink,   180
Pull'd the poor wretch from her melodious lay
To muddy death.

Laertes: Alas, then, she is drown'd?

Queen: Drown'd, drown'd.

Laertes: Too much of water hast thou, poor Ophelia,
And therefore I forbid my tears; but yet   185
It° is our trick,° Nature her custom holds,
Let shame say what it will; when these° are gone,
The woman will be out.° Adieu, my lord,
I have a speech a' fire that fain would blaze,
But that this folly drowns it.   (*Exit.*)

King: Let's follow, Gertrude.   190
How much I had to do to calm his rage!
Now fear I this will give it start again,
Therefore let's follow.

Exeunt.

ACT 5
SCENE 1°

Enter two Clowns° [with spades and mattocks].

1. Clown: Is she to be buried in Christian burial when she
willfully seeks her own salvation?

2. Clown: I tell thee she is, therefore make her grave straight.° The
crowner° hath sate on her, and finds it Christian burial.

1. Clown: How can that be, unless she drown'd herself in her own   5
defense?

2. Clown: Why, 'tis found so.

1. Clown: It must be [*se offendendo*],° it cannot be else. For here
lies the point: if I drown myself wittingly, it argues an act,
and an act hath three branches—it is to act, to do, to perform; [argal],° she drown'd herself wittingly.

2. Clown: Nay, but hear you, goodman delver—   10

1. Clown: Give me leave. Here lies the water; good. Here stands
the man; good. If the man go to this water and drown himself, it is, will he, nill he,° he goes, mark you that. But if the
water come to him and drown him, he drowns not himself;
argal, he that is not guilty of his own death shortens not his
own life.°   15

2. Clown: But is this law?

1. Clown: Ay, marry, is't—crowner's quest° law.

2. Clown: Will you ha' the truth an't? If this had not been a gen-
tlewoman, she should have been buried out a' Christian
burial.

1. Clown: Why, there thou say'st, and the more pity that great   20
folk, should have count'nance in this world to drown or
hang themselves, more than their even-Christen.° Come, my
spade. There is no ancient gentlemen but gard'ners, ditchers,
and grave-makers; they hold up Adam's profession.

2. Clown: Was he a gentleman?

1. Clown: 'A was the first that ever bore arms.   25

2. Clown: Why, he had none.°

1. Clown: What, art a heathen? How dost thou understand the
Scripture? The Scripture says Adam digg'd could he dig
without arms?] I'll put another question to thee. If thou an-
swerest me not to the purpose, confess thyself—

2. Clown: Go to.   30

1. Clown: What is he that builds stronger than either the mason,
the shipwright, or the carpenter?

2. Clown: The gallows-maker, for that outlives a thousand
tenants.

1. Clown: I like thy wit well, in good faith. The gallows does well;
but how does it well? it does well to those that do ill. Now thou 35
dost ill to say the gallows is built stronger than the church; argal, the gallows may do well to thee. To't again, come.

2. Clown: Who builds stronger than a mason, a shipwright, or a
carpenter?

1. Clown: Ay, tell me that, and unyoke.°

2. Clown: Marry, now I can tell.   40

1. Clown: To't.

2. Clown: Mass,° I cannot tell.

Enter Hamlet and Horatio [after off].

1. Clown: Cudgel thy brains no more about it, for your dull ass
will not mend his pace with beating, and when you are ask'd
this question next, say "a grave-maker" the houses he makes   45

°**askaunt** Sideways over. °**hoary** Grey-white. °**Therewith**
With willow branches. °**long purples** Wild orchids. °**liberal**
Free-spoken. °**cull-cold** Chaste. °**crownet** Made into coronets.
°**envious silver** Malicious branch. °**lauds** Hymns. °**incapable**
Insensible. °**indued** Habituated. °**It** Weeping. °**trick** Natural
way. °**these** These tears. °**The woman . . . out** My womanish
traits will be gone for good. °**5.1. Location** A churchyard.
°**Clowns** Rustics. °**straight** Immediately. °**crowner** Coroner.

°**se offendendo** Blunder for *se defendendo*, "in self-defense."
°**argal** Blunder for *ergo*, "therefore." °**Here . . . life** Alluding
to a very famous suicide case, that of Sir James Hales, a judge who
drowned himself in 1554; it was long cited in the courts. The clown
gives a garbled account of the defense summing-up and the verdict.
°**nill he** Will he not. °**quest** Inquest. °**even-Christen** Fellow-
Christians. °**none** No coat of arms. °**unyoke** Cease to labor,
call it a day. °**Mass** By the mass.

lasts till doomsday. Go get thee in, and fetch me a sup of
liquor.

[Exit Second Clown. First clown digs.]

      "In youth when I did love, did love,   *Song*
        Methought it was very sweet,
      To contract—O—the time for—a—my behove,°
      O, methought there—a—was nothing—a—meet."   50

Hamlet: Has this fellow no feeling of his business? 'a sings in
grave-making.

Horatio: Custom° hath made it in him a property of easiness.°

Hamlet: 'Tis e'en so, the hand of little employment hath the daintier sense.°

1. Clown: "But age with his stealing steps   *Song*
          Hath clawed me in his clutch,   55
          And hath shipped me into the land,
          As if I had never been such."

[throws up a shovelful of earth with a skull in it]

Hamlet: That skull had a tongue in it, and could sing once.
How the knave jowls° it to the ground, as if 'twere Cain's
jaw-bone, that did the first murder! This might be the pate   60
of a politician,° which this ass now o'er-reaches,° one that
would circumvent God,° might it not?

Horatio: It might, my lord.

Hamlet: Or of a courtier, which could say, "Good morrow, sweet
lord! How dost thou, sweet lord?" This might be my Lord
Such-a-one, that prais'd my Lord Such-a-one's horse when 'a   65
[meant] to beg it, might it not?

Horatio: Ay, my lord.

Hamlet: Why, e'en so, and now my Lady Worm's, chopless,° and
knock'd about the [mazzard]° with a sexton's spade. Here's
fine revolution,° and° we had the trick° to see't. Did these
bones cost° no more the breeding, but to play at loggats°
with them? Mine ache to think on't.   70

1. Clown: "A pickaxe and a spade, a spade,   *(song)*
          For and a shrouding sheet:
          O, a pit of clay for to be made
          For such a guest is meet."

[throws up another skull].

Hamlet: There's another. Why may not that be the skull of a law-   75
yer? Where be his quiddities° now, his quillities,° his cases,
his tenures,° and his tricks? Why does he suffer this knave
now to knock him about the sconce° mode with a dirty shovel, and will not tell him of his action of battery? Hum! This
fellow might be in 's time a great buyer of land, with his statutes, his recognizances,° his fines, his double vouchers, his
recoveries. [Is this the fine° of his fines, and the recovery of   80
his recoveries,] to have his fine pate full of fine dirt? Will [his]
vouchers vouch him no more of his purchases, and [double
ones too], than the length and breadth of a pair of indentures?° The very conveyances° of his lands will scarcely lie in
this box,° and must th' inheritor° himself have no more, ha?   85

Horatio: Not a jot more, my lord.

Hamlet: Is not parchment made of sheep-skins?

Horatio: Ay, my lord, and of calves-skins too.

Hamlet: They are sheep and calves which seek out assurance in
that. I will speak to this fellow. Whose grave's this, sirrah?°   90

1. Clown: Mine, sir.   *[sings]*

      "[O]", a pit of clay for to be made
        [For such a guest is meet].

Hamlet: I think it be thine indeed, for thou liest in't.

1. Clown: You lie out on't, sir, and therefore 'tis not yours; for my   95
part, I do not lie in't, yet it is mine.

Hamlet: Thou dost lie in't, to be in't, and say it is thine. 'Tis for
the dead, not for the quick; therefore thou liest.

1. Clown: 'Tis a quick lie, sir, 'twill away again from me to you.

Hamlet: What man dost thou dig it for?   100

1. Clown: For no man, sir.

Hamlet: What woman then?

1. Clown: For none neither.

Hamlet: Who is to be buried in't?

1. Clown: One that was a woman, sir, but, rest her soul, she's   105
dead.

Hamlet: How absolute° the knave is! we must speak by the card,°
or equivocation° will undo us. By the Lord, Horatio, this
three years I have took note of it: the age is grown so pick'd°
that the toe of the peasant comes so near the heel of the
courtier, he galls his kibe.° How long hast thou been grave
maker?

1. Clown: Of [all] the days i' th' year, I came to't that day that our   110
last king Hamlet overcame Fortinbras.

Hamlet: How long is that since?

1. Clown: Cannot you tell that? Every fool can tell that. It was the
very day that young Hamlet was born—he that is mad, and
sent into England.

°**contract ... behove** Shorten, spend agreeably ... advantage. The song, punctuated by the grunts of the clown as he digs, is a garbled version of a poem by Thomas Lord Vaux, entitled "The Aged Lover Renounceth Love." °**Custom** Habit. °**a property of easiness** A thing he can do with complete ease of mind. °**daintier sense** More delicate sensitivity. °**jowls** Dashes. °**politician** Schemer, intriguer. °**o'er-reaches** Gets the better of (with play on the literal sense). °**circumvent God** Bypass God's law. °**chopless** Lacking the lower jaw. °**mazzard** Head °**revolution** Change. °**and** If. °**trick** Knack, ability. °**Did ... cost** Were ... worth. °**loggats** A game in which blocks of wood were thrown at a stake. °**quiddities** Subtleties, quibbles. °**quillities** Fine distinctions. °**tenures** Titles to real estate. °**sconce** Head. °**statutes, recognizances** Bonds securing debts by attaching land and property. °**fines, recoveries** Procedures for converting an entailed estate to freehold °**double vouchers** documents guaranteeing title to real estate, signed by two persons. °**fine** End. °**pair of indentures** Legal document cut into two parts which fitted together on a serrated edge. Perhaps Hamlet thus refers to the two rows of teeth in the skull, or to the bone sutures. °**conveyances** Documents relating to transfer of property. °**this box** The skull itself. °**inheritor** Owner. °**sirrah** Term of address to inferiors. °**absolute** Positive. °**by the card** By the compass, punctiliously. °**equivocation** Ambiguity. °**pick'd** Refined. °**galls his kibe** Rubs the courtier's chilblain.

Hamlet: Ay, marry, why was he sent into England? 115

1. Clown: Why, because 'a was mad. 'A shall recover his wits there, or if 'a do not, 'tis no great matter there.

Hamlet: Why?

1. Clown: 'Twill not be seen in him there, there the men are as mad as he.

Hamlet: How came he mad? 120

1. Clown: Very strangely, they say.

Hamlet: How strangely?

1. Clown: Faith, e'en with losing his wits.

Hamlet: Upon what ground?

1. Clown: Why, here in Denmark. I have been sexton here, man 125 and boy, thirty years.

Hamlet: How long will a man lie i' th' earth ere he rot?

1. Clown: Faith, if 'a be not rotten before 'a die'—as we have many pocky° corses, that will scarce hold the laying in—°'a will last you some eight year or nine year. A tanner will last you nine year. 130

Hamlet: Why he more than another?

1. Clown: Why, sir, his hide is so tann'd with his trade that 'a will keep out water a great while, and your water is a sore decayer of your whoreson dead body. Here's a skull now hath lien you i' th' earth three and twenty years.

Hamlet: Whose was it? 135

1. Clown: A whoreson mad fellow's it was. Whose do you think it was?

Hamlet: Nay, I know not.

1. Clown: A pestilence on him for a mad rogue! 'a pour'd a flagon of Rhenish on my head once. This same skull, sir, was, sir, Yorick's skull, the King's jester. 140

Hamlet: This? [takes the skull]

1. Clown: E'en that.

Hamlet: Alas, poor Yorick! I knew him, Horatio, a fellow of infinite jest, of most excellent fancy. He hath bore me on his back a thousand times, and now how abhorr'd in my imagination it is! my gorge rises at it. Here hung those lips that I 145 have kiss'd I know not how oft. Where be your gibes now, your gambols, your songs, your flashes of merriment, that were wont to set the table on a roar? Not one now to mock your own grinning—quite chop-fall'n.° Now get you to my lady's [chamber], and tell her, let her paint an inch thick, to 150 this favor° she must come; make her laugh at that. Prithee, Horatio, tell me one thing.

Horatio: What's that, my lord?

Hamlet: Dost thou think Alexander look'd a' this fashion i' th' earth?

Horatio: E'en so.

Hamlet: And smelt so? pah! [puts down the skull] 155

Horatio: E'en so, my lord.

Hamlet: To what base uses we may return, Horatio! Why may not imagination trace the noble dust of Alexander, till 'a find it stopping a bunghole?

Horatio: 'Twere to consider too curiously,° to consider so.

Hamlet: No, faith, not a jot, but to follow him thither with mod-160 esty° enough and likelihood to lead it: Alexander died, Alexander was buried, Alexander returneth to dust, the dust is earth, of earth we make loam,° and why of that loam whereto he was converted might they not stop a beer-barrel? Imperious° Caesar, dead and turn'd to clay, Might stop a hole to keep the wind away. 165 O that that earth which kept the world in awe Should patch a wall t' expel the [winter's] flaw!° But soft, but soft, awhile here, comes the King,

Enter King, Queen, Laertes, and [a Doctor of Divinity, following] the corse, [with Lords attendant].

The Queen, the courtiers. Who is this they follow? And with such maimed rites?° This doth betoken 170 The corse they follow did with desp'rate hand Foredo° it° own life. 'Twas of some estate.° Couch we° a while and mark. [retiring with Horatio]

Laertes: What ceremony else?

Hamlet: That is Laertes, a very noble youth. Mark. 175

Laertes: What ceremony else?

Doctor: Her obsequies have been as far enlarg'd As we have warranty. Her death was doubtful,° And but that great command o'ersways the order,° She should° in ground unsanctified have lodg'd 180 Till the last trumpet; for° charitable prayers, [Shards,] flints, and pebbles, should be thrown on her. Yet here she is allow'd her virgin crants,° Her maiden strewments,° and the bringing home Of bell and burial.° 185

Laertes: Must there no more be done?

Doctor: No more be done: We should profane the service of the dead To sing a requiem° and such rest to her As to peace-parted souls.

Laertes: Lay her i' th' earth, And from her fair and unpolluted flesh 190 May violets spring! I tell thee, churlish priest, A minist'ring angel shall my sister be When thou liest howling.

Hamlet: What, the fair Ophelia!

Queen [scattering flowers]: Sweets° to the sweet, farewell! I hop'd thou shouldst have been my Hamlet's wife. 195 I thought thy bride-bed to have deck'd, sweet maid, And not have strew'd thy grave.

°**pocky** Rotten with venereal disease. °**hold...in** Last out the burial. °**chop-fall'n** (1) Lacking the lower jaw; (2) downcast. °**favor** Appearance. °**curiously** Closely, minutely. °**modesty** Moderation. °**loam** A mixture of moistened clay with sand, straw, etc. °**Imperious** Imperial. °**flaw** Gust. °**maimed rites** lack of customary ceremony. °**Foredo** Fordo, destroy. °**it** Its. °**estate** Rank. °**Couch we** Let

us conceal ourselves. °**doubtful** The subject of an "open verdict." °**order** Customary procedure. °**should** Would certainly. °**for** Instead of. °**crants** Garland. °**maiden strewments** Flowers scattered on the grave of an unmarried girl. °**bringing...burial** Burial in consecrated ground, with the bell tolling. °**requiem** Dirge. °**Sweets** Flowers.

Laertes: O, treble woe
  Fall ten times [treble] on that cursed head
  Whose wicked deed thy most ingenious° sense
  Depriv'd thee of! Hold off the earth a while,   200
  Till I have caught her once more in mine arms.

[leaps in the grave]

  Now pile your dust upon the quick and dead,
  Till of this flat a mountain you have made
  T' o'ertop old Pelion, or the skyish head
  Of blue Olympus.°   205
Hamlet [*coming forward*]: What is he whose grief
  Bears such an emphasis, whose phrase° of sorrow
  Conjures° the wand'ring stars° and makes them stand
  Like wonder-wounded hearers? This is I,
  Hamlet the Dane.°   210

[Hamlet leaps in after Laertes.]

Laertes: The devil take thy soul! *[grappling with him]*
Hamlet: Thou pray'st not well.
  I prithee take thy fingers from my throat.
  For though I am not splenitive° [and] rash,
  Yet have I in me something dangerous,
  Which let thy wisdom fear. Hold off thy hand!   215
King: Pluck them asunder.
Queen: Hamlet! Hamlet!
All: Gentlemen!
Horatio: Good my lord, be quiet.

[The Attendants part them, and they come out of the grave.]

Hamlet: Why, I will fight with him upon this theme
  Until my eyelids will no longer wag.
Queen: O my son, what theme?   220
Hamlet: I lov'd Ophelia. Forty thousand brothers
  Could not with all their quantity of love
  Make up my sum. What wilt thou do for her?
King: O, he is mad, Laertes.
Queen: For love of God, forbear him.   225
Hamlet: 'Swounds, show me what thou't° do.
  Woo't° weep, woo't fight, woo't fast, woo't tear thyself?
  Woo't drink up eisel,° eat a crocadile?°
  I'll do't. Dost [thou] come here to whine?
  To outface me with leaping in her grave?   230
  Be buried quick with her, and so will I.
  And if thou prate of mountains,° let them throw

Millions of acres on us, till our ground,
  Singeing his pate against the burning zone,°
  Make Ossa° like a wart! Nay, an thou'lt mouth,°   235
  I'll rant as well as thou.
Queen: This is mere° madness,
  And [thus] a while the fit will work on him;
  Anon, as patient° as the female dove,
  When that her golden couplets° are disclosed,°
  His silence will sit drooping.
Hamlet: Hear you, sir,   240
  What is the reason that you use me thus?
  I lov'd you ever. But it is no matter.
  Let Hercules himself do what he may,
  The cat will mew, and dog will have his day.°

Exit Hamlet.

King: I pray thee, good Horatio, wait upon him.   245

[Exit] Horatio.

  [to Laertes] Strengthen your patience in° our last night's speech,
  We'll put the matter to the present push.°—
  Good Gertrude, set some watch over your son.
  This grave shall have a living° monument.
  An hour of quiet [shortly] shall we see,   250
  Till then in patience our proceeding be.

Exeunt.

SCENE 2°

Enter Hamlet and Horatio.

Hamlet: So much for this, sir, now shall you see the other°—
  You do remember all the circumstance?
Horatio: Remember it, my lord!
Hamlet: Sir, in my heart there was a kind of fighting
  That would not let me sleep. [Methought] I lay   5
  Worse than the mutines° in the [bilboes°]. Rashly°
  And prais'd be rashness for it—let us know°
  Our indiscretion sometime serves us well
  When our deep plots do pall,° and that should learn° us
  There's a divinity that shapes our ends,°   10
  Rough-hew them° how we will.—
Horatio: That is most certain.
Hamlet: Up from my cabin,
  My sea-gown scarf'd about me, in the dark
  Grop'd I to find out them, had my desire,

°**ingenious** Intelligent. °**Pelion, Olympus** Mountains in northeastern Greece °**emphasis, phrase** Rhetorical terms, here used in disparaging reference to Laertes' inflated language. °**Conjures** Puts a spell upon. °**wand'ring stars** Planets. °**the Dane** This title normally signifies the king. °**splenitive** Impetuous. °**thou't** Thou wilt. °**Woo't** Wilt thou. °**eisel** Vinegar. °**crocadile** Crocodile. °**if...mountains** Referring to lines 203–205. °**burning zone** Sphere of the sun. °**Ossa** Another mountain in Greece, near Pelion and Olympus. °**mouth** Talk bombast (synonymous with rant in the next line). °**mere** Utter. °**patient** Calm. °**golden couplets** Pair of baby birds, covered with yellow down. °**disclosed** Hatched.

°**Let...day** Nobody can prevent another from making the scenes he feels he has a right to. °**in** By recalling. °**present push** Immediate test. °**living** Enduring (?) or in the form of a lifelike effigy (?). °**5.2. Location** The castle. °**see the other** Hear the other news I have to tell you (hinted at in the letter to Horatio. 4.6. 19–20). °**mutines** Mutineers (but the term *mutiny* was in Shakespeare's day used of almost any act of rebellion against authority). °**bilboes** Fetters attached to a heavy iron bar. °**Rashly** On impulse. °**know** Recognize, acknowledge. °**pall** Lose force, come to nothing. °**learn** Teach. °**shapes our ends** Gives final shape to our designs. °**Rough-hew them** Block them out in initial form.

Finger'd° their packet, and in fine withdrew 15
To mine own room again, making so bold,
My fears forgetting manners, to [unseal]
Their grand commission; where I found, Horatio—
Ah, royal knavery!—an exact command,
Larded° with many several sorts of reasons, 20
Importing° Denmark's health and England's too,
With, ho, such bugs and goblins in my life,°
That, on the supervise,° no leisure bated,°
No, not to stay° the grinding of the axe,
My head should be strook off. 25

Horatio: Is't possible?

Hamlet: Here's the commission, read it at more leisure.
But wilt thou hear me how I did proceed?

Horatio: I beseech you.

Hamlet: Being thus benetted round with [villainies],
Or° I could make a prologue to my brains, 30
They had begun the play. I sat me down,
Devis'd a new commission, wrote it fair.°
I once did hold it, as our statists° do,
A baseness° to write fair, and labor'd much
How to forget that learning, but, sir, now 35
I did me yeman's° service. Wilt thou know
Th' effect° of what I wrote?

Horatio: Ay, good my lord.

Hamlet: An earnest conjuration from the King,
As England was his faithful tributary,
As love between them like the palm might flourish, 40
As peace should still her wheaten garland wear
And stand a comma° 'tween their amities,
And many such-like [as's] of great charge,°
That on the view and knowing of these contents,
Without debatement further, more or less, 45
He should those bearers put to sudden death,
Not shriving time° allow'd.

Horatio: How was this seal'd?

Hamlet: Why, even in that was heaven ordinant.°
I had my father's signet in my purse,
Which was the model° of that Danish seal; 50
Folded the writ up in the form of th' other;
[Subscrib'd°] it, gave't th' impression, plac'd it safely,
The changeling° never known.° Now the next day

Was our sea-fight, and what to this was sequent
Thou knowest already. 55

Horatio: So Guildenstern and Rosencrantz go to't.°

Hamlet: [Why, man, they did make love to this employment,]
They are not near my conscience. Their defeat°
Does by their own insinuation° grow.
'Tis dangerous when the baser° nature comes 60
Between the pass° and fell° incensed points
Of mighty opposites.

Horatio: Why, what a king is this!

Hamlet: Does it not, think thee, stand me now upon°—
He that hath kill'd my king and whor'd my mother,
Popp'd in between th' election° and my hopes, 65
Thrown out his angle° for my proper° life,
And with such coz'nage°—is't not perfect conscience
[To quit him° with this arm? And is't not to be damn'd,
To let this canker° of our nature come
In° further evil? 70

Horatio: It must be shortly known to him from England
What is the issue of the business there.

Hamlet: It will be short; the interim's mine,
And a man's life's no more° than to say "one."°
But I am very sorry, good Horatio, 75
That to Laertes I forgot myself,
For by the image° of my cause I see
The portraiture of his. I'll [court] his favors.
But sure the bravery° of his grief did put me
Into a tow'ring passion. 80

Horatio: Peace, who comes here?]

Enter [young Osric,] a courtier.

Osric: Your lordship is right welcome back to Denmark.

Hamlet: I [humbly] thank you, sir.—Dost know this water-fly?°

Horatio: No, my good lord.

Hamlet: Thy state is the more gracious,° for 'tis a vice to know
him. He hath much land, and fertile; let a beast be lord of 85
beasts, and his crib shall stand at the king's mess.° Tis a
chough,° but, as I say, spacious in the possession of dirt.

Osric: Sweet lord, if your lordship were at leisure, I should
impart a thing to you from his Majesty.

Hamlet: I will receive it, Sir, with all diligence of spirit. [Put 90
your bonnet° to his right use, 'tis for the head.

°**Finger'd** Filched, "pinched." °**Larded** Garnished. °**Importing** Relating to. °**bugs . . . life** Terrifying things in prospect if I were permitted to remain alive; *bugs* = bugaboos. °**supervise** Perusal. °**bated** Deducted (from the stipulated speediness). °**stay** Wait for. °**Or** Before. °**fair** In a beautiful hand (such as a professional scribe would use). °**statists** Statesmen, public officials. °**A baseness** A skill befitting of men of low rank. °**yeman's** Yeoman's; solid, substantial. °**effect** Purport, gist. °**comma** Connective, link. °**as's . . . charge** (1) Weighty clauses beginning with *as*; (2) asses with heavy loads. °**shriving time** Time for confession and absolution. °**ordinant** In charge, guiding. °**model** Small copy. °**Subscrib'd** Signed. °**changeling** Hamlet's letter, substituted secretly for the genuine letter, as fairies substituted their children for human children. °**never known** Never recognized as a substitution

(unlike the fairies' changelings). °**go to't** Are going to their death. °**defeat** Ruin, overthrow. °**insinuation** Winding their way into the affair. °**baser** Inferior. °**pass** Thrust. °**fell** Fierce. °**stand . . . upon** Rest upon me as a duty. °**election** As king of Denmark. °**angle** Hook and line. °**proper** Very. °**coz'nage** Trickery. °**quit him** Pay him back. °**canker** Cancerous sore. °**come In** Grow into. °**a man's . . . more** To kill a man takes no more time. °**say "one."** Perhaps this is equivalent to "deliver one sword thrust"; see line 246 below, where Hamlet says. "One" as he makes the first hit. °**image** Likeness. °**bravery** Ostentatious expression. °**water-fly** Tiny, vainly agitated creature. °**gracious** Virtuous. °**let . . . mess** If a beast owned as many cattle as Osric, he could feast with the King. °**chough** Jackdaw, a bird that could be taught to speak. °**bonnet** Hat.

Osric: I thank your lordship, it is very hot.

Hamlet: No, believe me, 'tis very cold, the wind is northerly.

Osric: It is indifferent° cold, my lord, indeed.

Hamlet: But yet methinks it is very [sultry] and hot [for] my 95
complexion.°

Osric: Exceedingly, my lord, it is very sultry,—as 'twere—I
cannot tell how. My lord, his Majesty bade me signify to
you that 'a has laid a great wager on your head. Sir, this is
the matter—

Hamlet: I beseech you remember.

[Hamlet moves him to put on his hat.]

Osric: Nay, good my lord, for my ease,° in good faith. Sir, here is 100
newly come to court Laertes, believe me, an absolute° [gen-
tleman], full of most excellent differences,° of very soft° society, and great showing;° indeed, to speak sellingly° of him,
he is the card or calendar° of gentry;° for you shall find in
him the continent of what part° a gentleman would see.

Hamlet: Sir, his definement suffers no perdition° in you, though I 105
know to divide him inventorially would dozy° th' arith-
metic of memory, and yet but yaw° neither° in respect of° his
quick sail; but in the verity of extolment,° I take him to be a
soul of great article,° and his infusion° of such dearth° and
rareness as, to make true diction° of him, his semblable° is
his mirror, and who else would trace him,° his umbrage,° 110
nothing more.

Osric: Your lordship speaks most infallibly of him.

Hamlet: The concernancy,° sir? Why do we wrap the gentleman
in our more rawer breath?°

Osric: Sir?

Horatio: Is't not possible to understand in another tongue?° You 115
will to't, sir, really.°

Hamlet: What imports the nomination° of this gentleman?

Osric: Of Laertes?

Horatio: His purse is empty already: all 's golden words are
spent.

Hamlet: Of him, sir. 120

Osric: I know you are not ignorant—

Hamlet: I would you did, sir, yet, in faith, if you did, it would not
much approve° me. Well, sir?

Osric: You are not ignorant of what excellence Laertes is—

Hamlet: I dare not confess that, lest I should compare with him in 125
excellence,° but° to know a man well were to know himself.°

Osric: I mean, sir, for [his] weapon, but in the imputation laid
on him by them,° in his meed° he's unfellow'd.

Hamlet: What's his weapon?

Osric: Rapier and dagger. 130

Hamlet: That's two of his weapons—but well.

Osric: The King, sir, hath wager'd with him six Barbary horses,
against the which he has impawn'd,° as I take it, six French
rapiers and poniards, with their assigns,° as girdle, [hang-
ers°], and so. Three of the carriages,° in faith, are very dear 135
to fancy,° very responsive to° the hilts, most delicate carriages, and of very liberal conceit.°

Hamlet: What call you the carriages?

Horatio: I knew you must be edified by the margent° ere you
had done.

Osric: The [carriages], sir, are the hangers.

Hamlet: The phrase would be more germane to the matter if we 140
could carry a cannon by our sides; I would it [might be]
hangers till then. But on: six Barb'ry horses against six
French swords, their assigns, and three liberal-conceited
carriages; that's the French bet against the Danish. Why is
this all [impawn'd, as] you call it?

Osric: The King, sir, hath laid,° sir, that in a dozen passes between 145
yourself and him, he shall not exceed you three hits;° he hath
laid on twelve for nine;° and it would come to immediate
trial, if your lordship would vouchsafe the answer.°

Hamlet: How if I answer no?

Osric: I mean, my lord, the opposition of your person in trial. 150

Hamlet: Sir, I will walk here in the hall. If it please his Majesty, it
is the breathing time of day with me.° Let the foils be
brought, the gentleman willing, and the King hold his purpose, I will win for him and I can; if not, I will gain nothing
but my shame and the odd hits.

Osric: Shall I deliver you so? 155

°**indifferent** Somewhat °**complexion** Temperament. °**for my
ease** I am really more comfortable with my hat off (a polite insistence
on maintaining ceremony). °**absolute** Complete, possessing every
quality a gentleman should have. °**differences** Distinguishing
characteristics, personal qualities. °**soft** Agreeable. °**great showing**
Splendid appearance. °**sellingly** Like a seller to a prospective
buyer; in a fashion to do full justice. Most editors follow Q3 in reading
feelingly = with exactitude, as he deserves. °**card or calendar** Chart
or register, compendious guide. °**gentry** Gentlemanly behavior. °**the
continent . . . part** One who contains every quality. °**perdition** Loss.
°**dozy** Make dizzy. °**yaw** Keep deviating erratically from its course
(said of a ship). °**neither** For all that. °**in respect of** Compared
with. °**in . . . extolment** To praise him truly. °**article** Scope (?) or
importance (?). °**infusion** Essence, quality. °**dearth** Scarceness.
°**make true diction** Speak truly. °**his semblable** His only likeness or
equal. °**who . . . him** Anyone else who tries to follow him. °**umbrage**
Shadow. °**concernancy** Relevance. °**more rawer breath** Words too
crude to describe him properly. °**in another tongue** When someone

else is the speaker. °**You . . . really** You can do it if you try. °**nomination**
Naming, mention. °**approve** Commend. °**compare . . . excellence**
Seem to claim the same degree of excellence for myself. °**but** The
sense seems to require *for*. °**himself** Onself. °**in . . . them** In
popular estimation. °**meed** Merit. °**impawn'd** Staked. °**assigns**
Appurtenances. °**hangers** Straps on which the swords hang from the
girdle. °**carriages** Properly, gun-carriages; here used affectedly in place
of *hangers*. °**fancy** Taste. °**very responsive to** Matching well.
°**liberal conceit** Elegant design. °**must . . . margent** Would require
enlightenment from a marginal note. °**laid** Wagered. °**he . . . hits**
Laertes must win by at least eight to four (if none of the "passes" or
bouts are draws), since at seven to five he would be only two up.
°**he . . . nine** Not satisfactorily explained despite much discussion.
One suggestion is that Laertes has raised the odds against himself by
wagering that out of twelve bouts he will win nine. °**answer**
Encounter (as Hamlet's following quibble forces Osric to explain in
his next speech). °**breathing . . . me** My usual hour for exercise.

Hamlet: To this effect, sir—after what flourish° your nature will.

Osric: I commend my duty° to your lordship.

Hamlet: Yours. [*Exit Osric.*]. ['A] does well to commend it himself, there are no tongues else for 's turn.

Horatio: This lapwing° runs away with the shell on his head. 160

Hamlet: 'A did [comply], sir, with his dug° before 'a suck'd it. Thus has he, and many more of the same breed that I know the drossy° age dotes on, only got the tune of the time,° and out of an habit of encounter,° a kind of [yesty°] collection,° which carries them through and through the most [profound] and [winnow'd°] opinions,° and do but blow them to their trial,° the bubbles are out.° 165

Enter a Lord.

Lord: My lord, his Majesty commended him to you by young Osric, who brings back to him that you attend him in the hall. He sends to know if your pleasure hold to play with Laertes, or that you will take longer time.

Hamlet: I am constant to my purposes, they follow the King's 170 pleasure. If his fitness speaks, mine is ready;° now or whensoever, provided I be so able as now.

Lord: The King and Queen and all are coming down.

Hamlet: In happy time.

Lord: The Queen desires you to use some gentle entertainment° 175 to Laertes before you fall to play.

Hamlet: She well instructs me. [*Exit Lord.*]

Horatio: You will lose, my lord.

Hamlet: I do not think so; since he went into France I have been in continual practice. I shall win at the odds. Thou wouldst not think how ill all's here about my heart—but it is no matter. 180

Horatio: Nay, good my lord—

Hamlet: It is but foolery, but it is such a kind of [gain-]giving,° as would perhaps trouble a woman.

Horatio: If your mind dislike any thing, obey it. I will forestall their repair hither, and say you are not fit. 185

Hamlet: Not a whit, we defy augury. There's a special providence in the fall of a sparrow.° If it be [now], 'tis not to come; if it be not to come, it will be now; if it be not now, yet it [will] come—the readiness is all. Since no man, of aught° he leaves, knows what is't to leave betimes,° let be.

A table prepar'd, [and flangons of wine on it. Enter] Trumpets, Drums, and Officers with cushions, foils, daggers; King, Queen, Laertes, [Osric,] and all the State°

King: Come, Hamlet, come, and take this hand from me. 190

[*The King puts Laertes' hand into Hamlet's.*]

Hamlet: Give me your pardon, sir. I have done you wrong,
But pardon't as you are a gentleman.
This presence° knows,
And you must needs have heard, how I am punish'd°
With sore distraction. What I have done 195
That might your nature, honor, and exception°
Roughly awake, I here proclaim was madness.
Was't Hamlet wrong'd Laertes? Never Hamlet!
If Hamlet from himself be ta'en away,
And when he's not himself does wrong Laertes, 200
Then Hamlet does it not, Hamlet denies it.
Who does it then? His madness. If't be so,
Hamlet is of the faction that is wronged,
His madness is poor Hamlet's enemy.
[Sir, in this audience,] 205
Let my disclaiming from a purpos'd evil°
Free° me so far in your most generous thoughts,
That I have shot my arrow o'er the house
And hurt my brother.

Laertes: I am satisfied in nature,° 210
Whose motive in this case should stir me most
To my revenge, but in my terms of honor°
I stand aloof, and will no reconcilement
Till by some elder masters of known honor
I have a voice and precedent of peace 215
To [keep] my name ungor'd.° But [till] that time
I do receive your offer'd love like love,
And will not wrong it.

Hamlet: I embrace it freely,
And will this brothers'° wager frankly° play.
Give us the foils. [Come on.]

Laertes: Come, one for me. 220

Hamlet: I'll be your foil,° Laertes; in mine ignorance
Your skill shall like a star i' th' darkest night
Stick fiery off° indeed.

Laertes: You mock me, sir.

Hamlet: No, by this hand.

King: Give them the foils, young Osric. Cousin Hamlet, 225
You know the wager?

Hamlet: Very well, my lord.
Your Grace hath laid the odds° a' th' weaker side.

°**after what flourish** With whatever embellishment of language.
°**commend my duty** Offer my dutiful respects (but Hamlet picks up the phrase in the sense "praise my manner of bowing"). °**lapwing** A foolish bird which upon hatching was supposed to run with part of the eggshell still over its head. (Osric has put his hat on at last.)
°**comply . . . dug** Bow politely to his mother's nipple. °**drossy** Worthless. °**tune . . . time** Fashionable ways of talk. °**habit of encounter** Mode of social intercourse. °**yesty** Yeasty, frothy.
°**collection** Anthology of fine phrases. °**winnow'd** Sifted choice.
°**opinions** Judgments. °**blow . . . trial** Test them by blowing on them; make even the least demanding trial of them. °**out** Blown away (?) or at an end, done for (?) °**If . . . ready** If this is a good moment for him, it is for me also. °**gentle entertainment** Courteous greeting. °**gain-giving** Misgiving.

°**special . . . sparrow** See Matthew 10:29. °**of aught** Whatever.
°**knows . . . betimes** Knows what is the best time to leave it.
°**State** Nobles. °**presence** Assembled court. °**punish'd** Afflicted.
°**exception** Objection. °**my . . . evil** My declaration that I intended no harm. °**Free** Absolve. °**in nature** So far as my personal feelings are concerned. °**in . . . honor** As a man governed by an established code of honor. °**have . . . ungor'd** Can secure an opinion backed by precedent that I can make peace with you without injury to my reputation. °**brothers'** Amicable, as if between brothers.
°**frankly** Freely, without constraint. °**foil** Thin sheet of metal placed behind a jewel to set it off. °**Stick: . . . off** Blaze out in contrast. °**laid the odds** Wagered a higher stake (horses to rapiers).

King: I do not fear it, I have seen you both;
But since he is [better'd],° we have therefore odds.°

Laertes: This is too heavy; let me see another. 230

Hamlet: This likes° me well. These foils have all a length?
[*Prepare to play.*]

Osric: Ay, my good lord.

King: Set me the stoups° of wine upon that table.
If Hamlet give the first or second hit,
Or quit in answer of the third exchange,° 235
Let all the battlements their ord'nance fire.
The King shall drink to Hamlet's better breath,
And in the cup an [union°] shall he throw,
Richer than that which four successive kings
In Denmark's crown have worn. Give me the cups, 240
And let the kettle° to the trumpet speak,
The trumpet to the cannoneer without,
The cannons to the heavens, the heaven to earth,
"Now the King drinks to Hamlet." Come begin;

(*trumpets the while*)

And you, the judges, bear a wary eye. 245

Hamlet: Come on, sir.

Laertes: Come, my lord.

[*They play and Hamlet scores a bit.*]

Hamlet: One.

Laertes: No.

Hamlet: Judgment.

Osric: A hit, a very palpable hit.

Laertes: Well—again.

King: Stay, give me a drink. Hamlet, this pearl is thine,
Here's to thy health. Give him the cup.

(*Drum, trumpets [sound] flourish. A piece goes off [within].*)

Hamlet: I'll play this bout first, set it by a while. 250
Come. [*They play again.*] Another hit; what say you?

Laertes: [A touch, a touch,] I do confess 't.

King: Our son shall win.

Queen: He's fat,° and scant of breath.—
Here, Hamlet, take my napkin, rub thy brows.
The Queen carouses° to thy fortune, Hamlet. 255

Hamlet: Good madam!

King: Gertrude, do not drink.

Queen: I will, my lord, I pray you pardon me.

King [*aside*]: It is the pois'ned cup, it is too late.

Hamlet: I dare not drink yet, madam; by and by.

Queen: Come, let me wipe thy face. 260

Laertes: My lord, I'll hit him now.

King: I do not think't.

Laertes [*aside*]: And yet it is almost against my conscience.

Hamlet: Come, for the third, Laertes, you do but dally.
I pray you pass with your best violence;
I am sure you make a wanton of me.° 265

Laertes: Say you so? Come on.   [*They play.*]

Osric: Nothing, neither way.

Laertes: Have at you now!

[*Laertes wounds Hamlet; then, in scuffling, they change rapiers.*]

King: Part them, they are incens'd.

Hamlet: Nay, come again.

[*Hamlet wounds Laertes. The Queen falls.*]

Osric: Look to the Queen there ho!

Horatio: They bleed on both sides. How is it, my lord? 270

Osric: How is't, Laertes?

Laertes: Why, as a woodcock to mine own springe,° Osric:
I am justly kill'd with mine own treachery.

Hamlet: How does the Queen?

King: She sounds° to see them bleed.

Queen: No, no, the drink, the drink—O my dear Hamlet— 275
The drink, the drink! I am pois'ned.   [*Dies.*]

Hamlet: O villainy! Ho, let the door be lock'd!
Treachery! Seek it out.

Laertes: It is here, Hamlet. [Hamlet,] thou art slain.
No med'cine in the world can do thee good; 280
In thee there is not half an hour of life.
The treacherous instrument is in [thy] hand,
Unbated° and envenom'd. The foul practice°
Hath turn'd itself on me. Lo here I lie,
Never to rise again. Thy mother's pois'ned. 285
I can no more—the King, the King's to blame.

Hamlet: The point envenom'd too!
Then, venom, to thy work.   [*hurts° the King*]

All: Treason! treason!

King: O, yet defend me, friends, I am but hurt. 290

Hamlet: Here, thou incestuous, [murd'rous], damned Dane,
Drink [off] this potion! Is [thy union] here?
Follow my mother!   [*King dies.*]

Laertes: He is justly served,
It is a poison temper'd° by himself.
Exchange forgiveness with me, noble Hamlet. 295
Mine and my father's death come not upon thee,
Nor thine on me!   [*dies*]

Hamlet: Heaven make thee free° of it! I follow thee.
I am dead, Horatio. Wretched queen, adieu!
You that look pale, and tremble at this chance,
That are but mutes or audience° to this act, 300
Had I but time—as this fell° sergeant,° Death,
Is strict in his arrest—O, I could tell you—
But let it be. Horatio, I am dead,

°**is better'd** Has perfected his skill. °**odds** The arrangement that Laertes must take more bouts than Hamlet to win. °**likes** Pleases. °**a length** The same length. °**stoups** Tankards. °**quit . . . exchange** Pays back wins by Laertes in the first and second bouts by taking the third. °**union** An especially fine pearl. °**kettle** Kettle-drum. °**fat** Sweaty. °**carouses** Drinks a toast.

°**make . . . me** Are holding back in order to let me win, as one does with a spoiled child (*wanton*). °**springe** Snare. °**sounds** Swoons. °**Unbated** Not blunted. °**foul practice** Vile plot. °**hurts** Wounds. °**temper'd** Mixed. °**make thee free** Absolve you. °**mutes or audience** Silent spectators. °**fell** Cruel. °**sergeant** Sheriff's officer.

Thou livest. Report me and my cause aright   305
  To the unsatisfied.
Horatio: Never believe it;
  I am more an antique Roman° than a Dane.
  Here's yet some liquor left.
Hamlet: As th' art a man,
  Give me the cup. Let go! By heaven, I'll ha 't!
  O God, Horatio, what a wounded name,   310
  Things standing thus unknown, shall I leave behind me!
  If thou didst ever hold me in thy heart,
  Absent thee from felicity a while,
  And in this harsh world draw thy breath in pain
  To tell my story. *(a march afar off, [and shot within.]*
                    What warlike noise is this?   315

[Osric goes to the door and returns.]

Osric: Young Fortinbras, with conquest come from Poland,
  To th' ambassadors of England gives
  This warlike volley.
Hamlet: O, I die, Horatio,
  The potent poison quite o'er-crows° my spirit.°
  I cannot live to hear the news from England,   320
  But I do prophesy th' election lights
  On Fortinbras, he has my dying voice.°
  So tell him, with th' occurrents° more and less
  Which have solicited°—the rest is silence.   *[dies]*
Horatio: Now cracks a noble heart. Good night, sweet prince,
  And flights of angels sing thee to thy rest!   325

[march within.]

Why does the drum come hither?

[Enter Fortinbras with the [English] Embassadors, [with Drum,
  Colors, and Attendants.]

Fortinbras: Where is this sight?
Horatio: What is it you would see?
  If aught of woe or wonder, cease your search.
Fortinbras: This quarry cries on havoc.° O proud death,   330
  What feast is toward° in thine eternal cell,
  That thou so many princes at a shot
  So bloodily hast strook?
[1.] Ambassador: The sight is dismal,
  And our affairs from England come too late.
  The ears are senseless that should give us hearing,   335
  To tell him his° commandment is fulfill'd,
  That Rosencrantz and Guildenstern are dead.
  Where should we have our thanks?

Horatio: Not from his mouth,
  Had it th' ability of life to thank you.
  He never gave commandment for their death.   340
  But since so jump° upon this bloody question,°
  You from the Polack wars, and you from England,
  Are here arrived, give order that these bodies
  High on a stage° be placed to the view,
  And let me speak to [th'] yet unknowing world   345
  How these things came about. So shall you hear
  Of carnal, bloody, and unnatural acts,
  Of accidental judgments,° casual° slaughters,
  Of deaths put on° by cunning and [forc'd] cause,
  And in this upshot, purposes mistook   350
  Fall'n on the inventors' heads: all this can I
  Truly deliver.
Fortinbras: Let us haste to hear it,
  And call the noblest to the audience.
  For me, with sorrow I embrace my fortune.
  I have some rights of memory° in this kingdom,   355
  Which now to claim my vantage° doth invite me.
Horatio: Of that I shall have also cause to speak,
  And from his mouth whose voice will draw [on] more.°
  But let this same be presently° perform'd
  Even while men's minds are wild,° lest more mischance   360
  On plots and errors happen.
Fortinbras: Let four captains
  Bear Hamlet like a soldier to the stage,
  For he was likely, had he been put on,°
  To have prov'd most royal; and for his passage,°
  The soldiers' music and the rite of war   365
  Speak loudly for him.
  Take up the bodies. Such a sight as this
  Becomes the field, but here shows much amiss.°
  Go bid the soldiers shoot.

Exeunt [marching; after the which a peal of ordnance are
  shot off].

Related Works

"The Cask of Amontillado" (p. 190), "Young Goodman
Brown" (p. 320), *Words, Words, Words* (p. 697),
Oedipus the King (p. 701)

See Chapter 33 Review Card for Reading and Reacting questions
about William Shakespeare, *Hamlet*.

°**antique Roman** One who will commit suicide on such an occasion.
°**o'er-crows** Triumphs over (a term derived from cockfighting).
°**spirit** Vital energy. °**voice** Vote. °**occurrents** Occurrences.
°**solicited** Instigated. °**This . . . havoc** This heap of corpses
proclaims a massacre. °**toward** In preparation. °**his** The king's.
°**jump** Precisely, pat. °**question** Matter. °**stage** Platform.
°**judgments** Retributions. °**causal** Happening by chance.

°**put on** Instigated. °**of memory** Unforgotten. °**my vantage**
My opportune presence at a moment when the throne is empty.
°**his . . . more** The mouth of one (Hamlet) whose vote will induce
others to support your claim. °**presently** At once. °**wild**
Distraught. °**put on** Put to the test (by becoming king).
passage Death. °**Becomes . . . amiss** Befits the battlefield,
but appears very much out of place here.

Writing Suggestions: Character

1. In *Death of a Salesman*, each character pursues his or her version of the American Dream. Choose two characters, define their concept of the American Dream, and explain how each tries to make the dream a reality. In each case, consider the obstacles the character encounters, and try to account for the character's success or lack of success. If you like, you may also consider other works in which the American Dream is central—for example, "Two Kinds" (p. 336) or *Fences* (p. 724).

2. Many of the female characters in this chapter's plays—for example, Mrs. X (*The Stronger*), Linda (*Death of a Salesman*), and Ophelia (*Hamlet*)—are, in one way or another, in conflict with men. Focusing on female characters in two different plays, define each conflict, and consider whether it is resolved in the play. (If you like, you may also discuss a female character who appears in a play in another chapter.)

3. Minor characters are often flat characters; in many cases, their sole function is to advance the plot or to highlight a particular trait in a major character. Sometimes, however, minor characters may be of more than minor importance. Choose one minor character from *Death of a Salesman* or *Hamlet* (or from a play in another chapter), and write an essay in which you discuss what this character contributes and how the play would be different without him or her.

✔ CHECKLIST

WRITING ABOUT CHARACTER

- [ ] Does any character serve as a narrator? If so, what information does this narrator supply about the other characters? How reliable is the narrator?
- [ ] Who are the major characters? Do they change and grow during the course of the play, or do they remain essentially unchanged?
- [ ] What do the minor characters contribute to the play?
- [ ] Does the play include monologue or soliloquies? What do these extended speeches reveal about the characters?
- [ ] What is revealed about the characters through dialogue?
- [ ] Do characters use foreign words, regionalisms, slang, jargon, clichés, or profanity? What does such use of language reveal about the characters? About the play's theme?
- [ ] Is the characters' language formal or informal? Is the characters' language plain or elaborate?
- [ ] Do different characters have different styles or levels of language? What is the significance of these differences?
- [ ] How does language reveal characters' emotional states?
- [ ] Does the tone of any character's language change significantly as the play progresses? What does this change reveal?
- [ ] Does the play include verbal irony? Dramatic irony? How is irony conveyed? What purpose does irony achieve?
- [ ] What is revealed about characters through their actions?
- [ ] What is revealed about characters through the play's stage directions?
- [ ] How might different actors' interpretations change an audience's understanding of the characters?

Glossary Terms

aside Brief comment spoken by an actor to the audience (such as, "Here she comes. I'll play a fine trick on her now!") and assumed not to be heard by the other characters.

dialogue Conversation between two or more characters.

figures of speech Expressions that use words to achieve effects beyond ordinary language.

irony Literary device or situation that depends on the existence of at least two separate and contrasting levels of meaning or experience. **Dramatic** or **tragic irony** depends on the audience's knowing something the protagonist has not yet realized. **Situational irony** exists when what happens is at odds with what the story's situation leads readers to expect will happen. **Cosmic irony** (or irony of fate) exists when fate frustrates any effort a character might make to control or reverse his or her destiny. **Verbal irony** occurs when what is said is in contrast with what is meant.

monologue Extended speech by one character.

soliloquy Convention of drama in which a character speaks directly to the audience, revealing thoughts and feelings that other characters present on stage are assumed not to hear.

stage directions Words in a play that describe an actor's role apart from the dialogue, dealing with movements, attitudes, and so on.

staging Overall production of a play in performance: the sets, costumes, lighting, sound, music, and so on.

tone Attitude of the speaker or author toward a work's subject or audience, as determined by the word choice and arrangement of ideas.

34
Staging

Learning Outcomes
After reading this chapter, you should be able to do the following:

LO1   Identify stage directions

LO2   Understand the uses of staging

Timeline

c. 430 Sophocles, *Oedipus the King*

David Ives, *Words, Words, Words* **1994**

440 BC   **330 AD**   **1800 AD**   **1900 AD**   **2000 AD**

330 Construction is completed on Constantinople, the capital of the Byzantine Empire.

1830 Greece gains its independence from the Ottoman Empire.

The chimpanzee Ham completes a spaceflight after succesfuly carrying out assigned tasks. **1961**

404 The Second Peloponnesian War ends.

Freddie Mercury, lead singer of the band Queen, dies of AIDS. **1991**

The World Trade Organization is established. **1995**

eBAY is founded. **1995**

429 The Greek statesman Pericles is killed in the plague in Athens.

429 A major plague strikes Athens.

The computer Deep Blue defeats world chess champion Gary Kasparov. **1997**

1453 Constantinople, the capital of the Byzantine Empire, falls to the Ottomans.

431 The Second Peloponnesian War begins.

Staging refers to the physical elements of a play's production that determine how the play looks and sounds to an audience. It encompasses the **stage settings**, or sets—furnishings, scenery, props, and lighting—as well as the costumes, sound effects, and music that bring the play to life on the stage. In short, staging is everything that goes into making a written script a play.

Contemporary staging in the West has traditionally concentrated on re-creating the outside world. This concept of staging, which has dominated Western theatrical productions for centuries, would seem alien in many non-Western theaters. Japanese **Kabuki dramas** and **No plays**, for example, depend on staging conventions that make no attempt to mirror reality. Scenery and costumes are largely symbolic, and often actors wear highly stylized makeup or masks. Although some European and American playwrights have been strongly influenced by non-Western staging, the majority of plays being produced in the West still try to create the illusion of reality.

LO1 Identify Stage Directions

Usually a playwright presents instructions for the staging of a play in **stage directions**—notes that comment on the scenery, the movements of the performers, the lighting, and the placement of props. (In the absence of detailed stage directions, dialogue can provide information about staging.) Sometimes these stage directions are quite simple, leaving much to the imagination of the director. Consider how little specific information about the setting of the play is provided in these stage directions from act 1 of Samuel Beckett's 1952 absurdist play *Waiting for Godot*:

A country road. A tree. Evening.

Often, however, playwrights furnish more detailed information about staging. Consider these stage directions from act 1 of Anton Chekhov's *The Cherry Orchard*:

A room, which has always been called the nursery. One of the doors leads into Anya's room. Dawn, sun rises during the scene. May, the cherry trees in flower, but it is cold in the garden with the frost of the early morning. Windows closed.

Enter Dunyasha with a candle and Lopahin with a book in his hand.

These comments indicate that the first act takes place in a room with more than one door and that several windows reveal cherry trees in bloom. They also specify that the lighting should simulate the sun rising at dawn and that certain characters should enter carrying particular props. Still, Chekhov leaves it up to those staging the play to decide on the costumes for the characters and on the furniture to be placed around the room.

> **staging** Overall production of a play in performance: the sets, costumes, lighting, sound, music, and so on.
>
> **stage directions** Words in a play that describe an actor's role apart from the dialogue, dealing with movements, attitudes, and so on.

Some stage directions are even more specific. Irish playwright George Bernard Shaw's long, complex stage directions are legendary in the theater. Note the degree of detail he provides in these stage directions from his 1906 comedy *The Doctor's Dilemma*:

The consulting-room has two windows looking on Queen Anne Street. Between the two is a marble-topped console, with haunched gilt legs ending in sphinx claws. The huge pier-glass [a long narrow mirror that fits between two windows] which surmounts it is mostly disabled from reflection by elaborate painting on its surface of palms, ferns, lilies, tulips, and sunflowers. The adjoining wall contains the fireplace, with two arm-chairs before it. As we happen to face the corner we see nothing of the other two walls. On the right of the fireplace, or rather on the right of any person facing the fireplace, is the door. On the left is the writing-table at which Redpenny [a medical student] sits. It is an untidy table with a microscope, several test tubes, and a spirit lamp [an alcohol burner] standing up through its litter of papers. There is a couch in the middle of the room, at right angles to the console, and parallel to the fireplace. A chair stands between the couch and the window. Another in the corner. Another at the other end of the windowed wall. . . . The wallpaper and carpets are mostly green. . . . The house, in fact, was so well furnished in the middle of the XIXth century that it stands unaltered to this day and is still quite presentable.

Not only does Shaw indicate exactly what furniture is to be placed on stage, but he also includes a good deal of physical description—specifying, for example, "gilt legs ending in sphinx claws" and "test tubes and a spirit lamp" that clutter the writing table. In addition, he defines furniture placement and specifies color.

Regardless of how detailed the stage directions are, they do not eliminate the need for creative interpretations on the part of the producer, director, set designers, and actors (see "Actors' Interpretations," p. 600). Many directors see stage directions as suggestions, not requirements, and some consider them more confusing than helpful. Therefore, some directors may choose to interpret a play's stage directions quite loosely—or even to ignore them entirely. For example, in 2007, the Classical Theater of

props (short for properties) Pictures, furnishings, and so on that decorate the stage for a play.

 EXPLORE ONLINE >

To complete a tutorial of "Staging," visit your Literature CourseMate, accessed through www.cengagebrain.com.

Harlem staged Samuel Beckett's 1952 existentialist drama *Waiting for Godot* in New Orleans. The performances were held outdoors in areas of the city that had been seriously damaged by Hurricane Katrina, and the still-devastated setting gave new power to Beckett's drama of characters' search for meaning against a backdrop of emptiness and despair.

LO2 Understand the Uses of Staging

Various elements of staging provide important information about characters and their motivations as well as about the play's theme.

COSTUMES

Costumes establish the historical period in which a play is set and provide insight into the characters who wear them. For example, when Hamlet first appears on stage, he is profoundly disillusioned and quite melancholy. This fact was immediately apparent to Shakespeare's audience because Hamlet is dressed in sable, which to the Elizabethans signified a melancholy nature. In Tennessee Williams's classic play *The Glass Menagerie,* Laura's dress of soft violet material and her hair ribbon reflect her delicate, childlike innocence. In contrast, her mother's *"imitation velvety-looking cloth [coat] with imitation fur collar"* and her *"enormous black patent-leather pocketbook"* reveal her somewhat pathetic attempt to achieve respectability. Later in the play, awaiting the "gentleman caller," Laura's mother wears a dress that is both outdated and inappropriately youthful, suggesting both her need to relive her own past and her increasingly desperate desire to marry off her daughter.

PROPS AND FURNISHINGS

Props (short for *properties*) can also help audiences interpret a play's characters and themes. For example, the handkerchief in Shakespeare's *Othello* gains significance as the play progresses: it begins as an innocent object and ends as the piece of evidence that convinces Othello his wife is committing adultery. Sometimes props can have symbolic significance. During the Renaissance, for example, flowers had symbolic meaning. In act 4 of *Hamlet,* Ophelia, who is mad, gives flowers to various characters. In a note to the play, the critic Thomas Parrott points out the symbolic significance of her gifts: to Claudius, the murderer of Hamlet's father, she gives fennel and columbines, which signify flattery and ingratitude; to the Queen, she gives rue and daisies, which symbolize sadness and unfaithfulness. Although modern audiences would not understand the significance of these flowers, many people in Shakespeare's Elizabethan audience were aware of their meaning.

The **furnishings** in a room can also reveal a lot about a play's characters and themes. Willy Loman's house in Arthur Miller's *Death of a Salesman* (p. 605) is sparsely furnished, revealing the declining financial status of the family. The kitchen contains a table and three chairs and the bedroom only a brass bed and a straight chair. Over the bed on a shelf is Biff's silver athletic trophy, a constant reminder of his loss of status. Like Willy Loman's house, the Wingfield apartment in *The Glass Menagerie* reflects its inhabitants' modest economic circumstances. For example, the living room, which contains a sofa that opens into a bed, also serves as a bedroom for Laura. In addition, one piece of furniture highlights a central theme of the play: an old-fashioned cabinet in the living room displays a collection of transparent glass animals that, like Laura, are too fragile to be removed from their surroundings.

SCENERY AND LIGHTING

Playwrights often use **scenery** and **lighting** to create imaginative stage settings. In *Death of a Salesman,* the house is surrounded by *"towering angular shapes"* of apartment houses that emphasize the *"small, fragile-seeming home."* Arthur Miller calls for a set that is *"wholly, or in some places, transparent."* Whenever the action is in the present, the actors observe the imaginary boundaries that separate rooms or mark the exterior walls of the house. When the characters reenact past events, however, they walk over the boundaries and come to the front of the stage. By lighting up and darkening different parts of the stage, Miller shifts from the present to the past and back again.

The set of *The Glass Menagerie* is also innovative, combining imaginative backdrops with subtle lighting. As the curtain rises, the audience sees the dark rear wall of the Wingfield tenement, which is flanked on both sides by alleys lined with clotheslines, garbage cans, and fire escapes. After Tom delivers his opening narrative, the rear wall becomes transparent, revealing the interior of the Wingfield apartment. To create this effect, Williams used a **scrim,** a curtain that when illuminated from the front appears solid but when illuminated from the back becomes transparent. For Williams, such "atmospheric touches" represented a new direction in theater that contrasted with the theater of "realistic conventions."

Contemporary playwrights often use sets that combine realistic and nonrealistic elements. In his Tony

Award-winning play *M. Butterfly,* for example, David Henry Hwang employs not only scrims but also a large red lacquered ramp that runs from the bottom to the top of the stage. The action takes place beneath, on, and above the ramp, creating an effect not unlike that created by Shakespeare's multiple stages. At several points in the play, a character who acts as the narrator sits beneath the ramp, addressing the audience, while at the same time a character on top of the ramp acts out the narrator's words.

MUSIC AND SOUND EFFECTS

Staging involves more than visual elements such as costumes and scenery; it also involves **music** and **sound effects.** The stage directions for *Death of a Salesman,* for example, begin, *"A melody is heard, played upon a flute."* Although not specifically identified, the music is described as *"small and fine, telling of grass and trees and the horizon."* Significantly, this music stands in stark contrast to the claustrophobic urban setting of the play. Music also plays a major role in *The Glass Menagerie,* where a single recurring tune, like circus music, weaves in and out of the play. This musical motif gives emotional impact to certain lines and suggests the fantasy world into which Laura has retreated.

Sound effects play an important part in Henrik Ibsen's *A Doll House* (p. 562). At the very end of the play, after his wife has left him, Torvald Helmer sits alone on the stage. In the following stage directions, the final sound effect cuts short Helmer's attempt at self-deluding optimism:

HELMER: *(sinks down on a chair by the door, face buried in his hands)* Nora! Nora! *(Looking about and rising.)* Empty. She's gone. *(A sudden hope leaps in him.)* The greatest miracle—?

From below, the sound of a door slamming shut.

When you read a play, it may be difficult to appreciate the effect that staging can have on a performance. As you read, pay particular attention to the stage directions, and use your imagination to visualize the scenes the playwright describes. In addition, try to imagine the play's sights and sounds, and consider the options for staging that are suggested as characters speak to one another. Although careful reading cannot substitute for seeing a play performed, it can help you imagine the play as it might appear on the stage.

A Final Note

Because of a play's limited performance time, and because of space and financial limitations, not every action or event can be represented on stage. Frequently, incidents that would involve many actors or require elaborate scenery are only suggested. For example, a violent riot may be suggested by a single scuffle, a full-scale wedding by the kiss between bride and groom, a gala evening at the opera by a well-dressed group in box seats, and a trip to an exotic locale by a departure scene. Other events may be suggested by sounds offstage—for example, the roar of a crowd may suggest an athletic event.

David Ives (1950–   )

is the recipient of a Guggenheim Fellowship in playwriting and has published and produced numerous plays, many of which are one-act comedies. His plays are collected in *All in the Timing* (1994), *Mere Mortals* (1998), *Time Flies and Other Short Plays* (2001), and *Polish Joke and Other Plays* (2004). His play *Don Juan in Chicago* (1995) won the Outer Critics Circle Playwriting Award.

Words, Words, Words (1994)

Lights come up on three monkeys pecking away at three typewriters. Behind them, a tire swing is hanging. The monkeys are named Milton, Swift, and Kafka. Kafka is a girl-monkey. (They shouldn't be in monkey suits, by the way. Instead, they wear the sort of little-kid clothes that chimps wear in circuses: white shirts and bow ties for the boys, a flouncy little dress for Kafka.) They type for a few moments, each at his own speed. Then Milton runs excitedly around the floor on his knuckles, swings onto the tire swing, leaps back onto his stool, and goes on typing. Kafka eats a banana thoughtfully. Swift pounds his chest and shows his teeth, then goes back to typing.

Swift: I don't know. I just don't know. . . .
Kafka: Quiet, please. I'm trying to concentrate here. *(She types a moment with her toes.)*

Milton: Okay, so what've you got?

Swift: Me?

Milton: Yeah, have you hit anything? Let's hear it. ⁵

Swift (*reads what he's typed*): "Ping drobba fft fft fft inglewarp carcinoma." That's as far as I got.

Kafka: I like the "fft fft fft."

Milton: Yeah. Kind of onomatopoeic.

Swift: I don't know. Feels to me like it needs some punching up.

Milton: You can always throw in a few jokes later on. ¹⁰ You gotta get the throughline first.

Swift: But do you think it's *Hamlet*?

Milton: Don't ask me. I'm just a chimp.

Kafka: They could've given us a clue or something.

Swift: Yeah. Or a story conference.

Milton: But that'd defeat the whole purpose of the ¹⁵ experiment.

Swift: I know, I know, I know. Three monkeys typing into infinity will sooner or later produce *Hamlet*.

Milton: Right.

Swift: Completely by chance.

Milton: And Dr. David Rosenbaum up in that booth is going to prove it.

Swift: But what *is Hamlet*?

Milton: I don't know. ²⁰

Swift (*to Kafka*): What is *Hamlet*?

Kafka: I don't know. (*Silence.*)

Swift (*dawning realization*): You know—this is really *stupid*!

Milton: Have you got something better to do in this ²⁵ cage? The sooner we produce the goddamn thing, the sooner we get out.

Kafka: Sort of publish or perish, with a twist.

Swift: But what do we owe this Rosenbaum? A guy who stands outside those bars and tells people, "That one's Milton, that one's Swift, and that one's Kafka"—? Just to get a laugh?

>> Scene from the 2000 production of David Ives's *Words, Words, Words* by the English Theatre of Rome

---

° **mug's game** Pointless endeavor.

Kafka: What's a Kafka anyway? Why am I a Kafka?

Swift: Search me.

Kafka: What's a Kafka? ³⁰

Swift: All his four-eyed friends sure think it's a stitch.

Kafka: And how are we supposed to write *Hamlet* if we don't even know what it is?

Milton: Okay, okay, so the chances are a little slim.

> *Swift: But do you think it's Hamlet?*
> *Milton: Don't ask me. I'm just a chimp.*

Swift: Yeah—and this from a guy who's supposed to be *smart*? This from a guy at *Columbia University*?

Milton: The way I figure it, there is a Providence that ³⁵ oversees our pages, rough-draft them how we may.

Kafka: But how about you, Milton? What've you got?

Milton: Let's see . . . (*Reads.*)

"Of Man's first disobedience, and the fruit
Of that forbidden tree whose mortal taste
Brought death into the—"

Kafka: Hey, that's good! It's got rhythm! It really sings!

Milton: Yeah?

Swift: But is it Shakespeare? ⁴⁰

Kafka: Who cares? He's got a real voice there!

Swift: Does Dr. Rosenbaum care about voice? Does he care about anybody's individual creativity?

Milton: Let's look at this from Rosenbaum's point of view for a minute—

Swift: No! He brings us in here to produce copy, then all he wants is a clean draft of somebody else's stuff. (*Dumps out a bowl of peanuts.*) We're getting peanuts here, to be somebody's hack!

Milton: Writing is a mug's game° anyway, Swifty. ⁴⁵

Swift: Well it hath made me mad.

Milton: Why not just buckle down and get the project over with? Set up a schedule for yourself. Type in the morning for a couple of hours when you're fresh, then take a break. Let the old juices flow. Do a couple more hours in the afternoon, and retire for a shot of papaya and some masturbation. What's the big deal?

Swift: If this Rosenbaum was worth anything, we'd be working on word processors, not these antiques. He's lucky he could find three who type this good, and then he treats us like those misfits at the Bronx Zoo. I mean, a *tire swing*? What does he take us for?

Milton: I like the tire swing. I think it was a very nice touch.

Swift: I can't work under these conditions! No wonder ⁵⁰ I'm producing garbage!

Kafka: How does the rest of yours go, Milton?

Milton: What, this?

Kafka: Yeah, read us some more.

Milton: Blah, blah, blah . . .

"*whose mortal taste Brought
death into the blammagam.
Bedsocks knockwurst tinkerbelle.*"

Small pause.

What do you think?

Kafka: "Blammagam" is good.   55

Swift: Well. I don't know. . . .

Milton: What's the matter? Is it the tone? I knew this was
kind of a stretch for me.

Swift: I'm just not sure it has the same expressive
intensity and pungent lyricism as the first part.

Milton: Well sure, it needs rewriting. What doesn't? This is a
rough draft! (*A red light goes on and a buzzer sounds.*)

Light's on.

*Swift claps his hands over his eyes, Milton puts his hands
over his ears, and Kafka puts her hands over her
mouth so that they form "See no evil, hear no evil,
speak no evil."*

Swift: *This* bit.   60

Kafka (*through her hands*): Are they watching?

Milton (*hands over ears*): What?

Kafka: Are they watching?

Swift: I don't know, I can't see. I have got my paws over
my eyes.

Milton: What?   65

Kafka: What is the point of this?

Swift: Why do they videotape our bowel movements?

Milton: *What?!*

Swift: Light's off. (*They take their hands away.*)

Milton: But how are *you* doing, Franz? What've you got?   70

Kafka: Well . . . (*Reads what she's typed.*) "K.K.K.K.K.
K.K.K.K.K.K.K.K.K."

Swift: What is that—postmodernism?

Kafka: Twenty lines of that.

Swift: At least it'll fuck up his data.

Cultural Context

The basis for this play is the
"infinite monkey theorem," the idea that, given enough time
and enough monkeys, at least one monkey placed in front of
a typewriter will eventually produce William Shakespeare's
Hamlet. Credit for this idea is generally given to French
mathematician Émile Borel, whose 1913 essay explains the
theorem. Since then, numerous writers (including Richard
Russo and Douglas Adams) have alluded to this idea in literature, using it as a metaphor to explore the probability of random, spontaneous acts of artistic genius.

Kafka: Twenty lines of that and I went dry. I got blocked.   75
I felt like I was repeating myself.

Milton: Do you think that that's in *Hamlet?*

Kafka: I don't understand what I'm doing here in the first
place! I'm not a writer, I'm a monkey! I'm supposed
to be swinging on branches and digging up ants, not
sitting under fluorescent lights ten hours a day!

Milton: It sure is a long way home to the gardens of sweet
Africa. Where lawns and level downs and flocks
grazing the tender herb were sweetly interposèd . . .

Kafka: Paradise, wasn't it?

Milton: Lost!   80

Swift: Lost!

Kafka: Lost!

Milton: I'm trying to deal with some of that in this new
piece here, but it's all still pretty close to the bone.

Swift: Just because they can keep us locked up, they
think they're more powerful than we are.

Milton: They *are* more powerful than we are.   85

Swift: Just because they control the means of production,
they think they can suppress the workers.

Milton: Things are how they are. What are you going to do?

Swift: Hey—how come you're always so goddamn ready
to justify the ways of Rosenbaum to the apes?

Milton: Do you have a key to that door?

Swift: No.   90

Milton: Do you have an independent food source?

Swift: No.

Milton: So call me a collaborator. I happen to be a
professional. If Rosenbaum wants *Hamlet,* I'll give it
a shot. Just don't forget—we're not astrophysicists.
We're not brain surgeons. We're chimps. And for
apes in captivity, this is not a bad gig.

Swift: What's really frightening is that if we stick around
this cage long enough, we're gonna evolve into
Rosenbaum.

Kafka: Evolve into Rosenbaum?   95

Swift: Brush up your Darwin, baby. We're more than kin
and less than kind.

Milton: Anybody got a smoke?

Kafka: I'm all out.

Swift: Don't look at me. I'm not going to satisfy those
voyeurs with the old smoking-chimp act. No thank you.

Milton: Don't be a sap, Swifty. You gotta use 'em! Use   100
the system!

Swift: What do you mean?

Milton: Watch me, while I put my antic disposition on. (*He
jumps up onto his chair and scratches his sides, screech-
es, makes smoking motions, pounds his chest, jumps up
and down—and a cigarette descends.*) See what I mean?
Gauloise, too! My fave. (*He settles back to enjoy it.*)

Swift: They should've thrown in a Kewpie doll° for that
performance.

° **Kewpie doll** Style of doll based on magazine illustrations from the
early twentieth century.

Milton: It got results, didn't it?

Swift: Sure. You do your Bonzo routine and get a Gauloise out of it. Last week I totalled a typewriter and got a whole carton of Marlboros.

Milton: The trouble was, you didn't smoke 'em, you took a crap on 'em.

Swift: It was a political statement.

Milton: Okay, you made your statement and I got my smoke. All's well that ends well, right?

Kafka: It's the only way we know they're watching.

Milton: Huh?

Kafka: We perform, we break typewriters, we type another page—and a cigarette appears. At least it's a sign that somebody out there is paying attention.

Milton: Our resident philosopher.

Swift: But what if one of us really *does* write *Hamlet?* Here we are, set down to prove the inadvertent virtues of randomness, and to produce something we wouldn't even recognize if it passed right through our hands—but what if one of us actually does it?

Milton: Will we really be released?

Kafka: Will they give us the key to the city and a ticker-tape parade?

Swift: Or will they move us on to *Ulysses? (They shriek in terror at the thought.)* Why did they pick *Hamlet* in the first place? What's *Hamlet* to them or they to *Hamlet* that we should care? Boy, there's the respect that makes calamity of so long life! For who would bear the whips and scorns of time, the oppressor's wrong, the proud man's contumely—

Milton: Hey, Swifty!

Swift: —the pangs of despisèd love, the law's delay—

Milton: Hey, Swifty! Relax, will you?

Kafka: Have a banana.

Swift: I wish I could get Rosenbaum in here and see how *he* does at producing *Hamlet . . . That's it!*

Kafka: What?

Swift: That's it! Forget about this random *Hamlet* crap. What about *revenge?*

Kafka: Revenge? On Rosenbaum?

Swift: Who else? Hasn't he bereft us of our homes and families? Stepped in between us and our expectations?

Kafka: How would we do it?

Swift: Easy. We lure him in here to look at our typewriters, test them out like something's wrong—but! *we poison the typewriter keys*!

Milton: Oh Jesus.

Swift: Sure. Some juice of cursèd hebona° spread liberally over the keyboard? Ought to work like a charm.

Milton: Great.

Swift: If that doesn't work, we envenom the tire swing and invite him for a ride. Plus—I challenge him to a duel.

Milton: Brilliant.

Swift: Can't you see it? In the course of combat, I casually graze my rapier over the poisoned typewriter keys, and *(jabs)* a hit! A palpable hit! For a reserve, we lay by a cup with some venomous distillment. We'll put the pellet with the poison in the vessel with the pestle!

Milton: Listen, I gotta get back to work. The man is gonna want his pages. *(He rolls a fresh page into his typewriter.)*

Kafka: It's not a bad idea, but . . .

Swift: What's the matter with you guys? I'm onto something here!

Kafka: I think it's hopeless, Swifty.

Swift: But this is the goods!

Milton: Where was I . . . "Bedsocks knockwurst tinker-belle."

Kafka: The readiness is all, I guess.

Milton: Damn straight. Just let me know when that K-button gives out, honey.

Swift: Okay. You two serfs go back to work. I'll do all the thinking around here. Swifty—revenge! *(He paces, deep in thought.)*

Milton: "Tinkerbelle . . . shtuckelschwanz . . . hemorrhoid." Yeah, that's good. *That is good. (Types.)* "Shtuckelshwanz . . ."

Kafka *(types):* "Act one, scene one. Elsinore Castle, Denmark . . ."

Milton *(types):* "Hemorrhoid."

Kafka *(types):* "Enter Bernardo and Francisco."

Milton: *(types):* "Pomegranate."

Kafka *(types):* "Bernardo says, 'Who's there?' . . ."

Milton *(types):* "Bazooka."

Kafka continues to type Hamlet, *as*
The Lights Fade

Related Works

"Accident" (p. 103), "Two Questions" (p. 273), "The Value of Education" (p. 391), *Hamlet* (p. 644)

 See Chapter 34 Review Card for Reading and Reacting questions about David Ives, *Word, Words, Words.*

° **hebona** Type of poisonous plant.

Sophocles (496–496 B.C.)

is, along with Aeschylus and Euripides, one of the three great ancient Greek tragic dramatists. He lived during the flowering and subsequent decline of fifth-century b.c. Athens—the high point of Greek civilization. Born as Greece struggled against the Persian Empire and moved to adopt democracy, he lived as an adult under Pericles during the golden age of Athens and died as it became clear that Athens would lose the Peloponnesian War. Sophocles was an active participant in the public life of Athens, serving as a collector of tribute from Athenian subjects and later as a general. He wrote at least 120 plays, but only seven have survived, including three plays about Oedipus: *Oedipus the King* (c. 430 b.c.), *Oedipus at Colonus* (411? b.c.), and *Antigone* (441 b.c.).

Oedipus the King, or *Oedipus Rex* (sometimes called *Oedipus the Tyrant*), was performed shortly after a great plague in Athens (probably in 429 or 425 b.c.) and as Athens was falling into decline. The play opens with an account of a plague in Thebes, Oedipus's kingdom. Over the years, *Oedipus the King* has attracted impressive critical attention, from Aristotle's use of it as a model for his definition of tragedy to Freud's use of its power as evidence of the validity of the "Oedipus complex."

Oedipus the King* (c. 430 b.c.)

Translated by Thomas Gould

CHARACTERS

Oedipus,° *the King of Thebes*	**Tiresias,** *a blind seer or prophet*
Priest of Zeus, *leader of the suppliants*	**Jocasta,** *the queen of Thebes*
Creon, *Oedipus's brother-in-law*	**Messenger,** *from Corinth, once a shepherd*
Chorus, *a group of Theban elders*	**Herdsman,** *once a servant of Laius*
Choragos, *spokesman of the Chorus*	**Second Messenger,** *a servant of Oedipus*

MUTES

Suppliants, *Thebans seeking Oedipus's help*
Attendants, *for the Royal Family*
Servants, *to lead Tiresias and Oedipus*
Antigone, *daughter of Oedipus and Jocasta*
Ismene, *daughter of Oedipus and Jocasta*

The action takes place during the day in front of the royal palace in Thebes. There are two altars (left and right) on the proscenium and several steps leading down to the orchestra. As the play opens, Thebans of various ages who have come to beg Oedipus for help are sitting on these steps and in part of the orchestra. These suppliants are holding branches of laurel or olive which have strips of wool° wrapped around them. Oedipus enters from the palace (the central door of the skene).

---

*Note that individual lines are numbered in the following play. When a line is shared by two or more characters, it is counted as one line.

°**Oedipus** The name, meaning "swollen foot," refers to the mutilation of Oedipus's feet by his father, Laius, before the infant was sent to Mount Cithaeron to be put to death by exposure.

°**wool** Branches wrapped with wool are traditional symbols of prayer or supplication.

PROLOGUE°

Oedipus: My children, ancient Cadmus'° newest care,
why have you hurried to those seats, your boughs
wound with the emblems of the suppliant?
The city is weighed down with fragrant smoke,
with hymns to the Healer° and the cries of mourners.   5
I thought it wrong, my sons, to hear your words
through emissaries, and have come out myself,
I, Oedipus, a name that all men know.

Oedipus addresses the Priest.

Old man—for it is fitting that you speak
for all—what is your mood as you entreat me,   10
fear or trust? You may be confident
that I'll do anything. How hard of
heart if an appeal like this did not rouse my pity!

Priest: You, Oedipus, who hold the power here,
you see our several ages, we who sit   15
before your altars—some not strong enough
to take long flight, some heavy in old age,
the priests, as I of Zeus,° and from our youths
a chosen band. The rest sit with their windings
in the markets, at the
twin shrines of Pallas,°   20
and the prophetic embers
of Ismēnos.°
Our city, as you see
yourself, is tossed
too much, and can no
longer lift its head
above the troughs of
billows red with death.
It dies in the fruitful
flowers of the soil,   25
it dies in its pastured
herds, and in its women's
barren pangs. And the fire-bearing god°
has swooped upon the city, hateful plague,
and he has left the house of Cadmus empty.
Black Hades° is made rich with moans and weeping.   30

> *"Again now Oedipus,*
> *our greatest power,*
> *we plead with you, as*
> *suppliants, all of us,*
> *to find us strength . . . ."*

Not judging you an equal of the gods,
do I and the children sit here at your hearth,
but as the first of men, in troubled times
and in encounters with divinities.
You came to Cadmus' city and unbound   35
the tax we had to pay to the harsh singer,°
did it without a helpful word from us,
with no instruction; with a god's assistance
you raised up our life, so we believe.
Again now Oedipus, our greatest power,   40
we plead with you, as suppliants, all of us,
to find us strength, whether from a god's response,
or learned in some way from another man.
I know that the experienced among men
give counsels that will prosper best of all.   45
Noblest of men, lift up our land again!
Think also of yourself; since now the land
calls you its Savior for your zeal of old,
oh let us never look back at your rule
as men helped up only to fall again!   50
Do not stumble! Put our land on firm feet!
The bird of omen was auspicious then,
when you brought that luck; be that same man again!
The power is yours; if you will rule our country,
rule over men, not in an empty land.   55
A towered city or a ship is nothing
if desolate and no man lives within.

Oedipus: Pitiable children, oh I know, I know
the yearnings that have brought you. Yes, I know
that you are sick. And yet, though you are sick,   60
there is not one of you so sick as I.
For your affliction comes to each alone,
for him and no one else, but my soul mourns
for me and for you, too, and for the city.
You do not waken me as from a sleep,   65
for I have wept, bitterly and long,
tried many paths in the wanderings of thought,
and the single cure I found by careful search

° **Prologue** The portion of the play containing the exposition, or explanation, of what has gone before and what is now happening.

° **Cadmus** Oedipus's great-great-grandfather (although Oedipus does not know this) and the founder of Thebes.

° **Healer** Apollo, god of prophecy, light, healing, justice, purification, and destruction.

° **Zeus** Father and king of the gods.

° **Pallas** Athena, goddess of wisdom, arts, crafts, and war.

° **Ismēnos** A reference to the temple of Apollo near the river Ismēnos in Thebes. Prophecies were made here by "reading" the ashes of the altar fires.

° **fire-bearing god** Contagious fever viewed as a god.

° **Black Hades** Refers both to the underworld where the spirits of the dead go and to the god of the underworld.

° **harsh singer** The Sphinx, a monster with a woman's head, a lion's body, and wings. The "tax" from which Oedipus freed Thebes was the destruction of all the young men who failed to solve the Sphinx's riddle and were subsequently devoured. The Sphinx always asked the same riddle: "What goes on four legs in the morning, two legs at noon, and three legs in the evening, and yet is weakest when supported by the largest number of feet?" Oedipus discovered the correct answer—man, who crawls in infancy, walks in his prime, and uses a stick in old age—and thus ended the Sphinx's reign of terror. The Sphinx destroyed herself when Oedipus answered the riddle. Oedipus's reward for freeing Thebes of the Sphinx was the throne and the hand of the recently widowed Jocasta.

I've acted on: I sent Menoeceus' son,
Creon, brother of my wife, to the Pythian   70
halls of Phoebus,° so that I might learn
what I must do or say to save this city.
Already, when I think what day this is,
I wonder anxiously what he is doing.
Too long, more than is right, he's been away.   75
But when he comes, then I shall be a traitor
if I do not do all that the god reveals.

Priest: Welcome words! But look, those men have signaled that it is
Creon who is now approaching!

Oedipus: Lord Apollo! May he bring Savior Luck,   80
a Luck as brilliant as his eyes are now!

Priest: His news is happy, it appears. He comes, forehead
crowned with thickly berried laurel.°

Oedipus: We'll know, for he is near enough to hear us.

Enter Creon along one of the parados.

Lord, brother in marriage, son of Menoeceus!   85
What is the god's pronouncement that you bring?

Creon: It's good. For even troubles, if they chance
to turn out well, I always count as lucky.

Oedipus: But what was the response? You seem to say
I'm not to fear—but not to take heart either.   90

Creon: If you will hear me with these men present,
I'm ready to report—or go inside.

Creon moves up the steps toward the palace.

Oedipus: Speak out to all! The grief that burdens me
concerns these men more than it does my life.

Creon: Then I shall tell you what I heard from the god.   95
The task Lord Phoebus sets for us is clear:
drive out pollution sheltered in our land,
and do not shelter what is incurable.

Oedipus: What is our trouble? How shall we cleanse ourselves?

Creon: We must banish or murder to free ourselves   100
from a murder that blows storms through the city.

Oedipus: What man's bad luck does he accuse in this?

>> Christopher Plummer as Oedipus in a 1967 production

Cultural Context During the period in which
Oedipus was written, the Greeks were especially interested in the
relationship between greatness and *hubris*, the excessive pride and
ambition that leads to the downfall of a hero in classical tragedy.
They were fascinated by the idea that hubris can bring destruction:
that the same traits that can elevate a person to greatness can also
cause his or her ruin. This theme recurs throughout classical literature and was especially relevant between 431 and 404 B.C., when
the Second Peloponnesian War (which Athens lost) was being
fought between Athens and Sparta. After a Spartan army invaded
Attica in 431 B.C., the Athenians retreated behind the walls of their
city while the Athenian fleet began raids. Between 430 and 428 B.C.,
a plague (which the Athenians believed was inflicted upon them
by the gods) wiped out at least a quarter of the Athenian population. It was during this tumultuous time that Sophocles wrote of
Oedipus and his troubles.

Creon: My Lord, a king
named Laius ruled
our land before you
came to steer the
city straight.

Oedipus: I know. So I   105
was told—I never
saw him.

Creon: Since he was murdered, you must
raise your hand
against the men who killed him with their hands.

> **Creon: We must banish or murder to free ourselves from a murder that blows storms through the city.**

Oedipus: Where are they now? And how can we ever find
the track of ancient guilt now hard to read?

Creon: In our own land, he said. What we pursue,   110
that can be caught; but not what we neglect.

Oedipus: Was Laius home, or in the countryside—
or was he murdered in some foreign land?

Creon: He left to see a sacred rite, he said;
He left, but never came home from his journey.   115

Oedipus: Did none of his party see it and report—
someone we might profitably question?

Creon: They were all killed but one, who fled in fear, and he
could tell us only one clear fact.

Oedipus: What fact? One thing could lead us on to more   120
if we could get a small start on our hope.

Creon: He said that bandits chanced on them and killed him—
with the force of many hands, not one alone.

Oedipus: How could a bandit dare so great an act—
unless this was a plot paid off from here!   125

Creon: We thought of that, but when Laius was killed,
we had no one to help us in our troubles.

° **Pythian halls . . . Phoebus** The temple of Phoebus, Apollo's oracle
or prophet at Delphi.

° **laurel** Creon is wearing a garland of laurel leaves, sacred to Apollo.

>>Actors portraying Oedipus and Jocasta in 2006 production in Salzburg, Austria

Oedipus: It was your very kingship that was killed!
    What kind of trouble blocked you from a search?
Creon: The subtle-singing Sphinx asked us to turn   130
    from the obscure to what lay at our feet.
Oedipus: Then I shall begin again and make it plain.
    It was quite worthy of Phoebus, and worthy of you,
    to turn our thoughts back to the murdered man,
    and right that you should see me join the battle   135
    for justice to our land and to the god.
    Not on behalf of any distant kinships,
    it's for myself I will dispel this stain.
    Whoever murdered him may also wish
    to punish me—and with the selfsame hand.   140
    In helping him I also serve myself.
    Now quickly, children: up from the altar steps,
    and raise the branches of the suppliant!
    Let someone go and summon Cadmus' people:
    say I'll do anything.

Exit an Attendant along one of the parados.

                Our luck will prosper   145
    if the god is with us, or we have already fallen.
Priest: Rise, my children; that for which we came,
    he has himself proclaimed he will accomplish.

° **Parados** A song sung by the Chorus on first entering.

° **Strophe** Probably refers to the direction in which the Chorus danced while reciting specific stanzas. *Strophe* may have indicated dance steps to stage left, *antistrophe* to stage right.

° **Voice from Zeus** A reference to Apollo's prophecy. Zeus taught Apollo how to prophesy.

° **Pytho** Delphi.

° **Delian Healer** Apollo.

° **Artemis** Goddess of virginity, childbirth, and hunting.

° **god . . . sunset** Hades, god of the underworld.

May Phoebus, who announced this, also come
as Savior and reliever from the plague.   150

Exit Oedipus and Creon into the palace. The Priest and the Suppliants exit left and right along the parados. After a brief pause, the Chorus (including the Choragos) enters the orchestra from the parados.

PARADOS°
STROPHE 1°

Chorus: Voice from Zeus,° sweetly spoken, what are you
    that have arrived from golden
    Pytho° to our shining
    Thebes? I am on the rack, terror
        shakes my soul.   155
    Delian Healer,° summoned by "iē!"
    I await in holy dread what obligation, something new
    or something back once more with the revolving years,
        you'll bring about for me.
    Oh tell me, child of golden Hope,   160
        deathless Response!

ANTISTROPHE 1

    I appeal to you first, daughter of Zeus,
        deathless Athena,
        and to your sister who protects this land,
    Artemis,° whose famous throne is the whole circle   165
        of the marketplace,
    and Phoebus, who shoots from afar: iō!
    Three-fold defenders against death, appear!
    If ever in the past, to stop blind ruin
        sent against the city,   170
    you banished utterly the fires of suffering,
        come now again!

STROPHE 2

    Ah! Ah! Unnumbered are the miseries
    I bear. The plague claims all
    our comrades. Nor has thought found yet a spear   175
    by which a man shall be protected. What our glorious
    earth gives birth to does not grow. Without a birth
    from cries of labor
        do the women rise.
    One person after another   180
        you may see, like flying birds,
    faster than indomitable fire, sped
    to the shore of the god that is the sunset.°

ANTISTROPHE 2

    And with their deaths unnumbered dies the city.
    Her children lie unpitied on the ground,   185
    spreading death, unmourned.
    Meanwhile young wives, and gray-haired mothers with them,
    on the shores of the altars, from this side and that,
    suppliants from mournful trouble,
        cry out their grief.   190

A hymn to the Healer shines,
    the flute a mourner's voice.
Against which, golden goddess, daughter of Zeus,
    send lovely Strength.

STROPHE 3

Causing raging Ares°—who,   195
    armed now with no shield of bronze,
burns me, coming on amid loud cries—
to turn his back and run from my land,
with a fair wind behind, to the great
    hall of Amphitrite,°   200
or to the anchorage that welcomes no one,
Thrace's troubled sea!
If night lets something get away at last,
    it comes by day.
Fire-bearing god . . .   205
    you who dispense the might of lightning,
Zeus! Father! Destroy him with your thunderbolt!

Enter Oedipus from the palace.

ANTISTROPHE 3

Lycēan Lord!° From your looped
    bowstring, twisted gold,
I wish indomitable missiles might be scattered   210
and stand forward, our protectors; also fire-bearing
radiance of Artemis, with which
    she darts across the Lycian mountains.
I call the god whose head is bound in gold,
with whom this country shares its name,   215
Bacchus,° wine-flushed, summoned by "euoi!,"
    Maenads' comrade,
to approach ablaze
    with gleaming . . .
pine, opposed to that god-hated god.   220

EPISODE 1°

Oedipus: I hear your prayer. Submit to what I say
and to the labors that the plague demands
and you'll get help and a relief from evils.
I'll make the proclamation, though a stranger
to the report and to the deed. Alone,   225
had I no key, I would soon lose the track.
Since it was only later that I joined you,
to all the sons of Cadmus I say this:
whoever has clear knowledge of the man
who murdered Laius, son of Labdacus,   230
I command him to reveal it all to me—
nor fear if, to remove the charge, he must
accuse himself: his fate will not be cruel—
he will depart unstumbling into exile.
But if you know another, or a stranger,   235
to be the one whose hand is guilty, speak:
I shall reward you and remember you.
But if you keep your peace because of fear,

>> Actor portraying Oedipus in 2003 production in Vienna, Austria

and shield yourself or kin from my command,
hear you what I shall do in that event: 240
I charge all in this land where I have throne
and power, shut out that man—no matter who—
both from your shelter and all spoken words,
nor in your prayers or sacrifices make
him partner, nor allot him lustral° water.   245
All men shall drive him from their homes: for he
is the pollution that the god-sent Pythian
response has only now revealed to me.
In this way I ally myself in war
with the divinity and the deceased.°   250
And this curse, too, against the one who did it,
whether alone in secrecy, or with others:
may he wear out his life unblest and evil!
I pray this, too: if he is at my hearth
and in my home, and I have knowledge of him,   255
may the curse pronounced on others come to me.
All this I lay to you to execute,
for my sake, for the god's, and for this land

° **Ares** God of war and destruction.

° **Amphitritē** The Atlantic Ocean.

° **Lycēan Lord** Apollo.

° **Bacchus** Dionysus, god of fertility and wine.

° **Episode** The portion of ancient Greek plays that appears between choric songs.

° **lustral** Purifying.

° **the deceased** Laius.

>> Oedipus with members of chorus
in Tyrone Guthrie's 1957 film

now ruined, barren, abandoned by the gods.
Even if no god had driven you to it,   260
you ought not to have left this stain uncleansed,
the murdered man a nobleman, a king!
You should have looked! But now, since, as it happens,
It's I who have the power that he had once,
and have his bed, and a wife who shares our seed,   265
and common bond had we had common children
(had not his hope of offspring had bad luck—
but as it happened, luck lunged at his head);
because of this, as if for my own father,
I'll fight for him, I'll leave no means untried,   270
to catch the one who did it with his hand,
for the son of Labdacus, of Polydōrus,
of Cadmus before him, and of Agēnor.°
This prayer against all those who disobey:
the gods send out no harvest from their soil,   275
nor children from their wives. Oh, let them die
victims of this plague, or of something worse.
Yet for the rest of us, people of Cadmus,
we the obedient, may Justice, our ally,
and all the gods, be always on our side!   280
Choragos:° I speak because I feel the grip of your curse:
the killer is not I. Nor can I point
to him. The one who set us to this search,
Phoebus, should also name the guilty man.
Oedipus: Quite right, but to compel unwilling gods—   285
no man has ever had that kind of power.
Choragos: May I suggest to you a second way?
Oedipus: A second or a third—pass over nothing!
Choragos: I know of no one who sees more of what
Lord Phoebus sees than Lord Tiresias.   290
My Lord, one might learn brilliantly from him.
Oedipus: Nor is this something I have been slow to do.
At Creon's word I sent an escort—twice now!
I am astonished that he has not come.
Choragos: The old account is useless. It told us nothing.   295
Oedipus: But tell it to me. I'll scrutinize all stories.
Choragos: He is said to have been killed by travelers.
Oedipus: I have heard, but the one who did it no one sees.
Choragos: If there is any fear in him at all,
he won't stay here once he has heard that curse.   300
Oedipus: He won't fear words: he had no fear when he did it.

*Enter Tiresias from the right, led by a Servant and two of
Oedipus's Attendants.*

Choragos: Look there! There is the man who will convict him!
It's the god's prophet they are leading here,
one gifted with the truth as no one else.
Oedipus: Tiresias, master of all omens—   305
public and secret, in the sky and on the earth—
your mind, if not your eyes, sees how the city
lives with a plague, against which Thebes can find
no Saviour or protector, Lord, but you.
For Phoebus, as the attendants surely told you,   310
returned this answer to us: liberation
from the disease would never come unless
we learned without a doubt who murdered Laius—
put them to death, or sent them into exile.
Do not begrudge us what you may learn from birds   315
or any other prophet's path you know!
Care for yourself, the city, care for me,
care for the whole pollution of the dead!
We're in your hands. To do all that he can
to help another is man's noblest labor.   320
Tiresias: How terrible to understand and get
no profit from the knowledge! I knew this,
but I forgot, or I had never come.
Oedipus: What's this? You've come with very little zeal.
Tiresias: Let me go home! If you will listen to me,   325
You will endure your troubles better—and I mine.
Oedipus: A strange request, not very kind to the land
that cared for you—to hold back this oracle!

° **son . . . Agēnor** Refers to Laius by citing his genealogy.

° **Choragos** Leader of the Chorus and principal commentator on the
play's action.

>> 1945 London stage production with Laurence Olivier as Oedipus

Tiresias: I see your understanding comes to you
  inopportunely. So that won't happen to me . . .   330
Oedipus: Oh, by the gods, if you understand about this,
  don't turn away! We're on our knees to you.
Tiresias: None of you understands! I'll never bring
  my grief to light—I will not speak of yours.
Oedipus: You know and won't declare it! Is your purpose   335
  to betray us and to destroy this land!
Tiresias: I will grieve neither of us. Stop this futile
  cross-examination. I'll tell you nothing!
Oedipus: Nothing? You vile traitor! You could provoke
  a stone to anger! You still refuse to tell?   340
  Can nothing soften you, nothing convince you?
Tiresias: You blamed anger in me—you haven't seen.
  The kind that lives with you, so you blame me.
Oedipus: Who wouldn't fill with anger, listening
  to words like yours which now disgrace this city?   345
Tiresias: It will come, even if my silence hides it.
Oedipus: If it will come, then why won't you declare it?
Tiresias: I'd rather say no more. Now if you wish,
  respond to that with all your fiercest anger!
Oedipus: Now I am angry enough to come right out   350
  with this conjecture: you, I think, helped plot
  the deed; you did it—even if your hand,
  cannot have struck the blow. If you could see,
  I should have said the deed was yours alone.
Tiresias: Is that right! Then I charge you to abide   355
  by the decree you have announced: from this day
  say no word to either these or me,
  for you are the vile polluter of this land!
Oedipus: Aren't you appalled to let a charge like that
  come bounding forth? How will you get away?   360
Tiresias: You cannot catch me. I have the strength of truth.
Oedipus: Who taught you this? Not your prophetic craft!
Tiresias: You did. You made me say it. I didn't want to.
Oedipus: Say what? Repeat it so I'll understand.
Tiresias: I made no sense? Or are you trying me?   365
Oedipus: No sense I understood. Say it again!
Tiresias: I say you are the murderer you seek.
Oedipus: Again that horror! You'll wish you hadn't
  said that.
Tiresias: Shall I say more, and raise your anger higher?
Oedipus: Anything you like! Your words are powerless.   370
Tiresias: You live, unknowing, with those nearest to you
  in the greatest shame. You do not see the evil.
Oedipus: You won't go on like that and never pay!
Tiresias: I can if there is any strength in truth.
Oedipus: In truth, but not in you! You have no strength,   375
  blind in your ears, your reason, and your eyes.
Tiresias: Unhappy man! Those jeers you hurl at me
  before long all these men will hurl at you.
Oedipus: You are the child of endless night; it's not
  for me or anyone who sees to hurt you.   380
Tiresias: It's not my fate to be struck down by you.
  Apollo is enough. That's his concern.
Oedipus: Are these inventions Creon's or your own?
Tiresias: No, your affliction is yourself, not Creon.
Oedipus: Oh success!—in wealth, kingship, artistry,   385
  in any life that wins much admiration—

the envious ill will stored up for you!
  to get at my command, a gift I did not
  seek, which the city put into my hands,
  my loyal Creon, colleague from the start,   390
  longs to sneak up in secret and dethrone me.
  So he's suborned this fortuneteller—schemer!
  deceitful beggar-priest!—who has good eyes
  for gains alone, though in his craft he's blind.
  Where were your prophet's powers ever proved?   395
  Why, when the dog who chanted verse° was here,
  did you not speak and liberate this city?
  Her riddle wasn't for a man chancing by
  to interpret; prophetic art was needed,
  but you had none, it seems—learned from birds   400
  or from a god. I came along, yes I,
  Oedipus the ignorant, and stopped her—
  by using thought, not augury from birds.
  And it is I whom you now wish to banish,
  so you'll be close to the Creontian throne.   405
  You—and the plot's concocter—will drive out
  pollution to your grief: you look quite old
  or you would be the victim of that plot!
Choragos: It seems to us that this man's words were said
  in anger, Oedipus, and yours as well.   410
  Insight, not angry words, is what we need,
  the best solution to the god's response.
Tiresias: You are the king, and yet I am your equal
  in my right to speak. In that I too am Lord.
  for I belong to Loxias,° not you.   415
  I am not Creon's man. He's nothing to me.
  Hear this, since you have thrown my blindness at me:
  Your eyes can't see the evil to which you've come,
  nor where you live, nor who is in your house.
  Do you know your parents? Not knowing, you are   420
  their enemy, in the underworld and here.
  A mother's and a father's double-lashing
  terrible-footed curse will soon drive you out.
  Now you can see, then you will stare into darkness.
  What place will not be harbor to your cry,   425
  or what Cithaeron° not reverberate
  when you have heard the bride-song in your palace
  to which you sailed? Fair wind to evil harbor!
  Nor do you see how many other woes
  will level you to yourself and to your children.   430
  So, at my message, and at Creon, too,
  splatter muck! There will never be a man
  ground into wretchedness as you will be.
Oedipus: Am I to listen to such things from him!
  May you be damned! Get out of here at once!   435
  Go! Leave my palace! Turn around and go!

Tiresias begins to move away from Oedipus.

°**dog . . . verse** The Sphinx.

°**Loxias** Apollo.

°**Cithaeron** The mountain on which Oedipus was to be exposed as
an infant.

Tiresias: I wouldn't have come had you not sent for me.

Oedipus: I did not know you'd talk stupidity,
or I wouldn't have rushed to bring you to my house.

Tiresias: Stupid I seem to you, yet to your parents   440
who gave you natural birth I seemed quite shrewd.

Oedipus: Who? Wait! Who is the one who gave me birth?

Tiresias: This day will give you birth,° and ruin too.

Oedipus: What murky, riddling things you always say!

Tiresias: Don't you surpass us all at finding out?   445

Oedipus: You sneer at what you'll find has brought me greatness.

Tiresias: And that's the very luck that ruined you.

Oedipus: I wouldn't care, just so I saved the city.

Tiresias: In that case I shall go. Boy, lead the way!

Oedipus: Yes, let him lead you off. Here, underfoot,   450
you irk me. Gone, you'll cause no further pain.

Tiresias: I'll go when I have said what I was sent for.
Your face won't scare me. You can't ruin me.
I say to you, the man whom you have looked for
as you pronounced your curses, your decrees   455
on the bloody death of Laius—he is here!
A seeming stranger, he shall be shown to be
a Theban born, though he'll take no delight
in that solution. Blind, who once could see,
a beggar who was rich, through foreign lands   460
he'll go and point before him with a stick.
To his beloved children, he'll be shown
a father who is also brother; to the one
who bore him, son and husband; to his father,
his seed-fellow and killer. Go in   465
and think this out; and if you find I've lied,
say then I have no prophet's understanding!

Exit Tiresias, led by a Servant. Oedipus exits into the palace with his Attendants.

Stasimon I°

STROPHE 1

Chorus: Who is the man of whom the inspired
rock of Delphi° said
he has committed the unspeakable   470
with blood-stained hands?
Time for him to ply a foot

° **This day . . . birth** On this day, you will learn who your parents are.

° **Stasimon** Greek choral ode between episodes.

° **rock of Delphi** Apollo's oracle at Delphi.

° **son of Zeus** Apollo.

° **mantic** Prophetic.

° **earth's navel** Delphi.

° **interpreter of birds** Tiresias. The Chorus is troubled by his accusations.

° **house of Labdacus** The line of Laius.

° **Polybus** Oedipus's foster father.

° **winged maiden** The Sphinx.

mightier than those of the horses
of the storm in his escape;
upon him mounts and plunges the weaponed   475
son of Zeus,° with fire and thunderbolts,
and in his train the dreaded goddesses
of Death, who never miss.

ANTISTROPHE 1

The message has just blazed,
gleaming from the snows   480
of Mount Parnassus: we must track
everywhere the unseen man.
He wanders, hidden by wild
forests, up through caves
and rocks, like a bull,   485
anxious, with an anxious foot, forlorn.
He puts away from him the mantic° words come from earth's
navel,° at its center, yet these live
forever and still hover round him.

STROPHE 2

Terribly he troubles me,   490
the skilled interpreter of birds!°
I can't assent, nor speak against him.
Both paths are closed to me.
I hover on the wings of doubt,
not seeing what is here nor what's to come.   495
What quarrel started in the house of Labdacus°
or in the house of Polybus,°
either ever in the past
or now, I never
heard, so that . . . with this fact for my touchstone   500
I could attack the public
fame of Oedipus, by the side of the Labdaceans
an ally, against the dark assassination.

ANTISTROPHE 2

No, Zeus and Apollo
understand and know things   505
mortal; but that another man
can do more as a prophet than I can—
for that there is no certain test,
though, skill to skill,
one man might overtake another.   510
No, never, not until
I see the charges proved,
when someone blames him shall I nod assent.
For once, as we all saw, the winged maiden° came
against him: he was seen then to be skilled,   515
proved, by that touchstone, dear to the people. So,
never will my mind convict him of the evil.

EPISODE 2

Enter Creon from the right door of the skene and speaks to the Chorus.

Creon: Citizens, I hear that a fearful charge
is made against me by King Oedipus!

I had to come. If, in this crisis, 520
he thinks that he has suffered injury
from anything that I have said or done,
I have no appetite for a long life—
bearing a blame like that! It's no slight blow
the punishment I'd take from what he said: 525
it's the ultimate hurt to be called traitor
by the city, by you, by my own people!

Choragos: The thing that forced that accusation out
could have been anger, not the power of thought.

Creon: But who persuaded him that thoughts of mine 530
had led the prophet into telling lies?

Choragos: I do not know the thought behind his words.

Creon: But did he look straight at you? Was his mind right
when he said that I was guilty of this charge?

Choragos: I have no eyes to see what rulers do. 535
But here he comes himself out of the house.

Enter Oedipus from the palace.

Oedipus: What? You here? And can you really have
the face and daring to approach my house
when you're exposed as its master's murderer
and caught, too, as the robber of my kingship? 540
Did you see cowardice in me, by the gods,
or foolishness, when you began this plot?
Did you suppose that I would not detect
your stealthy moves, or that I'd not fight back?
It's your attempt that's folly, isn't it— 545
tracking without followers or connections,
kingship which is caught with wealth and numbers?

Creon: Now wait! Give me as long to answer back!
Judge me for yourself when you have heard me!

Oedipus: You're eloquent, but I'd be slow to learn 550
from you, now that I've seen your malice toward me.

Creon: That I deny. Hear what I have to say.

Oedipus: Don't you deny it! You are the traitor here!

Creon: If you consider mindless willfulness
a prized possession, you are not thinking sense. 555

Oedipus: If you think you can wrong a relative
and get off free, you are not thinking sense.

Creon: Perfectly just, I won't say no. And yet
what is this injury you say I did you?

Oedipus: Did you persuade me, yes or no, to send 560
someone to bring that solemn prophet here?

Creon: And I still hold to the advice I gave.

Oedipus: How many years ago did your King Laius . . .

Creon: Laius! Do what? Now I don't understand.

Oedipus: Vanish—victim of a murderous violence? 565

Creon: That is a long count back into the past.

Oedipus: Well, was this seer then practicing his art?

Creon: Yes, skilled and honored just as he is today.

Oedipus: Did he, back then, ever refer to me?

Creon: He did not do so in my presence ever. 570

Oedipus: You did inquire into the murder then.

Creon: We had to, surely, though we discovered nothing.

Oedipus: But the "skilled" one did not say this then? Why not?

Creon: I never talk when I am ignorant.

Oedipus: But you're not ignorant of your own part. 575

Creon: What do you mean? I'll tell you if I know.

Oedipus: Just this: if he had not conferred with you
he'd not have told about my murdering Laius.

Creon: If he said that, you are the one who knows.
But now it's fair that you should answer me. 580

Oedipus: Ask on! You won't convict me as the killer.

Creon: Well then, answer. My sister is your wife?

Oedipus: Now there's a statement that I can't deny.

Creon: You two have equal power in this country?

Oedipus: She gets from me whatever she desires. 585

Creon: And I'm a third? The three of us are equals?

Oedipus: That's where you're treacherous to your kinsman!

Creon: But think about this rationally, as I do.
First look at this: do you think anyone
prefers the anxieties of being king 590
to untroubled sleep—if he has equal power?
I'm not the kind of man who falls in love
with kingship. I am content with a king's power.
And so would any man who's wise and prudent.
I get all things from you, with no distress; 595
as king I would have onerous duties, too.
How could the kingship bring me more delight
than this untroubled power and influence?
I'm not misguided yet to such a point
that profitable honors aren't enough. 600
As it is, all wish me well and all salute;
those begging you for something have me summoned,
for their success depends on that alone.
Why should I lose all this to become king?
A prudent mind is never traitorous. 605
Treason's a thought I'm not enamored of;
nor could I join a man who acted so.
In proof of this, first go yourself to Pytho
and ask if I brought back the true response.
Then, if you find I plotted with that portent 610
reader,° don't have me put to death by your vote
only—I'll vote myself for my conviction.
Don't let an unsupported thought convict me!
It's not right mindlessly to take the bad
for good or to suppose the good are traitors. 615
Rejecting a relation who is loyal
is like rejecting life, our greatest love.
In time you'll know securely without stumbling,
for time alone can prove a just man just,
though you can know a bad man in a day. 620

Choragos: Well said, to one who's anxious not to fall.
Swift thinkers, Lord, are never safe from stumbling.

Oedipus: But when a swift and secret plotter moves
against me, I must make swift counterplot.
If I lie quiet and await his move, 625
he'll have achieved his aims and I'll have missed.

Creon: You surely cannot mean you want me exiled!

Oedipus: Not exiled, no. Your death is what I want!

° **portent reader** Apollo's oracle or prophet.

Creon: If you would first define what envy is . . .
Oedipus: Are you still stubborn? Still disobedient?   630
Creon: I see you cannot think!
Oedipus: For me I can.
Creon: You should for me as well!
Oedipus: But you're a traitor!
Creon: What if you're wrong?
Oedipus: Authority must be maintained.
Creon: Not if the ruler's evil.
Oedipus: Hear that, Thebes!
Creon: It is my city too, not yours alone!   635
Choragos: Please don't, my Lords! Ah, just in time, I see
          Jocasta there, coming from the palace.
          With her help you must settle your quarrel.

Enter Jocasta from the palace.

Jocasta: Wretched men! What has provoked this ill-
          advised dispute? Have you no sense of shame,   640
          with Thebes so sick, to stir up private troubles?
          Now go inside! And Creon, you go home!
          Don't make a general anguish out of nothing!
Creon: My sister, Oedipus your husband here
          sees fit to do one of two hideous things: 645
          to have me banished from the land—or killed!
Oedipus: That's right: I caught him, Lady, plotting harm
          against my person—with a malignant science.
Creon: May my life fail, may I die cursed, if I
          did any of the things you said I did!   650
Jocasta: Believe his words, for the god's sake, Oedipus,
          in deference above all to his oath
          to the gods. Also for me, and for these men!

KOMMOS°

STROPHE 1

Chorus: Consent, with will and mind,
          my king, I beg of you!   655
Oedipus: What do you wish me to surrender?
Chorus: Show deference to him who was not feeble in time past
          and is now great in the power of his oath!
Oedipus: Do you know what you're asking?
Chorus: Yes.
Oedipus: Tell me then.
Chorus: Never to cast into dishonored guilt, with an unproved   660
          assumption, a kinsman who has bound himself by curse.
Oedipus: Now you must understand, when you ask this, you ask my
          death or banishment from the land.

STROPHE 2

Chorus: No, by the god who is the foremost of all gods,
          the Sun! No! Godless,   665
              friendless, whatever death is worst of all,
          let that be my destruction, if this

° **Kommos** A dirge or lament sung by the Chorus and one or more of
   the chief characters.

° **them** The Chorus.

---

          thought ever moved me!
          But my ill-fated soul
              this dying land   670
          wears out—the more if to these older troubles
          she adds new troubles from the two of you!
Oedipus: Then let him go, though it must mean my death,
          or else disgrace and exile from the land.
          My pity is moved by your words, not by his—   675
          he'll only have my hate, wherever he goes.
Creon: You're sullen as you yield; you'll be depressed
          when you've passed through this anger. Natures like yours
          are hardest on themselves. That's as it should be.
Oedipus: Then won't you go and let me be?   680
Creon: I'll go.
          Though you're unreasonable, they know I'm righteous.

Exit Creon.

ANTISTROPHE 1

Chorus: Why are you waiting, Lady?
          Conduct him back into the palace!
Jocasta: I will, when I have heard what chanced.
Chorus: Conjectures—words alone, and nothing based on   685
          thought.
          But even an injustice can devour a man.
Jocasta: Did the words come from both sides?
Chorus: Yes.
Jocasta: What was said?
Chorus: To me it seems enough! enough! the land already
          troubled, that this should rest where it has stopped.
Oedipus: See what you've come to in your honest thought,   690
          in seeking to relax and blunt my heart?

ANTISTROPHE 2

Chorus: I have not said this only once, my Lord.
          That I had lost my sanity,
              without a path in thinking—
          be sure this would be clear   695
              if I put you away
          who, when my cherished land
              wandered crazed
          with suffering, brought her back on course.
          Now, too, be a lucky helmsman!   700
Jocasta: Please, for the god's sake, Lord, explain to me
          the reason why you have conceived this wrath?
Oedipus: I honor you, not them,° and I'll explain
          to you how Creon has conspired against me.
Jocasta: All right, if that will explain how the quarrel started.   705
Oedipus: He says I am the murderer of Laius!
Jocasta: Did he claim knowledge or that someone told him?
Oedipus: Here's what he did: he sent that vicious seer
          so he could keep his own mouth innocent.
Jocasta: Ah then, absolve yourself of what he charges!   710
          Listen to this and you'll agree, no mortal
          is ever given skill in prophecy.
          I'll prove this quickly with one incident.
          It was foretold to Laius—I shall not say
          by Phoebus himself, but by his ministers—   715

that when his fate arrived he would be killed
by a son who would be born to him and me.
And yet, so it is told, foreign robbers
murdered him, at a place where three roads meet.
As for the child I bore him, not three days passed   720
before he yoked the ball-joints of its feet,°
then cast it, by others' hands, on a trackless mountain.
That time Apollo did not make our child
a patricide, or bring about what Laius
feared, that he be killed by his own son.   725
That's how prophetic words determined things!
Forget them. The things a god must track
he will himself painlessly reveal.

Oedipus: Just now, as I was listening to you, Lady,
what a profound distraction seized my mind!   730

Jocasta: What made you turn around so anxiously?

Oedipus: I thought you said that Laius was attacked
and butchered at a place where three roads meet.

Jocasta: That is the story, and it is told so still.

Oedipus: Where is the place where this was done to him?   735

Jocasta: The land's called Phocis, where a two-forked road
comes in from Delphi and from Daulia.

Oedipus: And how much time has passed since these events?

Jocasta: Just prior to your presentation here
as king this news was published to the city.   740

Oedipus: Oh, Zeus, what have you willed to do to me?

Jocasta: Oedipus, what makes your heart so heavy?

Oedipus: No, tell me first of Laius' appearance,
what peak of youthful vigor he had reached.

Jocasta: A tall man, showing his first growth of white.   745
He had a figure not unlike your own.

Oedipus: Alas! It seems that in my ignorance
I laid those fearful curses on myself.

Jocasta: What is it, Lord? I flinch to see your face.

Oedipus: I'm dreadfully afraid the prophet sees.   750
But I'll know better with one more detail.

Jocasta: I'm frightened too. But ask: I'll answer you.

Oedipus: Was his retinue small, or did he travel
with a great troop, as would befit a prince?

Jocasta: There were just five in all, one a herald.   755
There was a carriage, too, bearing Laius.

Oedipus: Alas! Now I see it! But who was it,
Lady, who told you what you know about this?

Jocasta: A servant who alone was saved unharmed.

Oedipus: By chance, could he be now in the palace?   760

Jocasta: No, he is not. When he returned and saw
you had the power of the murdered Laius,
he touched my hand and begged me formally
to send him to the fields and to the pastures,
so he'd be out of sight, far from the city.   765
I did. Although a slave, he well deserved
to win this favor, and indeed far more.

Oedipus: Let's have him called back in immediately.

Jocasta: That can be done, but why do you desire it?

Oedipus: I fear, Lady, I have already said   770
too much. That's why I wish to see him now.

Jocasta: Then he shall come; but it is right somehow
that I, too, Lord, should know what troubles you.

Oedipus: I've gone so deep into the things I feared

I'll tell you everything. Who has a right   775
greater than yours, while I cross through this chance?
Polybus of Corinth was my father,
my mother was the Dorian Meropē.
I was first citizen, until this chance
attacked me—striking enough, to be sure,   780
but not worth all the gravity I gave it.
This: at a feast a man who'd drunk too much
denied, at the wine, I was my father's son.
I was depressed and all that day I barely
held it in. Next day I put the question   785
to my mother and father. They were enraged
at the man who'd let this fiction fly at me.
I was much cheered by them. And yet it kept
grinding into me. His words kept coming back.
Without my mother's or my father's knowledge   790
I went to Pytho. But Phoebus sent me away
dishonoring my demand. Instead, other
wretched horrors he flashed forth in speech.
He said that I would be my mother's lover,
show offspring to mankind they could not look at,   795
and be his murderer whose seed I am.°
When I heard this, and ever since, I gauged
the way to Corinth by the stars alone,
running to a place where I would never see
the disgrace in the oracle's words come true.   800
But I soon came to the exact location
where, as you tell of it, the king was killed.
Lady, here is the truth. As I went on,
when I was just approaching those three roads,
a herald and a man like him you spoke of   805
came on, riding a carriage drawn by colts.
Both the man out front and the old man himself°
tried violently to force me off the road.
The driver, when he tried to push me off,
I struck in anger. The old man saw this, watched   810
me approach, then leaned out and lunged down
with twin prongs° at the middle of my head!
He got more than he gave. Abruptly—struck
once by the staff in this my hand—he tumbled
out, head first, from the middle of the carriage.   815
And then I killed them all. But if there is
a kinship between Laius and this stranger,
who is more wretched than the man you see?
Who was there born more hated by the gods?
For neither citizen nor foreigner   820
may take me in his home or speak to me.
No, they must drive me off. And it is I
who have pronounced these curses on myself!
I stain the dead man's bed with these my hands,
by which he died. Is not my nature vile?   825

° **ball-joints of its feet** The ankles.

° **be . . . am** I would murder my father.

° **old man himself** Laius.

° **lunged . . . prongs** Laius strikes Oedipus with a two-pronged horse
goad, or whip.

Unclean?—if I am banished and even
in exile I may not see my own parents,
or set foot in my homeland, or else be yoked
in marriage to my mother, and kill my father,
Polybus, who raised me and gave me birth?   830
If someone judged a cruel divinity
did this to me, would he not speak the truth?
You pure and awful gods, may I not ever
see that day, may I be swept away
from men before I see so great and so   835
calamitous a stain fixed on my person!

Choragos: These things seem fearful to us, Lord, and yet,
until you hear it from the witness, keep hope!

Oedipus: That is the single hope that's left to me,
to wait for him, that herdsman—until he comes.   840

Jocasta: When he appears, what are you eager for?

Oedipus: Just this: if his account agrees with yours
then I shall have escaped this misery.

Jocasta: But what was it that struck you in my story?

Oedipus: You said he spoke of robbers as the ones   845
who killed him. Now: if he continues still
to speak of many, then I could not have killed him.
One man and many men just do not jibe.
But if he says one belted man, the doubt
is gone. The balance tips toward me. I did it.   850

Jocasta: No! He told it as I told you. Be certain.
He can't reject that and reverse himself.
The city heard these things, not I alone.
But even if he swerves from what he said,
he'll never show that Laius' murder, Lord,   855
occurred just as predicted. For Loxias
expressly said my son was doomed to kill him.
The boy—poor boy—he never had a chance
to cut him down, for he was cut down first.
Never again, just for some oracle   860
will I shoot frightened glances right and left.

Oedipus: That's full of sense. Nonetheless, send a man
to bring that farm hand here. Will you do it?

Jocasta: I'll send one right away. But let's go in.
Would I do anything against your wishes?   865

Exit Oedipus and Jocasta through the central door into the palace.

Stasimon 2

STROPHE 1

Chorus: May there accompany me
the fate to keep a reverential purity in what I say,
in all I do, for which the laws have been set forth

° **Olympus** Mount Olympus, home of the gods, and treated as a god
itself.

° **Earth's navel** Delphi.

° **Abae's** Abae was a town in Phocis where there was another oracle of
Apollo.

° **Olympia** Site of the oracle of Zeus.

and walk on high, born to traverse the brightest,
highest upper air; Olympus° only   870
is their father, nor was it
mortal nature
that fathered them, and never will
oblivion lull them into sleep;
the god in them is great and never ages.   875

ANTISTROPHE 1

The will to violate, seed of the tyrant,
if it has drunk mindlessly of wealth and power,
without a sense of time or true advantage,
mounts to a peak, then
plunges to an abrupt . . . destiny,   880
where the useful foot
is of no use. But the kind
of struggling that is good for the city
I ask the god never to abolish.
The god is my protector: never will I give that up.   885

STROPHE 2

But if a man proceeds disdainfully
in deeds of hand or word
and has no fear of Justice
or reverence for shrines of the divinities
(may a bad fate catch him   890
for his luckless wantonness!),
if he'll not gain what he gains with justice
and deny himself what is unholy,
or if he clings, in foolishness, to the untouchable
(what man, finally, in such an action, will have strength   895
enough to fend off passion's arrows from his soul?),
if, I say, this kind of
deed is held in honor—
why should I join the sacred dance?

ANTISTROPHE 2

No longer shall I visit and revere   900
Earth's navel,° the untouchable,
nor visit Abae's° temple,
or Olympia,°
if the prophecies are not matched by events
for all the world to point to.   905
No, you who hold the power, if you are rightly called
Zeus the king of all, let this matter not escape you
and your ever-deathless rule,
for the prophecies to Laius fade . . .
and men already disregard them;   910
nor is Apollo anywhere
glorified with honors.
Religion slips away.

EPISODE 3

*Enter Jocasta from the palace carrying a branch wound with wool
and a jar of incense. She is attended by two women.*

Jocasta: Lords of the realm, the thought has come to me
　　to visit shrines of the divinities 915
　　with suppliant's branch in hand and fragrant smoke.
　　For Oedipus excites his soul too much
　　with alarms of all kinds. He will not judge
　　the present by the past, like a man of sense.
　　He's at the mercy of all terror-mongers. 920

Jocasta approaches the altar on the right and kneels.

　　Since I can do no good by counseling,
　　Apollo the Lycean!—you are the closest—
　　I come a suppliant, with these my vows,
　　for a cleansing that will not pollute him.
　　For when we see him shaken we are all 925
　　afraid, like people looking at their helmsman.

Enter a Messenger along one of the parodos. He sees Jocasta at the altar and then addresses the Chorus.

Messenger: I would be pleased if you would help me, stranger.
　　Where is the palace of King Oedipus?
　　Or tell me where he is himself, if you know.

Chorus: This is his house, stranger. He is within. 930
　　This is his wife and mother of his children.

Messenger: May she and her family find prosperity,
　　if, as you say, her marriage is fulfilled.

Jocasta: You also, stranger, for you deserve as much
　　for your gracious words. But tell me why you've come. 935
　　What do you wish? Or what have you to tell us?

Messenger: Good news, my Lady, both for your house and
　　husband.

Jocasta: What is your news? And who has sent you to us?

Messenger: I come from Corinth. When you have heard my news
　　you will rejoice, I'm sure—and grieve perhaps. 940

Jocasta: What is it? How can it have this double power?

Messenger: They will establish him their king, so say
　　the people of the land of Isthmia.°

Jocasta: But is old Polybus not still in power?

Messenger: He's not, for death has clasped him in the tomb. 945

Jocasta: What's this? Has Oedipus' father died?

Messenger: If I have lied then I deserve to die.

Jocasta: Attendant! Go quickly to your master,
　　and tell him this.

Exit an Attendant into the palace.

　　　　　　Oracles of the gods!
　　Where are you now? The man whom Oedipus 950
　　fled long ago, for fear that he should kill him—
　　he's been destroyed by chance and not by him!

Enter Oedipus from the palace.

Oedipus: Darling Jocasta, my beloved wife,
　　Why have you called me from the palace?

Jocasta: First hear what this man has to say. Then see 955
　　what the god's grave oracle has come to now!

Oedipus: Where is he from? What is this news he brings me?

Jocasta: From Corinth. He brings news about your father:
　　that Polybus is no more! that he is dead!

Oedipus: What's this, old man? I want to hear you say it. 960

Messenger: If this is what must first be clarified,
　　please be assured that he is dead and gone.

Oedipus: By treachery or by the touch of sickness?

Messenger: Light pressures tip agèd frames into their sleep.

Oedipus: You mean the poor man died of some disease. 965

Messenger: And of the length of years that he had tallied.

Oedipus: Aha! Then why should we look to Pytho's vapors,°
　　or to the birds that scream above our heads?°
　　If we could really take those things for guides,
　　I would have killed my father. But he's dead! 970
　　He is beneath the earth, and here am I,
　　who never touched a spear. Unless he died
　　of longing for me and I "killed" him that way!
　　No, in this case, Polybus, by dying, took
　　the worthless oracle to Hades with him. 975

Jocasta: And wasn't I telling you that just now?

Oedipus: You were indeed. I was misled by fear.

Jocasta: You should not care about this anymore.

Oedipus: I must care. I must stay clear of my mother's bed.

Jocasta: What's there for man to fear? The realm of chance 980
　　prevails. True foresight isn't possible.
　　His life is best who lives without a plan.
　　This marriage with your mother—don't fear it.
　　How many times have men in dreams, too, slept
　　with their own mothers! Those who believe such things 985
　　mean nothing endure their lives most easily.

Oedipus: A fine, bold speech, and you are right, perhaps,
　　except that my mother is still living,
　　so I must fear her, however well you argue.

Jocasta: And yet your father's tomb is a great eye. 990

Oedipus: Illuminating, yes. But I still fear the living.

Messenger: Who is the woman who inspires this fear?

Oedipus: Meropē, Polybus' wife, old man.

Messenger: And what is there about her that alarms you?

Oedipus: An oracle, god-sent and fearful, stranger. 995

Messenger: Is it permitted that another know?

Oedipus: It is. Loxias once said to me
　　I must have intercourse with my own mother
　　and take my father's blood with these my hands.
　　So I have long lived far away from Corinth. 1000
　　This has indeed brought much good luck, and yet,
　　to see one's parents' eyes is happiest.

Messenger: Was it for this that you have lived in exile?

Oedipus: So I'd not be my father's killer, sir.

Messenger: Had I not better free you from this fear, 1005
　　my Lord? That's why I came—to do you service.

Oedipus: Indeed, what a reward you'd get for that!

Messenger: Indeed, this is the main point of my trip,
　　to be rewarded when you get back home.

Oedipus: I'll never rejoin the givers of my seed!° 1010

° **land of Isthmia** Corinth, Greek city-state situated on an isthmus.

° **Pytho's vapors** Prophecies of the oracle at Delphi.

° **birds . . . heads** Prophecies derived from interpreting the flights of birds.

° **givers of my seed** i.e., "my parents." Oedipus still thinks Meropē and Polybus are his parents.

Messenger: My son, clearly you don't know what you're doing.

Oedipus: But how is that, old man? For the gods' sake, tell me!

Messenger: If it's because of them you won't go home.

Oedipus: I fear that Phoebus will have told the truth.

Messenger: Pollution from the ones who gave you seed? 1015

Oedipus: That is the thing, old man, I always fear.

Messenger: Your fear is groundless. Understand that.

Oedipus: Groundless? Not if I was born their son.

Messenger: But Polybus is not related to you.

Oedipus: Do you mean Polybus was not my father? 1020

Messenger: No more than I. We're both the same to you.

Oedipus: Same? One who begot me and one who didn't?

Messenger: He didn't beget you any more than I did.

Oedipus: But then, why did he say I was his son?

Messenger: He got you as a gift from my own hands. 1025

Oedipus: He loved me so, though from another's hands?

Messenger: His former childlessness persuaded him.

Oedipus: But had you bought me, or begotten me?

Messenger: Found you. In the forest hallows of Cithaeron.

Oedipus: What were you doing traveling in that region? 1030

Messenger: I was in charge of flocks which grazed those mountains.

Oedipus: A wanderer who worked the flocks for hire?

Messenger: Ah, but that day I was your savior, son.

Oedipus: From what? What was my trouble when you took me?

Messenger: The ball-joints of your feet might testify. 1035

Oedipus: What's that? What makes you name that ancient trouble?

Messenger: Your feet were pierced and I am your rescuer.

Oedipus: A fearful rebuke those tokens left for me!

Messenger: That was the chance that names you who you are.

Oedipus: By the gods, did my mother or my father do this? 1040

Messenger: That I don't know. He might who gave you to me.

Oedipus: From someone else? You didn't chance on me?

Messenger: Another shepherd handed you to me.

Oedipus: Who was he? Do you know? Will you explain!

Messenger: They called him one of the men of—was it Laius? 1045

Oedipus: The one who once was king here long ago?

Messenger: That is the one! The man was shepherd to him.

Oedipus: And is he still alive so I can see him?

Messenger: But you who live here ought to know that best.

Oedipus: Does any one of you now present know 1050
about the shepherd whom this man has named?
Have you seen him in town or in the fields? Speak out!
The time has come for the discovery!

Choragos: The man he speaks of, I believe, is the same
as the field hand you have already asked to see. 1055
But it's Jocasta who would know this best.

Oedipus: Lady, do you remember the man we just
now sent for—is that the man he speaks of?

Jocasta: What? The man he spoke of? Pay no attention!

His words are not worth thinking about. It's nothing. 1060

Oedipus: With clues like this within my grasp, give up?
Fail to solve the mystery of my birth?

Jocasta: For the love of the gods, and if you love your life,
give up this search! My sickness is enough.

Oedipus: Come! Though my mothers for three generations 1065
were in slavery, you'd not be lowborn!

Jocasta: No, listen to me! Please! Don't do this thing!

Oedipus: I will not listen; I will search out the truth.

Jocasta: My thinking is for you—it would be best.

Oedipus: This "best" of yours is starting to annoy me. 1070

Jocasta: Doomed man! Never find out who you are!

Oedipus: Will someone go and bring that shepherd here?
Leave her to glory in her wealthy birth!

Jocasta: Man of misery! No other name
shall I address you by, ever again. 1075

Exit Jocasta into the palace after a long pause.

Choragos: Why has your lady left, Oedipus,
hurled by a savage grief? I am afraid
disaster will come bursting from this silence.

Oedipus: Let it burst forth! However low this seed
of mine may be, yet I desire to see it. 1080
She, perhaps—she has a woman's pride—
is mortified by my base origins.
But I who count myself the child of Chance,
the giver of good, shall never know dishonor.
She is my mother,° and the months my brothers 1085
who first marked out my lowness, then my greatness.
I shall not prove untrue to such a nature
by giving up the search for my own birth.

STASIMON 3
STROPHE

Chorus: If I have mantic power°
and excellence in thought,
by Olympus, 1090
you shall not, Cithaeron, at tomorrow's
full moon,
fail to hear us celebrate you as the countryman
of Oedipus, his nurse and mother, 1095
or fail to be the subject of our dance,
since you have given pleasure
to our king.
Phoebus, whom we summon by "iḗ!,"
may this be pleasing to you! 1100

ANTISTROPHE

Who was your mother, son?
which of the long-lived nymphs
after lying with Pan,°
the mountain roaming . . . Or was it a bride
of Loxias?° 1105
For dear to him are all the upland pastures.

° **She . . . mother** Chance is my mother.

° **If . . . mantic power** If I am a prophet.

° **Pan** God of shepherds and woodlands, half man and half goat.

° **Loxias** Apollo.

Or was it Mount Cyllēnē's lord,°
or the Bacchic god,°
      dweller of the mountain peaks.
who received you as a joyous find   1110
from one of the nymphs of Helicon.
the favorite sharers of his sport?

EPISODE 4

Oedipus: If someone like myself, who never met him,
      may calculate—elders, I think I see
      the very herdsman we've been waiting for.   1115
      His many years would fit that man's age,
      and those who bring him on, if I am right,
      are my own men. And yet, in real knowledge,
      you can outstrip me, surely: you've seen him.

*Enter the old Herdsman escorted by two of Oedipus's Attendants.
At first, the Herdsman will not look at Oedipus.*

Choragos: I know him, yes, a man of the house of Laius,   1120
      a trusty herdsman if he ever had one.
Oedipus: I ask you first, the stranger come from Corinth:
      is this the man you spoke of?
Messenger: That's he you see.
Oedipus: Then you, old man. First look at me! Now answer:
      did you belong to Laius' household once?   1125
Herdsman: I did. Not a purchased slave but raised in the palace.
Oedipus: How have you spent your life? What is your work?
Herdsman: Most of my life now I have tended sheep.
Oedipus: Where is the usual place you stay with them?
Herdsman: On Mount Cithaeron. Or in that district.   1135
Oedipus: Do you recall observing this man there?
Herdsman: Doing what? Which is the man you mean?
Oedipus: This man right here. Have you had dealings with him?
Herdsman: I can't say right away. I don't remember.
Messenger: No wonder, master. I'll bring clear memory
      to his ignorance. I'm absolutely sure
      he can recall it, the district was Cithaeron,
      he with a double flock, and I, with one,
      lived close to him, for three entire seasons,
      six months along, from spring right to Arcturus.°   1140
      Then for the winter I'd drive mine to my fold,
      and he'd drive his to Laius' pen again.
      Did any of the things I say take place?
Herdsman: You speak the truth, though it's from long ago.
Messenger: Do you remember giving me, back then,   1145
      a boy I was to care for as my own?
Herdsman: What are you saying? Why do you ask me that?
Messenger: There, sir, is the man who was that boy!
Herdsman: Damn you! Shut your mouth! Keep your silence!
Oedipus: Stop! Don't you rebuke his words.   1150
      Your words ask for rebuke far more than his.
Herdsman: But what have I done wrong, most royal master?
Oedipus: Not telling of the boy of whom he asked.
Herdsman: He's ignorant and blundering toward ruin.
Oedipus: Tell it willingly—or under torture.   1155
Herdsman: Oh god! Don't—I am old—don't torture me!

Oedipus: Here! Someone put his hands behind his back!
Herdsman: But why? What else would you find out, poor man?
Oedipus: Did you give him the child he asks about?
Herdsman: I did. I wish that I had died that day!   1160
Oedipus: You'll come to that if you don't speak the truth.
Herdsman: It's if I speak that I shall be destroyed.
Oedipus: I think this fellow struggles for delay.
Herdsman: No, no! I said already that I gave him.
Oedipus: From your own home, or got from someone else?   1165
Herdsman: Not from my own. I got him from another.
Oedipus: Which of these citizens? What sort of house?
Herdsman: Don't—by the gods!—don't, master, ask me more!
Oedipus: It means your death if I must ask again.
Herdsman: One of the children of the house of Laius.   1170
Oedipus: A slave—or born into the family?
Herdsman: I have come to the dreaded thing, and I shall say it.
Oedipus: And I to hearing it, but hear I must.
Herdsman: He was reported to have been—his son.
      Your lady in the house could tell you best.   1175
Oedipus: Because she gave him to you?
Herdsman: Yes, my lord.
Oedipus: What was her purpose?
Herdsman: I was to kill the boy.
Oedipus: The child she bore?
Herdsman: She dreaded prophecies.
Oedipus: What were they?
Herdsman: The word was that he'd kill his parents.
Oedipus: Then why did you give him up to this old man?   1180
Herdsman: In pity, master—so he would take him home,
      to another land. But what he did was save him
      for this supreme disaster. If you are the one
      he speaks of—know your evil birth and fate!
Oedipus: Ah! All of it was destined to be true!   1185
      Oh light, now may I look my last upon you,
      shown monstrous in my birth, in marriage monstrous,
      a murderer monstrous in those I killed.

Exit Oedipus, running into the palace.

STASIMON 4

STROPHE 1

Chorus: Oh generations of mortal men,
      while you are living, I will   1190
            appraise your lives at zero!
      What man
      comes closer to seizing lasting blessedness
      than merely to seize its semblance,
      and after living in this semblance, to plunge?   1195
      With your example before us,
      with your destiny, yours,
            suffering Oedipus, no mortal
      can I judge fortunate.

° **Mount Cyllēnē's lord** Hermes, messenger of the gods.

° **Bacchic god** Dionysus.

° **Arcturus** A star that is first seen in September in the sky over Greece.

ANTISTROPHE 1

For he,° outranging everybody,   1200
shot his arrow° and became the lord
    of wide prosperity and blessedness,
oh Zeus, after destroying
the virgin with the crooked talons,°   1205
singer of oracles; and against death,
in my land, he arose a tower of defense.
From which time you were called my king
and granted privileges supreme—in mighty
Thebes the ruling lord.

STROPHE 2

But now—whose story is more sorrowful than yours?   1210
Who is more intimate with fierce calamities,
with labors, now that your life is altered?
Alas, my Oedipus, whom all men know:
one great harbor°—
one alone sufficed for you,
as son and father,   1215
when you tumbled,° plowman° of the woman's chamber.
How, how could your paternal
    furrows, wretched man,
endure you silently so long.   1220

ANTISTROPHE 2

Time, all-seeing, surprised you living an unwilled life
and sits from of old in judgment on the marriage, not
a marriage,
where the begetter is the begot as well.
Ah, son of Laius . . . ,
would that—oh, would that   1225
I had never seen you!
I wail, my scream climbing beyond itself
from my whole power of voice. To say it straight:
    from you I got new breath—
but I also lulled my eye to sleep.°   1230

EXODOS°

Enter the Second Messenger from the palace.

Second Messenger: You who are first among the citizens,
    what deeds you are about to hear and see!
    What grief you'll carry, if, true to your birth,

° **he** Oedipus.

° **shot his arrow** Took his chances; made a guess at the Sphinx's riddle.

° **virgin . . . talons** The Sphinx.

° **one great harbor** Metaphorical allusion to Jocasta's body.

° **tumbled** Were born and had sex.

° **plowman** Plowing is used here as a sexual metaphor.

° **I . . . sleep** I failed to see the corruption you brought.

° **Exodos** The final scene, containing the play's resolution.

° **ball-joints of his eyes** His eyeballs. Oedipus blinds himself in both eyes at the same time.

---

    you still respect the house of Labdacus!
    Neither the Ister nor the Phasis river   1235
    could purify this house, such suffering
    does it conceal, or soon must bring to light—
    willed this time, not unwilled. Griefs hurt worst
    which we perceive to be self-chosen ones.

Choragos: They were sufficient, the things we knew before,   1240
    to make us grieve. What can you add to those?

Second Messenger: The thing that's quickest said and quickest
    heard:
    our own, our royal one, Jocasta's dead.

Choragos: Unhappy queen! What was responsible?

Second Messenger: Herself. The bitterest of these events   1245
    is not for you, you were not there to see,
    but yet, exactly as I can recall it,
    you'll hear what happened to that wretched lady.
    She came in anger through the outer hall,
    and then she ran straight to her marriage bed,   1250
    tearing her hair with the fingers of both hands.
    Then, slamming shut the doors when she was in,
    she called to Laius, dead so many years,
    remembering the ancient seed which caused
    his death, leaving the mother to the son   1255
    to breed again an ill-born progeny.
    She mourned the bed where she, alas, bred double—
    husband by husband, children by her child.
    From this point on I don't know how she died,
    for Oedipus then burst in with a cry,   1260
    and did not let us watch her final evil.
    Our eyes were fixed on him. Wildly he ran
    to each of us, asking for his spear
    and for his wife—no wife: where he might find
    the double mother-field, his and his children's.   1265
    He raved, and some divinity then showed him—
    for none of us did so who stood close by.
    With a dreadful shout—as if some guide were leading—
    he lunged through the double doors; he bent the hollow
    bolts from the sockets, burst into the room,   1270
    and there we saw her, hanging from above,
    entangled in some twisted hanging strands.
    He saw, was stricken, and with a wild roar
    ripped down the dangling noose. When she, poor woman,
    lay on the ground, there came a fearful sight: 1275
    he snatched the pins of worked gold from her dress,
    with which her clothes were fastened: these he raised
    and struck into the ball-joints of his eyes.°
    He shouted that they would no longer see
    the evils he had suffered or had done,   1280
    see in the dark those he should not have seen,
    and know no more those he once sought to know.
    While chanting this, not once but many times
    he raised his hand and struck into his eyes.
    Blood from his wounded eyes poured down his chin,   1285
    not freed in moistening drops, but all at once
    a stormy rain of black blood burst like hail.
    These evils, coupling them, making them one,
    have broken loose upon both man and wife.
    The old prosperity that they had once   1290
    was true prosperity, and yet today,

mourning, ruin, death, disgrace, and every
evil you could name—not one is absent.

Choragos: Has he allowed himself some peace from all this grief?

Second Messenger: He shouts that someone slide the bolts 1295
and show
to all the Cadmeians the patricide,
his mother's—I can't say it, it's unholy—
so he can cast himself out of the land,
not stay and curse his house by his own curse.
He lacks the strength, though, and he needs a guide, 1300
for his is a sickness that's too great to bear.
Now you yourself will see: the bolts of the doors
are opening. You are about to see
a vision even one who hates must pity.

*Enter the blinded Oedipus from the palace, led in by a household
Servant.*

Choragos: Terrifying suffering for men to see, 1305
more terrifying than any I've ever
come upon. Oh man of pain
what madness reached you? Which god from far off,
surpassing in range his longest spring,
struck hard against your god-abandoned fate? 1310
Oh man of pain,
I cannot look upon you—though there's so much
I would ask you, so much to hear,
so much that holds my eyes—
such is the shudder you produce in me. 1315

Oedipus: Ah! Ah! I am a man of misery.
Where am I carried? Pity me! Where
is my voice scattered abroad on wings?
Divinity, where has your lunge transported me?

Choragos: To something horrible, not to be heard or seen. 1320

KOMMOS

STROPHE 1

Oedipus: Oh, my cloud
of darkness, abominable, unspeakable as it attacks me,
not to be turned away, brought by an evil wind!
Alas! 1325
Again alas! Both enter me at once:
the sting of the prongs,° the memory of evils!

Chorus: I do not marvel that in these afflictions
you carry double griefs and double evils.

ANTISTROPHE 1

Oedipus: Ah, friend,
so you at least are there, resolute servant! 1330
Still with a heart to care for me, the blind man.
Oh! Oh!
I know that you are there. I recognize
even inside my darkness, that voice of yours.

Chorus: Doer of horror, how did you bear to quench 1335
your vision? What divinity raised your hand?

STROPHE 2

Oedipus: It was Apollo there, Apollo, friends,
who brought my sorrows, vile sorrows to their perfection,
these evils that were done to me. 1340
But the one who struck them with his hand,
that one was none but I, in wretchedness.
For why was I to see
when nothing I could see would bring me joy?

Chorus: Yes, that is how it was.

Oedipus: What could I see, indeed, 1345
or what enjoy—what greeting
is there I could hear with pleasure, friends?
Conduct me out of the land
as quickly as you can!
Conduct me out, my friends, 1350
the man utterly ruined,
supremely cursed,
the man who is by gods
the most detested of all men!

Chorus: Wretched in disaster and in knowledge: 1355
oh, I could wish you'd never come to know!

ANTISTROPHE 2

Oedipus: May he be destroyed, whoever freed the savage
shackles
from my feet when I'd been sent to the wild pasture,
whoever rescued me from murder
and became my savior— 1360
a bitter gift:
if I had died then,
I'd not have been such grief to self and kin.

Chorus: I also would have had it so.

Oedipus: I'd not have returned to be my father's 1365
murderer; I'd not be called by men
my mother's bridegroom.
Now I'm without a god,
child of a polluted parent,
fellow progenitor with him
who gave me birth in misery. 1370
If there's an evil that
surpasses evils, that
has fallen to the lot of Oedipus.

Choragos: How can I say that you have counseled well? 1375
Better not to be than live a blind man.

Oedipus: That this was not the best thing I could do—
don't tell me that, or advise me any more!
Should I descend to Hades and endure
to see my father with these eyes? Or see 1380
my poor unhappy mother? For I have done,
to both of these, things too great for hanging.
Or is the sight of children to be yearned for,
to see new shoots that sprouted as these did?
Never, never with these eyes of mine! 1385
Nor city, nor tower, nor holy images

° **prongs** Refers both to the whip that Laius used and to the two gold
pins that Oedipus used to blind himself.

of the divinities! For I, all-wretched,
most nobly raised—as no one else in Thebes—
deprived myself of these when I ordained
that all expel the impious one—god-shown   1390
to be polluted, and the dead king's son!°
Once I exposed this great stain upon me,
could I have looked on these with steady eyes?
No! No! And if there were a way to block
the source of hearing in my ears, I'd gladly   1395
have locked up my pitiable body,
so I'd be blind and deaf. Evils shut out—
that way my mind could live in sweetness.
Alas, Cithaeron, why did you receive me?
Or when you had me, not killed me instantly?   1400
I'd not have had to show my birth to mankind.
Polybus, Corinth, halls—ancestral,
they told me—how beautiful was your ward,
a scar that held back festering disease!
Evil my nature, evil my origin.   1405
You, three roads, and you, secret ravine,
you oak grove, narrow place of those three paths
that drank my blood° from these hands, from him
who fathered me, do you remember still
the things I did to you? When I'd come here,   1410
what I then did once more? Oh marriages! Marriages!
You gave us life and when you'd planted us
you sent the same seed up, and then revealed
fathers, brothers, sons, and kinsman's blood,
and brides, and wives, and mothers, all the most   1415
atrocious things that happen to mankind!
One should not name what never should have been.
Somewhere out there, then, quickly, by the gods,
cover me up, or murder me, or throw me
to the ocean where you will never see me more!   1420

Oedipus moves toward the Chorus and they back away from him.

Come! Don't shrink to touch this wretched man!
Believe me, do not be frightened! I alone
of all mankind can carry these afflictions.

Enter Creon from the palace with Attendants.

Choragos: Tell Creon what you wish for. Just when we
need him
he's here. He can act, he can advise you.   1425
He's now the land's sole guardian in your place.
Oedipus: Ah! Are there words that I can speak to him?
What ground for trust can I present? It's proved
that I was false to him in everything.
Creon: I have not come to mock you, Oedipus,   1430
nor to reproach you for your former falseness.
You men, if you have no respect for sons
of mortals, let your awe for the all-feeding

flames of lordy Hēlius° prevent
your showing unconcealed so great a stain,   1435
abhorred by earth and sacred rain and light.
Escort him quickly back into the house!
If blood kin only see and hear their own
afflictions, we'll have no impious defilement.
Oedipus: By the gods, you've freed me from one terrible 1440
fear,
so nobly meeting my unworthiness:
grant me something—not for me; for you!
Creon: What do you want that you should beg me so?
Oedipus: To drive me from the land at once, to a place
where there will be no man to speak to me!   1445
Creon: I would have done just that—had I not wished
to ask first of the god what I should do.
Oedipus: His answer was revealed in full—that I,
the patricide, unholy, be destroyed.
Creon: He said that, but our need is so extreme,   1450
it's best to have sure knowledge what must be done.
Oedipus: You'll ask about a wretched man like me?
Creon: Is it not time you put your trust in the god?
Oedipus: But I bid you as well, and shall entreat you.
Give her who is within what burial   1455
you will—you'll give your own her proper rites;
but me—do not condemn my fathers' land
to have me dwelling here while I'm alive,
but let me live on mountains—on Cithaeron
famed as mine, for my mother and my father,   1460
while they yet lived, made it my destined tomb,
and I'll be killed by those who wished my ruin!
And yet I know: no sickness will destroy me,
nothing will: I'd never have been saved
when left to die unless for some dread evil.   1465
Then let my fate continue where it will!
As for my children, Creon, take no pains
for my sons—they're men and they will never lack
the means to live, wherever they may be—
but my two wretched, pitiable girls,   1470
who never ate but at my table, never
were without me—everything that I
would touch, they'd always have a share of it—
please care for them! Above all, let me touch
them with my hands and weep aloud my woes!   1475
Please, my Lord!
Please, noble heart! Touching with my hands,
I'd think I held them as when I could see.

Enter Antigone and Ismene from the palace with Attendants.

What's this?
Oh gods! Do I hear, somewhere, my two dear ones   1480
sobbing? Has Creon really pitied me
and sent to me my dearest ones, my children?
Is that it?
Creon: Yes, I prepared this for you, for I knew
you'd feel this joy, as you have always done.   1485
Oedipus: Good fortune, then, and, for your care, be guarded
far better by divinity than I was!

°**I . . . son** Oedipus refers to his own curse against the murderer as well
as his sins of patricide and incest.

°**my blood** i.e., "the blood of my father, Laius."

°**Hēlius** The sun.

Where are you, children? Come to me! Come here
to these my hands, hands of your brother, hands
of him who gave you seed, hands that made
these once bright eyes to see now in this fashion.   1490

Oedipus embraces his daughters.

He, children, seeing nothing, knowing nothing,
he fathered you where his own seed was plowed.
I weep for you as well, though I can't see you,
imagining your bitter life to come,   1495
the life you will be forced by men to live.
What gatherings of townsmen will you join,
what festivals, without returning home
in tears instead of watching holy rites?
And when you've reached the time for marrying,   1500
where, children, is the man who'll run the risk
of taking on himself the infamy
that will wound you as it did my parents?
What evil is not here? Your father killed
his father, plowed the one who gave him birth,   1505
and from the place where he was sown, from there
he got you, from the place he too was born.
These are the wounds: then who will marry you?
No man, my children. No, it's clear that you
must wither in dry barrenness, unmarried.   1510

Oedipus addresses Creon.

Son of Menoeceus! You are the only father
left to them—we two who gave them seed
are both destroyed: watch that they don't become
poor, wanderers, unmarried—they are your kin.
Let not my ruin be their ruin, too!   1515
No, pity them! You see how young they are,
bereft of everyone, except for you.
Consent, kind heart, and touch me with your hand!

Creon grasps Oedipus's right hand.

You, children, if you had reached an age of sense,
I would have counseled much. Now, pray you may live   1520
always where it's allowed, finding a life
better than his was, who gave you seed.

Creon: Stop this now. Quiet your weeping. Move away, into
the house.

Oedipus: Bitter words, but I obey them.
Creon: There's an end to all things.
Oedipus: I have first this request.
Creon: Tell me. I shall judge when I will hear it.   1525
Oedipus: Banish me from my homeland.
Creon: You must ask that of the god.
Oedipus: But I am the gods' most hated man!
Creon: Then you will soon get what you want.
Oedipus: Do you consent?
Creon: I never promise when, as now, I'm ignorant.
Oedipus: Then lead me in.
Creon: Come. But let your hold fall from your children.
Oedipus: Do not take them from me, ever!
Creon: Do not wish to keep all of the power.   1530
You had power, but that power did not follow you through life.

*Oedipus's daughters are taken from him and led into the palace
by Attendants. Oedipus is led into the palace by a Servant.
Creon and the other Attendants follow. Only the Chorus
remains.*

Chorus: People of Thebes, my country, see: here is that Oedipus—
he who "knew" the famous riddle, and attained the highest
power,
whom all citizens admired, even envying his luck!
See the billows of wild troubles which he has entered now!   1535
Here is the truth of each man's life: we must wait, and see
his end,
scrutinize his dying day, and refuse to call him happy
till he has crossed the border of his life without pain.

Exit the Chorus along each of the parados.

Related Works

"Barn Burning" (p. 194), "Young Goodman
Brown" (p. 320), "Leda and the Swan" (p. 475),
Hamlet (p. 644)

 See Chapter 34 Review Card for Reading and Reacting questions
about Sophocles, *Oedipus the King.*

Writing Suggestions: Staging

1. Discuss the problems that the original staging of *Oedipus the King* poses for contemporary audiences, and offer some possible solutions.

2. Discuss and analyze the staging options for a play that is not in this chapter—for example, *Trifles* (p. 555) or *Tape* (p. 543).

3. Choose a short story that appears in this anthology, and explain how you would stage it if it were a play. What furnishings, props, costumes, lighting, and sound effects would you choose? What events would occur offstage? Possible subjects for this paper might include "The Story of an Hour" (p. 115), "A&P" (p. 131), or "The Storm" (p. 154).

 CHECKLIST

WRITING ABOUT STAGING

- ☐ What information about staging is specified in the stage directions of the play?
- ☐ What information about staging is suggested by the play's dialogue?
- ☐ What information about staging is left to the imagination?
- ☐ How might different decisions about staging change the play?
- ☐ Do the stage directions provide information about how characters are supposed to look or behave?
- ☐ What costumes are specified? In what ways do costumes provide insight into the characters who wear them?
- ☐ What props play an important part in the play? Do these props have symbolic meaning?
- ☐ Is the scenery special or unusual in any way?
- ☐ What kind of lighting is specified by the stage directions? In what way does this lighting affect your reaction to the play?
- ☐ How are music and sound effects used in the play? Are musical themes associated with any characters? Do music or sound effects heighten the emotional impact of certain lines?
- ☐ What events occur offstage? Why? How are they suggested?
- ☐ How does staging help to communicate the play's themes?

Glossary Terms

props (short for properties) Pictures, furnishings, and so on that decorate the stage for a play.

stage directions Words in a play that describe an actor's role apart from the dialogue, dealing with movements, attitudes, and so on.

staging Overall production of a play in performance: the sets, costumes, lighting, sound, music, and so on.

35

Theme

Learning Outcomes

After reading this chapter, you should be able to do the following:

LO1 Evaluate titles

LO2 Recognize conflicts

LO3 Evaluate dialogue

LO4 Evaluate characters

LO5 Evaluate staging

Timeline

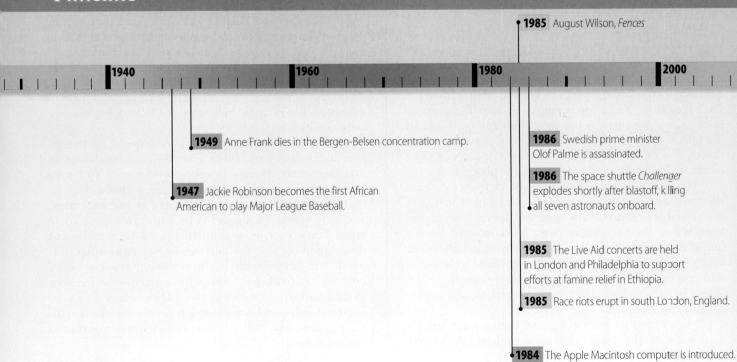

1985 August Wilson, *Fences*

1940   1960   1980   2000

1949 Anne Frank dies in the Bergen-Belsen concentration camp.

1947 Jackie Robinson becomes the first African American to play Major League Baseball.

1986 Swedish prime minister Olof Palme is assassinated.

1986 The space shuttle *Challenger* explodes shortly after blastoff, killing all seven astronauts onboard.

1985 The Live Aid concerts are held in London and Philadelphia to support efforts at famine relief in Ethiopia.

1985 Race riots erupt in south London, England.

1984 The Apple Macintosh computer is introduced.

Like a short story or a novel, a play is open to interpretation. Readers' reactions are influenced by the language of the text, and audiences' reactions are influenced by the performance on stage. Just as in fiction, every element of a play—its title, its conflicts, its dialogue, its characters, and its staging—can shed light on its themes.

EXPLORE ONLINE >

To complete a tutorial of "Theme," visit your Literature CourseMate, accessed through www.cengagebrain.com.

LO1 Evaluate Titles

The **title** of a play can provide insight into its themes. The ironic title of Susan Glaspell's *Trifles* (p. 555), for example, suggests that women's concerns with "trifles" may get to the truth more effectively than the preoccupations of self-important men do. Lorraine Hansberry's *A Raisin in the Sun* is another title that offers clues to the theme of a play. An allusion to Langston Hughes's poem "Harlem" (p. 409)—which asks, "what happens to a dream deferred? / Does it dry up / like a raisin in the sun?"—the title suggests what happens to an African-American family whose dreams are repeatedly crushed. Likewise, the title *Fences* (p. 724) offers clues to a major theme of August Wilson's play, suggesting that the main character is kept from his goals by barriers that are constructed by himself as well as by society. Finally, the title of Anton Chekhov's *The Brute* (p. 532) calls attention to the play's ideas about male-female relationships. The title may refer to Smirnov, who says that he has never liked women—whom he characterizes as "creatures of poetry and romance." Or, it may refer to Mrs. Popov's late husband, to whose memory she has dedicated her life despite the fact that he was unfaithful. Either alternative reinforces the play's tongue-in-cheek characterization of men as "brutes."

LO2 Recognize Conflicts

The unfolding plot of a play—especially the **conflicts** that develop—can reveal the play's themes. In Henrik Ibsen's *A Doll House* (p. 562), for example, at least three major conflicts are present: one between Nora and her husband Torvald, one between Nora and Krogstad (an old acquaintance), and one between Nora and society. Each of these conflicts sheds light on the themes of the play.

Through Nora's conflict with Torvald, Ibsen examines the constraints placed on women and men by marriage in the nineteenth century. Both Nora and Torvald are imprisoned within their respective roles: Nora must be passive and childlike, and Torvald must be proper and always in control. Nora, therefore, expects her husband to be noble and generous and, in a crisis, to sacrifice himself for her. When he fails to live up to her expectations, she is profoundly disillusioned.

Nora's conflict with Krogstad underscores Ibsen's criticisms of the class system in nineteenth-century Norway. At the beginning of the play, Nora finds it "immensely amusing: that we—that Torvald has so much power over . . . people." Krogstad, a bank clerk who is in the employ of Torvald, visits Nora in act 1 to enlist her aid in saving his job. It is clear that she sees him as her social inferior. For example, when Krogstad questions her about a woman with whom he has seen her, she replies, "What makes you think you can cross-examine me, Mr. Krogstad—you, one of my husband's employees?" Nora does not realize that she and Krogstad are, ironically, very much alike: both occupy subordinate positions and therefore have no power to determine their own destinies.

Finally, through Nora's conflict with society, Ibsen examines the destructive nature of the forces that subjugate women. Nineteenth-century society was male dominated. A married woman could not borrow money without her husband's signature, own real estate in her own name, or enter into contracts. In addition, all her assets—including inheritances and trust funds—automatically became the property of her husband at the time of marriage. As a result of her sheltered life, Nora at the beginning of the play is completely unaware of the consequences of her actions. Most readers share Dr. Rank's confusion when he asks Nora, "Why do you laugh at that? Do you have any idea of what society is?" It is Nora's disillusionment at finding out that Torvald and the rest of society are not what she has been led to believe they are that ultimately causes her to rebel. By walking out the door at the end of the play, Nora rejects not only her husband and her children (to whom she has no legal right once she leaves), but also society and its laws.

These three conflicts underscore many of the themes that dominate *A Doll House*. First, the conflicts show that marriage in the nineteenth century imprisons both men and women in narrow, constricting roles. They also show that middle-class Norwegian society is narrow, smug, and judgmental. (Krogstad is looked down upon for a crime years after he committed it, and Nora is looked down upon because she borrows money to save her husband's life.) Finally, the conflicts show that society does not offer individuals—especially women—the freedom to lead happy and fulfilling lives. Only when the social and economic conditions that govern society change, Ibsen suggests, can both women and men live together in mutual esteem.

LO3 Evaluate Dialogue

Dialogue can also give insight into a play's themes. Sometimes a character suggests—or even explicitly states—a theme. In act 3 of *A Doll House*, for example, Nora's friend, Mrs. Linde, comes as close as any character to expressing the central concern of the play when she says, "Helmer's got to learn everything; this dreadful secret has to be aired; those two have to come to a full understanding; all these lies can't go on." As the play goes on to demonstrate, the lies that exist both in marriage and in society are obstacles to love and happiness.

One of the main themes of Arthur Miller's *Death of a Salesman* (p. 605)—the questionable validity of the American Dream, given the nation's social, political, and economic realities—is suggested by the play's dialogue. As his son Biff points out, Willy Loman's stubborn belief in upward mobility and material success is based more on fantasy than on fact:

WILLY: (*with hatred, threatening*) The door of your life is wide open!

BIFF: Pop! I am a dime a dozen, and so are you!

WILLY: (*turning on him now in an uncontrolled outburst*) I am not a dime a dozen! I am Willy Loman, and you are Biff Loman!

Biff starts for Willy, but is blocked by Happy. In his fury, Biff seems on the verge of attacking his father.

BIFF: I am not a leader of men, Willy, and neither are you. You were never anything but a hard-working drummer who landed in the ash can like all the rest of them! I'm one dollar an hour, Willy! I tried seven states and couldn't raise it. A buck an hour! Do you gather my meaning? I'm not bringing home any prizes any more, and you're going to stop waiting for me to bring them home!

Although it does not explicitly state the theme of the play, this exchange strongly suggests that Biff rejects the desperate optimism to which Willy clings.

LO4 Evaluate Characters

Because a dramatic work focuses on a central character, or **protagonist,** the development of this character can shed light on a play's themes. Willy Loman in *Death of a Salesman* is developed in great detail. At the beginning of the play, he feels trapped, exhausted, and estranged from his surroundings. As Willy gradually sinks from depression into despair, the action of the play shifts from the present to the past, showing the events that shaped his life. His attitudes, beliefs, dreams, and dashed hopes reveal him to be an embodiment of the major theme of the play—that an unquestioning belief in the American Dream of success is unrealistic and possibly destructive.

Nora in *A Doll House* changes a great deal during the course of the play. At the beginning, she is more her husband's possession than an adult capable of shaping her own destiny. Nora's status becomes apparent in the first act when Torvald gently scolds his "little spendthrift" and refers to her as his "little lark" and his "squirrel." She is reduced to childish deceptions, such as hiding her macaroons when her husband enters the room. After Krogstad accuses her of committing forgery and threatens to expose her, she expects her husband to rise to the occasion and take the blame for her. When Torvald instead accuses her of being a hypocrite, a liar, and a criminal, Nora's neat little world comes crashing down. As a result of this experience, Nora changes; no longer is she the submissive and obedient wife. Instead, she becomes assertive—even rebellious—ultimately telling Torvald that their marriage is a sham and that she can no longer stay with him. This abrupt shift in Nora's personality gives the audience a clear understanding of the major themes of the play.

Unlike Willy and Nora, Laura in Tennessee Williams's *The Glass Menagerie* is a character who changes very little during the course of the play. Laura suffers from such pathological shyness that she is unable to attend typing class, let alone talk to a potential suitor. Although the "gentleman caller" draws her out of her shell for a short time, she soon withdraws again. Laura's inability to change reinforces the play's theme that contemporary society, with its emphasis on progress, has no place for people like her who live in private worlds "of glass animals and old, worn-out phonograph records."

LO5 Evaluate Staging

Various staging elements, such as props and furnishings, may also convey the themes of a play. In *Death of a Salesman*, Biff's trophy, which is constantly in the audience's view, is a prop that ironically underscores the futility of Willy's efforts to achieve success. Similarly, the miniature animals in *The Glass Menagerie* suggest the fragility of Laura's character and the futility of her efforts to fit into the modern world. And, in *Trifles*, the depressing farm house, the broken birdcage, and the dead canary hint at Mrs. Wright's misery and the reason she murdered her husband.

Special lighting effects and music can also suggest a play's themes. Throughout *The Glass Menagerie*, for example, words and pictures are projected onto a section of the set between the front room and dining room walls. In scene 1, as Tom's mother, Amanda, tells him about her experiences with her "gentlemen callers," an image of her as a girl greeting callers appears on the screen. As Amanda continues, the words *"Où sont Les Neiges"*—"Where are the snows [of yesteryear]?"—appear on the screen. Later in the play, when Laura and her mother discuss a boy Laura knew, his picture is projected on the screen, showing him as a high school hero carrying a silver cup. In addition to the slides, Williams uses music—a recurring tune, dance music, and "Ave Maria"—to increase the emotional impact of certain scenes. He also uses shafts of light focused on selected areas or characters to create a dreamlike atmosphere for the play. Collectively, the slides, music, and lighting reinforce the theme that those who retreat into the past inevitably become estranged from the present.

A Final Note

As you read, your own values and beliefs influence your interpretation of a play's themes. For instance, your interest in the changing status of women could lead you to focus on the submissive, almost passive, role of Willy's wife, Linda, in *Death of a Salesman*. As a result, you could conclude that the play shows how, in the post–World War II United States, women like Linda often sacrificed their own happiness for that of their husbands. Remember, however, that the play itself, not just your own feelings or assumptions about it, must support your interpretation.

August Wilson (1945–2005)

was born in Pittsburgh, Pennsylvania, to a German immigrant father and a black mother and lived in the African American neighborhood known as the Hill District. After leaving school at fifteen when he was accused of plagiarizing a paper, he participated in the Black Arts movement in Pittsburgh, submitting poems to local African American publications. In 1969, Wilson and his friend Rob Penny founded the Black Horizons Theatre Company, for which Wilson produced and directed plays. Although Wilson wrote plays while living in Pittsburgh, his work began to gain recognition only after 1978, when he moved to St. Paul, Minnesota. There, in 1982, Lloyd Richards, dean of the Yale School of Drama and artistic director of the Yale Repertory Company, staged a performance of Wilson's *Ma Rainey's Black Bottom*.

Wilson's achievement was epic. Beginning with *Ma Rainey's Black Bottom* in 1984, he wrote a ten-play cycle that chronicled the African American experience in the United States decade by decade. In addition to *Ma Rainey's Black Bottom,* a Tony Award winner, the plays in this cycle include *Fences* (1985), which won a Pulitzer Prize in 1987; *Joe Turner's Come and Gone* (1986); *Two Trains Running* (1989), which won Wilson his fifth New York Drama Critics Circle Award; *The Piano Lesson* (1987), which won a second Pulitzer Prize for Wilson in 1990; *Seven Guitars* (1996); and *Radio Golf*, the last play in the cycle, which opened in 2005, the year of Wilson's death. To honor his achievements, Broadway's Virginia Theater was renamed the August Wilson Theater.

Fences explores how the long-upheld color barrier in professional baseball affected the main character, Troy, who struggles with the pain of never realizing his dream of becoming a big-league player. Throughout the play, Troy retreats behind literal and figurative barriers that impair his relationships with his family.

Fences (1985)

CHARACTERS

Troy Maxson
Jim Bono, *Troy's friend*
Rose, *Troy's wife*
Lyons, *Troy's oldest son by previous marriage*

Gabriel, *Troy's brother*
Cory, *Troy and Rose's son*
Raynell, *Troy's daughter*

SETTING

The setting is the yard which fronts the only entrance to the Maxson household, an ancient two-story brick house set back off a small alley in a big-city neighborhood. The entrance to the house is gained by two or three steps leading to a wooden porch badly in need of paint. A relatively recent addition to the house and running its full width, the porch lacks congruence. It is a sturdy porch with a flat roof. One or two chairs of dubious value sit at one end where the kitchen window opens onto the porch. An old-fashioned icebox stands silent guard at the opposite end.
The yard is a small dirt yard, partially fenced, except for the last scene, with a wooden sawhorse, a pile of lumber, and other fence-building equipment set off to the side. Opposite is a tree from which hangs a ball made of rags. A baseball bat leans against the tree. Two oil drums serve as garbage receptacles and sit near the house at right to complete the setting.

Near the turn of the century, the destitute of Europe sprang on the city with tenacious claws and an honest and solid dream. The city devoured them. They swelled its belly until it burst into a thousand furnaces and sewing machines, a thousand butcher shops and bakers' ovens, a thousand churches and hospitals and funeral parlors and money-lenders. The city grew. It nourished itself and offered each man a partnership limited only by his talent, his guile, and his willingness and capacity for hard work. For the immigrants of Europe, a dream dared and won true.

The descendants of African slaves were offered no such welcome or participation. They came from places called the Carolinas and the Virginias, Georgia, Alabama, Mississippi, and Tennessee. They came strong, eager, searching. The city rejected them and they fled and settled along the riverbanks and under bridges in shallow, ramshackle houses made of sticks and tarpaper. They collected rags and wood. They sold the use of their muscles and their bodies. They cleaned houses and washed clothes, they shined shoes, and in quiet desperation and vengeful pride, they stole, and lived in pursuit of their own dream. That they could breathe free, finally, and stand to meet life with the force of dignity and whatever eloquence the heart could call upon.

By 1957, the hard-won victories of the European immigrants had solidified the industrial might of America. War had been confronted and won with new energies that used loyalty and patriotism as its fuel. Life was rich, full, and flourishing. The Milwaukee Braves won the World Series, and the hot winds of change that would make the sixties a turbulent, racing, dangerous, and provocative decade had not yet begun to blow full.

Cultural Context

The history of African Americans in baseball began in the period between emancipation and the civil rights movement. Banned from professional baseball by segregationist laws, African American players formed the Negro Leagues, with stars such as Satchel Paige and Josh Gibson emerging in the 1930s. Then, in 1946, Branch Rickey, the club president and general manager of the Brooklyn Dodgers, changed everything when he set out to sign the Negro Leagues' top players to his team. The first player he chose was Jackie Robinson, who broke the racial barrier and debuted at first base for the Dodgers on April 15, 1947, at the age of 28. Robinson's phenomenal performance earned him the Rookie of the Year award. In 1957, the year in which *Fences* s set, Robinson announced his retirement from baseball after he was traded to the New York Giants. In 1962, he was inducted into the Baseball Hall of Fame.

ACT 5
SCENE 1

It is 1957. Troy and Bono enter the yard, engaged in conversation. Troy is fifty-three years old, a large man with thick, heavy hands; it is this largeness that he strives to fill out and make an accommodation with. Together with his blackness, his largeness informs his sensibilities and the choices he has made in his life.

Of the two men, Bono is obviously the follower. His commitment to their friendship of thirty-odd years is rooted in his admiration of Troy's honesty, capacity for hard work, and his strength, which Bono seeks to emulate.

It is Friday night, payday, and the one night of the week the two men engage in a ritual of talk and drink. Troy is usually the most talkative and at times he can be crude and almost vulgar, though he is capable of rising to profound heights of expression. The men carry lunch buckets and wear or carry burlap aprons and are dressed in clothes suitable to their jobs as garbage collectors.

Bono: Troy, you ought to stop that lying!

Troy: I ain't lying! The nigger had a watermelon this big. *(He indicates with his hands.)* Talking about . . . "What watermelon, Mr. Rand?" I liked to fell out! "What watermelon, Mr. Rand?" . . . And it sitting there big as life.

Bono: What did Mr. Rand say?

Troy: Ain't said nothing. Figure if the nigger too dumb to know he carrying a watermelon, he wasn't gonna get much sense out of him. Trying to hide that great big old watermelon under his coat. Afraid to let the white man see him carry it home.

Bono: I'm like you . . . I ain't got no time for them kind of people.

Troy: Now what he look like getting mad 'cause he see the man from the union talking to Mr. Rand?

Bono: He come to me talking about . . . "Maxson gonna get us fired." I told him to get away from me with that. He walked away from me calling you a trouble-maker. What Mr. Rand say?

Troy: Ain't said nothing. He told me to go down the Commissioner's office next Friday. They called me down there to see them.

Bono: Well, as long as you got your complaint filed, they can't fire you. That's what one of them white fellows tell me.

Troy: I ain't worried about them firing me. They gonna fire me 'cause I asked a question? That's all I did. I went to Mr. Rand and asked him, "Why? Why you got the white mens driving and the colored lifting?" Told him, "what's the matter, don't I count? You think only white fellows got sense enough to drive a truck. That ain't no paper job! Hell, anybody can drive a truck. How come you got all whites driving and the colored lifting?" He told me "take it to the union." Well, hell, that's what I done! Now they wanna come up with this pack of lies.

Bono: I told Brownie if the man come and ask him any questions . . . just tell the truth! It ain't nothing but something they done trumped up on you 'cause you filed a complaint on them.

Troy: Brownie don't understand nothing. All I want them to do is change the job description. Give everybody a chance to drive the truck. Brownie can't see that. He ain't got that much sense.

Bono: How you figure he be making out with that gal be up at Taylors' all the time . . . that Alberta gal?

Troy: Same as you and me. Getting just as much as we is. Which is to say nothing.

Bono: It is, huh? I figure you doing a little better than me 15 . . . and I ain't saying what I'm doing.

Troy: Aw, nigger, look here . . . I know you. If you had got anywhere near that gal, twenty minutes later you be looking to tell somebody. And the first one you gonna tell . . . that you gonna want to brag to . . . is me.

Bono: I ain't saying that. I see where you be eyeing her.

Troy: I eye all the women. I don't miss nothing. Don't never let nobody tell you Troy Maxson don't eye the women.

Bono: You been doing more than eyeing her. You done bought her a drink or two.

Troy: Hell yeah, I bought her a drink! What that mean? I 20 bought you one, too. What that mean 'cause I buy her a drink? I'm just being polite.

Bono: It's all right to buy her one drink. That's what you call being polite. But when you wanna be buying two or three . . . that's what you call eyeing her.

Troy: Look here, as long as you known me . . . you ever known me to chase after women?

Bono: Hell yeah! Long as I done known you. You forgetting I knew you when.

Troy: Naw, I'm talking about since I been married to Rose?

Bono: Oh, not since you been married to Rose. Now, 25 that's the truth, there. I can say that.

Troy: All right then! Case closed.

Bono: I see you be walking up around Alberta's house. You supposed to be at Taylors' and you be walking up around there.

Troy: What you watching where I'm walking for? I ain't watching after you.

Bono: I seen you walking around there more than once.

Troy: Hell, you liable to see me walking anywhere! That 30 don't mean nothing cause you see me walking around there.

Bono: Where she come from anyway? She just kinda showed up one day.

Troy: Tallahassee. You can look at her and tell she one of them Florida gals. They got some big healthy women down there. Grow them right up out the ground. Got a little bit of Indian in her. Most of them niggers down in Florida got some Indian in them.

Bono: I don't know about that Indian part. But she damn sure big and healthy. Woman wear some big stockings. Got them great big old legs and hips as wide as the Mississippi River.

Troy: Legs don't mean nothing. You don't do nothing but push them out of the way. But them hips cushion the ride!

Bono: Troy, you ain't got no sense. 35

Troy: It's the truth! Like you riding on Goodyears!

Rose enters from the house. She is ten years younger than Troy, her devotion to him stems from her recognition of the possibilities of her life without him: a succession of abusive men and their babies, a life of partying and running the streets, the Church, or aloneness with its attendant pain and frustration. She recognizes Troy's spirit as a fine and illuminating one and she either ignores or forgives his faults, only some of which she

>> Viola Davis as Rose and Denzel Washington as Troy in 2010 Broadway production

recognizes. Though she doesn't drink, her presence is an integral part of the Friday night rituals. She alternates between the porch and the kitchen, where supper preparations are under way.

Rose: What you all out here getting into?

Troy: What you worried about what we getting into for? This is men talk, woman.

Rose: What I care what you all talking about? Bono, you gonna stay for supper?

Bono: No, I thank you, Rose. But Lucille say she cooking 40 up a pot of pigfeet.

Troy: Pigfeet! Hell, I'm going home with you! Might even stay the night if you got some pigfeet. You got something in there to top them pigfeet, Rose?

Rose: I'm cooking up some chicken. I got some chicken and collard greens.°

Troy: Well, go on back in the house and let me and Bono finish what we was talking about. This is men talk. I got some talk for you later. You know what kind of talk I mean. You go on and powder it up.

Rose: Troy Maxson, don't you start that now!

Troy: *(puts his arm around her)* Aw, woman . . . come 45 here. Look here, Bono . . . when I met this woman . . . I got out that place, say, "Hitch up my pony, saddle up my mare . . . there's a woman out there for me somewhere. I looked here. Looked there. Saw Rose and latched on to her." I latched on to her and told her—I'm gonna tell you the truth—I told her, "Baby, I don't wanna marry, I just wanna be your man." Rose told me . . . tell him what you told me, Rose.

Rose: I told him if he wasn't the marrying kind, then move out the way so the marrying kind could find me.

Troy: That's what she told me. "Nigger, you in my way. You blocking the view! Move out the way so I can find me a husband." I thought it over two or three days. Come back—

Rose: Ain't no two or three days nothing. You was back the same night.

Troy: Come back, told her . . . "Okay, baby . . . but I'm gonna buy me a banty rooster and put him out there in the backyard . . . and when he see a stranger come, he'll flap his wings and crow . . ." Look here, Bono, I could watch the front door by myself . . . it was that back door I was worried about.

Rose: Troy, you ought not talk like that. Troy ain't doing 50 nothing but telling a lie.

Troy: Only thing is . . . when we first got married . . . forget the rooster . . . we ain't had no yard!

Bono: I hear you tell it. Me and Lucille was staying down there on Logan Street. Had two rooms with the outhouse in the back. I ain't mind the outhouse none. But when that goddamn wind blow through there in the winter . . . that's what I'm talking about! To this day I wonder why in the hell I ever stayed down there for six long years. But see, I didn't know I could do no

>> Denzel Washington as Troy and Stephen McKinley Henderson as Jim Bono in 2010 Broadway production

better. I thought only white folks had inside toilets and things.

Rose: There's a lot of people don't know they can do no better than they doing now. That's just something you got to learn. A lot of folks still shop at Bella's.

Troy: Ain't nothing wrong with shopping at Bella's. She got fresh food.

Rose: I ain't said nothing about if she got fresh food. I'm 55 talking about what she charge. She charge ten cents more than the A&P.

Troy: The A&P ain't never done nothing for me. I spends my money where I'm treated right. I go down to Bella, say, "I need a loaf of bread, I'll pay you Friday." She give it to me. What sense that make when I got money to go and spend it somewhere else and ignore the person who done right by me? That ain't in the Bible.

Rose: We ain't talking about what's in the Bible. What sense it make to shop there when she overcharge?

Troy: You shop where you want to. I'll do my shopping where the people been good to me.

Rose: Well, I don't think it's right for her to overcharge. That's all I was saying.

Bono: Look here . . . I got to get on. Lucille going be 60 raising all kind of hell.

Troy: Where you going, nigger? We ain't finished this pint. Come here, finish this pint.

Bono: Well, hell, I am . . . if you ever turn the bottle loose.

Troy: *(hands him the bottle)* The only thing I say about the A&P is I'm glad Cory got that job down there. Help him take care of his school clothes and things. Gabe done moved out and things getting tight around here. He got that job . . . He can start to look out for himself.

° **collard greens** A leafy green vegetable.

> *"You can't tell me nothing about death. Death ain't nothing but a fastball on the outside corner. "*

Rose: Cory done went and got recruited by a college football team.

Troy: I told that boy about that football stuff. The white man ain't gonna let him get nowhere with that football. I told him when he first come to me with it. Now you come telling me he done went and got more tied up in it. He ought to go and get recruited in how to fix cars or something where he can make a living.

Rose: He ain't talking about making no living playing football. It's just something the boys in school do. They gonna send a recruiter by to talk to you. He'll tell you he ain't talking about making no living playing football. It's a honor to be recruited.

Troy: It ain't gonna get him nowhere. Bono'll tell you that.

Bono: If he be like you in the sports . . . he's gonna be all right. Ain't but two men ever played baseball as good as you. That's Babe Ruth° and Josh Gibson.° Them's the only two men ever hit more home runs than you.

Troy: What it ever get me? Ain't got a pot to piss in or a window to throw it out of.

Rose: Times have changed since you was playing baseball, Troy. That was before the war. Times have changed a lot since then.

Troy: How in hell they done changed?

Rose: They got lots of colored boys playing ball now. Baseball and football.

Bono: You right about that, Rose. Times have changed, Troy. You just come along too early.

Troy: There ought not never have been no time called too early! Now you take that fellow . . . what's that fellow they had playing right field for the Yankees back then? You know who I'm talking about, Bono. Used to play right field for the Yankees.

Rose: Selkirk?

Troy: Selkirk! That's it! Man batting .269, understand? .269. What kind of sense that make? I was hitting .432 with thirty-seven home runs! Man batting .269 and playing right field for the Yankees! I saw Josh Gibson's daughter yesterday. She walking around with raggedy shoes on her feet. Now I bet you Selkirk's daughter ain't walking around with raggedy shoes on her feet! I bet you that!

Rose: They got a lot of colored baseball players now. Jackie Robinson° was the first. Folks had to wait for Jackie Robinson.

Troy: I done seen a hundred niggers play baseball better than Jackie Robinson. Hell, I know some teams Jackie Robinson couldn't even make! What you talking about Jackie Robinson. Jackie Robinson wasn't nobody. I'm talking about if you could play ball then they ought to have let you play. Don't care what color you were. Come telling me I come along too early. If you could play . . . then they ought to have let you play.

Troy takes a long drink from the bottle.

Rose: You gonna drink yourself to death. You don't need to be drinking like that.

Troy: Death ain't nothing. I done seen him. Done wrassled with him. You can't tell me nothing about death. Death ain't nothing but a fastball on the outside corner. And you know what I'll do to that! Lookee here, Bono . . . am I lying? You get one of them fastballs, about waist high, over the outside corner of the plate where you can get the meat of the bat on it . . . and good god! You can kiss it goodbye. Now, am I lying?

Bono: Naw, you telling the truth there. I seen you do it.

Troy: If I'm lying . . . that 450 feet worth of lying! *(Pause.)* That's all death is to me. A fastball on the outside corner.

Rose: I don't know why you want to get on talking about death.

Troy: Ain't nothing wrong with talking about death. That's part of life. Everybody gonna die. You gonna die, I'm gonna die. Bono's gonna die. Hell, we all gonna die.

Rose: But you ain't got to talk about it. I don't like to talk about it.

Troy: You the one brought it up. Me and Bono was talking about baseball . . . you tell me I'm gonna drink myself to death. Ain't that right, Bono? You know I don't drink this but one night out of the week. That's Friday night. I'm gonna drink just enough to where I can handle it. Then I cuts it loose. I leave it alone. So don't you worry about me drinking myself to death. 'Cause I ain't worried about Death. I done seen him. I done wrestled with him.

Look here, Bono . . . I looked up one day and Death was marching straight at me. Like Soldiers on Parade! The Army of Death was marching straight at me. The middle of July, 1941. It got real cold just like it be winter. It seem like Death himself reached out and touched me on the shoulder. He touch me just like I touch you. I got cold as ice and Death standing there grinning at me.

Rose: Troy, why don't you hush that talk.

Troy: I say . . . what you want, Mr. Death? You be wanting me? You done brought your army to be getting me? I

° **Babe Ruth** George Herman Ruth (1895–1948), American baseball player. He played for the New York Yankees during the 1910s and 1920s and is remembered for his home-run hitting and flamboyant lifestyle.

° **Josh Gibson** (1911–1947), American baseball player. He played between the Negro Leagues between the 1920s and 1940s and was known as "the Negro Babe Ruth." An unwritten rule against hiring black players kept him out of the major leagues.

° **Jackie Robinson** John Roosevelt Robinson (1919–1972). He became the first African American to play major-league baseball when he was hired by the Brooklyn Dodgers in 1947.

>> Mary Alice as Rose, Ray Aranha as Jim Bono, and James Earl Jones as Troy in 1987 Broadway production

looked him dead in the eye. I wasn't fearing nothing. I was ready to tangle. Just like I'm ready to tangle now. The Bible say be ever vigilant. That's why I don't get but so drunk. I got to keep watch.

Rose: Troy was right down there in Mercy Hospital. You remember he had pneumonia? Laying there with a fever talking plumb out of his head.

Troy: Death standing there staring at me . . . carrying that   90
sickle in his hand. Finally he say, "You want bound over for another year?" See, just like that . . . "You want bound over for another year?" I told him, "Bound over hell! Let's settle this now!"

It seem like he kinda fell back when I said that, and all the cold went out of me. I reached down and grabbed that sickle and threw it just as far as I could throw it . . . and me and him commenced to wrestling.

We wrestled for three days and three nights. I can't say where I found the strength from. Every time it seemed like he was gonna get the best of me, I'd reach way down deep inside myself and find the strength to do him one better.

Rose: Every time Troy tell that story he find different ways to tell it. Different things to make up about it.

Troy: I ain't making up nothing. I'm telling you the facts of what happened. I wrestled with Death for three days and three nights and I'm standing here to tell you about it. *(Pause.)* All right. At the end of the third night we done weakened each other to where we can't hardly move. Death stood up, throwed on his robe . . . had him a white robe with a hood on it. He throwed on that robe and went off to look for his sickle. Say, "I'll be back." Just like that. "I'll be back." I told him, say, "Yeah, but . . . you gonna have to find me!" I wasn't no fool. I wan't going looking for him. Death ain't nothing to play with. And I know he's gonna get me. I know I got to join his army . . . his camp followers. But as long as I keep my strength and see him coming . . . as long as I keep up my vigilance . . . he's gonna have to fight to get me. I ain't going easy.

Bono: Well, look here, since you got to keep up your vigilance . . . let me have the bottle.

Troy: Aw hell, I shouldn't have told you that part. I should have left out that part.

Rose: Troy be talking that stuff and half the time don't   95
even know what he be talking about.

Troy: Bono know me better than that.

Bono: That's right. I know you. I know you got some Uncle Remus° in your blood. You got more stories than the devil got sinners.

Troy: Aw hell, I done seen him too! Done talked with the devil.

Rose: Troy, don't nobody wanna be hearing all that stuff.

Lyons enters the yard from the street. Thirty-four years old, Troy's son by a previous marriage, he sports a neatly trimmed goatee, sport coat, white shirt, tieless and buttoned at the collar. Though he fancies himself a musician, he is more caught up in the rituals and "idea" of being a musician than in the actual practice of the music. He has come to borrow money from Troy, and while he knows he will be successful, he is uncertain as to what extent his lifestyle will be held up to scrutiny and ridicule.

Lyons: Hey, Pop.   100

Troy: What you come "Hey, Popping" me for?

Lyons: How you doing, Rose? *(He kisses her.)* Mr. Bono. How you doing?

Bono: Hey, Lyons . . . how you been?

Troy: He must have been doing all right. I ain't seen him around here last week.

Rose: Troy, leave your boy alone. He come by to see you   105
and you wanna start all that nonsense.

Troy: I ain't bothering Lyons. *(Offers him the bottle.)* Here . . . get you a drink. We got an understanding. I know why he come by to see me and he know I know.

Lyons: Come on, Pop . . . I just stopped by to say hi . . . see how you was doing.

Troy: You ain't stopped by yesterday.

Rose: You gonna stay for supper, Lyons? I got some   110
chicken cooking in the oven.

Lyons: No, Rose . . . thanks. I was just in the neighborhood and thought I'd stop by for a minute.

Troy: You was in the neighborhood all right, nigger. You telling the truth there. You was in the neighborhood cause it's my payday.

Lyons: Well, hell, since you mentioned it . . . let me have ten dollars.

Troy: I'll be damned! I'll die and go to hell and play blackjack with the devil before I give you ten dollars.

° **Uncle Remus** The fictional narrator of *Uncle Remus: His Songs and His Sayings* (1880) and a number of sequels by Joel Chandler Harris. Uncle Remus tells tales about characters such as Brer Rabbit and the Tarbaby in exaggerated dialect, now widely considered to be a derogatory representation of African Americans.

Bono: That's what I wanna know about . . . that devil you done seen. 115

Lyons: What . . . Pop done seen the devil? You too much, Pops.

Troy: Yeah, I done seen him. Talked to him too!

Rose: You ain't seen no devil. I done told you that man ain't had nothing to do with the devil. Anything you can't understand, you want to call it the devil.

Troy: Look here, Bono . . . I went down to see Hertzberger about some furniture. Got three rooms for two-ninety-eight. That what it say on the radio. "Three rooms . . . two-ninety-eight." Even made up a little song about it. Go down there . . . man tell me I can't get no credit. I'm working every day and can't get no credit. What to do? I got an empty house with some raggedy furniture in it. Cory ain't got no bed. He's sleeping on a pile of rags on the floor. Working every day and can't get no credit. Come back here—Rose'll tell you—madder than hell. Sit down . . . try to figure what I'm gonna do. Come a knock on the door. Ain't been living here but three days. Who know I'm here? Open the door . . . devil standing there bigger than life. White fellow . . . white fellow . . . got on good clothes and everything. Standing there with a clipboard in his hand. I ain't had to say nothing. First words come out of his mouth was . . . "I understand you need some furniture and can't get no credit." I liked to fell over. He say, "I'll give you all the credit you want, but you got to pay the interest on it." I told him, "Give me three rooms worth and charge whatever you want." Next day a truck pulled up here and two men unloaded them three rooms. Man what drove the truck give me a book. Say send ten dollars, first of every month to the address in the book and everything will be all right. Say if I miss a payment the devil was coming back and it'll be hell to pay. That was fifteen years ago. To this day . . . the first of the month I send my ten dollars, Rose'll tell you.

Rose: Troy lying. 120

Troy: I ain't never seen that man since. Now you tell me who else that could have been but the devil? I ain't sold my soul or nothing like that, you understand. Naw, I wouldn't have truck with the devil about nothing like that. I got my furniture and pays my ten dollars the first of the month just like clockwork.

Bono: How long you say you been paying this ten dollars a month?

Troy: Fifteen years!

Bono: Hell, ain't you finished paying for it yet? How much the man done charged you?

Troy: Ah hell, I done paid for it. I done paid for it ten 125 times over! The fact is I'm scared to stop paying it.

Rose: Troy lying. We got that furniture from Mr. Glickman. He ain't paying no ten dollars a month to nobody.

Troy: Aw hell, woman. Bono know I ain't that big a fool.

Lyons: I was just getting ready to say . . . I know where there's a bridge for sale.

Troy: Look here, I'll tell you this . . . it don't matter to me if he was the devil. It don't matter if the devil give credit. Somebody has got to give it.

Rose: It ought to matter. You going around talking about 130 having truck with the devil . . . God's the one you gonna have to answer to. He's the one gonna be at the Judgment.

Lyons: Yeah, well, look here, Pop . . . let me have that ten dollars. I'll give it back to you. Bonnie got a job working at the hospital.

Troy: What I tell you, Bono? The only time I see this nigger is when he wants something. That's the only time I see him.

Lyons: Come on, Pop, Mr. Bono don't want to hear all that. Let me have the ten dollars. I told you Bonnie working.

Troy: What that mean to me? "Bonnie working." I don't care if she working. Go ask her for the ten dollars if she working. Talking about "Bonnie working." Why ain't you working?

Lyons: Aw, Pop, you know I can't find no decent job. Where am I gonna get a job at? You know I can't get no job.

Troy: I told you I know some people down there. I can 135 get you on the rubbish if you want to work. I told you that the last time you came by here asking me for something.

Lyons: Naw, Pop . . . thanks. That ain't for me. I don't wanna be carrying nobody's rubbish. I don't wanna be punching nobody's time clock.

Troy: What's the matter, you too good to carry people's rubbish? Where you think that ten dollars you talking about come from? I'm just supposed to haul people's rubbish and give my money to you 'cause you too lazy to work. You too lazy to work and wanna know why you ain't got what I got.

Rose: What hospital Bonnie working at? Mercy?

Lyons: She's down at Passavant working in the laundry. 140

Troy: I ain't got nothing as it is. I give you that ten dollars and I got to eat beans the rest of the week. Naw . . . you ain't getting no ten dollars here.

Lyons: You ain't got to be eating no beans. I don't know why you wanna say that.

Troy: I ain't got no extra money. Gabe done moved over to Miss Pearl's paying her the rent and things done got tight around here. I can't afford to be giving you every payday.

Lyons: I ain't asked you to give me nothing. I asked you to loan me ten dollars. I know you got ten dollars.

Troy: Yeah, I got it. You know why I got it? 'Cause I don't throw my money away out there in the streets. You living the fast life . . . wanna be a musician . . . running around in them clubs and things . . . then, you learn to take care of yourself. You ain't gonna

> "You living the fast life . . . wanna be a musician . . . running around in them clubs and things . . . then, you learn to take care of yourself."

>> Scene from 1987 production

find me going and asking nobody for nothing. I done spent too many years without.

Lyons: You and me is two different people, Pop. 145

Troy: I done learned my mistake and learned to do what's right by it. You still trying to get something for nothing. Life don't owe you nothing. You owe it to yourself. Ask Bono. He'll tell you I'm right.

Lyons: You got your way of dealing with the world . . . I got mine. The only thing that matters to me is the music.

Troy: Yeah, I can see that! It don't matter how you gonna eat . . . where your next dollar is coming from. You telling the truth there.

Lyons: I know I got to eat. But I got to live too. I need something that gonna help me to get out of the bed in the morning. Make me feel like I belong in the world. I don't bother nobody. I just stay with the music 'cause that's the only way I can find to live in the world. Otherwise there ain't no telling what I might do. Now I don't come criticizing you and how you live. I just come by to ask you for ten dollars. I don't wanna hear all that about how I live.

Troy: Boy, your mama did a hell of a job raising you. 150

Lyons: You can't change me, Pop. I'm thirty-four years old. If you wanted to change me, you should have been there when I was growing up. I come by to see you . . . ask for ten dollars and you want to talk about how I was raised. You don't know nothing about how I was raised.

Rose: Let the boy have ten dollars, Troy.

Troy: (to Lyons) What the hell you looking at me for? I ain't got no ten dollars. You know what I do with my money. (To Rose.) Give him ten dollars if you want him to have it.

Rose: I will. Just as soon as you turn it loose.

Troy: (handing Rose the money) There it is. Seventy-six 155 dollars and forty-two cents. You see this, Bono? Now, I ain't gonna get but six of that back.

Rose: You ought to stop telling that lie. Here, Lyons. (She hands him the money.)

Lyons: Thanks, Rose. Look . . . I got to run . . . I'll see you later.

Troy: Wait a minute. You gonna say "thanks, Rose" and ain't gonna look to see where she got that ten dollars from? See how they do me, Bono?

Lyons: I know she got it from you, Pop. Thanks. I'll give it back to you.

Troy: There he go telling another lie. Time I see that ten 160 dollars . . . he'll be owing me thirty more.

Lyons: See you, Mr. Bono.

Bono: Take care, Lyons!

Lyons: Thanks, Pop. I'll see you again.

Lyons exits the yard.

Troy: I don't know why he don't go and get him a decent job and take care of that woman he got.

Bono: He'll be all right, Troy. The boy is still young. 165

Troy: The *boy* is thirty-four years old.

Rose: Let's not get off into all that.

Bono: Look here . . . I got to be going. I got to be getting on. Lucille gonna be waiting.

Troy: (puts his arm around Rose) See this woman, Bono? I love this woman. I love this woman so much it hurts. I love her so much . . . I done run out of ways of loving her. So I got to go back to basics. Don't you come by my house Monday morning talking about time to go to work . . . 'cause I'm still gonna be stroking!

Rose: Troy! Stop it now! 170

Bono: I ain't paying him no mind, Rose. That ain't nothing but gin-talk. Go on, Troy. I'll see you Monday.

Troy: Don't you come by my house, nigger! I done told you what I'm gonna be doing.

The lights go down to black.

SCENE 2

The lights come up on Rose hanging up clothes. She hums and sings softly to herself. It is the following morning.

Rose: (sings)

Jesus, be a fence all around me every day
Jesus, I want you to protect me as I travel on my way.
Jesus, be a fence all around me every day.

Troy enters from the house.

Jesus, I want you to protect me
As I travel on my way.

(To Troy.) 'Morning, You ready for breakfast? I can fix it soon as I finish hanging up these clothes?

Troy: I got the coffee on. That'll be all right. I'll just drink some of that this morning.

Rose: That 651 hit yesterday. That's the second time this month. Miss Pearl hit for a dollar . . . seem like those that need the least always get lucky. Poor folks can't get nothing.

Troy: Them numbers don't know nobody. I don't know why you fool with them. You and Lyons both.

Rose: It's something to do. 5

Troy: You ain't doing nothing but throwing your money away.

Rose: Troy, you know I don't play foolishly. I just play a nickel here and a nickel there.

Troy: That's two nickels you done thrown away.

Rose: Now I hit sometimes . . . that makes up for it. It always comes in handy when I do hit. I don't hear you complaining then.

Troy: I ain't complaining now. I just say it's foolish. 10
Trying to guess out of six hundred ways which way the number gonna come. If I had all the money niggers, these Negroes, throw away on numbers for one week—just one week—I'd be a rich man.

Rose: Well, you wishing and calling it foolish ain't gonna stop folks from playing numbers. That's one thing for sure. Besides . . . some good things come from playing numbers. Look where Pope done bought him that restaurant off of numbers.

Troy: I can't stand niggers like that. Man ain't had two dimes to rub together. He walking around with his shoes all run over bumming money for cigarettes. All right. Got lucky there and hit the numbers . . .

Rose: Troy, I know all about it.

Troy: Had good sense, I'll say that for him. He ain't throwing his money away. I seen niggers hit the numbers and go through two thousand dollars in four days. Man bought him that restaurant down there . . . fixed it up real nice . . . and then didn't want nobody to come in it! A Negro go in there and can't get no kind of service. I seen a white fellow come in there and order a bowl of stew. Pope picked all the meat out the pot for him. Man ain't had nothing but a bowl of meat! Negro come behind him and ain't got nothing but the potatoes and carrots. Talking about what numbers do for people, you picked a wrong example. Ain't done nothing but make a worser fool out of him than he was before.

Rose: Troy, you ought to stop worrying about what 15
happened at work yesterday.

Troy: I ain't worried. Just told me to be down there at the Commissioner's office on Friday. Everybody think they gonna fire me. I ain't worried about them firing me. You ain't got to worry about that. *(Pause.)* Where's Cory? Cory in the house? *(Calls.)* Cory?

Rose: He gone out.

Troy: Out, huh? He gone out 'cause he know I want him to help me with this fence. I know how he is. That boy scared of work.

Gabriel enters. He comes halfway down the alley and, hearing Troy's voice, stops.

Troy: *(continues)* He ain't done a lick of work in his life.

Rose: He had to go to football practice. Coach wanted them 20
to get in a little extra practice before the season start.

Troy: I got his practice . . . running out of here before he get his chores done.

° **Archangel Gabriel** A messenger of God.

Rose: Troy, what is wrong with you this morning? Don't nothing set right with you. Go on back in there and go to bed . . . get up on the other side.

Troy: Why something got to be wrong with me? I ain't said nothing wrong with me.

Rose: You got something to say about everything. First it's the numbers . . . then it's the way the man runs his restaurant . . . then you done got on Cory. What's it gonna be next? Take a look up there and see if the weather suits you . . . or is it gonna be how you gonna put up the fence with the clothes hanging in the yard.

Troy: You hit the nail on the head then. 25

Rose: I know you like I know the back of my hand. Go on in there and get you some coffee . . . see if that straighten you up. 'Cause you ain't right this morning.

Troy starts into the house and sees Gabriel. Gabriel starts singing. Troy's brother, he is seven years younger than Troy. Injured in World War II, he has a metal plate in his head. He carries an old trumpet tied around his waist and believes with every fiber of his being that he is the Archangel Gabriel.° He carries a chipped basket with an assortment of discarded fruits and vegetables he has picked up in the strip district and which he attempts to sell.

Gabriel: *(singing)*
　　Yes, ma'am, I got plums
　　You ask me how I sell them
　　Oh ten cents apiece
　　Three for a quarter
　　Come and buy now
　　'Cause I'm here today
　　And tomorrow I'll be gone

Gabriel enters.

　　Hey, Rose!

Rose: How you doing, Gabe?

Gabriel: There's Troy . . . Hey, Troy! 30

Troy: Hey, Gabe.

Exit into kitchen.

Rose: *(To Gabriel.)* What you got there?

Gabriel: You know what I got, Rose. I got fruits and vegetables.

Rose: *(looking in basket)* Where's all these plums you talking about?

Gabriel: I ain't got no plums today, Rose. I was just singing that. Have some tomorrow. Put me in a big order for plums. Have enough plums tomorrow for St. Peter and everybody.

Troy reenters from kitchen, crosses to steps.

　　(To Rose.) Troy's mad at me.

Troy: I ain't mad at you. What I got to be mad at you 35
about? You ain't done nothing to me.

Gabriel: I just moved over to Miss Pearl's to keep out from in your way. I ain't mean no harm by it.

>> James Earl Jones as Troy and Courtney B. Vance as Cory in 1987 production

Troy: Who said anything about that? I ain't said anything about that.

Gabriel: You ain't mad at me, is you?

Troy: Naw . . . I ain't mad at you, Gabe. If I was mad at you I'd tell you about it.

Gabriel: Got me two rooms. In the basement. Got my own door too. Wanna see my key? *(He holds up a key.)* That's my own key! Ain't nobody else got a key like that. That's my key! My two rooms!

Troy: Well, that's good, Gabe. You got your own key . . . that's good.

Rose: You hungry, Gabe? I was just fixing to cook Troy his breakfast.

Gabriel: I'll take some biscuits. You got some biscuits? Did you know when I was in heaven . . . every morning me and St. Peter° would sit down by the gate and eat some big fat biscuits? Oh, yeah! We had us a good time. We'd sit there and eat us them biscuits and then St. Peter would go off to sleep and tell me to wake him up when it's time to open the gates for the judgment.

Rose: Well, come on . . . I'll make up a batch of biscuits.

Rose exits into the house.

Gabriel: Troy . . . St. Peter got your name in the book. I seen it. It say . . . Troy Maxson. I say . . . I know him! He got the same name like what I got. That's my brother!

Troy: How many times you gonna tell me that, Gabe?

Gabriel: Ain't got my name in the book. Don't have to have my name. I done died and went to heaven. He got your name though. One morning St. Peter was looking at his book . . . marking it up for the judgment . . . and he let me see your name. Got it in there under M. Got Rose's name . . . I ain't seen it like I seen yours . . . but I know it's in there. He got a great big book. Got everybody's name what was ever been born. That's what he told me. But I seen your name. Seen it with my own eyes.

Troy: Go on in the house there. Rose going to fix you something to eat.

Gabriel: Oh, I ain't hungry. I done had breakfast with Aunt Jemima. She come by and cooked me up a whole mess of flapjacks. Remember how we used to eat them flapjacks?

Troy: Go on in the house and get you something to eat now. 50

Gabriel: I got to sell my plums. I done sold some tomatoes. Got me two quarters. Wanna see? *(He shows Troy his quarters.)* I'm gonna save them and buy me a new horn so St. Peter can hear me when it's time to open the gates. *(Gabriel stops suddenly. Listens.)* Hear that? That's the hellhounds. I got to chase them out of here. Go on get out of here! Get out!

Gabriel exits singing.

> Better get ready for the Judgment
> Better get ready for the Judgment
> My Lord is coming down

Rose enters from the house.

Troy: He's gone off somewhere.

Gabriel: *(offstage)*

> Better get ready for the Judgment
> Better get ready for the Judgment morning
> Better get ready for the Judgment
> My God is coming down

Rose: He ain't eating right. Miss Pearl say she can't get him to eat nothing.

Troy: What you want me to do about it, Rose? I done did 55 everything I can for the man. I can't make him get well. Man got half his head blown away . . . what you expect?

Rose: Seem like something ought to be done to help him.

Troy: Man don't bother nobody. He just mixed up from that metal plate he got in his head. Ain't no sense for him to go back into the hospital.

Rose: Least he be eating right. They can help him take care of himself.

Troy: Don't nobody wanna be locked up, Rose. What you wanna lock him up for? Man go over there and fight the war . . . messin' around with them Japs, get half his head blown off . . . and they give him a lousy three thousand dollars. And I had to swoop down on that.

Rose: Is you fixing to go into that again? 60

Troy: That's the only way I got a roof over my head . . . 'cause of that metal plate.

Rose: Ain't no sense you blaming yourself for nothing. Gabe wasn't in no condition to manage that money. You done what was right by him. Can't nobody say you ain't done what was right by him. Look how long you took care of him . . . till he wanted to have his own place and moved over there with Miss Pearl.

Troy: That ain't what I'm saying, woman! I'm just stating the facts. If my brother didn't have that metal plate in his head . . . I wouldn't have a pot to piss in or a

---

° **St. Peter** Disciple of Christ, believed to be the guard at the gates of heaven.

window to throw it out of. And I'm fifty-three years old. Now see if you can understand that!

Troy gets up from the porch and starts to exit the yard.

Rose: Where you going off to? You been running out of here every Saturday for weeks. I thought you was gonna work on this fence?

Troy: I'm gonna walk down to Taylors'. Listen to the ball 65 game. I'll be back in a bit. I'll work on it when I get back.

He exits the yard. The lights go to black.

SCENE 3

The lights come up on the yard. It is four hours later. Rose is taking down the clothes from the line. Cory enters carrying his football equipment.

Rose: Your daddy like to had a fit with you running out of here this morning without doing your chores.

Cory: I told you I had to go to practice.

Rose: He say you were supposed to help him with this fence.

Cory: He been saying that the last four or five Saturdays, and then he don't never do nothing, but go down to Taylors'. Did you tell him about the recruiter?

Rose: Yeah, I told him.   5

Cory: What he say?

Rose: He ain't said nothing too much. You get in there and get started on your chores before he gets back. Go on and scrub down them steps before he gets back here hollering and carrying on.

Cory: I'm hungry. What you got to eat, Mama?

Rose: Go on and get started on your chores. I got some meat loaf in there. Go on and make you a sandwich . . . and don't leave no mess in there.

Cory exits into the house. Rose continues to take down the clothes. Troy enters the yard and sneaks up and grabs her from behind.

Troy! Go on, now. You liked to scared me to death. What was the score of the game? Lucille had me on the phone and I couldn't keep up with it.

Troy: What I care about the game? Come here, woman.   10 *(He tries to kiss her.)*

Rose: I thought you went down Taylors' to listen to the game. Go on, Troy! You supposed to be putting up this fence.

Troy: *(attempting to kiss her again)* I'll put it up when I finish with what is at hand.

Rose: Go on, Troy. I ain't studying you.

Troy: *(chasing after her)* I'm studying you . . . fixing to do my homework!

Rose: Troy, you better leave me alone.   15

Troy: Where's Cory? That boy brought his butt home yet?

Rose: He's in the house doing his chores.

Troy: *(calling)* Cory! Get your butt out here, boy!

Rose exits into the house with the laundry. Troy goes over to the pile of wood, picks up a board, and starts sawing. Cory enters from the house.

Troy: You just now coming in here from leaving this morning?

Cory: Yeah, I had to go to football practice.

Troy: Yeah, what?   20

Cory: Yessir.

Troy: I ain't but two seconds off you noway. The garbage sitting in there overflowing . . . you ain't done none of your chores . . . and you come in here talking about "Yeah."

Cory: I was just getting ready to do my chores now, Pop . . .

Troy: Your first chore is to help me with this fence on   25 Saturday. Everything else come after that. Now get that saw and cut them boards.

Cory takes the saw and begins cutting the boards. Troy continues working. There is a long pause.

Cory: Hey, Pop . . . why don't you buy a TV?

Troy: What I want with a TV? What I want one of them for?

Cory: Everybody got one. Earl, Ba Bra . . . Jesse!

Troy: I ain't asked you who had one. I say what I want with one?

Cory: So you can watch it. They got lots of things on TV.   30 Baseball games and everything. We could watch the World Series.

Troy: Yeah . . . and how much this TV cost?

Cory: I don't know. They got them on sale for around two hundred dollars.

Troy: Two hundred dollars, huh?

Cory: That ain't that much, Pop.

Troy: Naw, it's just two hundred dollars. See that roof   35 you got over your head at night? Let me tell you something about that roof. It's been over ten years since that roof was last tarred. See now . . . the snow comes this winter and sit up there on that roof like it is . . . and it's gonna seep inside. It's just gonna be a little bit . . . ain't gonna hardly notice it. Then the next thing you know, it's gonna be leaking all over the house. Then the wood rot from all that water and you gonna need a whole new roof. Now, how much you think it cost to get that roof tarred?

Cory: I don't know.

Troy: Two hundred and sixty-four dollars . . . cash money. While you thinking about a TV, I got to be thinking about the roof . . . and whatever else go wrong here. Now if you had two hundred dollars, what would you do . . . fix the roof or buy a TV?

Cory: I'd buy a TV. Then when the roof started to leak . . . when it needed fixing . . . I'd fix it.

Troy: Where you gonna get the money from? You done spent it for a TV. You gonna sit up and watch the water run all over your brand new TV.

Cory: Aw, Pop. You got money. I know you do.   40

Troy: Where I got it at, huh?

Cory: You got it in the bank.

Troy: You wanna see my bankbook? You wanna see that seventy-three dollars and twenty-two cents I got sitting up in there.

Cory: You ain't got to pay for it all at one time. You can put a down payment on it and carry it on home with you.

Troy: Not me. I ain't gonna owe nobody nothing if I can help it. Miss a payment and they come and snatch it right out your house. Then what you got? Now, soon as I get two hundred dollars clear, then I'll buy a TV. Right now, as soon as I get two hundred and sixty-four dollars, I'm gonna have this roof tarred. 45

Cory: Aw . . . Pop!

Troy: You go on and get you two hundred and buy one if ya want it. I got better things to do with my money.

Cory: I can't get no two hundred dollars. I ain't never seen two hundred dollars.

Troy: I'll tell you what . . . you get you a hundred dollars and I'll put the other hundred with it.

Cory: All right, I'm gonna show you. 50

Troy: You gonna show me how you can cut them boards right now.

Cory begins to cut the boards. There is a long pause.

Cory: The Pirates won today. That makes five in a row.

Troy: I ain't thinking about the Pirates. Got an all-white team. Got that boy . . . that Puerto Rican boy . . . Clemente.° Don't even half-play him. That boy could be something if they give him a chance. Play him one day and sit him on the bench the next.

Cory: He gets a lot of chances to play.

Troy: I'm talking about playing regular. Playing every day 55 so you can get your timing. That's what I'm talking about.

Cory: They got some white guys on the team that don't play every day. You can't play everybody at the same time.

Troy: If they got a white fellow sitting on the bench . . . you can bet your last dollar he can't play! The colored guy got to be twice as good before he get on the team. That's why I don't want you to get all tied up in them sports. Man on the team and what it get him? They got colored on the team and don't use them. Same as not having them. All them teams the same.

Cory: The Braves got Hank Aaron° and Wes Covington.° Hank Aaron hit two home runs today. That makes forty-three.

Troy: Hank Aaron ain't nobody. That what you supposed to do. That's how you supposed to play the game. Ain't nothing to it. It's just a matter of timing . . . getting the right follow-through. Hell, I can hit forty-three home runs right now!

Cory: Not off no major-league pitching, you couldn't. 60

Troy: We had better pitching in the Negro leagues. I hit seven home runs off of Satchel Paige.° You can't get no better than that!

Cory: Sandy Koufax.° He's leading the league in strikeouts.

Troy: I ain't thinking of no Sandy Koufax.

Cory: You got Warren Spahn° and Lew Burdette.° I bet you couldn't hit no home runs off of Warren Spahn.

> *"If they got a white fellow sitting on the bench . . . you can bet your last dollar he can't play! The colored guy got to be twice as good before he get on the team."*

Troy: I'm through with it now. You go on and cut them 65 boards. (Pause.) Your mama tell me you done got recruited by a college football team? Is that right?

Cory: Yeah. Coach Zellman say the recruiter gonna be coming by to talk to you. Get you to sign the permission papers.

Troy: I thought you supposed to be working down there at the A&P. Ain't you suppose to be working down there after school?

Cory: Mr. Stawicki say he gonna hold my job for me until after the football season. Say starting next week I can work weekends.

° **Roberto Clemente** (1934–1972), Major League baseball player for the Pittsburg Pirates, known as much for his humanitarianism as his unique batting style and ability. Clemente received the Most Valuable Player Award in 1966 and died in a plane crash in 1972 while shuttling supplies to Nicaraguan earthquake victims. ° **Hank Aaron** Henry Aaron (1934–   ), American baseball player who broke Babe Ruth's career home run record with a lifetime total of 755 home runs. The holder of 12 other Major League records, Aaron spent his Major League career with the Braves, first in Milwaukee and later in their hometown of Atlanta. ° **Wes Covington** John Wesley Covington (1932–   ), American baseball player known for his ability to frustrate pitchers by wasting time at the plate. In an eleven-year career, Covington played for six Major League teams, beginning with the Milwaukee Braves and retiring with the Los Angeles Dodgers in 1966. ° **Satchel Page** Leroy Robert Paige (1906–1982), American baseball player. He played in the Negro Leagues from the 1920s until 1948, when he joined the Cleveland Indians; he reportedly pitched 55 no-hit games during his career. Joe DiMaggio called him "the best pitcher I have ever faced." ° **Sandy Koufax** Sanford Koufax (1935–   ), left-handed pitcher who won 129 games and lost only 47 for the Los Angeles Dodgers in the six seasons between 1961 and 1966; he won three Cy Young Awards and pitched four no-hit games, the last of which (1965) was a perfect game.
° **Warren Spahn** (1921–2003), left-handed pitcher who at the time of his retirement in 1966 held the National League record of 363 wins; he won 20 or more games in four consecutive seasons (1947–1950) and in several other seasons during the 1950s. ° **Lew Burdette** Selva Lewis Burdette (1926–   ), American baseball player who pitched and won three games for the Milwaukee Braves against the New York Yankees in the 1957 World Series; for that Series, his ERA was an amazingly low .067.

Troy: I thought we had an understanding about this football stuff? You suppose to keep up with your chores and hold that job down at the A&P. Ain't been around here all day on a Saturday. Ain't none of your chores done . . . and now you telling me you done quit your job.

Cory: I'm going to be working weekends. 70

Troy: You damn right you are! And ain't no need for nobody coming around here to talk to me about signing nothing.

Cory: Hey, Pop . . . you can't do that. He's coming all the way from North Carolina.

Troy: I don't care where he coming from. The white man ain't gonna let you get nowhere with that football noway. You go on and get your book-learning so you can work yourself up in that A&P or learn how to fix cars or build houses or something, get you a trade. That way you have something can't nobody take away from you. You go on and learn how to put your hands to some good use. Besides hauling people's garbage.

Cory: I get good grades, Pop. That's why the recruiter wants to talk with you. You got to keep up your grades to get recruited. This way I'll be going to college. I'll get a chance . . .

Troy: First you gonna get your butt down there to the 75 A&P and get your job back.

Cory: Mr. Stawicki done already hired somebody else 'cause I told him I was playing football.

Troy: You a bigger fool than I thought . . . to let somebody take away your job so you can play some football. Where you gonna get your money to take out your girlfriend and whatnot? What kind of foolishness is that to let somebody take away your job?

Cory: I'm still gonna be working weekends.

Troy: Naw . . . naw. You getting your butt out of here 80 and finding you another job.

Cory: Come on, Pop! I got to practice. I can't work after school and play football too. The team needs me. That's what Coach Zellman say . . .

Troy: I don't care what nobody else say. I'm the boss . . . you understand? I'm the boss around here. I do the only saying what counts.

Cory: Come on, Pop!

Troy: I asked you . . . did you understand?

Cory: Yeah . . . 85

Troy: What?!

Cory: Yessir.

Troy: You go on down there to that A&P and see if you can get your job back. If you can't do both . . . then you quit the football team. You've got to take the crookeds with the straights.

Cory: Yessir. *(Pause.)* Can I ask you a question?

Troy: What the hell you wanna ask me? Mr. Stawicki the 90 one you got the questions for.

° **crackers** Derogatory term for white people, generally poor southern whites.

Cory: How come you ain't never liked me?

Troy: Liked you? Who the hell say I got to like you? What law is there say I got to like you? Wanna stand up in my face and ask a damn fool-ass question like that. Talking about liking somebody. Come here, boy, when I talk to you.

Cory comes over to where Troy is working. He stands slouched over and Troy shoves him on his shoulder.

Straighten up, goddammit! I asked you a question . . . what law is there say I got to like you?

Cory: None.

Troy: Well, all right then! Don't you eat every day? *(Pause.)* Answer me when I talk to you! Don't you eat every day?

Cory: Yeah.

Troy: Nigger, as long as you in my house, you put that sir 95 on the end of it when you talk to me!

Cory: Yes . . . sir.

Troy: You eat every day.

Cory: Yessir!

Troy: Got a roof over your head.

Cory: Yessir! 100

Troy: Got clothes on your back.

Cory: Yessir.

Troy: Why you think that is?

Cory: 'Cause of you.

Troy: Ah, hell I know it's 'cause of me . . . but why do 105 you think that is?

Cory: *(hesitant)* 'Cause you like me.

Troy: Like you? I go out of here every morning . . . bust my butt . . . putting up with them crackers° every day . . . 'cause I like you? You are the biggest fool I ever saw. *(Pause.)* It's my job. It's my responsibility! You understand that? A man got to take care of his family. You live in my house . . . sleep you behind on my bedclothes . . . fill you belly up with my food . . . 'cause you my son. You my flesh and blood. Not 'cause I like you! 'Cause it's my duty to take care of you. I owe a responsibility to you! Let's get this straight right here . . . before it go along any further . . . I ain't got to like you. Mr. Rand don't give me my money come payday cause he likes me. He give me 'cause he owe me. I done give you everything I had to give you. I gave you your life! Me and your mama worked that out between us. And liking your black ass wasn't part of the bargain. Don't you try and go through life worrying about if somebody like you or not. You best be making sure they doing right by you. You understand what I'm saying, boy?

Cory: Yessir.

Troy: Then get the hell out of my face, and get on down to that A&P.

Rose has been standing behind the screen door for much of the scene. She enters as Cory exits.

Rose: Why don't you let the boy go ahead and play football, Troy? Ain't no harm in that. He's just trying to be like you with the sports.

Troy: I don't want him to be like me! I want him to move as far away from my life as he can get. You the only decent thing that ever happened to me. I wish him that. But I don't wish him a thing else from my life. I decided seventeen years ago that boy wasn't getting involved in no sports. Not after what they did to me in the sports.

Rose: Troy, why don't you admit you was too old to play in the major leagues? For once . . . why don't you admit that?

Troy: What do you mean too old? Don't come telling me I was too old. I just wasn't the right color. Hell, I'm fifty-three years old and can do better than Selkirk's .269 right now!

Rose: How's was you gonna play ball when you were over forty? Sometimes I can't go no sense out of you.

Troy: I got good sense, woman. I got sense enough not to let my boy get hurt over playing no sports. You been mothering that boy too much. Worried about if people like him.

Rose: Everything that boy do . . . he do for you. He wants you to say "Good job, son." That's all.

Troy: Rose, I ain't got time for that. He's alive. He's healthy. He's got to make his own way. I made mine. Ain't nobody gonna hold his hand when he get out there in that world.

Rose: Times have changed from when you was young, Troy. People change. The world's changing around you and you can't even see it.

Troy: (slow, methodical) Woman . . . I do the best I can do. I come in here every Friday. I carry a sack of potatoes and a bucket of lard. You all line up at the door with your hands out. I give you the lint from my pockets. I give you my sweat and my blood. I ain't got no tears. I done spent them. We go upstairs in that room at night . . . and I fall down on you and try to blast a hole into forever. I get up Monday morning . . . find my lunch on the table. I go out. Make my way. Find my strength to carry me through to the next Friday. (Pause.) That's all I got, Rose. That's all I got to give. I can't give nothing else.

Troy exits into the house. The lights go down to black.

SCENE 4

It is Friday. Two weeks later. Cory starts out of the house with his football equipment. The phone rings.

Cory: (calling) I got it! (He answers the phone and stands in the screen door talking.) Hello? Hey, Jesse. Naw . . . I was just getting ready to leave now.

Rose: (calling) Cory!

Cory: I told you, man, them spikes° is all tore up. You can use them if you want, but they ain't no good. Earl got some spikes.

Rose: (calling) Cory!

Cory: (calling to Rose) Mam? I'm talking to Jesse. (Into phone.) When she say that? (Pause.) Aw, you lying, man. I'm gonna tell her you said that.

Rose: (calling) Cory, don't you go nowhere!

Cory: I got to go to the game, Ma! (Into the phone.) Yeah, hey, look, I'll talk to you later. Yeah, I'll meet you over Earl's house. Later. Bye, Ma.

Cory exits the house and starts out the yard.

Rose: Cory, where you going off to? You got that stuff all pulled out and thrown all over your room.

Cory: (in the yard) I was looking for my spikes. Jesse wanted to borrow my spikes.

Rose: Get up there and get that cleaned up before your daddy get back in here.

Cory: I got to go to the game! I'll clean it up *when I get back.*

Cory exits.

Rose: That's all he need to do is see that room all messed up.

Rose exits into the house. Troy and Bono enter the yard. Troy is dressed in clothes other than his work clothes.

Bono: He told him the same thing he told you. Take it to the union.

Troy: Brownie ain't got that much sense. Man wasn't thinking about nothing. He wait until I confront them on it . . . then he wanna come crying seniority. (Calls.) Hey, Rose!

Bono: I wish I could have seen Mr. Rand's face when he told you.

Troy: He couldn't get it out of his mouth! Liked to bit his tongue! When they called me down there to the Commissioner's office . . . he thought they was gonna fire me. Like everybody else.

Bono: I didn't think they was gonna fire you. I thought they was gonna put you on the warning paper.

Troy: Hey, Rose! (To Bono.) Yeah, Mr. Rand like to bit his tongue.

Troy breaks the seal on the bottle, takes a drink, and hands it to Bono.

Bono: I see you run right down to Taylors' and told that Alberta gal.

Troy: (calling) Hey, Rose! (To Bono.) I told everybody. Hey, Rose! I went down there to cash my check.

Rose: (entering from the house) Hush all that hollering, man! I know you out here. What they say down there at the Commissioner's office?

Troy: You supposed to come when I call you, woman. Bono'll tell you that. (To Bono.) Don't Lucille come when you call her?

° **spikes** Athletic shoes with sharp metal grips set into the soles.

Rose: Man, hush your mouth, I ain't no dog . . . talk about "come when you call me."

Troy: *(puts his arm around Rose)* You hear this, Bono? I had me an old dog used to get uppity like that. You say, "C'mere, Blue!" . . . and he just lay there and look at you. End up getting a stick and chasing him away trying to make him come.

Rose: I ain't studying you and your dog. I remember you 25 used to sing that old song.

Troy: *(he sings)*

Hear it ring! Hear it ring!
I had a dog his name was Blue.

Rose: Don't nobody wanna hear you sing that old song.

Troy: *(sings)*

You know Blue was mighty true.

Rose: Used to have Cory running around here singing that song.

Bono: Hell, I remember that song myself. 30

Troy: *(sings)*

You know Blue was a good old dog.
Blue treed a possum in a hollow log.

That was my daddy's song. My daddy made up that song.

Rose: I don't care who made it up. Don't nobody wanna hear you sing it.

Troy: *(makes a song like calling a dog)* Come here, woman.

Rose: You come in here carrying on, I reckon they ain't fired you. What they say down there at the Commissioner's office?

Troy: Look here, Rose . . . Mr. Rand called me into his 35 office today when I got back from talking to them people down there . . . it come from up top . . . he called me in and told me they was making me a driver.

Rose: Troy, you kidding!

Troy: No I ain't. Ask Bono.

Rose: Well, that's great, Troy. Now you don't have to hassle them people no more.

Lyons enters from the street.

Troy: Aw hell, I wasn't looking to see you today. I thought you was in jail. Got it all over the front page of the *Courier* about them raiding Sefus's place . . . where you be hanging out with all them thugs.

Lyons: Hey, Pop . . . that ain't got nothing to do with me. I 40 don't go down there gambling. I go down there to sit in with the band. I ain't got nothing to do with the gambling part. They got some good music down there.

Troy: They got some rogues . . . is what they got.

Lyons: How you been, Mr. Bono? Hi, Rose.

Bono: I see where you playing down at the Crawford Grill tonight.

Rose: How come you ain't brought Bonnie like I told you? You should have brought Bonnie with you, she ain't been over in a month of Sundays.

Lyons: I was just in the neighborhood . . . thought I'd 45 stop by.

Troy: Here he come . . .

Bono: Your daddy got a promotion on the rubbish. He's gonna be the first colored driver. Ain't got to do nothing but sit up there and read the paper like them white fellows.

Lyons: Hey, Pop . . . if you knew how to read you'd be all right.

Bono: Naw . . . naw . . . you mean if the nigger knew how to *drive* he'd be all right. Been fighting with them people about driving and ain't even got a license. Mr. Rand know you ain't got no driver's license?

Troy: Driving ain't nothing. All you do is point the truck 50 where you want it to go. Driving ain't nothing.

Bono: Do Mr. Rand know you ain't got no driver's license? That's what I'm talking about. I ain't asked if driving was easy. I asked if Mr. Rand know you ain't got no driver's license.

Troy: He ain't got to know. The man ain't got to know my business. Time he find out, I have two or three driver's licenses.

Lyons: *(going into his pocket)* Say, look here, Pop . . .

Troy: I knew it was coming. Didn't I tell you, Bono? I 55 know what kind of "Look here, Pop" that was. The nigger fixing to ask me for some money. It's Friday night. It's my payday. All them rogues down there on the avenue . . . the ones that ain't in jail . . . and Lyons is hopping in his shoes to get down there with them.

Lyons: See, Pop . . . if you give somebody else a chance to talk sometimes, you'd see that I was fixing to pay you back your ten dollars like I told you. Here . . . I told you I'd pay you when Bonnie got paid.

Troy: Naw . . . you go ahead and keep that ten dollars. Put it in the bank. The next time you feel like you wanna come by here and ask me for something . . . you go on down there and get that.

Lyons: Here's your ten dollars, Pop. I told you I don't want you to give me nothing. I just wanted to borrow ten dollars.

Troy: Naw . . . you go on and keep that for the next time you want to ask me.

Lyons: Come on, Pop . . . here go your ten dollars. 60

Rose: Why don't you go on and let the boy pay you back, Troy?

Lyons: Here you go, Rose. If you don't take it I'm gonna have to hear about it for the next six months. *(He hands her the money.)*

Rose: You can hand yours over here too, Troy.

Troy: You see this, Bono. You see how they do me.

Bono: Yeah, Lucille do me the same way. 65

Gabriel is heard singing offstage. He enters.

Gabriel: Better get ready for the Judgment! Better get ready for . . . Hey! . . . Hey! . . . There's Troy's boy!

Lyons: How are you doing, Uncle Gabe?

Gabriel: Lyons . . . The King of the Jungle! Rose . . . hey, Rose. Got a flower for you. *(He takes a rose from his pocket.)* Picked it myself. That's the same rose like you is!

Rose: That's right nice of you, Gabe.

Lyons: What you been doing, Uncle Gabe?   70

Gabriel: Oh, I been chasing hellhounds and waiting on the time to tell St. Peter to open the gates.

Lyons: You been chasing hellhounds, huh? Well . . . you doing the right thing, Uncle Gabe. Somebody got to chase them.

Gabriel: Oh, yeah . . . I know it. The devil's strong. The devil ain't no pushover. Hellhounds snipping at everybody's heels. But I got my trumpet waiting on the judgment time.

Lyons: Waiting on the Battle of Armageddon, huh?

Gabriel: Ain't gonna be too much of a battle when God get to waving that Judgment sword. But the people's gonna have a hell of a time trying to get into heaven if them gates ain't open.

Lyons: *(putting his arm around Gabriel)* You hear this,   75 Pop. Uncle Gabe, you all right!

Gabriel: *(laughing with Lyons)* Lyons! King of the Jungle.

Rose: You gonna stay for supper, Gabe? Want me to fix you a plate?

Gabriel: I'll take a sandwich, Rose. Don't want no plate. Just wanna eat with my hands. I'll take a sandwich.

Rose: How about you, Lyons? You staying? Got some short ribs cooking.

Lyons: Naw, I won't eat nothing till after we finished   80 playing. *(Pause.)* You ought to come down and listen to me play, Pop.

Troy: I don't like that Chinese music. All that noise.

Rose: Go on in the house and wash up, Gabe . . . I'll fix you a sandwich.

Gabriel: *(to Lyons, as he exits)* Troy's mad at me.

Lyons: What you mad at Uncle Gabe for, Pop?

Rose: He thinks Troy's mad at him cause he moved over   85 to Miss Pearl's.

Troy: I ain't mad at the man. He can live where he want to live at.

Lyons: What he move over there for? Miss Pearl don't like nobody.

Rose: She don't mind him none. She treats him real nice. She just don't allow all that singing.

Troy: She don't mind that rent he be paying . . . that's what she don't mind.

Rose: Troy, I ain't going through that with you no more.   90 He's over there cause he want to have his own place. He can come and go as he please.

Troy: Hell, he could come and go as he please here. I wasn't stopping him. I ain't put no rules on him.

Rose: It ain't the same thing, Troy. And you know it.

Gabriel comes to the door.

Now, that's the last I wanna hear about that. I don't wanna hear nothing else about Gabe and Miss Pearl. And next week . . .

Gabriel: I'm ready for my sandwich, Rose.

Rose: And next week . . . when that recruiter come from that school . . . I want you to sign that paper and go on and let Cory play football. Then that'll be the last I have to hear about that.

Troy: *(to Rose as she exits into the house)* I ain't thinking   95 about Cory nothing.

Lyons: What . . . Cory got recruited? What school he going to?

Troy: That boy walking around here smelling his piss . . . thinking he's grown. Thinking he's gonna do what he want, irrespective of what I say. Look here, Bono . . . I left the Commissioner's office and went down to the A&P . . . that boy ain't working down there. He lying to me. Telling me he got his job back . . . telling me he working weekends . . . telling me he working after school . . . Mr. Stawicki tell me he ain't working down there at all!

Lyons: Cory just growing up. He's just busting at the seams trying to fill out your shoes.

Troy: I don't care what he's doing. When he get to the point where he wanna disobey me . . . then it's time for him to move on. Bono'll tell you that. I bet he ain't never disobeyed his daddy without paying the consequences.

Bono: I ain't never had a chance. My daddy came on   100 through . . . but I ain't never knew him to see him . . . or what he had on his mind or where he went. Just moving on through. Searching out the New Land. That's what the old folks used to call it. See a fellow moving around from place to place . . . woman to woman . . . called it searching out the New Land. Can't say if he ever found it. I come along, didn't want no kids. Didn't know if I was gonna be in one place long enough to fix on them right as their daddy. I figured I was going searching too. As it turned out I been hooked up with Lucille near about as long as your daddy been with Rose. Going on sixteen years.

Troy: Sometimes I wish I hadn't known my daddy. He ain't cared nothing about no kids. A kid to him wasn't nothing. All he wanted was for you to learn how to walk so he could start you to working. When it come time for eating . . . he ate first. If there was anything left over, that's what you got. Man would sit down and eat two chickens and give you the wing.

Lyons: You ought to stop that, Pop. Everybody feed their kids. No matter how hard times is . . . everybody care about their kids. Make sure they have something to eat.

Troy: The only thing my daddy cared about was getting them bales of cotton in to Mr. Lubin. That's the only thing that mattered to him. Sometimes I used to wonder why he was living. Wonder why the devil hadn't come and got him. "Get them bales of cotton in to Mr. Lubin" and find out he owe him money . . .

Lyons: He should have just went on and left when he saw he couldn't get nowhere. That's what I would have done.

Troy: How he gonna leave with eleven kids? And where he gonna go? He ain't knew how to do nothing but farm. No, he was trapped and I think he knew it. But I'll say this for him . . . he felt a responsibility toward us. Maybe he ain't treated us the way I felt he should have . . . but without that responsibility he could have walked off and left us . . . made his own way.

Bono: A lot of them did. Back in those days what you talking about . . . they walk out their front door and just take on down one road or another and keep on walking.

Lyons: There you go? That's what I'm talking about.

Bono: Just keep on walking till you come to something else. Ain't you never heard of nobody having the walking blues? Well, that's what you call it when you just take off like that.

Troy: My daddy ain't had them walking blues! What you talking about? He stayed right there with his family. But he was just as evil as he could be. My mama couldn't stand him. Couldn't stand that evilness. She run off when I was about eight. She sneaked off one night after he had gone to sleep. Told me she was coming back for me. I ain't never seen her no more. All his women run off and left him. He wasn't good for nobody.

When my turn come to head out, I was fourteen and got to sniffing around Joe Canewell's daughter. Had us an old mule we called Greyboy. My daddy sent me out to do some plowing and tied up Greyboy and went to fooling around with Joe Canewell's daughter. We done found us a nice little spot, got real cozy with each other. She about thirteen and we done figured we was grown anyway . . . so we down there enjoying ourselves . . . ain't thinking about nothing. We didn't know Greyboy had got loose and wandered back to the house and my daddy was looking for me. We down there by the creek enjoying ourselves when my daddy come up on us. Surprised us. He had them leather straps off the mule and commenced to whupping me like there was no tomorrow. I jumped up, mad and embarrassed. I was scared of my daddy. When he commenced to whupping on me . . . quite naturally I run to get out of the way. *(Pause.)* Now I thought he was mad 'cause I ain't done my work. But I see where he was chasing me off so he could have that gal for himself. When I see what the matter of it was, I lost all fear of my daddy. Right there is where I become a man . . . at fourteen years of age. *(Pause.)* Now it was my turn to run him off. I picked up them same reins that he had used on me. I picked up them reins and commenced to whupping on him. The gal jumped up and run off . . . and when my daddy turned to face me, I could see why the devil had never come to get him . . . cause he was the devil himself. I don't know what happened. When I woke up, I was laying right there by the creek, and Blue . . . this old dog we had . . . was licking my face. I thought I was blind. I couldn't see nothing. Both my eyes were swollen shut. I laid there and cried. I didn't know what I was gonna do. The only thing I knew was the time had come for me to leave my daddy's house. And right there the world suddenly got big. And it was a long time before I could cut it down to where I could handle it.

Part of that cutting down was when I got to the place where I could feel him kicking in my blood and knew that the only thing that separated us was the matter of a few years.

Gabriel enters from the house with a sandwich.

Lyons: What you got there, Uncle Gabe?

Gabriel: Got me a ham sandwich. Rose gave me a ham sandwich.

Troy: I don't know what happened to him. I done lost touch with everybody except Gabriel. But I hope he's dead. I hope he found some peace.

Lyons: That's a heavy story, Pop. I didn't know you left home when you was fourteen.

Troy: And didn't know nothing. The only part of the world I knew was the forty-two acres of Mr. Lubin's land. That's all I knew about life.

Lyons: Fourteen's kinda young to be out on your own. *(Phone rings.)* I don't even think I was ready to be out on my own at fourteen. I don't know what I would have done.

Troy: I got up from the creek and walked on down to Mobile.° I was through with farming. Figured I could do better in the city. So I walked the two hundred miles to Mobile.

Lyons: Wait a minute . . . you ain't walked no two hundred miles, Pop. Ain't nobody gonna walk no two hundred miles. You talking about some walking there.

Bono: That's the only way you got anywhere back in them days.

Lyons: Shhh. Damn if I wouldn't have hitched a ride with somebody!

Troy: Who you gonna hitch it with? They ain't got no cars and things like they got now. We talking about 1918.

Rose: *(entering)* What you all out here getting into?

Troy: *(to Rose)* I'm telling Lyons how good he got it. He don't know nothing about this I'm talking.

Rose: Lyons, that was Bonnie on the phone. She say you supposed to pick her up.

Lyons: Yeah, okay, Rose.

Troy: I walked on down to Mobile and hitched up with some of them fellows that was heading this way. Got

---

° **Mobile** City and seaport in southwestern Alabama.

up here and found out . . . not only couldn't you get a job . . . you couldn't find no place to live. I thought I was in freedom. Shhh. Colored folks living down there on the riverbanks in whatever kind of shelter they could find for themselves. Right down there under the Brady Street Bridge. Living in shacks made of sticks and tarpaper. Messed around there and went from bad to worse. Started stealing. First it was food. Then I figured, hell, if I steal money I can buy me some food. Buy me some shoes too! One thing led to another. Met your mama. I was young and anxious to be a man. Met your mama and had you. What I do that for? Now I got to worry about feeding you and her. Got to steal three times as much. Went out one day looking for somebody to rob . . . that's what I was, a robber. I'll tell you the truth. I'm ashamed of it today. But it's the truth. Went to rob this fellow . . . pulled out my knife . . . and he pulled out a gun. Shot me in the chest. I felt just like somebody had taken a hot branding iron and laid it on me. When he shot me I jumped at him with my knife. They told me I killed him and they put me in the penitentiary and locked me up for fifteen years. That's where I met Bono. That's where I learned how to play baseball. Got out that place and your mama had taken you and went on to make life without me. Fifteen years was a long time for her to wait. But that fifteen years cured me of that robbing stuff. Rose'll tell you. She asked me when I met her if I had gotten all that foolishness out of my system. And I told her, "Baby, it's you and baseball all what count with me." You hear me, Bono? I meant it too. She say, "Which one comes first?" I told her, "Baby, ain't no doubt it's baseball . . . but you stick and get old with me and we'll both outlive this baseball." Am I right, Rose? And it's true.

Rose: Man, hush your mouth. You ain't said no such thing. Talking about "Baby, you know you'll always be number one with me." That's what you was talking.

Troy: You hear that, Bono. That's why I love her.

Bono: Rose'll keep you straight. You get off the track, she'll straighten you up.

Rose: Lyons, you better get on up and get Bonnie. She waiting on you.

Lyons: *(gets up to go)* Hey, Pop, why don't you come on down to the Grill and hear me play.   130

Troy: I ain't going down there. I'm too old to be sitting around in them clubs.

Bono: You got to be good to play down at the Grill.

Lyons: Come on, Pop . . .

Troy: I got to get up in the morning.

Lyons: You ain't got to stay long.   135

Troy: Naw, I'm gonna get my supper and go on to bed.

Lyons: Well, I got to go. I'll see you again.

Troy: Don't you come around my house on my payday.

Rose: Pick up the phone and let somebody know you coming. And bring Bonnie with you. You know I'm always glad to see her.

Lyons: Yeah, I'll do that, Rose. You take care now. See you, Pop. See you, Mr. Bono. See you, Uncle Gabe.   140

Gabriel: Lyons! King of the Jungle!

Lyons exits.

Troy: Is supper ready, woman? Me and you got some business to take care of. I'm gonna tear it up too.

Rose: Troy, I done told you now!

Troy: *(puts his arm around Bono)* Aw hell, woman . . . this is Bono. Bono like family. I done known this nigger since . . . how long I done know you?

Bono: It's been a long time.   145

Troy: I done know this nigger since Skippy was a pup. Me and him done been through some times.

Bono: You sure right about that.

Troy: Hell, I done know him longer than I known you. And we still standing shoulder to shoulder. Hey, look here, Bono . . . a man can't ask for no more than that. *(Drinks to him.)* I love you, nigger.

Bono: Hell, I love you too . . . I got to get home see my woman. You got yours in hand. I got to go get mine.

Bono starts to exit as Cory enters the yard, dressed in his football uniform. He gives Troy a hard, uncompromising look.

Cory: What you do that for, Pop?   150

He throws his helmet down in the direction of Troy.

Rose: What's the matter? Cory . . . what's the matter?

Cory: Papa done went up to the school and told Coach Zellman I can't play football no more. Wouldn't even let me play the game. Told him to tell the recruiter not to come.

Rose: Troy . . .

Troy: What you Troying me for. Yeah, I did it. And the boy know why I did it.

Cory: Why you wanna do that to me? That was the one chance I had.   155

Rose: Ain't nothing wrong with Cory playing football, Troy.

Troy: The boy lied to me. I told the nigger if he wanna play football . . . to keep up his chores and hold down that job at the A&P. That was the conditions. Stopped down there to see Mr. Stawicki . . .

Cory: I can't work after school during the football season, Pop! I tried to tell you that Mr. Stawicki's holding my job for me. You don't never want to listen to nobody. And then you wanna go and do this to me!

Troy: I ain't done nothing to you. You done it to yourself.

Cory: Just cause you didn't have a chance! You just scared I'm gonna be better than you, that's all.   160

Troy: Come here.

Rose: Troy . . .

Cory reluctantly crosses over to Troy.

Troy: All right! See. You done made a mistake.

Cory: I didn't even do nothing!

Troy: I'm gonna tell you what your mistake was. See . . . 165
you swung at the ball and didn't hit it. That's strike
one. See, you in the batter's box now. You swung and
you missed. That's strike one. Don't you strike out!

Lights fade to black.

Act 2

SCENE 1

*The following morning. Cory is at the tree hitting the ball
with the bat. He tries to mimic Troy, but his swing is
awkward, less sure. Rose enters from the house.*

Rose: Cory, I want you to help me with this cupboard.

Cory: I ain't quitting the team. I don't care what Poppa
say.

Rose: I'll talk to him when he gets back. He had to go see
about your Uncle Gabe. The police done arrested
him. Say he was disturbing the peace. He'll be back
directly. Come on in here and help me clean out the
top of this cupboard.

*Cory exits into the house. Rose sees Troy and Bono
coming down the alley.*

Troy . . . what they say down there?

Troy: Ain't said nothing. I give them fifty dollars and they
let him go. I'll talk to you about it. Where's Cory?

Rose: He's in there helping me clean out these cupboards. 5

Troy: Tell him to get his butt out here.

*Troy and Bono go over to the pile of wood. Bono picks up
the saw and begins sawing.*

Troy: *(to Bono)* All they want is the money. That makes
six or seven times I done went down there and got
him. See me coming they stick out their *hands.*

Bono: Yeah. I know what you mean. That's all they care
about . . . that money. They don't care about what's
right. *(Pause.)* Nigger, why you got to go and get
some hard wood? You ain't doing nothing but
building a little old fence. Get you some soft pine
wood. That's all you need.

Troy: I know what I'm doing. This is outside wood. You
put pine wood inside the house. Pine wood is inside
wood. This here is outside wood. Now you tell me
where the fence is gonna be?

Bono: You don't need this wood. You can put it up with 10
pine wood and it'll stand as long as you gonna be
here looking at it.

° **Joe Louis** Joseph Louis Barrow (1914–1981), American boxer known
as the "Brown Bomber." In 1937, he became the youngest boxer ever to
win the Heavyweight Championship, which he defended twenty-five
times; he retired undefeated in 1949.

Troy: How you know how long I'm gonna be here,
nigger? Hell, I might just live forever. Live longer
than old man Horsely.

Bono: That's what Magee used to say.

Troy: Magee's a damn fool. Now you tell me who you
ever heard of gonna pull their own teeth with a pair
of rusty pliers.

Bono: The old folks . . . my granddaddy used to pull his
teeth with pliers. They ain't had no dentists for the
colored folks back then.

Troy: Get clean pliers! You understand? Clean pliers! 15
Sterilize them! Besides we ain't living back then. All
Magee had to do was walk over to Doc Goldblum's.

Bono: I see where you and that Tallahassee gal . . . that
Alberta . . . I see where you all done got tight.

Troy: What you mean "got tight"?

Bono: I see where you be laughing and joking with her
all the time.

Troy: I laughs and jokes with all of them, Bono. You
know me.

Bono: That ain't the kind of laughing and joking I'm 20
talking about.

Cory enters from the house.

Cory: How you doing, Mr. Bono?

Troy: Cory? Get that saw from Bono and cut some wood.
He talking about the wood's too hard to cut. Stand
back there, Jim, and let that young boy show you
how it's done.

Bono: He's sure welcome to it.

Cory takes the saw and begins to cut the wood.

Whew-e-e! Look at that. Big old strong boy. Look
like Joe Louis.° Hell, must be getting old the way I'm
watching that boy whip through that wood.

Cory: I don't see why Mama want a fence around the
yard noways.

Troy: Damn if I know either. What the hell she keeping 25
out with it? She ain't got nothing nobody want.

Bono: Some people build fences to keep people out . . .
and other people build fences to keep people in. Rose
wants to hold on to you all. She loves you.

Troy: Hell, nigger, I don't need nobody to tell me my wife
loves me. Cory . . . go on in the house and see if you
can find that other saw.

Cory: Where's it at?

Troy: I said find it! Look for it till you find it!

Cory exits into the house.

What's that supposed to mean? Wanna keep us in?

Bono: Troy . . . I done known you seem like damn near 30
my whole life. You and Rose both. I done know both
of you all for a long time. I remember when you met
Rose. When you was hitting them baseballs out the
park. A lot of them gals was after you then. You had
the pick of the litter. When you picked Rose, I was
happy for you. That was the first time I knew you

---

had any sense. I said . . . My man Troy knows what he's doing . . . I'm gonna follow this nigger . . . he might take me somewhere. I been following you too. I done learned a whole heap of things about life watching you. I done learned how to tell where the shit lies. How to tell it from the alfalfa. You done learned me a lot of things. You showed me how to not make the same mistakes . . . to take life as it comes along and keep putting one foot in front of the other. (Pause.) Rose a good woman, Troy.

Troy: Hell, nigger, I know she a good woman. I been married to her for eighteen years. What you got on your mind, Bono?

Bono: I just say she a good woman. Just like I say anything. I ain't got to have nothing on my mind.

Troy: You just gonna say she a good woman and leave it hanging out there like that? Why you telling me she a good woman?

Bono: She loves you, Troy. Rose loves you.

Troy: You saying I don't measure up. That's what you   35
trying to say. I don't measure up 'cause I'm seeing this other gal. I know what you trying to say.

Bono: I know what Rose means to you, Troy. I'm just trying to say I don't want to see you mess up.

Troy: Yeah, I appreciate that, Bono. If you was messing around on Lucille I'd be telling you the same thing.

Bono: Well, that's all I got to say. I just say that because I love you both.

Troy: Hell, you know me . . . I wasn't out there looking for nothing. You can't find a better woman than Rose. I know that. But seems like this woman just stuck onto me where I can't shake her loose. I done wrestled with it, tried to throw her off me . . . but she just stuck on tighter. Now she's stuck on for good.

Bono: You's in control . . . that's what you tell me all the   40
time. You responsible for what you do.

Troy: I ain't ducking the responsibility of it. As long as it sets right in my heart . . . then I'm okay. 'Cause that's all I listen to. It'll tell me right from wrong every time. And I ain't talking about doing Rose no bad turn. I love Rose. She done carried me a long ways and I love and respect her for that.

Bono: I know you do. That's why I don't want to see you hurt her. But what you gonna do when she find out? What you got then? If you try and juggle both of them . . . sooner or later you gonna drop one of them. That's common sense.

Troy: Yeah, I hear what you saying, Bono. I been trying to figure a way to work it out.

Bono: Work it out right, Troy. I don't want to be getting all up between you and Rose's business . . . but work it so it come out right.

Troy: Ah hell, I get all up between you and Lucille's   45
business. When you gonna get that woman that refrigerator she been wanting? Don't tell me you ain't got no money now. I know who your banker is. Mellon don't need that money bad as Lucille want that refrigerator. I'll tell you that.

Bono: Tell you what I'll do . . . when you finish building this fence for Rose . . . I'll buy Lucille that refrigerator.

Troy: You done stuck your foot in your mouth now!

Troy grabs up a board and begins to saw. Bono starts to walk out the yard.

Hey, nigger . . . where you going?

Bono: I'm going home. I know you don't expect me to help you now. I'm protecting my money. I wanna see you put that fence up by yourself. That's what I want to see. You'll be here another six months without me.

Troy: Nigger, you ain't right.

Bono: When it comes to my money . . . I'm right as   50
fireworks on the Fourth of July.

Troy: All right, we gonna see now. You better get out your bankbook.

Bono exits, and Troy continues to work. Rose enters from the house.

Rose: What they say down there? What's happening with Gabe?

Troy: I went down there and got him out. Cost me fifty dollars. Say he was disturbing the peace. Judge set up a hearing for him in three weeks. Say to show cause why he shouldn't be recommitted.

Rose: What was he doing that cause them to arrest him?

Troy: Some kids were teasing him and he run them off   55
home. Say he was howling and carrying on. Some folks seen him and called the police. That's all it was.

Rose: Well, what's you say? What'd you tell the judge?

Troy: Told him I'd look after him. It didn't make no sense to recommit the man. He stuck out his big greasy palm and told me to give him fifty dollars and take him on home.

Rose: Where's he at now? Where'd he go off to?

Troy: He's gone about his business. He don't need nobody to hold his hand.

Rose: Well, I don't know. Seem like that would be the   60
best place for him if they did put him into the hospital. I know what you're gonna say. But that's what I think would be best.

Troy: The man done had his life ruined fighting for what? And they wanna take and lock him up. Let him be free. He don't bother nobody.

Rose: Well, everybody got their own way of looking at it I guess. Come on and get your lunch. I got a bowl of lima beans and some cornbread in the oven. Come and get something to eat. Ain't no sense you fretting over Gabe.

Rose turns to go into the house.

Troy: Rose . . . got something to tell you.

Rose: Well, come on . . . wait till I get this food on the table.

Troy: Rose!   65

She stops and turns around.

I don't know how to say this. *(Pause.)* I can't explain it none. It just sort of grows on you till it gets out of hand. It starts out like a little bush . . . and the next thing you know it's a whole forest.

Rose: Troy . . . what is you talking about?

Troy: I'm talking, woman, let me talk. I'm trying to find a way to tell you . . . I'm gonna be a daddy. I'm gonna be somebody's daddy.

Rose: Troy . . . you're not telling me this? You're gonna be . . . what?

Troy: Rose . . . now . . . see . . .

Rose: You telling me you gonna be somebody's daddy? You telling your *wife* this? 70

Gabriel enters from the street. He carries a rose in his hand.

Gabriel: Hey, Troy! Hey, Rose!

Rose: I have to wait eighteen years to hear something like this.

Gabriel: Hey, Rose . . . I got a flower for you. *(He hands it to her.)* That's a rose. Same rose like you is.

Rose: Thanks, Gabe.

Gabriel: Troy, you ain't mad at me is you? Them bad mens come and put me away. You ain't mad at me is you? 75

Troy: Naw, Gabe, I ain't mad at you.

Rose: Eighteen years and you wanna come with this.

Gabriel: *(takes a quarter out of his pocket)* See what I got? Got a brand new quarter.

Troy: Rose . . . it's just . . .

Rose: Ain't nothing you can say, Troy. Ain't no way of explaining that. 80

Gabriel: Fellow that give me this quarter had a whole mess of them. I'm gonna keep this quarter till it stop shining.

Rose: Gabe, go on in the house there. I got some watermelon in the Frigidaire. Go on and get you a piece.

Gabriel: Say, Rose . . . you know I was chasing hellhounds and them bad mens come and get me and take me away. Troy helped me. He come down there and told them they better let me go before he beat them up. Yeah, he did!

Rose: You go on and get you a piece of watermelon, Gabe. Them bad mens is gone now.

Gabriel: Okay, Rose . . . gonna get me some watermelon. 85 The kind with the stripes on it.

Gabriel exits into the house.

Rose: Why, Troy? Why? After all these years to come dragging this in to me now. It don't make no sense at your age. I could have expected this ten or fifteen years ago, but not now.

Troy: Age ain't got nothing to do with it, Rose.

Rose: I done tried to be everything a wife should be. Everything a wife could be. Been married eighteen years and I got to live to see the day you tell me you been seeing another woman and done fathered a child by her. And you know I ain't never wanted no

half nothing in my family. My whole family is half. Everybody got different fathers and mothers . . . my two sisters and my brother. Can't hardly tell who's who. Can't never sit down and talk about Papa and Mama. It's your papa and your mama and my papa and my mama . . .

Troy: Rose . . . stop it now.

Rose: I ain't never wanted that for none of my children. 90 And now you wanna drag your behind in here and tell me something like this.

Troy: You ought to know. It's time for you to know.

Rose: Well, I don't want to know, goddamn it!

Troy: I can't just make it go away. It's done now. I can't wish the circumstance of the thing away.

Rose: And you don't want to either. Maybe you want to wish me and my boy away. Maybe that's what you want? Well, you can't wish us away. I've got eighteen years of my life invested in you. You ought to have stayed upstairs in my bed where you belong.

Troy: Rose . . . now listen to me . . . we can get a handle 95 on this thing. We can talk this out . . . come to an understanding.

Rose: All of a sudden it's "we." Where was "we" at when you was down there rolling around with some godforsaken woman? "We" should have come to an understanding before you started making a damn fool of yourself. You're a day late and a dollar short when it comes to an understanding with me.

Troy: It's just . . . She gives me a different idea . . . a different understanding about myself. I can step out of this house and get away from the pressures and problems . . . be a different man. I ain't got to wonder how I'm gonna pay the bills or get the roof fixed. I can just be a part of myself that I ain't never been.

Rose: What I want to know . . . is do you plan to continue seeing her. That's all you can say to me.

Troy: I can sit up in her house and laugh. Do you understand what I'm saying. I can laugh out loud . . . and it feels good. It reaches all the way down to the bottom of my shoes. *(Pause.)* Rose, I can't give that up.

Rose: Maybe you ought to go on and stay down there 100 with her . . . if she's a better woman than me.

Troy: It ain't about nobody being a better woman or nothing. Rose, you ain't the blame. A man couldn't ask for no woman to be a better wife than you've been. I'm responsible for it. I done locked myself into a pattern trying to take care of you all that I forgot about myself.

Rose: What the hell was I there for? That was my job, not somebody else's.

Troy: Rose, I done tried all my life to live decent . . . to live a clean . . . hard . . . useful life. I tried to be a good husband to you. In every way I knew how. Maybe I come into the world backwards, I don't know. But . . . you born with two strikes on you before you come to the plate. You got to guard it closely . . . always looking for the curve ball on the inside corner. You can't afford to let none get past you. You can't afford a call strike. If you going down . . . you going down swinging. Everything lined up against you. What you gonna do. I fooled them, Rose. I bunted. When I found you and Cory and a halfway decent job . . . I was safe. Couldn't nothing touch me. I wasn't gonna strike out no more. I wasn't going back to the penitentiary. I wasn't gonna lay in the streets with a bottle of wine. I was safe. I had me a family. A job. I wasn't gonna get that last strike. I was on first looking for one of them boys to knock me in. To get me home.

Rose: You should have stayed in my bed, Troy.

Troy: Then when I saw that gal . . . she firmed up my backbone. And I got to thinking that if I tried . . . I just might be able to steal second. Do you understand after eighteen years I wanted to steal second. | 105

Rose: You should have held me tight. You should have grabbed me and held on.

Troy: I stood on first base for eighteen years and I thought . . . well, goddamn it . . . go on for it!

Rose: We're not talking about baseball! We're talking about you going off to lay in bed with another woman . . . and then bring it home to me. That's what we're talking about. We ain't talking about no baseball.

Troy: Rose, you're not listening to me. I'm trying the best I can to explain it to you. It's not easy for me to admit that I been standing in the same place for eighteen years.

Rose: I been standing with you! I been right here with you, Troy. I got a life too. I gave eighteen years of my life to stand in the same spot with you. Don't you think I ever wanted other things? Don't you think I had dreams and hopes? What about my life? What about me. Don't you think it ever crossed my mind to want to know other men? That I wanted to lay up somewhere and forget about my responsibilities? That I wanted someone to make me laugh so I could feel good? You not the only one who's got wants and needs. But I held on to you, Troy. I took all my feelings, my wants and needs, my dreams . . . and I buried them inside you. I planted a seed and watched and prayed over it. I planted myself inside you and waited to bloom. And it didn't take me no eighteen years to find out the soil was hard and rocky and it wasn't never gonna bloom. | 110

But I held on to you, Troy. I held you tighter. You was my husband. I owed you everything I had. Every part of me I could find to give you. And upstairs in that room . . . with the darkness falling in on me . . . I gave everything I had to try and erase the doubt that you wasn't the finest man in the world. And wherever you was going . . . I wanted to be there with you. 'Cause you was my husband. 'Cause that's the only way I was gonna survive as your wife. You always talking about what you give . . . and what you don't have to give. But you take too. You take . . . and don't even know nobody's giving!

Rose turns to exit into the house; Troy grabs her arm.

Troy: You say I take and don't give!

Rose: Troy! You're hurting me!

Troy: You say I take and don't give!

Rose: Troy . . . you're hurting my arm! Let go!

Troy: I done give you everything I got. Don't you tell that lie on me. | 115

Rose: Troy!

Troy: Don't you tell that lie on me!

Cory enters from the house.

Cory: Mama!

Rose: Troy. You're hurting me.

Troy: Don't you tell me about no taking and giving. | 120

Cory comes up behind Troy and grabs him. Troy, surprised, is thrown off balance just as Cory throws a glancing blow that catches him on the chest and knocks him down. Troy is stunned, as is Cory.

Rose: Troy. Troy. No!

Troy gets to his feet and starts at Cory.

Troy . . . no. Please! Troy!

Rose pulls on Troy to hold him back. Troy stops himself.

Troy: *(to Cory)* All right. That's strike two. You stay away from around me, boy. Don't you strike out. You living with a full count. Don't you strike out.

Troy exits out the yard as the lights go down.

SCENE 2

It is six months later, early afternoon. Troy enters from the house and starts to exit the yard. Rose enters from the house.

Rose: Troy, I want to talk to you.

Troy: All of a sudden, after all this time, you want to talk to me, huh? You ain't wanted to talk to me for months. You ain't wanted to talk to me last night. You ain't wanted no part of me then. What you wanna talk to me about now?

Rose: Tomorrow's Friday.

Troy: I know what day tomorrow is. You think I don't know tomorrow's Friday? My whole life I ain't done nothing but look to see Friday coming and you got to tell me it's Friday.

Rose: I want to know if you're coming home. | 5

Troy: I always come home, Rose. You know that. There ain't never been a night I ain't come home.

Rose: That ain't what I mean . . . and you know it. I want to know if you're coming straight home after work.

Troy: I figure I'd cash my check . . . hang out at Taylors' with the boys . . . maybe play a game of checkers . . .

Rose: Troy, I can't live like this. I won't live like this. You livin' on borrowed time with me. It's been going on six months now you ain't been coming home.

Troy: I be here every Friday. Every night of the year. That's 365 days.

Rose: I want you to come home tomorrow after work.

Troy: Rose . . . I don't mess up my pay. You know that now. I take my pay and I give it to you. I don't have no money but what you give me back. I just want to have a little time to myself . . . a little time to enjoy life.

Rose: What about me? When's my time to enjoy life?

Troy: I don't know what to tell you, Rose. I'm doing the best I can.

Rose: You ain't been home from work but time enough to change your clothes and run out . . . and you wanna call that the best you can do?

Troy: I'm going over to the hospital to see Alberta. She went into the hospital this afternoon. Look like she might have the baby early. I won't be gone long.

Rose: Well, you ought to know. They went over to Miss Pearl's and got Gabe today. She said you told them to go ahead and lock him up.

Troy: I ain't said no such thing. Whoever told you that is telling a lie. Pearl ain't doing nothing but telling a big fat lie.

Rose: She ain't had to tell me. I read it on the papers.

Troy: I ain't told them nothing of the kind.

Rose: I saw it right there on the papers.

Troy: What it say, huh?

Rose: It said you told them to take him.

Troy: Then they screwed that up, just the way they screw up everything. I ain't worried about what they got on the paper.

Rose: Say the government send part of his check to the hospital and the other part to you.

Troy: I ain't got nothing to do with that if that's the way it works. I ain't made up the rules about how it work.

Rose: You did Gabe just like you did Cory. You wouldn't sign the paper for Cory . . . but you signed for Gabe. You signed that paper.

The telephone is heard ringing inside the house.

Troy: I told you I ain't signed nothing, woman! The only thing I signed was the release form. Hell, I can't read. I don't know what they had on that paper! I ain't signed nothing about sending Gabe away.

Rose: I said send him to the hospital . . . you said let him be free . . . now you done went down there and signed him to the hospital for half his money. You went back on yourself, Troy. You gonna have to answer for that.

Troy: See now . . . you been over there talking to Miss Pearl. She done got mad cause she ain't getting Gabe's rent money. That's all it is. She's liable to say anything.

Rose: Troy, I seen where you signed the paper.

Troy: You ain't seen nothing I signed. What she doing got papers on my brother anyway? Miss Pearl telling a big fat lie. And I'm gonna tell her about it too! You ain't seen nothing I signed. Say . . . you ain't seen nothing I signed.

Rose exits into the house to answer the telephone. Presently she returns.

Rose: Troy . . . that was the hospital. Alberta had the baby.

Troy: What she have? What is it?

Rose: It's a girl.

Troy: I better get on down to the hospital to see her.

Rose: Troy . . .

Troy: Rose . . . I got to go see her now. That's only right . . . what's the matter . . . the baby's all right, ain't it?

Rose: Alberta died having the baby.

Troy: Died . . . you say she's dead? Alberta's dead?

Rose: They said they done all they could. They couldn't do nothing for her.

Troy: The baby? How's the baby?

Rose: They say it's healthy. I wonder who's gonna bury her.

Troy: She had family, Rose. She wasn't living in the world by herself.

Rose: I know she wasn't living in the world by herself.

Troy: Next thing you gonna want to know if she had any insurance.

Rose: Troy, you ain't got to talk like that.

Troy: That's the first thing that jumped out your mouth. "Who's gonna bury her?" Like I'm fixing to take on that task for myself.

Rose: I am your wife. Don't push me away.

Troy: I ain't pushing nobody away. Just give me some space. That's all. Just give me some room to breathe.

Rose exits into the house. Troy walks about the yard.

Troy: *(with a quiet rage that threatens to consume him)* All right . . . Mr. Death. See now . . . I'm gonna tell you what I'm gonna do. I'm gonna take and build me a fence around this yard. See? I'm gonna build me a fence around what belongs to me. And then I want you to stay on the other side. See? You stay over there until you're ready for me. Then you come on. Bring your army. Bring your sickle. Bring your wrestling clothes. I ain't gonna fall down on my vigilance this time. You ain't gonna sneak up on me no more. When you ready for me . . . when the top of your list say Troy Maxson . . . that's when you come around here. You come up and knock on the front door. Ain't nobody else got nothing to do with this. This is between you and me. Man to man. You stay on the other side of the fence until you ready for me. Then you come up and knock on the front door. Anytime you want. I'll be ready for you.

The lights go down to black.

SCENE 3

The lights come up on the porch. It is late evening three days later. Rose sits listening to the ball game waiting for Troy. The final out of the game is made and Rose switches off the radio. Troy enters the yard carrying an infant wrapped in blankets. He stands back from the house and calls.

  Rose enters and stands on the porch. There is a long, awkward silence, the weight of which grows heavier with each passing second.

Troy: Rose . . . I'm standing here with my daughter in my arms. She ain't but a wee bittie little old thing. She don't know nothing about grownups' business. She innocent . . . and she ain't got no mama.

Rose: What you telling me for, Troy?

She turns and exits into the house.

Troy: Well . . . I guess we'll just sit out here on the porch.

He sits down on the porch. There is an awkward indelicateness about the way he handles the baby. His largeness engulfs and seems to swallow it. He speaks loud enough for Rose to hear.

A man's got to do what's right for him. I ain't sorry for nothing I done. It felt right in my heart. (*To the baby.*) What you smiling at? Your daddy's a big man. Got these great big old hands. But sometimes he's scared. And right now your daddy's scared 'cause we sitting out here and ain't got no home. Oh, I been homeless before. I ain't had no little baby with me. But I been homeless. You just be out on the road by your lonesome and you see one of them trains coming and you just kinda go like this . . .

He sings a lullaby.

> Please, Mr. Engineer let a man ride the line
> Please, Mr. Engineer let a man ride the line
> I ain't got no ticket please let me ride the blinds

Rose enters from the house. Troy, hearing her steps behind him, stands and faces her.

She's my daughter, Rose. My own flesh and blood. I can't deny her no more than I can deny them boys. (*Pause.*) You and them boys is my family. You and them and this child is all I got in the world. So I guess what I'm saying is . . . I'd appreciate it if you'd help me take care of her.

Rose: Okay, Troy . . . you're right. I'll take care of your baby for you . . . 'cause . . . like you say . . . she's innocent . . . and you can't visit the sins of the father upon the child. A motherless child has got a hard time. (*She takes the baby from him.*) From right now . . . this child got a mother. But you a womanless man.

Rose turns and exits into the house with the baby. Lights go down to black.

SCENE 4

It is two months later. Lyons enters from the street. He knocks on the door and calls.

Lyons: Hey, Rose! (*Pause.*) Rose!

Rose: (*from inside the house*) Stop that yelling. You gonna wake up Raynell. I just got her to sleep.

Lyons: I just stopped by to pay Papa this twenty dollars I owe him. Where's Papa at?

Rose: He should be here in a minute. I'm getting ready to go down to the church. Sit down and wait on him.

Lyons: I got to go pick up Bonnie over her mother's house. 5

Rose: Well, sit it down there on the table. He'll get it.

Lyons: (*enters the house and sets the money on the table*) Tell Papa I said thanks. I'll see you again.

Rose: All right, Lyons. We'll see you.

Lyons starts to exit as Cory enters.

Cory: Hey, Lyons.

Lyons: What's happening, Cory? Say man, I'm sorry I 10
missed your graduation. You know I had a gig and couldn't get away. Otherwise, I would have been there, man. So what you doing?

Cory: I'm trying to find a job.

Lyons: Yeah I know how that go, man. It's rough out there. Jobs are scarce.

Cory: Yeah, I know.

Lyons: Look here, I got to run. Talk to Papa . . . he know some people. He'll be able to help get you a job. Talk to him . . . see what he say.

Cory: Yeah . . . all right, Lyons. 15

Lyons: You take care. I'll talk to you soon. We'll find some time to talk.

Lyons exits the yard. Cory wanders over to the tree, picks up the bat, and assumes a batting stance. He studies an imaginary pitcher and swings. Dissatisfied with the result, he tries again. Troy enters. They eye each other for a beat. Cory puts the bat down and exits the yard. Troy starts into the house as Rose exits with Raynell. She is carrying a cake.

Troy: I'm coming in and everybody's going out.

Rose: I'm taking this cake down to the church for the bake sale. Lyons was by to see you. He stopped by to pay you your twenty dollars. It's laying in there on the table.

Troy: (*going into his pocket*) Well . . . here go this money.

Rose: Put it in there on the table, Troy. I'll get it. 20

Troy: What time you coming back?

Rose: Ain't no use in you studying me. It don't matter what time I come back.

Troy: I just asked you a question, woman. What's the matter . . . can't I ask you a question?

Rose: Troy, I don't want to go into it. Your dinner's in there on the stove. All you got to do is heat it up. And don't you be eating the rest of them cakes in there. I'm coming back for them. We having a bake sale at the church tomorrow.

Rose exits the yard. Troy sits down on the steps, takes a pint bottle from his pocket, opens it, and drinks. He begins to sing.

Troy: 25

       Hear it ring! Hear it ring!
       Had an old dog his name was Blue
       You know Blue was mighty true
       You know Blue was a good old dog
       Blue treed a possum in a hollow log
       You know from that he was a good old dog

Bono enters the yard.

Bono: Hey, Troy.

Troy: Hey, what's happening, Bono?

Bono: I just thought I'd stop by to see you.

Troy: What you stop by and see me for? You ain't stopped by in a month of Sundays. Hell, I must owe you money or something.

Bono: Since you got your promotion I can't keep up with 30 you. Used to see you every day. Now I don't even know what route you working.

Troy: They keep switching me around. Got me out in Greentree now . . . hauling white folks' garbage.

Bono: Greentree, huh? You lucky, at least you ain't got to be lifting them barrels. Damn if they ain't getting heavier. I'm gonna put in my two years and call it quits.

Troy: I'm thinking about retiring myself.

Bono: You got it easy. You can *drive* for another five years.

Troy: It ain't the same, Bono. It ain't like working the 35 back of the truck. Ain't got nobody to talk to . . . feel like you working by yourself. Naw, I'm thinking about retiring. How's Lucille?

Bono: She all right. Her arthritis get to acting up on her sometime. Saw Rose on my way in. She going down to the church, huh?

Troy: Yeah, she took up going down there. All them preachers looking for somebody to fatten their pockets. *(Pause.)* Got some gin here.

Bono: Naw, thanks. I just stopped by to say hello.

Troy: Hell, nigger . . . you can take a drink. I ain't never known you to say no to a drink. You ain't got to work tomorrow.

Bono: I just stopped by. I'm fixing to go over to Skin- 40 ner's. We got us a domino game going over his house every Friday.

Troy: Nigger, you can't play no dominoes. I used to whup you four games out of five.

Bono: Well, that learned me. I'm getting better.

Troy: Yeah? Well, that's all right.

Bono: Look here . . . I got to be getting on. Stop by sometime, huh?

Troy: Yeah, I'll do that, Bono. Lucille told Rose you 45 bought her a new refrigerator.

Bono: Yeah, Rose told Lucille you had finally built your fence . . . so I figured we'd call it even.

Troy: I knew you would.

Bono: Yeah . . . okay. I'll be talking to you.

Troy: Yeah, take care, Bono. Good to see you. I'm gonna stop over.

Bono: Yeah. Okay, Troy.   50

Bono exits. Troy drinks from the bottle.

Troy:

       Old Blue died and I dig his grave
       Let him down with a golden chain
       Every night when I hear old Blue bark
       I know Blue treed a possum in Noah's Ark.
       Hear it ring! Hear it ring!

Cory enters the yard. They eye each other for a beat. Troy is sitting in the middle of the steps. Cory walks over.

Cory: I got to get by.

Troy: Say what? What's you say?

Cory: You in my way. I got to get by.

Troy: You got to get by where? This is my house. Bought 55 and paid for. In full. Took me fifteen years. And if you wanna go in my house and I'm sitting on the steps . . . you say excuse me. Like your mama taught you.

Cory: Come on, Pop . . . I got to get by.

Cory starts to maneuver his way past Troy. Troy grabs his leg and shoves him back.

Troy: You just gonna walk over top of me?

Cory: I live here too!

Troy: *(advancing toward him)* You just gonna walk over top of me in my own house?

Cory: I ain't scared of you.   60

Troy: I ain't asked if you was scared of me. I asked you if you was fixing to walk over top of me in my own house? That's the question. You ain't gonna say excuse me? You just gonna walk over top of me?

Cory: If you wanna put it like that.

Troy: How else am I gonna put it?

Cory: I was walking by you to go into the house 'cause you sitting on the steps drunk, singing to yourself. You can put it like that.

Troy: Without saying excuse me???   65

Cory doesn't respond.

    I asked you a question. Without saying excuse me???

Cory: I ain't got to say excuse me to you. You don't count around here no more.

Troy: Oh, I see . . . I don't count around here no more. You ain't got to say excuse me to your daddy. All of a sudden you done got so grown that your daddy don't count around here no more . . . Around here in his own house and yard that he done paid for with the sweat of his brow. You done got so grown to where you gonna take over. You gonna take over my house. Is that right? You gonna wear my pants. You gonna go in there and stretch out on my bed. You ain't got to say excuse me 'cause I don't count around here no more. Is that right?

Cory: That's right. You always talking this dumb stuff. Now, why don't you just get out my way?

Troy: I guess you got someplace to sleep and something to put in your belly. You got that, huh? You got that? That's what you need. You got that, huh?

Cory: You don't know what I got. You ain't got to worry about what I got. 70

Troy: You right! You one hundred percent right! I done spent the last seventeen years worrying about what you got. Now it's your turn, see? I'll tell you what to do. You grown . . . we done established that. You a man. Now, let's see you act like one. Turn your behind around and walk out this yard. And when you get out there in the alley . . . you can forget about this house. See? 'Cause this is my house. You go on and be a man and get your own house. You can forget about this. 'Cause this is mine. You go on and get yours 'cause I'm through with doing for you.

Cory: You talking about what you did for me . . . what'd you ever give me?

Troy: Them feet and bones! That pumping heart, nigger! I give you more than anybody else is ever gonna give you.

Cory: You ain't never gave me nothing! You ain't never done nothing but hold me back. Afraid I was gonna be better than you. All you ever did was try and make me scared of you. I used to tremble every time you called my name. Every time I heard your footsteps in the house. Wondering all the time . . . what's Papa gonna say if I do this? . . . What's he gonna say if I do that? . . . What's Papa gonna say if I turn on the radio? And Mama, too . . . she tries . . . but she's scared of you.

Troy: You leave your mama out of this. She ain't got nothing to do with this. 75

Cory: I don't know how she stand you . . . after what you did to her.

Troy: I told you to leave your mama out of this!

He advances toward Cory.

Cory: What you gonna do . . . give me a whupping? You can't whup me no more. You're too old. You just an old man.

Troy: *(shoves him on his shoulder)* Nigger! That's what you are. You just another nigger on the street to me!

Cory: You crazy! You know that? 80

Troy: Go on now! You got the devil in you. Get on away from me!

Cory: You just a crazy old man . . . talking about I got the devil in me.

Troy: Yeah, I'm crazy! If you don't get on the other side of that yard . . . I'm gonna show you how crazy I am! Go on . . . get the hell out of my yard.

Cory: It ain't your yard. You took Uncle Gabe's money he got from the army to buy this house and then you put him out.

Troy: *(advances on Cory)* Get your black ass out of my yard! 85

Troy's advance backs Cory up against the tree. Cory grabs up the bat.

Cory: I ain't going nowhere! Come on . . . put me out! I ain't scared of you.

Troy: That's my bat!

Cory: Come on!

Troy: Put my bat down!

Cory: Come on, put me out. 90

Cory swings at Troy, who backs across the yard.

What's the matter? You so bad . . . put me out!

Troy advances toward Cory.

Cory: *(backing up)* Come on! Come on!

Troy: You're gonna have to use it! You wanna draw that bat back on me . . . you're gonna have to use it.

Cory: Come on! . . . Come on!

Cory swings the bat at Troy a second time. He misses. Troy continues to advance toward him.

Troy: You're gonna have to kill me! You wanna draw that bat back on me. You're gonna have to kill me.

Cory, backed up against the tree, can go no farther. Troy taunts him. He sticks out his head and offers him a target.

Come on! Come on!

Cory is unable to swing the bat. Troy grabs it.

Troy: Then I'll show you. 95

Cory and Troy struggle over the bat. The struggle is fierce and fully engaged. Troy ultimately is the stronger and takes the bat away from Cory and stands over him ready to swing. He stops himself.

Go on and get away from around my house.

Cory, stung by his defeat, picks himself up, walks slowly out of the yard and up the alley.

Cory: Tell Mama I'll be back for my things.

Troy: They'll be on the other side of that fence.

Cory exits.

Troy: I can't taste nothing. Helluljah! I can't taste nothing no more. *(Troy assumes a batting posture and begins to taunt Death, the fastball on the outside corner.)* Come on! It's between you and me now! Come on! Anytime you want! Come on! I be ready for you . . . but I ain't gonna be easy.

The lights go down on the scene.

SCENE 5

The time is 1965. The lights come up in the yard. It is the morning of Troy's funeral. A funeral plaque with a light hangs beside the door. There is a small garden plot off to the side. There is noise and activity in the house as Rose, Gabriel, and Bono have gathered. The door opens and Raynell, seven years old, enters dressed in a flannel nightgown. She crosses to the garden and pokes around with a stick. Rose calls from the house.

Rose: Raynell!
Raynell: Mam?
Rose: What you doing out there?
Raynell: Nothing.

Rose comes to the door.

Rose: Girl, get in here and get dressed. What you doing? 5
Raynell: Seeing if my garden growed.
Rose: I told you it ain't gonna grow overnight. You got to wait.
Raynell: It don't look like it never gonna grow. Dag!
Rose: I told you a watched pot never boils. Get in here and get dressed.
Raynell: This ain't even no pot, Mama. 10
Rose: You just have to give it a chance. It'll grow. Now you come on and do what I told you. We got to be getting ready. This ain't no morning to be playing around. You hear me?
Raynell: Yes, mam.

Rose exits into the house. Raynell continues to poke at her garden with a stick. Cory enters. He is dressed in a Marine corporal's uniform, and carries a duffel bag. His posture is that of a military man, and his speech has a clipped sternness.

Cory: *(to Raynell)* Hi. *(Pause.)* I bet your name is Raynell.
Raynell: Uh huh.
Cory: Is your mama home? 15

Raynell runs up on the porch and calls through the screen door.

Raynell: Mama . . . there's some man out here. Mama?

Rose comes to the door.

Rose: Cory? Lord have mercy! Look here, you all!

Rose and Cory embrace in a tearful reunion as Bono and Lyons enter from the house dressed in funeral clothes.

Bono: Aw, looka here . . .
Rose: Done got all grown up!
Cory: Don't cry, Mama. What you crying about? 20
Rose: I'm just so glad you made it.
Cory: Hey Lyons. How you doing, Mr. Bono.

Lyons goes to embrace Cory.

Lyons: Look at you, man. Look at you. Don't he look good, Rose. Got them Corporal stripes.

Rose: What took you so long?
Cory: You know how the Marines are, Mama. They got to get all their paperwork straight before they let you do anything. 25
Rose: Well, I'm sure glad you made it. They let Lyons come. Your Uncle Gabe's still in the hospital. They don't know if they gonna let him out or not. I just talked to them a little while ago.
Lyons: A Corporal in the United States Marines.
Bono: Your daddy knew you had it in you. He used to tell me all the time.
Lyons: Don't he look good, Mr. Bono?
Bono: Yeah, he remind me of Troy when I first met him. *(Pause.)* Say, Rose, Lucille's down at the church with the choir. I'm gonna go down and get the pallbearers lined up. I'll be back to get you all. 30
Rose: Thanks, Jim.
Cory: See you, Mr. Bono.
Lyons: *(with his arm around Raynell)* Cory . . . look at Raynell. Ain't she precious? She gonna break a whole lot of hearts.
Rose: Raynell, come and say hello to your brother. This is your brother, Cory. You remember Cory.
Raynell: No, Mam. 35
Cory: She don't remember me, Mama.
Rose: Well, we talk about you. She heard us talk about you. *(To Raynell.)* This is your brother, Cory. Come on and say hello.
Raynell: Hi.
Cory: Hi. So you're Raynell. Mama told me a lot about you.
Rose: You all come on into the house and let me fix you some breakfast. Keep up your strength. 40
Cory: I ain't hungry, Mama.
Lyons: You can fix me something, Rose. I'll be in there in a minute.
Rose: Cory, you sure you don't want nothing? I know they ain't feeding you right.
Cory: No, Mama . . . thanks. I don't feel like eating. I'll get something later.
Rose: Raynell . . . get on upstairs and get that dress on like I told you. 45

Rose and Raynell exit into the house.

Lyons: So . . . I hear you thinking about getting married.
Cory: Yeah, I done found the right one, Lyons. It's about time.
Lyons: Me and Bonnie been split up about four years now. About the time Papa retired. I guess she just got tired of all them changes I was putting her through. *(Pause.)* I always knew you was gonna make something out yourself. Your head was always in the right direction. So . . . you gonna stay in . . . make it a career . . . put in your twenty years?
Cory: I don't know. I got six already, I think that's enough.
Lyons: Stick with Uncle Sam and retire early. Ain't nothing out here. I guess Rose told you what 50

happened with me. They got me down the work-house. I thought I was being slick cashing other people's checks.

Cory: How much time you doing?

Lyons: They give me three years. I got that beat now. I ain't got but nine more months. It ain't so bad. You learn to deal with it like anything else. You got to take the crookeds with the straights. That's what Papa used to say. He used to say that when he struck out. I seen him strike out three times in a row . . . and the next time up he hit the ball over the grand-stand. Right out there in Homestead Field. He wasn't satisfied hitting in the seats . . . he want to hit it over everything! After the game he had two hundred people standing around waiting to shake his hand. You got to take the crookeds with the straights. Yeah, Papa was something else.

Cory: You still playing?

Lyons: Cory . . . you know I'm gonna do that. There's some fellows down there we got us a band . . . we gonna try and stay together when we get out . . . but yeah, I'm still playing. It still helps me to get out of bed in the morning. As long as it do that I'm gonna be right there playing and trying to make some sense out of it.

Rose: *(calling)* Lyons, I got these eggs in the pan.   55

Lyons: Let me go on and get these eggs, man. Get ready to go bury Papa. *(Pause.)* How you doing? You doing all right?

Cory nods. Lyons touches him on the shoulder and they share a moment of silent grief. Lyons exits into the house. Cory wanders about the yard. Raynell enters.

Raynell: Hi.

Cory: Hi.

Raynell: Did you used to sleep in my room?

Cory: Yeah . . . that used to be my room.   60

Raynell: That's what Papa call it. "Cory's room." It got your football in the closet.

Rose comes to the door.

Rose: Raynell, get in there and get them good shoes on.

Raynell: Mama, can't I wear these? Them other ones hurt my feet.

Rose: Well, they just gonna have to hurt your feet for a while. You ain't said they hurt your feet when you went down to the store and got them.

Raynell: They didn't hurt then. My feet done got bigger.   65

Rose: Don't you give me no backtalk now. You get in there and get them shoes on.

Raynell exits into the house.

Ain't too much changed. He still got that piece of rag tied to that tree. He was out here swinging that bat. I was just ready to go back in the house. He swung that bat and then he just fell over. Seem like he swung it and stood there with this grin on his face . . . and then he just fell over. They carried him on down to the hospital, but I knew there wasn't no need . . . why don't you come on in the house?

Cory: Mama . . . I got something to tell you. I don't know how to tell you this . . . but I've got to tell you . . . I'm not going to Papa's funeral.

Rose: Boy, hush your mouth. That's your daddy you talking about. I don't want hear that kind of talk this morning. I done raised you to come to this? You standing there all healthy and grown talking about you ain't going to your daddy's funeral?

Cory: Mama . . . listen . . .

Rose: I don't want to hear it, Cory. You just get that   70
thought out of your head.

Cory: I can't drag Papa with me everywhere I go. I've got to say no to him. One time in my life I've got to say no.

Rose: Don't nobody have to listen to nothing like that. I know you and your daddy ain't seen eye to eye, but I ain't got to listen to that kind of talk this morning. Whatever was between you and your daddy . . . the time has come to put it aside. Just take it and set it over there on the shelf and forget about it. Disrespecting your daddy ain't gonna make you a man, Cory. You got to find a way to come to that on your own. Not going to your daddy's funeral ain't gonna make you a man.

Cory: The whole time I was growing up . . . living in his house . . . Papa was like a shadow that followed you everywhere. It weighed on you and sunk into your flesh. It would wrap around you and lay there until you couldn't tell which one was you anymore. That shadow digging in your flesh. Trying to crawl in. Trying to live through you. Everywhere I looked, Troy Maxson was staring back at me . . . hiding under the bed . . . in the closet. I'm just saying I've got to find a way to get rid of that shadow, Mama.

Rose: You just like him. You got him in you good.

Cory: Don't tell me that, Mama.   75

Rose: You Troy Maxson all over again.

Cory: I don't want to be Troy Maxson. I want to be me.

Rose: You can't be nobody but who you are, Cory. That shadow wasn't nothing but you growing into yourself. You either got to grow into it or cut it down to fit you. But that's all you got to make life with. That's all you got to measure yourself against that world out there. Your daddy wanted you to be everything he wasn't . . . and at the same time he tried to make you into everything he was. I don't know if he was right or wrong . . . but I do know he meant to do more good than he meant to do harm. He wasn't always right. Sometimes when he touched he bruised. And sometimes when he took me in his arms he cut.

When I first met your daddy I thought . . . Here is a man I can lay down with and make a baby. That's the first thing I thought when I seen him. I was thirty years old and had done seen my share of men. But when he walked up to me and said, "I can dance a waltz that'll make you dizzy." I thought, Rose Lee, here is a man that you can open yourself up to and be filled to bursting. Here is a man that can fill all them empty spaces you been tipping around the edges of. One of them empty spaces was being somebody's mother.

I married your daddy and settled down to cooking his supper and keeping clean sheets on the bed. When your daddy walked through the house he was so big he filled it up. That was my first mistake. Not to make him leave some room for me. For my part in the matter. But at that time I wanted that. I wanted a house that I could sing in. And that's what your daddy gave me. I didn't know to keep up his strength I had to give up little pieces of mine. I did that. I took on his life as mine and mixed up the pieces so that you couldn't hardly tell which was which anymore. It was my choice. It was my life and I didn't have to live it like that. But that's what life offered me in the way of being a woman and I took it. I grabbed hold of it with both hands.

By the time Raynell came into the house, me and your daddy had done lost touch with one another. I didn't want to make my blessing off of nobody's misfortune . . . but I took on to Raynell like she was all them babies I had wanted and never had.

The phone rings.

Like I'd been blessed to relive a part of my life. And if the Lord see fit to keep up my strength . . . I'm gonna do her just like your daddy did you . . . I'm gonna give her the best of what's in me.

Raynell: *(entering, still with her old shoes)* Mama . . . Reverend Tollivier on the phone.

Rose exits into the house.

Raynell: Hi.   80
Cory: Hi.
Raynell: You in the Army or the Marines?
Cory: Marines.
Raynell: Papa said it was the Army. Did you know Blue?
Cory: Blue? Who's Blue?   85
Raynell: Papa's dog what he sing about all the time.
Cory: *(singing)*
　　　　Hear it ring! Hear it ring!
　　　　I had a dog his name was Blue
　　　　You know Blue was mighty true
　　　　You know Blue was a good old dog
　　　　Blue treed a possum in a hollow log
　　　　You know from that he was a good old dog.
　　　　Hear it ring! Hear it ring!

Raynell joins in singing.

Cory and Raynell:
　　　　Blue treed a possum out on a limb
　　　　Blue looked at me and I looked at him
　　　　Grabbed that possum and put him in a sack
　　　　Blue stayed there till I came back
　　　　Old Blue's feets was big and round
　　　　Never allowed a possum to touch the ground.
　　　　Old Blue died and I dug his grave
　　　　I dug his grave with a silver spade
　　　　Let him down with a golden chain
　　　　And every night I call his name
　　　　Go on Blue, you good dog you
　　　　Go on Blue, you good dog you
Raynell:
　　　　Blue laid down and died like a man
　　　　Blue laid down and died . . .
Both: 90
　　　　Blue laid down and died like a man
　　　　Now he's treeing possums in the Promised Land
　　　　I'm gonna tell you this to let you know
　　　　Blue's gone where the good dogs go
　　　　When I hear old Blue bark
　　　　When I hear old Blue bark
　　　　Blue treed a possum in Noah's Ark°
　　　　Blue treed a possum in Noah's Ark.

Rose comes to the screen door.

Rose: Cory, we gonna be ready to go in a minute.
Cory: *(to Raynell)* You go on in the house and change them shoes like Mama told you so we can go to Papa's funeral.
Raynell: Okay, I'll be back.

Raynell exits into the house. Cory gets up and crosses over to the tree. Rose stands in the screen door watching him. Gabriel enters from the alley.

Gabriel: *(calling)* Hey, Rose!
Rose: Gabe?   95
Gabriel: I'm here, Rose. Hey Rose, I'm here!

Rose enters from the house.

Rose: Lord . . . Look here, Lyons!
Lyons: See, I told you, Rose . . . I told you they'd let him come.
Cory: How you doing, Uncle Gabe?
Lyons: How you doing, Uncle Gabe?   100
Gabriel: Hey, Rose. It's time. It's time to tell St. Peter to open the gates. Troy, you ready? You ready, Troy. I'm gonna tell St. Peter to open the gates. You get ready now.

Gabriel, with great fanfare, braces himself to blow. The trumpet is without a mouthpiece. He puts the end of it into his mouth and blows with great force, like a man who has been waiting some twenty-odd years for this single moment. No sound comes out of the trumpet. He braces himself and blows again with the same result. A third time he blows. There is a weight of

---

° **Noah's Ark** See Genesis 6.14–20.

impossible description that fails away and leaves him bare and exposed to a frightful realization. It is a trauma that a sane and normal mind would be unable to withstand. He begins to dance. A slow, strange dance, eerie and life-giving. A dance of atavistic signature and ritual. Lyons attempts to embrace him. Gabriel pushes Lyons away. He begins to howl in what is an attempt at song, or perhaps a songturning back into itself in an attempt at speech. He finishes his dance and the gates of heaven stand open as wide as God's closet.

That's the way that go!

Related Works

"Big Black Good Man" (p. 184), "Yet Do I Marvel" (p. 474), *Death of a Salesman* (p. 605)

See Chapter 35 Review Card for Reading and Reacting questions about August Wilson, *Fences.*

Writing Suggestions: Theme

1. In an interview, writer Lorrie Moore calls *Fences* "an African American *Death of a Salesman*." What do you think she means? Do you agree? Write an essay in which you examine the two plays in light of Moore's comment.

2. Write an essay in which you analyze the baseball images in *Fences*. How do the references to baseball help to develop the play's themes?

3. One of the themes of *Fences* is the dream a family has for its children. Compare the development of this theme in *Fences* and in another work in this book.

✔ CHECKLIST

WRITING ABOUT THEME

- [ ] What is the central theme of the play?
- [ ] What other themes can you identify?
- [ ] Does the title of the play suggest a theme?
- [ ] What conflicts exist in the play? How do they shed light on the themes of the play?
- [ ] Do any characters' statements express or imply a theme of the play?
- [ ] Do any characters change during the play? How do these changes suggest the play's themes?
- [ ] Do certain characters resist change? How does their failure to change suggest a theme of the play?
- [ ] Do scenery and props help to communicate the play's themes?
- [ ] Does music reinforce certain ideas in the play?
- [ ] Does lighting underscore the themes of the play?

Credits

Index of Authors and Titles

Index of Literary Terms

to BEN KATCHOR, "The Goner Pillow Company" (p. 113)

1. What actually happens during the course of "The Goner Pillow Company"? How much time do you think goes by from first panel to last?

2. In what sense does the first panel of the story provide exposition? Does the story include any foreshadowing? Does it include any flashbacks?

3. In panels 7–9, the narrator poses a series of questions. How do the illustrations answer these questions? How does panel 10 answer the questions?

4. How are the members of the Goner family different in terms of their attitude toward "the home entertainment industry"? Which family member's attitude is most like your own?

to KATE CHOPIN, "The Story of an Hour" (p. 115)

1. The story's basic exposition is presented in its first two paragraphs. What additional information about character or setting would you like to know? Why do you suppose Chopin does not supply this information?

2. "The Story of an Hour" is a very economical story, with little action or dialogue. Do you see this economy as a strength or a weakness? Explain.

3. What is the nature of the conflict in this story? Who, or what, do you see as Mrs. Mallard's antagonist?

4. Do you find the story's ending satisfying? believable? contrived? Was the story's ending unexpected, or were you prepared for it? What elements in the story foreshadow this ending?

to STEPHEN DOBYNS, "Kansas" (p. 117)

1. Paragraph 1 presents the story's exposition. List the specific information this paragraph reveals. How will each detail be important later in the story? Are any details unnecessary? Are any important details not introduced in paragraph 1?

2. What specific information are readers told in the story's first twenty-five paragraphs about the boy? the farmer? the couple in the blue Plymouth? Is all this information essential to the story's plot? What additional information might you want to know? Why?

3. The first twenty-five paragraphs present the story's basic plot; then, this section of the story is followed by three alternate versions of the boy's experience, each beginning with the sentence "The boy was standing by the side of a dirt road." How are the three alternate versions of events similar to and different from the boy's story as it is first presented? Which version is most satisfying? most logical? most believable? Explain.

4. What does the last sentence add to the story?

to WILLIAM FAULKNER, "A Rose for Emily" (p. 121)

1. Despite the story's confusing sequence, many events are foreshadowed. Give some examples of this technique. How does foreshadowing enrich the story?

2. Where does the exposition end and the movement toward the story's climax begin? Where does the resolution stage begin?

3. Emily is clearly the story's protagonist. In the sense that he opposes her wishes, Homer is the antagonist. What other characters—or what larger forces—are in conflict with Emily?

4. The narrator of the story is an observer, not a participant. Who might this narrator be? Do you think the narrator is male or female? How do you suppose the narrator might know so much about Emily? Why do you think the narrator uses *we* instead of *I*?

CHAPTER 11 CHECKLIST
for KATE CHOPIN, "The Story of an Hour"
(p. 115)

WRITING ABOUT PLOT

- ☐ What happens in the story?
- ☐ Identify the story's crisis or crises.
- ☐ Identify the story's climax.
- ☐ How are the story's events arranged? Are they presented in chronological order? What events are presented out of logical sequence? Are the causal connections between events clear? logical? If not, can you explain why?

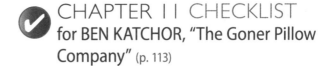

CHAPTER 11 CHECKLIST
for BEN KATCHOR, "The Goner Pillow Company" (p. 113)

WRITING ABOUT PLOT

- ☐ What do readers learn about characters in the story's exposition section? What do readers learn about setting? What possible conflicts are suggested here?
- ☐ What is the story's central conflict? What other conflicts are presented? Who is the protagonist? Who (or what) serves as the antagonist?
- ☐ How is the story's central conflict resolved? Is this resolution plausible? satisfying?
- ☐ Which part of the story constitutes the resolution? Do any problems remain unresolved? Does any uncertainty remain? If so, does this uncertainty strengthen or weaken the story? Would another ending be more effective?

CHAPTER 11 CHECKLIST
for WILLIAM FAULKNER, "A Rose for Emily"
(p. 121)

WRITING ABOUT PLOT

- ☐ What happens in the story?
- ☐ What do readers learn about characters in the story's exposition section? What do readers learn about setting? What possible conflicts are suggested here?
- ☐ Identify the story's crisis or crises.
- ☐ How are the story's events arranged? Are they presented in chronological order? What events are presented out of logical sequence? Are the causal connections between events clear? logical? If not, can you explain why?

CHAPTER 11 CHECKLIST
for STEPHEN DOBYNS, "Kansas" (p. 117)

WRITING ABOUT PLOT

- ☐ What do readers learn about characters in the story's exposition section? What do readers learn about setting? What possible conflicts are suggested here?
- ☐ What is the story's central conflict? What other conflicts are presented? Who is the protagonist? Who (or what) serves as the antagonist?
- ☐ Which part of the story constitutes the resolution? Do any problems remain unresolved? Does any uncertainty remain? If so, does this uncertainty strengthen or weaken the story? Would another ending be more effective?
- ☐ How are the story's events arranged? Are they presented in chronological order? What events are presented out of logical sequence? Does the story use foreshadowing? flashbacks? Are the causal connections between events clear? logical? If not, can you explain why?

to ART SPIEGELMAN, "Eye Ball" (p. 130)

1. According to the narrator of "Eye Ball," what are the major traits cartoonists must possess? How are these traits in conflict with the characteristics of a typical "boy in 1950s America"?

2. This graphic story is limited to two settings, the ballfield and the library. Are these two settings sufficient to illustrate the narrator's major problem, or would other settings be helpful?

3. The last panel alludes to Franz Kafka's "The Metamorphosis," a novella in which an alienated office worker turns overnight into a large bug. What do you think the narrator means by his final comment?

to JOHN UPDIKE, "A&P" (p. 131)

1. Summarize the information Sammy gives readers about his tastes and background. Why is this exposition vital to the story's development?

2. List some of the most obvious physical characteristics of the A&P's customers. How do these characteristics make them foils for Queenie and her friends?

3. How accurate are Sammy's judgments about the other characters? How might the characters be portrayed if the story were told by Lengel?

4. Given what you learn about Sammy during the course of the story, what do you see as his *primary* motivation for quitting his job? What other factors motivate him?

to KATHERINE MANSFIELD, "Miss Brill" (p. 135)

1. What specific details can you infer about Miss Brill's character (and, perhaps, about her life) from this statement: "She had become really quite expert, she thought, at listening as though she didn't listen, at sitting in other people's lives just for a minute while they talked round her" (par. 3)? Why do you suppose she doesn't interact with any of the people she observes?

2. In paragraph 9, Miss Brill realizes that the scene she observes is "exactly like a play" and that "Even she had a part and came every Sunday." What part does Miss Brill play? Is she a stock character in this play, or is she a three-dimensional character? Does she play a lead role or a supporting role?

3. What do you think Miss Brill means when she says, "I have been an actress for a long time" (par. 9)? What does this comment reveal about how she sees herself? Is her view of herself similar to or different from the view the other characters have of her?

4. At the end of the story, has Miss Brill changed as a result of what she has overheard, or is she the same person she was at the beginning? Do you think she will return to the park the following Sunday?

to CHARLES BAXTER, "Gryphon" (p. 138)

1. Describe Miss Ferenczi's physical appearance. Why is her appearance important to the story? How does it change as the story progresses?

2. How is Miss Ferenczi different from other teachers? from other substitute teachers? from other people in general? How is her differentness communicated to her pupils? to the story's readers?

3. Is Miss Ferenczi a round or a flat character? Explain.

4. Why does the narrator defend Miss Ferenczi, first in his argument with Carl Whiteside and later on the playground? What does his attitude toward Miss Ferenczi reveal about his own character?

✔ CHAPTER 12 CHECKLIST
for JOHN UPDIKE, "A&P" (p. 131)

WRITING ABOUT A CHARACTER

- ☐ What are the main character's most strongly held feelings and beliefs?
- ☐ What are we told about the major characters' backgrounds and prior experiences? What can we infer?
- ☐ Does the story include any stock characters? Does any character serve as a foil?
- ☐ With which characters are readers likely to be most sympathetic? least sympathetic?

✔ CHAPTER 12 CHECKLIST
for ART SPIEGELMAN, "Eye Ball" (p. 130)

WRITING ABOUT A CHARACTER

- ☐ What does the major character look like? Is his physical appearance important?
- ☐ What is the major character's most notable personality traits?
- ☐ What are the main character's most strongly held feelings and beliefs?
- ☐ What are we told about the major character's background and prior experiences? What can we infer?

✔ CHAPTER 12 CHECKLIST
for CHARLES BAXTER, "Gryphon" (p. 138)

WRITING ABOUT A CHARACTER

- ☐ What do the major characters look like? Is their physical appearance important?
- ☐ What are the major characters' most notable personality traits?
- ☐ Are the characters round or flat?
- ☐ Does the story include any stock characters? Does any character serve as a foil?

✔ CHAPTER 12 CHECKLIST
for KATHERINE MANSFIELD, "Miss Brill" (p. 135)

WRITING ABOUT A CHARACTER

- ☐ What are the major characters' most notable personality traits?
- ☐ Are the characters round or flat?
- ☐ Are the characters dynamic or static?
- ☐ Does the story include any stock characters? Does any character serve as a foil?

to MARJANE SATRAPI, from *Persepolis*
(p. 151)

1. What specific visual elements establish the setting of *Persepolis* as harsh and restrictive for Marji?

2. Compare the facial expressions of the "guardians of the revolution" (especially in the final four panels) with Marji's. How are they different? In what other respects does Marji look different from these women?

3. The two panels that show Marji purchasing the tapes are the only ones that have a dark background. Do you think Satrapi should have used dark backgrounds in any other panels? Why or why not?

to KATE CHOPIN, "The Storm" (p. 154)

1. How does the weather help to create the story's atmosphere? How would you characterize this atmosphere?

2. In Part I, the "sombre clouds . . . rolling with sinister intention" introduce the storm. In what sense does this description introduce the story's action as well?

3. In what ways does the storm *cause* the events of the story? List specific events that occur because of the storm. Is the presence of the storm essential to the story?

4. The weather is the most obvious element of the story's setting. What other aspects of setting are important to the story?

to SHERMAN J. ALEXIE, "This Is What It Means to Say Phoenix, Arizona" (p. 157)

1. In paragraph 1, readers are told that Victor lives on an Indian reservation. What details elsewhere in the story establish this setting? What associations does this setting have for you? Do you think the story could take place anywhere else?

2. In addition to various locations on the reservation, the story's settings include an airplane, a trailer in Phoenix, and a road through Nevada. What does each of these settings contribute to the story's plot?

3. How would you characterize the story's mood or atmosphere? How do Thomas's stories help to create this mood? How do they help to establish his character? Do you think Alexie should have included more of these stories?

4. Why do you suppose Victor and Thomas cannot be friends when they get back to the reservation? Why are they able to be friends when they are traveling to Phoenix?

to TILLIE OLSEN, "I Stand Here Ironing"
(p. 162)

1. "I Stand Here Ironing" focuses on incidents that took place in the "pre-relief, pre-WPA world" of the Depression (par. 9). In light of social, political, and economic changes that have occurred since the 1930s, do you think the events the story presents could occur today? Explain.

2. Who, or what, do you blame for the narrator's problems? For example, do you blame Emily's father? The Depression? The social institutions and "experts" to which the narrator turns?

3. Do you see the narrator as a victim limited by the times in which she lives? Do you agree with the narrator that Emily is "a child of her age, of depression, of war, of fear" (par. 55)? Or do you believe both women have some control over their own destinies, regardless of the story's historical setting?

4. Paragraph 28 describes the physical setting of the convalescent home to which Emily was sent. What does this description add to the story? Why do you suppose there is no physical description of the apartment in which Emily lived as a child? How do you picture this apartment?

✔ CHAPTER 13 CHECKLIST
for KATE CHOPIN, "The Storm" (p. 154)

WRITING ABOUT SETTING

- ☐ Is the setting just background, or is it a key force in the story?
- ☐ How does the setting influence the story's plot? Does it cause characters to act?
- ☐ What role do weather conditions play in the story?
- ☐ How does the setting influence the characters? Does it affect (or reflect) their emotional state? Does it help to explain their motivation?

✔ CHAPTER 13 CHECKLIST
for MARJANE SATRAPI, from *Persepolis*
(p. 151)

WRITING ABOUT SETTING

- ☐ In what time period does the story take place? How can you tell? What social, political, or economic situations or events of the historical period might influence the story?
- ☐ In what geographical location is the story set? Is this location important to the story?
- ☐ What kind of atmosphere or mood does the setting create? Does the atmosphere or mood change as the story progresses? Is this change significant?
- ☐ How does the setting influence the characters? Does it affect (or reflect) their emotional state? Does it help to explain their motivation?

✔ CHAPTER 13 CHECKLIST
for TILLIE OLSEN, "I Stand Here Ironing"
(p. 162)

WRITING ABOUT SETTING

- ☐ Is the setting specified or unspecified? Is it fully described or only suggested?
- ☐ Are any characters in conflict with their environment?
- ☐ In what time period does the story take place? How can you tell? What social, political, or economic situations or events of the historical period might influence the story?
- ☐ How does the setting influence the characters? Does it affect (or reflect) their emotional state? Does it help to explain their motivation?

✔ CHAPTER 13 CHECKLIST
for SHERMAN J. ALEXIE, "This Is What It Means to Say Phoenix, Arizona" (p. 157)

WRITING ABOUT SETTING

- ☐ Is the setting just background, or is it a key force in the story?
- ☐ Are any characters in conflict with their environment?
- ☐ In what geographical location is the story set? Is this location important to the story?
- ☐ How does the setting influence the characters? Does it affect (or reflect) their emotional state? Does it help to explain their motivation?

READING AND REACTING

to SHAUN TAN, from *The Arrival* (p. 174)

1. *The Arrival* was published as a book for children ages ten and up. In what respects does this excerpt seem like a story for children? In what respects does it seem like a story for adults?

2. *The Arrival* has no written text. Do you see this absence of words as a strength or a weakness?

3. The excerpt printed here (like the entire book) mixes realistic elements with elements of fantasy. What do the fantasy elements represent? What do they contribute to the story?

READING AND REACTING

to RICHARD WRIGHT, "Big Black Good Man" (p. 184)

1. Why do you suppose Wright presents events through Olaf's eyes? How would the story be different if Jim told it?

2. This story was published in 1957. What attitudes about race does Wright expect his American readers to have? Do these attitudes predispose readers to identify with Jim or with Olaf? Explain.

3. Why does Olaf dislike Jim? What does the narrator mean in paragraph 24 when he says that Jim's "intense blackness and ungainly bigness . . . frightened and insulted Olaf"?

4. In what ways do Jim's words and actions contribute to Olaf's fears? Do you think Olaf's reactions are reasonable, or do you believe he is overreacting?

READING AND REACTING

to EDGAR ALLAN POE, "The Cask of Amontillado" (p. 190)

1. Montresor cites a "thousand injuries" and an "insult" as his motivation for murdering Fortunato. Given what you learn about the two men during the course of the story, what do you suppose the "injuries" and "insult" might be?

2. Do you find Montresor to be a reliable narrator? If not, what makes you question his version of events?

3. What is Montresor's concept of personal honor? Is it consistent or inconsistent with the values of contemporary American society? How relevant are the story's ideas about revenge and guilt to present-day society? Explain.

4. Why does Montresor wait fifty years to tell his story? How might the story be different if he had told it the morning after the murder?

READING AND REACTING

to WILLIAM FAULKNER, "Barn Burning" (p. 194)

1. What is the point of view of the italicized passages? What do readers learn from them? How would the story have been different without these passages?

2. "Barn Burning" includes a great deal of dialogue. How would you characterize the level of diction of this dialogue? What information about various characters does it provide?

3. What conflicts are presented in "Barn Burning"? Are any of these conflicts avoidable? Which, if any, are resolved in the story? Explain.

4. What role does the Civil War play in "Barn Burning"? What does Abner Snopes's behavior during the war tell readers about his character?

CHAPTER 14 CHECKLIST
for RICHARD WRIGHT, "Big Black Good Man" (p. 184)

WRITING ABOUT POINT OF VIEW

- [ ] What is the dominant point of view from which the story is told?
- [ ] Does the story's point of view create irony?
- [ ] Is the story's third-person narrator omniscient? Does he have limited omniscience? Is the narrator objective?
- [ ] How might a different point of view change the story?

CHAPTER 14 CHECKLIST
for SHAUN TAN, from *The Arrival* (p. 174)

WRITING ABOUT POINT OF VIEW

- [ ] What is the dominant point of view from which the story is told?
- [ ] Does the story's point of view create irony?
- [ ] What are the advantages of the story's point of view? What are the disadvantages?
- [ ] Does the point of view remain consistent throughout the story, or does it shift? How might a different point of view change the story?

CHAPTER 14 CHECKLIST
for WILLIAM FAULKNER, "Barn Burning"
(p. 194)

WRITING ABOUT POINT OF VIEW

- [ ] What is the dominant point of view from which the story is told?
- [ ] Does the story's point of view create irony?
- [ ] Is the story's third-person narrator omniscient? Does he have limited omniscience? Is the narrator objective?
- [ ] Does the point of view remain consistent throughout the story, or does it shift? How might a different point of view change the story?

CHAPTER 14 CHECKLIST
for EDGAR ALLAN POE, "The Cask of Amontillado" (p. 190)

WRITING ABOUT POINT OF VIEW

- [ ] What is the dominant point of view from which the story is told?
- [ ] Is the narrator a character in the story? If so, is he a participant in the story's events or just a witness?
- [ ] What are the advantages of the story's point of view? What are the disadvantages?
- [ ] How might a different point of view change the story?

READING AND REACTING

to R. CRUMB, "A Hunger Artist" (p. 210)

1. How is the style—particularly the level of diction—used for the narrator's boxed comments different from the style used for dialogue?

2. How would you characterize this story's tone? What do the visual elements contribute to the tone?

3. Consider the story's visual style. How do visual elements—for example, the arrangement of images within panels, the relative size of the people depicted, and the use of white space—support the story's theme?

4. Do you see the hunger artist as a mentally ill fanatic or as a man of high principles? In what sense, if any, do you see him as an "artist"? How is he different from the crowds that come to see him?

READING AND REACTING

to JAMES JOYCE, "Araby" (p. 220)

1. How would you characterize the story's level of diction? Is this level appropriate for a story about a young boy's experiences? Explain.

2. Identify several figures of speech in the story. Where is Joyce most likely to use this kind of language? Why?

3. What words and phrases express the boy's extreme idealism and romantic view of the world? How does such language help to communicate the story's major theme?

4. How does the narrator's choice of words illustrate the contrast between his day-to-day life and the exotic promise of the bazaar?

READING AND REACTING

to (MARY) FLANNERY O'CONNOR, "A Good Man Is Hard to Find" (p. 224)

1. How are the style and tone of the narrator's voice different from those of the characters? What, if anything, is the significance of this difference?

2. The figures of speech used in this story sometimes create unflattering, even grotesque, pictures of the characters. Find several examples of such negative figures of speech. Why do you think O'Connor uses them?

3. What does the grandmother's use of the words *pickaninny* and *nigger* reveal about her? How are readers expected to reconcile this language with her very proper appearance and her preoccupation with manners? How does her use of these words affect your reaction to her?

4. How does The Misfit's dialect characterize him?

READING AND REACTING

to TIM O'BRIEN, "The Things They Carried" (p. 232)

1. Although the setting and the events described in "The Things They Carried" are dramatic and moving, its tone is often flat and emotionless. Give some examples. Why do you think the narrator adopts this kind of tone?

2. A striking characteristic of the story's style is its thorough catalogs of the concrete, tangible "things" the soldiers carry. Why do you suppose such detailed lists are included? What does what each man carries tell you about him? In a less literal, more abstract sense, what else do these men "carry"?

3. One stylistic technique O'Brien uses is intentional repetition—of phrases ("they carried"); people's names and identifying details (Martha's virginity, for example); and pieces of equipment. What effect do you think O'Brien hopes to achieve through such repetition? Is he successful?

4. Interspersed among long paragraphs crammed with detail are short one- or two-sentence paragraphs. What function do these brief paragraphs serve?

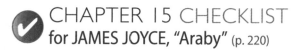

CHAPTER 15 CHECKLIST
for JAMES JOYCE, "Araby" (p. 220)

WRITING ABOUT STYLE, TONE, AND LANGUAGE

- [ ] Does the style emphasize the sound and rhythm of language? For example, does the writer use alliteration and assonance? repetition and parallelism? What do such techniques add to the story?
- [ ] What kind of imagery predominates? Where, and why, is imagery used?
- [ ] Do figures of speech reinforce the story's themes? reveal information about characters?
- [ ] Does the story make any historical, literary, or religious allusions? What do these allusions contribute to the story?

CHAPTER 15 CHECKLIST
for R. CRUMB, "A Hunger Artist" (p. 210)

WRITING ABOUT STYLE, TONE, AND LANGUAGE

- [ ] Is the level of diction generally formal, informal, or somewhere in between?
- [ ] What kind of imagery predominates? Where, and why, is imagery used?
- [ ] Does the story develop a pattern of imagery? How does this pattern of imagery help to convey the story's themes?
- [ ] Does the story make any historical, literary, or biblical allusions? What do these allusions contribute to the story?

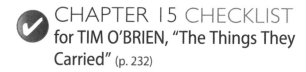

CHAPTER 15 CHECKLIST
for TIM O'BRIEN, "The Things They Carried" (p. 232)

WRITING ABOUT STYLE, TONE, AND LANGUAGE

- [ ] Does the writer make any unusual creative use of word choice, word order, or sentence structure?
- [ ] Is the level of diction generally formal, informal, or somewhere in between?
- [ ] Is there a difference between the style of the narrator and the style of the characters' speech? If so, what is the effect of this difference?
- [ ] Do any of the story's characters use regionalisms, colloquial language, or nonstandard speech? If so, what effect does this language have?

CHAPTER 15 CHECKLIST
for (MARY) FLANNERY O'CONNOR, "A Good Man Is Hard to Find" (p. 224)

WRITING ABOUT STYLE, TONE, AND LANGUAGE

- [ ] Does the writer make any unusual creative use of word choice, word order, or sentence structure?
- [ ] Is the story's tone intimate? distant? ironic? How does the tone advance the writer's purpose?
- [ ] Does the style emphasize the sound and rhythm of language? For example, does the writer use alliteration and assonance? repetition and parallelism? What do such techniques add to the story?
- [ ] Does the story make any historical, literary, or biblical allusions? What do these allusions contribute to the story?

to ALISON BECHDEL, from *Fun Home*
(p. 246)

1. The title of this story, *Fun Home*, is short for "funeral home," where the writer and her character grew up. In what sense is this title ironic?

2. Bechdel describes her father as a "Daedalus of décor." What does she mean?

3. Bechdel says that her father was both Icarus and Daedalus. What does this tell readers about her father?

4. What do the visual images add to the story? What would be lost if you disregarded the pictures and read just the narrative at the top of each frame?

to SHIRLEY JACKSON, "The Lottery"
(p. 251)

1. "The Lottery" takes place in summer, a conventional symbol that has a positive connotation. What does this setting contribute to the story's plot? to its atmosphere?

2. What, if anything, might the names *Graves*, *Adams*, *Summers*, and *Delacroix* signify in the context of this story? Do you think these names are intended to have any special significance? Why or why not?

3. What role do the children play in the ritual? How can you explain their presence in the story? Do they have any symbolic role?

4. What symbolic significance might be found in the way the characters are dressed? in their conversation?

to ALICE WALKER, "Everyday Use" (p. 256)

1. In American culture, what does a patchwork quilt symbolize?

2. What is the literal meaning of the two quilts to Maggie and her mother? to Dee? Beyond this literal meaning, what symbolic meaning, if any, do they have to Maggie and her mother? Do the quilts have any symbolic meaning to Dee?

3. How does the contrast between the two sisters' appearances, personalities, lifestyles, and feelings about the quilts help to convey the story's theme?

4. What does the name *Wangero* signify to Dee? to her mother and sister? Could the name be considered a symbol? Why or why not?

to RAYMOND CARVER, "Cathedral" (p. 261)

1. Who is the narrator? What do we know about him? Why does the impending visit by the blind man disturb him?

2. Toward the end of the story, the blind man asks the narrator to describe a cathedral. Why is the narrator unable to do so? What does his inability to do so reveal about him?

3. Why does the blind man tell the narrator to close his eyes while he is drawing? What does he hope to teach him? What is the narrator able to "see" with his eyes shut that he cannot see with them open?

4. In paragraph 96, the blind man observes that the men who began work on a cathedral never lived to see it completed. In this way, he says, "they're no different from the rest of us." What does the cathedral symbolize to the blind man? What does it come to symbolize to the narrator?

✔ CHAPTER 16 CHECKLIST
for SHIRLEY JACKSON, "The Lottery" (p. 251)

WRITING ABOUT SYMBOL, ALLEGORY, AND MYTH

- ☐ Are any universal symbols used in the work? any conventional symbols? What is their function?
- ☐ What possible meanings does each symbol suggest?
- ☐ How do symbols help to depict the story's characters?
- ☐ Does the story have a moral or didactic purpose? What is the message, idea, or moral principle the story seeks to convey? Is the story an allegory?

✔ CHAPTER 16 CHECKLIST
for ALISON BECHDEL, from *Fun Home* (p. 246)

WRITING ABOUT SYMBOL, ALLEGORY, AND MYTH

- ☐ Is any character, place, action, event, or object given unusual prominence or emphasis in the story? If so, does this element seem to have symbolic as well as literal significance?
- ☐ How do symbols help to depict the story's characters?
- ☐ How do symbols help to characterize the story's setting?
- ☐ What do the story's references to myth contribute to the story's plot or theme?

✔ CHAPTER 16 CHECKLIST
for RAYMOND CARVER, "Cathedral" (p. 261)

WRITING ABOUT SYMBOL, ALLEGORY, AND MYTH

- ☐ Is any character, place, action, event, or object given unusual prominence or emphasis in the story? If so, does this element seem to have symbolic as well as literal significance?
- ☐ How do symbols help to depict the story's characters?
- ☐ How do symbols help to advance the story's plot?
- ☐ Does the story have a moral or didactic purpose? What is the message, idea, or moral principle the story seeks to convey? Is the story an allegory?

✔ CHAPTER 16 CHECKLIST
for ALICE WALKER, "Everyday Use" (p. 256)

WRITING ABOUT SYMBOL, ALLEGORY, AND MYTH

- ☐ Are any universal symbols used in the work? any conventional symbols? What is their function?
- ☐ Is any character, place, action, event, or object given unusual prominence or emphasis in the story? If so, does this element seem to have symbolic as well as literal significance?
- ☐ What possible meanings does each symbol suggest?
- ☐ How do symbols help to depict the story's characters?

READING AND REACTING

to LYNDA BARRY, "Two Questions" (p. 273)

1. What are the "two questions" referred to in the story's title? Why do they matter so much to the narrator?

2. What is the central conflict of the story? How does the narrator resolve this conflict?

3. Look at the following characters in "Two Questions":

   - The octopus
   - The ghosts
   - The monkey
   - The cat

   How do each character's words and appearance help develop the central theme of the story? Which of these "minor characters" do you see as most important? Why?

4. What do you think the narrator learns about inspiration and creativity?

READING AND REACTING

to EUDORA WELTY, "A Worn Path" (p. 285)

1. How does the first paragraph set the scene for the rest of the story? How does it foreshadow the events that will take place later on?

2. Traditionally, a **quest** is a journey in which a knight overcomes a series of obstacles in order to perform a prescribed feat. In what way is Phoenix's journey a quest? What obstacles does she face? What feat must she perform?

3. Because Phoenix is old, she has trouble seeing. What things does she have difficulty seeing? How do her mistakes shed light on her character? How do they contribute to the impact of the story?

4. A **phoenix** is a mythical bird that would live for five hundred years, be consumed by fire, and then rise from its own ashes. In what way is the name of this creature appropriate for the main character of this story?

READING AND REACTING

to DAVID MICHAEL KAPLAN, "Doe Season" (p. 290)

1. The initiation of a child into adulthood is a common literary theme. In this story, hunting is presented as an initiation rite. In what way is hunting an appropriate coming-of-age ritual?

2. Which characters are in conflict in this story? Which ideas are in conflict? How do these conflicts help to communicate the story's initiation theme?

3. In the story's opening paragraph and elsewhere, Andy finds comfort and reassurance in the idea that the woods are "always the same"; later in the story, she remembers the ocean, "huge and empty, yet always moving. Everything lay hidden . . ." (par. 45). How does the contrast between the woods and the ocean suggest the transition she must make from childhood to adulthood?

4. How do the references to blood support the story's initiation theme? Do they suggest other themes as well?

READING AND REACTING

to D(AVID) H(ERBERT) LAWRENCE, "The Rocking-Horse Winner" (p. 297)

1. From what point of view is "The Rocking-Horse Winner" told? How does this point of view help to communicate the story's theme?

2. In what ways is "The Rocking-Horse Winner" like a fairy tale? How is it different?

3. Many fairy tales involve a hero who goes on a journey to search for something of great value. What journey does Paul go on? What thing of value does he search for? Is he successful?

4. The rocking horse is an important literary **symbol** in the story. What possible meanings might the rocking horse suggest? In what ways does this symbol reinforce the story's theme?

✓ CHAPTER 17 CHECKLIST
for EUDORA WELTY, "A Worn Path" (p. 285)

WRITING ABOUT THEME

- ☐ What is the central theme of the story?
- ☐ What other themes can you identify?
- ☐ Does the narrator, or any character, make statements that express or imply a theme?
- ☐ Do any symbols suggest a theme?

✓ CHAPTER 17 CHECKLIST
for LYNDA BARRY, "Two Questions" (p. 273)

WRITING ABOUT THEME

- ☐ What is the central theme of the story?
- ☐ What other themes can you identify?
- ☐ How does the point of view shed light on the story's central theme?
- ☐ Do any symbols suggest a theme?

✓ CHAPTER 17 CHECKLIST
for D(AVID) H(ERBERT) LAWRENCE, "The Rocking-Horse Winner" (p. 297)

WRITING ABOUT THEME

- ☐ What is the central theme of the story?
- ☐ What other themes can you identify?
- ☐ Does the narrator, or any character, make statements that express or imply a theme?
- ☐ Do any characters in the story change in any significant way? Do these changes convey a particular theme?

✓ CHAPTER 17 CHECKLIST
for DAVID MICHAEL KAPLAN, "Doe Season" (p. 290)

WRITING ABOUT THEME

- ☐ Does the title of the story suggest a theme?
- ☐ Does the narrator, or any character, make statements that express or imply a theme?
- ☐ In what way does the arrangement of events in the story suggest a theme?
- ☐ Do any characters in the story change in any significant way? Do these changes convey a particular theme?

to JANICE MIRIKITANI, "Suicide Note"
(p. 367)

1. This poem is a suicide note that contains an apology. Why does the speaker feel she must apologize? Do you agree that she needs to apologize?

2. What attitude does the speaker convey toward her parents?

3. Is the college student who speaks in this poem a stranger to you, or is her voice in any way like that of students you know?

to WILLIAM WORDSWORTH, "The World Is Too Much with Us" (p. 373)

1. What is the speaker's attitude toward the contemporary world? How is this attitude revealed through the poem's tone?

2. This poem is a **sonnet,** a highly structured traditional form. How do the regular meter and rhyme scheme help to establish the poem's tone?

to ROBERT HERRICK, "To the Virgins, to Make Much of Time" (p. 374)

1. How would you characterize the speaker? Do you think he expects his listeners to share his views? How might his expectations affect his tone?

2. This poem is developed like an argument. What is the speaker's main point? How does he support it?

3. What effect does the poem's use of rhyme have on its tone?

4. Whose side are you on—the speaker's or those he addresses?

to DUDLEY RANDALL, "Ballad of Birmingham" (p. 378)

1. Who are the speakers in the poem? How do their tones differ?

2. What kinds of irony are present in the poem? Give examples of each kind you identify.

3. What point do you think the poem makes about violence? about racial hatred? about the civil rights struggle?

4. This poem is a **ballad,** a form of poetry traditionally written to be sung or recited. Ballads typically repeat words and phrases and have regular meter and rhyme. How do the regular rhyme, repeated words, and singsong meter affect the poem's tone?

CHAPTER 21 CHECKLIST
for WILLIAM WORDSWORTH, "The World Is Too Much with Us" (p. 373)

WRITING ABOUT VOICE

- [ ] What do we know about the speaker?
- [ ] Does the speaker make any direct statements to readers that help establish his or her identity or character?
- [ ] Does the speaker address anyone? How can you tell? How does the presence of a listener affect the speaker?
- [ ] How do word choice, rhyme, meter, sentence structure, figures of speech, and imagery help to convey the attitude of the speaker?

CHAPTER 21 CHECKLIST
for JANICE MIRIKITANI, "Suicide Note" (p. 367)

WRITING ABOUT VOICE

- [ ] What do we know about the speaker?
- [ ] Does the speaker make any direct statements to readers that help establish his or her identity or character?
- [ ] Does the speaker address anyone? How can you tell? How does the presence of a listener affect the speaker?
- [ ] What is the speaker's attitude toward his or her subject?

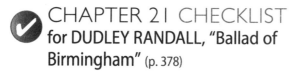

CHAPTER 21 CHECKLIST
for DUDLEY RANDALL, "Ballad of Birmingham" (p. 378)

WRITING ABOUT VOICE

- [ ] What do we know about the speakers?
- [ ] Are the speakers anonymous, or do they have particular identities?
- [ ] What are the speakers' attitudes toward their subject?
- [ ] Is the poem's tone consistent? How do you account for shifts in tone?

CHAPTER 21 CHECKLIST
for ROBERT HERRICK, "To the Virgins, to Make Much of Time" (p. 374)

WRITING ABOUT VOICE

- [ ] What do we know about the speaker?
- [ ] Does the speaker make any direct statements to readers that help establish his or her identity or character?
- [ ] Does the speaker address anyone? How can you tell? How does the presence of a listener affect the speaker?
- [ ] How do word choice, rhyme, meter, sentence structure, figures of speech, and imagery help to convey the attitude of the speaker?

to E. E. CUMMINGS, "in Just-" (p. 387)

1. In this poem, Cummings coins a number of words that he uses to modify other words. Identify these coinages. What other, more conventional, words could be used in their place? What does Cummings accomplish by using the coined words instead?

2. What do you think Cummings means by "far and wee" in lines 5, 13, and 22–24? Why do you think he arranges these three words in a different way on the page each time he uses them?

3. Evaluate this poem. Do you like it? Is it memorable? moving? Or is it just clever?

to GWENDOLYN BROOKS, "We Real Cool" (p. 392)

1. What elements of nonstandard English grammar appear in this poem? How does the use of such language affect your attitude toward the speaker?

2. Every word in this poem is a single syllable. Why?

3. Why do you think the poet begins with "We" only in the first line instead of isolating each complete sentence on its own line? How does this strategy change the poem's impact?

to GWENDOLYN BROOKS, "What Shall I Give My Children?" (p. 392)

1. Unlike "We Real Cool" (p. 392), also by Gwendolyn Brooks, this sonnet's diction is quite formal. Given the subject of each poem, do the poet's decisions about level of diction make sense to you?

2. Which words in this poem do you see as elevated—that is, not likely to be used in conversation?

3. Apart from individual words, what else strikes you as formal about this poem?

to A. E. HOUSMAN, "To an Athlete Dying Young" (p. 395)

1. Where does the poem's meter or rhyme scheme require the poet to depart from conventional syntax?

2. Edit the poem so its word order is more conventional. Do your changes improve the poem?

3. Who do you think the speaker is? What is his relationship to the athlete?

CHAPTER 22 CHECKLIST
for GWENDOLYN BROOKS, "We Real Cool" (p. 392)

WRITING ABOUT WORD CHOICE AND WORD ORDER

- ☐ Why is each word chosen instead of a synonym? (For example, is the word chosen for its sound? its connotation? its relationship to other words in the poem? its contribution to the poem's metrical pattern?)

- ☐ What other words could be effectively used in place of words now in the poem? How would substitutions change the poem's meaning?

- ☐ How would you characterize the poem's level of diction? Why is this level of diction used? Is it appropriate?

- ☐ Is the poem's word order conventional, or are words arranged in unexpected order?

CHAPTER 22 CHECKLIST
for E. E. CUMMINGS, "in Just-" (p. 387)

WRITING ABOUT WORD CHOICE AND WORD ORDER

- ☐ Why is each word chosen instead of a synonym? (For example, is the word chosen for its sound? its connotation? its relationship to other words in the poem? its contribution to the poem's metrical pattern?)

- ☐ What other words could be effectively used in place of words now in the poem? How would substitutions change the poem's meaning?

- ☐ Are any words repeated? Why?

- ☐ Is the poem's word order conventional, or are words arranged in unexpected order?

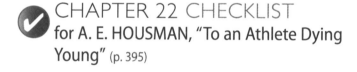

CHAPTER 22 CHECKLIST
for A. E. HOUSMAN, "To an Athlete Dying Young" (p. 395)

WRITING ABOUT WORD CHOICE AND WORD ORDER

- ☐ Which words are of key importance in the poem? What is the denotative meaning of each of these key words?

- ☐ Which key words have neutral connotations? Which have negative connotations? Which have positive connotations? Beyond its literal meaning, what does each word suggest?

- ☐ What is the purpose of the unusual word order? (For example, does it preserve the poem's meter or rhyme scheme? Does it highlight particular sound correspondences? Does it place emphasis on a particular word or phrase? Does it reflect the speaker's mood?)

- ☐ How would the poem's impact change if conventional syntax were used?

CHAPTER 22 CHECKLIST
for GWENDOLYN BROOKS, "What Shall I Give My Children?" (p. 392)

WRITING ABOUT WORD CHOICE AND WORD ORDER

- ☐ Why is each word chosen instead of a synonym? (For example, is the word chosen for its sound? its connotation? its relationship to other words in the poem? its contribution to the poem's metrical pattern?)

- ☐ What other words could be effectively used in place of words now in the poem? How would substitutions change the poem's meaning?

- ☐ Why might the poem use the level of diction that it does? Is it appropriate?

- ☐ Is the poem's word order conventional, or are words arranged in unexpected order?

to ROBERT FROST, "Nothing Gold Can Stay" (p. 404)

1. What central idea does this poem express?

2. What do you think the first line of the poem means? In what sense is this line ironic?

3. What is the significance of the colors green and gold in this poem? What do these colors have to do with "Eden" and "dawn"?

4. How do the various images in the poem prepare readers for the last line? Do you think the title spoils the impact of the last line?

to WILLIAM SHAKESPEARE, "My mistress' eyes are nothing like the sun" (p. 405)

1. What point does Shakespeare make in the first twelve lines of his sonnet?

2. What point does the rhymed couplet at the end of the poem make?

3. How is Shakespeare's imagery like and unlike that of traditional love poems?

4. How do you think the woman to whom the poem is addressed will react?

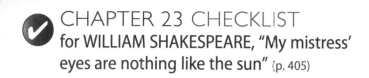

CHAPTER 23 CHECKLIST
for WILLIAM SHAKESPEARE, "My mistress' eyes are nothing like the sun" (p. 405)

WRITING ABOUT IMAGERY

- ☐ What details make the images memorable?
- ☐ What mood do the images create?
- ☐ How do the poem's images help to convey its theme?
- ☐ How effective are the images? How do they enhance your enjoyment of the poem?

CHAPTER 23 CHECKLIST
for ROBERT FROST, "Nothing Gold Can Stay" (p. 404)

WRITING ABOUT IMAGERY

- ☐ Does the poem depend on a cluster of related images?
- ☐ What details make the images memorable?
- ☐ What mood do the images create?
- ☐ How do the poem's images help to convey its theme?

to SYLVIA PLATH, "Metaphors" (p. 413)

1. The speaker in this poem is a pregnant woman. Do all the metaphors seem appropriate? For instance, in what sense is the speaker "a means, a stage" (line 7)?

2. If you were going to expand this poem, what other metaphors (or similes) would you add?

3. What are the "nine syllables" to which the speaker refers in the poem's first line? What significance does the number *nine* have in terms of the poem's subject? In terms of its form?

4. Would you say the speaker has a positive, negative, or neutral attitude toward her pregnancy? Which metaphors give you this impression?

to RANDALL JARRELL, "The Death of the Ball Turret Gunner" (p. 413)

1. Who is the speaker? To what does he compare himself in the poem's first two lines? What words establish this comparison?

2. Contrast the speaker's actual identity with the one he creates for himself in lines 1–2. What elements of his actual situation do you think lead him to characterize himself as he does in these lines?

3. Both this poem and "Dulce et Decorum Est" (p. 492) use figures of speech to describe the horrors of war. Which poem has a greater impact on you?

to ANDREW MARVELL, "To His Coy Mistress" (p. 419)

1. In this poem, Marvell's speaker sets out to convince a reluctant woman to become his lover. In order to make his case more persuasive, he uses hyperbole, exaggerating time periods, sizes, spaces, and the possible fate of the woman if she refuses him. Identify as many examples of hyperbole as you can.

2. The tone of "To His Coy Mistress" is more whimsical than serious. Given this tone, what do you see as the purpose of Marvell's use of hyperbole?

to ROBERT FROST, "Out, Out—" (p. 420)

1. The poem's title is an **allusion** to a passage in Shakespeare's *Macbeth* (5.5.23–28) that attacks the brevity and meaninglessness of life in very emotional terms:

> Out, out brief candle!
>
> Life's but a walking shadow, a poor player,
> That struts and frets his hour upon the stage
> And then is heard no more. It is a tale
> Told by an idiot, full of sound and fury,
> Signifying nothing.

What idea do you think Frost wants to convey through the title "Out, Out—"?

2. Explain why each of the following qualifies as understatement:
   - "Neither refused the meeting." (line 18)
   - "He saw all spoiled." (line 25)
   - "—and that ended it." (line 32)
   - "No more to build on there." (line 33)

   Can you identify any other examples of understatement in the poem?

3. Do you think the poem's impact is strengthened or weakened by its understated tone?

CHAPTER 24 CHECKLIST
for RANDALL JARRELL, "The Death of the Ball Turret Gunner" (p. 413)

WRITING ABOUT FIGURES OF SPEECH

- [ ] What figures of speech are present in the poem? Identify any examples of simile, metaphor, personification, hyperbole, understatement, metonymy, synecdoche, and apostrophe.
- [ ] What two elements are being compared in each use of simile, metaphor, and personification? What characteristics are shared by the two items being compared?
- [ ] Does the poet use hyperbole? Why? For example, is it used to move or to shock readers, or is its use intended to produce a humorous or satirical effect? Would more understated language be more effective?
- [ ] How do figures of speech contribute to the impact of the poem as a whole?

CHAPTER 24 CHECKLIST
for SYLVIA PLATH, "Metaphors" (p. 413)

WRITING ABOUT FIGURES OF SPEECH

- [ ] What figures of speech are present in the poem? Identify any examples of simile, metaphor, personification, hyperbole, understatement, metonymy, synecdoche, and apostrophe.
- [ ] What two elements are being compared in each use of simile, metaphor, and personification? What characteristics are shared by the two items being compared?
- [ ] Does the poet use hyperbole? Why? For example, is it used to move or to shock readers, or is its use intended to produce a humorous or satirical effect? Would more understated language be more effective?
- [ ] How do figures of speech contribute to the impact of the poem as a whole?

 # CHAPTER 24 CHECKLIST
for ROBERT FROST, "Out, Out—" (p. 420)

WRITING ABOUT FIGURES OF SPEECH

- [ ] What figures of speech are present in the poem? Identify any examples of simile, metaphor, personification, hyperbole, understatement, metonymy, synecdoche, and apostrophe.
- [ ] For what purpose does the poet use understatement? Would more emotionally charged language be more effective?
- [ ] How do figures of speech contribute to the impact of the poem as a whole?

 # CHAPTER 24 CHECKLIST
for ANDREW MARVELL, "To His Coy Mistress" (p. 419)

WRITING ABOUT FIGURES OF SPEECH

- [ ] What figures of speech are present in the poem? Identify any examples of simile, metaphor, personification, hyperbole, understatement, metonymy, synecdoche, and apostrophe.
- [ ] What is the effect of the poet's use of hyperbole? Would more understated language be more effective?
- [ ] How do figures of speech contribute to the impact of the poem as a whole?

to ADRIENNE RICH, "Aunt Jennifer's Tigers" (p. 433)

1. What is the dominant metrical pattern of the poem? How does the meter enhance the contrast the poem develops?

2. The lines in the first stanza are end-stopped, and those in the second and third stanzas combine end-stopped and run-on lines. What does the poet achieve by varying the rhythm?

3. What ideas do the caesuras in the first and fourth lines of the last stanza emphasize?

4. What is the speaker's opinion of Aunt Jennifer's marriage? Do you think she is commenting on this particular marriage or on marriage in general?

to GERARD MANLEY HOPKINS, "Pied Beauty" (p. 437)

1. Identify examples of onomatopoeia, alliteration, assonance, imperfect rhyme, and perfect rhyme. Do you think all these techniques are essential to the poem? Are any of them annoying or distracting?

2. What is the central idea of this poem? How do the sounds of the poem help to communicate this idea?

3. Identify examples of masculine and feminine rhyme.

4. Hopkins uses both pleasing and discordant sounds in his poem. Identify uses of euphony and cacophony, and explain how these techniques affect your reactions to the poem.

to GALWAY KINNELL, "Blackberry Eating" (p. 439)

1. What sounds does Kinnell repeat in the poem? How do they help to create the poem's rhythm?

2. This poem consists entirely of run-on lines. Why do you think the poet uses this technique instead of end-stopped lines?

3. One part of the poem deals with blackberries, and the other part deals with the poet's love for words. What is the connection between these two subjects?

4. How do alliteration and assonance help Kinnell convey his ideas?

to LEWIS CARROLL, "Jabberwocky" (p. 440)

1. Many words in this poem may be unfamiliar to you. Are they actual words? Use a dictionary to check before you dismiss any. Do some words that do not appear in the dictionary nevertheless seem to have meaning in the context of the poem? Explain.

2. This poem contains many examples of onomatopoeia. What meanings does the sound of each of these words suggest?

3. Summarize the story the poem tells. In what sense is this poem a story of a young man's initiation into adulthood?

✔ CHAPTER 25 CHECKLIST
for GERARD MANLEY HOPKINS, "Pied Beauty" (p. 437)

WRITING ABOUT SOUND

- ☐ How does the meter contribute to the overall effect of the poem?
- ☐ What is the effect of alliteration and assonance in the poem?
- ☐ How does rhyme unify the poem?
- ☐ How does rhyme reinforce the poem's ideas?

✔ CHAPTER 25 CHECKLIST
for ADRIENNE RICH, "Aunt Jennifer's Tigers" (p. 433)

WRITING ABOUT SOUND

- ☐ Does the poem contain repeated words and phrases? If so, how do they help to create rhythm?
- ☐ Does the poem use one kind of meter throughout, or does the meter vary from line to line?
- ☐ What effect do caesuras have in the poem?
- ☐ What effects are created by the presence or absence of pauses at the ends of lines?

✔ CHAPTER 25 CHECKLIST
for LEWIS CARROLL, "Jabberwocky" (p. 440)

WRITING ABOUT SOUND

- ☐ How does the meter contribute to the overall effect of the poem?
- ☐ Does the poem have a regular rhyme scheme?
- ☐ How does rhyme unify the poem?
- ☐ How does rhyme reinforce the poem's ideas?

✔ CHAPTER 25 CHECKLIST
for GALWAY KINNELL, "Blackberry Eating" (p. 439)

WRITING ABOUT SOUND

- ☐ Does the poem use one kind of meter throughout, or does the meter vary from line to line?
- ☐ How does the meter contribute to the overall effect of the poem?
- ☐ What effects are created by the absence of pauses at the ends of lines?
- ☐ What is the effect of alliteration and assonance in the poem?

to GWENDOLYN BROOKS, "First Fight. Then Fiddle" (p. 448)

1. What is the subject of Brooks's poem?

2. Explain the poem's rhyme scheme. Is this rhyme scheme an essential element of the poem? Would the poem be equally effective if it did not include end rhyme? Why or why not?

3. Study the poem's use of capitalization and punctuation carefully. Why do you think Brooks chooses to end many of her sentences in midline? How do her decisions determine how you read the poem?

4. What do you think Brooks means by "fight" and "fiddle"?

to MARTIN ESPADA, "Why I Went to College" (p. 452)

1. How is "Why I Went to College" different from Coleridge's and Blake's epigrams? How is it similar to them?

2. What function does the poem's title serve? Is it the epigram's "punch line," or does it serve another purpose?

3. What can you infer about the speaker's father from this poem? Why, for example, do you think he wants his son to go to college?

to MATSUO BASHŌ, "Four Haiku" (p. 453)

1. Haiku are admired for their extreme economy and their striking images. What are the central images in each of Bashō's haiku? To what senses do these images appeal?

2. In another poem, Bashō says that art begins with "The depths of the country / and a rice-planting song." What do you think he means? How do these four haiku exemplify this idea?

3. Do you think the conciseness of these poems increases or decreases the impact of their images? Explain.

4. "In a Station of the Metro" (p. 401) is Ezra Pound's version of a haiku. How successful do you think his poem is as a haiku? Do you think a longer poem could have conveyed the images more effectively?

to WALT WHITMAN, "From 'Out of the Cradle Endlessly Rocking'" (p. 456)

1. This excerpt, the first twenty-two lines of a poem nearly two hundred lines long, has no regular metrical pattern or rhyme scheme. What gives it its form?

2. How might you explain why the poem's lines vary in length?

3. Compare this excerpt with the excerpt from Whitman's "Song of Myself" (p. 520). In what respects are the forms of the two poems similar?

CHAPTER 26 CHECKLIST
for MARTIN ESPADA, "Why I Went to College" (p. 452)

WRITING ABOUT FORM

- ☐ Is the poem written in open or closed form? On what characteristics do you base your conclusion?
- ☐ How do the traditional conventions of an epigram suit the poet's language and theme? Does the poem follow the rules of the form at all times, or does it break any new ground?
- ☐ Are certain words or phrases isolated on lines? Why?
- ☐ How do elements such as assonance, alliteration, rhyme, and repetition of words give the poem form?

CHAPTER 26 CHECKLIST
for GWENDOLYN BROOKS, "First Fight. Then Fiddle" (p. 448)

WRITING ABOUT FORM

- ☐ Is the poem written in open or closed form? On what characteristics do you base your conclusion?
- ☐ Why did the poet choose open or closed form? For example, is the poem's form consistent with its subject matter, tone, or theme? Is it determined by the conventions of the historical period in which it was written?
- ☐ Are certain words or phrases isolated on lines? Why?
- ☐ How do elements such as assonance, alliteration, rhyme, and repetition of words give the poem form?

CHAPTER 26 CHECKLIST
for WALT WHITMAN, "From 'Out of the Cradle Endlessly Rocking'" (p. 456)

WRITING ABOUT FORM

- ☐ Why did the poet choose open form? For example, is the poem's form consistent with its subject matter, tone, or theme? Is it determined by the conventions of the historical period in which it was written?
- ☐ What determines the breaks at the ends of lines?
- ☐ Are certain words or phrases isolated on lines? Why?
- ☐ How do elements such as assonance, alliteration, rhyme, and repetition of words give the poem form?

CHAPTER 26 CHECKLIST
for MATSUO BASHŌ, "Four Haiku" (p. 453)

WRITING ABOUT FORM

- ☐ Are the poems written in open or closed form? On what characteristics do you base your conclusion?
- ☐ How do the traditional conventions of a haiku suit the poet's language and theme? Do the poems follow the rules of the form at all times, or do they break any new ground?
- ☐ Are certain words or phrases isolated on lines? Why?
- ☐ What use does the poet make of punctuation and capitalization? Of white space on the page?

to EDGAR ALLAN POE, "The Raven"
(p. 465)

1. Who is the speaker in the poem? What is his state of mind? How does the raven mirror the speaker's mental state?

2. "The Raven" contains a good deal of alliteration. Identify some examples. How does this use of repeated initial consonant sounds help to convey the mood of the poem?

3. The speaker refers to the raven in a number of different ways. At one point, it is simply "an ebony bird" (line 42); at another, it is a "prophet" and "a thing of evil" (85). How else does the speaker characterize the raven?

4. What is the symbolic significance of the raven? of the repeated word "nevermore"? of the bust of Pallas, the ancient Greek god of wisdom?

to ADRIENNE RICH, "Diving into the Wreck" (p. 469)

1. On one level, this poem is about a deep-sea diver's exploration of a wrecked ship. What details suggest that the poet wants you to see the poem as something more?

2. Explain the allegorical figures presented in the poem. What, for example, might the diver and the wreck represent?

3. Does the poem contain any symbols? How can you tell they are symbols and not allegorical figures?

4. In lines 62–63, the speaker says that she came for "the wreck and not the story of the wreck / the thing itself and not the myth." Explain this distinction. What do you think the speaker is really looking for?

to WILLIAM BUTLER YEATS, "Leda and the Swan" (p. 475)

1. What event is described in this poem? What is the mythological significance of this event?

2. How is Leda portrayed? Why is the swan described as a "feathered glory" (line 6)? Why in the poem's last line is Leda dropped by his "indifferent beak"?

3. The third stanza refers to the Trojan War, which was indirectly caused by the event described in the poem. How does the allusion to the Trojan War help develop the theme of the poem?

4. Does the poem answer the question asked in its last two lines? Explain.

to W. H. AUDEN, "Musée des Beaux Arts"
(p. 475)

1. Reread the summary of the myth of Icarus on page 473. What does Auden's allusion to this myth contribute to the poem?

2. What point does the poet make by referring to the "Old Masters" (line 2)?

3. Brueghel's painting Landscape with the Fall of Icarus is shown below. How does looking at this painting help you to understand the poem? To what specific details in the painting does the poet refer?

Musée D'Art Ancien, Brussels, Belgium
©Scala/Art Resource, NY

CHAPTER 27 CHECKLIST
for ADRIENNE RICH, "Diving into the Wreck" (p. 469)

SYMBOL, ALLEGORY, ALLUSION, MYTH

- [ ] How does your interpretation of each symbol enhance your understanding of the poem?
- [ ] What effect do the allegorical figures have in the poem?
- [ ] What do the allegorical figures signify on a literal level?
- [ ] What lesson does the allegory illustrate?

CHAPTER 27 CHECKLIST
for EDGAR ALLAN POE, "The Raven" (p. 465)

SYMBOL, ALLEGORY, ALLUSION, MYTH

- [ ] Are the poem's symbols conventional? Are they universal or archetypal?
- [ ] Are any symbols obscure or highly idiosyncratic?
- [ ] What is the literal meaning of each symbol in the context of the poem? Beyond its literal meaning, what else could each symbol suggest?
- [ ] How does your interpretation of each symbol enhance your understanding of the poem?

CHAPTER 27 CHECKLIST
for W. H. AUDEN, "Musée des Beaux Arts" (p. 475)

SYMBOL, ALLEGORY, ALLUSION, MYTH

- [ ] In what way do the poem's allusions deepen the poem's meaning? Does any allusion interfere with your understanding or enjoyment of the poem? If so, how?
- [ ] What myths or mythological figures are alluded to?
- [ ] How does the poem use myth to convey its meaning?
- [ ] How faithful is the poem to the myth? Does the poet add material to the myth? Are any details from the original myth omitted? Is any information distorted? Why?

CHAPTER 27 CHECKLIST
for WILLIAM BUTLER YEATS, "Leda and the Swan" (p. 475)

SYMBOL, ALLEGORY, ALLUSION, MYTH

- [ ] In what way do the poem's allusions deepen the poem's meaning? Does any allusion interfere with your understanding or enjoyment of the poem? If so, how?
- [ ] What myths or mythological figures are alluded to?
- [ ] How does the poem use myth to convey its meaning?
- [ ] How faithful is the poem to the myth? Does the poet add material to the myth? Are any details from the original myth omitted? Is any information distorted? Why?

READING AND REACTING

to SUSAN GLASPELL, *Trifles* (p. 555)

1. What key events have occurred before the start of the play? Why do you suppose these events are not presented in the play itself?

2. What are the "trifles" to which the title refers? How do these "trifles" advance the play's plot?

3. *Trifles* is a one-act play, and all its action occurs in the Wrights' kitchen. What do you see as the advantages and disadvantages of this confined setting?

4. All background information about Mrs. Wright is provided by Mrs. Hale. Do you consider her to be a reliable source of information? Why or why not?

READING AND REACTING

to HENRIK IBSEN, *A Doll House* (p. 562)

1. What is your attitude toward Nora at the beginning of the play? How does your attitude toward her change as the play progresses? What actions and lines of dialogue change your assessment of her?

2. List the key events that have occurred before the start of the play. How do we learn of each event?

3. Is Kristine Linde as much of a "modern woman" as Nora? Is she actually *more* of a modern woman? Is she essential to the play? How might the play be different without her?

4. Do you see *A Doll House* as primarily about the struggle between the needs of the individual and the needs of society, or about the conflict between women's roles in the family and in the larger society? Explain.

READING AND REACTING

to ARTHUR MILLER, *Death of a Salesman* (p. 605)

1. Is Willy a likeable character? What words and actions — both Willy's and those of other characters — help you to reach your conclusion?

2. How does the existence of The Woman affect your overall impression of Willy? What does she reveal about his character?

3. What does Willy's attitude toward his sons indicate about his character? How is this attitude revealed?

4. In the absence of a narrator, what devices does Miller use to provide exposition — basic information about character and setting?

READING AND REACTING

to WILLIAM SHAKESPEARE, *Hamlet* (p. 644)

1. What are Hamlet's most notable character traits? Do you see these traits as generally positive or negative?

2. Is Hamlet a sympathetic character? Where (if anywhere) do you find yourself growing impatient with him or disagreeing with him?

3. What do other characters' comments reveal about Hamlet's character *before* the key events in the play begin to unfold? For example, in what way has Hamlet changed since he returned to the castle and found out about his father's death?

4. List those in the play who you believe to be flat characters. Why do you characterize each individual in this way? What does each of these flat characters contribute to the play?

✅ CHAPTER 32 CHECKLIST
for HENRIK IBSEN, *A Doll House* (p. 562)

WRITING ABOUT PLOT

- ☐ Does the play contain a subplot? What is its purpose? How is it related to the main plot?
- ☐ How do characters' actions advance the play's plot?
- ☐ How does dialogue advance the play's plot?
- ☐ Does the play include flashbacks? foreshadowing? Does the play's dialogue contain summaries of past events or references to events in the future? How does the use of flashbacks or foreshadowing advance the play's plot?

✅ CHAPTER 32 CHECKLIST
for SUSAN GLASPELL, *Trifles* (p. 555)

WRITING ABOUT PLOT

- ☐ What happens in the play?
- ☐ What section of the play constitutes its rising action?
- ☐ What section of the play constitutes its falling action?
- ☐ How do characters' actions advance the play's plot?

✅ CHAPTER 33 CHECKLIST
for WILLIAM SHAKESPEARE, *Hamlet*
(p. 644)

WRITING ABOUT CHARACTER

- ☐ Does the play include monologue or soliloquies? What do these extended speeches reveal about the characters?
- ☐ Is the characters' language formal or informal? Is the characters' language plain or elaborate?
- ☐ Does the play include verbal irony? dramatic irony? How is irony conveyed? What purpose does irony achieve?
- ☐ How might different actors' interpretations change an audience's understanding of the characters?

✅ CHAPTER 33 CHECKLIST
for ARTHUR MILLER, *Death of a Salesman*
(p. 605)

WRITING ABOUT CHARACTER

- ☐ Who are the major characters? Do they change and grow during the course of the play, or do they remain essentially unchanged?
- ☐ What is revealed about the characters through dialogue?
- ☐ Does the play include verbal irony? dramatic irony? How is irony conveyed? What purpose does irony achieve?
- ☐ What is revealed about characters through their actions?

READING AND REACTING

to DAVID IVES, *Words, Words, Words* (p. 697)

1. Look up the names of the three monkeys in an encyclopedia. Why do you think Ives chose these names for his characters?

2. What personality traits define each of the monkeys? How are they alike? How are they different?

3. The monkeys sometimes use jargon typically used by writers for the movies or for television. Find several examples of this type of jargon. How does this use of language add to the humor of the play?

4. At various points in the play, the monkeys echo lines from Shakespeare's plays. Find several examples. What is the significance of this use of language?

READING AND REACTING

to SOPHOCLES, *Oedipus the King* (p. 701)

1. The ancient Greeks used no scenery in their theatrical productions. In the absence of scenery, how is the setting established at the beginning of *Oedipus the King*?

2. In some recent productions of *Oedipus the King*, actors wear copies of ancient Greek masks. What are the advantages and disadvantages of using such masks in a contemporary production of the play?

3. In the ancient Greek theater, the *strophe* and *antistrophe* were sung or chanted by the chorus as it danced back and forth across the stage. If you were staging the play today, would you retain the chorus or do away with it entirely? What would be gained or lost with each alternative?

4. How does Sophocles present information about what happened years before the play took place? If you were staging a contemporary version of the play, what additional ways could you use to present this information?

READING AND REACTING

to AUGUST WILSON, *Fences* (p. 724)

1. Obviously, fences are a central metaphor of the play. To what different kinds of fences does the play's title refer?

2. How are the fathers and sons in this play alike? How are they different? Does the play imply that sons must inevitably follow in their fathers' footsteps?

3. This play is set in 1957. Given the racial climate of the country at that time, how realistic are Cory's ambitions? How reasonable are his father's criticisms?

4. In what ways has Troy's character been shaped by his contact with the white world?

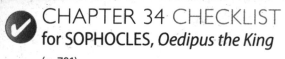
CHAPTER 34 CHECKLIST
for SOPHOCLES, *Oedipus the King*
(p. 701)

WRITING ABOUT STAGING

- [ ] What information about staging is specified in the stage directions of the play?
- [ ] How might different decisions about staging change the play?
- [ ] What events occur offstage? Why? How are they suggested?
- [ ] How does staging help to communicate the play's themes?

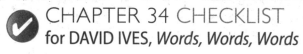
CHAPTER 34 CHECKLIST
for DAVID IVES, *Words, Words, Words*
(p. 697)

WRITING ABOUT STAGING

- [ ] What information about staging is specified in the stage directions of the play?
- [ ] How might different decisions about staging change the play?
- [ ] Do the stage directions provide information about how characters are supposed to look or behave?
- [ ] What costumes are specified? In what ways do costumes provide insight into the characters who wear them?

CHAPTER 35 CHECKLIST
for AUGUST WILSON, *Fences* (p. 724)

WRITING ABOUT THEME

- [ ] What is the central theme of the play?
- [ ] What other themes can you identify?
- [ ] What conflicts exist in the play? How do they shed light on the themes of the play?
- [ ] Do any characters' statements express or imply a theme of the play?